D0040771

KEY IDEAS
IN HUMAN THOUGHT

EDITED BY
Kenneth McLeish

Facts On File

Key Ideas in Human Thought

Facts On File, Inc.
460 Park Avenue South
New York NY 10016

Library of Congress Cataloging-in-Publication Data

Key ideas in human thought/Kenneth McLeish, general editor.
  p. cm.
  Includes bibliographical references.
  ISBN 0–8160–2707–2 (alk. paper)
  1. Philosophy—Dictionaries. 2. Humanities—Dictionaries.
3. Science—Dictionaries. 4. Social sciences—Dictionaries.
I. McLeish, Kenneth, 1940—
B41.K48   1993
031—dc20   93–24150
      CIP

A British CIP catalogue record for this book is available from the
British Library.

Facts On File books are available at special discounts when purchased
in bulk quantities for businesses, associations, institutions or
sales promotions. Please call our Special Sales Department in
New York at 212/683–2244 or 800/322–8755.

Compiled and edited by Book Creation Services, London
Typeset by August Filmsetting
Printed by Clays Ltd, St Ives plc

Printed in England

10 9 8 7 6 5 4 3 2 1

This book is printed on acid-free paper.

CONTRIBUTORS

Editor: Kenneth McLeish
Science Consultants: Dr Alexandra MacDermott,
Professor John P. Paul

Dr Jean Aitchison
Andrew Adams
Davina Allan
Dr Richard Burchmore
Dr Bernadette Casey
Andrew Cruden
Paul Duro
Teresa Fallon
Dr Tim Gordon
Rob Graham
Michael Greenhalgh
Dr Trevor Griffiths
Dr Andrew Jack
Dr E.M. Jackson
Jessica James
Mog Johnstone
Raminder Kaur

Tania Krzywinska
Cassandra Lorius
Catherine MacDermott
Dr Simon McLeish
Rabbi Rachel Montagu
Jeremy Musson
Dr Eleanor Nesbitt
Dr Brendan O'Leary
Ornan Rotem
Dr Philip Sarre
Matthew Saxton
Dr John Shepherd
Sue Smith
Dr Steve Stanton
Klaus-Dieter Stoll
Dr Elizabeth Stuart
Rosemarie Wedell

INTRODUCTION

In a lifetime, each human being can learn, ponder, marshal and apply some fifteen million million items of information. This is the process known, and thought about down the centuries, as thought. We are the only creatures able to do it, the only creatures able to imagine beings cleverer than we are, and to form (and communicate to others) ideas about their appearance and possible behaviour.

However, even today we still have astonishingly little understanding of how our species does all this. Early research into the workings of the brain was confined to crude physical experimentation (for example replacing with generated electrical current the nerve-impulses which jerked muscles or caused changes in skin-colour), and to the psychological testing of responses, emotions and opinions – testing which explained a great deal about the sorts of things people thought, and what influenced those thoughts, but virtually nothing about the processes of thought itself. Recent work with scanners has shown that when someone sets out to remember a series of simple facts (a sequence of half a dozen dates, for example, or the numerals from one to ten), waves of electrical energy flicker across the entire brain surface – but as yet the research has revealed nothing about why this should happen, what the patterns mean, where the 'memories' are stored, or what each 'memory' consists of. Is a 'memory', for example, an inert nugget of information, saved like a coin in a purse till needed, or is it something dynamic, triggered into active 'life' and restored to dormancy as soon as 'used'?

The vast majority of human brain-activity – 'thinking' – is reactive and instinctive. We may learn fifteen million million pieces of information in a lifetime, but it would hardly be possible to think about more than a fraction of them at any one time. Much of our awareness of the world, our subconscious 'thought' about the world, consists of 'givens' – that the sky is generally 'up' and the ground 'down', that a tree is a tree, that fire can burn, that certain things are poisonous to eat – and we pass our lives without giving them overmuch attention. As I write this, as you read it, our brains are simultaneously processing a dozen, a hundred, thoughts at each instant, and only a few of them are consciously related to this actual activity. We breathe; we maintain our posture; we digest our last meal or think about the next one; we feel comfortable or uncomfortable, secure or threatened; we remember something we have to do urgently or relax in the knowledge that we have nothing else to occupy us but this book; we remember how to use a word-processor, how to read. Such matters dip in and out of our conscious minds, tug our concentration this way or that. They are part of our experience of the thoughts being communicated in this introduction (about which you also have thoughts of your own); they are both essential to our experience of it, and irrelevant to that experience.

The bulk of such 'thinking' is hardly unique to the human species. To a greater or lesser extent, every living organism does it – to the point where we humans loftily dismiss it as hardly 'thought' at all. We assume, for example, that a scorpion never thinks 'I'm hungry' or 'Better avoid that mongoose'; that a basking lizard never rationalizes its enjoyment of the sun; that a sick cat neither feels woebegone nor consciously takes steps to improve its condition and its outlook on life. Yet when each of us humans hunts, or weeds, or seeks shelter, there is usually more than instinctive thought at work. We are probably the only creatures on Earth for whom the 'thoughts' required for survival can be mainly taken for granted, and who therefore continuously ponder other matters, to keep our brains in trim.

The subject of this book is this latter kind of thought – not what we use to survive, but what we think about while we are surviving, a process spurred by curiosity and communication. In a characteristic pattern, human thoughts usually begin with the observation of some phenomenon around us, and with questions about it. These are the start of an ever-expanding web of thought which spreads both in our own minds and in those of everyone we share it with. These edifices of thought are built not solely on the millions of facts we have inside our own heads, but also on the ideas and knowledge of other people, of our contemporaries, our predecessors and our progeny. In any given area of thought, growth is exponential: the analogy is not with a continuous line but with the unceasing division of cells in a growing organism. Some humans, in the fields of religion and science especially, like to believe that there is such a thing as absolute truth – and therefore, potentially at least, 'absolute' knowledge. But, as the history of human thought shows, every attempt to establish or declare an absolute is merely a staging post, one fixed point on a continuous intellectual journey.

An excellent example of the 'net' development of human thought is our attitude to (what we call) the supernatural. In origin, the idea of supernatural beings and powers is a straightforward solution to – or evasion of – some of the more complex questions of everyday life. It is a projection on to the unknown of the phenomena and behaviour we observe around us, and verify by experience. Thus, for example, the natures of Light and Dark are analogized with beings or forces in observed life, and their relationship (for so we perceive it to be) is imagined as opposition, a cosmic version of the observed opposition in the natural world between different creatures, or (more subtly) between different sides of the same creature.

Such simple ideas lead to the imagination of a vast hierarchy of supernatural beings and powers, and to the idea that human beings can have relationships with them modelled on those we construct in the natural world. Over time, ideas and attitudes accumulate about matters both tangible and intangible; processes of invention, abstraction and dogmatization may take over, leading to enormous systems of tradition, custom, philosophy and convention. These edifices, in turn, become 'what we know', and new ideas are constantly built on them, until they become so tangled with what we perceive to be the nature of human beings that it requires immense mental effort to imagine our species prised free of them, innocent of the assumptions and heedless of the artefacts and attitudes to which they have given birth. The end of the whole matter (so far) is a kind of benign intellectual bumble, in which the portion of the human race which believes in the supernatural tolerates the rest of the species, and vice versa. A Martian observer might find it astonishing that there are adherents of religion who nevertheless accept the discoveries of science, and scientists who are devout religious believers. But that is the case: the glories resulting from human thought in general, and about the supernatural in particular, were not achieved without the frequent, willing suspension not so much of disbelief as of logic.

At first glance, the scientific paradigm seems more rigorous. We have rationalized not the universe but the way we examine it; we have invented systems which provide (what seem to us to be) objective correlatives for thought itself. Deduction, induction, the experimental method, are triumphs of the human reasoning process, and for some who use them their appeal is even enhanced by the millennia-long opposition shown to them by those whose view of the world depends less on the application of logic than on the acceptance of authority. It may not be a 'scientific' attitude that nothing firms up conviction faster than opposition, but it is an attitude of many scientists.

The main difficulty in all this is that the universe keeps seeming to confound the rules we devise to explain it. It has, for example, been a view for 400 years or so that the 'laws' of the universe, after many wrong assumptions, are at last being properly discovered and codified, and that they are immutable – and no sooner is the idea established than new discoveries are made which challenge those laws. Scientists might claim that what is happening is not so much redefinition of the laws as refinement, that although we may veer now and then off course, the course is still a true one. In this world-view Boyle's chemistry in the 17th century was an 'advance' on alchemy, and meant that scientists never need again take account of alchemy. In the same way, modern medical knowledge renders obsolete many of the attitudes and practices of the past. But here again the universe seems to think otherwise. The more we discover about the nature of (say) carbon, the more we realize that the alchemists, for all their crude methodology and limited powers of expression, were aware of secrets we are only just rediscovering. Medicine, similarly, is so full of ideas and practices which are (a) hallowed by time, (b) outside modern 'scientific' medical logic, and (c) successful, that the whole idea of medicine as a rational science – rather than, say, an impressionistic and pragmatic system – is seriously undermined.

One of the most fascinating subjects for human curiosity has always been the human race itself: our nature as a species, ourselves as individuals, our neighbours, our forebears. The attempt to bring 'scientific' order to bear on the contemplation of such matters as how we think, what our emotions are, how we organize our societies and (in some cases) what we should do or think next has brought an entirely new dimension to human thought; 'new' disciplines, from anthropology to linguistics, from psychology to sociology, far more than such 'pure' sciences as genetics or particle physics, are creators and symbols of the 'modern' age we live in. Such disciplines lie on the interface between impression and experiment; they are human thought in a particularly creative and egregious form.

There remain the arts: the category of thought which some regard as the finest intellectual achievement of the species and others consider little more than a superb irrelevance, the category which feeds off all the others and seems to give little back, which is concerned not with reason but with imagination, which puts human wilfulness, playfulness, appreciation of beauty, in short emotion, right at the heart of every explanation and every prescription. When I invent a myth, carve a statue, write a poem or compose a string quartet, I am not abdicating from rigorous thought, I am concentrating it. The arts depend on selection and presentation, and part of their success is their controlled allusiveness, the way they show us one thing and invite us to remember and speculate about a hundred others. They are not the most subjective of all forms of thought, but they are the most overtly subjective. They hand the intellectual and emotional initiative right back to the spectators, invite us to put ourselves into the experience, to discover or develop attitude. When I look at a waterfall, my feelings are different from those when I hear a song about the same waterfall – and the reason is that, in the song, other human ideas have entered the equation, that communication with other people is modulating my thoughts about the waterfall even as I think them. This introduction began by conjuring up the nimbus of allusion, memory and association which accompanies every human thought and activity – and that nimbus, that evasive, ironic, suggestive and most demanding area of experience, is the province of the arts more than of any other kind of human thought.

There are shelves of books which survey this or that area of human thought – dictionaries of terms, glossaries of techniques, encyclopedias of specialisms, taxonomies of jargon. This guide attempts a different task. Our intention is to be not encyclopedic or dogmatic, but to show the networks of thought which govern our activities. We asked experts in the main disciplines first to select and then to write about the ideas in their fields which they considered of primary importance and influence, now and in the past. The thousands of entries in this book, then, are the distillation and presentation of their thoughts on human thought. This focus on idea and influence inevitably meant that *Key Ideas* had to ignore details of the practical applications, techniques or technologies. Some disciplines, such as linguistics and mathematics, lent themselves to the explication of -isms and -ologies, others to descriptions not so much of thoughts themselves as of a consensus about certain phenomena or areas of human experience. We cast our net wide, and left it wide-meshed. What escaped is in other books; what remains is an exploration of the sorts of concerns human beings have had in the whole course of their intellectual history, of how we got where we are, intellectually speaking, and – in an entirely open-ended way – of where we currently stand. The many cross-references in the book not only make essential links but also open up new avenues of ideas and thought. *Key Ideas* is a book in which connections are vital, in which the river matters more than each and every tributary.

My thanks, as editor, go first to my fellow-contributors. Their names appear in the front and in brief biographies at the back of the book; initials in the text indicate who took primary responsibility for each article. Kathy Rooney conceived the project in the first place, and guided it through the initial stages of planning and shaping. Gill Paul oversaw the physical progress of the book, collating the commissions as they went out and the work as it came in – an enormous task. Sam Merrell, as copy-editor, turned several dozen individual piles of paper, and the same number of computer discs (often in mutually incompatible systems – one of the major irritants in the making of modern reference books) into the single entity that is this book. To all of them, and to everyone else involved, my warmest thanks.

Kenneth McLeish

BIOGRAPHIES OF CONTRIBUTORS

EDITOR

Kenneth McLeish. MA, BMus (Oxford University). Author and theatre translator. Books (over 80) include *The Good Reading Guide, Companion to the Arts in the Twentieth Century, Shakespeare's Characters A-Z.* Translations include Aeschylus (all; with Frederic Raphael), Aristophanes (all), Euripides, Ibsen, Jarry, Feydeau, Labiche, Sophocles, Strindberg

CONTRIBUTORS

Andrew Adams. BEng in Electrical and Electronic Engineering, Strathclyde University.

Davina A. Allen. RGN, Addenbrookes Hospital, Cambridge. BA, Nottingham University. Nurse and Sociologist.

Richard Burchmore. BSc, PhD, AKC, King's College, London. Postdoctoral researcher in parasitology.

Bernadette Casey. BSc, MA, PhD. Head of Media Studies, College of St Mark & St John, Plymouth.

Neil Casey. BA, PhD. Head of Sociology, College of St Mark & St John, Plymouth.

Andrew Cruden. BENG, MSc, AMIEE, University of Strathclyde. Current research: Optical Sensors applied to electrical power system measurement.

Paul Duro. Lecturer in art history, Australian National University, Canberra. Joint author (with Michael Greenhalgh) of *Essential Art History*.

Teresa Fallon. BA, Leyola University, MA, University of Chicago. Current research: economics and politics of energy.

Tim Gordon. BSc, MB, BCh, University of Witwatersrand, London University, Rockefeller University. Head of Drug Metabolism Research unit; Medical Research Council (Headquarters Office).

Rob Graham. BA, MA. Head of Film & Television Studies, West London Institute of Higher Education.

Michael Greenhalgh. Professor of Art History, Australian National University, Canberra. Books include *The Classical Tradition in Art, Donatello and His Sources*, and the *Survival of Roman Antiquities in the Middle Ages*, with Paul Duro *Essential Art History*.

Trevor R Griffiths. BA, MA, PhD, (Warwick). Director of Media and Interdisciplinary Studies, University of North London. Books include *Stagecraft, Theatre Guide* (with Carole Woddis), *British and Irish Women Dramatists Since 1958* (with Margaret Llewellyn-Jones).

Andrew Jack. BA, BPhil, DPhil (London and Oxford). Visiting Lecturer in philosophy at King's College, London.

E M Jackson. BA, PhD, Birmingham University. Lecturer in Religious Studies, St Martin's College, Lancaster. Editor of *God's Apprentice: the autobiography of Bishop Stephen Neill* and *Unfinished Agenda: the autobiography of Leslie Newbigin*.

Jessica James. BSc, Victoria University of Manchester, in Physics. Current research: Theoretical Atomic Physics. Grateful thanks are due to the Institute for Nuclear Theory, Seattle, where she was working while the entries were written.

Margaret Johnstone. BA (philosophy) (Warwick); BPhil Social and Cultural Studies, Chelsea College, London University. Psychotherapist and writer.

Raminder Kaur. BA, Social Anthropology with Art and Archaeology, School of Oriental and African Studies, London.

Tania Krzywinska. MA in Modern Drama and Film, North London

University. Current research: Cinematic Hard Core Pornography.

Cassandra Lorius. BA, Social Anthropology, School of Oriental and African Studies, London. Journalist, writer and documentary researcher.

Alexandra J MacDermott. MA, DPhil, Somerville College, Oxford. Senior Lecturer in Physical Chemistry, Oxford Brookes University, and Lecturer in Physical Chemistry, St. Anne's College, Oxford.

Catherine McDermott. Teaches design history at Kingston University. Publications include: *Street Style*, *Essential Design*.

Simon McLeish. BA (mathematics) (Oxford), PhD (University of London). Current research: mathematical logic at Queen Mary and Westfield College, University of London.

Rabbi Rachel Montagu. Educated Newnham College, Cambridge and Leo Baeck College, London. Minister of Cardiff New Synagogue; assistant minister of the North Western Reform Synagogue.

Jeremy Musson. M.Phil, Warburg Institute London. Architectural Historian with special interest in 18th century and 19th century British art and architecture. Currently working for the Historic Buildings Department of The National Trust.

Brendan O'Leary. BA (politics, philosophy, economics), Oxford, PhD (economics), LSE. Reader in Political Science & Public Administration at LSE. Political scientist, lecturer and broadcaster. Books include *Theories of the State*, *The Asiatic Mode of Production*, *The Future of Northern Ireland*, *The Politics of Antagonism: Understanding Northern Ireland, and The Politics of Ethnic Conflict Regulation*.

Eur. Ing. Professor John P. Paul. BSc, ARCST, PhD, F Eng, FRSE.

Bioengineering Unit, University of Strathclyde, Glasgow.

Ornan Rotem. BA (Bristol), lecturer in the Department of Religious Studies, University of Bristol.

Philip Sarre. BSc (Southampton) MA (California), PhD (Bristol). Senior Lecturer in Geography, The Open University. Books include *The Changing Social Structure, Environment and Society* and *One World for one Earth!*

Matthew Saxton. MA, MSc, Edinburgh University. Current research: psycholinguistics. Lecturer in Psychology, Royal Holloway, University of London.

Dr John Shepherd. Educated at the Universities of Leeds and Lancaster. Current research: contemporary Islam and comparative religious ethics. Principal Lecturer, Dept of Social Ethics, St Martin's College, Lancaster

Sue Smith. BA (Reading). Subject Tutor, Theatre Studies, University of North London. Research interests in feminist theatre theories and practice. Publications include articles in *Studies in Theatre Production* and *Contemporary Theatre Review* (both with Lib Taylor).

Steve Stanton. BA, DPhil (York), ARCM. Ethnomusicologist and composer. Senior Lecturer in Music, City University, London.

Klaus-Dieter Stoll. Educated at the Gynasium Philippinum, Weilburg FRG and the University of Heidelberg. Editor and translator.

Elizabeth Stuart. BA, DPhil (Oxford), Diploma in Pastoral Care. Senior Lecturer in Theology at College of St Mark & St John, Plymouth.

Rosemarie Wedell. Read theology, lecturer at the Department of Comparative Religion, Manchester University; taught World Religions at Manchester College of Adult Education.

A

A PRIORI AND A POSTERIORI

A statement is a priori (Latin, literally 'from the former') just if it can be known to be true or false independently of experience. 'Two plus two is four' is a priori because it can be known to be true independently of experience.

A statement is a posteriori (Latin, literally 'from the latter') just if it cannot be known to be true or false independently of experience. 'The cat is on the mat' is a posteriori because it cannot be known to be true or false independently of experience. One can establish whether it is true or false only by having certain experiences, such as the experiences involved in looking at the cat and the mat. **AJ**

See also epistemology; rigid and non-rigid designators.

Further reading J. Dancy, *An Introduction to Contemporary Epistemology*; P. Moser, *A priori Knowledge*.

ABIOGENESIS

Abiogenesis (Greek, 'birth from the inorganic', i.e. spontaneous generation) is an ancient explanation for the origin of life, supported by superficial observation of events such as the emergence of maggots from rotting meat or the appearance of mice near a piece of old cheese. The idea that life arose, and continues to arise, spontaneously in mud was proposed by the Greek philosopher Anaximander (6th century BCE), who suggested that a spiny fish had been the first animal to emerge onto the land and had given rise to other animals by the process of transmutation (change of form).

This basic concept was recapitulated in a variety of forms (the 9th-century Arab biologist al-Jahic refers to the spontaneous generation of life in mud in his *Book of Animals*) until the 17th century when William Harvey, through his work on deer embryos, proposed that 'everything comes from the egg' in 1651. This was followed by the Italian physician Francesco Redi's demonstration, in 1668, that meat which was shielded from flies bore no maggots. It began to be accepted that higher organisms could not appear by spontaneous generation but the discovery of *animalcules* (microorganisms) by the early microscopist Antonie van Leeuwenhoek revived the theory. It was left to Louis Pasteur to resolve the problem in response to a challenge from the French Academy of Science in 1860. Pasteur showed that a sterile medium capable of supporting the growth of microorganisms remained sterile unless seeded with microorganisms.

Although Pasteur hammered some of the final nails into the coffin of spontaneous generation, the question of how the first living organism arose (**biopoiesis**) was not seriously considered until the 20th century. **RB**

See also biogenesis; germ plasm.

Further reading Paul Thompson, *Abiogenesis*.

ABSOLUTE

Philosophers often contrast objective reality and subjective appearances – how things seem from different points of view and how things really are. For example, one can contrast how the rock really is, independently of any subjective point of view, and the different ways it appears through a fish's eyes and through human eyes. In this context, the absolute is usually taken to mean the totality of objective reality, which transcends all subjective points of view upon it. **AJ**

See also objective and subjective.

Further reading B.Russell, *History of Western Philosophy*.

ABSOLUTE ADVANTAGE

Absolute advantage, in **economics**, is a concept of trade in which one country can produce a quantity of a product more efficiently (that is, with fewer resources of labour, land, and/or capital) than another country.

For example, in 1981, Japan produced a ton of steel with only 9.4 man-hours at a cost of only $502, compared with 16.5 man-hours and $622 in the UK. However, this statistic does not carry the implication that Japan should specialize in steel and the UK should not, because Japan might be even better relative to the UK at other things. The real guide to specialization and to maximizing the gains from trade is **comparative advantage**. Not only that, but neither absolute nor comparative advantage are necessarily static for all time: once, UK steel producers were more efficient than the Japanese. **TF**

Further reading Alfred D. Chandler, *The Dynamics of Industrial Capitalism*; Michael E. Porter, *The Competitive Advantage of Nations*.

ABSOLUTE MUSIC

Absolute music is music that exists simply for its own intellectual and emotional sake, for example, fugues, sonatas and symphonies (unless they have declared 'programmes'). Unlike **programme music**, it has no external references. By its nature, absolute music tends to be instrumental, or for voices making non-verbal sounds. However, some instrumental music, such as Indian classical music, is not 'absolute', because the melodic and rhythmic shapes on which the players improvise have recognized conventional associations. **KMcL**

ABSOLUTISM

Absolutism is rule not limited by any formal constraint, legal, constitutional or conventional; its power is unchecked, and its 'laws' are the commands of the ruler (the sovereign) who is not subject to law. Absolutism is necessarily an ideal, as no ruler ever fully controls all his or her subjects.

The theory of absolutism was embraced by the monarchs of early modern Europe who crushed aristocratic (political) and Roman Catholic (religious) constraints on their power. It was first articulated by the French thinker Jean Bodin, and the English philosopher Thomas Hobbes. They thought absolute government was not only preferable to **feudalism** but was also the only way to avoid the violence characteristic of human beings in 'a state of nature'. They believed that **sovereignty** must be centralized in the hands of the monarch. Absolutism was necessary for civilization.

Absolutist monarchy was condemned by its critics as merely despotic (see **despotism**). Absolutist régimes were found in **agrarian societies**, and today régimes with similar features are usually described as **authoritarian**. **BO'L**

Further reading Perry Anderson, *Lineages of the Absolutist State*; Thomas Hobbes, *Leviathan* (1651).

ABSTRACT ALGEBRA see Algebra

ABSTRACT DANCE

Abstract dance was the name of a specific style of **ballet**, devised in the 1920s and developed at the **Bauhaus**. Its aim was to remove from dance any external associations, so that the dancers could concentrate on pure movement and pure pattern. (Other dancers and choreographers, from Isadora Duncan and Martha Graham onwards, have used terms like 'expressive dance', 'free dance' and 'new artistic dance' to describe the same phenomenon.) In the wider sense, a great deal of dance is 'abstract'. Ballroom dancing, for example, is concerned with the pleasure the movement and pattern-making give to the dancers, and not with some external 'programme'. The main kinds of representational (that is, non-abstract) dance are religious dance, for example in India and Indonesia, and ballet – although, even with these abstraction is common, for example in the dancing of the Whirling Dervishes, or in modern ballet from Balanchine to Ailey, from Tetley to Bausch. **KMcL**

ABSTRACT EXPRESSIONISM

Abstract Expressionism was a term used by critics of Fine Art to describe a heterogeneous group of painters working in the late 1940s and early 1950s, loosely synonymous with the 'New York School'. The name 'abstract expressionism' had first been used in connection with Kandinsky's abstract painting of the 1920s, and indicates the movement's interest in personal expression as opposed to the dominant geometric abstraction descended from **Neoplasticism** and **Constructivism**. It is this alone that allows artists of such widely divergent styles to be grouped together. They may, however, be subdivided into the lyrical abstraction, colour field paintings of Robert Motherwell, Barnett Newman, Ad Reinhardt and Mark Rothko; the all-over, drip paintings of Jackson Pollock (which the critic Harold Rosenberg called 'action painting'); and the figurative expressionism of Willem de Kooning and Hans Hofmann. The critic Clement Greenberg coined the term 'American-style painting' to describe these trends. The movement quickly won acceptance and placed American art on a forward footing, enabling the US to dictate the terms of the modernist debate. **MG PD**

ABSTRACTION

Abstraction, the action of divorcing properties of physical objects from the objects themselves, is a fundamental concept, perhaps *the* fundamental concept, in **mathematics**. It marks off the beginning of mathematics from what went before. The discoverer of abstraction was the person who first realized that numbers are independent of the objects being counted, that two oranges and two apples (for instance) share a property, 'twoness', which is independent of what kinds of fruit they are. Ever since this discovery, abstraction has been a major theme in the development of mathematics, as those interested in the field have come up with ideas further and further divorced from their basis in the real world, and then sought ways to bring them back to tell us things about the real world which we might otherwise not have known.

Using abstraction, it is possible to reason directly about properties that hold in general; without abstraction, thought is limited to the particular. Intelligence itself has been linked by many to the ability to perform abstractions; the power of reasoning about the general by abstraction from the specific is the foundation of intellectual progress. Once, for example, the property of 'twoness' is isolated from the particular objects having that property, it becomes possible to determine properties of all objects having 'twoness' – such as the fact that two pairs taken together always

give a quartet – and to have such a thought, though infants can do it, is a highly sophisticated mental process.

Mathematics takes such thought-processes to lengths unimagined in ordinary life: indeed, mathematicians are often more interested in the abstraction itself than in any applications. The power of mathematics to abstract essential properties from the real world gives it its generality, and its power in its application to scientific problems. Without it, scientists would be unable to use mathematics to examine properties of the universe around them. (It is, of course, questionable whether a mathematics which was totally unrelated to the real world could ever have developed.) Each branch of the discipline is itself the product of abstraction: **geometry**, for example, is an abstraction of the calculations used in building and surveying. There are even branches of mathematics which are abstractions of other branches of mathematics: **category theory**, for example, is an abstraction of general properties of the objects studied in **algebra**.

Abstraction of a slightly different kind is a fundamental process in both **fine art** and **folk art**. It takes two main forms. In the first, the artist makes images which refer not to the visible world but to his or her own fancy. Typical examples are the whorls or zig-zags which adorn early pottery, or the rows and geometrical shapes made from beads which decorate Amerindian clothing. The appeal of such patterns lies in symmetry and repetition on the one hand, and on the other of interruptions in such symmetry. In fine art, main styles (of painting in particular) which use similar techniques are **Abstract Expressionism**, Geometric Abstraction, **Neoplasticism**, **Suprematism** and **Tachism**; the style is also a major feature of functional art and **design** throughout the world.

In the second kind of abstraction in art, the creator 'abstracts' images from the visible world, making (for example) the shapes of crosses, flower heads, hooks, leaves, pebbles and so on the basis for abstract patterns. The appeal here is two-fold: intellectual (appreciation of the pattern-making itself, as with the first kind of abstraction) and emotional (pleasure or challenge derived from the 'abstraction' of objects which still have a recognizable correlative, and non-artistic 'meaning', in the visible world.) This style is once again common in folk art – totemic art is a notable example – and in fine art is characteristic of those modernist movements which seek to break with the pictorial conventions of earlier art: examples are **Cubism**, **Expressionism**, **Fauvism** and **Futurism**. PD MG AJ KMcL SMcL

See also applicability of mathematics; artificial intelligence; scientific method; thought.

ABUSE see Child Abuse

ACADEME

Academe is named after a park in ancient Athens, sacred to the legendary figure Akademos. In the early 4th century BCE, Plato set up a teaching establishment there, to educate aristocratic students in **philosophy**, **politics** and **science** before they began careers in government. The school lasted for some 800 years, and was known not only for its teaching, but as a repository of intellectual knowledge, as the source of influential commentaries on the ideas of the past and as what we might nowadays call a 'think tank'.

All these functions have remained those of academe at large, right down to the present day. The great universities, from Isfahan to Oxford, from Peking to Wittenberg, from Alexandria to Harvard, have also been important physical collections of knowledge: the libraries at Isfahan and Alexandria, especially, were regarded in their time as containing all available human knowledge, and their collections (though vandalized and dispersed) are still the foundation of our written texts of the ancient past. Such universities were also important because they were, in theory at least, independent of religious or political bias. They may have been funded by princes and governments, and they may have been staffed by people of particular religious persuasions, but the central idea was never lost that intellectual thought

must, of its nature, stand aside from the pressures of the world or of faith, that it must be dispassionate and available to all.

From earliest times, the academic desire to remain uncontaminated was similar to one of the central ideas of religious **monasticism**. The monastics believed that true knowledge and worship of the divine could best be achieved in seclusion, by minds and spirits set free from the claims of everyday existence. In all the major faiths there was a strong sense that if a group of people removed themselves from the world and devoted their time to contemplation, prayer and spiritual exercises, they would engender a kind of pious intensity of feeling and understanding which would transcend ordinary perception. Augustine spoke of meditation in a *hortus conclusus*, 'enclosed garden' – the origin of cloisters; Persian scholars similarly believed that beautiful surroundings enhanced meditation, and worked in formal, peaceful gardens; Buddha advocated meditation every day in the same, quiet spot. Since, in the ancient world, the first entry to education was often through these monasteries, there came to be a blend or a confusion between such monastic ideals and those of academe. In some cases, the same people were both monks and academics; in all cases, the idea (shared by both traditions) that seclusion and intellectual exercise would lead to concentration, and thence to truer understanding, became a dangerous but guiding principle. Whether they realized it or not, academics became prey to two delusions: that the excellence of their studies somehow extended to their institutions or to themselves as people, lifting them above the common herd; and that intellectual activity and excellence were inadmissible or to be scorned if performed outside university walls.

There is, or was, perhaps some truth in this. Access to libraries, to precedent and to other like minds gave scholars of the ancient universities a start on their non-academic fellow-beings, and very often the separation of the learned from ordinary society allowed them, precisely, the opportunity to extend their research beyond the commonplace. In ancient Babylon, China and the Indus valley, for example, research into predicting and interpreting the movement of heavenly bodies, originally undertaken to facilitate the **astrological** systems required by religion or state, led to completely unrelated astronomical and mathematical discoveries, the foundation of all our present knowledge. Codes of behaviour, originally devised by practical people for common use, were elaborated by academics into huge (and, it must be admitted, self-regenerating) intellectual edifices, of which **Judaic** rabbinical lore and the **Islamic** *shari'a* are notable surviving examples, exploring such concepts as guilt and justice far beyond everyday concerns. 'Secret' studies (often punishable by death if pursued in society) led to advances in such subjects as **medicine**, and to the survival of knowledge and texts of which the religious or political authorities disapproved.

By the late Middle Ages, seclusion and self-satisfaction had led to the almost total ossification of academic study. Precedent and authority were what mattered; learning was a private fiefdom, and admittance was reserved for those willing to 'think like us'. In some areas of academe, this foolish and destructive attitude has persisted to the present day, and has resulted in the marginalizing, to a point near death, of what were once major areas of study. But by and large the rise, in the last 300 years, of rational science, mass education and universal literacy have had a magnificently cathartic effect, sweeping out the cobwebs of **scholasticism** and returning the open-mindedness and curiosity which were once academe's most crucial attributes. (That scientific academics, in some communities, have tended to become an exclusive, self-declared and self-protective élite just like any other is a deplorable, and hopefully transitory, phenomenon.) Despite the efforts of politicians, and (it must be said) of the dons in some university departments, human thought has once again, become universally available. It may be done more systematically, more skilfully and more comfortably in specialized institutions, but by and large it is once again, as it was when Plato started organizing discussion-groups in the Academy, accessible to anyone who has a brain. **KMcL**

ACADEMIES OF WESTERN ART

Towards the end of the 16th century, groups of European painters and sculptors, dissatisfied with the venality and artisanal aspects of the guild system, joined together into academies of art which sought to promote the intellectual and creative aspects of producing art over that of their craft-based predecessors. The aim was to capitalize on the rising status of the artist as the exponent of a liberal art. The first artists' academy (as opposed to the gathering of dilettanti, antiquarians and amateurs also called academies), was established in 1563 in Florence by the artist and historiographer Giorgio Vasari under the patronage of Cosimo de'Medici and with Michelangelo at its head. Other cities soon followed Florence's example, a notable case being Rome, where the Academy of St Luke was founded in 1593 with Frederico Zuccaro as its president. In France, the Académie royale de peinture et de sculpture was founded in 1648 around the ambitious and politically astute Charles Le Brun, who enlisted the royal support which was to make this academy the envy of Europe. In the 18th century, academies were established in, among other cities, Berlin (1696), Bologna (1709), Dresden (1750) and London (1768).

Wherever possible, the academies attempted to distance their own work from that of the guilds. They affected to despise the guilds as corrupt and self-seeking, and claimed that they stifled enterprise, freedom of choice and the rational order of creating art into precepts and rules open to the exercise of the intellect. To counter these perceived failings, the academy schools taught their students 'fine art' – which meant, primarily, not the practice of painting or sculpture but the theoretical aspects of anatomy, history and geometry. Students were taught **drawing** but not painting, as drawing was seen to be further removed from the manual application of paint reminiscent of the guilds.

Under state control for the most part, academies institutionalized art through competitions, exhibitions, lectures, discussions and treatises. The purpose of all this activity, which ultimately militated against the progress of the fine arts, was to show that painting and sculpture were worthy candidates for inclusion among the liberal arts. To the same end only history painting was regarded as an appropriate genre for the academic painter to practise. Thus a circular justification, that academic art needed an academy to defend its interests, while the academy would claim its *raison d'être* was to provide a fertile environment to train history painters, led academic painters into sterile, self-absorbed practices little suited to the needs of a changing environment.

By the 19th century the academies were regarded as anachronistic. Certainly they had no answer to the challenge of **Romanticism**, which held that an artist had nothing to learn from rules. In the face of this heresy, the academies reacted by using whatever influence they had to oppose innovation. The result was that in the course of the 19th century the academies declined from a position of considerable respect (in the 18th century, the French Academy welcomed almost all major, contemporary painters) to a position a century later where no significant artist deigned to accept nomination to the academy. In this climate, the academics were seen as offering little more than a certain kind of technical training, but none of the theoretical or intellectual leadership by which they had set such store two centuries earlier. **MG PD**

ACCOMMODATION THEORY

The accommodation theory, in **linguistics**, starts from the premise that speech accommodation takes place when people modify their speech so that it conforms more with the way their conversational partner speaks. A wide range of subtle adaptations have been observed, which tend to occur more or less unconsciously. For example, the speed at which people talk, the length of both pauses and utterances, the kind of vocabulary and syntax used, as well as intonation, voice pitch and pronunciation are all subject to the accommodation process.

This kind of convergence is by no means an automatic feature of all conversations, and we can discern certain social contexts in which accommodation can be predicted.

For example, accommodation tends to occur when the speakers like each other. Alternatively, accommodation has been observed when the need to be deferential arises, or when one person wants to put another person at their ease. Consequently, accommodation can be interpreted as a polite speech strategy, designed to convey the impression that the addressee's speech is legitimate and worthy of imitation. Interestingly, accommodation theory reinforces the view that women tend to be more co-operative conversational partners than men, with the finding that women display much more radical speech modifications than men, when switching from a formal interview situation to informal conversation with friends. **MS**

See also anthropological linguistics; ethnography of speaking; sociolinguistics.

ACCOUNTABILITY

Political accountability requires the actions of politicians, or public officials, whether they be administrative, ethical or financial, to be open to inspection, scrutiny and challenge. Political accountability is the hallmark of responsible and **representative government**. Régimes in which rulers cannot be held to account, either by representatives or by judges, are called arbitrary and authoritarian. In parliamentary systems ministers are held to account through oral and written questions – in some cases through 'interpellation', that is, through requiring them to give a detailed response to a question on policy or administration.

Managerial accountability, whether in the public or the private sector, similarly requires that managers be answerable for the tasks which they have contracted to perform, according to agreed standards of competence. Thus financial audits, narrowly construed, ensure that money has been spent as agreed and according to appropriate procedures, whereas efficiency and effective audits investigate whether managers achieve value for money and have developed appropriate programmes to achieve organizational goals. Managers are supposed to be accountable for: expenditure of funds, obeying laws, executing programmes and results. **BO'L**

See also administrative theory; democracy.

Further reading John S. Mill, *Representative Government* (1860).

ACCOUNTING

Accounting is the record of a firm's assets, liabilities and transactions, which reveals (and on occasion disguises) the company's financial state. Historic cost accounting, in which stocks, assets and liabilities are valued at their original cost, was unquestioningly used until the 1970s when rapid **inflation** made this unrealistic. A switch to current cost accounting was opted for by some, but due to the disinflation of 1981-85, historic cost accounting gained new respect.

Today's accounting methods are the result of technical progress of a profoundly important type. The commercial revolution could not begin until some form of rational money accounting had developed. Historically, accounting began as books of business opened on the market table, sometimes no more than notebooks of transaction. Calculations were made largely in Roman numerals, sums were often wrong, long division was considered something of a mystery, and the use of the **zero** was not clearly understood. By the 12th century, Venetians were using sophisticated accounting devices. The merchants in the rest of Europe, by comparison, were little better than schoolboys in their accounting ignorance. It took time for a recognition of the need for book-keeping to spread: not until the 17th century was double entry a standard practice. Only when money was rationally accounted for could large-scale business operations run successfully. **TF**

ACCULTURATION

Acculturation is the process of adoption, by one cultural group, of the customs, traits, **traditions** and **values** of another group with which it has been brought into contact. Studies of acculturation, especially among immigrant communities, usually focus on the effects of novel or different cultural conditions upon the original culture. Acculturation makes political **integration** much easier to accomplish. Acculturation can be distinguished from **assimilation** because it is one-sided: one group adapts its culture to another's, rather than a merger of identities taking place. Before acculturation is fully completed some affected individuals may protest and inaugurate an 'ethnic revival': attempting to revitalize their disappearing culture. **BO'L**

Further reading Nicholas Thomas, *Entangled Objects: Exchange, Material Culture and Colonialism in the Pacific*; Robert Carlson, *The Americanisation Syndrome: a Quest for Conformity*.

ACMEISM

Acmeism (from Greek *akme*, 'point') was a movement in Russian poetry of the 1920s led by the writers Nikolai Gumilev and Sergei Gorodetsky, and followed by Anna Akhmatova and Osip Mandelstam. Their aim was to write about everyday phenomena, and to use words and images for their primary, stripped-down meanings, without metaphor, clogged syntax or other forms of 'poeticizing'. The acmeists were particularly opposed to the mysticism and erotic suggestiveness of **symbolist** writing, and to the experiments of Mayakovsky and the **Surrealists**. The idea of cleansing language, of using words for words' sake alone, has been a recurring feature of poetry, not least in the 20th century (for example in the work of T.S. Eliot and William Carlos Williams); but the acmeists, in a way characteristic of artists in the 1910s, were the only ones to give it a name and a specific agenda. They published a magazine, *Apollo*, from 1909–17, and were denounced by the authorities as decadent and 'individualist': **socialism** demanded **realism** of a rather different kind. **KMcL**

See also socialist realism.

ACTION

We can distinguish between what someone does – their actions – and what merely happens to them. Punching John was an action of Janet's, but falling over was not an action of John's.

Not all bodily movements are actions. If someone else lifts my arm, then the rising of my arm is not an action of mine. A movement of a subject's body is an action only if it is preceded by an appropriate intention of theirs. But it is not enough, for a bodily movement to be an action, that it is preceded by an appropriate intention of theirs. Suppose a doctor asks me to raise my recently paralysed arm, that I intend to raise my arm and that the doctor then raises it. I intended to raise my arm and it rose. But the rising of my arm was not an action of mine, because my intention did not cause my bodily movement. A movement of a subject's body is an action only if it is caused by an appropriate intention of theirs. This is the central claim of the causal theory of action.

Not all actions are bodily movements, and the causal theory of action also applies to mental actions such as imagining and calculating. It is not enough for imagining a teddy bear that one has an image as of a teddy bear. If a hallucinogenic drug causes me to have an image as of a teddy bear, then I have not imagined a teddy bear, since my having the image as of a teddy bear is something that has happened to me, rather than an action of mine. Having an image is an action of mine only if it is preceded by my having an appropriate intention. And if, as a matter of complete coincidence, I intended to imagine a toy just before a hallucinogenic drug caused me to have an image as of a teddy bear, then I have not imagined a teddy bear. A mental event is an action only it is caused by an appropriate intention of the subject's. **AJ**

See also consequentialism; causal theories; freedom and determinism; responsibility and moral luck.

Further reading D. Davidson, *Essays on Actions and Events*; L. Davis, *Theory of Action*.

ACTION PAINTING see Abstract Expressionism

ACTION PERSPECTIVE

The action perspective is a general orienta-

tion to sociological analysis embraced by a number of branches of **sociology**: Weberian sociology, **symbolic interactionism**, and **ethnomethodology**.

Action is distinguished from behaviour by sociologists in that it involves meaning or intention – social activities make sense to those who participate in them. Proponents of this school of social thought believe social reality to be the product of the purposive, meaningful actions of societal members. The aims of sociological analysis, it is argued, should be to discover the meanings that those being studied give to their activities, and then to provide explanations for such social reality based on these meanings. A contrasting orientation to sociological analysis is **positivism**, which emphasizes the importance of social **structure** over individual action, and seeks to provide causal explanations of social reality which are located outside of individual societal members in the social structure. Meanings have no place in analysis for this school of thought.

All action theorists regard the first step in explanations of social life to be in terms of the meanings and purposes of those studied. There are differences, however, in the extent to which sociologists of this kind believe in the possibility of combining this with other types of complementary explanatory forms that is by reference to the social structure. **DA**

See also exchange; functionalism; generalized other; idiographic; individualism; naturalism; phenomenological sociology; rational choice theory; social construction of reality; social fact; social order; social self; structuralism; structure-agency debate; understanding.

Further reading P.S. Cohen, *Modern Social Theory*; A. Dawe, 'Theories of social action', in T.B. Bottomore and R. Nisbet (eds.), *A History of Sociological Analysis*.

ACTUAL

Philosophers distinguish between actuality and possibility, between how things are and how they might have been. I have short hair but could have let it grow rather than go to the barber's. Since the actual world is one of the ways it might have been, since the actual world is itself a possible world, philosophers more strictly distinguish actuality from non-actual possibility. **AJ**

See also modality.

Further reading D. Lewis, *Counterfactuals*; A. Plantinga, *The Nature of Necessity*.

ADAPTATION

In **biology**, the concept of adaptation (from Latin *ad*, 'towards' + *aptus*, 'fitting') refers to the process by which an organism increases its fitness to its environment, or to the change which increases this fitness. In the 17th and 18th centuries, the observation that organisms were so perfectly suited to life in their natural environment was frequently taken as evidence for the existence of a creator. The theologian William Paley argued, in his work *Natural Theology* (1802), that if a man were to find a watch on a deserted beach, he would naturally assume that such an intricate mechanism had a maker; Paley said that the existence of living creatures was, in the same way, evidence for the existence of God. Charles Darwin suggested instead that living organisms were not perfectly designed but were merely attempting to survive in a rapidly changing environment.

Adaptation is the process by which a species is modified, by **natural selection**, to fit an ecological **niche**. All living organisms are subject to natural selection, and as the environment is not stable, all species must be in a state of dynamic equilibrium caused by continuous pressure to adapt and become more competitive. All the inherited characteristics of a living organism are subject to this adaptation. If, for example, bacteria are grown in the laboratory in the presence of sub-lethal but inhibitory concentrations of an antibiotic, the organisms can be induced to undergo adaptation to produce individuals which are resistant to the effects of the antibiotic, and are thus more competitive than their predecessors. **RB**

See also adaptive radiation; Darwinism; evolution.

Further reading Richard Dawkins, *The Selfish Gene*; *The Blind Watchmaker*.

ADAPTIVE RADIATION

Adaptive radiation, in the **life sciences**, refers to the differentiation (or anagenesis) of one or a few species into many to fill a large number of related ecological **niches** by **adaptation**. Typically, a species adapts to colonize a new habitat and, this adaptation opening up a new range of niches, adapts again to fill the new niches which are presented. Thus the first bird species may have given rise to many more bird species by adaptive radiation. Fossil evidence suggests that the mammals underwent adaptive radiation to produce the range of mammal types extant today. **RB**

See also evolution; homology.

ADDITIVE RHYTHM

Additive rhythm is much used in folk music, especially in Africa and Eastern Europe, and has been standard in Western concert music since the beginning of this century. In music using non-additive rhythm, or 'divisive rhythm' (which is the most common form used in Western music) the rhythm is the product of binary or ternary divisions of a larger unit of time. (A waltz, for example, makes rhythmic patterns based on groups of three equal beats repeated regularly, with the main accent on the first beat; in 'common time', the main accent occurs on the first of every four equal divisions or beats.) In additive rhythm, by contrast, instead of large time-units being subdivided into regular beats, the beat, metre and melodic rhythm are all fashioned from multiples of the smallest unit.

One result of this aggregative procedure is that the beats need not be of equal length. In the Balkan regions in particular, rhythmic and metric patterns are often asymmetrical, comprising different combinations of binary and ternary multiples of a the basic small unit. In Bulgaria, for example, *paidushka* contains five basic units, with two stresses, in the ratio [2 + 3]; *rachenitsa* has seven units [2 + 2 + 3], and *gankino khoro* has eleven [2 + 2 + 3 + 2 + 2].

Combinations of these asymmetrical patterns also occur and are described as 'additive metres'. A typical example of such a pattern might be a repeated sequence of fourteen units, functioning as an aggregate of two accented patterns of five and nine units $[2+3]+[2+2+2+3]$.

The effect of additive rhythm on the ear is of a kind of organized anarchy, a rhythmic delirium. Folk players, trained in the method, find it easy to perform, but it can cause problems for classically-trained instrumentalists. In the Western concert tradition, therefore, additive-rhythm music is usually notated with constantly changing time signatures. A typical sequence of bars from the *Danse sacrale* which ends Stravinsky's *The Rite of Spring*, for example, has the time signatures $[2/16+3/16+3/16+2/8+3/16+3/16+5/16$ etc.]: that is, taking sixteenth-notes as the basic units for aggregation, a sequence of $[2+3+3+4+3+5]$. With practice, this kind of thing ceases to pose problems – and orchestras once had difficulty with the (non-additive, 'divisive') 'waltz' rhythms in Tchaikovsky's Sixth Symphony: a sequence of 5-beat bars instead of 3. **KMcL SSt**

ADLERIAN THOUGHT see **Individual Psychology**; **Inferiority Complex**; **Masculine Protest**

ADMINISTRATIVE DOCTRINES

Administrative doctrines are bodies of ideas which provide specific maxims about administrative 'whos, hows, and whats'. A simple example of an administrative maxim is the assertion that every member of the organization should wear the same uniform; another is the idea that pay should be related to seniority.

Administrative doctrines have developed both as cause and consequence of increasing organizational complexity: and many of them have their historical antecedents in the agararian empires. In contemporary Western civilizations, administrative doctrines usually cluster in distinct sets. The doctrines are often based on idealized conceptions of archetypal organizations, such as armies, businesses, religious communities, or democracies.

Administrative doctrines, according to Christopher Hood and Michael Jackson, are rarely neatly related to political beliefs or ideologies. For example, conservatives, liberals and socialists sometimes prescribe centralizing doctrines, albeit for different activities, and both conservatives and communists may organize their political parties like clans or churches of true believers. **BO'L**

See also administrative theory.

Further reading Christopher Hood and Michael Jackson, *Administrative Argument*.

ADMINISTRATIVE THEORY

Administrative theory should be distinguished from **administrative doctrines**. Administrative theory encompasses a wide variety of ideas about how organizations should be run, especially public administration. Administrative theorists develop explanatory and normative accounts of the roles **bureaucracies** do and should play in our social systems.

Classical administrative theory emphasized that bureaucracies should be organized according to the functional or purpose principle, and in clear scalar hierarchies which would facilitate political **accountability**. This idea was developed by the German sociologist Max Weber (1864–1920), who argued that modern or rational bureaucracies, as opposed to traditional or patrimonial bureaucracies, were distinguished by a clear hierarchical division of offices, impersonality in recruitment and procedure, continuity in form and files, and the primacy of functional expertise. These features guaranteed efficiency and inhibited corruption.

Recent administrative theorists have criticized the classical and Weberian defence of 'machine models of bureaucracy'. **Marxists** and **élite theorists** maintain that Weberian bureaucracies are agencies of domination and inhibit a more thoroughgoing democratization of society. Public choice critics argue that classical bureaux will be captured and bent to the will of 'budget-maximizing bureaucrats'; that bureaux should be exposed to competition from private sector agencies; and that the 'contracting-out' of public functions may be necessary to ensure efficient administration.

Organization theorists suggest that classical or 'line bureaucracies' are unsuited for turbulent and uncertain environments, and that professional organizations of a more collegial kind are essential for certain kinds of administrative task. **BO'L**

See also pluralism.

Further reading Patrick Dunleavy, *Democracy, Bureaucracy and Public Choice*; Stephen Robbins, *Organization Theory*.

ADVERTISING

Advertising was conceived essentially as a kind of social, consumer rhetoric: a way of publicly praising goods in order to encourage or persuade the public to use or buy them. It has clearly done much good by bringing many useful inventions, ideas and by-products of major research programmes to a wide number of people. But to say that this is still all it does would be too superficial. Advertising is arguably a main vehicle of social communication; and as such it has become the subject of much critical comment and even concern. When a **semiotic** analysis is applied to its products several other 'texts' often emerge which have little (or sometimes nothing) to do with the product being promoted. Judith Williamson, in *Decoding Advertisements* (1987), says that 'advertisements are one of the most important cultural factors moulding and reflecting our life today' and that '... in providing us with a structure in which we, and [the] goods are interchangeable, [advertisements] are selling us ourselves'. People are persuaded to identify themselves with what they consume. Advertisers sell dreams, ideal images and ways of life and values. The consumerist values and human images which advertising perpetually reinforces are simple stereotypes. It is pervasive and ubiquitous and that, in part, gives it its enormous power. Once, advertisers were associated only with promoting goods, skills or certain professional abilities. Now, they shape our political fortunes by running such things as election campaigns (see public relations below).

In addition it could be said that all forms of mass **media** rely on advertising for their existence. Newspapers have gone out of business through not being sufficiently attractive to advertisers (for example *The Daily Herald* in the UK in the 1960s). Advertising takes many forms, not all of them directly associated with selling a product. For example, governments 'advertise' that cigarettes are a health hazard. In sport and the arts a major development in recent years has been sponsorship. At face value this would appear to be a valuable form of support for cultural activities which benefit all people. But it is merely indirect advertising, and there is a danger that the recipients of such sponsorship come to rely on it and must constantly reveal and reflect their commercial allegiance or lose the support. To offer support 'without strings' is perhaps more of an ideal than a commercial reality.

The most pervasive forms of advertising are those which target the mass-consumer audience. Of these, television advertising is perhaps the most prestigious and powerful, since it commands the greatest audiences. And in this form quantity is far more important than quality. There is the advertising connected to public relations (PR), where corporate or personal images are created and marketed, sometimes subliminally. There is a PR division in every large company, and many freelance organizations whose central concern is to create or maintain the 'good name' of a company, a person or a political party. At the more mundane level, though no less powerful, are the trade and 'small ads' geared to specific sections of the community; these are the entire funding bodies for the incessant free papers which deluge letterboxes in the Western world.

Art has taken advertising seriously for many years now, the **pop** art movement of the 1960s being perhaps the most obvious example. Andy Warhol's paintings of soup tins have passed into popular mythology, becoming virtually synonymous with a widespread conception of 'modern art'. With supreme confidence, the advertising industry, no longer apologizing for its blatantly consumerist interests, regularly gives its best practitioners prestigious awards based on the aesthetic and artistic criteria traditionally reserved for so-called 'serious' drama. Advertising has amply repaid television and film for, as it were, feeding off those media by rechannelling into them many of its techniques developed for promoting consumer sales. Once regarded as the poor relative of 'real' art, advertising has had its contribution approved by some very eminent figures. The British writer and broadcaster Troy Kennedy Martin, for example, in the McTaggart Lecture at the Edinburgh Television Festival in 1986, put forward the idea of short 'micro-dramas' as a new television form. They would emulate commercials in structure and duration, and would be repeated many times. They would '... consist of dozens of fragments of dramas, shards of experience made and put out very quickly...[and]...would have "zero visibility" in the normal run of programming...[being]...part of a flow which would enhance their qualities...'. Such dramas are still in the future, though there are many more short films being produced and a video culture has developed to rival traditional dramatic structures. Also, whereas a few years ago work for television or film commercials was scorned by most serious actors and directors as a poor (though profitable) substitute for stage or screen plays, the product of many famous names are now seen or heard every night of the week. **RG**

AERODYNAMICS AND AIRCRAFT

Aerodynamics (Greek, 'study of the power of air') is the study of the flow of air or gases in motion. The main application of aerodynamics is in aviation. Aerodynamic analysis is also used to study the effect that wind will have on such artificial structures as bridges and tower blocks, on the flow of steam in turbines, or on the operation of wind-power generators.

The concept of flight was established by Leonardo da Vinci, who made sketches of devices similar to the modern helicopter and hang-glider. Although Leonardo's ideas were well ahead of their time, they were doomed to failure, as the principles of aerodynamics were unknown.

Aircraft flight is based upon the presence of four forces: thrust, drag, gravity and lift. As long as the forces of thrust are greater than drag, and lift is greater than gravity, the aircraft will stay up and move in the air. Thrust is provided by the engines and the lift is created by the wings of the aircraft. The lift is generated by increasing the pressure below the wing and decreasing the pressure above it by the shape of the upper and lower surfaces of the wing and its inclination to the direction of flight. These two forces combine to overcome gravity, and so make flight possible.

The first man-made flight took place, not in an aircraft, but by a balloon. The flight was made by the Montgolfier brothers in 1783. Initially hydrogen, which is the lightest known gas, was used to fill the balloon. Hot air was found to be cheaper and now helium is used for preference. Their flight was to herald the race to become the first man to fly. Work by people such as Otto Lilienthal, who constructed and flew gliders, opened up the way for first powered flight, which was achieved by the Wright brothers in 1903 at Kitty Hawk, North Carolina (the flight lasted just 12 seconds).

The aircraft remained in its infancy for the next 30 years as new developments took place. One major requirement was a light, reliable engine with good fuel economy, and the other was the availability of light material of suitable strength for the structure. During this time, the aircraft was given a wider and wider role, from delivering post to reconnaissance missions during World War I. It was also used for entertainment, especially with long-distance flights taking place in the hope that the pilot would collect major prizes. In 1927, Charles Lindbergh's single-handed crossing of the Atlantic was seen as a major technological breakthrough, and laid the foundations for long haulage **transportation** of people and goods.

By the start of World War II, the aircraft was at such a stage that its use in warfare was of paramount importance. It was also developed on the commercial side with the setting up of the first airline, KLM, in 1923. The original concepts of the use of the propeller driven by a piston engine remained until World War II when jet propulsion for military aeroplanes was first introduced. Commercial aeroplanes continued to use propellers driven by gas turbines until the introduction of the first commercial jet aircraft in 1949, the de Havilland Comet. Its introduction was to transform people's way of travelling, as foreign ports of call became more accessible. **AA**

See also jet engines.

Further reading J Christie, *High Adventure: the First 75 years of Civil Aviation.*

AESTHETIC JUDGEMENTS

Aesthetic judgements (from Greek *aisthanein*, 'to perceive' or 'sense') are judgements about the aesthetic status of objects, judgements about their beauty or ugliness. 'Michelangelo's David is beautiful' is an aesthetic judgement about a work of art. 'The Rockies are ugly' is an aesthetic judgement about a part of nature which is not a work of art.

Aesthetic questions of particular interest to philosophers include: are aesthetic qualities objective or subjective? Are objects beautiful or ugly independently of minds and the judgements they make? Or are objects beautiful or ugly only because minds judge them to be so? **AJ**

See also aesthetics.

Further reading V. Aldrich, *Philosophy of Art.*

AESTHETICISM

Aestheticism was a British **arts** movement which flourished briefly from the 1880s to the 1900s. Its main idea was that works of art should exist for their own sakes, without external relevance or meaning: 'the desire of beauty, the love of art for art's sake', as Walter Pater, a leading aesthete, put it. The aesthetes looked back to the ideal of beauty put forward in the paintings and writings of the **Pre-Raphaelites**. They also admired the dandyism and licence of the contemporary French **avant-garde**. Perhaps the most famous adherents of aestheticism were Aubrey Beardsley and Oscar Wilde in his green-carnation period. Those sympathetic to the movement included Swinburne, W.B. Yeats and Max Beerbohm. The movement was mocked in its own day (for example by Gilbert and Sullivan in *Patience*), and has, ever since, provided Philistines and comedians with a stereotype (accurate or not) of avant-garde artists as decadent, arrogant and dandified frauds. **KMcL**

Further reading Richard Aldington, *The Religion of Beauty*; Roger Scruton, *Art and Imagination.*

AESTHETICS

Aesthetics (from Greek *aisthesis*, 'perception by the senses') is a philosophical and critical study which attempts to define the concepts of **beauty** and **taste**. The idea itself is ancient – the first-recorded discussion of the nature of beauty is between Hippias and Socrates in Plato's dialogue *Hippias Major* (4th century BCE) – but the term itself was first coined by the 18th-century German philosopher A.G. Baumgarten, and was developed by Kant in his *Critique of Judgement* (1790), in which he argues that aesthetic appreciation reconciles the dualism of theory and practice in human nature, thereby leaving the way open to identify beauty as a profoundly subjective quality, not necessarily inherent in the work of art. Ever since then, aesthetics has been regarded as one of the major branches of **philosophy**.

Starting from the premise that there are a number of activities described as '**arts**' (**literature**, **music**, **painting**, **theatre** and so on), philosophers ask if there is a definition of 'art' that enables us to see what they have in common. One cannot say that a work of art is a beautiful *thing*, for there are beautiful things in Nature which are not works of art. But can one say that a work of art is a beautiful artefact? No: it seems that some works of art are not 'beautiful', but 'ugly'.

Can art be characterized in terms of its point or function? Some art represents: **novels** and certain paintings represent actual or merely imaginary states of affairs. But music and abstract paintings do not seem to be representative. And newspapers represent the world, but are not works of art.

Works of art may be said to express their creator's feelings. But this is at best a necessary and not sufficient condition for an artefact's being a work of art: spoken and written words are often expressions of feelings but are not works of art. Perhaps art is distinguished by its lack of external point or function. Art, it may be said, is just for art's sake.

What is the ontology of art? Are works of art identical with physical objects, or are they something else? Again, the variety of the arts precludes an easy answer. A picture or sculpture may be said to be a physical object. But a novel is not identical with any particular manuscript or copy of it: if all the original copies of a novel are destroyed, the novel will nevertheless exist if copies of the original are made. And what is the relationship between a score or script of a play and the performances of it?

Further questions concern the objectivity or subjectivity of aesthetic values. Are things objectively beautiful or ugly, or are beauty and ugliness in the eye of the beholder? (Note the difference between holding that aesthetic values are objective and that there is agreement about aesthetic values. A painting could be objectively ugly even though some, due to a desire to shock, hold that it is ugly. And there could be general agreement that a sculpture was beautiful, for social reasons, even though its beauty was a subjective rather than objective matter.)

Are **aesthetic judgements** simply a matter of taste? When you say that a picture is beautiful and I say that it is ugly, is there a genuine disagreement between us? Or are you merely saying that you like it, while I am merely saying that I do not in which case we are merely recording our own individual preferences? Is something beautiful just if it is disposed to produce a certain emotional response in minds which come into contact with it? Or is beauty something which *merits* those responses? **PD MG AJ KMcL**

See also art for art's sake; performing arts; supervenience.

Further reading V. Aldrich, *Philosophy of Art;* R. Wollheim, *Art and Its Objects.*

AETIOLOGY

Aetiology(Greek, *aitia,* 'cause' + ology), the study of the causes of disease, was first established when Hippocrates (4th century BCE) realized that disease was caused not by the actions of the gods but by earthly factors. Several hundred years later, the Greek physician/philosopher Galen ascribed the cause of disease to an imbalance in the four vital **humours**: blood, phlegm, and yellow and black bile. However, because so many of the causes of disease are unseen, the development of aetiology was delayed until the development of techniques such as microscopy and of knowledge about the principles of **genetics**. Nonetheless, observations linking causation to pathology were often made: the ancient Egyptians, for example, realized that there was a relationship between a blood-dwelling parasitic worm and the presence of blood in the urine. Furthermore the importance of a 'sound constitution' was recognized as important in the avoidance of disease. Modern aetiology encompasses the study of all diseases (genetic, metabolic and immunological, and diseases caused by environmental factors, pathogens, and poor nutrition) and the interactions of different disease states in the affected individual (study of the behaviour of diseases within communities is termed **epidemiology**). **RB**

Further reading Andrew Learmouth, *Disease Ecology.*

AFFECTIVE FALLACY

In literary criticism, the affective fallacy assumes that works can be read not as independent structures, but in terms of their emotional or other effects on their readers. In other words, the preconceptions we bring to our reading of any literary work – our cultural, emotional and verbal baggage, as well as that of our society and of the author – are part of the 'meaning' of the text as we perceive it, and cannot be dissociated from our perception. 'Non-affective' reading, by contrast, excludes all such external associations and concentrates solely on what is in the actual text. **KMcL**

Further reading W.K. Wimsatt, *The Verbal Ikon.*

AFFIRMATIVE ACTION

Affirmative action first emerged as a voluntary code of practice, later enshrined in the American Civil Rights Act of 1964. It prescribed ways to ensure that individuals from groups which had previously experienced discrimination would have better access to employment-opportunities. Affirmative action programmes have subsequently been widely adopted around the world, especially to counter discrimination based on race, sex, religion, national origin, age, physical disability and sexual orientation.

Weak affirmative action means deciding to hire (or promote) in favour of a candidate from a disadvantaged group when all candidates are otherwise equal on merit. Other forms of affirmative action involve 'outreach programmes', to encourage people to apply for jobs which people with their characteristics do not normally apply for, and monitoring the composition of workforces to ensure fair employment. The strongest forms of affirmative action involve setting goals and targets to ensure a better balanced employment profile in an organization.

Supporters of affirmative action contend that it is a just policy because (1) it compensates the victims of injustice at the expense of the beneficiaries of injustice; (2) it redistributes from the best-off to the worst-off; (3) it is socially useful, because it avoids the wasteful under-utilization of talent in a discriminatory society, and creates a fairer, and therefore more stable, society. Supporters of affirmative action usually believe that governmental intervention is necessary to counteract various forms of racial, religious, ethnic and sexual discrimination in both the public and private sectors of modern states. Critics of affirmative action claim that it amounts to reverse discrimination, and that it inevitably leads to 'quotas' being set by organizations. They believe that 'preferential hiring' policies, in favour of ethnic minorities and women: (1) discriminate against those who have never discriminated; (2) abandon the merit principle in favour of illiberal and ascriptive (racial, religious, ethnic or sexual) criteria; and (3) provoke a backlash amongst the previously privileged. The critics of affirmative action appear to believe that free-market societies naturally eliminate unjustified discrimination. **BO'L**

Further reading Robert K. Fullinwider, *The Reverse Discrimination Controversy: a Moral and Legal Analysis);* Michael Rosenfeld, *Affirmative Action: a Philosophical and Constitutional Inquiry;* Thomas Sowell, *Preferential Policies: an International Perspective.*

AFFLUENT SOCIETY

The concept of the affluent society, used to describe post–1945 democratic welfare capitalist societies, was pioneered by the Canadian economist, John Kenneth Galbraith. He argued that a long-term unintended consequence of economic growth in Western democracies was the simultaneous development of 'private affluence' and 'public squalor'. While very efficient in encouraging the demand for private goods and services, including consumer-durables, liberal-democratic capitalist societies are prone to under-supply public goods, like education, public health, environmental protection and public transport.

Galbraith later embellished this argument: because modern liberal democracies contain satisfied majorities, which have the skills and resources to avoid poverty, a 'culture of contentment' has developed, hostile to active and progressively redistributive big government. Whereas in the earliest electoral democratic systems the poor comprised (potential) electoral majorities, affluent or contented societies are likely to be content with tax-cutting conservative administrations. **BO'L**

Further reading John K. Galbraith, *The Affluent Society; The Culture of Contentment.*

AFRICANISM (PAN-AFRICANISM)

Africanism is the ideological belief that all

of the native peoples of the continent of Africa are a singular race or ethnicity. It is the first principle of a broad political and cultural movement which aims to promote the welfare of Africans worldwide. Among the African diaspora Africanism has historically been invoked to oppose **slavery** and racial discrimination, as well as to promote 'back-to-Africa' movements among American and Caribbean slaves, and their descendants.

Pan-Africanism is a movement whose goal is the establishment of a single, unified state of Africa. Influenced by the populist rhetoric of the Jamaican Marcus Garvey (1887–1940) and the more intellectual work of W.E.B. Du Bois (1868–1963) from the US, the Pan-African movement became a central pillar of the anti-colonial independence movements of the 1950s and 1960s. Fervently promoted by the 'Casablanca Group' of nations led by Kwame Nkrumah of Ghana, the Pan-African ideal of a single state was resisted by Haile Selassie's 'Monrovia Group' which preferred to emphasize political and economic co-operation between and among independent African states. The Organization for African Unity (OAU), formed in 1963, represented the institutional success of the more moderate goals of the Monrovia Group. Pan-Africanism today is an aspiration with little popular or governmental support. **BO'L**

See also nationalism; négritude.

Further reading P. Olisanwuche Esedebe, *Pan-Africanism: The Idea and Movement, 1766–1963*; W. Ofuatey-Kodjoe (ed.), *Pan-Africanism: New Directions in Strategy*.

AGGRESSION

Life scientists use the term aggression (Latin, 'assault') to describe behaviour (of an animal towards another) which serves to injure or provokes retreat. A workable definition of aggression is, however, difficult to achieve: for example, predatory aggression is sometimes excluded. Aggression may arise when there is competition for some requirement such as territory, food or a mate. It has been studied most thoroughly in mammals, where it can be broken down into attack and defensive threat patterns,

both of which may be quite rigidly mapped out in a given species. An aggressive response requires interaction with another individual and the course the aggressive behaviour follows may be modified by the response of the other individual. Thus aggression can elicit a submissive response, such as exposure of the throat, and this response can inhibit aggression. When aggression occurs between members of the same species or social group, one individual often backs down in this way before violence occurs. However, interspecies aggression can result in violence and even death if the pressure which initiated the behaviour is sufficiently strong. **RB**

See also ethology; mimicry.

Further reading Richard Dawkins, *The Selfish Gene*.

AGNOSTICISM

Agnosticism (Greek, 'not knowing'), in religious terms, is the view that evidence for God's existence is balanced by evidence against, and that the human intellect is too limited to form any judgement as to whether God exists or not. Although the actual term was coined by T.H. Huxley in the 19th century, it was Kant who did most to develop the theme in his *Critique of Pure Reason* (1781). In this work, he states that human beings are constantly tempted to use concepts which are both intelligible and indispensable to normal reasoning, and that where speculations go further than human experience they fool themselves into thinking that they can gain real insights. Agnostics of the 19th century, such as J.S. Mill and Leslie Stephen, added to this argument the use of scientific methods with regard to theological issues. **EMJ**

Further reading Bertrand Russell, *Why I Am Not a Christian*.

AGRARIAN SOCIETY

In **political science**, **sociology** and **anthropology**, agrarian society is contrasted on the one hand with hunter/gatherer society and on the other with **industrial society**. Agrarian societies are defined by the direct engagement of most of the population in the systematic production and storage of food, and by the minimal development of commercial agriculture. Although agrarian societies have varied considerably throughout history, especially in their religious cultures, they have shared deeply coercive and exploitative forms of rule and **caste**-based aristocracies. For these reasons agrarian societies are considered to have been inhospitable milieu for democracy, nationalism and equality; that is, the defining, or at least emergent, traits of most industrial societies. **BO'L**

Further reading Patricia Crone, *Pre-Industrial Societies;* Ernest Gellner, *Plough, Sword and Book: the Structure of Human History.*

ALCHEMY

Alchemy (Arabic *al-kimia*, 'the Egyptian art') was a form of investigation which arose in ancient China and was practised in Asia, the Middle East and Europe for millennia, until it gave way to modern **science** some 400 years ago. It took its cue from the idea that all matter on Earth was made from a mixture of four basic 'elements' air, earth, fire and water. Alchemists believed that if they could discover the proportions in which those elements were mixed, and change them, they would alter the nature of matter, creating or re-creating it to suit themselves.

Over the centuries, four quests became paramount. Alchemists searched for the 'elixir of life' (a potion to make mortal flesh immortal), the 'panacea' (a medicine to cure every disease), the 'philosopher's stone' (which would turn base metals into gold) and the 'alkahest' (which would melt anything else in creation: useful not only in the alchemists' experiments, but in war). To find these things, alchemists experimented with heating, pounding, mixing and testing every substance they could lay hands on, and in the process made many discoveries still valid in **chemistry** today.

Over the years, failure in all four quests led some alchemists to add black **magic** in their experiments. Their use of spells and incantations led outsiders to believe that they were in league with the Devil, and made alchemy disreputable. The end came in 1661, when Robert Boyle published *The Sceptical Chemist,* differentiating for the first time between true elements, compounds and mixtures and pouring scorn on the idea of four fundamental 'elements'. **KMcL**

Further reading Arthur Koestler, *The Sleepwalkers;* Jack Lindsay, *The Origins of Alchemy.*

ALEATORY (or ALEATORIC)

Aleatory (derived from the Latin word *aleae*, 'dice') is an adjective applied to any art form in which chance is allowed to play a part – although this can include 'finished' art: for example, in the 1920s the **Dada** artist Hans Arp made paper collages which depended on the random alighting of pieces of paper he dropped on to the base-paper from above, while the 1930s German sculptor Kurt Schwitters made 'rubbish houses' from whatever objects he came across.

The main application of aleatory techniques is in the **performing arts**, and particularly in **music**. In art music, 20th-century composers as significant as Pierre Boulez, Györgi Ligeti, Witold Lutoslawski and Karlheinz Stockhausen use aleatory techniques as an integral, and entirely accepted, component of their work. In aleatory music the players are encouraged to choose the sequence of movements, sections or individual chords and notes, or to improvise on a pattern or idea suggested by the composer – for example, in Ligeti's *Aventures*, on letters of the alphabet, and in Lutoslawski's *Preludes and Fugue*, on a series of lines, squares and triangles. Thus, the result differs from player to player and from performer to performer. Aleatory music is, in conception, similar to both Far Eastern art music and to **jazz** and **rock**, all of which involve **improvisation**, on an agreed basis, as a feature of the performance.

Aleatory procedures have been used in the **theatre**, and in the recitation of **poetry**; but there are few signs here that they have progressed beyond the experimental stage. **KMcL**

ALGEBRA

The original meaning of the word 'algebra'

was the solution, by mathematical manipulation, of simple equations (of the form now called linear equations, where only the unknowns appear and not their squares or cubes or other powers). It was a study originated by the Arabs, and the word itself is a corruption of the name of Al Jabr, an 8th-century Arab mathematician whose book was the first on the subject to be translated into Western languages. Algebra in this sense always aims to discover the number called the unknown and usually denoted by 'x' (though there can be more than one unknown) through arithmetical operations on a system of equations, which the unknown is supposed to satisfy all at once (this is why such systems are often known as simultaneous equations).

Algebra was able to develop because of the simplification of arithmetic caused by the development of a place dependent **number system** and the introduction of the number **zero** by Indian mathematicians. From this origin, algebra took two main turns.

The first is known as linear algebra, and is the study of systems of linear equations in greater generality than that described above; the aim is to say when systems of equations have any solutions and, if they do, when the solutions are unique. This is closely related to the concept of the **vector** in the **Cartesian co-ordinate system**, and led to the formulation of the concept of the vector **space** and of **dimension**. Much of the theory in this area has become associated with **analysis** and **topology**, in which context it is known as functional analysis, and has turned out to be a simple way to describe quantum mechanics mathematically. One of the most important concepts in this field is that of linear transformations, which are functions which preserve addition (in the sense that $f(a + b) = f(a) + f(b)$). (See **linearity**).

The second area is more diverse, and is generally given the title abstract algebra, though axiomatic algebra would perhaps be a better name. Here, those properties of number which are used in linear algebra to solve equations are treated as axioms (see **axiomatization**), and the properties of these systems of axioms are investigated. An example would be the commutativity of multiplication, the fact that for any two numbers $ab = ba$; it would be possible to study the properties common to all mathematical structures that have an operation which is commutative. The different branches of this kind of algebra are usually named after the system of axioms used; so we have group theory, ring theory and field theory (in which the objects of study are **groups**, **rings** and **fields** respectively). One of the main subjects of enquiry in this type of algebra, the homomorphism, is similar to the linear transformation in linear algebra. A homomorphism is a **function** from one group, ring or field to another, which preserves the properties of the operation(s) in the same way that a linear transformation preserves addition. A relatively new branch of study is that of **category theory**, which looks more generally at the properties of these algebraic objects; the objects of study here are classes (examples would be groups or rings) and functors, which are the homomorphisms between members of the same class. The results in the field are very powerful, but particularly difficult mathematically, because of their extremely general nature.

Algebra is important in mathematics because its use has revolutionized many other areas of the subject. For example, there are several branches of mathematics devoted to the use of algebra in other contexts, such as algebraic topology, algebraic **geometry** and algebraic **number theory**. It introduces standard notation to many other problems, and by doing this shows up similarities between branches of mathematics – a process which greatly eases the search for solutions to the problems. So its importance lies in the applications it has in other areas of mathematics. **SMcL**

Further reading L. Nový, *Origins of Modern Algebra*.

ALGEBRAIC GEOMETRY

This area of **mathematics** originated with René Descartes (1596–1650), after whom the **Cartesian co-ordinate system** is named. It has developed considerably since, but is still fundamentally concerned with co-ordinate systems, which have shown their importance in three main areas.

First, algebraic geometry demonstrated an intimate connection between two branches of mathematics which had previously seemed to be far apart, **algebra** and **geometry**. Equations from algebra define curves in the co-ordinate systems of the appropriate dimension. For example, the linear equation $y = 3x + 2$ defines the curve in which every point has a co-ordinate $(x, 3x + 2)$. This turns out to be a straight line (which is why such equations are called linear); more complicated equations give rise to more complicated curves; the equation $x^2 + y^2 = 1$ produces the circle of radius 1 centred at the origin. This connection led to the formulation of the idea of a **function**, which (in its original form) was an algebraic connection between x and y in the co-ordinates of the points in a particular figure.

Second, the Cartesian co-ordinate system was one in which the theorems of **Euclidean geometry** could be shown to hold by algebraic methods (which the original Greek methods of proof would not have allowed); they therefore showed that Euclidean geometry is consistent, that is, allowed of no contradiction, assuming that arithmetic is in its turn consistent. This is not, of course the same as showing that Euclidean geometry is true; there are co-ordinate systems which have **non-Euclidean geometries** (which, because they are curved, today are thought to give a truer reflection of the universe, which is also curved). For example, the system of latitude and longitude on the surface of the Earth is a co-ordinate system (except that the poles have no well-defined co-ordinates), but the theorems of Euclidean geometry are not all true in this system; for example, there are triangles which have the sum of their angles greater than two right angles (putting one corner at the north pole and the other two on the equator makes each angle a right angle). It is also the case that using algebraic co-ordinates measuring the length of lines, it is easy to do things which **Galois theory** later proved could not be done with Euclidean geometry.

The chief importance of algebraic geometry is in the way it clearly demonstrates the fact that clarity of notation is all important to mathematical development. **SMcL**

See also symbolism.

ALGEBRAIC NUMBERS

In the development of **numbers**, algebraic numbers come in generality between the **rational numbers** and the **real numbers**. A rational number is one that can be expressed in the form p/q, where p and q are **integers** and q is non-zero. The Greeks discovered the alarming fact (to them) that not all numbers are rational, through a classic use of the technique of **proof by contradiction**. Suppose that there was a rational number whose square was 2. It can be written in its lowest terms as p/q (this means that p and q have no common factors). So $(p/q)^2 = p^2/q^2 = 2$. Therefore, $p^2 = 2 \times q^2$, so that 2 divides p^2 and therefore p (this is because 2 is a **prime number**). So we write p as $2 \times r$, and, rewriting the original equation, $(2 \times r)^2 = 4 \times r^2 = 2 \times q^2$. So, cancelling by 2 we see that $2 \times r^2 = q^2$, which means that 2 also divides q. So 2 divides both p and q, contradicting that p/q was in its lowest terms. So the original assumption that the square root of 2 is rational must be false.

This fact was regarded by the Greeks as highly discouraging, because it went against all their ideas of what numbers should be like. They virtually abandoned the whole subject. It was not until the 16th century that Western mathematicians began to realize that the rationals were not the whole story. The next step is to construct the algebraic numbers. These are those numbers which are the roots of **polynomial** equations whose coefficients are integers, as for example the square root of 2 is the root of the equation $x^2 - 2 = 0$, or $ax^2 + c = 0$, where $a = 1$ and $c = -2$ are the coefficients. However, not all such equations are given roots; for example, the equation $x^2 + 1 = 0$ is not, for the simple reason that x^2 is always positive and so $x^2 + 1$ must always be greater than 0. The crucial property that a polynomial must have is that its sign changes. It will be given a root between a point where it has negative value and a point where it has positive value (for example, $x^2 - 2$ has value -1 when $x = 1$ and value 2 when $x = 2$, it has a root between 1 and 2).

Even this is not the end of the story. This became apparent when Joseph Liouville (1809–1882) discovered a criterion for when a number was algebraic (based on how quickly it could be approximated by a particular series of rational numbers), and, using this criterion, constructed the first known transcendental (non-algebraic) number in 1844. It was nearly 30 years before anyone showed that any useful number (that is, one not specifically constructed for the purpose) was transcendental. Charles Hermite (1822–1901) showed that e was transcendental in 1873. Almost immediately afterwards, Georg Cantor (1845–1918), using his new **set theory**, showed that there were vastly more transcendental numbers than algebraic numbers; that the algebraic numbers were countable (that is, of the smallest infinite size) but the real numbers were not. It remains a very difficult property to prove; it is not known, for many commonly used numbers in mathematics, whether they are algebraic or not. **SMcL**

ALGORITHM

Algorithm (from the Latinized form of the name Al Kwarizmi, the 9th-century Persian mathematician), in **computing**, is a set of rules determining how a task is to be performed. An example is the following algorithm for making a cheese sandwich: (1) open refrigerator door; (2) remove cheese from the second shelf from top; (3) peel back wrapping from cheese and place cheese on cutting surface; (4) cut four slices of cheese 0.5 cm thick with sharp knife; (5) butter two slices of bread on one side each; (6) place cheese slices on one of the slices of bread, on the buttered side; (7) place second slice of bread, butter side down, on top.

Most algorithms are vastly more complicated than this example. Any task a computer can be programmed to perform must be reduced to an algorithm beforehand.

Algorithms define both the limits and the scope of the activities of computers. It has surprised many to see just how many activities can be reduced to algorithms: some of the more unexpected include learning, games playing and even in some limited instances constructing algorithms. **SMcL**

ALIENATION

Alienation (from Latin *alienus*, 'outsider'), in **sociology**, refers to the sense that control over one's individual abilities has been taken over by outside agents. Originally it had philosophical and religious meanings: Ludwig Feuerbach (1804-72) used the term to refer to the establishment of gods and divine forces as distinct from human beings, and Marx originally used it to refer to the projection of human powers onto the gods. Marx later transformed it into a sociological concept by applying it to the experience of work.

For Marx, work was the most important human activity through which human beings expressed their individuality and creativity. The alienated worker finds work unsatisfying and unrewarding. Work has no creative value. Alienation is, however, far more than boredom at work. Alienation refers to workers' powerlessness and loss of control over the nature of their work tasks and the products of their labour – thus the term also denotes a specific set of social relations. In traditional societies, it is argued, though work may have been hard and exhausting, the individual worker still had a large measure of control over his or her daily labours. In contrast, the modern industrial worker has little control over his or her work situation. **Capitalism**, according to Marx, inevitably produces a high level of alienation. This is because in such a society a small number of individuals own the productive forces, individual workers rarely own the tools of their trade and have little control over what they produce. Production is for an abstract market rather than for self or for a specific customer. In these circumstances, alienation is heightened by mechanization and by a highly specialized **division of labour** (the separation of a job into simple constituent parts). Unlike the craftsmen of preindustrial societies, workers in industrial societies do not each produce a complete product. Rather, each may produce just one element of a fragmented whole. This may involve a routine task only and in this way many skills may be lost.

It is argued that workers in capitalist societies not only become alienated from their work and the products of their labour, but also from themselves and ultimately from each other. An alienated worker, Marx believed, is unable to find self-expression through work and this causes estrangement from self. Further, since work is a social activity, it is argued that alienation from work involves alienation from others and one becomes cut off from fellow workers.

Alienation as used by Marx, like **anomie**, is a concept which links explanations of individual behaviour to the wider social structure. Since Marx, alienation has been used to describe a wide range of phenomena. The subjective aspects of alienation were given emphasis by American sociologists in the 1950s and 1960s, in studies which, in effect, equated alienation with people's subjective feelings of dissatisfaction with life. This takes the meaning a long way from the original use by Marx. More recently some have pointed out that Marx, in his later work, abandoned the concept in favour of that of exploitation, and thus it is argued there is little need to preserve the concept.

In **drama**, alienation (*Verfremdung*) is a term used by the playwright Bertolt Brecht (1898–1956) to refer to the desired result of his **epic theatrical** practices. Generally, theatre characterized by alienation devices is opposed to **Naturalism** in its various manifestations. Brecht wanted audiences to achieve a critical and reflective distance from the onstage action, rather than be sucked in emotionally by the devices of the illusionistic theatre. His aim was thereby to facilitate the perception of underlying (political) structures and processes, which **ideology** normally hides in everyday life. Brecht himself wrote that such an 'alienation effect' occurred when, for example, someone saw his or her schoolteacher being hounded by bailiffs: that is, when a person

normally perceived as being in authority was suddenly seen in a completely different context.

Although some theatre workers mistook Brechtian incidentals (such as visible lighting equipment), designed to achieve distance in the face of a particular set of theatrical conditions, for a Brechtian method applicable in all circumstances, this does not detract from the importance of the general principle of which such incidentals were the original manifestation, that the familiar should be made unfamiliar. The theoretical point was that 'Alienation means historicizing, means representing persons and actions as historical, and therefore mutable'.

Unfortunately Brecht's relatively simple concept has, like so much else in his work, been bedevilled by confusion between aesthetic and political usages, and by issues of translation. Brecht's terms *Verfremdung* and *Verfremdungseffekt(e)* have been variously translated as Alienation and Alienation Effect(s), but also as Defamiliarization, Estrangement, Distancing, Distanciation and A-effect, E-effect and V-effect. The use of 'alienation' as a translation of *Verfremdung* has led to confusion with the Marxist use of 'alienation' (*Entfremdung* in German). While there are obvious links between the two forms of alienation, in that Brecht's theatrical approach is often intended to make clear those factors which lead to social and political alienation, Brecht's detractors and those who have confused the two senses of alienation have sometimes interpreted Brecht in such a way as to alienate (in the sense of 'turn off') audiences and readers. Brecht's use of the term *Verfremdung* (which he virtually invented) is clearly analogous to Shklovsky's *ostranenie* ('making strange' or 'defamiliarization'), a central concept in **Formalism. DA TRG SS**

See also bourgeoisie; capital; class; conflict theory; embourgeoisement thesis; labour process; Marxism; occupation; organization; rationalization; social stratification; structure; work.

Further reading Karl Marx, *The Economic and Philosophical Manuscripts of 1844*; Jan

Needle and Peter Thomson, *Brecht*; B. Ollman, *Alienation: Marx's Critique of Man in Capitalist Society*; John Willett (ed.), *Brecht on Theatre*.

ALLEGORY

Allegory (Greek, 'putting it another way') is a technique widely used in **fine art** (especially Western narrative painting) and in **literature**. In **narrative painting**, allegory involves an action being the vehicle for a covert meaning or interpretation. The 'real meaning' of a Renaissance nude, for example, may not be sensual pleasure but the personification of Truth. The presentation of **fable** and **myth** in **history painting**, and the presentation of dogmatic parable in religious painting, are clear examples of allegory, to the point where the 'meaning' of the painting can be entirely lost unless the allegory is understood. Such presentations are common throughout the history of Western narrative painting, from medieval depictions of the **Seven Deadly Sins** to the representation of Liberty as a semi-clad woman in Delacroix's *Liberty Leading the People* (1830), or the snakes, insects, lions, rats and other creatures into which our leaders are regularly turned in political cartoons. Other allegories are more occluded and need a more complicated set of references to decode them. Thus the representation of the story 'Hercules at the Crossroads' is allegorical, as he must choose between the rocky path of virtue or the broad plain of vice – each indicated by an alluring woman. Allegory in painting is not a genre, or even of itself a narrative. It relies on the beholder's ability to interpret devices such as the personification of abstract notions (for instance, good and evil as human figures) or the use of convention and symbol (for example the ant for industry or the lily for purity).

In Western art, three favourite sources of allegory were Ovid's *Metamorphoses* (perhaps the origin of the technique, as it consists of stories of people who change into objects such as trees or rocks), the Bible, and the various knight-errant epics and fables (such as George and the Dragon and the Holy Grail saga) which were a staple of medieval European imaginative literature.

Allegory largely disappeared from art with the advent of **modernism**, though 20th-century artists have since developed a variety of symbolic iconography of their own (for example, Giorgio de Chirico's and Salvador Dali's landscapes, and Joan Miró's eared ladders), which is as rich and complex as anything from the past.

In literature, allegory is a technique in which events or symbols of one kind stand for those of another. Examples are the way the physical journey and adventures described in John Bunyan's *The Pilgrim's Progress* stand for the journey and temptations of the Christian soul, and in J.D. Salinger's novel *The Catcher in the Rye* the way Holden Caulfield's exploration of the underbelly of New York stands for the emergence of adult sensibility from adolescent hope and angst.

Allegory is a form of **irony**; one in which the added meanings are generally more significant than the events onto which they are grafted. Religious allegory was especially popular in medieval Europe, when stories of love, descriptions of nature and tales of heroic adventure were all allegorized to have a deeper, Christian meaning. Typical examples are versions of the Holy Grail and Parsifal legends, in which knights stand for the beleaguered Christian soul, dragons and wizards for the Devil and his minions, and attainment of the goal is overlaid with images of transfiguration and ascension into heaven.

Allegories may also be philosophical and political. Philosophical allegory underlies works as diverse as Virgil's *Aeneid*, Edmund Spenser's *The Faery Queen*, Voltaire's *Candide*, Albert Camus's *The Plague* and William Golding's *Lord of the Flies* (in which the social degeneration of a group of boys marooned on a desert island allegorizes the author's view of the immanence of evil in human life). Political allegories include such works as Aristophanes' *Knights* (in which a contest between two slaves for their master's favour stands for the place-seeking of politicians), Geoffrey Chaucer's *Parliament of Fowls*, Joseph Conrad's *The Heart of Darkness* (reworked as an antiwar allegory in Francis Ford Coppola's 1979 film *Apocalypse Now*), Arthur Miller's *The Crucible* (in which the witch-hunts of Salem, Massachusetts in the 17th century symbolize the McCarthy anti-Communist hearings of the 1950s), and George Orwell's *Animal Farm* (in which a power struggle in a farmyard represents the rise of Stalinism in the USSR).

Outside the West, allegory has been used less overtly. For instance, Persian and Arabic literature consistently uses the image of a beautiful garden as an allegory for philosophical order and tranquillity of the soul. The Japanese writer Murasaki Shikibu's *The Tale of Genji* is, in part, a political allegory; Sufi preachers use anecdotes (similar to Aesop's *Fables*) to allegorize the religious, social and ethical problems human beings face, and the ways they should deal with them. **PD KMcL**

See also metaphor; symbolism.

Further reading J. MacQueen, *Allegory*.

ALTERED STATES OF CONSCIOUSNESS

'Altered states of consciousness' is an umbrella term for describing physical and mental states which are not considered part of ordinary experience. They occur in many societies in connection with mystical practices, ecstatic and trance states. Modern **psychology** locates these changes as arising within the psyche, while other cultures explain them in terms of changes in external reality, such as access to a spirit realm or extrahuman power. Trance states can be defined according to the degree of interaction believed to occur between the individual, who is in an altered state, and the spirit realm. In states of possession, the spirit is assumed to be in control of the person, who acts as the bodily vehicle by means of which the spirit can communicate. In **shamanism** the spirit or spirit world has been domesticated by the shaman, who uses his or her familiarity with the spirit realm in order to bring about changes in everyday life.

The word shaman originated in Siberia, where it referred to a religious specialist. Shamans are found throughout Asia and in many other cultures. They journey to the realm of the spirits in an altered state of consciousness, often induced by rhythmic drumming. Because of their ability to associate with the spirit realm shamans, as with other religious specialists, are often powerful figures in their society and are called on to mediate on behalf of humans, providing protective and curative services. The power shamans can tap into is also seen as potentially dangerous, so they may at times be marginalized by the rest of the community.

Anthropologists have examined the use of altered states to empower weak groups on the margins of society. The members of spirit-possession cults and religious ecstatic practices are usually drawn from weak, marginalized social groups. Ecstasy literally means 'standing outside [one's mind]', and reflects the spiritual transcendence from the mundane which they are trying to achieve.

The use of hallucinatory drugs, such as peyote, to induce ecstatic states as a means to explore the transcendental realm, was made famous by Carlos Castaneda in the 1960s. The authenticity of his anthropological accounts of initiation with a Yacqui Indian shaman in Mexico, however, have now been discredited. **CL**

See also indigenous metaphysics.

Further reading Carlos Castaneda, *The Teachings of Don Juan*; N. Drury, *The Elements of Shamanism*; I.M. Lewis, *Ecstatic Religion*.

ALTERNATIVE ENERGY

It has become apparent over the past thirty years that the total energy from a fuel source has to be maximized to its full potential, in order to save money and mineral resources. As this fact becomes clearer governments and individuals have begun to look at different propositions in order to save on energy costs.

At this present time the main sources of energy available to the Westernized culture are oil, gas, coal and nuclear power. With the environmental problems as well as the finite supplies of the four energy sources, more time and research is being spent on alternative sources of energy.

Direct or active solar energy may be exploited in various ways, including the direct production of heat for water and space, the growing of crops which can be processed into other forms of energy (biomass route) and the production of electricity using solar panels. The use of active solar-powered systems using collectors of one form or another are only viable in countries with warm climates and plenty of sun. Solar-powered power stations have been built, notably in southern France and California (where the largest solar power plant, 'Solar One', is in operation with a peak output of 10MW).

In northern European countries a more important facility is the use of passive solar power. This manipulates the form and fabric of the building to maintain comfortable internal surroundings for its users. As well as saving on energy costs, passive solar design frequently adds to the amenity of the structure of the building, such as the introduction of glass atriums in shopping malls.

As the Sun is the only source of energy (apart from fusion) at the present moment, the use of solar energy (passive or active) must be seriously considered. Another source of energy directly from the Sun is wind power. The driving force of the wind is the solar radiation interacting between the Earth's surface and atmosphere. It is this interaction that determines the character of high altitude winds. In the first few hundred metres above the Earth's surface there exists a turbulent layer, known as the boundary or mixing layer. All wind turbines operate within the boundary layer, and it is important that the turbines are sited as high as possible in order to capture as much energy as possible. The siting of wind farms on high hills has been the bane of many environmentalists who argue that natural beauty spots are being destroyed in order to supply energy.

Wave energy on the other hand overcomes the problem of scarring the landscape by placing the wave turbines far from shore. The advantage in using wave or wind power is that there is good seasonal matching between power supply and demand. The major drawback with wind and wave power is the lack of control engineers have over the power supplied.

The use of water is also seen in hydroelectric power stations and tidal power stations. A typical hydroelectric scheme uses a dammed river or lake to provide a reservoir that supplies a steady flow of water to drive turbines. In areas where the demand for power fluctuates, pumped storage plants may be installed, where the surplus power created during off-peak times is used to pump water back into the same or maybe a different reservoir. Tidal power uses reversible turbines that both manipulate the flood and ebb tides. At high tide sluice gates are closed, creating a reservoir in the tidal basin. The water can then be released at will. The largest tidal scheme in La Rance, France can produce 240MW, enough to satisfy the needs of a city of several hundred thousand inhabitants. Both systems (hydroelectric and tidal) can produce vast amounts of controllable energy, and the potential to use this renewable source energy must be maximized.

Another important source of alternative energy is the use of biomass (vegetable matter). Wood, crop residues and animal dung provide 40% of the energy used on the planet. In many developing countries they are the only source of energy with emphasis now being placed on the planting of fast-growing trees in order to supply firewood. Biomass is also being converted into alcohol which is being used as fuel for internal combustion engines when mixed with petrol.

As well as the use of biomass, domestic and commercial rubbish is being burned to provide heat for 'district heating schemes'. Such schemes are already in operation in Scandinavia where the energy produced in burning the refuse is used to heat water in pipes which eventually finds its way to nearby homes and offices. Even waste that is dumped into the ground yields useful energy. The decomposition of such material produces heat and methane, both of which can be used. Sewage when treated yields methane gas which can be used for cooking and heating. The sewage is deposited in 'biogas plants' and bacterial action produces the gas. Twenty million people in China use such a system.

Geothermal power is limited to countries where it is relatively easy to tap into the hot water that is heated by radioactive decay of elements below the Earth's surface. Places such as Iceland and New Zealand use their geothermic power to drive turbines and heat homes and factories directly. At present only such countries such as Iceland exploit this source of energy, but the technology exists to supply all the energy needs of the world for hundreds of years. Boreholes such as those drilled in Cornwall, in the UK, produce enough energy to drive turbines which generate electricity.

The use of renewable energy sources have to be taken seriously as the stocks of fossil fuels fall. With sensible conservation and the implementation of better insulation and waste heat recovery, it will be possible for the Earth to provide all of our energy requirements for centuries to come. **AA**

Further reading R.H. Taylor, *Alternative Energy Sources*.

ALTRUISM

In a biological context, altruism (from Italian *altrui*, 'someone else') describes any act by an individual which causes it to expend energy, but which brings it no direct benefit. An altruistic act usually enhances the chances of survival of another, genetically-related individual and rarely results in the death of the altruist, though some risk is often involved. A good example is the bird which gives a warning call upon sighting a hawk: it thus alerts its offspring while attracting the attention of the hawk to itself. It is probably incidental that the altruist, in this case, also warns any other potential prey, but John Maynard-Smith, in his book *The Theory of Evolution*, suggests that there is even a **kin selection** benefit in warning quite distant relatives.

Some authorities dispute the existence of altruism in instinctive situations: the concept of the **selfish gene**, a term coined by the biologist Richard Dawkins, ascribes an act of apparent altruism as beneficial to the gene if it protects copies of itself carried by relatives. For example, a worker bee that sacrifices itself to defend the hive is protecting its only chance of furthering its genetic line as it is sterile itself.

In **philosophy**, altruists believe that when we decide how to act we can, and should, take the interests of others into account as well as our own interests. They believe, for example, that we can, and should, sometimes give money to charity because of our concern for others, and not just because we wish to be thought well of by others, or to think well of ourselves.

Altruism contrasts in philosophy with ethical egoism. Ethical egoists (from Greek *ethikos*, 'of one's disposition'; Latin *ego*, 'I') think that we should not take the interests of others into account when we decide how to act, but should simply pursue our own interests. They may even insist that this is all we can do, that those, for example, who think they give money to charity because of their concern for others are simply deluding themselves. In reality, people only ever give money away for self-interested reasons. **RB AJ**

See also group selection; hedonism; morality; natural selection; sociobiology.

Further reading Richard Dawkins, *The Selfish Gene*; T. Nagel, *The Possibility of Altruism*.

AMBIENT MUSIC see Muzak

AMBIGUITY

Ambiguity (from the Latin for 'forked path'), in rhetoric or **literature**, is the use of words, or patterns of words, which lend themselves to more than one interpretation. The literary critic William Empson, in *Seven Types of Ambiguity* (1930), defined it as '...any verbal nuance, however slight, which gives room for alternative reactions to the same piece of language'. In all cases, from puns to the most complex **allegory** and **irony**, ambiguity invites the listener or reader, so to speak, to help create the full meaning of a group of spoken or written words. Unless the person responding to the words adds his or her understanding of the nuances involved, what is being heard or read remains inert, and it is largely in the use of ambiguity to awake and encourage that understanding, that rhetorical and literary subtlety consists. **KMcL**

AMENSALISM

Amensalism (from Greek *a-*, 'not' + Latin *mensalis*, 'one who shares the same table'), in the **life sciences**, is the relationship between two organisms in which one individual is harmed or inhibited by the other. Gause's principle of competitive exclusion states that two species cannot live in direct competition (for example, both requiring identical food) because one or the other will have a competitive advantage and will gain the upper hand through **natural selection. RB**

See also commensalism; niche; parasitism; symbiosis.

Further reading Philip Whitfield, *The Biology of Parasitism.*

ANAL STAGE see **Oral, Anal and Phallic Stages**

ANALOGY

Analogy, in the **life sciences**, is the comparison of two biological systems which have similarity of appearance or function but no genetic link. The concept was defined by Richard Owen, in the 19th century, to differentiate between cases of **homology** and those cases which were similar only at the level of superficial structure or function. The wings of an insect, for example, are analogous with those of a bird, because they have evolved separately to achieve the same function with a fundamentally different structure. **RB**

See also evolution; morphology.

ANALYSIS

Analysis (Greek, 'freeing up'), in **mathematics**, is the study of **calculus** and related topics. For a long time after calculus was revolutionized by Newton and Leibniz in the 17th century, when they discovered the fundamental theorem of calculus, it was regarded as something of a 'poor relation' of other branches of mathematics, some-

thing to be used only if absolutely necessary. The reason is that it was a subject which was not set up in any kind of rigorous way, and which used methods of proof depending on 'infinitesimals' and other vague and loosely defined concepts. (An infinitesimal was a number smaller in size than any other, but not actually zero; the existence of this kind of number seemed extremely unlikely.) The way that both the differential and integral calculi were derived also depended so strongly on infinitesimals (at least in Leibniz's formulation) that it did not appear that mathematicians would ever succeed in removing it. At any earlier time this would not have mattered much, but this was a period in which mathematicians began to seek ever increasing rigour. Michel Rolle (1652–1719) even taught that the calculus was a series of ingenious fallacies.

In the early years of the 19th century, Karl Weierstrass, Bernard Bolzano and Augustin-Louis Cauchy brought rigour to the subject by closer examination of the basic principles, and Weierstrass finally evolved a definition of the concept of 'limit' which did not involve the infinitesimal. Previously, the limit of a **function** at a point a was defined to be the value of that function infinitesimally close to a; the question was, how can a function be defined infinitesimally close to a point? By Weierstrass's new definition, the limit of the function f at the point a is the number y if for every t there is a w such that if the distance between x and a is less than w then the difference of f(x) from y is less than t. From this definition it becomes easy to define integration and differentiation; for example, the derivative of the function f at the point a is the limit at a (if it exists) of the quotient of the distance of f(x) from f(a) by the distance from x to f.

This success prompted an enormous growth in the subject of analysis in the 19th century. There were several different ways in which these ideas were generalized and developed. First, mathematicians began to experiment with generalizations of the concepts of the distance between two numbers and continuity (a function f is continuous at a if the limit of f at a is equal to f(a)); this led to the study of **metrics** (functions generalizing distance) and hence to **topology** and functional analysis (a marriage of the techniques of analysis and topology with those of **linear algebra**).

Second, Cauchy extended the specific generalization of analysis of real numbers to that of **complex numbers**. He proved the fundamental theorems of the new field of complex analysis, many of which seem extremely counter-intuitive, so that complex analysis is extremely powerful but a difficult technique to use. **SMcL**

ANALYTIC AND SYNTHETIC

A statement is analytic just if it is true or false solely in virtue of its meaning. The statement 'all bachelors are male' is analytically true because it is true solely in virtue of its meaning – 'bachelor' means 'unmarried adult male'. The statement 'some spinsters are married' is analytically false because it is false solely in virtue of its meaning – 'spinster' means 'unmarried adult female'.

A statement is synthetic just if it is not true or false solely in virtue of its meaning. The statement 'John is a bachelor' is synthetic because it is not true or false solely in virtue of its meaning. Whether this statement is true or false depends not only on what it means but also on facts about John – on whether or not he is married and an adult. **AJ**

Further reading A.J. Ayer, *Language, Truth and Logic*; J. Foster, *A.J. Ayer*.

ANARCHISM

The origin of the word anarchy is Greek: it means rule by nobody. Anarchists believe that governments and states are both unnecessary and exploitative: far from being an undesirable social condition of perpetual violence, anarchy offers the best hope of human emancipation. The most famous modern anarchist thinkers have been Pierre-Joseph Proudhon (1809–65), Mikhail Bakunin (1814–76) and Pyotr Kropotkin (1842–1921).

Anarchists can be either individualists or collectivists. Anarcho-capitalists are individualists, believing that societies can emerge spontaneously and be sustained solely through voluntary exchange and agreements between consenting individuals. Anarcho-syndicalists, by contrast, are collectivists, believing that collectively owned and managed enterprises could co-ordinate their activities in a decentralized and voluntary manner.

Critics of anarchism maintain that social co-ordination necessarily requires coercive organization (authority or the state) and that anarchists are naive to blame all or most evils in history upon the existence of **states**. The political naivety of anarchists has often taken the form of terrorist action against state authority, although anarchists would reply that large-scale terrorism has been the practice of states since their inception. **BO'L**

Further reading David Miller, *Anarchism*.

ANATOMY

Anatomy (from Greek, 'cutting up') is the field of **biology** concerned with the structure of organisms and the relationship of structure to function. The major technique in anatomy is dissection and the first recorded attempts to learn from dissection were made by the Alexandrian physician Herophilus who publicly dissected human cadavers at around 300 BCE, during the brief period of ancient Greek history when human dissection was permitted. Unfortunately, all his original work was destroyed with the library at Alexandria, but much of his work is known from the descriptions of others. Later, in the 2nd century CE, the gladiators' physician Galen was given the opportunity to investigate much human anatomy, but was unable to dissect cadavers.

The conclusions drawn by Greek anatomists remained largely unchallenged until the Renaissance when interest in anatomy was revived by artists such as Leonardo da Vinci, who made detailed anatomical drawings and recognized (among other things) the **homology** of the bone structures of human and horse legs, and by physicians such as Andreas Vesalius, who disagreed with his superiors at Paris and moved to Padua in Italy to teach anatomy. In 1543 he wrote *Seven Books on the Structure of the*

Human Body and established a new tradition of anatomy based on inquiring examination, a principle which set an example to other branches of science developing at the time.

The appearance of the microscope in the early 17th century enabled the study of microscopic anatomy and initiated the study of the anatomy of tissues (**histology**). Comparative anatomy, in which similarities in structure between differing species are studied and homologous structures such as wings and legs are identified, was pioneered by Edward Tyson who studied human and chimpanzee anatomy. The observations of comparative anatomists such as Tyson and Georges Cuvier, who studied the anatomy of fossil species (**palaeontology**), were a cornerstone of Darwin's evidence for his theory of **evolution**. RB

See also analogy; morphology.

Further reading Warren Walker, *Functional Anatomy of the Vertebrates.*

ANDROGYNY

Androgyny (Greek, 'man-womanness') is a term used to describe a person who has the characteristics of both masculinity and femininity. Androgynous figures appear in many art forms and in world mythologies. For example, in Greek myth, Teiresias lived life both as man and woman and so gained knowledge of sexual difference. The figure of the androgyne has occurred within **feminist** thought and is often used to embody the relation of biological sex type and gender. Many feminists have been fascinated with androgyny and have explored it theoretically and in practice.

In early feminism Virginia Woolf championed androgyny as a strategy to combat the unequal status of men and women. Later feminists have questioned the use of androgyny as a solution to male and female difference, believing that it does not take into account the way in which gender differences are imposed upon people. Some feminists argue that the figure of the androgyne in cinema (for example, Mar-

lene Dietrich or Greta Garbo) is the trangression of masculine and feminine dress and mannerism codes.

Contemporary feminists, such as Catherine Clement, have claimed that the androgynous figures of **myth** and **religion** are a means by which the dominant masculine order can use femininity on its own patriarchal terms. Androgyny often appears in contemporary feminist theory within work on cross-dressing, masquerade and film. **TK**

ANGER

Anger, in psychological terms, is a short-lived emotion, not an ongoing sentiment like love and hate. It is regarded as such because it is usually the response to some frustration or attack on self-worth. Anger may be seen as a release of locked responses, healthy in some instances, but also as an expression of thwarted feelings against some person or object, that avoids such deeper, more painful feelings as loss. **MJ**

ANGLICANISM

The Anglican Communion is a worldwide fellowship of Christian churches who recognize the Archbishop of Canterbury as their spiritual leader. Their representatives meet in conference at Lambeth in London every 10 years and they maintain the apostolic succession, while being independent of each other constitutionally. Anglicanism itself, however, is an ethos, a spirit, a shared history, a way of living and worshipping rather than a movement or an organization. Anglicans claim historical continuity with the first Celtic Christians in the British Isles, the Saxon monasteries and the medieval church, which often deviated significantly from Continental Christendom, and which, despite the martyrdom of Thomas à Becket in 1170, was usually dominated by the king. The break in 1532 between Henry VIII and Rome had more to do with his need for a son and heir than with religious reform, and the subsequent dissolution of the monasteries happened more because he needed ready money than for any religious principle. However, his loyal yet saintly archbishop, Thomas Cranmer, quietly prepared a Book of Common Prayer in English which has nourished public worship and private prayer to this day, and has been adapted and translated into many languages. It has established various liturgical principles for Anglicanism, for example use of the vernacular.

Everyone born in England is nominally Church of England and can call on its pastoral and educational services unless they declare otherwise. Actual membership is through baptism, confirmation, regular attendance at a local church and registration on its electoral roll. **EMJ**

Further reading Stephen Neill, *Anglicanism*.

ANGRY YOUNG MEN

In the period following World War II, there was a feeling among younger people in many Western countries that the entire fabric of society was rotten. It was felt that their elders had failed them, and that the values of society should be certainly questioned and probably swept away. This is, perhaps, a common, even healthy, feeling among the young, but it was particularly vehement from the mid-1950s, and was one of the forces that led to the rise, at about the same time, of 'teenage culture'.

In the UK it was given literary form by a group of writers nicknamed 'the angry young men'. The group included Kingsley Amis, John Osborne, Alan Sillitoe, John Wain and others. Their works attacked the Establishment not merely in thought and utterance, but in a social way (by letting us hear the voice of what one critic disparagingly called 'the bright working class'), and above all, by using techniques of popular culture (notably the routines of stand-up comedy) to subvert such hallowed Establishment forms as the 'novel of ideas' and the 'well-made play'. This streetsmart approach has been of lasting influence – more durable than the works of the Angry Young Men themselves, who, with the exception of Amis and Osborne, have proved to be literary men of straw. During the same period, many of the same writers, along with Philip Larkin, D.J. Enright and others, wrote flatly sardonic poems of a similar tone; they were nicknamed 'The Movement', though they were hardly cohesive or influential enough to justify the phrase. **KMcL**

Further reading Kenneth Allsop, *The Angry Decade*; Blake Morrison, *The Movement*.

ANIMA AND ANIMUS

Anima (Latin, 'spirit') and *Animus* (Latin, 'mind') correspond respectively to the psychological female element in a man and the male element in a woman. Jung believed that each of us carried in our psyche an unconscious image of ourselves as the opposite gender. He formalized symbols that he found in his patients' dreams as *anima* and *animus*.

The *anima* as the female element in the male unconscious is often symbolized as a hermaphrodite figure. Myths that illustrate the male need to rescue the female in himself are those where the hero rescues the damsel in distress. Mistress figures, who guide initiates through spiritual journeys, are also symbols of the *anima* – for example, Kwan-Yin in Chinese **Buddhism**, Sophia in Christian **Gnostic** doctrine or the ancient Greek goddess of wisdom Pallas Athene. These are known as the 'supreme feminine figure', what Goethe called the 'Eternal Feminine'.

The most frequent manifestation of the *anima* takes the form of erotic fantasy. The *anima* can be projected onto a woman until she appears to have its qualities. The *anima* is also often personified by a witch or priestess. *Anima* and *Animus* have dual aspects, life-giving or destructive.

There are four stages in the *anima*'s development. The first stage is exemplified by Eve who has instinctual, biological functions. The second stage, exemplified by Faust's Helen, is the romantic, aesthetic level. The third is exemplified by the Virgin Mary who is love and spiritual devotion. The fourth stage, exemplified by Sapienta, is wisdom transcending the most holy and pure. A man's complete and healthy development, according to Jung, should include these stages, but a man's *anima* is shaped by his mother and may have negative aspects instead.

The prince awakened by the kiss or love of a woman is the story of the reawakened *animus* in the woman. The qualities of the *animus* are the so-called masculine qualities of courage, initiative, intuition, objectivity and spiritual wisdom. The *animus* is hidden from consciousness, as is the *anima* in man, and is apt to take the form of a hidden conviction in women.

In its negative form this would be said to be manifest as a loud, insistent, brutal female personality, or as a woman whose personality relentlessly seeks for power. The *animus* of a woman is influenced by her father and may have negative effects which are said to lead to coldness, obstinacy and inaccessibility; in **myth** these attributes are symbolized by robbers, murderers and death demons.

The stages of the *animus* are: one, personification of physical power; two, initiative and capacity for planned action; three, the word, personified by the professor or clergyman; four, meaning and meditation in religious experience.

Psyche, in Greek myth, is the symbol of the *animus*. Loved by Eros, she was forbidden to look at him, but she did so and he left her. She regained her love only after a long search and much suffering. This story illustrates the negative *anima* rebuilding itself through creative activity. **MJ**

Further reading Carl Jung (ed.), *Man and His Symbols*.

ANIMAL MAGNETISM see Mesmerism

ANIMISM

The word animism (from Latin *anima*, 'spirit') was coined by the English anthropologist E.B. Tylor (1832–1917) to describe the religions of preliterate 'tribal' societies where the religious community was coterminous with the ethnic community. (Tylor was an expert on Central American society.) As he saw it, the predominant characteristic was the attribution of a soul or spirit to inanimate objects such as rivers, trees and mountains, and religion was directed to placating these spirits and those of the ancestors.

Tylor saw animism as the first stage of the education of the world, from which the higher religions and modern Western 'enlightened' civilization have progressed. Borrowing the 'three stages' theory of A. Comte (1798–1857), he divided the human race into the 'savage', the 'barbarian' and the 'civilized'; the implication was that it was the duty of the 'civilized' members of the species to enlighten the others and bestow the benefits of modern technology on them. It was the theory of **evolution** imported into the study of **religion**.

Tylor's theory of the gradual evolution of religion had a pernicious effect on Western perception of tribal religion, reinforcing the effects of racism and colonialism. There is no evidence of a progression from 'lower' to 'higher' in religions. Many religions contain so-called 'primitive' elements, and ideas such as **taboo** are found in one shape or form in most religions. Because of the pejorative associations of the word 'animism' it is usually replaced nowadays, in discussion of the faiths of the indigenous peoples of Africa, the Americas, Australia and elsewhere, with terms such as 'traditional religion' or '**tribal religion**'. **EJ CL KMcL**

ANNALES SCHOOL

The first name of the French journal *Annales: économies, sociétés, civilisations* was given to the group of French historians who founded it and shared common methodological principles. The most famous early members of the school were Marc Bloch and Lucien Febvre; more recent historians associated with the school include Fernand Braudel and Emmanuel Le Roy Ladurie. Braudel's *The Mediterranean and the Mediterranean World in the Age of Philip II* and his three-volume *Civilization and Capitalism* are among the most famous outputs of the Annales school.

There are four distinctive hallmarks of the school: their criticism of historians who focus too much on events; their belief that historians can and should use the methods of the **social sciences**; their rejection of the traditional historian's narrow focus on 'high politics'; and their focus on very long-term historical structures and dynamics (*la longue durée*). The emphasis on the long term, historical **geography**, material **culture** and the study of 'mentalities' is what most distinguishes current exponents of the school, as the belief that historians should employ the methods of the social sciences is now widely accepted by historians, at least outside the British Isles. **BO'L**

See also historical materialism.

Further reading Marc Bloch, *Feudal Society.*

ANOMIE

Anomie (Greek, 'lawlessness') is a concept that was initially brought into common usage by Émile Durkheim (1858–1917). It refers to a situation where the social norms that usually guide human behaviour no longer order individual actions. As with **alienation**, anomie is a concept which attempts to explain individual behaviour in terms of the wider social **structure**. It is assumed that human behaviour is constrained by the existence of explicit and implicit rules for social conduct, rules shared by all members of a given society. The existence of such rules enables individuals to carry on with their everyday life knowing how to behave in certain situations, and, equally, knowing what to expect of others' behaviour. Left to themselves it is believed that human desires are boundless, that there are no 'natural' or inbuilt limitations to the ambitions, desires or needs of individuals. Anomie exists when there are no clear standards to guide behaviour in a given area of social life. Durkheim asserted that in such a situation individuals would feel threatened, anxious and disoriented.

Durkheim believed anomie to be pervasive in modern societies. He believed an anomic division of labour to exist in those societies which failed to allocate jobs fairly according to talents. Durkheim also believed that anomie was one of the social factors causing **suicide**. Suicide, a quintessentially individual act, could, Durkheim maintained, be explained by reference to factors outside of the individual. He had noticed that suicide rates increased both at times of economic collapse and in times of economic boom. Durkheim attributed these variations in the rate to a single factor: anomie. He suggested that both economic boom and economic collapse are times of rapid social change, disrupting the lives of many individuals. Changing circumstances render irrelevant the rules and standards by which individuals guide their lives. It is argued that individuals can ultimately adjust to changes, but this takes time. In the interim there is a loss of meaning and purposefulness to life.

More recently the concept has been developed and used to illuminate other areas of social life. Merton has applied the idea of anomie to crime. He modifies the concept to refer to the strain caused when accepted standards of behaviour conflict with social reality. For example, in many Western societies it is claimed that anyone who works hard can be successful regardless of where they start from. The reality is that the majority of the disadvantaged have very restricted opportunities for advancement. In such a situation there may be pressure to get on by any means possible and this may lead to criminal acts. Merton argues that there are four possible responses to anomie used in this sense: innovation – the use of methods of which society disapproves to achieve one's desired goals; ritualism – going through the motions of pursuing goals by the socially approved means with little or no chance of succeeding; retreatism – opting out; and rebellion – efforts to change the system. **DA**

See also consensus theory; functionalism; internalization; norm; positivism; role; social integration; social order; structuralism; structure-agency debate; values.

Further reading É. Durkheim, *Suicide: a Study in Sociology;* S. Lukes, 'Alienation and anomie', in P. Laslett and W. G. Runciman (eds.), *Philosophy, Politics and Society.*

ANTHROPOLOGICAL LINGUISTICS

Anthropological linguistics is concerned with the way **language** functions as an integral part of human social institutions. This kind of research originated with Bronislaw Malinowski (1884–1942), whose technique of participant observation allows the investigator to observe communities from within, while maintaining an objective stance. Language is studied as it occurs in natural **discourse**, firmly embedded within its cultural context. There is, then, a heavy emphasis on the way language is used, and on the pragmatic knowledge speakers display in the production of speech in social settings (communicative competence). It is argued that the members of a particular speech community draw on a unique repertoire of communicative events. Different speakers may share a common language, but unless they also come from the same speech community, a breakdown in communication may well arise owing to conflicting views about the way communication should be structured. Evidently, speech communities vary widely in the way they construct conversations and deploy their knowledge of language in practice. For anthropological linguists, language is not merely a tool for gaining access to a storehouse of cultural knowledge. It is a fundamental aspect of that knowledge. **MS**

See also anthropology; ethnography; sociolinguistics.

ANTHROPOLOGY

The term anthropology (Greek *anthropos* + *logos*, 'discourse of humankind') was coined by Otto Casmann in 1594. Since its inception as a discipline in the 19th century, anthropologists have focused on the study of non-Western, small-scale, so-called **primitive** peoples. By the 1960s, the subject was broadened to investigate how people conduct their lives in various social and cultural contexts around the world, village and urban, including the anthropologists' own societies.

Remote and unfamiliar peoples have been a topic of interest since recorded times. In Europe, from the 15th century onwards, accounts from travellers about peoples encountered in distant territories were widely available. During the **Enlightenment**, the idea of 'primitive' man existing in a simple communal society became prevalent. In 1761, the French philosopher

Jean-Jacques Rousseau lauded the 'noble savage' who lived in a communal and dignified state – an ideal that was preferable, he claimed, to the economic iniquity and social deterioration of European societies.

The great thinkers of the 19th century viewed the 'primitive' in a different light. Their theories of **race** and **evolutionism** stressed the progressive development of societies from a state of 'primitive' savagery to the peak of contemporary European civilization. Physical anthropologists were engaged in documenting biological features of humans, in support of these theories. European colonial expansion created the means for wider contact between different societies, and anthropologists worked in colonized areas, such as Asia and Africa, where they conducted studies of social organizations, customs and religions. During this period, anthropology was established as a specialist discipline separate from European **sociology** and **philosophy**.

By the beginning of the 20th century, anthropologists rejected earlier theories of the 'primitive', established by evolutionism and physical anthropology, as ill-conceived and biased. In 1914, Bronislaw Malinowski ushered in a new era in anthropology, focusing on the way societies functioned in the present. He advocated that anthropologists engage in extended **field work** in order to gain clearer insights into the communities they were living with. This method, which he termed participant-observation, was the basis of his theory of **functionalism**. Functionalism concentrated on how present social practices and institutions were systematically linked together. By examining the internal logic of and relations between **kinship**, **ritual**, political and economic practices, each society was considered as a complex interrelated whole. Around the same time, American anthropologists established the discipline of Cultural Anthropology, which prioritized the study of **culture** as the system of values, ideas and beliefs, in contrast to British Social Anthropology which emphasized social roles, norms and organizations.

In the 1960s, the French anthropologist Claude Lévi-Strauss initiated a radical break with previous methods of analysing culture by applying **structuralist** models, derived from **linguistics**. With these models, he sought to investigate the conceptual structures of the mind through the observable pattern of social and cultural elements such as **myths**, **symbols** and **totemism**. His theories were widely influential. Nonetheless, they have been the target of several anthropological critiques. Structuralism, like its predecessor functionalism, did not adequately consider historical processes within each community or its **ethnohistory**. It also ignored the constructive role of the individual in society which to some extent was accommodated in later **transactionalist** theories.

Interpretative anthropology of the 1970s grew out of the American school of Cultural Anthropology to consider the way individuals assigned symbolic meanings in cultures. While maintaining the complexity of multi-layered, local interpretations about cultural symbols, these anthropologists believed meanings could be extracted from the world-views of the people in question. The interpretative project highlighted the process of **reflexivity** which examined the possibility of anthropologists imposing their own meaning in the process of translation from one culture to another. This has become central to contemporary anthropology's self-critical awareness of its role as mediator between different societies.

Prior to the 1960s, the political relations between the community and the anthropologist's own society, both historical and contemporary, were overlooked. **Marxist anthropologists**, originally from France, picked up on these concerns to offer more historical, political and economic orientated analyses of particular societies and their relation to countries with a colonizing history. The 1960s was a time in which most non-Western countries had shaken off their colonial rulers, but Marxist anthropologists claim that **neocolonialism** persists because ex-colonial countries still dominate world affairs by virtue of their political and economic **power**. Anthropologists began to re-evaluate their roles in these societies, considering whether anthropological research could be utilized to maintain or challenge the status quo

between different groups in societies or between nations. For instance, anthropology challenged assumptions about the universal subordination of women by showing that **gender** roles were cross-culturally subject to considerable variation.

Such global considerations mean that anthropology can no longer be described as the study of small-scale 'primitive' societies. It has expanded its field of enquiry, incorporating as well as influencing other disciplines such as sociology, pyschology, philosophy, political, economic and literary theories. This interdisciplinary domain is necessary to the consideration of societies, which involves an all-round understanding of human motives and capabilities. Anthropology is now in a strong position to make its arguments relevant to the contemporary world in which communities are connected in a complex of regional and global affairs.

These wider issues have led to a host of anthropological perspectives, all of which have in common the need to clarify and define concepts according to their particular social context. Life can be experienced and perceived in different ways which have led anthropologists to regard phenomena as culturally determined rather than as predetermined by **nature**. Anthropology has now become a discursive investigation into the different ways people organize their lives, beliefs and values rather than a discipline seeking ultimate 'truths' with which to explain them all. As such, anthropology has proved useful in drawing attention to **ethnocentric** assumptions about other peoples' ways of life.

Recent areas that have commanded anthropological attention have expanded the formerly limited horizons of both the discipline and the subject. Such areas include **development**, **tourism**, **visual anthropology**, **emotions**, **ethnicity** and global systems which concentrate on the way travel, migration, political, economic and media networks affect communities around the world. Anthropological discourse is now a dialogue between diverse cultural perspectives and aspires to a better understanding of others as well as of ourselves. **RK**

Further reading Roger Keesing, *Cultural*

Anthropology, A Contemporary Perspective; Adam Kuper, *Anthropology and Anthropologists;* I.M. Lewis, *Anthropology in Perspective.*

ANTHROPOLOGY OF RELIGION

Religion (Latin, 'that which binds') refers to rituals and beliefs which concern a supernatural 'other' world. Supernatural is a loose term to distinguish non-human realms and classes of beings. Beliefs in a supernatural realm could encompass such diverse religious practices as **sacrifice**, sorcery, **shamanism** and communal **cults**. Natural religions, in which deities are explained in terms of their relationship with nature, describe more holistic views about existence, rather than splitting the world into two distinct categories of natural and supernatural.

Anthropologists in the 19th century were concerned with finding the origins of religion, and creating a way of classifying the diverse religions found in 'primitive' societies. From the perspective of their institutionalized world religions, evolutionary anthropologists considered the earliest form of religion as ancestor worship, which evolved in to **animism**, **polytheism** and finally **monotheism**. Other models saw religion as an embryonic precursor to **science**. All these types of religion were regarded by evolutionists as fulfilling primary human needs in a utilitarian way. Religions provided an explanation for human existence, as well as attuning humans to a specific view of the cosmic order. As a cultural system, it provides the individual with the means to interpret personal experience. Religion often contains rituals whose express purpose is the maintenance of proper relationships with the 'other world'. When moral relations are not maintained a means of restoring balance must be sought through **ritual** and healing. In this way, religion plays a considerable part in reinforcing the moral and social order of the community.

The sociologist Émile Durkheim saw religion as a spatial and temporal realm set apart from everyday life, which helped to create a sense of solidarity among the members of a community. Deities were created in the image of society, rather than the other way round. This notion informed early studies of **totemism** as a form of ancestor worship.

In the 1960s, structuralists picked up the argument about **rationality** associated with science, technology and **economics** as being superior to other forms of explanation. They concluded that both religious and scientific modes of thought were parallel expressions of universal methods of classification that ordered the world around them.

Anthropologists now question the assumption that religion can be treated as a unitary category because of the multiplicity of interpretations and possible meanings ascribable to it. **Interpretative anthropology** redefined religion as a 'system of ideas about the ultimate shape and substance of reality'. This definition expressed the relationship between metaphysics and the social order.

Many African religions make a distinction between this world, the world of human society, and the 'other world'. The role of religious experts is to mediate between this world and the other. They gain their knowledge through bodily experience in the performance of rituals, rather than through scripture or faith, as in institutionalized, world systems of religion. In this context, religious knowledge is derived from a coherence of ontological conceptions and experiential reality. **CL**

See also symbolism; tradition.

Further reading A. Lehman and J. Myers (eds.), *Magic, Witchcraft and Religion;* Brian Morris, *Anthropological Studies of Religion.*

ANTHROPOMORPHISM

Anthropomorphism (Greek, 'giving human shape') is the technique of attributing human shape, ideas and feelings to non-human entities. It is a practice as ancient as the human race, and its root purpose seems to be not so much to 'dignify' non-human entities by imagining them like us, as to bring them within range of our own human understanding. Thus, at the simple level, one can say that clouds, for example, have 'faces', and at a more complex level that they 'frown' or 'race'. It may be claimed, initially as a poetic fancy, that Nature is empathetic to human emotions. One can talk of 'cunning' foxes or 'loyal' dogs, or imagine, for instance, a wildebeest cow mourning her newborn calf taken by lions. Sentient animals (and indeed trees, rivers, even rocks and buildings) are staples in **literature** of every kind. (Examples range from the frog in Aesop's fable who is ambitious to be an ox to the Houyhnhnms of Swift's *Gulliver's Travels*, from the trickster Coyote of African and American folk tale to Tolkien's Ents and George Orwell's pig-Napoleon.) One of the aims of **magic** is to allow human beings to enter into the condition of animals, to acquire, for example, 'second hearing' (the ability to understand all animal 'languages').

Anthropomorphism is particularly important to human beings trying to comprehend the supernatural. It is hard to come to terms with supernatural forces which have no shapes – with the ancient Greek Titans, for example, who became whatever they thought (fireball, hill, leaf, might, rage) for as long as they held that thought. It is much easier to project some kind of transcendent human identity on to supernatural 'beings' (the word itself is anthropomorphic), and then attempt to form relationships on the human model. The whole of **animism** depends on the view that the environment itself consents with human beings in a kind of shared perception and acceptance of existence. Many religions anthropomorphize their gods, either as beings with every human attribute magnified (as in ancient Greek or Nordic religion), or as beings that assume human nature in order to communicate with humans. Some religions go further, adding theriomorphism to anthropomorphism: their gods take on the shapes of beasts as well as of humans. For example, Sekhmet in ancient Egyptian religion, and Mother Earth in Aztec cosmology, had a crocodile shape; Ganesh in **Hinduism** has a human body and an elephant's head; the creator-god in much Australian native religion is a rainbow-snake. Even religions that attribute no physical human shape to their gods (such as **Christianity** and **Islam**) talk of

God as 'he', as a 'father', as 'wise', as 'merciful' and so on. **Shinto** shrines contain no visual images and yet Shinto **mythology** is full of anthropomorphic images. To the believer, all this is perfectly simple, an essential and unquestioned component of faith itself. To the nonbeliever, it might seem that whether we are dealing with the demon-masks of ancient native religions or with such comparatively sophisticated ideas as the Christian 'God made man', we are in the presence of something which tells us much less about the mysterious nature of the supernatural than about the imperatives of human psychology. **EMJ KMcL**

ANTI-CLERICALISM

Anti-clericalism is a liberal or socialist doctrine of opposition to the political authority, power and status of the clergy. In Europe the Catholic clergy were the special target of the currents of anti-clericalism which flourished in the post-**Enlightenment** era and influenced many European nationalist movements, including the French, Spanish, Italian and Irish revolutionary nationalist movements of the mid-19th century. In the 20th century, political cleavages between clericalists and anti-clericalists shaped electoral support for parties, especially in Italy and France. Anti-clericalist movements range from having particularist objectives (for example, getting rid of Jesuits) to general opposition to all types of clerical power (for instance, atheist campaigns in the USSR in the 1930s). A contemporary example of organized anti-clericalism is the movement in the US to prevent religious fundamentalists winning the right to practise religious activities in state schools. **BO'L**

Further reading José Sánchez, *Anticlericalism: a Brief History.*

ANTI-SEMITISM

Anti-semitism is intellectual hatred of, or prejudice towards, **Judaism** and Jews. Anti-semitism takes many forms: a hatred of Jews for their exclusivity and unique religious practices; a Christian hatred of Jews as the alleged killers of Christ; and in modern times is normally racist, suggesting that Jews are genetically inferior and inherently evil, and conspiratorial, suggesting that Jews control the world's finances, large-scale enterprises and communist parties.

Zionists claim that there is a modern political form of anti-semitism which rejects the idea that the state of Israel should exist. For them the question 'does Israel have the right to exist?' is equivalent to asking 'do Jews have the right to exist?'. Anti-Zionists vigorously reject the argument that opposition to Zionism is a form of anti-semitism, maintaining that the smear of anti-semitism is a rhetorical strategy designed to avoid criticisms of Israeli settler-colonialism in Palestine.

Religious anti-semitism has been prevalent in pre-Christian, Christian and Islamic cultures for over two millennia. Racist anti-semitism emerged in the form of a backlash against the legal emancipation of Jews which began in Europe at the end of the 18th century. In the 1870s, the writings of Germans like Marr, Stoecker and von Treitschke established a doctrine of Jewish racial inferiority which spread throughout central and eastern Europe, and to France in a somewhat milder form.

The political and economic crises in Germany and Austria in the 1920s and 1930s fostered anti-semitism, and it became an integral component of **Nazi** doctrine, in which Jews were scapegoated for the evils of capitalism and communism. Anti-semitism culminated in Hitler's Third Reich and the murder of six million Jews – his 'final solution' for the 'Jewish problem'. Today racist anti-semitism remains an important component of neo-fascist and integral **nationalist** movements in Europe and America. **BO'L**

See also race and racism.

Further reading Michael Curtis, *Antisemitism in the Contemporary World*; Léon Poliakov, *The History of Anti-semitism, I–IV*.

ANTIHERO see Hero

ANTIMASQUE see Masque

ANTINOVEL

An antinovel is a kind of fiction that chal-lenges our assumptions of what the **novel** ought to be. By subverting expectation, it focuses attention on the writer's underlying agenda rather than on superficial aspects of style or narrative. Cervantes' *Don Quixote* is not the adventure-saga whose structure it assumes; Thomas Mann's *Confessions of Felix Krull* is not the **picaresque** tale, and his *Buddenbrooks* is not the **bildungsroman** they purport to be. Subversion of formal expectation is often a feature of comic novels, from Laurence Sterne's *The Life and Opinions of Tristram Shandy, Gentleman* to Joseph Heller's *Catch-22*. The antinovel reached its apogee in the 20th century, when general awareness of past styles and forms liberated creative artists of all kinds. They were able to take elliptical, ironical or lateral approaches not just to their subject matter, but to the techniques of their art, in the certainty that their audience would follow them. Antinovels are often claimed to be the especial prerogative of the French **New Fiction** writers of the 1960s and beyond. In fact the style appears throughout the century. In the sense described above, Samuel Beckett, Italo Calvino, Günter Grass, Hermann Hesse, James Joyce, Pär Lagerkvist, D.H. Lawrence, Gabriel García Márquez and Virginia Woolf were all antinovelists – and by no means all of them were mere experimenters. **KMcL**

ANTIQUE, THE

Although antiquities (that is, 'antiques') have been described as 'rubbish old enough to be precious', 'the antique' is a shorthand term in art criticism for the whole package of Greek, Hellenistic and Roman art and architecture from the 5th century BCE to about the 4th century CE. Its study became of increasing importance for both the nature and the development of European art from the time of Charlemagne – an importance confirmed by the Italian **Renaissance**, the very name of which implies a 'rebirth' of art under the influence of ancient models. That painting, sculpture and architecture were all affected by the antique until the advent of **modernism** does not imply that the tradition is now dead, for **postmodernism** has seen to its resuscitation.

The profound importance of the antique in Western art is clearly illustrated by the number of articles touched by the concept in this book. Its works of art are the backbone of the classical tradition, and **academies** were set up to do that tradition honour. Great collectors, public museums and galleries focused predominantly on the antique. All were supplied in an almost systematic way by the young gentlemen who went on the Grand Tour – frequently nothing more than a more elegant version of plundering. It is, also, not the case that interest in the antique only began with the Renaissance: it is the core of Carolingian art, and much in evidence in the famous sketchbook of the 13th-century architect Villard de Honnecourt.

Although the antique can be a tyranny, the emotional richness and stylistic variety of the exemplars it provided have more usually made it an inspiration. Such richness and variety were given extra poignancy, in art, because they reflected and perpetuated the grandeur and attainments of the civilizations which had given them birth. **MG PD**

Further reading Michael Greenhalgh, *The Classical Tradition in Art*.

ANXIETY

Anxiety (Greek, 'racking'), that is distress of mind, disquietude and uneasiness, is not generally regarded in psychology as an irrational fear – a suggestion that may come from such common phrases as 'Anxiety was driving him out of his mind'. Anxiety does not have a clear source, unlike a phobia, but can be traced to unconscious processes (in **psychoanalysis**) and to faulty responses and thinking (**cognitive therapy**).

Psychoanalysis has focused on the unconscious sources of anxiety. Originally it saw anxiety as the outcome of repressed **libido**. Freud also thought at one time that anxiety was the result of an unconscious memory of the birth **trauma**.

The most recent view in psychoanalysis is that anxiety has two distinct characters. One signals towards changes in the environment, when the person makes an appraisal of internal or external danger. The other is the result of the **ego** not being able to defend itself from internal threats created by the tension between the ego and other subconscious and unconscious elements; an assessment is made of the ability to deal with the danger on conscious, subconscious and unconscious levels. Each is a system of defence. In mental disorders there is a distortion of the reality of the internal picture, which in turn distorts the external picture. People suffering from **neurosis** usually suffer much greater levels of anxiety.

Freud saw anxiety as a self-preservation instinct, and this is echoed in other psychological views which see it as an essential response to danger, part of the fight or flight reaction, a useful function, and part of the human condition. Others see anxiety as a disruptive element in dealing with danger. In cognitive models the external threat is seen as being followed by the appraisal of threat and then by coping behaviour. Anxiety comes in at the appraisal stage, and is usually based on a false picture. This causes unnecessary suffering in a misjudged situation, and more danger in a truly threatening encounter. The cognitive therapist, therefore, aims to address the unrealistic appraisal as a way of dealing with anxiety. **MJ**

Further reading S. Freud, *Inhibitions, Symptoms and Anxieties*.

APHASIOLOGY

Aphasiology (Greek, 'study of speech disorder'), in **linguistics**, is the study of language disorders which have been caused by brain damage. Injury can occur through serious accidents; via disease, such as tumours; or as the result of cerebro-vascular accident (stroke). As in many areas of science, the rationale behind aphasiology is that we can often gain valuable insights into the workings of a system when that system breaks down. It is hoped, then, that specific malfunctions in the speech of aphasic patients will shed light on the functioning of the unimpaired language system.

One of the earliest discoveries in aphasiology was reported by the French neurologist Paul Broca in 1861. Two of Broca's patients had severe language disorders (one of them was reduced to the two pronouncements *tan* and *sacré nom de dieu*). From a subsequent autopsy performed on these patients, it emerged that they had both suffered damage to a specific area in the front portion of the left hemisphere of the brain (later dubbed Broca's area). It has since been found that patients suffering from Broca's aphasia can generally understand what is said to them, but have considerable difficulty in producing speech. Sentences tend to be short and are produced intermittently, with long pauses in between. Broca's aphasia is also characterized by agrammatical sentences which arise from the omission of so-called function words, such as 'the', 'of' and 'to'.

Since Broca's pioneering studies, research in aphasiology has implicated several other areas of the brain as potential speech centres. One of the most important, located in the posterior part of the left hemisphere, was named Wernicke's area after Carl Wernicke in 1872. Patients suffering from Wernicke's aphasia possess fluent speech with generally intact grammatical structure. There may, however, be problems in attaching affixes, such as ing, in the appropriate context (for example, 'is louding' instead of 'is loud'). However, the most notable symptom of Wernicke's aphasia is a drastic reduction in the powers of speech comprehension.

A recurrent theme in aphasiology research has been the suggestion that damage to particular areas of the brain leads to specific language disorders. This finding would seem to suggest that certain language functions are highly localized. From the discussion of Broca's aphasia and Wernicke's aphasia above, for example, it might be tempting to conclude that Broca's area is crucial for the production of speech, whereas Wernicke's area controls the ability to process and understand speech. Although this localization hypothesis is still favoured by many researchers, others recommend caution since the effects of neurological damage, though seemingly highly localized, can in fact have unforeseen consequences in other areas. Most obviously, the immediate area leading to a brain lesion may be flooded with blood, while the area beyond the damaged section may be starved of blood. Thus, the normal functioning of otherwise unaffected regions can be seriously disrupted. Evidently, aphasiology can provide us with invaluable insights into the relationship between brain and language, but we should be aware that injured brains may not always be representative of normal ones. **MS**

See also neurolinguistics.

Further reading R. Lesser, *Linguistic Investigations of Aphasia.*

APOCALYPTIC LITERATURE

The root thought that gave rise to apocalyptic literature was the Judaeo-Christian idea that human life, indeed the life of the universe, is not random but an ordered progression from the Beginning through to the End. Some apocalyptic writers, for example William Blake, were particularly concerned with the End, and developed images, ideas and language directly from Revelation, the last book of the New Testament, which details the final days of the world.

Apocalyptic writers in general, however, are more concerned with the sequence of dire events, the crumbling of civilization, which precedes that end. Dystopian writing of this kind sees the human race as doomed (usually self-doomed). We are trapped like animals, laboratory specimens at the mercy of irresponsible powers; we are overbred, especially intellectually, and our own ingenuity is destroying us; we are too prolific; we are plundering the planet. Once such broadening of the idea is allowed, a huge range of writers can be described as apocalyptic, from Swift to George Orwell, from Zola to Wyndham Lewis. Critics have suggested that the apocalyptic imagination is a particular characteristic of 20th-century writing, both directly in **sf** (where writers such as J.G. Ballard, Harry Harrison and George Turner regularly depict the horrors of a future in which present-day problems – the **greenhouse effect**, over-population, too many cars – are multiplied in geometric progression towards oblivion), or in writers who have used sf ideas and techniques in a wider context, such as John Barth, Alasdair Gray, Thomas Pynchon and Kurt Vonnegut.

The New Apocalypse was a short-lived, 1940s movement, involving poets who wrote for a 1940s anthology with that title (edited by J.F. Hendry). Their interest was in 'love, death, and adherence to Myth and an awareness of war' – slightly wider than such earlier war-haunted poets as Wilfred Owen or Siegfried Sassoon – and they included such people as Vernon Watkins, Henry Treece and Norman MacCaig. KMcL

APPLICABILITY OF MATHEMATICS

Applicability is the real strength of **mathematics**: its relationship to the scientific method is the fact that it is so successful in explaining the real world.

Mathematics began with the **abstraction** of properties from the real world around us; it proves its usefulness when the results obtained from this abstraction are turned back again to the real world. This is how science works; scientists abstract the properties they wish to study from experimental evidence (for example, the observations of planetary motion over many years were used to find the positions of the planets); this abstraction is then manipulated mathematically, possibly with other assumptions thrown in (for example, Newton assumed that the attraction between the planets varied according to the inverse of the square of the distance between them), to find a mathematical way of describing this data (in Newton's case, that the planets move in elliptical orbits around the Sun), which can then be verified by further experimentation (which in this example, had already been done a century before by Kepler). The whole of **physics** and much of many other sciences depends on this procedure. It has been used also in unexpected places in fine **art** in the early **Renaissance**: for example, the science of **perspective** was developed mathematically as a method for producing pictures that looked more realistic.

The method of applying mathematics outlined above has proved greatly successful. Today, if the experiment to verify the mathematical conclusion does not give results that match up with the predictions, the scientist does not decide that mathematics is of no use. On the contrary, he or she checks the other parts of the procedure first: that false results are not being obtained because of something which was not originally taken into account, or because there was an error (such as over-simplification) in the abstraction. Even if neither of these is the case, there is enough confidence in the reliability of the mathematics that the conclusion that follows is not that this is a case where mathematics is not applicable, but that the extra assumptions which were made (possibly unconsciously) were wrong. SMcL

APPLIED LINGUISTICS

At present, the term 'applied linguistics' enjoys great currency, yet it is clear that any comprehensive description of the field might render the term vacuous, so disparate are the separate strands contributing to the whole. Speech therapy, for example, sits awkwardly alongside genre analysis, which must make room for research on **language planning**, computer-assisted language learning, language in education and so on, in a seemingly haphazard compilation of themes. Arguably, it has become all but impossible to recognize applied linguistics as a unified academic discipline. To add to the confusion, the term has become closely associated with the specific concerns of second and foreign language learning.

Nonetheless, a general attitude or approach to language can be discerned in applied linguistics. In particular, there is an overriding commitment to explore the manifestation of language as it actually functions in people's lives.

A key concept pervading many applied linguistic concerns is the notion of communicative competence, which augments our (intuitive) knowledge of grammatical rules with the idea that we also possess systematic knowledge about how language is deployed in order to fulfil its communicative potential. In this respect, therefore, knowledge of language use is regarded as an integral part of the language system. It is not separable from, nor in any way inferior to, our knowledge of **phonology**, **semantics**, **syntax** and so on. In many ways, therefore, we can discern a conscious reaction against the approach of linguistics proper, in which language is regarded as an abstract object, studied in isolation from the way it functions as a social phenomenon.

The concept of communicative competence is immediately applicable to applied linguistic studies of language learning and language teaching. A substantial body of research in recent years has been founded on the assumption that success in the acquisition of a second or foreign language is crucially dependent on the quality of communicative interaction experienced by learners. Hence the way communication is structured can affect the learner's ability, not only to convey and understand messages, but also to increase proficiency in the foreign language. There are obvious repercussions for pedagogy here, and they have determined that questions of how language is taught rank alongside questions concerning what is taught.

The concern with foreign language learning has also prompted interesting comparisons with the way a child acquires his or her mother tongue (see **psycholinguistics**). For an adult beginner in a foreign language, the concept of being taught the language in a classroom, according to the precepts of a consciously crafted syllabus, is not at all unusual. Infants, though, are never provided with explicit language lessons by their parents, yet arguably, they achieve a degree of linguistic mastery which adults can never hope to match. On the other hand, there are undoubted affinities between the processes of first and second language acquisition. In consequence, evidence from applied linguistic research has recently been marshalled in support of the concept of **universal grammar**, the genetic programme which dictates what both the adult and the infant know (and can possibly know) about language. Encouragingly, then, it is clear that research in applied linguistics can be relevant to abstract theoretical issues, in addition to its abiding concern with more tangible language-related issues. MS

Further reading D. Crystal, *Directions in Applied Linguistics*; R. Ellis, *Understanding Second Language Acquisition*.

APPLIED MATHEMATICS

Applied mathematics is the relating of mathematical concepts and results to the real world. Among researchers, it has always been the poor relation of **pure mathematics**, ever since the beginning of the latter as a systematic subject with the ancient Greeks. Pure mathematicians have tended to look down on their applied counterparts as being somehow sullied with the impurities of the world. (This is an attitude perhaps inherited from the Greeks, who viewed mathematics, and indeed all of science, as something that should take place as far away from the corruption of real life as possible.)

Needless to say, this contempt for applied mathematics does not permeate the whole of society. The average person might tend to look on all mathematics as equally abstract, uselessly divorced from the practical world. Governments have, however, usually favoured applied mathematics when it comes to giving research grants, mainly because it is easier to explain the goals of a research project of applied mathematics in terms of short-term material effects on society. This position is remarkably short-sighted; it overlooks the fact that applied mathematicians usually make use of pure mathematics that is already in existence; the only major advance in pure mathematics which was forced by the needs of applied mathematics or theoretical physics was Newton's development of the **calculus**, to enable him to solve the equations of planetary motion.

The two views need to be balanced. Applied mathematics, the ability to relate the abstract concepts of pure mathematicians to the world, is a gift which few pure mathematicians have. On the other hand, many of the major advances in science have come from making new applications of branches of pure mathematics which had already been developed with no thought of their possible application (and often, indeed, doubts that they would ever have any practical relevance). The prime example of this in the 20th century is Einstein's application of **non-Euclidean geometry** to the problems developing in late-19th-century physics to come up with his theories of **relativity**. SMcL

APPROXIMATION

Approximation, in **mathematics**, is the use of solutions to a problem when they are not exactly correct.

Approximation is all that **applied mathematics** can give to the true physical picture, for two reasons. First, in experiments in the physical world, an exact answer can never be obtained: this is due to the limits of accuracy of measuring machines and to human error. Second, it is usually the case that simplifying assumptions are made when the mathematical analysis is undertaken, in the processes of **abstraction** and application (see **applicability of mathematics**). Sometimes, only approximate mathematical solutions can be found, as in **chaos theory**.

The difference this makes from the real world does not really have a harmful effect on science, provided that the scientist always realizes that it is there. If scientists make allowances for the errors which have resulted when they test their theories experimentally (and a large body of mathematics helps them to work out how large the error might be), they will be truly following the **scientific method**, whereby they will attempt to find closer and closer approximations to the truth. In this way, Newton's theory of gravitation was superseded by a better approximation when Einstein formulated the theory of **relativity**. SMcL

ARABISM (PAN-ARABISM)

Arabism (Arabic *urubah*) is the founding ideology of the Arab nationalist movement, and emphasizes the Arabic language and culture as markers of a distinct national identity amongst the people of North Africa and the Middle East.

Arabism emerged during the decline of the Ottoman Empire in the second half of the 19th century, and spread rapidly after 1918. In the first half of the 19th century scholars like al Tahtawi advocated Arab patriotism as part of a larger Ottoman supra-nationalism to rival the nationalist organization of the Western European states, and to protect the Islamic faith from the incursions of Christendom.

Arabism emerged as a widely held separatist ideology before and after the 1914-18

war. The collapse of the Ottoman Empire in 1918 meant that Arabs no longer had a protective union against the Western European powers, and this change gave a decisive boost to Arabism. **Ba'athism** ('resurrection' in Arabic) was the primary pan-Arabic movement. It was influenced by the socialist organization of the Bolsheviks and was a reaction against the primacy of **Islam** as a unifying principle within the Ottoman Empire. Arabists do not reject Islam: they portray it as the fruit of Arab culture and history, and thereby assert the primacy of **nationalism** over religion.

Pan-Arabism seeks a unified state embracing all Arabic speaking peoples. Like the Pan-Africanist movement, the Pan-Arabic movement was divided between proponents of inter-governmental economic and political co-operation between sovereign Arab states (for example Lebanon), and advocates of the merger of existing Arab states into a single state (such as Syria). The Arab League was formed in 1945 with the aspiration to create eventual unity, but it has remained committed only to the moderate goals of inter-governmental co-operation. A short-lived United Arabic Republic (1958–61) of Syria and Egypt created temporary optimism that a broader pan-Arabic ideal could be achieved. Factions of the Ba'athist Party have held power in Iraq under Saddam Hussein, and in Syria, under President Assad. Their dictatorships have not led to pan-Arabist unity, but rather the converse.

Presently pan-Islamic movements may have superseded pan-Arabic movements in political importance in the Arabic world. BO'L

See also Africanism.

Further reading Albert Hourani, *A History of the Arab Peoples*; R Kalidi et al. (eds.), *The Origins of Arab Nationalism*.

ARBITRATION

Arbitration refers to dispute-settlement by a third party who attempts to negotiate a compromise or settlement between two or more antagonists. The concept of arbitration is normally contrasted with mediation. Arbitration implies that the arbiter has the capacity to impose a solution, and this capacity has normally been acknowledged by the antagonists in advance of the final settlement. Mediators, by contrast, normally lack the right and ability to impose a settlement. Because arbitration may involve flexible principles partially agreed in advance by the participants, it must be distinguished from adjudication, which follows firmly established procedures set by legal precedent.

Arbitration as a conflict-resolution mechanism in international relations began with the Jay Treaty between the USA and Britain in 1794. In 1899, the Permanent Court of Arbitration was established in The Hague, providing a pool of arbiters for international conflicts. While the Court has contributed to the resolution of several conflicts, the role of arbitration in international conflicts has been less prominent than originally envisaged, partly because of the transformation of the Court into a more strictly legal body. As a result, the Court of Arbitration competes (unfavourably) with other regional and international bodies, most notably the International Court of Justice and regional juridicial bodies such as the European Court of Human Rights and the European Court of Justice. However, the practice of placing arbitration clauses in treaties between and among states and corporate bodies is still common.

Arbitration more generally is increasingly used as a desirable dispute-settlement device in technical matters, because the parties to the dispute can nominate technical specialists as arbiters rather than rely on (expensive) lawyers. **BO'L**

Further reading J.G. Merrills, *International Dispute Settlement*; A.H.A. Soons, *International Arbitration: Past and Prospects*.

ARCHAEOLOGY

Archaeology (Greek, 'study of ancient things') is a comparatively recent study, dating from the rediscovery and first excavations of Pompeii in the 18th century. At first archaeology was little more than organized treasure-hunting, financed by rich Europeans anxious to own originals of the vases and statues previously only known from description or from **Renaissance** imita-

tions. But from the beginning of the 19th century (with Belzoni's work in Egypt), it became more and more systematic, and now adds a huge range of geographical, scientific, statistical and technological skills to the crude trowels and inspired guesswork which have been its main tools since the beginning. Also, nowadays, the reports of past excavations, and the presence in museums and university collections of the objects found in sites throughout the world, give archaeologists a huge weight of past experience and conjecture to draw on.

The archaeologist begins either with evidence (for example, documents or other historical accounts) or with an informed hunch about a particular site. (In modern urban societies, the first call can sometimes be an appeal by builders who have found ancient remains while excavating foundations, and want 'rescue archaeology' done to document the site and remove remains before they continue building over it.) The site is then prospected, surveyed and photographed before any digging takes place. Exacavation itself is systematic: a grid is prepared of the site, and each layer is carefully uncovered and documented before any lower ones are touched. (This is in contrast to the methods of earlier archaeologists, such as Schliemann, who cheerfuly dug up and threw away upper layers until they reached the one they wanted.) The prime task at this stage is to establish a **context** for every piece of evidence unearthed, by describing, drawing, mapping, numbering and photographing. Found objects may be in their primary position (that is, where they were placed or used by the original people of the site), or in secondary positions (for example on rubbish-heaps), or they may have been disturbed by natural phenomena or animals after their original owners left them. They are sometimes then removed for further analysis (for instance, dating by such methods as radiocarbon analysis or typology – comparing them with like finds from a known period), and sometimes left *in situ*. As the work proceeds, a stratigraphy of the site is built up: a vertical drawing of the layers, either a scale drawing or a matrix (graphic chart something like a family tree), with each layer and object meticulously entered and dated.

Archaeology is enormously expensive, and many sites remain only partially explored (Luxor in Egypt and Ankhor Wat in Thailand are cases in point) or not explored at all. Because of its costs, and because its activities impinge on land use of other kinds, it is a politically sensitive discipline. But in the 200 years of its existence, archaeology has united with work in **fine art**, **history** and the study of languages, literatures and religions to refocus, with scientific clarity and objectivity, our view of almost every aspect of the past. **KMcL**

Further reading Brian Hayden, *Archaeology: the Science of Once and Future Things.*

ARCHAISM

Archaism, in the **arts**, refers to the taste for the primitive and naive, and to an interest in the revival of such archaic models. It often predicates the belief in the innate value of the earlier model coming from a simpler, purer **golden age**, and that the revival of these forms will encourage a revival of the imagined quality of life of those former days. **JM**

See also classicism; Romanticism.

ARCHETYPES

Archetypes (Greek, 'originals') were discovered by Jung through the analysis of dreams. He discovered that images occur which are not always part of our own history or personal experience. He also discovered that these elements, which seemed to be inherited from somewhere else, had a tendency to organize themselves into predetermined patterns or symbols; these he called archetypes. Freud's analysis of dreams had come up with similar anomalies which he had called 'archaic remnants': part of our archaic past and biological development; a part of our mind that is close to animals. Each of us, in this sense, has an extremely old psyche, a deposit of collective images and primitive motifs. They are, according to Jung, fantasies and visual representations of our instincts. Each archetype is a recurring pattern of human development, which will represent itself as a mythical figure, image or motif. Six examples of archetypes we are

thought to live by are the Hero, the Orphan, the Wanderer, the Warrior, the Martyr and the Magician. **MJ**

Further reading Carol S. Pearson, *The Hero Within.*

ARCHITECT

The notion of the architect (Greek, 'master-builder'), essential to the understanding of the built environment, is relatively modern. The architect is usually understood to be both the designer of a building and the supervisor of its construction.

Writing about the architect in his treatise *De Architectura* in the 1st century BCE, the Roman theorist Vitruvius represented him as a polymathic ideal, one learned in all the arts, a scholar of history, philosophy, music and medicine, each field contributing to the architect's ability to design well. In the 4th century, Pappus of Alexandria provided a less rhetorical account, stressing the necessity of a theoretical background in up-to-date mathematical and mechanical science.

In medieval Europe it was traditionally the skilled master mason who was the most significant figure in the construction of a great building. In the later 15th and early 16th centuries, when most cultural life was characterized by the rediscovery of classical texts, the rediscovery of Vitruvius's treatise led to a reinforcement of the highest ideals of what contributed to the education and skill of an architect. Architects began to be appointed for their fame as artists (Giotto, for example, was appointed architect of Florence Cathedral), and while they might still come from the families of master masons, they often combined architecture with painting and sculpture. Leonardo da Vinci developed the theory of the 'ideal nature of art', by which he tried to prove that painting and architecture belonged to the **liberal arts** and not to the trades.

Formalized training in the classical principles characterized European education until the 19th century, when debate arose concerning 'architecture: art or profession?'. Its professional character was underlined by the introduction of qualifying exams, and by the gradual streamlining of the various tasks of other related professionals, requiring the skills of a structural engineer or a town planner. **JM**

See also craftsmanship; town planning.

Further reading A. Saint, *The Image of an Architect*; H.M. Colvin, *A Biographical Dictionary of British Architects 1600–1840*, chapter 2, 'The Architectural Profession'.

ARCHITECTURE

Architecture (Greek/Latin, 'skill of the master builder') was, until very recently, an activity more cognate with (say) surgery or shipbuilding than with any of the **arts**. That is to say, its skills were universally known and practised, and there were individual practitioners of genius (some of them even known by name, for example Imhotep, who designed the Great Pyramid at Gizeh and is the first 'known' architect in history), but there was no universal theory or critical consensus about it. Buildings were commissioned, built and used, as wounds were dressed or ships constructed: the work was functional, and it never occurred to anyone to assess its skills or measure its success or failure in other than functional terms.

The principal purposes of such 'architecture' are first, to provide shelter and security, and second, to dignify such activities as religious practice and rule. If aesthetic considerations impinged at all, it would be in choice of materials and of decoration – and even then, in early times, all but the most ornate buildings (**temples** or mausoleums, for example) were what one might call 'organic' architecture, made from locally available materials, 'growing' out of the surroundings as naturally as woods or hills. In such circumstances, 'thought' about architecture, even at its finest, must also have tended to be practical and undemonstrative – and not just in prehistoric times, but until well into the modern era. No doubt the people who planned and executed the Parthenon complex in Athens, the temples at Ankor Wat or Macchu Pichu and the palaces and streets of Fatehpur Sikri must have had anxious discussions about the overall planning of the sites and the place of the buildings in their environment; they must have made plans and discussed them;

they may well have felt a glow of creative satisfaction when the job was done. But their work was considered craft rather than art, and they were more likely to talk about foundations and materials than about such abstract notions as 'form follows function' or 'the built environment'. When the Roman writer Vitruvius, 'architect' to the Emperor Augustus, published his treatise *De architectura* in the 1st century BCE, he intended it not as an artistic statement but as a manual.

This lack of artistic pretension gave architecture a low-key image (despite the size and magnificence of so many of its artefacts) in most of the world through most human history. The architect was a craftsman, more at home with the surveyors and builders he worked with than in the salons of the patron. In the case of most buildings, the planners were as anonymous as the executors – indeed, they may well have been the same people. This is still the way of things in the greater part of the world: architecture may nowadays be taught as a practical art, with a codified set of theories and techniques and a libraryful of historical exemplars of style, but in the real world houses, shops, warehouses and so on are built as need arises, in a kind of consensus style determined by practicality and expense rather than by the designer's inspiration. It is only the wealthy – nowadays corporations more frequently than individuals – who can commission buildings to be works of art.

The concepts of the architect as an artist, and of architecture as fine art, is Western and dates from the **Renaissance**. A key idea was that beautiful works of art should be placed harmoniously in beautiful buildings, themselves grouped to enhance the overall effect. The environment itself was designed; each part had artistic significance not merely in its own right but as one component of a pre-planned whole. Architecture, being concerned with the enclosure of space, was a three-dimensional art form, but three-dimensionality was the only real distinction made between it and other kinds of art. The architects who enclosed the grandest spaces – individuals (as in the Square of Miracles in Pisa) or teams (as in the St Peter's complex in Rome) – were often painters or sculptors as well as architects; they shared the principles and ambitions of fine art, and the self-absorption and creative pretension of its practitioners. In their hands the planning of buildings, and of the space in which buildings were placed, for the first time took precedence over the actual brute activities of building: surveying, preparing the site, gathering materials and so on were relegated (on the ladder of creativity) in the same way as such practices as sizing a canvas, mixing colours, preparing a marble block or casting bronze did in the other arts.

This elevation of the architect from craftsman to genius – 'elevation', 'craftsman' and 'genius' are typical terms from the theoretical writing of the time – has persisted ever since, and has spread from the West throughout the world, at least at the expensive end of the market. Architects are now mainly designers and planners: the 'built environment' is their predominant sphere of interest. To some extent, their work programmes the way we live, and they take account of demographic, social and political factors as they plan. The architects of the 1920s USSR, of the Third Reich in Germany, of purpose-built towns and cities everwhere (from Peterlee in the UK to Brasilia in Brazil) went further, setting out quite deliberately to design not just buildings, but whole societies. Le Corbusier famously talked of a house as a 'machine for living' and planned 'radial cities' in which each activity – living, working, relaxing – would have its own area, separated off from all the others. In architecture and city planning, from the mid-19th century onwards, every single artistic 'ism' has been applied to the practicalities of living, often with minimal consent from the mass of the people who actually have to use, and live in the shadow of, the buildings which embody those 'isms'.

To say this is not to impute creative arrogance to architects as a profession, or at least to all of them. Because of the practical thrust of their work, not to mention in order to eat, they must temper their creative inspiration at least some way to the mood of the times, to the market place. Philanthropic – values the desire to provide healthy, secure environments for living and working, which have been part of architecture since its beginnings – still play their part. But the problem remains that, unlike the product of any other of the arts, what an architect creates, good or bad, is both enormous and permanent. No-one has to use a still life for shelter, or bring up a family in a figurine. If you hate it you can sell it or dump it. But if, as a 'consumer', you feel oppressed by the grid-system and skyscrapers of downtown Chicago, bemoan the regimentation and implicit imperialism of Chandigarh, or deplore the Guggenheim Museum, the Baubourg or the Hong Kong and Shanghai Bank headquarters, that is your tough luck. All these works have three things in common: they were conceived by people of 'vision' who behaved like creative dictators rather than democrats, they were enormously expensive and they will stand where they are, for better or worse, for centuries.

The standoff between pretension and appropriateness, in both architecture and **town planning**, is perhaps a predominantly 20th-century phenomenon, an unfortunate collision between reality and **modernism**. And 20th-century architects have created beautiful places and glorious buildings, works of art for living in, as well as monstrosities. In the days of **postmodernism**, they are also starting to listen again not just to their patrons but to the people who will actually use their creations, and we have also developed a healthy trend towards biting our lips against the financial loss and dynamiting the most disastrous of their creations (1960s tower-block slums come readily to mind). In short, if architects mislaid their humility at some stage in the last 500 years, there are signs that they are now, after a barrage of adverse criticism lasting nearly forty years, beginning to find it again – and that can only be good for all the rest of us. **KMcL**

See also architect; craftsmanship; functionalism; space and architecture.

Further reading Peter Collins, *Architectural Judgement*; Kenneth Frampton, *Modern Architecture: a Critical History*; Nikolaus Pevsner, *An Outline of European Architecture*; A. Soper and L. Sickman, *The Art and Architecture of China; The Art and Architecture of Japan*.

ARISTOTELIANISM

Aristotelian thinkers are followers of

Aristotle (384–322 BCE). Aristotle had a fundamental impact on the political thought and practice of Greek and Roman antiquity, not least through his teaching of rhetoric: the skill of persuading people when neither logical proof nor compelling empirical evidence are available in argument. Aristotle's political thought has also exercised a profound long-term impact on Western political philosophy, not least through his criticism of **Platonist Utopianism**. Aristotle devised the first typology of political régimes, distinguishing them by whether they were ruled by (a) a single ruler, (b) a few rulers, or (c) many rulers; and by whether the rulers ruled (1) in the interests of all or (2) in their own interests. This typology produces six types of régime, three good forms (a.1) monarchy, (b.1) aristocracy and (c.1) polity (or constitutional government); and three bad forms (a.2) tyranny, (b.2) oligarchy and (c.2) democracy. Later Aristotle distinguished Asiatic **despotism** as a peculiarly Oriental form of government. Aristotle supported a mixed constitution, which combined the best elements of kingship, aristocracy and popular government, which he called 'polity'. Aristotle's political thought anticipated modern **functionalism**. He argued that political life was biologically rooted and had *natural* forms; states should take natural forms, which he believed meant that they should be relatively small, and that individuals and social classes, particularly slaves, had natural functions to perform. These assumptions were used by him and subsequent thinkers to justify political institutions as natural which we now think of as abhorrent: such as slavery and the rule of men in domestic households. **BO'L**

Further reading Aristotle *The Politics; The Art of Rhetoric.*

ARITHMETIC see Integers; Number System; Number Theory; Rational Numbers; Real Numbers

ART AND CRAFT

Recognition of certain kinds of activity as 'artistic', and of the practitioner of those activities as an 'artist', is historically a relatively late development. It began in Europe during the **Renaissance**, when architects, musicians, painters, poets and sculptors were said by pundits to be practitioners of the 'fine arts', somehow creative in a different way from (for instance) actors, potters, prose writers, stonemasons and so on. The distinction became an article of faith in the 17th century with the founding of the **Academies**, and was finally transformed into a doctrine by **Romanticism**, when it became permissible for 'fine artists' to be people of genius, but the same appellation was seldom, or only ironically, applied to creative talents in other fields. 19th-century critics began an enthusiastic programme of revisionism, working out which of the artists of the ancient Greek and Roman past – Apelles? Homer? Praxiteles? Vitruvius? – was admissible to the pantheon of genius, a 'Gentleman' rather than a 'Player'. The notion tends to divorce 'artists' from any kind of ritual and social function, and would have baffled the ancient Greeks, just as it would be alien to the vast majority of artistic creators in the world, throughout history, for whom work is all and creative categories are irrelevant. Nonetheless, the notion of 'arts' and 'crafts', and the view that some useful distinction can be made between them, still persists in academic and critical circles, not entirely to the benefit of the **arts** themselves. **CMcD JM KMcL**

See also art(s), visual; connoisseurship; creativity; criticism; folk art; religious art.

Further reading A. Martindale, *the Rise of the Artist in the Middle Ages and Early Renaissance.*

ART DECO

Art Deco (derived from the phrase 'art as decoration') was a design style universally popular from late 1920s onwards. It was characterized by geometric forms, distinctive colour combinations, modern materials like stainless steel and in furniture smooth wraparound surfaces in luxurious veneers. Art Deco design was an amalgam of the changes affecting **fine art** and **design** in the interwar years, for example the bold colours of **Fauve** and **Cubist** painting, and the architecture of **modernism**. Populist application of the new Modernism influenced design across the board from cinemas to radios and vacuum cleaners. It also led to several important critics and designers criticizing Art Deco as a mere style without the intellectual rigour of hard-line Modern Movement thinking. In this context the term Moderne was used to suggest the Art Deco style as a much less serious version of Modernism. Nonetheless by the end of the 1930s, particularly in the US, Art Deco had become universally popular both for expensive custom-made objects and for cheap mass-produced ceramics and tableware. **CMcD**

ART FOR ART'S SAKE

The idea that works of art should exist for themselves, without political, social, religious or any other 'messages', was prevalent in 19th-century France as a response to **realism**. It was taken up in Britain at the end of the century by Walter Pater (who coined the phrase 'art for art's sake'), and by adherents of the **aesthetic** movement. Throughout the 20th century it has been a fundamental tenet (though seldom expressed in so many words) of **avant-garde** arts movements of every kind, from **Dada** to **Surrealism**, from **minimalism** to the **theatre of the absurd**. **KMcL**

ART NOUVEAU

Art Nouveau (French, 'New Art'), known in Germany as *Jugendstil* ('Youth Style'), was a style of decorative **art** and **architecture** practised throughout Europe and North America, and was prominent in the 1890s. It was the last great decorative design style of the 19th century. Art Nouveau relies on observed rather than formalized plant-forms and swirling, tendril-like patterns, which are applied not merely in painting and sculpture, but in furniture (for example, the work of Galle and Majorelle), cutlery, lamps, street signs and ironwork, such as the Métro stations in Paris. Its naturalism perhaps springs from the work of William Morris and the **Arts and Crafts** movement, but it lacks that movement's self-imposed restraint, derived from imitation of medieval styles and forms.

As a medium of artistic expression, Art Nouveau was largely dead by the 1920s, killed off by the postwar climate of austerity and classicism, not to mention its own excessive tendrilizing and exaggeratedly naturalistic forms. Its frivolity lived on in **Art Deco**, and had a major influence on the design of Hollywood musicals and comedies in the 1930s and early 1940s. Nonetheless, for all its exaggeration, some practitioners of the Art Nouveau style in its heyday during the 1890s and 1900s, such as Charles Rennie Mackintosh and Henry van de Velde, did design restrained pieces, whose simplicity chimed in well with industrial design and achieved for Art Nouveau a certain 'classicism' and dignity of its own. **CMcD KMcL**

Further reading Peter Selz and Mildred Constantine (eds.), *Art Nouveau: Art and Design at the End of the Century*.

ART(S), VISUAL

Visual art may be defined as the practice of shaping material, such as wood or stone, or applying pigment to a flat or other surface, with the intention of representing an idea, experience, or emotion.

However, in constructing a category called 'art' we are making assumptions which have a historical but not conceptual foundation. If today there is believed to be general consensus on what 'art' is and what its function might be, then this agreement dates only from the 18th century at the earliest, when the study of **aesthetics** was held to provide a methodology for the appreciation and understanding of art. Before this date there were *arts*, such as the art of **painting**, or of **sculpture**, but no discipline which might properly be considered as 'art'. If this is true of the Western world, then consideration of the art of Asia, Africa, the Americas and the Orient obviously renders our cosy assumptions about what art is, or should be, methodologically useless.

The theory and practice of the visual arts are ideologically constructed. To take the example of the Western world, the elevation from the **Renaissance** onwards of the arts of painting, sculpture and **architecture** into the domain of the **Liberal Arts** was the driving force behind an enormous number of developments in the 16th to 19th centuries, including the development of **academies** of art and the idea of the artist as genius which enjoyed its most unbridled successes during the age of **Romanticism**. Furthermore, from the 18th century, the separation of the fine arts (architecture, **music**, painting, **poetry** and sculpture – one might argue that the essential fine art object is an oil painting on canvas) from the decorative arts (such as fabric design, ceramics or jewellery) was also important to the way we nowadays construct the domain of 'art'. Yet such constructions pose more problems than they solve. They suggest that Western art has hived off certain 'fine' art practices from other areas which, in non-Western cultures, might be essential aspects of the visual within a given society.

The problem with this typology is highlighted if we turn to non-Western forms of art. There is not the same distinction in many cultures – one could cite India, Asia and pre-Columbian Latin America – between 'art' objects (for aesthetic pleasure and nothing else) and artefacts which are designed for some practical purpose yet which carry embellishment in the form of patterns, images or designs. In these societies, as well in the visual culture of peoples such as the Australian Aborigines or the tribes of New Guinea, mark-making, whether on the body or on some rock or other surface, is often intimately linked to patterns of **ritual**. Observations such as these demonstrate the futility of discussing art as if it were a category which could be delimited and defined.

A few comments may nonetheless be offered. In the first place, it is not axiomatic that non-Western visual culture has an essentially symbolic or ritual function, whereas the art of the West is free of these attributes. It goes without saying that a Florentine altarpiece of the Quattrocento, for example, has a ritualistic function (that of devotion). It is, however, true to say that the subsequent appreciation of 'art', and the development of the theory of the individualistic creative genius (on whom depends the autonomy of the work of art) has tended to separate (what we call) art as much as possible from its ritualistic, social or functional base, and to place it in a discrete category where its supposed immanent qualities (that is, its aesthetic value) may be appreciated.

But if we are ultimately unable to identify any objective criteria of what constitutes a work of art, we are at least able to point to qualities which seem to be common to all forms of artistic activity. Central to any artistic creativity are the working of the imagination, the play of the emotions and the operation of reason. It is likely that these qualities, in different combinations, contribute to the making of all forms of art, whether Western or other, as they allow the practitioner the opportunity to translate his or her experience of the world into a statement about the world.

The form such a statement takes is of course central to the art-creation process, and the study of form is part of the appreciation of art. Form is the plastic realization of the idea, translated into imagery (whether **abstract** or **figurative**) and given shape via the agency of paint, stone, wood or some other material. In this sense, to study form is to study the mind of the artist who created it, informed by our own preconceptions and prejudices and subject to the vagaries of the means of presentation, contextualization and environment.

This last remark indicates a central way in which 'art' *becomes* 'art'. The famous example of Duchamp's bicycle wheel mounted on a stool is a case in point. The object *becomes* 'art' by dint of its insertion into a fine-art environment, in this case a museum. While it would not arrest our attention for a moment if it were to be found on a rubbish tip, its situation within a controlled environment (an environment articulating difference as well as confirming the supposed intrinsic worth of the objects on display) is the means by which its transformation is achieved. This suggests that the notion of intrinsic quality (whether through the use of precious materials or the transforming skill of the artist) is not exclusively the hallmark of fine art, but that a sense of 'difference from' (not to be confused with uniqueness) is likewise part of the fine-art experience.

'Philosophical' considerations of this kind are, perhaps, chiefly the concern of the specialist. The general public is largely content to see the domain of art confirmed rather than questioned, and the art object presented in a way that makes it both intelligible and meaningful. In this, notions of appropriateness (for example, tradition, beauty or, to a lesser extent, acceptable eccentricity) are central. But here once again the essential difference is seen between Western and non-Western art forms. While in the West aesthetic appreciation is perhaps the most common response to the art object (that is, we value a work because it appeals to our **taste**, or confirms our opinions), in non-European cultures the idea of decorum is paramount. In such cultures, whether the imagery honours a local deity, cures a sick child or marks the turning of the seasons, it is the function of the ritual which is important, not whether the imagery conforms to some notion of 'beauty'.

Of course, such functions described above are not absent from European art, particularly if we think of the tremendous impetus given to sacred imagery by the Christian Church for at least 2,000 years. But today we have for the most part lost this original meaning, and have instead begun to invest the work of art with another form of 'religious' experience: art appreciation. Even so, for most people 'art' is more than this. Indeed, those schools of art, such as **Modernism**, which tend to be self-referential, eschewing the mimetic or referential quality present in so much visual imagery, are still among the least understood by the 'ordinary' consumer of art. In general, most people would expect art to tell them something about the world which was not immediately apparent in 'real' life. In this sense art has always had the function of widening our experience.

While the question of what constitutes the theory and practice of art cannot be solved as long as human society continues to set store by activities separate from the business of procuring the means to existence, and while societies differ in their conception of the purpose of human life, then 'art' identified as a means both to embellish daily life and as the repository of a form of knowledge not found in the same way in any other activity will continue to provoke discussion. **MG PD**

See also abstraction; Christian art; figurative art; folk art; religious art.

Further reading W. Benjamin, 'The Work of Art in the Age of Mechanical Production', in *Illuminations*; H. Honour and J. Fleming, *A World History of Art*; R. Wollheim, *Painting as an Art*.

ART, PHILOSOPHY OF see Aesthetics

ARTIFICIAL INTELLIGENCE

Artificial Intelligence (AI) is the most controversial area of computing today, an area beloved of **sf** authors – the duplication of human thought patterns by computer. It is an area in which much research has been done since the end of the World War II, beginning with the theoretical work of Alan Turing (1912–54) in the 1940s.

Thanks to our limited understanding of human **thought**, it is quite difficult to define what the goal of artificial intelligence actually is. For example, it is not possible to answer the question 'Do computers have knowledge of the data they process?' unless you can define the term **knowledge**. (This question also has consequences in the legal field – can a computer be allowed as a witness in court if it does not really know what it is talking about?) This kind of question is not really answerable in the present state of **philosophy** and **psychology**.

It is also difficult to know how you will tell that a computer is managing to duplicate human thought patterns. A common idea is that this is achieved when a computer can do something that only human beings can. Many candidates for this 'something' have already been achieved: computers can learn from experience (how to play chess, for example), come up with completely new ideas (a computer known as the Artificial Mathematician came up with a result in **number theory** no one had ever dreamed of before), reason from insufficient knowledge ('expert systems' have been developed which will come up with answers in terms of probabilities to questions about mineral surveying and organic chemistry) and so on. With these systems which use incomplete or inexact knowledge, however, the possibility of mistakes made by the computer is introduced – something long thought to be a purely human domain.

The most famous statement of the goal of research in artificial intelligence is the **Turing** test, in which a computer and a human being are kept separate from the tester, and he or she asks questions the answers to which will tell the human and the computer apart. The test ends when the tester gives up or decides which is the computer. The computer passes the test if the tester gives up or is incorrect; it is then judged to have sufficiently human intelligence to be artificial intelligence.

No computer has ever yet passed the Turing test. Present goals in artificial intelligence include making computers understand English, respond to statements correctly and reject nonsensical ones, or using computers in **fine art** and **music** as part of the creative element rather than just as tools or instruments. Some seemingly easy tasks have proved remarkably difficult for computers; it will be some time in the future before the first robot can be built that can cope with even the simplest non-laboratory situations, such as a home or office environment. **SMcL**

See also computer art; creativity; electronic music; epistemology.

Further reading T. Forester, *The Information Technology Revolution.*

ARTS AND CRAFTS

The Arts and Crafts movement was a group of British architects, artists and designers who sought to revive standards of design in the later 19th and early 20th century, principally by encouraging the revival of traditional handicrafts. It was in keen reaction to the cheap, mass-produced furniture and architecture of mid-19th century Europe.

The origins of the movement may be identified with the writings of the medievalist propagandist A.W. Pugin (1812–52) and of John Ruskin (1819–1900), for example *The Stones of Venice* (1851–53). This last work saw in the medieval architecture of Europe the condition of the craftsmen who created its great works, and compared it favourably with the condition of modern working people: freedom compared to slavery. This view had a profound influence on William Morris (1834–96) who may be regarded as the father of the Arts and Crafts movement.

Morris was educated at Oxford University, trained as an **architect** and was an associate of the **Pre-Raphaelites**. While still at university, he realized that his real talents lay in design, and in 1861 he established his own company called Morris, Marshall, Faulkner and Co. This company, and its products, remained at the centre of the Arts and Crafts movement until Morris's death.

The movement believed that a series of simple principles should be applied to the production of design. The first of these was truth to materials. Morris believed that every material had its own intrinsic quality, for example the abstract glaze of a pot or the natural colour of wood. With this in mind he tried to revive traditional methods of production – for example, at his printing works at Merton Abbey in Surrey he reintroduced traditional vegetable dyes (such as indigo) which had been superceded by the new synthetic dyes discovered in the 1830s. As well as reviving traditional craft techniques Morris also researched traditional patterns, spending long hours at the Victoria and Albert Museum studying Islamic carpets and tiles and Elizabethan textiles. These patterns Morris reworked into his wallpapers and textiles which still remain popular.

The young architects who were impressed with Morris's essentially pro-handicraft, anti-machine ethic established a number of associations, such as the Art Workers' Guild founded in 1884 by five architects, including Lethaby, E.S. Prior and Mervyn Macartney, pupils of Richard Norman Shaw (1831–1912). They were concerned with the idea of architecture as an art. The name 'Guild' was self-consciously a title identifying them with the medieval guilds. The other members of the Guild were painters and sculptors, craftsmen and designers, and while the Arts and Crafts Movement encompassed all their skills and interests, indeed was concerned with 'the unity of the arts', it would be as Alan Crawford writes: 'Impossible to imagine the Arts and Crafts Movement without architecture ...[because]... buildings can show the touch of the craftsman, the texture of materials and virtues of the old techniques.' In 1887 the Arts and Crafts Exhibition Society was founded to exhibit the work of the Art Workers' Guild and others in the field.

The final component of hardline Arts and Crafts beliefs was a commitment to social issues. Morris himself was a socialist who believed that the production of beautiful objects for all would enrich the spiritual quality of life. He wrote **Utopian** novels (the best known is *News from Nowhere*) predicting a happy, egalitarian, socialist future for humanity, was connected with the early **Fabian** Society, and toured the country lecturing and teaching. Many Arts and Crafts designers attempted social experiments based on the principles of communal living, for example C.R. Ashbee's Guild and School of Handicrafts, set up at Chipping Camden in 1888.

For all the busyness and intellectual consistency of the Arts and Crafts Movement, it did little to change the spirit of the time. Its anti-machine ethic was essentially anachronistic, and prevented its high design standards and strong moral qualities becoming a truly effective force in the contemporary world. Morris and his followers had wanted to make handmade products available to all, but in actuality, because production methods and the cost of materials meant that work could not be cheap, they were simply too expensive. Nonetheless, their ideas, products and writings were potent forces in challenging the purpose and function of design and the value of craft versus machine production, and, once the rationale was adapted to the machine age (for example in the **Bauhaus**), became a seminal influence on 20th-century Western design and, particularly, **architecture** (where ideas range from the concepts of the house as a 'total work of art' to the vernacular revival). **PD MG CMcD JM KMcL**

See also craftsmanship; functionalism; Gothic Revival.

Further reading E. Cumming, *The Arts and Crafts Movement*; P. Davey, *The Search for An Earthly Paradise: the Architecture of the Arts and Crafts Movement*.

ARTS, THE

Art (Latin *ars*) originally meant any innate skill or learned ability: speaking well, hairdressing, riding, acting. In Roman times 'work' was something done by slaves or people of the lower classes, and people with any opinion of themselves were eager to dissociate themselves with the term. As one (aristocratic) poet put it, *ars est celare artem*, 'the skill is in concealing the skill' – an early example of a 'gentlemen and players' snobbery about both arts and crafts, which is still quite widespread today.

In a somewhat narrower sense, the 'arts' later became what aristocratic children learned. They were ultimately derived from the subjects sponsored by the Muses in **myth** (astronomy/astrology, comedy, dance, history, music, poetry and tragedy), and were regarded as enhancements of life, adornments, as opposed to practical skills such as calculating, cooking or surveying, which were not the concern of the aristocratic employer and need therefore not be learned. This distinction was preserved in medieval Europe. Alcuin, the 8th-century scholar who devised for the emperor Charlemagne a syllabus for education throughout the Holy Roman Empire, based it on what he called 'the seven liberal arts' which together consistuted 'learning'. The *trivium* or 'triple road', the preliminary course, consisted of grammar, logic and rhetoric; the *quadrivium* or 'fourfold road', the advanced course, consisted of **arithmetic**, **astronomy**, **geography** and **music**. Once again, all these subjects were taught not as practical skills, but as those of the mind: servants existed to see to mundane matters, leaving the scholar free to let his, or more rarely her, mind roam at will – as Alcuin put it, 'like someone wandering in a beautiful garden, tending a plant here, savouring a scent there, plucking a bouquet of delight for his own and others' delectation'. This was not entirely snobbery. It was in keeping with the **monastic** idea that seclusion from worldly cares was helpful, if not essential, if one were to concentrate one's mind on 'higher things'.

Alcuin's classifications, astonishingly, were matched in other cultures which had no possible connection with or dependence on European ideas. In ancient China, for example, **literature** and music were regarded as 'cultivated arts', that is, skills reserved for people of sensibility, and were separated from more mundane skills such as painting or playing instruments or running households. The distinction was not one of brainpower: many mundane skills required high intellectual ability. It is, indeed, hard at this distance to see quite what the distinction was. Possibly it had something to do with a characteristic preoccupation of Chinese philosophers at the time, the idea that **beauty** was something which could be categorized, that there were hierarchies of 'the beautiful'. Most ancient Babylonian and Egyptian aristocrats, by contrast, left all intellectual matters to trained professionals, contenting themselves with enjoying the results (music and painting were to them commodities, to be bought like any others) and reserving their education for more practical upper-class skills, such as hunting and the observation of etiquette. Strikingly, **mathematics** was regarded as the highest 'art' in both societies, chiefly because it was essential for **astrology** and other forms of religious numerology. But it was a sacred and not a secular art, and was also utterly divorced from such practical number-based activities as surveying or commerce, placed on a much lower social plane.

Traditions such as these, which have more to do with social position than with the actual subjects of study or interest, are characteristic of all ancient societies, dependent on slave labour or on a rigid hierarchical structure. The higher your status, whether in sacred or secular circles, the more you needed to 'understand' the world, and the less you needed to know about how it was actually run. In the East, this was no barrier to the advancement of knowledge, since what we would now think of as **science** was an important study by educated people who were not aristocrats. In the West, by contrast, Alcuin's categories, and the implacable opposition of the Christian Church to any form of scientific enquiry which might contradict the teaching of the Bible, meant that practical learning remained stalled for centuries, being based on precedent rather than investigation, and that people devoted their creative energies to other matters. Humane letters (classics and **philosophy**) and **theology** were the principal subjects studied in most universities, with mathematics as a somewhat grudgingly admitted fourth.

Thus, when rational scientific explanation began at the time of the **Renaissance**, the gulf between practical and non-practical matters was centuries-old, and few people on either side saw any need to bridge it. The Renaissance also sponsored enormous interest in 'beauty' as a philosophical concept which could be discussed and compartmentalized, and this in turn led to the idea that creators of beautiful things – musicians, painters, poets – were working on some kind of abstract scale of excellence, that they could reach the heights. Thus, two developments coincided: the notion that 'science' was a separate study from 'the liberal arts', and the idea that the artistic creator was matching his or her effort against some kind of abstract ideal, that perfection was quantifiable and could be pursued.

Thus we come, in 18th-century Europe, to what might be called the modern idea of 'the arts' and 'the artist'. Diderot and the other **Encyclopedists** devoted much ink to assessing what these were, and how they related to 'science' and to 'craft'. The Arts, by and large, were such things as music, painting, poetry and theatre – bluntly put, entertainment with pretension. Artists were people who possessed not merely skill (as the root meaning of the word might suggest) but 'genius', innate sensibility of a higher order than that given to the rest of us. (Craftsmen and craftswomen had skill but no creative genius. Artistes were performers who had skill but no high aesthetic aspiration: a tragic actor or an orchestral cellist was an artist, a juggler or a clown was an artiste.) Drawing, engraving, painting and sculpture even formed a sub-category of their own, 'fine arts', as opposed to 'useful arts' (those crafts with a practical application).

Such categories have bedevilled the Arts for centuries, and continue to inform (or perhaps one should say deform) our attitudes today. The gulf between arts and science seems as wide as it has always been, with practitioners on each side being openly contemptuous of the other. The complexity of modern science, and the rise of what used to be called 'the practical arts' (that is, **technology**), have encouraged scholars and critics of the fine arts to adopt ever more pretentious and abstruse language to describe what creative people do in their field. For the ordinary person, who wants chiefly to be guided to enjoyable, stimulating, challenging, uplifting, 'great' literature, music, painting and so on, this Babel can seem as daunting as it is pointless. The Arts are still, as they have always been, hostages to critical **scholasticism**, gravestones of words. They are actually simple, among the most remarkable manifestations of the human intellect and human spirit, and available for the excitement, uplift and satisfaction of everyone who approaches them. **KMcL**

See also art and craft; criticism; drama; performing arts; sculpture; two cultures.

ASCETICISM

Asceticism (from Greek *askesis*, 'exercise') is the practice of self-denying exercises, of leading an austere way of life, in order to enhance one's mental powers or spiritual perception, to overcome vice and cultivate virtue. It has been practised worldwide and is particularly associated with early Western philosophy (for example the Greek **Stoics** and Cynics) and religion (where denial of the world was held to allow concentration on God or the gods). This latter is the view held particularly in **Hinduism** and **Buddhism**. Here, asceticism is seen as a way of detaching oneself from the world so that one can better contemplate the divine. It gives self-control and trains one to bear hardships for the cause. In Buddhism, it was also seen as a means of identification with or imitation of one's Lord.

It is significant that the Buddha and many other great figures in the world's religions began by practising lives of great austerity, but later modified or abandoned extreme asceticism. Christ was not an ascetic – on the contrary, he was criticized for enjoying parties – but demanded self-denial in terms of giving up home and family for the sake of the Gospel: inner discipline, not outward ascetic ostentation. This accords with the **Judaic** idea that the world was given by God to humankind for our enjoyment. Perhaps because of this last belief, asceticism in Judaism was rare, being confined mainly to prophets and mystics. In the Early Christian Church it was seen as an aid to prayer and meditation, and as a preparation for martyrdom. In the 3rd century, Origen and Clement of Alexandria began studying its theoretical basis, using Stoic ideas of the purification of the soul from passion (also a justification for asceticism in Buddhism). Their work paved the way, in theological terms, for the beginnings of Christian **monasticism**, of which asceticism was a main component. In the Reformation it reappeared as something for all lay people in Puritanism. The well-known Puritan ethic involving integrity, thrift, hard work (so that one has the resources for education and charitable work), fasting and renunciation of 'worldly' pleasures, has passed beyond religion into the secular world: it is now incarnate, for example, in the Green movement, and transcends the boundaries of nationality, **politics** and **religion**. **EMJ**

ASHRAMS

Ashrams are quite different from **Buddhist** or western-Christian monasteries. Essentially they are communities which grow up around a religious figure. The Upanisad tradition of sages going to the forest to meditate resulted in communities of disciples and devotees settling around their hut, following their teacher's guidance. Probably the most famous in modern times are Rabindranath Tagore's community at Shantinikitan, West Bengal, where he conducted his educational and cultural experiments (and which is now recognized as a university, although originally it was closer to deschooling, non-formal education and arts workshops), and Gandhi's *ashram* on the banks of the Sabarmati near Ahmedabad, which was a springboard for his independence campaign.

In a true *ashram*, there is no hierarchy. All depends on the guru's word. People come and go, according to their spiritual needs, and the only vows they take are of obedience to the **guru** (or swami) and that they will respect the community's conventions. These usually involve participating in a pattern of daily worship and meditation, sharing common tasks such as cooking and cleaning, living a life of great simplicity, wearing handloom cotton robes (sometimes of a distinctive hue), and abstaining from alcohol, meat and smoking. **EMJ**

ASIATIC MODE OF PRODUCTION

The Asiatic mode of production is both the most obscure and controversial of the 'modes of production' (economic systems) mentioned in Karl Marx's writings. Insofar as Marx's and Engels' writings can be decoded and clearly understood, the Asiatic mode of production refers to a system in which the vast majority of the population live in villages, in which there is no private property, complex division of labour or significant external trade. The villages are exploited by a despot and his officials, to whom they pay a combination of rent and taxes. The urban population, centred on the court aristocracy and the monarchy, are parasitic on the rural population. Marx described such Oriental societies, following in the tradition of British political economy, as incapable of development into more progressive social formations. They were arbitrary, despotic and stagnant, historical *culs-de-sac*, which could only be transformed by external intervention by more advanced societies.

The concept is controversial because (1) Marx and Engels wrote very little about it, (2) it appears to be a reflection of Eurocentric prejudices about Asia, (3) it was used by critics of Lenin and the Bolsheviks to warn against a premature assault on Tsarism, (4) it was hotly debated by Asian communists because of its alleged implications for their revolutionary politics, and (5) it was used, notably by Karl Wittfogel, as a parable for what would happen to societies under communist dictatorships. Wittfogel additionally claimed, wrongly, that Marx deliberately suppressed the idea because it threatened to subvert his own beliefs.

The Asiatic mode of production is intellectually contested because it does not fit easily with Marx's theory of history: it appears to deny that history is necessarily on a progressive path, suggests that the state rather than (private property based) class might be the locus of exploitation in some pre-modern societies, and also seems to be internally contradictory. For these reasons, among others, the concept was banned by Stalin from public discussion in the Soviet Union in the 1930s. As a result the concept was often used by dissidents as a coded way of criticizing Marxist-Leninist dictatorships in the USSR and Eastern Europe, and still is used in this way in China, North Korea and Vietnam. The long-term importance of the concept is as one of many failed ideas developed by historians and social theorists to explain the uniqueness of Western civilization. **BO'L**

See also agrarian society; Aristotelianism; despotism; historical materialism; Marxism.

Further reading Brendan O'Leary, *The Asiatic Mode of Production*; Karl Wittfogel *Oriental Despotism*.

ASSEMBLY-LINE PRODUCTION

Assembly-line production originated in the early automobile industry; Henry Ford was given credit for its development. Assembly-line production is a system of production in which the process is broken down into simple, single steps performed by each worker, such as tightening a bolt or spot-welding a joint. Materials to be assembled or processed move on a conveyor from work station to work station as the product is gradually put together from standardized parts. (In contrast with earlier, labour-intensive methods, in which each worker did a variety of tasks.)

In time the system was extended beyond assembly to manufacturing processes. The technique became widespread as scientific management applied time and motion study to minimize effort and increase man-hour output. It is a logical extension of Adam Smith's **division of labour** concept.

Charlie Chaplin, in his film *Modern Times*, caricatured the problems created for some people doing simple repetitive work on an assembly line. But as processing steps have been reduced to simpler and simpler elements, mechanization has become possible. Some of the problems of repetitive work have been mitigated by the growing use of robots to perform tasks more accurately than is possible by humans. Some completely automated plants have appeared. The problems of unemployment these cause are still being explored in most 'advanced' industrial societies. **TF**

ASSIMILATION

Assimilation (Latin, 'making similar to') refers to the process of convergence by which the culture of an ethnic minority group becomes similar to that of the culture dominant in society rather than remaining distinct from it. Increasingly, however, scholars have developed a preference for the more dynamic concept of **ethnicity**. **DA**

See also conflict theory; consensus theory; culture; norm; race; social integration; socialization; society; typifications; value.

Further reading M. Gordon, *Assimilation in American Life*; S. Patterson, *Dark Strangers*; J. Rex and D. Mason (eds.), *Theories of Race and Ethnic Group Relations*.

ASTROLOGY

Astrology (Greek, 'study of the heavenly bodies') is one of the oldest and most widely practised of all human activities. It is widely dismissed as a '**pseudoscience**' (that is, one which pretends to reliance on objective investigation and rational proof), and it has overtones of **magic** and charlatanry which do its reputation no good at all. But it persists in societies of all kinds throughout the world, and determines the lives of people who would otherwise have no truck with superstition or pseudoscience of any kind.

There are two kinds of astrology. 'Natural' astrology is the charting of heavenly bodies, and the making of numerical tables based on their position and movement in the heavens. It was a forerunner of **astronomy**, and is the source of such still-current time divisions as years, months, weeks, days, hours and so on. (The bypassing of the decimal system of counting in early **mathematics** is one result of this: the most convenient time divisions were not decimal, and so the mathematics based on them used units on a different base.) This astrology was connected with religious and social practice, and its skills were the (often jealously guarded) prerogative of priestly or other élites. Their charts and tables, based on observation and calculation, allowed them to predict such essential matters as (in very early societies) the fact that the Sun would return after night or spring after winter, and (in more developed societies such as Egypt or the Mayan kingdom) the imminence of floods, droughts and other such cataclysms. In the 8th century, to take just one example, the Venerable Bede devoted much of his time to working out and writing down calculations about the precise date of Easter and other 'moveable feasts' in the Christian year; his work still affects our perception of the calendar, worldwide.

Although, in many ancient societies, 'natural' astrology was the nearest thing to what we might nowadays think of as a 'proper' science, and its practitioners were among the most learned and intellectually sophisticated members of the community, two things fatally hampered its development. First was the lack of instruments to make precise observation of the heavens, and of mathematical systems or devices which would allow any but (in our terms) the crudest calculations. Second was the interdependence of astrology with **religion**. Because the astrologers dealt with heavenly bodies (which were thought to be under the control of the gods), and because they made predictions, they were thought to have supernatural contacts and abilities denied to less-learned people. Even in societies as sophisticated as ancient China and ancient Babylon, magic and esoteric jargon were essential tools of the astrologers, allying them with sibyls, soothsayers and other prophets rather than with surveyors, for instance, or merchants, the other main groups skilled in the use of numbers.

The second practice, 'judicial' astrology, was dependent on the first, but vitally different from it. Instead of merely observing, logging and calculating the positions of heavenly bodies, its practitioners tried deliberately to link their human clients to such movements. By asking questions about such things as the precise time of a person's birth, calculations could be made about the configuration of the heavens at that moment; these could then be compared with the state of the heavenly bodies at any later point in time (the moment of consultation, say, or some date and time in the future), and predictions made about what might happen and how the subject should behave. A direct causal link was claimed between the heavenly bodies and each individual's character and life-pattern: our exact moment of birth was considered as unique as a fingerprint, and allowed our entire lives to be tracked. The more people we met, the more complex such calculations became. In ancient China, for example, the emperor had a household of wives and concubines, and an entire college of astrologers to work out the most advantageous moment to have sex with each of them to guarantee the birth of a healthy, 'lucky' heir. The Carthaginian general Hannibal would not fight on a given day unless his astrologers declared it propitious – and put his eventual defeat as much down to choosing the wrong day as to Roman strategic superiority. (Lest we sneer, Napoleon and Montgomery were similarly superstitious, and in modern times at least one US president, Ronald Reagan, was said not to make a move unless his wife's astrologer approved it. Prudent or credulous, these men controlled the destinies of millions.)

In secular society, astrology of this kind has either retreated to an ivory tower, its practitioners becoming gurus to the rich and powerful, or has degenerated to the kind of mass predictions published in popular newspapers, in which tens of millions of people who share the same birth sign are blandly advised to keep calm under stress, or are reassured that the 15th will be a lucky day. But in several of the world's great belief-systems, including **Buddhism**, **Hinduism**, **Shinto** and **Daoism**, astrology is highly respected and an integral part of people's lives, both at such **rites of passage** as weddings and funerals, and in more mundane matters such as house-moving or the making of business deals. At this level, astrology is more than mere entertainment, and the same question is relevant as with any other belief-system which we may not share. Does its validity depend on objective verification, or do the

facts that millions of people, throughout history, have relied on it, that it has enabled their lives, give it credentials which rise above mere credence? **KMcL**

See also belief; divination; palmistry; witchcraft.

ASTRONOMY

The science of astronomy (Greek, 'naming the stars') was born when man began to observe and track the motion of the stars in the night sky. Initially, it was naturally assumed that the stars, Sun and Moon all circled the Earth. However, the behaviour of the planets, which appear as bright star-like objects moving against a background of fixed stars, does not fit this picture very well, and new explanations were sought.

Copernicus (Nikolaus Koppernigk, 1473–1543) was the first to realize that the motion of the planets can be explained if one considers them to be orbiting the Sun with the Earth, thus showing that the Sun is the centre of the solar system and demoting the Earth to satellite status. Johannes Kepler (1571–1630) described the system more fully, showing that they move not in circles but in ellipses with the Sun at one of the foci of the ellipse. This motion was shown to be a consequence of the nature of gravity by Newton.

Since Newton's time astronomy has increased in sophistication. Early telescopes observed only the visible light from the sky. Visible light, however, is only one small part of the **electromagnetic** spectrum, and today we utilize far more of it, from radio waves and microwaves to the ultraviolet and x-ray regions. Our atmosphere is an obstacle to observation; as well as confusing observations by shimmer, or blurring, it also attenuates all frequencies other than visible and radio waves. Thus many observatories are built in high places, where there is less atmosphere. This enables visible light to be detected with less distortion, and other frequencies to arrive at the telescope with greater intensity. Computers and electronics have revolutionized astronomy, greatly reducing the time needed to track and analyse objects.

Telescopes differ widely, depending upon the type of radiation that they are designed to detect. Radio telescopes are huge metal dishes, which need to be large because radio waves have wavelengths of the order of a metre. Light telescopes require mirrors and lenses of high quality; a mirror for a good telescope must be smooth enough that irregularities upon its surface are smaller than the wavelength of light, which is about one thousandth of a millimetre. Microwave dishes are typically a few metres across. The quest to observe the sky in other wavelengths has led to suggestions for space telescopes which would eliminate atmospheric distortion.

Astronomical observations reveal a wealth of information about the universe. From them we may learn about the early life of the universe, the evolution of stars and galaxies and the existence of bizarre objects like neutron stars and **black holes**. Because it is electromagnetic radiation, which travels at the speed of light, which we observe, the further an object is, the earlier in its history we are seeing it. If the light from a star takes 1,000 years to reach the Earth, then what we see is a picture of the star 1,000 years ago, not the star as it is today – it may not even exist at this time! Thus to see what the early universe was like, we look at very distant objects. **JJ**

ASTROPHYSICS

The traditional distinction between **astronomy** (Greek, 'naming the stars') and astrophysics (Greek, 'about the nature of stars') was that astronomers observe celestial objects, while astrophysicists seek to explain them. This division has now been superceded as both astronomy and astrophysics broaden in scope. Specifically excluded from astrophysics are the study and measurement of the motions and positions of the stars and planets. Topics which lie mainly within the domain of astrophysics are general **relativity**, **cosmology**, the evolution and structure of **stars**, the composition of interstellar matter, and the study of certain very high energy particles produced by violent events.

General relativity is tested by astronomy and astrophysics. Studies of the motion of Mercury and the deflection of light by the gravitational field of the Sun are examples of astronomical verifications; an example of an astrophysical one is the slowing down of a rotating binary system. The two stars are orbiting each other, and the rate at which their orbital speed reduces is exactly that predicted by general relativity.

To investigate cosmology and the early universe, various techniques are employed. One of these involves careful measurement of what is known as the three degree background. This is the remnant of the **Big Bang** – all that remains of the violent event that created the universe. We see it as a uniform energy background. Recent observations of slight irregularities in this background have given us important clues to how the galaxies evolved.

By observing the frequencies of the light emitted by stars, we may discover which atoms they are composed of, as each atom emits a characteristic set of frequencies. Thus we may learn how stars create elements and evolve themselves.

Interstellar matter is a subject of great interest, because we do not see enough of it. The way that stars and galaxies move indicates that there is far more matter around than we can actually see. It is thought that so-called 'dark matter', matter which emits no radiation and which we therefore cannot see, may provide the missing mass, and this matter may exist in the voids between the stars.

Sources which emit high energy particles are supernova remnants, radio galaxies, pulsars and quasars. Most of these are objects from the early universe, whose light has only just reached us. By studying them we may learn about the evolution of the universe. **JJ**

ATAVISM

Atavism (from Latin *atavus*, 'great-grandfather's grandfather'), in the **life sciences**, is the idea that an individual may bear features which are more typical of its ancestors than of its parents. Mendelian heredity provides a mechanism for this phenomenon, and it is not uncommon for characteristics to reappear after being absent from several generations. However, the term atavism has been associated with the appearance of what are seen as degenerate forms, or throwbacks, though these are in fact genetic aberrations. For example, Down's Syndrome is a congenital condition which was once thought to be a throwback to perceived ancestors; the facial characteristics associated with the syndrome thus led to the name 'Mongolism'. **RB**

See also genetic linkage; genetics; Mendelism.

ATHEISM

'The fool says in his heart, there is no God.' The Old Testament verse accurately sums up the attitude to atheism found in the Bible. But the question there is only whether one worships and obeys the true God or a false god. Even in the Book of Job (4th century BCE), it is not the existence of God which is questioned, but only his justice, mercy and love. When Job is finally vindicated, his hypocritical friends are said 'not to know' God, meaning that for all their protestations of faith, they understand nothing. In the ancient Greek world, to be *atheos* ('without God') similarly meant to hold false beliefs, and to fail to participate in the official cult, rather than to have no beliefs at all. In Roman times, the early Christians and Jews were frequently accused of atheism, because they did not make images of their deity and had no altars, temples or shrines, nor any recognizable priesthood. Their beliefs were treasonable because they did not join in public sacrifices, and though they prayed for the emperor, they would not offer libations to his 'genius' (indwelling spirit). Much the same attitude persisted in Christian kingdoms until the late 18th century; blasphemy is still an indictable offence in the UK. In some Muslim countries atheists are considered an insult to God by their very existence, and are punished accordingly.

Since false gods cannot be said to exist in the same sense as true gods, atheism, a negative, came to mean denial of belief.

Not only does God not exist, but to assert belief in him is wrong – a modern attitude which stands the theist's argument on its head. The Lisbon earthquake in 1752, in which thousands of faithful Catholics died, led many European intellectuals to adopt an atheist position of this kind. In the so-called Age of Reason, human reason was considered to be capable of solving the question of the existence of God, and the answer was increasingly negative. In the 19th century the discoveries of **science** were held to militate against **religion** because they undermined a literal interpretation of the scriptural narrative, especially of creation. In the 20th century 'theological atheism' holds that 'God' as a concept is dead, that theological language must be reinvented to take account of modern atheism, and that traditional arguments for the existence of God must be scrapped, just as divine intervention can no longer be used as the explanation for phenomena we do not understand. The consequence of this development is that belief in God supported by reason is no longer the norm, and theologians have abdicated the realm of metaphysics to philosophers.

Just as there were ancient Greek schools of thought (such as the Sophists and the Cynics) who attacked the prevailing theism, so in the ancient religions of the East, there were and are atheistic developments: schools of philosophy which teach atheism and schools of religion which, by emphasizing human effort, are *de facto* atheist. Nevertheless there is a danger, for Westerners, in categorizing Eastern religions as atheist when all they lack is the Western concept of a creator-God or a comparable belief system. They are still based on an experience of the numinous. This is particularly true of **Confucianism** and **Daoism** where moral law was held to govern the world like a natural process, and while there was controversy as to whether rituals were necessary to placate the spirits or not, the real question was whether such human attributes as benevolence could or could not be ascribed to this moral force.

It is rare to meet self-professed atheists in modern India, and when one does, it is usually because they have been influenced by the West. A famous example is Jawaharlal Nehru, who felt that India had 'too much religion' and that it was a great obstacle to social reform. The most radical objections to Hindu theism came from **Buddhism** and **Jainism**, but it has also been argued that a system which revolves around the concept of *dharma* (see **Dharmic religion**) is essentially atheist, since all depends on fulfilling one's *dharma* and thus achieving a better *karma* in the next existence. Jainism aims to free one from this system by **asceticism**, and though Jains accept the reality of the material world, they believe it exists eternally, and was not created. For Buddhists, the world is transitory, so it cannot have been created by a changeless God who has in any case no good motive to create the world. **KDS**

Further reading Gordon Stein (ed.), *The Encyclopedia of Unbelief.*

ATLANTEANISM see Utopianism

ATMOSPHERE AND LIFE

The Earth's atmosphere is made up of 79% nitrogen, 21% oxygen and a small but growing trace of carbon dioxide. Less well known but much more interesting is the fact that the present-day composition is totally different from that of the primitive Earth, which was hostile to life. How and why has the atmosphere changed so much?

The earliest atmosphere probably consisted of gases like hydrogen, helium, methane, ammonia and carbon dioxide (CO_2) – gases which occur in the atmospheres of the other planets. Most of these gases were lost and replaced by an atmosphere of gases emitted by volcanoes. Water vapour, CO_2, nitrogen, sulphur oxides, chlorine and fluorine would have been the main constituents emitted. Water vapour would be rapidly lost as rain and the more chemically active gases combined with other substances. Hence, the atmosphere for most of the Earth's history consisted largely of CO_2 with small amounts of nitrogen. The formation of the modern atmosphere required the removal of CO_2 and the liberation of oxygen as well as a large increase in the amount of nitrogen.

A clue to the beginning of the change can be found in Precambrian rocks. Some of the earliest of sedimentary rocks are the banded ironstones, which could only have been deposited in the absence of oxygen. Later in the Precambrian era, iron began to be deposited as 'red beds', which imply the existence of a small amount of oxygen. Between these sediments, from about three billion years ago, are found deposits of *stromatolites*, formed by fossilization of beds of blue-green bacteria. The significance of blue-green bacteria, which continue to occur in the coastal waters of Australia, is that they do not require oxygen for respiration but liberate it through photosynthesis. They were responsible for the first free oxygen, but this did not raise the atmospheric concentration very far as it would have combined with trace gases and with materials liberated by weathering. Only after this resistance had been overcome could other processes accelerate the liberation of oxygen and the removal of CO_2.

The first green plants were the phytoplankton, which lived in the surface waters of the oceans. Like other green plants, they liberated oxygen through photosynthesis but then reused it in respiration. However, because they lived in the deep ocean they caused a small net addition to oxygen levels because some of the carbon compounds incorporated in their cells sank to the bottom of the oceans and were locked into sediments which do not decompose because of the cold, dark and oxygen-free conditions.

As land plants grew larger and more elaborate, they provided another sink for carbon and another source of free oxygen. From 350 million years ago, especially in the period now called the Carboniferous, some land plants have been preserved from decomposition by being trapped in marshy conditions, and were eventually transformed into coal or petroleum. During this period, the oxygen content of the atmosphere reached 1%.

More recently, especially in the Cretaceous period from 145 million years ago, appeared the largest of the sinks for carbon. Small marine animals drew on dissolved CO_2 in the sea to build shells of calcium carbonate. When the animals died the shells, called coccoliths, sank to the sea floor and were transformed into chalk. The immense amounts of chalk – visible in rocks like those of the white cliffs of Dover – show that this was a major way of taking CO_2 away from the atmosphere.

The effectiveness of these processes is shown by the amounts of carbon now estimated to be locked into the various 'reservoirs'. If the amount remaining in the atmosphere is taken as one unit, there are 5 units in land vegetation and soil, over 14,000 units dissolved in the oceans or in ocean sediments and over 71,000 units in the rocks, mostly in the form of calcium carbonate. So natural processes have the capacity to remove huge quantities of CO_2, though probably too slowly to avert the prospect of **global warming** as a result of human activity, especially the burning of fossil fuels.

Plants and bacteria were also involved in the build up in levels of nitrogen, though the chemically unreactive nature of nitrogen also contributed. While other volcanic gases were removed from the atmosphere, nitrogen was more inert and thus more likely to remain. Some nitrogen was also derived from ammonia liberated by volcanoes. Today, nitrogen passes through soils and plants, but amounts fixed permanently into plant or animal tissues and preserved from decomposition are very small indeed. There is some loss of nitrate in solution, but this is taken up by algae and recycled. Overall, the losses no more than counteract the continuing emissions from volcanoes and consequently nitrogen has become the largest component of the atmosphere.

The development of the atmosphere to its current form has involved interlocking physical and biological processes, including the evolution of progressively more complex forms of life. The way these processes have produced an atmosphere ideal for complex forms of life has driven some interpreters to look for divine intervention and others to accept the concept of **Gaia. PS**

ATONALITY

Tonal music is music in which the listener can constantly relate the harmonies he or she hears to a tonal centre (in the case of many 18th- and 19th-century works, to a specific key, so that a piece can be said to be, for example, 'in C' or 'in G sharp minor'). In atonal music, this feeling of harmonic nucleus is replaced by that of a continuum of sound, in which each individual harmony is equal with all the others. Thus, although the word 'atonal' was once (wrongly) applied exclusively to **twelve-note music**, it can describe any music in which a feeling of harmonic vagueness, of ebb and flow, predominates. This would include not only works by such 20th-century composers as Olivier Messiaen, Michael Tippett or Edgard Varèse, but earlier pieces ranging from Bach's fugues to Wagner's *Tristan and Isolde* or Debussy's piano preludes. By the same token, much 20th-century music that was once regarded as 'atonal', for example Bartók's, can now clearly be heard to have a strong tonal drive, based on the departure from and return to the harmonies of a single, all-embracing 'key'. **KMcL**

ATONEMENT

Atonement ('at-one-ment'), originally a legal term for the reconciliation of two parties, has been annexed almost exclusively for theological use. In **Buddhism** and **Judaism**, atonement is thought to be initiated by the divine party, acting out of compassion and love, and despite the alienation caused by human sin and weakness. Christians believe that reconciliation between God and humankind took place through the sacrificial life and death of Jesus Christ. Humankind being too far sunk in sin and misery, and too restricted by the limitations of the human condition, to initiate reconciliation from the human side, the death of Christ was necessary to transform human awareness, to jolt humankind out of the consequences of sin, to vanquish death and to assuage God's wrath. **EMJ KMcL**

Further reading Leonard Hodgson, *The Doctrine of Atonement*.

ATTITUDE

Attitude (derived from Latin *aptitudo*, 'fitness'), when a quality of mind, is restricted entirely to the human race. Other creatures strike poses and follow particular sequences of action, but they seem, without exception, to be instinctive. When a cat stalks or a bowerbird displays, it seems not to be the result of considered choice, as it would be if a human being did so. There are some grey areas – dolphins 'playing' with or near humans, for example, or pets apparently modifying their behaviour to suit their owners' moods. But given the way wild dogs, for example, behave towards those higher up in the pack-hierarchy, even such responses to humans may be no more than instinct. A famous experiment in the early years of this century showed that 'Clever Hans', a horse which apparently added or subtracted numbers, tapping the answers with one hoof, was in fact merely responding to subliminal 'cues' from its trainer's body language, of which even the trainer was unaware.

Human beings behave instinctively in similar ways. But we are conscious of the world in a way other animals are not. We continuously review a range of responses to the situations we face. We plan, initiate and control events. We can project our minds into the past and the future, replacing actuality with imagination. The sum of all this is attitude. We constantly see ourselves, imagine ourselves, judge ourselves – no other creatures do this – and we modify our behaviour accordingly. Our behaviour is an intellectual construct, subject to the processes of reason. (Not to behave rationally, for us, is a rational choice.)

It can be argued that attitude is the vital component in every human activity, from democratic decision-making to the writing of poetry, from making love or making war to making gloves. Our decision to explore and explain our environment was initially narcissistic, and it is on that choice that the whole edifice of human knowledge, and much human fantasy, is built. Critics of the **Arts** talk of attitude as if it were a special quality of creative dancers, musicians, writers and so on. They look for (say) an author's 'stance' to his or her material, or a performer's 'stance' towards the audience; they consider influences and strategies, in an attempt to unpack the hidden attitudes within the work, and thus to refine our (the audience's) attitude towards that work. But

this is merely one refined (some would say over-refined) response to the fact of attitude in all human activity. Newton's or Einstein's work sprang from and depended on attitude just as much as did Hiroshige's or Beethoven's – or indeed, to move into more controversial areas, Buddha's or Christ's. The further human experience moves on, the more past experience we have to survey and this availability of all past human culture, and the range of present options it presents, are another possession unique to our species, at once our comfort and our glory. In short, to return to the root meaning of the word, attitude is what 'fits' us for what we are, and do, in the world. And the corollary is obvious: that if we behave in such a way as to wipe our species off the planet forever, that too is attitude, not instinctive or inbuilt behaviour but the result of choice. **KMcL**

AUDIENCE

The audience (from Latin *audire*, 'to hear'), in the sense of the potential recipients of experiences of **media** texts, has increasingly become a focus of debate within media studies. At one end of the spectrum is the model of a passive viewer helplessly *affected* by a text and at the other is the notion of an active viewer *using* the text for his or her purposes.

Much of the argument has centred on 'effects' analysis which claims that the mass media have the power unproblematically to impose their meanings onto audiences and that this causes direct social and political effects (the analogy of injection with hypodermic needles is sometimes used here). Thus in recent decades research has purported to show the link between television violence and subsequent violent behaviour in some categories of viewer. In the past, similar accusations have been levelled at comics, radio and gangster films. Much of this work is inconclusive but it has nonetheless proved powerful and popular in fuelling moral panics about the mass media.

This relative neglect of the audience's subjectivity is mirrored in the work of the **Frankfurt School**. They saw the burgeoning mass media as the generator, via film, **advertising**, pop music and television, of ideology which contributed to the reproduction of the capitalist system and the subordination of the working class. In recent decades some Marxists, particularly those working within British cultural studies, have replaced the concept of imposition with the idea of an active, conscious audience interacting with the text. Here audiences in the process of decoding (and to some extent this will be dependent on socioeconomic background) may conform by producing a dominant reading of a text, but equally they can resist domination by producing negotiated or oppositional readings. Thus, following the Italian Marxist Gramsci, the ruling bloc cannot impose its will on an audience but must struggle to 'win it over'.

Equally, effects analysis has been countered by research which asks not what effect the media have on people but what people do to the media. Uses and gratifications theory investigates how audiences use the media for their own purposes to satisfy existing needs. So, individuals will buy particular newspapers to confirm their political beliefs or they might install a satellite dish because they like watching sport on television. In neither case is the reader passive or, in the words of the American sociologist Harold Garfinkel, a 'cultural dope'. Critics of this approach have complained that the idea of a reader making a free choice is mythical, and argue that there should be a renewed focus on who produces media texts and why.

More recent work has sought to fuse the advances of uses and gratifications theory with the emphasis on decoding in Gramscian cultural studies, where the audience is restricted in its understanding by social position but free to decode in different ways within that context. Research has concentrated on the experience of viewing and the awareness that such apparently mundane issues as who we watch television with will fundamentally influence the act of viewing. BC

See also encode/decode; performing arts; pop culture.

Further reading D. Morley, *Television Audiences and Cultural Studies*.

AUGUSTAN AGE

The actual period of history known as the Augustan Age was the reign of the Roman Emperor Augustus (27 BCE-CE 14), which was perceived both at the time and since as a **Golden Age** for literature, during which Virgil, Horace, Ovid, Livy and others all flourished. Somewhat self-admiringly, English writers of the 18th century described their own time as a second Augustan Age, claiming for themselves the same 'Golden Excellences' they recognized in the ancient Romans: stylistic elegance, trenchancy and **taste**. The chief writers involved were Alexander Pope (who coined the analogy with Augustan Rome), Butler, John Dryden, Samuel Johnson and Jonathan Swift, but the expressed ideals, and assumed virtues, of 18th-century Augustanism could also have been claimed by Diderot, Voltaire, or any other writers of the **Enlightenment**. KMcL

AUTARKY

Autarky (Greek, 'self-sufficiency'), in **economics**, is a **Utopian** aim. It is an economic system that is totally self-sufficient, producing all that is consumed and importing nothing from outside. However, because no country is able to produce the whole range of goods demanded at competitive prices, in practice autarky condemns its disciples to inefficiency and relative poverty.

Some countries' leaders have attempted to achieve autarky in order to eliminate any reliance on foreign materials and better to defend the society in time of war. Others have pursued autarky together with social isolation to maintain the mores and genetic purity of the native population or to maintain the leaders' control. In today's world of high-tech production and minding one's neighbours' business, such efforts are virtually certain to fail. TF

AUTEUR THEORY

The auteur theory or principle has central importance in the critical analysis of cinema and film, and as such has been a contentious area of debate since the end of World War II. The term was coined by those French film critics who, deprived of Hollywood films during the occupation, enthusiastically embraced and re-evaluated them after the war had ended. Much of the debate was carried out in the pages of the journal *Cahiers du Cinéma* under the editorial guidance of André Bazin. The journal became a focus for a new generation of French critics, many of whom were, or later became, influential film-makers themselves (such as Jean-Luc Godard, François Truffaut and Claude Chabrol).

In 1954, Truffaut published a controversial article ('Une certaine tendence du cinema français') which damned traditional French cinema for its formal and stylistic conservatism, and especially for its over-reliance on literature as a source for its products. As part of this critique, previously disregarded Hollywood 'B' movies were given a new status and high praise. The basis of the *auteuristes'* argument was the visual style, flair and inventiveness shown by some film directors, despite the many constraints and limitations placed on them by the Hollywood studio system. Thus, it came to be argued that the film's director, rather than the writer of the original material, was the source of a specifically visual form of creativity.

Cahiers du Cinéma became known for its *politique des auteurs* ('the policy of authors') during the 1960s, and for some years was responsible for debates hinging on the worth or otherwise of particular film-makers. The journal was famous for its idiosyncracies and for the way it favoured certain directors, claiming for example that some directors were genuine auteurs, while others were merely clever technicians (or *metteurs*). Its contributors were seemingly particularly keen on those directors working within established genres, on location, and with an original screenplay or shooting script rather than an adaptation from a novel or play.

The auteur theory later took root in American and British criticism, most notably in the US via the work of Andrew Sarris. The approach has been criticized on a number of levels, including the arbitrary nature of its assessments and its potential for élitism. Nevertheless, it continues to be of use to media analysts and critics, and has

been especially appreciated as a means by which popular, commercial films can be re-evaluated. **BC**

See also criticism; new wave.

AUTHENTICITY

The 'authentic' was a key goal of the anthropologists' search for a true understanding of foreign cultures. This was particularly so from the 1920s on, when **field work** became standard practice. A society was seen as more 'authentic' if it had not come into contact with missionaries or colonial influence. Many early anthropologists set about trying to capture a picture of that society in its pristine, uncontaminated condition; what James Clifford termed the 'ethnographic present', a picture of society forzen in time. This image of static societies was often used as a contrast to ever-changing Western **culture**.

Modern **anthropology** borrowed from the philosopher Theodor Adorno the idea of examining how authenticity is applied in contemporary Western culture. For instance, tourism (see **tourism, anthropology of**) can be seen as a search for an authentic experience usually in an exotic place. For those who stay at home, contact with authentic pieces of culture, whether in films, books or museums, allows them to incorporate the authenticity of another culture into their own personal experience. The problem with authenticity is that it presupposes a compatibility between the object seen and what is being represented.

Authenticity is also a key concept in examining how artefacts from other cultures have been evaluated and appropriated by the West. The collecting and marketing of art objects has increased the value of the authentic object, as opposed to imitations. In the same way that the idea of authenticity was applied to whole cultures, it is, in this capacity, a criterion by which their artefacts are evaluated. **CL**

See also ethnohistory; visual anthropology.

Further reading James Clifford, *The Predicament of Culture*; Dean MacCannell, *Empty Meeting Grounds*.

AUTHORITARIANISM

Authoritarianism is the belief and practice
of a form of government in which the rulers
exercise authority without the consent of
the governed. By this definition most
régimes in human history and a majority in
our own time have been authoritarian. For
just this reason critics sometimes complain
that authoritarianism is a vague, 'catch-all'
or residual category, used to describe all
non-democratic régimes, such as **despotic**,
absolutist, **fascist**, **Marxist**-Leninist, military and **totalitarian** dictatorships.

More usefully, political scientists contrast authoritarianism with totalitarianism.
The two systems are both imposed on their
subjects and lack genuine political competition. However, authoritarian systems usually lack an over-arching single ideology,
need not be organized through a single
party system, and do not aspire to control
the entire social system, merely to disable
their oppositions.

During the Cold War between Western
liberal democracies and communist systems (1945–89) it was often argued by
Western right-wingers that authoritarian
systems were preferable to communist (or
totalitarian) systems, on the grounds that
the former could be reformed whereas the
latter could only be destroyed through war.
The foreign policy implication was that
Western democracies should (critically)
support right-wing authoritarian régimes
while opposing left-wing totalitarian
régimes, through war if necessary. The relatively peaceful internal collapse of **communism** in eastern Europe and the Soviet
Union (1989–91) suggests either that Western right-wingers were wrong or that communist systems were authoritarian rather
than totalitarian.

Some social scientists believe that authoritarian régimes, like empires, were very
probable in **agrarian societies**, because
power-resources were not widely distributed; by contrast in industrial and postindustrial societies the wider dispersal of
power-resources and skills among their
populations reduces the likelihood that
authoritarian régimes can be sustained, or
at least efficiently so. Let us hope they are
right. **BO'L**

See also Asiatic mode of production; industrial society.

Further reading Carl Friedrich and Zbigniew
Brzezinski (eds.), *Totalitarian Dictatorship and
Autocracy.*

AUTHORITY

Authority (Latin, 'power [of origination]')
refers to a type of **power** which when exercised is obeyed because it is considered to
be legitimate. Those who recognize the
'authority' consider it to be justified and
proper, and so the exercise of authority
tends to be effective in securing its objectives. Authority is also used to refer to the
established political rule within a community or state when this rule is politically
legitimate.

The sociologist Max Weber (1864–1920)
distinguished three 'ideal' types of authority. *Legal-rational authority* entails obedience to formal rules that have been
established by regular public procedures;
traditional authority involves the acceptance
of the rules which embody custom and
ancient practices; *charismatic authority* is
exercised because the followers or disciples
believe in the extraordinary capacities of
their leader. For Weber, any régime that
has minimum acceptance has some sem-
blance of legitimacy even if this is grounded
on the use of force.

The term authority has been employed
more loosely within **sociology** to refer to the
influence exercised by leadership. It is also
used in social psychology in research on the
dynamics of small groups to refer to influence over individual belief and behaviour.
DA

See also charisma; community; dominant
ideology; hegemony; ideal type; ideology;
legitimation; social control; society; state.

Further reading R. Nisbet, *The Sociological
Tradition*; F. Parkin, *Max Weber.*

AUTISM

Autism (Greek, 'selfness') is a mental condition which becomes apparent when a
young child fails to learn cognitive skills,
and appears not to have the thought processes which lead to communication and to

relationships with other people, including parents. Such children might be thought to be subnormal, were it not for their creative involvement with inanimate objects. The autistic state is thought to be present from very early on, possibly from birth. It leads to a permanent state of anxiety, creating an inability to relate to others and to develop social skills. The outcome of such limited contact with others is obsessive patterns of behaviour. Bettelheim, in his book *The Empty Fortress*, suggested that the condition was the result of very early lack of emotional support from the mother, but some autistic children have been found to be suffering from an oversensitivity to noise something which could be radically altered with training. **MJ**

AUTONOMY

Autonomy (Greek, 'law to oneself', 'being self-governed'), in **psychology**, is achieved by overcoming infantile dependence and creating adult independence. An adult can be neurotically dependent, imagining himself or herself to be dependent on others and not autonymous. Such neurotic reliance is the result of a belief that others have choices and they do not. There are different views in psychology as to how autonomy is gained, though all psychodynamic views would agree that autonomy necessarily includes autonomy from one's parents.

Autonomy in **psychoanalysis** comes through the successful completion of the Oedipal phase (see **Oedipus complex**). The first part of the Oedipal phase is when the child feels it should have the same-sex parental partner's place in the triangular relationship: at this stage, the parent in question is seen as the usurper. Then there is the discovery that it is dangerous to covet this position; the child sees itself as the usurper and fears retribution. This is resolved by sexuality becoming latent and being replaced by an identification with the parent of the same sex. The parent of the opposite sex is then rediscovered at puberty, when the person becomes attracted to the opposite sex. If not resolved this can result in father-or mother-fixated behaviour, as well as in neurotic dependent states.

Autonomy in Jungian psychology, seen through the myths created in fairy tales, views children as given symbolic gifts to help them, and finds children supported by special helpers, but the emphasis is on finding their way themselves and finally finding their own mates. If not resolved, the dependence on the parents is transferred onto the adult partners and autonomy is not achieved. Autonomy means assertion of our own needs, making choices and finding our own partner.

In politics autonomy is a relative concept which refers to the degree of freedom from coercion or outside influence which a state, a region, a group or an individual has over its own actions. The expression the 'autonomy of the state' when used by historians or political scientists may also refer to the ability of state officials to pursue state interests, rather than simply reflecting or reacting to the interests of dominant groups in society.

Theoretically all states which are recognized in the world system as sovereign are thought to be autonomous from other states. However, in practice, the autonomy of sovereign states is limited by international organizations, like the United Nations, NATO, ASEAN, supranational organizations, like the EC, and multiple forms of economic, cultural and political interdependence between states.

Regions and peoples within states may seek autonomy, rather than independence, that is, they seek self-government in domestic public policy rather than sovereignty in foreign affairs. Such autonomy may take the form of a developed government within a unitary state, a cantonal or provincial government within a federation, or indeed a nonterritorial form.

The idea of personal autonomy is a central value in most forms of Western liberalism, and in contemporary political philosophy is linked to debates about the justification of state, democracy and law, privacy and questions of distributive justice. Most recently it has played a central part in debates about multiculturalism. **MJ BO'L**

See also consociation; democracy; federalism.

Further reading Gerald Dworkin, *The Theory*

and Practice of Autonomy; Hurst Hannum, *Autonomy, Sovereignty, and Self-Determinism: the Accommodation of Conflicting Rights;* Charles Taylor, *Multiculturalism and 'The Politics of Recognition'.*

AVANT-GARDE

Avant-garde (French, 'front-line') is that section of any institution or movement in the **arts** which is judged, by its adherents or its enemies, to be ahead of the rest, in contrast to those who bring up the rear and are *rétardataire*, or at least in touch with the status quo. The term avant-garde is loaded with political and social undertones: 'I am stable, reliable and for the status quo'; 'you are a dangerous reactionary'; 'she is a left-wing avant-gardiste'. Its mixture of alienation of artistic creators and consumers who feel themselves to be outside current social norms makes the whole concept a spin-off from **Romanticism**. At the same time, it can be comforting (and perhaps creatively enabling) to imagine oneself not outside the mainstream but *as* the mainstream, if only the rest of the world would catch up and march in step.

The whole concept of an artistic avant-garde is scarcely older than the 19th century. Before then, the ostensible aim of artistic creators who required commissions was to conform to expectations or possibly to confound them in a predictable and unthreatening way. (These procedures stifled neither initiative nor innovation. To take one art at random, **drama**: both Aeschylus and Ibsen, in their day, followed the conventions of the age – the structures of Greek religious **tragedy** and of the **'well-made' play** respectively – and their work was just as fine, and just as admired by its audience, as the plays of such trumpeted radicals as, for example, Ionesco or Osborne in their day.) But it is true to say that 19th-century Europeans, influenced by the Romantic idea of the struggling artist (a measure of whose quality depended on his or her being against current trends or at least unappreciated by normal cognoscenti), developed the concept of the avant-garde not only to explain unappreciated innovation, but often to justify extreme radicalism in the arts.

In using labels like avant-garde, we are really talking less about the arts than about fashion in the arts. It is easier to decry as avant-garde something you fail to understand, or find threatening, than to try to get its measure. It is equally easy to cry up the novelty of your own or your favoured creators' art as avant-garde, and explain the indifference of the majority by saying that the work of art is simply ahead of its age. As with all fashions, time is the only true arbiter, and the chief purpose of labels and styles, if one takes the long view, is to act as an irritant and/or a stimulant both to creativity and to that presumptuous handmaiden of artistic creativity, appreciation. Perhaps, if we artists and consumers are to come to grips with the arts at all, to keep alert, we need the noise almost as much as we need the actual art. **KMcL**

See also taste.

AXIOM OF CHOICE

The axiom of choice has been one of the most hotly contested principles of 20th-century **mathematics**. Once the concept of the infinite had begun to be investigated by Georg Cantor (1845–1918), the axiom of choice was something it seemed obvious to formulate; it is (loosely) something that makes infinite sets behave far more like finite ones. Several different formulations of the axiom of choice have been made, among others by Ernst Zermelo (1871–1953) and Adolf Abraham Fraenkel (1891–1965), the inventors of modern axiomatic **set theory**.

Some of these equivalent formulations are as follows: (1) *The Classic Axiom of Choice* For every set A of non-empty sets, there is a set B (known as the choice set) which has one and only one member in common with each member of A. (2) *The Well-Ordering Principle* Every set can be well-ordered. (A set is well-ordered if for every element a,b,c we have $a < b$ or $b < a$ but not both; if $a < b$ and $b < c$ then $a < c$ and any non-empty subset has a minimal element.) (3) *Every Set has a Cardinality* This means that the notion of size is well-defined for infinite sets. There are several other, more complicated formulations of the same principle, one of the most commonly used being known as Zorn's Lemma.

Even once these definitions have been disentangled, there at first seems to be no problem. Some of the consequences of the axiom are much less desirable, being completely at odds with common sense. For example, it is possible (given the axiom of choice) to take a spherical object (such as an orange), cut it into a small finite number of pieces, which can then be reassembled to produce two spheres of the same size as the original one. This contradicts our understanding of how space works, but that in itself is not a sufficient objection to make mathematicians discard the axiom: it is not contradictory, but merely strange. Besides, the axiom of choice is vastly useful. A second objection is that it is often easy to use the axiom of choice to show the existence of some kind of mathematical object, but difficult to see what such an object looks like. An example of this is the well-ordering of the real numbers predicted to exist by the well-ordering principle (see below). This gives mathematicians a problem, for they like to be able actually to look at the objects they produce, and so try to produce them in a 'constructive' way.

Pure mathematicians collectively heaved a sigh of relief in 1939, when Gödel (1906–78) proved that the axiom of choice was consistent with the other axioms of set theory. He did not prove that it was necessarily true, merely that its use would never produce a result which contradicted the other axioms, which were all widely accepted. However, in 1963 Paul Cohen showed that the negation, or opposite, to the axiom of choice was also consistent with the rest of set theory. He demonstrated that there was a kind of set theory in which the set of real numbers was not well-orderable (this means that even if the axiom of choice is accepted, it is not possible explicitly to find a way of well-ordering the real numbers).

This demonstration left the axiom of choice in a kind of limbo. Today, mathematicians will use it if they can find no other way to prove a theorem, but its use still carries a stigma from the time when some thought it false, and it is always flagged when used. **SMcL**

Further reading W.V. Quine, *Set Theory and Its Logic.*

AXIOMATIZATION

Axiomatization is the process of taking a body of knowledge, usually but not exclusively in **mathematics**, and separating out certain sentences to describe it. These sentences are the axioms, and they will have the following useful properties: (1) They should be appear to be intuitively true. (2) Their meaning should be easy to grasp. (3) They should be consistent (that is, no contradictory result should follow from them as a logical consequence). (4) As much as possible of the body of knowledge (known as the theory) should be a logical consequence of them. (5) They should be as few in number as possible (that is, none of them should be a logical consequence of the others). (The reason for saying 'as much as possible' rather than 'all' in (4) is **Gödel's incompleteness theorem** which makes 'all' an unattainable goal in most reasonably powerful systems.) The mathematical sentences of the theory which are logical consequences of the axioms are called 'theorems'. Properties (4) and (5) together are usually coalesced as the property of 'productiveness' – a small number of axioms produce a large number of theorems.

Axiomatization has played an increasingly important role in mathematics. The original paradigm of an axiom system is the axioms for geometry of Euclid (*fl.* 295 BCE) (he actually called them 'postulates'). The search for increasing rigour in mathematics has led to the axiomatization of more and more theories, a process which culminated in the axiomatization of **set theory** by Ernst Zermelo (1871–1953) and Adolf Abraham Fraenkel (1891–1965). It is now common to start with a group of axioms and to see what can be deduced from them, rather than taking an existing body of knowledge and picking a group of axioms for it.

The role of axioms in mathematics has been to make far clearer exactly what is being said, particularly since the introduction of Gottlob Frege's **symbolic logic**. They expose exactly what is being assumed by particular mathematicians – the idea is never to assume something which is not an axiom. The success of axioms in many bodies of mathematics led to (not unreasonable) attempts to axiomatize the whole of mathematics, first in the *Principia Mathematica* of Bertrand Russell (1872–1970) and Alfred North Whitehead (1861–1947) and then in the **Hilbert programme**. The former was never finished, and the latter was proved impossible by Gödel. It has also led to attempts to duplicate the idea in other fields. Spinoza (1639–77) attempted to set up a system of **philosophy** which was axiomatic, and in the 19th century Marx tried to do the same in political theory. The problem that ruined the effectiveness of their work was that both of them failed to realize that unless the axioms are accepted, neither can the consequences of the axioms. The same problem has dogged others who have tried to bring 'mathematical' precision to areas other than mathematics.

One of the problems of formalization is that a series of formal proofs in symbolic logic soon becomes tedious; after a few theorems, the reader begins to scream for a less fussy approach. As a result, the tendency in modern mathematics has been to take what is known as a '**Platonic** viewpoint': to give informal proofs to convince a 'reasonable' person which can (theoretically, at least) be backed up with the more formal proof to counter objections. There are clearly disadvantages to this, as one person's idea of a convincing argument is different from another's. Also, the retreat from **formalism** makes it possible to hide mistakes (from oneself and others) in imprecise language and to make unstated assumptions. In an incorrect proof, it is usually the word 'clearly' that hides the error. SMcL

B

BA'ATHISM

Ba'athism literally means 'resurrection' in Arabic. It was the name coined by the Pan-Arabist movement which emerged in Syria in 1953. It was based on a combination of nationalist and state socialist ideologies, and distanced itself from **Islam** without utterly rejecting it, portraying the religion as a central product of Arab culture. The original Ba'athist movement was an amalgam of Akram Howrani's Syrian Arab Socialist Party and Michel Aflaq's Arab Resurrection Party. Ba'athism appealed broadly to the anti-aristocratic interests of the Arab peasantry and the newly emergent middle classes, creating, by 1960, a powerful network of parties in Iraq, Jordan and Lebanon.

In Syria the ba'athist ideal of Arab unity was partially realized with the formation of the United Arab Republic (UAR) between Syria and Egypt in 1958. However, ba'athism was banned by the Egyptian leader Gamal Abdel Nasser in 1960 in his attempt to consolidate power within the UAR. Ba'athist retaliation against the Egyptian putsch led to the dissolution of the UAR and the emergence of a radicalized ba'athist movement which seized control in Syria in 1963. By 1970 the radical wing of the movement under General Hafiz al-Assad consolidated its power by co-opting the Syrian communist movement, which led to the establishment of military and economic alliances with the former Soviet Union.

In Iraq, ba'athism emerged as a forceful political movement following the overthrow of the Hashemite monarchy in 1958. The pan-Arabist movement which led to the creation of the UAR accentuated divisions among Iraq's Sunni and Shi'ite Muslims as well as the Kurds and facilitated the emergence of the Ba'ath Party as a secular alternative to sustained religious and ethnic division. The Ba'ath Party achieved partial control in 1968 when General Ahmad Hassan al-Bakr seized power and invited the ba'athists to form a government. The ba'athist takeover was completed in 1980 when al-Bakr gave way to Saddam Hussein (a Sunni Muslim) who quickly consolidated power by systematically eliminating all his political rivals. Saddam Hussein's authority was challenged by the Ayatollah Khomeini in Iran who threatened to mobilize Iraq's Shi'ite Muslim majority against the secular ba'athist régime. This threat led to a preemptive strike by Iraq which escalated into a bloody and long war between the two countries (1980–88). Syria's support for

Iran in the eight-year war suggested that ba'athism had in practice become a form of national socialism in both Syria and Iraq. **BO'L**

See also Arabism; Islamic political thought.

Further reading Raymond Hinnebusch, *Authoritarian Power and State Formation in Ba'athist Syria: Army, Party and Peasant.*

BACTERIOLOGY

Bacteriology is the branch of **microbiology** dealing with the structure and properties of bacteria, particularly those properties which are important industrially or medically. Bacteria (named because they looked, to the first people to study them, like little sticks, *bacteria* in Greek) constitute a highly varied group of simple organisms, usually single-celled. They are difficult to classify in relation to plants or animals, but are usually considered to be more closely aligned to the plant kingdom than the animal kingdom. All bacteria are prototypes, meaning that they have a more simple cellular organization than plants and animals, which are eukaryotes. Prokaryotes have no chromosomes.

Ferdinand Cohn published the first classification of bacteria in 1872, but subsequent attempts to impose some kind of taxonomic order on the huge range of bacteria have met with great difficulty. Bacteria are classified by their shape, size and response to certain chemical stains. Robert Koch, a student of Cohn's, was a pioneer in the field who worked with the bacteria which cause important diseases such as anthrax and tuberculosis. Bacterial cells are much simpler in genetic and structural terms than the cells of larger organisms; they multiply extremely rapidly, by dividing every 20 minutes under suitable conditions, and they have the ability to adapt very rapidly to environmental changes. For these reasons they are extensively used in modern biochemical research. Pathogenic (disease-causing) bacteria represent the minority and induce their effects by their rate of growth and by the production of substances which are toxic to the body. **RB**

See also abiogenesis.

BALANCE OF POWER

Theories which describe conditions of equilibrium in political systems are called 'balance of power' theories. They can be divided into those which describe stability within internal (or domestic) political systems and those which refer to external or international systems.

Internal balance of power theories describe the political process through which certain parties and interest groups influence the allocation of resources or access to political power.

International balance of power theories focus on the mechanisms which are used to prevent war or aggression between and among sovereign states, the key idea being that wars are caused by a disruption of the existing balance of power. Debate among historians and political theorists has centred on whether or not a single hegemon (or dominant power) is necessary to prevent war and whether (and how) deterrence is essential to the preservation of stability in international relations. The relations between the 'great powers' between 1815 and 1945 remain the subject of controversy for balance of power theorists.

The development of deterrence theory underwent a significant change following the development of weapons of mass destruction such as hydrogen and atomic bombs. The emergence of two ideologically opposed nuclear superpowers (the USA and USSR) led to a change from a balance of power based on simple deterrence to an arms race based on each side's determination to hold a balance of terror, or an offensive capability to destroy or annihilate the opposing power. The escalating arms race led to a further development in deterrence theory known as 'mutually assured destruction' (MAD) in which each side was convinced that no pre-emptive nuclear strike would be sufficient to prevent the other from retaliating with a sufficiently massive force which would ensure total, immediate and mutual destruction.

The costs of this arms race, which appears to have ended in 1991, has been a significant factor in the economic decline of both superpowers; it left the US economically weakened and contributed to the disintegration of the USSR. Although the USA remains the world's dominant military power the decline in the ideological cleavage between **capitalism** and **communism** has led to a new form of balance of power, based primarily on economic interdependence rather than pure military strength. A multi-polar balance of power is emerging, based on a revitalized western Europe, Japan and China, economic superpowers which can partially offset the combined military and economic power of the US.

Whether the relative stability of the bipolar balance of power during the cold war, at least in the 'North' of the world, will be maintained in the emergent multipolar world remains to be seen. **BO'L**

See also pluralism.

Further reading Robert Keohane, *After Hegemony*; R. Pettman, *International Politics: Balance of Power, Balance of Productivity, Balance of Ideologies.*

BALLET

Ballet (Italian *balletto*, 'little ball') is a type of dramatic performance using dance and sometimes mime, to musical accompaniment. Except in a few cases, the performance tells a story or depicts a specific scene. The art of ballet, therefore, involves imposing an external intellectual correlative, a rationale, on particular kinds of physical activity. (If we took the individual components of athletics or gymnastics, and choreographed them to some predetermined narrative structure – as happened in the Spartakiads of Communist Czechoslovakia or the gymnastic displays of Communist North Vietnam – the process, if not the end-result, would be identical.) Dance-drama of this kind is one of the oldest of all dramatic forms – the earliest known cave paintings show dancers playing the parts of hunters and animals – and it survives in all cultures in religious celebrations, secular entertainments, or both. It has reached two peaks of extreme sophistication: religious theatre in the East, and 'classical' theatre-ballet in the West.

Using gesture, facial expressions and patterns of body-movement (both individual and group) to tell a story has led to the development of highly stylized and sophisticated forms of 'ordinary' movement in ballet, and in each form of the art there is a well-defined repertoire of meaning-through-movement. The Roman ballet-dancers who performed for (and sometimes with) the Emperor Nero used 32 hand-positions to indicate specific emotions, and temple-dancers in northern India train each muscle independently, so that even the flick of a finger joint or the twitch of an eyelid can speak volumes. Western theatre-ballet, though nothing like so complex, has a widely-understood repertoire of movement and gesture, which choreographers draw on and codify when they 'create' each new ballet. (In passing, the existence of choreography makes Western ballet utterly different from ballet in the East. Eastern dance-dramas are traditional, their movements unvarying from generation to generation; in the West, each choreographer draws on a pool of ideas and styles to create an original and individual work which remains his or her intellectual property. The difference is analogous to that between Eastern 'classical' music, which is traditional and improvised, and the strictly-notated and personally-copyrighted 'classical' music of the West.) Often, in both East and West, stylization has reached the point where the initial meanings of particular movements are lost, and the movements are retained for their own sakes alone: examples are the dancing on points and *fouettés* of Western theatre-ballet.

Of its nature, Eastern ballet has tended to be inward-looking and expressive: the movements are always subservient to the mood they invoke or the story they tell. In the West, by contrast, extroversion has increasingly become the rule. Ballet has become an art primarily of display, where the individual performer's technique is a perceived part of the attraction, and ballets are even created or re-choreographed specifically as star-vehicles. (The point is made if one contrasts ballet first with ice-dancing, where a similar development has happened, triple salchows and toeloops being applauded as if they were circus feats, and then with grand **opera**, where the dominance of star performers and directors has not yet entirely engulfed the form.) In the 20th century, largely because of the influence of Nijinsky and other dancers from Diaghilev's *Ballets russes* in the 1910s and 1920s, a new form of **abstract** ballet has even been devised, allowing concentration on dance and pattern alone, unencumbered by story.

By the mid-20th century, ballet throughout the world had become an esoteric and extravagant minority interest, exclusive and self-obsessed. But in the latter half of the century, with increased international travel and awareness of other cultures, ballet has been regenerated. It still has its purist corners, dazzling shrines to decadence – the Japanese court tradition and Bolshoi tradition come to mind. But elsewhere the influence of folk dance and popular dance from around the world, and even of athletics and gymnastics, has made ballet one of the most eclectic and dynamic of all **performing arts**. KMcL

BAROQUE

The origins of the word 'baroque' are obscure. Some authorities derive it from Italian *barocco*, the name of a particularly ornately-patterned kind of pearl; others say that it was a mnemonic coined by the 13th-century writer William of Shyreswood (a mnemonic for what, the pundits seem to have forgotten). It is a term used particularly in **architecture**, visual **art** and **music**. In architecture, it was first applied in the 18th century (by French **neoclassical** critics) as a term of abuse, meaning 'fantastic' or 'misshapen'. Late 19th-century art historians took up the term and used it more systematically to investigate (and to some extent categorize) work of the late-16th to mid-18th centuries. The architecture of this period, particularly perhaps that of Borromini (1599–1667) and Bernini (1598–1680), gives a sensation of the building treated as sculpture, particularly noticeable in the almost unprecedented use of curvilinear forms. (Fine examples are the front elevation of the Church of San Carlo Quattro Fontane and the colonnade of St Peter's, both in Rome.)

Baroque architecture is characterized by movement and drama. The principal elevations of baroque churches are often conceived in concave and convex planes, their interiors embellished with **sculpture** and painting. The expressionist qualities of the baroque are often ascribed to a particular phase in the history of the Catholic Church, after the readjustment and internal reform set in motion by the Council of Trent (1545–63) had given the Church both a renewed self-confidence, and a need to attract people away from the now established Protestantism.

In fine art, the term 'baroque' refers to work of the 17th and much of the 18th centuries in (especially) the Catholic countries of Europe, and to a style midway between **mannerism** and **rococo**. It implies grandeur, spatial complexity and an interest in the excesses both of decorative elaboration and of light and shade in short, a sense of theatre which often involves the manipulation of the spectator, whether the medium be painting or sculpture. By extension, the 'ringmaster' artist must co-ordinate all the arts in order to achieve the desired effect, so that baroque is frequently the union of the arts, working together (as in Bernini's 'control' of the crossing of St Peter's in Rome, mentioned above, or his arrangement of the piazza outside the building).

In music, baroque is used to describe European art-music from about 1600–1750: from the heyday of Monteverdi to the death of Bach, the period of such composers as Corelli, Handel, Telemann and Vivaldi. In the baroque period, the focus of attention shifted from church to secular music. Although church pieces continued to be written, secular **opera** became the vocal form most favoured by composers and patrons, and new forms of instrumental music (especially concerto, sonata and suite) were developed to replace the fantasias and ricercares of earlier times. There was a marked rise in the importance of virtuoso performers, opera singers and violinists in particular being in demand, and able to name their price (and the kind of music they would play) throughout the continent: this led to a homogenization of style which, by the end of the baroque period, had become pervasive. **PD MG JM KMcL**

See also Renaissance.

Further reading Anthony Blunt, *Baroque and Rococo*; John R. Martin, *Baroque*.

BARTOLOZZI SOUNDS

Bartolozzi sounds are named after Bruno Bartolozzi, who, in 1967, wrote a book describing them and explaining how to produce them from wind instruments. By using 'new' fingerings and ways of blowing, it is possible to produce, and control, all kinds of previously unorthodox sounds, such as chords, harmonics and microtones. These sounds were once considered freakish, but are now part of the standard repertory of composers, for example Luciano Berio or Karlheinz Stockhausen, and of performers, such as the oboist Heinz Holliger or the trombonist Vinco Globokar. **KMcL**

Further reading Bruno Bartolozzi, *New Sounds for Woodwind*.

BATTERIES

Batteries consist of one or more electric cells which produce electric currents directly from chemical reactions. The first battery was the Voltaic Pile, named after Alessandro Volta (1745–1827). Volta discovered that, by using dissimilar metals immersed in water with a little acid added, an electric current was produced. Batteries have come a long way since then and are now used in everything from a watch to powerful fuel cells.

The simplest form of electrical battery comprises a vessel containing an electrolyte such as a solution of salt in water and two dissimilar metals immersed in the electrolyte, but not touching. In this situation a voltage difference can be measured between the two plates which depends on the positions of the metals in the electrochemical services. (This is a list of metals in a specific order from most electropositive to most electronegative. The further apart the metals are in the series the greater the voltage developed). If a copper plate and a zinc plate are connected by a conductor current will flow.

The so-called dry battery replaces the liquid solution with a conducting jelly but the principle of its function is the same.

If high voltages are required a number, N, of such cells can be connected in series copper to zinc at each junction and the voltage between the ends will then be N times the voltage across one cell. The disadvantage of these batteries is that they cannot provide large currents due to the internal resistance of each cell and the energy stored is small. The cost per kilowatt hour of **electricity** from a battery may be several hundred times that of electrical mains energy.

Where electrical energy has to be available from a portable source the lead accumulator may be used. This is formed by two lead plates with a series of rectangular recesses on their surface. One of these plates has the recesses filled with lead oxide and the vessel is filled with sulphuric acid. If the cell has a constant voltage applied across the plates current flows and energy is stored. When the cell is fully charged it will retain this for long periods and deliver the energy when required. This is the basis of most batteries in motor cars. The charge in the battery developed by the generator when the engine is running is available to restart the engine when required even after periods of weeks or months. Several cells are joined together to form an accumulator to provide whatever voltage is required. The disadvantages of the lead accumulator restrict the areas in which it can be used. These are its weight, the presence of the corrosive acid which is dangerous if spilled, the fact that when charging hydrogen gas is produced which can be explosive in the presence of a flame, the fact that the lead plates will be irreparably damaged if too large a current is drawn from the battery and therefore that the battery can only be recharged at a slow rate. This slow rate of charge is also necessary because under rapid charging gas bubbles collect on the plates and prevent the acid from having free contact. **AA**

Further reading P. Dunsheath, *A History of Electrical Engineering*.

BAUHAUS

The Bauhaus (German, 'build-house') was a kind of design think-tank, founded in

Weimar in 1919 and broken up by the Nazis in 1933 (after which many of its members emigrated to the USA, to continue their work and brainstorming there). Its aims were to apply the best forms and styles of modern art to ordinary living, and in particular to marry mass-production techniques to the latest ideas in fine design – a kind of snappy 1920s **Arts and Crafts** philosophy. The Bauhaus itself was run like Edison's 'Invention Factory' a generation before, or like the Research and Development departments of many subsequent big businesses. Discussion, experimentation and development were everyday work, and production (especially mass-production) was a distinctly secondary activity.

In practice, Bauhaus creations (exemplified by tubular-metal furniture, variably-positionable desk-lamps and cuboid buildings) were stiff to look at and expensive to buy. The Bauhaus ideal, however, has influenced the design of consumer goods ever since, as anyone can testify who has sat in a moulded-plastic chair in a high-rise flat, or drunk from an extruded-polystyrene cup. The 'think-tank' method, too, has had enormous influence on the way 20th-century buildings, fabrics, furniture and fittings are designed and planned. Artists, architects and designers associated with the Bauhaus (and who went on to greater and less anonymous creation) included Marcel Breuer, Walter Gropius (its director for the first nine years), Vassily Kandinsky, Paul Klee, Mies van der Rohe (who succeeded Gropius as director in 1928) and Laszlo Moholy-Nagy. **KMcL**

Further reading H.W. Wingler, *The Bauhaus;* Tom Wolfe, *From the Bauhaus to Our House* (marvellously sour polemic against the whole concept of 'art-for-living').

BAYESIAN STATISTICS

Bayes's rule, formulated by Thomas Bayes (1702–61) sparked off a radical new direction in **statistics**, the application in **mathematics** of probability theory. The rule shows how to handle 'conditional probabilities', ones which show the effect of one event on another. For example, the probability that a patient has back trouble is higher if it is known that he or she claims to have back pains. We make one event (that the patient claims to have back pains) a condition of the other (that he or she has back trouble). It is usual to write the conditional probability of event A given that event B is known to have happened as $p(A B)$; Bayes's rule tells us that $p(A) = p(A B) \times p(B) + p(A \text{ not } B) \times p(\text{not } B)$.

Bayes's rule is used to find the probability of an event experimentally; the experimenter starts off with a degree of belief in each of his or her hypotheses, and uses Bayes's rule to modify these degrees of belief according to the results of experimentation (for example, an experiment could consist of asking a patient if he or she has back pains). The method is commonly used today by computers, providing 'expert systems' used in medicine, prospecting and fault diagnosis. **SMcL**

BEAR/BULL MARKET

A market in which prices are falling or are expected to fall is called by economists a bear market. It is a designation commonly used in securities markets and commodity markets and is the opposite of a bull market. Likewise, the term bear can be applied to a person who expects stock prices to fall and sells stock that he or she does not have for delivery at a future date. When the future date arrives the bear expects to buy in at a lower price to deliver the stock that had been sold under the future contract at a higher price.

Historically, the term bear for such a person appears early in the 18th century, first as bearskin jobber, which makes it probable that the original phrase was 'sell the bearskin', and that it originated in the well-known proverb, 'to sell the bear's skin before one has caught the bear'. The associated bull appears somewhat later and was perhaps suggested by bear. **TF**

BEAT GENERATION

The Beat Generation was prominent in US literary life in the mid-1950s. 'Beat' connects both with 'beaten' and 'beatified', because the writers felt crushed by the outmoded values of society and elevated by the headiness of their own revolt. (In this they were analogous to the **Angry Young Men** in the UK, though the style of their revolt, and of their actual work, was completely different.) Beat writers flouted the 'rules' both of society and of art, using a slangy, invented language (of which 'hip' is the best-known word to have reached ordinary usage) and blending fury with a Zen-inspired, free-floating anarchy of thought, which anticipated the Hippies of a decade later. The principal figures of the movement were the poets Allan Ginsberg and Gregory Corso and the novelists Jack Kerouac (who gave the movement its name) and (though he stood laterally to it) William Burroughs. Those influenced by Beat ideas, but not totally immersed in them, include Norman Mailer, Henry Miller, Kenneth Rexroth and a gallery of **sf** writers from Philip K. Dick and Frank Herbert to Gene Wolfe. **KMcL**

Further reading Jack Kerouac, *On the Road.*

BEAUTY

Beauty (from Latin *bellus*, 'pretty', and its French derivative *beau*) is a quality philosophers find hard to define. The standard definition is that it is the quality of things which pleases or delights the senses or intellect. However, being stroked can please and delight the senses, but it hardly seems right to say that being stroked is beautiful. Some philosophers hold that beauty is an intrinsic, mind-dependent quality of objects. Others hold that beauty is not objective, but consists in a disposition to produce a certain reaction (such as a feeling of approval) in mental subjects. In both these definitions, works of art are beautiful, and so are parts of nature (such as plants) which are not works of art.

Anthropologists say that beauty is not simply an essence embodied in the object or action itself, but derives from the values and ideas of the creator or observer, who is in turn affected by his or her cultural milieux. Therefore, concepts of beauty vary not just from person to person, but cross-culturally as well. Whether associated with physical attractiveness, artistic practices or products, graceful motions or other factors or attributes, ideas of beauty are closely entwined with values and expectations held in particular communities. They entail ideals of collective thought sustained by certain limitations. For example, ideas about a person's beauty are predetermined by the individual's gender.

Western ideas about beauty may be traced back to Plato. He proposed that what is beautiful is synonymous with the truthful and divine. Since then, various other theories have been offered. Beauty may be a property that evokes a special reaction in a person; it may also be a means of expressing non-possessive love and so forth.

Among the Tiv people in southern Nigeria the body was the primary context for ideas about beauty. Glowing after oil is rubbed over the body was considered particularly beautiful. Stylish dress, body scarification, and, in earlier days, teeth chipping, were also considered means of beautifying the body. Trends in these personal arts were noted, providing an index of variant notions of beauty and values between successive generations.

James Faris (see below) presented a picture of the Nuba peoples' views on personal beauty in the 1970s. Whereas Nuba women had their bodies scarred at key points in their life, particularly during puberty and after childbirth, Nuba men decorated their bodies with paint according to their progression through the age-grades. Ceremonial competition encouraged Nuba men to experiment with their personal arts in order to present themselves at their best for appreciation in the community. Only men who were initiated in the final grade were privileged to wear black all over the body. The important requirement for all Nuba people was that they wear a slim belt round the waist. Otherwise they would not be considered fully dressed. Thus Nuba ideas of beauty, whilst allowing for a great deal of individual variation and creativity, were considerably shaped by social and cultural values and expectations. **AJ RK**

See also body; aesthetics; visual anthropology.

Further reading James Faris, *Nuba Personal Art*; A. Rubin (ed.), *Marks of Civilisation.*

BEAUX-ARTS

The term Beaux-Arts, in European **archi-tecture**, is used to describe the rich, classi-cally inspired architecture of the practitioners trained in the École des Beaux Arts in Paris, in the 19th and early 20th centuries.

The central ideal of the school was **classi-cism**. It was subject to considerable inter-pretation, as students sought to apply 'classical' rules to what they perceived to be the essence of the building task, until they arrived at an appropriate compositional expression. This method of learning – pupils were lectured in mathematics, per-spective, stereotomy, construction and the history of architecture, while design was taught in the studios of practising archi-tects – produced an inventive, intentionally monumental and impressive style. Students competed for the Grand Prix de Rome, the prize for which was an extended period of study in Rome, in preparation for a career in the design of governmental commis-sions.

The grand **town planning** schemes carried out by Baron Haussmann (for example his redesign of Paris as a radial system of boulevards linked by transverse streets) also exemplify the architecture of the Beaux Arts, which is sometimes called 'Second Empire Style'. In the later part of the 19th century, it was widely used across North and South America, often translat-ing the inventive classical form into timber rather than stone.

As the École des Beaux-Arts was perhaps the most significant formal school of archi-tecture in Europe from 1819 to 1914, and was widely influential on architects from all over Europe and America, it served first as a prototype for architectural education, and then as a symbol for traditionalist architectural establishment against which the growing **modernism** movement would measure itself. In the later 20th century some **postmodernist** theorists have given considerable attention to the approach of the Beaux-Arts school. **JM**

See also neoclassicism.

Further reading R. Middleton (ed.), *The Beaux Arts and 19th century French Architecture*; A. Drexler (ed.), *The Architecture of the Ecole Des Beaux Arts*.

BEGGAR-MY-NEIGHBOUR

Beggar-my-neighbour, in **economics**, is a trade policy of competitive devaluation, where countries devalue their exchange rates in rapid succession in order to make export prices more competitive. This was prevalent in the 1930s. It is harder to achieve under floating rates, though the Japanese are often accused of trying to keep the yen artificially low to encourage their exports.

Although beggar-my-neighbour policies work for a short time to boost the domestic economy, there are several detrimental results: (1) the protected industry is ineffi-cient, so consumers have to pay higher prices; (2) trading partners are forced to retaliate with their own protectionist policies; and (3) they earn less foreign exchange, so buy less of the first country's exports. In effect, everyone is beggared. This happened in the 1920s and 1930s, but was partly outlawed by **GATT** (the General Agreement on Tariffs and Trade) after 1947. The slow-growing 1970s and 1980s and early 1990s have rekindled beggar-my-neighbour instincts. **TF**

See also devaluation; free trade.

BEHAVIOURALISM

In **political science** a strictly behavioural approach is one in which explanations are based on agents' overt, expressed and observable behaviour; on 'what is really going on' rather than on non-measurable values and motives. Behaviouralists emphasize that theories should be 'opera-tional', that is, capable of being empirically tested. For example, some psephologists claim that it is not possible to study scien-tifically the way people vote through focus-ing on their (non-observable) subjective feelings or attitudes, but it is possible to measure the impact of objectively defined **class**, **ethnicity** and religion upon the way in which people vote.

'Behaviouralism' is often used as a gener-ally dismissive description of the work of political scientists who hold crude **positivist** views or employ mathematical and statistical techniques. Normally such critics of behaviouralism are mathematically if not philosophically illiterate.

Behavioural political science was heavily influential in North American **social sciences** in the 1950s and 1960s. The skills of political scientists, both in data-collection and data-analysis, have been considerably enhanced as a result of the efforts of behaviouralists. However, few contemporary political scientists would now endorse behaviouralist psychology, the idea that the 'non-measurable' and the 'non-observable' are not worthy of analytical attention, or the thesis that the formal analysis of legal and constitutional documents has no place in their subject. **BO'L**

See also Chicago school.

Further reading Martin Landau, *Political Theory and Political Science: Studies in the Methodology of Political Inquiry.*

BEHAVIOURISM

Behaviourism means different things to philosophers and psychologists. In **philosophy**, Analytical Behaviourism is usually formulated as the doctrine that statements about the mental have the same meaning as (are analytically equivalent to) statements about behaviour. Those who contrast private, introspectible mental phenomena such as pains and publicly observable behaviour are mistaken. For, to give a crude example, the behaviourist holds that the statement 'she is in pain' means the same as (is analytically equivalent to) the statement 'she is manifesting aversion behaviour'.

If behaviourism were true it would solve the **mind-body problem**. For if statements about the mental have the same meaning as statements about behaviour, then (presumably) mental phenomena would just be behavioural phenomena. Being in pain would just be manifesting aversion behaviour. But the relation between behaviour and the body is unproblematic. So if behaviourism were true, the relation between mental phenomena and the body would be unproblematic.

Similarly, if behaviourism were true it would solve the problem of **other minds**. The problem of other minds is based on the assumption that one's beliefs about other minds are the result of an inference from publicly observable behaviour to private, introspectible mental phenomena such as pains. But if statements about the mental are analytically equivalent to statements about behaviour, there is no such inference. There is no 'epistemological gap' between behaviour and the mind.

Philosophers have two main objections to behaviourism. First, behaviourists hold that statements about the mental mean the same as statements about behaviour, but it seems obvious that mental phenomena *cause* behaviour. Pain cannot be identified with aversion behaviour, 'she is in pain' cannot mean the same as 'she is manifesting aversion behaviour', because pain causes aversion behaviour. The second objection depends on two thought experiments. Consider a race of 'Super Spartans' who do feel pain, but behave as though they do not. It will sometimes be true of a 'Super Spartan' that 'she is in pain', but false of her that 'she is manifesting aversion behaviour'. Therefore, these two statements do not have the same meaning. Now consider a group of perfect actors. They do not feel pain, but act as if they do. So it will sometimes be true of a perfect actor that 'she is manifesting aversion behaviour', but false of her that 'she is in pain'. Therefore, these two statements do not have the same meaning.

In **psychology**, behaviourism (founded by J.P. Watson in 1913) is the view that mental disturbances are reflex responses to the conditioning of past life; first and foremost it looks for explanantions of human psychology in terms of behaviour, that is, what can be observed. Unlike the psychodynamic theories of **psychoanalysis** and many psychotherapies, behavioural theory does not believe that emotional disturbance can be modified by simply knowing about such responses. Instead the behaviourist applies a counter-conditioning, and rejects any information or concepts obtained from the patient's reflections on his or her conscious experience. The behavioural therapist believes in the determining force of the environment and in working with observable behaviour patterns. He or she will attempt to lessen neurosis using external stimuli, administering rewards and punishments, or exposing the patient by degrees to situations or objects which frighten her or him. Examples of other techniques are systematic desensitization, relaxation training, flooding, positive reinforcement and assertiveness training.

Because the pure behaviourist view sees the subject as entirely passive, having no control over his or her life or destiny, being controlled by reinforcers in the environment and attaching no importance to personal meaning, it has found itself to be limited.

In the development of psychology in this century, behaviourism comes after psychoanalysis and before **cognitive therapy**. As a theraputic approach based on relearning, it is closer to cognitive therapy (which developed in the 1950s), and further away from psychoanalysis, which oversees change developing through interpretations and insight. Behaviourism therefore incorporates, or is incorporated into, such other approaches as cognitive therapy. **AJ MJ**

See also functionalism.

Further reading N. Block, *Readings in the Philosophy of Psychology*, vol. 1; G. Ryle, *The Concept of Mind*; B.F. Skinner, *Beyond Freedom and Dignity*; J.B. Watson, *Behaviourism*.

BEHOLDER, THE

Until recently the demands or expectations held by the spectator or viewer of a work of art were considered incidental to consideration of that work. In the search for the key to meaning, preference was given to the artist's intention. This attitude has recently been challenged by those who argue that the construction of meaning is a two-way process, and that the role of the beholder in the process is pivotal. The approach has been adopted by several factions in recent art history, from reception theorists to feminists, both of whom regard the social status, intellectual make-up, or gender of the beholder as central to the construction of meaning. **MG PD**

Further reading G. Pollock, *Vision and Difference*.

BELIEF

Belief (from old English *belyfan*, 'to hold dear') takes us into one of the largest and darkest areas of human **thought**. Belief is a function of thought; without rationality, without the abilities to create, learn and remember mental constructs, and to relate one's life-experience to them, it is impossible to believe.

Belief is the direct mirror image of **knowledge**. To know something is to have experienced proof of it; to believe something is to sidestep the need for proof. To know that black is white would be a very different thing from believing that black is white. And yet believers consistently behave as if what they have is knowledge, and claim their belief as such. This is the case in matters both great and small, but is particularly so in our attitude to the supernatural. If one believes in the existence of supernatural beings, the next stage is to make that belief into a faith (belief with imperatives for action), and the step after that is to claim that proofs exist (miracles, personal revelations and so on). A scientist can prove the existence of, say, black-body radiation or ripples in space – the process of proof may be laborious, but the end result is sure knowledge which the outsider is bound to accept. In the same way, religious believers down the ages have offered laborious and meticulous proofs – but here, in the final analysis, the outsider must share the revelation, accept the irrational, in order to share the belief. I do not need to believe in the existence of black-body radiation to know that it exists; I do need to believe in God to know that He exists. In the same way, unless I am a fool or a charlatan, disproof will change what I know; someone else's disbelief, by contrast, will have no effect at all on what I believe.

In rational thought, proof is an objective correlative against which to measure our ideas. In belief, the correlative is subjective and fanciful. Nonetheless, we take it just as seriously as, if not more seriously than, the proofs in an objective argument. In each case, it is as if we sidestep final responsibility for our ideas, or for our behaviour based on those ideas. For instance, I am, finally, not prepared to take responsibility for the systematic oppression of people of another skin-colour simply on the grounds that I feel like it; therefore I create a (sincere) belief-system to which I can appeal for justification, and which acts as a kind of intellectual scapegoat for my behaviour. I cannot personally guarantee happiness in a future life to those who share my ideas and way of life, but I can predicate (sincerely) a belief-system which offers it.

If we put it thus baldly, we are reducing human belief to playground level. Believers might make two arguments against such reductionism. First is the phenomenon of shared belief. There are certain unprovable ideas – for example the existence and nature of supernatural beings – which are universally shared by the human race, and have been so shared as far back as we can trace human consciousness. Is this a kind of mass delusion, a state (precisely) of mind, or is it as believers claim proof in itself that what is believed is true? Second is the intellectual ingenuity of the human species. Belief of one kind or another has led, and leads, to some of the most magnificent edifices of human creation, both intellectual and actual. They are one aspect, a major aspect, of our species' uniqueness and (we like to think) its glory. No other creatures write **symphonies**, create welfare states, believe in God. That being so, the argument continues, belief is not just something we have but is something we are. It is inherent to the human brain; it is an objective quality; one day, when we have developed enough reasoning skill, we will discover the proof that our belief is true, and instead of believing we will *know*. **KMcL**

BIG BANG

The Big Bang theory is humankind's attempt to answer that most fundamental question How did the universe begin? We believe that the universe started as an unbelievably dense point, and has been expanding ever since. The origin of this point may have been simply a random fluctuation, requiring no intervention from another source, but theories disagree about this.

The most successful version of the very early universe, known as the inflationary model, tells us that immediately after the formation of the point universe, it began an astonishingly rapid expansion, much faster than the **speed of light**. As information cannot travel faster than this speed, few parts of this primeval explosion could be affected by other parts, so instead of having a perfectly smooth distribution of matter, the universe, even at this early stage, became slightly 'lumpy' or granular. These irregularities eventually caused the formation of galaxies, millions of years later.

By the time one microsecond had passed, fundamental particles called quarks had formed and become bound to each other. After one millisecond, an asymmetry had arisen between matter and antimatter, leading to the situation we have today, with far more matter than antimatter. By a few seconds, none of the more exotic particles had survived and only electrons, neutrinos, photons and their antiparticles were important. A few protons and neutrons were formed, some of which combined to form the nuclei of the lightest elements hydrogen and, after about 100 seconds, helium and a few others.

After approximately one million years had passed, the universe had cooled sufficiently for electrons to be bound to the nuclei that existed, and the first atoms (mostly hydrogen) were created. The formation of atoms was the beginning of our familiar universe. Much later, these atoms combined in vast clouds to form stars and galaxies.

There are two important pieces of evidence for the Big Bang. One is that the radiation that remains from the explosion is still around today, although it retains little of its ferocious energy. We see it as a constant energy background, equivalent to space having a temperature of about 3 degrees above absolute zero, or −270 degrees Celsius. The other piece of evidence is that the Universe is still expanding. We know this because the light from distant galaxies is of a lower frequency than we would expect – it is said to be 'redshifted'. This means that those redshifted galaxies are travelling away from us at great speed.

One question that remains to be answered today is whether the universe will go on expanding, or whether it will eventually slow down and contract, due to the gravitational pull of all the matter inside it. If we knew how much matter the universe contained, we could answer this question, but we do not. It is believed that a lot of mass is located in so-called 'dark matter', which emits no radiation that we can detect. **JJ**

See also cosmology; particles.

BILDUNGSROMAN

Bildungsroman (German, 'formation-novel') is a type of fiction often used by European and North American writers. The central figure of such a work is seen as a kind of archetype of current society, and his or her life and adventures (the subjects of the novel) are made a framework or metaphor for wider social, ethical and moral comment. The form originated in Germany – Goethe's 'Wilhelm Meister' novels (1777–1829) are a supreme example – and was taken up elsewhere, in whole or in part, by such writers as Dickens, Flaubert and Gogol. It has been a particularly fruitful form in 20th-century North American writing: Louis Auchincloss, Robertson Davies, John Irving, Mordecai Richler, Philip Roth, John Updike and Jerome Weidman have made outstanding use of it. In Germany, Heinrich Böll, Günter Grass, Thomas Mann and others have used the form with savagery: Mann tearing into the bourgeois values of the early 20th century, Grass depicting the charnel house of **Nazism** and Böll the moral vacuity that followed it in ways that make the distinction still fuzzier between story and sermon. **KMcL**

BILINGUALISM

Linguistics experts reserve the term bilingualism for people who are proficient in two languages, and it is estimated that more than half of the world's population is bilingual to some extent. Most bilinguals have a preferred language in particular contexts; for example, they may use one language principally in the home, the second in the work place. The contexts in which the two languages are deployed can have far-reaching consequences on the degree and types of expertise achieved in each language. Certainly, the balanced bilingual (equally capable in both languages) is rarely encountered. Although many people learn a second language relatively late in life, the most intense focus of research interest has always been on the natural bilingual, who has acquired both languages spontaneously in the course of growing up. Bilinguals generally have no difficulty in keeping their two languages apart, but a common occurrence is the deliberate mixing of the two languages. While conversing mainly in one language, the speaker might insert one or two words (usually nouns) from the other language into the discourse. This 'code mixing' contrasts with 'code switching', in which entire phrases or sentences are intermingled throughout the conversation. **MS**

Further reading S. Romaine, *Bilingualism*.

BIMETALLISM

Bimetallism, in **economics**, as its name implies, is a monetary system using two metals rather than just one as a nation's money. (The metals are usually gold and silver.) Historically, bimetallism was supported by those who felt that the use of just one metal would unduly restrict the supply of money and depress the general price level, at a time when it was considered that money on intrinsic value was the only 'good' money. (In that view it is permissible, for convenience, to print paper money only so long as it is backed 100% by precious metal.)

An official exchange rate must be established between the two metals, represented by the weight of each metal in coins of the same denomination. When the USA was on a bimetallic standard for a time in the 19th century, complications arose when the market price ratio for the two metals differed from the official price ratio per ounce as used in coins. It proved impossible to keep both metals in circulation because the market price often differed from the mint price and people would melt down the dearer coins (to get the market value of the metal). Hence **Gresham's Law**: Bad money drives out good. **TF**

BIOCHEMISTRY

Biochemistry is the study of biological processes in terms of chemical interactions between the substances which make up living organisms. The chemical processes which occur within the body come under the general heading of **metabolism**, and are mediated by biological catalysts called **enzymes**. Enzymes are protein molecules and as such are **gene products**, so metabolism is under genetic control. The term biochemistry originated around the end of the 19th century, but the subject has its roots in early chemistry. The pioneering 18th-century French chemist Antoine-Laurent Lavoisier showed that there was a quantitative similarity between the respiration of living organisms and chemical oxidation. Then Jan Ingenhousz, also in the 18th century, showed that plants use sunlight to drive photosynthesis, a reaction which is the reverse of respiration. The development of structural organic chemistry in the 19th century paved the way for scientists to study first the important biological molecules (proteins, carbohydrates, fats, etc.) and their synthesis (anabolism) and degradation (catabolism) and later to study metabolic processes and their control. Modern biochemistry dominates many areas of biology, such as nutrition and genetics, principally because a complete understanding of all metabolic events involved in growth, reproduction and heredity should lead to a complete understanding of life itself, at least in mechanistic terms. **RB**

See also biophysics; biopoiesis; cytology; mechanism; molecular biology.

Further reading Robert Murray, *Biochemistry*.

BIOCLIMATOLOGY

Bioclimatology, in the **life sciences**, is the study of the interactions between living organisms and climate. Although the earliest people must have understood the important role of climate in determining the food available to them, bioclimatology is a modern science, not only because climatic conditions were until recently accepted as immutable but because the concept that the plants and animals could significantly affect the climate was not recognized. **RB**

See also ecosystem; Gaia hypothesis; global warming.

Further reading Stephen Schneider, *The Coevolution of Climate and Life*.

BIODIVERSITY

Biodiversity, in **ecology**, refers to the vast range of species types which exist in the natural environment. This diversity is a product of natural genetic variation under the influence of **natural selection**; organisms adapt to suit their environment and thus tend to become more specialized during **evolution**. The biodiversity of a given **ecosystem** is often seen as an indicator of its stability – **climax** communities tend to contain the greatest range of species while pioneer communities (which would be found on recently disturbed land such as an abandoned building site) are commonly composed of just a few species. Human-made environments also tend to contain very few species because of the degree of control which is exerted over them. As human activity becomes more intense in previously undeveloped areas, there is a tendency for the level of biodiversity to fall. This is seen as undesirable from a **conservation** point of view, and there have been recent attempts to preserve the biodiversity of complex habitats such as tropical rainforest. **RB**

See also adaptive radiation; Gaia hypothesis; pollution.

BIOGENESIS

The theory of biogenesis, in the **life sciences**, is the opposite of **abiogenesis**. It states that all living organisms are descended from other living organisms. Thus life comes from pre-existing life and is continuous rather than being spontaneously generated from non-living material. The concept of biogenesis is one of the central laws of modern biology. **RB**

See also biopoiesis; Darwinism; evolution.

Further reading William Day, *Genesis on Planet Earth*; Salvador Luria, *Life The Unfinished Experiment*.

BIOGEOGRAPHY

Biogeography, as its name suggests, is the study of how living organisms are distributed over the planet. Thus biogeographers might study the type of plant and animal communities found in arid zones. Climate is the most important external factor influencing the habitat. **RB**

See also bioclimatology; speciation.

Further reading P.L. Forey, *The Evolving Biosphere*.

BIOLOGICAL CONTROL

Biological control, in the **life sciences**, is the idea that pest organisms can be controlled by the manipulation of other living organisms, thus avoiding the use of indiscriminate, expensive and inefficient pesticides. Traditionally, this strategy has taken the form of the introduction of a potential predator or pathogen into the environment of the pest. This was often made possible because the pest organism itself had been introduced by man and had assumed a population of pestilential proportions precisely because it had been introduced without its natural enemies. The rabbit was introduced to Australia as a food and hunting resource but rapidly multiplied to become a serious pest, uncontrollable by shooting and trapping. It was controlled dramatically by the introduction to Australia of the virus which causes myxomatosis in rabbits.

Biological control often involves the use of insect predators, though careful studies must be carried out to ensure that the introduced species does not itself become an uncontrolled pest. Biological control can also be achieved by interfering with the reproduction of the pest, mainly by the introduction of huge numbers of sterile males. Chemicals called pheromones, which are the active components of animal scents, have been isolated and exploited to modify the behaviour of pest species; mole moths, for example, can be lured into traps baited with the pheromone which the female of the species normally releases to guide males towards her. It may also be possible to control pests using genetically engineered pathogens, provided the situation is sufficiently well understood. **RB**

See also niche; parasitism.

Further reading A.J. Burn, *Integrated Pest Management*.

BIOLOGICAL RHYTHM

Biological rhythm is the term used in the **life sciences** to describe the relationship between fluctuating biological phenomena and periodic changes in the environment, such as the regular passage of night and day and seasonal changes. Periodic phenomena, such as breeding seasons and menstrual cycles, and daily patterns, such as flowers opening in the morning and closing at night, are examples of biological rhythm. Cycles with a period of 24 hours are called circadian rhythms; they are influenced by the daily cycle of light and dark, but will continue if the organism is removed to a laboratory situation where light is continuous and temperature constant and will be adjusted, after a brief delay, if it is moved to a new time zone. Some periodic events are not clearly linked to environmental cycles: the 17-year cycle of the reproduction of the cicada, for example, always occurs at the same time of year but there is no clear environmental stimulus for the 16-year wait. **RB**

See also chronobiology; phenology.

BIOLOGISM AND BIOLOGICAL DETERMINISM

Biologism is a concept which claims to explain human behaviour in terms of physiological processes. Biological determinism uses this model to show that differences between men and women do not originate from culturally imposed gender characteristics but instead derive from physiological differences.

Feminists have taken up many different positions in relation to the biological model. Many would agree that women's bodies are different from men's and that as a result women's experience is different. Some feminists, for example Juliet Mitchell, have identified the main physiological difference between masculinity and femininity as reproduction and criticize the way in which reproduction has, through patriarchy, been seen as a biological reason for women's inferiority.

Mary Daly, and other radical, revolutionary feminists, argue that women have biologically determined psychological attributes and are naturally less aggressive than men. However, other feminists argue that the social determination of gender is equally or if not more important. Juliet Mitchell, for example, argues that women's 'lesser' capacity for demanding work and also for violence is a product of social coercion rather than a 'natural' biological tendency.

In contemporary feminist thought the use of a biological model to address female and male difference has come under attack. Parveen Adams argues that when children take up the position of masculinity or femininity they are adopting pre-defined roles within the system of representation of the dominant (patriarchal) order. The biological model is seen by many feminists as supporting patriarchy in constructing male and female difference as a 'natural' and 'provable' fact. Psychoanalytic feminists, amongst others, have questioned the way in which we categorize biological difference by asking, 'Whose interest does this serve?' This question makes what seemed, in biological terms, an easy distinction between men and women more problematic and complex, with the question of gender formation and representation as keys to the formulation of sex difference. **TK**

Further reading Shulamith Firestone, *The Dialectics of Sex*; Juliet Mitchell, *Women's Estate*.

BIOLOGY

Biology (Greek, 'study of life') is the study of living organisms in terms of the physical and chemical systems which they comprise. Broad aspects of study include origin, classification, structure, function and interaction with each other and with their environment. The term biology was coined by Karl Burdach (1776–1847) to describe the study of man, but was expanded by the German physiologist Gottfried Treviranus (1776–1837) to encompass the scientific study of life. **RB**

See also anatomy; biochemistry; botany; ecology; physiology; zoology.

BIOMASS

Biomass, in **ecology**, describes the total weight of living organisms of one species within a given area such as a habitat or **biome**. Biomass provides an indication of the energy stored within a community and the rate of change of biomass shows the productivity of the system under study. In a **food web** or chain, the biomass of the producers (green plants) greatly exceeds that of the consumers (herbivores and carnivores) because the transfer of energy between each link is inefficient. **RB**

See also community; competition.

BIOME

Biome, in **ecology**, is the term applied to the major biological communities which make up the **biosphere**. The concept is geographical and largely a function of human attempts to classify their environment into broad groups such as rainforest, though such categories are complex collections of smaller **communities** which interact at a number of levels. Communities respond to similar environmental conditions by parallel development in terms of the species types of which they consist: this gives rise to biome types such as mangrove swamp and coniferous forest.

Biomes of the same type are often seen on several different continents; for example, shrubland is a biome type found in different forms around the world. The species which make up geographically separate biomes of the same type are often different, but have evolved communities of similar structure as a result of parallel, independent responses to similar environmental conditions. Climate is the most important environmental factor in this convergent evolution and, as a result, given biome types are restricted to certain global areas: tropical rainforest, for example, is a biome type which is restricted to equatorial zones, while deciduous forest is found in more temperate areas to the north and south of the tropics. However, a number of other, more local factors such as soil type and altitude are also of importance in determining biome type. Furthermore, the biome and the physical environment interact and modify one another; the quality of soil is dependent upon the vegetation as well as on geology and climate, and humidity and rainfall are greatly affected by biome type. **RB**

See also biodiversity; ecosystem.

BIOMETRY

Biometry (Greek, 'measurement of life') is the study of biological systems using quantitative methods such as statistics. Biometry grew largely out of work on **evolution** and **genetics** by mathematicians such as Karl Pearson (1857–1936), who maintained that it was important to be able to measure biological phenomena which were based on events such as inheritance. Mendel's early genetic work is an example of biometric study; today biometry in the broad sense of statistical analysis of biological data is important in all areas of experimental biology. **RB**

See also epidemiology; taxonomy.

BIOPHYSICS

Biophysics is the application of the physical sciences to biology and living organisms. It is an interdisciplinary field which is largely a product of technical advances during the 20th century. However, the field has a historical basis with the general scientists of earlier times who felt free to apply their knowledge and intellect to the whole of science and beyond. Among early biophysical observations are the studies of the origin of bioluminescence in fireflies, of the electricity associated with electric eels and the connection between electricity and muscle contraction.

The age of technology has enabled great advances in the field of biophysics: techniques such as centrifugation, chromatography and electrophoresis have enabled the separation of biological molecules

according to physical attributes. Central to modern biophysics are the analytical techniques which enable the 3-dimensional structure of molecules to be determined. William and Lawrence Bragg, a father and son team, developed X-ray crystallography at the beginning of the century; it was used in work on virus structure, haemoglobin structure and, in the 1950s, it led to the elucidation of the structure of DNA, the molecule basis of the gene. Currently the field is expanding rapidly as techniques based on **genetics** and **immunology** are developed and exploited, with the potential to bring momentous advances to many fields of biology, genetics and medicine. Despite, and perhaps because of, its technical nature, biophysics is a very intellectual field which has produced a great number of Nobel laureates during the 20th century. **RB**

See also biochemistry; molecular biology.

Further reading James Watson, *The Double Helix*.

BIOPOIESIS

Biopoiesis (Greek, 'making life'), in the **life sciences**, is an explanation of how life on Earth originated from non-living matter. The age of the Earth is estimated at around 4.5 billion years while the Transvaal Fig Tree Chert fossils, estimated to be around 3.1 billion years old, contain bacteria and blue-green algae. Thus it seems likely that the first living organisms appeared within a few hundred million years of the Earth's formation.

Some scientists have proposed that life arrived on Earth from space (**panspermia**), but proponents of biopoiesis argue that this possibility does not invalidate their ideas since life, as it exists on Earth, must have arisen somewhere at some time. The theory has its roots in the 1920s, with J.B.S. Haldane in the UK and A.I. Oparin in the USSR who proposed that conditions on Earth at the time when life arose were very different from the modern environment. Oparin suggested that simple molecules in solution were able to interact under these conditions to form, at random, complex organic (carbon-containing) molecules, some of which were able to replicate themselves by acting as templates. Given sufficient time it was suggested that the components of this 'soup' would interact, again at random, giving rise occasionally to particular combinations which had special characteristics such as a membrane surrounding them and separating them from the environment. A living organism may be defined as a unit which is capable of reproducing itself and of interacting with its environment. Biopoiesis thus suggests how such a simple organism, called a *eobiont* (Greek, 'Dawn Life') might have originated and given rise to life on Earth today through the processes of **biogenesis** and **evolution**.

These ideas were largely hypothetical and as such were the target of criticism from many on the grounds that they were too far-fetched, and from **creationists** who claimed that they were blasphemous. However, starting in the 1950s a number of experiments were carried out which vindicated Haldane and Oparin. Reaction vessels containing solutions of chemicals thought likely to have be present on the primordial Earth were subjected to ultraviolet radiation or to electrical discharge and a wide variety of organic compounds was rapidly formed. Subsequently it has been demonstrated that many of the molecular prerequisites for life can be formed under similar conditions. **RB**

See also abiogenesis; biochemistry; natural selection.

Further reading Freeman Dyson, *Origins of Life*; Salvador Luri, *The Unfinished Experiment*.

BIOSPHERE

The biosphere is the area between the upper levels of the Earth's crust and the lower levels of the atmosphere, which is occupied by living organisms. Life scientists use the term collectively to describe all the Earth's habitats which can support life, or to describe the living organisms as a planet-wide, dynamic community. **RB**

See also ecosystem; biogeography.

BIOTECHNOLOGY

Biotechnology (Greek, 'science of the manipulation of life') is the application and exploitation of biological processes or organisms to man's own ends. It is a rapidly growing field. This expansion depends upon the new technologies of **molecular biology** such as **genetic engineering**, but the controlled use of biological processes by humans is by no means a modern phenomenon. For example, although yeast has been used for brewing and baking for thousands of years, the action of yeast was not understood until relatively recently. The possiblities of biotechnology have been realized as the biochemical and genetic mechanisms behind living processes have been elucidated. Louis Pasteur first demonstrated, in 1876, that the presence of microorganisms was responsible for the changes seen in fermentation. In 1897, Edouard Buchner showed that a cell-free extract of yeast could continue to support fermentation. The first **enzymes** were soon isolated and a wide range is now industrially harvested from specific microorganisms for use in a variety of products. A notable everyday example of the application of biotechnology is washing powder, which uses enzymes extracted from genetically engineered microorganisms adapted to life at high temperatures, so consequently the enzymes function best in the hot water used for washing.

The key processes in biotechnology are catalysis by enzymes, genetic transformation and biosynthesis. Biotechnology has been applied to **medicine**, in the production of penicillin, and to produce fuels such as alcohol. Agriculture has been revolutionized by the use of genetic engineering in crop breeding and in the development of new opportunities for food production, such as the use of fungi. Genetic engineering has been a reality since the 1970s and has enabled the production of drugs such as insulin and human growth hormone by fermentation of microorganisms which have had the specific human gene inserted into their genotype. The application of computers to the modelling of molecular interactions presents the possibility that molecules, such as drugs, may soon be designed for specific purposes and constructed using living cells. The future of biotechnology looks bright and the potential exists to improve nutrition, health care and the standard of living, and to use the new technologies to repair much of the damage done to the environment by previous technologies. The ethical implications of biotechnological progress must be seriously considered before new technologies are licensed for use, especially where the release of genetically modified organisms into the environment are involved. **RB**

See also transformation.

Further reading Steven Prentis, *Biotechnology*.

BITONALITY see Polytonality

BLACK COMEDY

Black Comedy is a type of **comedy** dealing with grotesque or unpleasant situations which attacks comfortable assumptions about social taboos, for example, by treating death as comic. The usage derives ultimately from the French dramatist Jean Anouilh (who categorized his plays as either *rose* or *noir*), and perhaps from André Breton's Surrealist *Anthologie de l'humeur noir* (1940). Although such earlier works as Aristophanes' *Knights* and Jonson's *Volpone* might be seen as black comedies because of their biting satirical approach, the term usually refers to one of the large number of 20th-century plays and films which operate within tragicomic patterns: the range is from Dürrenmatt to Orton, from Albee to de Almodóvar. **TRG SS**

Further reading J.L. Styan, *The Dark Comedy*.

BLACK HOLES

These are the remains of a very large stars after they have completed their life cycle. Small stars, about the size of our Sun, will end as white dwarfs: small, dense, cold lumps of matter which take no further part in stellar interactions. Larger stars several times the mass of the Sun have a far more spectacular ending. They die in a massive supernova explosion, losing about half their matter to space, and leave behind a neutron star, a tiny and extraordinarily dense object only a few miles across. But the even larger stars, whose mass after the explosion is still several times that of the Sun, will form black holes.

Some theories speculate that many tiny black holes could have formed in the early universe. None of these have yet been observed.

A black hole is an extraordinary object. Its edge or boundary is defined by what is called the 'event horizon'. The radius of this is determined by the mass of the black hole. The event horizon is the closest possible distance that light may approach the black hole and not be pulled into it. So strong is the gravity field of a black hole that, within the event horizon, not even light can escape. (This is the reason for their name.) However, Stephen Hawking has shown that some radiation may be emitted from the black hole, due to the 'stressing' of space and time at the boundary.

The event horizon is so called because we may never have any knowledge of events within it. If light cannot escape, then neither can information about the interior. Another bizarre effect that occurs near the event horizon is time dilation. Time is slowed down by large gravitational fields. This effect is just measurable upon the Earth, but becomes enormous near a black hole. At the event horizon, time stops completely. This means that if one observer sees another fall into a black hole, he will see his friend fall more and more slowly and finally stop. His friend will have no such illusion from her point of view, she will fall faster and faster until she passes through the event horizon. Beyond that point, however, she can never escape, and thus can never return to tell us about it. This is not a very likely scenario, in any case, as the gravitational forces would have stretched her into a long, thin thread long before she reached the event horizon.

Black holes, by their nature, are elusive objects. The most conclusive observations of objects thought to be black holes have come from binary x-ray systems, where a visible star is orbiting a massive, unseen companion. The mass and invisible nature of the companion mean that it is very unlikely to be anything other than a black hole. Three such binaries have been observed. Other possible black holes may be found in the centres of galaxies, such as our own Milky Way. **JJ**

See also stars.

BLACK MAGIC see Magic

BLACK POWER

Black power was a militant social movement which originated in the US in the 1960s. Black power emphasized the role of the white-dominated power structure in the subordination of black people. The movement advocated the removal of power from whites so that the condition of black people could be improved.

Although the Civil War ended slavery in the northern states this did not result in a dramatic advance in the fortunes of black people. Indeed, most remained in circumstances of dire poverty. A series of 'Jim Crow' laws passed in the south between 1890 and 1912 banned blacks from a number of 'white' amenities. The activities of the violent secret society the Ku-Klux-Klan ensured that this segregation was sustained.

The national Association for the Advancement of Coloured People (NAACP) and the National Urban League were founded in 1909 and 1910 respectively. Both fought a long struggle for black civil rights and finally, in 1964, a Civil Rights Act was passed by Congress banning discrimination in public facilities, education, employment and any agency receiving government funds. Attempts to implement the new act, however, met with ferocious resistance, leaders were beaten up and some even lost their lives.

The black power movement was a reaction to a perceived failure of the civil rights movement to make tanglible improvements in the situation of black people. Before the rise of the militant black power groups the ambition of black civil rights leaders was the integration of blacks into the wider American culture. Increasingly, however, black power helped to shift these ideals towards a stress on the dignity of being black and the intrinsic value of black culture. Black people began to demand an independent position in a plural society (a society in which there exists distinct racial, linguistic or religious groupings) rather than assimilation within the wider white culture.

The black power groups who advocated the use of violence as a means of achieving their ends either broke up into factions or were crushed by the authorities. Many blacks turned to the ballot box as a means of gaining political power. **DA**

See also assimilation; collective action; conflict theory; culture; ethnicity; power; race; social integration; social movements; subculture.

Further reading S. Carmichael and C. Hamilton, *Black Power: the Politics of Liberation in America*; W.J. Wilson Power, *Racism and Privilege: Race Relations in Theoretical and Sociohistorical Perspectives*.

BLACKMARKET

The blackmarket is the illegal exchange of goods at a free-market price when the product price is set lower by law or when exchange is legally forbidden. These transactions for goods and services are not declared to the tax man and therefore do not show up in the figures for **gross national product** (GNP). The black economy may thus mean that the country is actually richer than the figures suggest. One way of measuring the size of the black economy is by taking the difference between gross national product and gross national expenditure. As undeclared money is spent, it should turn up in the expenditure figures. The only snag is that this method misses money hidden away by individuals or companies, for instance in offshore tax havens.

Studies of the black economy suggest that in the UK in the mid-1980s it was worth perhaps 4–5% of GNP and in the US roughly the same. In Italy, by contrast, it could represent as much as a quarter of GNP in the same period. Optimists argue that black work keeps the unemployed off the breadline. However, it seems more likely that black work is performed by those who are already in employment and so possess the necessary tools, equipment and contacts. A more culturally sensitive term being substituted for black market is the term shadow economy. **TF**

BLENDING INHERITANCE

The idea of blending inheritance was almost universal among Life scientists until the general recognition of Mendel's work at the end of the 19th century. Although there was no clear evidence to support the assumption that parental characteristics were blended in the offspring, this appeared to be the obvious explanation for the observable inheritance of parental features. It appeared to be supported by observations of hybrids between species and was mathematically defined in terms of the fraction of the individual for which each ancestor was responsible a from a parent, from a grandparent and so on. However, if blending inheritance were the true situation, then interbreeding individuals would rapidly become homogeneous. This does not happen because genes are transmitted between generations as discrete units, enabling characteristics to be indefinitely conserved and giving each individual a unique combination of genes, some from each parent **RB**

See also gene; Mendelism; pangenesis.

BLOCK CONSTRUCTION

Block construction, in **music**, is a method of composing. Instead of structuring a piece by continually varying a few short motives or chord-patterns so that, in effect, the music is a stream of continuous variation (for instance the opening movement of Beethoven's Fifth Symphony) the composer begins by creating a number of short blocks of sound. These are then assembled, largely unvaried. Instead of proceeding by variation, the piece uses juxtaposition and contrast; each reappearance of a block is given new colour by, and gives new colour to, its surroundings. (Stravinsky's *Petrushka* is a case in point.) The method is much used in **folk music**, and was a favourite resource in European art music in the **baroque** period. It fell out of use in the late 18th and early 19th centuries, when developmental styles were preferred, but in the 20th

century it has once again become standard. It is one way of writing **serial music**, and was also favoured by such eminent 20th-century 'traditionalists' as Bartók, Messiaen, Stravinsky and Tippett. **KMcL**

BLUES, THE

The Blues (the name is possibly derived from the expression 'a fit of the blue devils', meaning depression) is a style of music which originated with black singers in the USA at the end of the 19th century. Its exact origins are obscure, but it may have emerged out of the rural folk and work songs of black Americans. 'The Blues' is a multifaceted term, and one which is largely determined by its social context. As a rural form, for example, it was not so much a musical object as a mode of performance, dependent on the singer's emotional response to personal circumstances of hardship and suffering. It combined elements of narrative, lament and complaint, and was essentially cathartic in intention. As the Blues spread throughout the southern states its poetic and musical structure became increasingly standardized: the words were organized in groups of three lines, and each line had four bars of music – hence the expression '12-bar blues'. (8-bar and 16-bar blues are occasionally found.) The music is a single line of melody over repeated chords. The harmonic content was fixed, and the style used syncopation of rhythm (especially dragging the beat) and 'blue' notes: slightly flattened versions of those degrees of the major scale which are usually sharpened to give brightness of sound, the 3rd and 7th.

The urbanization of black Americans, during the early part of this century, meant that other forms of Blues evolved. The so-called 'classic blues', featuring black female singers accompanied by small jazz bands, combined songs based on the rural form with material influenced by vaudeville and black entertainment music. Another urban form to emerge was the instrumental 'piano blues'. Stripped of the blues lyric, this retained the formal and harmonic structure of its rural counterpart; its players developed a variety of rhythmic idioms such as 'barrelhouse', 'boogie-woogie', 'stomp' and 'strut'. This last style became a major influence on **jazz** and, through its jazz-based derivative 'rhythm-and-blues', on all subsequent **pop** and **rock music**. Blues, therefore, not only survives in its own right, but is the bedrock of 20th-century Western popular music, one of the most influential ideas in the history of the art. **KMcL SSt**

Further reading Paul Oliver, *The Story of the Blues.*

BODY

All societies see the human body as more than just a physical organism. It is also the focus of a set of beliefs about its psychological and social significance. The culture in which we live determines the manifold ways bodily experience is perceived and interpreted. Current European ideas about the body are largely influenced by a Cartesian **dualism** in which it is seen as separate from the mind. Emotions are generally located in the body in Euro-American culture, in opposition to the rational mind. Other societies do not make the same distinction. Some may conceive three parts to the person, while others see the body as an integrated whole. A contrast to the mind-body distinction prevalent in Western thought is Michelle Rosaldo's study of head-hunting among the Ilongot in the Philippines. This demonstrates how passion and knowledge are inextricably linked in local explanations of the value of head-hunting to the person carrying out the act.

Anthropologists commonly see the body as a statement of identity. The way the body is marked, clothed and adorned often communicates information about an individual's position in society – their **status**, gender, ethnic or religious identity. Many **rites of passage** mark changes in social status by transforming the body. The wide-spread practice of body scarification in parts of central Africa is a means of literally marking the individual's transition through stages of his or her life cycle. Among the Nuba, for example, women are scarified with specific patterns at the onset of men-struation, at marriage and at the birth of their first child when they are assumed to have reached full maturity.

The body can be seen as a microcosm of society, the rules and taboos surrounding parts of the body mirroring social or cosmological principles. The prevalent notion that the left hand is unclean is an example of this.

The body can serve as a metaphor for society, and physical experience can actually be determined by social categories. The two bodies, the individual and the social, are closely linked to each other. According to the structuralist Mary Douglas, the body also represents the body politic. **Rituals** that express anxiety about the body and the maintenance of its boundaries through the control of orifices reflect a concern with defending the unity of the group. Good examples of this are Mediterranean and Middle Eastern preoccupations with honour and shame. Male honour (valour) and female shame (modesty) are seen to protect both the identity and integrity of a social group. In the Middle East, the honour of the individual reflects on the entire group. The widespread practice of female circumcision in Africa, to control women as a group, and their individual sexuality, is another example of this dual concern with social and bodily integrity. **CL**

See also beauty; mind-body problem; symbolism.

Further reading M. Douglas, *Natural Symbols*; B. Turner, *The Body and Society.*

BONAPARTISM

The expression 'Bonapartism' has been used in at least two different ways by historians and political scientists. In the liberal tradition, Bonapartism is seen (and criticized) as a system of government with a particular agenda. It owes its name to the rule of France by Napoleon Bonaparte during his Consulate and Empire (1799-1815). The perceived traits of Bonapartism are an active system of government dominated by the military; an **authoritarian** executive pursuing an aggressive, expansionist foreign policy; a domestic policy emphasizing ceremonial functions while practising enlightened despotism; and a centralized, meritocratic administration. French governmental institutions are still frequently accused of exhibiting Bonapartist tendencies, especially the degree of executive power maintained by the president, the large, bureaucratic administration, and the importance of monumental legacies maintained and constructed during each republic. However, the parliamentary republics and the non-expansionist, though independent, foreign policy of modern France would probably make Napoleon turn in his tomb in the Invalides.

In the **Marxist** tradition, Bonapartism similarly refers to a régime in which the executive part of the state, under the rule of one individual, achieves dictatorial power over all other parts of the social system. However, Marxists explain Bonapartism as the consequence of intense and evenly matched class struggle in capitalist societies: no class is sufficiently powerful to rule on its own and therefore an arbiter can impose himself on society and the state can acquire 'relative autonomy'. Marx thought that the régimes of Napoleon III and Bismarck's Germany exhibited common Bonapartist traits; later Marxists have applied his analysis to **fascist** régimes and Third World military dictatorships. **BO'L**

Further reading Hal Draper, *Karl Marx's Theory of Revolution: Volume 1: State and Revolution;* Pieter Geyl, *Napoleon: For and Against* (1949).

BOOLEAN LOGIC

The whole idea of **logic** (that sentences have a form that differs from their content) originated with the ancient Greeks, whose investigation of the subject culminated in the work of Aristotle (384–322 BCE). Even though his work was severely limited, only insignificant additions were made to it for 2,000 years, despite the fact that inferences outside Aristotelian logic were used all the time.

Gottfried Leibniz (1646–1716) was the first great modern mathematician who was interested in logic. He made the first attempts to find a systematic notation for logic. He failed to follow his work through,

and left it unfinished when he died. In the end, it was left to George Boole (1815–64) and Augustus de Morgan (1806–71) to come up with a fully worked-out notational system.

This notation (in its modern form) can perhaps best be demonstrated by breaking down a complex sentence into its symbolic form. Consider the sentence, 'If tomatoes or beans mean that the food is nasty, then the fact that the food is nice means that there are no tomatoes and no beans.' (The reason that this sentence reads rather fussily is that English is quite cavalier with logical pedantry, so one English sentence can express more than one logical form.) There are four concepts which give the content of this sentence: 'tomatoes', 'beans', 'food' and 'nice' ('nasty' is the same as 'not nice'). Nice describes the food. It acts as a **function** from the food to the pair true/false. Thus we write $N(F)$ for 'the food is nice'. We put T for 'tomatoes', B for 'beans'. Now, omitting words which serve no logical purpose, we have, 'If T or B mean not $N(F)$, then $N(F)$ means that not T and not B.' The sentence is of the form 'If ..., then ...', which is expressed by writing an arrow from the condition to the consequent, which are bracketed, to give '(T or B mean not $N(F)$) →($N(F)$ means not T and not B)'. Each bracketed clause is then analysed. 'T or B mean ...' is the same as 'If T or B then ...'; the second clause is similar. The sentence is now '((T or B)→(not $N(F)$)→ ($N(F)$→(not T and not B))'. The words 'not', 'or' and 'and' all have their own logical symbols ($\sim$, v and ˆrespectively), so the final version of the sentence is '((TvB)→ ($\sim N(F)$)→($N(F)$→(($\sim$T))ˆ($\sim$B))'.

The point of all this is that the truth of such a sentence depends only on its logical form and not on its content; any sentence with the same logical form is true under the same circumstances (the one above is always true). The symbols make the logical form clearer, and its truth or fallacy can be more easily seen. Moreover, it can be determined in a purely mechanical manner whether the sentence is true or false, once the truth values of the symbols T, B and $N(F)$ are known. Such logic is important, because it forms the basis of the way computers work. In a computer, the value true (or 1) is represented by a current flowing, and the value false (or 0) is represented by no current flowing. Circuits can be designed that transform the input values of A and B to an output value of A ˆ B, AvB, A→B or ∼A. The parts of a computer which perform calculations consist of very large numbers of such circuits. **SMcL**

See also symbolic logic.

BOTANY

Botany (from Greek *botane*, 'plant') is the study of all aspects of living plants; the first acknowledged botanist was Aristotle's student Theophrastus (*c*.371–287 BCE). He produced works entitled *Enquiry into Plants* and *Aetiology of Plants*, but these were not rediscovered by European philosophers until the **Renaissance**. Some of the earliest botanical work was based on the desire to classify medically useful plants in herbals. For example, Pesanius Dioscorides produced a herbal which referred to some 600 plants in the 1st century. In Europe, the Renaissance led to a great growth in scientific botanical study as botanical gardens and herbaria were established and stocked with plant species collected by travellers in the Old and New Worlds. In 1628, Caspar Bauhin produced his *Illustrated Exposition of Plants*, in which he used a binomial system to name some 6,000 plants, many of which were illustrated. The appearance of the lens and microscope in the 16th century promoted the establishment of plant anatomy as a new science, followed by **anatomy**, **biochemistry**, **physiology** and **taxonomy**. Botany led to great advances in the life sciences such as cell theory and **genetics**, and is continuing to contribute to scientific progress in agriculture, forestry and pharmacy. The original driving force behind botany continues as new plants, with unknown agricultural and pharmaceutical uses, are discovered daily. **RB**

See also ethnobotany; palaeobotany; photobiology; tropism.

BOURGEOIS DRAMA

Bourgeois drama is a term applied by theatre critics and scholars to plays about bourgeois people and/or plays aimed at bourgeois people. It is particularly used to describe serious drama about people of apparently unheroic status who were not traditionally seen, in Aristotelian terms, as potential tragic protagonists. There were some examples in Elizabethan drama but, unsurprisingly, bourgeois drama (in both senses) became established in the 18th century and continues to be highly significant. **TRG SS**

See also naturalism; realism.

Further reading R.B. Heilman, *Tragedy and Melodrama*; Raymond Williams, *Modern Tragedy*.

BOURGEOISIE

The term bourgeoisie (from a lost medieval Latin word which also gives the English 'burgess'), in **sociology**, is used in two senses based upon the definition described by Marx.

In one sense, it is applied loosely by sociologists to either the middle or ruling classes within capitalist society. Here bourgeoisie refers to those groups that have a vested interest in the preservation of **capitalism** and are thus in opposition to the working class. For Marx, the capitalist system of production involved two main classes: the bourgeoisie who owned the productive forces and the proletariat who did not. The proletariat are employed by the bourgeoisie and paid a wage, but this does not reflect the full value of the goods they produce. The difference or 'surplus-value' is creamed off by the bourgeoisie in the form of profit. According to Marx, the two classes are locked in a struggle over this surplus-value – a struggle which will ultimately result in the destruction of the capitalist system.

In its second usage, the term bourgeoisie is perhaps most accurately applied in a historical sense to the urban social class, which comprised the entrepreneurs, merchants and industrialists who were active in the earliest stages of capitalist development. Used in this way it refers to an actual historical group. **DA**

See also alienation; capital; class; conflict theory; labour process; Marxism.

Further reading T. Bottomore, *Classes in Modern Society*; T. Campbell, *Seven Theories of Human Society*, chapter 6.

BRAHMANIC RELIGION

Brahmanic religion (the religion practised and propagated by the Brahman **caste**) has been taken as normative **Hinduism** by scholars. The Sanskrit root *brm* from which the word Brahman is derived means 'to grow'. When applied to Brahmans it probably refers to their assumed spiritual powers to enhance life, deal with the gods, and to practise medicine and astrology. A Brahman (popularly Brahmin) is one entrusted with the power of sacred utterance, for example the ritual words of **sacrifice**. Brahman is the Word, the utterance itself, then the first principle of the universe, and hence a wholly abstract concept of God: the World Soul. This idea crystallized into that of Brahma the Creator, the first deity of the Hindu 'trinity' of Brahma, Siva and Vishnu. He is rarely worshipped individually, but he is the ultimate deity. Both concepts are integral to Brahmanic religion. Brahman resides in the human soul and becomes it.

Brahmanic religion divides life into four stages or *ashramas*. After the name-giving, rice-giving and finally the thread-giving ceremonies as childhood progresses, the first stage of life is entered when a teenage boy announces his intention to go to Varanasi to study the scriptures. His parents implore him to stay, give him presents and make arrangements for study, traditionally with a guru or teacher. When he returns, he takes a ritual bath in another ceremony, and (unless he was betrothed from childhood) a bride is quickly sought. The second stage is as householder, the principle purpose of marriage being to maintain domestic sacrifices and to raise children. When the Brahman sees his children's children, he may retire, with or without his wife (as she wishes), first to the forest to meditate and finally, when a widower, to devote himself to **asceticism** and self-knowledge in preparation for

death. At each stage he may put on the ochre-coloured robe of an ascetic and take a vow of celibacy to attain enlightenment more rapidly by austerities. Whichever pattern is followed, it is the way of knowledge, *gnana marga*. Women may also become nuns, or devotees of a particular guru, but generally they do not adopt an ascetic life until they are widowed grandmothers, no longer responsible for domestic arrangements at home. Nevertheless, there are some notable Brahman women saints and philosophers.

In addition to the theology of the Vedas and Upanishads, Brahmanic religion is shaped by the two great epics, the *Ramayana* and the *Mahabharata*, especially the teaching of the *Bhagavad-Gita* ('Song of the Adorable One'). **Vedic** worship was usually conducted in the open air, but possibly after contact with the Greeks temple worship began and with it temple art. It is said that because of the ascetic tradition, the Brahmanic religion is world-denying. Although some doctrines, such as that of *maya* ('illusion', better translated as 'transience') may give that impression, in actual practice the three aims of life, as set down in scripture and the marriage ceremony, are *dharma*, *arthi* ('wealth') and *karma* ('pleasure'). **EMJ**

BRETTON WOODS

Bretton Woods is the name given to the deal that spared the International Monetary System for 25 years after World War II, and set up the **International Monetary Fund** (IMF) and the **World Bank**. In 1944, officials from 45 non-Communist nations met at Bretton Woods in New Hampshire, USA, and agreed on a system of international liquidity and exchange rate management, to be administered by the IMF. This was the first time that a formal world agreement had laid down rules for the international monetary system.

Under Bretton Woods, exchange rates of IMF members were fixed in terms of gold, or the dollar; only the dollar was actually convertible into gold, at a fixed price of $35 an ounce. Members guaranteed to maintain their currencies' value (by buying and selling them) within 1% either side of parity, and were required to inform the IMF of any parity changes; they needed IMF permission for changes of more than 10%. The IMF rules required that changes should be made only if a country's balance of payments was in 'fundamental disequilibrium'.

For governments in payments difficulty, the Bretton Woods agreement envisaged two kinds of international reserves:

(1) Holdings at the IMF. These were (and still are) relatively small. IMF members deposit a 'quota' of national currency (and also, until 1976, gold) with the IMF, the quota being set according to the country's perceived 'importance'. The IMF then uses these deposits to lend to countries experiencing balance of payments difficulties. It can also use its holdings of special drawing rights.

(2) National currencies. Principally the dollar though, for large parts of the old British empire, also sterling. Because of the dollar's convertibility into gold, it had all the qualities that money requires: a stable value, convenience and widespread acceptability for transactions.

At first, the dollar's foreign obligations were fully backed by gold, but during the 1960s America's debt overtook its gold stocks. The stability of international money then depended on faith in the dollar itself. In August 1971 this faith was shattered: America's domestic economic troubles and problems paying for the Vietnam War led President Nixon to devalue the dollar against gold (to $38 an ounce) and hence against other major currencies. At a stroke, reserves of the central banks were reduced in value. After several months of instability, confusion and American arm-twisting, the leading industrial countries agreed in December 1971 to a new set of exchange rate parities under the Smithsonian Agreement, and by 1973 all the main currencies were floating. **TF**

BRUTALISM

Brutalism (from French *brut*, 'unadorned') was an architectural movement which had great vogue in the 1950s and 1960s: it seemed at the time as if every prize-winning new building was a monument to bare cement, breeze-blocks and unconcealed ducts and pipes. The chief architects of Brutalism included Paul Rudolph (born 1918) in the US and Alison and Peter Smithson (1920s-) in the UK. Among the movement's characteristic relics are several postwar British universitites and the graceless new towns in which they are placed; in each case the feeling that buildings come first and human needs nowhere (for all the architects' nobler convictions) is strong. Nonetheless, although pure brutalism was everything its name seemed to promise, the idea of unadorned beauty did lead distinction to several buildings in a more eclectic style, of which the Baubourg in Paris is a fine example. **KMcL**

BUDDHISM

The term 'Buddhism' was coined in the early 19th century by European Orientalists to denote a set of religious practices and sacred texts they observed in central and southeastern Asia. But in the 2,500 years of its existence, Buddhism has spread far more widely. It has covered most of East and Southeast Asia, and has at some time or other influenced the religious and cultural life of places as far afield as Burma, China, India, Japan, Nepal, Sri Lanka, Thailand, Tibet, and more recently, Europe and America.

The primary tenet of Buddhism is the cessation of 'suffering' (*duhkha*) in all its different forms. *Duhkha* is something more than the everyday suffering that most people encounter at some time or other. To Buddhists, the entire universe is subject to *duhkha*, and none – neither gods nor demons, neither those dwelling in hell or heaven – are exempt from it. Joys are always transient; life always ends in death and decay. Even death itself offers no salvation, since all sentient beings are constantly reborn into the endless cycle of death and rebirth. This understanding of the world is neither pessimistic nor nihilistic. Indeed, all the teachings of Buddhism point to the possibility of the cessation of *duhkha*. This cessation is what comprises the Buddhist notion of salvation – *nirvana*.

How is *nirvana* achieved? The Buddhist path to salvation or enlightenment is a matter of perfecting three essentials: (1) *Morality*, which involves the correct way of living, through the exercise of universal love and compassion toward all living beings. (2) *Wisdom*, which requires seeking an understanding and knowledge of things as they are, through thought and critical investigation. (3) *Practice*, involving mental development, through meditative exercises, concentration and insight aimed at a direct apprehension of reality.

These three essentials are not mutually exclusive. Morality, wisdom and practice are inseparably linked in Buddhism, not appended to each other like petals of a flower, but intertwined with one another like salt in the ocean (to evoke a famous Buddhist simile). They are basic ingredients of the path to salvation, which is open to all, and which is attained neither by blind faith nor by divine grace, but by 'seeing things as they really are'.

Traditionally, to be a Buddhist is to 'take refuge' in the 'Three Jewels' (*triratna*), also referred to as the 'Three Refuges'. These are: the Buddha (the 'Awakened One'), the *Dharma* (the 'Teaching') and the *Sangha* (the 'Community'). Through them one obtains release from *duhkha*. For worldly goals one may turn elsewhere, to local deities, **Brahmanic** rituals, **magic** and so on. Not surprisingly, Buddhism has always coexisted with other religious beliefs and has a clear tendency to accommodate the rituals of other 'local' religions. In most cases these 'local' beliefs were not seen as relevant to the spiritual quest, so could easily be tolerated. This inherent openness has facilitated the vast expansion and diversity of Buddhism.

The word *buddha* literally means 'one who has awakened'. But in the Indian religious context it has become an honorific title for an enlightened being. According to Buddhist belief there have been many Buddhas, and many are to follow. The most recent Buddha, and the one usually referred to historically, is Siddhartha Gautama. He was probably born in the second half of the 5th century BCE, of the Shakya clan residing in the northern part of India not far from the Nepalese border. Legend says that he was a prince, heir to his father's kingdom. Despite the worldly pleasures and luxuries of his royal upbringing, he sought a deeper understanding of life. His confrontation with the harsh realities of life prompted him to seek a way out of universal suffering. So he renounced family life and became an ascetic in search of the truth. For six years he wandered and studied under various religious teachers. Although he mastered all the known techniques, he did not find satisfaction. Then, at the age of 35 he decided to go his own way. Having taken a meal, he sat down under a tree (later to be known as the *Bodhi*-tree, 'Tree of Wisdom') and after deep contemplation came to the realization of the Truth. After this he became known as the Buddha, that is 'The Awakened (or Enlightened) One'. He delivered his first sermon to a group of five ascetics in the Deer Park near modern Sarnath.

Buddha's teaching recognized no differences of **caste** or class. (This was a revolutionary step, also taken by his contemporary, Mahavira: see **Jainism**.) His intention was to open the path of salvation to all humankind. In many respects, Buddha's life epitomizes cardinal elements in Buddhist doctrine and ethics. An important element is the emphasis on the 'middle way', a key motif throughout Buddhism. The Buddha experienced both sensual pleasure as a prince and the agony of self-mortification as an ascetic. Both rejected in favour of the middle way.

Another important feature of Buddhism, highlighted in the life and death of its founder, is its humanity. Although there is no doubt that Siddhartha is portrayed as fully human, over-emphasizing this has, at times, been somewhat misleading. It is true that the Buddha is not a god and that Buddhahood is attained in the human circumstances as the culmination of many lives. Nevertheless, being a Buddha is being neither human nor god, but going beyond the nature of both.

The Buddha's first sermon at the Deer Park is called 'The Setting-in-Motion of the Wheel of *Dharma*'. *Dharma*, the second of the 'Three Refuges', is a central term in Buddhism and in the whole development of Indian thought. It is both descriptive, meaning the way things are in reality, and prescriptive, referring to the way things should be; to stress this aspect it is often translated as '(natural) Law' or the 'Law of the Cosmos'. In Buddhism, to realize *dharma* is simultaneously to comprehend the Law of spiritual life and to achieve its goal.

The Buddha explained *dharma* in the form of the 'Four Noble Truths'. These 'Four Noble Truths' occupy a special position in Buddhism. They are:

(1) *Duhkha* (see above). It is said that everything is *duhkha*: birth, ageing, sickness, death, parting, not getting what one wants, change, decay – in fact any experience, whether pleasurable or painful. *Duhkha* has three elements: the *duhkha* of suffering in the psychological sense; the 'metaphysical *duhkha*' that reveals the perpetual flux of all that there is, and the *duhkha* of that which conditions the very essence of being. One might simplify by saying that *duhkha* embraces all possible non-*nirvanic* states of being in their psychological and ontological sense.

(2) *The Noble Truth on the Origin of Duhkha*. The cause of *duhkha* is the craving (literally 'thirst') for sensual pleasure, for something else, for more or for less, for being and for non-being. This craving is one link in a circular chain in which each element both begets and is begotten by its counterparts, ultimately locking one up in the prison of *duhkha*. This 'chain' is called 'Dependent Origination' and in it are embedded the principles of conditionality, reality and interdependence which form the core of the Buddhist explanation of all psychological and physical phenomena.

(3) *The Noble Truth on the Cessation of Dhukha*. Supreme and final liberation is the 'blowing out' (the literal meaning of *nirvana*) of the fires of craving, hatred and ignorance (sometimes referred to as greed, hatred and delusion). The Four Noble Truths are often explained through a medicinal allegory. The human condition is diagnosed as being *duhkha*. The reason for this malady is craving, and if the cause of this malady is removed health ensues. Health in this allegory is *nirvana*.

(4) *The Noble Truth of the Path* (leading to the Cessation of *Duhkha*). The path has eight factors: right views, right thought, right speech, right action, right livelihood, right effort, right mindfulness and right concentration. These eight reaffirm the three essentials of Buddhist spiritual training and discipline mentioned earlier (moral conduct, wisdom and practice). The fourth Truth thus covers the whole of Buddhist teaching, creating an intricate and harmonious whole.

The more historical sense of 'path' refers to the Order of monks and nuns who formally undertake to pursue the Buddhist life and to abide the Discipline (*vinaya*) of the Order. There has always been a place for lay followers in Buddhism, and salvation has never been reserved solely for monks and nuns. Nevertheless, right from its inception, Buddhism has been characterized by the heritage of monks and nuns who have renounced worldly life, and have decided to commit themselves to strict training within the community of other monks and nuns. This is the meaning of the word *sangha*, which otherwise generally means the community of those pursuing the Path. Monks and nuns give up all worldly belongings and possess only a bare minimum of personal goods (three robes, alms bowl, belt, razor, needle and not much else). Traditionally, the monks and nuns lived as wandering religious beggars, settling in one place only for the three months of the rainy season. They relied on **charity** for food, clothing, shelter and medicines. Expulsion from the *sangha* was, and is, rare and enforced only for extreme cases, though a monk or nun is always free to leave if they wish.

The *sangha* plays an extremely important role in Buddhism. It is the protector and maintainer of knowledge of the *dharma*. Unlike many other religions, Buddhism is not linked to a specific place or a society and does not control the **rites of passage**. The core of 'institutional' Buddhism has always been more preoccupied with preserving the *dharma* through the lineage of a committed community, rather than through political power structures, or control of social customs and lifestyles.

From its inception, *sangha* lacked a supreme authority. The Buddha refused to establish a functional hierarchy or a successor. Authority in the *sangha* is seen as collective and precedence is granted simply according to seniority, calculated by the date of ordination. Teaching is passed on to each novice only by an appointed and accomplished teacher, who in turn was trained by a master in his own right, standing in line right to the Buddha himself. The idea of a lineage is central to *sangha* and the dominance of the master/pupil relationship within it complements the absence of a central authority, shifting the burden of authority to the personal level.

The key ideas described above are shared by all traditions of Buddhism. However, these ideas, and the terms which embody them, have been interpreted differently among different traditions throughout the ages. Although schism and heresy are recognized in Buddhism (and would constitute grave departure from the Buddhist path) doctrinal differences are not seen as a sign of weakness, but as part of the legitimate progression of the path, and, on the whole, do not create rifts in the *dharma*. Yet the regional and doctrinal differences are such that it has been the practice, of both Buddhists and Western scholars, to divide the cumulative tradition into more manageable parts. There are three great 'vehicles' (*yana*) which emphasize different understandings of the process and goal of salvation: the Lesser Vehicle (*Hinayana*), the Great Vehicle (*Mahayana*) and the Diamond Vehicle (*Vajrayana*, usually referred to as *Tantra*). The major school of the *Hinayana* existing today is the Theravada, which is widespread among the countries of Southeast Asia. *Mahayana*, the dominant form of northern and eastern Buddhism, spread from India to China, Tibet and Nepal, and then from China to Japan. Contemporary Tibetan and Japanese Buddhism (including Zen Buddhism) is all *Mahayana*. It tends to be more accommodating to change and local influence, and its sacred texts are written in an enormous diversity and plurality of languages. *Vajrayana*, or *Tantra*, owes much to mainstream *Mahayana*, yet it has much in common with the Hindu form of Tantric

practice. At its core is a ritual system centred around the evocation of deities, the acquisition of supernatural powers and the attainment of enlightenment by means of meditation, 'incantations' (*mantra*), and yoga. **OR**

Further reading Christmas Humphreys, *Buddhism; Popular Dictionary of Buddhism.*

BUDGET DEFICIT

A budget deficit, in **economics** and politics, occurs when receipts for a budget period are less than expenditures. The deficit becomes indebtedness unless sufficient reserves have been built up in earlier periods from which to draw. In US federal finance, the **national debt** is the current net sum of all federal budget deficits over the years, counting those occasional surpluses as negative deficits.

Federal deficits may be a form of **fiscal policy** designed to expand economic activity in the economy by providing more government spending when private spending is deemed insufficient. For three decades in the US, however, federal budget deficits continued and grew, because the Administration and Congress were unwilling to raise sufficient funds by fees and taxation to pay for the expenditures they desired to make. The last federal budget surplus ($0.3 billion) was in 1960. Toward the end of the 1980s, deficits had grown to a range of $200–300 billion. The deficits were intended in the sense that they were budgeted, but in many years they were the opposite of appropriate fiscal policy because deficits are inflationary. They made the effort to control inflation by monetary policy much more difficult during the 1980s. **TF**

See also deficit spending.

BUREAUCRACY

Bureaucracy originally meant and still means 'rule by officials': the implication being that it is a possible, fully fledged system of government, just like democracy or aristocracy. However, bureaucracy has also required more neutral meanings, both as a synonym for public administration, and as a form of organization characterized by a hierarchy of offices, impersonality in its recruitment of staff and its procedures, contintuity in form and files, and the primacy of functional expertise.

Much political controversy still surrounds the first and original meaning of bureaucracy. Marxists and radical left-wing critics argue that bureaucracy subverts democracy, and prescribe participatory and egalitarian political systems to prevent this possibility. Their critics in turn maintain that such solutions are worse than the problems of bureaucracy. The German sociologist Max Weber (1864–1920) gloomily predicted the bureaucratization of the world, maintaining that all non-bureaucratic organizational forms would be displaced because they would prove less efficient. Weber and his precursor, the French political theorist Alexis de Tocqueville, thought that modern mass societies would be both the cause and consequence of bureaucratization. They saw strong liberal representative governmental institutions as the only effective means to prevent over-centralized states from crushing their civil societies.

It was Weber who produced what has become the classic model of bureaucracy. Bureaucratic organizations did exist in a limited form in traditional societies, but Weber believed the expansion of bureaucracy to be an inevitable feature of modern societies. The spread of bureaucracy in the modern world exemplified the process of rationalization. Weber suggested that a bureaucracy was the most efficient administrative form for the rational pursuit of organizational goals.

Weber constructed an 'ideal type' of bureaucracy – that is an abstract description which exaggerates certain features of real cases to underline their essential characteristics. Bureaucracies, as outlined by Weber, have the following fundamental features. (1) There exists a precise hierarchy of authority which can be depicted as a pyramid, with a chain of command stretching from the top to the bottom. (2) The conduct of the office holders at all levels is governed by written rules of procedure. (3) Officials are full-time, salaried and recruited on the basis of formal qualifica-

tions. Each job within the hierarchy has a fixed salary attached to it. It is expected that individuals will make a career within the organization. (4) The tasks of the officials within the organization are separate from their life outside. (5) In bureaucracies officials do not own the material resources – offices, desks, machinery – with which they work.

Studies have shown, however, that bureaucracies may not work in exactly the ways Weber described. The written rules can make workers inflexible and unable to respond to changing circumstances. It has also been suggested that informal practices developed by the workers themselves may be more efficient than adherence to written standards of procedure.

Economists, especially economic liberals in the public choice school, define bureaucratic public administration as hostile to the free market and enterprises. They claim that bureaucracies maximize their budgets or their staff, and crowd out, over-regulate and stifle the private sector: that is, they see bureaucracies as incipient forms of state socialism. They prescribe privatization, contracting-out and 'market-testing' as solutions to bureaucratization. Defenders of bureaucratic public administration maintain by contrast that it provides effective and accountable government and is the best known means of preventing public corruption. **DA BO'L**

See also accountability; authority; career; division of labour; élite theory; ideal type; occupation; organization; pluralism; profession; rationalization.

Further reading David Beetham, *Bureaucracy*; Patrick Dunleavy, *Democracy, Bureaucracy and Public Choice*; Stephen Robbins, *Organization Theory*.

BUSINESS CYCLE

Business cycles, in **economics**, are periods which alternate between prosperity and depression. They have occurred with varying amplitudes and periods of duration since the advent of the Industrial Revolution. Fluctuations in output are accompanied by fluctuations in employment and income. Cycles are not precisely repeated because their causes are complex and variable. Some students of the business cycle measure cycles from trough to trough or peak to peak. Joseph Schumpeter (1883–1950) argued that this was improper and inconsistent with the historical driving forces. He identified four stages of the cycle: *prosperity* (expansion from an equilibrium to the peak); *recession* (decline from the peak to the next point on the trend line); *depression* (further fall to the trough); and *revival* (expansion from the trough to the next equilibrium on the trend line). He measured the business cycle from equilibrium through the four phases to the next equilibrium. The National Bureau of Economic Research, on the other hand, identified two phases, expansion and recession, and measures business cycles from peak to peak or trough to trough.

The Kondratieff cycle is a business cycle named after a 19th-century Russian economist, Nikolai Kondratieff, who identified cycles of economic activity spanning 50 to 60 years. His book *The Long Waves in Economic Life* was published in 1925. It implied that **capitalism** had a secular stability, while Russia's Marxist leaders claimed it was self-destructively unstable. His work has attracted renewed interest recently as economists seek to explain the causes of the post-1973 recession. Unfortunately, Kondratieff does not prove very enlightening. His statistics established cycles from the later 1780s to 1844–51, from 1844–51 to 1890–96, and an upswing from 1890–96 to 1914–20 (which was followed, his adherents point out, by about 25 years of downswing, the 25 golden postwar years, and now by recession.) But Kondratieff's analysis was, at best, sketchy. **TF**

See also depression; gross national product.

Further reading Robert E. Lucas, *Models of Business Cycles; Studies in Business-Cycle Theory.*

BYZANTINE

In art history, the term Byzantine refers to the **art** and **architecture** of the Eastern Roman Empire, based, from the end of the 4th century onwards, on Constantinople, otherwise known as Byzantium. The architecture of the Christian Byzantine Empire combined the building traditions of Graeco-Roman **classicism** with the decorative traditions of the Arab world. It formed the basic style for church architecture in the Orthodox Christian World from the 5th century to the present day.

Perhaps the most significant building of this tradition was the church of Hagia Sofia, ('Divine Wisdom'), built in the 6th century, which still survives in present-day Istanbul. It is thought to be the greatest vaulted space, without the interruption of intermediate supports, ever constructed. A central dome seems 'suspended by a golden chain from heaven' over the church. Hagia Sofia became the model for most subsequent Byzantine church architecture. **JM**

Further reading R. Krautheimer, *Early Christian and Byzantine Architecture*; N. Pevsner, *An Outline of Western Architecture.*

C

CALCULUS

The word calculus is originally Latin for a small stone, referring to those used to perform calculations on an abacus or similar tool. Today in **mathematics** it has come to mean any system of rules for symbolic manipulation, something vastly important in a subject where the use of symbolic notation is crucial (see **symbolism**). The two major divisions in **logic** are known as the propositional calculus and the predicate calculus, and together these comprise the logical calculus. Calculi are also important in the study of **semantics** in the theory of computing.

Usually, the term is used to refer to the infinitesimal calculus unless qualified. Although this is often thought of as the invention of Newton (1642–1727) and Leibniz (1646–1716) (and to which of them it should be ascribed has been the subject of much debate), it was really the product of the work of many 17th-century mathematicians attempting to solve two major problems in applied mathematics. Newton and

Leibniz's fundamental contribution was to realize that the two problems were intimately connected.

The first problem is that of the differential calculus, to determine the tangent lines to a curve. For a particular point on a curve, there may be a straight line through the point which just touches the curve without crossing it. Such a line is called the tangent. (For some curves there are no such straight lines at some points.) The problem is, given a curve and a point on it, to discover whether the tangent exists and, if it does, to find its slope, which is known as the derivative of the curve at the point. This is important physically because the velocity of a moving body is always along the tangent to the curve described by its path. A knowledge of differential calculus is therefore essential to the study of mechanics.

The second problem, known as the problem of quadrature, is that of the integral calculus. The problem is to determine the area within a curve. In a **Cartesian co-ordinate system** in two dimensions (that is, with x and y co-ordinates), a curve is usually written as an equation, as $y = f(x)$, where f is a **function**. Then the integral of the curve (from a to b) is taken to be the area of the figure given by the curve itself between $(a,f(a))$ and $(b,f(b))$, and the straight lines joining $(a,f(a))$ to $(a,0)$, $(b,f(b))$ to $(b,0)$ and $(a,0)$ to $(b,0)$ along the x-axis. This is written as $\sim a\hat{\ }b\ f(x)dx$.

The intimate connection between the two problems, discovered independently by Newton and Leibniz, is known as the fundamental theorem of the (infinitesimal) calculus. A function $F(x)$ is defined to be the integral of the curve $f(x)$ between a and x (for some fixed number a), so that $F(x) = \perp\hat{a}x\ f(x)dx$. The fundamental theorem of the calculus is simply that $F'(x) = f(x)$, where $F'(x)$ is the derivative of F at the point $(x,F(x))$. In other words, the process of integration takes us from the function $f(x)$ to the function $F(x)$, and the process of differentiation takes us back from $F(x)$ to $f(x)$. There is in fact no difference between the two; there is only one calculus.

Newton and Leibniz used infinitesimal numbers (ones smaller in size than any other, but not actually zero); Leibniz connected the theorem with mystical ideas about infinitesimals that led to the calculus being regarded as not really a true part of mathematics with the same status as, say, algebra. This problem was eventually circumvented by Bolzano, Cauchy and Weierstrass in the early 19th century, and the mathematical theory of **analysis** was born. SMcL

CANNIBALISM

Cannibalism (derived from Canibales, the original old-Spanish name for the Caribs, a native people of the Caribbean) arouses a more extreme and instinctive response than almost any other human activity. To the people who ate other people – they seem, on available evidence to have been concentrated in the Southern hemisphere, in places as widely separate as Papua New Guinea, some parts of Polynesia, the Indonesian islands, southern Central Africa and Central America – it was probably a way of dealing with the Other: by eating other people, you took over their being, made them part of you. (Certainly economic necessity seems not to have been a compelling reason for the practice.) Cannibalism absorbed the strength of one's enemies; it was a way of simultaneously obliterating them from the world and celebrating their departure. In the cases of cannibalism widely reported in the West during the 1980s and 1990s, serial killers who were cannibals reported a similar kind of satisfaction: eating all or part of their victims was a form of possession, which some described in almost sexual terms.

Although in the abstract one might argue that eating human beings differs only in degree from eating any other animals, in practice cannibalism has been one of the longest and most widely-held of all **taboos**. Perhaps one reason is a kind of reverse of the Other theory: if we eat our Others, we are in a sense consuming part of our own selves. Extensions of this are the views in many religions that human beings are created in the image of God or the gods (so that consuming them will bring down supernatural wrath), or that the spirit is separated from the body at death (and therefore that eating the body will deprive the spirit of wholeness in the afterlife, and so bring its wrath down on the eater or the community). There is also a belief that dead people belong to other worlds, and that to consume them is to trespass where no living mortal is allowed. The rationale is complex, but the results are simple: almost every community, of almost every 'advanced' religious practice, has outlawed cannibalism.

Religion sanctions us to kill other people in war or by judicial execution, but once they are dead their bodies are to be disposed of with reverence – and for some reason (possibly displaced guilt) that reverence does not extend to eating them. The English author Barry Norman wrote a novel (*End Product*) about a future society in which one group of people (whites, as it happened) 'farmed' another group (blacks) for food, but took enormous care to remove their reasoning faculty (by lobotomy) soon after birth, so that they became a kind of sub-species, human-animal. It is a macabre premise, but focuses all the confused arguments about meat-eating in general and cannibalism in particular. For most people in the world, cannibalism has been a taboo for so long that it is no longer possible to explain it. Abhorring it seems not so much a willed act as part of our nature, part of what makes us human. (Other animals happily consume their own species, even their own offspring.) A corollary of this is that cannibals themselves are often regarded as in some way deficient, sub-human – a view which, however sympathetic, totally lacks logic. **KMcL**

CAPITAL

In popular usage, capital (from Latin *caput*, 'head', the unit of possession used in a Roman census) means money or wealth; to economists capital is the third factor of production (the others are labour and land), which are combined to produce goods and services. The proportions of capital and labour used to make a car, for example, depend on two things: (1) their *relative prices*, that is, labour costs and the rate of interest, which is one measure of the cost of capital; (2) the *state of technology* – processes that use a lot of capital relative to

labour are called 'capital intensive', while big labour users are called 'labour intensive'.

Although capital goods are normally taken as being machinery, buildings, planes, etc. – anything used to make something else – capital itself is further divided into two categories: *fixed capital*, that is, machinery, buildings and plant; and *working* or *circulating capital*, that is, stocks of raw materials and semi-finished goods, components and, crucially, money, that are used up quickly in the production process.

Certainly capital existed in the precapitalist world, in the sense of private wealth. But, although the funds existed, there was no impetus to put them to new and aggressive use. Writing in the 18th century, Adam Smith saw accumulation of capital as a vast benefit to society. For capital, if put to use in machinery, provided the division of labour which multiplies a people's productive energy.

In the 19th century, Marx used the term capital to refer to the privately owned wealth of the capitalist, which is used to create a surplus value. For Marx, all history could be divided into a number of time-periods which could be distinguished from each other in terms of their economic structure and associated social relationships. Marx argued that under a capitalist system of production the minority capitalist class owns the means of production and the majority working class does not. The value of wages paid to workers is less than the value of the goods they produce which are sold on the market for profit. This profit is creamed off by the capitalists and may be accumulated and reinvested in the productive process.

The term capital is used more loosely by some sociologists to refer to any 'asset' which is either immediately or potentially useable as a source of income, for example, 'cultural capital'. Used in this sense capital exists in all societies, whereas in the more restricted sense used by Marx it is a feature unique to capitalist society. **DA TF**

See also alienation; bourgeoisie; capitalism; class; conflict theory; labour process; Marxism; power; Protestant ethic; society.

Further reading A. Cutler, B. Hindess, P. Irst and A. Hussain, *Marx's 'Capital' and Capitalism Today.*

CAPITALISM

Capitalism is an economic system in which there is private ownership of natural resources and capital goods. The returns of rent, interest, and profit are paid to private individuals as owners who decide on the use of their natural resources and capital goods.

In practice, an economic system of private ownership has never existed in pure form – some public ownership and some public decision-making about the use of the means of production have existed in every society. The term, therefore, refers to economies in which the means of production (natural resources and capital) are predominantly privately owned and managed. Examples of rather pure forms of capitalism are the UK or the US during the 19th century.

As the 20th century has progressed, governments in capitalist countries have been taking on a growing role in ownership and/or management of natural resources and capital. On the other hand, socialist countries have increasingly permitted their farmers to sell at least part of their produce in markets for their own benefit, and socialist countries more and more have turned toward market direction of production to increase efficiency. It appeared that countries were moving at varying rates of speed from relatively pure capitalism and relatively pure **socialism** toward some combination of capitalism and socialism, becoming '**mixed economies**'. However, during the 1980s, the US, UK and France seemed to be moving toward less government ownership in the economy. And in 1989 and 1990, a bloodless revolution occurred in most of the socialist countries of Eastern Europe as the people deposed their Communist leaders: they have since attempted to adopt democratic forms of government, and continue to struggle to shift to market economies with private ownership of the means of production. **TF**

Further reading J. Scott, *Corporations, Classes and Capitalism;* A. Shonfield, *Modern Capitalism.*

CARBON DATING

Carbon dating is a method of determining the age of certain materials. The upper atmosphere of the Earth is constantly bombarded by cosmic rays from events in space. This bombardment creates a rare and unstable isotope of carbon, ^{14}C, from the nitrogen which comprises 80% of the atmosphere. Naturally occurring carbon has two stable isotopes, ^{12}C and ^{13}C. ^{14}C, however, is unstable, and decays to nitrogen with a half life of 5,700 years. The term half life indicates the time that it will take half the atoms in any sample to decay. Thus a sample containing, say, 32 atoms of ^{14}C, after 5,700 years will probably contain 16 atoms, in 11,400 years (2 x 5,700) there will be 8 atoms, and only after 100,000 years will the last atom decay. Of course, usually far more than 32 atoms are available.

All living things, and some soils, exchange carbon with the air, and therefore will contain the same percentage of ^{14}C as the atmosphere. This is constantly replenished as fast as it decays by the cosmic ray bombardment. As soon as a living organism dies, it ceases this exchange, and no more ^{14}C enters its body. The ^{14}C that it contains will decay, without being replenished. So if we examine a fossil that contains half as much ^{14}C as an equivalent living animal, we can say that it is probably 5,700 years old. Thus fossils may be dated by their ^{14}C content.

There are two ways of measuring the ^{14}C content of a sample. One method consists of waiting for the atoms to decay and detecting the decay products. This is not very useful for small samples which contain only a few atoms, as they would take a very long time to decay. A better way, high energy mass spectrometry, involves detection of the atoms themselves before they decay; with this method samples weighing only a few milligrams may be dated. This involves ionizing the atoms so they acquire charge, accelerating them, and deflecting them with a magnetic field. The path they take when deflected varies depending on their mass, and is used to detect the quantity of ^{14}C present.

We have assumed that the levels of ^{14}C

have remained constant throughout history. In fact, this is not quite true. It is certainly not true for the last century: future archaeologists will notice a very significant increase from the 1960s onwards due to nuclear tests. Concentrations of ^{14}C have varied in the past as well, probably due to changes in the Earth's magnetic field. But as long as we know how the concentrations of ^{14}C varied in the past, we may still accurately date samples. This data is provided by tree-rings in the bristlecone pine tree, which can live to the astonishing age of several thousand years. Each ring contains the concentration that existed in that year. From bristlecone pine studies, we may confidently date samples up to 6000 BCE. **JJ**

See also archaeology.

CAREER

The term 'career' (from Latin *carraria*, 'carriageway') refers to a sequence of jobs pursued by individuals in the course of their working lives, which may be structured or unstructured. Structured sequences of jobs form a hierarchy of increasing income and prestige. The term is also applied to progression in an non-occupational life course 'patient career'. **DA**

See also bureaucracy; division of labour; occupations; profession; social stratification; status; work.

Further reading R. Hall, *Occupations and the Social Structure*.

CARICATURE

The word caricature derives from the Italian *caricare*, 'to load', also the origin of the English word 'charge'. It means a form of artistic representation in which the normal appearance or traits of the person or institution caricatured are grotesquely exaggerated. In **literature** and **music**, caricature is often a single, if striking, effect rather than the basis for a whole work; in **drama** and **fine art**, by contrast, it can be the guiding principle of a complete composition. Nowadays, thanks especially to political cartoons and satire, we associate caricature with comedy, but – as Bosch's devils or Hogarth's rakes and whores show in art, or

such creations as Shakespeare's Richard III, the Struldbrugs in *Gulliver's Travels* or Big Brother in *1984* do in literature – its effects can also be deeply and disturbingly serious. **KMcL**

CARNIVAL

Carnival was a loosely theatrical if not dramatic form during the Middle Ages, a kind of **street theatre** through which the populace could entertain themselves and challenge the ecclesiastical and feudal hierarchies. There was no clear distinction between the actors and the spectators. Carnival was incorporated more formally into **Renaissance** drama, and has been particularly identified as a strategy in Shakespearean comedies, whereby the power of Elizabethan society could be challenged, but ultimately reabsorbed in order to reinforce that power. More recently, the idea of the carnivalesque has been used to produce theatre which can covertly oppose political power. **TRG SS**

See also theatre.

Further reading M. Bakhtin, *Rabelais and his World*; C.L. Barber, *Shakespeare's Festive Comedy*.

CARTEL

A cartel, in business terms, is an agreement, written or unwritten, between producers to fix prices, share out markets or set their production levels, in order to restrain competition and to raise profits. A cartel is used to regulate markets and fix prices as a monopolist would. Adam Smith believed that the temptation to create cartels to maximize profits was so naturally strong that he viewed all business contracts with the deepest suspicion, and wrote that 'People of the same trade seldom meet together, even for merriment and diversion, but the conversation ends in a conspiracy against the public or in some contrivance to raise prices'. In the US, cartels are outlawed by anti-trust legislation, but, at times, US firms have had permission to participate in international cartels, and in particular cartels which are government-sponsored commodity agreements.

Cartels became especially popular during the depression years of the 1920s and 1930s. In Germany, for instance, several steel companies formed the Rührstahl cartel and the three biggest chemical firms in the world at the time, Bayer, BASF and Hoechst, merged into a holding company called I.G. Farben (later to become notorious for its work on chemical weapons).

Success of cartels has been sporadic because of forces that tend to undermine them, particularly international ones. For example, one or more members will find it advantageous to shave price a bit and ignore quotas in order to sell more and reap even greater benefits from prices that are still artificially high. There is not much fear of market sanctions from the other cartel members because the latter have no way of imposing them. Buyers are happy to get even slightly lower prices, and suppliers of equipment are glad to support the expanded output. **TF**

See also monopoly.

CARTESIAN CO-ORDINATE SYSTEM

According to legend, René Descartes (1596–1650) saw the shadow of the lattice of a window falling on a table, and this inspired him to design the first co-ordinate system, which gives numerical values to points in space. His system is still used today, and is known as Cartesian in his honour.

In one **dimension** (in other words, on a line), Cartesian co-ordinates are defined by choosing a point known as the origin (with co-ordinate 0), and specifying a distance measure (how far away the point with co-ordinate 1 is from the origin). The points on the line now all have uniquely defined **real number** values; for example, if the point 1 is 1cm away from the origin, the point -243 is 243cm away from the origin in the opposite direction.

The two-dimensional system is a generalization from the one-dimensional system. Here, the aim is to define co-ordinates for the plane. As before, the origin is chosen, but this time also a line (known as the abscissa) through the origin. One-dimensional co-ordinates are then defined on the abcissa. A second line, the ordinate, is drawn through the origin at right-angles to the first line, and its co-ordinate system is defined in terms of that on the abscissa. If someone's right hand has thumb and forefinger extended, with the forefinger pointing along the abscissa from 0 to 1, then the point 1 on the ordinate is that at the same distance from the origin in the direction the thumb is pointing in. (This may sound confusing, but when drawn on a piece of paper it becomes easy to see what is going on.) Each point on the plane now has a unique co-ordinate, (x,y), where x is the length of the shortest straight line joining the point to the ordinate and y is the length of the shortest straight line joining the point to the abscissa.

The same process is repeated to give a third dimension, a co-ordinate system for space. It can also be generalized to any number of dimensions, something which originally seemed pointless but which now has many applications in today's theories of **cosmology**. It is worth noting that in order to co-ordinatize the motion of a body in space, such as the Earth, three dimensions are needed to give the position and three to give the velocity – six dimensions in all. In the same way cylindrical, spherical and other polar co-ordinates are developed using ideas of angular (as opposed to linear) measurements.

Algebraic geometry as a subject has advanced considerably since Descartes, but its importance to the development of mathematical thought stems mainly from the idea of the co-ordinate system. Cartesian co-ordinates are not the only ones which can be developed. **SMcL**

CARTOGRAPHY

At its simplest, cartography is the art and science of drawing charts and maps. It is a science because it requires scrupulous observation and recording of information and location, but it is also an art because the selection and presentation of the information in symbolic form involves aesthetic judgement. The nature of the map is guided by its purpose, which ranges from specific confidential information for limited circulation to general purpose series maps or atlases available to the public. Usually, presentation is guided by the need for accuracy, clarity and relevance to the purpose of the map, but sometimes maps are used for fictional or propaganda purposes.

Maps are known from very early societies, for example, recording plots of land on the Babylonian flood plain or showing distances and way stations on the Roman road network. Even the simplest societies had need for maps and used sketches drawn on the ground, wood or pieces of cloth, as well as stories or songs that carried information about other places and how to get there. The highpoint of cartography in the ancient world was Ptolemy's *Geographia* (2nd century CE): this included discussions of the principles of map making, details of several **map projections** and latitude and longitude of 8,000 places, as well as world maps. Unfortunately, this was later lost to Europe (though known to the Arabs) and for a thousand years maps of large areas were extremely distorted in shape and scale, perhaps most notably in the medieval maps showing a world centred on Jerusalem. Such maps were influenced by abstract ideas about the proper balance of continents and seas, and also suggested that the inhabitants of distant countries were less enlightened than those of Europe and the Mediterranean. Maps used for more practical purposes, especially sea charts, were more advanced and ultimately spurred a revolution in cartography.

The first major impetus in the development of cartography was provided by the European 'Voyages of Discovery' in the 15th and 16th centuries. Cartography was inspired by the rediscovery of Ptolemy and new information from navigation, as the use of compass, log, sextant and chronometer allowed both ships and coasts to be located with ever greater accuracy on the globe. Cartographers used the new printing technology to produce atlases which were works of art, but they also developed new map projections and it was no coincidence that the most famous, that of Mercator, equated a straight line on the map with a constant compass course. Even the errors of the past contributed: Columbus was encouraged to seek a western route to China because he was misled by maps based on Ptolemy and hence on Posidonius' 7,000 mile underestimate of the world's circumference. By the 18th century most of the world's coasts were mapped, but many inland areas remained *terra incognita*.

The major step forward in land surveying was the use of trigonometry to locate places by measuring angles rather than distances. This greatly increased the speed and accuracy of survey, and was first used by private map makers, such as Saxton, who produced the world's first national atlas in 1579. Two centuries later, the outstanding quality of the 182 sheets of the Cassini maps of France made the British army realize the importance of accurate mapping and led to the establishment of the Ordnance Survey to map the whole of Britain and then the Empire. During this century, subsequent advances were also pioneered by the military, from air photographs to satellites. The routine television weather report shows how dramatically cartography has progressed, with the ability to use satellite, radar and a global network of recording stations to provide the data for computer-generated maps of current and predicted weather conditions. The move from maps of isobars and fronts to maps of wind arrows, cloud cover and temperature zones shows the importance of presentation in making maps communicate with their users.

As we approach the end of the millennium, large amounts of information are available about many parts of the world – far more than can be included in a single map. Cartographers are now engaged in developing methods of linking information to location in ways which allow users to specify their own maps: these are **Geographical Information Systems**. PS

CASTE

Caste, in theory, is a rank in society combined with a specific occupation and ritual associations. It is a position that one is normally born into and broadly defines the group within which one can marry, although the reality may be a lot more complex.

Caste has usually been regarded as a **Hindu** phenomenon. The English word comes from the Portuguese *casta*, a term used to describe the people of India after the Portuguese settled there in the 16th century. (The Portuguese derived it from Latin *castus*, 'race', 'breed' or 'clan'.) Some anthropologists have questioned how far caste institutions are unique to Hindu societies. Communities, for instance, in West Africa, also appear to be ranked in ways similar to caste organizations. However, most attention has been directed to the nature of the caste system in India.

Several Hindu myths relate the origins of castes in a fourfold *varna* (literally 'colour') system. The most famous is the one about the bodily dismemberment of the god Purusha: his mouth gave rise to the Brahmins (priests and people of learning), his arms to the Kshatriyas (rulers and warriors), his thighs to the Vaisyas (traders), and his feet to the Sudras (cultivators, occupational and serving castes).

Conventional Hindu ideology considers the three higher castes – Brahmins, Kshatriyas and Vaisyas – as spiritually twice born. Outside of this *varna* system are the 'Untouchables'. These are the people conceived as ritually polluting and engaging in polluting occupations, such as the barber, sweeper and leather-worker. While 'Untouchables' are marginalized within the *varna* system, both are mutually dependent on each other for it is the 'Untouchables' that maintain the purity of the higher castes by removing polluting substances from the social system.

In practice, each *varna* is composed of a group of castes and sub-castes which show variation in different localities. Hindu ideas about castes also broadly define the castes who can dine, exchange food, water and services with each other. For instance, it is expected that a high-caste Brahmin does not receive cooked food or water in an earthenware pot from someone who is of a lower caste if ritual pollution and social disapproval are to be avoided.

A prominent scholar of the Hindu caste system, Louis Dumont, argued in his book *Homo Hierarchicus* (1966), that Hindu religious ideas about caste dominated all other aspects of society. A hierarchy of castes was therefore legitimate in traditional Hindu thought, contrary to Western ideas about equality. Later anthropologists have reappraised Dumont's views. Some argue that he has confused Hindu theory with practice, while others hold that he has given the dominant view of the Brahmins to the neglect of the lower castes. They accuse him of distorting and over-mystifying Hindu society to present a picture of a totally different and timeless place, thereby confirming **Orientalist** assumptions. Historical perspectives reveal that Hindu caste organizations were largely systematized by colonial administrative practices under British rule. Such analysts argue that colonialists 'imagined' caste as a system of racial typology which they could use as a label to categorize and govern the Indian people.

M.N. Srinivas (see below) has suggested some helpful caste-related concepts. He proposed the term 'dominant caste' for a caste group considered superior in a particular locality, and 'sanskritisation' to describe the aspirations of caste groups to raise their **status** in the eyes of society. 'Sanskritisation' could be effected by such measures as refraining from impure practices like alcohol and meat consumption.

It is evident that even in the case of Hindu society, ideas about caste are not agreed upon by all. In India, religious and political attempts have been made to eradicate it for the inequalities it demonstrates, both historically and in modern times. Industrialization and democratization have had considerable impact on the caste system, particularly this century. The mobility of class divisions based on economic achievements has cut across traditional caste occupations and hierarchies. Yet caste considerations continue to have great influence in Indian daily life, especially in the selection of marriage partners, allocation of temple priests, and in the political arena where, despite efforts to promote equality, positive discrimination favouring the position of 'Untouchables' in society has inadvertently led to a reinforcement of caste system allegiances. **RK**

See also colonialism and neocolonialism; ethnicity; race; structuralism.

Further reading B.S. Cohn, *Structure and Change in Indian Society*; Ron Inden, *Imagining India*; M.N. Srinivas, *Caste in Modern India and Other Essays.*

CASTRATION ANXIETY

Castration anxiety or complex is what makes the **Oedipal** stage of development, as described by Sigmund Freud, so intolerable. In Freudian analysis there are only two complexes, the Castration Complex and the Oedipal Complex. In the Oedipal stage, which happens roughly between the ages of 3 and 5 years, the child desires the opposite-sex parent and wishes to kill the same-sex parent. The boy-child at this stage is also aware of his father's penis (phallic stage) and is afraid of his superior size and power. He also knows that girls (his mother and sisters) do not have penises. There therefore seems to be a possibility that he could lose his. This is the castration anxiety, and it becomes so acute that all sexual thought and feelings are repressed to overcome this unbearable state. Freud saw this intense rivalry and fear of the father as a colossal psychic event, which forced the boy's sexuality into latency and simultaneously created the moral agency in the psyche, the Superego.

The events that lead to castration anxiety in the boy are not identical for the girl because of her different anatomy. Freud thought that when little girls observe their fathers' and brothers' penises they think that they have already been castrated. Their anxiety is therefore a state of resentment and envy called 'penis envy'. This resentment is directed at the girl's mother, according to Freud, and the girl compensates for this loss by wishing to have a baby by her father and thereby comes into Oedipal conflict with him. In this way the Oedipal pattern, and its consequences, latency and the development of the Superego, are set up in the girl-child. Basing these ideas about female sexuality on only a handful of cases, Freud concluded from the pattern of female Oedipal development that women have a weaker Superego and a weaker moral sense than men, and that 'anatomy is destiny'. This position was opposed by later psychotherapists. **MJ**

CATALYSTS

A catalyst (Greek, 'looser') is a substance which changes the speed of a chemical reaction without being changed or consumed in the reaction. Many substances act as catalysts, for example platinum silver and oxides such as vanadium pentoxide.

The application of catalysts in industry is enormous. One of the first uses of a catalyst was the use of iron ore magnetite to combine hydrogen and nitrogen to produce ammonia on an economical scale. The addition of this catalyst meant that hydrogen and nitrogen could now be combined using less energy than before, which in turn led to the process of an economic product.

Since the catalyst does not take part in the chemical reaction, it is only the surface area that does the work in speeding up the reaction. It is therefore important to expose as much of the surface area as possible, especially with precious metals such as platinum. This surface area can become 'poisoned' and therefore makes the catalyst less effective with use.

Catalysts are found in living organisms and are known as **enzymes**, which break down organic material. Enzymes are used to digest food, make food and beverages and are also used in the pharmaceutical industry. **AA**

CATEGORICAL IMPERATIVES see
Morality

CATEGORY THEORY

As modern **algebra** developed, mathematicians began to realize that the theorems proved in different branches were often very similar to each other. Category theory is the branch of algebra which studies these common properties of algebraic objects. A category consists of two objects: a class of underlying objects (such as **fields**, **groups** or **rings**) and a class of **functions** between these objects (such as group homomorphisms – those functions between one group and another which preserve multiplication). The reason that these notions have a great deal of generality about them is because they are designed to reflect the common elements between disparate branches of mathematics. The results that can be obtained by the use of category theory are powerful, because of their generality, but they are also very difficult, precisely because they are so general. **SMcL**

See also abstraction.

Further reading S. Maclane, *Categories for the Working Mathematician*.

CATHARSIS

One of the most contentious concepts used in **drama** and **theatre**, catharsis ('purgation') is a term used by Aristotle in his discussion of how **tragedy** works in his *Poetics*. His suggestion that tragedy 'through pity and fear purges such emotions' is generally assumed to refer to the sense of emotional release and satisfaction that accompanies the resolution of a tragic action, though the exact meaning has been hotly disputed. **TRG SS**

CATHOLIC POLITICAL THOUGHT

Catholic political thought has profoundly affected the development of Western political institutions. The systematization of Roman Catholic canon law from the 12th to the 15th centuries and its interpretation during the Middle Ages and after especially influenced the development of Western liberal constitutional and legal traditions. The canonists originated the systematic application of universal moral codes to legal questions, and were directly responsible for clarifying how constitutional monarchy, secular authority, elections, corporate bodies and consent could and should operate within a system of natural (as opposed to divine) law, and they were indirectly responsible for developing the idea of **sovereignty**. Even the idea of 'subsidiarity', the maxim that decisions should be carried out at the most appropriate level in the organizational hierarchy, is owed to the Catholic schoolmen. The synthesis of **Aristotelian** ideas and **Christian** revelation carried out by St Thomas Aquinas (1225–74) was the apogee of medieval Catholic thought. Aquinas argued that states had positive roles to play, not simply in preventing war, but as expressions of divine providence; politics could and should be guided by Christian ethics.

The primary changes in Catholic political thought since medieval times reflect the transformation of the relationship between the church hierarchy and the temporal authorities. The internal struggle between conciliarism and papalism represented reformist challenges to the church's authority. Conciliarism emerged as a means of solving the Great Schism in the early 15th century. However, papal supremacy returned following the crises of the Protestant Reformation. In the post-reformation era, following the Treaty of Westphalia, the partial restoration of Catholic influence in Europe led to a renewed challenge to papalism by the Gallican and Jansenist movements in 17th-and 18th-century France. The conciliarist challenge to papal absolutism was aided by the French Revolution after which Napoleon concluded a concordat with Pope Pius VII in 1801 in which the state assumed ultimate control over church property and administration.

In the 19th century, within the diminished temporal realm of the Vatican, papalism regained the ascendancy under Pius IX, who restated the doctrine of papal infallibility, and denounced socialism, non-denominational education and civil marriage and other products of democratic and secular political thought in the *Syllabus of Errors* (1864). However, a more modernist approach was articulated by some Catholic **corporatists** towards the end of the century, who recognized the need for the Church to adapt to **industrial society**, **democracy** and class conflict. Authoritarian Catholicism consolidated its position during the interwar years when key figures seemed to embrace the same conservative, anti-republican, anti-communist doctrines which gave rise to fascism in Italy, Germany and Austria. However, the tacit acceptance of the early fascist movements discredited the church when the excesses of the Nazi régime were made public. Once again, a crisis of legitimacy undermined papal authoritarianism and a new era of conciliarism emerged under the Second Vatican Council of Pope John XXIII and his successor Paul VI. The Second Vatican

Council (1963–5) represented not only a return to conciliarism within the church but also a significant liberalization of church doctrine from one of doctrinal absolutism to relativism, advocating ecumenism, subjective morality, a liberalization of the liturgy and the legitimacy of theological dissent; moreover Catholics now clearly accepted democratic and some types of socialist politics.

The new theology was a recognition of the declining acceptance of Catholicism's legitimacy as the universal Christian church. The influence of modern Catholic political thought within a given society is affected mainly by two factors: the level of modernization (or secularization) and the strength of competing ideologies or religions. But whatever their impact might be Catholics increasingly develop their political thinking under the influence of local and secular politics rather than papal or canonist influences. **BO'L**

Further reading J.H. Berman, *Law and Revolution: the Formation of the Western Legal Tradition*; N. Novak, *Catholic Social Thought and Liberal Institutions: Freedom with Justice*; W. Ullmann *Medieval Papalism: the Political Theories of the Medieval Canonists*.

CATHOLICISM

As with the **Orthodox** Christian Churches and some **Anglican** Churches, the Church of Rome claims to be the only true and universal church. In Vatican Council decrees, therefore, it calls itself 'the Holy, Catholic, Apostolic, Roman Church'. 'Catholic' (from which the term 'Catholicism' derives) means 'all-embracing, universal'. The present-day Roman Catholic Church is a world organization that, despite subtle variations from country to country, has the same basic structure, forms of worship and theological beliefs throughout the world. The words 'catholic' and 'catholicism' have also come to have a narrower, more sectarian (see **sect/sectarianism**) connotation, so that in the Lutheran churches, we find the phrase in the Nicene Creed, 'I believe in the holy, catholic and apostolic Church'. To confuse matters further, a *Catholicos* is a bishop of metropolitan rank in the Orthodox Churches.

Organization of the Roman Catholic Church, modelled on the colonial administration of the late Roman Empire, is both regional and territorial, being in the form of parishes grouped into dioceses, and then into archdioceses. A continuous line of bishops stretches back to the 1st century. The claims of the see of Rome are based on the tradition, not without historical foundation, that Peter and Paul were martyred there. That the pope could not err when speaking *ex cathedra* (i.e. from his throne in St Peter's cathedral, Rome) was popular belief since the Middle Ages, and was formally decreed in 1870. In controversy with the Orthodox since 1054 (when the pope excommunicated the patriarch of Constantinople) and with Protestant leaders, the Catholic Church is also held to be infallible.

Other distinctive features of Catholicism, apart from its claims to universality, undisputed authority and highly centralized episcopal government, are its **ecclesiology**, **Mariology** and doctrine of the real presence of Christ in the bread and wine at the Eucharist (**sacraments**). There is, also, a threefold ministry of bishops, priests and deacons, and since the 5th century, celibacy has been strictly enforced.

Because the Catholic Church expanded throughout Europe through the work of religious orders (who preserved civilization in the West in the so-called 'Dark Ages'), religious life has been highly esteemed, whether in communities of monks or nuns, as individual hermits grouped around a particular centre, or as individual consecration to follow a Rule while living in the world ('tertiaries'). This has led to the cult of innumerable saints. In modern times, Catholic theologians have been at the forefront of the **liberation theology** and **feminist theology** movements, while in many Third World countries the Catholic Church has moved from being a champion of the political status quo to a defender of human rights. **EMJ**

See also Catholic political thought.

Further reading Hans Küng, *Infallible?*.

CAUSAL THEORIES

Philosophers have given causal theories of various concepts, including the concept of action, knowledge and memory. The causal theory of action states that a movement of a subject's body (or an event in a subject's mind) is an action if and only if it is caused by an appropriate intention of theirs. So the movement of my arm is an action if and only if it is caused by an appropriate intention of mine, such as an intention to wave. The causal theory of knowledge states that a subject's belief counts as knowledge if and only if it is caused by that which makes it true. I know that it is raining if and only if my belief that it is raining is caused by that which makes it true – its raining. **AJ**

See also action; causation; knowledge; memory; perception.

Further reading S. Davis, *Causal Theories of Mind.*

CAUSATION

Certain events cause, or bring about others. But what is it for one event to cause another?

Some have attempted to explain the notion of causation in terms of constant conjunction. An event of one kind is said to cause an event of another just if all events of the first kind are constantly conjoined with events of the second. So, for example, lighting the match in the room full of gas caused the explosion because every event of the first kind – every lighting of a match in a room full of gas – is accompanied by an event of the second kind – by an explosion.

Others have attempted to explain the notion of causation in terms of counterfactuals. Given that two events actually occurred, then the first caused the second just if, counter to fact, the first event had not occurred, then the second would not have occurred either. For example, the lighting of a match in a room full of gas and an explosion actually occurred; the first caused the second because if, counter to fact, the match had not been lit, the explosion would not have occurred.

The counterfactual account of causation has the advantage that, unlike the account in terms of constant conjunction, it can allow that not all causes determine their effects. Smoking 20 cigarettes a day caused Tina to get lung cancer. But smoking 20 a day merely raises the probability, and does not determine, that one will get lung cancer. The constant conjunction account wrongly implies that smoking 20 a day did not cause Tina to get lung cancer, because smoking that many is not constantly conjoined with lung cancer. Not everyone who smokes that much gets lung cancer. In contrast, the counterfactual account correctly implies that smoking 20 a day did cause Tina to get lung cancer. For if, contrary to fact, Tina had not smoked, then she would not have got lung cancer.

However, while the counterfactual account can allow that some causes merely raise the probability of their effects, it faces other problems. One problem concerns overdetermination. Suppose that two assassins simultaneously score direct hits on the president's brain. Then his death is causally overdetermined. There were two independent causes – the first assassin's firing his gun and the second assassin's firing hers – each of which was causally sufficient for the death. So the first assassin's firing of his gun did cause the death. But if, counter to fact, the first assassin had not fired his gun, the president would still have died, because the second assassin would nevertheless have fired hers. The counterfactual account of causation thus seems to fail to accommodate cases of causal overdetermination. **AJ**

See also event.

Further reading D. Owens, *Causes and Coincidences*; R. Sosa (ed.), *Causation and Conditionals.*

CELL BIOLOGY

Cell biology is the study of the **physiology** of the cell and of its interactions with its environment. The interaction of a cell type with its neighbours and with the whole body of an organism is an important aspect. Some of the most extensively studied cell types are the lymphocytes, which are responsible for the cell-mediated immune response. Other cell types have been the focus of attention in cell biology because of peculiar characteristics or specializations: thus much work on nerve-cell biology has been performed on giant squid axons and work on cell behaviour has often concentrated on motile cells such as amoeba. **RB**

See also cytology; cytopathology; endocrinology; protozoology.

Further reading Stephen Wolfe, *Biology of the Cell*.

CELTIC REVIVAL

The revival of interest in Celtic literature began in the 18th century, when the Scots poet James Macpherson published poems purporting to be by a previously unknown bard, Ossian. They attracted huge attention and led to the publication of other Celtic material, both real (such as the *Mabinogion* and the Irish legends of Cuchulain) and imaginary (Tennyson's *Idylls of the King*). A chair of Celtic Literature was created at Oxford, the *eisteddfod* tradition was reinvigorated in Wales, and a scheme was projected to gather and publish all surviving Celtic stories and legends, much as the *Kalevala* collection in Finland had 'rescued' Nordic material. In 1893, W.B. Yeats published a set of folk-based stories and poems called *The Celtic Twilight*, and non-devotees of the movement fell on it as a name for the whole fey school.

In **music**, the Celtic revival involved figures as disparate as Mendelssohn (whose *Fingal's Cave* caught the mood as early as the 1830s) and Arnold Bax (an Englishman who wrote tone poems on Cornish and Irish themes), as well as such real Celts as Charles Villiers Stanford and Hamish McCunn. In the 20th century, true ethnographical and anthropological research has tended to sweep away the mists, and the whimsy has lingered on chiefly in such works as the musicals *Brigadoon* and *Finian's Rainbow*, and the acerbic comedies of Compton Mackenzie, especially *Whisky Galore*, and Eric Linklater. **KMcL**

CENTRAL BANK

A central bank acts as a banker to the commercial banking system and often to the government as well. It is usually a government-owned and operated institution that controls the banking system and is the sole authority for issuing money.

Every country has a central bank, or shares one (for example, in the French African Community). In the United States it is the Federal Reserve, in the UK the Bank of England, in Germany the Bundesbank and in Japan the Bank of Japan. Central banks stand uncomfortably at the point where **fiscal policy** and monetary control meet, ensuring that the government has the finances to meet its bills, and serving the public debt that results. Central banks have little or no control of fiscal policy; but they do operate monetary policy and oversee the financial system. The role of the central bank may be divided into four areas:

(1) As banker to the government. Public expenditure on goods and services typically accounts for 40% of gross domestic product (and more if transfer payments are included). A government deposits its revenues and reserve currencies with the central bank and pays its bills with central bank cheques. The central bank typically charges the government a fee for acting as its bank: this is one of its major sources of revenue.

(2) As banker to the banks. The central bank takes deposits from banks and lends to them. This function helps the central bank to control the supply of money, but also helps it to maintain the stability of the financial system. The central bank acts as lender of last resort, that is, it stands ready to provide any bank with cash should it be in difficulty, or if its customers want to withdraw their deposits. This safety net enables banks to borrow short and lend long, without losing sleep over it. Often central banks control bank lending by setting a fixed proportion of deposits that must be deposited at the central bank.

(3) As supervisor of the banks. Central banks usually have a say over who can operate as a bank or take the public's deposits. They regularly check the banks'

balance sheets and, either by law or by gentle persuasion, force financial institutions to toe the line.

(4) Issuing currency, and offering a guiding hand in foreign exchange markets. Designing, printing, issuing and withdrawing notes (and often coins as well) is the job of the central bank. In consultation with the government, and with other central banks, the central bank intervenes in currency markets to smooth fluctuation or to protect a target value. Central banks can also nudge currencies either way by shifting interest rates up or down relative to those prevailing in other countries. **TF**

CENTRALLY PLANNED ECONOMY

A centrally planned economy is one in which basic economic decisions are made by public authorities rather than by private persons. The key decisions involve investment in plant and equipment; this determines what will be produced. Other decisions usually include how to combine resources and how to distribute the product to households. The productive facilities (natural resources and capital) are held and controlled by the state rather than owned and controlled by private persons.

Central planning is a characteristic of **socialist** and **communist** economies. In theory, it could be more rational and equitable than the marketplace, but in practice it has always yielded inefficiency, a slothful **bureaucracy** and little incentive to work hard or innovate. In the People's Republic of China, for example, drawbacks in central planning have led the authorities to experiment with a compromise of free market dilutions, which have created specific geographic regions where free markets are allowed to operate and flourish.

The former USSR and the eastern European countries once under its influence operated under centrally planned economies. They began to introduce market direction of production in the 1970s on a very small scale, to try to overcome inefficiencies in their central planning. The struggle for change intensified in 1989 and 1990 with the peaceable overthrow of Communist governments in eastern Europe.

This is the first time in history that there has been a shift from a centrally planned economy to that of a market economy. There are competing schools of thought of what is the best route to achieve this transition. Current results have been shaky at best and at a high political cost. **TF**

See also capitalism; mixed economy.

CERTAINTY, INDUBITABILITY AND INCORRIGIBILITY

The passengers were certain, in the sense of feeling sure, that the plane would crash. But it did not. So certainty, in the sense of feeling sure, does not entail truth and, therefore, does not guarantee knowledge. The passengers felt sure that the plane would crash, but it wasn't true that the plane would crash and (since knowledge requires truth) the passengers did not know that it would. Philosophers often use the word 'certain' not in the sense of feeling sure, but in the sense of being indubitable, or in the sense of being incorrigible.

It is, for me, indubitable that I exist. I cannot doubt that I exist. (Similarly, it is, for you, indubitable that you exist.) So I am certain that I exist, not merely in the sense of feeling sure, but also in the sense that I cannot doubt that I exist. My evidence for the supposition that I exist – that I feel hot, or am trying to doubt that I exist – excludes the possibility that I do not exist. So I cannot doubt that I exist. The passengers in the plane felt sure that it would crash, but their evidence – the sudden lurching and the strange noise from one of the engines – did not exclude the possibility that it would crash. And, indeed, it did not. The passengers could doubt that the plane would crash and so, in this stronger sense, they were not certain that it would.

Another sense of the word 'certain' is being incorrigible. A statement is incorrigible just if it is such that, if someone believes it, then it is impossible for their belief to be false. Consider the statement 'I exist'. If someone believes that they exist, then they exist: it is impossible for someone falsely to believe that they exist.

We have already seen that certainty, in the sense of feeling sure, is insufficient for does not guarantee knowledge. Certainty, in each of the senses of indubitability and incorrigibility, does suffice for knowledge. If I cannot doubt that one of my beliefs is true, then my belief counts as knowledge. If a statement is incorrigible, and I believe it, then I know it. Some have supposed that certainty in one or other of these senses is also necessary for knowledge that a belief cannot count as knowledge unless it is indubitably true and incorrigible. Given that so little is indubitable or incorrigible, this claim has the sceptical consequence that we know almost nothing. **AJ**

See also belief; epistemology; knowledge; scepticism.

Further reading B. Williams, *Descartes*.

CHAMBER MUSIC

Chamber music (from Italian *camera*, 'room'), in European art music, uses substantial intellectual forms with small forces: string quartets instead of symphonies, sonatas or trios instead of concertos, *lieder* and other kinds of 'art song' instead of **opera**. By its nature, chamber music adds intimacy to intellectual density. This has, however, not prevented it from becoming a major concert form, played by virtuosi – much of it is beyond the ability of most amateurs in large concert halls just as often as in recital rooms. **KMcL**

CHANGE

Human beings are not the only inquisitive creatures in the world. Puzzlement and the urge to investigate are commonplace. It is what happens next that makes our case unique. Other animals satisfy their curiosity, and that is an end of it. When the same events happen again, they will be inquisitive again, and satisfied again. Their curiosity is part of the hunting instinct, and needs little or no intellectuality.

Human curiosity, by contrast, involves ratiocination – reflection, consideration, comparison, memory – and it often leads to creativity. As a species, we are seldom satisfied with the status quo for long. When we accept it, our acceptance is not instinctive but one choice from a range of options, an exercise of judgement. And we are quickly bored. The stimulus of change is essential to our mental well-being, and we ceaselessly strive either to bring it about or to make the choice to leave things as they are – where choice is involved, repetition is, each time, a form of change. There are no human activities which have not engaged our curious interest, and roused our eagerness for change. Even such instinctive quests as for food, shelter and reproduction are subject to incessant variation, and when it comes to such matters as social organization or **belief**, the difference between us and other animals, a difference created solely by our need for change, is overwhelmingly apparent. Other creatures have no need of fashion or **style**; they never establish or react to traditions (their behaviour patterns are instinctive); they create nothing (a weaver-bird's nest is not 'created' in the way a skyscraper or a tragedy is 'created'); they neither imagine nor criticize.

If the necessity to change things is one of the glories of humanity, it is also our curse. Throughout history (itself a continuum of change) the urge for change has led as often to destruction as to creation, and we may well end up changing ourselves and our planet until we exterminate ourselves. This thought has prompted many people to pursue such activities as introspection, meditation, or cries for help to non-human agencies and powers, real or imagined – and each of these activities is another facet of our dissatisfaction, our need for change: in short, of the unchanging human intellectual condition. **KMcL**

CHAOS THEORY

For almost all of its history, **applied mathematics** has been concerned with the solution of linear differential equations; most physical phenomena seemed to be approximately governed by such equations (see **linearity**). In such systems, the effect of a small change to the initial conditions makes only a small change to the system as a whole (for example, moving a snooker ball one millimetre makes little difference to the position in which it comes to rest after being struck by the cue-ball – all other things being equal).

However, during the 1970s and 1980s it gradually became apparent that for many systems (in particular, the Earth's weather), linear differential equations would not adequately model the system, particularly for some initial conditions. So attention was shifted to the use of non-linear differential equations, which predicted that small changes in the original conditions could sometimes make vast differences to the system. The famous example of this is that of a butterfly fluttering its wings and thereby causing a hurricane on the other side of the globe. (This does not, of course, happen every time a butterfly flutters its wings; it must be in exactly the right place at exactly the right time.)

The difficulty in this approach is that practically no non-linear equations can be solved with the methods of **analysis**. This has meant that the only way solutions can be found is through the use of computers that work out the effect of the equations over very short periods of time, and find approximate solutions. This has to be done very quickly, which means that computer scientists working in chaos theory are often pressing right up against the limits of the machines and software available today.

At the time of writing (early 1990s), chaos theory remains somewhat esoteric, of more significance in computing, mathematics and the physical sciences than in the world at large. There are signs, however, that it is beginning to make a mark in the **arts**, as part of the new pluralism of **postmodernism**. In the 1980s, artistic creators of all kinds began to explore the idea that chaos theory provided a rationale by which artists, instead of trying to impose order and structure, could exploit the random and unexpected. Examples range from the work of Boulez and his assistants at IRCAM (blending randomness with strict musical serialism) to improvised comedy in the theatre (where there was a huge 1990s upsurge throughout the Western world), from 'computer poetry' (in which the 'poet' programs the computer to create random word-patterns, and then selects from the results) to the work of such architects as Isozaki and Kuramata in Japan and Frank Gehry in California.

Work on the chaos theory and its implications is advancing so fast that it is impossible to predict future developments indeed to predict anything except that predictions and descriptions of the current state of the theory will be out of date almost as soon as made. **KMcL SMcL**

CHARACTER

Character is derived from the Greek word for the impression made in wax by a sealstone or seal-ring. This primary meaning is still used in typography and computing, where a 'character' is a mark with a single meaning, which can be varied only if it is modified in some way, or associated with another mark or marks. (Thus, *a* has a different significance from A or a; 1 is different from -1 or 11.)

In ancient Greek philosophy, the word 'character' came to have a second meaning: the 'stamp' of personality each of us possesses, as if we were wax imprinted by the gods or by circumstance. Greek philosophers used to teach about human nature by describing 'characters' of this kind, what we might think of (again, using an image from printing) as 'stereotypes'. The best-known surviving work of this kind is Theophrastos' *Characters* (3rd century BCE), which today is read less for its philosophical content than for its lively, witty descriptions of such marketplace personalities as the Bore, the Superstitious Person, the Gossip or the Boaster.

In medieval Europe, people often defined character as the results, in a person, of the pull of opposing forces – those of good and evil, or God and the Devil. This was an unconscious parallel to the Greek idea that characters were stamped on us at birth by the gods, but it also allowed the possibility of variation and change, as one resisted or accepted a particular kind of pull. In **literature**, writers followed this idea or played with the proposition (from **alchemy**) that all substances were a blend of earth, air, fire and water. The theory of 'humours' (best known in Britain from its use by Ben Jonson, but common in all European literature of the Middle Ages and Renaissance) says that human types are all blended from those four elements and seldom depart from them – a gift to **comedy** in particular.

In modern times, character has been explained more in psychological terms (particularly Freud's theories). In fiction, opaqueness and latency of character – anathema to earlier writers – have become important resources, and part of the enjoyment of much modern literature and **drama** is finding a character that develops or reveals himself or herself as the work proceeds. Some modern literature, for example the novels of Samuel Beckett and Franz Kafka, and many of the plays of the **theatre of the absurd**, have even centred on 'characters' who have no character at all. In terms of the original meaning of the word, this is a spectacular and creatively useful **irony**. KMcL

CHARACTER ANALYSIS

Character Analysis is one of the main concepts developed by Wilhelm Reich (1897–1957), who brought together in his work the theories of **psychoanalysis** and **Marxism**. Character traits, according to Reich, were the physical symptoms that the patient brought into therapy. The character was formed as a result of resistances to sexual (genital) longings and prohibitions. The **ego** or character armour had to be dissolved for the sexual person to emerge; Reich believed that if you cure the body the mind will follow.

Reich was able to identify symptoms, resistances and character traits as sharing the same source and mechanism. By retaining Freud's original concept of sexual **libido** as life's sole driving instinct, he supported a pan-sexual view of human nature. For Reich the Pleasure Principle was all; sexual energy and frustration explained all human neuroses. **Anxiety** arose from sexual frustration and aggression was a rechannelling of the libido. He disliked Freud's distinction between genitality and pre-genitality, and regarded the former as the only true sexuality. Fantasies during sex were regarded as abnormalities – he propounded the need to experience fantasy-free orgasmic potency. He disagreed with the idea of sublimation and thought creativity to be syn-

onymous with an uninhibited sexual life. Reich did eventually add Thanatos, the **death instinct**, and a return to the inert state as the other, opposite driving force.

Reich's writings attempted to show that psychoanalysis had a dialectical materialist nature and could be called a science in that sense. He wanted the social revolution to facilitate the sexual revolution.

Reich also conducted a search for the tangible source of life's energies. His resulting Orgonomic therapy was aimed at dissolving the musculature armature in a systematic way. He saw the body as divided into segments (like a worm) and said that his task was to release each section in turn so that life energies could be restored. **MJ**

Further reading Wilhelm Reich, *Character Analysis*; Charles Rycroft, *Reich*.

CHARACTER DANCE

The term character dance is used to describe all dance which is neither **ballet** nor ballroom, such as folk dance, religious dance, soft-shoe and other vaudeville dance, traditional dance and eccentric dance in **comedy**. In ballet, character dancers often appear in *divertissements*: displays of virtuosity lateral to the main action of the ballet, for example the suite of national dances in Tchaikovsky's *The Nutcracker* is typical. **KMcL**

CHARISMA

Charisma is a theological term (originally Greek) meaning 'gift of grace'. In a religious context it refers to individuals or groups of believers who claim to possess special powers.

Within **sociology** it is used to refer to the special qualities and powers claimed by, and attributed to an individual, making him or her capable of influencing large numbers of people who become followers. The charismatic leader may be a religious or a political leader.

Charismatic authority is one of three types of legitimate **authority** identified by Weber. Charisma refers to the authority vested in a leader by disciples and followers by virtue of a belief that the leader possesses special powers and extraordinary personal gifts. It is a form of authority which is based on an affective and emotional commitment to a leader. The authority of a charismatic leader may transcend existing authority. **DA**

See also church; power; religion; sect; social control; social movements.

Further reading R. Bendix, *Max Weber: an Intellectual Portrait*; R. Wallis (ed.), *Millennialism and Charisma*.

CHARITY

'Charity' is how the King James translation of the Bible renders the Latin word *caritas*, itself a considered, Biblical translation of the Greek word *agapé*. In Latin *caritas* is one of several words denoting 'love' of different kinds, and the distinctions between them greatly occupied the attention of medieval Christian scholars. Essentially, *caritas* was seen as a form of love untainted (as others were) with fleshly longings of any kind: it was the love God felt for humans, and which humans in return should aspire to feel for God and for all God's creation. It was not the same as love of country, love of virtue, or love of love itself. It was unselfconscious, altruistic and inspirational. Of the three pillars of Christian belief and practice declared by St Paul, faith, hope and 'charity', it was, in his word, the 'greatest'.

Having defined charity, Christian exegetists next went on to consider how it should be shown. Their conclusion was that human charity should model God's, who 'so loved the world that he gave his only begotten son...'. The giving which arises from love was not charity itself, but a product of charity. Nonetheless, this narrowing and crudifying of the meaning of the word became standard, and is now universal. Because we feel charitable, we give to those in need. In this sense, charity is close to *zakat*, the almsgiving which is the third of the five pillars of **Islam** (usually involving devout Muslims in giving 2.5% of their annual income to the poor); the difference is that *zakat* is a sacred obligation, whereas charity is not. In **Buddhism** almsgiving is also common, but here it is to support monks and nuns, and is regarded by most donors as a privilege rather than an obligation.

Secular forms of charity (in the sense of helping those less fortunate than oneself) sometimes take us into dark areas of motivation, conscience and guilt. Often, charity-giving is institutionalized: we prefer to give goods or money for others to disburse on our behalf, than to hand them over directly. In capitalist societies, charity has often been seen as a supplement to or replacement of the Welfare State, the so-called 'trickle-down' of wealth symbolizing a society 'at ease with itself'. In socialist societies, charity is often seen as unnecessary: in a state in which each contributes according to ability and receives according to need, the concept of 'charity', and the personal altruism of which it is a consequence, have no meaning. In the present-day politics of First and **Third Worlds**, 'charity' is often a hated concept, thought to contain overtones of patronage and **imperialism**, and to override ideas of equality and natural justice. In all such attitudes, we seem to have moved a long way from the original meaning of the word; is one right to infer, as some social anthropologists do, that 'conscience' and 'altruism' are not innate human qualities, and need some kind of **objective correlative**, some external imperative, if they are to work at all? **KMcL**

CHARIVARI

Charivari (from French *charivariser*, 'to deride') is a worldwide phenomenon, known also as *chiassio* ('uproar'), *katzenmusik* ('caterwauling'), 'rough music' and 'shivaree'. It consists of making a discordant racket with anything that comes to hand, such as kitchen utensils, sticks and stones, as well as the voice or the whistle. Originally intended to show possibly hostile supernatural powers that the people so derided were not worth attention, it was a popular accompaniment to wedding processions, harvest festivals and the like. It was and is also used to heap ridicule on people disapproved of by the community. For example, adulterers in the Appalachians in the USA and in Kenya were so treated.

Charivari was one of the accompaniments to the Dionysian processions from which Greek **comedy** (and hence all later Western comedy) originated. It is still standard in some Far Eastern religious practices, such as the celebrations of the Chinese New Year or Indonesian devil-exorcism, and is an integral part of voodoo ritual. In the West, a vestigial echo can be seen in the ribald hullabaloo which often accompanies a young man's 'stag night'. **KMcL**

CHASIDIM/HASIDIM

The Chasidic movement was established in the 18th century, in Eastern Europe, and should not be confused with a party of the same name who restored the Torah in Israel during the Maccabaean revolt (2nd century BCE). Its founder, Israel ben Eliezer, the Ba'al Shem Tov, ('Master of the Good Name', 1700–60), stressed the sincere and joyful performance of the commandments above the learning which was the usual source of religious prestige at the time. Although early Chasidim were criticized by their contemporaries for laxity in observance, innovations in prayer and study and alleged magical powers, their present-day successors are known for their stringency and conservative lifestyle. The Chasidim popularized mystic teachings which until then had been the preserve of small groups of initiates. Rabbi Dov Baer, the Maggid ('preacher') of Mezritch (1772–1827), was persuaded to join the movement, beginning a tradition of wandering charismatic preachers, but the strength of the movement was the belief in *saddikim* ('the proven ones' or 'righteous ones'), leaders who were like spiritual directors, mystics who could guide their followers and develop their spiritual powers. They were attacked for assuming the powers of mediators between God and ordinary people. As it developed, the movement split into local groups, each with a *rebbe*, who was revered as a leader, and perhaps as a miracle worker, another source of concern to their more rationalist critics.

Teacher-disciple rabbinic succession developed. Today, the best-known Chasidic dynasty is Lubavitch. The name derives from the small village in the south of Russia where their first *rebbe*, Scheur Zalman (1745–1813), came from. Based in New York since 1917, with a charismatic and saintly leader many regard as the Messiah, they actively seek to draw all Jews into stricter observance of the commandments and pursuits of wisdom and understanding. The movement is becoming so successful in so many countries that it has been compared with the Christian revival movements. They have always encouraged the Return to Israel. **RM**

Further reading H. Rabinowincz, *Hasidim and the State of Israel;* P. Signal, *Judaism; the Evolution of a Faith.*

CHAUVINISM see Prejudice

CHEMICAL COMPOUNDS

Chemical elements are usually never found in a pure state, but are generally combined with other elements and mixed with many others. The elements are linked together by means of chemical bonds. This bonding is haphazard but corresponds to the atomic structure of each element.

The ability of any atom to combine is determined by the number of electrons that occur in the atom's outer shell. If this outer shell is not full, the atom will try to attach itself to another atom in order to become stable. The 'inert gases' such as neon and krypton are stable since their outer shell has a full complement of eight electrons, not allowing interaction with other elements.

Since eight electrons give stability and a lack of structure with which to combine, the atoms with seven electrons will try to 'borrow' an electron from an atom which has one more than eight. Both atoms become stable as the electron from one has been 'borrowed' by the other, and so both now have eight electrons in their outer orbits. Two such atoms are sodium, which has only one electron in its outer shell, and fluorine which has seven; these readily combine to form a stable compound, sodium fluoride, where the two elements in the process of borrowing and giving now have the full quota of electrons in their respective outer shells.

Hydrogen atoms have one electron orbiting the nucleus and do not occur singly (except as short-lived intermediates during some chemical reactions or at high temperatures), but consist of molecules each having two hydrogen atoms joined together. This means that the molecule has now two electrons in the shared outer shell.

Since electrons carry a negative charge, an atom with too many electrons becomes a negative ion and too few a positive ion. Positive and negative ions combine in compounds to cancel each other out, so giving overall neutrality. Not all atoms ionize to form compounds but some, especially organic compounds, share electrons in covalent bonds and remain electrically neutral. **AA**

See also chemistry.

Further reading H.B. Gray, *Chemical Bonds*

CHEMISTRY

Modern chemistry has its origins in the practice of **alchemy**, which is over 6,000 years old. Alchemy was first practised in the Nile Delta, where it was discovered that the action of heat on minerals isolated the metal from the ore. Alchemy then spread throughout the Middle East and into Asia. One of its aims was to find the philosopher's stone which would convert base metals into the 'noble metal' gold. The philosopher's stone proved elusive, but the experimentation involved in trying to find it paved the way for modern chemistry. By the 12th century the availability of Arab writings on the subject of alchemy gradually led to the scientific study of chemical processes and reactions. With the publication of Robert Boyle's (1627–91) *Sceptical Chemist*, and his hypothesis that matter consisted of simple bodies, the science of chemistry was finally established.

During the 18th century various scientists, including Joseph Black and Henry Cavendish, began the systematic study of various elements and their compounds. Work by Antoine Lavoisier, the so-called founder of modern chemistry, demonstrated that any burning substance combines with oxygen. Among his other work Lavoisier undertook finally to separate alchemy and chemistry, by carrying out a wide-ranging series of experiments, and this is indeed what he achieved.

Lavoisier's new system was built on the concept of chemical elements, on which he derived a new nomenclature which scientists still use today. Once accepted, his theories gave chemists plenty to do. The introduction of John Dalton's atomic theory in the late 18th century made Lavoisier's theories even more exact; now that chemistry was logically based on sound principles, its progress was rapid.

Chemistry today can be broadly split into three main branches: *organic chemistry* (the study of carbon compounds) based originally on materials produced by living organisms, that is, bacteria, plants and animals; *inorganic chemistry* (the study of substances of mineral origin); and *physical chemistry*.

Because of the scarcity of some vegetable sources, and the variability of their quality, chemistry has been utilized to synthesize the complex molecules of some drugs. Originally 'synthetic' denoted a poor substitute but now it refers to the pure forms of drugs. The derogatory implication of 'synthetic' arose in the early use of fibrous manufacture from mineral oil bases. Nylon, being a simple fibre with little water absorption, could not reproduce the 'feel' of cotton and wool fabrics. Developments of new fabrics and changes in production of the fibres and methods of weaving now allow such desirable characteristics to be developed that 'synthetic' fibres are sometimes better than 'natural'.

In early civilization vegetable dyes were used to colour fabrics but the wide range of bright colours now used depends on a wide range synthesized from basic chemical materials. **AA**

See also catalysts; chemical compounds; metals and alloys; periodic table; science; scientific method.

CHICAGO SCHOOL

The Chicago School generally refers to social thought first developed at the University of Chicago in the 1920s and 1930s, particularly in the fields of **economics**, **sociology** and to a lesser degree **political science**.

In *economics*, the Chicago School, presently identified with writers like Gary Becker, Milton Friedman and George Stigler, is best known for its hostility to **Keynesian** economic policy, enthusiasm for monetarism and endorsement of *laissez faire* economics. Members of the Chicago School believe that economists should work with the assumption that individual behaviour is governed by rational decision-making (see **democracy**); make deductions based on this assumption; and test the merits of predictions based on this assumption. The predictions not the assumptions are open to testing. Exponents of the school have employed this method to topics previously considered outside the heartland of economics: like the demand and supply for marriage, crime and racism. The Chicago School has had an intermittent impact upon public policy, providing the back-up for New Right assaults on administrative discretion and the embracing of monetary policy as the sole means of controlling inflation. Today the doctrines of the School are looked on with a more sceptical eye in the UK and the US.

The Chicago School in *sociology* was influenced primarily by the work of Robert Park, Ernest Burgess and their colleagues who acted as mentors to a host of graduate students researching aspects of urban life in Chicago. They produced pioneering analyses of phenomena such as urban ecology, based on the application of behavioural studies of social process and symbolic interactionism.

The Chicago School of *political science* is primarily associated with the work of Charles E. Merriam and Harold Gosnell on political power, and especially voting behaviour. They drew heavily on the social psychological approach of Harold Laswell. The rigorous adaptation of political opinion polling and attitude surveys originated at Chicago, and represented the successful merger of methodological and conceptual approaches from **psychology**, sociology and economics. **BO'L**

See also behaviouralism.

Further reading M. Bulmer, *The Chicago School of Sociology*; M. and R. Friedman, *Capitalism and Freedom*; H. Simon, *Charles E. Merriam and the 'Chicago School' of Political Science*.

CHILD ABUSE

Abuse (Latin, 'counter-use') means making the wrong use of another person: reviling, ill-treating and violating them. It means the misuse of power within a relationship, and has become most strongly attached to the phenomenon of child abuse, the existence of which began to be more recognized as the social movements of the 1960s and the women's movement of the 1970s exerted an influence on **psychology**.

Freud, early in his career, acknowledged the existence of the sexual abuse of children. After analysing those of his women patients who were suffering from hysterical illnesses, he developed his seduction theory: that the symptoms were the result of these women having been seduced and molested as children, usually by their fathers or by family friends. The painful memory was avoided by being repressed and replaced instead by debilitating symptoms.

Freud abandoned this theory for three reasons. First, recollection of the sexual abuse did not usually relieve the symptoms. Second, he thought that childhood memory was unreliable. Third, he believed that the abuse happened too often to be plausible. He replaced the seduction theory with the idea that children fantasize rape in the Oedipal phase. Ferenczi, writing in his diary in the early 1930s, still privately believed that actual child abuse was a possibility, but it was not until the 1960s that therapists began once more to take the descriptions patients brought of child rape and abuse as recounts of real events.

Results of being sexually abused as a child are far-reaching and the effects can be inability to form intimacy, underlying anger, damage to self-esteem, self-abuse (such as drinking and taking drugs), and a deep sense of guilt and shame. If abused as a child, we can continue to allow others to abuse us or to be adult abusers ourselves –

an example of the way in which we carry both the child and parent we knew around in us as two aspects of ourselves. **MJ**

Further reading Alice Miller, *Banished Knowledge: Facing Childhood Injuries.*

CHILD ANALYSIS

Child Analysis was not conducted by Freud, even though he focused on childhood. His only child patient, 'Little Hans', was analysed through accounts given by the boy's father. The first analyst to conduct child analysis was Melanie Klein. Anna Freud later developed a varied technique for working with children.

The main differences in child analysis are that the parents and parent-figures are still actual external figures in the child's life, and not internalized parental figures. Children are really dependent, and so dependence is not a neurotic symptom for them. There is also a moral question involved, as the child does not give his or her consent.

In child analysis, play and toys replace **free association**. But it was only in this respect that Melanie Klein varied her approach between adults and children. She believed that even a 3-year-old child had a past which (like an adult) he or she lives in the present. Working in the Tavistock Clinic in London in the 1950s, Melanie Klein, D.W. Winnicot and Susan Isaacs developed the view that the infant's first object relationship to the mother is of vital importance. They were concerned with studying **psychosis** and located fixed points for this in the mother-child relationship.

Anna Freud, working with Dorothy Burlington, varied analytic technique with children. She shifted away from exploring psychic structures through studying neurosis and developed theories of normal and abnormal character structures. **MJ**

Further reading Melanie Klein, *Envy and Gratitude: a Study of Unconscious Sources.*

CHINESE REMAINDER THEOREM

This theorem, as the name suggests, is one of those known to Chinese mathematicians a long time before the West. It is closely related to the work of Euclid (*fl. c.*295 BCE) on number theory, and is usually proved with the use of Euclid's **algorithm**, though Euclid himself did not know the result. At first sight the theorem seems unlikely and counter-intuitive. It states that given any finite set of numbers with no factors in common (for instance, 3, 5, and 17) and another set of remainders (say, 2, 4 and 3) it is possible to find a number which leaves the first remainder when divided by the first number (here, remainder 2 when divided by 3), the second remainder when divided by the second number, and so on (here, such a number is 224). In fact, there are infinitely many such numbers, since adding the product of the original set of numbers ($3 \times 5 \times 17 = 255$) any number of times will give another number which works. **SMcL**

CHINOISERIE

Chinoiserie (French, 'Chinese-ing') denotes the influence of Chinese fine and applied art on European taste, especially during the 18th century. With the opening of trade routes by imperial powers like Great Britain and the Netherlands, Chinese ware became available in quantity for the first time in the West. The vogue for Chinese design particularly influenced interior furnishings, ceramics, architecture and landscape gardening. Chinoiserie properly refers not to Chinese artefacts, but to the products made by European manufacturers in emulation of the Chinese style, or by factories in the Far East which copied these European imitations. **MG PD**

Further reading H. Honour, *Chinoiserie: the Vision of Cathay.*

CHIVALRY

Chivalry (from French *chevalier*, 'horseman') was a system of values of considerable importance in the arts of medieval Europe and to some extent in aristocratic life as well. Its origins can be traced to the 8th century and the vows warriors made when they were accepted into Charlemagne's royal circle: to uphold the Christian church and the name of the Emperor, to defend the weak and challenge the strong, to avoid the **Seven Deadly Sins** and practise the **Seven Virtues**. In medieval literature and art, the distinction is often blurred between knights and saints: for example, St George is depicted as a knight vanquishing a dragon and rescuing a damsel, and Galahad as a saintly, even Christly, figure of purity with supernatural power. This blurring was particularly important, in real terms, at the time of the Crusades. It still promotes a misleadingly romantic image of the Crusades, which were, on the whole, no more than examples of violent adventurism and cultural **imperialism**.

The chivalric ideal inspired such medieval masterworks as the Grail and Arthur legend-cycles and the Roland epics. Its overspill into real life is apparent in the whole fabric of European feudal society, and in the constitution of many later European courts and aristocratic orders. Shakespeare's *Henry V*, and his English history plays in general, show how prevalent it was even in High **Renaissance** times. There was a somewhat pallid resurgence in 19th-century Europe, allied to the mock-medievalism of such people as Sir Walter Scott and the **Pre-Raphaelites**. Inchoate memories of chivalric ideas and behaviour haunt some of the rituals and practices of present-day aristocratic and establishment circles, both in Europe itself and in countries which were once European colonies or dependencies.

Very few value-systems are almost entirely invented by intellectuals and then taken over by real people as the basis of real behaviour and social culture. Chivalry's nearest parallel is, perhaps, the Japanese samurai code of *Bushido*, though that lacks the religious resonance which gave, and to some extent still gives, chivalric ideals such potency. **KMcL**

CHORUS

In ancient Greek **drama**, the chorus was a significant group of performers (usually 15 or 25), originally the main participants, whose singing and dancing played a major function in the production, either by commenting on or advancing the action of the major characters. Their performances took up between a third and a half of the total action, and contributed greatly to the mood and spectacle of the show as a whole. In later Western drama, the term was used to describe an individual who addresses the audience directly, often as a prologue, scene setter, or commentator on the action. Its most common contemporary usage is to describe a group of singers or dancers in **music theatre** who perform collectively. **TRG SS**

Further reading Oliver Taplin, *Greek Tragedy in Action*.

CHRISTIAN ART

Like all **religious art**, Christian art raises questions of purpose. Its original, and primary, functions were to aid devotion and to offer God the finest work a patron could commission or a craftsman or craftswoman could create. Aesthetic value was relevant, but by no means the most important factor: a plain wooden crucifix, or a scrawled outline on a wall, were just as effective as the most lavishly executed work of the finest artistic hands and minds. **Iconography** was more important than finish: the symbols contained in the work were what mattered, and devotional purpose outweighed anything which we might today recognize as artistic inspiration.

In most religions, art is a static phenomenon. Its styles and techniques were decided hundreds, even thousands, of years ago, and have changed little since. The art, like the symbols contained in it, is referential and eternal. But Christian art is different. From the very start it has mirrored the societies which created it, and although its symbols remain more or less the same, its appearance, styles and techniques have radically changed from century to century, country to country, almost artist to artist. This gives it a kind of richness different from the art of other religions, and has always made it particularly available to – or, depending on your point of view, the prey of – secular connoisseurs and commerce. It was a main focus for artistic and architectural patronage, productivity and development in the West and the orthodox East from the time of Christ himself until well into the 19th century, when encroaching secularism and consumerism (born of the Industrial Revolution) began to reduce its profile. (Even so, Christian iconography continued, and continues, to take its place in art, often in surprising ways – for example the use made of Christian symbols and of ideas parodied from earlier Christian artists by mid-20th century **Surrealists** or 1970s practitioners of '**junk art**'.) No one interested in Western art is therefore fully equipped without some knowledge of the Bible, of the iconographical traditions and transformations involved in the representation of its stories, and of Church ideas about the construction and furnishing of the House of God.

The transformation of iconography and form from the Graeco-Roman to Christianity was surprisingly smooth, no doubt because Graeco-Roman art was the natural model for Christians (themselves part of the same tradition) to adopt. Because the methodologies of Roman pagan art and architecture were adopted by the Christians (the emperor in triumph becomes Christ Triumphant, for example; the basilica becomes one layout for the church), the continuity between pagan and Christian is a long-lived strength, providing a repertoire upon which artists continue to draw.

We may view the adoption of pagan forms by Christian art alongside the transfer of power from the Roman emperor to the Papacy, in many ways its temporal as well as its spiritual successor. This provides one explanation for the bias towards continuity. An important element in the spread of Christian art is therefore the growing temporal power of the Church itself, and of monasteries, which grew in wealth and prestige during the Middle Ages. Piety (the attribute and practice needed to ensure the salvation of one's immortal soul) was paramount: building reflected not simply a desire to out-perform one's neighbours, but also to provide monuments to faith itself hence the 'age of the cathedrals'. Enormous buildings (often quite disproportionate to the size of the local population) were erected a process which often took several generations. Pilgrimage was an important medieval institution, and the routes to important sites (such as Rome and Santiago de Compostella) still boast their sumptuous shrines.

The Church, the monasteries and the pious laity were crucial in the provision of artistic patronage, which included everything from architecture, frescoes and monumental sculpture to Books of Hours, reliquaries, and souvenirs for pilgrims. Such structures long outlasted the Middle Ages, as chapels in the churches of Florence, Siena or Bavaria will attest.

The Reformation provided both a crisis and a fillip for Christian art and architecture. The Church of Rome commissioned buildings and decoration in an attempt (the Counter-Reformation) to stem the tide of Protestant propaganda. The reformers viewed 'catholic' iconography and power structures with contempt (witness the Wars of Religion, or the Commonwealth in England, both of which saw the destruction of much 'idolatrous' art). As a result, completely different styles of Protestant iconography were developed (for example, Rembrandt) which placed greater emphasis on the private reading of the Bible than on public demonstrations of faith.

The **Enlightenment**, at least in Protestant hands, provided a rational challenge to Christian art which decreased the apparent importance of the latter. Although it is probably not the case that the quantity of Christian art declined (as can be seen by the **Gothic Revival**, and the enormous number of devotional pictures and prints produced in 19th-century France), in our perception its relative importance declined before the onslaught of 19th-century positivism, itself a child of the Enlightenment. Courbet, for example, refused to paint what he could not see, and so never painted angels.

While there have been important revivals and commissions (many of them as a result of the devastation of two world wars), Christian art has now unquestionably lost its once-central position in the **hierarchy of genres**. **PD KMcL**

Further reading David F. Martin, *Art and the Religious Experience*.

CHRISTIAN DEMOCRACY

Originating in reaction to the 19th-century separation of church and state in Europe and Latin America, Christian **democracy** became an important political alignment in Europe only after World War II. As its name suggests it seeks to reconcile Christian values to liberal democracy, especially but not exclusively Catholic values. In practice Christian democracy has been an essentially centrist political movement, splitting the difference between the twin 'evils' of **socialist** collectivism and liberal individualism. The excesses of **fascism** and **communism**, and the outmoded nature of monarchical conservatism created a vacuum in western European politics which Christian Democratic parties were able to fill. They combined conservative, social welfare policies based on Christian family values in sexual, educational and cultural matters, with a progressive social welfare role for the state in health care, housing and industrial policy. Unlike economic liberals Christian democrats have been willing to work with trade unions in **corporatist** policy-making. The Christian Democratic parties have also historically been the most supportive of European integration.

The fortunes of Christian Democratic parties in Western Europe since World War II have followed a cyclical pattern broadly related to swings in class politics. In the immediate postwar years, Christian Democratic parties were dominant in Italy, West Germany, the Netherlands, Austria, Belgium and France. From the early 1960s to the mid-1970s their position was challenged by the re-emergence of modernized and moderated socialist parties across Western Europe. This trend was reversed towards the late 1970s as European politics shifted back towards the right. Since the early 1980s Christian Democratic parties have been the leading parties in Italy, Belgium, Germany, Luxembourg, and briefly in Ireland. However, as a bloc within the European Parliament the Christian Democrats (represented by the European People's Party) came second to the Socialists in the 1984 and 1989 European elections. The traditional strength of the Christian Democrats in Germany and Italy shows signs of fraying at the edges, threatened by economic crises, corruption, facilitated by their own long-term hegemony, and the collapse of communism.

Nevertheless, Christian Democracy is likely to remain at the centre of Western European politics. **BO'L**

See also conservatism.

Further reading R. Irving, *The Christian Democratic Parties of Western Europe*.

CHRISTIAN HUMANISM see Humanism

CHRISTIAN SOCIALISM

A moderate form of **socialism** which prescribes the integration of the Christian (specifically Protestant) principles of peace, brotherhood and non-hierarchical power structure with the socialist principles of equality, communality and non-competitiveness. Inspired by the work of Thomas Carlyle (1795–1881) the term was first used by members of the **Anglican** Church in support of aspects of the Chartist movement of the late 1830s. Although primarily a product of progressive **Protestantism**, similar movements have been inspired by radical clerics from the Catholic Church in France, the Netherlands and especially Latin America. **BO'L**

Further reading J. Marsden, *Marxian and Christian Utopianism: Towards a Socialist Political Theology*; E. Norman, *The Victorian Christian Socialists*.

CHRISTIANITY

Christianity is the name applied to the movement launched by the followers of Jesus of Nazareth after his death (*c*. AD 29) which has mushroomed into a **world religion**. Following the onslaught of **Islam** in the 7th century and setbacks in China in the 10th, Christianity, having spread northwards with the conversion of the Slavs and the Scandinavians in the early Middle Ages, became predominantly European. The religious intolerance and persecution which followed the Reformation in 16th-century Europe caused whole communities to migrate to America, while in the Southern Hemisphere vast areas became nominally Catholic under the *patroado* system (whereby the pope in 1378 divided the world into Spanish and Portuguese 'spheres of influence').

Sometimes Christian missionaries followed the colonializing forces, sometimes (like the Franciscan wandering monks of the 14th and 15th centuries or David Livingstone in the 19th century) they preceded them; but generally it is felt that although colonial development was an aid to evangelism in providing missionaries with transport and a degree of security, the cultural **imperialism** and the immoral lives of some settlers and traders proved a major obstacle to the incarnation of the gospel in non-Western cultures. Statistics are exceedingly unreliable, but nevertheless the majority of Christians are now Afro-Caribbean or non-Western; the proportion of Christians in the UK and India are practically identical (2–3 per cent of the population), although the former represents the major religion and the latter a small minority religion. In both cases practising Christians have a national influence out of all relation to their numbers, wealth and status. However, the demographical shift, which has come about partly because of the decline of Christianity in the West, following postwar demoralization and secularization, is going to have profound consequences for theology, spirituality and the ecumenical movement.

Originally there was little to distinguish the followers of Jesus from other great rabbis (teachers) of the 1st and 2nd centuries. They called themselves 'followers of the Way', that is, the way of life in a new community that Jesus had taught them, and claimed that the new covenant promised by the prophets Ezekiel and Jeremiah had materialized. They took Jesus' resurrection to mean that sin and death had been conquered, and after a charismatic experience on the day of Pentecost and subsequent experiences they felt compelled to preach Jesus' message of repentence as a response to the imminence of the Kingdom of God. They celebrated the resurrection by meals as Jesus had shown them, and made baptism the means of entry into the community.

When the movement reached the Greek-speaking city of Antioch, they were dubbed 'Christians' (Followers of Christ) as a pejorative term. Although the term is found in Tacitus in connection with the great persecution under Nero, and in Pliny (describing his interrogations of Christians in Trajan's reign), Christian writers avoided the term as pagan and political until the 3rd century.

It was the love of God for all humankind, Christians believe, which propelled them out of their Jewish cradle, into the Greek world on the initiative of Peter and Paul, then to penetrate the Roman administration and establish themselves in the Latin cities of the west and in North Africa, and to bring together Hebrew scriptures, Greek philosophy and Latin organization in a constant search for the truth. **EMJ**

See also Anglicanism; atonement; Catholicism; Christian art; covenant; ecclesiology; ecumenism; evangelicalism; feminist theology; gnosticism; Kingdom of God; liberation theology; monotheism; natural theology; orthodoxy; pentecostalism; Protestantism; sacrament; sect/sectarianism; syncretism; two kingdoms doctrine.

Further reading Owen Chadwick, *The Pelican History of the Church* (6 volumes); Bamber Gascoigne, *The Christians*; C.S. Lewis, *Mere Christianity*; Nathaniel Micklen, *A Faith for Agnostics*.

CHROMATICISM

Chromaticism (from Greek *chroma*, 'colour'), in Western **music**, is connected with **tonality**. The distance between any given sound and the same sound an octave lower or higher is conventionally divided into 12 equal semitones. Those semitones, in turn, are grouped to form scales. The 'major' scale, rising, consists of tone, tone, semitone, tone, tone, tone, semitone. The 'minor' scale, rising, consists of tone, semitone, tone, tone, tone, semitone, minor third. (1 tone = 2 semitones; 1 minor third = 3 semitones.) The same octave, if divided into regular semitones, would include 12 – and the semitones that appear in the 12, but not in the scale, are the chromatic notes which 'colour' the scale.

The game, for composers, has always been to see how much use can be made of chromatic notes, that is, how much chromaticism can be employed. Until the late

Middle Ages, chromatic notes were almost entirely forbidden: once your basic scale was established, you did not deviate from it throughout the music. However, in the late Middle Ages and **Renaissance**, composers began to experiment with 'modulation' (using chromatic notes to shift the music from one basic scale to another, 'changing key'). At first this was small-scale and was an extremely marked effect, used mainly for colouring the meaning of the text (for example at the words, 'he was crucified', in the Credo of the Mass). The madrigals of Gesualdo (late 16th century) are the most consistently 'experimental' pieces in this style. Other composers of the time wrote 'chromatic fantasies' for instruments as something of a novelty.

In the late 17th century, an 'equal temperament' tuning method was devised, making all 12 semitones of equal value. This meant, therefore, that music could be written (and, theoretically, played) in any key at all – a fact celebrated at the time by Bach, whose 'Well-Tuned Klavier' consists of 48 preludes and fugues, two each in each of the major and minor keys.

From this point on, more and more use was made of chromaticism. It still remained predominantly a colouristic device, but modulation became commonplace into and out of 'remote' keys (that is, keys far from the 'home' key). In the 19th century, advances in the manufacture of instruments made it possible for orchestras to play in even the most sharp-or-flat-filled keys, and instead of actually modulating from one key to another, composers began to use chromatic notes in passing, to give new colour and expressive power to melody and harmony. By the 20th century, this process had reached the point where almost any note or combination of notes was 'permissible', so long as it made sense in context, and total chromaticism (in which the music is 'in' a home key, but can move at will through any other chromatic regions the composer chooses) led to **atonality** and eventually to **twelve-note music**. KMcL

See also intonation, tuning and temperament.

CHRONICLE PLAY see History Play

CHRONOBIOLOGY

Chronobiology (from Greek *chronos*, 'time' + biology), in the **life sciences**, is the study of the control of living systems through time. All biological events occur over a course of time, but a great number occur in a cyclical fashion, with a period which can vary from microseconds (as in the beating of a wing) to a year (as in a mating season). There are two categories of such phenomena: those which are correlated with environmental periodicity (see **biological rhythm**), and those which appear to be independent of the environment. A characteristic of environmentally correlated rhythms is that they resist alteration, wether by drugs or the removal of environmental factors, they will arise spontaneously (in eggs laid in the laboratory, for example), and they are not dramatically affected by temperature. Evidence suggests the presense of an internal biological clock, in all plants and animals, which is capable of allowing rhythmic phenomena to be precisely controlled, provided the clock is regularly given the chance to synchronize itself with the environment. Investigation of the clock mechanism is particularly challenging because it is difficult to separate components of the clock from the functions it controls. **RB**

See also phenology.

CHURCH

The term church (from Greek *kuriakon* [*doma*], 'lord's house') refers to an assembly of people, social institutions and their associated beliefs and practices which comprise a distinct religious grouping. Churches, in contrast to sects (see **sect/ sectarianism**), claim a universal social membership based on birth and accept the importance of the state and other secular institutions in maintaining social order. **DA**

See also culture; Protestant ethic; religion; secularization.

Further reading M. Hill, *A Sociology of Religion*.

CHURCH'S THESIS see Computability

CIRCUIT THEORY

Circuit Theory, as the name suggests, enables a detailed mathematical study to be made of virtually any electrical circuit. This has formed the backbone of electrical study since its inception in the early 1800s, permitting engineers to design more efficient electrical apparatus.

In 1820, H.C. Oersted, from Copenhagen, discovered that the flow of electric current in a conductor would cause a magnetic field, thereby producing a deflection of a compass needle. This discovery led to research in the field of **electromagnetics**, the interaction between **electricity** and **magnetism**, an early pioneer of which was the Frenchman A.M. Ampère. Ampère gave clear definitions of electric current, the flow of electric charge in a conductor, and electric voltage, the tension of 'pressure' of electricity which would cause the flow of current in a closed circuit.

Ampère, however, saw no relationship between the current and voltage, and it was G.S. Ohm in 1827 who finally postulated that voltage was proportional to the current by a constant known as the resistance of the conductor. An analogy may be made between electricity and water flow in a pipe. Greater water pressure, or voltage, is required to overcome the resistance of the pipe, or conductor, to increase the water flow, or current.

Such was the impact of Ohm's Law that the main pioneers have been honoured by using their names as the terms of resistance and current. Current (I) is measured in units of Ampères and resistance (R) is measured in Ohms. If the voltage applied is V Ohm's law is written as $I = V/R$.

Following Ohm's Law and the recognition of resistance and the role it played, further circuit laws soon appeared. In 1841, J.P. Joule discovered that the rate of heating (P), expressed as Watts, produced by an electric current (I) flowing in a conductor of known resistance (R) was equal to the current in ampères squared times the resistance: $P = I^2R$.

Electrical engineering and the design and analysis of electrical circuits using circuit theory can be traced back to 1848, when G. Kirchoff discovered the current and voltage laws, subsequently named after him. Kirchoff applied Ohm's Law to circuits having several components and found that the sum of the currents at an interconnected point equalled zero, and that the sum of the voltages around a closed loop of the circuit equalled zero.

Including Kirchoff's Laws elementary circuit theory was essentially complete following the discovery of two other electrical concepts, *capacitance* and *inductance*, and their effect on the circuit behaviour. Capacitance relates to the ability of a condenser to store energy, and induction to a characteristic of electrical coils to resist rapidly changing currents. These concepts are necessary to analyse circuits in which the power supply is alternating, that is, varying at a fixed frequency between positive and negative (i.e. the direction of flow of current flow reverses in every cycle). William Thomson is credited with realizing the importance of capacitance through work on improving undersea cables, and Oliver Heaviside with inductance after early work with telegraphy.

From these early beginnings circuit theory now extends, through the application of **network theory**, to the analysis and design of the most complicated circuits, for instance those in **computer** silicon 'chips'.
AC

CIVIC CULTURE

The idea of a civic culture was developed by political scientists working within the **functionalist** tradition in the late 1950s and early 1960s. They were seeking to explain how the development of political culture affects the maintenance and legitimacy of states and régimes. Its exponents, Gabriel Almond and Sydney Verba, argued that a liberal democracy was 'congruent' with a civic political culture: one in which activity and passivity among citizens, civic obligation of citizens and performance by government, and social consensus and cross-cutting cleavages are combined in an appropriate mix. This argument was influenced by **behaviouralism** (it focused upon the determinants of an individual's psychological attitude towards political awareness and activism) and by intellectual reflection on the fragility of the interwar European democracies.

Critics of the civic culture approach to explaining democratic stability have argued that: (1) its conception of causation is wrong (institutions create culture rather than the other way around); (2) it is biased towards an élitist conception of democracy (presupposing the passivity of women and subaltern social classes); and (3) there are cases of functioning liberal democracies despite divided societies without cross-cutting cleavages (see **consociationalism**). The civic culture approach is also condemned as **ethnocentric**, taking Anglo-Saxon standards of liberal democracy as its implicit benchmark. However, as a pioneering attempt to map out an empirical exploration of political culture the approach still has its defenders. **BO'L**

Further reading G. Almond and S. Verba, *The Civic Culture: Political Attitudes and Democracy in Five Nations; The Civic Culture Revisited: an Analytical Study.*

CIVIL DISOBEDIENCE

Civil disobedience in general usage covers those forms of political protest against the state or régime which fall somewhere between physical force and constitutional opposition. The term was first articulated in Henry David Thoreau's essay 'On the Duty of Civil Disobedience' (1849), which justified refusal to pay taxes to a government that permitted slavery, and declared that 'the only obligation I have a right to assume is to do at any time what I think right'. However, the forms of action associated with civil disobedience have a longer history than Thoreau. Civil disobedience in the strictest form means that dissidents break the law (to protest its injustice or absurdity) but do not hide from or resist arrest by the authorities. Sometimes civil disobedience can be the prelude to revolutionary struggle against the state; and sometimes organizations may deploy a mixture of insurrectionary acts and acts of civil disobedience. Naturally civil disobedience stands little chance of success against a determined **authoritarian** or imperial régime, whereas in a democratic milieu it can be used to transform public opinion. In our century the non-violent mass-mobilizations of Mahatma Gandhi in South Africa and India, and of Martin Luther King in the US, are examples of the successful deployment of civil disobedience. Civil disobedience is meant to assist one or more of the following goals: (1) publicizing the cause of the movement; (2) emphasizing the illegitimacy of the law and the system which produces it; and (3) provoking acts of repression which undermine the **legitimacy** of the régime and, by contrast, portray the activists in a more favourable light. The early activities of the American and Northern Ireland civil rights demonstrators in the 1960s illustrate these primary functions. For example, the occupation by blacks of 'whites-only' lunch counters in Oklahoma and North Carolina provoked extensive and sensational media coverage, emphasized the absurdity of the racist laws segregating public amenities; and exposed the repressive nature of the local white police.

Political philosophers dispute the morality of civil disobedience, usually in their discussions of political obligation. Some argue that civil disobedience is only appropriate in an unjust state, and where all other means of remedy have been exhausted; others maintain that its use is a tactical rather than a fundamental issue; while conservatives reject it altogether because they are committed to the preservation of the authority of 'the powers that be'. **BO'L**

Further reading H. Bedau, *Civil Disobedience in Focus;* C. Villa-Vincencio, *Civil Disobedience and Beyond: Law, Resistance and Religion in South Africa.*

CIVIL ENGINEERING

Civil engineering is the designing and construction of public works. The building of permanent, large-scale works, requiring large numbers of people to construct, began with the first civilizations, most notably in the Nile valley, Mesopotamia and the Indus valley some five to six thousand years ago. The development of 'civil engineering' works could only be supported by a settled and organized society.

The first roads linked parts of Mesopotamia together, but it was not until the establishment of the Roman Empire that civil engineering and road-building in particular became an art as well as a science. The Romans built many bridges and viaducts that used the arch as support. With the demise of the Roman Empire, civil engineering in western Europe came to an abrupt standstill.

The next great impetus to civil engineering, in Europe, was the Industrial Revolution. Better transportation systems were required in order to supply the new industrial centres with cheaper raw materials and to create markets for finished goods. New roads, canals, bridges and tunnels were constructed on an unprecedented scale in order to achieve this.

As the urban populations have become larger, civil engineering has become of major importance – constructing faster roads, reservoirs to hold water and sewers to dispose of waste, with profound effects upon society. It is generally conceded that the increase in life expectancy during the 19th century was due not to advances in medical science but to the development of public water supply and sewerage systems. **AA**

Further reading G.E. Sandstrom, *Man the Builder*.

CIVIL LIBERTIES

Civil liberties are the freedoms, protected by law, generally considered to be essential features of liberal democratic government. The most important civil liberties prohibit governmental or state officials from unwarranted interference in the personal, political and economic activities of a citizen (see **liberalism**). The fundamental civil liberties include freedom of the person, of privacy, of movement, of expression, of association, and of worship. They are considered essential elements of a liberal civil society.

'Civil libertarians' resist novel incursions of the state which may lead to **authoritarian** government. Civil libertarians disagree

over which liberties are most crucial: right-wingers insist that the liberty to own and dispose of one's property is the most important freedom; while left-wingers insist that those liberties associated with democratic organization (such as freedom of expression and association) are in most need of protection. **BO'L**

See also civil rights; democracy.

Further reading R. Gastil, *Freedom in the World: Political Rights and Civil Liberties;* G. Phelps and R. Poirier (eds.), *Contemporary Debates on Civil Liberties: Enduring Constitutional Questions.*

CIVIL RIGHTS

The expression 'civil rights' has different meanings in different contexts and countries. In democratic Europe, civil rights are associated with the rights of persons as members of civil society, which emerged in the 18th century. They include the right to a fair trial, protection from cruel and unusual punishment, equality before the law, and freedom of expression, thought and worship. Many of them are now thought of as **human rights**, that is, rights which all persons should enjoy. Civil rights are sometimes distinguished from the political rights fought for in 19th-century Europe and America, although there is in practice much overlap between the two categories. Political rights guarantee citizens' participation in the formation and exercise of governmental power, through the right of free association, organization and the right to vote. Civil and political rights are usually entrenched in Bills of Rights in most liberal democratic constitutions (the UK is a notable exception). Civil and political rights together are often distinguished from social and economic rights. Some political thinkers, especially **socialists**, argue that substantive or social rights should be incorporated into law: such as the right to minimum nutrition, paid work, a certain number of years of public education and access to health care. They maintain that many civil rights are confined to procedural equality treating persons as equals and instead advocate the use of rights to set standards for citizenship. Civil rights may be distinguished from **civil liberties**, although the distinction is disputed by some. Not all civil rights are permissive in the way that civil liberties are. Civil liberties allow people to do some things without permission, whereas some civil rights prescribe standards. In the US, discourse about civil rights, although having some of the same connotations as it has in Europe, has become associated with the legal rights and protection of mal-treated racial and ethnic minorities; and the recognition that civil rights legislation did not stop *de facto* segregation and discrimi-nation led to the development of **affirmative action**. BO'L

See also democracy; liberalism.

Further reading D.C. Kramer, *Comparative Civil Rights and Liberties*; T.H. Marshall, *Class, Citizenship and Social Development*.

CIVILIZATION

Civilization (from Latin *civilis*, 'belonging to a society') is an ambiguous term. In its contemporary usage it refers to a unified social system, and is invested with notions of technological advances and cultural complexity characterized by hierarchical organization. The notion of civilization has, therefore, been used both to measure the sophistication of a society, and as a stick to beat those who seem to be less civi-lized.

Among the evolutionists of the 18th and 19th centuries, civilization was considered the summit of human achievement the pre-rogative of Western **culture**. Although ancient civilizations in Mexico, China, Egypt and India were recognized, the word acquired its ambiguity when used by evolu-tionists to talk about Western civilization. However, as Mahatma Ghandi wryly pointed out, the notion of a West that was civilized was a good idea, but it had cer-tainly not been attained.

Evolutionists described civilization as the end result of a process of development that started with their notion of savagery. This view was outlined in Henry Morgan's *Ancient Society* (1877), which described the evolutionary stages of social structure from 'savagery' and 'barbarism' to 'civilization'.

It was the opposition of civilization to notions of the 'primitive' which gave ideas like 'savagery' and 'barbarism' their dispar-aging tone. The connotations of the civiliz-ing force of Western civilization could be conveniently used to legitimize cultural and political dominance over others, as with the justifications about the welfare of 'natives' in colonized countries. Contemporary **anthropology** rejects such biased methods of comparing and evaluating societies, and is accordingly wary of using the term civili-zation. **CL**

See also colonialism; ethnocentrism; evolu-tionism; literacy/orality; primitivism.

Further reading A. Kuper, *The Invention of Primitive Society*; G. Stocking, *Victorian Anthropology*.

CLASS

The term class (Latin, 'assembly') refers to social and economic divisions between groups which create differences in wealth, prestige and power. The word is frequently used, but there is much debate as to its pre-cise meaning.

Marx used class to refer to the relation-ship of individuals to the productive forces of a society. He argued that there were two main classes – those who owned the forces of production and those who did not – and their interests were in conflict. The majority class shared a common situation in a system of production which exploited them, though each individual may not necessarily be aware of this fact. Marx called this 'false consciousness'. He thought that this conflict between the classes – the class struggle – was the driving force of social change. Under a capitalist system of production, for example, the continued exploitation of workers by the **bourgeoisie** eventually leads workers to develop an awareness of their common class position. He believed that when workers developed this class consciousness they would rise up, overthrow the ruling capitalist class and replace an exploitative and unequal capi-talist society with a fair and equal commu-nist society.

A more complicated model of class was developed by Max Weber. Weber believed classes were the reflection of differences of 'market capacity' which resulted in different 'life chances'. According to Weber, **capital** is only one of a number of sources of market capacity; other sources include skill and education. He identified four main classes: the propertied class; the administrative and managerial class; small businessmen; and the working class. Weber believed conflict would occur between groups whose interests were immediately opposed, for example between the propertied class and the managers. Weber also suggested that social divisions could also develop along the lines of **status** and honour.

In practice, a number of indicators of social class have been employed by social researchers. Income and occupation have been adopted as crude indicators of class position though neither is entirely satisfactory. Critics have pointed out that other social divisions may have important consequences for life chances which are not covered by these indicators, such as **gender** and **race**. Different classes are also characterized by distinct social habits, styles of speech and values. Class consciousness refers to the way people think about class and class divisions. Most agree that in the West class consciousness is strong – in the West the main groupings are upper, middle and working class. An individual who is class conscious has an awareness of the class system, his or her place in it, and the specific attributes associated with the different class groupings.

Studies have shown that class membership may crucially affect one's life chances. **DA**

See also conflict theory; culture; division of labour; embourgeoisement thesis; ethnicity; feminism; labour process; Marxism; occupation; power; profession; Protestant ethic; social closure; social mobility; social stratification; society; sociolinguistics; structure; values; work.

Further reading A. Heath, *Social Mobility*; E.O. Wright, *Classes*.

CLASS CONSCIOUSNESS see Class

CLASS STRUGGLE see Class

CLASSIC DESIGN

Classic design is a 20th-century term for objects which have stood the tests of time and critical approval. Although the phrase was not used in the 19th century, its sense was implied nonetheless – it was, so to speak, a design version of the principle of survival of the fittest. As a theory of design it was explored by those adherents of **modernism** who invested key examples of industrial production with qualities they described as 'classic'. To qualify as classic, an object has somehow to step outside issues of **taste** and **style**, and to retain its value and integrity. Le Corbusier, for example, selected the Thonet bentwood chair: its design, he said, had 'qualities' of 'relevance and permanence'.

More recently, the idea of classic design has come to reflect less ideological principles than issues of marketing and fashion. During the 1970s the concept of classic was exploited by furniture companies which identified a reproduction market for the work of famous 20th-century designers, including Gerrit Reitveld and Marcel Breuer. In the 1980s the word classic became a powerful marketing tool and shopping malls, department stores and high streets saw a proliferation of shops selling classic design, including objects ranging from lighting to toothbrushes.

Although the phrase 'classic design' and the value-judgement implied are a vital part of our late-20th-century consumer outlook, they are in the end no more than hype. The attitude to (certain aspects of) the past which they reveal is interesting; the concept of 'classic' design itself is less so. **CMcD**

CLASSICAL ECONOMICS

Classical economics was the dominant theory of economics from the 18th century until it was refined in the 20th century into neoclassical economics. Classical economists such as Adam Smith, David Ricardo and John Stuart Mill, held that the pursuit of individual self-interest produced the greatest collective benefits.

The classical school believed that an economy is always either in equilibrium or moving towards it. Equilibrium, the theory went, is ensured by movements in wages (the price of labour) and the rate of interest (the price of capital).

The rate of interest moves to ensure equality between savings and investment. If, for instance, entrepreneurs suddenly decide (perhaps because of technological improvements) that they want to invest more, then firms boost their borrowings, and so bid up interest rates. Higher interest rates have two effects. The first is that households are prepared to save more, and so, indirectly, lend more to the investing firms. The second is that some firms gradually reject the idea of investing more, because of the higher cost of borrowing. These two forces work on each other to produce a new equilibrium where savings equal investment.

This theory is founded on two assumptions: first, that the investment is highly sensitive to interest rates; and second, that the rate of interest is free to vary, so that savings and investment are quickly equalized. As for wages, they adjust to ensure that the equilibrium level of national income is that which produces full employment. If there is unemployment, then wages fall and so the demand for labour increases to mop up the unemployed. Conversely, if an economy is heading for unsustainable growth in national income wages rise to choke off the demand for labour.

The classical and neoclassical schools were eclipsed between the mid-1930s and the mid-1970s by the followers of John Maynard Keynes (see **Keynesian Theory**). Keynes attacked the two main classical tenets, arguing (1) that the rate of interest is determined or influenced by the speculative actions of bondholders; and (2) that wages are inflexible downwards, so that national income may be in apparent equilibrium at a point below full employment. Recently, attention has turned back towards some of the logic of classical and neoclassical economics.

CLASSICISM

Classicism, in the **arts** of the West, is a generic term for work which embodies the principles of order, harmony and reason supposedly underlying the **architecture**, fine art and **literature** of ancient Greece and Rome. It is an art primarily of the intellect, though morality – a particular world-view, as it were – is also involved, predicated on the Greek and Roman example. The classical impulse is 'Apollonian' (named after the Greek god of music, who took random Nature, and, by using intellect, tamed it and made it calm, cerebral, civic, generalized and moral); it contrasts with the personal, emotional and disorderly romantic impulse, which was 'Dionysian' (named after the Greek god of intoxication and hedonistic ecstasy). In each case, stylistic qualities match such perceived spiritual ones. Specifically, 'classical' or 'neoclassical' works use the same constructional techniques as those of the past.

Classicism is principally important in Western architecture. Classical architecture, as it is generally understood, is characterized by the use of a specific and defined range of architectural elements, a vocabulary of readily identifiable parts. The basic unit of classical architecture is the '**Order**', a standard variety of a column, supporting an entablature, based on the model of the classical temple colonnade. The relationship of the entablature to the column is sometimes described as 'post and lintel' architecture – the column being the vertical member (made up of capital, shaft and base), and the entablature being the horizontal, consisting of cornice, frieze and architrave. The **temple** in Greek society was the most significant building type, and for functional and ritual reasons was characterized by proportion and careful symmetry. A well-known example is the Parthenon complex in Athens; like most temples of its date, it is a rectangular space enclosed by structural columns, supporting the roof, which are arranged in colonnades on all sides.

The model of Greek architecture provided the basis, with certain modifications, for classical Roman architecture. The principal innovation of the Roman period was the combination of the column with the rounded arch, achieving technically a greater load-bearing capacity, as well as a new aesthetic combination, which can be seen in the structure of the Coliseum at Rome.

The 1st-century BCE architect and engineer to the Emperor Augustus, M. Pollo

Vitruvius, who wrote the only architectural treatise from classical antiquity to survive into the middle ages (*De Architectura*), set down both the theoretical and practical basis of architecture as practised in the late Roman republic, describing in detail the orders and requirements of an architect's education and such things as the most appropriate sites for towns, forts, etc. With the renewed interest in classical texts in the 15th century, this treatise became the basis for most written architectural theory in that period and in Europe this text, and texts modelled closely on it, dominated the subject for subsequent centuries. All architecture of a later period which derives from the classical, particularly in the employment of the order, and not only in terms of proportion, may be called classical, or **neoclassical**.

In **music**, 'neoclassical' has a different meaning. It refers to the style of composing that uses the 18th-century techniques of such composers as J.S. Bach or Mozart, but with 20th-century spikiness and harmony – a radical alternative to the romantic lushness of sound imagined by such men as Richard Strauss or Gustav Mahler.

The question of 'classicism' is bedevilled by a common misuse of the word 'classic' to mean a work of art which has become a 'standard', universally known and almost beyond the reach of criticism. Another common expression, originally confined to the West but now used worldwide, is 'classical music'. This was once taken to mean European art music from the end of the **Baroque** to the beginning of the **Romantic** periods, the time of Gluck, Haydn, Mozart and the young Beethoven, but is now universally used to mean European art music of the last four or five centuries. Sometimes Westerners talk of 'classical' Indian or Asian music with the same implication that there is a distinction between art music and more popular forms. All these terms are in wide currency, but none has any connection whatever with the traditions or artistic concepts of ancient Greece and Rome. **PD MG JM KMcL**

Further reading M. Greenhalgh, *The Classical Tradition in Art*; J. Summerson, *The Classical Language of Architecture*.

CLEAVAGES

Social cleavages differentiate groups by a clear social marker. Important cleavages may be marked by racial, ethnic, caste, religious, class, linguistic, sexual and age-cohort boundaries. The principal political significance of cleavages in democratic states is their effect on political alignments or attachments to parties. The impact of a given cleavage is affected by its 'salience', and its relationship with all other salient cleavages. The salience of a cleavage is its importance relative to other aspects of an individual's identity in a given society: it is used to predict individuals' attachment to political groups which claim to represent a particular cleavage or set of cleavages. For instance, the salience of religion as a cleavage varies considerably in its effect upon political alignments. In states such as Belgium and the Netherlands the existence of two or more significant religious (and anti-religious) communities led to the emergence of political parties which represented the confessional (and anti-confessional) cleavages; so much so that if a person's political party was known so was his or her religion (or lack of it). In the UK, by contrast, religion is not so salient a political cleavage because other cleavages (notably class, region and ethnic origin) take precedence, though religion may be correlated with these other markers. This latter possibility brings us to the importance of the structure of cleavages. Two (or more) cleavages are said to be 'coincident' when they encompass the same social group. For example, in a society where all middle-class people are Muslim, and all non-Muslims are not middle class the cleavages of class and religion exactly coincide. In contrast, social cleavages are 'cross-cutting' when members of one cleavage are widely distributed between the categories of another cleavage. For example, in a society where there are lower-, middle- and upper-class Muslims proportionate to their overall share of the population then the cleavages of religion and class are cross-cutting. Naturally there are a host of empirical possibilities between purely coincident and purely cross-cutting cleavages; and even when boundaries coincide or cross-cut each of them may not be equally important in their political impact. Some political scientists argue that numerous salient cleavages are associated with multi-party **democracy**, whereas a single dominant cleavage will be associated with a two-party system. Theories which view cleavages as the primary determinant of political alignments and electoral outcomes are criticized (1) for their inability to account for historical contingencies which alter the strength and formation of various cleavages; (2) for neglecting the importance of electoral systems in shaping political parties; and (3) because voting is increasingly based on specific issue-preferences with traditional cleavages allegedly losing their salience. **Pluralist** political scientists argue that cross-cutting cleavages are a fundamental source of democratic stability. They believe that where cleavages are coincident *and* based on racial, religious, ethnic or national markers, then a democratic accommodation is going to be very difficult. **BO'L**

See also consociationalism.

Further reading Arend Lijphart, *Democracy and Plural Societies*; S.M. Lipset and S. Rokkan, *Party Systems and Voter Alignments: Cross-national Perspectives*.

CLIMAX

The climax of a biological community is the ecologists' name for the equilibrium which is adopted when the process of succession has run its course and the species which make up the **community** are able to exist in a stable state of dynamic equilibrium, providing the environment (climate, soil, water supply, etc.) is also stable. Most communities which are undisturbed are said to be climax communities; where disturbance occurs, the return of environmental stability leads to a re-establishment of the climax community, via a series of transient community types. Thus oak forest, the climax community of much of the British Isles, is the natural end point for areas of disturbed land which are allowed to develop without interference. **RB**

See also conservation; succession.

CLINICAL PSYCHOLOGY see
Psychiatry

CLIOMETRICS

'Cliometrics' was the ironic name given to the 'new **economic** history', or 'quantitative economic history' developed in the 1950s and 1960s, principally in the US, but also in the UK and elsewhere in Europe. Clio is the muse of History and 'metrics' refers to measurement. Methodologically sophisticated economists abandoned the previous practices in the discipline of economic history (which primarily involved careful generalization after the accumulation of facts and historical case-studies) and instead behaved like econometricians (economists concerned with testing economic theory in a quantitative form). Their basic method was to develop a theory or hypothesis and test it against data to see if it could be verified or falsified through regression analysis. Whatever the deficiencies of particular works in this vein cliometricians have transformed economic history, imparting to it a degree of conceptual and empirical rigour it had previously lacked. However, cliometrics still has critics who claim that there is nothing new under the Sun. **BO'L**

See also econometrics.

Further reading D.N. McCloskey, 'The Achievements of the Cliometric School' in *Journal of Economic History*.

CLONING

Gene cloning (from Greek *klon*, 'twig' or 'graft') involves the production of many identical copies of a given **gene** or piece of DNA for use in **genetic engineering**. This is generally achieved by inserting the original DNA, often derived from a DNA 'library', into bacterium in the form of a plasmid (a small loop of DNA). The bacteria multiply and the plasmid duplicates itself many times, to produce a large number of gene clones contained within the daughter cells of the original bacterium. A DNA library is a collection of cloned fragments of DNA produced by digestion of the DNA of a specific organism using a restriction enzyme. The concept of cloning is often extended to whole organisms, though these are chiefly single-celled organisms or certain plants. In this context the term clone refers to all cells derived from a chosen parent; in cells which reproduce by binary fission, the genes carried by all the cells in a clone are the same, if the appearance of mutations is discounted. Since all the cells of an organism bear the entire gene complement, it is theoretically possible to produce a completely new individual from a single, non-germ line cell. This can be done with some plants and animals such as amphibians, but the cloning of humans remains firmly in the realm of science fiction. **RB**

See also immunology.

Further reading Zsolt Harsanyi, *Genetic Prophesy Beyond the Double Helix*.

CO-OPERATIVE PRINCIPLE see Pragmatics

COALITIONS

Coalitions are alliances of political rivals organized against a common foe or foes. Coalition governments are thus alliances of political parties which prefer to ally rather than compete, if only to share power. There have been coalition governments in the UK during World War I and between 1931 and 1945.

There is now a well-developed body of theory which attempts to explain the process by which coalitions form and their stability over time. It is important because coalitions are the primary form of political co-operation and decision-making among political parties, interest groups, states and international organizations.

The theoretical approach to coalitions is based on the mathematical postulates of **game theory** and focuses on at least four factors: (1) incentives or pay-offs which participants consider before joining a coalition; (2) the optimal size of a coalition for a given situation (should it be the minimum required to win?); (3) the shared characteristics of the participants (usually defined as shared values); and (4) the decision-making rules which the coalition will follow. Empirical tests of coalition theories applied to political parties, using computer models and laboratory simulations, support two general rules: first, coalition partners attempt to minimize the number of partners in order to increase their individual pay-offs (like access to ministries). This is called the 'minimal winning' rule. Second, coalitions tend to be formed between and among partners which differ least on policy questions. This is referred to as the 'policy-distance minimization' or 'minimal conflict' rule. The increasing complexity of coalition modelling to take into account factors such as variable pay-offs and variations in conditions over time have not deflected criticism from those who argue that the variability of real situations cannot be modelled adequately. However, alternative approaches based on the empirical analysis of actual coalitions rely on such a myriad of specific factors that they offer little predictive power beyond that derived from the common sense of experienced pundits. **BO'L**

See also electoral systems.

Further reading I. Budge and M. Laver, *Party Policy and Government Coalitions*.

CODE

A code, in the terminology of **linguistics**, **media** studies and **sociology**, is a system of signs employed by members of a culture to communicate meaning. A set of formal rules will enable the code to operate. Language is a code in as far as it is composed of symbols (words) which mean something and which can be used in accordance with a set of conventions to communicate. Similarly, Morse code, Braille, traffic light systems, dress codes and body language are all coded systems of communication.

Within media studies *code* is used to describe the systems of signs, images, sounds, technical methods and forms which work in conventional ways to create meaning in media texts. For example, television uses technical processes such as editing, lighting and framing of shots in a number of regular ways to communicate specific messages. A further instance might be provided by the work of the Russian formalist Vladimir Propp on narrative codes.

He showed how fairy tales have various recurrent types of character and categories of event which act to construct the story in understandable ways. This points to how the very creation and utilization of codes in particular ways can contribute to the placement of a text within a genre. However, codes do not necessarily operate in isolated ways, but combine within media texts in a complex fashion.

Codes are available for encoding a text with meaning but recent interest has centred on how far decoders (**audiences**) understand the meaning preferred by the encoder. **NC**

See also encode/decode; genre.

Further reading John Fiske, *Introduction to Communication Studies*.

CODING THEORY

Coding theory, in **mathematics**, is the study of the various ways information can be carried in codes. This is an area of increasing importance today, with more and more information of more and more kinds being transmitted over telephone lines, radio transmissions and the like; coding theory is used to determine the most effective way to send information and to avoid problems with corruption in transit. **SMcL**

See also information theory.

COGNITIVE THERAPY

Cognitive therapy has its origins in George Kelly's Personal Construct Psychology, the Rational-Emotive therapy of Albert Ellis and the Cognitive therapy of Aaron Beck. At least 17 other forms of cognitive therapy exist today. Cognitive therapists do not work with, or believe in, the idea of the **unconscious**. All mental activity, although not in awareness at any one time, is accessible directly, not part of some unconscious set of relations or drives. Cognitive therapy aims to assess and work with irrational patterns of thought that are confronted directly by asking the patient to report images and thoughts around irrational feelings and behaviours.

The core elements of a cognitive approach are the following: the alteration of the individual's maladaptive interpretations of their own life's events; the reconsideration of his or her way of interpreting their own environment; the development of coping patterns in order to change behaviour, environment and cognitions themselves; a commitment to monitoring of reactions and behaviour in order to increase comprehension. Cognitive therapy supports a methodological rigour and scientific approach using assessment, problem formulation, goal setting, regular monitoring and measurement of results.

Although there is no single model, Ellis's Rational-Emotive Therapy is used more widely in the US and Beck's Cognitive Therapy has a large number of practitioners in the UK. **MJ**

Further reading Aaron Beck, *Cognitive Therapy and the Emotional Disorders*.

COINS

Coins are money of intrinsic value. At one time each coin contained an amount of metal whose value as bullion was equal to the money value designated on the coin. For example, a dime contains 10-cents' worth of silver bullion; a silver dollar could be melted down and the silver sold for a dollar.

Obviously, problems could arise because of fluctuations in the market price of the metals used. When the market price of gold or silver rose above the minted value of coins, they would be melted down and sold for bullion and would thereby disappear from circulation. There was also difficulty because of clipping and 'sweating' coins to try to remove some of the metal value without losing the money exchange value. To keep coins in circulation and in good repair, monetary authorities reduced the amount of valuable metal in coins to a token amount. This meant that coins always have more value as a medium of exchange than as a metal. **TF**

See also bimetallism; Gresham's Law.

COLLAGE

Collage (from French *coller*, 'to stick') is an art-technique in which objects are stuck on to the surface of a work of art and incorporated in its composition. The technique is common in **folk art**, for example in the religious **sculpture** of some African and Caribbean peoples, created not by carving but by assembling pre-existing objects to make masks or totems. In **fine art**, collage was rare until Western painters began using it at the start of the 20th century. The **Cubists** incorporated pieces of newspaper, bus tickets, scraps of menus and other objects into their pictures, and the **Surrealists** went even further, creating whole pictures from an apparently random assemblage of 'found objects'. Picasso made collage-sculpture, turning such objects as bicycle handlebars, woodchips and screws into works of art. In the 1960s, Rauschenberg stuck car tyres, US flags, even a stuffed goat into his sculptures, making art out of the juxtaposition of objects which never lost their own identity rather than (as most earlier painters had done) using the scraps for their aesthetic qualities alone or for the effect they made in the whole montage.

In **music**, the term collage is used of works in which snippets of other compositions are inserted – not so much quoted and reworked (as in **parody**) as stuck on willy-nilly. The most often-quoted examples are the fragments of hymn-tunes and popular marches which pop up in the works of Charles Ives – a talking-point in their day because few other composers followed his example. But in electronic music, **musique concrète** and **postmodern** music, collage is standard practice, and a number of 'mainstream' classical composers, for example Copland, Shostakovich and Tippett, have also used it. Perhaps because of stringent copyright laws, the technique is rarely used in **pop** and **rock music**; more often, a line or chord sequence may be 'sampled' – that is, assimilated into the general texture and worked on in the same way as original material. Rap, however, often uses such sampling in a collage-like way, short bursts of the distorted sound of a pre-existing record being inserted into the backing texture.

In the 1980s, makers of television adverts experimented with collage. Using computer technology, they inserted modern actors into sequences of old film, or showed the actors in older films using the modern products; new soundtracks were often dubbed in to reinforce the message. A few mainstream film-makers have adopted the technique: examples are Woody Allen's *Zelig*, in which he inserts himself into a variety of famous historical scenes, appearing at Hitler's side during the Nuremberg Rally or with Churchill, Stalin and Roosevelt at the Yalta Conference, and Carl Reiner's *Dead Men Don't Wear Plaid*, in which Steve Martin, as a 1940s private eye, exchanges wisecracks with the likes of Humphrey Bogart, Peter Lorre and Myrna Loy. **KMcL**

COLLECTIVE BEHAVIOUR

Collective behaviour refers to the behaviour of people in groups or crowds. The most influential early sociological and social psychological theory of collective behaviour is that of Gustav Le Bon, writing in the late 19th century. Le Bon argued that in periods of social decline and disintegration, society is threatened by the rule of crowds. It is assumed that as a result of individual proximity, individual personality is subsumed in a crowd mentality, which radically transforms individual behaviour. The action of individuals tends to depart from routine standards of social demeanour and may be explosive and unpredictable.

In contemporary **sociology**, the term collective behaviour is used to refer to the mobilization of a mass of people with the aim of changing the social **structure**. Movements to change society involve secular and religious movements. N.J. Smelser, in *Theory of Collective Behaviour* (1962), produced one of the most influential generalized theories of collective behaviour, which emphasizes the importance of generalized beliefs and values in directing **social movements** in periods of rapid social change. **DA**

See also authority; conflict theory; consensus theory; corporatism; feminism; legitimation crisis; power; religion; subculture; values.

COLLECTIVE UNCONSCIOUS

The collective unconscious is a Jungian

term for the many symbols, chiefly relig-ious, which are collective and not individ-ual in nature. These collective symbols are natural, spontaneous products which cannot be made by an individual person.

A religious person might see these sym-bols as accessible to people who accept God. An atheist might think that they are invented; but they are impossible to invent. We are not able to place invention dates, times or authors for symbols. They seem to have no human source.

Jung's analytical psychology believed them to be collective representations, evolving from creative fantasies and dreams that existed in the first age of the human world – 'primeval dreaming'. They are therefore 'involuntary spontaneous manifestations', which were not, and could not have been, created intentionally. Jung saw dreams as the holding place of this col-lective unconscious, and read his patients' dreams symbolically from this point of view, rather than as elements which dis-guised repressed emotional meaning.

Dreams contain these archaic remnants in much the same way as the human body contains the history of its evolution. The human mind is seen to be organized in a similar way, containing traces of archaic man whose mind was closer to that of an animal. The old psyche is the basis of our mind, full of collective images and primi-tive motifs. This collective unconscious throws up **archetypes** which are primordial images and are not inherited representa-tions. **MJ**

Further reading C.G. Jung, *Four Archetypes: Mother, Rebirth, Spirit, Trickster*.

COLONIALISM AND NEOCOLONIALISM

Colonialism (from Latin *colonia*, '[farming] settlement of ex-soldiers in a foreign land') is the doctrine and practice of coloniali-zation, and is sometimes used as a synonym for **imperialism**. 'Administrative colonial-ism' is the control of a territory and its peoples by officials from an imperial or metropolitan centre. It may be combined with 'settler colonialism', the planting of settlers from the metropolis on the land of the native populations, as occurred, for example, in 17th-century Ulster and in 19th-century Algeria, and is presently occurring on the West Bank of the Jordan in Palestine. The practice of colonialism is as old as the first city-states. Colonialism is variously motivated by security considera-tions (settlers are planted to control strate-gic territories), economic avarice (exploiting the raw materials and labour of the native population), religious beliefs (spreading 'the true faith') and/or over-population (or unwanted population) in the metropolis.

The 'colonial era' describes the expan-sion of European states and peoples into the underdeveloped regions of the Ameri-cas, Africa and Asia from the late 15th cen-tury. European colonialists justified their projects through naked assertions of power, like the 'manifest destiny' pro-claimed by the young USA and the disse-mination of Western **civilization** to unfortunate heathens. Although the degree of empowerment of native peoples varied considerably, the uderlying rationale behind much European colonial policy was to develop local administrations which facilitated the free flow of resources to the mother country, while developing internal markets to absorb the mother country's exports and provide opportunities for capi-tal investment. However, there were exten-sive variations among the European powers in their patterns of administration and in the degree to which they exploited their colonies. The moral, political and economic justifications for colonialism dwindled, especially after 1945, when nationalist movements emerged and suc-cessfully challenged the legitimacy of imperialism.

An unexpected sidelight on colonialism is its relationship – often extremely fruitful – with the discipline of **anthropology**. It was, in fact, during the long period of European colonialism that anthropology first emerged as a scientific discipline, through the encounters with other cultures. In the Japanese colonization of Taiwan and Korea, anthropology was used fairly self-consciously as a means to manage its colo-nies. Anthropology has always had a strong presence in the countries which were colonized, while uncolonized communities have until recently been far less well-documented.

In British-ruled Africa during the 1930s, the government funded studies about the social structures of its subject people. These dealt with leadership, kinship, land usage and legal systems, all of which provided information which was ultimately helpful to colonial administrators. Anthropologists have been criticized for their unwitting complicity in allowing governments to gain a better understanding of how to rule native peoples. The crucial question is: for whom is anthropological knowledge produced? Today, even though indigenous anthropologists have been favoured in the former colonies, the central problem remains the 'privileged' position of the observer's point of view, arguably a form of ideological neocolonialism.

Since full-scale decolonization began at the end of World War I, a wider consideration of the power relations between anthropology and the subjects of its investigations has developed. This historical perspective has helped anthropologists to recognize similarities in present-day relationships between nations and the earlier colonial system. The neocolonialism system refers to relations between the West and many underdeveloped countries, which replicate earlier relations of political and economic exploitation and dependency.

The expression 'neocolonialism' is often used to describe the continuing political and economic dependence of some former colonies upon the powers which colonized them, as well as the increased economic control of allegedly sovereign states by economic powers such as the US and Japan. It is argued that the advanced industrialized states maintain this control through their leading economic position in world trade, and through the influence of large corporations operating on a global basis. By controlling the terms upon which trade is conducted Western countries perpetuate their privileged position. **CL BO'L**

See also dependency theory; diffusionism; globalization; world system.

Further reading T. Asad (ed.), *Anthropology and the Colonial Encounter*; S.C. Easton, *The Rise and Fall of Western Colonialism: a Historial Survey from the Early Nineteenth Century to the Present.*

COLOUR (as in quantum chromodynamics)

It is very important to realize that the quantum mechanical term colour has nothing whatsoever to do with the word colour in everyday use. It is simply a label used to provide a distinction between **particles**.

To understand why the concept of colour was introduced, it is necessary to understand the nature of fermions. Particles are divided into **fermions and bosons**. Fermions must obey the Pauli Exclusion Principle, which states that no two fermions in a system have the same set of quantum numbers. Thus, a particle made up of two or more identical fermions may not exist.

However, some particles composed of quarks appeared to violate this principle. An example is the particle which is made up of three seemingly identical strange quarks. In 1964, Greenburg proposed a solution to this problem, by suggesting that each quark possesses a property which he called colour. Thus the three quarks could each have a different colour quantum number (red, green or blue), but be identical in every other respect, and still remain fermions. This proposal means that there are three times as many quarks as were initially thought. However, this tripling has been tested in systems such as the neutral meson decay rate and found to be the case.

Colour was not detected before this because all quarks obey confinement. This means that quarks only combine in ways that are colour neutral overall. This is slightly analogous to charged particles. A negative particle and a positive one attract each other, and will combine to form a neutral one. Similarly, red, green and blue quarks combine to form colour neutral (white) particles. The essential difference is that we may observe positive and negative charges, but we never see 'coloured' systems. Some particles are colour neutral but have only two quarks. This is achieved by saying that each colour has a corresponding anti-colour, which cancels it out. Thus a particle could be composed of a red and an anti-red quark, and be colour neutral. **JJ**

COMEDY

Comedy (Greek, 'wedding-song') is one of the main dramatic genres. Although a truly inclusive definition of comedy remains a chimera, a number of persistent recurrent elements differentiate comedy from **tragedy, farce**, and **melodrama**. Historically, comedy has more often tended to be concerned with the social and the domestic rather than the political and the heroic, though a satirical strand mocking the pretensions of politicians and do-gooders has been sustained since the ancient Greek comedies of Aristophanes. Generally the human follies anatomized in comedy are ridiculed through a concentration on the excesses of fashionable behaviour and dress, bombast, and, above all, on pretension. Comedies tend, therefore, to deal in ordinary, even stereotypical, characters and in common social situations. Where tragedy may exalt the intellectual and the individual, comedy emphasizes our shared humanity, often particularly in terms of our shared bodily functions. While one of the functions of comedy is to make people laugh, many comedies work also through laughter to present views of the ways of the world which enable their audiences to understand more of themselves and the world through a recognition of their own as well as others' follies. **TRG SS**

See also bourgeois drama; carnival; comedy of manners; humours; irony; romantic comedy.

Further reading Northrop Frye, *Anatomy of Criticism*; Elder Olson, *The Theory of Comedy*; Wylie Sypher (ed.), *Comedy*.

COMEDY OF MANNERS

Comedy of Manners is a term generally applied to English comedies from the Restoration period – those of Etherege and Vanburgh are typical – and to similar works (such as Molière's plays or the comedies of Lonsdale or Coward in this century) in which the social conventions and customs of a leisured class sustain the dramatic impetus. Although it is often defined in terms which suggest a frivolous and superficial concern with fashions, decorum and etiquette, Comedy of Manners can be far more than a mirror-like re-creation of fashionable life held up on stage to an audience who can admire their own reflection. Its starting point is the view that human behaviour is patterned and consists of systems of codes and conventions (often implicit rather than explicit), which impose an order on experience by making it predictable and manageable; we send signals to others which they use (again often unconsciously) to 'place' us. Comedy of Manners is concerned with the gap between the outward conventional appearance of good order and the inner turmoil beneath the smooth surface. The discrepancy between outward appearance and inner reality can be a powerful means of investigating the relationships between the values enshrined in the code and the values people actually live by. **TRG SS**

See also bourgeois drama; comedy; humours; romantic comedy.

Further reading David L. Hirst, *Comedy of Manners*.

COMMEDIA DELL'ARTE

Commedia dell'arte (Italian, 'comedy of the profession') literally means the acting companies which operated in Italy from the 16th century, improvising plays round stock scenarios and characters (each with its own instantly recognizable mask and costume). The phrase has come to be used of the kind of performances such companies gave. Basically, their stock characters – Buffoon, Pantaloon, Harlequin, Columbine and so on – played out stories of seduction, impersonation and trickery with a wealth of physical, slapstick business which is one of the hallmarks of the style. (This business, the plots and the stock characters are all derived ultimately from the Roman comedies of Plautus and Terence, and from comedy devils and knockabout characters in the medieval **carnival** tradition.)

Commedia influences can be seen in **Pantomime**, in the works of Jonson, Shakespeare, Molière and Lope da Vega, and in the theatrical practice of 20th-century anti-naturalists such as Meyerhold. It had its widest 20th-century influence on Italian masters of the 1950s onwards (for example, Dario Fo and Franca Rame), and on the many companies which borrowed or imitated their techniques. It has a history, too, in puppet performances (for example, in the UK, Punch and Judy) and in circus and music-hall clowning from which its traditions travelled (in many cases little changed) into the routines of silent film comedy. **TRG KMcL SS**

See also comedy.

Further reading P.L. Ducharte, *The Italian Comedy.*

COMMEMORATION

Commemorative **architecture**, buildings constructed for remembrance, usually of the dead, has been a significant element in the buildings of most settled societies. The complex and often magnificent architecture of tombs, buildings constructed to both commemorate and house the dead, such as the famous pyramids of Gizeh in Egypt, is evidence of the continuing importance of philosophical and religious speculation on death from the earliest times.

The earliest tomb structures bear a close resemblance to contemporary domestic archetypes and it is assumed were conceived of almost literally as houses for the dead. As in many cultures the dead were believed to enter an afterlife, and many such tombs were furnished with the various necessities, either in actual, representational or symbolic form. In many developed cultures, areas were made for continuing ritual.

While tombs and other commemorative architecture come in any number of forms, the characteristic domed tomb of the ancient classical world is significant, for its origins, as it appears to evolve from a basic tumulus, a heap of stones over a grave, to a raised and enclosed round tower, surmounted by a domed roof – the model for many classical, **Romanesque** and **Renaissance** tombs.

It should be noted that the survival of tombs from early civilizations is often the greatest source available to the modern world of archaeological information. The spur to commemorate should not be taken as only associated with death. The distinctive triumphal arch of Roman antiquity, the great innovation of Latin architecture, otherwise so much in the shadow of Greek temple architecture, and many other buildings or structures erected to celebrate an event or an individual, have played a significant role in the built environment. The many aspects of commemoration are of course complex, many fine religious buildings in many cultures are erected to commemorate the deity, or holy men or women following a particular religion, many are built to commemorate a loved one or commend their soul to heaven, whereas the commemorative aspects of the patronage of some architecture may be for a far more down to earth desire to perpetuate a family name.

Even in funerary architecture, commemoration could often be called a part-motive, as even the most genuine religious motives are likely to have strong social and political significance, as well as providing the opportunity, throughout history, for the exercise of the skill of craftsman, designer and architect. **JM**

Further reading James Stevens Curl, *The Celebration of Death*; C. Brooks, *Mortal Remains.*

COMMENSALISM

Commensalism (Latin *commensalis*, 'sharing the same table') is a concept in the **life sciences**. According to the biologist Pierre-Joseph Beneden, writing in 1876, a commensal organism is one which benefits nutritionally from another without causing any harm. In the modern sense, the term encompasses organisms which benefit from shelter or transport. **RB**

See also amensalism; parasitism; symbiosis.

Further reading Philip Whitfield, *The Biology of Parasitism.*

COMMODITY

The term commodity (Latin, 'item of

stock'), in **economics**, usually refers to a raw material or primary product that is relatively homogeneous, and is traded on a free market. Examples are coffee, tin, sugar, wool, rubber, silver and cocoa. Commodities are bought and sold on a commodities exchange by dealers and commodity brokers or traders. The materials' homogeneity, fast communications and an efficient system of quality grading and control mean that commodities can be traded without an actual transfer of the goods. Speculators, hedgers and traders buy and sell rights of ownership in spot or forward (also known as futures) markets.

Commodity prices swing more violently than prices of manufactured goods. A small surplus of supply over demand can cause a dramatic slump in prices; floods or frost, for example, in a producing country can send a crop price soaring.

Commodities can be crucial for the welfare of developing countries dependent on one or two exports for most of their foreign exchange earnings – Zambia with copper, for instance, or Ivory Coast with coffee and cocoa. Consumers would prefer more stable prices, too. So two ways (both with faults) have been tried to stabilize commodity prices:

(1) International commodity agreements. These are agreements between producers and consumers which try to stabilize prices using buffer stocks and export or production quotas. They were in vogue in 1977 when the UN conference on trade and development (UNCTAD) recommended 18 commodities for agreements. But this plan got nowhere: the only agreements signed were for sugar, cocoa, tin, rubber and coffee. The trouble with the deal is that often the biggest producer or consumer does not join in. Also, when prices rise sharply, producers try to slide out of the agreement; when prices slump, consumers do likewise. No buffer stock has yet proved big enough to steady prices. The tin agreement, which managed to keep prices relatively stable over many years, collapsed spectacularly in 1986 when the buffer-stock manager ran out of money and the agreement's sponsoring governments refused to provide any more. Commodity agreements

benefit established (often high cost) producers at the expense of expanding (lower-cost) producers.

(2) Long-term contracts. These offer producers stable prices, but are negotiated with an eye to market prices; the more long-term contracts there are, the more marginal (and erratic) spot prices become. This has happened in the sugar market.

These attempts to stabilize prices have not worked well especially because commodity prices in 1980–85 all slumped at the same time, so swamping the money available, for example, for buffer stocks. So the **international monetary fund and European Economic Community** have tried to stabilize producers' export earnings too by compensatory financing making grants or loans to top up income. Here, too, the earnings slump in the early 1980s overstretched the cash on offer. **TF**

COMMUNICATION

A suitable phrase to define communication might be 'Social interaction through messages', which was coined by John Fiske in his book *Introduction to Communication Studies* (1990). Nevertheless it is a difficult word to define. The problem lies in its being a human activity so common that everyone recognizes it and takes it for granted. Not only does 'communication' take place when we talk or write to one another, it is also in how we dress, do our hair, or in what kind of car we drive. It is how we walk, stand, sit or dance. It is how we decorate our living spaces. It is what we perceive as important (and therefore choose to include within the camera frame) when we take a family snapshot.

However, despite such a range of inclusions, it is generally agreed that as a process, regardless of the stress put upon certain aspects and whatever the theoretical frames of reference employed, communication has five identifiable and fundamental elements: sender; receiver; channel (or mode); message; and effect. Thus, in the most basic terms, for any communication to take place a sender initiates a message, then encodes it (that is, translates it into a signal or signals, such as marks on paper – writing, drawing – Morse code or television signals). This is then sent, or transmitted, via a channel or medium (such as a book, telephone, television or clothes) to a receiver who decodes the message. In decoding the message, the receiver interprets it in some way and then usually returns a signal (answers) indicating whether the message has been understood or not. For example, a city executive (the 'sender') turning up for work in a grey suit and white blouse (the 'channel' or 'medium') is communicating something of her attitude to work. She may have intended to impress her boss (the 'receiver') with her seriousness and professionalism. Such an intention would be her message. Her communication would probably elicit (the 'decoding') a response of approval (the 'effect') from her boss. In the communication process this response constitutes a return signal, and in the example it might well be silent, even unconscious. If, however, the same executive arrived wearing studded leather jacket, jeans and a shaved head her boss's response signal might well be highly conscious, due to surprise (the 'effect') and confusion (the result of attempts to decode the message), and would probably be loudly articulated. Or the communication channel chosen for this might take the form of a written message, for example, her dismissal notice.

The central process of communication as detailed above has been subjected to study by two distinct methodologies of analysis identified (by John Fiske in the book named above) as the 'process' and 'semiotic' approaches. The 'process' school of study is linked particularly with **psychology** and **sociology**, while the semiotic school is more often linked with the **arts** and **linguistics**.

The 'process' school sees communication as the transmission of messages, a process by which, in Fiske's words, 'one person affects the behaviour or state of mind of another'. If the effect of the communication is different from that intended by the transmitter, the process school will examine the process to see why it produced a failure of communication. The 'semiotic' school sees communication as the transmission of messages, or texts. These are products of a specific **culture**, and are therefore subject to a variety of interpretations by the people concerned. That is to say that cultural differences between sender and receiver may alter the intended meaning in a communication and create misunderstanding. But such misunderstanding is not regarded as a measure of failure, rather as one of cultural difference; it may also create new meanings.

Communication is a subtle, complex and continuously fluctuating process, affected by a multitude of factors both external and internal. Two of the more important such elements are noise (either physical or semantic), and redundancy (together with its opposite, entropy).

'Noise' is anything which impedes or interferes with the message, and was not intended by the sender. Physical noise is interference to the communication channel: a hissing telephone line, for example, or 'snow' on a television screen. Semantic noise is any distortion to the message affecting its reception yet not intended by the sender. Thus it can refer to interference to the sender, the receiver, the message or the effect.

'Redundancy', in communication terms, means that part of a message which is predictable or conventional. It is an essential feature of our language. It exists to combat the effects of noise: by saying things more than once we reinforce the message, reducing the chances of misinterpretation. The opposite of redundancy is entropy, which refers to anything which is surprising or unpredictable. It can be seen, for example, in such artistic works as **poetry**, where the effect sought is one of unique and challenging expression.

Certain forms of communication receive specific attention. That described above is interpersonal communication. But when we talk to ourselves, either in an inner monologue or by processing impressions about the world around us, we are engaged in intrapersonal communication. All our inner thoughts, our responses to others, to the weather, to traffic, to television or print, to our wellbeing and our moods in general, all form a silent discourse which continually changes and in turn alters our **perception** of the world.

There is also a view that the communication process does not necessarily have to occur between two or more people. It might be argued that it also exists between a person and an inanimate object. We are not considering here some people's predilection for talking to pets or plants, but, for example, to the products made by artists. If no one sees a painting, can it be said that no act of communication has taken place in making that painting? Possibly, though the artist might argue that it had; that his or her communication was *with* the painting in an act of self-address. Thus the process would be artist ('sender') – subject matter ('message') – materials ('channel') – artist's self ('receiver') – artist's regard for product ('effect'). Not only that, but even if the painting is consumed by others, their interpreting ('decoding') of its 'message' may be different for each consumer. Each perceives the work according to his or her different values, culture and social background.

Finally, there seems to be common agreement that it is impossible *not* to communicate. Even remaining utterly immobile, straight-faced and 'expressionless' constitutes a form of communication, albeit a negative one. We may not want to think that we are influencing others by everything we do, but it is arguable that even by trying not to we are still exerting an influence, however unintended. Everything we do is open to interpretation; communication constantly takes place. **RG**

Further reading Len Masterman, *Teaching The Media.*

COMMUNISM

The core idea of communism, holding property in common, is very ancient. In **agrarian societies** communism was prescribed as the best way to realize ascetic or anti-materialist virtues, and to prevent the flourishing of selfish individualism or egoism. In early Western **Utopian** thought, from Plato's *Republic* to Thomas More's *Utopia*, communal holding of possessions was advocated to prevent rulers, and others, from becoming corrupt. The same ideals were present in early **Christian** social thought: poverty, chastity and obedience

were vital components of the monastic Christian life. Usually this kind of agrarian and ascetic communism was associated with respect for strong organizational hierarchies, in which the best would govern society.

Advocacy of the communist ideal in modern or industrial societies, by contrast, has not been associated with ascetic or hierarchical Utopias. Indeed, in **Marxist** thinking 'communism', the final stage of history, is envisaged as a society of absolute material abundance in which class division and the division of labour are no longer necessary because the production problems of the human race have been resolved. In this **ideology** the full realization of equality, liberty, community and abundance are all considered possible after the capitalist mode of production, having fully developed the productive forces, has been abolished.

Critics of modern communism maintain that the protection of some minimal private property rights are in fact preconditions of **democracy**, liberty and efficiency, and that in practice so-called communist régimes have betrayed their own egalitarian ideals establishing dictatorial and corrupt élites who effectively control an atomized and dependent population. **BO'L**

See also historical materialism; socialism and social democracy.

Further reading Émile Durkheim, *Socialism and Saint-Simon*; A. Ryan, *Property and Political Theory.*

COMMUNITY

Community (Latin, 'association'), in **ecology**, is the term applied to all the organisms in a given environment or habitat, interacting with each other in such a way as to confer distinct characteristics which enable it to be qualitatively distinguished from other communities. The concept of the community is largely a convenience term used by ecologists to denote a biological system under study. No living community can truly be isolated from those which surround it – the community of an oak forest, for example, is composed of smaller communities which live on particular tree types, animal corpses and so on.

Each species in a community lives in its **niche**, a mode of life which is defined largely by other species within the community. Species interact with one another and individuals react with other members of their species. These interactions are studied principally in terms of energy flow and the factors which affect it: thus, predator/prey relationships and territorial behaviour are of interest to the ecologist, as is the flow of nutrients through the **ecosystem**. A biological community is not a closed system and is therefore not stable, though a dynamic equilibrium may often exist if environmental conditions permit. Environmental disturbance causes a shift in the equilibrium and the community returns to stability, or **climax**, by the process of succession. This phenomenon has been likened to the **homeostatic** control exhibited by individual organisms, and there is a school of thought which maintains that biological communities are complex organisms. (This holistic outlook is epitomized in James Lovelock's **Gaia hypothesis**, which suggests that the entire community of the biosphere acts as a single, complex organism.)

In **sociology**, community is one of the most elusive and vague terms in use. At the very least it refers to a set of relationships operating within certain boundaries, locations or territories. The term may also be used to refer to relations which do not operate in a clearly defined location, such as the 'Gay community'. The term is often used in a prescriptive sense.

It is possible to distinguish three main uses of the term community within sociology: (1) it is described as a locality. (This closely approximates the geographers' use of the term.); (2) it has also been used to denote a network of relationships, which can be characterized by conflict as well as mutuality; (3) it may refer to a particular type of relationship which has certain qualities. In this, its popular usage, it is associated with positive connotations, as 'community spirit'. This is a romanticized view of 'traditional society' which has given rise to the concept of community with the associated features of cohesion, support and intimacy.

Whatever the difficulties of definition, communities all operate within boundaries or territories. Boundaries serve to demarcate membership from nonmembership. Some community boundaries are rigidly maintained – for example, some religious communities. Others are more fluid and open. **DA RB**

See also assimilation; biome; competition; culture; ethnicity; food web; race; sexuality; social integration; society; subculture; urbanism/urbanization.

Further reading C. Bell and H. Newby, *Community Studies*.

COMPARATIVE ADVANTAGE

Comparative advantage, in **economics**, is a principle of trade which holds that there is a benefit to specialization and trade where there are differences between countries in the relative efficiency of producing two products, even though one country has an **absolute advantage** in producing both products.

This principle, first described by Ricardo, demonstrates how countries can gain from trading with each other even if one of them is more efficient in every activity. For example, suppose nation A could use its resources to produce wheat or cotton or some combination of the two. Suppose further, that nation A can produce both wheat and cotton cheaper (with less resources) than nation B, so that nation A has an *absolute advantage* in the production of both wheat and cotton. Nation A can benefit, nevertheless, from specialization in the production of that product whose relative cost is lower and then trade that product with nation B for the other product.

Comparative advantage arises from the uneven distribution of the world's resources together with the requirement of different proportions of factors of production to produce different commodities and services. Resources in this context include natural resources, capital goods, size and training of the labour force, and technical knowledge. **TF**

COMPARATIVE-HISTORICAL LINGUISTICS

For centuries now, **languages** have been studied by systematically comparing one language with another, and by extension, linguists have tried to establish the relations between whole groups, or families, of languages. A notable stimulus was provided in the late 18th century by Sir William Jones, with the surprise discovery that the ancient Indian language, Sanskrit, shared certain fundamental properties with many European languages, including Latin and Greek. In the wake of this finding, a biological metaphor was adopted: genetic relationships between languages were sought and family trees were drawn to reveal the pattern of antecedent languages from which later forms of language evolved.

In the process of change, it was assumed that a single, parent language split, gradually but irrefutably, in such a way that subsequent developments followed separate routes in the creation of new language systems. While this process of divergence precipitates quite distinct languages, a family resemblance is nevertheless maintained, owing to the common origins and the systematic nature of the changes involved. The process of divergence is repeated continuously, resulting in a tree diagram comprising numerous divisions and subdivisions, which eventually terminate in well-attested languages and dialects. In the case of Sanskrit and Greek, for instance, it was reasoned that, ultimately, they must both stem from a common ancestor known as Proto-Indo-European. Clearly, this ancestor language is no longer extant, so the historical linguist must undertake a reconstruction (in part at least) which will provide a plausible description of the parent language.

A major difficulty is that languages embody numerous idiosyncrasies which could militate against an accurate reconstruction. Furthermore, languages can change in several different ways, not simply through the influence of historical processes (see, for example, **pidgins and creoles**). All of these extraneous influences must be carefully sifted out in the course of a reconstruction concerned with the genetic links between languages. In this regard, a fundamental problem is to identify items in different languages which are essentially equivalent. Equivalence tends to be established in terms of the structure of particular words (see **morphology**) as well as the sound patterns in evidence (see **phonology**). The kinds of changes which occur are not random or arbitrary, which means that the ambition to reconstruct long-deceased languages is less daunting than it appears to be on first inspection.

The concern with how languages change is underpinned by the complementary desire to explain why languages change. One approach argues that certain configurations of speech sounds are inherently more robust than others. Thus, a sort of 'natural phonology' dictates that particular sounds will remain immutable, and furthermore, be implicated in the changes which do occur in neighbouring sounds. A quite distinct approach regards language change as a socially motivated phenomenon. Systematic variation is regarded as a natural characteristic of language (consider, for example, the different ways of pronouncing 'grass' in English). The origins of language change are then explained on the basis that people systematically choose one variant rather than another, according to a complex range of social factors, including age, gender, class, level of formality, and so on. **MS**

Further reading T. Bynon, *Historical Linguistics*; H.H. Hock, *Principles of Historical Linguistics*.

COMPETITION

Life scientists define competition as the interaction which occurs between living organisms when there is demand for a common resource such as food, space or a mate. Competition is an important type of interaction between the members of a biological community: in a hypothetical situation where there are limitless resources, the population increases indefinitely. Since, in reality, resources are finite and variable, a point is inevitably reached at which competition occurs. The individuals or species which are more successful in this competition will have a better chance of reproducing successfully than their competitors; this is the principle behind **natural selection**. Between species, competition for a **niche** appears inevitably to result in success for only one species – this is the competitive exclusion principle. Where two or more species do appear to occupy the same niche, it is usually found that minor habitat differences enable the two to avoid direct competition. Animals have evolved complex behavioural strategies for competition; this is well illustrated by competition for mates. Human manipulation of the environment is often based in removing competitors so that a desirable species can flourish in a niche which would normally be occupied by a different species. In some cases, **biological control** has been facilitated by the introduction of new competitors from geographically distant communities.

In **economics**, competition arises in situations where there is more than one seller in a market or, on the buyer's side, more than one buyer in a market. Competition is not black and white; there are shades between pure competition and pure **monopoly**. Perfect competition, for economic theorists, is an idyllic state with a large number of sellers and buyers, with a homogeneous good and free entry to the market. No buyer or seller is big enough to affect the price through his or her purchases or sales, so all are price takers. If firms make supernormal profits (that is, more than the minimum needed to keep them in business) more firms enter, competing the price down. In the real world there are few perfectly competitive markets. **RB TF**

See also guild.

Further reading Joseph Moran, *Introduction to Environmental Science.*

COMPLEX NUMBERS

In **mathematics**, the complex numbers are the final stage in the search to extend the number system to obtain all the numbers that might be needed. The process began with the natural numbers, then the **integers**, then the **rational numbers**, then the **algebraic numbers** and then the **real numbers**. (This is the order in which they were discovered and used; today textbooks usually skip the algebraic numbers.) The real numbers are a **field**; the problem is that they are not algebraically closed ('algebraically closed' means that every **polynomial** equation has a solution; in the real numbers, the polynomial equation $x^2 + 1 = 0$ has none). The complex numbers are formed by adding in an extra number i, which is defined to be a solution of $x^2 + 1 = 0$ ($-i$ is also a solution) it is the square root of -1. This number can be multiplied by any real number; this gives rise to numbers known (somewhat unfortunately) as imaginary. Complex numbers are those which are sums of real and imaginary ones, such as $3 + 4i$.

It turns out that the complex numbers are algebraically closed; any polynomial equation has a complex number solution. This fact is known as the fundamental theorem of algebra, and shows that the complex numbers are as far as we need to go. The name this result was given shows its perceived importance; it ranks it with the fundamental theorem of the **calculus** discovered by Newton and Leibniz, which precipitated some of the most important developments leading to modern mathematics. However, the theorem has failed to live up to this promise; it is a direct consequence of some of the deeper theorems of complex analysis. Although it is often used, it has not really expanded the horizons of mathematics.

Complex analysis, mentioned above, was developed by Augustin-Louis Cauchy (1789–1857). He sought to extend the methods of **analysis** of **functions** of real numbers, recently made rigorous by himself, Karl Weierstrass (1815–97) and Bernard Bolzano (1781–1848). The definitions they came up with for such concepts as the limit were translated into the terms of complex numbers with much ease. The results of complex analysis are, however, very different from those of real analysis; they all stemmed from the theorem which is named after Cauchy, and some of them were very different from what was expected. The concepts of differentiation and integration are even more closely linked for complex numbers than they are for real numbers. Complex analysis is difficult, partly because the functions are hard to conceptualize.

It certainly seemed as though complex numbers would never be used for anything concrete they did, after all, involve imaginary quantities. Electrical engineers discovered that alternating currents and the properties of circuits associated with them could most easily be represented by the use of complex numbers. This is another example where mathematical research produced something apparently totally abstract that eventually turned out to be extremely practical. **SMcL**

COMPLEXITY

In **computing**, it is vital to have some idea of how long a program will take to execute before it is run. If it is going to take the whole of the lifetime of the universe before the computer comes up with the answer to a problem, then it is pointless to tie up valuable hardware to try and solve it. The concept of how long an **algorithm** will take to solve a given problem is that of complexity. It is usual to take some number obviously connected with the problem (for example, if the problem is to check if n is a prime number, n would be an obvious number to choose) and examine how the length of an algorithm to solve the problem for n varies with n. In the case of the prime, the complexity is n, multiplied by some constant. (It is usual to ignore constants, because the constant is dependent on the particular computer on which the program is run.)

One of the most studied problems in this field is the 'salesman problem'. Given n towns and a distance, is it possible for a travelling salesman to visit all the towns via some route which has length less than the given distance? This problem is the best-known example of ones which are known as NP-complete; that means that it is not possible to *solve* the problem in **polynomial** time (NP stands for 'no polynomial') but a solution, a path given as a response, can be *checked* in polynomial time. **SMcL**

COMPLEXITY THEORY

The complexity theory, in **science**, is a development from **chaos theory** and the **law of nature**. It states that if random happenings in Nature are left to themselves, they will settle not into the simplest possible pattern (as was once thought), but into complex patterns. In computer simulations of ants carrying eggs in a nest, for example, it has been discovered that left to themselves they will gradually arrange the eggs in concentric circles, largest on the outside and smallest on the inside. When this abstract model – which imported no outside 'intelligence' of any kind, merely charting an unprogrammed series of random movements – was tested by observing real ants, they did exactly the same. The theory has implications for the process of **evolution** and for **cosmology** – and it suggests, as **Euclidean geometry**, **quantum mechanics** and **relativity** did before it, that our concepts of the 'laws of physics' or the 'laws of the universe' still need refining. **KMcL**

COMPOSITION AND STRUCTURE OF THE EARTH

Since the Earth is approximately 6,370 km in radius and geologists have access only to the outer few kilometres, it is remarkable that they can claim to identify the structure and composition of the interior. Although natural processes have brought up material (including diamonds) from several hundred kilometres deep and scattered meteorites over the surface, the main means of knowing what is at the centre rest on an understanding of **seismology**. Fortunately, observation and inference yield a consistent picture, and one which implies how the present structure has come about. In the small amount of space available here, the easiest way of presenting this material is to describe what is known, then say how it is known and then conclude by outlining how it came about.

Geologists divide the solid Earth into three main layers. At the surface is the *crust*, ranging from 6 km thick in the oceans to 90 km in major mountain ranges, The continents are heterogeneous, as described under **rock cycle**, but the overall composition is andesite to granite (that is, mainly potassium and sodium aluminosilicates with some free silica). The ocean crust consists of basalt (mainly calcium/sodium aluminosilicates, with considerable pyroxene and olivine). Beneath the crust lies the *mantle*, reaching 2,900 km below the surface. Mantle rocks have been brought to the surface and are known to consist of peridotite, composed of the minerals olivine (85%) and pyroxene (15%). The form of the peridotite varies with depth, becoming more compact as pressure increases. Between 50 and 250 km is a zone where up to 5% of the rock is molten and the molten fraction has the composition of basalt. Below 2,900 km is the Earth's *core*, which is now believed to have two components: an inner core of radius 1,215 km, a solid ball made of a 20/80 nickel iron mix; an outer molten layer of 88% iron and 12% sulphur. The density of the core (10–13 tonnes per cubic metre) is very much higher than that of the mantle (3.3–5.4 tonnes per cubic metre).

The existence of the core was deduced from observations of earthquake vibrations, using knowledge of the effects of different states and densities on the speed and direction of travel. Earthquakes generate two kinds of vibration which travel through the Earth: P waves vibrate in the direction of travel, while S waves vibrate at right angles to it. P waves move faster and both travel faster in more dense material, except that S waves will not travel through a liquid. The absence of S waves from earthquakes on the opposite side of the world from the recorder is the clearest indication of the liquid core. There are other zones where P waves are not detected as a result of the effects of refraction when entering or leaving more dense layers. The central, solid core was inferred from the faster than expected arrival of P waves from earthquakes directly opposite the observatory and from others apparently reflected from the surface of the core. Confidence in these inferences about the interior was greatly strengthened when other researchers investigating the Earth's magnetic field showed that it could best be explained as the result of electrical currents flowing in a liquid metallic core.

The characteristics required to carry both seismic waves and electric currents in ways consistent with the observations also coincide with the indications from a study of meteorites. There are three kinds of meteorites, iron, stony/iron and stony, especially a group called 'chondritic' after the droplet-shaped particles in them. Chondritic mete-orites consist of peridotite, nickel/iron, iron sulphide and olivine in the chondrites. This is also the composition of the solid components of other astronomical objects, including the Sun. It is now believed that the Earth formed by the accretion of particles similar to chondritic meteorites and was composed largely of iron (35%), oxygen (30%), silicon (15%) and magnesium (10%).

As gravity forced these particles together, the temperature rose so that the iron melted and settled toward the centre as a result of its greater density. Just as slag in a blast furnace rises to the surface, so the lighter metal silicates and oxides rose to form an upper layer – the mantle.

However, the early Earth had no crust, and an account of just how this was formed has been gained by insights from **plate tectonics** combined with known chemical differences. At hot spots in the upper mantle, convection currents formed, as they now do at mid-ocean ridges. Basaltic magma was lighter and more mobile than the peridotite and so rose to the surface, solidified and spread across the sea floor to form the ocean crust. At destructive plate margins this basalt was drawn below the surface, compressed and heated. Less dense and more mobile minerals would be left at the surface, as they are today in island arcs composed of andesite. Over hundreds of millions of years these island arcs would be progressively built up into continents, with associated erosion, deposition and mountain building. Beneath mountainous zones, melting occurred, with selective mobilization of some minerals and recrystallization of granite at depth. Subsequent erosion has revealed granite at the surface, including extensive areas like the Canadian shield.

This process, with selective mobilization of some elements and minerals, is consistent with observed differences between peridotite, basalt and granite. Olivine and magnesium are more plentiful in peridotite and so were left behind. Silica and aluminosilicates were progressively enriched, except that calcium is richer in basalt than granite. The result of these processes was to give the crust a different chemical composition from that of the mantle, with less magnesium and iron and more of the other metals, especially aluminium. Nevertheless, the crust is predominantly made of only a small number of elements: oxygen (47%), silicon (28%), aluminium (8%), iron (5%), calcium, sodium, potassium and magnesium – taking the total to 99%, so that the other 80 odd elements make up about 1% in total. In practice, these few elements are combined in complex and stable minerals, especially feldspars (aluminosilicates), which make them difficult to use as anything but stone. Fortunately other internal and surface geological processes have created local concentrations of many minerals which can be used as sources of useful elements. Biological processes have also contributed to these local concentrations, most notably in modifying the **atmosphere**. **PS**

COMPULSION

Compulsion (from Latin *compulsum*, 'driven together') suggests the act of an irresistible compelling force, or an involuntary action which is the result of constraint: something not chosen by free will. Its Latin root suggests more than one hidden source for an action.

In **psychoanalysis**, compulsive thoughts and actions are those which the person feels compelled to carry out, or otherwise risk **anxiety**; involuntary actions are the result of the failure of the mechanism of unconscious repression, or, alternatively, a manifestation of feeling of alienation, as the person feels that the actions are not part of themselves. Although compulsion seems to happen spontaneously, it cannot be defined as a spontaneous act because there is no element of creativity or growth involved.

An example of a compulsion (given by D.W. Winnicott) is that of a young boy who ties objects in his home together with string. This worries his family especially when he eventually ties the string around his sister's throat. The compulsion is analysed as covering up his anxiety and fear of separation. He has been separated from his mother many times, for example when she has been ill in hospital and when she gave birth to his sister. **MJ**

COMPUTABILITY

A **function** is computable if there is a method by which a computer can be programmed to calculate the function. This is not a precise definition, and several attempts to sharpen it have led to definitions which have all been proved to be the same. One approach was to look at the functions themselves, and to ignore the computer completely; this approach gave the computable functions their other commonly used name, the recursively enumerable functions. Another definition was that devised by Alan Turing (1912–54), the true pioneer in the field of theoretical computing. He came up with the notion of a **Turing machine**, a simple mathematical model of the insides of a computer. His definition of computable was simply that a Turing machine could find the value of the function in a time that could be proved to be finite. A computer programmer can be confident that any computer can calculate a computable function in a finite time, though he may not be able to know in advance how long the calculation will take (see **complexity**).

From the definition of recursively enumerable functions, it can be shown that there are countably many computable functions (in other words, that they can be arranged in an infinite list). This means that there are functions which are not computable. The fact that functions exist which are not computable puts limits on the abilities of computers, which has implications in the field of **artificial intelligence** if, as some think, non-computable functions are inherent to intelligent thought.

A third way of looking at computability is Church's thesis, named after its originator, Alonso Church (1903–). This states that any function for which an informal **algorithm** can be written to compute the value of the function is computable. For example, the function that is 1 for values of n which are multiples of two and 0 elsewhere is computable, and can be calculated by the informal algorithm that counts from 0 in steps of 2 until either n has been reached or $n + 1$ has been reached; if the former then the function is 1 and if the latter then it is zero. This is a very simple example of a computable function, and it is not difficult to turn this informal algorithm into a formal proof that a Turing machine carrying out that process must terminate. For more complicated functions it is not obvious that this will be the case. The reason that Church's thesis is not really a mathematical idea is that it is about the relationship between informal reasoning and the formalized approach of the mathematical arguments, something that is the domain of **philosophy**. It is also a statement which cannot be proved, for exactly the same reason: the evidence is purely scientific nobody has ever managed to find an function for which it fails. **SMcL**

Further reading T.H. Crowley, *Understanding Computers*.

COMPUTATIONAL LINGUISTICS

For perhaps the majority of linguists, and other researchers interested in **language**, computers have come to be seen as a valuable analytical tool. Traditionally, language-related topics, such as the study of grammar, have relied on a corpus of sentences which, though constantly increasing, is nevertheless pointedly small in comparison to the sheer quantity of authentic language data which can now be scrutinized. Undoubtedly there will continue to be valid reasons for focusing on a limited and carefully selected body of data, but equally clearly, new insights on the very nature of language are emerging simply through the study of vast corpora of language samples.

A major branch of computational linguistics has been involved with the attempt to produce computer systems which can effectively simulate the way we both understand and produce natural language. However, it is one thing to programme a computer so that its language outputs resemble those of natural human language. It is quite another to devise a computational system which processes language in the same way as human beings do, and it is this latter aim to which many researchers aspire. A fundamental problem in this approach has been how to accommodate the common phenomenon of breakdowns in the natural process of communication. If we want a computer to be able to interact effectively with people, then it will have to be able to cope with the multifarious range of minor interruptions, reworkings, signs of incomprehension and so on which characterize natural linguistic interaction.

Computers have also become influential in the preparation of dictionaries. It is becoming increasingly common for the initial stages of dictionary-making to be based on the computational analysis of enormous collections of authentic language samples, comprising several million words, both written and spoken, from a wide variety of sources. The guiding concept has been the use of concordancing, in which an enormous language corpus is scanned for every example of a particular word, along with its linguistic context. (The computer highlights several words on either side of the desired word.) The great advantage of such concordancing is that it allows the lexicographer to establish which words are consistently associated together. Thus, our knowledge of collocations has been vastly improved and is now beginning to provide many new insights on the inner workings of lexical and syntactic organization.

Without doubt, the age of the computer has opened up new vistas for research on a wide range of language-related topics. Machine translation, computer-assisted language learning, speech synthesis, **stylistics**, **lexicography** and **lexicology**, speech processing, **syntax**, **artificial intelligence** are characteristic areas. **MS**

Further reading R. Grishman, *Computational Linguistics: an Introduction*.

COMPUTER

Few technological advances have had such a decisive effect on human society as the invention of the computer (it has been described as a second industrial revolution), and yet **computing** is still in its infancy. Ever since computer technology became portable and cheap with the invention of the silicon chip in the late 1960s, the industrialized way of life has been completely revolutionized. Everything has changed, from the factory floor to music, from banking to the prevention of crime.

The reason that the computer has been able to cause such far-reaching changes is that it is so versatile. The whole story of the industrial revolution until the computer has been that of the production of more and more specialized machines, to the point where car assembly lines need to be substantially altered when the model of car to be produced is changed. Now, the computer can not only be used for millions of different applications (so that, for example, the same computer could run accounts and check production standards), but the computer system itself does not usually need to be changed; just the **program** that tells it what to do.

There are essentially two types of computer (others are hybrids of these types). Analog computers have as their inputs physical quantities (such as a voltage down a wire or pressure on a lever) which the internal workings process to give an output in the form of other physical quantities. They have major drawbacks. First, their accuracy is low and is limited by insuperable physical problems such as friction. Second, the accuracy of the results also depends on the apparatus used to measure them (such as a voltmeter) and on the observer's ability to use them correctly. Third, they are often designed with a specific problem in mind and are useless once that problem is solved. (An example would be the model used by a civil engineer to see if the bridge he intends building will collapse in high winds – it is totally pointless once the bridge is built.)

Such devices have been rendered virtually obsolete by the successful design of digital computers since the 1940s. A digital computer accepts input in the form of numbers, processes them inside by means of a program, and presents the output in terms of numbers. Such computers solve (or at least alleviate) all the problems with analog computers mentioned above. The results can be presented in an easy to read form such as a numerical display or printout; their accuracy is limited only by the accuracy of the figures entered in and the amount of time the operator wishes to spend allowing the computer to improve the accuracy of the result; and they can solve other problems by means of altering their internal program, which is far easier than on those analog machines which were designed to solve general problems. **SMcL**

Further reading T. Forester, *The Microelectronics Revolution.*

COMPUTER ART

As there is no longer anything sacred about a paintbrush, and thanks to the development of digital imaging, artists may now use computers as tools for the production of art, and do so relatively cheaply and to increasing effect. So long as the work of art is on the computer screen, it is just a collection of points of light. Each point is controllable through software and various input devices (mouse, joystick, electronic pen), so that it can be infinitely modified; modification is also made by executing various computer processing convolutions (for example, reverse, enlarge, make smaller, sharpen, blur, change all colours, turn into fine art, and so on). The image may be printed out at any stage (either as a computer bit map or, on some systems, as a video signal), and its development can be further continued while copies of the 'printing stage' images can be stored on disk (computer disk or video disk).

Such flexibility is exciting, and useful in the graphic arts, but at present (mid-1990s) tends to be held back by the high cost and relatively low quality of suitable output devices. One intriguing development is interactive art, where you can sit at a computer, load whatever image you want from your own creation to any work of art from the present or the past and modify it and play with it to your heart's content. **MG**

Further reading J. Lansdowne and R. A. Earnshaw (eds.), *Computers in Art, Design and Animation;* Caron Ward and Rhonda O'Meara (eds.), *Towards a New Aesthetic: Exploring Computer Aided Art & Design.*

COMPUTER GRAPHICS

One of the major ways that computers have made an impact on today's culture is in the field of entertainment. They would never have been able to do this except for their ability to produce images on screens or on paper – their graphics capability.

The first computer graphics were produced manually (using the computer basically to print out what was typed into it).

They consisted of pictures drawn using the characters available on computer keyboards. Once computers began to be connected to monitor screens, by directly causing the electron gun at the back of a television screen to light up points on a screen at the direction of the computer, it became possible to produce much more detailed and (eventually) coloured images; **computer art** packages began to be developed. The operator could input an image and have it appear on the screen; better methods were developed to do this rather than typing in the colour of every spot on the screen, by using instruments such as scanners (which take an image on paper such as a photograph and automatically store it in the computer's memory) and light-pens (which allow the operator to draw on a pad and have the result appear on the screen as if it were a piece of paper).

This was still only using the computer as a drawing tool; the next step was to use the computer to help create the design. The earliest steps in this direction led to the first computer games: drawing a pair of bats and a ball on a screen, and moving them according to the instructions of players using keyboards or joysticks was the first example. There are again two divisions in this, which might be called interactive graphics and non-interactive graphics.

Non-interactive graphics use the computer to produce just one image; today's computers will often be programmed to perform tasks like drawing charts and graphs from tables of data. A computer can also be used to take a start picture and an end picture and draw a series of images moving successively away from the start and towards the end (a process from the animation industry known as in-betweening), or to combine two images in one (used in the movie *Star Wars* to produce backgrounds for scenes using models). These techniques and others like them have had a major influence on the special effects departments in the film industry. Images of **fractals** created by computer have turned out to look very like natural phenomena such as coastlines. Non-interactive graphics are also used for more serious purposes; there are artists who create pictures which are partly the creation of the computer (a phenomenon which leads to the question, can computers be artists?).

Interactive graphics have had serious spinoffs as well as providing ever more sophisticated games. The main limitation of such systems is the complexity of the images; a convincing picture on a screen has thousands of items of information which need to be updated very fast. The needs of the entertainment industry have financed much research on faster computation, which has been of great importance in many other areas. **SMcL**

COMPUTER SIMULATION

One of the major problems in 20th-century science and engineering is the expense of experiment. It costs money to build a model of a bridge to test a new design, for example, and such a model may not be very accurate as a mimic of the behaviour of the actual bridge. In another example, some investigations of the very early universe cannot be performed using telescopes. The answer to both of these problems is the computer simulation. The programmer inputs the relevant parameters (for the bridge it could be the average wind speed or the strength of the steel used for example) into the computer, which contains a program to mimic the behaviour of the real bridge or the real universe. In the second example, the results would be compared with the appearance of the universe today; for the engineer designing the bridge, unworkable designs will be eliminated without the need to build costly and time-consuming models. **SMcL**

See also computer.

COMPUTING

The **computer**, as a tool for the processing of information, has had a vast impact on 20th-century life. It has been said that there have only been three inventions to deal with information: writing, printing and the computer. The third is of a different order from the first two, because it deals with the processing of information as well as with its storage.

Computers can have such a great effect because of their versatility. With different **programs** running, the same computers can perform vastly different tasks; their applications are endless. The versatility of today's digital computers (compared with their analog ancestors) is dependent on two insights. The first, made by Claude Elwood Shannon (1916–), is that the two states of **Boolean logic** (true and false) can be represented using circuits, current flowing for true and not flowing for false. They can also represent numbers, using the binary **number system**, with current flowing for 1 and not flowing for 0. The second insight was made by John von Neumann (1903–57), who realized that programs, being made up of symbols, could be interpreted in the computer in the same way that data could, leading the way towards programs stored in memory (see **von Neumann model**).

A computer, though versatile, is not omnipotent. There are definite limits to the tasks that computers can perform. The first step towards designing a program to solve a problem is to work out an **algorithm** (a set of rules for performing a task) to solve it. The study of those tasks which computers can perform (strictly speaking, the functions computers can calculate) is known as **computability**. The study of this began with the work of Alan Turing (1912–54) on the **Turing machine**, a theoretical model of a computer. Other approaches include the philosophical idea of **Church's thesis**, which basically is that any function for which an algorithm to calculate it can be devised informally can be computed in practice. Related to this is the study of how fast computers can perform those tasks they can perform, because for practical purposes a task that takes thousands of years to complete is not worth attempting; this study is known as **complexity**.

Once an algorithm for a task has been developed, it is necessary to program it into the computer so that the computer can perform it. Originally, computers only understood a small number of instructions (typically a dozen) related to the manipulation of the locations in which memorized items are stored and their contents. These instructions are known as machine code. However, it is difficult for a human programmer to understand these instructions and to visualize what is going on. For this reason, **high level languages** were developed in which each instruction represents many machine code instructions, and which allow a far more structured approach to programs. Such structuring is perhaps furthest developed in **functional programming**.

One of the major industrial uses of computers is the control of **robots**. Although these are not the rapacious monsters of science fiction, they do pose ethical and political problems, as they replace human beings in the workplace. The jobs they can undertake are presently very limited, owing to the difficulty of designing a robot which can cope with unpredictable items in its environment. All the problems which might occur have to be foreseen beforehand, and solutions explicitly programmed in, and this is difficult outside very limited and controlled environments, such as laboratories. One of the major thrusts in research in computing is in the field of **artificial intelligence**, the (long-term) aim being to build a computer which can perform to or beyond the level of a human being.

Apart from in the workplace and as a research tool, one of the main ways that computers have affected lives this century has been through entertainment. From the earliest days when computers were first programmed to control television screens, people began to design games with more and more sophisticated **computer graphics**. The ability to use the computer to create images has also been exploited by film and television to memorable effect.

As a research tool, **computer simulations** have been the most useful applications of computers. Their ability to perform tedious and complicated calculations far quicker than human beings can (and without grumbling) has meant that a mathematical model of a situation (such as the position of particles in the early universe, or the design of a bridge) can be programmed into the computer which will then perform experiments (changing the position of the particles with time, or varying wind speed) to see what happens. This eliminates a large part of the need for expensive building and testing of physical models to destruction in engineering, and makes it possible to perform experiments dependent on conditions impossible to re-create on Earth.

The computer is the most versatile tool which humankind has ever developed. Like all tools, it has the potential for misuse. Many foresee a society dominated by a few who use computers to control the many; others see computers as the instrument which will one day free humankind from the slavery to physical effort (and maybe even some degree of mental effort), to concentrate on leisure and the pursuit of enjoyment. Whatever happens, the one thing that is reasonably certain is that with the development of computers society will never be the same again. **SMcL**

Further reading J. Weizenbaum, *Computer Power and Human Reason*.

CONCEPT see Idea

CONCEPTUAL ART

Conceptual art was a loose umbrella term which gained currency in Western arts **criticism** during the 1960s. It described a variety of art forms which placed emphasis not on the material presence of the work of art but on its 'conceptual' meaning. (The approach was analogous to **new criticism** in **literature**.) In practice, this threw up a variety of activities from Performance Art and Body Art through to **minimalism**. Much of this work was directed at exploring the conventional limits of art through the deployment of a range of anti-art practices. Conceptual art is often abstruse, uninterested for the most part in audience comprehension, and designed to inspire indifference. The intention is that experimenting with unorthodox art forms will turn attention away from questions of representation and **mimesis** towards the reality of the work's conceptual framework. The sceptic may still want to ask what the conceptual artist will despise as irrelevant questions: (1) What is 'art' for?, and (2) Does conceptual art fulfil that purpose, whatever it may be? **KMcL MG PD**

Further reading D. Krishna, *The Art of the Conceptual: Explorations in a Conceptual Maze over Three Decades*.

CONCERTO

Concerto (Italian, 'concert'), in European art music, means a work in which one or more solo instruments perform in such a way as to contrast or blend with the accompanying orchestra. The form was devised in the 17th century, at first for church use and then as vehicles for secular soloists, in particular violinists. At this early stage, the idea of display, common in later concertos (notably the barnstormers of the 19th and 20th centuries) was hardly apparent. The feeling, whether in solo concertos or *concerti grossi* ('fat concertos'), for a group of soloists and orchestra, was one of contrast – and this has persisted, quieter concertos being written (and enjoyed by the public) as often as virtuoso show-pieces. **KMcL**

CONFEDERATION

A confederation (Latin, 'those who league together') is a political structure which consists of independent states or entities joined by agreement into a union of equals. The main distinction between a confederation and a federation is that the power of the central authority is delegated in a confederation but is autonomous in a federation; or, to put matters another way, in a confederation **sovereignty** rests with the constituent states, whereas in a federation it is shared between the federal government and the states (or provinces). This distinction is much clearer in the German language in which a *Staatenbund* is a confederation while a *Bundesstaat* is a federation.

Another way of distinguishing a confederation from a federation is that the former is usually a union for specific purposes (for example free trade or defence), whereas a federation is all-purpose. In its current form, the European Community is mostly confederal in character. For instance, the executive authority of the Community is shared collectively among the member-states in the form of the Council of Ministers in which each state's minister is formally equal. Moreover, the European Community does not have a mandatory common defence or foreign policy. Yet many argue that the legal institutions of the Community have acquired federal characteristics, and that (albeit qualified) majority voting in the Council of Ministers suggests incipient **federalism**; and some even claim that the Maastricht Treaty has established a federal European Union. **BO'L**

Further reading M. Forsyth, *Unions of States: the Theory and Practice of Confederation.*

CONFLICT THEORY

Sociologists use the term conflict theory to refer to any theory or collection of theories which emphasize the role of conflict in human societies. More specifically conflict theory refers to a collection of theories of the 1960s, which provided an alternative model of social life to that of the then dominant branch of sociology, structural-functionalism.

The structural-functionalist school of thought portrayed societies as governed by a consensus of values. Conflict theorists argued that functionalist sociology disregarded conflict of value and interest in society, or at best regarded them as of secondary importance. As an alternative to functionalism, conflict theorists offered a model of society and social change which gave primacy to the role of **power**, coercion and the pursuit of economic and political interest.

Some versions of conflict theory were based on the ideas of Marx. For Marx, the whole of society was divided into two basic classes representing the interests of **capital** and labour. The conflict between these two interests, he argued, would eventually transform society. Some, however, drew on the work of Simmel, who believed that conflict had positive functions for social stability and helped to preserve groups and collectivities. **DA**

See also alienation; authority; bourgeoisie; class; consensus theory; dependency theory; discourses; dominant ideology; ethnicity; feminism; hegemony; ideology; Marxism; race; social control; social order; sociology of knowledge.

Further reading L. Coser, *The Functions of Social Conflict;* R. Dahrendorf, *Class and Class Conflict in Industrial Society;* J. Rex, *Social Conflict: a Conceptual and Theoretical Analysis.*

CONFUCIANISM

Confucianism is named after Confucius, the Latin form of Kong Fu Zi ('Master Kong'). Little is known for certain of Kong himself. He lived in the 6th-5th centuries BCE (*c.*551–479 BCE), and is said variously to have been a civil servant, a government minister, a provincial ruler and a teacher. After his death he acquired a reputation not unlike that of Socrates in the West: a 'method' was attributed to him, a body of anecdote was created by followers, and 'his' teachings became the basis for a vast philosophical system. Unlike Socrates, however, he became personally revered, as a semi-divine being: temples were built to him, and pilgrims visited his tomb, right down to the present day.

Confucius was not a religious teacher, but an ethical philosopher. He became associated with religion because he edited the the *Wu Jing* ('Five Classics'), a repository of Chinese religious and ethical thought and history, and because his followers produced a collection of dialogues and sayings purportedly his, the *Lun Yü* ('Collected Sayings' or 'Analects'), which became a central text of the Confucian **religion**, and is still treated with the reverence due to holy scripture. His disciples Meng-zi (Mencius, 372–389 BCE) and Xun-zi (*c.*300–238 BCE) further codified the system of thought and belief, something Confucius himself would probably have deplored now attached to Confucius' name. Until the outbreak of World War II, knowledge of this system, and of the Confucian scriptures (collectively known as 'The Great Learning') which enshrined it, were compulsory parts of all tertiary education and civil service training in China.

Essentially, Confucius was uninterested in religion. He spoke of a supreme being

(*Tian*, 'heaven'), but was entirely happy with the vast pantheon of gods and supernatural beings of traditional Chinese religion. Although later Confucianism had, and has, temples, priests and a creed-like codification of belief, none of these are essential. There is no **fundamentalism** in Confucianism, any more than in Platonism or Jungianism.

In the absence of a religious hierarchy, Confucius taught that the solution to the problems of life lay in the practice of *li* (a combination of what we might call custom, propriety and ritual observance). The practice of *li* ensures continuity; without it there is chaos. *Li* is concerned with maintaining the balance of the universe, a balance which was not created but which exists of itself and because we tend it. In this balance, supernatural beings and mortals all have their place; institutions, whether in the supernatural or mortal worlds, depend on it and guarantee its survival as it guarantees theirs; past, present and future are a continuum in which all actions take their place, affecting not just the present but the future and the past.

Insofar as religious practice is concerned, the main duty we owe to the continuum is to our ancestors. They live in the afterlife as we live in the presentlife, and they have needs and problems just as we do. *Li* involves looking after these needs and trying to help with these problems. We attend to our ancestors' physical needs by making paper models of the objects they will need in the afterlife (everything from food and drink to toys and radiograms); we burn the models ceremonially, and the real objects are re-created for our ancestors in the afterlife. We attend to our ancestors' emotional and intellectual needs by constantly talking to them, involving them in our affairs and ourselves in theirs. Simple in essence, this practice grew, over the centuries, into an enormous edifice of duty, in which families might easily bankrupt themselves in the here-and-now in order to ensure their ancestors' well-being in the afterlife, and in which **sacrifice** and other interaction with the supernatural became main components of every waking hour.

Confucius and his immediate disciples seem to have regarded *li* as a moral and ethical force for social engineering. The Analects put it bluntly: 'If you lead people with legal measures and regulate them with punishment, they will have no sense of honour and shame. If you lead them by the power of *de* (virtuous example) and regulate them by the rules of *li*, they will have a sense of shame and will thus rectify themselves.' To be truly moral, a person and a society should possess *ren* ('humanity'), and to acquire this was the main goal of all Confucian teaching and practice. A person who has it, by self-discipline, contemplation and behaviour of integrity, is *zhun-zi* (a word which originally simply meant 'aristocrat', but which Confucius developed to mean 'person of superior merit'). Such a person should be open-minded, compassionate and not concerned with self; provided that he – Confucianism never refers to females – has these qualities, his actual status in life, whether prince or beggar, is unimportant.

Like many ethical and moral systems predicated on continuity and stability, Confucianism was fine so long as it was confined to a small group of people and maintained its pure form, but as soon as it was universally applied, it became grossly simplified and corrupted. In particular, the idea of *li* was applied to society and to intellectual thought, with stultifying results. Reverence for one's forebears is one thing, but obsession with intellectual precedent is quite another (and unrelated). 'Official' Chinese learning became a matter of the mastery of ever-larger amounts of dead facts, the accreted wisdom of the past; invention was allowed (because technology was regarded as an activity for lower-class persons, beneath the notice of the intellectual élite), but novelty of thought was discouraged. The observance of ritual became an all-consuming passion, from the ancestor-devotions of ordinary households to the grand processions, prayers and sacrifices with which the emperor and his officials guaranteed the continuity of the state. Hierarchies applied to every facet of life, and movement from one level to another was difficult and often a punishable offence. In short, the dynamism inherent in Confucius' own teaching (or at least the teaching attributed to him) was replaced by forms of etiquette, which determined Chinese life and culture for two millennia, until they were abolished by the Communist government in 1949. The problem is not (as with some other ethical and religious systems) that modern societies are trying to base their whole way of life on systems devised for small groups in ancient or medieval times, without modifying them, but that Confucius' teaching has been, from the start, disastrously misinterpreted and misapplied. Its entanglement with religious practice perhaps lies at the heart of this and is something which Confucius himself (as a soul mate, so to speak, of Socrates) would surely have deplored. KMcL

See also Buddhism; Daoism.

Further reading Arthur Waley, *The Analects of Confucius* (contains good introduction and notes); Herbert Fingarette, *Confucius – the Secular as Sacred*.

CONNECTIONISM

Connectionism, in **linguistics**, is a theory of cognition which provides a model of how learning takes place. The model draws inspiration from the way the billions of neurons in the brain are interconnected in complex ways to produce a network of associations. It is suggested that during brain activity the neurons convey signals to associated neurons, causing the latter to be either aroused or inhibited. The arousal of one neuron by another reinforces the connection between them, while inhibition causes the connection to be weakened. The overall pattern of connection strengths is taken to represent the knowledge of the system at a given time. And as the relative strengths of connections alter with progressive reinforcement and inhibition, the state of knowledge changes accordingly.

In connectionist theory, computer models are designed to mimic genuine neurological processes, by using numbers to represent the relative strengths of connections between neurons, or units, in a network. However, since very little is known about what actually happens at the neurological level in the brain, it is a moot point whether connectionism does in fact provide a valid metaphor for cognitive processes. Furthermore, it is quite conceivable that there is more to cognition than can be explained by neurological activity alone. MS

See also thought.

CONNOISSEURSHIP

Connoisseurship (from French, 'one who knows' or 'one who understands'), as a methodology within art history, is inseparable from notions of quality and authenticity, which form part of that discipline's construction of 'the work of art'.

The appreciation of works of art for their intrinsic qualities (aesthetic value) rather than for their functional or devotional purpose (cult value) led to their being considered in a different way, at least by experts in the West. By the **Renaissance** it was commonplace to value works for the skill they exhibited rather than the materials used, and it follows that the connoisseur's interest in 'fine' art is an interest in the skills and practices used. From the 16th century to the 18th century connoisseurship implied both discrimination and knowledge, not much different in fact from the skills of the 18th-century amateur (a word which in those days meant 'enthusiast'). The 18th-century connoisseur made the same kind of value judgements common in, but not synonymous with, those of **criticism**: the difference lay in the connoisseur's specialized knowledge of the subject, without the subjective and perhaps excessive enthusiasms of the amateur or the impersonal pronouncements of the critic – although it must be noted that connoisseurship has often confused personal enthusiasm with the disinterested appraisal of competence. The most striking example of this in recent times was the acceptance, against the signal evidence (at least to modern eyes), of the work of the forger van Meegeren as authentic 'Vermeers'.

A second meaning of connoisseurship, closer to today's, is that of the art expert able to distinguish between the authentic and non-authentic, for example between an original and a **copy**. This implies that an authentic work of art demonstrates qualities or – and this is not the same thing – *quality* which an imitation cannot. As a consequence of this some works of art are called 'authentic' (meaning original works by a given artist), while others are called copies. This definition of the work of the connoisseur is narrow, but it has had great impact on the study of art history and museology, where collections have long been valued for the integrity (that is, authenticity) of their holdings. In this limited sense connoisseurship goes little beyond attribution or establishing the provenance of a work.

Today the meaning of connoisseurship retains at least an element of the critical/aesthetic interests of earlier centuries. And while it is not correct to imply, as one might with the phrase 'art expert', an element of commerce (and the valuation, rather than *evaluation*, of works of art), limiting connoisseurship to the narrow confines of authentication has proved a regrettable restriction. While in the past connoisseurship provided many of the parameters still regarded as the norms of art history, the continued uncritical application of such notions today does little to advance the study of the history of art. **MG PD**

Further reading M.J. Friedländer, *On Art and Connoisseurship* (1942).

CONSCIENCE

Conscience is the (supposed) faculty by which one is aware of the moral status of one's own actions. It is the faculty by which one is aware that one morally ought, or ought not, to have acted as one actually did, and by which one is aware that one morally ought, or ought not, to perform some possible action. **AJ**

See also ethics.

CONSCIOUSNESS

Consciousness (from Latin, *conscire*, 'to be aware'), in psychological terms, describes the state of being awake to our surroundings: neither asleep, nor in a coma, nor drugged in any way, even if we have more, or less, limited consciousness or awareness.

It is the state of paying attention to what we are doing, or to our own mental process: faculties which are not possessed by animals.

According to Freud, consciousness is distinct from unconsciousness in that it takes account of space and time, is intolerant of contradiction and gives constant meanings to images. The **unconscious** constantly switches the meaning of symbols in dreams, and uses contradictions, such as displacement, as defence-mechanisms. The unconscious becomes conscious by being verbalized, and in this sense consciousness also has the function of creating integration of feelings and ideas into externalized language. Freud had less to say about conscious activities than about unconscious ones, and the neglect of conscious material, in Freudian analysis, is criticized by those working with existential, phenomenological, cognitive or behavioural approaches.

Philosophers distinguish two sorts of consciousness (which they roughly equate with 'awareness'). I am conscious that I am in **pain** and that I wish I were not. That is, I am aware that I am in each of these mental states. The two sorts of consciousness correspond to two types of mental state. Mental states such as pains, and sensory experiences (visual and auditory experiences, for instance) are phenomenological: they feel a certain way. Consciousness of being in a phenomenological state is a matter of being aware of how it feels, is a matter of feeling it. Indeed, such mental states seem to be necessarily conscious: one cannot be in pain without being aware that one is in pain simply because pain necessarily feels a certain way, and one cannot be in pain without being aware that one is in a state that feels that way. So one sort of consciousness is awareness that one is in a state that feels a certain way. And phenomenological states seem to be necessarily conscious.

Not all mental states are phenomenological, however. Propositional attitudes such as beliefs and desires are not phenomenological. Having a **belief** or desire is not a matter of things feeling a certain way. And non-phenomenological mental states are not necessarily conscious. As Freud taught, there are unconscious beliefs and desires.

Since having a belief or desire is not a matter of things feeling a certain way, consciousness of having a certain belief or desire is not a matter of being aware of how things feel, is not a matter of feeling which beliefs or desires one has. So what is it to be conscious of certain of one's beliefs and desires but not others? Some hold that consciousness of beliefs and desires is a matter of having beliefs about one's beliefs and desires. I am conscious of my belief that Cambridge is beautiful and of my desire to be a better actor because I believe that I believe Cambridge to be beautiful and I believe that I desire to be a better actor. And I am not conscious of my repressed belief that my mother is evil or of my desire that she be dead because I do not believe that I believe that my mother is evil and I do not believe that I desire her dead. **AJ MJ**

See also mental phenomena; stream of consciousness; thought.

Further reading Albert Ellis, *Growth Through Reason: Verbatim Cases in Rational Emotive Therapy*; C. McGinn, *The Character of Mind*.

CONSCIOUSNESS RAISING

Consciousness Raising groups grew out of the Women's Liberation Movement of the 1960s. The aim of these groups was to give women the opportunity to talk about and understand their experience of oppression, and to recognize through listening to other women the commonality of the experience of sexual oppression. The methodology of Consciousness Raising groups was summed up in the phrase, 'The personal is political'. The groups offer women a non-hierarchical space and practice in which to speak for themselves, and also a platform from which women can speak out as a group. Some feminists criticized the search for commonality, arguing that it denied the different experience of women of colour and lesbian women. Consciousness Raising groups placed value upon women's everyday experience which was often considered 'banal' and marginalized within traditional patriarchal academic discourse.

Sheila Rowbotham has argued that insights derived from Consciousness Raising groups have led to the diversity of political, theoretical and anti-theoretical positions within feminism. For many feminists, Consciousness Raising has added the dimension of women's experience to theoretical work and has helped women to find the voice to speak out for themselves against oppression. **TK**

Further reading Juliet Mitchell, *Woman's Estate*; Women's Studies Group, *Women Take Issue: Aspects of Women's Subordination*.

CONSENSUS THEORY

Consensus theory refers to the branch of **sociology** that emphasizes the role of shared **values** as the basis of any persisting **social order**. The problem of social order is a central one in sociology: what is the basis of the tendency for societies to cohere in a stable pattern of relationships, expectations and social structures, rather than disintegrating into the chaotic pursuit of individual self-interest?

Within sociology a distinction can be made between those who emphasize coercion as the basis of social order and those who emphasize a consensus of shared values and expectations. In practice most sociological theories recognize the role of both. The school of sociology which follows the ideas of Parsons, however, provides the central explanation for the problem of social order in terms of a consensus of values, which are adopted and shared by all members of the population as a result of common experiences of **socialization**.

The nature and extent of consensus has been a subject much debated within sociology. Research suggests that dominant social values are not entirely accepted by large sections of the population. Even when common values are accepted this may be only pragmatic and partial. **DA**

See also assimilation; authority; conflict theory; culture; discourses; dominant ideology; functionalism; hegemony; ideology; internalization; legitimation; norms; power; social control; social integration; social movements; subculture.

Further reading P.S. Cohen, *Modern Social Theory.*

CONSEQUENTIALISM

Consequentialism is the doctrine that we ought to do whatever will have the best consequences. We are morally responsible for all of the foreseeable consequences of our actions and should take all foreseeable consequences into account when deciding how to act. So when deciding whether to give money to a beggar, I must weigh the increase in the well-being of the beggar against the possible costs, such as encouraging vagrancy. Consequentialists differ as to how to evaluate the consequences of actions. Some hold that we ought to do whatever will create the greatest amount of pleasure for humanity taken as a whole, while others emphasize different values (such as beauty, well-being or equality). But they all agree that the right thing to do is whatever will create the most desirable state of affairs.

There are two main kinds of objection to consequentialism. First, we are sometimes obliged to bring about a very undesirable state of affairs even when we could bring about a better one. I may be obliged to spend my dead father's money on an expensive gravestone because of a death-bed promise I made to him, even though the money would be far better spent helping his grandchildren. Actions may be intrinsically right even if they have bad consequences (like my keeping my promise) and intrinsically wrong even if they would have good consequences (like breaking my promise).

The other main objection to consequentialism is that it is too demanding. There are many starving people in the world and my money would be of far more use to them than it is to me. Am I obliged to give my salary to the starving, retaining only enough of it to prevent my starving? The trouble here, some say, is that consequentialists fail to respect the common-sense distinction between acts and omissions.

Many philosophers and lawyers distinguish cases in which one allows a bad thing to happen from cases in which one brings that bad thing about, claiming that allowing a bad thing to happen is less blameworthy than bringing that bad thing about. Suppose I hear of a starving family who will die within a week if I do not send a food parcel. If I do not send them anything, I am allowing the family to die. Such indolence may well be reprehensible but it is not as bad as murder. On the other hand, I may send them a poisoned food parcel that will kill them in a week's time. Here the end result is the same – the family dies a painful death in a week's time. But in the second case I am guilty of murder since I have actively killed the family and not merely allowed them to die. The consequentialist would see no difference here – the family's death is a foreseeable consequence of both my action and of my inaction. So if I am a murderer in the one instance, I am as bad as a murderer in the other as well. **AJ**

See also deontology; double effect, doctrine of; utilitarianism.

Further reading S. Scheffler (ed.), *Consequentialism and its Critics*; B. Steinbock (ed.), *Killing and Letting Die.*

CONSERVATION

Conservation describes the use of the resources of the Earth in a way that is not wasteful or destructive. It involves environmental management by humans to sustain the status quo or equilibrium which is seen by us to exist in our environment; this management often involves attempts to repair the damage caused by **pollution**.

It has long been recognized that humans depend upon the Earth for those resources which have enabled the development of civilizations. As human populations have expanded it has become clear that many of these resources are not finite. Thus, in modern terms, conservation encompasses the rational use of resources, their restoration and reuse through recycling. Technology plays an increasingly important part in these processes but conservation is by no means a novel concept. Historically, it was thought that primitive humans lived in harmony with nature, but archeological evidence shows that this was far from the truth. Prehistoric peoples had few of the technologies which today cause large-scale pollution yet they managed to modify their environment dramatically by using their most powerful tool, fire. Fire was used indiscriminately by many prehistoric groups to change much of the Earth's landscape from woodland to pasture or arable land. As the human population grew, the demand for natural resources grew with the ability to harvest them, yet the concept of conservation is not a modern phenomenon as we have long realized the benefit of preserving resources, even if competition has often prevented people from adopting such a strategy.

Science has brought a better understanding of the complexity of the **ecosystem** and of the far-reaching effects of disturbing the ecological balance. This has led to the exploitation of renewable resources such as solar energy and to the imposition of a degree of control over the exploitation of finite resources such as oil. Conservation in the sense of preservation has also become popular in recent times: national parks and similar conservation areas exist in many countries as zones where environmentally disruptive activity is tightly controlled by law. There have also been moves towards the establishment of global conservation authorities. However, humans continue to modify the environment to their own ends, often with little regard for the ecosystem as a whole and the most effective conservation measures are still legislative controls upon polluting activities. **RB**

See also Gaia hypothesis; greenhouse effect; ecology.

Further reading Robert Arvill, *Man and Environment*; Rachel Carson, *Silent Spring*; Joseph Moran, *Introduction to Environmental Science*.

CONSERVATISM

Four core values lie at the heart of conservative or right-wing political thought: authority, hierarchy, property and community. These values are generally defended in a 'common-sensical' philosophy which rejects the idea that human beings can be perfected.

Authority Conservative political thought began as a defence of authority in all social domains. The French Revolution prompted what became known as the 'reactionary' right to defend the old European order. Its French exponents, most famously Joseph de Maistre, defended traditional religious authority against radical scepticism and liberal secularism; supported established monarchies against the enthusiasts for liberal republicanism; and rejected any querying of patriarchal authority in the family. Authority was defended because it preserves order: questioning authority threatens social chaos, so obedience to traditional and religiously sanctified rulers is imperative. De Maistre asserted that Europe required the restoration of the authority of 'the pope and the executioner'. In our times religious **fundamentalists** of the Christian and Islamic faiths embrace a similarly theological **authoritarianism**. If the European reactionary conservatives, like de Maistre and his co-thinkers Bonald and Lamennais, were Catholics and monarchists, conservatives in Britain could not be. They defended a Protestant faith, an aristocratic political order, and, at most, a limited monarchy. The Irishman Edmund Burke provided the most coherent articulation of conservative philosophy in his *Reflections on the French Revolution* (1790). There he predicted that the French Revolution would degenerate into terror and dictatorship. The revolutionary destruction of hallowed customs would not improve the world but fragment it, and encourage – license – the unbridled abuse of freedom. Authority preserves traditions which contain the accumulated wisdom and experience of past generations. It is tampered with at our peril. Frenzied 'theorizing' revolutionaries waste these treasures. Authority permits human beings to evolve while preserving the inheritance of past civilization. Legitimate authority, founded on centuries of evolution, is preferable to the system of naked power manufactured by rationalist revolutionaries. The authoritarian preservation of established morality is superior to the license of permissive **libertarianism**.

The tension between the absolutism of de Maistre's reactionary conservatism and

Burke's evolutionism illustrates a standard division among conservatives. Reactionaries seek to restore a vanished and frequently wholly-imagined past, offering the politics and religion of a better yesterday; whereas evolutionists argue against radical change, not against *all* change. European and North American liberals, who reject the reactionary conservatives' assumptions about the unquestionable merits of ancient authority and religious tradition, have, nonetheless, often found common cause with conservatives in defence of authority, sharing the belief that order, stability and traditional family values are essential for the rule of law and the development of a free but disciplined market order. However, a fundamental chasm endures between conservatives and liberals. Conservatives have no qualms about unlimited government, as expressed, for example, in the doctrine of 'parliamentary sovereignty' in the UK, whereas **liberalism** has always been a political philosophy which has sought to limit and fragment governmental authority through such devices as the separation of powers and bills of rights.

Hierarchy Conservatives like Burke and de Maistre unite in defence of traditional hierarchies. The hereditary principle whether understood as a title to property or status is considered sacrosanct. Conservatives therefore support monarchy and aristocracy as well as private property rights. By contrast, liberals reject the universal application of the hereditary principle. They believe in hereditary property rights, but not in hereditary political rights or titles. In much conservative thought hierarchy is considered the natural form of human existence, equality, by contrast, is artificial. Hierarchy is defended because it provides continuity and encourages diversity. Conservatives tended to approve 19th-century Social Darwinist ideas in which existence was seen a struggle for survival of the fittest and hierarchy the natural outcome of this struggle. Today they are inclined to believe **sociobiologists** who argue that there are fundamental and immutable cognitive and emotional differences between the races and sexes. Such thinking easily slips into **racism**, the belief that certain peoples

are innately superior to others, or sexism, the belief that men are superior to women. These dispositions have led many conservatives to defend racial domination and segregation (as practised in the South African system of apartheid or in Nazi Germany), and to demand the return of women to their traditional roles of child-rearing and domestic labour. It is mistaken to assume that all conservatives share such views, or that all who hold such views are conservatives, but there is no gainsaying the historic association between conservative hierarchical political thought and racism and sexism.

Hierarchicalism also explains why conservatives have generally been suspicious of **democracy**, because of its levelling consequences and its rejection of caste principles in favour of the presumption of the political equality of all adult citizens. For example, the English conservative philosopher Roger Scruton (see below) asserts that democracy is a 'contagion'. Conservatives gradually accepted democratic institutions, such as universal suffrage, only when they became persuaded that they would not automatically imply the eradication of privilege. Modern conservatives, such as the Austrian philosopher Friedrich von Hayek, have supported representative democracy because they see it as the best system of government for a free-market society. Representative democracy in other words is defended as a means rather than an end.

Property Conservativism shares with liberalism a firm commitment to individuals' rights to private property in contradistinction to **socialism** and **communism**. Conservatives make two key arguments for the justice of strong private property rights. The first, deriving from John Locke (1632–1704), suggests that individuals have a natural right to property in whatever they have mixed their labour with, and this right is transferable. In principle all property rights can therefore be traced back to their original acquisition to see whether or not they are just – a proposition which creates some easily imagined difficulties. The second, developed in the work of the German philosopher Hegel (1770–1831), suggests that private property rights are essential if individuals are to be free, and able to exercise their freedom. Without strong private property rights there are no real individuals only members of tribes or the serfs of collectivist states. Conservatives part company with liberals, however, because they recognize that the claims of authority or community must sometimes have precedence over the rights of individuals. This difference explains why conservatives, especially in the European Christian Democratic tradition, sometimes accept the principles of the welfare state including progressive taxation and public provision of basic social goods which economic liberals think of as despotic intrusions on property rights. In the last two decades economic liberalism has been on the ascendant among conservatives, and political exponents of this philosophy, known as the 'New Right', have been especially vigorous in the English-speaking advanced liberal democracies.

Community Conservatives, unlike liberals, advocate the maintenance or the building of solidaristic unitary communities, united by bonds of affection, blood, **ethnicity**, language and **culture**. They argue that liberals are merely concerned to build associations on the basis of **utilitarian** standards – self-interested egoistic individuals who conduct all their social relations on a contractual basis. Romantic conservatives argue, like socialists, that industrialized economies ordered on liberal principles produce atomized individuals and rootless, bloodless cosmopolitans disconnected from history. In the past, identities were expressed in localist loyalties: to the king, the lord or the 'village communities' of feudal times. Subsequently conservatives have displaced such loyalties towards the nation. Having once suspected **nationalism** conservatives have sought to appropriate its doctrines as their own. To paraphrase Burke, the idea of the nation cuts across class distinctions to unite all in community with the dead, the living and the as yet unborn. Conservatives are rarely internationalists. They support **capitalism** because they see it as a good means of preserving order, hierarchy and property rights, but insist it must be regulated in the national interest. Where capitalism threatens the core values of conservatives then intervention by the authorities is considered justified. This fact explains why conservatives sometimes justify protectionism as opposed to free trade; it also explains why conservatives experience no contradiction in rejecting consumer choice in matters of sexual preference, literature and the dramatic arts. Censorship and moral regulation are considered essential to preserve a stable national community.

Anti-rationalism Conservatives, from Edmund Burke in the 18th to Michael Oakeshott in the 20th century, argue that liberals and socialists produce abstract, unfeeling, ideological and rationalist doctrines. Rationalists are accused of seeking to evaluate all social practices by the yardstick of reason alone, and thereby remorselessly corrode the complex web of habits and customs that preserve social order. They are accused of benevolent but simple-minded conceptions of human nature, which stress our cognitive abilities, our instrumental reason and our potential for altruism, but which neglect the spontaneous drives and emotions that can only be tempered by the discipline of traditional civilization. This distrust of human capacities and lack of belief in the prospects for human progress is distinctive to the conservative temperament. **BO'L**

Further reading T. Honderich, *Conservatism*; R. Scruton, *The Meaning of Conservatism*.

CONSOCIATIONALISM

A consociational (from Latin *cum*, 'with' + *socius*, 'ally') or power-sharing **democracy** is characterized by four traits: (1) executive power-sharing, incorporating representatives of the major groupings in a segmented (or divided) society; (2) proportional allocation of legislative, executive, judicial and bureaucratic posts according to the electoral strength of the major groupings; (3) community self-government on cultural matters (for example, language, education and religion); and (4) constitutional veto powers for minorities. The term consociationalism was invented by the Dutch political scientist Arend Lijphart to distinguish the optimum form of democracy in a segmented society from the majoritarian model of democracy.

The conditions required to achieve a stable consociational democracy are controversial. Among the factors which Lijphart claims are important are: a history of political accommodation among cultural élites; the absence of a majority segment; a small number of cultural communities (between three and five); a common enemy or shared external threat; and relative economic equality between or among communities. As a result of the restrictiveness of these and other qualifications examples of successful consociational democracies are limited. Consociationalism has been practised in Belgium and Switzerland since 1945 and 1943 respectively, and to a lesser extent in Canada and Malaysia, despite the existence of salient ethnic cleavages. It was successful in easing the transition to modern secular politics in the Netherlands from 1917 to 1967. However, in political systems where cleavages are deeper, and nationalist in character, attempts at consociationalism have failed, at least so far (for example, Cyprus, Northern Ireland and the Lebanon).

Critics of consociationalism focus on three alleged shortcomings: first, that it is 'undemocratic' because the majority must abdicate the right to govern on its own; second, that power-sharing is ineffective because of the inherent difficulties of government-by-committee; and finally, that it maintains or even deepens cleavages by institutionalizing them. Its proponents claim that consociationalism is nevertheless the most promising democratic method of resolving conflict in deeply divided societies, and less likely to provoke protracted conflict than other alternatives. They argue that in many parts of the world majoritarian democracy is the problem not the solution, and the real choice is between consociational democracy or no democracy. **BO'L**

See also ethnicity.

Further reading A. Lijphart, *Democracy in Plural Societies: a Comparative Exploration.*

CONSTRUCTIVISM

Constructivism is a loosely defined move-ment in **architecture**, **design** and fine **art**, associated particularly with the decade following the 1917 Revolution in Russia. It was seen as a political movement which sought its aesthetic expression in mechanical structures, celebrating structural and technological advances, and attempting to remove the traditional distinctions between art and life.

In architecture, the first phase of Constructivism in Russia was associated with temporary timber constructions used for exhibitions and street art, and the second phase with buildings proper. Buildings were conceived of as part machine form and part biological structure; an influential work being that of Vladimir Tatlin (1885–1953) who designed the Monument to the Third International of 1920, a slanting tower, a distorted frustum in spiral form, which would contain a cubic hall for the legislative council of the Third International, a pyramidal executive block above, and on the top a cylindrical information centre. Each of these separate blocks would rotate at different rates, and the structure was made of steel and glass. A contemporary account spoke of 'by the transformation of these forms into reality, dynamics will be embodied in unsurpassable magnificence'. However, although its model was paraded through the streets, it was never actually built for there was a shortage of steel. Also notable is the radical work of Konstantin Melnikov (1890–1974) who worked both in timber, in a reinterpretation of traditional Russian agrarian construction, and later in a sophisticated concrete construction. He built five workers' clubs in Moscow in 1927–29, each of which revealed externally the auditoria and circulation spaces. In the later 1920s, the influence of Constructivism was felt in Poland, Czechoslovakia, Germany and the Netherlands, in almost 'translucent' buildings of the 1920s and 1930s in which most of the internal workings were exposed, often revealing the movement of lifts or conveyor belts.

In **painting**, **sculpture** and the other fine arts, constructivism, to some extent, opposes its contemporary movement **expressionism** through its promotion of the reasoned deployment of the principles of 'pure' art. It articulates dimension in terms not of mass but of volume in space. In this sense it is the sculptural equivalent of **suprematism** in painting or the **cubist** assemblages of Picasso. Constructivism's early exponents in Revolutionary Russia championed it as a socially relevant art (as exemplified in the title of Tatlin's *Monument to the Third International*, described above), but the revolution soon turned against abstraction in favour of **socialist realism**, disillusioning many of its principle adherents and sympathizers (such as Gabo, Antoine Pevsner, Kandinsky, Lissitsky and Maholy-Nagy), and forcing them to flee Russia. This emigration had the effect of spreading the principles of Constructivism throughout Europe and the US. **PD MG JM**

Further reading J.M. Nash, *Cubism, Futurism and Constructivism.*

CONSUMPTION FUNCTION

Consumption treated as a function of income. The consumption function is C-f(y), where C is consumption expenditure and Y is income. The analysis of John Maynard Keynes (1883–1943) focused on the absolute level of current income as the determinant of consumption expenditure. Others have introduced modifications, such as the relative income hypothesis of James Duesenberry, the life-cycle hypothesis of Franco Modigliani, or the permanent income hypothesis of Milton Friedman. Each of these concepts analyses the relationship between household consumption expenditure and income and then aggregates it for the economy. **TF**

Further reading Milton Friedman, *A Theory of the Consumption Function.*

CONTEMPORARY HISTORY

Contemporary history is the name given to history of the very recent past normally the history of the last half century or less. Some historians argue that there can be no such history, because the lack of free access to governmental official documents prevents informed historical judgements, and because events are too recent to be seen in proper perspective. These arguments are rejected by contemporary historians, who maintain that the idea that historical truth is necessarily to be found in official documents or state archives is risible, and who believe that through interviews (oral history) and the techniques of the **social sciences** (for example, social surveys and **content analysis** of the media) contemporary analysts can generate valid sources to sustain their arguments. **BO'L**

Further reading G. Barraclough, *An Introduction to Contemporary History.*

CONTENT ANALYSIS

Content analysis is the empirical study of **communication** through the systematic analysis of words, texts and symbols. With its strict classificatory form and emphasis upon empirical analysis, content analysis can be interpreted as a **behaviourist** adaptation of the earlier practice of **hermeneutics**, the interpretation of underlying meaning. As a tool in **political science**, content analysis was first applied by Harold Laswell and others to the study of the effects of political propaganda upon public opinion. The content analysis of open-ended responses remains an important application in public opinion analysis because it provides more rigorous data on actual attitudes than the answers given to closed questions or structured multiple-choice responses.

Content analysis is also applied to the study of negotiation in diplomacy and conflict management in order to specify which factors are influential in the outcome of negotiations. The study of political records of speeches, statements, campaign pledges, news broadcasts and election coverage are all important sources of information to which content analysis is applied. For example, content analysis of statements in Hansard (the record of the House of Commons in the UK) is a useful tool for analysing significant changes in political beliefs, or as a way of tracking changes in the behaviour of prime ministers in Parliament. **BO'L**

Further reading R.P. Weber, *Basic Content Analysis.*

CONTEXT

Context (from Latin *contextus*, 'weaving

together') is the setting which can modify our view of an idea, phenomenon or statement. The difference is between placing things in a sequence of **logic** (in which case they have one identity only, a kind of objective identity as one link in a chain of reasoning), and placing them in a context (in which case contingent meanings spread out from them like ripples in a pool, blurring and enriching the individual significance rather than articulating it). This is the sense in which the significance of a word or note of music is modified by the other words or notes surrounding it, the significance of a find on an archaeological site is modified by the artefacts and structures which surround it, or the significance of a historical event or political act depends on contingent circumstances.

In several disciplines, this basic idea of context is developed. In **linguistics**, for example, context is the 'non-linguistic environment of an utterance' – everything about its circumstances, its utterer and its audience, that is every determinant of meaning except the contents of the utterance itself. In **lexicography**, similarly, contextual definition or implicit definition is a way of showing what words mean, not by using synonyms or giving derivations but by referring (with examples) to the circumstances in which the words are or have been used.

Context, or contextualism, in **architecture** is an important precept of **postmodernism** in the late 20th century. It is the understanding of a new building's design in its many relative concepts (that is, time, landscape, culture and so on), and refers not only to the design of individual buildings by reference to their surroundings but also to the importance of such context (the existing physical and cultural environment) for **town planning**.

Contextualism could be said to bear some relation to the principles held by the architects of the **Arts and Crafts** movement of the late 19th century, who, when required to build in a sensitive historic context, might remark, as did Robert Weir Schulz, 'There is a workable, reasonable, commonsense solution to every problem, and here I would say that it consists in adhering, as near as may be, to the general type of the district

and not using materials that will jar'. Perhaps one of the best known examples of self-consciously contextual architecture in Europe is Robert Venturi's Sainsbury Wing, an extension to the National Gallery in Trafalgar Square, London: this attempts to harmonize the demands of a new building placed in a sensitive position against a well-known public building, with a frontage onto an important public space.

In **geography** and the **social sciences**, contextuality is a version of the same idea: no phenomenon (for example the mortality rate in a given area) can be considered without studying the whole network of relationships and circumstances contingent on it, however remote or irrelevant they may initially seem. **KMcL JM**

See also ethnomethodology.

Further Reading K. Ray, Contextual Architecture: Responding to Existing Style.

CONTEXTUALISM see **Context**

CONTEXTUALITY see **Context**

CONTINENTAL DRIFT

Anyone with an atlas can see the coincidence between the shapes of South America and Africa, indeed scholars first speculated about it as early as the 17th century. Early explanations tended to involve floods or the drowning of continents, but these were rejected by the middle of the 19th century. At that time, the Earth was thought to be cooling and shrinking, and the idea that the continents could move was unthinkable, as it remained for most geologists for centuries. The problem with the idea of continental drift was that the mounting evidence that the continents had changed their positions remained unconvincing in the absence of a mechanism which seemed adequate to move them.

The main advocate of the idea of continental drift was a German meteorologist, Alfred Wegener, who first published in 1915. He recognized the difference between continental and oceanic crust and believed that the continents were floating on the ocean crust. He noted that isostatic adjustment (for example, after a period of glaciation) required vertical movement and argued that this implied that horizontal movement must be possible. His main contribution was in going beyond the fit of the coastlines to present evidence of other kinds of fit.

Three of his lines of argument are still regarded as sound. First, he showed that mountain ranges of the same age existed in North America and the British Isles, as they did in South Africa and Argentina, and that when the coastlines were brought together the alignment fitted perfectly. Similarly, there were rocks on each side of the Atlantic with identical fossils, including those of freshwater fish. Third, he suggested that geological features distinctive of particular climatic conditions, such as desert sandstones, showed that all the continents had moved relative to each other and the world's climatic zones. He suggested that the existence of glaciated areas of similar age in South America, South Africa, India and Australia could only be explained as the result of their combination into a huge supercontinent. Indeed, he went further, suggesting that all the continents had once formed a single land mass, which he called Pangaea.

Wegener's ideas were slow to impress most geologists; for example, his work was not translated into English until 1925. Most preferred to regard the distributions as coincidental or as the result of earlier connections by 'land-bridges' rather than accepting the movement of continents. But Wegener did have some supporters, most notably du Toit, a South African who not only assembled further evidence in the southern continents, but also suggested that the mechanism must be convection currents in the mantle. In this he was following a British expert on radioactive dating, Arthur Holmes, who had also suggested that convection currents could have pulled apart the supercontinents. Even without such a mechanism, studies of mountain ranges were showing that very large horizontal movements were required to account for the observed pattern of faulting and folding.

From the 1950s onward, new evidence from several areas of research revived the debate. Studies of palaeomagnetism – the magnetic field locked into certain rocks at the time of their formation – showed that these rocks had changed their orientation to the magnetic poles and to each other. To account for the changes required accepting that the continents must have moved. Measurements of heat flow through the Earth's crust showed that the flow was highest at mid-ocean ridges and lower in the ocean trenches, where there were also negative gravity anomalies. These observations seemed consistent with the existence of convection currents in the mantle. The scene was set for a revolution. The final irony was that when the revolution did occur, it did not do so under the old banner of continental drift but under a new banner **plate tectonics**. PS

CONTINGENCY see Modality

CONTRACEPTION

Contraception (Latin, 'against fertilization') offers women the means to prevent or plan pregnancy. For most **feminists** the availability of contraception is central to the project of freeing women from patriarchy. It is also considered by many feminists that the right to choose if and when to have children also enables women to disassociate reproduction from **sexuality**, allowing women choices about expressing sexuality without being coerced into the patriarchal family structure. The availability of safe and free birth control is an ongoing struggle and a vital element of feminist activism and thought.

Where contraception is freely available to women there remains a crucial issue in the way that partriarchy theorizes and defines the female body. Feminist thinkers have argued that the patriarchal bias of medical science has meant that there is not sufficient testing of the long-term effects of birth control. They have also argued that where contraception is available, in either the family or constitutionally, responsibility for birth control is very often placed on the woman. Feminists consider that one of the reasons for this is that if women decide to break out of the sole role of motherhood they are opting out of the patriarchal family structure, and are not, in patriarchal terms, 'entitled' to male support. This continues even though the function of barrier methods of contraception has changed since the identification of the AIDS virus. Contraceptive methods are often criticized by feminists for not being an ideal choice but a choice between risks. In many parts of the world the fight to obtain contraception still continues. **TK**

Further reading Sue O'Sullivan (ed.), *Women's Health: The Spare Rib Reader;* Margaret Sanger, *Motherhood in Bondage.*

CONTRASTIVE ANALYSIS

Contrastive analysis, in **applied linguistics**, is a method first proposed by Uriel Weinreich in the 1950s. It highlights the structural differences between two languages, with the aim of identifying potential sources of difficulty for people learning a foreign language. On the basis of the behaviourist idea that old habits can interfere when learning new habits, it was suggested that knowledge of one's first language (L1) might interfere with the learning of a second language (L2). Interference creates difficulties for the L2 learner, leading to an increase in the production of errors. And the likelihood of interference increases as the level of difference (linguistic distance) between two languages increases.

However, the assumption that linguistic difference can be equated with the psychological concept of learning difficulty is not supported. An enormous number of errors predicted by the contrastive analysis hypothesis simply do not occur. For example, English L1 speakers learning L2 Japanese have to contend with the fact that verbs go at the end of Japanese sentences. However, this fundamental difference rarely provokes learners of Japanese L2 into using English word order when speaking Japanese. The difficulties with contrastive analysis stem mainly from the inappropriate application of behaviourist concepts. However, the idea that learner difficulties may be predicted on the basis of structural differences between two languages is of value and continues to guide research (see **universal grammar**). In particular, contrastive analyses based on the sound systems of different languages can provide highly reliable predictions concerning the difficulties which may face learners in the pronunciation of a particular foreign language. **MS**

CONTROL THEORY

Control Theory, in electrical engineering, is a mathematical theory which provides a method for assessing a systems response, or output, for a specific input, and will also determine whether the stability of the system is affected.

The theory relies on the use of **circuit** and **network theories** to provide equations which model the performance of the electrical circuits. The idea of modelling electrical circuits dates back to 1827 when G. Ohm first defined the relationship between voltage and current.

An important category of control systems is automatic control systems, which require a feedback signal from the output to a controlling device which provides a self-regulating function (see **feedback principle**). In general, the controller will compare the output signal to some reference or preset signal, and will take any correcting action necessary to maintain the output within limits defined by the reference.

In 1932, in the USA, H. Nyquist invented a graphical technique which analysed feedback systems and allowed designers to check whether an automatic system would become unstable during operation. The control of electricity supply networks, where the frequency and power outputs of large generating machines must remain within statutory limits, is one modern example of the everyday application of control theory. **AC**

CONVERGENCE THEORY

The convergence theory, in **history** and **sociology**, states that all industrial systems, whether capitalist or communist, would converge in their social, political and economic systems because of the determinant effects of technological development. It is a view first put forward by Clark Kerr and colleagues in the 1960s. It is located in the tradition of functionalist analysis which assumes industrialism to be a particular type of society with specific needs for which like solutions will be found resulting in the development of similar types of society; it is a modern version of Max Weber's theory of the importance of bureaucratic structures in the management of production and distribution of services. It also suggests that it is the forms of technology to be found in a given society which determine the nature of that society.

Convergence theorists believe that the whole world is entering an era of complete industrialization. According to this theory a 'logic of industrialism' ensures that all social developments result in definite changes in social institutions. All industrialized countries tend to become more alike. It is claimed that it is only through industrialization that the countries of the **Third World** will be able to break out of their poverty.

Proponents of this view believe that in a number of respects industrialized countries will become more alike. Modern industrial systems of production, it is argued, create a highly complicated **division of labour**, incorporating wide-ranging skills and competencies. Furthermore, unlike preindustrial societies, industrialized societies are more open there are greater opportunities and freedom for people to choose their work and improve their social status, rather than this being determined by traditions and the family they were born into. In industrialized countries specialist education is believed to become more important, and a higher level of literacy and skills is found among the population as a whole. A further feature convergence theorists claim that industrialized societies have in common is that the majority of the population live in cities rather than in rural areas. Proponents of the convergence theory argue that as industrialized societies become more alike, they then develop networks of interdependence. Because such societies will gradually come to share the same outlooks and interests it is argued that the possibilities of war diminish.

The capitalist revolution in the former USSR, the success of **mixed economies** such as Japan and Germany, and the decline of pure **market economies** such as the UK and US might appear to offer support for convergence theory. However, historical contingencies – particularly the devastation and reconstruction of both Japan and Germany following World War II – are important factors in explaining the development of these states. Moreover, convergence theory neglects the possibility that political and social institutions may be significantly autonomous from technological 'imperatives'.

In recent years the theory has been modified in recognition of the fact that industrial countries become more alike in certain respects than others. Most significant are the use of similar industrial technologies and the similarities of the daily lives led by the population. Other aspects of life, such as political systems, religious beliefs and patterns of economic organization, it is conceded, are more variable.

The originator of the theory did not go so far as to endorse convergence as a means of helping humanity resolve some of its major problems, though others have reached this conclusion. Andrei Sakharov, once a prominent Soviet dissident, advocated the active furtherance of convergence. He argued that the greater the similarities between the Soviet Union and the United States then there would be a reduction in global tensions. It remains the task of history to test the accuracy of this argument. **DA BO'L**

See also bureaucracy; capitalism; culture; dependency theory; diffusionism; evolutionism; globalization; socialism; society; theories of modernity; urbanism/urbanization; world system.

Further reading J.K. Galbraith and S. Menshikov, *Communism and Co-existence: from the Bitter Past to a Better Prospect*; Clark Kerr, *Industrialism and Industrial Man*; *The Future of Industrialized Societies*.

CONVERTIBILITY

Convertibility, in **economics**, is the concept that currencies can be readily exchanged for gold, or for another currency. The major modern currencies – the dollar, the Deutschmark, the pound and so on – are fully convertible, the last vestiges of nonconvertibility having been abandoned in 1958. This oils the wheels of international trade, because countries can pay for their imports in any convertible currency, not one specified by the central bank.

Minor currencies in beleaguered economies such as the Mexican peso may be convertible only under strictly regulated circumstances. Such minor currencies nevertheless form the majority; more often than not, currencies are not fully convertible and/or are protected by exchange controls. Withdrawing convertibility, as happened in Mexico in September 1982, is one way to halt a run of speculation on a currency. To allow convertibility, a country must have sufficient reserves of foreign exchange or gold to back likely demands on the currency, or must have trust from the money markets. **TF**

COPY

'Copy', to the Western **art** critic, means a non-fraudulent manual imitation produced by a third party of another work of art. Thus the copy is not a version or replica, which properly refers to a copy made by the artist of the original or under his/her control. Neither is the copy the product of mechanical means of duplication such as a reproduction, nor is it identical with a fake or **forgery**, where the intention is to deceive.

Multiplication of a prototype has been a motivating force in the creation of copies since antiquity. The excellence of Greek sculpture was admired by the Romans who invented little but perfected mechanical means of copying, which allowed for the duplication of the chosen original. Many Greek sculptures, such as the *Laocoön*, are today known through their Roman copies. Medieval guild practice in Europe encouraged the repetition of workshop formulas and of successful prototypes rather than the invention of new artistic solutions. Medieval artists were less interested in notions of originality in the design or execution of the work as in the use of genuine (authentic) materials of the first quality.

During the **Renaissance**, a more conscious sense of rivalling antiquity meant that artists measured themselves against past art, while acknowledging that antiquity embodied a near-perfect formal solution to the representation of human form.

Michelangelo won prestige by imitating antiques which were taken for originals. However, artists soon became careful to show that their copies were works created in the spirit of homage or for the purposes of study, because the public now demanded of practitioners a sense of individuality hitherto not part of the artistic persona. The need to differentiate between original and copy led to the rise of **connoisseurship** (often erroneously regarded as synonymous with the work of the art historian).

Copying thus became for artists a means to study the art of the past. Artists as markedly original as Rubens advocated the emulation of antiquity. With the rise of the **academies** in the 17th century, a system of values, which antiquity was held to best embody, was taught primarily through the study and execution of copies. Sir Joshua Reynolds, in the *Discourses*, professed the doctrine that imitation, for the purposes of instruction, was far removed from slavish copying of appearances. Instead the aim was to re-create the conditions of the making of the original even if in practice this tended to mean literally copying the models prescribed by the academics.

By the 19th century art training adhered rigidly to the doctrine of the imitation of past art. This attitude engendered in students the dangerous belief that past art had accomplished everything and little remained to be done. The advent of **modernism**, however, meant that artists ceased to regard copying as an essential part of training. The copy made for the purposes of study was superseded by the interpretative copy, such as Francis Bacon's *Portrait of Pope Innocent X* (1953) or Picasso's reworking of compositions after Manet or Velásquez, which challenge the original by refusing to regard it as authoritative.

However, the copy is not absent from contemporary art practice. **Pop** Art, for example, challenged the notions of originality: are Andy Warhol's prints of the *Mona Lisa* copies, parodies, or original works of art? Today postmodern interest in intertextuality, where rigid notions of original/copy, or indeed authentic/inauthentic have ceased to have meaning, is restructuring fundamental notions of what constitutes the domain of art. **MG PD**

CORPORATISM

Corporatism is the name given to the theory of the 'corporate state' which was first extensively articulated in Catholic social thought, and in **fascist** Italy. It supposed that the political community is composed of diverse functional and economic corporate bodies, and argued that representation of interests should take place on the bases of such autonomously organized corporations (or syndicates), rather than on individualist or territorial principles of representation. In fact, corporatist bodies in Italy were controlled by the state so the expression 'authoritarian corporatism' is often used to describe fascist practices.

In many of the postwar liberal democracies policy formulation and implementation became highly dependent upon organized business and trade unionized labour, and governments tacitly recognized that these corporate bodies had effective representational monopolies. These practices are variously described by political scientists and economists as liberal corporatism, neo-corporatism or corporate **pluralism**. Extensive debate exists over whether such liberal corporatist practices are a transitory or permanent feature of modern democracies. **BO'L**

See also Catholic political thought.

Further reading A, Cawson (ed.), *Organised Interests and the State*; P. Williamson, *Corporatism in Perspective*.

COSMOLOGY

Cosmology (Greek, 'study of the universe') was, until only about 400 years ago, a matter of speculation and religious assertion. Lacking any idea of **scientific method**, and any technology to assist either investigation or calculation – not to mention never conceiving of the need for any of those things – the ancients invented explanations of how the universe came into being, what it was like and how it worked.

God or the gods created it: if pressed, experts could give a specific date, for example by tracing generations back in time to the 'prime mover' or movers. Those few experts who did speculate about the heavens in what we might now call a scientific manner tended to place intellectual reasoning above the investigation and analysis of actual phenomena, and so made pictures and gave descriptions of universal phenomena and their causes which were as fanciful as any **myth**.

The consensus of opinion, in all societies, was that the universe was centred on the Earth – indeed, in some cases, that the Earth *was* the universe – and that all living beings in it, including the supernatural beings who managed it, were somehow projections of our own human selves. (Supernatural beings were bigger, existed outside mortal time, had magic powers, but were still essentially refractions of ourselves.) Above all, the universe was held to be controlled by sentient beings, on the human plan. Various forms of these ideas still persist among the adherents of some religions, either (uneasily) side by side with the discoveries of modern scientific cosmology or (triumphally) in opposition to them. **Pseudoscience**, too, draws heavily on such ideas: it was only 100 years ago that people were excitedly talking about irrigation canals on Mars, and there are still people who believe that such things as the Nazca lines in Peru are landing strips for extraterrestrial astronauts.

Rational cosmology began some 400 years ago with the work of Copernicus and Galileo. Their observations of the heavens showed that the facts did not fit existing theories of cosmology. Newton and others next began exploring the physical laws of Nature, studying such matters as planetary motion and the nature and properties of light. The third foundation stone of scientific cosmology came in the late 18th century, when Hutton and others demonstrated that the Earth – and by implication, the universe of which it was part – was almost inconceivably older than anyone had previously imagined. From this point on, scientific knowledge progressed at an exponential rate, and every new discovery in **astronomy, biology, chem-**

istry, **geology** and **physics** refined and clarified a factual picture of the origins, nature and functioning of the universe.

At the time of writing – and the picture still changes with each piece of new research – the consensus is that the universe began some 15,000–20,000 million years ago with a single explosion, the 'Big Bang'. Reverberations from this can still be sensed, and debris from it is still spreading outwards, so that the universe is both constantly expanding and infinite. Some scientists predict that expansion will end when the gravitational pull of the heavenly bodies already existing balances the velocity of the debris still in motion, and stasis occurs. This possible event will be the 'Big Crunch', and no one can foresee what will follow it, except possibly another build-up of energy leading to another 'Big Bang', and so on to infinity. **KMcL**

Further reading John McLeish, *Cosmology;* Stephen Hawking, *A Brief History of Time;* Carl Sagan, *Cosmos* (breathlessly written, but interesting on both the science and the pseudoscience of the cosmos).

COUNSELLING

Counselling, in **psychiatry**, has taken the therapeutic skills developed in various areas of **psychology** which correspond most closely to the helping skills of caring, listening and reflection. With the aim of creating a trusting relationship and being supportive, while giving little or no direction or advice, counselling endeavours to enable people to develop insight into their problems and to find resources within themselves by looking at their lives in a fresh way.

Whereas **psychotherapy** tends to look at more deep-seated problems, counselling tends to focus on specific current problems. It is a concentrated kind of help, using human skills like questioning to explore personal distress and to make sense of unhappiness. It has been found that this simplified approach can reduce **anxiety** and relieve **depression**. Both counsellors and therapists take on the traditional role once filled by elders and priests. **MJ**

Further reading Carl R. Rogers, *Counselling and Psychotherapy.*

COUNTER-TRANSFERENCE

Counter-transference was the term first used by Freud for unforeseen and unanalysed feelings on the part of the analyst for the patient. Because of the recurring nature of counter-transference, the conviction grew within the psychoanalytical movement that personal analysis was as important for analysts as it was for their clients. Personal analysis is now a requirement of any psychoanalytic training. The analyst's own transference of feelings and projections onto his or her patient is still recognized as a distorting element in treatment. Counter-transference is also used as a positive aspect of analysis, as it is understood that the feelings the patient provokes in the analyst are part of that person's interaction with other people and can be useful material in the analysis. The analyst's emotional attitudes and responses towards his patient and his patient's behaviour is used as clinical evidence: these responses of the analyst or therapist are seen as a reflection of the patient's own intention and meaning. **MJ**

Further reading A. Alexandris and G. Vaslamatizis (ed.), *Counter-Transference, Theory, Technique, Teaching.*

COVENANT

Jews believe that they are in an eternal relationship with God who made a covenant with Noah after the flood, promising that there would never again be a comparable flood upon the Earth. Jewish tradition believes that implicit in that covenant are seven commandments which, if kept by the righteous the world over, ensure them a share of life everlasting. These commandments forbid murder, adultery and incest, idolatry, false oaths, theft and cruelty to animals, and require every society to set up systems of just laws. Then God made a more specific covenant with the Jewish people, the descendants of Abraham.

The concept of covenant was taken over by the first Christians, who maintained that Jesus had instituted a new covenant sealed in his blood, a sign of which was the sacramental meal when they broke bread together and shared a cup of wine, as Jesus had commanded them to do. The Christian Scriptures came to be known as 'The New Covenant' in Greek (English translation; 'Testament'). In 1638, the radical Presbyterian party in Scotland opposed Charles I, his bishops and the Book of Common Prayer, revived the concept of covenant, getting their supporters to sign a covenant, hence their name, 'The Covenanters'. **EMJ RM**

See also Judaism.

Further reading John Bright, *Covenant and Promise*; G.D. Henderson, *Religious Life in Seventeenth-Century Scotland* (1937); Norman Snaith, *The Distinctive Idea of the Old Testament*.

CRAFTSMANSHIP

Craftsmanship (the term predates such egalitarian usages as 'craftworker') is the work of a skilled artisan, a practitioner of skilled manual labour, such as a stonemason, carpenter or joiner. The attempt to define the 'craftsman', particularly perhaps as distinct from the 'artist', has a distinguished pedigree. In Plato's *Republic*, in his discussion on 'The Theory of Art', he describes three makers: God who makes the ideal Form (which exists in its perfect quality in a different world); the craftsman who makes, say, a bed, 'with his eye on the form'; and the artist who copies what the craftsman has created. The skills represented are user, maker and artist. The craftsman is the maker of objects, who takes his instructions from the user.

In the history of the construction of great buildings of all periods it is clear that a master builder often had the role of an **architect**, surveyor and engineer in the process of construction, and it should be noted that the word 'architect' itself derives from the Greek word for a master builder, or overseer of craftsmen (*tekton*). The architects of the early modern period of Western history were often the sons of master masons, who by virtue of education and social preferment were seen as professional designers of buildings, as distinguished from the craftsman who works with his hands.

With a fine disregard for (or ignorance of) such notions, or of Plato's categorizations, many 'fine-art' pundits from the **Renaissance** onwards – and indeed, many craftworkers themselves – tended to see craft as hand labour devoid of intellectual content. A typical attitude is that of the 17th-century founders of the French Academy of Painting and Sculpture, who denigrated guild artists as 'craftsmen' lacking 'invention and learning'. The distinction was accentuated by the almost total disregard of the fine-art establishment for **folk artists** of all kinds, whom (if they considered them at all) they categorized as people of craft rather than of art.

In the 19th century, such attitudes persisted in European art establishments, and in architecture a similar distinction grew between 'craftsman' and 'architect', thanks in part to the establishment of professional architectural associations and examinations, and partly by the increasing rise of civil engineering and surveying as distinct professions. Several groups of the period, for example the **Arts and Crafts** Movement in Britain, did attempt to bridge the gap between 'craft' and 'art' through the promotion of handcrafts, aiming to recapture, in the face of machine production, the traditional cratsman's understanding of materials – as the motto of one influential group, the Art Workers' Guild, put it, 'to use materials aright'. Characteristic examples are William Morris's printing and bookbinding activities (using methods which Gutenberg would have immediately understood) and Ernest Gimson's Cotswolds workshop in the late 19th century, using traditional methods of furniture design.

Unfortunately, such **Utopian** schemes tended to founder in the face of economic necessity, and the old idea of 'craftsmanship' failed to make an impression. Indeed, developments in both architecture and design in the 20th century, from the work of the **Bauhaus** and Le Corbuiser onwards, have brought machine processes to a level of skill and beauty which seems to need nothing from former styles or ideas. In contemporary usage, the idea of 'crafts-manship' has lost its dignity, becoming an advertizer's word for a kind of fuddy-duddy traditionalism. Recently, however, female artists and feminist critics have rehabilitated the idea of 'craft', seeing in its subservient position to fine art a mirror of their own equally unjust social and political subjection. **PD MG JM KMcL**

Further reading H.M. Colvin, *A Biographical Dictionary of British Architects 1600–1840* (especially chapter 1, 'The Building Trades'); M. Greensted, *Gimson and the Barnsleys;* Lionel Lambourne, *Utopian Craftsmen: the Arts and Crafts Movement from the Cotswolds to Chicago.*

CREATIONISM

Creationism is the view that the universe and everything in it were created by God, as stated in the book of Genesis in the Bible. **Fundamentalist** Christians hold that creation happened exactly as described, in six days. More seriously, scientific crea-tionists argue that the complexity and diversity of the universe are such that it cannot have arisen by chance or by such processes as **natural selection** and **uniformi-tarianism**, that these factors point to a pur-pose and therefore to a purposer: a single 'first cause'. Although insertion of the supernatural into the debate is anti-rationalist and anti-science, and though all the scientific evidence so far collected favours the anti-creationist point of view, very many people, including scientists – and including those otherwise not predis-posed to religious belief or practice – still hold to it. **KMcL**

Further reading Hugh Montefiore, *The Prob-ability of God* (the religious, indeed Christian, side of the argument); Richard Dawkins, *The Blind Watchmaker* (the scientific side).

CREATIVITY

Creativity (from Latin *creare*, 'to make [from nothing]'), in the sense of producing something which expresses one's own orig-inal genius or talent, used to be regarded as the province of God or the gods alone. Only the Creator could create; human

beings (themselves created in the divine image) could merely imitate, not initiate, creation. Thus, works of the imagination were a reflection or a by-product of the divine-human relationship, and any beauty or intellectual or emotional power they possessed came from that relationship. Indeed, in many societies the very impetus to creativity was sacred: artists worked either directly to serve the gods or in festi-vals and other social rituals with religious overtones. Even when the arts were secu-larized – as in the court painting of Mughal India, for example, or Japanese dance-drama – an element of religiosity remained, creators often regarding themselves, and behaving, as acolytes not of gods but of some kind of quasi-sacred mystery.

This respectful spirit is the one in which even creators as individually minded, 'talented', as (for instance) Homer or Phei-dias went to work. When the Roman poet Horace wrote that his work would be a 'tomb-monument more lasting than bronze', the phrase was a straightforward metaphor with no overtones of arrogance or self-awareness. Horace was not claiming genius for himself, but comparing himself to the smith who crafts a tomb-monument or the client who commissions it; just as other people's monuments were bronze, so was his verse. The artists of antiquity – from Exekias to Omar Khayyám, from Vatsayan to Lady Murasaki – seldom or never intrude ideas of their own impor-tance into their work. If the work is beauti-ful or significant (their silence seems to imply) those are the qualities innate in the material, in the subject or in the treatment, and not facets of their own creative powers. The only ancient artists who boast about their own excellence are people such as Aristophanes and Ovid – and the refer-ences are comic, made to put down oppo-nents and raise a laugh. Japanese painters and sculptors, even those (the majority in ancient times) who worked anonymously, used to put a deliberate 'mistake' into each of their creations – a line slightly askew, a dip, a fold, a minute modulation of colour. This was not self-assertion; its purpose was to make the work, not the artist, stand out from its fellows as unique. In a similar way, when medieval European masons and woodcarvers 'signed' their work, by depicting themselves as gargoyles, or among the worshippers at Christ's manger, or among the crowds of souls clamouring for mercy at the Last Judgement, they were not so much declaring that the work they had made belonged to them as that they belonged to it; they were, in a sense, inserting themselves into the universal worship or supplication which the work both represented and encouraged.

This feeling, that artists (however individually interesting and talented) were part of a continuum of creation, persisted in Europe until the **Renaissance**, and for centuries longer in the East, until they began to take in and modify Western ideas. Renaissance practitioners and pundits of the arts talked of creativity as a rare, innate quality which set the possesser apart from (indeed, above) the brute instincts of ordinary people. Philosophers and critics (such as Vasari) agonized about the 'artist's shaping hand' as evinced in the work of almost anyone from Praxiteles to Giotto; the 16th-century poet Tasso put it more roundly, 'There are two creators, God and the poet'. Attempts to determine what made works of the imagination 'great' (that is, challenging and satisfying to a degree matched by few others) led inevitably to the notion that the creators of such works could themselves be 'great' and unique individuals. Creators divided into two camps: those (such as the 16th-century Italian composer Palestrina or the Renaissance architect Brunelleschi) who regarded themselves chiefly as skilled craftworkers, servants of their patrons and of their art as creators had always been, and those (such as Michelangelo or Monteverdi) who felt and said that they stood apart from the common herd even of creative artists, and that they had to wrestle not merely with the materials of the art, but with their own creative spirit, to produce their work. Shakespeare and his contemporary creative artists had a lively sense of their own genius, and were not loath to express it so that a kind of artistic swagger, a creative swashbuckle, is intrinsic to the arts of Elizabethan England (and indeed to the behaviour of such people as Drake or Raleigh, who claimed, in so many words, that their very lives were works of art).

From the Renaissance to our own time, the tendency has increased to create a gulf between art and artisanship, between the 'creative' and the 'practical'. People in professions which would once have been regarded as pure craft – architects and garden designers, for instance – are now routinely described as if they were artists, and of genius. For example, Gaudí and Mies van der Rohe are considered as closer to Picasso than to the anonymous masons who built Notre Dame or the Forbidden City. Almost every art form, from choreography to **sculpture**, from **poetry** to **pop**, is beset with hierarchies and categories of creative excellence, discussion of which sometimes replaces appreciation of created works themselves. Modern creative artists also have to come to terms with a vast weight of past 'work of genius' before they can begin. In short, although the change has made little difference to the work artists do, or to the rewards they receive, it has completely changed the way 'creative' people view themselves. Once, they were mirrored, defined, fulfilled, in the work they did; now, before you create, you must establish an **attitude** to your art, to its actuality, theory, past, present and marketplace – in fact, you must establish yourself. **KMcL**

See also aesthetics; culture; genius; taste.

CREATIVITY AND PLAY

Defining **creativity** has posed an interesting challenge to psychologists and pyschoanalysts. Freud, for example, saw it as an act of sublimation of sexual instincts – an explanation which falls frustratingly short of a satisfactory definition of a highly-regarded human attribute. D.W. Winnicot, from the British school of psychoanalytical objects-relations thought, put forward a more complex theory: that there is a potential space between mother and baby which is where the baby learns to play; playing is seen as a prerequisite for creativity. Winnicott thought that a healthy relationship to reality was a creative one. Those of his patients who were compliant with reality and felt that they had no impact on it were mentally ill and full of feelings of futility and that nothing mattered.

Having located play as an important aspect of illness and recovery, Winnicot also discovered that the psychoanalytic ideas of inner and outer reality did not adequately cover the experiences of playing and creativity. For Winnicot playing leads to cultural experience, appreciation and creation and is the missing link between inner and outer reality. The mother creates the potential space by giving the baby sensitive, loving management when the child is separating out from the mother – the phase when the baby moves from experiencing the world as an extention of itself to realizing its separateness. If the baby has a poor experience, then Winnicot sees that there is little space left for anything but **introversion and extraversion**. The job of the psychoanalyst or therapist is to give the patient back this area to play in. **MJ**

Further reading D.W. Winnicot, *Playing and Reality*.

CRITICAL PERIOD HYPOTHESIS

According to the critical period hypothesis in **linguistics** (CPH), the ability to learn languages is confined to a biologically circumscribed period, ranging from the age of about 18 months up to the age of adolescence. The notion of a critical period finds its inspiration in the biological concept of maturation, whereby development is programmed to follow a genetically-determined sequence. However, the expression of the genetic programme requires appropriate environmental conditions. Hence, it is argued that in the absence of normal exposure to language during the critical period, it would subsequently be biologically impossible to acquire language normally.

The CPH predicts that brain damage which would cause language loss in adults should not have such catastrophic effects in infancy. This is because the child's brain is still being moulded by maturational forces and the concomitant flexibility allows other regions of the brain to take over and proceed with development more or less normally. However, it has emerged that specific brain injuries in infancy can result in permanent language impairment. Furthermore,

the flexibility of younger brains does not entirely disintegrate in adulthood. Currently, in fact, there is no convincing evidence for a decisive cut-off point at adolescence, beyond which language learning is impossible. **MS**

CRITICAL REGIONALISM

The idea of critical regionalism in **architecture** is essentially a **postmodernist** precept stressing, in the design of a new building, the attention that must be given to the existing physical context of that building's region.

Critical regionalism is not an equivalent of the later 19th-century vernacular revival, because it does not call for a return to vernacular building type. Nor is it in opposition to modern technology. It is a reaction to the global uniformity of **modernism**, a conscious feature of the International Style which sought to break down nationalist barriers. Later observers noted that if people from different localities did not travel, for whatever reason, then they would be unable to identify with international style, but would only regret the loss of any attention to their indigenous culture. The term 'critical regionalism' was coined in the early 1980s by Alex Tzonis, and is identified with the theoretical writings of the critic Kenneth Frampton, who describes it thus: 'Regionalism upholds individual and local architectonic features against more universal and abstract ones.' **JM**

See also contextualism.

CRITICAL THEORY

Critical theory is a form of sociological analysis associated with the 20th-century Frankfurt School of critical **sociology**. The notion of **criticism** is rather older than this though. It refers to the exercise of negative judgement.

During the Reformation, in the 16th century, textual criticism developed as a weapon of religious conflict – biblical criticism entailed the negative but objective judgement of ecclesiastical practice and dogma. For G. Hegel, criticism meant the process of uncovering hidden assumptions, the questioning of claims to **authority** and thus a way of emancipating society. Marx took the idea of criticism a step further and argued that to merely interpret the world was insufficient, efforts should be made to try and change it.

The critical theory of the Frankfurt School arose out of a dissatisfaction with the use of 'criticism' by institutionalized **Marxism** to legitimate the political decisions of the Communist Party. Critical theory rests on the assumption that in order to understand and explain social reality one cannot avoid evaluating and criticizing society's own self-understanding. A principle exponent of critical theory is Habermas. Habermas dismisses the idea of a neutral, apolitical science, based on a separation of facts and values, as untenable. He argues that questions of truth are inextricably bound up with political problems of freedom of communication and the exchange of ideas. **DA**

See also discourse; dominant ideology; hegemony; ideology; legitimation; positivism; social construction of reality; sociology of knowledge.

Further reading Connerton (ed.), *Critical Sociology*; T. McCarthy, *The Critical Theory of Jurgen Habermas*.

CRITICISM

Criticism (from Greek *krites*, 'judge') is an activity about which diametrically opposite opinions can be held. It can be seen either as an essential component of human thought, a major guarantor of our cultural existence, or as lateral to true intellectual activity, not to say parasitic upon it. Aristotle's writings on **drama** demonstrate the point. Writing in the 4th century BCE, and seeking not to criticize the writing of plays, but to draw conclusions about the types of plays being written and to extrapolate from them a kind of definition of what the purpose of drama was and how it might be achieved, Aristotle put forward some general opinions, which were subsequently taken as rules by generations of playwrights and connoisseurs of drama. Indeed, they are still mentioned with care whenever abstract discussion of drama is attempted.

On the one hand Aristotle's work did enormous (unintended) harm, by closing off avenues of thought and creative exploration. To this day, academic appreciation of ancient Greek drama is straitjacketed by attempts to relate the plays to his comments rather than to any other correlative. On the other hand, attempts by later generations to understand and abide by his 'rules' have led to some of the West's finest drama. Aristotle's work has been a springboard for new creativity of kinds one can hardly imagine without it. This is, perhaps, how what is self-admiringly called 'higher' criticism should operate – the activity defined by the 19th-century poet and critic Matthew Arnold as 'a disinterested endeavour to learn and propagate the best that is known and thought in the world'.

This kind of criticism is a form of **scholasticism**, and as such has been almost entirely squeezed out of scientific thought. It persists in the **arts**, and many critics have followed in Aristotle's footsteps, with equally dynamic and energetic effect on the creative community. The best of such critics are aware, however, that to 'endeavour...to learn and propagate the best that is known and thought in the world' must be a self-correcting exercise, that opinions should be transitory, that humility should be a quality not of creators but of critics. This view is, alas, not common, either in critics or in those who read them. The writer Eduard Hanslick, in 19th-century Vienna, saw himself (and was seen by others) as a kind of Napoleonic music critic, leading the armies of rational common sense against the Wagnerian enemy. In the UK during the 1930s, T.S. Eliot spoke like Moses delivering the Ten Commandments, articulating views about 'high' culture which have bedevilled English **literature** ever since. (Eliot himself, a creative artist as well as a pundit, came to deplore and repudiate his own views in later life.) The worst example of all, also in the UK, was an attempt, in the early 1970s, by the art historian Kenneth Clark to define 'civilization' in a series of television programmes entitled *Civilization*. He defined it quite emphatically as the paintings, buildings, sculptures and (grudgingly) music, theatre and literature of western Europe between about 1400 and 1900. The problem was not the programmes, but the title and the fact that millions of people throughout the world took it at face value, and formed a ludicrously distorted, exclusive and patrician view of what 'civilization' is.

Clark's programmes, an egregious example of a flea setting out to describe the elephant it feeds on, are symptomatic of what is wrong with much of the 'criticism' currently practised throughout the world. (The rest of the world has accepted the Western view of what criticism is and how it should be done. Even in countries whose culture is precisely not prescriptive and definitive – India and China spring to mind – the search for fundamental principles in artistic creation, and the fundamentalist propagation of orthodox opinion in the matter, are as common as in countries used to precriptivism, whether social, religious, political, or, as in this case, artistic.) We have transformed critics into soothsayers, and hang on their every word. There is nothing wrong with reading X's views on the death of tragedy, at the 'high' level, or Y's opinion of last night's harp recital, at the 'low' level so long as we never mistake them for a branch of the activities they seek to describe. **KMcL**

CROSSING OVER

In the **life sciences**, the concept of crossing over is at the heart of the recombination of genetic information which occurs during sexual reproduction. Crossing over takes place when gametes (sperm or eggs) are produced from specialized gamete-forming cells which, in common with other cells of the organism, have two of each chromosome; when a sperm fuses with an egg the resulting cell has two of each chromosome, paired as alleles (23 pairs in humans). This cell (the zygote) can then divide many times to produce all the cells which make up the individual, all of which have paired chromosomes.

Crossing over occurs before the pairs of chromosomes are separated in the gamete-forming cells. Before the paired chromosomes are separated, they are aligned closely together, giving the DNA strands the opportunity to break and re-link. During this process, strands from opposite alleles may join with one another rather than rejoining to the chromosome they broke from. Thus, when the alleles are sep-

arated each will contain some stretches of DNA which were formerly part of the other, and the gametes formed will possess, in a single set of chromosomes, genes derived from both the alleles carried by the gamete-forming cell.

The process of crossing over increases the degree of difference between offspring and is thus the single most important source of the variation which is required for **evolution. RB**

See also gene; genetic linkage; meiosis.

CRYPTOGRAPHY

Since World War II, one of the most important military uses of **mathematics** and **computers** is in the field of cryptography (Greek, 'writing down the hidden', or 'hidden writing'). Until this century, the codes used in warfare were usually simple substitution codes, where the same letter in the cipher always stands for the same letter in the original. From the advent of radio, which meant that the signal sent out could be intercepted by anyone with a receiver set to the same wavelength without even the knowledge of the sender, codes became far more important, and led to an immense increase in the complexity of the codes used. For example, the letter in the cipher which stood for a particular letter in the original could depend on many other things than which letter it represented – the date and time, the position in the message, the length of the message, the identity of the sender and receiver and so on. This presented a great challenge to code-breakers, and increasingly sophisticated statistical methods began to be used to solve the new codes. Code-breaking was the first major application for digital computers, with the Enigma code being cracked in the 1940s by a team including Alan Turing (1912–54).

Cryptography does not only have military uses. It is also important in today's world of digital communication. The major needs are for methods to encode information as sequences of 0s and 1s which are as short as possible and secure from corruption if mistakes are made in transmission, and, in some cases, secure from interpretation by competing firms. **SMcL**

See also coding theory.

CUBISM

Cubism, one of the quintessential styles of 20th-century Western painting, was prefigured in the late, increasingly geometric works of Cézanne, and was energetically developed in the 1900s and 1910s by Braque and Picasso (whose *Les demoiselles d'Avignon* (1907) is generally cited as one of the first 'official' cubist pictures). Cubism aimed to restructure representation through a redefinition of **realism**, to show the solid reality of objects and not merely their appearance. Its technical starting point, the division of the objects the artist wishes to depict (houses, trees, fruit, musical instruments, faces, whatever) into planes of light and colour, is identical to that of any earlier art. In cubism, however, the planes are stressed, separated one from another and even outlined until geometric shapes dominate the finished picture. (As well as the cubes which give the style its name, cylinders, pyramids and spheres are common.) Thus, in its first phase, 'Analytical Cubism' (1908–12), cubism abandoned the conventions of **Renaissance** pictorial space in favour of a multi-viewpoint exploration of the motif, showing from many different angles objects disposed in shallow picture space, articulated through overlapping and interlocking planes which respect the planimentric nature of the picture surface. In its second phase, 'Synthetic Cubism', it moved away from the representation of the object in Nature to focus on the material nature of the object in relation to other objects or materials. Synthetic Cubism emphasizes its non-illusionistic agenda through the inclusion of 'real' elements, such as fragments of wallpaper or journals of photographs. (Thus Braque's *Still Life on a Table* (1913) includes a strip of newspaper, the primary meaning of which is the fact that it is a newspaper, but one which by extension 'represents' a newspaper in a painting, and lastly provides a structuring device within the picture space.)

At its most extreme (for example, in Picasso's *Man Smoking a Pipe* or Duchamp's *Nude Descending a Staircase*), a cubist picture can seem to the unconvinced observer little more than a tumble of shapes which are difficult to relate to the picture's title. At its most representational (for example, in the check tablecloths, plates and fruit of a Gris still life), a cubist work can be little more than a pleasant emphasis of form over content. Although at its finest (for instance, in Picasso's 1930s and 1940s portraits of Jacqueline) it becomes just as much the means towards an end as, say **perspective** was in the hands of the Old Masters. Its importance resides in its potential to construct works of art that no longer hold up Nature as an ultimate appeal, but in which relationships between the constituent parts are central to the meaning. In this, it confirmed the general direction of **modernism** in fine art from Manet onwards, and anticipated the development of **abstraction** and Clement Greenberg's ideas on 'pure' painting. There is little cubist **sculpture**, and what there is – such as the work of Lipchitz – suggests that paint on a flat surface remains the ideal vehicle for this apparently three-dimensional style. **PD MG KMcL**

Further reading R. Rosenblum, *Cubism and 20th-century Art*.

CULT

Cult (Latin, 'worship' or 'devotion') has two distinct meanings in English religious and theological writing. The first sense is similar to the use of the word *bhakti*: intense worship of or devotion to a particular saint or deity, who is credited with miracle-working powers. Examples include the cults of Our Lady of Fatima (**Mariology**), of Muslim saints in India (whose graves are venerated as shrines), or of Satya Sai Baba, who has a living incarnation in Bangalore, India. Such a cult is often local, based on a particular shrine or the memory of a local person, and members remain part of a mainstream **church** or **religion**.

The second sense is as a description of what is now known as a neoreligious movement, or in older writings, a heterodox **sect** outside the mainstream churches, often with secret doctrine and worship. An example is the cult of Dionysus in the ancient Greco-Roman world. This sense has become pejorative and, because practitioners object to it, it is falling into disuse among serious researchers. Also, cult used in this sense has a tenuous connection with **occultism**. EMJ

CULTURAL GREY-OUT see Musical Acculturation

CULTURAL RELATIVISM

Cultural relativism was introduced by the American anthropologist Franz Boas, who founded the Cultural School of Anthropology in the early 1900s, to emphasize the particularistic nature of differences between cultural systems. He criticized the evolutionist tendency to overgeneralize, and instead believed that each society should be documented in detail before any attempts were made to draw conclusions about perceived similarities. At the beginning of this century, anthropologists in the USA were engaged in trying to preserve the remnants of the Indian communities that had survived virtual extinction through war and disease, by recording what was left of their ways of life. The meticulous recording of customs and traditions, along with a concern with material objects and artefacts, provided the basis for the style of exhibition one finds in modern ethnographic museums.

In its heyday, cultural relativism radically challenged evolutionary modes of thinking about 'primitive' societies, and came to represent an emphasis on the 'particulars' of a society rather than making broad cross-cultural comparisons about concepts that were presumed to be universal. In anthropological debates of the last few decades, the concept of cultural relativism has been opposed to that of cultural universalism, questioning the extent to

which Western criteria can be used to evaluate other social systems. Cultural relativists argue that the diversity of cultural systems means that each one can only be evaluated according to its own values and belief systems. Taken to its logical extreme, the concept of cultural relativism can be used to uphold the status quo in a community, by not stepping outside a system in order to make any broadly comparative evaluations, or not locating the current state of play in a historical context. Cultural relativism has been criticized for resting on the assumption that communities can be considered as naturally demarcated like the remaining American Indian communities who were literally 'enclosed' on reservations. **CL RK**

See also culture; evolutionism; language.

Further reading Stocking, G (ed.), *Franz Boas, The Shaping of American Anthropology*.

CULTURE

Culture (from Latin *colere*, 'inhabit', 'cultivate', 'protect', 'honour with worship') is one of the most widely used, and abused, words in English. Its meaning blurs and varies according to its context and who is describing it. In straightforward scientific terms, a culture is a living cell or group of cells encouraged to multiply in a medium outside the body. In **archaeology**, a culture is a collection of artefacts related to each other through the closeness of the region they were found in or the period they were believed to be from. Material culture has been associated with particular social groups as a means of ordering material data, although contemporary archaeologists are more sceptical of straightforward equations between artefact and societies.

All the senses above filter into the predominant meaning of 'culture' in **anthropology** and the **social sciences**: the way of life particular to a given group of people. In 1871 the anthropologist Edwin Tylor defined it thus: 'Culture or civilization...is that complex whole which includes knowledge, belief, art, morals, law, custom and any other capabilities and habits acquired by man as a member of society.' The problem with Tylor's definition is that it takes European culture as the prototype for all other cultures. The idea of culture – to describe the general development of the group in terms of intellectual, spiritual and aesthetic qualities – is implied, but on Western terms. It suggests that 'primitive' cultures have to undergo a developmental process in order to be as 'civilized' as European culture.

Such evolutionary schemes were later abandoned; anthropologists now treat culture as a neutral term used to describe a system of ideas, values and behaviours. For a considerable period early this century, British social anthropologists contrasted culture with society. In their aspirations for a social scientific approach, culture was regarded as an arbitrary and vague term while 'society' was used to refer to functional roles, structures and organizations. For American cultural anthropologists, however, culture was treated as synonymous with society.

More recently, anthropologists and sociologists have attacked the idea that cultures exist as discrete, unified things on the grounds that it is an invention that does not correspond to the actuality of social life. It does not allow for differences in views within a community, or properly account for relationships between communities. Similarly, the assumption that societies function as bounded systems composed of integrated roles and institutions has also been discredited. Cultural differences are reflected in current distinctions between *subculture* associated with divergent values, appearance and behaviour of groups that identify themselves in contradistinction to the wider or dominant society; *counter-culture* to describe those who defy majority norms and values; and *personal culture* to describe how an individual makes use of and relates to his/her cultural environment.

When coupled with nature, culture is treated like nurture, which considers the degree to which human thought and behaviour are affected by their environmental conditions rather than their biological make-up. Within structuralist theory, which attempts to discover the ordering principles of the mind, the nature-culture

distinction has been transposed to chart the ways people make boundaries between what is considered a part of society and what is seen to lie beyond it. It is humans that determine what is nature for it is not something that is determined by itself. On this point, Marshall Sahlins has offered the useful remark: 'Nature is to culture what culture makes of nature.'

In the last half-century, two fascinating sociological phenomena have been, first, the interpenetration (especially in the West) of such phenomenological views of culture – that is, that it comprises the whole experience of everyday life – with the old critical notion that it was inherently to do with the **arts**, and with 'high arts' at that; and second, the extraordinary way in which Western mass culture (with all its ephemeral and transitory 'output': television, **advertising**, fashion, pastimes, social activities) has colonized the entire world far more successfully than the earlier 'high culture' of the imperialist West. Mass communications, mass-production of artefacts and global marketing are the reasons, and they have begun to dictate the 'cultural agenda' of the entire world.

Until recently (and still in some universities and among other literary subcultures) the mass culture which emerges from such developments has been despised as somehow inferior to the 'high arts' which alone embody the notion of cultural excellence. The fear is ever-present that, in any society, because culture is absorbed by a socialization process, and because the mass media occupy a central and powerful role in that process, the output of the media may only reflect the culture of the dominant group who control it or consume it. This would suffocate the cultural values of many people who do not subscribe to the dominant view. This would be a tragedy, not because of its effects on the chattering class (who, ironically, would now find their culture marginalized and made second best in exactly the way they formerly treated the culture of the mass of the population) but, more seriously, because it led to the erosion and obliteration of minority attitudes and the habits of mind of minority groups throughout the world.

Perhaps in the end, culture is not what

we discuss but what we live. As a set of value-judgements about beliefs and ways of life, particularly in the areas of social behaviour and intellectual activity, it is a particularly human phenomenon (unless one assumes that other creatures make such judgements), and can never be objective. It is an example of the hierarchical, categorizing impulse which is such a characterstic feature of the human mind and also of our love of defining ourselves and others, and by defining, excluding. In ancient Greece, Greek-speakers proclaimed that they were 'cultured' compared to 'barbarians' (those whose speech sounded like 'bar-bar'); it is not recorded what barbarians thought of Greeks. In other areas, at one time or another, to be 'cultured' has involved being a member of the Japanese Imperial household, following **Islam**, being a middle-European intellectual, not being a Westerner, preferring Beethoven to the Beatles, studying Arts rather than Sciences, rejecting all artefacts (physical or intellectual) created by 'dead, white, European males', observing particular rules of social etiquette or, in each case, being or doing just the opposite.

The 19th-century English poet and critic Matthew Arnold wrote (in *Culture and Anarchy*) that culture was a 'study of human perfection' – which he went on to define as the exercise of rationality as opposed to instinct. (To be rational, in this definition, includes the rational awareness of the power, and 'usefulness', of instinct.) A cultured person, for Arnold, enhanced his or her individual awareness, striving towards the goal of moral and spiritual perfection. Seventy years after Arnold's book was published, and in the course of pursuing 'perfection' of a different kind, Hermann Goering said (misquoting the poet Heinz Johst), 'When I hear the world "culture" I reach for my gun'. This perhaps epitomizes the 'practical' (uncultured?) person's reaction to the narcissistic and fashion-bound **scholasticism** of which redefinitions of culture are such a persistent, and egregious, example. **BC RK KMcL**

See also assimilation; criticism; cultural relativism; diffusionism; dominant ideology; ethnicity; evolutionism; functionalism; hegemony; ideology; internalization; interpretative anthropology; kinship; media; naturalism; nature/culture; norms; religion; role; sexuality; social control; social integration; socialization; social/sociological problem; society; sociolinguistics; structuralism; subculture; taste; tourism, anthropology of; values; work.

Further reading T.S. Eliot, *Notes Towards the Definition of Culture*; George Steiner, *Bluebeard's Castle: Notes Towards the Redefinition of Culture*; George Stocking Jnr, *Race, Culture and Evolution*; Raymond Williams, *Culture*.

CYTOLOGY

Cytology (Greek *kutos*, 'vessel' + ology), in the **life sciences**, is the study of the living cell, the basic unit of all life according to the cell theory stated in 1839 by the German biologists Theodor Schwann and Matthias Schleiden. They postulated that all living organisms are composed of one or more cells – and, in 1855, Rudolf Virchow added that cells can only arise by the division of pre-existing cells. Cytology was established as a science in 1892 when the German anatomist Oscar Hertwig proposed that the function of the organism reflects the function of its constituent cells. Modern cytology involves the study of cellular metabolism and of the genetic control of the cell.

The living cell is divided from its environment by a membrane, composed of fatty molecules, and the space within is filled with an aqueous solution (the cytoplasm) of molecules including proteins and carbohydrates. Discrete membrane-bounded regions of this cytoplasm, termed **organelles**, are found within all cells and have varying functions, including energy storage, energy transduction and protein production. Higher cells (eukaryotes) possess nuclei which are membrane-bounded organelles, containing the chromosomes which bear the genetic material as DNA. Communication between the nucleus and the cytoplasm is by RNA which passes out of the nucleus bearing genetic information in usable chunks. Simpler cells (prokaryotes), such as bacteria, have fewer organelles and no nucleus or chromosomes: genetic information, in the form of DNA or

RNA, exists in the cytoplasm. Plant and bacterial cells have rigid cell walls in addition to the plasma membrane; animal cells have no cell wall but the plasma membrane is reinforced by networks of filaments which act as a scaffold and which may also be contractile, allowing the cell to move. A feature of cells is that they are specialized according to function, especially where they are part of a complex multicellular organism; thus a muscle cell is rich in contractile fibres and mitochondria, organelles which produce usable energy from sugars. **RB**

Further reading Christian de Duve, *Blueprint for a Cell.*

D

DADA

Dada ('hobbyhorse') was an anti-art art movement of the 1910s to 1920s. It began in Zürich with the collaboration of a group of artists seeking refuge from World War I, and included the Romanian poet Tristan Tzara, the French fine artist Hans Arp and the German writer Hugo Ball. In 1916 Ball founded the Cabaret Voltaire, where Dada 'manifestations' took place, backed up by the publication of manifestoes, pamphlets and magazines (whose anarchic graphics later became influential in **avant-garde** circles). In 1917 Dada spread to the rest of Europe and beyond (notably to Australia and the Americas). Tzara and Ball opened the Galerie Dada in Zürich, Francis Picabia published the magazine *391* in Barcelona, and Marcel Duchamp brought out the magazines *The Blind Man* and *Wrong-Wrong* in New York. After the war Dada became influential in Germany round Kurt Schwitters, Hans Arp and Max Ernst, and in France where Paris Dada was animated by André Breton and Louis Aragon.

The name Dada, reputedly selected at random by sticking a knife in a dictionary, was adopted to symbolize the antirational, anarchic and anti-traditionalist stance of its members. The idea was to demolish bourgeois standards in the arts by mocking them. The Dadaists printed nonsense poetry set in a random selection of typefaces, exhibited such 'found objects' as Duchamp's *Fountain* of 1917 (a urinal signed 'R. Mutt') or a bicycle wheel mounted on a stool, and performed anti-music consisting of rude noises and random shouts. Such tactics of shock and unreason challenged accepted values in the arts (such as the cult of **beauty**), which the group regarded as hypocritical and out of keeping with 20th-century militaristic and industrial civilization.

The Dada movement itself was short-lived, a matter of a few dozen exhibitions, publications and cabaret performances. After 1919 its nihilistic principles were moderated under the dual influence of a nascent institutionalization of the Dadists' work (for example, Dada was incorporated into the Paris Salon des Indépendants in 1920), and a replacement of the shock of disjunction with an interest in juxtaposition as an aesthetic principle – notably, after 1923, in **Surrealism**. Although Dada's life was little more than an artistic mayfly dance, the feeling of alienation, of challenge, of art as a 'happening', which it restored to our experience of the arts was seminal to the **theatre of the absurd, Cubism, neoclassicism** and Surrealism – in fact, to just about every major development in the arts this century. **PD MG KMcL**

Further reading H. Richter, *Dada: Art and Anti-Art.*

DANCE

Dance can be simply defined as patterned movement. The anthropological contribution to the study of dance has been its focus on the dance as a social event, rather than as a bodily or aesthetic experience. In traditional societies, dance has been treated as one manifestation of **ritual**, analogous to oratory. The Marxist anthropologist Maurice Bloch suggested that all forms of ritual behaviour are formulaic and repetitive, and that their fixed quality embodies messages which can be interpreted as bolstering traditional forms of authority.

Many **functionalist** approaches treated dance as a static cultural expression, neglecting the aspect of its spontaneous creativity. Not only has dance been seen as a means of transmitting messages or a form of social control, it has also been analysed as a safety valve for pent-up feelings, or as a means of transcending the physical realm as in trance states. By looking at the message transmitted, the feelings and the social context, **anthropology** can locate particular dances in the social realm. Dance also reflects class and gender classifications in society. Belly dancers at weddings in Egypt, for example, embody a sexuality which socializes brides into their new role as sexually active beings. Egyptian men dance in communal Sufi rituals, in which the emphasis on achieving ecstasy underlines the importance of the internal condition of the individual. Here the dance is mirroring cosmological rather than social classifications.

Recent concerns with **phenomenology** and embodiment look at the body itself as a medium which both participates in, and makes its mark on, society. Disco dancing, for example, restricted by legislation in China, provides a forum for youth to express their disaffection with the state. **CL**

See also body; ethnomusicology.

Further reading Paul Spencer (ed.), *Society and the Dance*; Victor Turner, *Dramas, Fields and Metaphors*.

DAOISM

Daoism (or Taoism) derives its name from the book *Dao de jing* ('Classic of the Way and its Power'). This was formerly attributed to a sage of the 6th century BCE, Lao-zi ('the old philosopher'), but is now thought to have been compiled in the 3rd century BCE. Nonetheless, tales of Lao's miraculous powers continued to circulate, at least at a popular level, for centuries. He was 62 years (or 82) years in the womb, and was born with snow-white hair and able to speak. When he was 160 years old (or 200), disgusted with the world, he mounted a chariot drawn by a black ox and galloped off to paradise. On the way, stopped by a tollkeeper and asked to leave some remnant of his wisdom to ordinary mortals, he sat down and wrote the *Dao de jing*.

Dao means 'the way', and Daoism began as a mystic religion practised by ascetics. It

was not until the 1st century CE that it was codified into a popular religion of practice, in a form which has lasted, practically unchanged, to the present day. *Dao* is the way of things, the primal force in the universe, omnipresent, all-controlling, unfathomable and indescribable. Our aim in life should be to become one with the *dao*, and this is done by living a harmonious life, by meditation, simple living and openness of spirit. There are close links with **Confucian** thought in all this, and the two systems have become inextricably linked in Chinese philosophical and religious practice.

The harmony of the *dao* depends, in part, on an exact balance of opposites: good and evil, light and dark, motion and stillness, negative and positive, feminine and masculine. This harmony is shown in the symbol of Yin and Yang: a circle formed by two intercoiled, tadpole-like shapes, one dark, one light. The Yin is dark, feminine and negative; the Yang is light, masculine and positive. Everything which exists is a balance of Yin and Yang, and only so long as that balance is maintained can there be universal harmony. Enlightenment involves both perception and acceptance of that balance. (In popular religion, the balance can be upset by hostile forces, natural or supernatural, and restored by prayer and sacrifice.)

In the Middle Ages, it was thought that oneness with the *dao* conferred immortality. This in turn led to the notion that our earthly bodies could be transmuted to their supernatural, immortal forms by **alchemy**, and alchemical research was a central interest of Daoists for centuries. Similarly, **divination** was considered a way to find out more about the inscrutable nature of *dao*, and to investigate those aspects of it which lay outside mortal time and space. A favourite form of divination was to consult the *Yijing* (or *I ching*, 'book of changes'), a collection of oracular statements which you read in accordance with chance numerological patterns discovered by such means as tossing handfuls of sticks on the ground. **Astrology** became an inextricable part of Daoist practice, to the point where its true purpose (to explore the *dao*) was blurred into mundane futurology. The *Dao de jing* itself contains what is perhaps the definitive argument against all such foolishness. Chapter 40 begins 'Reversal is the movement of the *dao*' – that is, whatever we perceive to be the *dao*, the opposite is true (and continues to be so even if we move to take the opposite view); truth and falsity are opposites, and the harmony between them is paradox.

If Confucianism was the practical aspect of Chinese philosophy and religion for two millennia, Daoism was its esoteric and mystical branch. A grossly simplified form of it became popular in the West in the 1960s, and still distorts the Western perspective of what it was, is, and means. Virtue (*de*), for the true Daoist, is a quality not of individuals but of the *dao* itself: we find ourselves by losing ourselves. With virtue, as the *Dao de jing* puts it, 'everything returns to its original, natural state, and total harmony is reached'. **KMcL**

See also Buddhism.

Further reading C.K. Chang, *Religion in Chinese Society*; Arthur Waley, *The Way and its Power* (translation, with good notes and introduction, of the *Dao de jing*); Richard Wilhelm and Cary F. Baynes, *The I Ching or Book of Changes* (translation, with good notes and introduction).

DARWINISM

Charles Darwin (1809–82) proposed a theoretical explanation for **evolution**, based on his studies of similar species and their **biogeographical** relationships with one another. The concept of evolution was first mooted in the 18th century, by, among others, Darwin's grandfather Erasmus Darwin, but no satisfactory cause was suggested. Darwin observed great similarities between certain organisms and explained them by proposing common ancestry. Where similar organisms differed, he suggested that **adaptation** had occured in response to pressure from the environment, leading to the establishment of a new but related species. The inheritance of characteristics ensured that offspring were very similar to their parents – thus Darwin recognized heredity as improving stability on the process of reproduction. This stability was modified by variation, a liberalizing force which permits limited change to arise in the population. Although Darwin was unable to explain the mechanism behind these two forces (he was a proponent of **pangenesis**), he realized that they were important to the evolution of species through the process of **natural selection** in which variants of a species compete for survival. The outcome of this competition is determined by a selective death rate, dependent on the **fitness** of each individual. Those individuals best adapted to the environment would thus survive to pass their advantageous characteristics to their offspring.

Darwinism, the chief ideas of which were set out in Darwin's book *On the Origin of the Species* in 1859, stimulated a major re-evaluation of **biology** despite intense criticism from contemporary scientists and theologians, who protested that he was unable adequately to explain the mechanisms behind heredity and variation, and could not deliver proof that evolution had happened. Experimental support for his ideas grew through the remainder of the 19th century, but it became apparent, particularly as **genetics** began to be understood, that the theory was over-simplified. Today, conventional explanations for evolution are termed Neo-Darwinism, in which the principles of Darwinism are retained. Thus Neo-Darwinism does not accept that acquired characteristics can be inherited, an idea which was prevalent at the time of Darwin. The concept of natural selection is more precisely defined in terms of reproductive success or fitness. **RB**

See also creationism; homology; Lamarckism; Mendelism; morphology; palaeontology; speciation.

Further reading Douglas Futuyma, *Evolutionary Biology*.

DATING THE EARTH

Most societies have a creation myth which explains how and when the Earth was formed. For European societies, in the Christian era, the Book of Genesis was taken as a literal description of the creation until the 19th century. Not only did this state that the Earth had been formed in a week, it implied that the accounts of human events in the Old Testament covered the whole of the Earth's history. Archbishop Ussher of Armagh, writing in the 17th century, calculated that the genealogies given in the books of the Old Testament gave the date of the Creation as 4004 BCE.

This extremely short period gave little time for geological processes to have any effect, though Noah's Flood was taken literally and used to explain the existence of fossils of animals and plants now extinct. But as geologists studied rates of erosion and deposition, let alone contemplated the possibility of mountain building, it was clear that much longer timescales must be involved. This was described by James Hutton's principle of **uniformitarianism** and his dictum, 'no vestige of a beginning, no prospect of an end'. The work of William Smith in assembling rocks from different areas into the stratigraphic column suggested that hundreds of thousands of feet of rocks had been laid down in the UK, in climatic conditions ranging from hot desert and tropical marshland to permafrost and ice sheet. From 1859, Darwin's work on **evolution** added another pointer to a long timescale. So the scientific community came to accept Genesis as allegorical, and that the age of the Earth had to be measured in hundreds or thousands of million years.

Towards the end of the 19th century, this consensus was rudely shattered, not by a backlash from the church, but by one of the most distinguished scientists of the day. Lord Kelvin used one of the most advanced sciences to construct what appeared to be an unimpeachable case for a rather short lifetime for the Earth. Measurements were made of the heat loss from the surface of the Earth – most obvious at volcanoes, but detectable elsewhere. It was assumed that this heat was the remainder of that present when the Earth formed as a molten ball of rock. Experiments in furnaces showed how much heat was required to raise rock to melting point, so the starting point could be calculated. Then the laws of thermodynamics could be used to calculate the time required to cool from the starting point to the observed temperatures. The calculation was done several times with slightly different assumptions, but Kelvin argued that the

Earth could not be much more than 24 million years old. This was clearly insufficient to allow the theories of the geologists and biologists to be true, so there was a disabling lack of consensus.

The problem was solved shortly after Kelvin's death by the discovery of **radioactivity**. This both provided a means of generating heat within the Earth, so making possible a much longer lifespan, and a means of measuring the time. There are some 65 naturally occurring radioactive isotopes on Earth. These are unstable and spontaneously break down by emitting neutrons to form a daughter product, which may be another isotope of the same element or a lighter element. Each isotope breaks down with a constant half-life – a constant time to halve the amount present at the start of the period. If the half-life is known and mother and daughter products remain together it is simple to calculate the duration of the decay process. In practice it has proved very complex as the daughter product may itself be radioactive or may be more mobile, but the problems can be overcome by the use of more than one decay process. Even the first measurements, by Boltwood in 1906, using the decay of uranium to lead, were enough to refute Kelvin and vindicate the geologists. Boltwood's estimates for different rocks ranged from 400 million to 2.2 billion years, so he indicated that the Earth is a hundred times older than Kelvin's estimate. His measurements are now thought to be about 20% too long, but modern methods have found even greater ages for other materials.

The oldest rocks so far dated are calculated to be 3.5 billion years old, but the Earth itself is probably about a billion years older. This is indicated by measurements of the age of meteorites, 4.5 billion, and of Moon rocks, 3.7–4.6 billion years. Since the Earth originated simultaneously with the Moon, 4.6 billion years is now thought to be the most probable estimate. **PS**

DE BROGLIE WAVES

Louis Victor de Broglie (1892–1987) was one of the pioneers of early quantum mechanics. It had been realized that light, for many years considered to be purely a wave, interacts as a particle. De Broglie made the conceptual leap of realizing that the fact that waves have a particle-like nature could imply that particles have a wave-like nature. He defined the wavelength of a particle by

$$\lambda = \frac{h}{p}$$

where λ is the wavelength, h is equal to 6.62×10^{-34}, known as Planck's constant, and p is the momentum of the particle. The truth of this hypothesis has been confirmed by innumerable experiments; particles such as electrons have been shown to travel as waves exactly in accordance with this formula.

We do not notice the wave nature of large particles (such as billiard balls) because Plank's constant is such a small number. The wavelength of a billiard ball is so small that we could never devise an experiment to test it. But when the momentum of a particle is very small (such as an electron) the wavelength may be large enough to detect. JJ

DEATH

Philosophers have difficulty in establishing a definition when considering death. If death is the termination of one's existence, then one cannot survive death. But many people deny that we do in fact die in this sense, holding that we survive the demise of our bodies. They believe that death is not the termination of one's existence, but merely the end of the continuous biological functioning of one's body.

There are various theories about how people can survive their death, that is, the demise of their bodies. Those who believe in bodily resurrection seem to believe that we are our bodies and, therefore, cannot exist without them. When one's body ceases to function, one ceases to exist. But on the day of judgement, God will resurrect our bodies and we will thereby return to life. We will have died – our bodies will have ceased to exist – but when God resurrects our bodies he will thereby have resurrected us.

Others believe, by contrast, that people are not their bodies, but immaterial souls which can survive the destruction of their bodies. The doctrine of transmigration of the soul seems to be such a view: my immaterial soul is currently intimately (causally) related with this human body, but when it is destroyed I – my soul – will persist and become intimately (causally) related with some other human or nonhuman animal body. My identity is that I am an incorporeal soul, and when this body ceases to exist I will be re-embodied in another body – I will be **reincarnated**.

Still others hold that my immaterial soul will survive the demise of this body and will not be reincarnated. At death I will become disembodied, I will cease to have a body, and in this state I will remain. A belief in the personal survival of death does not require a belief in immortality. One might believe that one will survive the end of one's (current) body, while still expecting to cease to exist altogether at some time after that.

For anthropologists, attitudes to death, and **rituals** associated with death, are major areas of research. Cultural evolutionists of the late 19th and early 20th centuries devoted much attention to mortuary rituals, ancestor worship and beliefs in an afterlife. These were all seen as a result of 'primitive' peoples' need for reassurance in the face of the inevitability of death. Ancestor worship not only secured humans a place in the afterlife, but was also a useful means of bolstering tradition in the here-and-now.

Property and inheritance laws to some extent determine the importance which society attatches to the death of an individual. There is generally less ritual in hunter-gatherer societies as there is less property to be disposed of – unless the individual's death raises questions about handing down authority and leadership. Notions about the individual and his or her place in society or the cosmos are reflected by death rituals. Death rituals vary according to the class and gender of the deceased, or the presumed state of his or her spiritual development. Accordingly, for example in India, the appropriate way of dying and burial differs for a Hindu ascetic and a secular householder.

Following the sociologist Émile Durkheim, who asserted that funeral rituals strengthen social solidarity, Robert Hertz focused on the way mortuary rites were a means of repairing the fabric of social life damaged by death. The powerful forces manifested after death could be used in the regeneration of social life. Hertz also argued that the emotions of the individual are formed by social context, just as are conceptions of death. Deaths that are somehow anomalous sometimes cannot be dealt with. For example, in the Sudan, a Nuer man who was presumed dead, and for whom mortuary rites had been performed after a long absence, was not reincorporated into village life when he returned to the community, manifestly alive and not dead. 'Bad' deaths, or unnatural deaths through accidents or homicides, are often believed to create another class of malevolent spirits, which may come back to create problems for the living.

Mortuary rites reflect the nature of beliefs; for example, if there is a belief in an afterlife, death rituals will elaborate this. In 1905, Hertz published an essay on death rituals in Indonesia and Malagasy which examined the relation between the state of the corpse, the fate of the soul, and the ritual condition of the mourners. In many cultures, if the flesh has not completely decomposed the bones must be scraped clean before undergoing a second burial, symbolizing the final release of the spirit from its mortal remains. As well as re-establishing the cohesiveness of the social group such second burials reincorporate the mourners into full social life. Life values of fertility and **sexuality** are often associated with death rituals and work to reaffirm the social order. Among the Gimi of New Guinea, women (associated with birth and rebirth) consume dead men's flesh out of compassion so as to free their spirit. **AJ CL**

See also personal identity; rites of passage; self; spiritualism.

Further reading R. Bloch and P. Huntingdon Metcalfe, *Celebrations of Death*; M. and J. Parry, *Death and the Regeneration of Life*; T. Penelhulm, *Disembodied Existence*; Bernard Williams, *Problems of the Self*.

DEATH INSTINCT

The death instinct was first discussed by Freud in his book *Beyond the Pleasure Principle* (1920). It was a brand new theory of the instincts. In the book he asserted for the first time that the death instinct existed and that it and the sexual instinct were the prime motivators of human behaviour. Freud, in his theories of instincts, had always included the existence of conflict and compromise because these are such an essential part of human **psychology**. He felt the need to postulate opposing instincts to explain these aspects of human nature. The single driving force of the **libido** was unsatisfactory in this respect.

The theory of the death instinct was a result of Freud's reflections on the necessity his patients felt to repeat bad experiences. This compulsion to repeat was particularly marked in shell-shocked soldiers returning from World War I. He felt that this compulsion had an instinctive quality. The necessity to go back over what had happened before was seen by him to be 'an urge inherent in organic life to restore an earlier stage of things' and 'the expression of inertia inherent in organic life'. He went on to say that the aim of all life was to return to the inert material it came from in death (a straightforwardly mechanistic view). He called the death instinct Thanatos and the sexual instinct Eros. **MJ**

Further reading S. Freud, *Civilisation and its Discontents*.

DECADENCE

Decadence (Latin, 'falling off') was a late-19th-century movement in the **arts** in Europe. Its guiding spirit was a feeling of moral and aesthetic exhaustion, as if there were nothing more to contribute to the sum of (pointless) human knowledge and experience. In such circumstances, the artist (so the Decadents believed) could only make the best of things, living for the moment, sating himself or herself on experience and drinking deep of superficiality. (To the outsider, if not to Decadents themselves, it was apparent that the relationship between the abandoned standard and the ensuing decadence is symbiotic, that decadence is impossible without consciousness of the standard being undermined, and that decadence therefore relies extensively on the very standards it affects to despise.) The chief artistic monument to Decadence itself is Huysmans's novel *A rebours* (1884), but the 'philosophy' influenced the **aesthetic** movement in Britain (Oscar Wilde's *Salome*, with Aubrey Beardsley's illustrations, is a characteristic work), and its ideas also lie behind the work of many 20th-century artists, including Lawrence Durrell, André Gide, Henry Miller, Gertrude Stein, the **Dadaists**, the **Surrealists**, the world-weary German writers, painters and performers of the Weimar republic and after – not to mention such later sophisticates as the **Angry Young Men**, the **Beat Generation** and 1970s Punks. **KMcL**

Further reading Richard Gilman, *Decadence: the Strange Life of an Epithet.*

DECONSTRUCTION

Deconstruction is a technique in **criticism** and **philosophy**, dating back to the ancient Greeks but now mainly associated with the name of Jacques Derrida (1930–). It is a school of thought of extreme scepticism, rejecting the accepted claims made by all existing systems. In the criticism of **literature**, for example (the most controversial area to which the technique has been applied), one starts from the assumption that a literary text has not one meaning but many, that 'meaning' itself is a fragmentary and diffuse phenomenon. Detailed examination of a text, so far from narrowing down what it is saying until one central 'meaning' becomes apparent, releases all kinds of latent, fragmentary and often contradictory 'meanings', not necessarily anything like the one(s) the writer of the text may have had in mind. The method involves 'deconstructing' the text as one might disassemble a jigsaw puzzle: that is, not looking for corespondences which would help to fit pieces together to make a single unit, but concentrating on individual elements and on the gaps, dislocations and disjunctions between them. The technique is not confined to literature: it has, for example, been successfully applied to the traditional critical categories of **architecture** (beauty, form, function, harmony, meaning and order) and to the work of anthropologists and sociologists – and it is also used, though in a less

rigorous way than Derrida and his followers had in mind, as part of the decision-making process in business and politics. **JM KMcL**

Further reading G. Broadbent, *Deconstruction: a Student's Guide*; C. Norris, *Deconstruction: Theory and Practice.*

DECORATION

Decoration (from Latin *decorare*, 'to beautify'), in the field of architectural ideas, concerns the varied embellishment of built structures for aesthetic effect, bringing them beyond the strictly utilitarian and functional. The term is used synonymously with 'ornament', although in 20th-century, Western discourse the idea of 'decoration' is given special prominence in the field of 'interior' decoration, that is, the treatment of interiors with different paints, fabrics and objects.

Although from earliest times a built structure may depend for aesthetic effect on its shape, the 'modelling' of its mass or weight of the articulation of related spaces, it is a characteristic of most settled societies that enormous emphasis has been placed on the addition of ornament, such as colour, by the different use of materials, or as with carving, by the application of pattern and design. In many cases such ornamentation might be abstract, such as the geometric forms which we associate with Mayan culture, and achieved by carving and the treatment of the building materials. Abstract ornament, and much of the figurative carving of early cultures, drawn from the animal or vegetable world, was in some way related to mythical or religious beliefs.

Painting and **sculpture** are throughout history seen as the 'sister' arts to architecture, but in the 20th century, due to the **modernist** doctrine of **functionalism** (the belief that beauty must necessarily follow from a building or object functioning well), there was a dramatic rejection of those sister arts which traditionally supplied surface decoration to the built form. It is a claim of the **postmodernist** architects that they attempt to revive this traditional relationship. **JM**

Further reading J. Barnard, *The Decorative Tradition.*

DECORATIVE ARTS see **Art(s), Visual**

DECORUM

Decorum, a Latin term, is the standard of appropriateness or propriety applied to all matters of human conduct in classical antiquity, and in **architecture** refers to the principles and standards of design appropriate to a particular building for its particular function. The idea derives from the application of the Aristotelian Mean and the consequent avoidance of extremes, as a notion of conduct, and particularly of speech, and in the formation of a rhetorical argument. Vitruvius in *De Aedificatoria* (1st century BCE) recommends, for example, the use of particular orders for **temples** to particular gods, and also that where a building has a magnificent hall, it must not have a mean entrance but one appropriate to the magnificence within. As a precept influencing design it also governed the type of **decoration**, and became of enormous influence after the rediscovery of Vitruvius in **Renaissance** Europe. JM

DEDUCTION

Deduction (from Latin *deducere*, 'to lead from') is a form of logic in **philosophy** and **mathematics**. In philosophy, a deductive argument is such that if all its premises are true, then its conclusion must be true. It is impossible for all the premises of a deductive argument to be true and yet its conclusion be false. The following argument is deductive: Gabriel is a man; all men are mortal; therefore, Gabriel is mortal. This argument is deductive because if its premises are true, then its conclusion must be true. Its premises may not be true, of course: Gabriel may be an angel rather than a man. But if all its premises are true, then its conclusion cannot be false.

Deduction forms the lifeblood of mathematics, which in its essence consists of various sets of rules (axioms) and the deductions which can be made from them. In a sense, it is impossible to find new information by deduction: all the deductions that

can be made are implicit in the original axioms. Mathematics seeks to find all the deductions that can be made, especially those which are not obvious consequences of the axioms. (A recent result, the classification of the finite simple groups, is so non-obvious that its proof takes thousands of pages of argument.)

Deduction in mathematics can be formalized, but it is usually done in an informal, more accessible manner. (This will still use some symbolic language for clarity, at least to the specialist: symbolic language is what makes it inaccessible to the non-specialist.) **AJ SMcL**

See also axiomatization; formalism; induction.

Further reading N.W. Gowar, *Basic Mathematical Structures*; M. Sainsbury, *Logical Forms.*

DEFENCE MECHANISM

Defence mechanism, in **psychology**, is another term for the process of repression by which an unacceptable idea is made unconscious. Defence is a psychoanalytical concept on which Freud and his daughter Anna spent much time. It is the mind's mechanism for dealing with unwanted sexual impulses or by which the ego is defended from engulfment by the id. In defence mechanism, the sexual drive is given symbolic expression. These defences deal with uncomfortable conflict between the sexual instinct and the **ego** (reality) instinct; in this sense they are also symbols of compromise.

Denial as a defence mechanism can simply mean the denial of obvious reality which is too painful. Denial of internal events is illustrated by the reaction of a person who has just lost a spouse and continues to act as if he or she is still living in the same house.

Another common defence mechanism is displacement, found in dreams and hysterical symptoms. It is the process where something which creates painful feelings is transferred onto another image or symptom away from the original anxiety. In dreams, one image can symbolize another and hysterical symptoms (such as paralysis) can be the result of repressed memories of a sexual nature. Displacement, for example, can be not hitting the boss who makes us angry but hitting the children when we get home. Another example is the displacement of **Oedipal** wishes towards the mother in choosing a partner who resembles her.

Other defence mechanisms are repression itself, and disassociation. The latter is also called splitting. In splitting, internal mental structures, under the pressure of trauma, split in two, one part being retained in consciousness and the other split off into unconsciousness. If the ego splits in this way, then the part which remains conscious is usually experienced as the self. Splitting usually also entails dividing the emotional aspects into good and bad, retaining one or the other for the self and relegating the other to a part of the **unconscious**, the Superego. This can result in dual or multiple personalities.

Rationalization is when a person creates a plausible but false rationale for something they wish to deny or avoid. A soldier, for example, may assist in war crimes and then say that he was only doing his duty.

Projection is also a defence mechanism. Here a person will attribute to somebody else impulses which they in fact hold. A wife, for example, may accuse her husband of rejecting her when in fact she is rejecting him.

The defence of introjection could also be called identification. Rather than feel hostile feelings towards a neglectful parent, the child (and then the child as an adult) takes on the mother's character as a way of protecting her- or himself against this distress.

Reversal is the taking of an attitude from a past relationship and using it in a present one, for example, taking the hatred of a parent and using it as an attitude against the self. Isolation is the detachment of emotional feeling from its source and directing it elsewhere, an example being the detached way people can talk about traumatic events which have happened to them. Reaction Formulation is turning a feeling into its opposite, for example hatred of the father into love for him.

Sublimation is also characterized as a defence mechanism, but is slightly different in that it is seen to be working for a good purpose. Sublimation (according to psycho-analytical theory), like other defence mechanisms uses the drive of instincts to create patterns of behaviour. In sublimation, productive work takes the place of repressed sexual feelings, therefore, this mechanism is seen as a useful adaption towards reality. For example, Freud considered Cézanne's achievement as a painter as the result of sublimation. **MJ**

Further reading Sigmund Freud, *Inhibitions, Symptoms and Anxieties in the Problem of Anxiety*; Anna Freud, *The Ego and the Mechanisms of Defense.*

DEFICIT SPENDING

Deficit spending, in **economic** terms, may be a part of **fiscal policy** in which the government plans deficits in order to stimulate the economy during recession or **depression**. In prosperity, a balancing fiscal policy would call for a government surplus to retard **inflation**. The US has not pursued such a balanced fiscal policy. Generally, deficits have occurred in the US because of the unwillingness of Congress and the Administration to face the political heat required to balance the budget, that is, to raise taxes and fees to pay for the desired expenditures or to reduce the level of spending to coincide with revenues. In fact, the US Treasury has run a **budget deficit** through prosperity and recession in all but 5 years between 1949 and 1989. The most recent surplus was $.3 billion in 1960. **TF**

DEISM

Deism (from Latin *deus*, 'God') describes, in general, belief in God without belief in supernatural revelation – that is, belief in a God and religious practice based only on reason. The use of the term varies widely and it can stand for a belief in a God who has no personality at all, or does not take part in the affairs of the world, or for the belief in God but not in an afterlife, or even the belief in God but the rejection of all doctrines of faith. The term was first used by the Calvinist theologian Pierre Viret in his *Instruction Chrétienne* (1564). During the 17th century exponents of Deism suffered harsh persecution and imprisonment, especially in England. However, it continued to attract many thinkers and philosophers, and by the 18th century it had become a prominent movement both in Europe and America. Deistic views were held by many notable figures, such as Edward Herbert, John Tolant and Matthew Tindal in England, Giordano Bruno, Rousseau and Gotthold Lessing in Europe, and Benjamin Franklin and Thomas Jefferson in America. **EMJ**

Further reading Leslie Stephen, *History of English Thought in the Eighteenth Century, vol. 1.*

DEMOCRACY

Democracy originally in ancient Athens meant rule by the *demos*, that is, the citizens. Today, in Abraham Lincoln's words we use democracy to mean rule 'of the people, by the people, for the people': the people being the sane and adult population of a state.

Theorists of democracy differ radically in their conception of popular rule and democratic practices. On the one hand there are advocates of direct or participatory democracy. In ancient Greece it was literally true that citizens (free-born males over the age of 30, which was about a quarter of the resident population in 5th-century Athens) ruled: they were appointed to public offices by lot, public policy was made in meetings of the assembly which all citizens were expected to attend, and elected officials were subject to vigorous popular scrutiny. There was no separation of powers and no constraints on popular **sovereignty**. This version of democracy was most famously propounded in the 18th century by the French philosopher Jean Jacques Rousseau, although he defended what he called republican rather than democratic government. The critics of direct democracy in the ancient world, including Socrates, Plato and Aristotle, had condemned pure democracy as dangerous and advocated a mixed constitution, combining elements of monarchy, aristocracy and democracy. In the long interlude between classical Greece and early modern Europe most political systems were imperial or feudal, and élites crudely caricatured democracy as 'mob rule' – which is why the revival of democratic

thinking before and after Rousseau was initially defended in republican language. Today, however, advocates of direct and participatory democracy are found everywhere. They argue that the best decision-making occurs through organized debate, deliberation and voting by all those affected by a given organization. Radical or participatory democrats are by definition egalitarians, believing that people can only be independent citizens if legal, economic and political institutions are not hierarchical or unaccountable.

On the other hand there are advocates of indirect or representative democracy, who define democracy as a system in which there is genuine competition to win popular support for the right to form the government. Democracy, therefore, minimally requires universal suffrage and competitive political parties. Defenders of representative democracy, most famously John Stuart Mill, maintain that direct democracy becomes inefficient beyond a certain size of decision-making unit, and believe that there is a trade-off between the benefits of direct democracy and effective decision-making. They maintain that leaders should be elected by and accountable to the people, but that the people themselves should not rule directly except insofar as their votes determine the outcome of elections or constitutional referendums. Some conservative advocates of representative democracy maintain that it must expressly prevent the dangers of direct democracy: for them property rights and civil rights must be constitutionally protected from the rule of the majority.

There are of course many types of representative democracy. They can assume **federal**, confederal or unitary forms; they can be organized around majoritarian or **consociational** principles; and they are found with a wide variety of **electoral systems**.

The nature of representative or liberal democracy has led to a great deal of intellectual controversy. One key question has been 'who really governs in a democracy?' European **élite theorists** like Michels, Mosca, and Pareto asserted that representative democratic institutions are merely a façade: the real control over government is held by a ruling class or 'power élite'. **Marxists** similarly contended that popular rule in capitalist democracies is an illusion: a capitalist class makes all the effective decisions which shape people's lives. In contrast, critics of Marxists and élite theorists maintain that representative democratic institutions, for all their faults, are never unilaterally controlled by one set of interests: a plurality of influences operate on representative government. For this reason the influential American political scientist Robert Dahl describes most modern representative democracies as 'polyarchies' (systems in which many rule). Another key question about democracy is 'what explains the partial democratization of the world?' or 'why have some countries democratized but not others?' One answer, popular until recently, and most famously associated with the historical sociologist Barrington Moore, was that 'bourgeois democracy' was the outcome of unique historical configurations in western Europe and North America. Another answer, recently enforced by the collapse of **authoritarian** rule in eastern Europe, suggests that democratization is caused by **modernization**: processes which lead to a more equal dispersal of resources (education, skills and rights) among the people than in pre-modern societies. Modernization therefore makes aristocratic or oligarchic rule increasingly more difficult to sustain. A still more recent answer, associated with Francis Fukuyama, suggests that the gradual historic success of liberal democracy, against its rivals, is proof of the power of democratic ideas and the exhaustion of alternative ideologies. **BO'L**

See also confederation; liberalism; pluralism; republicanism.

Further reading R. Dahl, *A Preface to Democratic Theory*; P. Dunleavy and B. O'Leary, *Theories of the State: the Politics of Liberal Democracy*; F. Fukuyama, *The End of History and the Last Man*; T. Vanhanen, *The Process of Democratization: a Comparative Study of 147 States*.

DEMOGRAPHY

Demography (Greek, 'writing about peoples'), in **ecology**, **geology**, the **life** sciences and **sociology**, is the study of the structure of human populations by the application of statistical techniques. The information which is gathered about human populations by censuses can be used to examine trends and enables social planning to be modified according to predicted population changes. The data produced are vital to sciences such as **epidemiology** which depend upon the analysis of trends and correlations. Studies of the structure of human communities in terms of the individuals from which they are composed became popular in the 17th century, and regular censuses in the USA in 1790 and in Britain and France in 1801. Prior to this, information about human populations was patchy and irregular, often based on investigations of land ownership and thus biased toward certain elements in society. Where statistics were collated, investigators tended to be preoccupied with mortality. Modern censuses enable the collation of much more information and can be very accurate if well designed and supported by the registration of birth, marriage and death. **RB**

See also population biology.

DEMONISM

'Demon' comes from the Greek word *daimon*, which meant a kind of intermediate supernatural being between gods and mortals. Some *daimones* were the souls of people from the **Golden Age**, whose function in the afterlife was to take interest in specific places or human beings. Others were the indwelling spirits of rivers, woods, hills and so on. Others again were the souls of one's own dead friends and relatives – or in the case of wicked demons, one's enemies and rivals.

This kind of demon is part of every supernatural belief-system in the world. **Animist** belief depends on it; Roman **Catholic** saints and **Buddhist** great souls are kinds of demon; demons are the main spirits controlling life in religions as far apart as those of China and pre-Christian Scandinavia. In many religions – those of the ancient Middle East are a case in point – demons are not inherently good or bad, benevolent or hostile. They are not aloof, beyond understanding, like the gods; they are changeable, influencable, like mortals. They can be persuaded to help us (more easily than gods can be persuaded) and conversely, they can more easily and quickly turn against us. Thus, a large part of the practice of many religions is the propitiation and celebration of demons, or the attempt to dislodge or avert their evil powers. Many festivals and ceremonies, even in the world's most 'developed' religions, grew out of demonism of this kind, and it remains one of the most colourful, and most personal and deeply-felt, aspects of much religious practice.

The position of demons in **Judaism** and **Christianity** is particularly interesting. **Monotheism** in early Judaism involved the denial of all other supernatural beings but God. The gods of non-Judaic worshippers were dismissed as idols; spirits and demons were categorized as the shock troops of evil, always waiting to infiltrate the mind and body of unwary believers and turn them away from God. If people fell ill or went mad, this was demons' work; if your children misbehaved or your neighbour cheated you, they were afflicted by demons. The way to put matters right was not to address the demons directly, but to ask God to deal with them for you. In this belief-system, all demons are by nature evil, servants of the Devil (the arch-demon). Later, the souls of the faithful departed were assumed to become angels, but their function never quite became that of benign demons (since only God can be benign). Angels praise and rejoice in the majesty of God; even saints, when they entered Christian practice, were thought not to work miracles by themselves alone (as demons did in other religions), but only by the power of God, or by intercession on our behalf with God.

Demonism, which is an exclusively religious phenomenon, has a secular parallel in **spiritualism**. The spirits of the departed are thought, in the same way, to retain an interest in the mortal world, to be prepared to listen to us, talk to us and help us – or, if they feel like it, play mischievous and hurtful tricks on us. The chief differences from demonism are that there is no real hierarchy among spirits (they have no God to intercede with on our behalf), and they move towards us or away from us more or less at will, needing cajoling or exorcism only in the most extreme cases. **KMcL**

See also magic; Satanism.

DENDROCHRONOLOGY

Dendrochronology (Greek, 'study of time by trees') is the use of tree rings to date past events which modified the structure of the tree rings. Trees lay down annual rings, the width of which in cross-section indicates the length and quality of the growing season when the wood was laid down. Thus the age of a tree can be determined by counting the total number of rings, and deductions can be made about climatic conditions during historical periods by the thickness of rings of known age. Certain trees can live for thousands of years and can therefore reveal information about climate in prehistoric times. Rings from different trees can be matched up so that the rings found in ancient timbers can be matched with rings in trees felled at a known date. This enables an absolute chronology of climatic changes to be determined, data which is of great use in archaeology. The term was coined by the founder of the science, the astronomer Andrew Douglass, who first investigated tree rings while looking for evidence of past sunspot cycles in vegetation. **RB**

See also bioclimatology; palaeobotany.

DENIAL see Defence Mechanism

DEONTOLOGY

In a deontological (from Greek *dei*, 'it is right' plus 'ology') system of ethics, there are certain moral rules and the righteous person is one who follows those rules. According to the rules, certain actions are absolutely forbidden, regardless of the consequences of not performing them. I may not kill an innocent child, even if the whole world would be saved by its death. So deontologists think that the rightness or wrongness of an action is independent of its consequences. In that, they are anti-consequentialist. **AJ**

See also consequentialism; ethics; virtues and vices.

DEPENDENCY THEORY

Dependency theory, in **history** and **sociology**, is the thesis that a number of countries, in particular in the **Third World**, are unable to control major aspects of their economic life, because of the dominance of industrialized countries in the world economy.

Dependency theory was first developed by economists in Latin America in the 1950s. It was established to oppose the prevailing view that Third World countries could achieve modernization and industrialization if they followed the example of those countries that had already industrialized. Proponents of dependency theory underline the uneven development of global society, which they argue, has cast the main core of the industrialized world (US, Europe and Japan) in a dominant central role, rendering the position of the Third World countries peripheral and dependent upon them.

Dependency theorists maintain that a 'surplus' is extracted by advanced capitalist countries from poor underdeveloped countries. The first examples of this 'surplus extraction' occurred when metropolitan capitalist countries plundered their colonies. Since then, however, surplus extraction is alleged to have been institutionalized normally through the repatriation of profits to the metropolis. Dependency theory has been used to explain neocolonialism in which formal political and administrative control over former colonies is replaced by economic control through the exploitation of raw materials and monopolization of import markets.

Proponents of dependency theory view economic aid and technical assistance as tools of manipulation which generate cultures of dependency. Another application of dependency theory is found in literature on the capitalist world-system which adapts **Marxism** to argue that dependency is an inevitable consequence of **capitalism** because 'core' economies need weaker 'peripheral' economies from which to extract raw materials and develop export markets

for finished products. Most forms of dependency theory are overly deterministic, are both logically and empirically questionable, and no longer enjoy the intellectual currency which they once had among the Western left many of whom now recognize that it is often the lack of capitalism rather than its presence which is responsible for poverty in underdeveloped countries. **DA BO'L**

See also colonialism; convergence thesis; diffusionism; evolutionism; globalization; imperialism; society; theories of modernity; world system.

Further reading S. Amin, *Unequal Development: an Essay on the Social Formations of Peripheral Capitalism*; R. Munck, *Politics and Dependency in the Third World: the Case of Latin America*.

DEPRESSION

Depression is commonly used as a definition of an emotion like despondency, dejection or gloom. As a diagnosis, depression is part of a cycle or syndrome (also called a depressive illness) which used to be called melancholia because of its association with low spirits. In depression, thoughts about life are towards the pessimistic. Depressives see events always as having little meaning for them. It is also a condition where people blame themselves mercilessly for everything that happens whether it is really connected to them or not. Psychiatrists distinguish between endogenous depression (which is the result of there being something unspecified in the constitution of the person which is the cause) and exogenous depression (which is the result of response to a disturbing event).

Psychoanalysis sees depression as the result of ambivalent feeling towards the mother, who may herself be depressed or not able to give good enough interaction with and care to the baby. The child is both dependent and angry with the 'absent' mother. The ambivalent feeling leaves the child with the idea that it has destroyed the internal mother, as it is easier to deal with one catastrophic view than with an ambivalent one. Having destroyed the internal mother, there then follows mourning because of the dependence. This mourning is what characterizes the depression. Depressive anxiety is a belief that one's innate aggression would destroy other internal objects. **MJ**

DEPRESSION, ECONOMIC

A depression, in **economic** terms, is a long-lasting recession in economic activity. Over a prolonged period, there is a low level of economic activity with very high unemployment and high excess capacity. Companies close, demand falls, unemployment rises and people get poorer.

It is the bottom, or trough phase of the **business cycle** when that bottom is unusually low. Some economists, such as Joseph Schumpeter (1883–1950), reserve the term for the phase of the cycle form trend line to trough, with the other three phases being revival from trough to trend line, prosperity from trend line to peak, and recession from peak to trend line. Today the term generally is reserved for a state of the economy which has very substantial unemployment of labour, many factories idle or producing well below capacity, and strong downward pressure or prices. The period from 1929 to 1933 in the USA is an extreme example of depression.

Less-severe downturns in economic activity are called recessions, a label that is not as scary and so might be less likely to cause further constriction in spending by households and businesses. Such sensitivity toward possible adverse psychological effects was evident when, at the end of 1990, Federal Reserve Chairman Alan Greenspan even avoided use of the term 'recession' and instead spoke of 'a meaningful downturn aggregate output'. **TF**

DEPRESSIVE POSITION

The Depressive Position is a concept of Melanie Klein's, a further development in her object relations **psychoanalysis**, and is the developmental phase in the infant that occurs after the **Paranoid-Schizoid Position**. It begins when the baby recognizes its mother.

In the early months the baby lives in a dream-like world of sights and sounds, pleasant and unpleasant experiences, where the mother is a series of parts particularly breasts, hands, voice, etc. This is the time of the Paranoid-Schizoid Position when the baby can split off the unconscious objects that are too threatening.

Out of this emerges the mother as a whole object. This brings about a gradual understanding of separation: that this person, the mother, contains good and bad parts which the baby can love and hate. This separation brings up the feeling that the child is responsible for the separation and its hateful feelings have brought it about. The baby suffers guilt and pain and experiences it as a kind of death, imagining that it has caused irreparable harm to the love-object. This is followed by a phase of reparation which is facilitated by the supported mourning of the infant. This phase is brought up again in adult depression, and the painful separation is relived through a therapeutic relationship with the analyst and, given the depressive position, the termination of the therapy and its mourning phase are seen as a most important part of that process. **MJ**

Further reading Hannah Segal, *Klein*.

DEREGULATION

Deregulation is the reduction or elimination of governmental controls and rules regulating the behaviour or firms in an industry. Deregulation is one strand of **supply-side economics**. Regulatory reform and deregulation developed momentum in the US in the Nixon administration and continued apace in the administrations of Ford, Carter and Reagan. The deregulation that occurred during those years has been referred to as economic deregulation because it involved returning to a reliance on competition in markets to control prices and quantities, rather than reliance on laws and commission rules. At the same time that economic regulation was declining a new regulatory movement was under way in the form of protective regulation, designed to protect people from the social consequences of production with legislation to provide clean air, clean water, occupation safety and health, etc.

Perhaps the best example of deregulation came in the American airline industry in the late 1970s, when rules on which airlines could fly which routes and at what price were abolished. The result was a surge of activity, with new airlines setting up – and by the time the cycle was properly advanced many new routes had settled back into a pattern not dissimilar to the original. The cut-price innovators like People Express had failed to survive or had been taken over by bigger, older competitors. **TF**

DESCRIPTIVISM AND PRESCRIPTIVISM

Consider a word such as 'healthy'. According to prescriptivists, we can analyse the meaning of this word into two components: descriptive and evaluative. The first is some description of a physical condition which will be different in the case of different creatures. For humans, it will be having a functioning heart and liver, not having cancer or AIDS, etc. For plants, it will be something else. The second component is a prescriptive meaning, in this case usually a mark of approval. When we say someone is healthy this is ordinarily a commendation, an expression of approval of their physical condition. According to the prescriptivist, these two components can be separated: we can say that someone is 'healthy' in a sneering tone of voice, thus ascribing a certain physical condition to them while withholding our approval. But when we use the word in a standard way we are commending the physical condition in question to ourselves and everyone else.

Descriptivists think it impossible to discern an evaluative element in the meaning of 'healthy'. 'Healthy' means something like 'in a physical condition suitable for the life of the creature in question'. This suitability is an objective matter, a function of the creature's characteristic life, rather than a matter for approval by us. One may or may not approve of people who have functioning hearts, but that has nothing to do with whether it is healthy to have a functioning heart. Furthermore, one does not express any such attitude merely by calling a physical condition 'healthy'. The sentence 'I don't like health' makes perfect sense.

Descriptivists and prescriptivists also apply their analyses to ethical terms like 'courageous'. On the prescriptivist view, courageous behaviour is behaviour which has certain characteristics of which we approve and we can specify these characteristics (the descriptive meaning of the term) without evaluating them. We can abstract a non-evaluative meaning from the word 'courageous'. On the descriptivist view, it is impossible to specify the characteristics which make certain behaviour courageous, other than by using words like 'brave' which the prescriptivist would regard as evaluative. But on the descriptivist's view, words like 'brave' and 'courageous' are not evaluative, for it makes perfect sense to say 'I do not approve of bravery'. Rather the meaning of 'courageous' is purely descriptive and so also for other ethical terms such as 'generous', 'kind' and 'sympathetic'. **AJ**

See also emotivism; ethical relativism; ethics; fact and value.

Further reading R. Hare, *The Language of Morals* (part two); P. Foot, 'Goodness and Choice', in *Virtues and Vices*.

DESCRIPTIVIST LINGUISTICS

The descriptivist approach to linguistic science is most closely associated with the American linguist Leonard Bloomfield (1887–1949). Descriptivism originated in America at the beginning of this century and was a major paradigm for research right up until the 1960s. The inspiration for descriptivism was the urgent need to produce a lasting record of the native languages of North America, since many of them were under immediate threat of extinction. To this end, the American anthropologist Franz Boas spearheaded an early survey and published the results in the classic *Handbook of American Indian Languages*, in 1911. Nowadays, it is no surprise to learn that linguists study all manner of strange and exotic languages from around the world. Yet it was only with the pioneering work of Boas that such languages were accorded equal status with more familiar objects of study like Latin, Greek and German. In this respect, descriptivism represented a sharp break with the traditions of European linguistics.

The initial surprise, which never ceased to impress descriptivists, was the enormous range of linguistic diversity they unearthed. Seemingly, each new language they came across possessed quite unique structures and categories. For example, it was discovered that in Kwakiutl, a language indigenous to British Columbia, verbs are not inflected to indicate the time of action, as in most European languages, but to indicate whether or not the speaker actually witnessed an event in person, or only learned of it from another person, from the available evidence, or even from a dream. Remarkably, these differences of perspective are encoded in the **syntax** of the language. In English we would require long, possibly unwieldy phrases to convey what, in Kwakiutl, would be encoded in the grammar via verb inflections.

In order to cope with the barrage of alien concepts and constructions in their analyses, descriptivists made strenuous efforts to set aside their preconceptions about language. Methods of analysis appropriate for Latin and Greek could easily give a distorted picture when applied to a native American language. A fundamental aim was to devise an objective approach, a set of 'discovery procedures', which could be applied to any language, in order to interpret it correctly and produce an accurate description. This technique failed in its assumption that any set of procedures or techniques of analysis are entirely independent of the object studied. In fact, it will always be the case in any science that the methods of investigation employed will reflect to some extent the expectations and prejudices of the scientist.

In contrast with current preoccupations in linguistics (see **universal grammar**), a notable feature of descriptivism is its disdain for the idea that certain universal linguistic concepts and categories are inherent in all human languages. Bloomfield asserted the opposing 'infinite diversity' view with the observation that the very next language one came across might well contradict any universal tendencies hitherto observed, and that it was therefore futile to study languages with a view to discovering underlying universal characteristics. **MS**

Further reading R.A. Hall, *Leonard Bloomfield: Essays on His Life and Work*; D. Hymes and J. Fought, *American Structuralism*.

DESPOTISM

Despotism is now largely an archaic concept in the **social sciences**, mostly supplanted by concepts like **totalitarianism** and **authoritarianism**. However, like the expressions **absolutism** and tyranny, despotism is used in political rhetoric to describe governments which exercise arbitrary and apparently total power.

Since the time of Aristotle despotism has been associated in Western political thought with the Orient. Until the 18th century four core ideas recurred in Western political speculation about despotic régimes. Such systems were believed to be presided over by a despot, untrammelled by legal or political restraints in the exercise of power; found principally in the Orient, in the land-based empires of Asia, especially Persia, India and China; administered by an élite, dependent upon the despot for their authority, office and revenue (unlike the more autonomous nobility of Western feudalism); and so oppressive that their subject populations were to all intents and purposes slaves.

The French philosopher Voltaire pointed out that the Greek word for despot had a double meaning, covering both 'head of the family' and 'master of slaves', and these connotations have remained with the concept of despotism from the time of classical antiquity. The Greeks, in particular, contrasted their freedom with the despotism of barbarian peoples. Aristotle's typology of political régimes was based on the idea that the bad or deviant forms of rule – tyranny, oligarchy and democracy – were characterized by despotic behaviour by rulers who governed in their own interests rather than that of their subjects. He also distinguished Asian despotisms by the existence of hereditary succession and royal bodyguards.

The Romans used the term tyranny when expressing contempt for autocratic rule, but in early medieval Europe, after Aristotle's *Politics* was rediscovered, the term despotism came back into intellectual currency, especially in attacks on the medieval papacy, and later in polemical conceptions of Turkish government. Aristotle's ideas became the basis for a flourishing European stereotypical classification of all Oriental and African systems of government, and reached their apogee in the 18th century work of Montesquieu, one of the most famous philosophers of the French **Enlightenment**.

Montesquieu argued that despotism was capricious government, based on organized fear, and maintained that it was geographically more likely in large-scale agrarian empires, especially in hot and arid regions. Voltaire, his best-known French critic, argued by contrast, in favour of 'enlightened despotism' suggesting that Montesquieu's arguments were mere apologias for the interests of the redundant feudal aristocracy and rested on the questionable foundation of unreliable 'travellers' tales'. Like several other philosophers of his era Voltaire was a Sinophiliac, believing that in China the emperor governed through a meritocratic bureaucracy which rationally administered his subjects. China could therefore be commended as a model of a progressive polity.

The idea that despotism was (or could be) enlightened did not survive into the 19th century. Liberal discourse was hostile to unaccountable rulers, and philosophies of progress developed in which despotism, especially the Oriental variety, was periodized as a backward stage in human development. In the writings of the French economist Turgot and the philosopher Condorcet, and the German thinkers of the late Enlightenment, like Kant, Herder and Hegel, Asiatic régimes were condemned as despotic and stagnant, fossilized and incapable of progressive development from within their own resources. These notions became commonplace amongst the classical political economists, like the Mills, who conceived of despotic 'Oriental society' as an obstacle to capitalist development; and, in an altered form, they also formed the basis of Karl Marx's idea of a distinctive **Asiatic mode of production**. In the 1950s, at the height of the Cold War, the idea of a distinctively Oriental despotism was revived by Karl Wittfogel, a Sinologist and ex-Marxist. He argued that despotism in

Oriental societies could be functionally explained by the need for large-scale and centrally planned irrigation in arid or semi-arid regions – a thesis which was vigorously rejected by many historians of Asia. Even more controversially, Wittfogel maintained that communist régimes were the direct successors and the industrial equivalents of the 'hydraulic despotisms' of Asia. **BO'L**

Further reading R. Koebner, 'Despot and Despotism' *Journal of the Warburg and Courtauld Institutes* (1951); B. O'Leary, *The Asiatic Mode of Production*; K. Wittfogel, *Oriental Despotism*.

DETERMINISM

Determinism (from Old French *déterminer*, 'to fix') is the philosophical doctrine which regards everything that happens as determined by what preceded it. From the information given by a complete description of the world at time t, a determinist believes that the state of the world at time t + 1 can be deduced; or, alternatively, a determinist believes that every event is an instance of the operation of the laws of Nature. The wide acceptance of this view, at least in the Western world, was a result of the work of mathematical physics in the 18th and 19th centuries. At this point, it looked as if Newton and his successors had reduced the universe to systems of equations, through which the position of any particle in the universe could be predicted forever, provided that sufficent information was known about the factors affecting its motion (in other words, providing that the position of all other particles in the universe was known). Determinism is not a position of which Newton himself would have approved, since it denies any need for the existence of God, and seems to reduce human beings to the status of predictable machines. It was, however, regarded by others (for example the 18th-century mathematicians Laplace and Lagrange) as the triumph of **science**, showing that, through the laws of cause and effect, the future was as fixed as the past.

In science, determinism as a serious philosophy could not survive the demise of the Newtonian view of the universe. As the quantum theory of Planck and his associates brought chance into physical theory at the beginning of the 20th century, as the **uncertainty principle** of Werner Heisenberg (1901–76) showed that some events were inherently unpredictable, and as Einstein's theory of **relativity** so changed the concept of **time** that physicists could no longer be certain which events came before or after others, determinism became more and more untenable, and many philosophers (for example Russell) began to feel that the concept of cause and effect was itself just an illusion. Not only that, but in the meantime Kant's view that **mathematics** (and in particular **Euclidean geometry**) was *a priori* truth had been shattered by the construction of **non-Euclidean geometry** by Lobachevsky, Bolyai and Reimann – an event which made scientists far more inclined to accept that mathematical equations were not necessarily the arbiters of what goes on in the universe.

The new non-determinism which resulted from all this has led to the view, held by many scientists and others throughout the 20th century, that the universe is inherently chaotic, that actions do not lead to consequences. This view was a major influence on **existentialism**, a world-view which (it could be argued) has come to prevail in the Western world. In this, all actions are equally meaningful (or meaningless); what matters is to validate one's existence by taking action, though what that action is is not important. A third point of view is 'compatibilism', which holds that it is possible to give an account of human freedom without invoking non-determinist explanations of human action.

As applied to political and historical thought determinism describes the views of those who think that individual 'choice' is (a) determined by conditions beyond the individual's control, and/or (b) that it is the result of free will. Historical determinism emphasizes the limits imposed by antecedent and long-term economic, political and social conditions, as in the writings of exponents of the **Annales school**. Economic determinism is the theory which attributes all major social and political interests and actions and their organization to the prerogatives of economic causes. In **rational choice** writings, economic determinism takes the form of assuming that individuals are always seeking to maximize their utility functions, and are always engaged in 'rent-seeking'. In Marxist thought, economic determinism is supported by the doctrine of **historical materialism** which attempts to explain history as the product of changes in material conditions rather than as the product of changes in ideas, values and **culture**. Economic reductionism is frequently used as a pejorative label for determinist arguments which ignore or subsume non-economic factors in their accounts of phenomena like culture, **nationalism** and political **power**.

In philosophy, the distinction is made between determinism and indeterminism. Determinism is the doctrine that every event has a determining cause: is one which causally suffices for its effect. Some causes may merely raise the probability of their effects without causally determining them. Smoking causes lung cancer, but smoking merely raises the probability that one will get lung cancer, rather than causally determining that one will.

Indeterminism is the view that some events do not have determining causes. So indeterminism is true only if some events are uncaused, or some events have only probabilistic rather than determining causes, or both.

Philosophers have long worried about whether freedom and responsibility are compatible with determinism: see comments on existentialism above. They have more recently begun to worry about whether freedom and responsibility are compatible with indeterminism. Clearly, if freedom and responsibility are incompatible with both determinism and indeterminism, then it is impossible to be free or responsible.

In **psychology**, those, like Freud, who believe in psychic determination in **psychiatry**, assume that all mental events have causes. Freud believed that the existence of unconscious forces proved psychic determinism to be a fact of mental life, but he also recognized that consciousness, far from being just the result of unconscious forces, had its part to play in mental phenomena. Nevertheless, he regarded **psy-**

choanalysis as a science based on causal-deterministic assumptions and this makes difficulties for psychoanalytic theory when describing aspects of what we call free will, choosing, deciding, etc.

One aspect of psychic determination in psychoanalysis that has been severely criticized by women is the notion that their egos and superegos (the I and the moral conscience) are biologically determined; that girls experience the two main complexes of childhood, the Oedipus complex and castration anxiety, differently because of their lack of a penis. Simone de Beauvoir and later feminists objected to Freud's determinism, and put descriptions of female sexuality into social and political contexts without eschewing the psychological ones.

Freud also invented the concept of over-determinism. This is the theory of multiple causation, where various factors reinforce a position or action a much more complex notion than simple determinism. An example of over-determinism is when emotional states like anger are over-determined by past anger, at other objects and events, being brought in to a present situation. AJ MJ SMcL BO'L

See also chaos theory; dualism; mind-body problem.

Further reading Karl Popper, The Open Universe; T. Nagel, The View from Nowhere; P.F. Strawson, Individuals; R. Weatherford, The Implications of Determinism.

DETERRENCE THEORY

The idea of deterrence, in politics, is really a general theory of social control, which assumes that the threat of retaliation can prevent an individual, group or state from committing an act of aggression. The primary criterion for effective deterrence is assumed to be the establishment of a credible threat of retaliation. Credibility is determined by whether (a) the threat is understood by the potential aggressor, which requires clear communication of the intention to retaliate; (b) the potential aggressor realizes that the potential target values its strategic position sufficiently to

retaliate; and (c) the aggressor has confidence in the potential target's capability to retaliate effectively.

The most elaborate developments in deterrence theory have been produced in the fields of criminology, jurisprudence and strategic studies. In criminology and jurisprudence deterrence provides a utilitarian justification for punishment. Punishment is alleged to serve as a deterrent to both the individual criminal as well as to society at large: punishment is supposed to give credibility to the state's intent to retaliate against criminal behaviour. In strategic studies a distinction is made between the application of deterrence on a limited scale, for example, between two states or on an extended scale in a regional or even global level, for example, the Strategic Defence (or Star Wars) Initiative. Another is made between fixed-response deterrence tactics where the threat of retaliation is predetermined, and flexible-response deterrence where the degree of retaliation is determined by the extent of aggression. The latter was adopted by the US under President Kennedy's defence secretary Robert McNamara who encouraged NATO to maintain a credible conventional force deterrent in Europe in order to pre-empt the rapid escalation to the nuclear level of any initial conflict with forces of the Warsaw Pact. BO'L

See also balance of power; game theory.

Further reading M. Charlton, From Deterrence to Defence: the Inside Story of Strategic Policy; J.P. Gibbs, Crime, Punishment and Deterrence; B. Moller, Common Security and Nonoffensive Defence: a Neorealist Perspective.

DEVELOPMENT

Intrinsic to current Western ideas of development are notions of economic growth, socioeconomic transformation and modernization, all of which are associated with the wealthy industrialized nations. Development in this sense is as old as the expansion of Europe, under which imperialism created unequal economic relations between colonial and colonized nations. In order for there to be developed countries, there must be those considered in a state of underdevelopment.

Development is one of the few fields for applied **anthropology**. Anthropologists often participate in aid programmes, looking at the way specific projects affect and alter the lives of the recipients. Basing their views on **field work** in the community, or on their general understanding of how small-scale communities work, anthropologists can often contribute detailed knowledge of social relations something which development planners lack. The anthropologist's role is thus to act as mediator between developers and developees, with the goal of modifying the project to meet local needs or aspirations in as favourable way as possible.

Anthropologists have also looked at indigenous technical knowledge: practical knowledge about favourable conditions, risks and limitations. This knowledge is often handed down orally through the generations, and may be overlooked by developers unduly focused on scientific and statistical objectives to the neglect of vital social and cultural factors. **CL**

See also economic anthropology; modernization; Westernization.

Further reading Robert Chambers, *Rural Development: Putting the Last First.* Mark Hobart, *An Anthropological Critique of Ignorance: the Growth of Ignorance.*

DEVELOPMENTAL BIOLOGY

Developmental biology is the study of the processes by which organisms develop. The science has its roots in **embryology** but modern developmental biology encompasses the genetic control of cell differentiation, specialization and multiplication which leads to the formation of tissues and whole organisms. **RB**

See also germ layer theory; germ plasm; ovism; pangenesis; phylogeny; teratology.

DEVELOPMENTAL CYCLE

The developmental cycle was a concept introduced by the anthropologist Meyer Fortes in 1958, to replace an ideal notion of a household. Domestic groups fluctuate over a lifetime, expanding after marriage when children are born or other dependents share the household, and later fragmenting when the adults reach old age. The domestic group may expand to include members who are not kin, and are sometimes given fictive kinship to normalize their relationships in the group. The exploration of the notion of a developmental cycle in domestic groups has drawn attention to the fluctuating nature of the domestic group, which had previously been treated as a stable producing unit in statistical analyses. By rejecting kinship studies that were frozen in time, Fortes introduced a much-needed dynamic to their analyses.

The concept of cyclical change has also been useful in analysing the life course of an individual. Each person must go through particular stages – often marked by **rites of passage** – in order to realize their full social status. This cycle has been used to explain how changes in status serve to maintain the status quo. By having specific privileges attached to each stage in life, individuals are induced to accept the constraints as well. For instance, among the Maasai of Kenya, unmarried men form a distinct age-set which separates them from everyday community life. The young warriors are dominated by the elders, yet when members of this age-set graduate to the status of elders, they relish the opportunity to dominate the young men in their turn. The dependent relationship of women on men in the Middle East has been discussed in terms of a bargain. Women get power and prestige through their elder sons, and so come to accept their relatively insignificant status as newlyweds, often dominated by their husband's mother living in her household. The birth of a son signals the beginning of their rise in authority. **CL**

Further reading J. Goody (ed.), *The Developmental Cycle in Domestic Groups;* P. Spencer, *The Riddle of the Sphinx.*

DEVELOPMENTAL LINGUISTICS

Developmental linguistics provides a reaction against the otherwise enormously influential distinction, drawn by Ferdinand de Saussure (1857–1913), between synchronic and diachronic approaches to **language**. In the 19th century, linguistic science was predominantly diachronic in orientation: concerned with explaining how languages evolve over time. A synchronic approach, on the other hand, stresses that for the native speakers of a language, the history of the language is irrelevant. If we examine a language at a particular point in time, it can be regarded as a self-contained system which can be analysed in isolation from the historical processes which shaped it. In fact, the synchronic approach advocated by Saussure has in this century become by far the dominant paradigm in linguistic research.

In the 1970s and 1980s, developmentalists began to challenge the heavy bias towards synchronic linguistics, because it presents an artificial view of languages as static phenomena. Dynamic processes of language change are only accommodated with the contrived notion of a series of discrete linguistic systems placed one after the other like beads on a string. For developmentalists, though, languages exhibit great variety and are subject to numerous forces of change which will be missed by a purely synchronic approach. Hence, developmental linguistics focuses on the manifold processes of growth and change which help explain how a language came to be the way it is. First and second language acquisition, creolization, language change and dialectal variation are therefore of particular relevance. A natural outcome of this approach is the rejection of the view that linguistic science constitutes an autonomous discipline. It is believed that evidence from other fields of enquiry, including neurology, anatomy, social history and **anthropology**, are of direct relevance for an explanation of how languages evolve.

A weak version of developmentalist theory would assert that static models of language are incomplete, since they do not accommodate processes of language change and variation. A strong version would argue that static, synchronic models totally misrepresent the intrinsically dynamic nature of language. In both cases, it is suggested that languages maintain a balance between the shaping influences of both socio-communicational and neuro-biological factors. The socio-communicational aspects of language arise from numerous social variables, including social status, **gender**, **ethnicity**, **discourse** structure and pragmatic context, to create so-called abnatural developments. The neuro-biological aspects of language, on the other hand, stem from the genetic endowment of the human species and determine so-called connatural developments. The notion of naturalness in language is often invoked to explain connatural developments, with the suggestion that some linguistic features are closer to the prototypical nature of language than others. Languages will clearly differ in terms of their proximity to the prototype in certain specified domains. As a result, the members of a linguistic category can be placed on a scale of markedness, with those closest to the prototype being described as unmarked. Developmentalists, therefore, reject the orthodox view that all linguistic systems are equivalent in terms of the communicative resources they offer their speakers; in principle, one language can be judged better than another for certain purposes. **MS**

See also comparative-historical linguistics; descriptivist linguistics; dialectology; generative grammar; pidgin and creole linguistics; psycholinguistics; structuralism; transformational grammar.

Further reading C-J Bailey, *On the Yin and Yang Nature of Language*.

DHARMIC RELIGION

Dharmic religion is the name given by Chaturvedi Badrinath, and other radicals, to **Hindu** religion which centres on the performance of *dharma*. The word is difficult to translate, but is perhaps best rendered as 'duty', as in 'England expects...' and the Victorian concept of 'filial duty'. Significantly, the Latin *pietas* (as exemplified by Aeneas in Virgil's *Aeneid*) is very similar, because both involve reverence for the gods and for one's ancestors, respect for elders, obedience to parents, loyalty to one's ruler and justice in dealings with fellow human beings. The difference is that in *dharma* people realize their *dharma* by fulfilling their appropriate roles in society according to their **caste** – a status determined by *karma*, the reward for doing one's *dharma* in a previous life. One can change neither that nor one's *dharma*, but faithfulness will be rewarded in a future life and an improved *dharma*. This is the theme of the *Bhagavad-Gita*, where Krishna appears to Arjuna, the king's warrior brother, and persuades him to be true to his *dharma* as a warrior and slaughter his cousins, despite his qualms of conscience about *ahimsa* ('nonviolence'). God himself has a *dharma*, which is to emanate, to sustain and to reabsorb Himself. We are not free agents; our only choice is whether to fulfil our *dharma* or not, and even that choice is influenced by *karma*. A woman has no *dharma* of her own, generally speaking her thread is her husband's, which makes remarriage after his death impossible. A wife's loyalty and a widow's faithfulness are necessary for his salvation, not hers. **EMJ**

Further reading R.C. Zaehner, *Hinduism*.

DIALECTICS

Dialectics (Greek, 'discussion') was a method of philosophical reasoning first described in ancient Greece. It consisted of talking logically about abstract matters. The Socratic dialogues of Plato and Xenophon show the method as it was practised in Athens in the 5th century BCE. There are two approaches, refutation and induction. In the first, the main speaker (in the surviving dialogues, Socrates himself) gets his interlocutors to begin with a statement, and then makes them tease out every possible consequence of it in logical sequence until they reach the point where the statement is shown to be untrue. In the second, the main speaker starts with a general statement and persuades his interlocutors to agree that it is true in a number of specific instances, and therefore (by implication) likely to be true overall. A century later, Aristotle refined the dialectical system (in his book *Topics*). Now discussion starts from a stated position, or thesis ('something put forward'), for example 'virtue is good' or 'water is wet'. Arguments are then produced for and against the statement, and a conclusion is reached on the balance of the evidence produced. This is a similar method to that used by debating societies and adversarial systems of **law** or government in later times, and its drawback is similar, that it is limited not by the objective number of proofs available, but by the knowledge, temper and disposition of those taking part. Aristotle himself recognized this problem, and drew a distinction (in *Analytics*) between true demonstration (what we might call logical, objective proof) and dialectic itself, which is reasoning from opinion.

In the **philosophy** and law of many great religions, dialectic is a main method of approach. The discussion, however, is not merely between contemporaries: it takes in the entire weight of statement and opinion of the past, and involves present thinkers considering and commenting on precedents which in some cases stretch right back to statements by the founder of the religion in person. This method gave rise to two systems of religious-based ethics in particular, those of **Islam** (the *shari'a*) and **Judaism**. From Judaism the dialectical method spread to **Christianity**, and from there was perverted to the arid **scholasticism** which passed for intellectual thought in the European Middle Ages. A favourite kind of scholasticism was the 'disputation', a system of examination for degree or office in which the candidate reasoned for and/or against selected theses and was rewarded for rhetorical ability rather than for insight. (The prevalence of this method partly explains the hostility to Galileo of his university colleagues: he was abandoning argument by disputation in favour of argument from observation, a process of which they had no experience.)

In more modern philosophy, Hegel described dialectic not merely as a process of reasoning, but as a constant movement in history, in life, in thought, in the working of the universe, from thesis to antithesis and thence to synthesis. It is thus not a human construct but an objective phenomenon, and human reasoning is just one paradigm of a greater whole. One can easily imagine the fun Socrates might have had discussing this unprovable idea. **KMcL**

DIALECTOLOGY

Dialectology, in **linguistics**, has brought about the consideration of dialects as **language** systems in their own right. It is in fact notoriously difficult to distinguish between language and dialect in an entirely objective way. In practice, most dialectologists employ definitions which tend to comprise a bundle of features typically associated with dialects. Thus, dialects normally have fundamental phonological, lexical and syntactic similarities with at least one other language. In addition, the region in which a dialect is spoken typically does not subsume another language (the reverse cannot be said for many languages). Many definitions also acknowledge the widespread absence in dialects of those features which contribute to the standardization of a language (established writing conventions, dictionaries, written grammars and so on).

Dialects can be studied in isolation, but it has long been recognized that many fruitful insights on the nature of language can be revealed via a systematic comparison of the way dialects vary from region to region. Indeed, large-scale surveys based on regional variation constitute the central focus of research in dialectology. Studies of regional dialectal varieties demonstrate that linguistic variation is not simply a superficial, geographically determined aspect of language. Instead, variation is revealed to be a fundamental feature of human language. It has been demonstrated, for instance, that the existence of regional dialectal variants plays a crucial role in the historical process of language change.

Traditional dialectal surveys aimed to determine the core features of a given dialect, which is the indigenous language of a community, acquired in childhood and used regularly by adults. In this situation, so-called NORMS (non-mobile older rural males) are often selected as informants, since they tend to provide the most reliable source of conservative speech forms. It is a relatively straightforward task to examine the dialect of a community if there is a stable population and relatively little contact with the outside world. But the 20th century has witnessed unprecedented levels of population movements, with a concomitant increase in contact between disparate languages and cultures, along with a dramatic increase in the power of communication systems. As a result, many of the dialects associated with isolated rural communities in the 19th century are now dying out. Nowadays, therefore, dialectal surveys often take on the nature of a **taxonomic** exercise, designed to record language varieties which are in imminent danger of extinction.

An alternative, **sociolinguistic**, approach to dialectology does not expect to encounter this kind of linguistic purity. This difference of emphasis is motivated by the realization that linguistic variation is often strongly associated with certain social factors, rather than simply a geographical region. Thus, it has been found that social status, gender, the social setting of conversation and the type of conversation are all important factors. The stability and predictability of the language used in given contexts has led to the concept of distinct styles or registers, each of which is characterized by its own special vocabulary and structural conventions. Thus, the register used by lawyers in court is quite different from that used by football players in the changing room. Each person typically has command of a whole range of particular registers, providing individuals with the ability to speak appropriately in a given setting. Hence, variation is not merely confined to inter-dialectal comparisons from one region to another. It is an inherent feature within the speech of each individual. **MS**

Further reading L. Davis, *English Dialectology: An Introduction*; J.K. Chambers and P. Trudgill, *Dialectology.*

DIATONICISM

Diatonicism (from Greek *dia tonikos*, 'at intervals of a tone') is an (artificial) acoustical system which underlies most Western music. The distance between a sound and the same sound an octave lower or an octave higher is divided into groups of tones and semitones: these groups are modes or scales. (A mode divides the octave into six or seven units, counting the starting-note, and a scale into eight.) The diatonic scales are major (tone-tone-semitone-tone-tone-tone-semitone) and minor (tone-semitone-tone-tone-tone-tone-semitone – often nowadays with the last two tones replaced by semitone-minor third).

In diatonic music, every sequence of notes in a melody – jump from note to note – or chord in the harmony must conform to the basic scale, and the music is said to be 'in' the mode or key named after the note on which that scale begins and ends. Originally, notes outside the system were not allowed, but as music became more elaborate, the idea of modulation was introduced: using notes outside the basic system to shift the music briefly or for longer periods into other systems (see **chromaticism**).

The ancient Greeks, who used modes – which are like scales, except that each of the seven modes has a slightly different arrangement of tones and semitones from all the others, and therefore a slightly different 'character' – assigned specific subjective 'meanings' to each mode. The doric mode was warlike, the lydian mode amorous, the phrygian mode pastoral, and so on. Music with certain associations had, by convention, to use the appropriate mode. Scales, because apart from their starting-point, they are identical to one another, have no such associations. However, in Europe in the 17th and 18th centuries, when the comparatively simple nature of brass instruments meant that they could only play 'in' certain scales, those scales were associated with music using brass instruments, and the occasions for which it was written. Hunting and military music, for example, was usually in B flat, C or D. By the same token, pastoral music, using flutes, was often in G (their natural scale). These associations persisted, to some extent, even after instruments were developed which could play all the chromatic notes with equal ease. At the end of the 19th century, the composer Scriabin and others experimented with assigning (or pretending to discover) specific psychological associations with this key or that, and composing music accordingly, but the idea had only a brief vogue.

Diatonic music has been standard in the West at least since ancient Greek times, and perhaps longer (none survives, so no one knows). It has constantly been nudged by other systems – **folk music**, for example, often divides the octaves into units smaller than tones and semitones – and it has been enriched and modified by a continual expansion of the use of chromaticism. But it has never been displaced, and is the root of most of the Western musical experience, in all forms. At various times, attempts have been made to show that it is endemic to sound itself, that it is acoustically validated. But modern scholars say that this is wishful thinking, and that we assume it simply because our ears have been conditioned to it over thousands of years. In our pluralist modern age, diatonicism is beginning to be subverted both by our increasingly familiarity with non-diatonic music from other traditions (especially from Africa and East Asia), and by the use of electronics (which allow infinitely varied divisions of the octave). The process, however, is still not far advanced, and may, like chromaticism, end up as an enrichment of diatonicism rather than its replacement. **KMcL**

See also intonation, tuning and temperament; tonality.

DICTATORSHIP

Dictatorship is a form of government in which an individual or small group assumes complete executive and legislative power without the constraints imposed by a constitution. Although the term is now used pejoratively to describe tyrannical authority figures, dictatorship initially referred to the constitutional appointment of an individual to take temporary charge of the Roman Republic during times of military emergency. (The Latin word *dictator* implied one who gave orders without needing to spend time in consultation.) Echoing the Roman custom modern dictators usually attempt to legitimize their assumption of power by emphasizing the necessity of autocratic control in times of instability. Modern dictatorships are more likely to occur where constitutional traditions are not strong, where the military has traditionally had an interventionist role in government, and where crises of **modernization** have become acute.

The 'dictatorship of the proletariat' was the name envisaged by Karl Marx for the period immediately following the overthrow of capitalism, during which he thought the working class would have to seize control over the means of production and do what was necessary to smash the remnants of the bourgeois state apparatus. Marx thought that this dictatorship would, like the Roman model, be temporary, and after the success of the proletarian revolution the state would wither away. In practice however, the 'dictatorship of the proletariat' in Communist régimes has been a dictatorship of the Communist party. **BO'L**

See also authoritarianism; Marxism.

Further reading R. Chilcote et al., *Transitions from Dictatorship to Democracy*; J. Ehrenberg, *Dictatorship of the Proletariat: Marxism's Theory of Socialist Democracy*.

DIFFERENTIAL CALCULUS see **Analysis**; **Calculus**

DIFFUSIONISM

Diffusionism (from Latin *diffunder*, 'to pour out') is the term used by anthropologists and sociologists to account for the spread, through time, of aspects of **culture** – artistic traditions, **language**, **music**, **myths**, religious beliefs, social organization, technological ideas – from one society or group to another. The term was first used by the anthropologist Edward Tylor, in his book *Primitive Culture* (1871), to explain the presence of elements of culture in societies where they could not have originated.

Tylor's work initiated a debate among anthropologists which continued for most of the succeeding 50 years. Diffusionists used evidence for similar cultural elements from diverse areas to map out geographical distributions, forming what were called 'culture areas'. With the increase in Egyptian archaeological finds from the 1920s onwards, Elliott Smith and others proposed the spread of Egyptian culture as a model, saying that cultural traits diffused from this 'cradle of civilization' to other parts of the world, as ripples spread when a stone is thrown into a pond – a process effected, they said, by cultural contact, by trade or by movement of populations. Evolutionists, by contrast, claimed that if similar cultural traits were observed in diverse communities, they could equally well be the result of coincidence, that different peoples could experiment and invent on similar lines without need of actual contact.

In the latter half of the 20th century, the diffusionist-evolutionist debate was dropped in anthropology, mainly because its historical arguments could not be properly substantiated. Instead, anthropology concentrated on data collected from field work among communities in the present. However, the debate continues in speculation about archaeological finds, and is helped by the method of radiocarbon dating (pioneered by W.F. Libby in 1946). This discussion has centred on the geographical origins and spread of humankind (a study supported by skeletal discoveries), and on speculations about the origins of material cultures (a study supported by the remains of artefacts and the evidence of such things as crop cultivation and metal technology).

Sociologists generally come down on the diffusion side of the evolution-diffusion argument. Some go so far as to claim that by the present day cultural diffusion has occurred on such a large scale that all modern societies exist as part of a single world-system. There is a body of opinion which holds that the diffusion of social institutions and cultural values characteristic of Western capitalist systems was essential if development was to occur in the **Third World**; their critics point out that the diffusion of Western cultures to the Third World, which has been occurring for centuries, has resulted in under-development rather than development.

Sociologists also use the term diffusion in a more mathematical sense to refer to the spread of ideas. Models show a pattern of spread which proceeds slowly at first, then more rapidly, then slowing down as there are fewer people still to be involved. These models are similar to those for the spread of disease, but social diffusion is assumed to be more varied than that of disease. **DA RK**

See also archaeology; assimilation; civilization; convergence thesis; dependency theory; ethnoarchaeology; evolutionism; field work; globalization; norms; society; syncretism; theories of modernity; values; world system.

Further reading J. Goody (ed), *The Developmental Cycle in Domestic Groups*; P. Spencer, *The Riddle of the Sphinx*.

DIGITAL LOGIC

Digital Logic (Greek, *logica*, 'reasoning') is a method by which electrical circuits are provided with a limited ability to make decisions. The most common use of digital logic today is in the control and arithmetic functions of digital **computers**, without which modern life would grind to a halt.

Digital systems operate using discrete values to represent the information to be conveyed. The simplest example would be one in which the only permitted values were '0' meaning 'off', or '1' meaning 'on'. Such as system is termed a binary system or a system having two states.

The first digital logic system applied to electrical circuits was proposed by Shannon in 1938 in America, when he applied Boolean algebra (see **Boolean logic**) to electrical switching circuit design. The switching circuits were a form of binary system as mentioned above. Boolean algebra allowed mathematical manipulation of logic statements such as 'AND' or 'OR' functions. A Two-input 'AND' function, for example, would only output a '1' or 'on' state if both input states were '1' or 'on'. In this case it required one input *and* the other input to be '1' to produce a '1' on the output. Any other combination of inputs including both '0' or 'off' gave a '0' or 'off' output.

Shannon implemented this reasoning to give initially simple electrical circuits an element of decision-making. For example, a circuit could be constructed which required two switches to be in a closed state, before a lamp was lit. In such an instance the logic is inherent in the switching layout: that the lamp remains 'off' until both switches are 'on'. Logic functions such as 'AND' and 'OR' and many others, could then be physically constructed using electrical switch layouts. These switching circuits were termed logic gates.

It was soon realized that simple arithmetical tasks such as addition could be performed by implementation of the necessary logic gates, configured in a manner determined by Boolean algebra. This development led to the production of the first electrical calculators at the time of World War II.

Following inventions in other areas of electrical science, such as **electronic** theory and **semiconductor device theory**, memory units were invented using logic gates, as well as by magnetic tape drive and digital integrated circuit memory. This allowed results from arithmetical operations using logic gates to be stored and allowed computer programs to operate. (Computer **programs** step through a series of instructions, some of which may perform arithmetic operations using logic gates, while others may use logic gates to determine whether certain switches are 'on' or 'off' and therefore to determine whether certain conditions are satisfied.) The memory units permitted automatic operation of a program, enabling the results of logic operations to be stored and recalled whenever necessary.

The modern digital computer is the summit so far of achievement in digital logic. A computer will take an input signal and process that signal under the control of a program stored in its memory. Such programs today mean that millions of arithmetical calculations can be performed per second, feats that could not possibly be achieved by other means. **AC**

DIMENSION

Dimension (Latin, 'measuring across'), in **mathematics**, is one of the most fundamental concepts of **geometry**. The dimension of a mathematical object is the least number of co-ordinates needed to describe every possible member of the object (see **Cartesian co-ordinate systems**). For example, a line has dimension 1 (because one number is all that is needed to express the position of a point on the line), whereas the system describing the movement of the Earth around the Sun has twelve (three each for the positions of the Sun and the Moon, and another three each for their velocities). There are systems that need infinitely many co-ordinates (some complex descriptions of the flow of fluids, for example).

Recently, mathematicians have also discovered **fractals**: objects which have fractional dimensions. It is perhaps one of the most paradoxical-sounding ideas in modern mathematics, that some objects take, for instance, one and a half numbers to describe the position of points in them. Because of the way that fractals are generated from (usually) lines of dimension one, they are too complex to be described by just one number, but they do not fill space in the way they would have to in order to be of dimension two. **SMcL**

DISCOURSE

Discourse (middle English, '[verbal] communication') is an important idea in critical theory, **linguistics**, literary theory and **sociology**. The term is especially associated with the French philosopher Michel Foucault (1926–84) and others, who used it to describe the way systems function in **culture**, **ideology**, **language** and society, and the way in which that functioning reflects and sustains **power** and those who wield it. For sociologists, discourses are specialist systems of knowledge and sustain practices which are united by a common assumption and which function to close off the possibility of other ways of thinking, talking or behaving. Often, their power is maintained by the terms used to describe things: a simple example is lawyers' jargon and more complex examples are scientific classification and the patterns of religious **ritual**. Foucault and his followers advocate the use of 'intellectual archaeology': studying phenomena such as the structure of a society or its attitudes to such things as madness or **sexuality** by deconstructing the discourse involved.

In literary theory, the study of discourse is a way to examine creative work in the light of the mind-set of past societies and of groups or individuals within them: this sheds light on the content and meaning of the works created within those societies. Thus, for example, Homer's *Odyssey* is not fully understood in terms of its images or narrative or poetic qualities alone, but also in light of the assumptions in Homer's mind as he wrote, in the inventors and elaborators of the myths on which he based his work, on the hierarchies and ideas of the society for which he wrote, and of ours as we read his work. Knowledge of such matters can radically change our view of a work of art – as has been shown, for example, by feminist assessments of the novels of Jane Austen.

In linguistics, until quite recently, enquiry into the nature of language was almost entirely confined to the analysis of individual sentences or parts of sentences. However, it has become increasingly apparent that extended sequences of language are worthy of our attention, since discourse is more than just a random jumble of unconnected sentences. In fact, both spoken and written texts have structures and functions of their own which are entirely missed unless we look beyond the level of the sentence. And once we begin to explore the way language is organized as discourse, the focus necessarily shifts away from the treatment of language as an abstract object, to a consideration of the way language is used as a socially situated phenomenon.

An adequate discourse analysis must take into account who is saying (or writing) the words of a text to whom, and in what social context. Despite a multiplicity of theoretical orientations, there is an overarching concern in discourse analysis with the way language functions in speech or writing. An influential model which adopts this basic tenet investigates the language of the classroom in terms of the patterns of interaction between teacher and students. In a deliberate move away from an analysis based purely on linguistic forms, it was argued that discourse could be described in terms of a series of units defined according to their function in the discourse. For example, it emerged that a common interaction sequence in the classroom comprised three so-called moves, each with a different discourse function: Initiation, Response and Feedback:

Teacher: 'What's two plus two?' = Initiation
Student: 'Five.' = Response
Teacher: 'Not quite, I'm afraid.' = Feedback

Individual moves are composed of one or more lower order units, known as acts, while moves combine in turn to create a higher order unit, termed an exchange. Thus the combination of the three moves, Initiation, Response and Feedback, together constitute a single exchange typical of classroom interaction. In this model, exchanges combine together to make transactions, which combine in turn to give the lesson as the highest unit of classroom discourse.

Crucially, the structure of discourse is revealed to be hierarchical in nature, since units at one level, or rank, combine together to make a single unit at the rank above. The notion of a hierarchy of discourse ranks has been adapted in various ways to render it applicable far beyond the narrow scope of classroom interaction. Clearly, this kind of analysis views discourse as a series of actions which describe the structure of interaction without recourse to the particular linguistic forms employed. Various other models of discourse analysis emphasize that the ability to convey and understand messages can often be understood by taking into account the social context of the discourse, in addition to the way the language forms are organized above the level of the sentence. **DA KMcL MS**

See also dominant ideology; hegemony; social construction of reality; social control; sociology of knowledge.

Further reading M. Coulthard, *An Introduction to Discourse Analysis*; Michel Foucault, *The Order of Things*; A. Sheridan, *Michel Foucault, the Way to Truth*.

DISCRIMINATION

Discrimination literally refers to judging or differentiating between objects, persons or attributes. In politics it refers to the unfavourable or unequal treatment for appointment or promotion of individuals or groups, normally by reference to criteria which are irrelevant or prejudicial for the proposed task or function. The purpose of discrimination can either be positive or negative. Negative discrimination is used unjustly to deny an individual or group access to some privilege or opportunity normally based on their race, sex, age, language, religion, ethnicity or sexual orientation. For example, the denial of a black person the right to vote in South Africa denied that person access to power based upon a criterion, race, which has nothing to do with that person's ability to exercise a political choice. Positive or reverse discrimination, by contrast, attempts to compensate for past instances of negative discrimination by rewarding an individual or group with a privilege or opportunity (see **affirmative action**).

Discrimination can be exercised either directly or indirectly. Direct discrimination may be the most obvious and apparently harmful, but in fact its overtones also makes it more difficult to defend in the light of public scrutiny. Indirect discrimination is potentially more harmful because its covert nature allows it to pervade institutions. Examples of indirect discrimination include tacit cultural biases against poor people in college entrance exams, questions about the care of children in interviews, the 'gerrymandering' of electoral boundaries to ensure the under-representation of representatives of certain communities, and hiring people who come from certain schools which just happen to have disproportionate numbers of pupils with a given physical or cultural background. **BO'L**

See also conservatism; equality; liberalism; socialism and social democracy.

Further reading R.J. Cormack and R.D. Osborne (eds.), *Discrimination and Public Policy in Northern Ireland*; P. Figueroa, *Education and the Social Structure of 'Race'*.

DISEASE

Disease is impairment of any function of person. The term has come to mean the sum total of perception of impairment by the person (symptoms), the disorder observed by the physician (signs), and the discernible biochemical or cellular changes (pathology). The quality and practical value of the description of disease is much improved if the cause is known, and further improved if there is a well-established and proven means to prevent or to treat the disease.

Western medicine has focused upon external causes of disease, such as injury or harmful agents. An early observation, in 19th-century Britain, was the common occurrence of scrotal cancer in chimney-sweep boys, leading to coal tars being called toxic and carcinogenic. The science of **microbiology** has revealed many causes of disease bacteria, fungi and later viruses. Koch, the discoverer of the cause of tuberculosis also postulated four conditions which must hold in order to link a microorganism with a disease. One hundred years later, Koch's postulates are still valid, but are, of course, disregarded when convenient. Although, for example, the description of the disease tuberculosis includes the means to prevent and to treat the condition, the incidence or commonness of the disease has remained unpredictable and this suggests that factors other than the causal agent need to be taken into account.

Another group of diseases are caused by deficiencies of essential substances – for example, blood loss can lead to iron-deficiency anaemia, which is treated by stemming the loss and replacing the iron. In pernicious anaemia one fails to absorb an essential substance (vitamin B_{12}) – here the absorption defect is difficult to treat and the vitamin can easily be injected to cure the disease. The attribution of diseases to dietary deficiencies is no longer scientifically supportable except in rare circumstances. Dietary disease is most commonly undernutrition or starvation or our very own Western malady, overnutrition. Disordered function of the endocrine glands can cause disease by over- or under-function.

There is still a large proportion of diseases in which the model or description does not include cause, or the means to prevent or to treat.

An examination of diabetes provides a rewarding example in interaction between human thought and doctors' action. The name of the illness means 'siphon' and it was first known as the 'pissing evil'. The frequently passed and abundant urine was found to be sweet tasting by pre-biochemical, 17th-century physicians. (Fortunately for researchers such unsavoury duties have always been well rewarded.) The abundant sweet urine is due to an excess of glucose in the blood which passes into the kidney tubule where it draws water from the person to try to achieve a 'normal' concentration. The excess of glucose is the prime observable phenomenon about diabetes. In the late 19th century, experimental animals whose pancreases had been removed were found to have diabetes. Insulin was discovered by Banting and Best in 1921 and came to be used to treat diabetic people. However, those who survived the acute effects of the disease developed the chronic effects which were also life threatening. Biochemical information accumulated and many Nobel prizes later a most elegant and beautiful picture of metabolic processes emerged. Diabetes proved to be a profound and pervasive metabolic disorder in which the 'burner' which produces our energy seemed to splutter for many accountable reasons some of which could be set in train by an insulin deficiency. Another aspect of treatment of diabetes is by regulation of diet. Because of the excess of glucose, carbohydrates (the part of diet which includes sugars) were assumed to be 'bad' and diabetics had to eat a diet low in carbohydrates, that is to say, a diet high in proteins and fats. This diet is similar to what was eaten by people reacting to the privations of the war and in whom a rise in heart attack rate was observed. It is also the diet which was experimentally fed to rabbits, with the same result.

The next change in thinking came with the recognition of the value of vegetable fibres in diet, derived from the observation of a low bowel cancer rate in Ugandan people who ate a high-fibre diet. This led to clinical trials of high-fibre and whole-grain-based diets as part of the treatment of diabetes. The trials proved the preventive effect of such a diet on many complications. Thus, after the discovery of insulin, the evolution of the rational treatment for diabetes was influenced only minimally by the elegant biochemical model explaining the disease. The clinical trials which revealed the information of fundamental importance were intuitively derived from the distantly related information about high-fibre diets which influenced the fashion of thinking about the effect of what we eat. Much effort has been expended on futile efforts to isolate the protective factors in grain. The high, whole-grain diet has a clearly proven therapeutic value, but the way in which it works is not known.

Western medicine has tended to emphasize external causes of disease. When, for example, the emotions are assumed to have a role in the cause or manifestation of disease there is still a trend to group such situations under a 'stress-related disease' or external heading. By contrast the classical Chinese system lists 14 causes of disease, seven external (heat, cold, dryness etc.) and seven internal (the emotions). **TG**

See also epidemiology; health; medicine.

DISPLACEMENT see Defence Mechanism

DISSOCIATION OF SENSIBILITY

Dissociation of sensibility was a phrase coined by T.S. Eliot, writing about the activity of writing **poetry**. In brief, he drew a distinction between 'reflective' poets, (who used words and images as the 'mechanism of sensibility' which allowed them to 'devour any kind of experience'), and 'intellectual' poets (who dissociated their sensibility from the activity of writing poetry). To write about the scent of a rose was a different matter entirely from experiencing the scent of a rose. The idea was fashionable in literary criticism for half a century, but even Eliot came to deplore the way in which it had been taken as a view about poets in general to whom it is clearly not applicable rather than about Milton, Dryden and their followers, to whom he originally applied it. **KMcL**

Further reading T.S. Eliot, 'The Metaphysical Poets', *Selected Essays*.

DIVINATION

Divination (Latin, 'predicting from evi-

dence') has always been a popular human activity, allowing us to feel in contact with, if not precisely in control of, the one aspect of existence which human beings know about but can never comprehend: time (see **space and time**). Divination is, simply, the interpretation of existing phenomena to predict the future. The ancient Romans, for example, one of the most fanatically superstitious of all ancient peoples, used to divine the future by watching the flight of birds, listening for thunder, interpreting chance remarks by passers-by or the unexpected hoots and howls of domestic pets, and examining the colour and shape of the organs of specially-sacrificed animals; pragmatists (such as the admiral who threw a flock of sacred chickens overboard when they failed to predict the time he wanted for his battle) were rare. Of the thousands of other methods of divination used in human history, some of the most popular have been **astrology** (prediction from heavenly bodies), bibliomancy (randomly picking quotations from books – in the West the Bible and Virgil's *Aeneid* were favourites – and relating them to the questions asked), casting lots (choosing objects at random from a collection, assuming that one's choice will have supernatural guidance), crystallomancy (predicting from the patterns seen in rocks or crystal formations), nephelomancy (interpreting cloud-shapes), oneiromancy (prophesying from dreams), **palmistry** (interpreting the lines on people's hands), phrenology ('reading' the bumps on people's heads), phyllomancy (hearing messages in the rustling of leaves in the wind), pyromancy (interpreting the shapes seen in fire), rhabdomancy (dropping matchstick-like rods in a random way, and interpreting the patterns they made) and xylomancy (observing the knotholes and gnarls in wood). The most common of all forms of divination is **numerology** (consulting mathematical charts and configurations). The ancient Babylonians, Chinese, Egyptians, Mayans and a dozen other peoples used it to predict the future, and we still do this today, making statistical models and computer simulations and assuming or pretending (just as ancient numerologists did) that they are more than informed guesswork. **KMcL**

See also magic numbers; necromancy.

DIVISION OF LABOUR

The concept of division of labour is the basis of modern **economics**. It was first developed as a theory by Adam Smith (1723–90), and refers to the specialization of work by tasks. Smith saw division of labour as an outgrowth of increases in the size of markets and the consequent growth in the size of production units. In economic theory, it is identified as a cause of **economies of scale**.

In **sociology**, the term is used in three different senses. First, it may refer to a technical division of labour and describes the productive process. Adam Smith used the term to mean specialization as a result of subdividing work into simple operations performed by separate workers. Organized in this way, worker productivity was raised and labour costs lowered. For Marx, work lost its creativity and meaning for workers when subdivided in this manner.

Second, 'division of labour' is used to refer to a social division of labour and in this sense it is applied to society as a whole. Here it is used to refer to social differentiation more generally, that is the separation of different areas of social life such as family and work.

Third, 'sexual division of labour' refers to the division of tasks between women and men. The sexual division of labour is often explained on the basis of biology. Feminists, however, explain it with reference to the domination of men in general and the separation of the domestic domain from the public sphere. **DA TF**

See also alienation; bureaucracy; career; comparative advantage; evolutionism; feminism; gender; globalization; labour process; occupation; organization; profession; rationalization; social closure; social stratification; society; status; work.

Further reading D.M. Gordon, R. Edwards, M. Reich, *Segmented Work, Divided Workers*; A. Oakley, *The Sociology of Housework*; T. Parsons, *Societies: Evolutionary and Comparative Perspectives*.

DIXIELAND

Dixieland (after a nickname for the Southern United States) is a kind of **jazz**, known as 'traditional' or 'trad' in Europe. It was a development from **New Orleans** jazz, distinguished by a 'wilder', freer style, both in solos and in the ensemble **improvisations** which framed them. **KMcL**

DOCUMENTARY DRAMA

Documentary **drama** refers to plays and theatrical events based directly on, and often incorporating quotations from, factual material. As with **history plays** questions of authorial point-of-view often determine critical response, since the purpose of documentaries is to raise public awareness of the issues presented theatrically. Documentary drama, as practised by Piscator in the Living Newspapers and in the work of Joan Littlewood, has been a significant sub-genre in 20th-century US and European drama. **TRG SS**

Further reading D. Paget, *True Stories? Documentary Drama on Radio, Screen and Stage*; R. Stourac and K. McCreery, *Theatre as a Weapon*.

DODECAPHONIC MUSIC see Serial Music

DOMINANT IDEOLOGY

The term dominant ideology means the principal ideas, values and morals in a given society. It is a particular version of reality but only one of a number of possible versions. These ideas may, however, be so well-established that members of society believe them to be naturally given and beyond question. It is possible for different ideologies to exist within a given society different versions of reality but they lack the persuasive power and generalized acceptance enjoyed by the dominant ideology.

Marxist sociologists have pointed out that ideologies are rarely neutral, and serve to justify and support the interests of a powerful social group over less-powerful groups. The dominant ideology thesis asserts that working-class subordination in capitalist societies is largely the outcome of the cultural dominance achieved by the capitalist class. For Marx, the ruling ideas in a given society are always the ideas of the ruling social group. Feminist sociologists make a similar point, but starting from a different premise.

Sociologists such as Abercrombie criticize the dominant ideology thesis, arguing that its proponents overestimate the extent to which different groups are integrated into the dominant culture, and underestimate the extent to which different groups can generate ideas which run counter to dominant ideologies. **DA**

See also assimilation; class; conflict theory; critical theory; culture; discourse; hegemony; ideology; internalization; Marxism; norms; power; social control; social integration; socialization; social movements; sociology of knowledge; subculture; values.

Further reading N. Abercrombie, S. Hill, B.S. Turner, *The Dominant Ideology Thesis*; J. Larrain, *The Concept of Ideology*.

DOUBLE ASPECT THEORY

This is the theory, in **philosophy**, that while mental and physical aspects or properties are radically different, they are nevertheless aspects or properties of the same things. Mental and physical properties are distinct, and neither can be reduced to the other. They are fundamentally different from each other, and neither should be regarded as more real than the other. But they are nevertheless aspects of the same things. Those who infer from the radically different nature of mental and physical properties to the claim that minds are non-physical, having no physical properties, and that bodies are non-mental, having no mental properties, are mistaken. **AJ**

See also dualism; mind-body problem.

Further reading T. Nagel, *The View from Nowhere*; P. F. Strawson, *Individuals*.

DOUBLE EFFECT, DOCTRINE OF

The doctrine of double effect, in **philosophy**, says that actions are morally permissible even if we can foresee that they will have bad consequences, provided these consequences are not intended by us. For instance, a nation at war may bomb enemy cities with the intention of destroying military targets.

These targets are known to be close to areas where civilians live and many civilians will die in the bombardment. But since the intention is only to destroy the military targets and not to kill the civilians, the bombing is permissible.

The doctrine of double effect is popular with some moral theologians, but it is difficult to reconcile with ordinary notions of responsibility. I don't intend to drive my neighbours to distraction by playing loud music all the time; I only want to enjoy myself. I am nevertheless held responsible for the discomfort I knowingly cause them. The doctrine of double effect is anti-consequentialist in that it claims that we are not to be held responsible for all of the foreseeable consequence of our actions, but only the ones we intended. **AJ**

See also consequentialism.

Further reading H. Hart, 'Intention and Punishment' in *Punishment and Responsibility*; G. Williams, *The Sanctity of Life and the Criminal Law*.

DRAMA

The word 'drama' (Greek, 'action', 'enactment') was first used in a technical sense to refer to staged performances of previously-written plays by Aristotle in his *Poetics* (4th century BCE), and much theorizing about the art of drama, especially in its literary form, also begins with his work. But in modern times, as **anthropology**, **archaeology** and palaeography have revealed more and more about human activity in the world, the idea of 'drama' contained in the second definition above, 'enactment', has been shown to have far wider scope than Aristotle could possible have imagined.

The essential ingredient of drama, as Aristotle pointed out, was *mimesis*, the imitation or representation of reality. A palaeolithic cave painting of an antlered dancer at Trois Frères in France gives the clue to one kind of such representation in earliest times – a clue backed up by evidence throughout the world. The dancer is representing an animal, mimicking its movement in dance. Perhaps he is part of some **ritual**, designed to persuade watching spirits to bring success to a hunt; perhaps he is part of a re-enactment of the hunt afterwards, to celebrate its success; perhaps he is part of what might be called an abstract representation of hunting, performed for no other purpose than entertainment. When, in ancient Israel, a goat was ceremonially loaded with the sins and guilt of the entire human community, and driven out into the desert to be eaten by wild animals, this ritual was both real and symbolic, 'drama' in both senses. When the priest in a Christian mass gives each worshipper bread and wine, he is simultaneously re-enacting Christ's actions at the Last Supper and creating a new action, real and of its moment. In both cases, the ritual element, the real action, perhaps predominates over the dramatic. But when Indian temple dancers (for instance) parade as teeth-flashing, high-leaping demons and the gods who vanquish them, or welcome an invisible Lord Krishna with submissive movements and flirtatious, caressing glances (re-enacting the story of his seduction of the cowgirls), emphasis has moved the other way, and performance is more dominant than ritual. The fights and seductions in Noh drama, or the apparitions of ghosts and demons in Chinese classical drama, clearly have links with ritual, but exist – that is, have meaning – almost entirely at the moment of performance only, and for the entertainment of the spectators. They are drama not ritual, in the same way as fights in Shakespeare or mad-scenes in Schiller are performance pure and simple.

To call a dramatic performance 'pure and simple' is, in fact, to sidestep another of the large issues first raised by Aristotle: the purpose and effect of dramatic performance. In a phrase which has become cant, he said that the function of drama – he was talking specifically about the awesome (literally awful) events depicted in such Athenian tragedies as *King Oedipus* – was to 'purify' the spectators by arousing 'pity and terror' (that is, identification with the characters and their dilemmas, and horror both at the events shown and at the possibility that one's own inner feelings or thoughts might lead to similar catastrophe). At one level this is a ritual function and Athenian drama was part of a huge religious festival, full of rituals of all kinds from dance to sacrifice, from procession to public prayer. But at another level Aristotle was hinting at the

feeling of exaltation, of psychological repleteness, which entertainment (and not just drama) can induce. (It is this exaltation, the moment of surrender, the door between rational self-control and abandonment to the 'higher reality' and 'higher perception' of instinct, of which Dionysus was god. To bring about such exaltation, in the **myth**, he gave mortals two unique gifts: sacred dance and wine.)

The festivals of Dionysus in Athens were concerned most specifically with this ecstasy. The drama competitions were merely one way among many of inducing and celebrating it. Performance-spaces were so arranged that, in the open air, all spectators could see other spectators: the audience was itself part of the occasion, and identification was not just with the characters depicted in the drama, not just with the professional actors and singers who depicted them, not just with the **Chorus** (amateurs, selected representatives of each area of the town), but also with the other watchers, other participants. This identification still happens in performances of religious drama throughout the world, and it can still occur in our secular theatres today, with spine-tingling effect.

Aristotle was neither a priest nor a practitioner of theatre. He was an academic, formulating theories and relying on evidence. For this reason he had far less to say about what we might nowadays think of as the anthropological and psychological functions of drama (about which one can merely assert, not prove, one's views) than he did about actual, extant plays. He proved his points by references to specific plays, all of them comparatively recent (written about a century before his time) and still in the current repertoire. (Even then, he was selective: his theories fit the plays of Sophocles which he adduces as evidence, but have little relevance to much other surviving Greek tragedy, notably the work of Euripides.) He dealt with written plays only; orally-transmitted traditions were of merely passing interest, perhaps because he felt that they were inaccessible to his hearers and readers, or were mutable evidence, in a way which written texts were not. This factor has led, in drama studies ever since (at least until this century), to the view that written drama is somehow a different art form from any other kind and, in the West at least, that it is superior. (In Western comedy, written drama is even called 'high' comedy, and improvised comedy 'low' comedy, as if the possibility of scholarly attention had somehow elevated the form.) The word 'drama' is still sometimes claimed to mean the tradition of written theatre only and the result, given the oral, accretive traditions of most Eastern art forms, is that for Western scholars it has tended to mean just Western plays and methods of performance.

Aristotle divided drama into two main hierarchical genres, **tragedy** and **comedy**. Although the section of *Poetics* dealing with comedy is lost or fragmentary, and most of his surviving writing is therefore to do with tragedy, his views have nonetheless tended, in the West, to be applied to drama of every kind. Because the precedent he set for thinking about drama was founded on the philosophical basis of logic, it imposed on the plays he analysed the logical values he deemed necessary for life. Embedded in his hierarchy of genres was a reflection of moral and social status (which the Roman writer Horace later conflated in his poem about why and how to write, *The Art of Poetry*; 'poetry' here really means 'literature'). With increasing literacy and the desire for classical knowledge, which marked Western intellectual life during the **Renaissance**, it was inevitable that these ideas would influence the development of drama; a strong awareness of generic distinctions, formal structures and social status determined the way plays were written and perceived. Generally, for example, tragedy was assumed only to afflict the highly-born; comedy covered a broader social range. **Poetry** was the language of tragedy, elevated above everyday utterance as the emotions and dilemmas depicted were thought to be elevated; prose was for everyday speech, and for comedy.

Such distinctions – as well as comparatively minor ideas derived from Aristotle and the plays he described, such as the five-act structure – affected much Western drama in the Renaissance and beyond, both fine work (such as that of Racine) and a slew of dull, rule-rigid and formulaic plays. But there was a vigorous alternative tradition, an almost **postmodernist** eclecticism, which can be seen in the work of such writers as Calderón, Shakespeare, and Molière. They drew inspiration partly from classical theory, partly from vernacular tradition, and partly from their own imagination and the needs of each individual play as they wrote it. The *commedia dell'arte* and the *auto da fé* are the two best-known traditions which underlie such drama, and they now have the melancholy distinction of being less well-known than the dramatic styles they influenced. Other theories such as the **alchemical** idea of the four **humours** which inspired Jonson's comedy of humours led to dramatic experiment as fascinating as any of the theories of the absurd or **alienation** which dramatists have used in our own time.

Although there were technical developments in theatre practice over the following hundred years (in such matters as scenery design, lighting and make-up), there was little advance in dramatic ideas. Classical Greek and Latin drama, and the plays of Shakespeare, and to a lesser extent Molière, were principal influences even on such literary giants as Schiller and Hugo; thousands upon thousands of 'perfect' dramas were written, much admired, and died – good examples are the opera librettos of Metastasio, made with strict adherence to Aristotelian rules and the practices of Sophocles and Seneca, but devoid of stage life to the point where not even the music of such geniuses as Gluck or Mozart can redeem them as dramatic spectacle. Change came in the 19th century, when adherents of **naturalism** advocated the application to drama of scientific techniques of observation and analysis, in deference to Darwin's theory that environment conditions behaviour. (This approach had been prefigured in novels, especially in France, since the beginning of the century; it began to permeate drama in the middle of the century, and was given impetus in 1880 when Zola published his influential essay 'Naturalism and the Art of the Theatre'.) Strict application of such theories was often as unsuccessful, in dramatic terms, as had been rigid **neoclassicism** in preceding centuries. Formulaic and sententious melodrama, 'well-made plays' in which cardboard characters enacted their own downfall (a downfall caused not by the Aristotelian 'tragic flaw' but by their own wretched circumstances or some terrible inheritance such as poverty or syphilitic madness) in scenes to which no self-respecting computer would nowadays admit authorship, became the dismal norm. More successful naturalistic dramatists – the range is from Ibsen, at the top of the tree of quality, to such men as Sardou, Scribe and Jones, on the lower branches – exceeded naturalist conventions while still representing the everyday concerns of (middle-class) society rather than the neoclassical conflicts of love and duty.

Essential to naturalistic drama was the concept of **illusionism**, which aimed to give the illusion that 'real' events were happening onstage, to disguise the artifice of their production. The dramaturgy of naturalistic plays took this into account, specifying recognizable domestic settings and using apparently colloquial forms of speech. (This is the point, perhaps, at which Western dramatic practice is most remote from anything current in the East. Until the present century, when Eastern audiences began to see Western plays, and some Eastern writers for example Mishima began writing plays in Western styles, naturalism played no part whatever in Eastern dramatic art.) It is not essential, if illusionism is to be fully effective, that plays should be naturalistic, but it is necessary that the spectator participate in the exchange, imaginatively accepting whatever is represented, however supernatural or fantastic it may be. This participation, which Coleridge called '**willing suspension of disbelief**', is both an extension of, and something entirely different from, the reaction of 'pity and terror' predicated by Aristotle on his fellow Athenians at festivals of Dionysus.

In the 20th century, Brecht set out to challenge this apparently uncritical response from audiences by developing a drama which was anti-illusionist, and which exposed the artifice of its production; the **epic drama** which he created did not represent a political position, it was intrinsically political. The modes of production became as important as the playscript, thus countering the long-held primacy of the written text. At the same time, other dramatists drew on the vigorous vernacular tradition (for example music-hall), and on techniques from film and experimental fiction, to create other kinds of non-illusionist drama. Although 'well-made plays', **history plays** and their progeny still pullulated on the stage, a whole new kind of drama, fast-moving, constantly innovatory and challenging by its very unexpectedness, became the norm. Instead of purging the spectators by pity and terror, plays now used incongruity, absurdity (in the wide sense) and a kind of shared connivance in the spectacle, a shared awareness of the whole dramatic tradition of the past (shown, for example, in the **parody** of all kinds and at all levels) which has reinvigorated the form. Growing awareness of the rest of the world, in societies everywhere, has also brought Eastern ideas to bear on Western drama, and vice versa, in ways which have pluralized, eclecticized and transformed the art. **TRG KMcL SS**

See also dance; performing arts; theatre.

Further reading Aristotle, *Poetics*; J.L. Styan, *Drama, Stage and Audience*; Eric Bentley (ed.), *Theory of the Modern Stage*; Raymond Williams, *Drama from Ibsen to Brecht*.

DRAMATURGICAL MODEL

This is an approach within the branch of **sociology** known as **symbolic interactionism** which is particularly associated with Erving Goffman. In this approach to social analysis the theatre is the basis of an analogy with everyday social life. Social action is conceived of as a 'performance', and individuals play parts, stage-managing their behaviour in order to control the impression they wish to convey to others. This is a process Goffman terms 'impression management'. He argues that actors aim to present themselves always in a favourable light and in ways appropriate to the particular roles they are playing, and to the particular social setting they find themselves in. For Goffman, much of social life can be divided up into front and back regions. Front regions are 'on-stage performances', whereas back regions resemble the backstage area of the theatre. Goffman also examines the ways in which social actors co-operate as teams in order to preserve front region performances, and hide from view certain 'backstage' behaviours.

Goffman emphasizes the precarious nature of social order which is always at risk of disruption by embarrassment or breaches of the front. **DA**

See also action perspective; career; generalized other; role; social construction of reality; social self; structure-agency debate; understanding.

Further reading J. Ditton (ed.), *The View from Goffman*; E. Goffman, *The Presentation of Self in Everyday Life* (1959) and *Relations in Public: Microstudies of Public Order* (1971).

DRAWING

Drawing, in European fine **art**, means a composition of line and shade, usually on paper and executed in pencil, pen, charcoal, chalk or a similar graphic medium. Drawings traditionally have served as the preparatory stage of picture-making, from the first sketch to transferring the composition to canvas, panel or wall. Drawing was first appreciated as a medium in its own right during the Renaissance, when working drawings became sought-after and valued for the insights they offered into artists' powers of invention. In the 17th century, academic theory drawing was valued over **painting** as the literal transposition of the idea, distant from the 'mechanical' work of grinding and applying colour, which recalled the artisanal approach of the guilds. From this stemmed the belief in the superiority of line over colour (Poussinistes v. Rubenistes) – an assertion which assumed that colourists neglected drawing. While many artists such as Rubens, Rembrandt, Fragonard and Turner made drawings, artists such as Ingres went further and made drawing the touchstone of art. (Two of Ingres's favourite aphorisms were 'Drawing is the probity of art', and 'I can teach you painting in a week, but drawing takes a lifetime'.) In the 20th century, drawing has been liberated from its predominantly subservient role to find expression in the work of such consummate artists as Rodin, Matisse and more recently Hockney. **MG PD**

Further reading Susan Lambert, *Reading Drawings: an Introduction to Looking at Drawings*.

DREAMS

Dreams were believed, by the 19th century Romantics, to be messages from 'the Beyond' with personal significance. The Rationalists denied that dreams had any sense at all, while the Materialists claimed that dreams were no more than the results of body activities and sense stimuli during sleep. Freud reasserted the more traditional view that dreams had a personal meaning; he compared them to messages and letters.

In sleep, according to Freud, the mind is in a state of relaxed censorship. Dreams are disguised representations of unconscious wishes which are not accessible in a waking state. What Freud called the 'dream work' employs further displacements of direct imagery, condensation of images, representations and concrete symbolism. These are the manifest forms of the latent content (the wishes). Freud called dreams the 'royal road to the unconscious'.

For Jung, dreams were the main source of our knowledge of symbolism. The individual symbols in dreams are natural and spontaneous products of the unconscious. They are not signs: a symbol is something which stands for more than its obvious immediate meaning, whereas a sign is something that means less than the object it stands for. Many dream symbols are not individual but collective in their nature, and these are chiefly religious symbols. Jung discovered that ancient symbols, of which his patients had no prior knowledge, turned up in their dreams. Dreams, therefore, demonstrated to him the existence of a **collective unconscious**. **MJ**

Further reading Sigmund Freud, *On Dreams*; Jung, *Psychology and Alchemy*.

DUALISM

Dualists hold that the mental is not physical and that the physical is not mental. They have usually held that there are mental things which are not physical (such as my mind) and physical things which are not mental (such as my body). **AJ**

See also epiphenomenalism; idealism; interactionism; materialism; parallelism.

Further reading J. Foster, *The Immaterial Self*; W.D. Hart, *Engines of the Soul*.

DUTY

A duty (Old French, 'what is owed') or obligation (Latin, 'something which binds') is, **philosophically**, something one morally ought or ought not to do. One ought not to inflict suffering on others, which is to say that one has a duty not to inflict suffering on others. One is obliged not to do so. Duties or obligations may conflict. One has a duty not to inflict suffering on others, but one also has a duty to tell the truth. These duties conflict when truthfully answering a question will inflict suffering. **AJ**

DYSLEXIA

The term dyslexia derives from the Greek for 'difficulty with words and language' and came into common usage in 1887, replacing the earlier, more emotive, phrase 'word blindness'. Dyslexia is by no means a rare phenomenon, and although estimates vary, something of the order of ten per cent of people are affected.

Dyslexia can arise as a result of brain damage, either around the time of birth or possibly later in life, following a stroke. The pattern of dyslexia witnessed as a result of birth trauma is often compounded by hyperactivity, poor concentration and inherent clumsiness. However, this group of traumatized dyslexics are generally held to be in the minority, and the main focus of research has been a second group known as developmental dyslexics. Developmental dyslexia arises from a distinct pattern of neurological development which is almost certainly genetically determined. It is widely known that dyslexics experience difficulty in learning to read, but there are a number of underlying factors which contribute to this outcome. A major problem for some dyslexics is a general asymbolia, in which the ability to recognize words as coherent, symbolic entities is disturbed. The normal capacity to identify each word globally in terms of its symbolic value is impaired. Other symptoms include failure to perceive linguistic patterns such as intonation, stress and rhyme; disfluencies in the motor skills required for writing; difficulties in processing sound and letter sequences; short-term memory dysfunction in processing symbolic series; and even problems with spatial orientation and time judgements.

In most people, **language** is processed in the left hemisphere of the brain, in conjunction with analytic and symbolic skills such as the ability to manipulate numbers. Consequently, the problems experienced by dyslexics can sometimes be traced to impaired left hemisphere functioning. In these cases, the right hemisphere skills, which include face recognition, emotional expression, visuo-spatial and integrative skills, can be highly developed in dyslexics. Thus, it is not uncommon to find dyslectic people succeeding in the fields of architecture, art, design, technology and so on.

In the majority of cases, there is by now an overwhelming body of evidence to implicate deep-seated neurological causes for dyslexia. However, educational psychologists have been signally reluctant to treat dyslexia as an inherited condition and, instead, factors external to the child have often been blamed. Low socioeconomic status, general social maladjustment and emotional disturbance and poor teaching methods have all been cited as causes for dyslexia. Very often, these views appear to be more politically than scientifically motivated, and unfortunately they have tended to hinder rather than advance the treatment of dyslexics. Acknowledging the underlying neurological causes of dyslexia can help in the early diagnosis of specific disorders and thus lead to the design and implementation of appropriate teaching programmes. For example, some dyslexic children are more proficient at processing information aurally, in terms of sound patterns, rather than visually. For such children, a typical programme might concentrate on games involving sound patterns, rhyme, repetition, recitation and so on. In other words, the child's individual skills are exploited as a means of overcoming the language difficulties created by dyslexia. **MS**

Further reading F.R. Vellutino, *Dyslexia: Theory and Research*.

DYSTOPIANISM see Utopianism

E

EARTH ART

Earth Art (also known as Land Art or Environmental Art) was a 1960s movement related to **conceptual art** and against the urban sophistication of **minimalism**. It was an attempt to broaden the accepted boundaries of sculpture, making the environment more than simply a context but the material for the work itself. Thus Robert Smithson constructed a 500 m *Spiral Jetty* in the Great Salt Lake, and Walter de Maria inscribed two white lines in the Nevada Desert in *Mile Long Drawing*. **MG PD**

Further reading A. Sonfist, *Art in the Land: a Critical Anthology of Environmental Art.*

ECCLESIOLOGY

Ecclesiology (Greek *ekklesia*, 'church' + ology), is the doctrine of the nature of the Christian Church. After its virtual extinction among liberal Protestants *c*.1830–1930, and replacement among others by **eschatology**, the 'rediscovery of the nature of the Church' has been one of the most significant developments in Christian theology this century. It was possible because of modern scholarship recovering the literature of the Early Church, and the consensus on liturgical reform, and came about as much because of pressure from secularism, **fascism** and **communism** as because of the growing momentum of the ecumenical movement. The influence of Karl Barth, who in 1929 changed his planned 'Christian Dogmatics' to 'Church Dogmatics', and Père Congar on the Catholic side, was decisive, but theologians with a seminal influence, such as Dietrich Bonhoeffer, have also produced major ecclesiological works. The role of the churches as agents for liberation in some Third World countries, combined with a general appreciation of the need for humankind to live in communities and contribute to them, gave a new impetus to these studies in the 1950s and 1960s. Now the crisis produced on the one hand by the ordination of women and on the other by **fundamentalism** and the house church movement will demand further theological developments. **EMJ**

See also Christianity; ritual; sacrament.

Further reading M.J. Congar, *Divided Christendom* (1939); J.H. Oldham and W.A. Visser't Hooft, *The Churches Survey Their Task* (1937).

ECLECTICISM

Eclecticism (from Greek *eklegein*, 'to pick out') was an ancient Graeco-Roman philosophy whose adherents picked and chose from ideas in other philosophical systems, without following any of them totally: the exponents best remembered today are Cicero and Seneca. Pliny the Elder took a similar approach to the investigation of phenomena, studying and writing about everything from military tactics to the age of rocks, from the life-cycle of seaweed to the best way to educate children. In the **arts**, eclecticism is a similar principle: taking your ideas, magpie-like, from wherever you fancy, and adapting them to fit your inspiration. It was a (rather self-conscious) movement in the **architecture** and fine art of the **Renaissance**, perhaps in reaction against the vast number of 'isms' described and prescribed at that time. In the same way, and perhaps for similar reasons, it has been a governing principle of **postmodernism** in all the arts, creators reacting against the straitjacketing 'methods' and reforming programmes which were such characteristic features of the first half of the 20th century.

The problem with eclecticism (if it is a problem) is that most geniuses are eclectic and most geniuses have imitators: therefore, what begins as eclecticism very quickly becomes a style, and then, when critics and scholars get their hands on it, a school. The truth is, perhaps, that artistic innovation is an organic process, and that what we perceive as schools and movements are merely descriptive labels, irrelevant to true creators but handy for also-rans. **KMcL**

ECOFEMINISM

In ecofeminism concern for the environment and the welfare of the planet are combined with feminist analysis and reaction to the power of the patriarchy. The image of 'Nature' as a supine, passive entity cultivated by 'man' who ploughs, sows, begets and controls and dominates, is rejected in favour of a conciliatory non-interventionist approach involving equal contributions from both sexes. Feminists are convinced that if attitudes can be changed (and generally they seem to believe that they can be), then the posioning of creation will cease. There is, however, no questioning of the assumption that the natural world in some way is feminine, and congenial, rather than hostile, dangerous, and 'red in tooth and claw'.

Ecofeminism is world-affirming, with a 'green' approach to life. The radical critique of **gender** roles in the natural world requires a revision of **medicine, ethics** and theology, with, for example, women reclaiming control over their bodies instead of doing what (male) doctors tell them to do. It involves an integrationist approach to work/ housework, home/workplace, gender roles, etc., in a way which recalls William Morris and the **Pre-Raphaelites**. Some ecofeminists have moved on to embrace **goddess** theology and the **Gaia hypothesis**. TK

See also feminism; feminist theology.

Further reading J. Plant (ed.), *Healing the Wounds: the Promise of Ecofeminism*; Mary Daly *Gyn/Ecology*.

ECOLOGY

Ecology (Greek, 'study of the home') is the study of how organisms relate to their environment and to each other in the biological communities of which all living organisms are a part. As such, ecology is a major division of **biology** and also has relevance to all fields of the **life sciences** as all living systems are meaningless unless studied in the context of their environment. The ecologist looks at whole organisms and their organization into communities.

Prior to the 19th century, most scientific study had been concerned with individual organisms, viewed in isolation from their natural environment. Classifications of species sometimes referred to typical habitats, but it was investigations of the geographical distribution of plant types according to climate which initiated the first scientific study of ecology. The term ecology was coined in 1866 by Ernst Haeckel (1834–1919) after Charles Darwin's (1809–82) publication of *Origin of Species* in 1859 stimulated great interest in the study of organisms in relation to their environment. Interest in ecology was initially strongest among botanists, but 20th-century biology has been permeated by ecology at all levels and has, incidentally, served to unite seemingly disparate fields.

Modern ecology has not abandoned the field study as the source of data, but the advent of the computer brought new possibilities to ecological modelling, enabling complex data to be collated and used to support the extrapolation of trends as a means to predict the consequences of environmental changes. **Computer simulations** of the behaviour of ecological processes such as the **greenhouse effect** and of more localized systems, such as polluted rivers, have enabled reasonably accurate forecasts to be made. The ecologist plays a central role in applied biology and in the monitoring of the effects of **pollution**, though it must be borne in mind that the systems under study are almost infinitely complex and therefore inherently unpredictable. Ecology has also provided scientific weight to those who promote environmental **conservation** and, from the 1960s onwards has been one of the most politically important areas of science. **RB**

See also community; ecosystem, population biology; competition.

Further reading Paul Colinvaux, *Why Big Fierce Animals are Rare*; Joseph Moran, *Introduction to Environmental Science*.

ECONOMETRICS

Econometrics (from the Greek for, 'budget-measurement technique') is **mathematical** and **computer** skills applied to **economics**. The econometrician's best-known activity is building mathematical 'models' of the relationships in the economy, using equations that embody those relationships between, for example, investment, interest rates and economic growth. Once built, the model can be used (with a computer) to forecast the economic future.

Econometrics clearly has a valuable role to play in quantifying economic relationships; a computer can now handle such quantities of data that econometric analysis has become practical and accessible. However, it does have its critics. The economist Joan Robinson of Cambridge University put it this way: 'I don't know any mathematics. I have to think.' Unless econometric seeds are sown on soil that has been thoroughly and thoughtfully prepared, they will provide information and conclusions lacking coherence and relevance. **TF**

See also game theory.

ECONOMIC ANTHROPOLOGY

Economic anthropology emerged as a recognizable field in the 1950s. Its predominant aim was to integrate conventional **economic** issues with anthropological perspectives, to place these issues in their wider contexts of social relations, concepts and values. This included subjects such as the way labour is divided, the means for producing and distributing goods and services, and questions of ownership, property and inheritance. It was realized that in a Western **market economy**, economic institutions are separated from other spheres in social life, and that this distinction was not an appropriate framework within which to consider other societies. Prior to this period, non-monetary economies had largely been overlooked: they were an area which lay outside the agenda of economic theorists (who concentrated on monetary economies). Economic anthropologists contributed by offering finer analyses on agricultural, horticultural and hunting gathering economies. They later considered how these economic organizations interacted with factors like colonial rule, industrialization and the global spread of capitalism.

Karl Polyani initiated a prominent debate in the 1950s by criticizing those economic anthropologists who, in his view, applied inappropriate market economy based concepts, such as supply and demand, profit maximization, etc., to societies not dominated by such principles. He proposed three types of goods distribution systems that could be prevalent in any society: one that featured 'reciprocity', the return of gifts, which was associated with societies organized by kinship relations. The second was based on 'redistribution', the pooling of goods for later distribution a system typical of those societies with a central institution of authority. The third was that of market exchange, in which goods were distributed at prices determined by supply and demand as is present in **capitalist** societies.

Supporters of Polyani were referred to as the 'substantivists' while 'formalists', in contrast, maintained that certain universal economic principles were relevant for all economies. This formalist-substantivist debate reached little reconciliation. Other anthropologists under the influence of Marxist theory, shifted the focus to study the economic forces and social relations determining the production of material goods as opposed to considering how these material goods are distributed in society. Marxist anthropologists (see **Marxist anthropology**) also considered ideas about reproduction. Not only was material production essential to the economic organization, but reproduction provided the means to perpetuate them by supplying a workforce.

A related issue in this area is the theoretical construct of 'economic man'. This portrays individuals as decision-makers acting in their own interest within the economic system. The ability to gain maximum benefits for the minimum of input is considered paramount and an index of rational behaviour. However, the concept of 'economic man' overlooks non-market factors in decision-making. Nor does it adequately account for the social context, particularly when economic organizations are inseparable from the larger society typical of pre-capitalist societies. These societies lack a distinct economic sphere for it is more likely to be embedded in kinship, religious, ceremonial or other such social values. **RK**

See also colonialism; development; exchange; gift; modernization; rationality; scarcity; urban anthropology.

Further reading Raymond Firth (ed.), *Themes*

in Economic Anthropology; LeClair & Schneider (eds.), Economic Anthropology; Stuart Platter (ed.), Economic Anthropology.

ECONOMIC DEVELOPMENT

Economic development is the process of increasing output per capita, so potentially improving economic well-being. It is potential because well-being depends upon what the greater productivity is used for. Given the land area of a country, economic development can occur with increases in the quality and quantity of capital goods, and the quality of the labour force. Education and technological change are great driving forces of **economic** growth.

Less-developed countries can experience great strides in economic development by acquiring more and better capital goods as well as by more education and training of the labour force. They usually lack social-overhead capital, such as efficient transportation and communications systems, and need more as a prerequisite for growth. Economically developed countries already have a substantial capital base and tend to rely more upon invention and discovery, translated into innovation, as the sources for further development. **TF**

Further reading Alexander Gerschenkron, *Economic Backwardness in Historical Perspective;* W.W. Rostow, *Stages of Economic Growth.*

ECONOMIC GROWTH

Economic growth is the process by which an economy increases its ability to produce goods and services as measured by output. Immediate causes of economic growth are: (1) an increase in the quantity of capital goods; (2) the introduction of new techniques of production and new kinds of machines. Long-term causes of growth are research and invention, population growth and improved education. Population growth may increase total output, but the other causes also increase productivity (labour-hour output) and provide the potential for increases in per capita growth, hence economic well-being. Numerous theories of economic growth include those

by Adam Smith, Karl Marx, Joseph Schupeter, Roy Harrod, E.D. Domar and Franco Modigliani **TF**.

See also economic development.

Further reading Karl Marx, *The Marx-Engels Reader* (1848); Adam Smith, *An Inquiry into the Nature and Causes of the Wealth of Nations* (1776).

ECONOMICS

Economics (Greek, 'controlling a household') is the study of the way society allocates resources for the production, distribution and consumption of goods and services. It is concerned with how societies answer the three, basic economic questions: What goods and services to produce? How to produces them? For whom in society are the goods and services to be produced?

The subject is normally divided into **microeconomics** and **macroeconomics**. In both branches, certain operating standards are pursued: theorizing, collecting and analysing facts, and then re-examining theory in the light of them. Throughout this (never-ending) process, economics is concerned to develop general propositions that can be applied in a variety of countries, periods, and circumstances and still hold good. That is why it claims to be a 'science', even though it is almost impossible to set up a laboratory experiment in the way that physical scientists can arrange every day. **TF**

ECONOMIES OF SCALE

Economies of scale refers to the benefits of mass production. In many industries, big is beautiful (or anyway cheaper) because unit costs of production fall; for example the mass-production of cars; giant shipbuilding yards; steel works, where initial investment costs are heavy and can be lightened only if output is expanded.

All processes have an optimal level of output beyond which efficiency falls, however, often because of managerial problems. Large-scale production can become inflexible, and can be slow to innovate because of heavy investment costs.

Decreases in average costs occur as manufacturing plants and firms grow larger, that is, falling long-run, average costs when all factor inputs are increased. This situation may occur because certain kinds of equipment are very large in their minimum efficient size. Or, different and more efficient arrangements and techniques of production may be utilized as the plant or firm grows larger. Adam Smith identified specialization and **division of labour** as causes of economies of scale. **TF**

Further reading Alfred D. Chandler, *Scale and Scope: the Dynamics of Industrial Capitalism*; Michael E. Porter, *The Competitive Advantage of Nations*.

ECOSYSTEM

An ecosystem (Greek *oikos*, 'home' + system) is an interdependent **community** of living organisms, united by the environment in which they live. It is essentialy a human concept, useful for the study of the **ecology** of biological communities, but of limited use as a definition because no community lives entirely in isolation from others; the **biosphere** itself is probably the only complete ecosystem. However, in order to study the complex interactions which make up the web of life it is necessary to break down the biosphere into extremely simple units; thus an ecosystem may be a rotting log and the living organisms which base their lives around it, or the intestines of a cow and the various organisms that live within it. Ecosystems are best studied in terms of the interactions between individual organisms – these interactions can be described as energy and/or material exchange along the food chain. In this way ecosystems can be broken down into trophic levels, of which each is composed of individuals which derive nutrition in a certain basic way such as by harvesting sunlight or by hunting animals.

The basic trophic levels in any ecosystem are producers (the green plants), consumers (herbivores and carnivores) and reducers (bacteria, fungi and other organisms which reduce organic matter to an inorganic form. Material is transferred with energy and is thus cycled within the ecosystem, returning to the non-living environment where it becomes available once more to producers. The cycles of transfer of elements such as nitrogen and carbon can also reveal much about the characteristics of a given ecosystem. The environment is the non-living surroundings which support the biological community; in the case of terrestrial ecosystems it can be broken down into soil and climate. The environment provides physical support and is the reservoir for the basic materials which are required by the producers. The continuous nature of the environment illustrates how it is unrealistic to consider any ecosystem in isolation from those which surround it. **RB**

See also biome; conservation; food web.

Further reading Joseph Moran, *Introduction to Environmental Science*.

ECUMENISM

Ecumenism (from Greek for 'the inhabited world' and then 'the community of those who believe as we do'), is a predominantly Christian, European movement. From the time of the Reformation irenical spirits, such as Erasmus and Leibnitz, lamented the disunity of Christendom. The modern ecumenical movement, however, only began properly in the 19th century, when Evangelical Anglicans, Congregationalists and Baptists began collaborating in Britain and India. Their aims were to create missions, to translate the Bible into Oriental and Continental languages, to fight slavery and illiteracy, the appalling factory conditions of the Industrial Revolution and the illtreatment of children. This concern with evangelism and social reform continued to bring Christians together throughout the 19th century, most notably in the founding of the Y.M.C.A. (1844) and the Y.W.C.A. (1855), the Evangelical Alliance (1846) and the Student Volunteer Movement (1886). It formed the basis for the International Missionary Council (1910) and the Life and Work Movement (1920), both of which came together in the World Council of Churches (1948).

As its Greek origin suggests, the word 'ecumenical' implies something of universal application and comprehensiveness. It is the force that makes things cohere. While there can, therefore, be 'secular' ecumenism, Christians assert that it is Christ in whom all things cohere. Christian unity is only the beginning of a wider unity of humankind. Hence current ecumenical concern with issues of justice and peace, ecology and the conservation of the planet. **EMJ**

Further reading Ruth Rouse and Stephen Neill (eds.), *The History of the Ecumenical Movement 1517–1948*; Ans van der Bent, *The Utopia of World Community.*

EGO see **Id, Ego and Supergo**

EGO PSYCHOLOGY

Ego Psychology is a variety of psychoanalytical theory developed from Freud's book *Ego and the Id* (1923) by his daughter Anna Freud. Her book, *The Ego and the Mechanisms of Defence* (1936), contrasts with the instinct theory which preceded it and with the Kleinian **object relations** theory which was developed at the same time. It aims to pay attention to the nature of reality through the structure and strong building of the ego. The ego was seen as having four distinct parts. One was autonomous and was responsible for actions like speech, breathing, and walking. Another area was seen as topographically separate from the others, and able to remain free from neurotic conflict. The other two were concerned with two different forms of sublimation. One desexualises, first the infantile libido, and then the pre-genital sexual impulses. The second deals with aggressive aspects of the libido. Ego psychology works to complete these last two processes if they have been resolved in the growing child or adult. Its intention is to merge the development construct with the self, as in, for example, the Self Theory of H. Kohut. **MJ**

EGO STATE see **Transactional Analysis**

EGYPTOLOGY

Egyptology, as the Greek derivation of the word suggests, is the study of ancient Egyptian civilization and antiquities. Ancient Egypt was the first-known major civilization, emerging 6,000 years ago at the same time as the (lesser) Sumerian and Chinese civilizations. According to the priest Manetho, who produced the 30-volume *History of Egypt*, King Menes (around 3100 BCE) was the First Dynasty ruler responsible for uniting the diverse population of ancient Egypt into a culture that eventually reached great heights in **architecture**, the **arts**, **astronomy**, **mathematics**, **medicine**, **music** and **religion**. Egyptian ideas about social organization influenced the Greeks and through them much of contemporary society. Manetho's work was destroyed by the fire at the great library at Alexandria when it was captured by Julius Caesar (1st century BCE), destroying much of the textual documentation concerning Pharaonic Egypt. The remaining texts were wilfully burnt in 391 CE, an act hampering Egyptology's current attempts to reconstruct and understand this ancient civilization.

In 1799, a black basalt stone covered with inscriptions was found in Rosetta, near Alexandria, during military operations by the French. A text in Greek was accompanied by a passage both in hieroglyphic script, and in demotic (a kind of shorthand used by scribes in ancient Egypt). A talented French linguist, Jean-François Champollion, set out to decipher the 'lost' languages, and 1822, the date when he sent his findings to the Academie des Inscriptions et Belles-Lettres, is the point most generally accepted as the start of Egyptology as a science.

Reports by early Greek and Roman travellers and the work of the Greek historian Herodotus, who was fascinated by the ancient world, were followed in the 17th century by descriptions of the archaeological marvels throughout Egypt, abandoned or desecrated first under **Christianity** and later under **Islam**, and often submerged in sand. **Archaeology** was the first discipline to pay attention to these ruins. Amateurs dug where they wanted, often destroying much in the process, until the Frenchman Auguste Mariette founded the Egyptian Antiquities Service in 1858, along with the Cairo Museum. From this point on, Egyptology gradually assumed a more scientific character, through the painstaking work of enthusiasts like Flinders Petrie, George Reisner and Howard Carter.

From the 17th century explorers, collectors, and European consuls continued a tradition started by Roman and Byzantine emperors of making off with Pharaonic statues, sphinxes and pillars. The flow of antiquities was only partially stemmed when Mariette established the Cairo Museum and the Egyptian Antiquities Service. Tomb robbing had been a widespread phenomenon even at the time tombs were built to house royalty and nobility with their jewel-encrusted gold possessions, amulets and mummy casings. Howard Carter's discovery of the largely intact tomb of Tutankhamun in 1922 astonished people with the extraordinary wealth and craftsmanship of the buried objects, bringing knowledge of the achievements of ancient Egypt to the Western world. (The resulting Egyptomania spawned a fashion for an imaginary ancient Egypt that has influenced design and styles in architecture, films, and fashions from the 1920s to the present day.)

In the wake of his military campaigns in Egypt, Napoleon commissioned a group of scholars to study and record the monuments, resulting in the publication of *Description de L'Egypte*. The same two methods are still largely used by Egyptologists. Archaeological excavations and epigraphy (the study of inscriptions) are used in an analysis of monuments and remains in their attempt to reconstruct a picture of ancient civilization. Egyptology is still a young science, and new finds are being unearthed all the time.

The Egyptologists' overriding concern with description may have hindered them at first from developing a more holistic understanding of Pharaonic Egypt. Until recently, there has been little change in the way scholars have attempted to comprehend this ancient civilization, and no attempt to question the premises on which these assumptions are made. As Barry Kemp writes in *Ancient Egypt*, it is at best an imagined world, and current speculations may have more to do with our contemporary understandings of what constitutes **civilization**. Egyptologists have posited a highly bureaucratic society led by a kingship propped up by elaborate religious institutions, characterized by continuity and rigid resistance to change. While contemporary scholars argue that they were a pragmatic race little inclined to philosophical speculation, in classical times early Egyptians were credited by the Greeks with great knowledge and wisdom. As well as the mystery cults reported by Herodotus, there was a highly developed and ritualized mortuary cult, dealing with death and metamorphosis. A number of texts guiding the dead through the afterlife were found in the many excavated tombs, the most well-known being *The Book of the Dead*.

The advanced knowledge evident in the findings dated from the First Dynasty bears witness to an astonishing degree of civilization, without any evidence of earlier precursors. This has led to speculation about the origin of this knowledge, evidenced in the astonishing precision of proportions and measurements. The self-styled Egyptologist R.A. Schwaller de Lubicz spent his life studying the mathematical laws according to which the temples were built, concluding that these principles constituted a sacred science. He claimed that the Egyptian priesthood's understanding of the harmonious relationship between man and nature was expressed in art and architecture. The sophisticated use of irrational rations *phi* and *pi* to express proportion was generally assumed to have been 'discovered' by the Greeks. Schwaller de Lubicz showed that they were abundantly used and argued that in fact Greek civilization was a pale shadow of that of the ancient Egyptians, and that much vital esoteric knowledge was lost with the decline of Egypt. His theories have been rejected by scholars reluctant to revise the received view that Greece is the birthplace of civilization as we know it. Yet it is through the work of such enthusiasts that Egyptology has progressed beyond a discipline that is concerned merely with documentation of an ancient culture, to one that attempts to understand a world-view from within its own parameters, rather than those imposed in hindsight by a very different society. **CL RK**

See also ethnoarchaeology.

Further reading J.R. Harris, *The Legacy of Egypt*; John West, *Serpent in the Sky*.

ELECTORAL SYSTEMS

Electoral systems are one of the most important social inventions, yet one of the least discussed by the general public. They are methods of translating votes (for candidates) into seats (or offices) for representatives, although they can also be used, directly and indirectly, to translate policy preferences into decisions in referendums or multiple-choice 'preferendums'.

In principle, electoral systems are infinite in number, but are usually classified in three categories: as proportional, majoritarian or plurality-rule systems. *Proportional* representation systems are the most common in modern democracies. They aim to achieve proportionality between the share of the vote won by political parties (or candidates) and the share of seats they win in the relevant assembly, and some of their intricacies are discussed below. *Majoritarian* systems are designed to guarantee that a candidate can only be elected if she or he wins a majority of the vote cast (i.e. 50% + 1). If no candidate wins a majority on the first count, then, as happens in Australia under the alternative vote, the second preferences of eliminated candidates may be counted to ensure that one candidate has a majority *or*, as happens in France, a second (or run-off) ballot may be held between the two highest placed candidates. *Plurality-rule* systems are the crudest electoral systems, and award seats to the candidates with the most votes (which may well be less than a majority).

This classification of proportional, majoritarian and plurality systems refers only to the electoral formula used in each case, that is, the principle behind translating votes into seats. However, the impact of all these systems is decisively affected by the district magnitude (or 'size' of the constituency). Under simple plurality-rule, elections take place in single-member constituencies, but it is also possible, as in Japan, to combine plurality rule with multi-member constituencies. Majoritarian systems operate with single-member constituencies. By contrast, proportional systems normally operate with multi-member constituencies. It is possible to combine single-member constituencies with proportionality – as in the German 'additional member system' – though such systems involve two sets of representatives being elected by different methods. Plurality, majoritarian and proportional rule systems obviously affect the way in which voters make their choices. In plurality rule systems voters are pushed towards choosing a government, and the system encourages two-party competition, although it is also compatible with long periods of dominance by one party. Plurality rule is criticized for under-representing minority parties which may be dramatically under-represented if their candidates usually come second or third in most constituencies. 'The winner takes all' is the logic of simple plurality rule. Majoritarian systems also push voters into choosing a government, but at least with their first-preference vote (or in the first ballot vote) they can safely vote for their most preferred candidate or party, even if they stand little prospect of being elected. Proportional systems, by contrast, normally encourage voters to express their authentic electoral preferences, and seek to ensure that the relevant assembly roughly mirrors popular preferences. They are therefore more likely to lead to multi-party systems.

Proportional systems differ in the manner and extent in which they achieve proportionality. No system achieves perfect proportionality and in real-world cases the number of parties (or candidates) winning seats is less than the number of parties (or candidates) winning votes. Proportionality is radically affected by whether or not thresholds exist (for instance, requiring parties or candidates to obtain a minimum of 5% of the vote before being assured representation); by the magnitudes of electoral districts; and by the mathematical formulae used for the allocation of seats (examples of which include the d'Hondt, Hagenbach-Bischoff and Sainte-Laguë methods) which vary considerably in the extent to which they help large or small parties. The closest approximation to proportionality is achieved through having an entire country vote as a single district, without thresholds, and awarding percentage shares of seats directly in proportion to percentage shares of votes won by parties (with 'rounding off' to allow for the fact that legislators cannot be found in the form of decimal points).

The most basic division between proportional systems is that between list systems, which aim to ensure the proportional representation of parties, and the single transferable vote (STV), which aims to ensure that voters have greater choosing power than political parties and can express their preferences across candidates. The most extreme party list systems leave the rank ordering of candidates for a given party entirely in the hands of the party: so if you vote for party A you must accept party A's slate of candidates in the order it prefers. However, in practice most proportional list systems give voters some degree of choice, enabling them, in Switzerland for example, to vote for candidates from more than one party list (*panachage*). The single transferable vote (STV), by contrast, empowers voters to rank order their preferences across candidates (ordering them 1, 2, 3 ...n on their ballot papers). Candidates stand in multi-member constituencies, and to be elected must obtain a quota, which is given by the Droop formula, that is,

$$\left\{ \frac{V}{(S+1)} + 1 \right\}$$

where V is the total number of valid votes cast and S is the total number of seats to be filled. A candidate who obtains more than the quota after first-preference votes are counted is declared elected, and her or his 'surplus' votes are then transferred to other candidates, according to the voters' second-preferences. If no other candidates are elected the bottom-placed candidate is eliminated the the second-preferences of his or her voters are distributed. These procedures, or counts, continue until the appropriate number of seats have been filled. STV enables voters to choose across parties, and to discriminate between candidates of the same parties. Plurality, majoritarian and proportional systems all have their exponents and critics. Plurality and majoritarian systems are defended on the ground that they produce strong and accountable governments, and, it is

claimed that voters can identify who is likely to form a government. They are criticized for giving power to parties which actually lack majority support and under-representing opposition and minority parties; and are condemned as especially inappropriate in ethnically or deeply divided societies. Proportional systems are defended on the grounds that they produce fair outcomes which more accurately express popular preferences. They are criticized for allegedly leading to fragmentation of the party system and for encouraging multi-party coalition government.

Proportional systems have been chosen by most of the new democracies established since World War II: STV has not proven as popular as party-list systems, because, after all, it is usually political parties which devise and implement new electoral systems.

Plurality rule is used in countries like the UK and, with the exception of Japan, only by countries which were once governed by the British empire like Canada, India and the USA. All the member-states of the European Community, except the UK, use proportional systems. There also appears to be a general trend across many democracies to converge on a version of the German 'additional member system' which combines some of the features of single-member constituencies found under plurality and majoritarian systems with the proportionality of list systems. The political consequences of electoral laws remain a subject of heated controversy among politicians and political scientists although it is usually more difficult to engage the general public in the more arcane aspects of electoral studies. **BO'L**

See also consociationalism; democracy; party system; representative government.

Further reading A.M. Carstairs *A Short History of Electoral Systems in Western Europe;* D.W. Rae *The Political Consequences of Electoral Laws;* R. Taagepeera and M. Schugart, *Votes and Seats.*

ELECTRICITY

Electricity (from Greek *electron*, 'amber';

the rubbing of which causes electrostatic phenomena: see below) is the generic term used to describe the science of electrical conduction, attraction and repulsion, **electromagnetics** and other electrical phenomena. Although electrical sparks were being studied as early as the 1700s, electricity as a major science has only been under way for just over a century. In this relatively short time electricity utilization has spread epidemically.

The earliest known reference to an electrical phenomenon was to that of electrical attraction by the ancient Greeks, who noted that a piece of amber when rubbed would attract light objects such as leaves or straw. The Greeks believed that amber contained some magical power by which it attracted objects and it was not until the 17th century that a more scientific explanation was produced. In 1600, William Gilbert published a paper giving details about magnetism and electrical attraction. Later, in 1670, a German, Otto Van Guericke, charged a sulphur ball causing electrical sparks to be produced and verifying that opposite charges attract. In 1729, Stephen Gray discovered that the charge could be transferred from one body to another by connecting it with a conductor, usually metallic, but could not be transferred when using an insulated connection, usually non-metallic. Thus electric conduction was discovered.

Up to this time, the only source of electricity was the friction generator, where a body was rubbed to produce an electrical charge on it. However, in 1800 Alessandro Volta invented the **battery**, a source of electricity that did not require more rubbing to recharge. The battery produced electricity by chemical action between two metals and a liquid. Volta also noted that by stacking the batteries he could produce enough electric charge to cause sparks. The battery also enabled a continuous electric current to flow, compared with the momentary currents produced when friction generators discharged. An electric current was determined to be the movement of charge analogous to the flow of water in a pipe, and electric voltage was considered the 'pressure' required to cause the current to flow.

The advent of continuous current sources enabled measurement of electric current and voltage, and led to the **circuit theory** of today. The first step was Ohm's Law which related the current and voltage to the resistance of the conductor. In 1820, Hans Oersted discovered that an electric current produced a magnetic field and in 1831, Michael Faraday showed that a magnetic field can produce an electric current. This was the beginning of electromagnetism, which united the previously separate theories of electrical and magnetic phenomena.

Practical applications for electricity soon began. The incandescent light bulb had been produced by Thomas Edison and the beginnings of an electric power network to supply the new electric street lamps was under way by the 1880s. Electric telegraphy was started around the 1840s and the following introduction of the telephone in the late 1870s heralded the start of the modern communications era.

The theory of electricity progressed rapidly during the 19th century and culminated with James Maxwell's electromagnetic theory. This theory, among other ideas, predicted that electricity could be transmitted without the use of wires. This so called 'wireless electricity' was shown to exist by Heinrich Hertz in Germany, and is now known as radio.

However advanced the theory had become by this time, there were still several observable electrical effects that the theories could neither explain nor predict. This was to alter following the discovery of the electron by J.J. Thomson in 1897, and the classification of the electron as a fundamental charged particle. The electron was shown to be negatively charged and an electric current was subsequently thought of as being electrons in motion through a conductor. After this discovery, **electronic** devices which used the properties of the electron appeared in rapid succession, such as the diode and a later derivative the triode.

The discovery of the electron produced great changes in the way human beings studied the materials and interactions of the materials they knew of. The realization that **quantum theory** provided an explanation of those phenomena where classical theory failed, hastened the age of quantum mechanics and with it the semiconductor age (see **semiconductor device theory**). Semiconducting materials were shown to have unique electrical properties and in particular allowed the manufacture of reliable electronic devices, such as the transistor.

Transistors and other electronic devices marked the beginning of the **computer** age, as digital logic circuits were made which could perform arithmetic functions or make simple decisions. The first electronic calculators were produced around the time of World War II, and following the invention of integrated circuit techniques, producing silicon 'chips', the first microcomputer was produced in the mid-1970s. **AC**

ELECTROLYSIS

Electrolysis (New Latin *electricus*, 'like amber' and Greek *luein*, 'to loosen') is the chemical change produced in an electrolyte by an electric current. Generally an electrolyte is a solution in water of certain salts, for example, common salt, sodium chloride, dissolved in water is an electrolyte. For instance, aluminium is produced from ore by electrolysis using carbon electrodes.

Electrolysis is a redox (REDuction/ OXidation) process where an atom or molecule loses electrons to another atom or molecule. When an electric current is passed through an electrolyte the positively charged ions in the solution are attracted towards the cathode (the negative electrode) while the negatively charged ions in solution are attracted towards the anode (the positive electrode). On reaching the electrodes the ions acquire or lose charges and may be deposited or appear as gas from the solution and form elements or similar compounds. An example of this is a solution of Copper Chloride (CuC_{12}) which when subjected to electrolysis forms copper and chlorine gas.

Electrolysis is the basis of electroplating in which a thin layer of valuable metal is deposited upon cheaper and less valuable metal. Chromium plating on steel is accomplished by first depositing a thin layer of copper by electrolysis and then a more substantial layer of chromium. In this way the component receives a cohesive non-corroding polished surface. By con-

trast galvanized steel is produced by dipping steel into molten zinc – not by electrolysis.

In certain chemical processes molten metal may be used as an electrolyte. **AA**

ELECTROMAGNETISM

This force has long been familiar to humankind. Possibly the first to learn about its properties were the Chinese, who discovered that a magnetized needle always points north. Later, static electricity and electric sparks fascinated a generation, and the discovery of current electricity produced primitive electric motors. It soon became obvious that electricity and magnetism were inextricably linked; a moving charge, or current, creates a magnetic field, and moving charges can be deflected with the use of magnets.

In the late 19th century, James Maxwell unified all these phenomena in four equations, known as Maxwell's equations, which described the entire gamut of electricity and magnetism, and moreover, showed that light, infrared radiation, ultraviolet radiation, radiowaves and x-rays are all exactly the same kind of waves, differing only in wavelength. They are electromagnetic waves, composed of an electric and a magnetic wave oscillating at right angles to each other. Maxwell's equations predicted the speed of light from other well known constants. This triumphant theory was perhaps the first example of the unification of forces, showing that electricity and magnetism are merely different aspects of the same force. Unification of all known forces is one of the ultimate aims of 20th-century physics.

There 's an asymmetry in the equations, due to the non-existence of a magnetic monopole. Positive and negative electric charges may exist on their own, but we never see the north end of a magnet without the south end. If a magnet is broken in two, it merely forms two new north and south poles in the middle, so that one end never exists without the other. However, some modern theories suggest that magnetic monopoles may exist, and so the magnetic monopole term is sometimes included in the equations.

We now believe that the electromagnetic force operates by exchange of photons – the photon is the field carrier for the electromagnetic force. Current theories suggest that, just as electricity and magnetism may be unified as the electromagnetic interaction, so may the weak force and the electromagnetic force, as the electroweak interaction. The weak interaction has the Z and W **bosons** as its field carriers. At very high energies, such as those produced in particle accelerators, the photon and the Z boson look very similar.

Electromagnetic phenomena pervade our lives. All electrical apparatus, static electricity, magnets, motors, dynamos and natural phenomena such as lightning may be understood by the use of Maxwell's equations. **JJ**

ELECTRONIC MUSIC

As its name implies, electronic **music** is generated not by human performers, but by electrical impulses. At first it was recorded on disc or tape, but modern machines such as the computer and synthesizer now produce it to order, and so allow an element of 'live' performance. Such machines also allow techniques to be used which are not so readily available to composers using human performers: instantly slowing the music down or speeding it up, playing it backwards, mixing, delaying or enhancing reverberation, and above all modulating the signal. The synthesizer alters the frequency of the generated sound at the operator's will, and the computer digitalizes instructions for sound-generation in the same way as it does any other input, creating information which can then be processed in any way the operator chooses.

The initial sounds on which electronic methods are used can be generated either as 'white noise' (pure signal from a tone generator), or by 'sampling'. In sampling, a single sound from any source (instrument, natural sound, voice) is digitally recorded, fed into the computer and modulated in the normal way. Computers can thus mimic any sound the operator chooses, from symphony orchestras to skylarks and can subject them to every conceivable kind of electronic alteration. Music can be pro-

grammed to be in 'real time', that is with the computer imitating the nuances and inflexions a live human performer might employ; or it can be 'step-time composition', using strict rhythmic accuracy based on equal time-divisions of the computer clock. The composer Iannis Xenakis invented what he called 'stochastic music', building up huge structures from tiny individual units whose organization depended on (often computer-generated) mathematical sequences.

Electronic methods, and electronic instruments, are standard in modern **rock** and **pop**. They are vital to composers of film, radio and television music. But apart from the *ondes martenot* (whose sound is a pure, clear squeal like that of a musical saw) few electronic instruments have found their way into any but the most **avant-garde** art music, and electronic techniques of composition are still generally resisted in favour of more traditional methods. The avant-garde minority, however, is vigorous. Several composers of note have consistently produced electronic works, either 'composing' them on tape in the studio (as Milton Babbitt, John Cage, Herbert Eimert and other pioneers used to do) or using synthesizers and sound mixers to blend with 'orthodox' performers in live concerts (as Pierre Boulez and Karlheinz Stockhausen do). Others who use electronic techniques as part of a wider repertoire include such key names as Luciano Berio, Györgi Ligeti, Henri Pousseur and Xenakis. But because the electronics industry moves ahead so far so fast, the whole field remains more suited to constant experiment than to the production of established masterworks, and raises the issue of whether machines, however sophisticated, can ever rival the emotional power generated by human performers making natural sounds. **KMcL**

Further reading P. Griffiths, *A Guide to Electronic Music.*

ELECTRONICS

Electronics is the study of devices in which the movement of electrons is controlled, usually within a vacuum or semiconducting material. An electron (Greek, *electron* 'amber') is the fundamental particle of electrical charge and gives rise to an electric current when the electrons are set in motion travelling through a material.

Electronics is one of the fastest growing areas of electrical science and engineering and has a tremendous impact on our everyday lives, from the television sets we watch at home to the computers we use at work. The formal discovery of the electron in 1897 by J.J. Thomson in Britain, and its classification as a charged particle, have led to greater understanding of all materials around us, by stimulating research which led to the formalization of **quantum theory**. Prior to Thomson's work, there was a general acceptance that a fundamental unit of electric charge existed, originating from work with **electrolysis** and cathode rays. Modern cathode ray tubes are used to provide the picture in television sets.

The first commercial electronic device was Edison's diode, or thermionic valve, discovered in 1880 through Edison's work with incandescent light bulbs. At the time, the electron had still not been 'discovered' and explained, though Edison later realized that this was what caused his diode to function. The light bulbs, which contained a filament of wire enclosed in a vacuum, were found to conduct electricity from the filament, through the vacuum, to another wire suspended in the vacuum and connected to the positive end of the filament. The 'Edison effect', as it became known, permitted current to flow in one direction only, from the filament to the wire, and was to find use in early radio receivers (see **radio transmission**).

The next major development in electronics was an extension of the diode, by Lee De Forest; it was called a triode as it had three pieces of wire in it. De Forest proved that a triode could be used as an amplifier, that is, it received weak radio signals, boosted them electronically and output a much stronger reproduction of the input signal. This greatly improved the quality of radio receivers.

The early electronic devices, although successful in their own right, were handicapped primarily by unreliability and fragile construction. With the advent of semiconductor devices, which in most cases had greatly improved reliability and performance, the electronics explosion of the post World War II period began. The first significant semiconductor electronic device was the transistor, or 'transfer resistor', which was developed, along with the theory of **semiconductor devices**, to be a semiconductor 'copy' of a triode. The transistor functioned as a very good amplifier and was, and still is, used in millions of radio sets.

As the manufacturing of semiconductor devices was improved and refined, miniaturization of transistors became possible and a new era of electronics began: **microelectronics**. Microelectronics has permitted the construction of electronic circuits having tens of thousands of transistors in pieces of semiconducting material no larger than a fingernail. Technology such as this has allowed previously obscure areas of engineering and science such as digital logic to be physically realized, and **computers** today all use microelectronic circuitry. **AC**

ELIMINATIVISM

Eliminativists, in **philosophy**, think that we should abandon certain ontological claims, that we should eliminate certain claims from our account of what exists.

Superstitious people used to make the ontological claim that witches exist. Most people today have eliminated the claim that witches exist from their theory of what reality contains. They are eliminativists about witches. There are more controversial versions of eliminatism. Roughly put, materialists believe that everything is physical. Most materialists believe that mental things do exist, that reality contains mental things, merely claiming that every mental thing is physical. Eliminativist materialists also hold that everything is physical. They also deny that the mental could be physical. So, they infer that there are no mental things: there are no minds, plans or intentions. We should eliminate the claim that mental things exist from our theory of what reality contains. We should be eliminativists about the mental. **AJ**

See also materialism.

Further reading P. Churchland, *A Neurocomputational Perspective; Matter and Consciousness.*

EMBOURGEOISEMENT THESIS

The embourgeoisement (French, 'making middle class') thesis was a popular **economic** argument in the UK in the 1950s and 1960s. It asserted that the working class in modern capitalist societies have adopted the lifestyle and political attitudes of the middle class. Contrasts were drawn, for example, between the conditions of the working classes in the UK in the 1930s and their situation after 1950. It was assumed that the establishment of the welfare state, almost full employment, actual improvements in living standards, and the mass production of consumer goods had eliminated the material and cultural differences between the classes. This increased affluence was supposed to have resulted in a decline in working-class support for radical political movements, which was believed to have contributed to the success of the Conservative party during this period.

Some sociological studies seemed to support the embourgeoisement thesis, but the most direct response to the thesis was the Affluent Worker Studies by Goldthorpe and Lockwood which refuted it by reference to worker attitudes. Other studies suggested that a still greater number of people did not enjoy a middle-class standard of living. **DA**

See also bourgeoisie; class; culture; occupation; profession; social mobility; social stratification.

Further reading J.H. Goldthorpe, D. Lockwood, F. Bechhofer and J. Platt, *The Affluent Worker: Industrial Attitudes and Behaviour; The Affluent Worker: Political Attitudes and Behaviour; The Affluent Worker in the Class Structure.*

EMBRYOLOGY

Embryology (from Greek *bruon*, 'swelling' + ology) is the study of the growth and development of the embryo of an animal. In the 4th century BCE, Aristotle hypothe-sized that the embryo was formed by gradual assembly from menstrual fluid, but little investigative work was done until the 17th century with the rise of **anatomy**. René Descartes dissected embryos and noted elements of their structure, and William Harvey studied the embryos of chicks and deer and formulated his hypothesis that the egg is the origin of the embryo in all living things. Also common at this time was the ideas of preformation, in which the precursor of the embryo is a miniature adult called the homunculus, and epigenesis, where the environment in which the embryo is housed shapes its development.

The 18th-century German anatomist Caspar Wolff set the ball rolling for modern embryology with his observation that undifferentiated material became specialized as the embryo developed. Karl von Baer (1792–1876) compared the development of vertebrate embryos and noted that the embryos resembled each other very closely, so that embryonic reptiles could hardly be distinguished from those of bird or mammals. This stimulated the idea, popular in the 19th century, that 'ontogeny recapitulates phylogeny': in other words that a developing embryo passes through the forms of its evolutionary ancestors until it reaches the shape of its parent. It is true that closeness of evolutionary relationship is reflected in embryological development and embryology is important in the study of **phylogeny**. Modern embryology is concerned with the control of cell differentiation and the development of the embryo from the zygote (the single-celled product of the fusion of the sperm and egg) to the developed offspring. **RB**

See also developmental biology; germ layer theory; germ plasm; ovism.

Further reading Salvador Luria, *A View of Life.*

EMERGENCE

Emergence, in the **life sciences**, is the doctrine that a complex of species or structure can arise as part of **evolution** without being predictable from preceding conditions. The idea arose because of the contradiction between the predicted course of evolution and the picture presented by the actual fossil record. Essentially, evolution is not a smooth progression from less to more highly adapted, but is punctuated by huge leaps in complexity, such as the appearance of nucleated cells. Although it is very unlikely that such events could have occurred by the conventional mechanisms of variation and **natural selection**, it is frequently assumed that they must have done so. It is also possible that the fossil record is incomplete, though this seems unlikely due to accurate radioisotopic dating techniques now available. The subject of emergence is recurrent in 20th-century scientific philosophy where it is conceptually linked to organistic thinking as a result of the perceived levels of organization it produces in evolution, but has had little impact on the doctrines of Neo-**Darwinism**. **RB**

EMOTIONS

It is fairly clear what 'emotions' (from Latin *emovere*, 'to move out') mean in English: the inward experience of strong feeling, often accompanied by physiological changes. However, further investigation presents difficulties. How should emotions be labelled? How do similar emotions (for example anger and frustration) differ from each other? How do emotions relate to the inner states of those who experience them?

Psychologists study the way unreal or unrealistic expectations of an event produce inappropriate emotions or responses. In classical **behaviourism**, there is a stimulus response model. An external event leads directly to an emotional response, a result of previous conditioning. In this theory, thinking does not enter the interaction; the stimulus is seen as always coming from outside and meaning is rejected.

From the perspective of **cognitive therapy**, events with special meaning determine emotional responses. Meaning is encased in an image or thought. Reports of observations or feelings will always be attached to a thought. This being the case, it is possible to ask what kind of thoughts

lead to which emotions. Differing emotional situations lead to the same emotional response leading to generalizations.

In **psychoanalysis** an internal stimulus occurs: an impulse or unconscious wish which is generally unacceptable and whose emergence imposes a threat. If the person is unable to ward off the taboo impulse, they will experience the emotions of guilt or anxiety. The stimulus is internal and unconscious and the emphasis is on unconscious meaning. For example, in the **Oedipus complex** the boy reacts to the sight of his mother (stimulus) with an unconscious sexual impulse towards her. The wish threatens to break into the conscious and the boy feels anxious because of possible punishment (the father).

In **anthropology**, the study of emotions in other societies is complicated by the task of translating languages and concepts. It is an area closely related to recent concerns in varying concepts about **personhood**. Both have received attention and have raised several issues for consideration.

Conventionally, as in the behaviourist model described above, emotions have been seen as separate from reason and logic. Careful consideration, however, reveals that emotions often overlap with value-related or reasonable conduct. For instance, passion may be used instrumentally in speech to make some kind of gain. In fact, the distinction between reason and emotion depends on the Cartesian idea of there being a separation of the mind and body. This idea locates the mind as the seat of rational thought and the body as the location of emotions. In contradiction to this are the views of, for example, the Taita people of Kenya. Their beliefs relate the head as being equivalent to the mind, the liver as the seat of the will and the heart as associated with emotions and the mystical capacity to affect others through these emotions.

Anthropological perspectives on emotions have ranged from the study of social or public display of emotions to a more psychological approach attempting to find what it is that defines human nature. Some anthropologists interpret public displays of emotions, such as those at funerals, as more of a socially learned obligation than an indication of the person's inner state. Related to this theme is the way social expectations about emotional behaviours hinge on the position of the person in society, in terms of age, gender, status, etc. and how this varies for different contexts.

Other anthropologists, under the influence of Sigmund Freud's psychoanalytic theories, have interpreted emotional experiences and displays as a safety valve to discharge disturbances of various kinds. This view has been criticized for reducing all other dimensions in society to this supposed primary cause, and it also depends on the idea that each person is an autonomous individual who subjectively feels emotions. In other societies, to impose such an assumption is possibly to distort their world-views. Traditional Hindu ideas about emotions, for example, derive from the theory of *rasa* ('juice', 'extract', 'flavour'). This describes emotions in terms of social situations or practices instead of in terms of individual feelings. The metaphor of taste and nourishment is widely used rather than the hydraulic metaphor (of discharging or letting off steam) familiar in the West.

Historical overviews have provided further insights into varying senses, concepts and behaviours concerning emotions. The current understanding of fear as equivalent to dread, terror and horror, and as an emotion that is unpredictable, uncontrollable and unknowable, is very different from the 19th-century usage embodying the idea of respect and reverence, as, for instance, in the fear of God. Each categorization reflects on the social and cultural fabric of its times.

Even though emotional states, terms and behaviours may vary widely, anthropologists generally agree that there is a basic commonality of experiences that defines us all as sentient human beings. An anthropology of emotions, to the extents possible, is valuable in that it affords an insight into how people interpret visible and unseen states and how this relates to the social and cultural context, while compelling one to review our own assumptions on what is 'natural' about emotions or about the person. **AJ MJ RK**

See also death; interpretative anthropology; rationality; ritual; self.

Further reading M. Arnold, *Emotion and Personality*; Owen Lynch, *Divine Passions*; Catherine Lutz and Lila Abu-Lughod, *Language and the Politics of Emotion*; David Parkin, *Towards an Apprehension of Fear*.

EMOTIVISM

Emotivism is the view, in **philosophy**, that when one makes a moral judgement, one is expressing an emotional reaction to the object of the judgement. So when I say 'the Nazis were evil', I am expressing my feelings of revulsion towards them by using the word 'evil' and this is the only function of that word. Emotivism denies that by saying the Nazis were evil I give some reason for my feeling of revulsion towards them. Rather, to say that the Nazis are evil is just to express my revulsion.

Prescriptivism is a descendent of emotivism. It agrees that moral judgements express emotional reactions of approval and disapproval, but also claims that moral terms do latch onto certain nonmoral features of the thing in question, features which explain my reaction. **AJ**

See also descriptivism and prescriptivism; ethical relativism; fact and value.

Further reading A.J. Ayer, *Language Truth and Logic*; C. Stevenson, *Facts and Values*.

EMPIRICISM

Empiricism (from Greek *empeirein*, 'to experience'), in **philosophy**, is the doctrine that all knowledge is derived from experience. Before one has any experience, before one perceives or introspects, one has no knowledge at all. There are different versions of empiricism, however. We can get an understanding of two of them by considering what different empiricists have meant by the phrase 'is derived from'. Some empiricists have held that all knowledge causally originates from and is justified by experience. Others have merely held that all knowledge is justified by experience.

Consider the first version. Some empiricists have claimed that all ideas causally derive from experience and, therefore, that before one has any experiences one has no ideas. Before it has any experiences, the mind is a *tabula rasa*, a white sheet devoid of any ideas, upon which experience has yet to leave its mark. There are no innate ideas, that is, ideas which the mind possesses before it first has experiences.

However, one can hardly have beliefs before one has any ideas or concepts, and it is only beliefs which may attain the status of knowledge. So if possessing ideas causally depends upon having experiences, possessing beliefs and, therefore, knowledge also causally depends upon having experiences. Experience does not merely justify one's knowledge claims, but is also causally necessary for possessing the beliefs which may attain the status of knowledge.

The first version of empiricism, with its claim that all ideas causally derive from experience is vulnerable to the objection that it is difficult to see how all of the ideas or concepts we possess could causally derive from experience. Consider the concept of necessity, the idea that such and such must be the case. It is difficult to see how the idea that things must be a certain way could be derived from one's sensory or introspective experience of how things actually are.

The second version of empiricism avoids this objection. It does not claim that all ideas originate from experience. It can thus allow that the mind has innate ideas, and even innate beliefs. But, it insists, all knowledge is justified by experience, so no belief can count as knowledge until it has been justified by experience. So the second version of empiricism holds that all knowledge is justified by experience, but is neutral on the question of whether all ideas and beliefs causally depend upon experience. It can thus allow that we have ideas and beliefs before we have any experiences, that we have innate ideas and beliefs. **AJ**

See also innate ideas; rationalism.

Further reading A.J. Ayer, *Language Truth and Logic*; R.S. Woolhouse, *The Empiricists*.

ENCODE/DECODE

Within **media** studies the encode/decode couplet is used in two related but separable ways. First, it refers to the twin *processes* by which producers of media texts can use a communicative **code** to embody, or *encode*, a text with specific meanings, and by which **audiences** interpret or *decode* that text. But second it refers to a particular approach within media studies to the difficult question of the relationship between text and audience.

Implicit within certain media perspectives – for instance much 'effects' theory and some crude **Marxism** – is the idea that media messages can be precise and 'anchored', and that furthermore audiences will understand the message in accordance with the encoder's specific aims. For such Marxists this process is a central aspect of the generation of a **dominant ideology**. The neglect, though, of the audience's role has prompted a renewed interest in how people relate to, act upon and thus decode texts.

At the core of this critque is the idea that media text and its constituent parts is polysemic. That is, while meaning is in some senses constrained – television news is not presented in cartoon form, for example – it still can be understood in multiple ways. David Morley has observed how decoding will depend at least in part on socioeconomic identity of the decoders; gender, class and race have attracted particular interest in this context.

Stuart Hall's revised Gramscian Marxism, rejecting the assertion that the mass media simply encode a dominant ideology, explores the complexity of both encoding and decoding. In his analysis, encodings and decodings can be in line with dominant ideology but they can also negotiate or oppose that ideology. **NC**

Further reading S. Hall et al (eds.), *Culture, Media and Language*, Stuart Hall's chapter on 'Encoding/Decoding'.

ENCYCLOPEDISTS

The Encyclopedists were a group of French intellectuals who collaborated, between 1751 and 1776, in the production of the *Encyclopedia* edited by Denis Diderot. They believed that human beings were enchained by ignorance and superstition, and that the way to free them was to provide them with true knowledge. The 35-volume *Encyclopedia* was intended to be a compendium of all human knowledge up to that point, a rational survey of existence excluding opinion and dogma of every kind. Apart from Diderot himself, and his assistant d'Alembert, the principal Encyclopedists were Buffon, Montesquieu, Rousseau, Turgot and Voltaire. **KMcL**

See also Enlightenment.

ENDOCRINOLOGY

Endocrinology (Greek *endo*, 'inside', *krino*, 'sift' + ology), in the **life sciences**, is the study of the systems of internal body secretions, which are collectively termed hormones. These chemical messenger substances are secreted into the blood by endocrine glands and circulate throughout the bloodstream; where they come into contact with tissues which are sensitized to them (target organs) they produce an effect. A wide range of functions is under a degree of hormonal control, from menstruation to lactation and from thirst to the formation of urine. Some hormones act on endocrine glands so that the system may be partly self-regulating. Other endocrine systems are regulated by negative feedback, in which hormone secretion is inhibited by some product of the changes which the hormone initiates.

The first hormone, adrenaline, was isolated by the Japanese chemist Jokiche Takamine (1854–1922), after it had been observed that extracts of the adrenal gland could raise blood pressure. As the 20th century has progressed many other hormones have been discovered, often during the course of investigations into human disorders. Most important of all was the discovery of insulin in 1921 by the Canadian physician Frederick Banting. Insulin is a hormone that plays a central role in the control of sugar metabolism; lack of insulin results in diabetes mellitus, a disease which was usually fatal before insulin replacement was possible. Today, insulin and many other hormones, such as human growth hormone and steroid hormones, can be synthesized artificially and used in medicine and research. Contraceptive pills are based on the steroid sex hormones progesterone and oestrogen. **RB**

See also homeostasis; metabolism; phenology; synergism; tropism.

Further reading Mac Hadley, *Endocrinology*.

ENLIGHTENMENT

The Enlightenment is the blanket term for one of the dominant movements in 18th-century, European intellectual activity. Its roots can be traced back earlier, to the thinking behind the Reformation in the 16th century and **humanism**, the rise of 'true' **science** prefigured by such figures as Paracelsus and carried on by Francis Bacon, Robert Boyle (author of *The Sceptical Chemist*), Galileo, Newton and others, and the writings of Descartes and Pascal. Its prime impulse was in pre-Revolutionary France, in the work of such people as Buffon, Condorcet, Diderot (whose *Encyclopedia* was its first monument), Montesquieu, Rousseau and Voltaire. The basic premises of the Enlightenment were liberal, pro-science, anti-superstition, and that the state was a proper vehicle for improvement of the human condition. Its thinkers – a roll of honour in 18th-century thought and writing, including Benjamin Franklin, Edward Gibbon, Herder, David Hume, Thomas Jefferson, Kant, Lessing and Adam Smith – took it as self-evident that the human race had for too long been intellectually shackled. People's habits of thinking were based on irrationality, polluted by religious dogma, superstition, an overadherence to historical predecent and irrelevant tradition and that the way to escape from this, to move forward, was to seek for true knowledge in every sphere of life, to establish the truth and build on it. People's minds were, literally, to be 'enlightened': freed from murk.

Along with the contemporaneous Industrial Revolution (from which it obtained much inspiration and ammunition), the Enlightenment occasioned the profoundest change in the mind-set of the largest number of people in Europe since the advent of **Christianity** itself. Its basic principles and objectives, which became the matrix of the modern age, led to a ferment of activity in politics (ranging from the Declaration of Independence to Equality and the abolition of slavery) and in the scientific work of such people as Darwin, James Hutton and Joseph Priestley. It led to a new self-confidence (or self-importance) in European ideas about **civilization**, and the need to spread such ideas to 'less-favoured' peoples throughout the world. In the **arts** it resulted in the view that **literature**, **music**, **painting** and **theatre** were tools for the moral and social improvement of humankind, and from there to expressive and individually-assertive experimentation of all kinds, most notably the **Stürm und Drang** and **Romantic** movements which followed it. **KMcL**

Further reading J. Redwood, *Reason, Ridicule and Religion: the Age of Enlightenment in England*; B. Willey, *The Eighteenth-century Background*.

ENTOMOLOGY

Entomology (from Greek *entomon*, 'cut up', 'segmented' + ology) is the biological study of insects, by far the most numerous and most widespread class of animals. Aristotle was an early entomologist, noting that the body of an insect is divided into three segments. The Italian naturalist Ulisse Aldrovandi revived interest in entomology at the beginning of the 17th century, further stimulated by the advent of the microscope which was immediately put to use by entomologists. In the 17th century, Marcello Malpighi, one of the first microscopists, carried out pioneering investigations of insect neuroanatomy and Jan Swammerdam described the microscopic anatomy and life histories of a great range of insects and attempted to classify them. Modern entomology continues to involve a large amount of traditional **taxonomy** as new species are described continuously. Pest biology is an important area of entomology since many important pests are insects (for example, aphids) and many insects are important biological control agents (for example, ladybirds eat aphids).

Many insect groups undergo metamorphosis between larval and adult stages (for example, caterpillar to butterfly) and are thus of great interest in **developmental biology**. **RB**

See also anatomy; biological control; sociobiology.

ENTROPY

Today, entropy (Greek, 'transformation') can be thought of in three ways. It is intimately related to the fact that naturally occurring processes have a direction. On a microscopic level, it is related to the number of ways in which a system can arrange itself. And in modern-day communication theory, it is a measure of information.

The first aspect of entropy is concerned with the second law of **thermodynamics**. This law has been stated in various forms, but it can be summarized by saying that nothing ever works with perfect efficiency. Any engine, motor or other system which converts energy from one form to another will not convert 100 per cent of the energy. Some will be lost by friction, or heat loss, or other forms of wastage. Examples of such systems are power stations (converting chemical energy in fuel to electrical energy), living creatures and petrol engines. The entropy change of such a system is defined as being equal to the energy change divided by the temperature of the system.

All systems attempt to maximize their entropy. Entropy should not be confused with energy; the energy of the world is constant, but the entropy tends towards a maximum value.

On a microscopic scale, entropy is a measure of the number of ways that a system can arrange itself. This statement implies **quantum** mechanics; only a system with a finite number of available 'positions' or energies for the particles to occupy can have a finite number of arrangements of the particles.

To see why entropy tends towards a maximum, consider several particles in a box. We can arrange them so that they are all in a corner, or more evenly distributed around the box. There are far more ways to arrange them so that they are evenly distributed. This makes sense; if we put some gas into a box, it is unlikely to condense in a corner, but spreads out to fill the box. The entropy of the disordered, evenly distributed arrangement is much higher than an orderly bunching of particles in a corner, thus the system finds the state of highest entropy.

Entropy is a measure of disorder within a system. A system with all its particles neatly in one place is an ordered system, while one that has its particles randomly spread out is far more disordered.

Entropy may also be considered as a measure of information. If we know that all the particles are in the corner, we have considerable information about them. However, if they are spread out, all we know about a particular particle is that it is in the box somewhere! Paul Shannon has shown that entropy and the transmission of information are closely related.

The last quantity that entropy is closely linked with is the direction of time. Entropy always increases with time. Taken to its logical conclusion, this means that the universe is tending toward a state of maximum entropy. **JJ**

ENVIRONMENTAL ART see Earth Art

ENVIRONMENTALISM

Environmentalism (from Old French *environner*, 'to surround') is a term whose meaning has changed dramatically since 1970. Before that it was used in the **nature/culture** debate in **psychology** to identify the school of thought that believed the environment had a substantial effect on human personality and behaviour. Since 1970 it has been used to identify the broad argument that human societies should give a higher priority to the natural environment. This was not a wholly new argument, indeed a large part of the message had previously been advocated by the conservation movement, but it gained some new aspects and much greater salience. However, it is not enough to consider pre-and post-1970 meanings because the concept of environmentalism could only be meaningful in a large-scale society where society and Nature are alienated.

In small-scale societies, such as the groups of hunter-gatherers in which all humans lived until 10,000 years ago, long-term survival required that people lived off the fruits of Nature without destroying the plants and animals they depended on. Agricultural societies could support larger populations, often with large proportions of nobles and priests, but avoided major environmental problems, with the exception of the breakdown of irrigation systems in Mesopotamia. The major religions founded in such societies, notably **Hinduism** and **Buddhism**, advocated inner development and harmony with nature. Even the Judaeo-Christian tradition, which is often criticized by environmentalists for its belief that God had chosen mankind to have dominion over Nature, taught that we should act as God's stewards on Earth. In the Middle Ages, growing populations and increasing trade did begin to have some impact on the natural environment, but this was only a faint precursor of future developments.

In the 19th century, the Industrial Revolution in western Europe and the USA dramatically increased human impacts on the environment. The new economic doctrine of *laissez-faire* led to the pursuit of profit and a disregard of **pollution** and waste. Improved transport allowed a greater exploitation of distant resources where the interests of local people were often ignored. Large, industrial cities were built on an unprecedented scale and with equally unprecedented effects upon the environment. These cities stimulated both practical responses, such as pollution controls and sewage systems, and pioneer environmentalist ideas.

Three movements or schools of thought, developed in response to the upheavals of industrialization, were directly related to environmentalism. The most extreme was **Romanticism**, which advocated the spiritual benefits of contact with Nature, but in a way which seemed to be available only to a minority and which, unrealistically, left the cities out of account. An alternative, and perhaps more attractive to conservatives, was a revival of the concept of stewardship. More explicitly political was the concept of **utilitarianism**, a doctrine which sought to maximize pleasure and minimize pain, with implications for environmental policy, but with the limitation that all decisions were to be taken in human terms. In practice, the difficulty of measuring pleasure meant that demand was often used as an indicator, so utilitarianism was largely absorbed into the market economy.

The earliest practical effect of environmentalism was in the USA where the conservation movement was very influential in the development of the West, including the dedication of National Parks from the 1870s. However, conservation was defined as 'wise use' so it sanctioned some developments that more single-minded preservationists deplored. In the UK, the establishment of National Parks did not occur until after 1945, and the parks were given the role of promoting recreation as well as preservation, with powers hardly greater than those available to any planning authority. With the exception of controls over smoke and chemical emissions, early environmentalism mainly consisted of local reaction to particular activities.

The new environmentalism of the 1970s was increasingly holistic in content and global in coverage. Issues like the **population explosion**, nuclear hazards, whaling and resource shortages spread far beyond the local and seemed to require radical changes in values and priorities. New types of international pressure groups appeared, most notably Greenpeace and Friends of the Earth, initially in North America, but soon spreading to many countries. The first UN conference on Environmental Pollution was held in Stockholm in 1972 and the UN Environmental Programme was set up. In the 1980s **global warming** and ozone depletion were added to the environmentalists' agenda, and it became apparent that the atmosphere could only be stabilized by restricting energy and material use at levels that seem to require the reversal of industrialization. At the time of writing, few governments are prepared to consider anything but reducing the rate of growth of energy use.

As a political movement environmentalism aims to affect governmental decision-making – either directly by electing 'green' candidates or indirectly as a lobby group. Public awareness is now widespread, and the increased public concern caused by the accumulation of apparently impressive, but not always conclusive, scientific evidence on environmental matters has led to the proliferation of environmental organizations, and to some electoral successes for 'green' political parties – though these successes have been eroded by mainstream political parties. Significant international agreements, such as the Montreal Protocol, which aims to limit the production of substances which deplete the world's ozone layer, demonstrate the new level of international concern for environmental issues.

In the last few years of the 20th century, fully fledged green political philosophies are emerging, some of which claim that there is a distinctive green theory of value. 'Dark greens' argue that preserving the Earth's **ecosystem** for its own sake, not because it is beneficial to humans, should be at the centre of political activity. Some of them are known as Gaia theorists because they believe that the Earth (Gaia) will survive our adapatations of nature, but argue that we may not be able to survive the changes that the Earth will make in response to our interventions (see **Gaia hypothesis**). 'Light greens', by contrast, argue for environmentalist public policies because they are confident that they will ultimately benefit our species. Greens of all hues remain uncertain about whether they favour the creation of a powerful global government with the ability to enact the coercive measures required to enforce green public policies, or radically decentralized political communities as means of achieving their objectives. They have also not resolved whether or not they favour greater albeit sustainable economic growth, or a radical reduction in global consumption (population). They also remain understandably ambivalent about most of the achievements of Western **civilization**, as many green theorists appear to think that human organizations, like the state, and human cultural productions, like the positivistic sciences, have been catastrophic.

The seriousness of environmentalist arguments are often occluded by the proponents of 'green lifestyles' which can involve eccentric 'New Age' religions. **BO'L PS**

Further reading R. Eckersley, *Environmentalism and Political Theory: Toward an Ecocentric Approach*; J. Gibson, *Green Illusion: Critique of Modern Environmentalism*; R. Goodin, *Green Political Theory*; D. Pepper, *The Roots of Modern Environmentalism*; Theodore Roszak, *The Voice of the Earth: an Explanation of Ecopsychology.*

ENZYMES

Enzymes are proteins derived from living cells, the function of which is to mediate the chemical reactions which occur in the **metabolism** of living organisms. Enzymes perform this function by acting as catalysts; catalysts need not be made of protein, but enzymes make extremely efficient catalysts and are also very specific in that they will only catalyse certain reactions. Enzymes greatly increase the rate of chemical reactions which would often not proceed at all without catalysis. They achieve their function by providing a 'rendezvous' for the chemicals (called substrates) which are the starting point for the reaction. The enzyme binds the substrate(s) in such a way that the reaction can readily proceed; the chance of these conditions being met without the intervention of an enzyme are greatly reduced. This concept of enzyme function has been called the 'lock and key hypothesis'.

Enzymes are sensitive to their environment, particularly temperature and acidity, and will not function optimally if their environmental conditions are not tightly regulated, as they are within living cells and organisms. They are sensitive to such factors because they are composed largely of protein, which is a chain-like molecule. Protein is made from subunits (amino acids) which are linked in a specific order to form a chain which folds up in a pattern dependent upon the sequence of amino acids in the chain. This 3-dimensional structure is, as the term 'lock and key' suggests, essential to the function of the enzyme but is not rigid. Changes in temperature or in other conditions can cause shifts in the structure of the enzyme so that it can no longer bind its substrates. Substrates are bound in a binding site, and the range of structures which are bound is very limited because of the 3-dimensional shape of the binding site (analogous to a keyhole). This is the explanation for enzymes specificity, but chemicals with a molecular structure which is very similar to that of the substrate may also bind to the enzyme, sometimes more strongly than the substrate itself. This blocks the enzyme's function and is the mechanism by which many drugs and poisons work, modifying the metabolism of the substrate by blocking enzyme function. Studies of enzyme structure in 3-dimensions present the possibility of designing specific enzyme inhibitors for use as drugs; currently, most drugs are discovered by serendipity.

Enzyme-mediated reactions were first recognized by Eduard Buchner who, in 1897, showed that a cell-free extract of yeast could catalyse the fermentation which was previously thought to require the presence of living yeast cells. The first enzyme was purified as a crystal of protein in 1926, and all enzymes subsequently purified have been found to be based upon protein molecules. Enzymes, which are the product of the genes, are thus the mechanism by which the DNA controls the function of the organism; the direction taken by metabolism is dependant upon the enzymes present. **RB**

See also biochemistry; biotechnology; fermentation; pharmacology.

Further reading Robert Murray, *Biochemistry*; John Smith and Hywell Williams, *Drug Design*.

EPIC

Epic (Greek, 'formal utterance') is a narrative of events, usually of a mythic or heroic nature and often involving the supernatural. Most early epics are in verse and many stem from the **myths** and **legends** of the society in which they arose. The origins of such epics are in oral **literature**, and their verse forms and structures have traditional roots. Some epic cycles have no acknowledged author and many, for example those from Aztec and Inuit myth, or the cosmologies of Africa, Australasia and the ancient Middle East, remain inchoate and regional. Others are more ordered, but still anonymous. For instance, even the Hindu *Mahabharata*, the grandest to acquire 'literary' form, was said to have been assembled not by an author but by a legendary sage, Vyasa, who dictated it to the god Ganesa. There are epics, however, that do show the influence of a single, shaping mind, giving order and sequence to disparate traditional elements. Homer's *Iliad* and *Odyssey*, and the *Kalevala* (assembled by Zacharias Topelius in the 1820s) are outstanding examples.

Literary authors have quarried epics of all these kinds, or written epics of their own. Some outstanding examples include, Virgil's *Aeneid* (building complex historical and political allegory on a framework of half-traditional, half-invented myth), Milton's *Paradise Lost* (treating biblical myth in part-Homeric, part-allegorical style) and Camoens's *Lysiads* (a Portuguese national epic based on the voyages of Vasco da Gama). In more modern times, the epic manner has been used in prose, giving density to such novels as Tolstoy's *War and Peace* and Herman Melville's *Moby Dick*.

Mock-epics are an almost equally popular form. They use epic techniques to deal with subjects which are frivolous rather than grand, sometimes just for fun (as in the Sindbad stories in the *Arabian Nights*), sometimes with ironical or satirical purpose (for example, Alexander Pope's *The Rape of the Lock*). Mock-epics include such ancestors or precursors of the novel as Petronius' *Satyricon*, Cervantes' *Adventures of Don Quixote* and Rabelais' *Gargantua and Pantagruel*. The mock-epic style is common in Western fiction: Gogol's *Dead Souls*, Mark Twain's *Huckleberry Finn*, Proust's *Remembrance of Things Past*, James Joyce's *Ulysses*, Jaroslav Hašek's *The Good Soldier Švejk*, Thomas Mann's *Confessions of Felix Krull* and Joseph Heller's *Catch-22* all make individual, and selective, use of it. **KMcL**

EPIC THEATRE

Epic Theatre is a term used by theatre scholars to describe dramatic and theatrical practices originally associated with Brecht and Piscator. The idea is to combat audiences' tendencies to empathic reactions (such as were demanded by the theatre of **naturalism**). Brecht developed a range of strategies to achieve an **alienation** effect, whereby the audience remained aware of the processes of the theatrical event and were thus able to reflect on its intellectual and emotional implications as it happened, rather than be consumed by it. Very little contemporary dramaturgy and staging is unaffected in some way by Epic Theatre. **TRG SS**

See also drama; theatre.

Further reading J.L. Styan, *Modern Drama in Theory and Practice 3: Expressionism and Epic Theatre*; John Willett, (ed.), *Brecht on Theatre*; John Willett, *The Theatre of Erwin Piscator*.

EPICUREANISM

Epicureanism is named after Epicurus (341–270 BCE), a Greek aristocrat who founded what was essentially a philosophical mystery-cult, which was practised initially by a group of people who lived in his high-walled garden in Athens. (Epicureanism is the modern name; in ancient times the cult, and the philosophy, were called 'The Garden'.) The Epicureans' goal was to achieve *ataraxia*, 'freedom from disturbance' – a quality they defined as 'happiness of soul', and which they sought through seclusion from everyday bustle, contemplation, the avoidance of emotional commitment and the quiet enjoyment of life's pleasures.

Epicureanism had enormous appeal for the less assertive aristocrats of ancient Greece and Rome, setting themselves apart from the political turmoil of the times. But because of its secretive nature, and because there were no prescribed canons of **belief** or practice – Epicureanism was in no sense a religious cult – its adherents came to be accused of every kind of hedonistic and orgiastic excess. The early Christians, in particular, vilified Epicureans for saying that the world was (a) transient and (b) all that we had, and for (as Christians thought) equating 'the good life' with pleasure and not with ethical, moral and theological ambition or excellence. To modern eyes, there are palpable similarities between Epicurean ideas and those of Far Eastern philosophies and religions; that these were never explored in ancient times, not so much because there was no contact between East and West as because the Epicureans avoided 'becoming involved' with anyone else at all, is a matter of historical fascination if not regret. The Roman Empire, for one thing, and the subsequent history of western Europe, might have been entirely different if its rulers had followed the enlightened paganism of men such as the poet Horace (perhaps the best-known today of all Epicureans) or the Emperors Hadrian and Julian, rather than the **Stoic** severities of Augustus Caesar (in secular affairs) or St Paul (in spiritual matters). **KMCL**

EPIDEMIOLOGY

Epidemiology (Greek *epidemia*, 'prevalence of disease' + ology), in the **life sciences**, is the study of factors which determine the behaviour of a **disease** within a community. The epidemiologist is thus interested in the complex interactions between the host and parasite populations (see **parasitism**). Statistical techniques are used to determine factors such as frequency of infection, efficiency of transmission and susceptibility of subpopulations and to assess the significance of a wide range of associated factors such as dietary habits, social position, seasonal influences, etc. In a famous example, the discovery of infectious hepatitis was worked out by a Yorkshire family doctor who collated the information about the cases in his village and linked them all with a children's tea party. In another famous study doctors' life histories were logged and followed, and it emerged that smoking cigarettes and lung cancer were linked. In the first example subsequent studies revealed a viral cause for the disease; in the second subsequent studies have strengthened the predictive value of the observation of the link between smoking and lung cancer although the causal agent has never been isolated.

Such data, collected and collated worldwide, builds up a picture of the relationships between causes of disease and behaviour-patterns, and enables the design of strategies to deal with disease. The World Health Organization uses such global epidemiological information to plan programmes of vaccination and health education of the type which led, in this century, to the eradication of smallpox.

In field trials, epidemiology could be used to test (for example) if vaccination alters the incidence of a disease, or to compare vaccination with a different intervention, like ensuring a supply of purified water. Epidemiology could also be used to test the effectiveness of a treatment, for example, the use of a specific drug to treat a particular illness. The process is to choose two comparable groups of patients of adequate size, to give the drug to one group and an indistinguishable preparation (the placebo) to the other group. In due course the results are tallied and if the test group fared better than the control group, then the treatment has been effective. (However, it has been observed that if the operators of the trial know the content of the preparation being dispensed they are able to influence the outcome of the trial, by unwittingly showing enthusiasm, compassion or over-inquisitiveness. Thus was devised the double-blind controlled trial in which neither prescriber nor recipient knew what was in the medicine. Not many medical or other treatments have been tested in this way, and even after trials have been concluded and published, uses of treatments are not necessarily altered.)

Epidemiological studies can be used to test the utility and effectiveness of any treatment or intervention: that is to say, it is not necessary to know how a given treatment works, but it is possible to design a study to find out if it works well enough to be worthwhile doing. Epidemiological studies can also be used to test the validity of information about factors causing or influencing disease, thereby suggesting potentially useful paths to investigate. **RB TG**

See also aetiology; medicine; parasitology; toxicology; virology.

Further reading Craig Jones, *Anthropology and Epidemiology*.

EPIPHENOMENALISM

Epiphenomenalists (Greek *epi*, 'additional', *phenomenon*, 'happening'), in **philosophy**, are dualists, holding that the mental is not physical and the physical is not mental. They further hold that while physical events (such as damage to the body) have mental effects (such as pains) mental events (such as pains) do not have physical effects (such as winces). This is because while they hold that the mental is non-physical, they deny that non-physical events have physical effects. Only physical events have physical effects, and the mental is non-physical, and therefore causally impotent with respect to the physical. **AJ**

See also dualism; interactionism; parallelism.

Further reading K. Campbell, *Body and Mind*; T. Huxley, 'On the Hypothesis that Animals are Automata', in *Method and Results*.

EPISTEMOLOGY

Epistemology, in **philosophy**, as its Greek derivation makes clear, is the theory of knowledge. There are various (apparent) sources of knowledge. The various faculties by which we perceive the world (vision, hearing, touch, taste and smell) seem to furnish us with knowledge of how the world currently is. Memory seems to furnish us with knowledge of how the world was. And imagination seems to furnish us with knowledge of how the world might have been.

Two central concerns of epistemology are the nature of knowledge – what knowledge is – and the extent of knowledge – how much, if anything, we know.

What is knowledge? One traditional answer is this: knowledge is true justified belief. I know that London is big because my belief that London is big is true and justified. Another requirement for knowing seems to be that one's belief was acquired by a method which was, in the context, reliable. My belief that London is big satisfies this requirement, for it was acquired by a method which was, in the context, reliable: I trusted what my geography teacher said.

Philosophers have often distinguished two forms of knowledge. I know a priori that two plus two is four, for one can know that two plus two is four independently of experience. In contrast I know a posteriori that London is big, for one cannot know that London is big independently of experience: one must listen to what an expert says on the topic, travel through London, or look at it from above.

How much, if anything, do we know? Not a lot, according to sceptics. Sceptics hold that one cannot attain knowledge in various areas. Limited versions of scepticism hold that one cannot attain knowledge of the minds of others, of the unobserved, or of the external world. Global scepticism is the doctrine that we know (almost) nothing.

The issue of what knowledge is is not independent of the question of how much, if anything, we know. If indubitability were a necessary condition for knowledge, if one could know that London is big only if one could not doubt that London is big, then we would know almost nothing. In particular, I would not know that London is big, for I can doubt that it is: perhaps my geography teacher was lying, or perhaps my entire life is a dream and London does not even exist.

Attempted rebuttals of scepticism, attempts to show that we do know what we think we know, have often been foundationalist. It has been held that there is a set of foundational beliefs, beliefs which justify all other beliefs which count as knowledge but which do not themselves require justification in order to count as knowledge. Perhaps the foundational beliefs are about the given, the supposed raw data of one's own experience, uncontaminated by theoretical interpretation or cognitive interpretation. This foundation justifies all other beliefs which count as knowledge, concerning, for example, the external world and other minds. Coherentists hold that foundationalism is mistaken. There are no foundational beliefs, and beliefs all hang together, mutually adjusted, in a single, coherent web. **AJ**

See also a priori and a posteriori; causal theories; certainty; empiricism; foundationalism and coherentism; given; idealism; illusion; imagination; induction; introspection; knowledge; memory; naive realism; other minds; perception; rationalism; representative theory of perception; scepticism.

Further reading J. Dancy, *An Introduction to Contemporary Epistemology*; K. Lehrer, *Theory of Knowledge*.

EQUAL TEMPERAMENT see **Intonation, Tuning and Temperament**

EQUALITY

Equality is one of the central ethical, moral and political values of liberals and socialists. They know, of course, that all women and men are not created equal, if equal is taken to mean identical. One way of interpreting equality as a principle, one with its roots in the thought of Aristotle, is as a consistency-requirement: no discrimination should be made between persons who are equal in all respects relevant to the decision in question. However, this formal principle allows for great inequalities where people are not equal in all relevant respects. A more substantive conception of equality, found in Christian and Western political philosophy, supposes that all persons, by virtue of their common humanity or common needs, are fundamentally equal. So, it is said by **utilitarians** that no person should count for more than one, and, by followers of Immanuel Kant (1724–1804), that no person should be treated as a means to satisfy the ends of some other person.

This substantive conception of equality proscribes racism and sexism, and prescribes legal and political equality – at least for sane, adult citizens – and these presumptions are now accepted in all modern democracies. However, political disagreement centres on whether egalitarianism requires a moral commitment to ensuring that people experience equal levels of income, or utility, or welfare. Most philosophers would agree that those who favour 'equality of results', or of 'outcomes' have to give reasons why they favour such policies. Relevant reasons might include the belief that without economic equality people would not be

capable of acting as independent citizens, as Rousseau argued, or the thesis that human fellowship cannot be freely founded without extensive equality in resources, as the ethical socialists maintained. The philosopher John Rawls has argued both that people do not deserve many of their advantages, and that inequalities have to be justified – in particular inequalities may be justified if they increase the welfare of the worst-off people in a society.

Most controversy about what equality requires arises from disputes over the meaning and mechanisms for enforcing equality of opportunity. On the one hand there is debate over whether or not equality of opportunity simply means a fair opportunity to enjoy unequal rewards and positions. On the other hand the procedures required for producing 'equal opportunity' are widely disputed. For example, redistributive policies or policies to produce **affirmative action** are criticized on the grounds that they deny the better-off and non-minorities their rights to equality of opportunity. **BO'L**

See also conservatism; feminism; human rights; liberalism; socialism and social democracy.

Further reading J. Baker, *Arguing For Equality*; J.A. Rawls, *Theory of Justice*.

EQUALITY AND EQUAL RIGHTS FOR WOMEN

Mary Wollstonecraft's *A Vindication of the Rights of Women* (1792) and Harriet Taylor's *The Enfranchisement of Women* (1851) were early works that demanded women's equality. Liberal feminists of the 19th century campaigned for legislation for women's rights, believing that legislation would solve the problem of women's subordination. In the early 20th century, militant activists such as the Women's Social and Political Union took collective action for equal rights and opportunities for women, in the form of votes for women. In 1968, a strike by women workers at Ford in the UK demanded equal pay. Even after the introduction of the Equal Pay Act (1970) and the Sex Discrimination Act (1975) in the UK many activist groups continue to campaign for equal pay and equal opportunity, which are not sufficiently covered in the legislation.

A criticism that some feminists have levelled against legislation for equal pay and opportunity is that, although in theory this legislation should grant economic equality for women, it does not legislate against the structural inequality that occurs before women enter the work arena. Some feminists have argued that the patriarchal organization of society resists any real reform of inequality, but relies on tokenism to try to vindicate itself from claims of discrimination. One area that has been researched by feminists is education. Here it has been proved that boys take 'masculinzed' subjects, science etc. and girls take 'feminized' subjects. The result is that girls and boys are not then equal in the work market.

Kate Millet's book *Sexual Politics* states that in the USA in 1970 women were better qualified than men doing comparable work, and in the UK the Equal Opportunity Commission in 1992 states that women have more GSCEs and more degrees than men. The Equal Pay Act (UK, 1975) was amended in 1984 to require equal pay for equal value. The problem with this is that in many of the jobs held by women there are no men doing comparable work so that enforcement of the law is impossible. The Equal Pay Act does not take into account the fact that many women are engaged in unpaid domestic work or part-time work, nor does it provide child care for working women, in so doing women are still disenfranchised.

It should be noted that Equal Pay and Sex Discrimination laws are not worldwide, and where they are in place they do not successfully deal with class, racial discrimination, or with the many aspects of patriarchy that inform women's lives. **TK**

Further reading Olive Schreiner, *Women and Labour* (1911); Harriet Taylor, *The Subjection of Women* (1869).

ERGONOMICS

Ergonomics (Greek, 'work-organization') is the relationship of **design** to the way men and women actually use objects. Its purpose is to increase efficiency, comfort and safety. As an intuitive process ergonomics has always been a factor in design. A spade or a knife, for example, must be designed in such a way as to do its work, or there is no purpose in making it at all. (In recent years we have seen 'ergonomically designed furniture', which suggests that traditional chair-shapes and table-shapes completely misfitted the needs of the users – and which baffles as many present-day users as it benefits.)

A notable exponent of good ergonomic practice is the 18th-century English pottery manufacturer Josiah Wedgwood, who tested his teapots in his own kitchen for balance, stability, ease of pouring and other such practical properties. As a 'science', however, ergonomics developed during World War II when ergonomists studied the working environment of such people as fighter pilots and submarine crews. They studied the most efficient way of using the available space and operating the controls, and applied scientific research to matters such as the range of the human eye or the power of the hand grip. After the war the same research techniques began to be applied to the design of domestic appliances, factory machinery, vehicles and so on. However, in spite of the huge amount of literature and research into the subject, many believe that ergonomics is not an exact science but only a small component in the design process. But it has undoubtedly improved the areas of comfort and use, and is particularly beneficial in designing for the old, sick and handicapped. **CMcD**

EROTICISM

Eroticism comes from Eros, the Greek god of sexual desire, and means either the erotic spirit or nature (in which case it is the same as 'erotism') or works of art designed to produce a sexual stir (in which case it is the same as 'erotica').

The first meaning is interesting because of the questions it raises about the state of human beings compared with other creatures. So far as is known, most living species use sex for the purpose of procreation only: however rampant and frequent their coupling, it is the result of an instinctive urge to replenish the species, and nothing more. Human beings seem to be one of the very few species to use sex also for pleasure and to celebrate loving relationships – in some circumstances, to the point where the possibility of procreation is an unwanted inconvenience. We know, because we can see them doing it, that monkeys masturbate, but we have no idea what they think as they do so, much less if it at all resembles human thoughts in a similar situation. Furthermore, eroticism seems to be more about *anticipation* or *remembrance* of sexual pleasure than about actuality. It seems to be about an idea – and as such, it must be restricted to humans, the only creatures (again, so far as we know) that have ideas.

Eroticism in the sense of erotic art poses questions of a different kind. It is clear that **pornography** can be erotic (that is, cause sexual arousal), but it is equally the case that by no means all erotic art is pornographic. To think this would be to bracket a Donne love-poem (for instance) or a Renoir nude with *Raped on the Railway: a True Story of a Lady who was first Ravished and then Flagellated on the Scotch Express* (popular reading, the British Library assures us, with its gentlemen readers in Victorian England). A simple distinction might be to say that pornography is crude eroticism, eroticism subtle pornography. But this (though a standard view among 'anti-permissiveness' campaigners) again seems to miss the essential nature of eroticism. Pornography is explicit, eroticism celebrates a mystery; thus, the contract with the reader or spectator is different. Pornography uses sexual images to incite the consumer to orgasm; eroticism incites him or her to think about sexual relationships, those being described or suggested and those of his or her own.

Such a distinction fits many cases: the temple art of India is erotic, not pornographic, the descriptions of sex in the average airport 'bonkbuster' are pornographic, not erotic. But it still leaves many works of art trembling in no-man's-land. Is a girlie calendar erotic or pornographic (or possibly neither, falling into that large and dismal category of 'soft' that is, not-quite

'porn')? What of works of 'high' literature? (The last pages of *Ulysses* or the whole of Nabokov's *Ada*, not to mention his *Lolita*, come to mind.) Is there any difference, apart from social context, in the performances of a Turkish belly-dancer and the stripper at a Western stag night? There are a million erotic encounters in films, and the erotic qualities of actors are a key ingredient in a film's success. But these are not the same as the encounters, and the qualities, of performers in blue movies. Fairy tales often have erotic undertones, but this hardly makes them pornographic.

Perhaps the answer is as before, that pornography evokes an objective response (essentially, voyeurism) and eroticism a subjective one (reflection on the mysteries and pleasures of one's own sexual nature and relationships). A group of seven-year-olds in the US on whom, unbelievably, experiments in this area were done in the 1950s reacted to hardcore pornography (scenes from blue movies) by laughing, to erotic material (it was Douanier Rousseau's picture of the tiger in the jungle, and a scene from Cocteau's film *Beauty and the Beast*) with bafflement and, in some cases, alarm. This seems to confirm that if the difference is, truly, one of subtlety, then the subtlety lies not in the pornographic or erotic material itself, but in the response it evokes in each one of us. **KMcL**

See also gender; self.

Further reading Anne Carson, *Eros the Bittersweet*.

ESCHATOLOGY

The doctrine of eschatology, 'last things' (Greek, *eschaton*, 'the end'), in **Christianity**, is now recognized as being central to the teaching of Jesus and the message of the New Testament. The fact that the word itself was not invented until 1844 indicates that its significance had long been ignored or discounted. Until then, Jesus' teaching about the imminent arrival of the Kingdom of God – or even the picture of the Son of Man coming in judgement – was interpreted as something that would happen at the end of history, in God's good time. (Luther had believed that the world would end in 1535, but after him apocalyptic beliefs became the monopoly of fringe dissidents.) Alternatively, Jesus' parables and sayings were considered to have been fulfilled by events in church history. There was no appreciation of the eschatological tension in Paul's letters nor of the way that belief that Jesus would return within a few years governed the liturgy, ethics and expectations of the first Christians. This meant that scholars also missed the crisis caused by the delay of the *parousia* ('coming') of Jesus. History was simply progressing smoothly from creation (soon to be questioned by **Darwinism**) to salvation, with a paradigm shift caused by the death and resurrection in the middle.

Three things happened to revolutionize this perspective: the Evangelical revivals, with their ardent longing for the end and a consummation of the personal relationship with Jesus, hit the educated classes through the YMCA and the Student Volunteer Movement; the demolition of belief in Jesus' omniscience by critical scholarship demanded a radical reassessment of his teaching; finally, the horror of World War I, an experience that seemed like the end of the world, or at least the end of 'civilized' society. The old liberal theology appeared destroyed for ever. Modern warfare replaced Roman occupation as the catalyst for eschatology.

Early attempts at reinterpretation spiritualized the concept of the Kingdom of God, saying that teaching about this ideal 'last age' of God's direct rule on Earth (found also in the Old Testament, they noted) related to the spiritual condition of those who surrendered their lives to Jesus and was the product of the Early Church. It did not emanate from the historical Jesus. Although it was Rudolf Bultmann who most directly confronted the question that Jesus was mistaken in his expectations of an imminent end, it was Albert Schweitzer (later to sacrifice an academic career to work as a doctor in Congo) whose books, published from 1902 to 1904, initiated the modern appreciation of eschatology as the key to the life and teaching of Jesus. Schweitzer believed that Jesus tried to precipitate a crisis which would inaugurate the Kingdom of God first by sending out his disciples to preach the Gospel and then by entering Jerusalem on a donkey and submitting to crucifixion to fulfil the prophecies. Schweitzer was also the first to appreciate the impossibility of disentangling the early church belief in eschatology from the beliefs in the historical Jesus. Schweitzer's Jesus is a Promethean figure who threw himself against the wheel of history and was crushed, but he effectively rehabilitated eschatology even if he made mistakes in his assessment of the context of Jewish apocalyptic literature.

In the debate that has raged since then, three broad positions have emerged in British theology, slow as it was to absorb the full impact of Karl Barth's theology. First, there is the strictly futuristic view that in the near or distant future, cataclysmic events will occur, natural disasters, wars, famines and plagues will smite the Earth, and the church will be fearfully persecuted. Then the Lord will appear, judge the living and the resurrected dead and the righteous will enter his Kingdom. In a variation found from the 2nd century onwards (for example, in the writings of Papias and Irenaeus) Christ and his saints would first reign for a thousand years before the end (**millenarianism**). This, in general, is the position adopted by conservative Evangelicals. Then there is the realized eschatology of C.H. Dodd, whose work has had almost as much impact as Schweitzer's. He noted the transformation of the Kingdom of God of the Synoptic Gospels into 'eternal life' in John's Gospel, and advanced the theory of 'realized eschatology'. Emphasizing the 'now' in Jesus' teaching and the way in which the Kingdom is a present force in Pauline epistles, he concluded that the essential kingdom was already present, constituted in this life by Jesus' life, death and resurrection. Life has already been transformed by Jesus, it is only a question of entering into it. Between these two poles are those who believe that in Jesus' life and death a process was begun which will be completed on the last day. The Kingdom has been inaugurated but not completed. The early church thus lived in a hiatus between resurrection and return, sustained by the Spirit (see **pneumatology**). There are a number of variations and refinements of this crude statement. R.H. Fuller has argued strongly for what might be called 'inaugurated' eschatology, in which Jesus is considered to have believed that the progress of the kingdom was connected to his ministry, but would not be finally established until after his death and return.

It will be perceived that eschatological beliefs of whatever kind depend on a linear view of history – eschatology as an imminent reality is impossible in **Buddhism** and **Hinduism** – and on one's view of who Jesus of Nazareth was, or at least who he thought he was.

In **Judaism**, since the 8th century BCE and the prophecies of Amos and Micah, there has been a strong belief in 'The Day of the Lord' when judgement, not necessarily a vindication, would be meted out on Israel and the nations. The Essene communities and the community at Qumran retired to the wilderness to await the Messiah, but were disappointed when the revolutionary Bar Kochba ('Son of the Star') was captured and executed by the Romans (135 BCE). There have been many disappointments since then, but hope has never been extinguished. It has been fuelled by the modern restoration of the state of Israel (see **Zionism**). FMJ

Further reading A. Schweitzer, *The Quest of the Historical Jesus* (1910); *The Mystery of the Kingdom of God* (1925); C.H. Dodd, *The Parables of the Kingdom* (1935); *The Apostolic Preaching and its Development* (1936); O. Cullmann, *The Christology of the New Testament*; J. Moltmann, *The Theology of Hope*; Joachim Jeremias, *The Parables of Jesus*.

ESP see **Parapsychology**

ESSENCE

John Locke distinguished between the real and nominal essence of substances such as water. The real essence of a substance is its hidden 'inner constitution': we now know that the real essence of water is H_2O. The nominal essence of a substance is its observable properties: the nominal essence of water is the way it looks, tastes, feels, etc.

Something is an instance of a substance just if it has the essence of that substance.

Locke held that something is water just if it has the nominal essence of water, just if it tastes, feels and looks like water. If something has the nominal essence of water, but is not H_2O, it is nevertheless water. And if something is H_2O, but does not have the nominal essence of water, it is not water. Part of his reason for holding this was his view that we cannot know the real essence of a substance – its hidden 'inner constitution'.

The view that we cannot know the real essences of substances has been overturned by the progress of science. After all, we now know that the real essence of water is H_2O. Contemporary philosophers hold that something is water just if it has the real essence of water, just if it is H_2O. If something has the real essence of water, but does not look, taste, or feel like water, it is nevertheless water. And if something looks, tastes, and feels like water, but is not H_2O, then it is not water. AJ

See also essentialism.

Further reading J.L. Mackie, *Problems from Locke*; S. Kripke, *Naming and Necessity*.

ESSENTIALISM

Essentialism, in **philosophy**, is the doctrine that things have essential properties, properties without which they would not be the things that they are. Many philosophers hold that the essence of water is its real essence; the essence of water is H_2O. So the stuff in my glass has an essential property, a property without which it would not be the stuff that it is; if the stuff in my glass did not have the property of being H_2O, then it would not be water.

Anti-essentialists hold that there are no essential properties (properties without which things would not be the things that they are) independently of our definitions and ways of classifying things. Being a rational animal is an essential property of humans, but this is merely because we have chosen to define 'human' as 'rational animal', because we have chosen to classifying something as a human just if it is a rational animal. And things do not have essential properties independently of our definitions and ways of classifying things. **AJ**

See also essence.

Further reading S. Kripke, *Naming and Necessity.*

ETHICAL INTUITIONISM

Ethical intuitionists, in **philosophy**, deny that moral judgements are merely expressions of emotion or approval. They argue that there is a special faculty of moral intuition which gives us access to moral truths, to facts about what we ought and ought not to do. This intuitive faculty may render certain rules of conduct self-evidently correct and then moral conduct will be a matter of following those rules. Ethical knowledge, so conceived, has been compared to mathematical knowledge, where the latter consists of knowing the consequences of certain self-evident axioms, axioms grasped by some form of mathematical intuition. On the other hand, the faculty of moral intuition may be more like our sensory organs. It may enable me to see the goodness in my brother helping an old person across the road, just as we can see that the road is wide. **AJ**

See also ethical relativism, in **philosophy**, fact and value.

Further reading H. Sidgwick, *The Methods of Ethics,* vol. 3; G. Warnock, *Contemporary Moral Philosophy.*

ETHICAL RELATIVISM

Ethical relativism, in **philosophy**, is the view that ethical judgements are true or false only relative to a particular context. So if I say that eating people is wrong, while you say it is right, we may both be speaking the truth. For **cannibalism** may be wrong in my context and right in yours. Relativists disagree about what the relevant context for us is. Some would say it is a particular cultural or historical setting, so cannibalism may be permissible among 'primitive' natives of a Pacific Island but not in a modern European city. Other relativists claim that the relevant context is that of a specific individual, so that cannibalism may be right for you and wrong for me simply because we are different people with different inclinations. But all relativists deny that there is any way of formulating moral claims that will make them true in all conceivable contexts. In this they depart for the common-sense view that we can reasonably make moral assessments of the behaviour of other people, even when they come from a rather different social or historical context. **AJ**

See also emotivism; ethical intuitionism; fact and value.

Further reading B. Williams, *Morality,* chapter 3; *Ethics and the Limits of Philosophy.*

ETHICS

Ethics (from Greek *ethikos,* 'dealing with [human] nature'), in **philosophy**, can roughly be characterized as dividing into three parts: normative ethics; practical ethics; and meta-ethics.

Normative ethics is the study of general normative principles or virtues. There are various doctrines concerning general normative principles. **Altruists** hold that when deciding how to act one ought to take the interests of others into account, as well as one's own. **Hedonists** hold that one ought to pursue only pleasure or happiness for oneself and others. The Golden Rule states that one should act towards others as one wants them to act towards oneself.

Consequentialists believe that one ought to do whatever will have the best consequences. (**Utilitarianism,** the doctrine that one ought to do whatever will maximize well-being or happiness is one version of **consequentialism.**) **Deontologists** hold that the rightness or wrongness of actions is a matter of how they accord with moral rules, *not* of their consequences. One must obey the rule that one ought to tell the truth, even if the consequences of breaking the rule would be better. Others hold that rightness or wrongness cannot be captured by a set of moral rules at all, and that it is not simply the consequences of an action which determine its moral status. Rather, one ought to be a virtuous person, one who has certain emotional reactions to various situations, reactions which lead one to behave in ways which are virtuous, honest, generous or kind.

Practical ethics is the study of specific, practical ethical problems such as abortion, euthanasia, war and our treatment of animals. Clearly, the study of practical ethical issues is not independent of the study of general normative principles. General normative principles have implications for specific practical ethical problems, so acceptance of a general normative principle may lead one to change one's opinions about a specific practical issue, and one's firm conviction concerning a specific practical issue may lead one to see the failing of a general normative principle.

Meta-ethics is not concerned with which moral principles we should follow, or how they relate to specific practical problems, but investigates abstract conceptual and metaphysical issues which arise for *any* moral principle. One meta-ethical claim is this: any moral judgement concerning a particular is universalizable to all similar particulars. **Emotivism** claims that moral judgements are simply expressions of emotions. Descriptivism claims that moral terms are purely descriptive. Prescriptivism claims that moral terms have two independent components of meaning: descriptive and evaluative. (See **descriptivism and prescriptivism**). **Ethical relativism** is the doctrine that moral judgements are true or false only relative to a particular context. Some hold that murder is wrong because God has commanded us not to commit murder. **Ethical intuitionism** is the doctrine that there is a special faculty of moral intuition which gives us access to moral facts, to facts about how we ought to behave.

The **naturalistic fallacy** is the supposed fallacy of inferring an 'ought' from an 'is': the issue being whether ethics is objective or subjective. **AJ**

See also fact and value; God's commands; morality; objectivism and subjectivism; practical ethics; universalizability; virtues and vices.

Further reading J.L. Mackie, *Ethics: Inventing Right and Wrong*; P. Singer, *Practical Ethics*; B. Williams, *Morality: An Introduction to Ethics*.

ETHNICITY

Ethnicity can be broadly defined as a collection of shared traits (both objective and subjective) which define a human collectivity in relation to other collectivities. Ethnic markers are perceptible physical or social characteristics displayed by persons – such as 'race', **language**, **religion**, customs, geographic origins, dialect – that identify them as members of a recognizable ethnic category. Someone is either a member of a certain ethnic category or he or she is not, although they may have overlapping membership of more than one ethnic category. Ethnic markers possess objectivity even if they are denied by individuals who inherit them. An ethnic group, as opposed to an ethnic category, consists of people who think of themselves as members of the group as well as being defined by others as members of the group. Endogamous marriage preserves the identity of the ethnic group, and ethnicity assumes (real or fictional) common descent amongst members of a group, although the doctrines used to define group membership vary between those which emphasize kinship or race, and those which stress an inherited shared culture, based, for example, on a common language, history, or religion. For the latter ethnicity is metaphorical or imagined kinship.

This division defines the basis for alternative theories of ethnicity. Primordialists, who may embrace the ideas of sociobiologists, define ethnicity as requiring actual common descent: ethnic loyalty, for them, is like nepotism, being loyal to those who share the same gene pool. They emphasize the 'givens' of ethnic identity: traits which have physical markers, such as skin colour, or phenotypical characteristics, like body shape. They believe that ethnic identity and emotional attachments are more powerful than those based on shared interests. Instrumentalists (or situationalists), by contrast, assume that shared culture, interests and self-definitions are of prime importance in defining a person's ethnic identity, which they think is much more flexible and the result of social invention than primordialists allege. They emphasize that ethnic groups can emerge and split, and even be invented complete with newly minted fictions about their 'common origins'.

In 19th- and 20th-century political and social theory the belief was widespread that ethnic groups and identities would 'wither away' under the pressures of **modernization** (liberal integration theory) or advanced **capitalism** and **socialism** (Marxist theory). Today confidence about the withering away of ethnicity is less likely to be expressed. Indeed, some put the converse thesis that modernization (or capitalist or socialist industrialization) makes ethnic identity more important and more likely to be the cause of conflict because **colonialism**, imperialism, mass migration, and nation-building combine to bring ethnic groups into competition for scarce resources.

The relationship between ethnicity and **nationalism** is the subject of much dispute in **anthropology**, **political science** and **sociology**. Some argue that nationalists invent nations, constructing a myth of a common ethnic past, while others maintain that to be credible and successful nationalist movements must be built on a genuine sense of ethnic identity among the target-audience. The test-cases for such arguments are the extent to which multi-ethnic states are successful in forging shared national identities.

Ethnocentrism, the tendency of people to employ their cultural criteria as benchmarks for judging the worth of other communities, is held by some to be the primary source of ethnic conflict, whereas others stress economic or even genetic foundations for ethnic antagonism.

Ethnic conflict may seem ubiquitous in the contemporary world, but there are also many instances of relatively amicable relations between ethnic groups. A simple distinction can be drawn between states in which strategies are developed to eliminate relevant differences between ethnic groups (through policies like genocide, mass population-transfers, partition or **secession**, and **integration** or **assimilation**) and states which seek to regulate or manage

ethnic differences without aiming to terminate or abolish existing ethnic identities (through policies like control, **arbitration**, **federalism** or **consociationalism**). BO'L

See also community; conflict theory; ethnohistory; social closure; social conflict; social integration; social stratification; society; tradition; tribalism; typifications; urban anthropology.

Further reading D. Horowitz, *Ethnic Groups in Conflict*; J. McGarry and B. O'Leary (eds.), *The Politics of Ethnic Conflict Regulation*; J. Montville (ed.), *Conflict and Peacemaking in Multiethnic Societies*; A.D. Smith, *The Ethnic Origins of Nations*.

ETHNOARCHAEOLOGY

Ethnoarchaeology (Greek, 'the study of ancient communities') involves the combination of anthropological **field work** in a particular community and **archaeological** research and findings. Methods and choice of community vary according to the particular research problem investigated, but are generally chosen so that a similarity in environments and technologies may be established. For instance, from the study of hunting and gathering communities of North America, South Africa and Australia, observations of tool manufacture, butchering techniques, settlement patterns, etc. may provide working models by which to interpret material remains from the hunter-gatherers of the past. In this way, archaeology does not limit itself solely to the description and classification of finds, but widens the possibilities of constructing a reasonable set of models and insights into how people treated these artefacts in the past.

In the 19th century such approaches were used to construct an evolutionary framework in which it was argued that contemporary 'primitive' communities were 'fossils' from the past. In modern times, it has been acknowledged that this is not the case. Such communities have not lived in isolation from agricultural peoples, but have been considerably influenced by the surrounding societies and state policies, and are affected by the increasingly restricted amounts of land to habitate. In some cases, for example, the Muria Gonds of India, hunting and gathering may prove to be an economically beneficial means of livelihood in their provision of honey and leather to settled communities. In cases such as the Venda people of Sri Lanka, a hunting and gathering lifestyle may be assumed by the members as a means to attract tourists.

Another problem with ethnoarchaeology is that not all past behaviours have parallels today. Additionally, the symbolic and institutional complexes of any society are not easily clarified from investigating the material remains alone. A common presumption to avoid is that uncomplicated material artefacts are evidence for a 'simple' society.

However, the premise that underlies ethnoarchaeology is that some of our behavioural relationships revolve around material artefacts, and that this behaviour is an important part of all human relationships in **space and time**. Therefore, despite the problems of substantiating propositions, ethnoarchaeology suggests richer models that may encourage and refine insights into past behaviours and technologies. **RK**

See also culture; diffusionism; ethnohistory; evolutionism; scarcity; symbolism.

Further reading Ian Hodder, *Symbols in Action: Ethnoarchaeological Studies of Material Culture*; Carol Krame (ed.), *Ethnoarchaeology*.

ETHNOBOTANY

Ethnobotany (Greek *ethnos*, 'people' + *botanikos*, 'of plants') is the scientific reevaluation of traditional botanical knowledge. The field covers plants which produce food, materials and drugs. James Cook was a pioneering ethnobotanist when he suggested that that the breadfruit plant, which he had encountered in the Pacific islands, would make an ideal food for slaves in the West Indies. The modern science is primarily concerned with the search for new drugs in plants from areas such as the Far East and the South American rainforests. Investigation of traditional medicines and medical folklore can lead to plants which have potential medical uses. Conventional scientific drug-screening techniques are then employed and have turned up a wide range of natural compounds which have activity against many of the major diseases from cancer to malaria. **RB**

See also pharmacology; toxicology.

ETHNOCENTRISM

The term 'ethnocentrism' ('nation-centred' from the Greek *ethnos*, 'nation') was introduced in 1906 by the sociologist William Sumner, to describe the tendency to see one's own culture as superior to others, and to gauge other societies by those criteria which are significant in one's own society. The idea of rationality and progress is implicit in ethnocentric attitudes. It is a product of evolutionary ideas about 'primitives' and 'civilization', which often served to legitimize the kinds of statements made about others. Paradoxically, it was books written by anthropologists about the peoples among whom they had lived that seriously challenged ideas about the 'primitive'. The explicit aim of field work in the 1920s was to try to see the world of others, through their own eyes.

Yet early anthropological studies were full of consciously and unconsciously ethnocentric judgements about **cannibalism**, violence, or **sacrifice** in other societies. Contemporary anthropologists use their understanding of the problems of ethnocentrism to avoid the pitfalls of making value judgements about the systems established by other communities to the problems they face. Anthropology is unusual among the social sciences for openly examining its own underlying premises, and this has given it a certain resilience in the fast-changing arena of social enquiry. **CL**

See also cultural relativism; Marxist anthropology; reflexivity.

Further reading Robert LeVine and D. Campbell, *Ethnocentrism: Theories of Conflict, Ethnic Attitudes and Group Behaviour*.

ETHNOGRAPHY

Ethnography generally refers to the written

description of the customs and lifestyle of a specific community in which the anthropologist has lived for a period of years; such an account is called an ethnographic monograph.

Ethnography also refers to the methodological basis of **anthropology**, that of participant-observation: living among a community and gathering information from people in their own language. These experiences provide the basis on which theoretical issues can be debated. The importance of ethnographic research was established by Bronislav Malinowski, who lived amongst the Trobriand Islanders in Melanesia for the duration of World War I. The books he wrote about them gained popularity among a wide audience.

The recent book *Writing Culture* by Clifford and Marcus has problematized the idyllic situation described by Malinowski. They argued that the discrepancy between the idealized world of social theory and the actual problems of daily life often compromises the neat and tidy conclusions drawn by anthropologists. The limitations of writing as a medium for conveying experience further hampers scientific pretensions to obtain neat social facts. **CL**

See also field work; reflexivity.

Further reading Claude Lévi-Strauss, *Tristes Tropiques*; G. Stocking (ed.), *Observers Observed*.

ETHNOGRAPHY OF SPEAKING

The ethnography of speaking is a branch of **anthropological linguistics** which stresses the role of **language** as a social institution, in accord with the **Prague School** concept of linguistic function. Ethnographers of speaking highlight the various ways in which the social functions of **language** vary quite markedly from one speech community to the next. Consequently, great emphasis is placed on the analysis of language skills as they are manifested in naturally-occurring social interaction. In this way, a range of speech events can be identified, which reveal how communication is made meaningful through the interaction of language with socio-cultural factors, including the role and status of participants and the discourse strategies adopted.

The ethnography of speaking is central to any discussion of cultural diversity, since speech communities are partially defined according to the particular configuration of speech events in evidence. An explanation is thus provided for the prevalence of miscommunication across cultural boundaries, even where there is a shared code, or language, since fundamental differences may exist in the reasons for conversation and the way it is organized. **MS**

ETHNOHISTORY

Ethnohistory (Greek, 'research into communities') usually refers to the history of nonliterate peoples. It may also be used to describe the method of combining **anthropology** and the study of people's historical representations through their oral traditions, or the re-evaluations of documents produced by travellers, missionaries, conquerors or colonialists commenting on other societies.

Clark Wissler first coined the term in 1909 as a synonym for documentary. It came into anthropological usage, with its present associated meanings, in the 1950s. Prior to this, British anthropologists had concentrated on how societies functioned as social systems in the present. This in turn was a reaction to earlier anthropologists fallaciously speculating on how societies evolved from the past.

However, Edward Evans-Pritchard's 1950 paper reproached contemporary anthropologists for neglecting **history** altogether. He commented on the need to integrate a 'good' history into anthropological approaches. Both disciplines contained fundamental similarities, since both history and anthropology were about interpretations and translations of individual and social practices removed in either time or space. Together, they provided the means for a wider and dynamic field of enquiry; their combination would help to form a fuller picture of 'the thoughts of living men' in their interpretations of their pasts and the way they distinguish between different types of pasts such as 'myth', 'legend', 'history', 'fact' and 'fiction'. It would act to correct the fallacy of the 'ethnographic present' which described the tendency to portray communities living in a static and timeless place. The misleading idea that 'primitive' communities only undergo change with European contact would also be undermined.

One major problem with Evan-Pritchard's directives was that the kind of 'good' history he was proposing sought to construct the kind of chronology of events typical in the West. Other senses of how events are constituted and how the past is conceptualized may show a different pattern, incompatible with this model. For instance, the Australian aborigines' version of history as expressed in their 'dreamtime' narratives, for example, is very different to chronological views of history, yet it is no less significant to the Aborigines' sense of reality and values.

Some anthropologists have considered the way constructions of the past relate to the individual's or community's identity and interests in the present. A history may be constructed to fulfil such aims. Therefore, instead of asking how the past leads to the present, anthropologists ask how the present creates the past. Linked to this view are concepts about the person, **space and time**, religious views and how different or rival versions of the past relate to economic or political competition in contemporary times. **RK**

See also diffusionism; ethnicity; evolutionism; Marxist anthropology; myth; Orientalism.

Further reading Bernard Cohn, *An Anthropology among the Historians*; Edward Evans-Pritchard, *Anthropology and History*; Elizabeth Tonkin (ed.), *History and Ethnicity* (1989).

ETHNOMEDICINE

Ethnomedicine is the exploration of indigenous health systems. The efforts of people to deal with problems, accidents and illnesses give rise to a number of overlapping systems that can be broadly compared to the 'developed' notion of medicine; but ideas about what constitutes a healthy or sick person vary greatly.

Ethnomedicine has replaced the term medical anthropology to emphasize the study of beliefs and practices other than those embodied in conventional scientific medicine. Medical anthropology draws on both **medicine** and **anthropology** to interpret cultural understandings of health in different cultures. Originally focused on the health practices and ways of explaining disease in technologically primitive communities from the perspective of a Western biomedical model, it now looks at the multiplicity of explanations for individual and collective misfortune, and at how healers and patients are socialized in the context of these systems of thought.

These systems often borrow elements from each other, and cannot be seen as mutually exclusive – particularly since the introduction of the Western system of biomedicine, which has generally had profound implications for local knowledge. For instance, the increasing professionalization of the healer has significantly changed power relations in some societies. The perceived need to create specialists along the lines of Western medicine, who have access to a body of knowledge (usually contained in written texts), has changed the relationship between religious specialist and client, who previously may have shared a body of common knowledge according to which the client could actively influence the therapeutic process.

Humoral systems of medicine, which are practised virtually worldwide, and were once the basis of European medicine, view individual and collective dysfunction as a result of lack of harmony in the fundamental forces believed to make up the natural world including humans. Traditional Chinese medicine, for example, treats this imbalance of yin and yang energy through dietary adjustment, herbal preparations and treatments such as acupuncture which are designed to rebalance the vital energy, or *chi*, within the body. (The government in China is consciously seeking to preserve traditional Chinese medicine from the influence of biomedicine.) **CL**

See also ethnopsychiatry; humours.

Further reading A. Kleinman (ed.) *Patients and Healers in the Context of Culture.*

ETHNOMETHODOLOGY

Ethnomethodology, in **sociology** and **sociolinguistics**, is the study of the lay methods used by people in everyday life in order to construct, account for and make sense of what is happening in the social world. In short it means 'the people's methodology'. The term was coined by the father of the discipline Garfinkel at the beginning of this century. The focus of study for the ethnomethodologist is the properties of practical common-sense reasoning employed in mundane, everyday situations of action, an area largely ignored by other branches of sociology.

This school of thought developed as a reaction to the implicit assumption of sociologists that they had a privileged understanding of the social world by virtue of the methods that had been developed in the field. Conventional sociology treats the accounts of ordinary people as deficient and replaces them with those of their own. Garfinkel argued that this marginalized the everyday knowledge of lay people. He maintained that lay folk also possess procedures (of which they are largely unaware), that, for all practical purposes, enable them to make sense of the social world and create a sense of orderliness.

Ethnomethodologists use two main techniques for study. The first method aims to disrupt the smooth running of everyday routines in order to reveal the bases of social order. Garfinkel, in what have become known as 'the Breaching Experiments', instructed his students to go home and behave as if they were lodgers. The reaction of parents and relatives was dramatic – puzzled, bemused, even hostile. Garfinkel believed that this revealed the careful and delicately constructed order of everyday life.

As an overwhelming number of everyday activities are carried out through speaking, ethnomethodologists have given a lot of attention to the study of conversation. The second method of ethnomethodological investigation is conversation analysis which, it is believed, reveals the shared understandings necessary for social life and the practical skills that are used by people in order to make sense of reality.

Ethnomethodology has highlighted the role of **context** in everyday understanding. An important feature of everyday life, it is argued, is the indexical character of conversation. Ethnomethodology points out that conversation depends for its intelligibility on the characteristics of the situation in which it is taking place. The meaning of conversation or talk is never unproblematic, it has to be worked out and there are immense skills involved in this.

A further feature of social life identified by this school of thought is the reflexivity of accounts. This view suggests that it is not possible to separate a social act from the account that is given of it. The accounts made by people of a given situation may also act to reproduce or transform those social situations to which they refer.

Critics of ethnomethodology have suggested that it deals with trivia; it presents an over-ordered notion of everyday life which is really fraught with conflict and misunderstanding; it contains no notion of wider social structures and thus cannot explain how activities are constrained; and it adopts the same methods of enquiry that it has criticized in others. **DA MS**

See also action perspective; individualism; microsociology; phenomenological sociology; social order; structure; structure-agency debate; symbolic interactionism.

Further reading D. Benson and J. Hughes, *The Perspective of Ethnomethodology*; H. Garfinkel, *Studies in Ethnomethodology*; J. Heritage, *Garfinkel and Ethnomethodology*.

ETHNOMUSICOLOGY

The term ethnomusicology (Greek *ethnos*, 'nation' + musicology) literally means the study of music from different cultures. It was originally coined in 1950, by the Dutch musicologist and authority on Indonesian music Jaap Kunst, as a more appropriate name for an area of scholarly investigation previously known (by Europeans) as 'comparative musicology'. Comparative musicology was understood to be the study of 'exotic' music, that is of musical cultures outside the European tradition, and was therefore thought of as the primitive and Oriental branch of music history. As a scientific discipline it was regarded as fundamentally distinct from conventional, European **musicology**. Non-European music was handed down orally, without the means of writing, and because of its improvised nature and the immense variety of tonal and tuning systems, its investigation required methods other than those used for Western art music.

The idea that there exists a universal definition of music and that this is easily distinguishable from non-music was also challenged. Consideration of one's own society raises the problem of the fine line between music and non-music. In other societies, for instance in a Bulgarian village context, vocal but not instrumental performances are considered as music. Other ethnomusicological studies have discovered that musical thought and classifications vary widely. Linguistic models have been used to enquire into such matters. The most common construct is that of the emic-etic distinction. This was first coined by Kenneth Pike in 1967 to designate the subjective viewpoint shared by a group, emic, and the analytical models applied by the outside, etic. Even though hard and fast lines between insider's and outsider's viewpoint are difficult to draw, the emic-etic dimensions have provided a useful way of clarifying and comparing musical concepts across societies.

In 1950 Kunst wrote that, 'The study-object of comparative musicology is mainly the music and musical instruments of all non-European peoples, including both the so-called primitive peoples and the civilized Eastern nations'. By 1959, however, he had revised and extended his definition: 'The study-object of ethnomusicology is the traditional music and musical instruments of all cultural strata of mankind, from the so-called primitive peoples to the civilized nations. Our science therefore investigates all tribal and folk music and every kind of non-Western art music. It studies as well the sociological aspects of music, as the phenomena of **musical acculturation**, i.e. the hybridizing influence of alien musical elements.' However, he added that Western art music and popular or entertainment music should be excluded from this field.

There is still no real consensus as to the precise meaning of the term ethnomusicology. But the main debate has centred on two points of scholarly view. The anthropological view sees ethnomusicology as the study of music in culture, within the context of its society, and as the study of music as a universal aspect of human social behaviour. If this stance places emphasis on the rules of a particular culture or society, of which music-making is an active feature, the musicological view prefers as its objective the rules of that society's musical system, working towards an understanding of the music studied in terms of itself.

Even though many have accepted ethnomusicology as a borderline area between musicology and **anthropology**, emphasis continues to remain on the study of musical cultures outside the investigator's own background. Although Westerners might describe the study of, for example, Javanese *gamelan* (a type of orchestra) music as ethnomusicology, that is to say music outside our own culture, how would Javanese scholars view it? After all, European scholars are unlikely to regard the study of a Beethoven symphony as ethnomusicology, even though the Javanese might. The term could, therefore, be construed as ethnocentric. More recently, however, some ethnomusicologists have extended the term to include the study of various kinds of music found on their own doorsteps, bringing into focus the social and popular music of urban subcultures and the music-making of so-called ethnic minority groups.

In 1977, Alan Lomax developed a system of musical notation that was intended to apply to all musical cultures. It was called cantometrics and used to relate features of musical performance to the social and cultural context. Examples included how the complexity of economic and political organizations might relate to the styles of music people produced. He also remarked that the degree to which women sing in a shrill, high-pitch voice, was dependent on the severity of their sexual subordination in the community. Critics have pointed out that although Lomax's theories are illuminating, they are

no more substantial than chance correspondences, for though there are plenty of
cases that support his cantometric theories,
there are just as many that subvert them.
In addition, they do not take into account
the perspectives of the musicians and performers.

Lomax also warned of a 'cultural greyout' the more cultural and musical systems
come under the spread of the widening
travel and communication networks. His
particular fear was that they may be submerged by the influences of Western music.
However, detailed ethnomusicological studies have refuted these forecasts. Musical
developments show myriad paths of
changes and fusions with other musical
systems. Sometimes Western music is
appropriated by the practitioners into their
own genres of musical styles. At other
times it is the technological innovations
that are used to modernize different forms
of music, while its distinctive musical elements are retained. Occasionally, musical
styles may be hybridized with other forms
of music, such as Hindi film music or
reggae. These three broad dimensions are
illustrated by the changes undergone in the
UK since the mid-1980s with the traditionally rural Punjabi musical performance
called Bhangra.

Ethnomusicology has now emerged as
an approach to the study of any music,
providing it does so not only in terms of
itself, but also in relation to its cultural
context. Music often forms an essential
part of the kinds of identities individuals
construct for themselves – identities which
may transcend divisions in society. In addition, musical forms and styles are often
identifiable with the traditions of particular
social groups. This is the main driving
force in the late-20th century broadening
of the scope of ethnomusicology to include
studies of Western genres of music in their
social and cultural contexts – indeed, to
embrace all kinds of music not included in
conventional, historical musicology (that is
to say, the study of cultivated music in the
Western European art tradition). **RK SSt**

See also culture; dance; ethnicity; gender;
syncretism; traditions, Westernization.

Further reading Marcia Herndon and Norma
Mcleod, *Music as Culture;* Alan Merriam, *The
Anthropology of Music;* Bruno Nettl, *The Study
of Ethnomusicology: Twenty-nine Issues and
Concepts.*

ETHNOPSYCHIATRY

Ethnopsychiatry refers to indigenous conceptions about mental states and mental
illness in different cultures. The term itself
is ambiguous, reflecting Western assumptions about the divisibility of mind from
body, and notions about a particular dis-
ciplinary approach to dealing with mental
illness. Mind and body can be seen as
totally interconnected in the case of
Voodoo death in Arnhem, Australia,
where the belief in the power of a sorcerer's
curse literally causes the person to die.

Society plays a considerable role in the
definition of what we would call mental illness. It defines what is considered normal
or abnormal behaviour, and labels it as
either appropriate or socially unacceptable.
Social factors also determine the way
mental disturbances manifest themselves,
and the way they are perceived and treated
within a community.

In contemporary Western society, it is
doctors, psychiatrists and jurists who
define what is healthy, insane, or criminal.
A medical 'discipline' has been created in
both senses of the word. According to
Michel Foucault (*Birth of the Clinic*), it is
difficult to distinguish the discipline of psychiatry from the social control of individuals. Because of this **ethnocentric** bias,
anthropological studies focused on
whether religious specialists or healers,
such as the shaman, could be considered
'psychotic' in Western psychiatric terms,
because they were frequently initiated after
undergoing strange out-of-body experiences. However, their skills were not directed at creating social order through the
management of individuals' deviant behaviour, but were described in a completely
different idiom. (See **altered states of con-
ciousness**.)

By looking at the various systems which
account for, and deal with, different types
of misfortune, the conceptual systems
underlying indigenous approaches can be
uncovered. Misfortune covers religious and

ritual elements as well as therapeutic approaches dealing with it. Of course these systems are not always about therapeutics, and may also be a form of social control – as in the case of **witchcraft**. An African shaman among the Hehe of Tanzania, for example, treats the persons he considers disturbed by a variety of means: magical, herbal, physical or social. Conditions are recognized by their causation; through **divination** the shaman establishes whether the causation is due to moral wrong-doing, incest, witchcraft, spirits, or natural causes.

This attempt to understand mental disturbances in their own cultural context has proved more fruitful than have earlier examinations of mental illness from a Western psychiatric perspective. **CL**

See also emotions; ethnomedicine; mind-body problem.

Further reading C. Helman, *Culture, Health and Illness*; S. Kakar, *Shamans, Mystics and Doctors*.

ETHOLOGY

Ethology (Greek *ethos*, 'characteristic' + ology) is the study of animal behaviour. It is a modern science but was studied by natural historians, though often with an anthropocentric bias, long before the 20th century. In the 19th century, the term ethology was used by John Stuart Mill to describe the 'Science of characters'; it was first used to describe the study of animal behaviour by Oscar Heinroth (1871–1945). Behaviour is studied both in the laboratory, where environmental stimuli can be controlled, and in the field. Two zoologists, Konrad Lorenz and Nikolaas Tinbergen, pioneered the controlled study of behaviour in the mid-20th century, and since then the field has grown rapidly. Much ethology has been restricted to non-learned responses in animals, partly because of the complexity of learned behaviour, and ecologists have become deeply involved with instinctive animal behaviour because of its importance in **natural selection**. Ethology is applied to problems of pest control, but many studies are driven by the far more complex problem of unravelling human behaviour, both learned and instinctive. To

this end social groups of mammals, particularly the higher primates, have been extensively studied. **RB**

See also aggression; altruism; instinct; mimicry.

Further reading Nikolaas Tinbergen, *Social Behaviour in Animals*; E.O. Wilson, *Sociobiology The New Synthesis*.

EUCLIDEAN GEOMETRY

Euclidean geometry, in **mathematics**, is the term used to describe the whole of classical geometry, that is, everything that was known about the relationships between points and lines until the 18th and 19th centuries. It was called Euclidean because only insignificant advances had been made since the time that Euclid (3rd century BCE) catalogued all that was known in his time in the field in his *Elements*, a book which became the standard for rigorous mathematics until the 19th century. In it, Euclid derived the results known in his time (such as **Pythagoras' theorem**) from a small number of rules (axioms) and definitions (see **axiomatization**).

Although most of Euclid's axioms were accepted without quibble, the axiom of parallels was not. A parallel is a line which passes through a given point and does not cross a given line; Euclid's axiom states that for any line and any point not on the line, there is exactly one parallel to the line through the point. The reason it was not accepted is that in some situations it does not seem to be true in the real world: a pair of railway lines, for example, appear to meet on the horizon. Even Euclid does not seem to be convinced of the truth of the axiom, for he derived all the results he possibly could from the other axioms before the axiom of parallels was used at all.

For 2,000 years after the production of the *Elements*, mathematicians attempted to show that the parallel axiom could in fact be deduced from the other axioms proposed by Euclid, without success: it turned out to be an impossible task. Several mathematicians from the 16th century onwards tried to do this by assuming the opposite (that there were no parallels or at least two) and trying to derive a contradiction to show that the supposition was absurd. In the case where there were assumed to be no parallels, a contradiction was found, but in the other case, none was. None of the mathematicians who studied this took the next step of announcing the discovery of **non-Euclidean geometry**, being afraid of the derision they would receive from other mathematicians. In the end, it was left to two obscure mathematicians, Johann Bolyai (1802–60) and Nicholas Lobachevsky (1792–1856), to publish their conclusions: that assuming the existence of at least two parallels was equally valid to assuming exactly one. Mathematicians slowly began to accept this work, as models were devised which had exactly the properties of Bolyai-Lobachevsky geometry. As the 20th century began, the position of Euclidean geometry as that which governed the universe was displaced, especially after Einstein used non-Euclidean geometry to formulate his general theory of **relativity**.

Greek geometry had also come up with three problems, which no-one could solve. Every construction in the *Elements* can be carried out with a straight edge and compasses; no measuring implement was allowed for either angle or distance. The first is known as squaring the circle; it is to construct (using only compasses and straight-edge) a square of the same area as a given circle. The second is, given an arbitrary angle, to construct (using only compasses and straight-edge) the angle which is one third the size of the given one. The third is, given a cube, to construct (using only compasses and straight-edge) a new cube of exactly double the volume. Using the tools of **Galois theory**, it is now known that all these problems are impossible within the rules; unfortunately that does not stop mathematical societies from receiving hundreds of incorrect constructions every year. **SMcL**

EUGENICS

Eugenics (Greek, 'science of good breeding') is the science of improving offspring and is generally applied to humans. The idea that scientific approaches might lead to an improvement in human stock became popular after the publication of Charles Darwin's *Origin of the Species* (1859), in which the concept of **natural selection** was proposed. The term eugenics was coined in 1883 by Francis Galton who conducted research into human genetics and intelligence, and, on the basis of this, campaigned vigorously on behalf of eugenic breeding. Eugenics is often divided into positive and negative categories: the former deals with the possibilities of breeding superior humans by encouraging reproduction between individuals with particular 'desirable' qualities; the latter is concerned with preventing the reproduction of those individuals who are perceived to carry inferior genes. Extreme measures, such as compulsory sterilization, were often countenanced by otherwise liberal individuals who believed that their ideas were supported by genetic facts.

In reality, proponents of eugenics are rarely objective or scientific in their opinions. In the early 20th century, eugenics was enormously popular in the UK and this interest spread, notably to the USA and Germany. Prior to World War II, compulsory sterilization of inmates in mental institutions was permitted in many American states. The rise of **Nazism** in Germany meant that compulsory negative eugenics programmes were directed against certain ethnic minorities, disabled people and other 'undesirables'. Millions of people were murdered in the name of 'genetic cleansing', while those who bore 'Aryan' characteristics were encouraged to reproduce and their offspring given preferential treatment. As a consequence of these events, the use of the term eugenics has since been avoided, but even so the ideas are often still espoused for political reasons. Furthermore, when the frequency of harmful genes in the human population is calculated, the proportion of individuals carrying one or more is very high; even if such genes could be identified, the scale of a eugenics programme would be so vast that it could never be implemented without the use of force.

In a medical context, voluntary eugenics is beneficial provided that objective advice is given; people with a family history of certain serious genetic disorders may decide not to have children. In the future, such people may be helped by **gene therapy**, a developing medical technique which has great potential for the alleviation of suffering, but also for misuse by supporters of eugenics. **RB**

See also atavism.

Further reading D.H. Labby, *Life or Death*; S. Trombley, *The Right to Reproduce*.

EUPHUISM

Euphuism is an exaggeratedly fancy English style. It was invented by John Lyly for his novel *Euphues* (1578), and involves the use of abstruse classical allusion and figures of speech of every kind, particularly similes, extravagant metaphors, alliteration and assonance. Lyly's books were enormously popular and his style was widely imitated. Indeed, even Shakespeare (who sends it up in the utterances of Fluellen and Pistol in *Henry V* and the Sir-Topas swanking of Feste in *Twelfth Night*) was not immune to it. In later English literature, the most successful uses of it are Sir Thomas Urquhart's magnificently engorged, 17th-century translation of Rabelais, and the 19th-century, poetical extravagance of Swinburne and his imitators (such as James Elroy Flecker). It also underlies the dandified utterance of Restoration comedy, and is most satisfyingly mocked by Sheridan (for example in Mrs Malaprop's assaults on the language in *The Rivals*) and by Joyce (in the parodies of romantic literature in *Ulysses*). **KMcL**

EUROPEAN ECONOMIC COMMUNITY (EEC)

The European Economic Community is an economic union among 12 western European democratic countries formed to integrate their economies by reducing and removing trade barriers among members, by adopting a common trade policy toward the outside world, and by providing for the free movement of labour and capital within the group. The EC has a Council of Ministers, a Commission, a European Parliament, and a Court of Justice.

The Community was founded on 25 March 1957, when six countries – France, the former West Germany, Belgium, Holland, Luxembourg and Italy – signed the Treaty of Rome. It was a direct development from the European Coal and Steel Community, founded by the above six at the Treaty of Paris in 1951, which still exists as an adjunct to the EEC. In 1973, three more members joined the club, the UK, Ireland and Denmark, and in 1981 Greece joined, then Spain and Portugal in 1986.

The EC is moving toward even more economic integration than the goals above suggest. There is now agreement to merge into a single trading block. Businesses in countries outside the group anticipate that it may become more difficult to enter the EC market and are actively developing branch or joint production facilities within in at as well as searching for ways to export into it. In addition to economic integration, the EC has an ultimate goal of political union.

The European Monetary System (EMS) is an organization whose members agree to hold their exchange rates in a relatively fixed relation to the currencies of the other members. Not all of the EC members have joined this monetary system, indeed, some members have pulled out of it, but even so the EC members are discussing how to achieve a single Eurocurrency and a European central bank.

In the 1980s, the pressures of recession, and the difficulties of decision-making by 12 countries with often divergent national interests, has meant that progress in economic fields has largely stagnated. **TF**

EUTHANASIA

Euthanasia (Greek, 'good execution') is the act of killing a hopelessly ill person on grounds of mercy. It is expressly forbidden in the West on legal and Judeo-Christian religious grounds. It is also rejected by doctors when they declare their ethical intent in the Hippocratic oath.

Individuals can declare their wish that life should not be unnecessarily sustained but any person aiding in the performance of the request is in danger of prosecution.

It is also illegal to provide help to a person wanting to commit **suicide**. Other societies have more flexible attitudes, simply allowing people to die, for example, by exposure to the elements.

In recent years, the enormous cost of life-sustaining procedures in the hopelessly ill has been found to endanger the economics of health care in industrially 'advanced' societies. This may encourage some reconsideration of the moral and legal issues, as was the case with slavery when other forms of trade were found to be more lucrative and the moral issue was resolved for economic reasons. **TG**

EVANGELICALISM

Evangelicalism is derived from the Greek for 'telling of good news', but, over the centuries, the terms 'evangelicals' and 'evangelicalism' have been subject to many changes and reflect the convergence of a number of traditions. Erasmus used them to describe what he saw as the narrowness and fanaticism of **Lutheranism**. Luther used them to describe all those who accepted the doctrine of 'justification through faith alone', which he saw as the core of the gospel. By 1700 the terms had become synonymous with 'Protestant' or 'Lutheran'. In Britain, the Methodist religious awakening around 1750 was described as the evangelical revival, and revivalists of a slightly later period inside the Anglican and Free Churches also claimed the term.

Evangelicals of all kinds came together to support William Wilberforce's crusade against the slave trade, to found the modern missionary societies and to collaborate in the work of the British and Foreign Bible Society. In 1846, Europeans and North Americans whose **ideology** was founded in Reformation Protestantism, early pietism and the evangelical revival formed in London the Evangelical Alliance to co-ordinate their activities. However, by the late 1910s the Reformed tradition was in upheaval. On one side was the liberal tradition and on the other a revivalist, confessional coalition of parties under the names 'conservatives', 'evangelicals' and **fundamentalists**. The final split between evangelicals and fundamentalists came when Billy Graham accepted the help of liberal church leaders for his New York Crusade in 1957. Prominent fundamentalists accused Graham and his evangelical followers of being 'traitors from within'. The evangelicals are today organized worldwide in the World Evangelical Fellowship and the Lausanne Committee for World Evangelization. **KDS**

Further reading D.W. Dayton, *Discovering an Evangelical Heritage*.

EVENT

An event (Latin, 'what comes about') is an occurrence, change or happening. Intentional actions, in **philosophy**, are events – my action of steering the car round the hole in the road was an event. But not all events are actions – the explosion of the star was an event, but not an intentional action. Events enter into causal relations, they are causes and effects of one another. Flicking the switch caused the light to go on; the first event caused the second. **AJ**

See also action; causation.

Further reading D. Davidson, *Essays on Actions and Events*; D. Lewis, *Philosophical Papers*, vol. 2.

EVOLUTION

Evolution (from Latin *evolutio*, 'unrolling') is a theoretical explanation for the mechanism by which species change and have changed since the origin of life on Earth. The overall evolutionary trend has been diversification of species, coupled with increases in complexity of structure and function; the theory of evolution explains these observations. Aristotle (4th century BCE) noted that variations on a living theme do not often appear to be generated independently, and he argued that this suggested that gradual changes of form had occurred. Creationist explanations of the origins of the species were dominant throughout the Middle Ages and **Renaissance**. It was generally held that the species had been created as immutable and could not change or interbreed. The idea of evolution was not seriously considered until the 18th century, though it was accepted that extinctions could occur because the fossil evidence for this was overwhelming.

In the 18th century, the French philosopher Charles-Louis Montesquieu examined the issue of the species and declared that in the beginning there were very few species, and that these had multiplied since. The French naturalist Georges-Louis Buffon suggested that the horse was related to the ass because they could interbreed, and he also noted similarities between man and the apes. Erasmus Darwin (Charles Darwin's grandfather) summed up the views at the end of the 18th century in his poetical work *Zoonomia* (1796), concluding that evolution had occurred but proposing no serious mechanism.

In the early 19th century the idea that species might change as a result of pressures from their environment began to be considered. In 1809, Jean-Baptiste Lamarck proposed an evolutionary tree, indicating common ancestry, and stated that life tended to increase in complexity. The driving force behind this was the benefit that the organism could accrue if it became better suited to its lifestyle – Lamarck, along with most other naturalists at the time, thought that characteristics acquired by individuals during life could be inherited by their offspring. Although Lamarck's mechanism of evolution was in error (and this was realized by many of his contemporaries) he was the first to present a systematic idea of the course of evolution.

The modern concept of the mechanism of evolution was pioneered by Charles Darwin (1809–1882), who had observed the relationships between similar species which were geographically adjacent and attempted to relate these differences to the lifestyles of each species. He also studied fossil remains in the light of his knowledge of geology and began to draw conclusions concerning the transmutation of species. Over a similar period the Scottish naturalist Alfred Wallace was engaged in a similar study. In 1858, the two read a paper to the Linnaean Society and the following year Darwin's *The Origin of the Species* was published, to a storm of controversy. However, by the end of the 19th century Darwin's ideas had been accepted and they have stood the test of time, becoming clarified by the advent of **genetics** and reinforced by observations in all fields of biological study.

The evidence for evolution comes from the fossils of extinct species and the comparative study of existing species. When rocks are arranged in order of age, the fossil records show that simple organisms preceded complex ones; for example, the first fish appeared well before reptiles, which appeared before birds and mammals. When Darwin and Wallace were constructing their theories, comparative anatomy and **embryology** provided important evidence on the relationships between different species, while the **biogeographical** distribution of species was important as supporting evidence. Modern techniques of **biochemistry** and **molecular biology** allow evolutionary relationships to be quantified because metabolic pathways and similarities between the genes themselves can be compared.

Darwin's principal ideas on evolution were based on his observation that living organisms have the capacity to multiply, yet their populations tend to be fairly stable so a proportion of each generation must fail to reproduce. Furthermore, all individuals vary from one to another. He concluded that those offspring which are best able to compete for available resources will be more likely to survive and reproduce, passing the characteristics which made them successful to their own offspring. This is the theory of **natural selection** and is central to the conventional Darwinian theory of evolution. The process of natural selection is entirely automatic, driven and regulated by the environment. It leads to diversification and increases in the overall number of species because it tends to produce and favour specialized adaptations among groups of organisms; the many species of mammal which exist today evolved from a few ancestral mammals by adapting to live in more diverse habitats, such as trees, burrows, water, etc. The theory accepted that variation occurred and explained it by the theory of **pangenesis**, which was disproved and replaced first by the **germ plasm theory** and later by **Mendelian** genetics. At first it seemed that the idea of random mutations occurring within genes was incompatible with natural selection because of the influence of chance. However, experimental work and mathematical studies showed that the possibilities for variation which Mendelian genetics permitted were just what was required for Darwin's theories, and served only to reinforce the theory of natural selection.

Modern **biology** is based upon evolutionary theory and it is a common thread which unites diverse areas though the theory is continually re-examined in the light of fresh evidence, and there is dispute over the relative importance of natural selection, mutation and sexual recombination. Evolution resulting in the formation of new species is too slow to be observed in action, but the **genetic drift** of existing species can be observed; for example, the famous case of the butterflies which became darker in colour so that they were still camouflaged in polluted, smut-covered industrial areas. **RB**

See also adaptation; adaptive radiation; analogy; creationism; Darwinism; emergence; extinction; group selection; hybridization; homology; kin selection; Lamarckism; morphology; niche; palaeontology; sexual selection; speciation; taxonomy; uniformitarianism.

Further reading P.L. Forey, *The Evolving Biosphere*; Salvador Luria, *A View of Life*; John Maynard-Smith, *The Theory of Evolution*.

EVOLUTIONISM

Evolutionism (from Latin *evolvere*, 'to roll out') is a movement in **anthropology** and **sociology** which was much in vogue in the 19th and early 20th centuries. It refers to theories of change in which development is seen to go through stages of increasing complexity and diversification. It is closely related to the idea of progress and technology, which is most prevalent in capitalist society.

Evolutionism gained currency in the 19th century with Charles Lyell's geological theories, Herbert Spencer's sociological ideas and especially with Charles Darwin's 1859 work *On the Origin of Species*. It was thought that organisms and human populations pass through the same stages of progression. Human society was compared to a biological organism and the notion of 'the survival of the fittest' was used to explain the development from one stage to the next. Around this time, physical anthropology (focusing on human beings) and social anthropology were also closely linked together. Notable anthropological advocates of evolutionist theories in the 19th century include Louis Henry Morgan and Edwin Tyler. They elaborated upon a scheme from hunting/savagery, through herding/barbarism to **civilization**. Marx and Engels, influenced by the works of Morgan, applied evolutionary theories in positioning their own stages of social and economic relations, principally that of 'primitive', ancient or 'slave', feudal and capitalist modes of production. James Frazer concentrated his evolutionist theories on **magic**, **religion** and **society**, which are synthesized in his famous work *The Golden Bough* (1926–36).

In sociology, the starting point for classical evolutionary thought was the observation that historical comparisons of different types of human society suggests a movement towards increasing complexity. Classical evolutionists assumed that social change was inevitable, universal and progressive. Only one path of development was believed to exist: each society would pass through a linear sequence of developmental stages. Sociological evolutionists developed the comparison between societies and biological organisms: both grow and develop, and as they do so they become increasingly complex and internally differentiated (as societies become more complex areas of social life which were formally intermingled become clearly separated). Social change results in an increasingly complex but more tightly integrated society.

Neo-evolutionism developed in the 1960s as a response by functionalist sociologists – in particular Talcott Parsons – to the criticism that functionalist theory, which emphasized social integration and harmony, was unable to explain social change. Sociologists returned to the classical evolutionism of the 19th century. However, neo-evolutionists part company from their classical predecessors on two main counts: they propose multiple paths of social development (as opposed to a single one); and they place greater emphasis on the mechanics of change between evolutionary stages (which, they argued, the classical evolutionists had neglected). The neo-evolutionist school believes that the process of change is intimately linked to a given society's social institutions – these are the fabric of social life and include the political and economic systems, religion, family, education and so on. The mechanisms of social change, it is argued, can be explained in terms of the needs of a given society to maintain these structures.

Neo-evolutionist accounts of social change contain three main elements. They argue that all social change is the result of the processes of *differentiation* (the idea that as societies develop all aspects of life become increasingly diverse and separated from each other), *reintegration* (regulatory mechanisms which counteract the tendency towards disintegration entailed by differentiation and change) and *adaption* (the direction of differentiation and reintegration is determined by the need of society to adapt to its environment).

One of the main neo-evolutionist contentions is that human civilization has increased in its efficiency and mastery of the environment, so that the kinds of societies which have emerged in later periods of history are more efficient and powerful than earlier types. Critics have questioned such assumptions, and most recently environmentalists drawing attention to human destruction of the planet have seriously questioned the so-claimed 'adaptive' capacity of modern societies. **DA RK**

See also convergence thesis; culture; dependency theory; diffusionism; functionalism; historical sociology; holism; Marxist anthropology; primitivism; scarcity; sociobiology; structuralism; structure; system; systems theory; theories of modernity.

Further reading J.W. Burrow, *Evolution and Society;* P.Q. Hirst, *Social Evolution and Sociological Categories;* T. Parsons, *Societies: Evolutionary and Comparative Perspectives;* Elman R. Service, *A Century of Controversy: Ethnological Issues From 1860–1960;* George Stocking Jnr, *Race, Culture and Evolution: Essays in the History of Anthropology.*

EXCHANGE

Exchange (from Latin *cambiare*, 'to barter') is a fundamental concept in **anthropology** and **sociology**. It has been defined as a form of social interaction concerned with 'returning the equivalence', and the Exchange Theory claims that in their interactions with each other, individuals always attempt to seek to maximize their rewards. Exchange systems may include words and communication, goods and services, even spouses in marriage arrangements. They are fundamental for establishing and maintaining relationships. Two main strands can be identified: individualistic and collectivist exchange systems and theories.

The individualistic school is epitomized by the work of the sociologists G.C. Homans and P. Blau. The basic model is a two-person one. Social life is compared to economic life, and it is assumed that in social interaction, as in market transactions, there is an expectation that there will be an equivalent return on an investment. All partners in the exchange are expected to try and maximize their own rewards. (For example, Blau suggested that people only marry partners able to provide equal social assets.) Critics argue that this theory over-emphasizes the self-seeking elements of the personality, and point out that it is unable to go beyond the two-person model and explain such social features as domination or more generalized social values, and as such is only a partial theory of social life. Exchange theorists are also accused of focusing on trivia.

The collectivist model of exchange is associated with French anthropology and in particular with the ideas of Mauss and Lévi-Strauss. In his 1925 work on the **gift**, Mauss looked at exchange systems through the idea of 'reciprocity'. This considered the way gift giving in different societies created, altered and maintained relationships between individuals and groups. Lévi-Strauss, developing this idea in terms of his **structuralist** theory, applied the principle of exchange to the circulation of women in marriage systems. He described two types of exchange prevalent in marriage arrangements: complex (as found in Western societies); and elementary (as found in non-Western societies). His aims were to show that exchange systems underlying social behaviour and thought in all societies were essentially the same for all things exchanged, whether words, goods or women. This was critical to his structuralist agenda which sought to demonstrate that all human beings experience phenomena in a fundamentally similar way.

Many have criticized Lévi-Strauss's chauvinistic bias in viewing women as objects of exchange rather than as persons. The universalism of structuralist models in attempting to explain all human behaviour has also been undermined. Structuralism is particularly inadequate in accounting for the use of exchange items for strategic or political gains. Transactionalism, which takes account of people maximizing and calculating in some of their social relationships provides a more useful methodology for these instances. Both structuralist and transactionalist angles have been integrated in a theory called 'adaptive strategies'. This approach considers plans of actions made by a group of people to deal with internal or external constraints in society, but acknowledges that it need not always be consciously realized by all the persons.

Other, more economically-orientated, anthropological analyses have focused on the relationships and comparisons between market exchange and non-monetary exchange systems. Related to this is the topic of 'spheres of exchange': a concept that refers to the way certain exchange items are freely exchangeable within social and moral constraints. Spheres of exchange are more often a characteristic of non-monetary societies. For example, before the introduction of European goods and money in the 1950s, the Tiv society of southern Nigeria contained three spheres

of exchange. One was to do with locally produced commodities, such as foodstuffs. The second was to do with prestige items like slaves, cattle, horses and brass rods. The third was the most prestigious and concerned rights in women and children: as evident in marriage arrangements.

There is also evidence for 'spheres of exchange' operating in modern societies that use money, commonly thought of as an all-purpose exchange item. For instance, services within a family or religious objects cannot be measured in monetary terms without upsetting moral values. The articulation of changes within 'spheres of exchange' is therefore an essential component in the consideration of exchange and moral systems in societies. **DARK**

See also community; culture; economic anthropology; individualism; marriage; norms; rational choice theory; reciprocity; transactionalism; social integration; society; structure-agency debate; values.

Further reading P. Blau, *Exchange and Power in Social Life*; P. Ekeh, *Social Exchange Theory: the Two Traditions*; G.C. Homans, *Social Behaviour: its Elementary Forms*; M. Mauss, *The Gift*.

EXCHANGE RATE

The exchange rate is the price at which one currency can be converted into another. Currencies freely traded on the foreign exchange markets have a sort rate for immediate exchange, and a forward rate for dealing at some date in the future.

The ratio of the value of one country's money to the value of another country's money is expressed, for example, as dollars per pound sterling, or francs per dollar, or yen per francs. When the world is on a fixed standard such as the **gold standard**, each currency is related to gold by law, for example, the US declares that one ounce of gold equals $35, and France declares that one ounce of gold equals F175. Thus each currency is related to others by a legal ratio to gold (which is $1.00 = F5 in this example). If trade imbalance were to create a surplus of dollars relative to what the French want to hold, francs would be used from the US stabilization fund to purchase dollars, and ultimately gold would flow from the US to France in exchange for remaining surplus dollars. The exchange rate might vary from the legal rate slightly, depending upon the cost of gold shipment.

When the world is on a fluctuating exchange-rate system, each exchange rate is established by the buying and selling of currencies in the world's money markets and can change over a very short period of time, even second by second when markets are open. **TF**

EXISTENCE

People exist but fairies do not. What is the difference between existing and not existing? Some philosophers have held that existence is a property. It is a property that everything which exists has. So, for example, some have argued that God exists on the grounds that existence is a property, a property which it is better to possess than not, and that God, a perfect being, can hardly lack a property which it is better to possess than not. This argument obviously collapses if existence is not a property.

One reason given for thinking that existence is not a property is this. A property distinguishes entities from one another, enabling us to pick out similarities and dissimilarities, to contrast the things which possess the property from those which do not. But if existence is a property which everything which exists has, one cannot contrast the things which possess the property from those which do not.

Considerations such as this have led philosophers to deny that existence is a property. We often ascribe properties to entities. To say that George is pink is to ascribe a property, the property of being pink, to an entity, George. But to say that George exists is not to ascribe a property to him. Rather, it is to say that there is a thing and that thing is George. **AJ**

See also metaphysics.

Further reading W. V. Quine, *From a Logical Point of View*; M. Sainsbury, *Logical Forms*.

EXISTENTIAL PSYCHOLOGY see **Phenomenology**

EXISTENTIALISM

Existentialism is a non-rigorous form of philosophical enquiry into human nature and the human 'predicament' (as existentialists see it). Everything else in existence merely exists; humans are aware of their existence, and therefore have the potential to understand it and (perhaps) control it. We are self-creating creatures: we can choose what we want to be, and choose to be it. The moment of choice, the leap into existence, comes between two fixed points: the nothingness from which we come and the nothingness to which we return after we die. Our glory is the self-defining choice; our agony is that we need to make it. The idea was formulated by Kierkegaard in the first half of the 19th century, was developed by Husserl a century later, and had enormous prominence in the 1940s and 1950s, particularly in the work of Jean-Paul Sartre.

The main significance of existentialism today is not as a philosophical programme, but as the matrix of a strain of intellectual creativity which dominated the arts and preoccupations of the chattering classes in Europe between the end of the Spanish Civil War in 1936 and the student riots of 1968.

In **literature**, the chief existentialist writer was Jean-Paul Sartre. In his (autobiographical) novels *Nausea* and the three-volume *The Roads to Freedom*, and in such plays as *The Flies* and *Huis Clos*, he examined the idea that 'Man is a useless passion' and the plight of the passive hero longing but unable to contrive some self-defining act. Other French writers took up the style, notably Albert Camus. The quest for identity underlies much European **drama** and prose fiction of the 1950s and beyond, and existentialist thinking underlies (but does not dominate) works as diverse as Günter Grass's *The Flounder*, John Updike's *Rabbit* tetralogy and the plays of Samuel Beckett and Dürrenmatt.

Existentialist themes also surfaced in films in the 1940s and 1950s, particularly those of the Italian neorealists and by such

Japanese directors as Ichikawa and Kurosawa. Indeed, Japanese artists, particularly after the shocks of Hiroshima and Nagasaki, gave existentialist ideas a particularly savage and nihilistic edge. There are few bleaker explorations of existentialist dilemmas than Oshima's film *In the Realm of the Senses* or Mishima's novel *Confessions of a Mask*. Comedians, especially in the US, had a wonderful time sending up existentialist angst – and in two notable cases, those of Tony Hancock in the UK and Woody Allen in the US, Sartrean ponderings blossomed into a complete and agonizingly plausible comic persona. **KMcL**

Further reading W. Barrett, *Irrational Man*.

EXOBIOLOGY

Exobiology (Greek, 'study of life out there'), a term coined by the US geneticist Joshua Lederberg, is the study of, or search for, extraterrestrial life. Biologists assume that, as life has evolved on Earth, it will also have evolved, though possibly very differently, on any number of other planets. No compelling evidence for the existence of extraterrestrial life has so far been recognized and there are many critics of the field and its theories, not least because of its perceived associations with **sf**.

The prime aim of the exobiologist is to devise a means of detecting alien life, however radically different it may be from terrestrial life. The great distances involved mean that such investigations have largely been limited to scanning for unusual thermodynamic patterns at the surface of other planets.

Theoretical predictions suggest that there are a great number of inhabited planets, most home to civilizations far more advanced in time than those of humans. Attempts have been made to communicate by placing unambiguous pictorial messages on satellites and sending coded radio messages. Radio telescopes can detect signals from over 1,000 light years distant and have been used, notably by Soviet scientists, to listen for messages from distant stars. The SETI (Search For

Extraterrestrial Intelligence) programme represents a concentrated effort to scour the radio waves for patterns which might have originated from a sentient source. Such signals would not necessarily have been sent as deliberate attempts at communication from other planets, but would nevertheless be recognizable as evidence of extraterrestrial life. Radio waves have been emitted unintentionally from Earth for some 100 years and may ultimately be received by a similar SETI programme on a distant planet.

The detection of life by chemical means is also a highly developed science, but is limited by the space probe technology available for collecting samples. Although the presence of organic molecules may be taken as circumstantial evidence for the existence of life, it has been shown experimentally that certain physical conditions can promote the abiotic formation of organic molecules. **RB**

See also biogenesis; biopoiesis; panspermia.

Further reading Henry Cooper, *The Search for Life on Mars*; Francis Crick, *Life Itself*.

EXPERIMENTATION

Experimentation (from Latin *experiri*, 'to test') is one of the first signifiers of active intelligence, as opposed to instinct. When, for example, a rat in a maze learns the sequence of moves needed to win the reward or avoid punishment, it does so by trial-and-error, gradually eliminating error until the 'correct' behaviour-pattern is established. This is a form of willed imprinting, and it is not done by 'lower' creatures such as seaslugs or ants, whose behaviour is instinctive and does not depend on learning or memory. At a 'higher' level still, computers can be built which experiment along the rigorous lines which are part of the **scientific method**: thesis, testing-by-experiment, conclusion. At what is so far the 'highest' level known, experimentation is not merely a testing process but a creative one, throwing up side-issues, suggesting possibilities and leading to conceptual and practical breakthroughs which were no part of the original idea. No rat, no computer, but almost every single human being, does this. **KMcL**

See also artificial intelligence; thought.

EXPLANATION

An explanation of a phenomenon accounts for it, making it intelligible. Thus an explanation of an event tells us why it occurred, and an explanation of a **law of nature** tells us why it obtains.

According to the covering law model of explanations in **philosophy**, phenomena are explained by subsuming them under a general law, and perhaps by mentioning certain initial conditions. One explains a law of nature by subsuming it under more general laws of nature. Kepler's laws of planetary motion are explained by Newton's more general laws of mechanics. And one explains the occurrence of an event by reference to a general law and certain initial conditions: the falling of the glass is explained by the laws of gravity and my letting go of it at a height.

The covering law model faces various objections. One is as follows. It is not sufficient for explaining a phenomenon that one subsumes it under a general law linking it with an initial condition which did in fact obtain. So, for example, it is a law of nature that men who do take birth control pills do not get pregnant; however, if a man did take birth control pills this is hardly the correct explanation of him not becoming pregnant. **AJ**

Further reading C. Hempel, *Aspects of Scientific Explanation*; E. Nagel, *The Structure of Science*.

EXPRESSIONISM

Expressionism was a style in the Western **arts** which straddled the latter half of the 19th century and the first half of the 20th. Until the 19th century, the arts had been principally concerned with the depiction of reality, and artists used emotion – their own or their subject's – as one component of expression and not its guarantor. Expressionist art, by contrast, dealt directly with the transmission of emotion. It

was subjective and incoherent rather than objective and precise. The urge towards the overt expression of feeling began with the **Romantic** movement at the end of the 18th century, but true expressionism was only liberated a century later, when Freud's work made complexes, neuroses and private obsessions acceptable subjects for polite study and for the arts.

In **music**, though earlier compositions like Berlioz's *Symphonie fantastique* or Wagner's *Tristan and Isolde* are clearly concerned above all with emotion, the term 'expressionist' is generally reserved for such works as Scriabin's *Poem of Ecstasy*, Richard Strauss's *Salome* or Schoenberg's *Verklärte Nacht* and *Erwartung* (high peaks of the style).

In **literature**, though the chief expressionists are turn-of-the-century writers, such as Mallarmé, Huysmans and Maeterlinck, expressionist aims and techniques also influenced later writers, for example André Gide, Proust, Franz Kafka and, in his blunter way, Hemingway. In **drama**, expressionism was the style of men such as Strindberg, Frank Wedekind and Georg Kaiser, and hardly survived the 1920s. It can still be found in the cinema, in the work of such directors as Murnau or Fritz Lang and more modern exponents of Gothic or horrific mystery, for example Hitchcock's *Psycho* and Ingmar Bergman's *The Seventh Seal*, both of which use expressionist techniques.

The most lasting expressionist work has been in fine art. Here, creators sought to give pictorial expression to states of mind, religious or social convictions, in images which in their roughness of execution and simplicity of line and plane broke with the conventions of academic art. In their place they favoured a frame of reference influenced by naive and **folk art**. The two most thorough-going exponents of the style were the Bridge Group (Dresden, 1905), whose members carried expressionism to extremes in violent and aggressive compositions, and the Blue Rider Group (from 1911 onwards), whose members evolved a more structured style. More generally, expressionist painting ranges from the harsh canvases of Munch and Kokoschka (which show recognizable people in states of nightmare psychological alarm) or the paintings of Kandinsky (whose aim was to paint abstract emotion, and whose results often seem experimental and chaotic rather than exact) to the much later **Abstract Expressionism** of painters such as de Kooning, Dubuffet or Robert Motherwell. Many other artists (for example, Francis Bacon, Marc Chagall and Georges Rouault), though not full-hearted expressionists, have used the emotional fervency and gaudy colour characteristic of the style.

In fine arts, neoexpressionism was a label used in the 1980s and beyond to describe the work of narrative-based expressionist painters, principally in Germany, who reacted against the banalities of **conceptual art** and the impersonality of **minimalism**. Typical examples are the work of Anselm Kiefer, who depicted his country's past in such works as *To the Unknown Painter* (a commentary on the tragedy of the Nazi period in Germany), and Georg Baselitz's paintings of people literally upside-down, designed as a comment on the human condition. Other leading neoexpressionists include Francesco Clemente, Jörg Immendorff, A.R. Penck and Julian Schnabel.

In **architecture**, expressionism was identified with the works of architects in Germany, Holland and Scandinavia from the end of World War I until the 1920s. The expressionist buildings are characterized by unusual angular or organic forms and internal volumes, to some extent made possible by the imaginative use of reinforced concrete. The historian Pevsner saw the style as a deviation from the development of the Modernist movement, working under the influence of **Art Nouveau** in the political crisis following World War I. The prewar work most closely identified with expressionism is probably that of Peter Behrens (1868–1940), particularly his factories for A.E.G. in Berlin (1908–13), and certainly the postwar work of **Bauhaus**, during the Weimar period, is felt to have absorbed the principal features of expressionism, visually the stark expressive simplicity and theoretically a sense of architecture's ethical obligation, as a tool for raising social standards. The best-

known examples of postwar expressionist architecture are the Chilehaus in Hamburg of 1923, the work of Fritz Hoeger (1877–1949) and the interior of the Grosses Schauspielhaus in Berlin of 1919 by Hans Poelzig (1869–1936). Perhaps one of the most striking of all buildings in the expressionist idiom was an early work of Erich Mendelson (1887–1953), the 'Einstenurm', an observatory tower, built at Potsdam in 1920, an organic form with a motif of streamlining which was to become so important in Western industrial design. **PD MG JM KMcL**

Further reading K. Honnef, *Contemporary Art*; W. Pehnt, *Expressionist Architecture*; D. Sharp, *Modern Architecture and Expressionism*; John Willett, *Expressionism*.

EXPRESSIVE DANCE see Abstract Dance

EXTENSIONALITY see Intensionality and Extensionality

EXTINCTION

Extinction (Latin, 'being wiped out') is the disappearance of all members of a formerly living species. It was acknowledged by early palaeontologists who found fossil remains which were clearly dissimilar to extant species of the known world. Most scientists and laypeople believed, up to the 19th century, that extinction was impossible because all living organisms were in the care of God. In the 19th century it became clear, with the reconstruction of dinosaur remains, that extinction was a fact; many put this down to catastrophies such as flooding and accepted that this implied that the number of species on Earth was in steady decline. When Charles Darwin proposed a mechanism for the formation of new species it was explained how this process would render others uncompetitive and thus liable to gradual extinction. **RB**

See also evolution; fitness; natural selection; speciation.

EXTRAVERSION see Introversion and Extraversion

ÉLITE THEORY

Élite theorists, in historical and political studies, maintain that all forms of complex social organization inevitably become dominated by a small group, an élite (literally 'the elect', or 'chosen'). In a normative sense élitism suggests that the skills needed to manage a complex organization, like the state, require the elevation of a select group to positions of control. The classical élite theorists, like Vilfredo Pareto, Gaetano Mosca and Roberto Michels, argued that it is an empirical fact that governments and societies throughout history have been controlled by a 'ruling class' or power élite. Michels' '**iron law of oligarchy**' described the process whereby an élite, once in a position of leadership, is able to accumulate more power through the control of access to information and through the manipulation of the decision-making process. The iron law of oligarchy dovetails neatly with the conservative (see **conservatism**) belief in the necessity and virtue of hierarchy in human affairs.

As a theory of **history**, élite theory emerged as a reaction against **Marxists** who claimed that history has been the history of class struggle, but that after the socialist revolution there would no longer be any objective need for a ruling class. Élite theorists maintained that if Marxists were ever successful they would in turn form a new political élite. Indeed Pareto argued that political change is measured by the ability of an established élite to withstand challenges from the inevitable emergence of new élites. In Pareto's scheme the control of information, coercion and conciliation, and the management of bureaucratic power constitute determinants of the cycles of political change; he also detects a cycle in the psychological character of élites, in which 'lions' alternate with 'foxes'.

The difficulty in defining where élite power begins and ends, especially in a democracy, is one focus of criticism of élite theory, especially by thinkers from the pluralist tradition (see **pluralism**). Modern élite theorists argue that though most liberal democracies superficially appear to be open to competition and influence by non-élites, in fact, this competition is managed from above by a small group, usually representatives of government, big business and the military, sometimes referred to as the 'military-industrial complex'. Their critics maintain that this argument is unfalsifiable. The most prominent applications of élite theory in the social sciences analyse the background characteristics of élites (for example, their education and family history), and their social and professional networks. **BO'L**

See also historical materialism; liberalism; socialism and social democracy.

Further reading P. Dunleavy and B. O'Leary, *Theories of the State: the Politics of Liberal Democracy*; S.J. Eldersveld, *Political Elites in Modern Societies: Empirical Research and Democratic Theory*.

F

FABIANISM

Fabianism is the name of both a socialist intellectual organization which originated in Britain in 1884, and of a general type of **socialism**. The Fabian Society took its name from the Roman general Quintus Fabius Maximus Cunctator (known as the 'delayer') who defeated Hannibal through a battle of attrition, striking at the appropriate moment, and avoiding wasteful direct battle. However, the British Fabians have never been very much enthused by battle: they have been intellectual.

In politics, the principal authors of the Fabian agenda were Beatrice and Sidney Webb. The slogan 'the inevitability of gradualness' became the Fabians' guiding theme, as they commended the gradual development of socialism, engineered not by revolution, but by the application of rational analysis to problems of government, and by socialists deliberately working within liberal and capitalist institutions.

Gradualism as opposed to 'revolutionism' would educate the public in the merits of socialist solutions.

Writers associated with the movement from the beginning included Annie Besant, Bernard Shaw and H.G. Wells. However, each had private obsessions and interests, which ran hand in hand with their socialist beliefs, and resulted in their own, idiosyncratic views of Fabianism – somewhat to the dismay of pure politicians like the Webbs. Besant was interested in religious mysticism (she later became a leading **theosophist**); Shaw was an ardent advocate of such things as naturism, reformed spelling, teetotalism and **vegetarianism**; while Wells was convinced that **science** was not an objective study, but a beneficent and redemptive force in human affairs.

Ideas such as these tended to give Fabianism an aura of crankiness, both in popular opinion (it was much mocked in tabloid newspapers) and in the minds of the 'governing classes' whose influence the Fabians aimed to subvert, but who nevertheless idolized Shaw, Wells and the others even as they sidelined their ideas. In the end, many Fabian politicians moved on to support the newly-formed Labour Party. The society, however, remains in existence. Unlike some of its early members, contemporary Fabians are resolutely hostile to **Marxism**, especially in its Leninist variants, believing that revolution is counterproductive for the advancement of democratic socialist ambitions. They are also critical of producer-based socialism, believing that socialists must pursue the public interest rather than that of narrow or sectional interest-groups. They also maintain that socialism, or social democracy, is the logical completion of liberalism, rather than its ideological enemy.

The Fabian Society continues to influence political debate in the UK (especially in the Labour Party), although many other think-tanks and policy organizations now rival it in significance. Fabian socialism has also been influential in the countries of the British Commonwealth. **KMcL BO'L**

Further reading Margaret Cole, *The Story of Fabian Socialism*; B. Pimlott, *Fabian Essays in Socialist Thought* (especially the chapter by R. Barker); P. Pugh, *Educate, Organize: a Hundred Years of Fabian Socialism*.

FABLE

A fable is a short tale illustrating a moral point. Many come from, or imitate, **folk literature**. A favourite method of fable is to tell a tale using animals as characters, and anthropomorphizing them in the process. This happens, for example, in the Roman satirist Horace's story of the Town Mouse and the Country Mouse, the Brer Rabbit stories from the USA and George Orwell's *Animal Farm*. Fables, by combining entertainment and moral instruction, have always been favoured forms of writing for children. Even in a more elaborate, literary guise, for example Swift's *Gulliver's Travels* or the anecdotes used by Sufi preachers to expound their philosophy of life, they tend to a kind of self-conscious reductionism which can irritate as many adults as it seduces. **KMcL**

FACT AND VALUE

Philosophers often distinguish between statements of fact such as 'there are three chairs in the next room' and evaluative statements such as 'the chairs in the next room are beautiful'. The former simply describes the contents of the next room while the latter evaluates them. Evaluative judgements may involve ethical terms ('good', 'generous'), assessments of rationality ('prudent', 'wise', 'justified'), points of etiquette ('polite', 'crass'), as well as aesthetic and other vocabulary ('pretty', 'funny'). However, it is not entirely clear why counting the chairs is just stating the facts while saying that they are beautiful is to go beyond the facts. The distinction between fact and value has been further explained in a number of different ways.

First, it is said that people must agree on the facts about the chairs (such as their number), while they need not agree on whether they are nice-looking chairs. People can have different opinions about whether the chairs look good without anyone being wrong, but there is only one right answer to the question: 'how many chairs are there in the next room?' But this way of contrasting facts with values seems to presuppose the truth of relativism about values, a controversial doctrine.

Second, it is said that anyone who can see the chairs can see how many of them there are while they cannot simply see whether they are nice looking or not – one needs to evaluate their appearance. In general, we can discover the facts through our senses, but an evaluative judgement requires more than sensory input, it also requires that we apply our aesthetic or other values to assess our experience. However, one could equally well say that in order to learn how many chairs there are, we have to apply our understanding of what a chair is. One could reply that a chair is objectively a chair while a chair is only subjectively nice-looking, but this way of making the distinction presupposes that value judgements are subjective, another controversial doctrine.

Third, it is said that a statement of fact is not, by itself, a reason for doing anything, while an evaluative judgement is. Knowing the number of chairs in the next room will not drive me to act unless I want to do something with those chairs, while knowing that the chairs are nice-looking gives me reason to prefer them to other chairs when furnishing my room. But someone might respond that knowing the chairs in the next room are nice will give me reason to prefer them only if I want nice-looking chairs in my room. This way of distinguishing facts from values presupposes that value judgements are prescriptive rather than descriptive, another controversial doctrine.

It seems that the distinction between facts and values arises only when we adopt one of a number of doctrines about so-called evaluative judgements; it is not a neutral datum. **AJ**

See also emotivism; ethical intuitionism; ethical relativism; descriptivism and prescriptivism.

Further reading J.L. Mackie, *Ethics*, chapter 1.; B. Williams, *Ethics and the Limits of Philosophy*, chapter 8.

FACTION

A faction (i.e. 'fact-fiction'; no connection with other meanings of the word) is a work of **drama** or **literature** treating facts in a fictional manner, or applying the techniques of documentary or other factual narrative to wholly fictional material. Shakespeare's history plays and Daniel Defoe's novels are faction of the first kind. **Realist** novels, such as Zola's *Germinal* or Theodore Dreiser's *An American Tragedy*, are faction of the second kind. The name 'faction' could equally be applied to some ostensibly documentary material, for example much autobiography and emotively-coloured sociological writing, such as Mayhew's *London Labour and the London Poor* or George Orwell's *Down and Out in London and Paris*.

Today the commonest use of the word is in film and television, where 'faction' is a recognized form, making **drama** of recent events. Its authors often weave into their fictional narratives transcripts of real speeches and conversations and news film of the people and events involved. Trials, scandals, political machinations and wars are favourite subjects. Faction of this kind is increasingly the main way in which many people get to know about history or current affairs. Some social commentators claim that a reverse effect is now noticeable. Conditioned by such powerful factions as *Apocalypse Now*, *Silkwood*, *All the President's Men* in the cinema, or *Cathy Come Home*, *Tumbledown* and innumerable films about historical figures such as Churchill on television, many viewers (and reporters) are tending to treat real news events as if they have been edited and presented, even created especially, for home consumption, as if real life itself is some kind of imaginative construct. **KMcL**

FAÇADISM

Façadism, in European **architecture**, refers to the practice of building anew behind a retained front elevation. In certain contexts, such as Brighton in 18th-century England, terraces were constructed to give a classical conformity to the street while each individual dwelling might be designed to suit an individual occupant. Façadism refers perhaps most specifically to situations of redevelopment, and often represents a failure to appreciate the three-dimensional integrity of a built structure's original design. **JM**

FAITH

In many languages, for example Greek and German, the same word is used for both belief (an intellectual assent to a statement of fact or a doctrine, or a reasonable assumption, such as 'I believe that the Sun will shine tomorrow') and faith (unconditional trust or confidence in someone or something, as in 'I have faith in my doctor's ability to cure me). To add to the confusion, 'faith' in English can also refer to **religion** (as in 'the Christian faith' or 'interfaith dialogue'), although a Hindu would use the word *dharma* or duty, and others would see their religion as a way of life (or rather, *the* way of life), not merely the way one thinks. Therefore faith is something one does, not something one passively accepts. Yet at certain times in some religions one's salvation, as in a political party, has depended on holding correct beliefs, which one can adopt as a matter of will-power rather than in loving response to a power beyond oneself. In **Hinduism** there is both the *gnana marga*, the way of knowledge, which informs belief and is reserved to the few, and the *bhakti marga*, the way of loving devotion, which is akin to faith.

Within **Christianity**, there is a difference between the Roman Catholic position that 'the faith' is a deposit of doctrine handed down infallibly by the Church from generation to generation, which one accepts as a voluntary (though predestined) act of will, as it is credible if not fully comprehensible, and the Protestant position that faith arises in response to God's love revealed to the believer by divine grave, the work of the Holy Spirit. Interestingly, Paul's first letter to the Corinthians (chapter 13), gave priority to love or **charity** over faith and hope, though it is doubtful if the three can be separated from each other. **EMJ**

Further reading John Hick, *Faith and Knowledge*.

FANTASY LITERATURE see sf

FANTASY/PHANTASY

Fantasy is viewed in various ways by different psychological schools. Sexual desires and aggressive impulses can be satiated by conscious fantasy; they can be as pleasurable, explicit or frightening as we want to make them. They are seen as a safety net which holds bad parts of the inner self, and are used this way in **literature**, **science** and everyday action.

Psychoanalysts distinguish between 'fantasy', daydreaming, imagining (which is synonymous with neurotic daydreaming) and unconscious 'phantasy', an imaginative activity which underlies all thought and feeling. All psychodynamic schools agree that conscious mental activity is accompanied, supported and enlived by unconscious phantasy. In Freudian analysis phantasies might be oral, anal, libidinal, infantile, or hysterical. Kleinian psychoanalysis works with the unconscious phantasies based on observance of object relations that the patient brings, and examines how these relate to past and present experience.

Jung also saw that phantasy, developed in childhood, prevented growth. Phantasy occurs in childhood as a way of dealing with real conflicts in the family which are too difficult and painful to deal with directly.

Gestalt sees fantasy as a middle zone of awareness. In fantasy we are trying to actualize our self-image, not our actual self, and growth is distorted and inauthentic. Characterized by internal debates and talking to oneself, it is a substitute for engaging with the real situation. Fantasy neutralizes the future by creating catastrophic or optimistic scenarios, and such mental activity will often provoke anxiety. **MJ**

FARCE

Farce (Latin, 'stuffing') is a genre of comic **drama**, characteristically presenting an anarchic world in which authority, order and morality are under threat, and in which ordinary people are caught up in extraordinary goings-on or extraordinary people are caught up in ordinary goings-on. At its best it gives subversive expression to our wilder imaginings and rebellious instincts. Although farces may steal from **comedy** and comedy may incorporate the farcical, farce on the whole devotes less attention to character, and has more manic physical activity and accelerating momentum in its plots.

In farce at its best, the successive discoveries, reversals, coincidences and repetitions are worked into an intricate and completely satisfying pattern, which persuades an audience of the logic of each successive step along the way, even if the final result seems supremely illogical. Disguise, role-playing and frantic improvisation are forced upon the characters to keep them one step ahead of disaster, or enable them to keep up appearances as events spiral out of control. A degree of manic activity results, drawing extensively on the physical skills of the actor. Farces often rely heavily on stereotypes – stuffy matriarch, henpecked husband, bimbo, apoplectic military man, etc. Inventively handled, these can be very funny and an essential part of the farcical mechanism. Uninventively handled, they can reinforce prejudice and create easy laughs. Some contemporary farces effectively challenge stereotypes, as Stoppard does in *Dirty Linen* (1976), where the 'dumb blonde', Maddie Gotobed, turns out to be far from dumb, or as Orton does in his general onslaught on sexual compartmentalization.

Many of the plays of Aristophanes and Plautus offer fine examples of farcical techniques and structure, and it was also a characteristic feature of much medieval secular and religious drama. Since the **Renaissance**, three periods of particular creative activity in farce may be distinguished. The first is **Commedia dell'arte** in 16th-and 17th-century Italy, with its stock characters, situations, improvisations and comic routines. The second is France between the mid-1800s and the 1920s, where such prolific writers as Labiche and Feydeau satirized bourgeois life and the institution of marriage. Recently farce techniques and episodes have been extensively used for their subversive potential in 'serious' plays, which seek to challenge conventional sexual, political or social responses, for example, (in the UK) Caryl Churchill's *Cloud Nine* (1979) and Edward Bond's *Early Morning* (1968), and (in the US) Albee's and Kopit's plays of the absurd. **TRG SS**

See also theatre of the absurd; tragedy.

Further reading Jessica Milner Davis, *Farce*.

FASCISM

Fascism is a term used to describe historically specific interwar (1919–45) European political movements and doctrines. Its derivation is from *fasces*, the ceremonial bundles of rods containing an axe with its head protuding, symbolizing the authority of the ancient Roman republic (which many Fascist governments wished to emulate). Fascist is also used more loosely to describe any form of right-wing authoritarian régime which is not explicitly **socialist**. In its most loose usage fascism is employed to denigrate people espousing either right-wing or left-wing views with which the speaker or writer disagrees.

Interwar European fascism is easiest to define by what its exponents opposed. They were anti-democratic, anti-Marxist, anti-liberal and anti-conservative: although they were prepared to make temporary alliances with their enemies, normally with conservatives. They rejected cultural and economic conservatism, including its Christian foundations, but also the internationalism, pacifism and materialism of liberals and the left. They invariably embraced an extremely chauvinistic form of **nationalism**, usually in a form which emphasized the racial or ethnic foundations of national identity, and committed them to imperial aggrandisement of their nations and to militaristic doctrines and practices. They were generally in favour of **totalitarianism**: the total control of the polity, economy and society by a fascist party which would create a new national and secular culture, and indeed a new (or revived) people. Fascists were élitists, emphasizing the role of charismatic and authoritarian leaders: although they claimed that fascism represented the interests of all the nation and they mobilized mass political parties.

Many of the characteristics of interwar European fascist ideas and movements have been found elsewhere, in Europe, both before and after the interwar period, and in Latin America, Asia and South Africa. However, most historians and political scientists tend to see fascism as a uniquely interwar European phenomenon, and one utterly discredited by the defeat of Nazi Germany and fascist Italy. Whether they are right to be so sanguine remains a moot point. **BO'L**

See also conservatism; liberalism; Marxism.

Further reading W. Laqueur (ed.), *Fascism: a Reader's Guide*; S.G. Payne, *Fascism: Comparison and Definition*; S.J. Woolf (ed.), *Fascism in Europe*.

FASHION see Change

FAUVISM

Fauves (French, 'wild animals') was the disparaging term given by the French critic Vauxcelles to a group of artists including Derain, Rouault and Vlaminck who exhibited at the Paris autumn Salon of 1905. What disconcerted him – he was comparing their work with Donatello's sculpture – was the dazzle of colour that filled their canvases: large areas of flat, unmodulated colour, often thickly applied and with little resemblance to Nature. In fact the Fauvists used colour, not as the **Impressionists** had done, to transcribe the 'reality' of surface appearance, but to fix the expressionistic properties of brilliant colour as a structural device. Thus, Matisse in *Green Stripe (Madame Matisse)* (1905) used olive green to project his wife's nose and brow away from the warm flesh tone of her cheeks without recourse to orthodox devices of modelling or delineation. The brushstrokes, boldly applied across the picture surface, serve to draw further attention to the non-recessional nature of the implied picture space. (In this respect, Fauvism had been anticipated centuries earlier, by such such artists as Mantegna, Rembrandt and El Greco.) Apart from colouristic brilliance – which had great influence on such **Expressionists** as Munch and Kokoschka – the Fauvists had very little else in common,

and soon went their separate ways. Their immediate predecessors include van Gogh and Gauguin; later painters influenced by their style range from Dufy and Kandinsky to Bacon, Rauschenberg and Soutine. **MG PD**

Further reading J.E. Muller, *Fauvism*.

FEDERALISM

Federalism (from Latin *foedus*, 'covenant') is a political arrangement where several states choose to join together for mutual advantage, while retaining an amount of autonomy: the analogy is less with a body or a pack of animals than with stockholders in a company. Often such federations are successful: the United States and the German federation are prime examples. But often they fail: notable examples are the United States of South America, which Simón Bolívar attempted and failed to establish in the early 19th century, and the former USSR which so spectacularly unravelled after the Cold War. In each of the last two cases, the attempt was to federate not states but whole countries, with long-established ethnic and political identities of their own.

In a federation **sovereignty** is shared between the central or federal government and the sub-federal governments (known as cantons, Länder, provinces, republics or states). Each of these two levels of government is sovereign in its own domain, and the relations between the two levels are normally regulated by constitutional law which specifies the appropriate competencies (separate or joint) of the federal and sub-federal units. Federations are usually accompanied by a written constitution. Democratic federations also normally provide for bicameral representation at the federal level: a popular chamber, or house of representatives, and a provincial chamber or senate in which *either* each of the sub-units of the federation are equally represented *or* the less populous sub-units are over-represented. Constitutional change in a federation is distinguished by the fact that the sub-federal units have the right to participate in amending (or vetoing change of) the federal constitution, and to change their own constitutions. Disagreements remain legion among political scientists and constitutional lawyers about the precise necessary and sufficient conditions to define a federation. At one extreme are those who see any system of decentralization as displaying federal characteristics, at the other are those who require numerous highly specific institutional arrangements to be present.

Federalism has developed in various parts of the world (for example, as well as Germany and the US, in Australia, Belgium, Canada, India and Switzerland), and has been vigorously espoused elsewhere for various reasons. The latter have included the desire to promote a single market and/or strong defence and foreign affairs capability out of an existing **confederation**; the wish to integrate diverse ethnic, linguistic, religious, racial or regional communities without imposing uniform centralization; and the ambition to disperse and balance sovereign power in what used to be a unitary state.

Critics of federalism condemn it for being too weak, and not sufficiently responsive to the will of the majority (the argument made by exponents of a unitary state); or, conversely, federalism is criticized for being too centralist (the argument made by confederal opponents of greater European integration). Others observe, with either approval or disapproval, that federal systems are almost always engaged in constitutional renegotiations of competencies, and complex bargaining over redistributive issues.

Federalist ideas have long antecedents in Western political thought, especially in the dispersed patterns of authority characteristic of European **feudalism**, but the first detailed defence of a modern federal system of government was published in 1787 in the USA by Alexander Hamilton, James Madison and John Jay. Their opponents, the anti-federalists, were mostly confederalists. Similar arguments now surround the creation of a deeper 'European Union'. **BO'L**

Further reading A. Hamilton, J. Madison and J. Jay (ed. I. Kramnick), *The Federalist Papers;* K.C. Wheare, *Federal Government.*

FEEDBACK PRINCIPLE

The Feedback Principle, in **electronics**, is implied when a measure of the output signal from some system is applied, or fed back, to the input of the same system. By this means the system input can be controlled to compensate for undesired output states or signals, and the system stability is improved. The principle may be considered as a way in which a mechanical or electrical system 'learns from its errors'.

Feedback is used in a myriad of diverse applications. The concept first appeared as the mechanical governor for a steam engine, where the centrifugal force on rotating weights was used to control the supply of steam to the cylinders. Since the centrifugal force depended on the rotational speed, the engine was controlled to run at a constant speed. The cruise control in motor cars, for example, applies the principle of feedback to maintain a steady cruising speed. If the cruise control detects that the car's speed is increasing, for instance because it is going downhill, then the electronic sensors will send a signal back to the control system which will reduce the fuel flow and therefore the power developed by the engine, causing the car to slow down until the required steady speed is achieved.

A great deal of the early work concerned with understanding and controlling the use of feedback was applied to telephony and electronic amplifiers. The early vacuum amplifiers were among the first electronic devices to be commercially used, and had produced significant advances in the area of long-distance telephony and improving the quality of radio reception. However, it had been found that quite severe distortion occurred in some amplifiers, resulting in audible hum or unintelligible speech being reproduced. In 1927, H.S. Black invented the concept of 'negative feedback', whereby controlling the amount and phase of the feedback signal greatly reduced the distortion, at the cost of a small reduction in amplification. The invention of the negative feedback amplifier greatly improved telephone communication at this time, and other applications of feedback soon followed.

In 1932, H. Nyquist analysed a generic feedback system and devised a mathematical and graphical method to establish general rules of stability for the system. By this time it was recognized that distortion was due to instability or unwanted oscillations in the output signal, caused in most instances by unsuitable levels of feedback. By investigation of the Nyquist Diagram, as it became known, much improved electronic amplifiers were built, and complex control system behaviour could be modelled and assessed.

Around the 1930s and 1940s, work on oscillators, where positive feedback is used, created effective signal generators which have become standard pieces of electrical communication test equipment, and crystal oscillators. Positive feedback occurs when the output signal is fed back to increase the input signal, which in turn increases the output signal and so on. Oscillators apply this principle but effectively limit the maximum value that can be reached. Crystal oscillators, for example, use positive feedback to produce the very accurate high frequency waveforms, or oscillations, that are used in modern radio tuners to enable demodulation of incoming radio signals. Crystal oscillators are also used in accurate timing circuits and in modern quartz watches.

The development and application of the feedback principle, along with **electromagnetism** has led to atomic models and theories giving much greater understanding of the materials we use today. **Quantum** mechanics has led to many other related discoveries, including **wave-particle duality** of matter and the use of semiconducting materials; it has also helped scientists to understand and harness nuclear energy. The application of dependent technologies, such as semiconductor materials providing silicon 'chips' and electronic computers, has led to quantum mechanics becoming the cornerstone of modern **physics** and has heralded a new generation of science. **AC**

FEMINISM

Feminism is variously defined as 'advocacy of the right of women to equality with men in all spheres of life' and 'women's struggle' to gain that right. The distinction reflects its dual nature: it is at once a sociopolitical theory and a social movement. Feminists have used many different methods to enable the vision of equality to be realized, and feminists do not always agree on the causes for women's oppression. Consequently, many contemporary feminists prefer to use the plural 'feminisms' to reflect the different perspectives that must, necessarily, be given voice.

In both theory and practice, women's resistance to male domination may well predate the formation of fully-articulated, or fully-acknowledged, **ideology** and practice; many feminists argue that 'women's history' has always been present, but is invisible in the history books of patriarchy. Conventionally, however, feminism as a movement is traced back to the late 18th century in Europe, immediately following the French Revolution. Taking their inspiration from the Revolutionary ideals, several women's clubs were formed in Paris and other cities to promote women's rights. Political programmes were elaborated calling for equal rights in education, employment and government. The reception was hostile and the clubs were dissolved by government decree. (This hostility set the pattern for the treatment of women's movements in all countries, in succeeding generations.)

In the 19th century, it was in the USA that feminism developed most, becoming a model for women's movements in other countries. American feminists were closely involved with groups committed to the abolition of slavery and to temperance. Perhaps such activity was one reason why comparatively few gains were made in this period in improving women's own social or political position. In Europe, a petition signed by 1,500 women was presented to the British Parliament in 1866, demanding full voting rights for women. It was ignored, and in response the organizers set up the National Society for Women's Suffrage, which for the rest of the century continued to struggle for full voting rights. By the early 20th century marches and demonstrations were standard throughout Europe and the USA, and by the end of the 1920s, voting rights were achieved in many countries, though by no means all.

At this stage it became clear that the question of equality was far more wide-ranging than voting-rights. One of the key texts for modern feminism, Mary Wollstonecraft's *Vindication of the Rights of Woman*, had put the issue clearly as long ago as 1792, and in the 1920s feminists such as Vera Brittain and Virginia Woolf began exploring and campaigning on the ideas it raised. Wollstonecraft had said that oppression was not primarily a matter of laws and exclusions; it was custom and attitude, arose in the home, and imposed femininity on women (a process she described as a woman being made 'the toy' of a man). Woolf and Brittain wrote of women's need for employment and financial independence, and other writers and activists of the period fought for equal pay, child care and reproductive rights. The time was ripe: the experience of European women in World War I, running homes and businesses, working in factories and down mines, making decisions and engaging in activities formerly reserved for men, had raised a huge popular hunger for such equality once the war was over and the men came home. A movement that had until then been predominantly middle class and educated now found new roots among women of all types and in all areas. The work was still chiefly in the Western world, though there were stirrings of feminist revolt in some Islamic countries (in Egypt, the campaign for women to be allowed to choose whether or not to wear the veil – an important symbol of equality – was won at this time), and in Japan (where suffrage societies were founded on the Western model).

During the 1920s and 1930s, many feminists still assumed that legislation, economic independence and a political voice would end women's oppression in all its aspects. But experience proved otherwise, and consequently, in the 1960s, feminist writers (again, initially, in the UK and the US) broadened the critical domain, considering it necessary to look at the construction of **gender** and **sexuality** for the reasons and also the solution of women's oppression. Julia Kristeva in her essay 'Women's Time' divides feminism into three stages. Early feminism demanded equal access to the 'symbolic' (the place in which meanings are assigned) order. In post-1960s feminism, women rejected the male symbolic order in the name of difference – this form of radical feminism highlighted and celebrated femininity. Tori Moi argues that the project of radical feminism must continue to counteract **patriarchy**, but metaphysical gender identities must be deconstructed so that radical feminism does not become an inverted sexism.

Feminism has used many different critical methodologies to identify and challenge women's oppression. By looking at the diverse methodologies used by feminism it is possible to form a skeletal picture of what feminism means for contemporary women. During the 1960s, **Consciousness Raising** groups gave feminism a very powerful tool for using women's experience as the cornerstone for theoretical discourse. Feminists pointed out that patriarchal academic discourse had neglected to include the experience of women as it was considered banal and not 'objective'. In order to counteract this patriarchal denial of women's experience feminists used the phrase 'the personal is political' to show that no element of experience is outside of ideological discourse. On the basis of consciousness raising feminists were able to theorize why women were excluded or written out of academic thought. Juliet Mitchell, for example, reassessing the Freudian view of femininity, argued that it was better not to reject Freud's view as patriarchal, but to use Freud's texts as a means of measuring how patriarchy worked to construct femininity as negative and passive. It is through the critical use of such theories that feminism has greatly contributed to the recent impact of postmodernist thought. Some feminists have rejected what they call the 'tools of the father' and radical feminists have aimed at re-conceptualizing theory from a female perspective. Radical feminism is characterized by the theoretical practice of uncovering what is taken to be 'natural' and making visible the patriarchal investments that lurk within.

As well as measuring and identifying patriarchal structures many feminisms have formulated strategies and campaigns for combating patriarchy and oppression. Such strategies depend on what particular feminists believe to be the main vehicles of oppression. Radical feminists have thought that 'separatism' enabled women to withdraw from male-dominated institutions, both to flourish outside the male domain and to articulate, through withdrawal, women's dissatisfaction with the patriarchal status quo. Some feminists have argued that the only way to escape patriarchy is to reject heterosexuality and take on a lesbian identity. Others have devised strategies for highlighting women's position in relation to cultural phenomena, developing strategies for reclamation and acknowledgement of women's cultural output which had been, and often still are, buried under male control of the institutions of cultural production. Books have been devoted to women as spectators of films, books and art. Some feminists have looked at the way in which popular culture can be read in a subversive way, for example, Hollywood films of the 1940s and 1950s made specifically with a female audience in mind. Feminist publishers have republished forgotten or unpublished novels by women as well as providing the means by which contemporary feminist texts can be published. Many film-makers and writers have been introducing into the cultural agenda the notion that women, as well as men, have sexualities. Feminist thought has also become an important critical tool for diverse academic subjects as well as within specific women's studies courses. Despite claims that we in the West now live in a 'postfeminist' society feminism still has many indispensable questions to ask.

'Postfeminism' is a term used to suggest that the project of feminism has ended, either because it has been completed or because it has failed and is no longer valid. Contemporary feminists strongly disagree with either of these arguments and most would see 'postfeminism' as a term that has been imposed upon feminism from patriarchal sources. Many contemporary feminists set out to assess and challenge what has been termed the 'backlash' against femininsm.

Susan Faludi's book *Backlash: The Undeclared War* (1992), for example, documents the way in which the fight for equal rights for women has throughout history been subject to 'fits and starts'. Faludi puts forward the example of US magazines in the 1920s, which claimed that young women

were not interested in feminism. Similar arbitrary statements have appeared in contemporary magazines. By placing modern notions of 'postfeminism' within a historical framework in this way, Faludi is able to identify patterns of 'masculinity in crisis' produced by patriarchal fears that arise during peaks of feminism. She also describes the ways in which disagreements and rivalries within the strands of feminism have often been exploited and used to support the patriarchy's backlash.

Tania Modleski addresses and challenges postfeminism by arguing that within academic work there seems to be an increasing assumption that the goals of feminism have been achieved. She argues that the recent rise of gender studies and the study of masculinity is, once again, emphasizing male issues at the expense of feminism. Modleski also suggests that within critical theory many theorists do not adequately differentiate between feminism and feminization (that is, patriarchal construction of femininity). For her, and for other feminists, these factors are the effect of patriarchy's defensive attempt to incorporate female power. She also believes that recent postfeminists play with gender, in particular differences are negated, and this will 'lead us back into our "pregendered" past where there was only the universal subject: man.' **DA TK BO'L**

See also class; power; social construction of reality; social stratification; sociology of knowledge; typifications.

Further reading H. Eisenstein, *Contemporary Feminist Thought*; A. Oakley, *Housewife*; Gayle Rubin, *Thinking Sex: Notes for a Radical Theory of the Politics of Sexuality*.

FEMINIST CRITICISM

Feminist **criticism** is an arts and political movement which began in the US and western Europe during the 1960s and has continued to the present day, though it is still more active in the West than in the East. At first it was principally confined to **fine art** and **literature**, but in the 1980s it spread to such other areas as film, **music** and **theatre**, though progress in these fields has been slower than in other arts.

The starting point of feminist criticism is that women creators have been systematically marginalized by a male-dominated tradition, and that there is a current of 'women's experience' which should no longer be hidden, but should surface and be recognized as of equal importance to 'men's experience'. There are three main ways to do this. First is the rediscovery and restoration to circulation of works by women of the past, and the sponsoring of new work. Second is the critical examination of 'women's experience' as depicted by both women and men – often involving a refocusing of our views about past creators and their works. Third is the search for and discussion of a specific 'gender' in literary or artistic work, in the grain of thought processes and style themselves.

The second and third of these approaches are of most significance. If only the first applied, feminist criticism would be no more than just another revisionist agenda devoted to the rehabilitation of derelict reputations. The broader approach, however, has led to the development of the view that the works of both men and women are legitimate subjects of study, and, more importantly, to the use of notions of **discourse**, **ideology** and **power** to study the motivations of artistic creativity itself. This approach has revealed hitherto overlooked areas of interest (such as the representation of women, the gendered 'gaze', institutional bias, sexuality and patronage), and has led some critics to argue that **feminism** is not simply another ism (like **Marxism** or **structuralism**), but, because it challenges male-defined parameters of artistic creativity, is a new discipline altogether. For example, received notions of 'greatness' and 'genius' are so constructed that they exclude all but a handful of women creators. (This is particularly so in the creation of classical music and of plays.)

The feminist conclusions are that only the overthrow of this canon and its replacement with a broader constituency will allow women the place they deserve and that this in turn should lead to a new evaluation of the nature of artistic creativity itself. This last point suggests that we are in a transitional and revolutionary stage, in which political agendas are more urgent than the

cause they serve. But that cause, a refocusing of our whole idea not of men or women but of the arts, is of far more significance than any of the activities which serve it, and (with apologies to those currently lined up on this or that side of the barricades) can only make us eager for the day when ideologies of all kinds, in Marx's phrase, have 'withered away'. **KMcL**

FEMINIST THEATRE

Ideas within feminist theatre have developed from the incorporation of new content and spectacular imagery in the agitprop performances of the early 1970s to a feminist critique of and concern with the **postmodernist** issues of theatrical representation and writing. **TRG SS**

See also political drama; theatre.

Further reading Sue-Ellen Case, *Feminism and Theatre*; Helene Keyssar, *Feminist Theatre*.

FEMINIST THEOLOGY

Women theologians bring very varied perspectives and church traditions to their theology, so that it is better to talk of an approach to theology than of a theology itself. Nevertheless, they are not only restructuring theological language and reconstructing the image of God, but changing the understanding of the nature of theology itself. Women are retrieving their heritage – what Jewish women call 'the half empty bookshelf' – because women's contributions to historic events have been ignored, with (in **Judaism** and **Christianity**, for example) Abraham, Isaac and Jacob being commemorated in the liturgy and not the equally courageous Sarah, Rebecca, Rachel and Leah. They are also developing their own distinctive rituals and spirituality.

Although there have always been pioneering women in religious life, whether saints or not, and religious women such as Christabel Pankhurst and Emily Davidson in the suffragist movement, women were at first reluctant to join the feminist movement because of its pro-abortion and anti-motherhood stand, but they were becoming increasingly aware of the weight of prejudice against women seeking to understand their faith for themselves, instead of accepting (male) authority. For, in common with other theologies of liberation, feminist theology starts where women are today, and analyses their social situation, the religious pressures they are under (for example, that women are Eves, tempresses, responsible for leading men into sin, etc.), the taboos they must observe and the degree to which they are excluded from sacrament and priesthood. They use the feminist concept of the **patriarchy**. Most feminist theologians, if they believe in the work of the faith community, are in favour of the ordination of women to the priesthood (in Christianity) and the rabbinate (in Judaism). Many, having been excluded from career advancement in secular professions, are sensitive to the structural discrimination of religious institutions, and the way motherhood is exalted in the abstract and exploited to keep mothers in inferior positions. Some women have become so alienated that they have left the mainstream religious movements to join groups worshipping the Goddess. Others are working on liturgies and translations of scriptures in non-sexist language. Interest has centred on **pneumatology**, while the evolution of feminist ethics, especially in matters relating to female biology, has been paralleled by women's work in the field of moral theology.

The ultimate aim of feminist theology is to liberate women and men from centuries of oppression, and to enable them to contribute as fully as possible to contemporary developments in research, spirituality and the expression of their faith. A number of flourishing networks exist to assist this, some denominational and some interdenominational or inter-faith (tackling common concerns such as the rise of **fundamentalism**). EMJ

See also god; goddess; feminism.

Further reading Mary Grey, *The Wisdom of Fools*; Ann Loades, *Feminist Theology*.

FERMAT'S LAST THEOREM see Number Theory

FERMENTATION

The process of fermentation (from Latin *fervescere*, 'to boil') was used by ancient civilizations in the production of bread and wine. It was thought by the ancient Greeks to be a process of maturation. It was investigated by **alchemists** and early chemists, notably Antoine Lavoisier, in the 18th century, who observed that it could be represented by a chemical equation. Theories explaining the mechanism behind the process were proposed only in chemical terms until Louis Pasteur's famous experiments, in 1876, showed that fermentation could not occur unless a sterile medium was contaminated by microorganisms. Fermentation plays a central role in modern **biotechnology** where single-cell organisms, particularly yeast and bacteria, are grown on a large scale for the synthesis of gentically engineered products. **RB**

See also enzymes.

FERMIONS AND BOSONS

To discuss the similarities and difference between fermion and boson particles, the concept of intrinsic spin, or angular momentum, must be introduced. In current understanding, all particles possess intrinsic angular momentum, which is a fundamental property of the particle. This angular momentum is quantized in units of $\frac{h}{2}$, where h is a physical constant with the value 1.054×10^{-34}.

The Standard Model, the currently accepted description of how particles interact, leads us to believe that there are two types of particle: particles which constitute matter, and particles which are used as intermediaries of forces. The first type are fermions, and have half-integral values of h for intrinsic spin; the second are bosons, with integral values.

These particles interact very differently. Fundamental requirements of symmetry lead to the Pauli Exclusion Principle, which states that no two fermions in a system may have the same set of **quantum** numbers. This is identical to the statement that no two fermions may occupy the same place at the same time. For bosons, these symmetry requirements have more subtle consequences, which lead to macroscopic quantum phenomena such as superfluidity and superconductivity.

Bosons behave differently, and have no exclusion principle. This difference in behaviour may be seen when two fermions interact together to form an effective boson, which occurs in superconducting metals. Electrons are fermions, which is why they form ordered shells around the nucleus of an atom. If they were bosons, they would be at liberty to all fall down to the lowest energy level, and if this were the case, **chemistry** and therefore life would never have existed. **JJ**

See also quantization.

FEUDALISM

Feudalism comes from the medieval Latin word for 'fee'. It may be broadly defined as an agrarian political order in which coercive and judicial power is decentralized among an aristocratic ruling class (as opposed to a centralized monarchy), and as an economic order in which peasants produce most output (and are exploited by aristocrats). By implication, feudalism is characteristic of societies with low levels of urbanization, mercantile trade, and industrial production. On this broad definition feudal systems have existed during many periods of post-tribal human history, and in all major continents of the world (except Australasia). They are considered typical of **agrarian societies** in which imperial or despotic authority is absent – that is, rulers with the ability to treat aristocrats as their dependents. In **historical materialist** thinking feudalism is the last mode of production in human history which precedes capitalism.

However, some historians and social scientists define feudalism as an historically-specific European phenomenon, covering the centuries succeeding the collapse of Charlemagne's empire, and confined to areas of Latin Christendom. On this narrow conception feudalism (as its Latin derivation suggests) centrally involved hierarchically organized service, in which a grant of land bound a feudal lord to his sovereign, and tied subordinate knights to more powerful nobles in a system of vassalage.

This definition explains the origins of the term 'feuding' – armed conflicts between autonomous lords and their retinues. The narrower conception of feudalism also mandates the presence of other social practices: castle-based structures of lordship, a distinctive warrior caste committed to an honorific conception of chivalry, serfdom, a caste-based social order, and a separation between religious and political authorities. However, even this narrower conception of feudalism cannot be defended as unequivocally European as régimes displaying these traits can be found in historical India and the Middle East. **BO'L**

See also Asiatic mode of production; despotism; sovereignty.

Further reading M. Bloch, *Feudal Society*; J.H. Kautsky, *The Politics of Aristocratic Empires*; R.S. Sharma, *Indian Feudalism c.300–1200 AD*.

FIBRE OPTICS

Fibre optic cables are manufactured from glass or transparent plastic and used to transmit light and optical images. This medium of transmission may be used to transmit digital data over long distances avoiding the need for expensive copper electrical cables.

Fibre optic cable works on the principle of total internal reflection of light. This principle was first understood in the 1870s, but major developments in this field have occurred since the 1950s. Light enters at one end of the cable and has multiple reflections from one side of the cable to the other until the light appears at the far end. For transfer of sound or information the light is encoded in a series of binary pulses (1 or 0) and is then decoded at the receiving end. If the light is to travel long distances, repeaters are used to boost the signal at regular intervals.

The first experimentation with light with a transmission medium began with scientists trying to send light down long hollow pipes, which had mirrors and lenses to guide the light straight down the pipe. The pipes were then buried for protection. This method worked well as long as the pipes were not disturbed, but failed as soon as the pipes were bent. Fibre optic cables overcame this problem in allowing light to travel down its length without the need for mirrors or lenses. In fact, fibre optic cables can be bent into any shape required, even around sharp corners.

Fibre optics are used widely in medicine to transmit images of the internal organs to a camera outside, so eliminating the need for exploratory surgery. Even if surgery is required (for example, removal of cartilage), fibre optics can reduce the severity of the operation. Only small incisions need to be made and armed with a fibre optic cable attached to a camera and a **laser** or small shears or scalpels operated by slender cables passing down the tube, the surgeon may cut or sew cartilage together. Thus the patient may be remobilized in days instead of weeks.

The advantages of fibre optic transmission systems include, weight and cost reduction, much improved signal to noise ratio and the use of lower cost materials. **AA**

Further reading N.S. Kapany, *Fibre Optics: Principles and Applications.*

FICTION

The creation of fiction is an activity unique to the human race. Other creatures may dissemble (for example to lead predators from eggs in a nest), but none tell lies. Embroidering the truth, moving from reality to meta-reality, requires not merely imagination but intellectual objectivity: the powers to decide what effects we are aiming for and what ways will best or most enjoyably achieve those effects, and the ability to eavesdrop on ourselves, as it were, to assess our performance even as we give it. People with a tin ear for the **arts** often affect to despise fiction, on the grounds that making up reality is a denial of the true analytical and logical powers of the human mind. On the contrary, making fiction uses those powers in a precise, and precisely calculated, way. Anyone can pigeonhole, but to invent your pigeonhole before you start and then modify it as you go along to suit what you choose to put into it: that takes thought. **KMcL**

FIELD WORK

Field work is the research undertaken by an anthropologist in a particular community. When **anthropology** emerged as a discipline, such societies tended to be tribal or remote, but field work is now often undertaken in urban societies or among minority groups or subcultures.

Field work relies on the principle of participant-observation – the anthropologist shares the life of a community, participating as well as observing, in order to experience and understand it in as much detail as possible. An anthropologist is expected to learn the language proficiently and spend at least a year 'in the field'. Presuming that problems of translation, both linguistic and cultural, can be overcome, field work produces careful descriptions of specific communities. Anthropological facts are actually lived experiences turned into sociological facts through the process of observing and questioning. The anthropologist gleans information through a select number of people (termed informants).

Despite the anthropologist's status as both participant and observer, understanding is inevitably limited to some extent by the personal views of the informants. Male anthropologists, for example, often fail to elicit the alternative models of society proposed by women, as well as other interest groups in the community. Unless the anthropologist is careful, the views represented in his or her writing exclusively reflect the views of an élite, or those of marginal groups, depending on their choice of informants. The multiplicity of versions or models of reality tend to be reduced to a one-dimensional study of society.

Anthropologists are increasingly aware of the problems inherent in the methodology of participant-observation. Most anthropologists now write explicitly about their own position within the community, so that readers can evaluate the information for themselves. **CL**

See also ethnography.

Further reading M. Griaule, *Conversations with Ogotemmeli*; P. Rabinow, *Reflections on Fieldwork in Morocco.*

FIELDS

Fields are among the fundamental mathematical structures studied in **algebra**. A field is a **ring** in which each non-zero member of the field has a multiplicative inverse. The structure is that a field is a **group** under the operation of addition and (if the zero is left out) also a group under multiplication. Examples of fields include most of the commonly used kinds of numbers: **algebraic numbers**, **complex numbers**, **rational numbers** and **real numbers** are all fields. Real numbers, in fact, can be uniquely characterized as they are the only field which has an ordering and the property of completeness. **SMcL**

FIGURATIVE ART

Figurative art, also known as representational art, is the mirror image of **abstract** art. That is, it portrays figures or objects as they might appear in nature: the **objective correlative** is something real rather than (as in abstract art) a pattern, geometrical shape or other intellectual construct. Whatever distortions or fantasies the artist builds into the representation, this real correlative keeps it representational. Thus, even the most angular **cubist** statues (such as those of Lipchitz), even the most diagrammatic of **folk-art** religious paintings, so long as they depict real things or are based on what we can see in real life, are figurative.

Folk art often shows, in simple forms, both extremes of the figurative approach. On the one hand are faithful portrayals of people, animals, plants, and so on; on the other are shapes which reduce the object portrayed to its basic elements, to a symbol, and which can be hard for the untutored eye to recognize. Thus, Mother Earth is represented both as the statuette of a beaming, fecund woman, fertility and motherhood personified, and as an oval with a dividing line from top to bottom (symbolizing the female genitalia) or as a single, nippled breast. In depictions of hunting scenes, animals or enemies can be shown in recognizably lifelike forms, or as stick-like representations (sometimes reduced to as little as a single line). Supernatural beings are often imagined, and depicted, as hybrids of real objects: their faces are half human, half gnarled tree-root; they have snakes for hair; they have knives for teeth and fires for eyes.

The tendency to pattern-making in all folk art often blurs the boundary between the figurative and the abstract – lightning-zigzags, fish-ovals, snailshell-coils and tree-trunk forks are built into the texture, offering the eye the satisfaction of pattern and the brain the pleasure of association with the story, **legend** or scene alluded to. This tendency has been adopted by the fine art of **Islam** (where figurative representation is discouraged): representation becomes pattern and pattern representation, in a combination of directness and allusion whose complexity is often increased by specific and overt religious references.

In most cultures, figurative art begins with religion, and specifically with human-like or beast-like representations of the divine. These are often meticulously lifelike – there are no more naturalistic sculptures of the human body than those of Aphrodite in the Greek tradition, for example, or of Shiva dancing in the Indian – and the artists take the opportunity to show 'idealized' forms of **beauty** for beneficent deities, and self-consciously grotesque beasts and humans for demons. In many cases – for example in the canopies and wings which surround depictions of *apsaras* in Buddhist art, or the Edenic tendrils and petals of medieval **Christian art** – the figurative is extended to provide a semi-abstract pattern, a practice which, again, perhaps began as an attempt to depict the meta-reality of the supernatural world, but surely continued out of sheer artistic exuberance.

Secular figurative art often uses the same or similar forms as sacred, but removes the mystical element. Instead, artists often go for detail of the everyday, carving veins and wrinkles on human figures, painting every fleck of dew on a cobweb, fold in a fabric or ray of light through the leaf-canopy in a forest. In second-rate hands, this attention to detail can be tiresome, bleeding life from the work as in the all-engulfing battle scenes favoured in 19th-century European boardrooms, or the equally overwhelming corporate portraits or cityscapes hung in their contemporary Japanese equivalents. But where genius is at work, meticulousness gives the art a kind of richness which seems to remove it from the world, in much the same way as the decoration of religious art transcends reality. In a Rembrandt portrait, for example, or an Exekias pot-painting, it is as if not just the particularity of the person or thing represented, but its entireness, its metaphysical identity, has been captured and represented. This is one quality of figurative art, the power to focus the general through the particular, is one to which abstraction can never aspire. **KMcL**

FIN DE SIÈCLE

Fin de siècle (French, 'end of century') is a bizarre artistic offshoot of **millenarianism**, that inexplicable psychic unease engendered by the approaching end of each millennium. Only one century has so far had a *fin-de-siècle* in the **arts**, the 19th – perhaps because it was the first century in which, thanks to the arrival of the Industrial Society, people in the developed world at least were governed by clocks and watches, and the passing of time units larger than a day or a harvest season was universally perceived. Certainly the passage from (say) 400 BCE to 399 BCE, or 1599 to 1600, took place without fluttering anyone's sensibilities. Even the move from 999 to 1000 was marked by only a few Christians, whose zeal in Bible study was matched only by mathematical ignorance, and who convinced themselves that at 12.01 am on the first of January, 1000, Gabriel would blow his horn and the Day of Judgement would begin.

Throughout the Western world, the passage from the 19th to the 20th century roused extremely strong feelings of a different kind, fanned (and in some cases originated) by popular newspapers and by authors (such as H.G. Wells in the UK and Jack London in the USA) who should have known better. The general thesis was that advanced society had reached a point of exhaustion, of stagnation, and that all its institutions (save possibly commerce, then more immune to fashion than it is today) desperately needed an injection of new ideas if they were to survive. The first day of the new century was perceived as a good moment to aim for such an injection, and accordingly, for a couple of decades beforehand, pundits and commentators began assessing situations, discussing possibilities and making forecasts.

Politically and socially, the turn of the 20th century happened to coincide with (rather than triggered) a general feeling of dissatisfaction and radical experiment frantically opposed by the conservative. Republicanism, women's suffrage, educational and penal reform, changes in work practices all were feverishly discussed. Anarchy was suddenly no longer the idea of a lunatic few, but was a serious possibility, seriously discussed and even attempted in most of the university towns in Europe. New machinery (such as motor cars and moving-picture cameras) and 'new' ideas (such as modular construction in buildings) suddenly began to suggest that the future (that is, the new century) would look, and be, radically different from the past. The scientific community – by this period it was beginning to think of itself as a community – was no longer reeling under the implications of **Darwinism**, but was beginning to cope with the possibilities of the 'new' physics: **quantum** mechanics and the theory of **relativity** were well on the horizon.

Throughout the 18th and 19th centuries, the arts of the West had been particularly subject to fads and fashions, responsive to social and intellectual change as at no previous time. The *fin-de-siècle* atmosphere of the 1880s and 1890s therefore had a profound effect on artists of every kind. This was partly due to the fact that in most of the arts, major creative bombshells had been detonated in the previous few decades, so that musicians, for example, were still coping with the fallout from Wagnerism, dramatists with that of Ibsenism, painters with the collapse of the **Academy** tradition and the rise of such 'movements' as **Impressionism**. The Paris Exhibition of 1889, held to celebrate the centenary of the French Revolution, had attracted exhibitors from throughout the world, and for many Western creative artists their first experience of Eastern techniques (for example, Mughal Indian painting, Japanese print-making, Chinese poetry, or Balinese *gamelan* music) had indicated realms of possibility previously unimagined. Oriental visions and versions of reality chimed with the then-current Western interest in 'other' states of being, from dreams to the spirit world, and encouraged artists to believe that each exploration of 'reality', each personal refraction, was as valid as any other. The new medium, film, all the rage in Europe from the mid-1890s onwards, also suggested that 'surreal' happenings (for example, speeded-up time, or the unexpected juxtapositions achieved by jump-cuts) were not so much signs of a disordered mind as perfectly legitimate versions of 'reality'.

Artists reacted to all this ferment in two different ways, or rather three, if one counts aggressive philistinism and refusal to have any truck with the new as an 'artistic' reaction. Some were inspired by the feeling of exhaustion, of the impotence and perceived irrelevance of art to life, and produced work notable for its aloofness, its dandyism, its refusal to take any responsibility or make any references beyond itself. Exquisite decadence, in such people as Beardsley, Maeterlinck, Satie, Whistler and Wilde, was more than the pose its detractors imagined: it was an energetic and creative force. Its surviving manifestations – Debussy's and Maeterlinck's *Pelléas et Mélisande*, Wilde's *The Portrait of Dorian Gray* and the designs of Charles Rennie Mackintosh are notable examples – may seem somewhat peripheral to the mainstream of art, or of artistic masterwork, but the impact of decadence was crucial to the development of almost every major art movement of the succeeding century, from **Dada** to **minimalism**, from **expressionism** to the the **twelve-note system**, from **surrealism** to the **theatre of the absurd**.

The second response was eager innovation. Artists everywhere began devising agendas and writing manifestoes for the 'art of the future'. This usually involved three things: complete junking of any ideas or methods regarded as valid in the past, confrontation (for which 'outraging the bourgeoisie' was a less polite alternative name) and political activism based on the feeling that art had the power to remake, and if necessary redeem, society. To some extent, the entire history of 'modern art' in the 20th century, and our perception of artists, has suffered from this attitude, the outraged bourgeoisie turning away from art in far greater numbers than those which supported it, and the 'proletariat' (whose lot most of the early programmes were devised to 'better') remaining as aloof from the arts as

when they started. It may seem a paradox that the 'hard' programmes of the reformers had such negative results (most, from **futurism** to **serial music**, from **vorticism** to **structuralism**, had a deadening rather than an invigorating effect on the arts at large), while such 'soft' artistic manifestations as those of the decadents had and still have such insidious and lasting influence. But such remains the case. The 20th century, artistically speaking, has been a battleground between the two approaches, and the seeds of the conflict (which has occupied our best creative minds and energies ever since) lies in work produced, in Europe especially, 100 years ago. *Fin-de-siècle* may be an accurate temporal designation for what was going on, but in terms of influence, we are talking far more of the 20th century than of the 19th, and of beginnings far more than ends. **KMcL**

Further reading C. Paglia, *Sexual Personae: Art and Decadence from Nefertiti to Emily Dickinson*; R. Shattuck, *The Banquet Years*; D. Silverman, *Art-nouveau in Fin-de-siècle France: Politics, Psychology and Style*.

FINE ARTS see Art(s), Visual

FISCAL POLICY

A fiscal policy (from Latin *fiscus*, 'rush basket' or 'purse') refers to the changes in federal government spending and taxation in order to affect the general level of economic activity. Such policy was urged by John Maynard Keynes, the British economist, in the early 1930s when it appeared that monetary policy would not bring the UK or the US out of deep depression. The US Employment Act of 1946 adopted fiscal policy as a means of fighting unemployment.

In order to manage public expenditure and raise the revenue to pay for it, governments have to decide on forms of taxation and the volume of spending. Taxation can influence spending and working behaviour, and the distribution of income in a society. So governments choose a balance between direct and indirect taxation (for example, income tax versus value added tax); progressive or regressive taxation; taxing companies or individuals; the balance between earned and unearned income. Fiscal policy aims to plug loopholes, and must constantly adapt to new tax dodges. In addition, one eye has to be kept on other countries' policy, as more favourable taxation policy elsewhere may lure away tax revenue producing multinational companies.

In addition to taxation, governments choose the volume of their spending. Spending is divided between current (pens, textbooks, salaries) and capital items, (roads, hospitals, sewers). Bids to cut spending usually focus on capital spending which can be cut more quickly and easily than current. It is easier to scrap a planned project then someone's salary. The drawback is that capital spending, as investment, may have a bigger multiplier effect on total spending; also, the infrastructure must be maintained and if neglected will collapse and cause further economic turmoil.

To slow an 'overheated' economy, fiscal policy would reduce government spending and/or raise taxes. Governments find either policy very difficult to adopt. Either action is likely to lose votes and financial support for legislators. Even when people agree generally that belt-tightening is required each of us prefers that it be someone else's belt. **TF**

See also deficit spending.

FITNESS

Fitness, in the **life sciences**, is a term used in Neo-Darwinism (see **Darwinism**) to describe the possession of inherited characteristics which render the organism in question more competitive and thus more likely to leave more descendants. Organisms that possess these characteristics are described as more fit than those of their competitors which do not. This gives them an advantage in the process of natural selection, which has been described as 'the survival of the fittest'. **RB**

See also adaptation; natural selection.

Further reading John Maynard-Smith, *The Theory of Evolution.*

FIXATION

The term fixation was used by Freud to describe a state of emotional arrest of part of a person's psycho-sexual development, a state of being fixed in the past. It is visible in attachments to objects which represent one of the three earlier stages of sexual development before the genital phase, called the **oral, anal and phallic stages**. Freud quoted the case of the girl who continued to suck her thumb right through childhood, into and after puberty and into adulthood. She commented that even the best of kisses was never as satisfying as sucking her thumb. This girl was fixated at the oral stage. The miser who hoards money, the collector who hoards pictures, or people who dwell long and unproductively on uncompleted tasks, may be fixated at the anal stage. Even after a stage is outgrown and other activities take its place, it will resurface during times of anxiety and stress. Freud called this reversal regression, and in some cases the fixation was so absolute as to hinder further development of the individual.

The term fixation is also used more generally outside psychoanalysis as a term to describe any state where a person is fixated on a person or object in such a way as to prevent development or change, or as a way of avoiding other issues which may demand change. **MJ**

FOLK ART

Folk art may be identified loosely as the visual production of those communities whose approach to the making of imagery can neither be considered to be 'primitive' (in the ethological sense) on the one hand, nor 'academic' (in the sense of a sophisticated and somewhat narrow fine-art production) on the other. In practice folk art may thus be loosely associated with those rural communities which articulate through visual means the rituals, religious observance, folk wisdom, folklore, social mores, or heritage of their society.

The area is vast. But if we take folk art to mean either the product of such societies, or an art which exhibits qualities which fine art would label as unsophisticated, then we can make some incursion into the subject. The nature of folk art is extremely diverse, but may generally be considered to be the visual outcome of the conditions under which it was produced, displayed, or otherwise utilized. In this sense, the very label folk 'art' is itself problematic, in that it opposes the quality of 'folk' to the category of 'art' often with the assumption that folk art is a 'primitive' version of 'academic' art.

The rise of academic study of folk art can be associated with the early 19th century, a period when the interest in the untutored, the individual and the non-canonical was being enshrined in the **Romantic** aesthetic. From this time on, folk art has usually been seen as the opposite of an art which posits its existence on rules, order and artificiality. From this perspective folk art had the virtue of simplicity, directness and honesty. (It hardly needs saying that the attribution of these qualities to folk art says far more about the way the Age of Romanticism – and to some extent the Age of **Enlightenment**, as expressed in Jean Jacques Rousseau's myth of the primitive conceived of the category of art than it does about the nature or purpose of folk art itself.)

For the 19th century, the attribution of folk art to the untutored spirit (with the assumption that such a spirit speaks truer than does artifice), was close to associating folk art with the spirit of the people, the **collective unconscious** in whose 'art' were to be found the fundamental values of society. This form of cultural nationalism has been part of the study of folk art ever since – an association which has done little for the understanding of the subject, especially as it is not clear where this association stands in relation to discourses on fine art.

Folk art, then, may be seen as an essentially social art, responding to immediate and localized needs in an immediate and localized way. Within this broad definition, the various and diverse forms folk art has taken are legion. It may manifest itself in abstract pattern making or realistic representation, although the former tends not to be self-consciously abstract in the way **modernist** painting may be so described, and the latter may not exhibit the sophisticated use of representation which we associate with the **naturalism** of the **Renaissance**. In fact, both Renaissance and modernist painting are conceptual in so far as they use a theoretic construction in order to give form to their ideas, whereas it has been observed that a characteristic of folk art is that its practitioners do the opposite, and begin with the particular to arrive at the whole.

One could continue with observations of this kind almost indefinitely, but certain similarities may be tentatively ascribed to folk art. They would include the simplification of the means of representation down to its essentials; a propensity to pattern making; the exaggeration, for the sake of clarity or expression, of the image; and the attempt to visualize the intangible. It could of course be argued that these are the properties of visual imagery worldwide, that what in fact we are here discussing is not folk art but art. While this is a persuasive argument, for the moment the 'fine' conception of art still holds sway, at least in art-critical circles, and this form of image-making has, for the time being, usurped the art discourse. This has resulted in all other forms of art production being marginalized, whether geographically/racially (as, for example, 'Third World' art) or aesthetically, where folk art is seen to be an inferior form of the quintessential (fine) art practice. **MG PD**

See also religious art.

Further reading N. Graburn (ed.), *Ethnic and Tourist Arts*; S. Hiller, *The Myth of Primitivism: Perspectives on Art* .

FOLK LITERATURE

Folk **literature** may seem to be a contradiction in terms: folk arts, one might think, are fluid, traditional, self-regenerating and anonymous, whereas literary works are fixed, anchored to individual creators and specific occasions of authorship. In fact folk literature can be just as sophisticated, in themes, form and content, as any attributable work, and so far from being fluid, it is often quite remarkably fixed and internationally so, in a way which defies explanation except in terms of something like Jung's theory of the **collective unconscious**. The 'Cinderella' story alone illustrates this. It is told on every continent, in over 200 known versions, some as much as 1,000 years old (that is, from times before inter-continental travel could reasonably have carried them), and all with recognizable details and themes in common. It is hardly surprising that cosmological myths from different traditions have themes in common; that a simple folk tale should do so is remarkable.

Folk literature, from **myths** and **legends** to the simplest nursery rhymes, is fundamental to human **culture**, a matrix for all our imaginings. It began in preliterate cultures and shows no sign of diminishing vigour despite the growth of literacy. It offers endless possibilities for anthropological, sociological and psychological research, and – as any library catalogue will show – is a bottomless well for anthologists. It has provided themes, attitudes, forms of verse and prose, turns of speech and inspiration to all manner of literary creators. It is a purely human phenomenon – no other creatures have the imagination to make up stories or the language to transmit them – and it is human thought in one of its most mysterious, most pervasive and most seductive forms. **KMcL**

FOLK MUSIC

Folk **music** is a term used by musicologists to distinguish types of 'vernacular' music from 'art' or cultivated music, and usually means orally-transmitted music as opposed to notated or 'literate' music. However, in a society which has no written or separately identifiable art music the term is irrelevant. In general, therefore, the term folk music has validity when referring to the non-literate music of Western cultures, and to those musical traditions of Asia and the Orient which are not recognized as art music. It is, however, largely inapplicable to the traditional music of Africa and some South American countries. At its congress in 1955, the International Folk Music Council passed the following resolution defining folk music:

'Folk music is the product of a musical tradition that has evolved through the process of oral transmission. The factors that shape the tradition are: (1) continuity that links the present with the past; (2) variation which springs from the creative impulse of the individual or the group, and (3) selection by the community which determines the form or forms in which the music survives.

The term can be applied to music that has been evolved from rudimentary beginnings by a community uninfluenced by popular and art music, and it can likewise be applied to music which has originated with an individual composer and has subsequently been absorbed into the unwritten tradition of a community. The term does not cover composed popular music that has been taken over ready-made by a community and remains unchanged, for it is the refashioning and re-creation of the music by the community that gives it its folk character.'

At the time (the 1950s) the scope of folk music was generally understood to embrace narrative songs and ballads, erotic and courtship songs, seasonal and festival songs, work and trade songs, and dance and instrumental music. The IFMC's definition was therefore subsequently thought to be too restrictive and too heavily weighted in favour of Western culture, and the meaning of the term 'folk music' has since continued to be the subject of heated academic debate. Indeed, who the 'folk' are is something upon which folklorists have seldom agreed. For some, folk music was simply rural, peasant music; for others it has meant the indigenous music of a particular ethnic group, or of a specified section of a society regardless of its rural or urban context. It was the acceptance that folk music can exist in towns and cities, in forms, for example, such as black American **Blues** or Jewish *klezmer* music, that broadened the concept of folk music and prompted the IFMC to change its name in 1981 to the International Council for Traditional Music. A further distinction must be made between *oral* and *aural*, particularly in an age where technological advances in communications and broadcasting media permit learning by hearing rather than by a direct word-of-mouth tradition. Consequently, the term 'folk music' can only be used loosely and arbitrarily, for the distinctions between folk, popular and art music are becoming increasingly fuzzy.

Another problem facing the folk music historian is the question of authenticity in the early song collections. It is now assumed that many collectors were guilty of some form of mediation, for example, in the rewriting and rearrangement of the song's text, rendering its publication suitable for an educated and critical reader, in the expurgation of lewd, bawdy lyrics, in the censorship of tunes in a musician's repertoire that did not conform to the predefined notion of what constituted 'folk', and in the modification of melodic and rhythmic elements to suit 'cultivated', European musical taste.

In European culture, the general public's view of folk music has been conditioned largely by the concerted effort of the collectors and revivalists who, in wishing to promote their nation's folk music as a socially beneficial tool, often painted a romantic and idealized picture of rural life. There is a popular belief that a nation's folk music must somehow embody the essential traits of that nation's culture and people. This conviction has at times provoked a politically nationalistic view of folk music, and one not only held by the general public but also by some folk song scholars. Cecil Sharp, an eminent collector of English folk songs in the early 1900s, concluded that: 'The discovery of English folk-song places in the hands of the patriot, as well as the educationalist, an instrument of great value. The introduction of folk-songs into our schools will not only affect the musical life of England; it will also tend to arouse that love of country and pride of race, the absence of which we now deplore.' Lamentably, this concept of folk music has, at times, been exploited by dictatorships and authoritarian governments. For example, in Nazi Germany folk songs were used to emphasize the 'purity' or superiority of its cultural heritage in contrast to the 'degenerate' and 'culturally contaminated' music of its European neighbours. In the USSR during the 1950s, traditional folk tunes from all its ethnic groups were adapted to verses praising Stalin, collectivism and the rule of the proletariat. At the same time in England, another revivalist movement emerged which, supported by the Communist Party of Great Britain and other left-wing organizations, spawned numerous 'folk clubs' where semiprofessional singers performed the songs collected at the turn of the century.

In American society, folk songs have been used for various social and political causes, especially as protest songs. The American view of folk music, in contrast to the European, was deeply affected by the songs of the poor and oppressed segments of its society, in particular by Afro-American forms such as the Blues. The use of folk song to voice protest became increasingly popular with white Americans, especially during the 1950s and 1960s, when causes such as the civil rights movement and the pacifist campaign opposing the Vietnam War bred a new generation of singer-songwriters, including the internationally successful Bob Dylan, who mixed traditional Anglo-American folk styles with elements of urban popular music.

In the 1960s, the term 'folk music' was adopted by the commercial recording industry as one of its marketing labels. Using the superficial paraphernalia of what passed by popular belief as 'folky', it promoted a prestigious and stereotypical image of the 'professional' folk singer whose self-penned songs consciously avoided the saccharine sentiments of the **pop** music ballad. The public came to revere the solitary, in-touch-with-Nature minstrel-poet, juggling with surreal imagery and symbolism, or the protesting hobo-troubadour whose menu of complaints has since become today's ecologically 'green' agenda. In the late 1960s a new brand of commercial folk music emerged as a fusion of traditional Anglo-American elements with amplified Western **rock** and Blues, marketed as 'folk-rock'. By the end of the 1980s much of the world's folk music, whether genuine or contrived, had been subsumed under the recording industry's new banner '**World Music**'.

If, according to the IFMC, one of the characteristics of folk 'is the refashioning and re-creation of the music by the community', then it appears that the term itself has been widely subjected to the same process of variation. SSt

Further reading Dave Harker, *Fakesong; the manufacture of British 'folksong' 1700 to the present day*; Bruno Nettl, *Folk & Traditional Music of the Western Continents*.

FOLK ROCK see Rock Music

FOOD WEB

The food web of a biological **community** describes the flow of energy between the species types which make up the community. Complex interactions occur between individuals and species, and these are important in defining the community as a whole. The term 'food chain' is also used for this purpose, but 'web' more usefully illustrates the intricacy of the interactions involved. Any biological community may be broken down into producers and consumers. The primary producers are green plants, which use sunlight as an energy source to construct complex, energy-rich molecules such as proteins, fats and carbohydrates: used for structure and energy storage. The consumers are those organisms which derive their energy from that trapped by producers: thus consumers include herbivores, predators and organisms such as fungi which feed upon rotting biological material. The energy transfer is inefficient, so the producers and lower consumers are much more abundant in terms of numbers and material than the higher consumers; this gives the web or chain a pyramid shape. In most communities the species diversity is such that a number of herbivores can feed on a number of plants, while being preyed upon by a variety of carnivores. The energy stored within the bodies of consumers which have few predators is trapped at this stage because the bodies of the animals, and indeed all other organisms, will ultimately be made available as a food source for other consumers. This produces the web structure of energy flow; nutrients such as carbon and nitrogen also flow within the food web in such a way as to be recycled. The pathways of energy and nutrient transfer may be mapped by the ecologist but are dynamic and fluctuate with populations and environmental conditions. **RB**

See also biomass; biome; competition; ecosystem.

FORDISM see **Labour Process**

FOREIGN EXCHANGE RESERVES

Foreign exchange reserves are made up of foreign currencies and gold, and these resources are held by a country's **central bank** or treasury department. These reserves may be used to buy and sell the country's currency on foreign exchange markets the purpose being to affect that country's exchange rates. On occasions it may occur that, by agreement, several governments may enter exchange markets, at the same time in order to influence a particular country's exchange rates. An example of such a concerted action occurred near the end of the 1980s, when the central banks of several countries entered foreign exchange markets to sell dollars from their reserves to try to help the US prevent the value of the dollar from rising. Under the post-World War II **gold standard** countries were called upon to maintain stabilization funds to maintain the international value of their currency short of transferring gold. **TF**

FORGERY

Forgery, in **art** terminology, is a **copy** of someone else's creation passed off by the forger as an original work by the original creator. A forgery (or fake, the law makes no distinction) may, therefore, be distinguished from the various forms taken by the copy, for example studies after the art of the past, emulations, or replicas. Vasari recounts the story of the young Michelangelo making a marble Cupid and then artificially ageing it in order to convince a collector of its antique origin. Although Michelangelo's patron, Lorenzo de' Medici, remarked that in passing it off as an antique Michelangelo would get far more money for it, a mercenary motive seems less important here than the young man's pretension to rival the sculptors of antiquity.

A forgery may be perpetrated through imitating the style of an artist or period, or counterfeiting the materials typical of that period (either through reusing old materials or ageing modern ones). In practice forgery most often involves employing both deceptions at once. Having obtained or made materials similar to the object to be imitated, the artist then takes care to imitate the appearance of the work copied, often through reassembling characteristic passages into one new work. This form of copying, known as a pastiche, has the advantage for the forger of allowing the forgery to fit in to an artist's oeuvre without duplicating any one work. A further sophistication is when the forger makes a work sufficiently unlike the artist copied in order to tempt the historian to construct a connection between the two, thereby legitimizing the forgery.

Passing off a work as being by the hand of another, inevitably more famous, hand has long been the stock in trade of unscrupulous dealers. However, amateurs and art historians have often allowed their enthusiasm for their chosen artists to sway their judgement. Van Meegeren's rather poor forgeries of Vermeer made in the 1940s could only convince an art historian desperate to expand Vermeer's slender oeuvre.

Artists have attempted to control the proliferation of forgeries of their work. Albrecht Dürer instigated court actions to prohibit the fraudulent use of his monogram or the unauthorized copying of his work. Claude Lorrain kept a studio book, the *Liber Veritas*, in which he recorded all his compositions and their location. Likewise the art market and museums, both with a vested interest in protecting their reputations for unimpeachable integrity, have attempted to distinguish the original from its copy. This is done in one of two ways, either with the aid of science, through laboratory tests, x-rays and chemical analysis, or through **connoisseurship**, which is the ability of an art expert to assess the authenticity of a work from the handling, style, or, more vaguely, the 'feel' for the quality of the work. Until quite recently, the approach of the connoisseur has been confounded in the public's mind with that of the art historian.

Aesthetically there are several problems with the notion of forgery. It contrasts the 'genuine' or authentic work too strongly with its 'fraudulent' imitation. The effect of attributing positive qualities to an original, only to contrast it with the negative values of the imitation – lack of quality, skill, conviction – is a normative one which adds little to the understanding of either imitation or model. In fact the inferiority of the copy is not intrinsic but implied on the basis of this binary opposition. **MG PD**

FORMALISM

Formalism is an exclusive concentration on form or forms, in any field from **religion** to **science**, from social behaviour to the **arts**.

In the criticism of fine art, formalism was a movement which flourished in the early part of this century, and then again from the 1960s onwards, in the work of such writers as Clement Greenberg. It offers a corrective to the obsessive interest in **authenticity** and individuality of **connoisseurs**, who label anything they are unable positively to identify as either 'after X', 'School of X' or a **forgery**. Formalism treats the characteristic appearance of, for example, **romantic** painting, as an expression of 'a way of seeing' special to that period. It seeks to subsume the many different stylistic expressions of a period into a kind of meta-style, a dominant mode of seeing whose validity is confirmed by examples of the art of the period in question. There are two main problems: first, that this stance is too narrow to encompass a complete explanation of the meaning of any given work of art, and second, that only those works which support the formalist construction are considered important, the rest tending to be marginalized – a formalist equivalent of the connoisseurs' 'inauthentic' label. Nonetheless, formalism was and is a salutary discipline, and was an important component in the development of **modernism** at the beginning of this century, when the notion was prevalent that artistic styles could be codified, and when artists themselves were more fascinated by such programmes and 'isms' than in almost any other period in history.

In **literature**, formalism was a critical theory developed in immediately post-Revolutionary Russia, by a group of writers and academics led by Roman Jakobson. The basic idea was that 'literature', as distinct from any other kind of writing, is achieved by the use of certain artificial formal devices, specific to it alone. For the original formalists, this theory had political and social overtones as well as literary: the structures of written communication were directly relevant to the objectives of such communication. In particular, the Formalists said that 'literature' never depicts reality in a straightforward way, but always mediates, organizes and presents it by the use of language, 'defamiliarising' it in the process. The idea of 'defamiliarization' (in Russian *stranenie*, 'making strange') interested later literary theorists, particularly Jacques Derrida and his followers: it is, precisely, the creative process which **deconstruction** sets out to investigate and sidestep.

In **mathematics**, formalism is a school of thought that all work in mathematics should be reduced to manipulations of sentences of **symbolic logic**, using standard rules. It was the logical outcome of the 19th-century search for greater rigour in mathematics. Programmes were established to reduce the whole of known mathematics to **set theory** (which seemed to be among the most generally useful branches of the science). First attempts to do this included those of Bertrand Russell and A.N. Whitehead in *Principia Mathematica* (1910), and the later **Hilbert Programme**. It was hoped that such programmes would be the culmination of all mathematics, not only setting the discipline on a strong formal foundation, but making it possible to write out a proof or disproof of any formal sentence totally mechanically. In other words, every mathematical result would be known or not known. Kurt Gödel, however, proved this impossible with his Incompleteness Theorem, dooming Hilbert's programme as unattainable (see **Gödel's incompleteness theorem**), and formalism is today something of a backwater in mathematical philosophy. Mathematicians tend to avoid the complication of constantly working in formal symbols, and to work informally – though arguments should be capable of being backed up with their formal versions if required.

In **music**, formalism is the use of specific musical forms – for example, fugue, passacaglia and ritornello – to give external order to works whose main intellectual rationale comes from something else. Thus, romantic symphonists, drawing the threads of their works together in last movements, often treated non-fugal material in the manner of fugue. Christian church composers, faced with the task of giving musical coherence to settings of enormously long liturgical statements such as the *Gloria* or *Dies Irae*, often used fugal or sonata techniques, sometimes to the point where musical logic, and attractiveness, obliterated the original devotional function of the work. **Opera** composers, from Purcell (in *Dido and Aeneas*) and Mozart (in his act-finales) to Verdi (in *Falstaff*) often underlaid emotional and dramatic flow with such forms as chaconne or fugue. **Twelve-note** composers (for example Berg in *Wozzeck*, Schoenberg in his concertos and chamber works, or Webern in almost every piece) used 18th-century forms to give a sense (real or ironical) of familiar order to work which was otherwise radical and innovatory: a process analogous to, if subtler than, the **collage**-like use of 18th-century forms by **neoclassical** composers. **PD MG KMcL SMcL**

See also axiomatization.

Further reading Cedric Greenberg, *Art and Culture*.

FORMATION NOVEL see **Bildungsroman**

FOUNDATIONALISM AND COHERENTISM

Foundationalists hold that there is a category of beliefs which justify all other beliefs which count as knowledge, but which do not themselves require justification in order to count as knowledge. All beliefs that count as knowledge are either part of this foundation, or are built upon and justified by it. These foundational beliefs may concern subjects' own experiences. So, beliefs about one's own experiences will not require justification in order to count as knowledge, but beliefs about anything other than one's own experiences – beliefs about supposedly more theoretical matters, such as beliefs about the laws of Nature – will require justification by beliefs about one's own experiences in order to count as knowledge. The beliefs that form the foundation of all other knowledge need not be certain, but they can only be undermined by reference to beliefs of the same class. That is, beliefs about one's own experiences do not need to be certain in order to count as knowledge, but they can only be undermined by other beliefs about one's own experiences.

Coherentists deny that there is any such class of foundational beliefs. The belief that a certain experience occurred can be overturned by beliefs about supposedly more theoretical matters. For example, the belief that a certain experience occurred can be overturned by a sufficiently well-justified belief that such an experience would violate a law of Nature. So it is not the case that while beliefs about laws of Nature are justified or undermined by beliefs abut one's own experience, beliefs abut one's own experience cannot be undermined by beliefs about laws of Nature. All beliefs hang together, and beliefs abut experiences and supposedly more theoretical matters such as the laws of Nature are mutually adjusted. Beliefs must be adjusted all together, in a single, coherent, holistic web. It is not the case that one sub-set of beliefs justifies all others, but cannot be overturned by those other beliefs. **AJ**

See also epistemology; knowledge.

Further reading Bonjour, *The Foundations of Empirical Knowledge*; J. Pollock, *Contemporary Theories of Knowledge*.

FOUR COLOUR THEOREM see
Provability; Topology

FOUR FORCES, THE

The ultimate aim of 20th-century **physics** is to show that the four forces are all different aspects of the same force.

They are **gravity**, **electromagnetism**, the **weak force** and the strong force. They are believed to be the only forces in Nature, although some suggestions that a fifth exists have been made. Sensitive experiments to detect this fifth force have not discovered it, although its existence has not been entirely ruled out.

The forces differ widely in every respect. The weak force and the strong force have such short ranges that they only interact when the separations involved are smaller than the width of an atom, but gravity and the electromagnetic force take effect at intergalactic distances.

The strength of each force is another factor by which they are distinguished. Gravity is the weakest of the four, needing a mass the size of the Earth for us to feel its effects. The weak force is the next strongest, followed by the electromagnetic and then the strong force.

We are familiar with the concept of forces diminishing with distance, but there is an exception to this rule. The strong force, acting between quarks, grows greater with distance, rather as if the objects were connected by elastic.

Under the right circumstances all forces except gravity can repel. Gravity only attracts objects together, never pushing them apart.

All forces are 'carried' by field particles. The force affects objects by exchange of these particles. A common conceptual difficulty is encountered when one attempts to understand how attractive forces can operate in this way.

Physical scientists believe that at the beginning of the universe, when very high temperatures existed, there was only one force and one field particle. As the universe cooled, the forces became differentiated, and 'branched away' from each other. Gravity separated very early, which is why it is very different to the other forces. The next to go was the strong force, followed by the weak force. This leaves us with the electromagnetic force which we see today.

Scientists hope to show that all the forces are aspects of one fundamental force by attempting to re-create the conditions at the beginning of the universe in high energy particle accelerators. Today, due to these experiments, we can say that the weak force and the electromagnetic force are indeed aspects of a single force, known as the electroweak interaction. The theory which combines the weak and the electromagnetic forces into the electroweak interaction is called the Standard Model, and was discovered in the 1960s.

An early example of the unification of forces was provided by James Maxwell (1831–79). He showed that electricity and magnetism are intimately related, and combined the separate ideas about the two into electromagnetic theory, without which no electrical apparatus would be understood today. We now consider electricity and magnetism as different aspects of the electromagnetic force. **JJ**

See also unified field theory.

FRACTALS

A fractal (from Latin *frangere*, 'to break'), in **computing**, is a geometric figure which has fractional **dimension**, usually between 1 and 2. Fractals are constructed by continually repeating changes to originally simple figures; for example, a method of constructing a fractal would be to start with the line |, then replacing | by >, to give two straight lines; then replacing each of those straight lines by >; and keeping on doing this. At each stage, the figure constructed so far is one-dimensional, but the fractal itself is too complex to be described with only one co-ordinate, though not filling the plane (which it would need to do to be two-dimensional). Such figures are easily produced using computers; they continue the process until the changes made are smaller than the resolution of the screen or printer on which the result is to be displayed. They have today proved important for **computer graphics**, particularly for the entertainment industry. **SMcL**

FRANKFURT SCHOOL

The Frankfurt School is the name given to a group of **Marxist** social theorists who fled Hitler's régime to work within **academe** in the USA, returning to Frankfurt in 1949. Otherwise known as critical theorists, the group included such figures as Herbert Marcuse, Theodor Adorno and Max Horkheimer.

These thinkers were influenced by Hegelian philosophy as well as by Marxist politics and economic analysis. They are noted too for their incorporation of some of Freud's ideas into their work. Although there are important differences between the individual figures in the school, they were united in their fear and hatred of **fascism**, and shared a certain degree of cultural pessimism which may be attributed to their prewar experiences.

Although broadly left-wing in orientation, these thinkers were by no means followers of Stalinism and are perhaps best known for the way they tried to refine Marxist theory in the light of developments in both communist and capitalist states. They attempted to move away from what they saw as the over-deterministic and economistic tendencies in some of Marx's writings, and to account for the complexities of modern culture and new forms of consciousness.

The significance of the Frankfurt School for students of the mass **media** or **popular culture**, has been in relation to their focus on the development of a mass consumer culture. The possible effects of advertising, mass-produced popular music and the technical reproduction of images via cinema, television, etc., were seen as intrinsically bound up with the needs and values of entrepreneurial **capitalism** and the capitalist state, (though they applied their analysis to communist régimes too). It was argued that modern societies were becoming increasingly dehumanized through the increase of technology (especially those forms connected to the mass media), and that individuals were manipulated by mass media that were bound to work, ultimately, in support of the status quo.

Horkheimer and Adorno took a particularly pessimistic view, while Marcuse suggested ways in which, despite the unlikelihood of any form of proletarian revolution, new groupings, such as students, might begin to challenge the manipulations of mass culture. As such, Marcuse became for a while in the 1960s a guru of the youthful 'counter-culture'.

The Frankfurt School disbanded at the end of the 1960s, and their ideas on mass culture and 'cultural decline' have been superceded by writers who have focused more on the way popular media and cultural forms may be seen as a process of struggle and negotiation, rather than as a subtle form of coercion. Nevertheless, the influence of critical theory has been immense and the echoes of its work continue to be heard. **BC**

Further reading D. Held, *Introduction to Critical Theory.*

FREE ASSOCIATION

Free association, in **psychiatry**, is a mental exercise where the patient first turns his or her attention to a subject which is meant to be analysed because it is causing questions or anxiety, and then allows thoughts to run freely from there. Special attention must be taken to avoid censoring, modifying or omitting anything. If this difficult process can be kept going by the analyst, the hidden meaning behind the subject in question will eventually show itself. Freud discovered that many unimportant lapses in memory could reveal hidden thoughts through free association. The apparently random forgetting of a word, for example, would be found through this process to have a definite meaning and be caused by complex psychological factors. Importantly, not only was the technique able to bring pathogenic ideas to the surface, it also had the effect of relieving symptoms and obsessions at the same time.

Because of these discoveries Freud held that no psychological event was random. In this sense everything a person does is determined. This general principle is called psychic **determinism**.

One source for the free association technique may have come from Freud's Jewish heritage. There are numerous **meditation** techniques, employed in Jewish **mysticism**, which bear a striking resemblance to free association: ways for example to find the true meaning of a sacred text by employing a similar kind of word play, looking for key words and searching for anagrams. **MJ**

Further reading Sigmund Freud, *The Psychopathology of Everyday Life.*

FREE DANCE see Abstract Dance

FREE JAZZ

Most jazz improvisation is based on pre-existing material, either from the general repertoire or specially composed or agreed by the band in question. The 'pull' between individual creation and our knowledge of the original material is one of the main components of the show. In free jazz, the players use no pre-existing material – except possibly an agreement among themselves about the length and sequence of each section or each piece – but improvise at will. Harmony, melody and rhythm are subject to no pre-conditions. There have been many free-jazz solo artists, and solo work may seem to be the natural way to perform free jazz. But in group work, the players' interaction and mutual inspiration (a feature of all jazz) is particularly important, and contributes to the feeling of vertiginous excitement, of creative tightrope-walking, characteristic of the style. **KMcL**

See also improvisation.

FREE TRADE

Free trade, in **economics**, is open trade between countries without any barriers imposed by governments, such as **tariffs**, quotas, subsidies or bureaucratic tangles (for example, safety rules designed to favour domestic manufacturers). Advocates of free trade think that an open trading system encourages a fast growth in world trade which generates fast growth in output, and, by increasing competition, fast improvements in efficiency. Most economists favour free trade because the benefits can accrue to all as total world output increases according to the principle of **comparative advantage**.

Historically, free trade has been a rare commodity. In the 1930s retaliatory increases in tariffs cramped trade and led to worldwide recession. With this in mind, in 1945, the Western powers set up the General Agreement on Tariffs and Trade (**GATT**), to negotiate and regulate commercial policies and gradually reduce tariffs and other barriers.

Thanks to successive 'rounds' of GATT negotiations, tariffs on manufactured goods have fallen quickly, with the average tariff for industrial goods by 1982 at 5% for the EEC, 4.5% for the US and 4% for Japan. World trade grew by, on average, 5.9% a year in the 1950s, 8.5% a year in the 1960s and 6.4% a year in the recession-hit 1970s. But growth then slowed to 2.3% in 1980, and trade actually shrank in 1981. There was a swing back towards protectionism in the US and Europe in the early 1980s; not actually going so far as to restore tariffs, but by raising administrative barriers to trade, and demanding 'voluntary restraint agreements' on exports from Japan and other Far Eastern suppliers. However, in 1986 governments agreed on a new round of GATT negotiations, which may slow or halt the drift to protectionism. Note, also, that protectionism ebbs and flows with movements in **exchange rates** if these do not reflect trade competitiveness. Two periods when the dollar became overvalued – 1970–71 and 1981–84 – coincided with the fiercest bouts of US protectionism since 1945, because other countries' exports, especially Japan's, became super-competitive.

Arguments against free trade and for protection generally are political and lack an economic basis, the primary exception being the infant industry argument. In order to nurture a new, 'infant' industry, and to allow time for a country to build up the infrastructure necessary to make the industry internationally competitive takes time, and heavy fixed costs, so short-term protection can be justifiable. The question is when should a country decide to dismantle trade barriers and force its protected industry to compete. **TF**

See also subsidy.

FREEDOM AND DETERMINISM

Is determinism the doctrine that every event has a determining or sufficient cause compatible with freedom of action and freedom of will? If determinism is true then everything that happens has a determining cause. My giving money to charity has a determining cause, perhaps my wanting to give money to charity. And my wanting to give money to charity has a determining cause. And that event has a sufficient cause, and so on back to the beginning of time. So if determinism is true, then right back at the beginning of time it was causally determined that I would want to give money to charity and that I would do so. So it would seem that if determinism is true, my want and my action

are not free. Determinism seems incompatible with freedom of will and freedom of action.

There are two versions of incompatibilism, the theory that freedom and determinism are incompatible. **Libertarians** hold that freedom and determinism are incompatible, that we are free and, therefore, that determinism is false. One problem for the libertarian is that indeterminism, mere randomness, seems no more compatible with freedom than determinism. If it is merely up to chance, rather than causally determined what decisions we will make and what actions we will perform, can we really have freedom of will and freedom of action?

Hard Determinists are also incompatibilists. They hold that determinism is true and infer that we are not free.

In contrast, compatibilists or Soft Determinists hold that freedom and determinism are compatible. They give accounts of freedom of action and freedom of will according to which both are consistent with determinism. Compatibilists often hold that freedom of action is the ability to do what one wants to do. Those who are constrained by chains or prison walls are unable to do much of what they want to do. If they want to go to the seaside, they cannot. But those who are not constrained can do what they want to do, even if their wants and actions are causally determined. If I want to go for a day trip, I can. If I want to stay at home, I can. The (supposed) fact that it was causally determined many millennia ago that I would want to go to the seaside and that I would go is irrelevant. I can do what I want to do, so my actions are free.

One natural objection to this is that there seems to be little advantage in having freedom of action unless one also has freedom of will. And if it was causally determined many centuries ago that I would want to go to the seaside, can my will really be free? One is responsible for one's actions only if they are free. **AJ**

See also causation; determinism and indeterminism; responsibility and moral luck.

Further reading J. Foster, *The Immaterial Self*; P. Van luwagen, *An Essay on Free Will*; G. Watson, *Free Will*.

FREUDIAN THOUGHT see Castration Anxiety; Counter-transference; Death Instinct; Defence Mechanism; Determinism; Dreams; Fixation; Free Association; **Id, Ego and Superego**; Infant Sexuality; Instincts; Interpretation; Libido; Oedipus Complex; **Oral, Anal and Phallic Stages**; Transference.

FRONTIER TRADITION

The frontier tradition was a 19th-century phenomenon in the **literature** particularly of Australia, Canada, New Zealand and the USA. White settlers in the frontier regions of these countries – or certainly those who wrote about them – regarded the untamed wildness almost with mystic reverence. They were seen as places where life was reduced to its essence, where 'men were men' and people were in a state of harmony, rarely found elsewhere, with other animals and with Nature.

At one level, the frontier tradition deals with harsh beauty, rugged emotion and a severely simplistic moral and ethical code. It spans novels (for example from authors ranging from James Fenimore Cooper to Jack London and Ernest Hemingway), ballads, pulp literature of all kinds, and the films and television series inspired by such works. At another level, it involves a kind of transcendental identification of, for example, 'the American spirit' with the urge to push actual, physical frontiers further and further back. Writers as diverse as St-Jean de Crèvecoeur, Bret Harte, Louisa M. Alcott, Chuck Norris and Willa Cather made use of this.

Outside the USA, the tradition is descanted on, often with savage irony, by such writers as Peter Carey and Patrick White in Australia, Margaret Atwood in Canada, and Keri Hulme in New Zealand. Women writers have found it particularly useful 'decomposing the outback myth', as Miles Franklin put it: taking the macho stereotypes of the outback style and adding psychological and physical verisimilitude.

In all of this, attitudes of native peoples are ignored or patronizingly misrepresented. It would be fascinating, if such a thing existed, to read their literature about this frontier world. **KMcL**

FUNCTIONAL PROGRAMMING

Functional programming, in **computer** studies, provides a somewhat different way to look at computing than normal programming, which concentrates on the task to be solved. It is the method of programming which is closest to being mathematical, and thus lends itself to such applications as proving that a given program will perform the job it was intended to do, fulfilling its specifications. Essentially, a functional programming language will contain some basic definitions of **functions** (such as addition and multiplication), and the computer evaluates expressions containing these and additional functions defined by the programmer. A program consists of a list of definitions and then expressions to be evaluated.

The importance of functional programming is principally that by reducing a computer program to its mathematical essentials it is possible to tell very easily whether a program will run without producing errors (in most languages, it takes many times as long to find and correct errors than it does to write the program in the first place) and whether it meets its specifications. **SMcL**

FUNCTIONALISM

Functionalism (from Latin *fungere*, 'to perform') is a main, and controversial, branch of **anthropology** and the **social sciences**. It seeks to explain the features of a society in terms of the functions they perform or the consequences they have for society as a whole. The word 'function' itself is used to mean the impact for a social system or society of an occurrence or institution which is assumed to make a significant contribution to the operation and support of the system as a whole.

Functionalism was founded in the late 19th century by the sociologists Herbert Spencer and Émile Durkheim. They compared human society to a biological organism: a system of interdependent parts all of which make a contribution to the overall working and sustenance of the system. Social phenomena are explained in terms of the functions they perform or the contribution they make to the system as a whole. A distinction is usually made between the consequences of social behaviours which are intended and recognized by the individual members of the social system (manifest functions), and those which are hidden and unintended (latent functions). (For example, R.K. Merton's analysis of the rain dances of the North American Hopi people suggests that although the rain dances were intended to have the effect of bringing rain, they may also be seen as having the unintended consequence of facilitating the social integration of the community.)

Spencer and Durkheim were chiefly interested in Western industrial society, and functionalism was chiefly a sociological discipline until the 1910s, when Bronislaw Malinowski took the lead in applying functionalist models to non-Western societies – in his case, the Trobriand islanders in Melanesia. Malinowksi concentrated on social and cultural phenomena such as patterns of **kinship**, **marriage** and residence, and argued that they fulfil primary psychological and biological needs, which then contribute to the functioning of society.

Malinowski's approach involved a fundamental difference in methodology. Earlier anthropologists had based their work mainly on reports and documents produced by travellers and colonial administrators, and their conclusions were therefore somewhat speculative and inadequately documented. Malinowksi and his followers, by contrast, spent time with the societies they were studying, on the assumption (which now seems self-evident) that to understand a given society fully, it must be studied as a total unit. This approach underlay such pioneering work as Edward Evans-Pritchard's study of **magic**, oracles and **witchcraft** among the Azande people of Sudan in the 1930s. Evans-Pritchard showed that though the Azande viewed these belief-systems in a different way from their common associations in the West, the systems nonetheless performed understandable functions in that they were both systematic mechanisms of social control and a means of explaining personal fortune and misfortune. Finally, in the early 1950s, Alfred Radcliffe-Brown developed 'structural functionalism', focusing on structures in society, that is the networks of social relations and institutions (for example, kinship systems, political organizations and **rituals**) that reinforced collective sentiment and social integration.

In the 1950s and 1960s, under the aegis of such scholars as Talcott Parsons and R.K. Merton, functionalism became a fundamental part of sociological and political explanation. It influenced theoretical and methodological attempts to explain the conditions and factors which make a political system work. For example, **systems theory**, as expounded by David Easton and others, modelled the political decision-making process as a system of inputs, outputs and feedback loops which lead to the creation of binding agreements. Other political scientists developed functional frameworks for the comparative analysis of different political systems by distinguishing between system, process and policy functions which institutions perform.

Functionalist 'explanation' is criticized on philosophical and normative grounds. Philosophical critics complain that functional explanation is circular. It confuses the consequences of an action with its causes. They also complain that functional explanations lack causal mechanisms to give them plausibility. For example, if a political scientist declares that the fragmented pattern of quasi-governmental agencies is explained by its functional consequences for a capitalist economy, he or she has given us no account of how, or why, this result is achieved. Even if functionalist accounts do provide causal mechanisms they are then subject to a second criticism: if they are valid they are usually redundant. For example, if priests conduct rain-dances because they believe it will produce social cohesion among tribal members we have an *intentional* explanation of the phenomenon, and we do not require a functionalist account.

According to Jon Elster (see below) a valid functional explanation takes the following form: a social activity is explained by its function for a group if and only if the function is an effect of the activity, if the activity is beneficial for the group, and if the effect is unintended and unrecognized by the agents producing the effect. He maintains that very few so-called functionalist explanations meet these requirements.

Normative criticism of functionalism, in the social sciences, takes two forms. First, it is considered as being normatively biased towards conservativism, because it assumes that social systems are well integrated and stable, organic wholes, where everything has a purpose and role, and, by implication, discounts the viability of replacing any given existing system by another. Second, it is argued that functionalists went too far in rejecting the importance of the state and political agency in classical political science and sociology.

In **philosophy**, functionalism is the view that mental states can be characterized in terms of their functional or causal role. So, for example, the mental state of being in pain might be said to be the state which has the causal role of being typically caused by damage to the body, typically causing the belief that one is in pain, and typically causing aversion behaviour.

The main objections to functionalism concern **consciousness**. Experiences have a phenomenology: they feel a certain way. But, it seems, the phenomenology of experiences is not captured by functional characterizations of mental states. This claim is illustrated by means of the following thought-experiments. Imagine two people Tim and Sue whose internal states have exactly the same functional roles. Green traffic lights cause in both of them a state which causes them to believe that the lights are green, and to move their cars forward. Red traffic lights cause in both of them a state which causes them to believe that the lights are red, and to stop their cars. But their colour experiences are inverted, in the sense that the experience that Sue has when she sees a green light feels exactly the same as the experience Tim has when he sees a red traffic light. And the experience Sue has when she sees a red light feels exactly the same as the experience Tim has when he sees a green one. So there is a difference between them – a difference in how their experiences as of red traffic lights feel – which is not captured by the functional characterization of their experiences.

In **psychology**, functionalism views mental phenomena not as states or structures, but as activities. Function leads to structure; phenomena are explainable in terms of the functions they fulfil. *Mutatis mutandis*, the same idea applies in **architecture** and the visual **arts**. It is assumed that if one creates an artefact which serves the purpose for which it is made, one creates a thing of beauty. The idea, present in the writings of Plato and Aristotle, engaged 18th-century European writings on **aesthetics**, though there a distinction tended to be drawn between fitness for the purpose as a *component* of beauty, and fitness as being *all* of beauty. Functionalism in the modern sense makes a connection between function and form, as in the famous aphorism of the early–20th-century architect Louis Sullivan that 'form follows function'. For Sullivan and other exponents of **modernism**, the beauty of a structure is revealed through the logical way in which it expresses the inherent qualities of the materials used and the purpose for which it is designed. In this sense, a skyscraper and an **abstract expressionist** painting may both be said to be 'functional' or 'expressive'.

Such concepts played a guiding role in the **Bauhaus**, but more recently the doctrine of functionalism in the arts has come to be questioned, particularly since the 1960s, when it seemed that modernism had confused it totally with **brutalism**. There is after all no reason why a highly-decorated, **Art-Nouveau** teapot, say, may not pour tea as well or better than one embodying a rigorously austere machine aesthetic. The artists of **postmodernism** have reacted against functionalism, reintroducing decoration, whimsy, colour and a sense of play, without losing the advances made by the application of fundamentalist principles. **DA PD MG AJ CMcD RK JM KMcL BO'L MS**

See also consensus theory; evolutionism; field work; holism; political anthropology; primitivism; social conflict; structuralism.

Further reading D. Easton, *A Systems Analysis of Political Life*; Adam Kupfer, *Anthropologists and Anthropology*; R. Merton, *Social Theory and Social Structure*; B. Reyner, *Theory and Design in the First Machine Age*.

FUNCTIONS

A function, in **mathematics**, was originally a relationship between numbers, such as that relating a to a^2. The value of the function at the number a was the number related to a. This definition of a function emphasizes the fact that it is an operation: take a number, and find the value of the function there.

However, by the end of the 19th century, this kind of definition was not rigorous enough. As part of the search for the ultimate foundations of mathematics, mathematicians wanted to be able to reduce everything else to **set theory**, and this definition of a function was too loose to work. The new definition was that a function is a set of pairs, where for each a there is exactly one b such that the pair (a,b) is a member of the function. This definition does obscure the operation element of the previous one, but it has proved to be the standard. The set a such that for some b (a,b) is a member of the function is the domain of the function, and the set b such that for some a (a,b) is in the function is the range of the function. It is also more flexible, because a function does not only have to have numbers in the domain and range as it did originally. **SMcL**

FUNDAMENTALISM

Fundamentalism derives from the Latin word *fundamentum* ('base'). Its chief use today is to describe extreme conservatism in any faith, especially in **Christianity** (see below) and **Islam** (where it involves strict obedience to the letter of the Qur'an and to *shari'a*).

In Christianity, modern fundamentalism developed in the 1910s, when the Conservative Wesleyans and Reformed Evangelicals joined in a war against liberal secularization, which was in their opinion challenging the 'fundamentals', that is the inerrancy of Scripture, the deity of Christ, Virgin Birth, Resurrection and Second Coming. In the US one of the main battles of the fundamentalists was and continues to be against the teaching of **evolution** in public schools. Another fierce battle is fought against the spread of **pornography** (or what

a particular fundamentalist group defines as pornography) and the moral laxity and social corruption to which it is said to lead. While large sections of the evangelical groups and mainline churches developed a broader base, the fundamentalists pursued a militant, separatist line. However, in the late 1970s and 1980s certain elements, such as the television-evangelist Jerry Falwell and his 'Moral Majority', entered the political arena, supporting an ultra-conservative agenda which included opposition to abortion, Catholicism, **equal rights** of men and women, homosexual rights, evolution and **communism**. **KDS**

FURNITURE MUSIC see Muzak

FUTURISM

Futurism was a European artistic movement of the early 20th century, devised by Filippo Marinetti and others, and announced in the *Futurist Manifesto* of 1909. The idea was to create works of art for a new century, reflecting and programming modern ideas without reference to concepts or methods of the past. The Futurists were in favour of **modernity**, speed, technology and the power of the machine. Because the idea of movement is inherent in all these aims, Futurist artists developed the concept of 'dynamism': the representation of human beings or machines in action. (Characteristic examples, both from the early 1910s, are Boccioni's *Unique Forms of Continuity in Space*, a sculpture which shows a striding bronze figure whose limbs transform, and are transformed by, space, and Balla's *Dynamism of a Dog on a Leash*, which shows a dog whose legs blur, cartoon-like, imitating the forward momentum of its owner.) The Futurists were also interested in 'simultaneity', representation of multiple viewpoints, similar to **cubism**, but with the addition of movement, for example in Carra's *Simultaneity, Woman on a Balcony* (1913).

The ideals of Futurism were taken over and modified in other arts. In **literature**, vocabulary and syntax were to be stripped of the clutter of the centuries: short words, sentences without redundant adverbs, adjectives (or even, if possible, verbs), single ideas in single expressions. In **music**, the 'sounds of life' (particularly machines and industrial processes) were to be welded to such modern styles as **jazz**, without 19th-century harmonic or formal baggage. In **theatre**, short scenes were favoured, with a tumble of progress analogous to the cutting and montage of film. (Film is the quintessentially Futurist **performing art**.)

Futurist concepts were rapidly absorbed by **politics**: the style became the favoured artistic idiom of both 1920s **fascism** and **communism**. Perhaps because of this, and its wide use in propaganda, it passed into popular culture more readily than most other types of modernist art, affecting advertising and design of all kinds, from buildings to teacups and from fabrics to film sets. Its uncluttered severity, and mass popularity, made it an important influence on artists of all kinds in the second half of the century. **PD MG JM KMcL**

Further reading M.W. Martin, *Futurist Art and Theory*.

G

GAIA HYPOTHESIS

As the name Gaia is understood today, it is the translation into modern ecological **myth** of the concept of the ancient goddess Mother Earth (known in Greek as *Gaia* or *Ge* as in 'geology'). According to the Greek writer Hesiod (8th century BCE), Gaia was the mother or grandmother of Zeus, and his rule depended on her consent. Modern **anthropologists** think that this idea may be a recollection of the mother goddess who lies in the prehistory of many ancient religions – and perhaps it is the subconscious recollection of this which gives the modern 'theology' of Gaia its appeal to ecologists, feminists, New Age mystics and others.

The Gaia hypothesis was proposed by James Lovelock in 1972. It suggests that the whole Earth functions as a living being and that the biota regulate the atmosphere, oceans and crust to sustain conditions ideal for life. Gaia is at least 3.6 billion years old, and living things and physical conditions have evolved together. Lovelock began to develop this idea when working for NASA as part of a team designing equipment to seek life on Mars. He realized that the composition of the atmosphere was the most obvious sign of life on Earth, and concluded that since the Martian atmosphere was close to chemical equilibrium, this proved that life was absent – a conclusion later confirmed by the two Viking spacecrafts.

The Gaia hypothesis makes an attractive contrast to a mechanistic view of the universe, in which human beings analyse a 'dead', objectified universe, compartmentalize it and superimpose their will on it. Refinements and criticisms of the concept have produced ideas of a thermodynamic pathway regulating all things. There are various theories as to what the regulatory mechanism is: is it perhaps just 'life' itself? Sometimes it sounds similar to 'divine providence', and indeed one is reminded of the 'Paley's watch' theory of the nature of the universe, governed by laws and free from divine interference.

The problem is that although a number of dedicated biologists have produced data to support the hypothesis, there is no way of testing it as one cannot test the planet from outside the system. Some biologists, while accepting that the **biosphere** does have feedback mechanisms which affect atmospheric composition and temperatures, criticize Lovelock for overemphasizing the role of living things, for theorizing too far ahead of the evidence, and for implying that Gaia is teleological. He responds by demonstrating simple mechanisms which could automatically counter fluctuations in solar radiation, and by insisting that the purpose of a hypothesis is to stimulate investigation rather than to follow it. For theologians, another difficulty is that the Gaia concept leaves no room for moral choice: Gaia is neutral, simply a living organism. If humankind persists in excessive disruption, Gaia will eliminate the source of the trouble; if humankind destroys itself (for example in a nuclear holocaust), Gaia will continue unconcerned. This is an assertion of exactly the same kind as the religious believer's assertion that God cares for creation; it is an example of our modern tendency to abandon faith in the supernatural as a source of myth, and replace it with an equally potent, and equally irrational, faith in the laws of **science** as we perceive them. **RB EMJ PS**

See also community; ecofeminism; god; goddess; greenhouse effect; homeostasis; pollution.

Further reading James Lovelock, *Gaia: a New Look at Life on Earth; The Ages of Gaia;* Anne Primavesi, *From Apocalypse to Genesis.*

GALOIS THEORY

Galois theory, in **mathematics**, originated in response to the problem of solving **polynomials**. Methods of solving quadratics (polynomials of the form $ax^2 + bx + x = 0$) were known, at least in part, to the ancient Babylonians, and are now commonly taught in school. A method of solving cubics (equations of the form $ax^3 + bx^2 + cx + d = 0$) was discovered (probably rediscovered) by Tartaglia (Niccolo Fontana; 1500?–57) and published by Girolamo Cardano (1501–76) in 1545 in his *Ars Magna*, which also included a method to solve quartics (equations of the form $ax^4 + bx^3 + cx^2 + dx + e = 0$) discovered by Ludovico Ferrari (1522–65). The obvious next step was to find a solution of the same kind for the quintic; many mathematicians attempted to do so over the next 280 years, with a growing feeling that the task was impossible. This was finally proved to be the case by Niels Henrik Abel (1802–29) in 1824.

So the question mathematicians were now considering was to determine when a given equation could be solved in the same way as the quadratic, cubic and quartic. Évariste Galois (1811–32) was a French mathematician who, during a life which sounds like the plot of a romantic novel, was ignored by the Academy of Sciences in Paris, who failed to understand his highly original and, for the time, highly abstract work. After his death (in a duel over a woman) an extremely elegant solution to this problem was found among his papers. The method is to use the theory of **groups** in a very advanced way to attack the problem:

and the concept of a group was one which Galois had to invent for the purposes. His work was really the beginning of abstract **algebra**. Many other problems in mathematics can be reduced to the question of solving a polynomial equation, so Galois theory has thrown light in many areas of the subject. **SMcL**

GAME THEORY

Game theory is perhaps the most important 20th-century development in the formal (or mathematical) **social sciences**. The landmark work in game theory was John von Neumann and Oskar Morgenstern's *Theory of Games and Economic Behaviour*, which was published in 1944. The insights of game theory are constantly being refined and elaborated, and it remains one of the most vibrant fields in the social sciences.

Game theory is the mathematical study of games and strategy. Its purpose is, essentially, to determine from a given set of rules the likely strategy to be used by each player, and to find the best. In this sense, the theory of games is the analysis of the strategic elements of a game rather than that of the chance elements, which mathematicians have studied over a much longer period in **probability**. But game theory is not an abstract activity, not pure mathematics. Nor is it a game, though it is useful for explaining the **logic** of many social games. It is mostly deployed to explore such complex and serious topics as the logic of arms races, the behaviour of agents in imperfect markets, and the behaviour of political parties and coalitions. Game theory studies the logic of interdependent decision-making between individuals or groups on the suppositions that the agents involved in a game are rational, that is, that they have well-formed preferences and pursue their interests efficiently, and that they have strategies, which requires them to have more than one possible course of action. In this sense the whole of economic theory, and much political theory, are subsets of game theory.

Game theorists classify games by their nature and their pay-offs. Co-operative games are those in which the players can communicate and bargain with one another; in non-co-operative games these features are absent. Non-co-operative game theory is the more fundamental and rigorous: it calls for a complete description of the rules of the game so that the strategies available to the players can be studied in detail. The aim of the analyst is to find the equilibrium solutions to the game. Game theorists also classify games by whether or not they are zero-sum or not. In zero-sum games what the winner gets (in whatever units) is exactly equal to the loss of the loser. Non zero-sum games include those in which all players benefit (positive-sum games) or lose (negative-sum games), although not necessarily by the same amounts, and ones in which some players win and others lose, but not by the same amounts (variable-sum games).

In the social sciences most focus has been on non zero-sum games. The most famous is the two-person *prisoner's dilemma* which has an apparently paradoxical property. In this game each player has a dominant strategy, that is, one course of action which leads to the best possible pay-off against whichever of two options the opponent chooses. So both players, if they are rational, must choose these strategies. However, the pay-offs of the game are such that both players would be better off if they co-operated and chose 'dominated strategies', that is strategies that would leave them vulnerable to being 'suckered' by their opponent. This game has been seen by many as a paradigm illustration of the central problems of conflict and co-ordination in **politics**, **economics** and **psychology**.

The prisoner's dilemma, like other games, has been formally modelled and used in experimental situations by psychologists, and has been used to explore the logic of arguments used by great political theorists of the past, such as Hobbes, Hume and Rousseau. In the 1970s and 1980s, the use of game theory was increasing across the social sciences, and was perhaps most fruitful in the field of evolutionary biology where it is used to model genetically determined animal behaviour on the assumption that genes behave as if they were rational maximizing agents.

The nature of the problems game theory sets out to solve is such that it is hard to determine in a reasonable amount of time. It is pointless, for example, discovering that the best strategy would have been to raise interest rates six months ago! Analyses of even 'simple' games, for example, poker, can only be done for versions of the game which are so simplified that no real-world enthusiast would play them. Another problem is that in most of the game-like situations which interest social scientists, the interest is not in the best thing to do but in the usual thing people do, something about which mathematical game theory can say nothing. In many political or economic situations, the question is what the best thing to do would be assuming that the other players continue to play as usual. (This is also a question to which professional gamblers would like to know the answer.) Because game theory is really about what should be done if every player is playing as well as they can, the number of practical applications of game theory has turned out to be far more limited than those who wish to apply it would desire. **TF SMcL BO'L**

See also monopolistic competition; oligopoly.

Further reading K. Binmore, *Fun and Games: a Text on Game Theory*; R.D. Luce and H. Raiffa, *Games and Decisions*.

GANDHIANISM

Gandhianism is a term derived from the life and teaching of Mohandas Karamchand Gandhi, which has become institutionalized in India, because every 'serious' politician feels obliged to appear in *khadi* (handwoven cotton) and to support such Gandhian causes as handloom industries. Publication of Gandhi's works is subsidized, as the works of Marx used to be in Eastern Europe. In the 1970s his name was used to endorse birth control policies, when he insisted on continence as the only remedy. Nevertheless, the Gandhi Peace Foundations near Delhi and Gandhigram, Tamil Nadu, were involved in supporting civil rights issues to the irritation of the governments of Indira Gandhi (no relation) and her sons. Both institutions emphasize rural reconstruction and experimentation with ways of working with the poor, as Gandhi did.

Gandhi saw himself essentially as a religious reformer. He was a man of great personal piety as well as charisma. He belonged to the Vaishya class (see **caste**) and while his strict vegetarianism, abhorrence of sex, pursuit of self-control and personal **asceticism** may derive from the mores of his caste, he was also greatly influenced by local **Jain** priests near his home, for example in his doctrine of nonviolence, and by Christians who befriended him when he studied law in London and then went to work in South Africa. Despite such eclecticism, Gandhi was always a thoroughgoing **Hindu**, deeply opposed to conversion. He claimed that God is truth and truth is God. He followed *dharma* (see **Dharmic religion**) as a force based on nonviolence, truth, renunciation and absence of passion. This approach made it possible for those who loved India to join his movement regardless of their religion. He came to represent a moral force, to which the British had no answer, and the death knell of conservative **Brahmanic religion**. EMJ

Further reading Percival Spear, *A History of India*, vol. 2.

GATT (GENERAL AGREEMENT ON TARIFFS AND TRADE)

Despite the designation 'agreement' in its title, GATT is an international organization created in 1947 to provide a continuing basis for nations to negotiate and regulate commercial policies. The principal activity is multinational negotiation for **tariff** reductions. Its articles of agreement provide principles of behaviour and a general set of rules governing the conduct of trade among nations. GATT was signed by 22 countries in 1947, in a bid to encourage free trade and avoid the protectionism prevalent in the 1930s. Now more than 100 countries have signed.

GATT is based on two principles: reciprocity in liberalizing trade; and nondiscrimination. GATT helped to provide substantial progress in reducing quotas in the 1950s and 1960s. GATT has also helped

to reduce tariffs in a series of negotiating 'rounds'. By the seventh round (the Tokyo round), completed in 1979, tariffs applied to industrial products were down to 6.6% for the EEC, 6.4% for the US and 5.5% for Japan, and were set to be reduced to 4.7, 4.4 and 2.8% respectively by 1 January 1987.

GATT has two weaknesses that have thwarted its efforts in other areas: it has precious few weapons; and it depends on countries being aware of mutual self-interest. In particular, GATT has had to resort to toothless 'codes' for trade issues like government procurement, subsidies and anti-dumping action. Agriculture and services have been virtually untouched. Tariffs are relatively easy to police, but hidden, non-tariff barriers are more difficult. TF

GAY THEATRE

Gay theatre, as a particular aesthetic and practice, emerged from the anti-naturalist and political activism of Western theatre in the 1970s, and sought to place in the foreground the histories and experiences of gay men and lesbians. It was founded on similar liberation concepts to those which informed **feminist** and community theatres, and was initially aimed at a specific constituency, though it rapidly achieved a wider audience. TRG SS

Further reading Philip Osment, *Gay Sweatshop*.

GEARING SYSTEMS

The invention of pulleys and gearing systems is subject to some mystery, but it is known that by the 1st century BCE that the mechanical advantage in using gears was well documented. People such as Archimedes, Vitruvius and Hero of Alexandria all worked at improving these mechanical systems.

A simple spur gear system comprises a pinion A of small diameter having possibly 20 teeth engaging with a larger one B having perhaps 80 teeth. Thus the pinion will rotate at 4 times the speed of the wheel. In spur gears the efficiency may be as high as 98% and therefore next to no power is lost in the transmission. The power P transmitted is proportional to the rotational speed S and the torque or turning action T. Thus P = constant × T × S,   P = constant × TA × SA, P = constant × TB × SB.

Thus $TB = TA \dfrac{SA}{SB}$ But $\dfrac{SA}{SB} = \dfrac{1}{4}$
so $TB = 4 \times TA$

This illustrates the use of gears by changing the rotational speed to a lower value a higher torque is transmitted.

The gear box of a motor car has 4 or 5 sets of gears for forward motion and usually one for reverse. The feature of a single pair of gears in mesh is that the shafts turn in opposite directions. Thus to get shafts to turn in the same direction an intermediate shaft is used carrying for instance wheel B and another pinion C which engages with wheel D. In this way pinion A and wheel D rotate in the same direction, and this concept is used to produce forward or reverse movement in the automobile gear box.

In cars of traditional design the drive from the gearbox is transmitted by the propeller shaft to the rear axle, which is perpendicular to it. The special type of pinion and gear wheel is used here called a hypoid drive. Each wheel has teeth which are spiral in form and special oils are needed to reduce friction and wear as the teeth slide over each other.

In large ships driven by steam turbines the economical recovery speed of the turbine is much faster than the economical recovery speed of the propeller. The mismatch in speeds is accommodated by reduction gears where the pinion may be 0.5 metres in diameter and the gear wheel 3 metres in diameter. These gears and those in an automobile require specialist machines for their manufacture since each tooth of the pinion must be identical and match identically the teeth on the gear wheel. Errors in the profiles of the teeth lead to noise and vibration which may break the teeth or fracture the shafts. **AA**

GEBRAUCHSMUSIK

Gebrauchsmusik (German, 'utility music'), in the wider sense, means any **music** conceived as a support for other activities (film music is a prime example), and the whole *gebrauchsmusik* concept is analogous to commercial art. In the narrower sense, it was a type of music written in the 1920s by a group of German composers led by Paul Hindemith and Kurt Weill, and influenced by the views of Brecht and the **Bauhaus**: that art of all kinds, graphic art, music, **poetry**, **theatre**, should be useful as well as beautiful, should serve practical needs and speak to the widest possible audience a direct negation of the earlier **art for art's sake** ideal. Utility music consisted of songs, marches and cantatas with patriotic or political texts (exhorting people to work hard was a favourite theme), of teaching pieces for both children and adults – some of Hindemith's most appealing short compositions – and of larger-scale concert and music-theatre works with a wide popular appeal (Weill's *The Threepenny Opera* is typical).

Gebrauchsmusik, as a movement, died at the time of World War II, though its ideas lived on in the utilitarian music demanded of composers in the then East Germany. Weill, Hindemith and the others turned to other things, though even there the ideals of usefulness and accessibility persisted in Weill's Broadway musicals on patriotic themes, for example, or Hindemith's set of sonatas, one for each orchestral instrument. **KMcL**

GENDER

In its everyday usage, gender (from old French *gendre*, derived from Latin *genus*, '[biological] type') refers to the distinction between females and males according to anatomical sex. Women and men are assumed to be distinct biological entities. But anthropologists, feminists and sociologists use the term in a completely different way. They focus on cultural variations in the construction of gender, looking at concepts of the body, ideas of **sexuality**, procreation and reproduction, and the way gender roles are conditioned by society. In these terms, gender does not refer to the biological and physical differences between the sexes, but to to socially constructed notions of femininity and masculinity. Even despite this work, the old notion that biology defines sexuality (which in turn defines gender roles) still surfaces from time to time, for example in the idea (common among male thinkers) that the female personality is determined by anatomy and by women's reproductive function, or the idea (common among female thinkers) that the male sex hormone testosterone is associated with a male propensity to violence.

The discrediting of biological theories has led to many studies of how gender differences develop. Gender socialization begins the day a child is born, and continues as a learned strategy of adaptation or repression, depending entirely on the way each person sees herself and himself (and others) in relation to changing (or unchanging) circumstances. In early anthropological studies of gender roles, a major (though at first unrealized) problem was that research was carried out by men, and that they often relied exclusively on the explanations given by men about social systems. To redress the balance, an 'anthropology of women' set out to elicit what were called women's 'muted models'. The problem, however, lay deeper, in presuppositions (by people of both sexes) that certain roles and behaviour were 'natural' for women or for men. **Feminism** opened the debate in anthropology about whether women could be considered universally subordinated and if so, whether their subordination was due to their biological nature or was the product (as Engels suggested in the mid-19th century) of specific social institutions linked to the way labour was divided. Leaving aside gender politics, exactly similar questions can be asked about men.

At this stage in human history, it is almost impossible to untangle the knot of cultural conditioning, motivations and politics which underlie the assignment and acceptance of roles in society. Cutting the knot is, as many feminists claim, perhaps the only way forward. Anthropologists, by contrast, see the problems as not political but scientific, concerned with the nature and interpretation of evidence. To give just one example: studies of gender roles in different societies show that they are not always asymmetrical, but are often seen as complementary within the society and – furthermore, that they are not always predicated on biological difference. This evidence undermines notions of the univer-

sal subordination of women, and indeed of the existence of a universal category of 'women' which can be assumed to be the same in all societies.

The range of socially constructed gender roles is diverse, often based on occupation rather than social activity. In industrialized societies women are under-represented in positions of power and influence; their average wage is considerably below that of men; they take a disproportionate share of responsibility for domestic work and childcare. In agricultural societies the situation is often entirely different. Some societies even create 'in-between' categories, or 'third genders'. The eunuchs of India, for example, who are frequently invited to bring spiritual blessings at the birth of a baby, are often not perceived in terms of gender at all. Such categories challenge the idea of a universal opposition between female and male. In sum, the evidence suggests diversity rather than universality; the only thing it seems to do for sure is dissolve categories based on notions of a 'natural', biological gender essence.

Feminist theorists bypass or dismiss all such matters, as irrelevant to the main issue. They argue that the imposition of gender ideology is particularly oppressive to females, because the characteristics linked with femininity are usually negative and passive. Feminists argue that women's oppression is a result of men's categorization of women as an inferior **class**. Some see femininity as a wound inflicted upon women. For Shulamith Firestone, for example, the battlefield of gender is not just about **partriarchy** but also about reproduction. Other feminists have celebrated women's gender difference and taken the nonaggression of femininity as a political position.

French feminist thought is strongly concerned with language. Hélène Cixous, for example, has shown how language itself is built on a structure of oppositions that assign the negative to femininity: sun/moon, activity/passivity. French feminists use the term *écriture féminine* to describe women's writing that emphasized the body and tries to break free of the oppositional structure of language, through plurality and fluidity. Although the term describes women's writing, it is not a biological definition but is used as a metaphor to describe that which lies outside the dominant 'phallocentric' discourse and does not depend upon the presence of a female body.

Many contemporary feminists use psychoanalytical theory to help identify the construction of gender difference in the process of infant development. Nancy Chodorow, for example, rejects the Freudian notion that gender roles are assigned through the **Oedipus complex** and stresses the role of mothering in the formation of gender differences. She argues that, given female parenting, girls internalize the caring role and boys reject the aspects of caring and empathy. Other feminists point out that some gender theories do not adequately explain femininity in men and masculinity in women. Contemporary lesbian theorists ask the question: if we are genderized into femininity and heterosexuality then how do we account for 'femme' lesbians, heterosexual 'butch' women and bisexuals? Clearly, theories of gender are still problematic and a vital area of enquiry. **DA TK CL KMcL**

See also culture; division of labour; evolutionism; field work; kinship; norms; primitivism; ritual; role; social conflict; social construction of reality; socialization; sociobiology; stratification; sociology of knowledge; typifications.

Further reading Judith Butler, *Gender Trouble: Feminism and the Subversion of Identity*; P. Caplan (ed.), *The Cultural Construction of Sexuality*; C. MacCormack and M. Strathern (eds.), *Nature, Culture and Gender*; A. Oakley, *Sex, Gender and Society*; S. Weitz, *Sex Roles; Biological, Psychological and Social Foundations*.

GENE

The gene is the unit of inheritance. The word was suggested in 1909 by the Danish geneticist Wilhelm Johannsen as an abbreviation of the term pangene (Greek, 'source of everything'), which was originally used by Hugo de Vries in 1889. Johannsen thought of the genes as the characteristics specified in the gametes, but he deliberately avoided the temptation to hypothesize as to their nature. Gregor Mendel's work, in the 19th century, showed how characteristics

were inherited as discrete 'factors', without blending. As the 20th century progressed, the relationship between genes and chromosomes was elucidated, and chromosome maps appeared, showing the positions of individual genes, calculated according to the degree of genetic linkage between them. As biochemical techniques improved, it was revealed that genes were made of a large molecule called DNA, contained within chromosomes.

Molecular biology was founded on the ability to determine the sequence of nucleic acid subunits which make up the DNA molecule. This sequence is codes for an amino acid sequence in a protein, which is the gene product. The gene is the genetic information which specifies a protein; by its modern definition, one gene codes for one enzyme (protein) and it is by this pathway only that the genetic information contained in the DNA can exert control over the living cell. Thus the concept of the gene refers to both a structure and a function. The gene is the unit of transfer of genetic material between generations; typically, the offspring bear two copies of each gene (two alleles), one derived from each parent. Where the alleles are different, the individual is said to be heterozygous (with respect to the gene concerned) and one of the genes is dominant and is expressed in the individual – this is the most common situation in normal populations. Where the two alleles are the same, the individual is said to be homozygous. **RB**

See also blending inheritance; genetic code; genetic linkage; genetics; Mendelism; polymorphism.

Further reading Bruce Alberts, *Molecular Biology*.

GENE POOL

When geneticists talk of the 'gene pool' of a population, they mean the genetic resources available. The greater the gene pool, the larger the number of combinations which can arise through sexual reproduction. If a gene pool is very small, then the rate of **genetic drift** is enhanced and the likelihood of inbreeding is increased. **Evolution** acts upon the gene pool through the mechanism of **natural selection**, and produces changes in the frequency of occurrence of specific genes. **RB**

Further reading Richard Dawkins, *The Selfish Gene*.

GENE THERAPY

There are over 4,000 genetic disorders recognized in humans and most cannot be completely alleviated by conventional treatment. The idea behind gene therapy is to introduce healthy genes into patients who carry faulty or undesirable genes; thus the root cause of the disease can be treated by genetic engineering rather than by simply attempting to alleviate symptoms with drugs. There are two possibilities for gene therapy, though one, germ line therapy (in which the genome of the gamete-producing cells is altered) has far-reaching ethical implications and is therefore unlikely to be countenanced by regulatory authorities, at least in the near future. Many scientists consider that germ line therapy can never be permitted as the long-term implications to the human genome cannot be calculated.

Gene therapy of somatic (non-gamete-producing) cells is a much more realistic prospect as it affects only the individual patient. At present it is only feasible in diseases where a gene is absent or faulty, in that it underproduces its protein product; in this case the replacement gene can alleviate the disease by augmenting the production of protein. In practice, the large number of new cells to which such a gene must be introduced, in order to have a significant effect, means that it is necessary to use a virus vector to insert the gene into the genome of each cell by a process known as transduction. Such viruses can be produced in the laboratory and modified so that they do not complete their life cycle. This is essential to avoid the spread of the virus, and with it the gene, to other individuals. Cells that received the new gene would then multiply it by dividing to produce new cells. The number of cells which would need to receive the gene, therefore, depends upon the rate at which the cell type multiplies. If the absence of the gene reduces the life span of the cell, then the proportion of genetically altered cells will steadily increase. In diseases such as cystic fibrosis, where one important gene is absent, the gene therapy could have a life-saving effect even if only a small minority of cells were genetically altered. At present it is necessary to remove the affected cells for gene therapy; for this reason most success has been seen with tissues such as bone marrow, the cells of which can be readily removed and replaced. **RB**

See also eugenics; genetic engineering; transformation.

Further reading Zsolt Harsanyi, *Genetic Prophesy Beyond the Double Helix*.

GENERAL WILL

The general will (or *volonté générale*) was a pivotal concept in the political thought of Jean Jacques Rousseau (1712–78). He defined the general will as the common good that a well-formed citizen would recognize, as opposed to his own particular will (*volonté particuliere*). (Rousseau meant 'his', precisely. There was no place, in his thought, for women as citizens.) Rousseau believed that the full expression of positive **liberty** is only possible in a society where each individual's conception of liberty is compatible. For that reason he emphasized the need to develop a common and well-developed system of civic education in order to transform each individual into a citizen. In a community of educated citizens each individual will will be able to discern the general will or common good, and in supporting it will display the rational exercise of their freedom. Rousseau's conception of a good social order also presupposed both economic equality among citizens and the superiority of small-scale participatory democracy: otherwise there would be too many divisions of interests to sustain a shared conception of the common good.

In the eyes of his critics, Rousseau's ideas, especially those governing the general will, are the source of **totalitarian** conceptions of democracy which seek to force people to be free. For his supporters Rousseau carefully identified the conditions of a workable and free democratic society (even if he had sexist blindspots) and cannot be blamed for the abuse of his ideas at the hands of Jacobins and Bolsheviks. **BO'L**

See also liberalism.

Further reading M. Cranston, P. Riley, *The General Will Before Rousseau: the Transformation of the Divine into the Civic.*

GENERALIZED OTHER

The term 'generalized other' was originally coined by G.H Mead (1863–1931), but its major influence has been on the branch of **sociology** known as **symbolic interactionism**. It refers to the individual's conception of the general attitudes and **values** of those people within society with whom he or she interacts.

According to Mead the generalized other emerges during the 'game-stage' of childhood development. Through the playing of games, for example, 'mothers and fathers' children imaginatively assume other social roles, and in so doing become aware of their own position and social roles within the general scheme of social activity.

Mead believed this shared perspective of the generalized other enables individuals to engage in social interaction. It is through social interaction with others that one's sense of 'self' becomes established.

The concept of the generalized other is important because it attempts to bring together the individual self and the larger society in order to explain how social order is established. The generalized other acts as an important constraining influence on individual behaviour in that it will be regulated in terms of the supposed opinions and attitudes he or she attributes to others. **DA**

See also action perspective; dramaturgical model; idiographic; individualism; internalization; norms; role; socialization; social order; social self; structure-agency debate.

Further reading G.H. Mead, *Mind, Self and Society* (1934) and *The Philosophy of the Act* (1938); A. Strauss, *George Hebert Mead on Social Psychology* (1964).

GENERATIVE GRAMMAR

The generative approach to grammar orig-inates with the most influential linguist of the 20th century, Noam Chomsky. Although revolutionary, Chomsky's theorizing did carry forward several linguistic traditions, including the **Descriptivist** aim to study language in an objective manner. For Chomsky, this aim was achieved with the adoption of recently formulated terms and concepts from mathematical **logic** and recursive function theory. As a result, it became feasible for the systematic properties of syntactic relations to be expressed in formal terms.

A grammar that generates sentences should not be viewed as some kind of sausage machine, churning out, or generating, grammatical strings of words (sentences). The grammar itself is entirely neutral with respect to matters of sentence production and comprehension (see **psycholinguistics**). In fact, the term generate, in a formal sense, refers simply to an abstract ability to be explicit about the status of a given sentence, namely, whether it is grammatical or not.

The generative approach redefined the very object of enquiry in linguistics. Previously, a limited body of language data was analysed to produce a list of structural regularities. The problem, though, is that the insights derived from this approach cannot be transferred automatically beyond the confines of the particular sentences chosen for analysis. The more challenging goal, taken on by generativists, is to explain the linguistic competence of a native speaker, that is, the knowledge of language present in the minds of individuals. There is an attempt, then, to describe the grammars of specific languages, as known to their native speakers, in addition to specifying the knowledge of language shared by all human beings.

A striking property of linguistic systems, noted by Chomsky, is that an infinite number of different possible sentences can be produced and understood by the native speakers of a language on the basis of a finite set of grammatical rules or principles. Chomsky showed how this infinite formal power derives from the recursive property of grammars. **Recursion** is possible when part of the outcome of a linguistic rule can feed back into the original rule again, and set in train a potentially infinite cycle.

A central aim in generative grammar, then, is to capture those properties which allow the generation of all (and only) the possible sentences of a language. Additionally, the grammar provides each sentence with a description which outlines the construction type and the relevant relationships obtaining with other kinds of construction. Given the complexities of language, it is perhaps not surprising that it is a matter of some considerable controversy as to which particular rules or principles provide the best account of grammar. Nevertheless, the influence of Chomsky's concept of generativism is so pervasive that almost all syntactic theories developed since the late 1950s have shared the basic assumptions of the generative approach to grammar. **MS**

See also theories of grammar; universal grammar.

Further reading G. Horrocks, *Generative Grammar*; F.J. Newmeyer, *Linguistic Theory in America*.

GENETIC CODE

The genetic code is the phrase used by life scientists to describe the form in which information is carried by DNA. The information carried by a gene instructs the cell to produce specific protein. The basic structure of a protein is a string-like molecule which is constructed from units called amino acids; the sequence of amino acids in this string gives each protein its special physical and chemical properties. This basic structure of protein molecules has similarities to that of the DNA, which is composed of a chain of subunits called nucleotides. The gentic information which the DNA carries is encoded in this nucleotide sequence, and the process of protein synthesis is thus called translation, from the genetic code of the nucleotides in the DNA to the sequence of amino acids in the protein.

Only four types of nucleotide – called A, T, G and C – make up DNA, while there are more than 20 types of amino acids which can make up a protein. The four 'letters' of the DNA alphabet are grouped into three-letter 'words' to signify the amino acids: for example, CGT in the DNA code stands for the amino acid alanine. Thus the genetic code is a triplet code in which three nucleotides in sequence (a codon) code for one amino acid type. Some nucleotide triplets do not appear to code for anything, while others act as the punctuation in the genetic 'script'. In order for the information contained in the form of DNA to be translated into a protein, the DNA sequence must itself be transcribed into an RNA molecule. RNA is closely related to DNA and is constructed from four nucleotides. This 'messenger' RNA molecule is small enough to diffuse out of the nucleus into the cytoplasm where special structures called ribosomes read the code and synthesize the protein.

The idea that chemical units might encode genetic information was first suggested in the 19th century, but it was not until the 1950s that it was suggested that a nucleotide sequence might act as a template for amino acid sequence. By the 1970s the code had been cracked so that genetic information could be read in terms of the protein for which it encodes; this knowledge is central to **molecular biology** and the many disciplines to which it is related. The flow of information is unidirectional – it appears to be a law of biology that an amino acid sequence cannot give rise to a nucleotide sequence. **RB**

See also genetic engineering.

Further reading Bruce Alberts, *Molecular Biology of the Cell*.

GENETIC DRIFT

Life scientists use the phrase 'genetic drift' to describe the phenomenon in which the frequency of individual genes varies within a population. When a **gene** is present at a low frequency, there is a chance that none of the individuals carrying it will reproduce successfully and the gene will be lost. The **gene pool** is thus changed over time by genetic drift. Genetic drift is distinct from both **natural selection** and **mutation**, and is a feature of small populations where the number of potential mates is limited. **RB**

See also speciation.

GENETIC ENGINEERING

Genetic engineering is the deliberate

alteration of the genome of an organism, involving the insertion, deletion or substitution of sections of DNA. The DNA that is inserted may have been designed to code for a specific amino acid sequence in a protein or it may have been extracted from the genome of a different organism with particular desirable characteristics. The biological tools used by the genetic engineer are **enzymes**, which cut DNA (restriction enzymes), and bacteriophage viruses, which can be used to insert DNA into bacterial genomes. Once the required **gene** is inserted it can be cloned by multiplication of the bacterium, producing a quantity large enough for manipulation with restriction enzymes.

The products of the genetic engineer are of increasing commercial importance in **biotechnology**; for example, the human hormone insulin is now produced for medical use by bacteria which have the human gene for insulin inserted into their genome. The bacteria are grown on an industrial scale by fermentation and the gene product (the insulin) is harvested and purified. When an animal bears additional genes, which were inserted at the stage of the fertilized egg, all the daughter cells which make up the body carry the genes and the individual is said to be transgenic. Such animals are used extensively for research but also have great potential in agricultural biotechnology. **RB**

See also cloning; gene therapy; transformation.

Further reading Bruce Alberts, *Molecular Biology of the Cell*; Steven Prentis, *Biotechnology*.

GENETIC LINKAGE

Certain characteristics may have a tendency to be coinherited; that is they are often transmitted together. Gregor Mendel, in the 19th century, concluded that all characteristics were inherited independently of all others, but it emerged early in the 20th century that this was not always the case. As the structural nature of **genes** became understood, the mechanism for this phenomenon became clear. Genes are arranged in a linear fashion along chain-like DNA molecules, which are coiled within chromosomes. Genes that are positioned close to one another within a chromosome are less likely

to be separated when the chromosomes pair and recombine by **crossing over**, a process in which fragments of DNA are exchanged between paired chromosomes during the production of gametes. Sex linkage occurs when genetic determinants are found on sex chromosomes – diseases which only manifest themselves in one sex (such as haemophilia) may be sex-linked. **RB**

See also meiosis.

Further reading Bruce Alberts, *Molecular Biology of the Cell*.

GENETICS

Genetics (Greek, 'study of basic creation-units') is the study of heredity. The term was introduced by William Bateson in 1905 to refer to the rapidly expanding field which had emerged after the rediscovery of Gregor Mendel's work. The science of genetics was founded on the idea that inheritance and variation are the result of the same process rather than the result of two opposing mechanisms. At this time, experimental genetics was concerned with the study of offspring from particular matings. It rapidly became clear that, though Mendel's results were correct, some of his conclusions were oversimplified; this was largely due to his restricting his studies to the pea plant. The use of the microscope and of techniques such as radioisotopic labelling enabled the genes to be localized to the chromosomes which are found in the cell nucleus. The American geneticist T.H. Morgan elucidated the role of the chromosomes in heredity. Biochemical approaches to genetics enabled a structure for DNA to be determined which was compatible with the known pattern of DNA replication. This led to a massive expansion of **molecular biology**, a field which is now synonymous with biochemical genetics, and to the application of this knowledge to industry, **medicine** and agriculture. The genetic make-up of a group of individuals is termed population genetics and is closely related to **evolution**; Darwin's theory of evolution recognized the existence of heredity but his explanation for the mechanism (**blending inheritance**) was incorrect. Genetics has filled this gap and the study of populations of plants and animals appears to bear out the principles of evolution. **RB**

See also Darwinism; gene; genetic code; Mendelism; mutation; natural selection.

Further reading Bruce Alberts, *The Molecular Biology of the Cell*; Richard Dawkins, *The Selfish Gene*.

GENOTYPE

Genotype, in **genetics**, is the material inherited by an individual from its parents, not all of which is necessarily expressed but all of which has the potential to be transmitted to future generations. The genotype of an individual is fixed for the duration of its life, except for any mutations which may occur. **RB**

See also gene pool; genome; Lamarckism; phenotype.

GENRE

Genre may be French (for 'type', 'kind' or 'form') but the roots of its meaning go back to Plato, who drew distinctions between major forms of **drama**. However, in more recent times, genre has been used as a system of classification in **art**, **literature** and the **media**. For instance, science fiction films, womens' magazines and television soap operas are examples of popular genres within the mass media.

As a means of understanding the media, genre analysis has some advantages and limitations, and this has been reflected in the variability of its use and popularity at different times. Genre analysis emphasizes the ways in which certain patterns, themes, structures and styles may be identified, despite differences in storyline or plot. In this way, we can understand genre as a kind of scaffolding which 'contains' and shapes individual variations. The key elements of a genre text, therefore, are repetition, recognition and familiarity. Given these factors, the part played by the audience or reader in recognizing and responding to generically identifiable texts is seen as crucial.

A major problem within genre analysis concerns the genesis of any genre and the problem of circularity. We can recognize a Western film by its landscape, the presence of guns and stetsons, and by such themes as the struggle between civilization and the wilderness, but how do we come by this classifying list in the first place? Could it be that this can only occur by watching a number of films that contain such elements and attaching the label later? Whatever their origins, genres are seen as capable of shifting and developing over time, sometimes by commenting on earlier examples. The evolution of a genre can produce cross-genres and other variations. These are often linked to changing social attitudes.

Much has been written on the ways in which Hollywood film genres developed within a specific cultural and commercial context (the studio system), which encouraged repetition on the basis of prior box-office success. Some critics have blamed the studio system for lack of artistic vision and experimentation, while others have pointed to the ways in which talented film-makers were able to develop a personal style within the constraints of the genre film.

Recently, structuralists and feminist theorists, among others, have focused on the way in which generically defined structures may operate to construct particular ideologies and values, and to encourage reassuring and conservative interpretations of a given text. **BC**

Further reading R. Allen, *Channels of Discourse*; S. Neale, *Genre*.

GENRE PAINTING

Genre painting depicts scenes of daily life, animals or still life. While such themes have long been represented in **art** – for example, in the statuettes of gossiping women or busy slaves which were popular in Hellinistic Greece – the advent of Christian **iconography** meant that, in painting, they were pushed to what might be described the decorative sidelines, into the background of scenes of grander significance: a trend followed also in the paintings with historical subjects. In contrast to the subject matter of these works, genre paintings as such usually encompass low-key, domestic portraiture without any dynastic, doctrinal or heroic pretensions. This style of genre painting first became important, in its own right, in 17th-century Holland, where it fulfilled the desire of the middle classes for representational painting that reflected their everyday, secular and commercial lives. Prominent among the Dutch genre painters were de Hooch, Metsu, Steen and Vermeer.

In the 18th century, genre painting had two flowerings: one in the Imperial court of Japan (where domestic scenes, typically showing animals, children and beggars were popular); and in France, where Chardin's still lifes and interiors were particularly outstanding, imbued as they were with a reverent attention to the commonplace, which transcends mere representation. In the 19th century, genre painting formed only a significant minority at exhibitions, such as those of the Paris salon. Indeed, genre subjects were largely dealt with by photographers – further sidelining the art. The advent of **Impressionism**, however, challenged and defeated the need to essay an 'important' subject in order to make an 'important' painting. This meant that artists were able to find the full range of aesthetic and intellectual possibilities within very simple still-life motifs. A concern with form rather than content, which became a hallmark of **modernism**. In the 20th century, collapse of the hierarchy of **genres** has finally put paid to the lowly status accorded to genre painting in academic critical esteem. **MG PD**

GENRES, HIERARCHY OF

The term 'hierarchy of genres' refers not to **genre painting** but to the genres of painting (from French, *genre* 'type', 'category'). The notion that some works of art, because of their subject matter, are automatically more important than others is alien to contemporary thinking, but until at least the middle of the 19th century it had real force. The **academies of Western art**, which practised an elevated form of painting in the grand manner, ranged painting in ascending order from still life (inanimate objects) through genre and animals (peopled, but only by peasants) and landscape through portraits (for the most part of sitters of some social standing) to religious and history painting. These last two were considered the most

important categories, because they encompassed all other genres. The genre painter could only paint one kind of scene, but the history painter was also a landscape/genre/still-life painter, as all these skills were needed to represent the dramatic narrative of history.

This system militated against such genre painters as Chardin, who found himself fulsomely praised by the critic Diderot but denied access to comparison with **history painters**. Greuze, by contrast, who failed to enter the French Academy as a history painter, was awarded the dubious privilege of being received as a genre painter. **MG PD**

Further reading J. Harding, *Artistes pompiers: French Academic Art in the 19th Century.*

GEOGRAPHIC INFORMATION SYSTEMS

Geographic information systems were a part of the information technology revolution of the 1980s. They brought together a number of previously separate technologies and promised to transform the provision of information to governments, businesses and utilities, as well as to academics and other private citizens. A geographic information system locates information in geographic space and has five elements: data capture; data preparation; data storage; analysis and output. As such, it brings together the interests of data collecting organizations such as national censuses, databases, for example Ceefax, geographers and other spatial analysts, and cartographic organizations in public and private sectors. Indeed, one of the problems has been the proliferation of different systems as specialized organizations extend their areas of interest: for example, the US census developing map production or Bartholomews setting up databases to simplify map preparation.

Ideally, a geographic information system allows an organization or individual to access a large variety of data, which has been collected and updated by private and/or official sources, to process it in ways they specify and to output it as maps, diagrams or tables. The problem is that different data-collecting organizations use different spatial bases for different purposes. Some data may be continuous, some may relate to points or lines and much relates to areas which vary in scale, shape and regularity. As a result, even simple tasks such as bringing together two kinds of data and mapping their association pose complex problems. The large databases and heavy processing demands require more sophisticated systems to be run on mainframe computers, though desktop machines can be used for simpler systems. No doubt the technical problems will be overcome, but the standardization of areas between organizations is a slow process. At present the demands of assembling data and presenting it in graphic form is sufficiently demanding to satisfy most users and few systems offer much ability to carry out statistical analyses of the resulting patterns. But, in spite of reservations, ease of access to information has improved dramatically. A pioneer British system of the mid-1980s, the Domesday disk, claimed to offer any purchaser more geographic information on one laser disk than had previously been available to any government department. In future, it is likely that more and more varied information will become available, but it is probable that access will be determined by cost factors resulting from the expense of building up these systems and the value of up-to-date information. **PS**

Further reading D. Martin, *Geographic Information Systems and their Socioeconomic Applications.*

GEOGRAPHY

The Greek roots of the word 'geography' (*ge*, 'Earth', *graphia*, 'drawing') suggest that this is a discipline concerned with 'description of the Earth', but geographers have always insisted that it studies 'the Earth as the home of Man'. This apparently simple definition has a number of implications: (1) the concern is with the surface of the Earth not with its deep structure, which is the domain of **geology**; (2) geography includes physical, biological and social phenomena, and ideally seeks to show how they are integrated together; (3) because of its interest in

the surface of the Earth, geography is very much concerned with location, place and distance.

The very wide range of phenomena studied by geographers, from landforms and climate to human cultures, has led different practitioners to adopt different emphases. Some have emphasized its role in linking natural science with the humanities, others its focus on man and Nature (or as we would now say 'society and environment'), yet others its emphasis on relationships in geographic space. At worst, different geographers have drifted apart and become more interested in the specialist disciplines such as geology, meteorology, **botany**, **sociology** or **economics** than in other parts of geography. At best, and in aspiration, geography remains a holistic and humane discipline concerned to make sense of our lives in the context of nature and the whole of human society.

In the sense that geography deals with the practicalities of life in the home place, the ability to travel to neighbouring places and to find out about more distant places, all societies must have had a vital interest in the subject. As a recognizable academic discipline its roots lie in ancient Greece, though it was not clearly separated from **astronomy**. Two themes can be traced: some geographers, notably Strabo, sought to satisfy curiosity about exotic places, while others, led by Ptolemy, sought to measure and map the globe. Like other branches of learning, knowlege of Greek geographers was lost to western Europe, but preserved by Arab scholars.

Interest in geography was revived in western Europe in the 16th century by the voyages of discovery. These voyages stimulated the production of better maps (see **cartography**) and also created a strong interest in knowledge of the origins of commodities including spices, Oriental craft products and precious metals. Major advances came in the 19th century as scientific exploration moved beyond a focus on the commercial to take an interest in natural history. The leading geographical explorer was a German, Alexander von Humboldt, who travelled widely in South America and Asia. As well as cataloguing the variety of habitats and species, he argued that there was a 'unity in diversity' among the inhabitants of the Earth's surface. He was the main inspiration of the first university professor of geography, Carl Ritter, who ascribed this unity to divine purpose. But for nearly all of the 19th century most geography was pragmatic, a vital part of the spread of commerce and empire, and of the creation of the **international division of labour**. It was not until the latter part of the century that geography emerged as a self-conscious academic speciality in the universities of Germany, France and Britain.

While the academics were beginning to try to explain what makes **places** different, the promotion of their subject was still influenced by practical motives. The French government did so because it ascribed its defeat in the Franco-Prussian war to the Germans' better knowledge of geography. Britain's first professor of geography, H. Mackinder, was not accepted as a member of the Royal Geographical Society until he had led an expedition to climb Mount Kilimanjaro. But as geography became an accepted part of the school and university curriculum, a new problem appeared: how to organize and subdivide a subject whose scope was so wide?

Although understanding the Earth as 'the home of Man' was regarded as the ultimate purpose of geography, the task was soon seen as too big for any one person and so geographers began to specialize. For much of the 20th century the major division was between *regional* and *systematic* specialists.

Regional geography attempted to show how the physical, biological and social characteristics of an area combined to give it a unique way of life or personality. The art of 'regional synthesis' was particularly well developed in France before 1939.

The proponents of a systematic approach argued that it was premature to ask what was unique about a region until it had been established how particular features varied over the world. In turn, that required knowledge of the disciplines that specialized in particular phenomena. The result was the fragmentation of geographers' interests and a major division between *physical* and *human* geography.

Physical geographers took an approach influenced by natural science. Geomorphology studies landforms and is influenced by geology and hydrology. Climatology studies the variation of climate over the world and blends into meteorology. **Biogeography** and soil geography map and explain the variability of plants, animals and soils. At a global scale it is clear that there is some coincidence of climate, plants, soils and landforms – but only very recently have attempts been made to model how change in one sphere will affect the others.

Human geography has become increasingly influenced by the social sciences. Consequently, historical geographers have been joined by economic, social and political geographers, and population geographers have interacted with demographers. Recently, cultural geography has gone beyond a quasi-anthropological concern with 'primitive' cultures to begin to investigate the symbolic and ideological processes which hold modern societies together.

The divisions of geography reflect more than just the practical difficulties of tackling the discipline's agenda. They also reflect the pressures of university organization and academic prestige. The division between physical and human geography became very real for students admitted to science or arts faculties, and in some universities, especially in the USA, geomorphology became a very minor part of geology.

During the 1960s a new approach to geography moved the subject a long way from its traditional concerns. A small number of geographers in the USA and UK became convinced that the discipline should not pursue questions of regional uniqueness, but model itself on the **scientific method** as applied in the physical sciences. The aim would be to seek for laws governing the phenomena of geography. There was a problem in that these phenomena also belonged to other disciplines. This was overcome by emphasizing that geography was concerned with the spatial patterns on the surface of the Earth, and that it was rendered distinctive by this 'spatial perspective'. The approach was christened *spatial analysis* and soon became dominant, though always criticized by regional geographers, advocates of a humanistic approach and political radicals.

The key insight of spatial analysis was that certain spatial patterns resulted from the minimization of transport costs. So agricultural zones and urban land use could be shown to approximate to concentric bands, market towns to be ideally distributed in hexagonal patterns and industrial plants to be at the least cost location relative to major raw materials. So social processes had their own geometry. Unfortunately, this geometry was often obscured by other influences so the ambition to establish laws, in the sense of repeatedly observable patterns, was rather unsuccessful. It began to be realized that what was really needed was explanations which could account for what was observed, and could allow for the complex combinations of influences which geographers usually find to be present. Spatial analysis lost its dominance of theory, though it has subsequently been revived as part of the new information technology known as **geographical information systems**.

The next step was to go beyond the long-standing concern of geographers with issues of practical relevance, and to develop Marxist explanations for geographical phenomena. This gave geography a more sophisticated view of social processes than had previously been available, but as the 1980s progressed it became clear that abstract categories, such as **capitalism**, could not account for the complexity of situations in different places. So geographers began once more to emphasize the effects of localities as well as global differences in levels of development.

Perhaps the greatest disappointment for the discipline of geography came in the early 1970s when environmental problems came on to the public agenda. The discipline whose historic role had been to identify the links between natural and human processes was then fragmented into physical and human subdivisions, and preoccupied with a debate between spatial analysts and Marxists. Only a small minority had maintained their global perspective on society-Nature relationships and, though they provided a nucleus around which many geographers regrouped to tackle urgent environmental issues, those issues seem now to be regarded as 'ecological' rather than as geographical. In practical terms, scientists and especially climatologists have found themselves on the forefront of studies which attempt to assess the causes and consequences of major environmental problems, such as **global warming**.

The discipline may be given a second chance because the Brundtland Report has identified **sustainable development** as the way forward. Geographers have done a great deal to show how the international division of labour has created **uneven development** at scales from local to global, and it has described how current economic and political systems generate social and environmental problems. They are, therefore, well placed to show how those systems need to be changed to make development sustainable. That is the challenge for the 21st century. **PS**

Further reading D.N. Livingstone, *The Geographical Tradition.*

GEOLOGY

Geology (Greek, 'Earth-study') is the scientific study of the Earth. There is a very long history of practical knowledge of the rocks, minerals and structures found at the surface and used for building, pigment or metallurgy, but, in spite of some tentative steps by the Greeks and Romans, scientific geology hardly began before the 19th century. Geology's problem, which is also the reason for its fascination, is that it asks fundamental questions about the origin, development, structure and behaviour of the solid Earth. For most of human history such questions have been beyond the reach of **science** and were seen as too important to be left to rational investigation. The situation has been transformed in the last two centuries, but only in the last few decades have convincing answers emerged.

A key figure in the emergence of modern geology was a Scot, James Hutton (1726–97). His contribution was to put forward a theory of the Earth which was rooted in his own observations. His explanations of what he observed were not all correct, but they embodied an approach that became dominant in the 19th century, which was **uniformitarianism**.

Hutton lived most of his life in Edinburgh, then one of the great intellectual centres of Europe. He developed an early interest in chemistry which he maintained while studying law, medicine and agriculture. He travelled in Scotland and Europe and preferred field and laboratory investigation, often in collaboration with other investigators, to reading existing texts. As a result, his *Theory of the Earth*, first read in 1785, published as a paper in 1788 and only extended into a book in 1895, was highly original. He discussed rock formation, uplift, erosion and deposition (first proposing what we now call the **rock cycle**), and even anticipated later views of the role of glaciation in transporting boulders and of the relations between river systems and their basins. Some of his conjectures later proved wrong, but he had already shown himself willing to test his ideas against observation and change them if they did not fit the facts. It is ironic that the generation which followed him were more impressed by the Neptunist arguments of Werner and the catastrophist beliefs of Cuvier. Those arguments were gradually abandoned, though Werner's work on mineralogy and crystallography was an important forerunner of the later work of Berzelius (1779–1848) on the chemical principles of mineralogy.

A crucial practical contribution to the development of geology was made by William Smith, who worked as a surveyor, first in the Somerset coalfield and later on canals, turnpike roads and estates throughout England and Wales. His work both stimulated detailed local studies of geological structure and clarified the sequence of rocks in the *stratigraphic column*. He recognized that the same sequence of rock strata could be found in different places and that a particular stratum would have a distinct set of fossils. As a result he was able to add together the local sequences of rocks to build up the whole stratigraphic column, showing all the sedimentary rocks of the UK from the oldest to the youngest. His observations, plus the principle of *faunal sequence* could then be used by other geolo-

gists to refine the overall picture. With this knowledge, field geologists could both map the outcrops of rocks on the surface and begin to identify the three-dimensional geological structure which underlay them. They were able to show that layers of rock had been tilted and folded, that faults marked where layers of rock had been torn apart and displaced vertically, and that in places there were unconformities between older rocks and much younger ones, marking periods when deposition had either not occurred in that location or had been removed by erosion. Smith and his followers were showing that the Earth has a long and dynamic past rather than a short static one. He published the first geological map of England and Wales in 1815 and went on to produce more detailed county maps. This work was developed by the Board of Ordnance from the 1820s and later by the Geological Survey of Great Britain.

Much of the later work in the 19th century was an extension and elaboration of the work of these pioneers, whether in more painstaking survey and analysis of geological structure (often in association with mining activity), exhaustive investigation of mineralogy (aided by new instruments like the polarizing microscope) or in the analysis of surface processes. A Swiss, Louis Agassiz, showed that glacial features could be found in much of northern Europe and America and so identified the extent of the recent Ice Age. American geomorphologists began the investigation of fluvial processes in both shorter and longer terms. But for most of the century the knowledge of geologists was restricted to the outer layers of the planet.

The key advances in the 20th century stemmed from the development of *geophysics*, which offered a number of new ways of investigating the internal structure of the Earth. **Seismology** had a long history as the observation and recording of earthquakes but from the 1880s it progressed rapidly and in 1906 R.D. Oldham was able to deduce the internal structure and composition of the Earth, especially the existence of the Earth's dense core and less dense mantle and crust. Measurement of gravity anomalies had begun to show variation in the strength of gravity at different places, and that mountain ranges did not exhibit the positive gravity anomalies which would be expected if their extra mass was simply piled on top of the underlying rock. As a result it was proposed that the extra mass must be counterbalanced by 'roots' of less dense rock, suggesting that the continental rocks are 'floating' on the underlying rock. This idea, formalized as the concept of *isostacy*, was proposed in 1899 and supported by studies of gravity anomalies and rates of uplift in areas recently covered by thick ice sheets.

The notion of substantial vertical movement of parts of the Earth's crust was supported by studies in experimental petrology: Bridgeman showed that at the sorts of temperatures and pressures which would occur 30 to 40 km below the surface rock would be more plastic and possibly able to flow. Bowen's studies of silicate melts and rates of cooling did much to clarify the origins of igneous rocks.

The discovery of **radioactivity** and the existence of a constant half-life for the transition of a radioactive isotope to its daughter product was soon recognized as both a method of heating the Earth from within and a possible method of giving absolute dates to the rocks of the stratigraphic column. Boltwood used ratios of uranium to lead to date samples in the range 410–2,200 million years. Later, this was shown to be about 20% too high, but the method finally refuted Kelvin's thermodynamic argument for ages as little as 20 million years (see **dating the Earth**).

In 1912, Alfred Wegener published a theory which was as startling as Hutton's had been a century earlier. He proposed that the continents had moved over time, and indeed that they had once formed a single super continent. He was able to produce a lot of evidence, including the fit in shape (most noticeable for the two sides of the Atlantic), the evidence of climate change provided by geological deposits (for example the red sandstones of the UK show it experienced a desert climate and was thus well to the south of its current latitude), many geological structures and fossil assemblages appear as if torn apart and separated by thousands of miles. In spite of the evidence, most geologists regarded **continental drift** as a new form of catastrophism because no current mechanism seemed to exist.

From the 1960s new observations of the mid-ocean ridges showed that ocean spreading was occurring at rates of 2–10 cm per year, and geologists began to accept a new view of the Earth. The theory of **plate tectonics** brings together many previously disparate observations and explains how they result from the movements of about 20 crustal plates. In its way it is a change similar to the Copernican revolution. No longer do we stand on a static Earth whose surface is a complex riddle. Now we stand on a mobile Earth whose past movements have created the pattern of rocks and structures that past geologists described and present-day geologists can explain. **PS**

GEOMETRY

Geometry (Greek, 'land-measurement'), is the mathematical investigation of the relationship between points and lines. Euclid (3rd century BCE) catalogued the existing state of geometrical knowledge in his day in his book *Elements*, and made the study of geometry the science which the ancient Greeks found most pleasing (as being the one in which pure reason could play the most part). His work laid the basis of **Euclidean geometry**. The methods of the *Elements* were embedded in **algebraic geometry**, based on the co-ordinate systems of René Descartes (1596–1650). Euclid's work in geometry was not superseded until the 19th century, when the work of Johann Bolyai (1802–60) and Nicholas Lobachevsky (1792–1856) showed that there were consistent versions of geometry in which the axioms of Euclid did not hold; this led to the development of **non-Euclidean geometry**. **SMcL**

GEOPOLITICS

Geopolitics is the analysis of power relations between countries. It is often viewed from the perspective of the superpowers, or at least major powers or alliances, rather than that of the minor powers, and it is more concerned with strategic military issues than with those of **democracy** or **human rights**. In the long run, geopolitical power relates to size of population and territory and to economic development, but military power tends to lag behind economic power: for example, compared to Japan the UK and the US are militarily stronger but economically weaker.

One of the pioneers of geopolitical ideas was the first British professor of geography, Halford Mackinder, whose analysis of 1904 was summed up in the dictum: 'Who rules East Europe commands the heartland; who rules the heartland commands the world island; who commands the world island commands the world.' In coded language this identified Germany and Russia as well placed for world domination, and sought to justify Britain's imperial activities in the fringes of Eurasia and in the oceans and islands as a way of blocking the continental powers. It was a perspective which fitted the priorities of the USA after 1945, and probably one which created the USSR's fear of encirclement and attack.

In fact the USA had experience of geopolitics dating back at least to 1823, when it adopted the Monroe Doctrine, which committed it not to intervene in European affairs so long as the European powers avoided colonial intervention in Latin America. In 1947, the Truman Doctrine changed the commitment to one of 'active support for free people' – which meant active opposition to Soviet and Chinese influence, even if this meant support for dictatorial régimes or even breaking the law. This led to intervention over Berlin, Korea, Vietnam and the Lebanon and to paranoia over Castro's Cuba and the destabilization of Allende's Chile. In 1979, influenced by US reliance on imported oil, the Carter Doctrine identified the Persian Gulf as vital to the USA and contributed to conflict with revolutionary Iran, support for Iraq and the sudden reversal of view over Iraq's occupation of Kuwait.

As we approach the end of the millennium, the collapse of the USSR has left the US as the sole superpower. The only immediate counter forces are Europe and Japan, but in neither case is the potential power being realized, Europe because of fragmentation and Japan because of distaste for past geopolitical adventures. In the longer term China and India have great potential because of their huge populations, but will be of limited influence until they achieve a higher level of development. In the shorter term the pattern looks likely to be one of smaller scale conflict, whether in the fragments of the eastern bloc or from heavily armed oil states such as Iraq. Such a world will not encourage broad geopolitical concepts, but this is probably a good thing, because the cynical concern for power makes geopolitics unable to contribute to solving international issues like **sustainable development** or the inequalities of the **international division of labour**. **PS**

GERM LAYER THEORY

The germ layer theory, in the **life sciences**, is the idea that all embryos are composed of distinct layers which give rise to particular tissues in the adult. It was proposed by Karl von Baer (1792–1876) and represented a departure from the previous idea of preformation (see **embryology**). The theory was extensively modified with the advent of cell theory and **evolution** theory, but it is still accepted that an embryo has three germ layers. However, these do not originate or develop in the same way in all organisms. **RB**

GERM PLASM THEORY

The germ plasm theory, in the **life sciences**, was formulated by August Weismann and presented as 'The germ plasm: A theory of heredity' in 1893. It envisaged the segregation of sex cells (germ plasm) from somatic (body) cells at an early stage in the development of the embryo so that they remain unaffected by the external and internal environment. It was thus a rejection of the idea that characteristics which are acquired during the life of an individual can be inherited by the offspring. The germ plasm is essentially immortal while the somatic tissues live only in one generation, for the lifetime of the individual; in the case of single-celled organisms which divide by binary fission (the production of two individuals from one), the organism itself is immortal. The germ plasm theory, correct in essence but not in detail, was the precursor to the **gene theory** and set the scene for it by producing an intellectual environment which was ripe for the acceptance of Mendel's work on **genetics**, published in 1866 but overlooked until 1900. **RB**

See also embryology; pangenesis.

GESAMTKUNSTWERK

Gesamtkunstwerk (German, 'united-art work') was an ideal put forward in late-19th-century Germany, and was concerned above all with the **performing arts**. The theory was that works of art should be created in which all the participating arts should have equal status: not just words and **music** (about whose status in **opera**, relative to one another, there had been centuries of argument), but design, lighting, production and any other activity essential to the show. Wagner proclaimed that his music-dramas were *gesamtkunstwerk* – and perhaps in his own Bayreuth theatre, performed under his direction and with his designs, they were. A generation after Wagner, Alexander Scriabin wrote large-scale concert works in which light shows and musical sounds were carefully integrated to induce (he hoped) specific psychological and mystical states (he even had perfumes sprayed on the audience at appropriate moments in the performance). In the modern era, this kind of approach has been widely used by **pop** and **rock** groups, electronics and lasers making possible effects which neither Scriabin nor Wagner could have imagined even in their most technicolor dreams. Together with film, live rock shows are perhaps the most convincing realizations, so far, of the *gesamtkunstwerk* ideal. **KMcL**

GESTALT

Gestalt (German, 'form', from Old High German *stellen*, 'to shape') was developed in the 1950s in New York by Frederick and Laura Perls. Frederick was a psychoanalyst who disliked the passivity and rigidity of the psychoanalytic practice, and Laura was already working with the old Gestalt school, which saw human beings as perceiving the world as meaningful configurations, called *gestalts*. Integration, existential and phenomenological respect for experience and concentration therapy were all taken by the Perls from the earlier Gestalt school. The Perls adopted the Reichian view that the body was as involved as the mind in constructing resistances. Their Gestalt therapy was linked to the human potential movement in the 1960s. The therapy works to heighten awareness and enhance the quality of interactions. It holds a holistic view that a person relates to the environment: humans are not self-sufficient, but engage with the environment and surroundings in order to work and grow. The Gestalt view of the personality is that it has a number of functions, bodily, perceptual, verbal and cognitive. The inborn goal is self-actualization in biological, physical, psychological, social and spiritual needs, and exists in open-ended creativity in adjusting to situations. **MJ**

Further reading Hefferline, Perls and Goodman, *Gestalt Theory*.

GIFT

Gift (from Old Germanic *geb*, 'to give') first received detailed anthropological attention in Marcel Mauss's book *The Gift* (1925). He was influenced by other anthropologists' work and literary texts. These included the *kula* exchange of the Trobriand Islanders (a Melanesian custom of ceremonial exchange in which special necklaces and shell armbands are exchanged between islands in opposite geographical directions), North American Indians' *potlatch* (exchange of items at extravagant feasts held at births, weddings, deaths, etc.), and ideas about gift-giving amongst the Eskimos of North America, Hindus in India and the Maori community in Polynesia.

Mauss's classic text has been subject to numerous interpretations. The conventional version relates Mauss's claims for fundamental aspects of gift exchange in 'archaic' or 'primitive' societies – the obligation to give, to receive and to repay. Such instances Mauss called 'total presentations' referring to a complex of econo-mic, aesthetic, religious, moral and legal qualities acting to create relationships between groups of people. This is exempli-fied by *potlatch* feasts amongst North American Indians in which gifts are pre-sented to all the guests in recognition of their positions through inheritance or achievement. The more generous and extravagant the *potlatch*, the more prestige attaches to the hosts. The recipients of the gifts are then expected to return the com-pliment by holding a *potlatch* that is equal or better in generosity at a later date.

An evolutionist framework is offered by Mauss in which 'total presentations' between groups of people develop to gift exchange between persons representing groups. Giving a gift initially is linked up with the person's social identity, status and prestige in society. A notable example at this stage concerns ideas about gifts amongst the Maori community. Mauss termed their beliefs as the 'spirit of the gift'. This entailed the idea that the thing given embodies some part of the original owner's personality and therefore must eventually be returned to him.

This stage of gift-giving in which the person represents a group is then thought to be eradicated by modern market exchange in which individuals act in their own interests. The concept of gift is con-trasted with the idea of commodity. Gifts create debts with people in which they come to be associated with one or other of the participants (inalienable), whereas commodities depend on being able to be converted with other things and can be passed on without being associated with the former owner (alienable). That is, a personal or social relationship is a pre-condition for gift-giving whereas com-modities such as money are impersonal in that they do not symbolize a caring rela-tionship, yet are appropriate for particular motivations.

Later anthropologists offer a more plausible interpretation of Mauss's writ-ings by saying that in modern societies the concept of gifts is not eradicated by market exchange, but comes to represent the pure or moral counterpart of commodity exchange in a market economy. As market

exchange becomes increasingly dominant and lacking in a moral code, then the idea that gifts should be pure and ethical becomes more urgent. Gifts here are thought of as something quite different to their exchange in non-monetary societies, such as was present in North American Indian societies and Maori communities before they were brought under the ambit of a market economy. **RK**

See also economic anthropology; exchange; gender; reciprocity.

Further reading Chris Gregory, *Gifts and Commodities*; Jonathon Parry, *The Gift, the Indian Gift, and the 'Indian Gift'*.

GIVEN, THE

In the arts, 'the given' (or as Henry James described it, the *donnée*) is the single semi-nal idea, the seed from which an entire work germinates. Tracing the creator's thought process back to this 'given' is a recognized critical technique in all the **arts** and for critics and consumers of the arts in general, tracing the thought process for-wards from the 'given', treading in the creator's footsteps as it were, is one of the most satisfying ways to experience a created work.

In **philosophy**, 'the given' means the sup-posed raw data of experience, uncontamin-ated by theoretical interpretation or cognitive inferences.

The argument from illusion suggests that when we perceive objects in the external world, all we are ever directly aware of are sensory experiences as of objects and not the objects themselves. This leads to the problem of scepticism: if one is only ever directly aware of sensory experiences as of objects and not objects themselves, how can one know that the objects really are as they seem to be? One's beliefs about the external world go beyond one's immediate experience. So if one's beliefs about the external world are justified, they must be justified by inferences from the raw data of one's experience. One's beliefs about the external world have the status of hypotheses, and these hypotheses are justified by inferences from 'the given': the raw data of one's experience. **AJ**

See also illusion, argument from; scepticism.

Further reading J. Dancy, *An Introduction to Epistemology*; J. Ross, *The Appeal to the Given*.

GLAM ROCK see Rock Music

GLOBAL WARMING

The possibility of significant warming of the Earth's atmosphere over the next century is arguably the most important environmental problem facing humanity. If it does occur, it will disrupt human settlements and agriculture throughout the world, as well as destabilizing natural processes which have taken billions of years to reach their present state. To prevent it would require radical changes in human activities, including a redefinition of the idea of 'progress'. At present, atmospheric scientists expect a rise of some 4°C over the next 50 years, but they are uncertain what this will mean for certain areas. Such a rise would be a temperature change of the same order as the change from glacial to interglacial, so any additional warming would be an unprecedented interference with the atmosphere.

Global warming is sometimes blamed on the **greenhouse effect**, but it is important to realize that the natural greenhouse effect is a vital contributor to life on Earth. Without the warming effect of the absorbtion of heat in the atmosphere, the Earth's surface temperature would be similar to that of the Moon ($-18°C$). What is at issue is an enhanced greenhouse effect as a result of changes in the composition of the atmosphere, notably increases in carbon dioxide, CFCs (chlorofluorocarbons), methane, nitrous oxide and water vapour. These greenhouse gases are particularly effective in absorbing radiation from the Earth's surface and so warming the atmosphere. Even a small overall warming could change climatic patterns and melt snow, ice and permafrost, with unpredictable effects on ecosystems and sea levels. However, though these gases have been increasing in concentration for a century or more, it is by no means certain that they have caused any warming yet. The Earth's average temperature has risen by .5°C since 1860, but that is within the normal range of variability. So all current worries are based on predictions of the response of the atmosphere to expected increases in emissions of greenhouse gases. The Second World Climatic Conference brought a high level of consensus among scientists that warming was probable and would be best avoided, but responses from politicians were muted.

There are two major problems for politicians seeking to respond to the threat of global warming – leaving aside that it is a problem involving timescales far greater than political terms of office. First, the causes of increased emissions include the key activities which sustain life and promise affluence. Second, an effective response must be global and is prevented by sharp differences in the interests of different countries. The main sources of carbon dioxide emissions are fossil fuel burning (in power stations, smelters and vehicles) and deforestation. Methane is produced by rice paddies and cattle, as well as leaks from gas pipelines. Nitrous oxide comes from vehicles, deforestation and agriculture. Only CFCs are relatively easy to control, but they are extremely persistent once emitted. Apart from CFCs, controlling emissions of greenhouse gases would require huge increases in energy efficiency and the transformation of agriculture as well as reversal of deforestation. Agreement to implement such huge changes would have to overcome differences between countries. The more developed countries use much more energy than the less-developed, so they are arguably responsible for the problem. But they are reluctant to reduce coal or oil burning appreciably. The less-developed countries have plans to increase power generation and therefore emissions. Most east European countries use energy very inefficiently, but lack capital to invest in more modern plant. Agriculture and deforestation will probably be even harder to change, because it will involve changes to the diet of whole populations, including a sharp reduction in consumption of intensively-reared cattle. An international agreement was reached at the 1992 Earth Summit, but the policies agreed will only reduce the rate of increase of greenhouse gases.

In the US, one factor that has reduced the willingness of politicians to take action is that industrial lobbies have been arguing that global warming is a left-wing plot intended to block economic growth. This, coupled with a fear that American voters regard their right to drive large cars as on a par with the constitutional right to bear arms, made the administration of President Bush very obstructive in international negotiations. Given the economic and political power of the US, and their consumption of energy, this stance has reduced other countries' readiness to respond. This seems particularly unfortunate when the risks are so high, and most of the preventative measures make sense for other environmental reasons, and some, especially, energy efficiency, are also economically advantageous. It is true that tackling global warming has major implications, but if it requires a change toward **sustainable development** rather than exploitative and unequal methods this would appear to most people to be a gain rather than a loss.

Finally, it is worth noting that any suggestion that global warming threatens life on Earth is highly exaggerated. The changes in atmospheric composition are significant in relation to changes in the last few million years, but are very small compared with the changes brought about by life (see **atmosphere and life**). PS

GLOBALIZATION

The term globalization, in **economics**, refers to the development of worldwide social and economic relationships. The world, in many crucial respects, has become a single social system as a result of the many ties of interdependence between the various countries. In recent history, men and women find that their lives are influenced by organizations and networks which are located many miles away from them. Consider, for example, the range of products available in Western supermarkets which depend on a complex system of relationships between various countries.

It is only in relatively recent times that it has been possible to speak of forms of social association which stretch across the globe. The total world-view now taken for granted is a fairly recent development. Globalization started two or three centuries ago with the expansion of Western influence as Western adventurers began to explore different parts of the globe. The gulf that then existed between different parts of the world led to the development of some bizarre beliefs about peoples from foreign parts. The Chinese, for instance, believed that the English would die of constipation if they did not eat rhubarb; 19th-century Western missionaries displayed extraordinary arrogance when they saw their task as one of 'civilizing' the 'savages' they encountered in Africa.

Globalization has, however, not taken place evenly and the development of world social relations has resulted in marked inequalities between the industrialized and **Third World** countries. Most Third World countries are in areas which once underwent Western colonial rule. Sufficient food may exist to feed the world population, but still millions of people die of hunger and starvation every year. Large amounts of food are destroyed or stored indefinitely in Western countries and businesses operating in the Third World are geared to export to the West rather than to satisfy local food needs.

The process of globalization has been greatly facilitated by developments in communications and transport. An important feature of globalization is the development of **multinationals** – companies operating in two or more countries across national boundaries. As a consequence of globalization multinational companies are able to take advantage of the diverse tax and wage rates and levels of unionization in different countries, forcing employees to compete in the world labour market. The final product can be assembled from many different units, made in a large number of different countries. Countries in the world have become largely interdependent as a result of these multinational companies. **DA**

See also convergence thesis; dependency

theory; diffusionism; division of labour; historical sociology; labour process; society; world system.

Further reading H. Bull, et al. (eds.), *Expansion of International Society*; P. Worsley, *The Three Worlds: Culture and World Development*.

GLOTTOCHRONOLOGY

One of the major aims in **historical linguistics** is to chart the sources of common heritage obtaining between individual languages. Among the numerous methods available, one technique which gained some currency from the 1950s to the 1970s is a statistical procedure known as glottochronology (Greek, 'study of tongue time'). A formula is applied to provide an estimation of the time when two related languages split away from a common parent. A fundamental assumption is that the original vocabulary of a given language decays over time, being steadily supplanted by borrowings from other languages. In particular, there is supposed to be a core vocabulary, common to all languages, which comprises such semantic categories as family terms, body parts and pronouns. In one version of the formula, it is estimated that the replacement rate for this core vocabulary is 19% per millenium. When we wish to determine the time at which two languages parted company, we must enter into the formula a number of factors, including the number of cognates, that is, the number of core vocabulary items they have in common. Despite early enthusiasm, the popularity of glottochronology has waned greatly in recent years, since the original formula made too many unwarranted assumptions and simplifications about the way languages actually change. **MS**

GNOSTICISM

Gnosticism (from Greek *gnosis*, 'knowledge') denotes systems of special philosophical and religious knowledge which enlighten the individual and guarantee salvation to those who attain it. In this it resembles *gnana marga* ('way of knowledge') of **Brahmanic religion**, though gnosticism was almost invariably a secret doctrine disclosed by a great teacher and involving a considerable element of self-knowledge. Until the *Nag Hammadi MS* (Coptic, 4th–5th century) was published in the last 20 years, gnosticism was known mainly from the writings of its opponents, principally the Church Fathers Irenaeus (*c*.130–200) and Tertullian (*c*.160–200), and fragments of non-canonical gospels. They represented an intellectual movement which challenged the theology and ethics of the Christian Church. But from the gnostic scriptures themselves, it seems that the principal appeal lay in a religious experience and in moral strength to survive a turbulent, hostile world.

There has been scholarly debate about the origins of gnosticism, but it seems to originate in Jewish and Christian depression after the fall of Jerusalem (CE 70), its utter destruction (135) and the disappearance of the Jewish state, and in disillusion with **eschatology**. Hence the basic gnostic doctrine was redemption from the material world. The soul escaping from matter is reunited with the *Pleruma* ('perfection') or fullness of God (possibly also 'fulfilment'). Elements of gnosticism can be found in Greek philosophical movements, Chasidic **Judaism**, Orphic **cults** in Babylonia and Indo-Aryan religion.

Christian Gnosticism drew some ideas from all these movements. In the writings of the Church Fathers, its founder was said to be Simon Magnus of Samaria who was alleged (Acts 8:9f) to have offered Peter money for spiritual power (hence the word 'simony'). He rescued a woman, Helen, in Tyre, from 'bondage' and declared that she was Sophia, 'Divine Wisdom', who could similarly liberate her devotees. The Supreme Being, Simon claimed, was remote from this transitory world, but, either directly or through Sophia, sent Jesus to show the way of salvation and to defeat death. To Gnostics, Jesus was not actually human but only appeared so, as Greek gods did when they walked the Earth. The risen Christ, however, was a living presence for Gnostics, giving new revelations. These frequently took the form of Gospels allegedly by Jesus' friends. In them Mary Magdalene is often shown as the chief interlocutor and leader of the community. This mirrors the equality women enjoyed among Gnostic sects, and the challenge they presented to the Church hierarchy as typified by Peter.

Gnostics tended to extreme **asceticism** (as contact with worldly things was defiling), or else they were antinomian, rejecting all morality and restraint. When Christianity became the official religion of the Roman Empire, in the 4th century, repression was savage. Gnosticism resurfaced, however, in the Cathars ('the pure') and Albigensians of medieval France, when again the challenge was as much political as theological. Gnosticism has recently been the subject of close scrutiny by **feminist theologians** because of the prominent role given to women and to Divine Wisdom. **EMJ**

Further reading H. Jonas, *The Gnostic Religion*.

GOD

When the **Christian** bishop J.A.T. Robinson caused a furore in Britain with his book *Honest to God* (1963) it was because he argued that the word, image and concept were bankrupt. Ordinary people no longer believed in God as, for example, an old man in the sky, or someone 'out there' watching over them, or a hypothesis to explain gaps in scientific knowledge. His book pointed to a difficulty in English – that the generic term for deity is also used as a personal name for the divine power worshipped in the Judaeo-Christian tradition (since God's name was considered too holy for human use). Ironically, *Dios*, from which deus/god, di/divinity comes, was the name of an ancient pre-Hellenic pantheon god – it comes from the same root as 'sky' – and the overwhelming majority of humankind still, today, has no difficulty whatsoever in believing in God. The evidence, they would say, is all around in the natural world.

The Apostle Paul argued that all people seek after God, who has left signs by which he can be found. Later Christian thinkers developed this into a series of arguments for the existence of God. Anselm (*c.*1033–1109), for example, maintained that if one means by God 'that than which a greater cannot be conceived', then one must necessarily conceive also that the entity exists, because what exists is greater than what does not exist, and a non-existent God would be a contradication in terms. Since what exists is greater than the mere idea of it, then God must exist.

Existence is generally taken to be an essential attribute of God – a non-existent God is a contradiction in terms which may be why in so many religious traditions the existence of God or gods is taken for granted, and not debated.

Another category of arguments for the existence of God centres on the design of the universe. Before the concept of **evolution**, the universe was seen as a perfect mechanism designed by God the Creator. The most famous version is known as 'Paley's Watch' after William Paley, who argued that the existence of a 'clockwork' world demanded the existence of a watchmaker. The idea of an absentee impersonal watchmaker suited 18th-century thought, but it left no room for 'miracles' or for God's personal involvement in the world. This is one of the big divisions within and between religions: is God an impersonal force, an unmoved Mover, Uncreated Creator, or simply above and beyond the world, time and space? Or does He or She condescend to be known on human terms, as Father, Mother, Lover, possessed of personality, even if it is beyond comprehension? Are the people who appear to have a 'hotline to heaven' deluded, and what are the natures of worship and **prayer** if a direct relationship is not possible?

These dilemmas raise a further question as to whether one can talk about God using human analogies and metaphors. Can one use human language at all? If not, what happens about **myth**, that important source of theological insight and religious self-awareness? Other arguments for the existence of God include the epistemological, which is based on the nature and origin of human knowledge, the moral argument which asks whence comes human conscience and morality and finds a moral purpose in the universe, and the aesthetic argument (which is perhaps more of a gut feeling), that such a beautiful world points to a benevolent creator. If the use of analogy is not justified, then it becomes increasingly difficult to defend the traditional arguments from accusations of **anthropomorphism**. As it is, God is often described in categories heavily coloured by contemporary culture and politics – God as King, Judge, Lord, etc. – which are found in many faiths. Similarly, defining God in abstract terms (such as Truth, Wisdom or the Supreme Good) can reveal more about society's values than about God without necessarily invalidating the assertion. What is dangerous is to say that Truth or Love is God.

In many religious traditions, for example, **Islam** and Orthodox **Christianity**, God is always described aphatically (that is, in negatives), as one cannot find adequate adjectives. He (always He!) is immortal, invisible, ineffable, impassible, unknowable, beyond comprehension, etc. This raises the questions of how one can know He exists at all, or if He does what relevance He has to the human condition? For the 'religions of the book', God is known by what he has chosen to reveal of himself. The nature of revelation as divine communication has been thoroughly investigated by modern theologians, especially by Karl Barth who emphasizes God's transcendence and Rudolf Bultmann, who applied an **existentialist** philosophy to biblical exegisis. Both were concerned with the Bible as the Word of God, but Barth's insight was to turn the traditional question round, making God the subject not the object of human thought, making God a 'Thou' rather than an 'It'. In this hypothesis, human existence is dependent on justification before God rather than on God's existence needing justification to the world. But the approach raises the question of what is meant by faith. How can one know one is not deluded?

Perhaps it is inevitable that after two hundred years of scientific discoveries and an expanding universe, and the impact of **Marxism**, with a mechanistic view, that highly personal understanding of God should develop, with many retreating into **fundamentalism**. When Christian missionaries opened colleges in India in the 1820s to 1830s, they were convinced that modern scientific education would banish the myths and superstitions of **Hinduism** and the bigotry, as they saw it, of Islam, not appreciating how a generation later, Darwin would wreck the Christian faith of thousands, or how the Hindu mind would accommodate modern science. The tragedy, for Christians at least, is that **science** and **religion** have been increasingly compartmentalized and specialized to a degree where it is rare to find someone who understands both. However, while it is now generally acknowledged that one cannot scientifically prove the existence of God, equally, scientists cannot claim to be objective researchers, working without recourse to value-judgements and non-scientific presuppositions and leaps of imagination. Humankind needs **faith** and science – which proves, at least, that theology is also at bottom **anthropology**.

Separating God from the world enabled scientists to pursue their work without accusations of blasphemy, but now both **pantheism** and panentheism are enjoying a revival in the West as attempts to relate God to the world when the traditional Christian option of incarnation is rejected. Hence also the concept of **Gaia**. EMJ

Further reading John Hick, *The Existence of God*; E.L. Mascall, *Existence and Analogy*; Hugh Montefiore, *The Probability of God*.

GOD'S COMMANDS (AND ETHICS)

What makes murder wrong? Some consider that murder is wrong because God has forbidden it, because He has commanded us not to murder and will punish us if we do. But as Plato pointed out, this seems to get things the wrong way around. Surely God commanded us not to murder, and will punish murderers, because murder is wrong – wrong before God forbade us to murder. If God had commanded us to murder, and punished those who did not, this would surely not make murder right. Further, it is difficult to see why, if God commanded us not to murder, and promised to send murderers to Hell, this would make murder wrong, rather than merely imprudent. **AJ**

Further reading Plato, *Euthyphro*; P. Quinn, *Divine Commands and Moral Requirements.*

GODDESS

It has long been argued, on the basis of archaeological evidence, that the original deity, or form given to the creative power behind the world, was the mother goddess. Cultic figures of pregnant women have been found at the oldest layers of ancient Near Eastern civilization, in Egypt and in the Indus Valley. Pregnant women were vital to the survival of society and the ability to give life pointed to a creator goddess. Simply known as the Devi, Goddess, she is still the most powerful god in villages in southern India, while tribal goddesses such as Kali ('The Black One') became national deities. A mother goddess (Gaia, 'mother Earth') was the focus of worship in pre-Hellenic Greece, but as in India, the invading Aryans brought male deities. Goddesses were the subject of powerful myths such as those of Isis, Demeter and the Babylonian moon goddess, having the power to resurrect their husbands, renew the earth, and grant fertility and health. Some were married off to the invaders, as in the case of Meenakshi, 'the fish-eyed' Tamil goddess of Madurai (now said to be an incarnation of Parvati), a mountain goddess and consort of Shiva.

Goddesses are often manifestations of Nature – mountains, rivers or astral bodies – or have the power to inflict illnesses such as cholera or smallpox. Here they verge on the demonic. (Perhaps because of male fear of uncontrollable female sexuality, demons are often female.) Women and female deities are seen as empathic with Nature or part of it, whereas male deities engage in battle, dominate storms and are generally 'macho'. There are famous war-like exceptions, Durga, Kali and the huntress goddesses, but they have a tender side as well. On the other hand, particularly in Vaishnavite **Hinduism**, male deities such as Vishnu were felt to be incomplete and had to have

a female consort to complete the fullness of deity. Sakti, the female power in the god, is of great importance in Tantricism.

The Sakti principle points to another development, the emergence of female deities who personify abstract principles, such as Wisdom, Good Fortune, Love, etc. The archetypal example of this is the Greek goddess Athene, who sprang fully grown, clothed and armed from Zeus's head as the goddess of wisdom and valour. A female principle, Wisdom exists as a separate entity in the later writings in the Hebrew Scriptures.

The questions are whether these female deities are meant to be or act as role models, whether they reflected the role of women in societies, or whether, as in the case of the Virgin Mary, it is a question of compensatory deification, in which female deities are honoured by a male priesthood while women are kept in submission.

Two trends have emerged among women theologians and worshippers today, alienated by male-dominated churches and synagogues. First, there is the attempt to revive knowledge and worship of the ancient mother goddess, especially (in the UK, at least) the Celtic goddess: this is sometimes combined with a 'green' approach, and with interest in Gaia (see **Gaia hypothesis**). Second, there is a restructuring of mainstream **religion**, as when words like 'God/Ess' are used to symbolize a non-patriarchal deity, or God is addressed as 'She' in the liturgy. **EMJ**

Further reading Asphodel Long, *In a Chariot Drawn by Lions*; *The Search for the Female in Deity*; Margaret Murray, *The Genesis of Religion.*

GÖDEL'S INCOMPLETENESS THEOREM

At the beginning of the 20th century, mathematicians were beginning to feel that it was going to be possible to unify the whole of **mathematics**, and to catalogue the complete subject. An attempt was made by Bertrand Russell (1872–1970) and Alfred North Whitehead (1876–1947) in their *Principia Mathematica*, where they attempted to reduce the whole of known mathematics to **set theory**. Slightly later, David Hilbert (1862–1943) outlined the **Hilbert programme** for mathematics, in which an attempt was to be made to classify the whole of mathematics and to give a method by which the truth or falsity of theorems written in **symbolic logic** could be determined in a purely mechanistic way. This programme was ambitious – it would mean the end of the task of mathematics if it were to be completed. (The idea that it might be possible was suggested by the similarity of the proofs of theorems from many disparate parts of mathematics.)

However, the Hilbert programme was hardly started when it was dealt a deadly blow. A young mathematician, Kurt Gödel (1906–78) proved his incompleteness theorem, which showed that the programme was impossible to complete. Gödel was studying the logic of **Peano arithmetic**, an **axiomatization** of the arithmetic of the natural **numbers**. He realized that every sentence of symbolic logic could be encoded with a unique number, and that it was therefore possible to write down sentences in symbolic logic that would mean things like '$2 + 2 = 4$ is provable'. He then looked at sentences of the form 'The sentence with number n is true' and found that, using the method of **recursion**, it was possible to find a sentence with number n which, when translated, essentially said, 'the sentence with number n is true but not provable', in other words, 'this sentence is true but not provable'. So he had shown that there were some true statements which it was impossible to prove, in Peano arithmetic. The same is true of any reasonably powerful mathematical system, and so the Hilbert programme is completely unattainable. SMcL

Further reading D. Hofstadter, *Gödel, Escher, Bach*; E. Nagel and J.R. Newman, *Gödel's Proof*.

GOLD STANDARD

The gold standard is a monetary system in which the monetary units are equated by law to ounces of gold at an official exchange rate, and currency is readily exchangeable for gold. When other countries also equate their money to gold, then gold becomes an international common denominator, establishing the legal **exchange rate** of each currency with all others in the system. For example, if 1 ounce of gold equals 19 UK pounds and 1 ounce of gold equals 38 US dollars, then 1 pound equals 2 dollars.

When a disequilibrium occurs in the international balance of payments, the exchange value of a deficit nation's currency will tend to fall. Countries are most reluctant to devalue their currency (by legally fixing a larger amount of currency equal to 1 ounce of gold) in recognition of its lower value. Instead, foreign exchange reserves may be used by the deficit country in exchange for its currency held by foreigners.

The gold standard was the benchmark for exchange rates before 1914, and returned briefly to prominence in the 1920s and 1930s. Currencies were convertible into gold, at a fixed price, and international debts were transacted in gold; gold itself was then usable as a currency.

In 1914, World War I disrupted world trade and payments, and most industrialized countries left the gold standard. Along with others, the UK returned to the standard in 1925. The pound was set at its prewar parity against gold, which had not been changed since Isaac Newton set it in the 17th century. This anachronistic approach to economics forced the UK to abandon gold and devalue in 1931, floating the pound from 1931 to 1939. The gold standard broke down generally in 1930–33, under pressure of slump and the huge cutbacks in international lending. The US suspended the dollar's convertibility to gold in March 1933, returning to it, with restricted convertibililty, in January 1934.

After World War II, a limited form of gold standard survived, but only for the dollar. Even that was abandoned in 1971. TF

See also Bretton Woods; international monetary fund.

GOLDEN AGE

Ancient Greek and Roman writers divided

the history of the universe into a number of Ages. In sequence, these included the Golden Age (a time of perfection), the Silver Age (a time of self-indulgence), the Bronze Age (a time of heroic endeavour) and the Iron Age (the present – usually categorized as dismal). Critics of Latin **literature** fell on the first two of these Ages, using them to pigeonhole works according to perceived stylistic or thematic merit. 'Golden' authors included Cicero, Horace, Ovid, Virgil and others from the 1st century BCE and early 1st century CE. 'Silver' authors were those immediately following, such as Lucan, Martial, Tacitus and others. The categories tell more about the minds of their inventors than of the authors concerned; inexplicably, the labels are still in use today. **KMcL**

GOLDEN SECTION

Golden Section (or Golden Mean) was the 19th-century name given to a system of mathematical proportion, which had been discussed since ancient Greek times and had been in use for even longer (examples have been found in the planning of Stone Age temples in Britain and in Egyptian pyramids of the 3rd millenium BCE). The Golden Section is a way of dividing a line so that the ratio of the smaller section is to the larger as that of the larger is to the whole; or a way of dividing a rectangle into two areas in such a way that the ratio of the smaller area is to the larger as that of the larger is to the whole. It can be expressed as: 5:8 : : 8:13 or as a:b : : b:c (a + b).

The Golden Section is the only ratio that is also a proportion. This uniqueness led early Greek numerologists (who thought that the entire universe was founded on number relationships) to assign to it a kind of philosophical perfection. The Pythagoreans, for example, were fascinated by the isosceles triangle (in which the base forms a Golden Section with the longer side) and the pentagram, which is formed from three triangles, contains many Golden Sections, and was assumed by them (and by numerologists and black magicians ever since) to have mystical properties. Later writers, including Plato, Omar Khayyám (in his role as astronomer and mathematician)

and the 16th-century Italian mathematician Luca Paccioli, devoted much attention to the Golden Section. Their interest was in finding some kind of relationship between its mathematical nature and its assumed philosophical or mystical 'perfection': Plato, indeed, assigned to it a kind of moral force, claiming that works of art and buildings using it exerted a calming influence on the beholder.

This may not be as far-fetched as it seems. Sculptors and architects, not only in the West, where it has been taught since Greek times, but throughout the world, have used the Golden Section in works that are regarded as particularly harmonious and pleasing to the eye. In painting, again worldwide but consciously in the West since **Renaissance** times, it is used to form relationships between different areas of the painting surface. In Japanese landscape painting, for example, the division is often diagonal across the picture area, the 'upper' triangular area forming a Golden Section with the 'lower'. In Western landscape painting the division can be horizontal or vertical. The break between land and sky, for example, or the disposition of a stand of trees, is often so organized. In all such work – and this, perhaps, bears out Plato's contention – the effect of the Golden Section is greatest when it is subliminal, when we seem to discover harmonious proportion in the painting for ourselves without analysing it to see how it is achieved.

In a similar manner, musical form was sometimes organized in the **Baroque** period in Europe to make what were claimed to be the sound equivalents of the Golden Sections (for example, Purcell's 'Golden' Sonata). Such pieces have a perceptible and carefully organized proportion between the various blocks of sound which comprise each movement's form, but since the Golden Section is a visual and not an aural phenomenon, the use of the name in music is purely fanciful. **MG PD KMcL**

Further reading H.E. Huntley, *The Divine Proportion: a Study in Mathematical Beauty.*

GOTHIC

Gothic **architecture** is the architecture of

western Europe of the medieval period, 12th to the 16th century, generally characterized by the use of the pointed arch, the vault and the flying buttress. It succeeds the round-arch style, known as **Romanesque**, and is in its turn succeeded by the architecture of the **Renaissance**, which sought to revive the architecture of Latin Antiquity. The term 'gothic' seems to have originated as a term of abuse in the Renaissance period, referring to that which was not classical, and later has come to be a general term to cover the arts of the medieval period. Gothic is seen to be an important break from **classicism**, but this was undoubtedly not self-conscious.

Gothic architecture and ornament varied widely across Europe, but its principal expression is in church architecture, its aesthetic innovation and experiment principally inspired by the creative and impressive settings from the Christian liturgy. There is general agreement that the first important Gothic building is the choir of the Abbey of St Denis, Paris, designed for, and quite possibly by Abbot Suger, in the early 12th century. The effect of the new choir was visually, dramatically different to the heavy and monumental quality of Romanesque architecture. It was light, its masonry seeming almost skeletal, and offered a splendid focus for the high altar of Christian liturgy. At Chartres and Bourges in France the next principal structural innovation, allowing a much greater degree of spatial integration (compared to the compartmentalization of Romanesque architecture of the previous centuries), was the use of the flying buttress, to provide structures which had previously depended on galleries as supports for the vaulting. Gothic churches tend to be characterized by a strong sense of verticality, lightness and movement towards the eastern end of the church – as Nikolaus Pevsner puts it: 'Activity held in suspense'. In later gothic architecture, great emphasis is also laid on scale, with enormous churches and cathedrals dominating towns, often with tall soaring spires.

The Gothic style was favoured by one of the more important reformed monastic orders, the Cistercians, apparently on grounds of structural soundness rather than beauty, and it soon became the dominant style across Europe for ecclesiastical architecture. Needless to say there are variations of the Gothic style in different European countries.

The naturalistic carved stone ornamentation of Gothic churches, particularly their entrance portals, was extremely important, and they have been referred to as 'encyclopedias in stone', associated partly with a scholastic tendency to systematize knowledge and to see the natural world as systematically ordered towards God. JM

See also Gothic Revival.

Further reading R. Branner, *Gothic Architecture;* B. Fletcher, *A History of Architecture,* chapter 12; E. Male, *The Gothic Image;* N. Pevsner, *An Outline to European Architecture,* chapters 3 and 4.

GOTHIC LITERATURE

Gothic **literature** was a vogue in Britain in the 1790s. Its connection with Gothic art seems remote, except that it is often set in crumbling, ancient castles. In essence, Gothic novels and poems subjected their heroes (and especially their heroines) to jeopardy in dark, old houses and other sinister locations. Grimness of the physical environment was matched by darkness and panic in the emotions. The **eroticism** of dread has never been so consistently or deliberately exploited. The style leaned heavily on earlier folk tales, and was a harbinger of **Romanticism**. Later writers who employed it, notably Edgar Allan Poe, Mary Shelley and Robert Louis Stevenson, took it to heights of horror undreamed of by its original exploiters 'Monk' Lewis, Mrs Radcliffe and Horace Walpole. The Gothic influence is evident throughout literature written in English, from Dickens, the Brontë sisters and H.G. Wells to such modern masters of the macabre as James Herbert and Stephen King. All modern fantasy and **sf** has learned from it – and from there its influence has spread to such authors as Angela Carter, Bernice Rubens,

Salman Rushdie and Jeanette Winterson, and to many German and South American exponents of **magic realism**. **KMcL**

GOTHIC REVIVAL

'Gothic revival' was the name given to a rebirth of interest in medieval Europe, especially its **architecture** and decorative arts. The revival began in 18th-century Britain and became widespread in Germany and then North America. Its earlier manifestations have the decorated appearance of the **rococo** seen through historicizing spectacles, and the resultant filigree of such works is often called 'gothick' to distinguish it from the later, more 'archaeological' imitations and re-creations of Pugin, William Morris and others in the 19th century.

In England certain buildings, for example Westminster Abbey and some universities, had continued to be constructed in a continuation of Gothic traditions right up to the 17th century. Architects such as Wren worked in respect of the greatness of the building, in what might be called 'Gothic Survival'. The 'Gothic Revival' proper derives from the late 18th and early 19th century historicist interest in the Middle Ages as a source for inspiration and style, and is part of a reaction, in all the **arts**, to the dominance and rationality of **neoclassicism**. (Characteristic and highly influential literary works, for example, are the poems of such pseudo-medieval bards as 'Ossian', and the 'medieval' novels of Walter Scott.)

If the taste for 'Gothic' began with literature, and was fuelled by fashionable antiquarianism (such as Walter Scott's 'reconstruction', actually invention, of 'traditional' Scottish dress, music and ceremonial to mark the 1822 royal visit to Edinburgh, or the huge upsurge in interest in King Arthur and Robin Hood at the same period), one of its most-lasting inspirations was genuine medieval architecture, especially the great cathedrals. To the early Romantics these were awesome in scale, picturesque, thrilling for their scale, height, command of internal space, and not least for their associations with Europe's ancient Christian and chivalric past. Such build-

ings, and the style of their construction, seemed to symbolize a kind of European dignity and solemnity, and the result was that Gothic architecture came to be perceived as a national style, particularly in the countries furthest from the centre of Roman classical civilization, and for whom therefore classical revival might be considered alien. In England, for example, the national significance of Gothic can be shown by the choice of the style for the rebuilding of the Houses of Parliament in 1836–7.

The association with Europe's ancient Christian past was also significant since classically inspired church architecture had come to be perceived as yet another sign of the secularization of the Christian church, and the return to Gothic forms, now subject to the careful scrutiny and analysis of antiquarians and historians, was felt to have a religious purpose. As the century progressed architects such as A.W.N. Pugin (1812–52) began to champion the functional qualities of Gothic architecture, and the 'honest expression' of its construction, as opposed to 'false' classical architecture, which hid a variety of functions behind a symmetrical façade. Nonetheless, the buildings of such men reflect a stylistic dilemma: though they are clearly Gothic, there is nevertheless a 'classical' severity and balance to their elevations.

The architecture of the Gothic Revival in England spans almost a century and changes to reflect the tastes and interests of different generations. What is now called 'High Victorian Gothic' was the phase of the 1850s and 1860s in English architecture which was dominated by an interest in continental Gothic. John Ruskin (1819–1900) championed the north Italian Gothic of Venice and Verona, in his works *The Seven Lamps of Architecture* (1849) and *The Stones of Venice* (1851–53), as well as promoting the interest, also advocated by Pugin in 'constructional polychromy', that is, the use of different colours and textures of building materials. Other architects such as William Burges (1827–81) were attracted by the simplicity of early French Gothic.

In a broader context – epitomized in the work of Morris, Millais and the **Pre-Raphaelites** generally – the Gothic Revival was an early episode of Romanticism, of the reaction of North against South, of spirit against flesh, of the intricate and vegetative against antique-based formalism. Hence arguments in favour of Gothic (in Germany and France as well Britain) often emphasized its 'home-grown' character (which was visible in monuments from earlier ages) as against the dry imports from the classical South. **PD MG JM KMcL**

See also Arts and Crafts.

Further reading C. Eastlake, *A History of the Gothic Revival*; Georg Germann, *Gothic Revival in Europe and Britain: Sources, Influences and Ideas*.

GOTHIC STYLE

The term 'Gothic' was originally one of abuse. Italian **Renaissance** art theorists used it contemptuously to describe the styles of European building and fine art common in the Middle Ages. They associated such works with the Goths and Vandals who had (it was claimed) swept away both the Roman Empire and the more 'sophisticated' artistic styles which characterized it. It was not until the 19th century that serious study began of medieval styles and techniques, and Gothic came to be recognized as a consistent style in its own right, and one of the most significant in the artistic history of northern Europe.

In **architecture**, the chief surviving Gothic buildings are Christian churches and abbeys, and the castles and palaces of the nobility. Whatever humbler buildings may have been like, all these survivors are distinguished by their massiveness. Their characteristic feature is that they are structured on natural forms, those of the skeleton or tree (a method also used at the time in the analogous craft of shipbuilding). Huge 'trunks' or 'backbones' support branch-and rib-like stems, which in turn support lighter infilling. Where the structure is particularly huge, for example in fortifications or cathedrals, buttresses are used to add extra strength. The most glorious examples of this monumental style still in existence are northern Europe's cathedrals, notably Nôtre Dame, St-Denis and Chartres in France, Cologne and Freiburg in Germany, and Durham, Canterbury and York in England.

In secular buildings, the interiors had characteristically rectangular rooms with high, narrow windows, joined by long corridors and spiral, stone staircases between floors. The stone walls were sometimes plastered, but more usually were panelled in wood or hung with tapestries. Floors were of hewn stone, sometimes overlaid with earth or wood. Heating was by enormous hearths supplemented by braziers.

In **fine art**, the term 'Gothic' is usually applied to the paintings, tapestries, sculptures and above all jewellery and furniture made in the medieval period. Gothic painting and weaving, compared with both earlier and later styles, can seem both chunky and naive; carving (both in wood and stone) and metalwork, by contrast, have a grace and delicacy belying the uncouth image projected on the style by Renaissance critics. The apogee of Gothic art can be seen in the filigree stonework and wooden screens in many churches, in stained-glass windows, in bejewelled, inlaid goldwork and weapons, and especially in illuminated manuscripts, whose illustrations and scripts alike stand comparison with anything created before or since. **KMcL**

Further reading Alain Erlande-Brandenburg, *Gothic Art*.

GOVERNMENT AND BINDING THEORY see Universal Grammar

GRADUALISM

Gradualism is the name given by historians to the strategy advocated by those socialists who argue that a socialist society can and should be achieved gradually when socialists are operating within a liberal democratic society. Gradualists commend participation in the electoral process and education and persuasion of the public as to the merits of **socialism**. Gradualism is closely associated with **Fabianism** in Britain, with social democracy in the European

Continent, and reformed or euro-communist parties, like the former Italian Communist Party.

Gradualists criticize revolutionary socialists on the grounds that revolutionary strategies are not likely to succeed, either in precipitating a revolution within liberal democratic societies, or in bringing about a democratic socialist society. Indeed they maintain that Marxism-Leninism, and the dictatorial Marxist régimes it has produced have been the primary obstacles to the electoral success of democratic socialism. Their revolutionary critics reply that gradualism in practice prevents socialism from being realized. They believe that social democrats become managers rather than transformers of capitalism, and that the ruling class will never permit a democratic transition to socialism. **BO'L**

GRAHAM TECHNIQUE

The Graham Technique, in **ballet**, developed from the work and teaching of Martha Graham (1893–1991), and is the starting point for most modern **dance**. In essence, it is an amalgam of the fluidity and free-form grace of ancient Greek dance (as interpreted by Isadora Duncan) and the disciplines of classical ballet technique. Graham's work also affected the story-lines of ballet. She brought in folk themes (and the folk styles of dance which went with them), non-Western dance styles and a new awareness of the gymnastic aspect of dance. If ballet has lost much of its 19th-century whimsy, and become intellectually more rigorous and stylistically more eclectic, that is a development which began with Graham. **KMcL**

GRAMMATOLOGY

Grammatology (Greek, 'study of the written symbol'), in literary criticism, is the name given by Jacques Derrida and his followers to the 'general science of writing'. The idea is that spoken words have a natural relationship with what they mean, and that writing is separate from or lateral

to this. (This is different from the traditional view, that writing is an instrument or conduit of the spoken word.) **KMcL**

See also deconstruction; formalism.

GRAPHIC SCORE

The graphic score is an attempt by 20th-century composers to involve each performer more closely in creating, as opposed to interpreting, the **music**. Conventional scores meticulously notate as many details as possible of the composer's intentions for the music: pitch, duration, method of attack, the exact place of every note in the overall structure. All the performer has to do, essentially, is play what's there, and his or her personality, as expressed in the performance, is of secondary (though not negligible) importance. This is quite different from the performance of most music in the world, where the work itself is created, in whole or in part, by the performers on each occasion.

A graphic score replaces notes, slurs, rests and so on with other images: lines (sinuous or jagged, like the lines on a graph), geometric shapes, letters of the alphabet, patterns, pictures of actual people or objects. There is usually also a rubric, suggesting the kinds of meditative or emotional state the composer has in mind for the performer at any given moment. In graphic scores using computers or other electronic means, instructions for this are laid along the staves. Rehearsal of such music involves the discovery not just of what the composer had in mind (as in conventionally-notated music), but also of the intentions and feelings of each performer, and of the group. (This, again, is what happens in the preparation of Chinese, Indian or Japanese classical music, **jazz**, **rock** and **folk music**.) In performance, the discoveries made in rehearsal are allied to new statements and new group interaction.

Most graphic scores are written for solo performers (with or without electronic modulation), or for small groups. But there have been experiments for larger forces, including Györgi Ligeti's *Aventures* (an **opera** in which each performer's basic 'score' was a letter of the alphabet), and the 'scratch orchestra' works by such composers as Cornelius Cardew (in which people could bring along any score, or any object, they wished, and interpret it in any way they chose). Many more mainstream composers, for example Witold Lutoslavski, Krzysztof Penderecki and Karlheinz Stockhausen, use graphic techniques in sections of longer, more conventionally-notated scores. **KMcL**

See also improvisation.

GRAVITY

The force of gravity was discovered by Newton in the 17th century. He showed that the same force that makes an object fall to the Earth keeps the planets in their orbits. The theory of General **Relativity**, propounded by Einstein at the beginning of the 20th century, further enhanced our understanding of this force.

Any two objects which have mass will be attracted to each other. This does not agree with our everyday experiences. We do not notice the force of gravity between, say, two tennis balls. However, this is because gravity is very weak, and only very large masses (such as the Earth and the Moon) have an appreciable effect.

Gravity decreases in strength as we move away from the massive object. Again, we do not notice this there is no perceptible lessening of gravity, for example, as we climb up a mountain. However, with sensitive enough equipment, we would be able to tell that the pull of gravity does indeed get less as our distance from the Earth increases.

Our Earth is not large enough to show some of the more spectacular gravitational effects. Only large stars can do this. When a star is large enough, the force of gravity is sufficient to crush the atoms together to make a neutron star. An even larger star forms the ultimate end-product of gravity a **black hole**. This is so called because its gravity is strong enough to ensure that no light may escape it.

Gravity slows down time, in a similar fashion to relativistic speeds. Sensitive experiments have shown that a clock at high altitude, where gravity is slightly weaker, goes faster than one at sea-level. This effect is tiny upon the Earth, but much larger close to a very massive body like a neutron star. As we approach the surface of a black hole, Einstein's theory of General Relativity tells us that time slows and finally stops. **JJ**

See also relativity.

GREEN POLITICS AND DESIGN

The burgeoning Green movement has had unexpected and striking spinoffs in **design**. The history of green design goes back to pioneers like Victor Papanek whose popular book *Design For The Real World*, published in 1971, stressed low-technology, recycling and a social role for the designer. In general, however, the environmentalist lobby viewed designers with suspicion regarding them as part of the consumer culture that lay at the heart of environmental problems. That position has seen a radical shift in the 1990s. Nowadays designers take on board the long-term implications of their designs and the materials they use. These concerns range from furniture designers refusing to use rare hard woods to graphic designers exploring the possibilities of recycled paper and non-toxic printing inks. More importantly legislation by the EC and US will force designers and manufacturers to change design practice and thinking. As we approach the end of the century a new green aesthetic for design will influence the whole of our visual culture. **CMcD**

See also ecology; pollution.

GREENHOUSE EFFECT

The greenhouse effect is a simile for the action of the Earth's atmosphere as a trap for energy which arrives as sunlight. Sunlight passes readily through the various layers of atmosphere and reaches the surface of the Earth to have a localized warming effect. The Earth's crust re-radiates much of this energy as infrared light, of a much longer wavelength than that of sunlight; various gases found in the atmosphere are opaque to infrared light so that the energy is absorbed rather than dissipated into space. The temperature of the atmosphere and the surface of the Earth are raised. This is the greenhouse effect and the gases which are responsible are called greenhouse gases: they include water vapour, carbon dioxide and methane. The levels of these gases in the atmosphere seems to be naturally regulated and the greenhouse effect is an important mechanism by which the temperature at the surface of the Earth is maintained within the fairly narrow limits suitable for life. It is thought that human activity has altered the atmospheric levels of certain greenhouse gases such as carbon dioxide and methane, and there appears to be a correlation between small increases in the level of atmospheric carbon dioxide and a slight increase in global temperatures over the past century. The consequences of continued increases in temperature could prove disastrous for human civilizations and, in the light of this there has been recent interest in the various options for reducing the upward trend in carbon dioxide levels. However, it is likely that the **biosphere** will be able to adjust to higher temperatures even if humans cannot. **RB**

See also conservation; Gaia hypothesis; global warming; pollution.

Further reading Michael Gottlieb, *Energy Policies and The Greenhouse Effect*; James Lovelock, *Gaia: A New Look at Life on Earth*; Crispin Tickell, *Climatic Change and World Affairs*.

GRESHAM'S LAW

Gresham's law was named after Sir Thomas Gresham, master of the mint in England under Queen Elizabeth I in the 16th century. Basically, the law is that bad money drives out good. When more than one kind of money is in circulation (for example, gold and silver coins), the money which is overvalued at the official price will tend to remain in circulation because it is worth more as a medium of exchange than as bullion in the market. The money which is undervalued will disappear from circulation to be hoarded or to be melted down because it has higher value as metal than as

legal tender. The undervalued coins might also disappear from domestic circulation by being used for foreign payments, where the higher market value (relative to the domestic legal tender value) would be effective.

'Bad' money may also be paper money in which people have little confidence because too much is issued at a time of inflation. If it is legal tender, people will pay it out as they receive it, while hoarding coins of intrinsic value ('good' money) that they receive. Before the US Civil War, private bank notes were not legal tender, but Gresham's Law applied as people kept the bank notes of reputable banks and tried to spend the bank notes of more obscure banks. **TF**

See also bimetallism.

GROSS DOMESTIC PRODUCT (GDP)

The calculation of gross domestic product is the best measure of economic activity in a country. Normally abbreviated to GDP, it is arrived at by adding the total value of a country's annual output of goods and services. GDP equals private consumption + investment + government expenditure + the change in stockbuilding + (exports minus imports). It is normally valued at market prices; by subtracting indirect taxes and adding subsidies, however, it can be calculated at factor cost. This measure more accurately reveals the incomes paid to factors of production. To avoid double counting of goods and services produced for intermediate use, only final production for consumption and investment is aggregated. To eliminate the effect of inflation, GDP growth is normally expressed in constant prices. However, one school of economists believes that the nominal GDP expressed in current prices is the best guide for **macroeconomic** policy, because it reminds governments that both inflation and real economic growth matter.

GDP can be measured in three ways: by adding incomes of residents, both individuals and firms, derived directly from the production of goods and services; by adding the output contributed by different sectors; by adding expenditure on the goods and services produced by residents, before allowing for depreciation or capital consumption.

Since one person's output is another person's income, which in turn becomes expenditure, these three measures ought to be identical. Because of statistical imperfections, they rarely are. In addition, tax dodgers and the black economy escape the output and income measures but should, if the earnings are spent, turn up in the expenditure measure.

Although GDP is flawed, it is the best available measure of economic activity. Activities that are not paid for and so cannot be priced, such as housework or voluntary work, are excluded as well as the black economy. **TF**

See also gross national product.

GROSS NATIONAL PRODUCT (GNP)

Gross national product (GNP) is the value of the total output of final goods and services in the economy for a particular time period, such as a year, plus the value of any net increase of goods-in-process. GNP measurement enables economists and politicians to quantify economic growth a process useful for policy decisions as well as a tool used to compare states to one another. GNP is measured by adding up the value of all consumer goods and services sold, or the value of all of the capital goods produced and sold plus net changes in inventories, the value of all government expenditures, and the value of net foreign trade known as net exports. The term 'final goods' means only those goods at the last set of transactions the sale to the final user omitting all intermediate production and distribution transactions. This technique is used in order to avoid double counting. **TF**

See also consumption function.

GROTESQUE

Grotesque (from Italian *grottesca*, 'little cave'), in **architecture**, was a system of fanciful decoration based on Roman wall-paintings discovered in 1488 in the buried ruins (grottoes) of Nero's palace, the *Domus Aurea* ('Golden House'). Painters of the **Renaissance** period made expeditions to the ruins to study them. Revived as a form of architectural decoration, incorporating scrolls and fantastic animals and birds, it proved remarkably adaptable in decorative work to classical architecture from the Renaissance onwards. **JM**

GROUP SELECTION

Group selection, in the **life sciences**, is the idea that behaviour which is beneficial to a group but not to an individual can arise by **natural selection**. Group selection was proposed to explain ostensibly altruistic behaviour which did not appear to be explained by the traditional view of **kin selection**. However, it is a controversial concept because Darwinian natural selection can only act upon the individual, conserving genes which confer benefits. Group selection is an attractive concept in sociological terms but does not appear to occur in biology, where behavioural adaptations are studied in terms of **genetics**. An individual **gene** can only be selected if it is advantageous and therefore the situation in which one gene reduces its likelihood of selection, while enhancing the chances of a different gene, cannot arise; in other words, a gene which might promote an altruistic act is likely to be selected against and to be deleted from the gene pool. Apparent cases of group selection can be adequately accounted for when the genetic relationship between the individuals is investigated. Often, apparent instances of group selection are the result of **anthropomorphic** observation of a non-human system. **RB**

See also altruism.

Further reading Richard Dawkins, *The Selfish Gene*; John Maynard-Smith, *The Theory of Evolution*.

GROUPS

A group is one of the most important ideas in abstract **algebra**. Many structures turn out to be groups, and the investigation of the properties of groups in general ('group theory') has turned out to be one of the most fertile areas of 19th- and 20th-century mathematics.

A group consists of a set of some kind, and an operation, which is designed to mimic some of the properties of + on the **integers**. The operation is a **function** taking pairs of elements in the set to a third element in the set. The operation satisfies four axioms. (1) If a and b are in the set, then a + b is defined and in the set. (2) If a, b and c are in the set, then $(a+(b+c))=((a+b)+c)$. (Brackets show which operations should be performed first; this axiom amounts to saying that the order in which operations are calculated does not matter. This property is known as associativity.) (3) There is an element e in the set such that for every a in the set, $a+e=a$. (The element e is known as the identity, and mimics the function of 0 in the numbers.) (4) For every element a there is an element b, written a^{-1}, such that $a+b=e$. (The element b is known as the inverse of a, and takes the place of − a in the integers.) **SMcL**

See also category theory; fields; Galois theory; Hilbert's problems; rings.

GROWTH

Growth, in **economic** terms, means an increase in real **gross domestic product**, which implies higher output and incomes. Economists are unable to describe the precise causes of growth; but technical progress has much to do with it. From 1950 until 1973 growth accelerated in most of the 'developed' world; in the rest of the 1970s, the industrialized countries found the path to growth more difficult. Slow growth results in increased unemployment, slower rising incomes and disgruntled voters. **TF**

GUILD

An ecological guild describes a group of species, plants or animals, which have a similar habitat or lifestyle. The members of such a group live in overlapping **niches**; an example can be seen in a group of fish which have a highly specialized mode of nutrition. Called cleaner fish, all members of the guild feed by removing parasites and other unwanted organic material from other fish. The various species of cleaner

fish have avoided coming into direct competition with one another by adopting species-specific behavioural patterns. Examples of guilds are common in most ecosystems and illustrate how the process of evolution permits the survival of species which differ only in very subtle ways. **RB**

See also community; competition.

GUILD SOCIALISM

From 1915 until about 1930 Guild Socialism was one of the leading intellectual doctrines of non-Marxist **socialism** in Western Europe. Initially an off-shoot of British trade unionism, Guild Socialists developed a critique of the wage-labour system which was then expanded by various thinkers into a general theory of **democracy**. Briefly stated, the theory argued that traditional medieval guilds, based on crafts and specific industrial sectors, should be resurrected, albeit on a democratic basis, to form the building blocks of modern political, economic and social organization. As articulated in the theoretical writings of G.D.H. Cole, the leading guild socialist, the role of the central state was to be reduced to that of co-ordinator of the various guilds, and functional representation would replace individual or territorial representation. In these respects guild socialism resembled **corporatist** thinking.

As a 'middle way' between revolutionary **Marxism** and the **gradualism** of the **Fabians**, Guild Socialism was neither radical enough to appeal to Leninists, nor pragmatic enough to entice Fabians. Moreover, the guild socialists had no rigorous economic theory, either of socialist public management or market-steering. However, the legacy of guild socialism survives in the importance attached to functional representation in the British Labour party and other European socialist parties. **BO'L**

Further reading G.D.H. Cole, *Guild Socialism Re-stated* (1920); G. Foote, *The Labour Party's Political Thought: a History*.

GUILT

Guilt, in past civilizations, was seen as the cause of mental illness (as well as of physical illness and catastrophe), and sins had to be confessed to make possible a cure. This was the case for the Aztecs of ancient Mexico, the Semitic civilizations of the ancient Orient and the Emperors of China. In modern **psychology** guilt feelings must also be relieved if patients are to get better.

Modern psychologists perceive guilt as a state in which a person feels a guilt about some past event which he or she had little power to control or prevent, and about which powerful guilt-feelings remain which can cause states of depression and anxiety. This is distinct from the definition of guilt which attributes fair blame and responsibility to an individual for a criminal action, though both senses are connected to fear of retribution and punishment. Freud looked specifically at this former kind of neurotic guilt. He saw guilt as arising from conflict between the person's Superego, the internalized moral agency, and the expression of infantile wishes and desires – this is like an internal continuation of conflict between the child and the parents in the adult person's history.

Shame is closely related to guilt, as it is an emotion of self-assessment. But guilt, unlike shame, cannot be avoided by concealment. It has been suggested that guilt is done *by* the self on account of a specific (harmful) action, while shame is done *to* the self by the (imagined) views of others. **MJ**

Further reading H.B. Lewis, *Shame and Guilt in Neurosis.*

GURU MOVEMENTS

The guru (Sanskrit, 'teacher') is both the supreme teacher and also a spiritual master. Particularly in **Shaivism**, one requires a guru to lead one to enlightenment. The disciple may search for years before he finds his guru through a sudden insight and submits to him in total obedience, performing the most menial tasks for him. In return he is initiated into the guru's spiritual discipline, and year by year is brought to enlightenment. He is given his own special secret *mantra* to recite. Later, partly because of the Vedanta identification of God and the soul, the guru came to be imbued with divine attributes as well

as human holiness. Even today in rural areas, families under the guidance of a particular guru will wash his feet when he visits them and drink the dirty water afterwards as a holy drink. The guru is supported by the offerings of such families.

In the so-called guru movements, a personality cult has sprung up and the guru is seen as divine, or as a reincarnation of a saint or deity. Gurus are generally *sannyasi*, that is they have renounced the world, and they wear the ochre robes of the ascetic. But a guru may have his own residence, or **ashram**. They are deemed to have no personal history before they took their vows and no **caste**, but in practice they are usually Brahmans.

Among ordinary Hindus, gurus are often held to be figures of fun, like Anglican vicars in English comedy. One of the most popular Tamil classics is the *Strange Surprising Adventures of the Venerable Guru Simple, and his Five Disciples, Noodle, Doodle, Wiseacre, Zany and Foozle.* (This was actually written by a Jesuit, C.J. Beschi.) **EMJ**

Further reading Khushwant Singh, *Gurus, Godmen and Good People.*

H

HAGIOGRAPHY

Hagiography (Greek, 'writing about holy things') is a Judaeo-Christian phenomenon. The original *hagiographa* ('holy writings') were the so-called 'poetical' books of the Bible – Psalms, Proverbs, Job – as distinct from the Books of the Law or the Prophets. The content of these books was held to be exemplary rather than didactic.

In the Christian era, the same function was assigned to biographies of saints and martyrs. Their lives and their thoughts and utterances were set out as examples. Literary texts, aimed at the reading public, often dwelled on the 'meaning' of the events of a saint's life, drawing it out in prose which was often flowery, philosophical and devotional – a relative of such great medieval **allegories** as *The Romance of the Rose* or Chrétien de Troyes' Arthurian romances. Hagiography for ordinary (that is, at this time, illiterate) people, by contrast, was largely done in pictures – and paradoxically, the religious meaning of the torments and revelations depicted was not drawn out, but left to be deduced. John Foxe's *Book of Martyrs* (1563) is a characteristic example – and typical as much of the Gothic imagination of the genre as of its assertive pietism.

That such writings survived well into the present can be attested by the present writer, who can remember as a child of six or so (in the 1940s) being shown a prized, leather-bound book of saints' stories, and who still has nightmares based on the pictures of dis-embowellings, gougings and burnings at the stake which seized the attention despite, rather than because of, the images of parting clouds and beckoning angels at the top of every scene. Hagiography also survives in a bastardized, secular form: fan magazines and articles in popular papers, magazines and film biopics, which treat famous people with the same kind of breathless, uncritical – though usually less sadistic – idolization. **KMcL**

HAPPENINGS

Happenings in the 1960s were multimedia events animated by artists such as the composer John Cage and the painters Claes Oldenburg and Allan Kaprow. An offshoot of **Dada**, they emphasized the spontaneous and transient elements in performance while manipulating performers, props and audience in ways designed to break down barriers between creator and spectator. A Happening was neither an exhibit nor a theatrical event, but the site of an experiment in perception and as such was linked to Conceptual Art. As part of the **Pop** phenomenon, Happenings championed the development of art forms away from the formal traditions of fine art and the exhibition space. Thus they might be sited in parking lots, factories or in the street, and might involve materials not associated with fine art, for example rubber tyres, water, fat, ice cubes, and, in the case of Joseph Beuys's *Fluxus*, live and dead animals. Its emphasis on transient effects, and its challenge to

notions of the permanence of art and of aesthetic values, made the Happening one of the most dynamic forms of artistic expression of the 1960s. **MG PD**

Further reading M. Kirby, *Happenings: an Illustrated Anthology*.

HAPPINESS AND PLEASURE

Philosophers have often equated happiness with pleasure. Pleasure can be a sensation: an agreeable feeling. But it is not always a sensation. 'I'm pleased to be top of my class' does not seem to mean the same as 'Being top of my class causes me to have agreeable sensations'. It seems that pleasure and happiness can sometimes be cognitive, rather than a sensation. Perhaps pleasure can sometimes be a matter of having one's desires satisfied, and this pleasure is not the same as having an agreeable feeling.

Pleasures can be compared and ranked in terms of quantity and quality. Some pleasures are better than others in purely quantitative terms: they are more intense, last longer, or both. And perhaps some pleasures are better than others in qualitative terms. The intellectual pleasure involved in doing **philosophy** or solving a mathematical problem, for example, may be perceived as 'higher' or better than the merely sensual pleasures that we feel after a good meal. **AJ**

See also hedonism.

Further reading R.M. Hare, *Freedom and Reason*.

HARD ROCK see Rock Music

HARD-EDGE PAINTING

Hard-edge Painting was an aspect of geometric **abstraction**, which, in the 1960s, reacted against the gestural and painterly canvases of the **Abstract Expressionists**. The style emphasized geometric, rectilinear compositions, which respected the 'flatness' of the picture surface. Rendered with a sharp, 'hard' edge, the machine-like application of colour likewise stressed the impersonality of the canvas and the artist's desire to avoid the autobiographical or subjective references inherent in **expressionism**. Major practitioners of the movement included Ellsworth Kelly, Kenneth Noland and Al Held. **MG PD**

HEALTH

Health, in medical terms, is the harmonious and efficient working of the entire person. The definition does not sit comfortably in post-Cartesian science and needs to acknowledge the description of person as body-mind or body-mind-spirit.

The Western scientific description of the structure and function of the **body** has achieved great elegance. Since the invention of the microscope the constituent parts have been revealed in increasingly great detail. Microscopists have been worthy companions of painters and textile-makers in the skilful use of dyes and pigments to reveal the parts of tissues and cells. Biochemical studies have complemented the observations of structure, and have explained how the parts are constructed and maintained, how biological information is stored and transmitted, and how the energy to maintain life is derived and stored. The full picture explains the roles of the parts of our diet the contribution of the Earth to our health.

The construction of this picture has been, at least aesthetically, one of the great triumphs of human thought. All this notwithstanding, Western medical science has no means of measuring or defining health other than as the absence of signs or symptoms of disease. The large and elegant mass of information has also proved difficult to translate into means of providing a health-promoting regimen, or, with a few notable exceptions, of explaining the basis of illnesses. The science of nutrition is particularly disappointing in providing information which can survive critical evaluation.

Medical advice about health seems to be derived from a consideration of *risk factors* which enable the prediction of likelihood of, for instance, heart attack – that is to say, sedentary lifestyle, smoking, high cholesterol levels, diabetes melitus and high blood pressure are the factors which make a heart attack more likely in proportion to the number you have. Of these factors, giving up smoking and doing some strenuous exercise seem to have the most clearly proven benefit. If you have high blood pressure it must be reduced by 'lifestyle' changes, or by drugs. If you have diabetes the illness must be controlled, and you must also eat a diet high in grains and pulses. What to do about high cholesterol levels remains unclear. Reducing cholesterol by drugs does not alter the heart attack rate, and increases the chance of other life-threatening illnesses. Altering the kind of fats eaten has not been shown to be of proven benefit. The most extensively exploited and most well-known advice is doubtful. Advice about health has had to be advice of doubtful scientific value about illness. In apparently comparable countries in the 'developed' world the heart-attack rate is rising in some and falling in others, for unexplained reasons.

By contrast classical Chinese medicine was based firmly upon the maintenance of health: it is said that the physician was paid only when the person was well. If the person had complaints or symptoms, the thrust of the treatments was to enable the re-emergence of health-regulatory mechanisms. Health was maintained by harmonizing with Nature, tempering activity according to the seasons, basing diet upon the grains, not being dominated by an excess of emotions and being moderate about all things. If the physician was required to intervene the intent was the ennabling of harmonious flow and distribution of *chi* or *qi* – a substance not unlike the structure and function of blood which transports and manifests everything to do with person. The calligraphic character for *chi* consists of 'breaths' and 'the steaming grain of rice'. Health could also be encouraged by meditative exercises like *Chi Kong* (or *Qi Gong*) and *Tai Chi Chuan* (or *Tai Ji Chuan*).

In the years preceding and following World War II, there developed in Western medical practice a remarkable and innovative idea, that a doctor should know the members of the community as healthy people, and that illness should be regarded as an intercurrent event and not as the sole reason for doctor-patient encounter. The idea was that doctors, with a team of helpers nurses, home visitors, social workers, industrial hygenists, etc. should provide day-to-day health care services to everyone, also utililizing 'well-person' clinics. As the people got to know each other there would be an emerging database about the state of health of the community, and over time, medical interventions could be evaluated, compared and reported upon. The advantages of the system are that doctors and their helpers are all members of a team acknowledging the value of all contributors, and that people in the community deal with people they come to know, each respecting the other. Not least, the database accumulates information of increasing quality enabling critical evaluation of medical interventions.

Health Centres were first set up and successfully operated in Peckham, London, England in the 1930s and in Polela, Natal, South Africa in the 1940s. The idea was to have been the model for the British National Health Service, but too many medical planners seem to have found it threatening. The term Health Centre is now sometimes used to describe the building in which General Practitioners work, but this has no link with the original concept. **TG**

See also Daoism; disease; medicine.

HEAVY METAL see Rock Music

HEDONISM

Ethical hedonism (from Greek *hedone*, 'pleasure') is the doctrine, in **philosophy**, that when acting one morally ought to pursue only pleasure or happiness, for oneself and (perhaps) others. Psychological hedonism is the doctrine that, as a matter of fact, agents only ever do pursue their own pleasure or happiness.

These doctrines are very different. The first states that pleasure or happiness is the only good, and is a theory about how we *ought* to act rather than about how we do act. It is consistent with ethical hedonism that people sometimes actually act in pursuit of goals other than pleasure, and that people sometimes actually put the pleasure of others before their own. Neither of these are consistent with psychological hedonism. Further, one cannot conclude from the (supposed) fact that agents actually only ever pursue pleasure or happiness that agents ought only to pursue pleasure or happiness.

Ethical hedonists may hold that when acting one morally ought to pursue pleasure or happiness for others as well as oneself. They may hold that one should sometimes put the pleasure of others before one's own. So ethical hedonists need not be ethical egoists. **AJ**

See also altruism; happiness and pleasure.

Further reading J.S. Mill, *Utilitarianism*; G.E. Moore, *Ethics*.

HEGEMONY

Hegemony (from Greek *hegemon*, 'chief', 'leader' or 'ruler'), in **sociology**, **political science** and international relations, is generally used to describe dominance or control rather than leadership. Thus 'hegemonism' describes the policies of states which control or bully those within their sphere of influence; 'hegemonic control' refers to a system of ethnic domination in which the political élite controls a subordinated ethnic community (or communities) in such a way that it is incapable of effective revolt; and 'hegemonic party' refers to a political party which is the only effective party in control of a particular society.

The widespread popularity of the concept of hegemony in the 1970s and 1980s derived from the western Marxist rehabilitation of the *Prison Notebooks* of the Italian Communist leader, Antonio Gramsci, who died at the hands of Mussolini's Fascists. Drawing upon the work of Machiavelli and the élite theorist Pareto, Gramsci used the concept of hegemony to describe the way in which he believed the bourgeoisie established and maintains its control even in a democratic system in which workers and peasants might make up an electoral majority. The dominance of the bourgeoisie was not based upon their control of the coercive power of the state, but rather rested upon their ability to exercise moral and political leadership, and to win consent for their vision of what was possible and worthwhile.

In Gramsci's thought, each successful political system requires the creation of an 'historic bloc', unified around an 'hegemonic project', in which the dominant class builds alliances beyond itself, and wins consent for its institutions and ideas. The appeal of this idea for western Marxists was twofold: it helped account for the failure of revolutionary Marxism in western Europe, and it suggested that intellectuals played a key role in building hegemony for a historical bloc. By implication the role of western Marxist intellectuals was to create a 'counter-hegemonic project', that is, an alternative form of political and moral leadership.

In recent years the word 'hegemony' has come to be used more loosely, in studies of working-class youth **subcultures**, the production of television news and the development of state education. Some historians deplore this development, claiming that while the obscurities, difficulties and contradictions in Gramsci's writings on hegemony owed something to his conditions of imprisonment, his latter-day disciples in western Europe and North America have no similar excuse for lack of clarity. **DA BO'L**

See also authority; bourgeoisie; capital; class; conflict theory; critical theory; culture; discourses; dominant ideology; élite theory; ideology; knowledge; legitimation; Machiavellianism; Marxism; norms; party system; power; social construction of reality; social control; sociology of knowledge; values.

Further reading J. Femia, *Gramsci's Political Thought: Hegemony, Consciousness and the Revolutionary Process*; A. Gramsci, *Prison Notebooks*; S. Hall and T. Jefferson, *Resistance Through Rituals Youth Cultures in Post War Britain*.

HELMINTHOLOGY

Helminthology is the study of parasitic worms (helminths), responsible for a number of serious diseases of humans and food animals. The single most important helminth parasite of humans is the blood-dwelling fluke *Schistosoma*, which infects several hundred million people worldwide, causing death and disability for its human hosts and serious economic problems for the countries where it occurs. Other helminth diseases of humans include river blindness and tapeworm infection, while the

liver fluke is a serious problem in sheep. The study of helminths is a relatively recent science and was initially involved in the elucidation of other life cycles of important worms; these are often complex, involving several hosts. Modern studies have focused on the **immunology** of helminthological infections and it has emerged that these pathogens, which are unusual parasites in that they are complex multicellular organisms, have evolved special techniques for evading and disrupting normal host defences. These studies are important in the search for treatments but are also fascinating models of **evolution**. **RB**

See also aetiology; epidemiology; parasitology.

Further reading Philip Whitfield, *The Biology of Parasitism*.

HEREDITY/ENVIRONMENT

The debate between heredity and environment reiterates the earlier debate about nature and nurture. Following the publication of work by the behaviourist J.P. Watson, there was a widespread assumption that environment and conditioning were all-important; this view ignored biological and genetic determinants, disregarding strong evidence for genetic factors. Geneticists, such as Mather and Jinks, observe gene behaviour but do not say that a **gene** type is identical with behaviour. They look at the interaction between genetic and environmental aspects, as this accounts for individual variation. A new discipline, **sociobiology**, attempts to combine both approaches, looking at goals directed by both genetic and environmental pressures. **MJ**

HERMENEUTICS

Hermeneutics (from Greek *hermeneuein*, 'to track down'), in theology, is the technique of interpreting writings held to contain divine truth. In ancient times such writings might be the utterances of oracles or prophets, and hermeneutics consisted of 'translating' them into the vernacular. The Christian Church took over the idea because it fitted well with the doctrine of a faith once delivered in the Scriptures. In early Christian hermeneutics, three different methods were employed: allegorical, analogical and literal. In the 19th century, due to the rise of the methods of historical criticism (which led to the view that one should understand an author against the background of his or her environment), hermeneutics became less and less the art of discovering divine inspiration, and more and more that of relating it and one result was an opening and widening of the gap between biblical exegesis and dogmatics. The 20th century, however, brought a revival of biblical hermeneutics, notably in the work of Martin Heidegger and Rudolf Bultmann and his school. For Heidegger, language was the method through which 'being' itself was communicated; an author became the true priest of humankind because through him 'being' was mediated.

In the wider field of literary criticism, hermeneutics is the attempt to discover, by systematic examination, the true meaning of a text (which is assumed to exist, as a specific entity, and to have been in the mind of its author as he or she composed the text). As a critical approach it is directly opposite to **deconstruction**. EJ KMcL

Further reading C.E. Braaten, *History of Hermeneutics*; R. Bultmann, *The Problem of Hermeneutics*.

HERMETIC

Hermetic is an adjective derived from the name of Hermes, the Greek god of deception who guided the souls of the dead to the Underworld. 'Hermetic writings' are those thought to contain hidden truths, usually of a cabbalistic or metaphysical kind. They are often in gibberish, or in codes accessible only to initiates. In medieval Arabia and Europe they were widely held to contain the secrets of all knowledge, and they and those who could understand them were regarded with almost superstitious awe. The prophecies of Nostradamus (15th century) are the most widely-known hermetic writings still to survive.

'Hermetic poetry' is something completely different. It was an Italian movement of the 1930s, whose practitioners attempted to use words on a page, and the spaces between and around them, for their own evocative sakes, without the distortions of logic, rhetoric or other externals. The idea was to take poetry beyond the reach of (especially Fascist) censorship, to tap into true feeling. The movement itself was of its period and short-lived, but its aesthetic influenced such poets of importance as Montale, Quasimodo and Ungaretti. KMcL

HERO

In Greek **myth**, a hero was the offspring of one mortal parent and one immortal – an example is Herakles, son of Zeus and the mortal queen Alkmena. Because of their half-human, half-divine nature heroes had difficulty adapting to the demands of mortal life, and their personality disorders – not to mention their divine attributes – often caused trouble in the mortal world. (For instance, Herakles periodically went mad and at one stage murdered his own children; Helen's superhuman beauty was a direct cause of the Trojan War.) Such problems, and the more-than-mortal appeal of heroes generally, led to heroes playing the main roles in most myth-based stories and hence to the word being applied to the protagonist of a piece of **fiction** generally. The Romans, making over Greek myth for their own purposes, sometimes allegorized the hero's conflicts in what we would think of as psychological terms: Aeneas's dilemmas in Virgil's *Aeneid*, for example, are caused not so much by the struggle between divine and mortal sides to the same nature as by (for instance) the conflict between love and duty.

In later fiction of the simpler kind (for example folk tales), heroes lost the dual mortal/immortal identity, but kept their ability to move between the human and superhuman worlds. Favourite types of hero-stories are those involving quests and those involving 'making something of oneself' (usually moving from rags to riches as a result of application, cunning, superhuman intervention or all three at once). In more complex fiction, the Roman model is often followed and the hero is the figure in whose character and actions some moral, ethical or other dilemma is worked out. In 'formation novels' (see **Bildungsroman**) the hero often stands for a whole society, and his or her development dramatizes larger political, social or psychological concerns.

Some pieces of fiction centre on an *antihero*: someone whose qualities are the last we would expect from a person in such circumstances. A favourite kind of antihero is the bland, characterless individual in whom the venalities and follies of a whole society are mirrored. Notable examples of this type include, Švejk in Jaroslav Hašek's *The Good Soldier Švejk*, Zeno in Italo Svevo's *The Confessions of Zeno*, Franz Kafka's anonymous heroes, even Marcel in Proust's *Remembrance of Things Past*. Other antiheroes are more assertive and take an anarchic, satirical view of the society in which they live. This is often the case with the 'heroes' of comedies, from the outrageous old men of Aristophanes to Yossarian in Joseph Heller's *Catch–22* or Kingsley Amis' *Lucky Jim*. Writers in the 20th century have taken an especial delight in subverting our expectations of what heroes in **literature** and **drama** are 'supposed' to be – proof, if nothing else, that the stereotype still has life. **KMcL**

HETEROPHONY

Heterophony (Greek 'other voice') is a style of **music** which uses no harmony or counterpoint: there is one line of melody only. This line is performed, sometimes on its own, sometimes with a rhythmic and/or drone accompaniment. The key element is that several voices or instruments all perform the line, not in absolute unison (as the sopranos in a choir or the viola section in a symphony orchestra might), but with all the possibilities of deliberate or chance variation: individual phrasing, spontaneous ornament, independent rhythmic variation. The line is thus subtly blurred and varied even as we hear it.

Heterophony occurs most frequently in orally-transmitted vocal traditions. For example, in some forms of African, Polynesian and black American Christian hymnody, each member of the congregation sings his or her own independent and highly embellished version of the hymn, producing a complex web of vocal strands. Heterophony is also a fundamental technique in many Asian and Oriental musics. In Indonesian gamelan, for example, several instruments of the ensemble play rhythmically and melodically divergent versions of the same basic melody, according to predetermined conventions for each instrument. In the last decade or so of the present century, heterophony has become an important element in **electronic music** (where computers modulate the sounds we hear, or the same line is played 'live' and enhanced at the same time). It is also a feature of **minimalist** music.

Heterophony is not so much a technique as an indication of the importance, in many musical cultures, of the expressive and aesthetic quality of each individual part, and of the personal, often improvised contribution to the musical whole as well as to the performance itself. (In a similar way, it has been suggested that the Christian heterophony described above arises more from religious than musical conviction, reflecting each worshipper's wish to bear witness, freely and individually, to a personal relationship to God.) Heterophony is relatively unfamiliar to Western ears, but is, nevertheless, the world's predominant musical style, and has so been since remote antiquity. **KMcL**

HETEROSEXUALITY

Heterosexuality (partner choice of the opposite sex) as an institution has been questioned and examined by radical and revolutionary feminists. Adrienne Rich's essay 'Compulsory Sexuality and Lesbian Existence' argues that **feminism** needs to ask how heterosexuality as an economic institution is based upon the absence of any alternative for women. The presence of choice, Rich argues, would allow women to determine the meaning and place of **sexuality**. Rich deplores the way in which feminist theory has contributed to lesbian invisibility and marginality, and calls for a broader definition of what is considered 'lesbian' which is not limited to clinical definitions of 'lesbianism'. Rich's strategy offers a way of breaking down rigid patriarchal definitions of heterosexuality, which devalue women's relationships with one another.

Anne Koedt and Charlotte Bunch argued that heterosexuality was an ideological construction and needed to be examined in the same way that feminists had looked at other areas of women's oppression. Ann Koedt believes that through heterosexuality **patriarchy** divides women from one another. Lesbians who questioned heterosexuality and heterosexism were considered by some as a threat to feminism. Charlotte Bunch argued that heterosexuality was basic to women's oppression, and also argued that feminist theory must ask itself difficult questions to lead to effective strategies in the future.

Gayle Rubin has put forward the view that very often feminism has buried lesbianism under a heterosexist agenda. For Rubin the separation of sexual and gender oppression is vital and she considers that in criticizing the sexual oppression of heterosexuality feminism will become richer. Many women have criticized feminism for being the view of the Western, white, middle-class, heterosexual. Rubin and Rich have offered feminism a means to criticize its own methodologies and assumptions.

In the UK, Sue Ardhill and Susan O'Sullivan have argued that the psychoanalytic model of the development of the feminine position, which was thought by some feminists to create the psychic conditions for later female heterosexuality, does not adequately address women who are 'femme' lesbians. This seems to suggest that more work is needed in the analysis of the construction of femininity and, what was thought to be an intrinsic part of femininity, heterosexuality. **TK**

Further reading Charlotte Bunch, *Not by Degrees: Feminist Theory and Education*; Gayle Rubin, *Thinking Sex: Notes for a Radical Theory of the Politics of Sexuality*.

HIERARCHY

Hierarchy is any structured system of values in which the elements are unequally rank-ordered from the most superior to the most inferior. In an organizational hierarchy, authority is distributed so that distinctions of function (and prestige) are rank-ordered between superordinates and subordinates.

The **caste** system in India represents an exemplary hierarchical form of socioreligious organization and values, utterly at odds with the values of Western egalitarianism and liberalism.

The etymological origin of hierarchy is Greek: it means 'sacred rule'. Its historical origin is ecclesiastical reflecting the managerial principles of the Christian church (see **Catholic political thought**), in which the pope and bishops were at the apex of the church with privileged access to sacred truths, and the laity at the bottom. During the Reformation, in 16th-century Europe, the legitimacy of hierarchy was challenged by Protestant thinkers, notably Calvin, who argued that individuals did not need the church hierarchy to mediate between them and God. Nevertheless, church organization in the Catholic church and many Protestant churches has remained hierarchical.

In religious organizations functional distinctions represent ascending gradations of access to divine authority where those at the top are alleged to be closer to the god or gods. In secular organizations the rank-ordering of functional distinctions may be ascriptive, that is hereditary, or achievement-oriented, that is based on merit and ability to perform specific tasks. Modern armies, public bureaucracies and large-scale business organizations are examples of hierarchical organizations where positions of leadership are largely determined by performance and experience. Contemporary examples of hierarchical organizations based on hereditary distinctions of prestige include the British Monarchy and House of Lords.

Liberals and socialists accept hierarchies, like bureaucracies, provided they are based on merit and instrumentally useful for the achievement of goals. However, they remain prone to rejecting hierarchical authority, either on egalitarian or individualist grounds. Conservatives, by contrast, embrace hierarchism as a principle, which they believe is consonant with the natural order of the world. **BO'L**

See also conservatism; liberalism; socialism and social democracy.

Further reading L. Dumont, *Homo Hierarchicus*.

HIGH LEVEL LANGUAGES

The heart of any digital **computer** is the Central Processing Unit (CPU), which performs the work of calculation. It will understand a preset group of instructions (known as 'op-codes'), to tell it what to do. These op-codes are strings of 0s and 1s. A **program**, from the point of view of the CPU, is a sequence of these instructions, executed consecutively (taking into account 'jump' instructions, which tell it to leave out several instructions). The total set of all possible instructions is called the 'machine language'.

In essence, the machine language is very simple; there may only be a few dozen different instructions (to ensure that the CPU is cheap, efficient, fast and reliable). It is very powerful; the **Turing machine**, an even simpler theoretical model of a computer, can do everything that the most sophisticated super-computer can do (though not as fast). The problems of machine language are that the set of instructions understood by the CPU is specific to the make of computer being used, and that it is very difficult, given a machine language program, to understand what it is doing and to change and debug it (remove errors) and, indeed, to write it in the first place.

To overcome these problems 'assembly language' is used. Although not very different from machine language, this does solve some of the obvious faults; mnemonics are used instead of binary op-codes, and labels can be used (so that, for example, the exact number of instructions to be skipped by a jump instruction does not have to be calculated beforehand), and so on. Assembly language cannot be directly understood by the CPU; it needs a program (the 'assembler') to translate for it.

Assembly language does not move forward very far. One instruction in assembly language represents one instruction in machine language, so that the program will still not be comprehensible to the human user without a lot of special training. This problem is solved by using any one of a large number of higher level languages, in which one instruction can represent many machine language instructions, and which can therefore be made comprehensible to a human user. Common examples of such languages are FORTRAN, BASIC, PASCAL, LOGO and C. In most of these languages, it is possible, given a little ingenuity, to gain some idea of what a program will do with no actual formal understanding of the language itself.

Once again, higher level languages need to be translated so that the CPU can understand them. There are two main methods by which this can be done. An 'interpreter' is a program that operates when the program you wish to run (the 'source' program) is executed: it translates each instruction one at a time as needed into machine (or assembly) language. This approach takes no account of whether an instruction has been encountered before; it will just translate it again, so that one line of source program may be translated thousands of times. This makes it a slow method of running software. However, it does have the advantage that the full translated version of the program does not need to be stored, so it tends to be the method used when memory space is at a premium. The alternative, a 'compiler', takes the source program as a whole and creates a version in assembly language, which can be stored and run at a later date. This means that programs, once compiled, can run much faster. Many compilers 'optimize' as they compile the source program, eliminating inefficiencies (caused by the very nature of high level languages) to produce even faster running compiled programs. **SMcL**

HIGH TECH

High Tech is a 20th-century attitude to industrial materials which influenced **architecture** and **design**. The name was a 1970s invention for fashionable attitudes to designing buildings and objects for the home, and the cult was the title of a best-selling 1978 book by Joan Kron and Suzanne Slesin, *High Tech: The Industrial Style and Source Book for The Home*. This book illustrated how to integrate into the home industrial products such as warehouse shelving systems and factory floor coverings. It sparked off a fashion for such products all over the world. The roots of High Tech can be traced back to the ideals of the Modern Movement during the 1920s. In the 1920s, for example, the French architect Pierre Chareau used industrial glass bricks and shop steel ladders in several of his buildings; in the 1930s the Museum of Modern Art in New York put on exhibitions showing the public the beauty of industrial products such as laboratory glass. Later examples include Charles Eames's house in Santa Monica, built using off-the-peg factory components, and the 1970s Pompidou Centre in Paris (by Renzo Piano and Richard Rogers), which revealed heating ducts and utility conduits as decorative features for the outside of the building. In the 1980s, High Tech became part of the language of **postmodernist** design. **CMcD**

HILBERT'S PROBLEMS

In 1900, one of the most distinguished mathematicians of the day, David Hilbert (1862–1943), gave a lecture in Paris looking ahead to the new century in **mathematics** and attempting to define the areas in which future developments would lie. 'We know that every age has its own problems, which the following age either solves or casts aside as profitless and replaces by new ones. If we would obtain an idea of the probable development of mathematical knowledge in the future, we must ... look over the problems which the science of today sets and whose solution we expect from the future.' Hilbert went on to list twenty-three such problems. Some were specific mathematical problems, others more general questions (such as the sixth, the application of the method of **axiomatization** to physics). The remarkable things about these problems were the breadth of mathematics covered (from **set theory** to **number theory** to **algebra** to **topology** to mathematical physics), and the effect they have had on modern mathematics. A couple were trivial, but the others generated whole new branches of the subject in the efforts made to solve them or to show that they were insoluble (as some were). **SMcL**

HILBERT'S PROGRAMME

Hilbert's programme was an attempt by David Hilbert (1862–1943) to define the remaining task left to **mathematics** and to set up a programme to carry this out. The aim of Hilbert's programme was to find a way, given a sentence in **symbolic logic**, to mechanically determine whether that sentence was true or false. This aim was shown to be impossible by **Gödel's incompleteness theorem**. **SMcL**

HINDUISM

Hinduism (Old Persian, 'what Indians do') is the collective term given today to the majority **religion**, **philosophy** and **culture** of the peoples of India. However, this usage is problematic. In the first place, the concept is foreign to those labelled as 'Hindus', and is used indiscriminately to embrace both local cults and highly sophisticated and complex religious, as well as philosophical systems and social customs. There are also misleading political and social connotations. In addition, so-called 'Hindus' do not accept the Western definition of what religion is. It is wrong to view Hinduism as being like any other religion, that is (Latin *religio*, 'that which binds') as a force which unites people and enables them to relate to the supernatural, to the force which supplies morality to society and assuages individual longings for immortality. 'Hinduism' is not the cement of society, but the building itself. It is a total world-view, a way of looking at life and experiencing it, of understanding society as a whole, and one's place in it as a member of a family, profession or trade, caste and people. It defines what a person is and how they should behave, so it is highly ethical, yet a Hindu cannot be said to 'practise faith' in the same sense that a Christian or Muslim does. A Hindu *is* his or her faith: born a Hindu and remaining one.

The term 'Hindu' was originally a Persian word denoting a person of Indian religion and race, and was used by the Mohammedan conquerors of 'India'. The independence struggle and political developments since 1947, especially since the death of Jahawarlal Nehru in 1964, have led to 'being Indian' becoming synonymous with 'being Hindu'. Despite the presence of **Christianity** in India for at least

1,500 years, and of **Islam** for about 1,000 years, to adhere to these faiths is, in some quarters, considered unpatriotic. Yet much of contemporary Hindu faith was brought into India from Iran by Aryan invaders, and Hinduism has shown a remarkable capacity to absorb foreign cults and ideas.

The writer Niraud Chaudhuri, in his book *Hinduism*, defined Hinduism as: 'a civilised amplification of the primitive man's way of living in the world by accepting the conditions which he believes are inextricably laid down by the supernatural spirits who really own and govern it. It is also an elaboration of the primitive man's corollary that by accepting the conditions it is possible to establish a relationship of mutual dependence which will be stable.' This definition indicates the points of contact of classical Hinduism with traditional religion as found among tribal peoples. Thus it was possible for the beliefs of the Aryan invaders to relate to the religious experience of the indigenous, 'aboriginal' people, Dravidians and so on, while they were at the same time being refined and developed by priest and king to preserve the racial distinction between Aryan and Dravidian or tribal, and to prevent assimilation. To what extent Aryan culture was imposed on the tribal peoples so that the process of 'sanskritization' began, or to what extent Dravidian, especially Tamil, ideas filtered upwards (in the same way as Christianity moved from slaves upwards in Rome), is a matter of considerable scholarly debate – a debate coloured by political agitation, resistance to the spread of the Hindi language in southern India and the influence of the anti-Brahman movements. There is also considerable controversy about the exact dating of Hinduism. The Sanskrit language is used not as vernacular but rather like ecclesiastical Latin as a *lingua franca* for the educated classes all over India. It is related to Old Persian of the 9th century BCE, but as an artificial language, it is extremely difficult to date. **EMJ**

See also ashrams; Brahmanic religion; caste; Dharmic religion; Gandhianism; guru movements; moksha; Saivism; sakti; Tantrism; Vaishnavism; Vedic religion; yoga.

Further reading Nirad Chaudhuri, *Hinduism*.

HISTOLOGY

Histology (Greek *histos*, 'web' + ology), in the **life sciences**, is the microscopic study of tissues, which are collections of cells with the same function (for example, muscle or nervous tissue). The science was originally concerned with the structure and its relationship to function, but the advent of tissue- and enzyme-specific stains, byproducts of the dye and pharmaceutical industry, have enabled histologists to identify tissues by biochemical means. **RB**

See also cytology; biochemistry.

Further reading Carlos Junqueira, *Basic Histology*.

HISTORICAL LINGUISTICS see Comparative-Historical Linguistics

HISTORICAL MATERIALISM

The philosophy of history of **Marxism** is known as historical materialism. It is most sharply stated by Karl Marx in his Preface to a *Contribution to the Critique of Political Economy* (published in 1859). As traditionally understood, historical materialists follow Marx and Engels in believing that there is progress in human history, characterized by humankind's progressive mastery of Nature, and the accumulation of technological capacities. They believe that forms of organizing work, and the political and belief systems which accompany them, persist as long as they encourage technological progress. Five progressive 'modes of production' have existed according to Marx and Engels. Beginning with primitive communism history has witnessed the succession of the Asiatic, slave, feudal and capitalist modes of production. They predicted there would be two more, **socialism**, followed by advanced **communism**.

The Marxist theory of class struggle and revolution arguably is consistent with historical materialism although there are critics who suggest otherwise. Excepting primitive and advanced communism, each mode of production is characterized by fundamental class division and exploitation in which the ruling class owns the means of production (land or capital or people) and extracts 'surplus labour' from subordinate classes. These structural conditions are the material foundations of class struggle. Asiatic peasants, slaves and serfs were exploited by being directly forced to work for others, whereas workers in capitalist societies are forced to work on pain of starvation. Marx and Engels believed that the historical evidence suggested that the ruling class within each mode of production would be challenged and replaced by a new ruling class as and when their rule ceased to advance the productive forces (technology and knowledge). Thus the feudal nobility, who had been dominant because they owned the land, were overthrown by the capitalist class (the **bourgeoisie**), who gained ascendancy because of their control of capital and new industrial technologies. In their turn the bourgeois class was doomed to be replaced by the industrial working class (the 'proletariat'), which was now capable of advancing the productive forces without the redundant and increasingly parasitic class of capitalists.

Historical materialists therefore insist that revolutionary changes in modes of production, that is, transitions from one mode to another, occur after class struggle and polarization, but are always materially rooted in the changing relations between the level of development of the productive forces (technology) and property systems ('relations of production').

Historical materialism is in sum a theory of history which: (1) assumes progress in human history, defined as increasing technical progress and progressive reductions in the labour time required to produce basic necessities; (2) functionally explains property, political and ideological systems by their consequences for the advancement of the productive forces; and (3) connects the definition of social classes and class struggle to the modes of material production and their transformation.

Critics maintain that historical materialism is false or one-sided because it is economistic, that is, it neglects the autonomous role of non-materialist factors (like culture and ideas) in explaining historical change; that it is **historicist**, because it claims to possess knowledge of laws of historical progress; and that it is teleological, because it assumes that there is going to be an end to history (advanced communism). They also point to multiple inconsistencies and ambiguities in historical materialism. In particular they maintain that it is unclear whether Marx and Engels believed in a unilinear (single) path to historical progress or a multilinear one, and whether they thought that all regions of the world had to go through the same preordained stages of history, or whether 'stage-skipping' was possible.

However, for all its multiple faults even the severest critics concede that historical materialism has deepened the scope of historical inquiry, and some maintain that the insights of historical materialism can be detached from the rest of the Marxist system and used as a set of heuristics. **BO'L**

See also Asiatic mode of production; capitalism; feudalism; functionalism; idealism; slavery; state.

Further reading G.A. Cohen, *Karl Marx's Theory of History: a Defence*; B. O'Leary, *The Asiatic Mode of Production*.

HISTORICAL SOCIOLOGY

Historical sociology means a merging of the two disciplines of **sociology** and **history** in terms of their interests and methods of study.

Historical sociology can be used in a general sense to refer to any sociology focused particularly on the study of past societies or using historical sources. More specifically the term is used to refer to a certain form of comparative sociology, which focuses on historical societies and the order and change within these societies. Historical sociology in this second sense fell out of favour for some time, though more recently interest has been rekindled.

There is a sense in which all general theories of social change are historical sociologies. This has led some sociologists, for example P. Abrams, to assert that historical sociology forms the core of traditional sociology, and that its importance should be reaffirmed in modern sociological thought. Abrams argues that history is at the heart of sociology because sociology is expressly concerned with the transition to industrialism as a specific historical process; concerned with the life-histories of individuals in social contexts; and concerned with the relationship between human action and social structure as an empirical issue in world history. **DA**

See also bourgeoisie; evolutionism; globalization; Marxism; theories of modernity.

Further reading P. Abrams, *Historical Sociology*; Fernand Braudel, *On History*.

HISTORICISM

Historicism (from German *Historismus*), in **history** and **political science**, is a controversial and ambiguous concept with at least three distinct meanings.

(1) Historicism initially described a philosophical approach to history, originating in Germany, which assumed that all historical events are unique, unrepeatable and ungoverned by any general laws of nature. This historicism was a reaction against **positivism** as it came to be applied to the study of history towards the end of the 19th century. Contrary to the positivist doctrine that all human behaviour was explicable and law-like, historicists argued that the attempt to depict the 'reality' of a given historical period based on the analysis of surviving evidence or contemporary ideas is a dangerous simplification. Historicists like Wilhelm Dilthey asserted that each epoch should only be interpreted within its own ideas, values and context rather than those of contemporary analysts. Critics have wondered whether this injunction is feasible or coherent. In the study of political thought such historicism has led analysts to reject the idea that the 'classics' contain general, universal or timeless arguments or hypotheses. Instead they decode or 'read' such books as conversations between contemporaries. In effect, such historicists reject the social sciences in favour of **hermeneutics** and literary **criticism**.

(2) The second, and very different, conception of historicism is that of a negative common trait allegedly shared by a series of 19th- and 20th-century thinkers (such as Hegel, Comte, Marx and Spengler). Historicists are accused of believing in 'historical laws of necessity', and that they could predict the future course of events on the basis of a 'science of history'. Following World War II philosophers like Raymond Aron, Karl Popper and Hannah Arendt argued that attempts to define general laws of historical development are merely ruses, components of ideologies which justify forms of **totalitarian** domination. Popper was the most famous critic of 'historicisms'. He argued that the ideologies which underpinned fascism and Marxism falsely claimed to possess general knowledge of the laws of historical processes and of the future – an argument which he refuted particularly on the grounds that historicists could not predict the content or course of future acquisitions of knowledge, although he deployed other refutations as well. Popper also maintained that historicist determinism simultaneously suggests the impotence of politics or of human agency while providing cover for **Utopian** and totalitarian government. Popper's criticisms of historicism are devastating but are arguably indiscriminate. In particular, his treatment of Hegel – who actually shared Popper's view that 'historicist knowledge of the future' was not possible – has been condemned as unfair.

(3) A third conception of historicism, of more recent vintage, is that criticized by the French Marxist philosopher Louis Althusser. It has curious but imprecise affinities with the other two meanings of historicism. Althusser asserted that **historical materialism** was not an historicism. He meant that **Marxism** was not teleological, that is, he did not believe that history was inexorably working towards a given end or goal. Moreover, unlike Hegel, he argued that Marx regarded history as 'a process without a subject' and did not consider each historical epoch as an 'expressive totality', in which each social practice (economic, cultural, political and theoretical) is an expression of a single essence. Althusser's description of historicism came very close to Popper's, and his description of what historical materialism is not looked suspiciously like what its

exponents and critics had always assumed it was.

Recent neo-Hegelian philosophies of history, like that proposed by Francis Fukuyama (see below), declare that history is at an end, that is, has culminated in liberal democratic **capitalism**, have been seen as new historicisms by their critics.

The term Historicism is an important concept in the graphic arts, **design** and **architecture**. In art criticism, the term has two diametrically opposite meanings. The original use of the term defines a given historical epoch as unique and unrepeatable, and, therefore, only to be understood through its own concerns. In opposition to this Popper used the word to mean the application of quasi-scientific world-views, such as Marxism, to historical development with the aim of not only of explaining the past, but also offering a perspective on the present and a blueprint for the future. A new approach called 'New Historicism' has been recently developed, rejecting both these positions to focus on the 'intertextuality' of historical artefacts (the way guild practice, for example, may 'refer' to medieval panel painting and vice versa).

In architecture, historicism refers to styles which draw inspiration and vocabulary from a past period; it is the opposite particularly of **Modernism**, which refers to a style of building free of such reference. The late-19th-century German word which it derives from, *Historismus*, was a derogatory term used to describe what was felt to be the overemphasis then given to history, and was later used to describe the philosophy of history associated with Hegel. In more recent usage it refers most often to respect for the past and the deliberate revival of past styles, treated almost as a matter of social and moral responsibility. A characteristic example is the **Gothic Revival** and its associations with medieval Christianity and religious piety, where the association with what was imagined as a former stable Christian Society acted as a powerful metaphor for contemporary societies. In this century, which has been mostly characterized by attempts to move away from dependence on the historicist 'approach', the period after World War II and the debates surrounding the reconstruction of

cities mostly destroyed in the war, such as Warsaw, brought further prominence to the issue of the need for historical continuity and imitative reconstruction.

Applied to design, historicism describes the practice of selecting the ideas and styles of past periods of visual culture. Borrowing from the past has long been accepted as a legitimate creative activity – for example, Roman sculptors borrowed from the Greek tradition, while the Renaissance painter Raphael quoted from Roman wall paintings. During the last 150 years, however, historicism has come to represent an important design debate. In the 19th century, historicism was a central and legitimate area for the designer. There were simply hundreds of books reproducing the ornaments of many different cultures, ranging from Aztec to Indian and they were intended to provide the designer and the manufacturer with a diversity of source material with which to decorate their products. However, in the 20th century the Modern movement took a very different view of using the past. They wanted to create a new language of design and for the Modernist any form of historical borrowing was a crime. This puritanical position was not effectively challenged until the 1960s when **pop** designers freely explored the past. With the advent of **postmodernism** historicism offered a freedom of selection and choice of imagery that was irresistible to contemporary designers. Borrowing from the past is now an integral part of contemporary visual culture, and once again historicism is a respectable area of creativity. **PD MG CMcD JM BO'L**

See also classicism; determinism; parody; Romanticism.

Further reading Francis Fukuyama, *The End of History and the Last Man*; N. Pevsner, *An Outline of European Architecture* (chapter 8); Karl Popper, *The Poverty of Historicism*.

HISTORY

History may be the queen of the **humanities** but it is the bastard child of the **social sciences**. Recognizable history in the form of written chronicles of kings and peoples is as old as the first literate empires but self-conscious historical inquiry received a notable impetus in the works of the Greek 'fathers', Herodotus (?485-?425 BCE) and Thucydides (?460-?395 BCE). The word 'history' itself is derived from the title of Herodotus' book *Inquiry into the Causes and Events of the War between Greece and Persia*: *historia* is Greek for 'knowledge discovered by inquiry'.

As a modern field of scholarship, education and professional vocation, history flowered in Europe between the 16th and 19th centuries, exemplified in masterpieces like Edward Gibbon's *Decline and Fall of the Roman Empire* and David Hume's *History of England*. In these centuries history was regarded both as story-telling, providing narratives of entertainment, and as a source of moral guidance and salutary lessons on what should not be done. Much history narrated the achievements and follies of monarchs and high political élites, or the tales of saints. By the mid-19th century many Western historians began to work as cultural nationalists, constructing epic narratives of the origins, tragedies and triumphs of their nations, and many saw their primary task as that of narrating the constitutional, diplomatic, military and administrative history of their nation-states.

Towards the end of the 19th century history became professionalized as an academic discipline: history departments were established in universities, professional associations formed, and PhD programmes launched. State archives were established and historians became more systematic about their collection, citation and critical inspection of primary source materials. This professionalization had positive consequences: the successful outlining of the broad contours of the political evolution of the major Western states since early medieval times and a dramatic improvement in the historiography of the ancient European world. However, professionalization also had negative consequences. History, especially in the English and German languages, was infected by an incredibly impoverished empiricism, in which novel fact-finding and minute attachment to detail replaced the concern of earlier historians to fit their researches into broader interpretations.

Naturally these historians wrote largely for one another rather than for a wider public who preferred to digest the old-style history or updated popular versions of it. Such historians were rightly accused by their critics of neglecting to think about the purposes of historical inquiry; being slaves to (usually state) archival material; overly focused on narrow 'high politics' or 'history from above'; and arrogantly ignorant of other social science disciplines such as **anthropology**, **demography**, **economics**, **political science** and **sociology**. There were exceptions to the decline of history into impoverished empiricism, notably in the work of historians like Arnold Toynbee, but their writings were often deficient in an equal but opposite way being overly speculative, visionary, historicist and disrespectful of evidence.

The reintegration of history and historians with the social sciences has occurred fitfully since the 1930s, beginning with the **Annales school** of historians in France, and culminating in the work of the 'new historians' of the 1960s who were more philosophically conscious and willing to learn from the social sciences. The empiricist idea of 'value-free' history has been questioned, conceptual precision has become more frequent, model-building and testing is no longer frowned upon, and **quantitative history** has become recognized as methodologically central to sound historical scholarship. This reintegration has been assisted by the recognition of anthropologists, economists, political scientists and historians that a great deal of their work and hypotheses could be usefully validated through historical investigations and not simply through present-centred research.

The 'new history' according to one of its most exemplary exponents, Lawrence Stone (see below), is characterized (1) by its analytical rather than narrative structure; (2) by the fact that it seeks causal explanation rather than mere accounts of what happened, when and how; (3) by its concern with the past of human beings and society in the broadest possible ways: demography, **geography** and **ecology**, social history and social institutions, social mobility, and the history of culture and communications; (4) by its focus on the masses, the poor, the subaltern, the oppressed and not least women. The fruits of the new history are best seen in distinct new fields of inquiry: the history of the family, science, demography and the history of mass cultures. However, history as a field of inquiry is never likely to become one in which investigation of the particular and the construction of narratives are abandoned. **BO'L**

See also hagiography; legend; saga.

Further reading L. Stone, The Past and the Present Revisited.

HISTORY PAINTING

History Painting, in Western **art**, is a **genre** of painting in which scenes taken principally from the Bible, mythology and classical literature are treated in an elevated and morally edifying way. The historical genre, which stylistically is associated with, but not identical to, the Grand Manner, was the preferred genre of academic artists who regarded it as the highest expression of art. Notable practitioners include Poussin, Charles Lebrun, Benjamin West and David. **MG PD**

HISTORY PLAY

A History Play is a play that draws on historical events and characters, rather than imaginary ones, as the primary source of its plot. The historical material is usually shaped in order to influence audiences' understanding both of their own assumptions about their history and of their own contemporary existence by drawing analogies between contemporary and historical experience. Inevitably, history plays, given the nature and conventions of theatre, are selective and may rearrange chronology and amalgamate characters in the service of the design of the play: this sometimes gives rise to controversy with literal-minded commentators and with political figures sensitive to the analogies plays and audiences might make. The term Chronicle Play is generally used to describe plays that are less sophisticated in their presentation of historical material and which demand less complex reactions. **TRG SS**

Further reading I. Ribner, The English Play in the Age of Shakespeare; H. Lindenberger, Historical Drama.

HOLISM

Holism (from Greek *holos*, 'whole'), in medical practice, refers to intentions or procedures which relate to body-mind-spirit, rather than to the post-Cartesian divided parts. It must also be the opposite of reductionist, and therefore be incompatible with any procedure which follows the rules of Western **science**. A scientific proposal must be reduced in size to enable it it relate to the body of preceding knowledge, and be testable by available techniques. Although a holistic procedure cannot be explained in scientific terms, the effectiveness of any procedure, holistic or otherwise, used for the treatment or aleviation of illness can be tested in clinical trials and shown to be useful or not.

The first use of the word is attributed to the South African politician J.C. Smuts in his book *Holism and Evolution* (1926). However, it is one of many attempts to resolve the problem of **dualism** in science and philosophy, which has been under active consideration by more serious thinkers since the dawn of time.

Holism, in **sociology**, is the belief that societies should be seen as wholes, or as systems of interrelated components. Societies are believed to have properties which cannot be deduced from the characteristics of individuals; proponents argue that analysis should thus start with large-scale social institutions. Social **structure** is given primacy in explaining social outcomes. **DA TG**

See also action perspective; evolutionism; functionalism; individualism; structuralism; structure-agency debate; system; systems theory.

Further reading A.O. Lovejoy, The Revolt Against Dualism; René Descartes, Meditations on First Philosophy.

HOMEOSTASIS

Homeostasis (Greek, 'equilibrium'), in the **life sciences**, is the maintenance of a constant internal environment in which conditions are the optimum for life. It is the self-regulating mechanism by which the dynamic equilibrium of all biological systems is maintained. In order for an organism to function, it must continually undergo physical and chemical changes; these must be controlled within fairly narrow limits by a co-ordinated process. The concept of an internal environment was proposed by the French physiologist Claude Bernard in the 19th century, and the actual term homeostasis was coined in 1939 by Walter Cannon. The principle of homeostasis permeates all levels of biology and extends beyond the internal environment to the external in the control of population interactions, and the control of the **biosphere** as a whole. It is also applicable to mechanized systems such as automatic pilots and thermostats. Two forms of control exist: feedback, where the output of a system modifies its activity; and simple on or off control.

All living cells control their internal environment by pumping chemical requirements and waste into and out of the cell by behavioural responses. In multicellular organisms the process is extended to the environment within the organism but outside the constituent cells, which co-operate to control their environment. Birds and mammals have developed some of the most complex homeostatic systems, controlling body temperature, for example, within narrow limits by physiological and behavioural responses. Populations are controlled by homeostatic processes, such as the feedback response in which the size of the predator population limits that of the prey and vice versa. The control of conditions throughout the biosphere, such as the level of atmospheric carbon dioxide, is homeostatic in principle. **RB**

See also endocrinology; Gaia hypothesis; humours; metabolism.

Further reading W.B. Cannon, *The Wisdom of the Body* (1932); Margaret Stanier, *Physiological Processes*.

HOMOLOGY

The concept of homology (Greek, 'study of sameness'), in the **life sciences**, refers to the study of **evolution** where a homologous structure in two or more species indicates commonality of ancestry. The degree of homology is related to the closeness of genetic relationship, though gross structural homologies are difficult to quantify. Leonardo da Vinci first noted the homology between the bone structures of human and horse legs, which superficially look very different but which consist of the same bones adapted for different modes of locomotion. In the 19th century, the paleontologist Richard Owen defined the term along with the concept of **analogy**, noting that the two may occur in the same structure and may be difficult to separate. However, Owen denied the existence of evolution and the first to postulate that homology indicated a genetic connection between species was Karl Gegenbaur. The identification of homologous features was very important in the post-Darwinian debate on evolution, and in the development of classification systems based on ancestry. Modern techniques have shown that the concept of homology can be extended to the physiological and molecular level: the vertebrate oxygen-carrying protein haemoglobin has conserved homology in that substantial pieces are the same in different species. Gene sequencing has allowed homology to be quantified, as the proportion of the DNA in a gene which is homologous to another can be directly measured. **RB**

See also adaptive radiation; anatomy; morphology; palaeontology.

HOMOPHONY see **Polyphony**

HUMAN RIGHTS

Human rights are rights which all human beings should possess because they are human beings irrespective of their citizenship, nationality, race, ethnicity, language, sex, sexuality, or abilities. They are therefore distinguishable from **civil rights** which are conferred on individuals because they are citizens of a state. Unless human rights are specifically embodied in constitutional provisions they are not legal rights.

The doctrine that there are human rights is a lineal descendant of the doctrine of natural rights proposed by the founders of liberal political thought, notably John Locke (see **natural law** and **liberalism**). They argued that although individuals necessarily sacrifice some freedoms to enter into a social contract there remain certain rights which are inalienable – such as the right to life, and freedom from arbitrary and oppressive government.

The modern doctrine of human rights is primarily concerned with the protection of individuals from persecution by the state, and is used as a normative base-line for criticizing the standards of governmental conduct throughout the world. A list of human rights was expressed in the United Nations Universal Declaration of Human Rights (1948) which included political, economic and social rights, but excluded collective rights. The UN Declaration influenced other statements of fundamental rights, including the European Convention for the Protection of Human Rights and Fundamental Freedoms. Although human rights are not enforced by the UN its agencies frequently report on their absence or violation in member-states; and non-governmental agencies such as Amnesty International and Human Rights Watch (including Helsinki Watch in Europe) are effective in publicizing human rights violations and putting moral pressure on the relevant states.

While the language of fundamental human rights has been associated with the spread of liberal and democratic ideals, it has its critics. Some maintain that there are no such things as universal human rights. They claim there are likely to be major differences of cultural interpretation, for instance, as to which freedoms should be constitutionally entrenched. Controversy also surrounds the content of human rights. Should they be restricted to feasible and enforceable civic and political rights, or should they be extended to include social and economic rights, like the right to employment, or the right to a basic income? **Utilitarian** critics complain that to establish some rights as inviolable is to ignore the fact that most governmental activity involves judgements as to the weight to be given to potentially contesting values. Finally some political scientists argue that to reduce all questions of politics to questions of rights means that all public policy questions will eventually become 'juridified', that is, decided by judges rather than by more directly democratic processes. **BO'L**

Further reading A. Gewirth, *Human Rights: Essays on Justification and Applications;* J. Waldron (ed.), *Theories of Rights.*

HUMANISM

Humanism (from Latin *humanus*, 'centred on human beings') was an intellectual movement in Europe which began in the 14th century and reached its peak at the time of the Reformation and **Renaissance**. Humanists reacted against medieval **scholasticism** by emphasizing human intellectual and cultural achievements rather than such things as divine intervention, the brevity and misery of life and the need for escape. The movement began in Italy with a strong emphasis on study of the classics of ancient Greek and Roman civilization. Characteristic figures were the 14th-century poet Petrarch (one of the first European writers to make a proper study of ancient Roman literature and to imitate its forms and themes), and the 15th-century thinkers Lorenzo Valla (who developed literary criticism in the light of newly-discovered classical manuscripts) and Marsilio Ficino and Giovanni Pico della Mirandola (who tried to unite secular philosophy with Christianity). In 1458, when the noted humanist and scholar Enea Silvio de Piccolomini was elected Pope (Pius II), the success of the humanist movement was assured.

The attempt, particularly in northern Europe (where such rulers as Francis I of France and Henry VIII of England encouraged the spread of the new learning) to unite evangelical piety with classical scholarship resulted in a 'Christian humanism', with the goal of returning to the sources of the Scriptures and of faith. Erasmus (who edited the works of the Church Fathers and the Greek New Testament) was the most important figure in this work. The influence of the humanist movement on the Reformation is important. Many Reformers, including Calvin, Melanchthon and Zwingli, had a humanist background and their thinking is clearly influenced by humanism, as were many of those who led the movement for reform within the Roman Catholic Church. The spread of all such ideas was greatly aided by the invention of new printing techniques, and humanists, such as R. Estienne and John Froben, published thousands of books and pamphlets.

The rediscovery of classical writings (not least the work of the Greek philosophers and scientists), and relaxation of the intellectual censorship which had been so characteristic of the medieval Church, led to a huge increase in philosophical, scientific and social study. It was not so much that God was marginalized, as that study of human beings, and of natural phenomena, was now possible without the need to kowtow to dogmatic, biblical explanations. It is no accident that the peak of humanist activity coincides with the first great period of European scientific research, with the work of such observers and thinkers as Bacon, Copernicus, Galileo, Harvey and Paracelsus.

In the **arts**, the rediscovery of classical (that is, pagan) literature sparked a fascination with the thoughts, emotions and preoccupations of ordinary people, as opposed to allegorical figures, aristocrats or religious intellectuals. This trend was particularly noticeable in **drama**, which was now permissible again after a millennium of church repression. The humanistic age is the time of the **commedia dell'arte**, of Calderón, Lope de Vega and above all Shakespeare.

The second, great humanist period in European intellectual life was the 18th-century **Enlightenment**. Once again, the motivating idea was to prise intellectual activity away from the shackles of religion and to irradiate human life not with the assurance of God's mercy but with knowledge. This process continued throughout the 19th and 20th centuries, the age of scientific rationalism. **Darwinism**, Freudianism, **quantum** mechanics and the like were merely peaks along a continuous onward path. The shift was from intellectual hierarchies to pluralism, from certainty to enquiry (and often, disillusion), from artistic realism imbued with guilt (as shown in the fiction of, for instance, Dostoevsky or Zola) to documentary realism (as shown in the novels of such writers as Theodore Dreiser and H.G. Wells). At this point, the word 'humanism' first began to denote an avowedly antireligious stance where human beings were not only 'the measure of all things', but the only measure. Auguste Comte, in the 19th century, revived the term in his 'religion of humanity', which came to be associated with scientists defending Darwinism. Walter Lipmann, in his *Preface to Morals* (1929), introduced the concept of 'scientific humanism', a philosophy based on science and morals without religion. Secular humanism today emphasizes human worth and the rights of human beings, and its **atheism** is as dogmatic and uncompromising as the religious **fundamentalism** which led to its rise in the first place. **EMJ KMcL**

Further reading A.R. Hall, *The Scientific Revolution;* E.H. Harbinson, *The Christian Scholar in the Age of the Reformation.*

HUMANITIES

The humanities, or *litterae humaniores* (Latin, 'humane studies'), in medieval education, were the classics, **philosophy** and contemporary **literature**. 'Humane' in this context means 'relevant to the study of human beings'. The classics were studied because it was thought that they demonstrated most human secular knowledge at its best; philosophy was studied because it showed how human beings think, and what their thought has been at its most elevated; contemporary literature was studied to show what the 'best' minds of the time were thinking. These studies, it was thought, would prepare people for life, or if they had to enter a profession, would fit the mind for the army, diplomacy or government (none of which needed further study), or for professions wich needed postgraduate, specific work, such as the Church or the Law. The concept may seem either naive or breathtakingly arrogant, but the humanities were the most highly regarded course of study in most European universities from their foundation in the late Middle Ages right through to the middle of the 20th century. KMcL

HUMOURS

The term humour (Latin *umor*, 'liquid'), in the life sciences, refers to any fluid in an animal or plant, but the ancient Greeks supposed that there were four basic humours: yellow and black bile, phlegm and blood. Various imbalances of these four could account for a wide range of disorders and their properties were central to the ideas of Hippocrates (*c*.450-*c*.370 BCE). The four humours are often equated with the ancient Greeks' idea of the four elements (earth, fire, water and air) and represent an important step away from the previous belief that diseases were the result of devils, divine displeasure, etc. and therefore inexplicable in mechanistic terms.

The concept of the four humours persisted until the 18th century and was a prime force in the development of Western **medicine**. The theories increased steadily in complexity to allow the humours to fluctuate slightly with season and age and to affect **psychology**. Treatments were based on their supposed effects in boosting or reducing the relative levels of each humour and certain procedures such as bloodletting became extremely popular for diverse symptoms. When, in the 19th century, great advances were made in understanding the cause of disease the concept of vital humours was not abandoned completely as it found shelter in the idea of **homeostasis** and the maintenance of an internal physiological balance.

In **drama**, Comedy of Humours is a term used to describe a Renaissance European dramatic form, drawing on traditional medical beliefs in the influence of the four 'humours' on individual character. Characters dominated by blood are sanguine, those dominated by phlegm are phlegmatic, yellow bile makes the personality choleric and black bile leads to melancholy.

In dramatic terms this leads to unbalanced stereotypical characters dominated by a single trait. **RB TRG SS**

See also aetiology; alchemy; character.

Further reading Ann Barton, *Ben Jonson, Dramatist*.

HYBRIDIZATION

Hybridization (from the Greek for the offspring of a tame sow and wild boar, or the offspring of one free parent and one slave) is the breeding of members of different species with one another to form a hybrid. In the 18th and 19th centuries many scientists and horticulturalists were fascinated by hybridization. Species do not normally interbreed and the offspring of such matings are often sterile, but plants can often be reproduced vegetatively (that is, without sexual reproduction, as in the propagation of new plants from cuttings). Many new species are formed by the crossbreeding of existing species, usually of the same genus. In the 18th century, Linnaeus investigated hybridization in plants and attempted to reproduce existing species by crossing different members of the same genus. He was interested in showing how a few divinely created species could give rise to many more by crossbreeding. In the 19th century, Gregor Mendel studied hybridization and it was this that stimulated his investigation of **genetics** in different varieties of pea plant (see also **Mendelism**). However, Darwin's theories on **evolution** distracted attention from hybridization by providing new explanations for the appearance of new species. **RB**

See also speciation; thremmatology.

HYDROBIOLOGY

Hydrobiology (Greek, 'study of life in water') is the study of the interactions between living organisms and water. Water is generally a very stable environment for life, indeed, it is where life is thought to have originated. Organisms that live in or on water can profoundly affect its suitability for use by humans, while our use of water has an all too frequently deleterious effect upon the life which it supports. **RB**

See also biogeography; homeostasis.

HYPNOSIS

Hypnosis (from Greek *hupnos*, 'sleep') was discovered by a French nobleman Puysegur while investigating the phenomenon called **mesmerism**. An English physician, James Braid (1795–1860), made a scientific investigation of mesmerism and the results of suggestibility on the part of human subjects; he called this phenomenon neuro-hypnotism, and this was later shortened to hypnotism. By the mid-19th century studies into hypnotism had established a number of genuine hypnotic effects including amnesia, hypnotic suggestion, paralysis and anaesthesia. These were later discovered to have a marked similarity to the condition of hysterical patients suffering from paralysis, and was further investigated by such people as Jean Charcot, the French neurologist, and Sigmund Freud.

The phenomena of hypnosis were concrete examples of the **unconscious** at work, and its discovery was to enable Freud, working with Breuer, to posit an unconscious in an empirical scientific framework, based on clinical observation. From these beginnings a complex theory of mind, and consequently **psychoanalysis**, were progressively developed. **MJ**

HYPOTHETICAL IMPERATIVES see Morality

HYSTERIA

Hysteria is a word from ancient Greek which was used purely to describe diseases in women which were thought to be a result of a malfunction of the uterus (*hysteron*). The Greeks thought that the uterus travelled around the body and pressed on other organs, and that sexual frustration caused the womb to shrink, or to harbour animal spirits which could pass from there to other organs and cause such severe physical disturbances as paralysis or fits.

Freud's theories retained the sexual importance of the phenomena in hysteria; he explained pathological symptoms as the result of repressed sexual wishes. The publication in 1885 of Freud and Breuer's *Studies in Hysteria* marked the beginning of **psychoanalysis** as the exploration of physical conditions which resulted from repressed memories. Although Freud never actually did a definitive study of hysteria, modern psychoanalysts consider that hysteria has its fixed point in the **Oedipus Complex**, and that it is a condition which uses the **defence mechanisms** of repression and disassociation to create the symptoms. For Fairbairn, and his version of **objects relations** theory, hysteria is a result of externalization of the good object and internalization of the bad one.

Hysteria as an illness is still characterized by having physical symptoms which have no physical cause; the cause is psychological, not pathological. The women suffering from hysteria who were Freud's middle-class, Viennese patients are often regarded as a social phenomenon which has passed into psychoanalytical history; the phenomenon nonetheless exists in all members of society, of all classes, who seek therapeutic help. **MJ**

Further reading L. Veith, *Hysteria: the History of a Diseas.*

I

ICONOGRAPHY

Iconography (Greek, 'writing about images') is the study of subject matter in **art**. The iconographer employs knowledge of symbolic imagery to interpret works of art. The art historian Erwin Panofsky was a pioneer of iconographical studies and is now their leading exponent. In his own words, iconography is 'that branch of the history of art which concerns itself with the subject matter or meaning of works of art, as opposed to their form'. For example, a painting in which a woman is placed next to a spiked wheel is a representation of St

Catherine, martyred on such a wheel and whose attribute it is. This is a simple example; usually the study of iconography is far more complicated, requiring an extensive knowledge of the related culture and intellectual climate before analysis can take place. A classic example is Panofsky's analysis of van Eyck's *The Marriage of Arnolfini and his Wife* (1434) in his book *Early Netherlandish Painting*.

Panofsky established an important distinction between iconography and iconology. In *Studies in Iconology* (1939) he defined 'iconography' as the study of subject matter, and 'iconology' as the study of meaning. His definitive example illustrating this difference is that of the man who raises his hat as a polite gesture. While the action is straightforward (taking off a hat) its meaning derives from the practice of medieval knights removing their helmets to express peaceful intent. As Panofsky states: 'To understand [the] significance of the gentleman's actions I must not only be familiar with the practical world of objects and events, but also with the more-than-practical world of customs and cultural traditions peculiar to a certain civilization.' Thus the action has two meanings, primary or apparent, and secondary or conventional. This latter quality points toward hidden meaning in a work of art.

Other eminent exponents of an iconographic approach include Emile Mile, Aby Warburg and Randolph Wittkower. **MG PD**

Further reading W.J.T. Mitchell, *Iconology: Image, Text, Ideology.*

ID, EGO AND SUPEREGO

Id, Ego and Superego are the essential components in Freud's final model of the mind. A fourth component was Pcpt-Cs (short for perception-consciousness), which provided the window onto external reality.

The Ego (a term Freud derived from the Latin for 'I' and used as early as 1895) is an agency of mind which civilizes the Id, organizing translations between the Id (which does not work on the reality principle) and the outside world. Its function is to control behaviour, taking into account reality as well as the instinctual impulse. Although it is reality-oriented it is part unconscious, part pre-conscious (unconscious at a particular moment but not repressed), and performs the disciplined activities of thinking and judging.

The Id (Latin, 'It') is the **unconscious**, the undifferentiated psychic source of instincts and passions. Freud saw the whole mechanism of human development as a move from undifferentiated primitive states to differentiated and structured ones. The human infant is seen as virtually all Id. Repressed ideas move from the Id through the Ego and undergo distortions in dreams, displacement and neurotic presentation.

The Superego was initially thought to be part of the Ego. Eventually Freud saw this mechanism as being formed by the **Oedipus complex** into a separate function. The intensity of those conflicts in the child and the defensive action that they precipitate creates the Superego, an area which prohibits the expression of Oedipal wishes. It is an enforcing mechanism, with an energy of its own, and inhibits moral behaviour. **MJ**

Further reading Raymond E. Fancher. *Psychoanalytic Psychology: the Development of Freud's Thought;* Merton M. Gill, *Topography and Systems in Psychoanalytic Theory.*

IDEAL TYPE

Ideal type, in the **social sciences**, refers to an artificially constructed 'pure type' which emphasizes certain traits of a social item which do not necessarily exist anywhere in reality.

Attention was first drawn to the ideal type in **sociology** by Max Weber (1864–1920) in order to make explicit the procedures by which he believed social scientists formulated general abstract concepts. Weber believed that social scientists selected as the defining features of an ideal type certain aspects of behaviour or institutions which were observable in the real world, and exaggerated these features to construct an abstract model. Not all the characteristics present in this model would actually be present in the real world, but a better understanding of any given situation could be reached by means of a comparison with the 'ideal type'. The ideal type should not be confused with the notion of an ideal in a moral sense – that is, an exaggeration of those traits considered desirable.

For Weber, ideal type analysis was the sociological counterpart to the experimental method in the natural sciences. In contrast to the physical sciences, however, he did not envisage that a general agreement could be reached on ideal type concepts in sociology, or that such concepts would become the basis of generalized laws. **DA**

See also authority; bureaucracy; positivism; social fact.

Further reading R.E. Rogers, *Max Weber's Ideal Type Theory*.

IDEALISM

The word idealism (derived ultimately from the Greek for 'to see') is used in at least four distinct ways in human thought. In everyday language it means moral or principled conduct (as opposed to pragmatic or 'realistic' conduct) – a usage preserved in the discipline of international relations. In **history** and the **social sciences**, it refers to the views of those who believe that ideas (or more broadly, 'cultures') are the most important explanatory sources for human conduct.

In **philosophy**, idealism is a theory first put forward by George Berkeley (1685–1753) and developed by Georg Wilhelm Hegel (1770–1831). The theory is that all that exists is the product of minds or ideas, that physical objects have no existence outside of the mind that is conscious of them: so understood, idealism is the opposite of **materialism**.

What rationale is there for such a surprising view? The argument from illusion suggests that when one sees a mountain the immediate object of one's experience is a visual image as of a mountain, and that this image is distinct from the mountain itself. Our perceptual experiences as of objects are distinct from the objects we perceive. Plausible as this is, it seems to lead to the sceptical problem that all one ever directly experiences are images as of objects, and not objects themselves. So how can we know that the objects really are as they seem to be? When one seems to see a mountain, how can one be sure that the mountain is there and that one is not merely hallucinating or dreaming it?

Berkeley's initial view, that physical objects are ideas in finite minds (such as ours and those of other animals), seems to solve this problem. If the mountain is just my visual experience as of it, then asking how I can be sure that the mountain is there seems to make no more sense than asking how I can be sure that I am having a visual experience as of a mountain. If physical objects are identical with my experiences as of them, then there appears to be to be no gap between seeming to see a mountain and really seeing a mountain.

So the view that physical objects are ideas in finite minds seems to have the advantage of dissolving the problem of **scepticism**. Unfortunately, it has two unacceptable results. The first is that physical objects only exist when they are perceived by a finite mind. The coin exists when I see it as I put it into the piggy bank, and it exists when you see it as you take it out. But it ceases to exist in between, because no finite mind is perceiving it.

The second objection is this. If physical objects are identical with my experiences of them, then there appears to be to be no gap between seeming to see a mountain and really seeing a mountain. This appears to have the advantage of dissolving the problem of scepticism. But it also obliterates the common-sense distinction between hallucinating or dreaming a mountain and seeing one. Surely there is a difference between seeming to see a mountain (when one hallucinates or has a dream about a mountain) and really seeing a mountain. The claim that physical objects are ideas in finite minds seems to obliterate this distinction.

Berkeley later held that physical objects are ideas not in finite minds but in the one infinite mind – God's. This avoids both the above problems. The coin in the piggy bank exists when no finite mind is perceiving it, because it exists as an idea in God's mind whether or not a finite mind is perceiving it. And there is a difference between hallucinating a mountain and really seeing a mountain. When I hallucinate an object which does not exist, I have a sensory idea as of it, but it does not exist because there is no idea of it in God's mind and objects are ideas in God's mind. When I see a mountain which does exist, I have a sensory image as of a mountain, a mountain which does exist because there is an idea of it in God's mind.

Thus, the second form of Idealism, according to which objects are ideas in God's mind, avoids the problems of the first version. Unfortunately, it also lacks the attraction of the first version noted above. The first version was attractive because it seemed to dissolve scepticism, by obliterating the gap between appearance and reality, between its seeming to me that the mountain exists and the mountain's really existing. But the second version respects this common-sense distinction. It may seem to me that the mountain exists when the mountain does not really exist. So the sceptical worry returns. If reality may be different from the way it appears to me, how can I know how things really are rather than merely knowing how they seem to be?

The fourth use of 'idealism', in the fine **arts**, originated in ancient Athens. Plato said that everything we see in reality is merely a shadow, a simulacrum, of its own ideal form, and Aristotle said that painters and sculptors, as they did their work, often had the ideal form in mind rather than the reality before their eyes. Art, therefore, might be truer to the ideal than reality itself. This was certainly the aim of Greek sculptors such as Praxiteles and Myron: they worked out complex theories of 'ideal' proportion, and modelled their works accordingly. (They were usually depicting gods and other supernatural beings, and saw them as the 'ideals' of beauty, dignity and so on, of which the same human attributes were simulacra. Therefore, to try to show the ideal, a statue of a god would take the best available versions of each human quality and try to embody them.) This approach was characteristic of Greek art (especially **sculpture**) until the late 3rd century BCE, when artists replaced it with **realism**, showing human beings and animals as they were, and in poses characteristic of real life (for example a beggar with hand outstretched or a slave gri-

macing as she carried a heavy pot) rather than in emotionally neutral, idealized poses (prototypes of modern photographic pinups).

The distinction between idealism and realism in art was maintained, in Roman Europe and beyond, in a distinction between sacred and secular art. Sacred images aimed to show the ideal (both 'good' qualities and the 'bad' ones which were to be purged by true devotion and belief); secular images – unless they were concerned to show idealized versions of such qualities as leadership in a prince or benevolence in a patron – tended to be realistic views of the here-and-now. (This was so even if imaginary scenes were shown: Bosch's Hell, for example, is a nightmare, but its components are nasty ingredients from ordinary Flemish life of the time, stage-managed by gargoylish devils who are hybrids of perfectly ordinary, if horror-inspiring, creatures from reality.) The same is true of other 'fine-art' traditions: Indian, Persian and Far Eastern art, for example, all make a distinction between idealized human and animal forms in religious art (coupled in some cases with idealized depictions of plants and landscape), and an earthly, indeed often earthy, realism in the presentation of the secular. **Folk art** traditions, by and large, stand aside from idealism: their depictions of the supernatural tend more to (what sophisticated Western critics would describe as) **surrealism**, and the tendency to pattern-making and abstraction takes the 'reality' out of their depictions of secular phenomena. Idealism, as a guiding principle, is irrelevant.

During the **Renaissance**, European artists and theorists rediscovered and once again promoted idealism as a guiding principle of art with a slight but significant difference from the Platonic or Aristotelian approach. Now the driving theory was that art should be an uplifting experience for the observer, and that the artist should seek to achieve this uplift by representing not the natural world as seen, but an improvement of it shaping Nature, as it were, by a process of discerning selection. Bellori, lecturing at the Academy of St Luke in Rome in 1664, said that the artist gives flesh to ideal forms a promotion of the artist from the ancient Greek notion, that he or she simply strove to depict an ideal which was already there. In Neo-Platonic terms, the artist's pursuit of beauty is nothing more or less than a veneration of the Godhead visible in all creation an argument which should be considered before believing (as some Christian critics did) that the use during the Renaissance of originally pagan subject matter, a criterion of beauty, was in some way impious. **PD MG AJ KMcL**

See also materialism; naive realism; representative theory of perception.

Further reading J. Foster, *The Case for Idealism*; J. Foster and H. Robinson, *Essays on Berkeley*; Erwin Panofsky, *Idea: a Concept in Art Theory*.

IDEAS

Since Descartes, philosophers have assumed that all ideas (Greek, 'look', 'form' or 'kind') are 'in' the mind. Some philosophers, such as Locke and Hume, seem to have thought that all ideas are sensory images. Whenever one perceives, remembers, thinks, imagines or dreams one has a sensory image 'before' one's mind. When one thinks of a cat, for example, one has a visual image similar to, though somewhat less vivid than, the visual image one has when one sees a cat. One problem here is this: if all ideas are sensory images, how can one have an abstract idea, an idea not of this or that particular cat, but of 'cat' in general? A sensory image of a cat is inevitably an image of a cat with some determinate colour and size, and how can an image of a cat with some determinate colour and size serve as our general idea of 'cat', when cats come in a variety of shapes and colours?

Contemporary philosophers insist that thinking of a cat need not involve having a mental picture or sensory image of a cat similar to the image one has when one perceives a cat. This seems right. But if having an idea is not a matter of having a sensory image before the mind, what is it to have an idea? Some hold that one possesses the idea 'cat' if one can distinguish cats from things which are not cats. One problem for

this suggestion is that there are machines which can distinguish between damaged and undamaged tins of beans – machines which will throw out the damaged cans. But such machines seem not to have minds or ideas. **AJ**

Further reading J.C. Mackie, *Problems from Locke*; Wittgenstein, *The Blue and Brown Books*.

IDENTIFICATION see Defence Mechanism

IDENTITY

My copy of *Wuthering Heights* may be the same as my sister's in two different ways. If we each possess our own copy of the same print run of *Wuthering Heights* then our copies are qualitatively identical (from Latin *identitas*, 'sameness'). The colour, size, typeface and spelling of my sister's copy is exactly the same as the colour, size, typeface and spelling of mine, so our different copies have the same qualities or properties. Alternatively, we may have been given a joint Christmas present. If there are not two copies with the same qualities or properties, but only one copy which we share, then they are numerically identical.

Leibniz's principle of the indiscernibility of identicals states that if *a* is numerically identical with *b*, then *a* and *b* are indiscernible: every property of *a* is a property of *b*, and vice versa. This intuitively obvious principle needs to be distinguished from the more controversial principle of the identity of indiscernibles, which states that if every property of *a* is a property of *b*, and vice versa, then *a* is numerically identical with *b*. The plausibility of the second principle depends on which properties are considered relevant. It seems that if *a* and *b* have exactly the same properties, including spatio-temporal properties, then they must be numerically identical. But if spatio-temporal properties are not considered relevant, the principle is less plausible. It seems that there could be two books exactly alike in all their properties, except that one exists at a different time or place to the other. **AJ**

See also rigid and non-rigid designators.

Further reading D. Wiggins, *Sameness and Substance*.

IDENTITY THEORY

The identity (Latin, 'sameness') theory, in **philosophy**, holds that mental events are numerically identical with physical events. There are two versions of this view.

The type identity theory holds that mental types or properties are numerically identical to physical types or properties. So, for example, the mental property of being in pain is identical to the physical property of being a C-fibre stimulation. (C-fibre stimulations are neural events in the brain.) This has the consequence that every pain is a C-fibre stimulation, that every thing with the property of being a pain also has the property of being a C-fibre stimulation.

In contrast, the token identity theory holds that every event which has a mental property has a physical property, but denies that mental properties are physical. Every pain has some physical property or other. But while some pains may be C-fibre stimulations, others may not have the property of being a C-fibre stimulation, but the different physical property of being a D-fibre stimulation. An analogy is this. Every piece of furniture is physical, but furniture properties are not physical properties. Every chair has some physical property or other, but there is no physical property which all chairs have: some are made of wood, some of plastic and yet others of metal. **AJ**

See also dualism; identity; materialism; mind-body problem; types and tokens.

Further reading D. Davidson, *Essays on Actions and Events*; C. McGinn, *The Character of Mind*.

IDEOLOGY

The term ideology (French *idée* + ology) was coined by the philosopher Destutt de Tracy to describe his proposal for 'a science of ideas'. Today the concept of ideology has multiple usages and definitions. On epistemological definitions ideological thought refers to sets of ideas which are not scientific: that is, illogical conjunctions of ideas and/or ideas which are not amenable to empirical verification or falsification and have to be taken on trust. On this conception **astrology**, political doctrines, **psychoanalysis**, **religions** and theologies are examples of ideological thinking.

On **Marxist** definitions ideologies refer *either* to systems of ideas which reflect and functionally support the dominant economic system, *or*, relatedly, to patterns of ideas shaped by people's class interests. Marxists believe that the '**dominant ideology**' in a given historical period reflects the interests of the dominant class. One implication of the Marxist approach is that ideologies may distort a person's perceptions of his or her interests, or lead to what Marxists call 'false consciousness'.

More broadly in the **social sciences** ideologies are regarded as systems of **belief** which provide a coherent and relatively consistent explanation of a given social or political order, or a programmatic vision about how to achieve a new social or political order. They usually have core conceptions of human nature and philosophies of history which explain how we got where we are and where we should now go. Used in this way an ideology means a simplified (and sometimes simplistic) political philosophy, doctrine or world-view (or *Weltanschauung* in German).

Non-Marxist studies of ideology can be divided on the one hand into those which critically analyse the logical content of bodies of social and political theory, and more empirically oriented investigations which seek to establish the existence of ideological thinking and the effects of ideological thinking on the political behaviour of individuals and groups. These studies reach radically different conclusions concerning the ways in which ideology affects political action: ranging from those who think nearly all political activity is ideologically (or discursively) based to those who think that only a minority of people act because of ideological thinking or are ideologically conditioned.

Twice in this century social scientists have predicated the 'end of ideology' and the arrival of more pragmatic and rational approaches to politics: once in the early 1960s and again in the aftermath of the collapse of the USSR. Decoded, these were in fact claims that the appeal of Marxism had terminally diminished in Western liberal democracies.

In ordinary usage, ideology now has both positive and negative connotations: positively, ideology may be commended when a person or an organization is behaving in accordance with a coherent world-view (as in 'ideologically correct'); negatively, ideological thinking is condemned because it leads a person or an organization to behave with a morally blinkered or factually distorted conception of reality. **BO'L**

See also critical theory; class; conflict theory; culture; discourses; hegemony; historical materialism; legitimation; norms; power; social construction of reality; social control; social stratification; sociology of knowledge; state; values.

Further reading N. Abercrombie, S. Hill and B. Turner, *The Dominant Ideology Thesis*; D. Bell, *The End of Ideology*; L. Feuer, *Ideology and Ideologists*; J. Larrain, *The Concept of Ideology*.

IDIOGRAPHIC INVESTIGATION

Idiographic investigation, in **sociology**, is concerned with the individual or unique experience rather than with generalities. It contrasts with a nomothetic approach which seeks to establish general laws following a model of investigation derived from the natural sciences. **DA**

See also ethnomethodology; naturalism; phenomenological sociology; positivism; social realism; symbolic interactionism; understanding.

IDOLATRY

Idolatry (from a neutral Greek word meaning 'image', with the same root as the verb 'to see') has come to mean the veneration of images, and has generally had a pejorative sense during its chequered history, especially when used by Jews, Christians and Muslims to describe the practices of other faiths.

From the earliest times and in all civilizations representations of gods have been made, whether in the ancient Middle East, Egypt, the Indus valley civilization, ancient China or Africa, or the pre-Hellenic civilizations in Greece and Crete – that is, since at least 4000–5000 BCE. The earliest 'idols' are invariably little models of Mother Earth (see **goddess**) and the sky gods. Clearly a very deep, basic psychological need is supplied by the provision of a tangible sign of divine power. As civilizations and their technology advanced, these representations became more and more sophisticated and beautiful, reaching great heights in, for example, the arts of classical Greece (6th–3rd century BCE) and the Chola and Pandyan eras of Tamil Nadu. But in one area of the world, the ancient Middle East, there was a reaction against idolatry in the 15th century BCE, when the Israelites whom Moses led from Egypt adopted an austere **monotheism**. Although they carried around the tablets of stone on which the Ten Commandments were engraved with the awe, reverence and pomp normally associated with idols, they were strictly forbidden to make graven images. They did not always live up to this high ideal, but since the surrounding peoples used images, idolatry quickly became equated with apostacy.

Excavations of synagogues in the Roman period have uncovered murals and mosaics with graphic representations, but there is no hint of veneration. (In the same way, in India under the Moguls, art, especially miniature painting, flowered, in contravention of **Islamic** law.)

At first **Christianity** followed its Jewish parent, but in the 2nd century CE, Christian sarcophagi have scenes depicting biblical stories, and when Christianity became a mass religion and the official faith of the Roman Empire, images – not least the central image of Christianity, the cross (with or without the form of Christ himself), were sometimes assumed to have miraculous powers, a belief which the Reformers did not hesitate to castigate as idolatry. In the violent upheavals and wars which accompanied the Reformation, religious statues were smashed, cathedrals wrecked, and the treasures of the **Renaissance** vandalized in a popular protest which hardened into puritanism. In **Protestantism** there is still considerable ambivalence about **religious art** (though the cross retains its symbolic potency), and the reforms of the Second Vatican Council (1962–65) have led to a reaction in Roman **Catholicism** against holy images and miracle-working statues.

In the East the Orthodox Church was rent by the iconoclastic controversy (c.725–842), saying that it was the veneration of icons (see **iconography**) and statues which prevented the conversion of Jews and Muslims. The Byzantine Emperor Leo III the Isaurian (?675–741) totally forbade their use as idolatrous. Great persecution of monks, who were the main icon painters, ensued, while the deposed patriarch appealed to Rome. Successive popes condemned the policy, upheld by Leo's son and grandson in turn, but two empresses, Irene, who instigated the Seventh Ecumenical Council at Nicaea (787), which upheld the icons, and Theodora, who got a pro-icon patriarch elected in 842, got the policy reversed despite the iconoclastic stance of the army. However, to avoid charges of idolatry, Orthodox art henceforth remained two-dimensional, though icons are venerated as images of heavenly reality.

The iconoclastic controversy was undoubtedly due in part to the influence of Islam, where all image-making is forbidden. The position in **Hinduism** is complex. On the one hand, educated Hindus are convinced that images of the deity are not worshipped, but are simply aids to worship, and some movements which reject sacrifice and the concept of a personal god, reject images altogether. For the majority, however, the deity is present in a very real way in the 'idol'. When a statue of the deity is completed, a special ceremony is held to call down numinous power into the image. Then it is treated as god, that is, as a king or queen: daily washed, clothed, fed, taken out in procession and offerings made before it. Interestingly, the word 'idol' has been taken into Indian English and indology as a neutral, almost technical word for the divine image, depite the fulminations of missionaries against idolatry. There are still many Indian Christians who will not enter a temple because of the presence they feel there as represented by the devotions shown to the idols. It is the presence of idols which makes a building into a temple.

Both in Hinduism and African traditional religion, God is present in everything. It is therefore a question of taking something already infused with divinity in some way and making it a special channel of divine power. A tree or rock, for example, can be as much an idol as a statue or carving (see **Shinto** and **totemism**). Probably the best way to view the use of idols is as lifelines to the deity, something to hold on to, something to bring one into direct contact with the divine. However, the question is always whether the object of veneration does not become the subject of worhsip. Idolatry is often seen in the West as a possessive kind of love, following Paul's strictures about 'covetousness which is idolatry'. Idolatry has thus become equated, in general parlance, with obsession: we 'idolize', for example, people, money, power or sex. **EMJ**

ILLUSION, ARGUMENT FROM

There are, in **philosophy**, a number of versions of the argument from illusion. All versions attempt to establish that when one perceives an object, all one can be immediately aware of is one's sensory experience as of it, and not the object itself.

One version of the argument from illusion begins with considerations concerning hallucinations. When Macbeth asks whether there is a dagger in front of him, the answer is 'no'. Macbeth clearly is not perceiving a dagger, because there isn't a dagger there. But he is having a visual experience as of a dagger in front of him. When someone hallucinates an object, they have a sensory experience as of an object which is not there. Further, seeing an object is phenomenologically indistinguishable from (that is, feels just the same as) hallucinating it. So even when Macbeth does see a dagger, even when there is a dagger before him and it causes him to have an experience as of it, all he is immediately aware of is his experience as of a dagger, not the dagger itself.

Another version of the argument begins with considerations concerning the perception of distant objects. One can perceive a distant star which no longer exists. The light now striking one's retina and causing one to 'see' the star left the star millennia ago, and the star has since ceased to exist. So what one currently sees cannot be the star, but a sensory experience as of it. And, more generally, when one perceives an object, all one can be immediately aware of is one's sensory experience as of it, and not the object itself.

The claim that all we are ever directly aware of are sensory experiences as of objects and not objects themselves seems to give rise to the problem of scepticism. If one is only ever directly aware of sensory experiences as of objects and not objects themselves, how can one know that the objects really are as they seem to be? **AJ**

See also idealism; naive realism; representative theory of perception; scepticism.

Further reading D. Armstrong, *Perception and the Physical World*; A.J. Ayer, *The Central Questions of Philosophy*.

ILLUSIONISM

Art thrives on illusion when it attempts to convince that what is factitious is real. A painted landscape on a wall is a real landscape; the figures in the dome of a church are part of a real vision of Heaven vouchsafed to the viewer; a portrait actually breathes; the fly which the apprentice paints on the work and the teacher tries to brush away; the bunch of grapes is so lifelike that a bird tries to eat them. Such *trompe l'oeil* work is characteristic of all areas and of all periods: the examples above, for example, are based on anecdotes from ancient Greece, Mogul India, Edo Japan and medieval Europe.

In a sense, all artists are magicians, because when they 'imitate nature' they conjure up a new world which has many features of the 'real' one. Hence works of art have often been the subjects of miracu-

lous claims: wooden Madonnas cry, Ganesh's image dictates answers to a studying schoolchild, a statue comes to dinner and leads Don Giovanni to Hell. Such stories testify less to the existence of the supernatural than to the power of art or to the **beholder**'s willingness to suspend what in theatrical circles would be termed disbelief.

The viewer's 'consent' with a work of art, his or her willingness not merely to enter into its world but to surrender to it, is a feature of our human eagerness to play, to make believe. We may believe entirely (as people do who see Christ's wounds bleeding as he hangs sculptured on the cross), or we may take a kind of ironical delight in pretending to believe, colluding with the artist. Artists have taken diametrically opposing views of their role in the process. Some claim, high-mindedly, that the 'illusion' of art is in fact a kind of meta-reality, that no kind of deception is practised. Others gleefully admit and parade their sleight of hand: the range is from Mantegna's use of *sotto in su* in the **Renaissance** ('from below upwards', painting figures on a church ceiling so that they look foreshortened), or the fake doors (sometimes half open, sometimes with servants disappearing through them, or gardens or other rooms just visible beyond) painted on the panelling of **Baroque** palaces such as Versailles, to those present-day portraits of spaniels and horror-film characters whose eyes 'seem to follow you round the room'. **PD MG KMcL**

Further reading M. Battersby, *Trompe l'oeil; the Eye Deceived*.

IMAGE

This commonly-used term (from Latin *imago*, 'immature form' or 'representation') has a range of meanings within **media** studies and in common parlance. On one level, image refers to a representation or likeness. For instance, a photograph, a print or a moving film is said to to capable of reproducing something that exists in reality. This reproduction is termed the image and has both a physical existence (a photograph, say, of a footprint in the snow) and a physical referrent (the object being photographed or the foot that stepped on to the snow). In media usage, there is a technical language around the quality of the image produced.

On a different level, 'image' can have a mental or symbolic conception. In this sense the notion of image is more metaphorical and is often used in **literature** (the imagery of a character, for instance). Image here invokes ideas or feelings about something or someone.

A third, recent, and now very common utilization of the term draws heavily on the latter of these previous understandings. It is used in **advertising**, in public relations and in the construction of identities for celebrities, politicians, products and organizations. 'Image' here is connected to the artificial construction of a public identity. It links to the idea of an attempted control over the way others regard us and to the idea of reputation. A whole industry has been built around brand-image, public-image and image-management to the extent that it is possible to talk of a person's, product's or company's image.

Interestingly, the way individuals present themselves in day-to-day interaction was a subject of intense academic study before it was subject to major commercial application. Specifically, the Canadian sociologist Erving Goffman has written extensively on behaviour in public places and 'impression management'. **BC**

Further reading E. Goffman, *The Presentation of Self in Everyday Lifef*.

IMAGERY

The ability to objectivise experience by envisaging it, and then to subjectivise it by processing those images in a deliberate and personal way, is (so far as is known) unique to humans. The imaging process can be replicated, to some extent, by machines, but so far no mechanical brain has been created which can handle images proactively and creatively. Machines may be able to analyse light more sensitively than any human, but none can formulate a Theory of **Relativity**. Machines can perceive and modulate sound in every conceivable way –

except to write a **symphony**. The creation, modulation and communication of images, and ideas about images, lies at the heart of all human social interaction, technology, science and the arts. **KMcL**

IMAGINATION

Imagination (Latin, 'forming images') is the (supposed) faculty by which we acquire knowledge of non-actual possibilities. Just as I know that bananas are actually yellow by the faculty of sight, so I know that it is possible for bananas to be purple by the faculty of imagination. I know that bananas could be purple because I can imagine a purple banana.

But what is it to imagine a purple banana? Imagination seems to involve forming sensory images; imagining a purple banana seems to involve forming a sensory image as of a purple banana.

However, imagination must involve more than merely forming sensory images. After all, one may form an image of exactly the same sort when imagining a purple banana and imagining hallucinating a purple banana. One is obviously imagining something different when one imagines a purple banana and when one imagines hallucinating a purple banana, but one may form an image of exactly the same type when doing these different things. So more than merely forming a sensory image is involved in imagining these things.

The extra element involved seems to be a cognitive supposition. When one imagines a purple banana, one forms a certain sensory image and then supposes that it is a purple banana. When one imagines hallucinating a purple banana, one forms a certain sensory image and then supposes that it is an experience as of an object which does not in fact exist. So imagination seems to involve both forming sensory images and making cognitive suppositions. **AJ**

See also actual; modality.

IMAGISM

Imagism was a poetic movement founded primarily by Ezra Pound in 1912. Its purpose was to dispense with the superfluous, to present clear images in simple words nd comprehensible **syntax**, and generally to sweep away the emotional grandiosities of 19th-century **poetry**. As well as Pound himself, the Imagists included Hilda Doolittle, James Joyce, Amy Lowell and William Carlos Williams (who developed the style in the 1930s into an even more rarefied style of his own, objectivism, in which the poet tries to keep personality rigorously out of what he or she describes). The work of the Imagists was often no more than tersely coy, and 20th-century poetry has never really recovered from the aura of pretentious preciousness with which they invested it. At its best, however, for example much of Pound's early poetry, it transcends affectation and genuinely achieves the stripped-down clarity of expression and emotional exactness to which it aspires. Not only that, but the stylistic experiments of the Imagists had an incalculable effect on most of the great English-language poets of the the century, from W.H. Auden and T.S. Eliot to John Berryman, Robert Graves and Robert Lowell. **KMcL**

Further reading J.B. Harmer, *Victory in Limbo: Imagism 1907–1917.*

IMITATION

The concept of imitation in **art** stretches back to antiquity, and few terms in art theory have been more misunderstood. The concept has been out of favour since **Romanticism** wrongly equated imitation with copying and made it the hallmark of lack of **originality**. While the Latin term *imitatio* is associated with the Greek *mimesis*, in art theory it tends to mean not just the copying of nature but the emulation of the best of the existing canon of works and was so discussed in Quintilian's *Institutio Oratoria*. It was never a question of slavishly copying older art, but rather of engaging in dialogue with the best of the past.

In artistic traditions that depend on tradition and conservatism, such as those of the Middle and Far East, 'imitation' in this sense was the central creative procedure. 'Originality' was hardly an issue, and an individual artist's excellence was measured more in terms of his re-creation of existing forms and styles than of the creation of new ones. In the West, this approach was followed until the **Renaissance**, though some individual artists, for example Apelles, Praxiteles and Dioscorides, did make a name for the excellence of their contribution. But the idea of an individual artist having something personal to say, within or outside the tradition, hardly became prominent until the end of the Middle Ages. Therefore, while imitation was at least an issue throughout the Middle Ages, it was only from the Renaissance on that it became central to many theories of art, and was institutionalized by the **academies** (which needed to reconcile a belief in rules and precedent with a sense of invention, which, they claimed, was absent in the craft-dominated guilds).

Thus the doctrine of copying the great artists of the past was, at first, successful, but later became ossified into a mindless, unquestioning veneration of the past. A dogma that influenced training throughout a student's apprenticeship and became a straitjacket for all but the strongest creative personalities. Those who did escape (for example Rubens) gained great profit from studying older art. However, those who remained under its yoke were drained of originality. Beginning with the Romantics' veneration of originality as an essential rather than learned quality, imitation in the 20th century has become the site of **parody** and pastiche, and as such forms an important aspect of **postmodernism**. **MG PD**

Further reading K.E. Maison, *Art Themes and Variations: Five Centuries of Interpretations and Re-creations.*

IMMUNOLOGY

Immunology (Latin *immunis*, 'exempt' + ology) is the study of the immune system, which is a complex set of biological processes which act co-operatively to prevent invasion by other living organisms (pathogens) and to regulate the growth and differentiation of the cells of the body. The immune system is divided into two functional parts, called the innate and adaptive arms.

The innate system provides defence against invasion by maintaining barriers such as skin, toxic secretions, acids in the stomach and enzymes which destroy bacteria in tears, mucous, etc. Phagocytic cells are capable of enveloping and digesting foreign cells and particles, and are present in the blood and in organs such as the brain, the lungs and the skin. Killer cells circulate in the blood along with molecules which can cause clotting of blood and which can combine to puncture the membranes of foreign cells. When activated, killer cells and phagocytes produce hormones which attract more of their own kind, producing the symptoms of inflammation.

Despite this defensive barrage, foreign cells can penetrate the body and begin to multiply; at this stage the adaptive immune response becomes important. This arm of the immune response centres around a class of molecules called antibodies which act as specific receptors for molecular structures such as proteins. Antibodies can be produced against millions of structures which are foreign to the individual; these structures are called antigens and are frequently proteins found at the surface of pathogenic organisms. Antibodies are produced by specialized cells called lymphocytes which bear a specific antibody at their surface; when this antibody binds to an antigen the lymphocyte is stimulated to divide and produce large quantities of antibody which are released into the blood. The antibody serves to label foreign material in the body so that it may be recognized by cells such as the phagocyte. Antibodies can also act alone to agglutinate foreign particles, inhibiting their growth and causing them to precipitate. When an individual is exposed to an antigen which it has not encountered before, a specific antibody is produced in large quantities and the immune response can be targeted efficiently against the threat. If the same antigen is experienced again, the immune system is already primed and can respond much more rapidly; this is the basis of vaccination, in which the individual is exposed to the antigen without the pathogen, priming the immune response without the risk of causing pathology. Vaccination was pioneered by Edward Jenner (1749–1823) who discovered that humans could be made resistant to smallpox by inoculation with blood serum from animals infected with cowpox.

Self antigens are ignored by the immune system because they have been experienced from the outset of life and the cells which produced antibodies against self antigens have been deleted from the complement of lymphocytes at an early stage of development. When self antigens which are not normally found in the extracellular environment are encountered by lymphocytes, the immune response removes them; this is the mechanism by which abnormal body cells are controlled. Occasionally, the immune response becomes sensitized against normal self antigens and autoimmune diseases such as rheumatoid arthritis occur. The discrimination of self from non-self by the immune system is efficient and, while this is important in the control of tumour cells, it is also the reason for the rejection of transplanted organs. The immune response of organ transplant patients is suppressed with drugs to prevent rejection – and such patients must be monitored carefully to avoid the establishment of infections against which they have no defences. More commonly, immunopathology occurs when the immune response produces an inappropriately severe response to an innocuous foreign particle, such as pollen, and inflammation occurs leading to symptoms of allergy. **RB**

See also bacteriology; endocrinology; helminthology; homeostasis; molecular biology; natural selection; network theory; parasitology; toxicology; virology.

Further reading Robert Desowitz, *The Thorn in the Starfish*; Ivan Roitt, *Immunology*.

IMPERIALISM

Imperialism (from Latin *imperare*, 'to command'), in **history** and **political science**, literally refers to the expansion or consolidation of an empire, and to doctrines which support such activities. Empires are characterized by the fact that they are not culturally or territorially contiguous entities, and involve the political domination of some peoples and territories by a core dominant civilization or class. In this sense imperialism is as old as agrarian civilization, and is not yet a purely historical phenomenon. However, all the evidence of this century suggests that **nationalism** and the democratization of the world are leading to the collapse of the world's surviving empires.

The 'age of imperialism' is usually more narrowly defined by historians to cover the period from the 16th century, when European powers competed to expand their empires in Africa, the Americas and Asia, until the early 20th century when competition among the imperial powers led to the outbreak of World War I. The imperialism of the Great Powers of this period can be distinguished by two formal types: administrative imperialism, in which outlying regions of the empire were indirectly ruled, and settler **colonialism** in which settlers held a region for the imperial power.

The academic study of imperialism divides into economic and political schools of thought. Economic theories are primarily **Marxist** in origin. In their simplest forms they explain empires as driven by the urge to create wealth by force. By contrast some classical Marxists argued that late-19th-and early-20th-century European imperialism was a means of temporarily forestalling the inevitable crises of **capitalism** by creating new markets and outlets for capital investment a view expounded by Lenin among others. In this perspective imperialism was an outgrowth of monopoly capitalism. Dependency theorists of imperialism, influenced by Marxism, suggest that the uneven nature of capitalist development led to the formation of a core of wealthy and powerful empires which competed for control over the less developed states of the periphery, a process which resulted in the purposeful 'non-development' or 'underdevelopment' of the peripheral states.

The economic approach to explaining imperial formation is not universally accepted. Others maintain that cultural and political motivations are essential elements in the construction of empires: Joseph Schumpeter, for example, argued that landed aristocracies were far more likely to embrace imperialism than were capitalists.

Moreover, a great deal of historical inquiry surrounds the subject of whether or not formal empires 'paid'; and some maintain that economic explanations fare better in accounting for the decline of empires than they do in interpreting their rise. The political approach to interpreting imperialism emphasizes two features of the latter stages of the 'age of imperialism': first, the geopolitical competition among the great powers in the second half of the 19th century which created a race for empire, which had more to do with political and military rivalry than with the need for markets and resources; and second, the problems faced by imperial powers in establishing and maintaining authority in new territories. The difficulty of balancing a costly centralized authority over distant territories with the need to maintain economic and political stability in the centre proves a herculean task for all great imperial powers and is normally the root cause of imperial decline. BO'L

See also agrarian society; dependency theory.

Further reading A. Brewer, *Marxist Theories of Imperialism: a Critical Survey*; D.K. Fieldhouse (ed.), *The Theory of Capitalist Imperialism*; P. Kennedy, *The Rise and Fall of the Great Powers*.

IMPLICIT DEFINITION see Context

IMPRESSIONISM

The best-known form of impressionism is the French fine-**arts** movement begun in the 1870s and embracing such painters as Cézanne, Degas, Monet and Renoir. The movement was named soon after Monet's painting *Impression: Sunrise* was first exhibited in 1874. Impressionism was radical in three main ways. First, since the artists preferred to exhibit their work independently, it broke with the authority of the Salon. Second, seeming indifference to subject matter removed one of the major props to the 19th-century theory of aesthetic value (in which, for example, historical subjects were deemed more important than **genre** themes). Third, the Impressionists' close observation of nature and of the effects of light cut through academic practice, and rendered obsolete much art education based on academic 'know-how' and respect for the past.

As the title of Monet's painting suggests, the object was to depict not 'photographic' reality, but an impression of reality, the prismatic view of the artist's own eye. Above all, Impressionist painters were concerned with representing light, often dappled by leaves, reflected in water, or scattered into myriad dots like a newspaper photograph. In his studies of La Grenouillère, near Paris, Monet also fused two formerly discrete stages of painting: the sketch and the execution of the finished canvas. Painting for at least part of the time on the spot, Monet sacrificed studio finish for the advantages of loosely-handled paint, primarily in order to retain in the one canvas elements of 'preparation' formerly lost in execution of a finished painting. (He was followed in this technique by others, notably Renoir.) Not surprisingly, the Impressionists were accused of making sketches, not works of art. But this was to miss the point. They broke with academic practice in order to present the viewer with a spontaneous interpretation of the world, unclouded by the application of academic formulae. In fact Impressionist paintings were not for the most part made at a single sitting, but were often reworked. But, thanks to the use of broken brushstrokes, high-keyed colour, thick, opaque impastos and little preparatory painting, the pictures retain the freshness of studies.

In breaking with the formulae of academic art practice, with subject-based Salon painting and with the tyranny of official exhibitions, the Impressionists created a climate for the rapid advance of **modernism**. In exploring the potential of painting to capture the effects of light, and in allowing the medium – the paint itself – to become the painting (rather than merely the means to depict the subject), they laid the foundations for almost all subsequent styles in art. Although there is no single 'impressionist' style (Turner, Gauguin, Manet and Seurat, for example, were all in their quite different ways Impressionists), impressionist techniques and ideas underlie **cubism**, **expressionism**, **minimalism**, and in

fact every ism save those following harsher, more politically or philosophically oriented paths, such as **constructivism** and **futurism**.

Impressionism is also apparent in the arts of **literature** and **music**. In both, it implies an evocative, subjective and somewhat misty conjuration of atmosphere, of which Stéphane Mallarmé's poem of adolescent eroticism *L'aprés-midi d'un faune*, and Debussy's tone poem based on it, are archetypes. However, Debussy was not really a musical impressionist, his works are too formal and objective, and yields that particular distinction to such composers as Delius and Respighi. In literature, impressionism was largely absorbed into other movements, from the dewy-eyed mysticism of the **Pre-Raphaelite** poets to the more exotic (and erotic) fancies of such minor writers as Frederick William Rolfe and Ronald Firbank (and one major writer, André Gide). As in art, it very soon evolved, and became the basis for writing of many other kinds, from the precise imprecision of the **imagists** (and through them, of much later verse) to the very different novels of Hermann Hesse, James Joyce and Virginia Woolf, the plays of Samuel Beckett and the film scripts directed by Marcel Carné, Cocteau, Kurosawa and Mizoguchi.

In fine art, the term ncoimprcssionism was coined in 1886 by the critic Félix Fénéon to describe the paintings of Seurat and his followers. The neoimpressionists sought to follow impressionist aims while introducing a new 'scientific' rigour into the representation of light. They based their theories on a selection of ideas from science and **aesthetics** (ideas themselves based on discoveries made in **optics** in the first half of the 19th century). The fundamental principle was that two colours juxtaposed on the canvas will mix optically to produce a tone brighter than the one the artist physically mixed on the palette. This resulted in a technique known as 'divisionism' (sometimes called **pointillism**), in which the application of small touches of pure paint offer the eye of the beholder a brilliance, harmony and luminosity absent from conventional paintings.

In fine art, postimpressionism is the term, more handy than informative, usually applied to those European artists, from van Gogh to Cézanne, who were influenced by, or reacted to, impressionism in ways which would otherwise be difficult to group. Their work shows neither stylistic unity nor a common agenda; if they are a 'group' at all it is purely in temporal terms, as a link between the 19th and 20th centuries and a conduit connecting the early modernists to cubism, **fauvism** and beyond. **PD MG KMcL**

Further reading P. Pool, *Impressionism*; J. Rewald, *Postimpressionism: from van Gogh to Gauguin*.

IMPROVISATION

Improvisation is the chief way in which **music** is, and always has been, performed. The performers invent what they play or sing as they go along, either with complete freedom or conforming to some pre-arranged or preselected idea. They respond creatively to one another, to the mood and atmosphere of the occasion and to the ideas contained in the basic material.

It is important to distinguish between improvisation in which a piece of music is created during its actual performance, and improvisation in which an existing piece of music is subjected to interpretation, elaboration and variation. A further distinction lies in whether improvisation is the trained response to a given sign, the development of a musical idea held in memory, or an impulsive musical action during the performance itself. It is a term not easily defined, since there are as many meanings as there are different musical traditions in the world. However, improvisation is an essential element in all orally-transmitted music, from the social music of aboriginal peoples to such major art traditions as Indian classical music.

In Western music, improvisation is most commonly understood to be the musical invention that takes place within a familiar or predefined formal framework. This may simply be an abstract, structural model involving melodic, harmonic or rhythmic elements, as in the performance of **Blues** or the cadenza of a classical **concerto**, or it can even be an existing piece of music in its most basic skeletal form, as in the practice of **jazz**. Another form of improvisation is the musical realization of codified symbols and their interpretation or elaboration within the stylistic conventions of the musical idiom. They are generally used to represent either a melodic outline, as in the cipher notation of Indonesian *gamelan* music and the ideographic notation of ancient Chinese zither music, or to give harmonic guidance, as in the use of chord symbols in **pop** music and jazz.

Improvisation is central to the art-music traditions of many Asian cultures, such as Arabian *maqâm*, Indian *râga* and Persian *dastgâh*. The performer undergoes a programme of training, which is as long and demanding as that for a Western performer of notated music, the objective being to acquire a rich musical vocabulary of melodic and rhythmic patterns, with which new compositions may be created. The framework for Asian improvisation is less structured than that of Western models, and is more a scheme for musical development governed primarily by aesthetic, expressive conventions. In musical cultures of this kind, the bases for improvised performances are often traditional, some of enormous antiquity. In religious music-drama, for example (such as that of Indonesia), each character or moment in the story has its own kind of music, hallowed by tradition – demon-music, fight-music, praise-music – and the performers improvise on ideas well known to both themselves and the audience. A similar technique is used in Japanese classical **drama**, where declamation and song (often to pre-composed texts, also extremely ancient) is accompanied by a group of musicians improvising music on traditional ideas, but keeping in phase with the mood and style of the particular performer. Classical Indian musicians draw from a vast repertoire of traditional melodic sequences (*râgas*) and rhythmic patterns (*talas*), each of which has conventional associations: times of day, patterns of weather, emotions and so on. By improvising on these patterns, sometimes for hours at a time, they seek to induce a kind of transcendental state in their hearers, in which the suggestions in the music fuse with the promptings of the hearers' own individual selves and with those of the audience as a whole.

Throughout the world, jazz and **rock** musicians use pre-existing songs, the words and melodic and harmonic patterns of which give a kind of objective correlative to the improvised performance. Traditional 'wedding bands' in Eastern Europe play processional music, and dance music, based on patterns of melody and rhythm which can be as much as 2,000 years old. Church music, from Tibetan Buddhist chanting to the Shaker songs of North America, is improvised in a similar way – and as with jazz and rock, the use of specific words gives particular colour and associative power to each performance.

The major exception to the idea of improvised music is the Western classical tradition. In this, music is meticulously notated, and the performers' task is to interpret the composer's marks as faithfully as possible, accommodating their own creative and emotional impulses to the ideas unlocked from the written score. (This is particularly useful in the creation of large musical forms such as **symphony** or **opera**. It could be argued, indeed, that neither orchestral music nor opera could exist, in the extraordinary subtlety we know them, unless the scores were written down. A *gamelan* is a largish group of players (sometimes over 60); a Noh play can involve several dozen performers; but the overall intellectual and emotional control is different, and certainly less varied, than in, say, a Mahler symphony or a Wagner opera.) An element of improvisation has always been built into Western classical music, but in a small way. Performers in **Renaissance** church music – and 18th-century music added ornaments and short cadenzas to the printed score; continuo players in the 18th-century improvised accompaniments based on chords notated by figures under a bass note ('figured bass'); concerto soloists in the 18th and 19th century improvised cadenzas to show off their technique. But in Western society, a performer who improvises or is musically illiterate now tends to be looked on as less accomplished than the performer of composed, notated music – a direct consequence, some say, of musical élitism prac-

tised by the conservatoires of music, with their insistence on musical literacy. Equally, highly-trained conservatoire musicians can be so accustomed to relying on the printed page that they are unable to improvise or perform 'by ear'. Such matters pose the fundamental questions of what exactly musical competence is, and who should be its judge. It is only in the last few decades, with jazz and rock becoming accepted subjects for study alongside 'classical' music, and with the advent of **aleatory** techniques, **graphic scores** and the like, that improvisation in Western art music has achieved anything like the importance it has always had elsewhere. **KMcL SSt**

INCEST

The incest taboo prohibits sexual relations between certain categories of kin. Certain kinds of incest taboo are universal, yet even in the immediate nuclear family the categories are not uniform. The taboo varies from culture to culture, whether including the father, all or some of the offspring and siblings, or even larger groups. For example, a Kachin tribesman in Burma is prohibited from sexual relations with his daughter or sister because of incest taboos, but in the case of his mother it would qualify as adultery.

Incest categories were incorrectly assumed to be due to a natural repugnance for sexual relations between members of a family because of their close physical proximity. Sigmund Freud suggested that there was in fact an unconscious inclination towards incest precisely because it was forbidden.

The structuralist Claude Lévi-Strauss argued that though the incest taboo manifests itself in different forms, it is a universal rule. It was a fundamental way of classifying the world, and could be related to his distinction between **nature** and **culture**. It was a crucial step in the establishment of 'culture' to renounce one's own women in order to create wider social links through exchange. He saw the incest taboo as a way of demarcating separate marriage groups in complementary relationship to each other. By exchanging sisters for wives in exogamy – the practice of spouses marrying outside a specified group – wider social networks could be created based on a principle of reciprocal exchange. However, incest is only one aspect of the rules which regulate **marriage** and sexual relations. Exogamy prohibits marriage within a specified group but not necessarily sexual relations. It appears that marriage partners are confused with sexual partners in Lévi-Strauss's analysis.

Anthropologists have tended to neglect rules regarding sexual relationships in favour of **kinship** patterns. They have also neglected to examine the behaviour that is classified as incest in each society, assuming it to be a universal category close to the concept of **child abuse** as it is applied to Western society. Anthropologists are currently engaged in an exploration of the categories and conceptions of incest. **CL**

Further reading Claude Lévi-Strauss, *The Elementary Structures of Kinship.*

INCOME

Income is the flow of money (or goods in the case of income in kind) to the three factors of production: wages for labour; profit and interest for capital; rent for land. Incomes are not exclusive in an economy. Incomes move in a circular flow: labour earns wages which it spends on goods and services produced by firms; firms pay interest for capital, rent for land and wages for labour, all of which are again spent in some form on goods and services. Yet although incomes flow in this way, they do not all pass through all hands: one central problem of **macroeconomics** is how the income flow is determined, and how it is allocated between factors.

National income is a snapshot of this circular flow, and is the aggregate of all factor incomes – rent, wages, interest and profits – during any one period. More conventionally, it is determined statistically as the value of the economy's output (see **gross domestic product**).

One way of measuring the degree of equality in a society is by its income distribution: the way total personal income is divided between rich and poor. This is best depicted by a Lorenz Curve, which plots the shares of different groups of the population in total income. Governments use taxation to try to close this gap, but the biggest shifts in distribution in the industrialized world have been outside direct government control: for example, the transformation from mass unemployment in the 1930s to full employment in the 1950s brought with it a large redistribution of income. **TF**

INCOMPLETENESS THEOREM see **Gödel's Incompleteness Theorem**

INCREMEMENTALISM

Incrementalism (Latin *incrementum*, 'increase' + 'ism'), in **political science**, is the theory of decision-making developed by Charles Lindblom (see below). It suggests that decisions are necessarily circumscribed by experience and are subject to cognitive and information-processing costs. It also implies that most successful decision-making is conservative with a small 'c': that is, based on small deviations from the status quo. The theory was developed in reaction to the theory of comprehensively 'rational' decision-making, which asserts that rational decision-makers should evaluate all available options before selecting that option which optimizes their goals.

Incrementalism assumes that in most political and policy-making circumstances this kind of decision-making is not possible because it presupposes what cannot be (for instance, perfect information, perfect knowledge, low-cost time to evaluate all possible options, and decision-makers who know exactly what they want). In most circumstances the best predictor of what policy-makers do today is what they did yesterday (plus or minus a small change, an increment or decrement). They cannot optimize, so they focus on a few feasible options, and they frequently proceed within an existing consensus rather than by radically deviating from the status quo. Moreover, incrementalism assumes that democratic decision-makers generally proceed through 'partisan mutual adjustment', rather than through centralized and heroic planning. Less grandly they 'muddle through'.

Incrementalists say that their case is demonstrated by the way in which most states make their budgets: programmes are not rationally and comprehensively evaluated, instead policy-makers focus on marginal additions or reductions to programmes. There is a natural affinity between **pluralism** and incrementalism, but Lindblom, the pioneer of reflection on incremental decision-making, has become progressively more critical of incrementalism both as a positive account of decision-making and as a normative guide to decision-making, although he remains sceptical of the claims of the policy sciences and practitioners of what he calls 'professional social inquiry'. **BO'L**

See also game theory.

Further reading C. Lindblom, *The Intelligence of Democracy; Politics and Markets;* C. Lindblom and D. Cohen, *Usable Knowledge: Social Science and Social Problem Solving.*

INDEPENDENCE

Independence, as an idea in **history** and **political science**, is both a value and a descriptive concept, suggesting lack of dependence on others. Thus an independent state is a sovereign state it possesses the maximal degree of internal autonomy which a state may possess. In (what is called) international **law** the recognition of a state's independence means that the state is supposedly legally protected from external interference in its domestic affairs. In practice the autonomy of independent states is limited by the **geopolitical** interests of world and regional powers, and all states are characterized by some level of interdependence: 'no state is an island', that is, unaffected by events and processes beyond its borders.

Since the 19th century (when the legitimacy of **self-determination** and **nationalism** became widely recognized) independence movements have been the most important foci of political change throughout the world. The Versailles Treaty (1919) entrenched the concept of self-determination in international relations although it was usually granted only to existing states. One reason for the proliferation of independence movements is that independence represents the ultimate protection and recognition of a group's collective identity. However, multiethnic or multicultural independence movements have been common, especially in territories formerly governed by colonial or imperial powers. **BO'L**

See also sovereignty.

INDIGENOUS METAPHYSICS

Indigenous metaphysics describes conceptions among various peoples about the universe, the role of humans, and their relationship to unseen powers. **Anthropology** has shown that different metaphysical schemes about existence and ontology refer not to universal truths, but to cultural presuppositions. Not only do individuals experience reality in different ways; so do communities. The 'dreamtime' of the Australian aboriginal, for example, relates the mystical dreamtime of the past to the visible world. The dislocation of normal spatial and temporal qualities in the dreamtime situates it parallel to the visible world, and means that it is only accessible to those who have been initiated into its mysteries. Many indigenous philosophies similarly situate humans within, or complementary to, the processes of the natural world rather than in opposition to it, or attempting to control it.

In the early part of this century, Lucien Lévy-Bruhl started a long debate among anthropologists about the **rationality** of human thought. (It began with the publication of his book *Primitive Mentality* in 1922.) He saw 'primitive' people as governed by feelings rather than reason, and saw their conceptual frameworks as 'pre-logical' mystifications of reality. The debate about whether there were two modes of thought, one magical/mystical and the other rational/scientific, continued until recently. These two realms are not, however, mutually exclusive. The fact that death is blamed on **witchcraft**, for example, does not exclude the observation that it was caused by a collapsing hut.

A more fruitful approach than seeing indigenous ontologies as irrational mystifications, is to view them as conceptual frames that both explain and determine perceptions of reality. They do not refer to stable, immutable realities or reflect assumptions shared by everyone in a community. Members of a spirit-possession **cult**, for example, have theories about spirit bodies which impinge on their physical bodies to varying degrees. Spirit possession is related to beliefs in various categories of both good and mischievous **demonism**; or malevolent spirits (see **spiritualism**).

Recent anthropological concerns with conceptions of **personhood** have examined the way individuals interact with cosmic forces. Hindus have a theory of partibility which sees the individual as made up of immaterial substances which interact and mingle with the essences of other persons and objects. **CL**

See also death; religion; space.

Further reading P. Heelas and A. Lock (eds.), *Indigenous Psychologies*; P. Hountondji, *African Philosophy*; G. Lienhardt, *Divinity and Experience, The Religion of the Dinka*.

INDIVIDUAL PSYCHOLOGY

Individual Psychology is the name of the work of Alfred Adler. His was a pragmatic, concrete **psychology**, based on principles and methods for the acquisition of practical knowledge about our environment. Adler's principle of unity assumes the indivisibility of the mind/body relationship. His principle of dynamism emphasizes the aim and intentionality of psychic processes and goals. We are free to choose, but determined insomuch as choices are self-imposed laws. Adler put forward the principle of cosmic influence: man cannot be considered separate from the thousands of universal influences and, following on from that, community feeling is a reflection of this. His definition of community was familial and social ties, creative activities and ethical function; these feelings can extend to plants and animals, inanimate things and the universe.

A further principle was that of the spontaneous structuring of parts in a whole, that is, that the mind organizes itself according to individual goals. Every aspect of mind, including memories, fantasies, dreams, perceptions and sensations does this. His principle of action and reaction between the individual and the environment described how the individual constantly adjusts and readjusts to the environment. His law of absolute truth describes a fictitious norm of optimal balance between the needs of the individual and those of the many varied communities; this was the unattainable goal for which we strive psychologically. **MJ**

Further reading Alfred Adler, *In Freud's Shadow*; P.E. Stepansky, *Adler in Context*.

INDIVIDUATION

Individuation was Jung's term for the pattern of human growth. **Dreams** are part of the web of psychological factors which create an individual's life pattern. Dreams, watched over a period, reveal these patterns, in their own repeated patterns. Jung saw development as unique to each individual. He uses the example of the tree. No pine, he says, grows in an identical way; the impulse of growth is towards unique realization and cannot be systematically described; it is a living experience, charged with imagination, irrational and ever-changing. There is a central psychic nucleus (the seed) from which the whole structure of consciousness stems. Jung believed that if one person started on the course of individuation then it would affect and benefit other people around them, and that this in turn would have its effect on external events. **MJ**

Further reading Anthony Stevens, *On Jung*.

INDIVIDUALISM

Individualism, in the **political sciences**, is the opposite of collectivism, and is commonly understood as a political doctrine which declares that the aim of a political order should ultimately be to satisfy individual needs, wants and goals rather than the common good, the **general will**, or the 'public interest'. For this reason its critics tend to accuse individualists of being 'egoists' or of embracing 'atomism'. The most influential 19th-century analyst of individualism was Alexis de Tocqueville who detected its virtues and flaws in his writings on *Democracy in America* (1835 and 1840).

In the **social sciences**, 'methodological individualism' asserts that ultimately social scientific explanations must be grounded in the actions of, or facts about, individuals: that is, the actions of social collectivities must be ultimately decomposable into acts, intended or otherwise, of individuals. Methodological individualism is thought by some to be a necessary ingredient of political **liberalism**, and an essential safeguard against **totalitarianism**; others believe that it must be rejected if the social sciences are to understand properly the social nature of human life. **BO'L**

See also action perspective; ethnomethodology; exchange; libertarianism; phenomenological sociology; rational choice theory; social fact; structure-agency debate.

Further reading S. Lukes, *Individualism*; J. O'Neill, *Modes of Individualism and Collectivism*.

INDUCTION

Induction (Latin, 'leading on'), in **philosophy**, is the method of reasoning by which we move from premises concerning what we have observed to a conclusion concerning what we have not. Every emerald that has been observed has been green. From this we infer that the next emerald to be dug out of the ground will be green. Indeed, from the fact that every emerald that has been observed has been green we infer that every emerald, observed or unobserved, is green. Each of these is an inference from premises concerning what has been observed to a conclusion about something that has not.

Inductive arguments are not deductive. A deductive argument is such that if its premises are true, then its conclusion must be true. It is impossible for all of the premises of a deductive argument to be true and yet its conclusion be false. The following argument is deductive: Gabriel is a man; all men are mortal; therefore Gabriel is mortal. This argument is deductive because it is such that if its premises are true, then its conclusion must be true. Its premises may not be true Gabriel may be an angel, not a man, but it is impossible for all of its premises to be true and yet its conclusion be false.

Inductive arguments are not deductive. No inductive argument is such that if its premises are true, then its conclusion must be true. It is possible for all of the premises of an inductive argument to be true and yet its conclusion be false. The claim that every emerald that has been observed was green is consistent with the claim that the next emerald dug out of the ground will not be green. And the statement that every emerald that has been observed was green is consistent with the claim that not every emerald is green. It may just be coincidence that every emerald that has been observed was green, that we have not yet stumbled upon buried deposits of non-green emeralds.

It is possible for all of the premises of an inductive argument to be true and yet its conclusion be false. So if one believes the conclusion of an inductive argument on the grounds that its premises are true, it is always possible that one has acquired a false belief. If one infers from one's true belief that every emerald that has been observed was green that every emerald is green, it is always possible that one has acquired a false belief. This raises the worry that a method of inference which can lead one from true beliefs to false ones cannot be rational.

Is induction rational? That is, do the premises of an inductive argument ever give one reason to believe its conclusion? Since the truth of the premises of an inductive argument is compatible with the falsity of its conclusion, the premises of an inductive argument cannot decisively establish that its conclusion is true. The truth of the premises of an inductive argument cannot make its conclusion certain. But can the truth of the premises of an inductive argument nevertheless give one good reason to believe its conclusion?

Some philosophers claim that induction is rational because it is a form of inference to the best explanation. Given certain phenomena, it is legitimate to infer to the best explanation of those phenomena. There are various competing attempts to explain the fact that every observed emerald has been green. One is that it is simply coincidence that every emerald that has been observed was green, and that we have not yet stumbled upon the buried deposits of non-green emeralds. Another is the explanation that, as a matter of natural law, every emerald is green. Every observed emerald is green because the laws of nature make it necessary that every emerald be green.

Of these two attempted explanations, the second seems best. Indeed, the first is not so much an explanation of the fact that every observed emerald was green as the claim that this fact is just an inexplicable coincidence. So we can infer that the best explanation of the fact that every observed emerald was green is that, as a matter of natural law, every emerald is green. But clearly, if the laws of nature make it necessary that every emerald be green, we can also infer that the next emerald to be dug out of the ground will be green, and that every emerald, observed or unobserved, is green. Induction is rational, because it is a form of inference to the best explanation.

In **mathematics**, induction is one of the major methods used to prove results. (Another is **proof by contradiction**.) Induction only applies to certain kinds of sets, and is typically used to prove results about the natural **numbers**, which form the prototypical example of an inductive set (one in which induction can be carried out).

For the natural numbers, induction works as follows. Suppose P(n) is a statement about the natural number n in **symbolic logic**, and we wish to show that P(k) is true for every possible value of k (so P(0) is true, and P(1), and so on). What we actually show is that P(0) is true, and that if P(n) is true, then so is P(n + 1); the principle of induction is then invoked to tell us that P(k) is true for every natural number k. So induction is used to go from a large set of particular statements to a single general statement.

This use of the principle of induction as a means of mathematical proof is based on the idea of induction in the **philosophy of science**. This idea is that the universe is basically uniform, so that, for example, it is a scientific 'fact' that the Sun will rise tomorrow, because it has done so every day in your experience so far. The idea is that the universe in the near future will be like the universe is now, and is the basis for the idea of the **scientific method**, in which only those experiments which are repeatable are to be studied. Unlike induction in science, however – which is not so much a proof that the Sun will rise tomorrow as a suggestion that this is the most likely hypothesis – proof by induction in mathematics is absolute. **AJ SMcL**

See also deduction; law of nature.

Further reading David Hume, *Enquiries Concerning Human Understanding*; Bertrand Russell, *Problems of Philosophy*; N.W. Gowar, *Basic Mathematical Structures*.

INDUSTRIAL COMMUNISM see **Communism**

INDUSTRIAL DEMOCRACY see **Democracy**

INDUSTRIAL SOCIETY

Industrial society (a society composed of industrielles, industrious workers), in **political science** and the **social sciences**, was a term first coined by the French socialist Saint-Simon. However, the prototype of the idea of industrial society was developed in the work of the Scottish political economists who distinguished 'commercial society' as the most advanced state of human history. Explicit recognition of the distinctiveness of industrial society, as compared with **agrarian society** (or **feudalism**) was widespread among the classical 19th-century sociologists (Herbert Spencer, Auguste Comte, Émile Durkheim, Max Weber and Karl Marx). Any distinct conception of industrial society is normally part of a philosophy of **history** in which industrial society is contrasted with its predecessors, tribal and agrarian societies.

The most distinctive feature of industrial society is that material production of goods and services is its outstanding social activity. Agriculture gives way to industry as the key source of employment and social stratification. Industrial societies are characterized by an extensive **division of labour**, historically unprecedented social and geographical mobility among their workforces, explosive urbanization, the breakdown of **caste** hierarchies in favour of egalitarianism (or at least 'substitutability' among workers), and the centrality of an impersonal and large-scale market or planning mechanism in organizing the production and exchange of goods and services. Industrial societies are also literate, and thereby, at least according to some social theorists, prone to democratization. Above all industrial societies are characterized by the systematic application of cognition, especially the natural sciences, to the organization of work and other social activities.

Theorists of industrial society agree that industrial society fundamentally shapes all economic, social and cultural relations, even if it does not determine them. They focus on five debates: (1) whether industrial societies are subject to breakdown and transformation through class conflict (as Marx hoped and Durkheim feared); (2) whether industrial societies are more militant, or warlike, than agrarian societies (the evidence of our century does not seem to favour Saint-Simon or Spencer's view that they are naturally pacific); (3) whether industrial society is naturally democratic or hierarchical; (4) whether all industrial societies (be they capitalist or communist) must converge on a single type; and (5) whether industrial societies are being displaced by a novel electronic, information-based, postindustrial (or postmodern) order, which some think is emerging in our own time, in which services displace industry, and the social class structure is considerably modified; others see these allegedly novel trends as merely the completion of the logic of industrial principles. **BO'L**

See also capitalism; convergence theory; democracy; environmentalism; historical materialism; modernization; nationalism; mass society; urbanism/urbanization.

Further reading R. Aron, *Eighteen Lectures on Industrial Society*; E. Gellner, *Plough, Sword and Book: the Structure of Human History*.

INFANT SEXUALITY

Infant sexuality had not been thought to exist until Freud came across many images, dating from childhood, through the process of **free association**, involving the mouth and anus as well as the genitals in childhood recollections. The genitals figure less frequently than the mouth and anus, as young children were not equipped for genital sexuality. Freud thought even the youngest children are subject to strong impulses that are repressed. These discoveries shocked the Victorians who believed that children were non-sexual until puberty. From these insights he constructed a whole theory about the nature of **sexuality**. The infant is polymorphously perverse and is transformed by experience into an adult with a highly individual sexuality. **MJ**

Further reading Sigmund Freud, *Three Essasys on the Theory of Sexuality*.

INFERIORITY COMPLEX

The Inferiority Complex was an important concept in Alfred Adler's **individual psychology**. He made a distinction between the natural feelings of inferiority and a subjective complex of inferiority. He defined a mentally healthy person as someone who moves on a horizontal plane and is task-oriented (that is, adjusting his or her behaviour to situations, using common sense). This would deal with three major life tasks: work, friendship and love. (Dreikurs later added a fourth to this: becoming at one with oneself and relating to the cosmos.) Psychological disturbances occur when individuals feel inferior and that they do not have a place. These inferiority feelings are substituted with compensatory striving for personal superiority. Those who feel inferior and act superior cannot do tasks adequately, as neurotic inferiority feelings sabotage the progress. Psychotic individuals distort reality to escape feelings of inferiority; psychopaths, rejecting common sense, have only self-interest, so that no conscience interferes with delusions of grandeur.

Adler thought that inferiority feelings could be the result of educational errors, pushing the child too hard, or of a socially and economically inferior environment. He saw two ways in which people dealt with them: the feeling of superiority already described, and a retreat behind the barricades of weakness while projecting feelings of superiority. **MJ**

Further reading Alfred Adler, *In Freud's Shadow;* P.E. Stepansky, *Adler in Context.*

INFINITY

Before the 19th century, the idea of the infinite was dismissed by mathematicians. Although they knew that there were infinite sets, they felt that nothing interesting could be said about them. Something was either infinite or not, and that was all that could be said.

Towards the end of that century, the German mathematician Georg Cantor (1845–1918) began to think somewhat about the idea of the infinite in mathematics. He tried, for example, to come up with a definition of the concept of the infinite. (Previously, such definitions as 'bigger than any number' were used, but that is in fact a circular definition, because the set of numbers is infinite, so that it amounts to a definition of infinite as 'as big as infinite'.) He also set out to categorize infinite sets.

One of the first things that Cantor realized was that some infinite sets were bigger than others. He defined when two sets were to be of the same size: his definition was based on the intuitive behaviour of the numbers which were already familiar. Two sets are 'equinumerous' (equal in number) if there is a mapping between them which is a bijection, that is, a **function** where the two non-equal elements in the first set have non-equal images, and where every element in the second set has an element which the function maps to it. For example, the sets 1,2 and 5,7 are equinumerous, because the function mapping 1 to 5 and 2 to 7 is a bijection.

The smallest infinite set is that of all the natural **numbers**, and any set which is equinumerous with them is called countable or enumerable, because it is possible to write any such set as an infinite list (as the bijection between it and the natural numbers effectively gives you a first element, and a second element, and so on). Many kinds of numbers are countable, such as the **integers** and the **rational numbers**, while others are not (the way that the **real numbers** are shown to be uncountable is in **algebraic numbers**). It came as a big shock that there were such things as uncountable sets; previously it had seemed that you must be able to list the elements of any set. The reaction was so strong that many mathematicians condemned Cantor's results.

The same ideas give a non-circular definition of the infinite. An infinite set is defined to be one which is equinumerous with some subset of itself (other than the whole thing). For example, the set of natural numbers is equinumerous with the set of even numbers.

Today, however, the infinite is very much part of mathematics, and much of the work in **set theory** in this century has been to do with the various properties of infinite sets; see **axiom of choice** for a discussion of one of the most important. **SMcL**

Further reading R. Rucker, *Infinity and the Mind.*

INFLATION

Inflation occurs when prices rise rapidly for goods and services. A classic case of extreme inflation was the hyperinflation in Germany after World War I, when prices rose so rapidly that printing presses could not keep up by printing new currency of larger denominations; larger numbers were stamped on top of already issued currency. Money to buy everyday items literally required a wheelbarrow to carry it around. The entire monetary system collapsed.

In the US, consumer price index increases of 5% or 6% are considered inflationary, while double-digit increases such as those in the late 1970s cause grave concern. In the 1980s, a number of countries experienced inflation rates of 50%, 80%, 100% and some more than 1000%, rates which were economically and politically destabilizing. Prices of consumer goods and services in an inflation usually outrun most prices of factors of production.

Rises in consumer prices steadily erode the purchasing power of a given currency unit. Inflation would matter little if it was smooth, uniform, and all incomes were adjusted perfectly in line. But it does not work like that. Creditors and those on fixed income, such as many retired persons, lose purchasing power during inflation. Debtors gain by paying back money of lesser purchasing power than when the money was borrowed.

Economists differ in their analysis of the causes of inflation, and therefore in their prescribed cures. **Monetarism** holds that inflation can be reduced only by slowing down the growth of the money supply: in the words of the economist Milton Friedman, 'inflation is always and everywhere a monetary phenomenon'. Many Keynesians (see **Keynesian Theory**), by contrast, tend to believe that inflationary pressures can exist independently of monetary conditions; to run a modern economy at low inflation and low unemployment, they say, governments need an incomes policy. **TF**

Further reading J.M. Keynes, *A Tract on Monetary Reform*; Thomas Sargeant, *Inflation*.

INFORMATION THEORY

Information theory is the branch of **mathematics** concerned with the analysis of communication. Like games, communication is an ancient characteristic of the human race; like **game theory**, information theory was not developed until the 20th century. The first work in the field was that of Claude Elwood Shannon (1916-). There are three major aspects of communication: the actual passing of information from one device to another (via a telephone line, for example, or along the nerves between the ear and the brain); the semantic content of that information (understanding the meaning of what is said); and the effective content of that information (the emotional content of what is said – the use of propa-

gandist words or the tone of voice, for instance). These three areas all affect one another, and there is considerable overlap between them.

The efficiency of the passing of information is obviously crucial to making any assessment of the meaning of the information in the other two parts of communication. Shannon principally investigated the first, engineering aspect, because it was most susceptible to mathematical analysis. Shannon's work revealed a great deal about the way that we communicate and also about what it is possible to communicate (or what it is possible to know about A given knowledge about B and the connections between A and B). For example, about half of the content of spoken English is redundant, which is why it is possible easily to correct spelling errors caused by inefficient transmission.

Information theory has had a massive effect on the way that electronic communications have been developed during the 20th century, particularly through **coding theory**. It also has applications, often unrecognized, in other fields such as **economics. SMcL**

INNATE IDEAS

An innate (Latin, 'inborn') idea, in **philosophy**, is an idea in the mind before it has any sensory experiences. Empiricist philosophers such as Locke argued that before it has any sensory experiences the mind is a *tabula rasa* or 'blank tablet', empty of all ideas. One of Locke's objections to the hypothesis of innate ideas is that if there were any innate ideas, they would be universal – they would be possessed by adults and infants, and by members of different tribes and cultures. But no idea has ever been established as universal in this sense. **AJ**

See also empiricism.

Further reading John Locke, 'An Essay Concerning Human Understanding'; J.L. Mackie, *Problems from Locke*.

INNATENESS

The thesis of innateness, in **linguistics**, has

been reworked and brought to prominence since the 1960s by Noam Chomsky. However, the idea that human beings are born with certain aspects of knowledge already in place is in fact very old, stretching back at least as far as Plato. Chomsky asserts that several specific aspects of linguistic knowledge must be inborn in the child. Without this genetic headstart, it is argued that children would be unable to learn their native **language** as quickly and efficiently as they patently do.

Currently, the most important argument advanced in favour of innateness is the so-called argument from the poverty of the stimulus. The 'stimulus' is taken to be the language of parents and care-givers which provides a model of the grammar which the child must learn. It is asserted that there are certain highly abstract principles of language which are simply not present in the input stimulus. Yet even very young children, nevertheless, have a clear grasp of this kind of linguistic knowledge. The necessary conclusion for Chomsky is that the child must be genetically 'pre-wired' with just those aspects of language knowledge which are absent from the input. In fact, empirical demonstrations that the stimulus genuinely is impoverished have never been provided, since it is extraordinarily difficult to show that the child's knowledge could not just as easily be explained by a general ability to deduce the structure of a given linguistic principle. Even so, current debate is centred not so much on whether aspects of language and language learning could be innate, as on precisely what is innate. **MS**

INSPIRATION see Thought

INSTINCT

In the **life sciences**, the term instinct (Latin, 'pricked in') is generally used to describe animal behaviour which is not learned. In antiquity, it was considered that most animal behaviour was governed by innate impulses. Although many conceded that animals could show intelligence, most philosophers denied that animals reasoned when performing functions such as nest-building in birds or web-weaving in spiders. Avicenna (980–1037) defined instinctive

behaviour as that which was performed invariably; this definition persisted into the 17th century. In the 18th and 19th centuries some, such as Erasmus Darwin, admitted that animals could reason. This developed into the idea that animals exhibited habitual behaviour because their environment was relatively constant. This was explained by Charles Darwin as the action of **natural selection** on inheritable behaviour patterns. In the modern context, ethologists (see **ethology**) recognize that instinct is represented by behaviour which is substantially determined by genetic information, and thus under the influence of natural selection, but that there is an element of environmental stimulation in all behaviour.

Instincts are a vital part of Freud's psychological theories. He assumed that all human behaviour is governed by instinct. Before 1920, he thought that the two instinctual drives in man were the sexual instinct (a general drive towards physical pleasure) and the ego instinct (which strives towards self-preservation. Hunger and fear, for example, are responses to reality made possible by the ego instinct.) Freud regarded psychological phenomena as being the result of conflict between these two opposing instincts. The sexual, instinctual wishes strive for realization and the ego instinct acts to repress them.

The phenomenon of **narcissism** upset this picture because it did not fit neatly into either category. Narcissism was seen as an over-active ego instinct striving for self-preservation and aggrandisement, but it also led to a lack of sexual drive. Freud could no longer satisfactorily separate out the instincts into the two categories: sexual and ego instincts. He solved the problem by subdividing the sexual instinct into object and ego libido. In this way the instincts came from the same libidinal force and the two aspects of narcissism could be accounted for. But this now meant that sexual libido and object (ego) libido came from the same source of energy: human beings were motivated by a single drive. This no longer accounted adequately for the conflict and compromise in human nature. In 1920, therefore, Freud postulated a new instinctual drive: the **death**

instinct. There were once again two opposing instincts, the sexual instinct and the death instinct. **MJ RB**

See also sociobiology; thought.

Further reading Raymond E. Fancher, *Psychoanalytical Psychology, The Development of Freud's Thought.*

INTEGERS

Integers (Latin, 'unbroken') are the first step onwards from the natural **numbers**. They arose much later, not really being accepted by mathematicians until after the Middle Ages, and they extend the natural numbers by the concept of owing. In the natural numbers, many equations of the form $a + b = c$ can be solved. For example, the solution of $a + 2 = 4$ is $a = 2$. However, there is no solution of the equation $a + 4 = 2$; a ends up 'owing' 2. In the integers, the solution of such equations always exists; in this case, it is written -2.

If the natural numbers are viewed as an infinite line 0 1 2 3 and so on, the integers are an infinite line extended in both directions rather than only one (the natural numbers have a beginning, 0, while the integers do not), so that we have ... -3 -2 -1 0 1 2 3 ..., the '...' representing indefinite continuation of the sequence in both directions.

In the integers, then, there is a solution to every equation involving addition of integers. However, when multiplication is brought in, there are once again equations which do not have solutions. For example, $x \times 2 = 4$ has a solution, but $x \times 4 = 2$ does not. The integers were therefore not powerful enough, and so the **rational numbers** were constructed. **SMcL**

INTEGRAL CALCULUS see Analysis; Calculus

INTEGRATION

Integration (from Latin *integrare*, 'to make one'), in **political science** and the **social sciences**, refers to the processes by which members of different groups are incorporated into a society, organization, institution or **state**. Integration may occur socially, politically or economically, but the term is most precisely used to refer to political or civic integration treating everybody with citizenship rights as equal citizens. Social integration involves coming to share a common **language** and **culture**, which may be described as **assimilation** if the original cultural differences between peoples completely disappear, or **acculturation** if one group adapts to the culture of another. Political integration may involve the incorporation of existing states, territories or communities into a larger structure. Thus, for example, the European Community represents an experimental attempt to create a new political union out of existing states and peoples. Economic integration usually involves the integration of markets, either to control production and price levels, for example OPEC (the Organization of Petroleum Exporting countries), or to create conditions for free trade as exemplified by NAFTA (the North American Free Trade Agreement) which partially integrated the markets of Canada, the US and Mexico.

In psychoanalytical theory, integration is part of development. According to classical (Freudian) **psychoanalysis**, the psyche starts as an unintegrated id and becomes inegrated through ego development.

According to later **objects relations** theory, the child starts off with a primary integrated ego; **defence mechanisms**, reacting to anxiety, act to split off repressed parts of the self. Psychoanalysis is then a process of retrieving lost parts of the self and reintegrating them into a more whole self.

Jung saw integration as a process of **individuation**, where movements between introversion (nearer the **unconscious**) and extroversion (nearer the conscious) turned cyclically to create periods of integration. **MJ BO'L**

See also nationalism.

Further reading K. Deutsch, *Nationalism and Social Communication*; Freida Fordham, *An Introduction to Jung's Psychology.*

INTELLECT see Thought

INTENSIONALITY AND EXTENSIONALITY

A sentence is intensional, in **philosophy**, if substituting co-referring terms in it may change its truth value. Suppose that Mary is the mass murderer. Then 'Mary' and 'the mass murderer' are co-referring terms: both refer to the same thing. Further suppose that Fred admires Mary. Then the statement 'Fred admires Mary' is true. Substituting co-referring terms – replacing 'Mary' with 'the mass murderer' – we get the sentence 'Fred admires the mass murderer'. So substituting co-referring terms has taken us from a true sentence to one which may well be false. After all, Fred may not know that Mary is the mass murderer.

In contrast, a sentence is extensional if substituting co-referring terms in it is guaranteed to preserve its truth value. Consider the sentence 'Mary is blonde'. Substituting co-referring terms, we get the sentence 'the mass murderer is blonde'. If the original sentence is true, the second must be true. And if the original sentence is false, the second must be false. For the first sentence is extensional, and the second is derived from it simply by substituting co-referring terms. **AJ**

See also intentionality.

Further reading S. Haack, *Philosophy of Logic*; M. Sainsbury, *Logical Forms*.

INTENTIONALITY

Intentionality (Latin, 'tend onto'), in **philosophy**, is aboutness, or object directedness. The history book is intentional because it is about the development of the steam engine. And the picture is intentional because it is a picture of Windsor castle, because it is 'directed at' the object Windsor castle.

Most types of mental state are intentional. One cannot have a **belief** that is not a belief about something. Desires, hopes, fears and love are also essentially intentional. My intention to go to the shops is intentional; it is about something. But not all intentional mental states are intentions; beliefs are intentional but are not intentions. Nor should intentionality be con-

fused with intensionality. A sentence is intensional just if substituting co-referring terms in it may change its truth value. But not all intentional phenomena are sentences; consider pictures and books. The sentence 'Mary is blonde' is intentional, it is about something, but it is not intensional. So intentionality is clearly different from intensionality. **AJ**

See also intensionality and extensionality; mental phenomena.

Further reading R. Cummins, *Meaning and Mental Representation*; J. Searle, *Intentionality*.

INTERACTIONISM

Interactionists, in **philosophy**, are dualists, holding that the mental is not physical and that the physical is not mental. They further hold that the mental and physical causally interact. Bodily damage, which is physical and not mental, causes pain, which is mental and not physical. And pain, which is mental and not physical, causes aversion behaviour, which is physical and not mental. The non-physical mental and the non-mental physical causally influence each other. **AJ**

See also dualism; epiphenomenalism; parallelism.

Further reading J. Foster, *The Immaterial Self*; W.D. Hart, *Engines of the Soul*.

INTERFEROMETRY

Interferometry, the study of interference effects in optical systems, helped prove that light both behaves as a wave function and had a particle nature. The wave character implied that in-phase components of separate light rays would constructively interfere, or sum their intensities and become brighter, whereas out of phase components would destructively interfere or cancel their intensities and become duller.

Thomas Young performed an experiment in 1800 demonstrating the interference of light by passing sunlight through pinholes in an opaque material, and observing light and dark interference fringes on a screen. Young used this experiment to calculate the wavelength of light waves and subsequently discovered that interferometers can be used as very accurate measurement instruments. Indeed the metre standard length is defined as 1,650,763.73 wavelengths of light from the Krypton 86 isotope, the measurements being performed using an interferometer.

Applications of interferometry include x-ray crystallography, where diffraction or 'bending' of x-rays around atoms in a crystal produces an interference pattern which presents details of the material's structure. The invention of crystallography helped prove that crystals had a regular molecular structure. Holograms, first produced by Gabor in 1948, record and reproduce 3-dimensional images by application of interferometry techniques. AC

See also wave-particle duality of light.

INTERNAL COMBUSTION ENGINE

There are basically two kinds of internal combustion engine. In one the fuel burns within a cylinder, exerting pressure on a piston which is generally connected to a crank to produce rotation; the other is the gas turbine where the combustion produces hot gases under pressure which are guided by vanes to the impellers of the turbine, producing rotation according to the same fundamental laws as govern the windmill.

Gaseous hydrocarbon from oilfields, or produced from coal and liquid fuels from oil wells, coal or fermented sugar, can be used in both kinds of engines. On a small scale sewage gases and methane from cattle manure have been used.

Credit for inventing the internal combustion engine is generally given to Nikolaus Otto who in 1867 designed and produced the Otto reciprocating engine. In this, a mixture of gas and air is drawn into the cylinder on the downstroke. The valves close and the piston moving upwards compresses the mixture heating it until combustion starts at a 'hot spot' on the cylinder head. The mixture then burns, increasing the cylinder pressure four- or fivefold, pushing the piston down in the 'working stroke' and giving a power output. After this stroke the inlet valve opens, the piston

moves up again ready to restart the cycle with air/fuel induction. Benz in 1885 developed the use of petrol, producing the first internal combustion powered wheeled vehicle. The operation of these engines was greatly simplified by the development of the carburettor to give a uniform mixture of air and fuel vapour, ascribed to Maybach in 1892, and the application by Daimler of the sparking plug to ignite the fuel and air mixture at a precise time in the engine cycle.

The compactness of the internal combustion engines and its high power-to-weight ratio were big advantages over the **steam engine**, which had dominated industry and transport until this time. In the USA, Ford produced the Model T automobile, making personal powered vehicles widely available at low cost. Buses had existed from the early 19th century and progressed from horse traction to steam, but they only really made headway with the application of electrical power in tramways and the internal combustion engine as we know it now.

Present-day buses, trucks and lorries are generally powered by the engine developed by Diesel (1892). This has no electrical ignition system. Air is drawn into the cylinder and compressed to a pressure of up to $600lb/in^2$ (4MPa; 40 atmospheres). Diesel fuel oil is then injected into the cylinder where it burns immediately and rapidly because of the temperature of the compressed air. Because of the high pressures developed Diesel engines require to be stronger and therefore heavier than petrol or gas engines. Their virtues however are long life, less frequent maintenance requirements, rugged construction, and economy due to use of cheaper fuel.

The first aircraft used internal combustion petrol engines, initially with the cylinders in line as in present cars but soon in a more compact lighter form with the cylinders placed on the radius of a circle centred on the crankshaft. During World War II the UK and Germany developed almost simultaneously the concept of the gas turbine. This has proved so successful that nearly all planes are now powered by 'jets' rather than reciprocating combustion engines. Gas turbines are used also for ships and for electric power production.

The advantage of the gas turbine over conventional coal-fired steam turbine generators is its compact size and its very rapid start up time, allowing it to be brought into service quickly to keep the electrical supply in balance with sudden changes in the power requirements. There will always be controversy over the use of gas turbines which are dependent on the availability of limited supplies of natural gas compared to the much greater stocks of coal. **AA**

See also transportation.

Further reading D.I. Ruquhart, *The Internal Combustion Engine and How It Works.*

INTERNALIZATION

Internalization, in **sociology**, means the process by which an individual learns and accepts the social **values**, rules and **norms** of conduct relevant to his or her social group or wider society. In **psychology**, internalization is a basic concept in Freud's theory of personality development. **DA**

See also assimilation; culture; functionalism; socialization; social control; social integration; social order; social structure; society.

Further reading K. Danziger, *Socialization.*

INTERNATIONAL DIVISION OF LABOUR

In the 1970s, it became increasingly common for problems of unemployment and industrial closure in the UK and other Western countries to be blamed on the advent of a new international division of labour. As part of this, it was often asserted that manufacturing jobs were being exported to developing countries. The concept extends Adam Smith's classic theory of the **division of labour** to deal with the industrial and employment structure of whole groups of countries. It was used for the capitalist world and excluded the Soviet bloc, which was economically independent until recently. However, before it is possible to discuss the new concept, it is necessary to understand the old.

The old international division of labour (OIDL) existed between 1850 and 1950. The key point was that manufacturing industry was heavily concentrated in western Europe, the USA and later Japan. These countries were industrialized, both in the sense that they dominated the main industries of the period – textiles, iron and steel – and in the sense that they became developed in terms of incomes, education and consumption. The rest of the world was increasingly linked to the metropolitan countries, mainly as a source of agricultural products but also minerals, and as a market for manufactured products. Much of international trade was channelled by the colonial empires of the time, which added political dominance to economic dominance. However, the USA was reluctant to take the colonial route and relied mainly on economic power, especially in the independent countries of Latin America. As the heavy engineering industries were complemented by manufacture of consumer goods, the industrialized countries moved towards mass consumption and welfare systems, which gave their whole populations a high standard of living compared to the mass of the population in the colonies, though this advantage was shared by the Europeans in a few settler colonies.

The long established pattern of the OIDL changed from the mid-1960s, for reasons which are still being debated. The **Bretton Woods** system of fixed exchange rates crumbled and rates of profit fell, especially in the US, which also went into balance of payments deficit and financed it by exporting dollars and creating inflation. Manufacturing companies sought ways of restoring profitability, and many of them chose to do so by 'going multinational': that is, internationalizing production to lower costs and open new markets. This led to the salient feature of the new international division of labour (NIDL), the emergence of the newly industrializing countries (NICs), notably Brazil, South Korea, Taiwan, Hong Kong and Singapore. The obvious attraction was cheap labour, but investors also sought some experience of industry and an adequate infrastrucure as well as political reliability. As a result, the new industrialization involved a small group of middle-income countries rather than a general spread of industrialization into the less-developed countries. Another new group of countries emerged as OPEC quadrupled oil prices in 1974. These countries included Mexico and Nigeria as well as the familiar oil exporters of the Middle East. Their economic growth was even faster than that of the NICs and some became more affluent than the developed countries, but the sale of oil did not bring about the industrialization of the whole society.

The degree of change involved should not be overstated: the previous groups of developed and less-developed countries continued to exist in spite of the emergence of the NICs and oil exporters. By 1980 the multinationals employed 44 million people and American multinationals employed as many people outside the US as the whole US labour force but only 4 million were in NICs, and total employment in the developed countries was 300 million. So the main change was internationalization of the economies of the developed countries rather than a move to the NICs. Nor was the growth that did occur in the NICs unequivocally beneficial: much of the new industry of the NICs was owned or financed from developed countries and only South Korea seems to have developed sufficient locally-owned industry to aspire to economic independence. By the 1980s, indiscreet bank lending in NICs and some oil exporters had created a huge debt problem which was magnified by interest rate rises until countries like Brazil and Mexico could not pay even the interest on their loans. Although many debts have been renegotiated, no debtor has reneged on the debt and many countries are now following austerity programmes imposed by the IMF. Whatever this may do for their credit rating, it does not help to achieve the incomes and infrastructure which would challenge for developed country status.

A development since the late 1980s is that the former Soviet bloc, which was previously regarded as developed, though at a lower level than the First World, has now been opened to the capitalist world economy and experienced dramatic loss of industry and jobs. It is too soon to assess what will happen, but it is far from certain that their developed status will be retained.

It is ironic that these countries have chosen to join the capitalist world economy at a time when, in spite of two decades of rapid change, the problems of employment and profitability have not been solved. Indeed, at the time of writing (1993) one of the key elements of the internationalization of the world economy, the General Agreement on Tariffs and Trade (GATT), is on the verge of breakdown. If the future is one of increased protectionism by trading blocs, the international division of labour may be heading for another period of slow change. PS

INTERNATIONAL MONETARY FUND (IMF)

The International Monetary Fund (IMF) is the supervisor and safety net for the international monetary system: an international organization created in 1944 to eliminate foreign exchange restrictions, provide convertibility of currency and encourage **exchange rate** stability to promote trade. The Fund was set up at **Bretton Woods**, along with its sister institution the **World Bank**, to supervise the fixed exchange rate system.

The original IMF agreement was created to assist the functioning of an international **gold standard** system following the end of World War II. Each nation set an official par value for its currency in terms of gold or in terms of the US dollar. The US pledged to maintain the value of the dollar at $35 per fine ounce of gold by buying and selling gold at that price internationally. Some nations did not have enough gold for their currency to exchange freely for gold. Those nations set the par value of their money in terms of US dollars, using dollars for their currency reserves. Thus they were indirectly on the gold standard. Market exchange rates were to be kept within 1% of par value by the use of each nation's stabilization fund. If a nation developed a chronic deficit in its balance of payments and a steady drain on its foreign exchange reserves, it could propose a change in its official par value. It happened that, in practice, countries would devalue their currency without prior approval by the IMF, to prevent speculator profits from the advance notice that an approval process would provide.

The IMF provided for a fixed exchange-rate system based on a gold exchange standard in the short run, while in the long run, some flexibility was provided through a mechanism for changes in official par values. The IMF could also lend to countries with balance-of-payments deficits with funds from the IMF holdings of gold and currency. The holdings arose from subscriptions of member nations determined by their quotas, which reflected each nation's economic importance in the world economy.

On 1 January 1970, the IMF was authorized to create Special Drawing Rights (SDRs) as a reserve asset that countries could use to settle international accounts. This potentially turned the IMF into a world central bank with the ability to create international reserves. But SDRs are allocated among participating countries according to their quotas, so they have been of limited help in coping with balance-of-payments problems.

In 1971, the US stopped honouring its obligation to sell gold at $35 per ounce, an action which broke the dollar loose from its gold moorage. In 1973, European countries and Japan began to let their currencies float against the dollar, and the world was on a flexible exchange system.

With the end of fixed exchange rates, the International Monetary Fund lost an important part of its purpose and its mechanism for achieving its goals. The IMF continues to pursue foreign exchange stability by being a source of short-term credit to acquire foreign exchange to pay for imports when exports and capital movements are insufficient to generate enough foreign exchange. The borrowing country is expected to take steps to correct the imbalance and, also, countries with persistent trade surpluses are encouraged to take steps to correct this imbalance. **TF**

INTERNATIONAL RELATIONS

The name international relations is a misnomer shared by the mistitled multidisciplinary academic subject of inter-national relations and the sub-discipline of international law. The real meaning of 'international' is 'inter-state': that is, relationships between states, rather than nations – thus, 'internationalism', properly employed, expresses solidarity and equality among nations rather than states.

The relations between polities and states were not of central concern to the earliest political theorists and lawyers (although Aristotle and Machiavelli wrote on the subject) but from the 1600s onwards jurists like Grotius, Pufendorf and Vattel addressed the question of whether there was a 'law of nations' co-equal to the domestic law of states, and political philosophers like Rousseau and Kant addressed the possibility of moral conduct in war and the need for a stable and just international order. It was the distinctive dynamics of the European states' systems which gave rise to the distinct theoretical discipline of international relations, although this did not develop institutional expression until the aftermath of World War I led academics to focus on the questions of why the war had occurred, and how a war of such magnitude could be avoided in future. This approach, based on a liberal view of human nature, was subsequently labelled **idealist** because it assumed that rational actors could agree that war was both unwanted and avoidable. This thinking was reflected in the formation of the League of Nations. Renewed challenges to world peace by the rise of Japan and Germany in the 1930s led to a reappraisal of the assumptions of the idealist school.

The self-proclaimed realist school, spearheaded by the English historian E.H. Carr and followed in the 1940s by Hans Morgenthau, was heavily influenced by **Machiavellianism**. The realists denied that a liberal conception of human nature could become the basis of world peace. Morgenthau declared that 'peace and security' is the **ideology** of satisfied powers. Realists assume that relations between states are governed by interests which are largely immune from morality. Power is central to this approach: the primary interest of the **state** and the primary means of fulfilling secondary interests. On this view the stabilization of the inherently anarchic world system is a result of the achievement of a balance of power.

In the 1950s and 1960s, the realist approach was challenged but ultimately reinforced by thinkers from the **behaviourist** school, who adopted more inductive, and empirical methodologies, which were especially influenced by theories of decision-making and **game theory**. Realism remains the most dominant of the Western schools of thought in international relations. However, another theoretical approach has challenged the realist's view of the state as the most important unit of analysis. Thinkers broadly classified as **pluralists** emphasize the influence of groups at the sub-state and transnational levels on the diplomacy and foreign policies of states. The influence of arms industries upon strategic balances is an example of the policy-shaping capacities exerted by non-state agents.

A third school of thought in international relations can be defined as structuralist or neo-Marxist. Work in this tradition emphasizes the globally systemic character of international relations in contrast to the state- or group-centred approaches described above. **Structuralists** tend to adopt models in which international capital is the primary determinant of relations between states. Although the realist school remains the dominant approach to the study of international relations, notably in foreign policy analysis, pluralist political thinking, especially that which emphasizes the importance of social and political movements and ideas like **nationalism**, **ethnicity**, **feminism** and **environmentalism** is likely be particularly influential in the post-Cold War era. **BO'L**

Further reading Hollis, Martin and Steve Smith, *Explaining and Understanding International Relations.*

INTERPRETATION

Interpretation, in **psychiatry**, a method developed by Freud for the analysis of material brought up in **free associations** and **dreams**, consists of looking at two types of context: latent and manifest content. The manifest content is what is actually said to

the analyst or what is actually seen in the dream; the ideas behind these are the latent content. Freud's masterwork *The Interpretation of Dreams* spends much of its large volume looking at the relationship between the latent and manifest content, and the systems of defence which operate in the presentation of ideas or the memories of dreams. The latent content in dreams, for Freud, consists of wish-fulfilling phantasies, compared with the reporting of everyday occurrences, and of neurotic symptoms which could be the outcome of actual experiences; all of which can be the focus of interpretation.

Memories, recollections of recent events, reports of feelings and the telling of dreams are examined by someone with a knowledge of symbolism and an understanding of unconscious processes. Accuracy is tested by the patient's response: he or she will either confirm it by relating some other experience which corresponds to the interpretation, or will not respond to, or accept, the interpretation for reasons of resistance, or because the analyst has not interpreted correctly. The function of interpretations is to increase self-awareness and to aid integration by making the patient conscious of his or her internal unconscious workings and motivation. **MJ**

Further reading Sigmund Freud, *The Interpretation of Dreams;* C. Rycroft, *Imagination and Reality.*

INTERPRETATIVE ANTHROPOLOGY

Interpretative anthropology was introduced by the American anthropologist Clifford Geertz, whose influential book *The Interpretation of Culture* (1973) defined **culture** as a system of meanings in terms of which people interpreted their experiences and guided their actions. The way to understand these meanings was to elicit the full range of associations generated by objects and events. Culture was seen as a network of shared symbols, whose meanings were created by the significances they accumulated in daily life. These 'networks of significance' serve to locate individual experience in some kind of framework, as well as to explain it. A famous example used by Geertz is borrowed from the philosopher Gilbert Ryle: a wink and an involuntary eye twitch are physically identical events, but one is loaded with a code of meanings, while the other is not intended to convey any information.

Interpretative anthropology borrowed from **hermeneutic** trends in **philosophy**. In anthropology, hermeneutics considers the role of the observer in the interpretation of knowledge. One of Geertz's primary concerns was how to avoid imposing meaning from outside. Despite the complexity of cultural systems, he saw them as amenable to interpretation. By paying much more attention to the explanations given by locals, he could synthesize both perspectives.

Interpretative anthropology has led to an increased interest in 'insider' explanations over the theorization of 'outsider' anthropologists. Earlier functional analysis had tended to impose its own models on the societies under study. Interpretative anthropology emphasized actual descriptions and the significance of the specific terms used, as well as how they could be translated into terms comprehensible to the anthropologist's own culture without misrepresenting local interpretations. Despite this, critics have argued that an emphasis on local viewpoints is still problematic if culture is treated as a homogenous whole. **CL**

See also field work; symbols.

INTERSUBJECTIVE

Something is intersubjective, in **philosophy**, if it is not objective, but there are ways of reaching agreement upon it between different subjects. It is not an objective (that is, mind-independent) fact that mud tastes horrible, but different subjects agree that mud tastes horrible. **AJ**

See also objective and subjective.

INTONATION, TUNING AND TEMPERAMENT

Intonation is the degree of precision with which a singer, or a performer on an instrument without fixed tuning, can pitch a musical note according to standards of accuracy agreed within a musical culture. The musical language of a culture not only influences the concept of what is 'in tune' and 'out of tune', but also determines the tuning and temperament of its instruments. Temperament is a system of tuning in which small, almost imperceptible adjustments are made to the notes of the 'natural' musical scale (that is, the scale determined by the physical laws of sound), so that the distances between certain similar or successive pairs of tones are identical. Many ancient societies, such as the Chinese, Greeks and Hindus, evolved their theories of tuning and temperament according to mathematical principles associated with their religious and philosophical beliefs, including **cosmology**, numerology and sacred proportions.

The system of tuning modern, Western musical instruments with fixed pitch is known as 'equal temperament'. In this, all the intervals between the consecutive notes of, for example, a piano are tuned equally, so that when a melody is played commencing on any of the 12 different notes it will always possess identical tonal characteristics. Contrary to this Western practice of standardization, in Bali, for example, not only does each *gamelan* have its own individual tuning, but also pairs of similar instruments within each orchestra are tuned slightly differently to one another, creating a distinctive musical colouring or timbre.

In many folk, popular or non-European musical traditions the concept of intonation is concerned less with accuracy of pitch than with its subtle variation or inflection. This indicates that pitches can exist between the notes of the musical scale or between the

Table of cents

	C	D	E	F	G	A	B	C
Equal temperament	200	200	100	200	200	200	100	
Ancient Greek	204	204	90	204	204	204	90	
Indian	218	164	109	218	218	164	109	
Javanese	167	245	125	146	249	165	103	

notes of a piano, and that this tonal material is also culturally conditioned. For example, whereas the note-bending on a Western **rock** guitar, on a **jazz** trombone or by a **Blues** singer may be perfectly acceptable to Western ears, similar inflections on an Indian sitar, a Japanese flute or by a Moroccan *muezzin* may seem totally alien. Music is often described as a 'universal language', but it is the intonation, tuning and temperament of each musical culture that creates its own dialect.

The diversity of tunings between different societies may be best demonstrated using the system of measurement created by A.J. Ellis in the 1880s. In his system the distance between each adjacent note on an equally-tempered piano is calculated as 100 cents. Using only the white keys of the piano, the table of cents provides comparisons of typical tunings from ancient Greece, India and Java. **SSt**

See also chromaticism; tonality.

Further reading Hugh Boyle, *Intervals, Scales & Temperaments: Introduction to the Study of Musical Intonation.*

INTROJECTION see Defence Mechanism

INTROSPECTION

Introspection (Latin, 'looking inwards') is the faculty by which one is aware of one's own mental states and not other people's. One introspects that one is in pain, that one is hungry, and that one is becoming angry although one has yet to express one's anger behaviourally. One does not always acquire knowledge of one's own mental states by introspection. One may learn that one is angry with a friend by inferring this from the way in which one keeps avoiding them, and not by introspecting the anger one has repressed, in just the way that one can infer how someone else is feeling from their behaviour. **AJ**

Further reading G. Ryle, *The Concept of Mind.*

INTROVERSION AND EXTRAVERSION

Introversion (Latin, 'turning in') and Extraversion (Latin, 'turning out') are part of Jung's theory of types which he postulated to help create a focus within the complexity of human growth. They are types but not dogmatic descriptions of individuals. Each individual can be more or less categorized as having both 'types'. Ghandi, for example, was described by Jung as both ascetic (introvert) and politician (extrovert). Jung thought that we needed both qualities in balance. Being too introverted is an over identification with the internal innate potential. Extraversion is an over identification with the environment. Each in extreme is seen as a pathological imbalance: schizoid withdrawal and the hysterical personality. **MJ**

Further reading Jolande Jacobi, *The Psychology of C.G. Jung.*

INTUITION see Ethical Intuitionism

INTUITIONISM

Scepticism in **mathematics** over the new **set theory** of Georg Cantor (1845–1918) (and in particular his work on **infinity**) led to the formation of the school of mathematics known as intuitionism in the early years of the 20th century. The main thesis of the school was that the basis of mathematics should be in thought rather than in **logic** or symbols, and in particular, the basic intuitions of the construction of an infinite series of numbers. The chief proponent of this idea was Luitzen Egbertus Jan Brouwer (1881–1966). Intuitionists felt that the idea of the infinite in the work of Cantor was counter-intuitive, and that it should therefore be avoided. Their main argument was that in order to meaningfully assert the existence of something (for example, a number satisfying certain properties), it is necessary to give a definite method of (at least theoretically) constructing this object. They rejected the ideas of **formalism** and **logicism** (which were mainly to do with the language in which mathematical thought should be expressed), to say that mathematical concepts have an existence independent of the language used to express them, and therefore that the only important property a language should have is that it should express mathematical ideas clearly.

They argued, to counter Cantor's set theory, that it is never actually necessary to look at the whole of an infinite set at once; only finite parts of it are used at any one time. The set of numbers, for example, is only a 'potential infinity'. The followers of this school attempted to show the results that other mathematicians proved using only finite and constructive methods (that is, by direct construction); many of their proofs were forced to be much longer and more difficult to follow. Intuitionism tended always to follow behind the mainstream of mathematics, rather than to produce its own results. In the end, intuitionism perished under its own weight as mathematicians turned to the increasingly easier methods of mainstream mathematics; professional mathematicians became more confident about handling infinite sets, and so very few mathematicians still have any philosophical or intuitive quarrels with the idea of infinite sets. **SMcL**

INVISIBLE HAND

The 'invisible hand' is the economist Adam Smith's (1723–90) characterization of the way the capitalist system works or ideally might work. Smith put forward his ideas in his book, *Inquiry into the Nature and Causes of the Wealth of Nations* (1776), which is still regarded as a bible of **classical economics**. According to Smith, when all individuals act from self-interest, spurred on by the profit motive, then society as a whole prospers, with no apparent regulator at work. It is, wrote Smith, as if an 'invisible hand' guided the actions of individuals to combine for the common wealth. Unfortunately, visible hands are also needed, since some individuals' pursuit of self-interest overlaps or conflicts with others' self-interest. Examples of visible controllers include policemen, governments and anti-trust agencies. Governments sometimes have to aid the invisible hand by passing anti-trust legislation and breaking up monopolies. Too much regulation, on the other hand, can disrupt the market and give the invisible hand arthritis.

Adam Smith would never have thought of himself as a revolutionary; he was only explaining what to him was very clear, sensible and conservative. But he gave the world the image of itself for which it had been searching. After *The Wealth of Nations*, people began to see the world about themselves with new eyes. They saw how the tasks they did fitted into the whole of society, and they saw that society as a whole was proceeding at a majestic pace toward a distant but clearly visible goal. **TF**

IRON LAW OF OLIGARCHY

The **élite theorist** Roberto Michels formulated the 'iron law of oligarchy' in his book *Political Parties* (1911). In simple terms, he asserted that 'who says organization, says oligarchy'. Michels argued that all political parties, including those which profess democratic values, become the instruments of their leaders who eventually become a self-interested and self-satisfied oligarchy.

Michels' arguments were primarily derived from his study of the German Social Democratic Party at the turn of this century. Using ideas from the then fashionable 'crowd psychology', he claimed that any mass of citizens is psychologically incapable of complex decisions. Masses need leaders who can stir them out of apathy, and once organized they continue to defer to their leaders. Moreover, the large size and complex tasks of mass political parties create the need for leaders with expertise who enjoy stable tenure of office, but this organizational logic further increases oligarchic tendencies. Finally, Michels thought that it was in the nature of things for élites to advance their own interests and power at the expense of those of their followers. His personal pessimism about the prospects for **democracy** hastened his intellectual evolution towards **fascism**.

Critics of the 'iron law of oligarchy' make three key observations. First, Michels' law is a truism if it merely says that leaders are different from the led and that key decisions are normally made by minorities. Second, Michels does not establish that there is no countervailing 'iron law of democracy', whereby leaders who stray from the wishes of the led are overthrown by revolts from below. He simply neglects the possibility that party leaders are kept in check by their activists and the possibility that rivals will displace them if they betray the cause. Third, Michels' arguments are time-bound. An 'iron law of emulation' did operate in early 20th-century Europe, where socialist parties had to mimic the centralized authoritarian state to which they were opposed. However, it does not follow that all political parties have to display unremediable oligarchic traits in all political systems. **BO'L**

IRONY

Irony (Greek, 'dissimulation') is a technique used in everyday speech, in **literature** and most especially in **drama**. Simple irony involves two people only: the person using irony (or being the subject of it) and the person perceiving it. Complex irony involves more than two people: the person(s) using irony, the subject(s) and the perceiver(s). In all cases, irony consists of a statement being made which, whether or not so intended by the maker, has a hidden layer of meaning to the perceiver. Thus, if someone says to a slugabed, 'You're up early', this is simple irony; if someone says to a third party, about a slugabed, 'He's up early', this is complex irony.

Irony can be apparent only to the user, so that outsiders are unaware of it. In that case the user is also the perceiver, and the satisfaction is entirely solipsistic. But most irony involves a kind of collusion between the user and the perceiver: a collusion against the world or other people which is a form of bond. In 'serious' literature and drama, collusion is usually between author and audience. The author lets us into a secret not shared by the characters in a given situation, allowing us to take a lateral view, as it were, to see nuances and overtones not superficially present. In Homer's *Odyssey*, when Odysseus' elderly dog Argos greets his long-lost master – the only creature in Ithaka to recognize – him our appreciation of the scene is deepened by the knowledge, already planted for us by Homer, but not apparent to Odysseus, that the dog is on the point of death. Romeo's last speeches over the body of Juliet, in Shakespeare's *Romeo and Juliet*, are suffused with irony for us, the audience, because we know what Romeo does not, that Juliet is not really dead. The whole of Thomas Mann's *The Magic Mountain* is deepened by our ironical knowledge that the people in the TB sanatorium are clutching at false hopes, that they are doomed to die – and not least of them the central character, who, in Mann's most ironical stroke of all, recovers from TB and leaves the asylum joyfully, only to enlist for service in World War I.

Comic irony can also be of this kind. The author's lateral viewpoint to his or her material is made apparent from the start, and gives apparently deadpan utterances and straightforward situations overtones of ridiculousness. Often this is done by language. In P.G. Wodehouse's novels or Oscar Wilde's plays, for example, the peacock style constantly intrudes the author into the material, inflecting everything said or done. The same thing is done with situation and character. People take part in sequences of events, or behave or speak in certain ways, which we know are fraught with silliness but they do not. The more doggedly and more innocently they persist, the more we laugh. Satirical **comedy** often makes use of this form of irony. It is also a feature of bawdy comedy, in which the perceiver is encouraged to see sexual or scatological overtones in utterances or behaviour which the performers appear to think quite innocent.

In comic drama, another kind of irony often exists between comedian and audience. The comedian steps momentarily out of character, so to speak, makes a comment, makes a gesture, raises an eyebrow, sending up the very performance he or she is giving, then returns instantly to the role inside that performance. This is the stock-in-trade of stand-up comedians and it is a recurring feature of a huge range of satirical comedy, from the improvised farces of the **commedia dell'arte** or the plays of Aristophanes or Dario Fo to the films of Buster Keaton or Woody Allen and to radio and television 'sketch' comedy of almost every kind. **KMcL**

ISLAM

The term 'Islam' means submission, and a 'Muslim' is one who submits. One submits to the will of God, of Allah, which was revealed to Muhammad, the last in the line of prophets, and is preserved in the Qur'an, the Muslims' sacred text. Islam has the second largest number of followers worldwide after **Christianity**. The predominantly Muslim regions are North and West Africa, Arabia and the Middle East extending through Turkey, Iran and Afghanistan up into the central Asian republics and down into Pakistan, India and Bangladesh, and finally Malaysia and Indonesia (the country with the largest number of Muslims in the world).

Muhammad was born in Mecca in Arabia in approximately CE 570. Mecca contained an important religious shrine, a cube-shaped building called the Ka'ba, and was also a prosperous trading centre. Muhammad was a merchant and married a wealthy business woman, Khadija. He was given to withdrawing from Mecca to reflect in the solitude of the surrounding hills. On one such occasion, in a cave on Mount Hira, he was overwhelmed by a sense of being addressed by the angel Gabriel, and was told to 'read' or 'recite'. Other experiences of a similar nature followed and he began to preach in the streets of Mecca. He spoke of a coming Day of Judgement, of the resurrection of the dead, and of the need to obey God in a life of faith and good works. His ideas earned him the scorn of his fellow citizens, followed by anger when he criticized the affluent for neglecting their obligations to the poor, and warned them in dramatic terms of the fate which would befall them in consequence. Above all, he denounced the veneration of idols in the Ka'ba and proclaimed that God is One. In 622, he and his followers were forced to move to Medina, an oasis town about 320 km north of Mecca. This year of the Hijra, or 'Emigration', later marked the start of the Islamic calendar.

After Muhammad's death in 632, the records of his revelations were collected to form the Qur'an. Muslims believe this to be a perfect copy of an original in heaven and accordingly revere it as revelation. Such was the respect Mudhammad's first followers had for him that they also sought to preserve the records of his sayings and actions. These are called *hadith*. Unfortunately, countless fabricated *hadith* also appeared, causing great confusion, but eventually those judged to be authentic were brought together in authoritative collection. They show the believer the path or way (*sunna*) of the Prophet, and are second only to the Qur'an in importance.

The emphasis in Islam on the one true God and, therefore, on the unforgivable nature of the sin of *shirk* (assigning partners to God) leads Muslims to stress the difference between their beliefs and those of Christians for whom Christ is divine. Nevertheless, Muhammad is the central figure in their faith and criticism of him is considered intolerable. (Hence the sensitivities aroused in the Salman Rushdie affair.) Although Muhammad is 'just a man', he is regarded as the perfect model to imitate. Many believers pray to him for miraculous intervention, or beseech him to intercede with Allah on their behalf. Such practices are frowned upon by the learned, but they continue, and have undoubtedly contributed to the spread of the faith.

'The learned' are known collectively as the *ulama*. They are not, except in **Shi'ism**, organized in a formal, structured hierarchy, but an informal hierarchy exists based on reputation for learning. This learning in turn is based heavily on extensive study of past theologies and law, to the extent that the *ulama* are sometimes referred to as the lawyer theologians. Many are indeed judges (*qadis*) in Islamic religious courts, or legal experts (*muftis*) offering guidance on legal interpretations. In Islam as in **Judaism**, the law is of enormous importance.

The obvious authorities were first the Qur'an and then the collections of *hadith*. From them Muslim thinkers evolved an authoritative system of Islamic law, *shari'a*. The *shari'a* is not a comprehensive legal code in the modern Western sense. In most Muslim countries today, a modern, Western-type code has been adopted to complement the *shari'a*, and in some countries it has replaced it entirely, despite the objections of so-called Islamic fundamentalists. Yet historically, the ruler's (or state's) law has always existed alongside the *shari'a* as its necessary complement. In Islam there is no clearly defined division between what is 'religious' and what is 'secular'.

There is no contradiction in the fact that as well as being experts in law and jurisprudence, the *ulama* are trained in theology. Muslim theology developed in opposition to philosophy, rejecting the free play that the latter allows to reason. The early traditions of Islamic philosophy were eventually defeated, leaving theology, with its insistence on **faith**, supreme. Innovation was distrusted, or virtually excluded. The excitement of early explorations in theology was replaced with the safe rehearsal of tradition.

This development is of more than historical interest, because it is a major contributory factor to the contemporary ferment in Islam. Once the systems of law and theology had emerged, it was widely believed that the intellectual task for Islam was essentially complete. The view prevailed that the 'gates of *ijtihad*' were closed. *Ijtihad* is the exercise of reason and a spirit of enquiry, and this was no longer necessary.

Within the overall, central framework of the Qur'an, Sunna, *shari'a*, law and theology, the 'ordinary believer' had and continues to have a more immediate basis on which to practise his or her faith – the Five Pillars.

First is the *shahada*, the confession of faith. 'I bear witness that there is no god but God; I bear witness that Muhammad is the Apostle of God.' These words are breathed into a newborn baby's ear so that they may be the first intelligible utterance heard; and they are often a Muslim's dying words.

Second is *salat*, the set prayers said five times a day (as opposed to informal prayer which may be uttered at any time). They may take place at home, at work, in the mosque, in the street – wherever one happens to be at dawn, midday, mid-afternoon, sunset and at night. Believers all face Mecca to pray, symbolizing their unity with the *umma* and their recognition of the significance of Muhammad. Congregational prayer in the mosque at noon on Friday is a duty for men in particular, and is followed by a sermon.

Third is the duty of *zakat*, alms-giving. Detailed amounts are specified in the *shari'a*; a figure in common use is 2.5% of one's savings over the year. This 'pillar' symbolizes the concern for the poor and underprivileged that is a recurrent theme in the Qur'an, which also emphasizes the importance of purity of motive in giving.

Fourth is the fast of Ramadan, involving abstinence from food and drink between dawn and sunset for a month. This is obligatory for all healthy adults, but not for the old or pregnant women. The end of Ramadan is marked by one of the main Muslim festivals, 'Id al-Fitr, when presents are exchanged.

Fifth is the *hajj*, the pilgrimage to Mecca. It is obligatory to make it once in a lifetime, if possible. In order to symbolize equality before God, pilgrims wear simple, white garments, which they may continue to wear afterwards. A person who has made the pilgimage may incorporate the title *hajji* into their proper name. For most of the hundreds of thousands who go, it is the event of a lifetime, but unfortunately excitement in Mecca has on occasion been difficult for the Saudi authorities to control, with tragic results. Since the Iranian revolution in 1979 there have also been political demonstrations in Mecca by Iranian pilgrims.

The end of *hajj* is commemorated by a four-day festival held worldwide. This is the 'Id al-Adha, the 'Festival of Sacrifice'. Animals are sacrificed and the meat distributed to the poor.

There is considerable diversity of opinion and belief among Muslims. Roughly, fundamentalists differ from the conservatives (as typically exemplified by the *ulama*) in being willing to reject much of the tradition and go back to the Qur'an and Sunna, and they differ from modernists in rejecting the West's preoccupation with reason and **science**. They advocate the establishment of Islamic states, with some version of Islamic law in place.

A controversial issue is the status of women. Liberal Muslims advocate equality of the sexes, sometimes arguing that just as the provisions in the Qur'an concerning slavery need to be reinterpreted in support of abolition, so the teaching about women needs to be reassessed. Fundamentalists agree with conservatives that there is spiritual equality between the sexes, but say that this should not be translated into social equality. The roles assigned to the sexes are different, they claim, and it is part of the role assigned to men that they should exercise overall authority in society.

Contention also surrounds the use of violence and the right to freedom of religion. Muhammad used force, and holy war is a legitimate concept in Islam. It was invoked by both Iran and Iraq in their eight-year war (1980–88). In traditional Islamic law it is forbidden to renounce one's faith on pain of death. Apostasy invites the death penalty and is a crucial element in the Salman Rushdie affair. Clearly this view is incompatible with the Universal Declaration of Human Rights, which liberal Muslims would uphold and fundamentalists reject.

The division between Shi'ite Muslims and the majority Sunni Muslims has been brought into prominence by events in Iran and Lebanon. The name 'Sunni' derives from *sunna*, 'the way' as set forth by Muhammad. The Shi'ites also follow this way, but with their own traditions and laws. From one of the Shi'ite sects the Baha'is emerged and formed a separate religion. The Ahmadiya are an active proselytizing group with members throughout the world. However, they are denounced as apostates by other Muslims because of the claims of their founder, Ghulam Ahmad (1839–1908), to be a prophet. JS

See also Islamic political thought.

Further reading A. Rippin, *Muslims*; Rafiq Zakaria, *The Struggle Within Islam: the Conflict Between Religion and Politics*.

ISLAMIC POLITICAL THOUGHT

Like all the major world religions Islam has inspired reflections on politics. The Qur'an, as 'revealed' to the prophet Muhammad, is not, however, a treatise on political philosophy, so Islamic political thought derives from creative interpretations of the Qur'an, sometimes synthesized with other traditions such as Greek **philosophy** in medieval times, and Western philosophy in modern times.

With some exceptions most modes of Islamic political thought have embraced authoritarianism, and are inconsistent with democratic philosophy. The earliest Muslim jurists had to grapple with two immediate legacies of their charismatically founded religion: the belief that all law is present in the Qur'an as the sacred and revealed word of God; and the existence of the office of the imam-caliph; that is, the divinely sanctioned ruler who was or who claimed to be the successor of the prophet Muhammad. The Sunnis maintain that the political and religious authority of the imam-caliph is held by a person belonging to the Quaraish (Muhammad's tribe), while the Shi'ites assert it belongs to descendants of Ali (Muhammad's cousin).

The Sunnis have been dominant in most parts of the Islamic world, and not surprisingly Sunnism is associated with conservative doctrines of government. The Sunnis accepted early in the history of Islam that the caliphate could be held by somebody who was not religiously virtuous. In most of the Islamic world the imam-caliph was soon stripped of military and political authority, although the separation of religion and politics, the spiritual and the temporal, was never clarified in the manner of Christian political thought. Most Sunni jurists' answer to the problem of **political obligation** was simple, authoritarian and absolutist: absolute obedience to the existing ruler was imperative if anarchy was to be avoided even if the ruler was impious or tyrannical. However, this thesis sat uneasily with another theme, the competing authority of Islamic law, the *shari'a*: that is, the divine legislation explicit or implicit in the Qur'an, capable of clarification and codification only by the *ulama* (the religious scholars and legal jurists). In the hands of a minority of Islamic writers the insistence that the ruler be religiously virtuous became the basis for a right of rebellion. Multiple medieval Muslim scholars produced books advising princes, sultans and sovereigns on the art of statecraft – sometimes known as the 'mirrors-for-princes' literature. The ruler's obligations were both religious and practical – to respect and enforce the Holy Law, defend or expand the frontiers, wage war against unbelievers, dispense justice, and provide order. In return the ruler was entitled to expect the obedience of the subject in all things except sinful conduct.

The Shi'ites, by contrast with the Sunnis, never accepted that a true Imam could be impious. The world, in their view, can only be maintained in order if there is a true Imam present in the world, to whom all obedience is owed. This belief is one of the origins of Mahdism, the belief that the twelfth Imam who disappeared in a cave in the 9th century will return one day to create a virtuous order before the end of the world.

The classic text of Islamic political thought was produced by the 14th-century scholar, judge, warrior and diplomat, Ibn Khaldun, whose *Muqadimma* still provides the best means of understanding the cyclical pattern in the rise and fall of régimes in the classical Arab world.

In more recent times efforts have been made to modernize Islamic political thought – including attempts to legitimize a conception of popular **sovereignty** through extending the traditional requirement that rulers engage in consultation with the community of believers; and to elaborate the idea that every individual shaped by a just Islamic state can behave as if they are a pious jurist. Such democratizing trends in Islamic political thought are made somewhat plausible by the fact that Islam is formally a religion which embraces the equality of the community of believers and formally is hostile to caste hierarchies and to racism (all can be converted to Islam). However, on the other hand, Islam historically accepted and codified three stark inequalities: between masters and slaves, between men and women, and between Muslims and non-Muslims – although the extent to which slaves, women and unbelievers were excluded from political influence has varied dramatically across Islamic régimes. Democratizing trends in Islamic political thought compete directly with those contained in certain versions of Shi'ite doctrines such as that articulated by Ayatollah Khomeini and his followers in contemporary Iran who declare that sovereignty is possessed by God alone, although, for the time being Earthly authority is possessed by his vice-regents, the Shi'ite religious officialdom. **BO'L**

See also democracy; Catholic political thought.

Further reading E. Gellner, *Muslim Society*; B. Lewis, *The Political Language of Islam*.

J

JACOBINISM

The Jacobin Club was a society of deputies during the French Revolution, led by Robespierre. It took its name from the Jacobin monastery at Versailles, where it held its first meeting. The Jacobins stood for the establishment of a single, uniform, rational and centralized nation-state, which would be a democratic republic, expressing the sovereignty of the people. Jacobins were entirely hostile to aristocratic privileges and to all feudal forms of government. The sense of Jacobinism, as a belief in a nationally uniform and centralized government, hostile to the division of parcellization of sovereignty remains in current political usage, especially in France.

Robespierre's Jacobins established a revolutionary dictatorship when France was at war with and encircled by the reactionary European powers. Their conduct of government, through the Committee of Public Safety, gave rise to a different meaning of Jacobinism in which the Reign of Terror from 1793 to 1794 was seen as the logical end-product. In this sense Jacobinism is understood as a form of élitist insurrectionary politics, in which an élite, possessed of true social and political knowledge, believes itself entitled to seize and hold political power in the name of the people. Thus Jacobinism is used pejoratively to describe groups which advocate the overthrow of the state or régime without regard to the will of the people or the majority and in this sense, Jacobinism is often seen as a forerunner of Bolshevism.

Jacobinism is also sometimes used to describe the practice of those who engage in nation-building, forging national homogeneity out of diverse peoples, without much regard to their consent. **BO'L**

See also Marxism; nationalism; sovereignty.

JAINISM

The Jain, or Jaina, **religion** of India developed from the ancient sect of Jinas ('those who overcome'). The founding of the present Jain community in India can be traced back to Vardhamana Mahavira ('Great Hero'), who lived in eastern India *c.*540–468 BCE. Mahavira's historicity is established by the fact that he is named in **Buddhist** scriptures; he came from the same martial clan as the Buddha and had been educated as a prince. He was married with a daughter when he left home to live as an **ascetic**. After 12 years he attained enlightenment, then wandered along the Ganges teaching, until his austerities killed him at the age of 72.

During the Mauryan dynasty (*c.*320-*c.*185 BCE) the small community of monks and lay followers enjoyed royal patronage, but a serious famine caused them to migrate to the Deccan plateau in southern India. There they established important centres of faith. During their migration a division occurred between those Jains who insisted that no clothing at all should be worn, who became known as Digambaras ('sky-clad'), and those who wore plain white robes, the Shvetambaras ('white clad') Jains. Today both groups wear white robes in public, although the division persists and each group has its own body of literature.

Jains are strict vegetarians and their doctrine of *ahimsa* means that they reject violence and killing. It is because of this that Jains have been unable to follow agricultural occupations for fear of hurting the small creatures in the soil. Similarly, one may not light or extinguish a fire.

Jainism is basically a system of psychic discipline and **meditation** supported by its own metaphysical doctrine. In this it is not unlike Buddhism since both represent a strong reaction to the extreme forms of Hindu ritualized, sacrificial practices. The Jain doctrine of *ahimsa* rules out the practice of animal **sacrifice** since every being is inhabited by a soul and the universe is made up of infinite and separate individual souls. The goal of Jain life is the escape of the soul from the body in order to dwell in eternal bliss (**moksha**). In order to achieve it *karma* must be avoided. In the Jain view, *karma* is a substance adhering to the soul: human activities, especially cruelty and violence, produce a kind of solid encrustation around the soul and must be dissolved by ascetic discipline and meditation in order to set the soul free.

Jains, like Buddhists, are basically atheistic in their doctrines, although they do not deny the existence of gods. Since the universe in their system is eternal, governed by immutable law, there is no need or place for the concept of an omnipotent, divine creator. There is no universal destruction, as in **Hinduism** and Buddhism; the ages roll on through improvement and decline. The chief distinction between Jains and Buddhists consists in the Buddhist rejection of even the concept of soul or of an immortal ingredient in the human being. *Karma* in Buddhism arises from the system of ethical relationships between human beings which determine the state of future rebirths.

The Jain community in India continues to flourish. Its three million members have great influence, especially in Gujarat and Rajasthan. Austere but beautiful medieval statues commemorating Jain ascetics have been found as far south as Madurai. Gandhi is believed to have derived his doctrine of *ahimsa* from Jains in his native Guyarat (see **Gandhianism**). **RW**

JAPONISME

Japonisme (or French *Japonaiserie*, 'Japonizing') refers to the influence of Japanese art and crafts on the West, which followed the opening up of that country to the West in the 1850s. In the decorative **arts**, the influences are similar in kind, if not in extent, to those of the **chinoiserie** craze of the 18th century. In painting and applied arts, Japanese systems of design, well known in the West through imported prints, offered artists of the later 19th century (such as Degas, Manet and Toulouse-Lautrec) a way of 'balancing' works through masses of colour and a robust linearity. Such methods were radically different from the traditional, 'renaissance' techniques, and were crucial factors in the whole development of modern art in the West. **MG PD**

Further reading Siegfried Wichmann, *Japonisme: the Japanese Influence on Western Art since 1858.*

JAZZ

Jazz (from the 19th-century American slave slang – reference books are often mealy-mouthed about this – for 'fuck') is both a kind of **music** and a style of performing. It originated in the Southern USA, at first on slave plantations as a mainly vocal form (of which **spirituals**, the songs of Stephen Foster and the **blues** are the main surviving relatives), and then, after the American Civil War when people picked up and began using band-instruments abandoned in the fighting, as a mainly instrumental form. The instruments were primarily those of a military band clarinet, drums, trombone, trumpet with banjo or piano and double bass. The performers played and improvised on music current at the time: hymns, marches and such popular dances as polkas and quadrilles. White music-historians make great play of the African origins of the slaves, claiming that the rhythmic alertness and melodic waywardness of jazz are legacies from Africa. This would be more convincing if African music, as recently revealed, showed anything like the same characteristics. In fact such things as syncopation and blue notes are common in all **improvised** performance (in Norwegian folk fiddling, for example, as far away as can be imagined from Africa or New Orleans), and they may have come into jazz simply because that's how people wanted to play the music.

Jazz went through several periods of development. At first it was little more than a do-it-yourself version of the vaudeville, folk and church music of the time. (Blues and **ragtime**, a syncopated, cheekily harmonized dance-style, were particularly influential.) Then, in New Orleans and elsewhere, the formula was developed for what is now called **Dixieland** jazz. This spread north, in particular to Chicago in the 1920s, and became popular with white audiences as well as black, partly through the prolific recordings made by some early bands. In the 1930s 'big band jazz' or 'swing' evolved, setting virtuoso instrumental soloists and singers in the context of large groups (usually from about 16 to 30). As swing became more and more anodyne and commercial in the 1940s, jazz soloists developed 'bebop' (named after the wordless vocalizations of Dizzie Gillespie). With the rise of **pop**, and subsequently of **rock**, from the 1950s onwards, jazz and popular music took different directions. Jazz performers began to experiment with free forms, and to draw inspiration from classical music – of the past; listening to jazz became a more esoteric activity; critics and jazz writers began overintellectualizing their response, so that jazz itself became polarized. Performers, however, have kept it alive and particularly, now that singers have more or less deserted en masse to rock, jazz is primarily the province of instrumental virtuosos whose invention and technique fear nothing in comparison with the giants of the past.

Jazz shares with film the distinction of being one of the few art forms whose whole history is still available: recordings, from Edison's cylinders onwards, exist of almost every performer of any distinction (and a fair number of also-rans). It has always been an eclectic form of music, happy to take in instruments from all traditions electric guitars, marimbas, sitars, synthesizers, violins and to draw on techniques from other kinds of music (for example, Debussyan harmony, neoclassical spikiness or the minutely varied repetitions of **minimalism**). In turn, jazz has influenced performers in other areas, not only in popular music, pop and rock, but in the development of an 'attitude' in 20th-century classical music – a kind of street-smart, self-aware sureness of utterance which is in direct contrast with the drawn-out harmonic angst of most **atonal** music and is far more than just a matter of bright rhythms and crisp articulation. **KMcL**

Further reading Rudi Blesh, *Shining Trumpets* (a comprehensive introduction to the history and aesthetics of jazz); Marshall Stearns, *The Story of Jazz.*

JET ENGINE

The jet engine became a reality in 1930

when Frank Whittle designed and patented the essential elements of the modern turbojet. His design was first tested in 1937 but similar work in Germany led to the first turbojet powered aircraft, the Heinkel HE–178 in 1939.

The turbojet works on the following principles. Air enters the engine and is immediately compressed, whereupon heat is added by burning fuel, usually kerosene. This leads to a build up of hot gases which expand in the turbine, where energy is extracted to drive a rotating compressor. Further expansion of the gases through the the nozzle causes the energy of this gas stream to produce thrust that acts as the propulsion power for the engine. Extra power can be extracted by adding more heat in the afterburner.

Its development has led to jet **transportation** that has shrunk the size of the planet. The first commercial jet aircraft, the Comet, flew in 1949 and in less than 30 years, the design and building of Concorde has seen passengers travel at twice the speed of sound.

The jet engine is still being developed by aircraft manufacturers as they seek better power to weight ratios and new fuel saving devices. **AA**

Further reading J.E. Treager, *Aircraft Gas Turbine Engine Technology.*

JINGOISM see **Prejudice**

JUDAISM

Judaism is the name originally given to the **religion** not by its own practitioners but by others. It is derived from the name given in 933 BCE to the Southern Kingdom of Judah, formed from the ancestral lands of the tribes of Judah and Benjamin when the other Hebrew-speaking tribes of Israel refused to accept the harsh rule of Solomon's son Rehoboam, and withdrew to form the Northern Kingdom of Israel with its own centres of worship. But the Kingdom of Judah survived until 587 BCE, when it became a province first of the Babylonian Empire, then of the Greek warlords who succeeded Alexander, and then of the Romans, with only a brief period of independence under the Maccabees (*c*.165–87 BCE). These upheavals and the effect on agriculture led to migration to all the major cities of the ancient world, so that what had originally been the name of a tribe became the name of a whole people, their ancestral land and their religion, with a fine literary tradition evolving into a scriptural canon and a sophisticated social system with strong moral cohesion.

Judaism, as a religion, puzzled the ancient world. There was only one temple, in Jerusalem, and no idol or image of God was to be found anywhere. Calling themselves the Children of Israel, Jews refused to work on the seventh day, refused to sacrifice to other gods, and while they were prepared to pray for the well-being of the Roman emperor, they would rather die than worship him. Contact with **Zoroastrianism**, reaction to the early **Christian** church and incessant persecution led to modifications in the Jewish faith, but there is a continuity and consistency from earliest times to the present day.

The origins of the Jewish faith have been a matter of controversy for scholars since methods of modern textual and literary criticism were applied to the Pentateuch (the first five books of the Bible) in the middle of the 19th century, and archaeologists uncovered the civilizations contemporary to the Children of Israel. For Christians, who had apropriated the Hebrew Scriptures as their 'Old Testament', this archaeology was a vital quest for the foundations of faith: to know, for example, what really happened to Moses on Mount Sinai. But for Jews, who had a living tradition of interpretation, who always felt themselves in dialogue with their forebears, and who certainly did not see themselves as an anachronistic survival from the past, this kind of validation was less important than such matters as religious revival and the birth of modern **Zionism**. That the question should be asked at all is an indication of the importance of the understanding of history in first Judaism and then Christianity. If God were not perceived as acting in history to redeem his people, there would simply be no Jewish faith. If a slave race had not been liberated and led out of Egypt to a new homeland in

Palestine, assimilating related clans already settled there, there would be no Jewish people, and if there had not been charismatic leaders appearing as prophets, priests, kings and military leaders, and teachers whose words and deeds were enshrined in scripture and tradition, neither the people nor their faith would have survived until today. In the liturgy of Temple and synagogue the story of the Exodus from Egypt was continually rehearsed. In every Jewish home at the ritual Passover meal the youngest child asked why this night of all nights was special, and was told the story, while at other great festivals such as Purim and Chanukah other occasions of deliverance were celebrated. However, the dynamic of this belief is not the glory of the past but the hope of the future. Belief in resurrection and the last judgement came relatively late into Jewish faith, in the 2nd century BCE, as a response to the mass slaughter of innocent Jewish people by their Syrian rulers. The important questions, rather, were the continuity of one's family within Israel and the apotheosis of Israel within history.

The controversy referred to above concerns the identity of the God of Israel, and the extent of borrowings from surrounding tribes. This God has no personal name in the sense that Jupiter or Vishnu do. In the earlier strands of the Pentateuch, God is referred to as El, of the honorific plural Elohim, a word for God found in surrounding culture c.2000 BCE, with a suitable epithet and title, such as 'Lord God of Hosts'. He made himself known to the patriarchs, Abraham, Isaac and Jacob, and as their personal deity was known as 'the God of Abraham, the Fear of Isaac and the Mighty One of Jacob', but more usually (and always in liturgy) as 'The God of Abraham, the God of Isaac and the God of Jacob'. There is debate among Christian theologians as to whether this is not a merging of three separate tribal deities as well as three separate theophanies, but already before anything was written down (c.1000 BCE) there was a rich tradition of stories involving the nomadic patriarchal family as successive generations rather than separate tribes.

The turning point came with Moses' experience. The fugitive Hebrew adopted by an Egyptian princess encountered God in the wilderness, but when asked the name of the God who was sending him back to his people, he was told YHWH, which can be translated as 'I am who I am', 'I was who I was', 'I will be who I will be'. In other words, God is who he is, and his name is no business of his people. However, a new relationship was established. God was now to be addressed as Lord, and the appellation YHWH is considered too sacred to use. He is bound to those whom he had called by a **covenant**, whereby he protected them, and they obeyed him, giving service and worship in lives dedicated to the pursuit of justice, peace and the responsible stewardship of his creation.

Judaism emphasizes the importance of creating a just society, with the cry of the prophet Amos echoing down the centuries: 'Let justice roll down like waters, and righteousness like a mighty stream.' His successors, Hosea in Israel, the Northern Kingdom, and Isaiah and Jeremiah in Jerusalem (8th–7th century BCE), did not hesitate to blame the nation's misfortunes on the refusal to give justice to the poor or mercy to the debtors. The commandments in Deuteronomy frequently repeat the injunction to protect the widow and the orphan, and to love the stranger. 'For you too were strangers in the land of Egypt until I took you out with a mighty hand and an outstretched arm.' The corners of the field were to be left for the poor to come and harvest, and the gleanings of harvest and vineyard were to be left for them as well. These laws from Leviticus and Deuteronomy can be seen in practice in the Book of Ruth. Later, when Jews were no longer living an agricultural life, and a money economy had developed, financial support replaced this, and every Jewish community developed a network of institutions to facilitate this. Orphanages, dower societies and credit unions proliferated to meet changing social needs. The Hebrew word for giving to charity, *sedakah*, comes from the same root as the word for justice; that is, it is the right of the poor that the rich share with them, and they are not the recipients of favours. Maimonides, the medieval philosopher and jurist, said that there are eight degrees of charitable giving, and ranked them in a hierarchy, preferring the recipient to be self-supporting thereafter. The principle of Leviticus 19, 'You shall be holy, as I the Eternal, your God, am holy', undergirds Jewish ethics. Later Judaism said that creating a just society is part of the process of *tikkun olam*, bringing the world into a state of perfection, which is the Jewish people's task on Earth.

Observance of the Jewish faith depends much on women, because it is family-based, and because they oversee obedience to the complex rules of purity and **taboo**. A Jew is someone with a Jewish mother (not necessarily a Jewish father), though conversion is possible in Reform Judaism. Judaism has been continually as risk from assimilation into the religions of the countries in which Jews live – since about twenty-five per cent of Jew marry non-Jews – and to massacre: about one third of the Jewish world population, for example, perished in the Holocaust during the 1930s and 1940s. The establishment of the state of Israel has therefore been crucial to the survival of Judaism; second in importance is the existence of a strong community in North America. **EMJ RM**

See also chasidim/hasidim.

Further reading Michael Fishbane, *Judaism; Revelation and Traditions*; E. Kedourie (ed.), *The Jewish World*; Herman Wouk, *This is My God*.

JUDGEMENT see Style; Taste

JUGENDSTIL see Art Nouveau

JUNGIAN THOUGHT see Anima and Animus; Archetypes; Collective Unconscious; Dreams; Individuation; Introversion and Extraversion; Libido; Shadow.

JUNK ART

Junk Art was a 1950s and 1960s movement which used industrial junk, urban debris and the detritus of the consumer society as the raw material for art. In both its examination of the accepted limits of fine-art practice and its use of junk as raw material it is related to Braque's and Picasso's Synthetic **Cubist** collages, the found objects of

the **Dadaists** and the Arte Povera group. In one of the definitive creative acts of Junk Art, the sculptor César assembled synthetic sculptures from car bodies crushed in a hydraulic press into grotesque building blocks. **MG PD**

JUST WAR

The 'just war' doctrine, in **history** and **political science**, attempts to define moral criteria for the initiation of war (*jus ad bellum*: Latin, 'justice prior to war') and the conduct of war (*jus in bello*: Latin, 'justice during war'). Attempts to develop just war criteria can be traced to classical Roman **law**, itself influenced by Greek and Hebrew philosophy. These ideas were systematized in European, Christian canon law (see **Catholic political thought**) in the early Middle Ages, and then developed further in the 16th and 17th centuries by jurists like Grotius. Key figures in the elaboration of criteria for a just war include St. Augustine in the 5th century, Thomas Aquinas in the 13th century, and Reinhold Niebuhr in the 20th.

The criteria for *jus ad bellum* are fourfold: first, the party who wages war must have sufficient authority to do so; second, there must be a just cause of offence, such as unprovoked aggression; third, there must be an intention to wage war solely for the sake of peace, or 'for the suppression of the wicked' and 'the sustenance of the good'; and fourth, there must be a reasonable prospect that the war can be won. The criteria for *jus in bello*, concern appropriateness of means to ends, and centre on notions like proportionality and discrimination.

The definition of a just cause for war is problematic because its legitimacy can be based on circular reasoning. Who has the authority to declare whether a war is just? The ruler? The people? What is the status of just war standards in a civil war? Even the justification of war to repel an unprovoked act of aggression is problematic because most acts of aggression or intervention are justifiable according to some moral or political claim – for example, an historic national-territorial claim, or the protection of a stranded ethnic minority.

The traditional criteria for *jus in bello* are no less ambiguous. The decision to use force must be proportional – that is, force must do more good than harm – but this criterion assumes that those who engage in war know how much destruction will occur before the war commences. The concept of proportionality attempts to limit the use of force to the amount necessary to achieve peace, yet such issues are inherently contestable: President Truman, for example, justified the use of atomic bombs against Japan in World War II by arguing that more lives would be saved if the war were brought to a sudden end. While Truman's argument may have been correct, the subsequent proliferation of weapons of mass destruction has significantly limited the scope of justifiable means because the potential destructiveness of war has increased significantly, and is much more likely to result in large-scale suffering for non-combatants.

The potentially anarchic nature of relations between states and the unpredictability of conflict-escalation may make moral criteria necessarily ambiguous and of limited (thought not insignificant) use in actually preventing or managing the conduct of war. However, just war criteria affect the decisions and actions of potential combatants, and have guided the Geneva Conventions, and the arbitration mechanisms imposed by the UN Security Council. **BO'L**

See also pacifism; utilitarianism.

Further reading J.T. Johnson, *Can Modern War be Just?*; M. Walzer, *Just and Unjust Wars*.

JUSTICE

Justice (Latin, 'theory and practice of just law') is perhaps the central moral and political value which polities and states are meant to express. Conceptually there are two types of justice: legal justice and social justice. Legal justice mandates procedural fairness in treating people alleged to have broken the law and in arbitrating disputes between aggrieved parties. It also involves debates over what punishments, if any, may be justly imposed on those who break the law (see **deterrence theory** and **law**). Social justice, by contrast, refers to the 'fairness' or 'rightness' of the overall distribution of benefits and burdens in society.

In Western political philosophy, great controversy has always surrounded the interpretation of social justice. There are cynics who argue that social justice is merely a name given to existing distributions of welfare by the powerful (an argument first advanced by Thrasymachus in Plato's *Republic*); and there have been those who argue that only legal justice is possible whereas social justice is, allegedly, a mirage, an impossible ideal with which to burden public officials (an argument made by Friedrich von Hayek).

The mainstream of philosophical debate about social justice has pursued three questions. First, which values, or combination of values, should have primacy in deciding issues of distributive justice? Should 'right' (legal or customary entitlement) always prevail, or should merit (or desert, or 'equality of opportunity') prevail as a way of enhancing economic efficiency; or should 'need' (however defined) ground a substantively egalitarian standard of distributive justice? Or should we combine these criteria and apply them differently in particular circumstances? Second, controversy surrounds the question of whether theories of social justice should be based on conceptions of fairness or conceptions of impartiality (or what rational agents would choose as the most just arrangements in circumstances where they could not use their bargaining power to seek their own advantage)? Third, there remain major controversies about whether states should seek to ensure procedural fairness before human agents engage in economic and other activities, or whether states should seek to regulate and change the outcomes of free decisions by agents. There is an extensive and related debate, among socialists, liberals and conservatives, over the extent to which governments can and should regulate the activities of citizens to ensure social justice, and over the patterns (procedural or substantive) which any justified interventions might follow. **BO'L**

See also conservatism; liberalism; socialism and social democracy.

Further reading D. Miller, *Social Justice*.

K

KANTIAN ETHICS

Kantian ethics are based on the system developed by Immanuel Kant in the 18th century, which had an inestimable impact on Christian theology, particularly on Anglicans and Lutherans. Kant taught that **natural theology** was an illusion, but that the voice of conscience would establish truth where reason could not. A sense of duty assures one that the idea of freedom is real, and since God is required to establish justice and freedom, there must be another world in which he can redress the balance.

Kantian ethics are based on three fundamental ideas. First, moral principles are **a priori** knowledge. One is not taught the difference between right and wrong; one knows by instinct what is right. How one does what is right, the application of moral principles, may depend on experience and observation. Such moral principles, or rather the sense of duty, should be obeyed for their own sake, and from love of one's neighbour, but, ultimately, duty is more important than motive. This idea made Kant an implacable opponent of the views that ends justify means, and that making a mistake is less serious if one had the right intentions. In Kantian ethics, for example, if it is wrong to lie, as conscience declares it is, then it is always wrong to lie even if someone will be injured if the truth is known.

Second, Kant stated 'Act so as to treat humanity both in your own person and that of every other man always as an end and never only as a means.' The high value set on every individual treating fellow human beings as ends in themselves meant the death knell of slavery, exploitation and the denial of human rights.

The third principle was 'the idea of the will of every rational being as a universally legislating will'. This is the pinnacle of the **Protestant** principle, that each individual is responsible for making his or her own ethical decisions in the light of their conscience, and is little more than the restatement of the principle of universalism.

In 1793 Kant wrote a treatise on **religion**, relating his ethical principles to traditional Lutheran theology. He handled this under four headings: the existence of radical evil in human nature, the conflict between good and evil principles, the victory of the good and the foundation of a Kingdom of God on Earth, and religion and priestcraft. He asserted that religion was no more than the recognition of all our duties as divine commands. The moral law had no purpose beyond itself, there was no need of a personal saviour, and a moral person had no need of prayer. In view of such opinions, it is hardly surprising that he found himself in trouble with the authorities. **EMJ**

Further reading A.D. Lindsay, *Kant*.

KEYNESIAN THEORY

Keynesian theory, in **economics**, was developed by the English economist, John Maynard Keynes (1883–1943), and was presented in 1936 in his book, *The General Theory of Employment, Interest and Money*. Keynes rejected large parts of neoclassical economics and his ideas have had a profound effect on economic analysis and policy in the Western world. His theory attempts to explain how the level of economic activity is determined. He asserted that economies could be in equilibrium at less than full employment, and that it was therefore for governments, through their taxing and spending policies, to ensure enough effective demand to produce full employment. He believed that monetary policy is ineffective relative to the more direct fiscal policy in efforts to bring an economy out of deep depression. Keynes therefore switched the emphasis of policy from **microeconomics** to **macroeconomics**, where it remained for almost 40 years. His influence was enormous; governments everywhere came to accept responsibility for full employment. His critics were not silent, however; as **inflation** rose in the late 1960s and early 1970s, their claim that Keynesian policies were inevitably inflationary began to receive new attention. From 1973 on, governments ceased to be Keynesian in any literal sense. They allowed unemployment to rise without trying to expand **budget deficits** enough to prevent it.

Most economists today accept the broad framework of Keynes' analysis, but have refined and revised the detail and emphases of the theory. Monetary policy (see **monetarism**) has been restored to a position of importance for coping with the milder recessions experienced since the 1930s. Keynes emphasized aggregate demand, but today some consider the supply side as important for economic policy (see **supply-side economics**). Many disagree with applying his particular policy recommendations to today's economic problems. **TF**

Further reading A. Leijonhufvud, *On Keynesian Economics and the Economics of Keynes.*

KIN SELECTION

The term 'kin selection' was coined by John Maynard-Smith (in his work, *The Theory of Evolution*, 1966) to describe the apparently altruistic situation where **natural selection** acts upon an individual in such a way as to benefit its relatives without benefit to itself. Thus a worker bee is genetically preprogrammed to remain sterile throughout her life, which is spent caring for her relatives, some of whom will become queen bees and multiply many of the genes which the sterile worker herself carries. **RB**

See also altruism; evolution; group selection; selfish gene.

Further reading Richard Dawkins, *The Selfish Gene.*

KINETIC ART

Kinetic art (from Greek for 'concerned with the relationship between moving bodies') consists either of three-dimensional mobiles and constructions which operate in a predetermined or random way, driven by a motor or by natural energy such as wind, or **Op Art** paintings which use optical illusion to cause the picture surface to appear to move before the eye. Examples of the former are the mobiles of Alexander Calder and the powered constructions of Yves Tinguely, while Victor Vassarély's geometric abstrac-

tions exemplify the latter. Other artists who have experimented with kinetic art include Marcel Duchamp and Pol Bury. **MG PD**

KINGDOM OF GOD

From earliest times in the religions of the ancient Near East, God has been represented as a king presiding over his court or leading his hosts in battle. This imagery became stronger with the rise of a monarchy in Israel, as the evidence of many of the psalms shows. From a heavenly warlord intervening on behalf of his people, the concept was enlarged to make God ruler of all nations. The problem was that the nations did not acknowledge his sovereignty, though ultimately they would have to, according to the prophets. As Jewish political power waned so the conviction grew that there would be a day of judgement at God's hands, but originally the Kingdom of God was a political and historical event, establishing peace and justice.

Jesus began his ministry proclaiming the advent of the Kingdom of God and preaching preparation by repentance and reform as John the Baptist had done. The miracles he performed displayed the power of God's kingdom, but it is a matter of dispute how soon he expected the new age to come when creation would be redeemed. He was executed as a political agitator, but the Early Christian Church held his resurrection to be a vindication of his teachings and the beginning of a process that would transform life. At first Jesus's return in the glory of the Kingdom was expected imminently, but by the close of the 1st century it was seen as eternal life, a new dimension, a new quality of life which begins now. Jesus' teaching was reassessed in such a way that three solutions to the problem of the Kingdom arose.

First, it was seen as a future reality, when the sin, illness, evil and death which corrupt creation would be abolished. Second, the Kingdom was seen as a present reality, though hidden from all but the faithful. Finally, there is the view that the Church is the anticipation of this heavenly kingdom, and in the centuries when Christianity was supreme in Europe, the Church was regarded as the only bulwark against heathen hordes, the identification of Church and Kingdom was complete. (In the East, the Kingdom was identified with the Byzantine Empire).

After the epoch-making writings of Albert Schweitzer (see below), no Christian theologian has been able to ignore the relationship of Jesus to the Kingdom of God, itself the subject of fierce controversy. Just as a synthesis concerning the present and future reality of the Kingdom was being worked out in the 1950s and 1960s, a polarization of 'liberal' and 'Evangelical' Christians took place, with the former supporting 'realized' **eschatology**, or the kingdom present here and now, and the latter extreme apocalyptic. With the upsurge of **liberation theology** interest has tended to focus again on establishing peace and justice now as part of God's plan. **EMJ**

Further reading A. Schweitzer, *The Mystery of the Kingdom of God* (1925); W. Pannenberg, *Theology and the Kingdom of God.*

KINSHIP

Kinship (derived from Old Norse *kyn*, 'produce'), in **anthropology**, refers to a system of social relations. It is the bedrock of all societies derived from descent and marriage relations, and kinship terms, behaviours, duties and organization vary greatly between different communities. Studies of these differences have formed a defining part of anthropology ever since the discipline emerged in the 19th century.

The first systematic account of kinship was provided by Lewis Henry Morgan in 1871. Morgan considered kinship terms in various societies and attempted to link their differences to the patterns of social organizations. He was particularly concerned with why certain native American peoples used terms such as 'father' and 'mother' for people other than their biological father and mother. His conclusion was that it represented a kinship system in which relationships through descent were not distinguished from relationships through marriage, so that a mother's brother, sister and their children were treated in the same way as the person's father, mother and siblings respectively.

Morgan's terminological studies on kinship initiated numerous other interpretations and critiques. In 1913, Bronislaw Malinowski shifted the focus away from what he described as 'kinship algebra', to concentrate on kinship's part in integrating society. The family was considered as the 'initial situation' which fulfilled individual needs as well as being a building block for the functioning of societies.

In 1949, Claude Lévi-Strauss considered kinship terms and systems of attitudes, not according to what function they performed in society, but how they could be interpreted to illuminate structures of the mind. He applied linguistic theories to kinship systems and extended earlier assumptions of the elementary kinship unit as composed of husband, wife and children to include the wife's brother. Thereby, brothers that gave away women in marriage systems were also included as part of the primary kinship atom. The circulation of women between wife-giver (the brother) and wife-taker (the husband) was compared to the exchange of words. Marriage was therefore considered as the elementary feature of kinship solidarity rather than relationships through blood descent.

For a considerable amount of time afterwards, debate raged between those advocating theories of descent as the primary feature of kinship systems and those alliance theories that favoured marriage as the more significant factor in establishing solidarity within society.

Another perspective on kinship relations considered the extents to which they are premised on moral duties and obligations. Meyer Fortes, from his study of the Tallensi people in Ghana, called this factor the 'moral amity of kinship'. Most people grow up in families, and therefore conceive relations of kin as an elementary organizing principle of their world. For instance, we may see family resemblances and relationships in plants and animals. Kinship may also be extended to other social relations, as is apparent with adoption, religious brotherhoods, and the use of words like 'brother' and 'sister' to members of political movements based on common backgrounds and goals.

Some social theorists have noted the political and economic self-interests of members related to each other by kin. From this perspective, the moral aspects of kinship are stripped to their material foundations. Others have considered the way the wider political and economic climate moulds the character of the family. For instance, in capitalist societies, the domestic family is ideally considered as the hearth for sentiments and mutual assistance. This acts as the counterpart to the wider market economy in which people tend to act in their own self-interest.

Numerous anthropological accounts have reported on the variations of kinship terms and organizations. Whereas, in a Western context, no distinction is made between relations through the father (patrilineal) and mother (matrilineal) as is apparent with uncle and aunt, other societies (for example in India) have separate terms for each line of descent. Even the supposition that the family of wife, husband and siblings is the basic unit of all societies has fallen short of accounting for all societies. A common distinction has been to call this type of kinship organization as the nuclear family and household units which comprise a wider network of kin, the extended family. **DA RK**

See also community; culture; economic anthropology; ethnicity; exchange; gender; marriage; norms; role; socialization; society; status; structuralism.

Further reading M. Anderson (ed.), *Sociology of the Family*; C.C. Harris (ed.), *The Family: An Introduction*; Roger Keesing, *Cultural Anthropology*.

KITSCH

Kitsch (a word invented in Munich in 1870, from *verkitschen*, 'to make money'), is **art** or **design** which is aesthetically 'worthless' (in terms of the 'high' art from which it is derived), and which is designed to appeal to the lowest common denominator of appreciation and therefore to sell. Distinguishing it from 'art' is difficult since, jesuitically, the matter might be argued to rest on intention and/or judgement, and this brings up questions of **revivalism** and of high camp. A photograph of Cabbage-patch dolls posed like the figures in Leonardo's Last Supper (such a thing exists) is undoubtedly kitsch but what of objects like Warhol's multiples or Oldenburg's floppy-toilet or giant clothes-peg 'statues'? Kitsch follows taste and does not set it, so its products are always recognizable and therefore 'safe'. High styles, if 'wrongly' used, or used to follow taste rather than to set it, perhaps also constitute kitsch – this is where the Warhol/Oldenburg 'problem' becomes acute. Is a French château, meticulously reconstructed in every detail and with perfect craftsmanship, but set down in the Sahara or in Disneyland, kitsch or art? **PD MG CMcD KMcL**

See also culture; style.

KLEINIAN PSYCHOANALYSIS see Child Analysis; Depressive Position; Object Relations; Paranoid-Schizoid Position; Reparation.

KNOWLEDGE

I know that the Battle of Hastings was in 1066 and that $2 + 2 = 4$. But what, in **philosophy**, is knowledge?

Knowledge requires **belief**. One can only know that the Battle of Hastings was fought in 1066 if one believes that it was. But there is more to knowledge than belief. For one can believe a falsehood, whereas one cannot know a falsehood. John believes that Mary loves him, but cannot know that she loves him because she does not. And there is more to knowledge than believing a truth. Mary egoistically believes that everyone loves her, and infers that John loves her. And, completely coincidentally, he does. So Mary's belief that John loves her is true, but she does not know that he loves her.

What more than true belief is required for knowledge? Many philosophers have thought that the answer is justification. Mary's belief that John loves her is true, but unjustified. She does not have good reason to suppose that John loves her, but believes he does because she egoistically believes that everyone loves her. Knowledge, then, is true justified belief. I know that the Battle of Hastings was fought in 1066 because I believe that it was fought in that year, my belief is true, and I have good reason for my belief, perhaps because I read the information in a trustworthy history book.

The claim that knowledge is justified true belief was, however, refuted by Gettier. He showed that having a justified true belief is insufficient for knowledge. Suppose that Helen, one of my sisters, tells me that she is pregnant, on the grounds that her pregnancy test at the clinic was positive. I infer that one of my sisters is pregnant. I believe that one of my sisters is pregnant, and I have good reason to believe that one of my sisters is pregnant; my belief is justified. Further suppose that my belief is true, but not because Helen is pregnant. There was a mix up at the clinic and she is not pregnant, but my belief is true because, as a matter of complete coincidence, Christine, my other sister, is pregnant. My belief that one of my sisters is pregnant is true and justified. But I do not know that one of my sisters is pregnant. True justified belief is insufficient for knowledge.

What more than true justified belief is required for knowledge? One answer is this. A belief counts as knowledge only if it was acquired by a method that was, in the context, reliable. A method for acquiring beliefs is reliable just if it leads one to acquire beliefs which are true and does not lead one to acquire beliefs which are false. Trusting one's sensory experience is a reliable method for acquiring beliefs in most contexts. If one trusts one's sensory experience, one will acquire beliefs about the external world which are true; one will not acquire beliefs about the external world which are false (unless, say, one is on a hallucinogenic drug).

Trusting hospital pregnancy tests is also an example of what may seem, in most contexts, a reliable method for acquiring beliefs. But in the above example, the context of the mix-up at the hospital meant that it was not a reliable method. And this is why my true justified belief that one of my sisters is pregnant does not count as knowledge. For a belief counts as knowledge only if it was acquired by a method that was, in the context, reliable.

What, then, is knowledge? One answer is this: knowledge is true justified belief that was acquired by a method that was, in the context, reliable. A subject's belief counts as knowledge when they have good reason to have that belief, the belief is true, and it was acquired by a method that was, in the context, reliable. **AJ**

See also a priori and a posteriori; epistemology; scepticism.

Further reading J. Dancy, *An Introduction to Epistemology*; J. Foster, *A.J. Ayer*.

L

LABOUR PROCESS

The term labour process originally derives from Marx, and refers to the process of production: human labour power is applied to raw materials and machinery in order to produce commodities.

Marx concentrated his attention on the labour process under **capitalism** in which labour (the workers) is subordinate to the capitalists who own the forces of production. Marx made a distinction between the 'formal' and the 'real' subordination of labour. 'Formal' subordination, he argued, occurred in the early stages of capitalism where ownership of the means of production did not also entail direct control of labour in the production process. It was the development of the factory system of production that entailed a 'real' subordination – this involved the loss of the traditional craftsman, strict worker discipline, and the tying of workers to the machines with which they worked.

Marx's ideas have been developed by Braverman, who argues that 'real' subordination of labour was only fully realized in the 20th century. Braverman considers that control over the labour process by the owners of capital has been extended by modern management techniques, widespread mechanization and the computerization of tasks – which has resulted in a deskilling of workers.

A development believed to be particulary important in the deskilling process is that of Scientific Management. Scientific management originated in the USA in the late 19th century. One of its main proponents was Frederick W. Taylor (1856–1915). It involves an approach to job design which entails the separation of mental and manual work, a specialized **division of labour** (the division of work into simple, routine constituent parts each performed by a different worker), close management control of work effort and the payment of incentive wages. In practice, the need for flexibility and the opposition of workers, meant the principles of scientific management were never fully implemented, though many elements of Taylorism remain.

Scientific management was also linked with the revolution in manufacturing methods introduced by Henry Ford. Fordism is a system of production which entails manufacture of a standardized product, carried out on large plants, produced for mass markets employing an assembly line process. The assembly line was one of Ford's most famous innovations. Instead of workers moving between tasks, the flow of parts is achieved as much as possible by machines so that the assembly-line workers are tied to their own work position and have no need to move about the workshop. An important consequence is that the pace of the work is controlled mechanically and not by the workers themselves or by supervisors. Ford pushed job fragmentation to extreme limits.

Subsequent technological developments have led some to refer to post-Fordism – the new economic possibilities that have been made possible with the development of microchip technology, computers and robotics. The distinguishing feature of the post-Fordism era is the foundation of smaller productive units, catering for specialized markets using flexible productive methods. An important element of this is the development of an **international division of labour**. DA

See also alienation; anomie; bourgeoisie; capital; class; globalization; Marxism; occupation; organization; rationalization; work; world system.

Further reading C.R. Littler, *The Development of the Labour Process in Capitalist Societies*.

LABOUR THEORY OF VALUE

The labour theory of value, in **economics**, is the notion that the value of any good or service depends on how much labour it incorporates. The labour theory of value was used as an approximation by English classical economists Adam Smith (1723–90), who suggested it, and David Ricardo (1772–1823), who developed it. The theory was adopted and assumed a central place in the philosophy of Karl Marx (1818–83) and was used to develop the theory of surplus value, in which the capitalist takes all of the value produced by labour beyond that amount needed for the labourer's subsistence. These classical economists spawned a school of neoclassical dissenters the main cause of dissent being the latter's disagreement with the labour theory of value. They argued that price was independent of how much labour had gone into producing something, being determined solely by supply and demand. TF

LACANIAN PSCHOANALYSIS see Mirror Phase

LAFFER CURVE

The Laffer Curve, in **economics**, relates average taxation rates to total tax revenues. The curve was named after Arthur Laffer, an academic at the University of Southern California, who received acclaim in the 1970s for a theory devoid of empirical content. Legend has it that in November 1974, in a Washington bar, Laffer first drew his curve on the back of a beer mat. Since then his curve has been drawn a thousand times.

The Laffer Curve illustrates a theory about the relationship between tax rates and total tax revenues. As the tax rate rises from zero toward 100%, tax revenues will rise, reach a maximum and decline to zero. To increase tax rates beyond that which produces maximum tax revenues will only cause tax revenues to fall because of the adverse effect upon individual and business incentives. In the hands of advocates of supply-side tax cuts (see **supply-side economics**), the curve 'proves' that most governments could raise more revenue by cutting tax rates. Drawn by those of a different persuasion, it 'proves' that raising tax rates will bring more revenues. In the early 1980s, some supply-siders argued that the US had gone beyond the maximum tax revenue on the curve, so that a reduction in taxes would actually increase tax revenues. President Ronald Reagan and a majority in Congress succeeded in reducing tax rates and the economy began to recover from recession. Whether the reduction in tax rates caused an increase in tax revenues is doubtful, because the issue is clouded by the myriad other changes that occurred simultaneously in the economy, including growing federal budget deficits. **TF**

LAINGIAN THOUGHT see
Phenomenology

LAMARCKISM

Lamarckism is a theory, proposed by the French naturalist Jean-Baptiste Lamarck in 1809, which suggested that **evolution** occurred as a result of beneficial characteristics, acquired by an individual during its life, being passed on to its offspring. Moreover, the individual acquires new characteristics and abilities as a result of effort to satisfy new challenges from the environment. Thus, for example, the giraffe has evolved a long neck as a result of stretching to reach high leaves, and the blacksmith's son will inherit his father's strong arms. Lamarck's ideas were entirely hypothetical, but, though recognized as such, they influenced many 19th-century scientists, including Darwin. By the early 20th century Lamarckism was largely discredited but was perpetuated in the USSR by the influential biologist Trofim Lysenko who denied the existence of **genes**. Lysenkoism was officially endorsed because it appeared to corroborate the socialist ideals of equality, and between the 1930s and the 1960s many of its opponents were 'executed', to the great detriment of Soviet science.

Neo-Lamarckism allows the idea that natural selection may act upon the acquired characteristics of an individual.

However, Lamarckist doctrine is entirely contradicted by **molecular biology**, which states that information encoded in genes can pass to gene products but that this information flow is unidirectional. **RB**

See also pangenesis.

Further reading Arthur Koestler, *The Case of the Midwife Toad.*

LAND ART see Earth Art

LANDSCAPE PAINTING

Landscape painting is the representation of Nature in art, with or without the depiction of human or animal figures. In European art, landscapes are present, often in a very stylized or idealized form, in the background to many paintings of the **Renaissance** and earlier. In Asian art, landscape painting existed much earlier.

As a genre in its own right, worthy of a painter's attention, pure landscape painting in Europe cannot be traced back much earlier than the 16th century, specifically to Aldorfer's *Landscape with a Footbridge* (*c.*1520). This painting differs from its predecessors in that there is no subject matter other than Nature, a factor which was negatively to influence critical reaction to the genre until the end of the 19th century. Thus while landscape was important for later European **pastoral** painters such as Giorgione, or in the **narrative painting** of Brueghel and the reveries of Watteau, none of these artists may be said to embody the true landscape tradition. In the same way, the ideal landscapes of Claude in the 17th century are properly speaking a variant on **history painting** (known as Historical Landscape). On the other hand both the **Picturesque** movement in the later 18th century and **Romantic** painting placed the representation of landscape at the centre of their philosophy.

In the art of ancient Greece and Rome, landscape painting was not an independent genre, but formed part of the representation of the pastoral myths of **literature**. As such it may properly be described as background to narrative painting, as an essential yet subservient part of the representation. Yet within Roman art in particular, there emerged in the decoration of villas wall painting whose primary function can be interpreted as enjoyment of depictions of the countryside for their own sake. (A favourite idea was to juxtapose a wall-painting of (say) a garden with a window opening on to a real garden: the juxtaposition made the art.)

In Post-Imperial Europe the development of landscape was an essentially northern phenomenon – in Germany in the 16th century, the Netherlands in the 17th century, and Britain in the 18th and early 19th centuries; the 19th century saw the development away from studio painting (perhaps after sketching direct from nature) to plein air painting in the Barbizon School. In Holland, in the 17th century in particular, the taste for landscape knew no limits. This was due in part to the influence of **Protestantism**, which proscribed 'idolatory' (hence dethroning the Scriptures from the pinnacle of the hierarchy of **genres**) and in part perhaps to the Dutch taste for describing the world around them.

In China, the representation of landscape has always been central to its art, rendered in a non-scientific form of **perspective** which attempts to reconcile distance and foreground through the judicious use of devices such as meandering rivers. While this tradition continued for centuries, it fell into academicism and sterility which was broken when China was rudely confronted by the economic and cultural power of the West at the beginning of the 20th century. During the height of Communist power in China traditional landscape painting fell victim to the imposition of **socialist realism**, a genre which focused on the human figure. In Indian and Persian painting, landscape tended to be 'idealized', showing the perfect idyllic background to human activity, creating mood and atmosphere rather than making statements of its own. Islamic art, by and large, has eschewed landscape art (in favour of real landscapes, for example beautiful gardens); this is due partly to the prohibition against creating images, and partly to the vigorous and elaborate traditions of abstract and geometric art.

Landscape has played an important part not just in giving identity to societies such as that of 17th-century Holland, but also to those parts of the globe which Europeans colonized in the 18th and 19th centuries. Both in North America and Australia, the visual appropriation of the land by white settlers (whose art opposed the abstract, non-representational imagery of the native peoples) was accomplished largely through the genre of landscape painting, and interesting if not always successful confrontations between, for example, European Romanticism and the Australian bush gave landscape a political as well as aesthetic importance during the 19th century.

In Europe, in the later 19th century, the **Impressionists** finally succeeded in winning acceptance for landscape as a genre worthy of critical attention. This was accomplished less by confronting the bankrupt genre of narrative painting than by simply ignoring it, and by building up a constituency of patrons and critics who appreciated the directness and freshness of Impressionism after the stultifying and rule-bound productions of the **academies**. For a time, landscape painting was central to the **modernist** endeavour, in part at least because its subject matter was seen to be value free, and thus open to the development of stylistic innovation denied to more traditional genres. Within modernism, landscape has continued to play a significant role from the formal analysis of Cézanne to the **fauves**, **expressionism** and **surrealism**, though its importance to the modernist project has naturally tended to decline in the face of Abstraction. **MG PD KMcL**

Further reading K. Clark, *Landscape into Art*; W. Stechow, *Dutch Landscape Painting in the Seventeenth Century*; M. Sullivan, *The Birth of Landscape Painting in China*.

LANGUAGE

Language (medieval Latin *linguaticum*, 'tongue-equipment') is a way of communication by symbols. Feelings, ideas, thoughts and wishes are encoded, sometimes manipulated (for example by **syntax**) and passed on by the utterer; the receiver then decodes them. In simple languages (such as semaphore) the code is simple, and there is little scope for misunderstanding; in complex languages, the state of mind and the circumstances of utterer and receiver, and the nuances of the code used all affect the 'meaning' of the message. (The English language, for example, has many hundreds of thousands of individual words, even before grammar and syntax, never mind such further subtleties as **irony** or metaphor, are deployed on them.)

Until recently, it was commonly held that 'language' exclusively meant symbolic communication by means of patterns of words, either spoken or written, and that its use was confined to human beings. Rousseau famously said that we differ from the rest of the animal kingdom in two main ways, the use of language and the prohibition of **incest**. Other forms of communication, for example Morse Code or the sign language used by the deaf, were considered to be dependent on 'real' language, and to need conscious or subconscious translation into 'real' language before they could be understood. It was believed that language was one of the principal survival-attributes of the human race (the only beings able to think in the abstract, and to pass on those thoughts), and that the ability to learn a language – usually something done subconsciously, as a young child – was one of our species' most remarkable achievements. Some 5,000 languages are currently spoken in the world, and there is thought to have been a similar number of now-'dead' languages.

In the 20th century, the narrow meaning of the word 'language', as sketched above, has been widely challenged. If language is a code for the communication of ideas, should the term not include (for instance) the warning-calls of birds, the purring of cats, and at a more complex level the 'song' of whales or dolphins and the honey-dance of bees? Are such things as camouflage or the use of pheromones not 'languages', fulfilling a similar purpose to patterns of spoken or written words? In short, is it not a (characteristic) example of human speciesism to claim that language is exclusively what we possess, and what we do with it? Such questions are not merely examples of political correctness. They raise the fundamental issues of where the boundary blurs between communication in general and language in particular, and of whether encoding and decoding complex messages (either sent by other people or received from our surroundings or our memories) is not, in fact, the way we think. Perhaps calling bee-dances and monkey-shrieks 'languages' is merely playing with words – an activity which is itself a function of human language and human thought, and therefore restricted to our species.

Teasing out such conundrums is the work of philosophers of language, and perhaps more **scholasticism** than **science**. In the practical world, language studies concentrate on the human encodification of ideas in words, on the use of verbal symbols. One sub-branch of this work has been the attempt to see whether animals can be taught to understand, and use, human language. It has been shown that pets, for all the wishful thinking of their owners, do not 'understand every word I say'. Their apparent response to verbal signals is actually to tone of voice and body language: it is instinctive, and no different from the response they make to similar stimuli in the wild. By contrast, scientists have had some success learning, and using, dolphin 'language', though communication is restricted to practical and immediate matters, with no transmission of abstract ideas. Chimps have been taught human language – not spoken (their larynxes are the wrong shape to make human sounds) but signed – and have achieved vocabularies in the low hundreds, and the construction of 'sentences' involving concepts of past and future and the description of emotional and physical states. But a barrier seems to arise at about the language-level of a human toddler, and whether the breakthrough is into more self-aware abstract reasoning, or into a wider concept of what language is and what can be done with it, chimps fail to surmount it, whereas toddlers move on to more complex linguistic abstraction in a matter of weeks or months.

The scientific study of language, **linguistics**, is concerned above all, in hierarchical sequence, with phonetics (the sound of language), **phonology** (the significance of sounds in a given language), **morphology** (language structure), **semantics** (meaning) and **pragmatics** (context). Language studies also take in varieties of language (for example, dialects and foreign languages) and **translation**. A related study is the development and use of artificial languages (such as **computer** 'languages'). Some authorities say that this is cognitive science or computer science rather than linguistics; others claim that useful comparisons can be made with human language, and that the way computers use 'language' gives valuable insights into the way human beings think and communicate.

The study of language is of particular importance in **anthropology**. The way people speak, and spoke, is a clue to the way they see and saw their world, and linguistic analysis is one of the anthropologist's most vital skills. The simplest problem to solve is actually learning the language involved, and much useful work was done in this area by 19th-century anthropologists and missionaries, writing dictionaries and transcribing oral narratives from aboriginal languages throughout the world. The hardest problem is that of assessing **context**, taking into account the circumstances of the speaker or writer, the envelope of ideas in which each utterance is contained, and, not least, the circumstances and preconceptions of the receiver, that is the anthropologist himself or herself. For example, it was only late this century that Margaret Mead and others realized that the people from some of the 'remote' societies they visited, often societies unvisited by outsiders ever before, were fabricating or embroidering accounts to fit what they thought their visitors would like to hear: in short, in an all-too-human version of the Heisenberg **uncertainty principle**, the observer was unconsciously affecting and therefore distorting what was being observed.

Anthropologists in the 19th century were concerned, above all, to study the historical development of language and language families, especially those of exotic peoples. In the 20th century these interests were largely abandoned in favour of treating language as an essential part of communication in the society under investigation, and so making language studies a central way of understanding that society. Cultural anthropologists, espec-

ially in the US, focused on the way language encodes ideas about people's physical and conceptual universe. When, for example, Benjamin Whorf studied the Hopi language in the 1950s, he concluded that the Hopi people had a very different sense of reality, **space and time** from English-speaking people. (This led to his development of Edward Sapir's 1920s theories into the 'Sapir-Whorf hypothesis', that every language creates and represents a distinct way of thinking.)

In the 1960s, Claude Lévi-Strauss adapted theories about language structures in a different way. He was interested in Ferdinand Saussure's view that language is a set of systematic relations between elements, and attempted to apply it to social and cultural practices. His intentions were to use linguistic models to illuminate structures of all human minds. In his study of **myth**, for example, and on the analogy of phonemes (the minimal sound-units in language, without any intrinsic meaning of their own), he coined the word 'mythemes' to describe the basic components present in myths from diverse cultures and different times. From this work, he evolved the theory that human minds use pairs of contrasts (for instance, hot/cold, male/female, nature/culture) to order all phenomena. A fascinating offshoot of this work, by others, was the attempt to reconstruct (from computer analysis of mythemes in the world's myths and phonemes in the world's languages) the original language of the entire human race. A couple of hundred words have so far been suggested, for such concepts as 'god', 'fire', 'mother' and 'sky'. The parallels with and implications for Jung's theory of the **collective unconscious** are intriguing to contemplate.

Since the 1950s, some anthropologists have begun to query how far linguistic models can in fact be applied to social and cultural systems or to the structures of the human mind. Instead, they investigate language for the kinds of metaphors it contains, metaphors which reflect but do not determine people's world-views. (A typical such metaphor in English is that of time as a commodity to be budgeted, saved or wasted.) Even in theoretical or literal language and thought, metaphors are central.

For instance, the idea of knowledge as a landscape is conveyed in phrases such as 'landmarks in history' or 'intellectual horizons'; understanding is rooted in the metaphor of seeing, as in 'I focus on this point' or 'I see what you mean'. Comparison with metaphor-use across languages leads to valuable insights. The Maori language, for example, metaphorizes knowledge in terms of how it is inherited from ancestors and is a precious part of the individual, not to be shared with strangers.

Other anthropological perspectives on language concentrate on how it is not just a reflection of the world, but is used to give directions and commands, to make changes. This is shown, for example, in the precision of the language used in religious **ritual**, **magic**, **prayers** and curses. Another field is the **ethnography of speaking**: the study of language codes present in communities. The choice of words we make indicates the degree of familiarity between us and the people with whom we are communicating; it also reflects our social status and the situation we (and the other members of the group) are in. Anthropologists borrow the linguists' terms dialect (the language characteristic of regions or social classes) and idiolect (the language characteristic of an individual speaker). **KMcL**

See also artificial intelligence; exchange; fiction; folk literature; interpretative anthropology; literacy/orality; structuralism; symbolism; thought.

Further reading David Crystal, *Encyclopedia of Language*; George Lakoss and Michael Johnson, *Metaphors We Live By*; Edmund Leach, *Culture and Communication*; David Parkin, *Semantic Anthropology*.

LANGUAGE PLANNING

Linguists observe that natural processes of linguistic change are complemented, on occasion, by more direct, consciously motivated intervention in the form of language planning. Numerous sociopolitical factors can give rise to a need for language planning, including the relocation of international boundaries, the withdrawal of colonial powers, or the creation of new nations. Language corpus planning can be contrasted with language status planning, although the two approaches are by no means mutually exclusive. In language corpus planning, attention is paid to the formal aspects of language. A language variety is selected to function as the norm in society, prior to being codified and standardized. A writing system may have to be developed, in addition to conventions for spelling, **morphology** and **syntax**. Modernization, via the creation of new lexical items, may also be needed to cope with the demands of science, technology and international commerce. The next step is to gain acceptance for the language reforms and encourage the diversification of the social functions fulfilled by the language. Language status planning, on the other hand, is characterized more by the development of national identity through language. The rights of minority languages within a society have to be balanced with the need to promote a language which will be accepted both nationally and internationally. **MS**

LANGUAGE UNIVERSALS

Broadly speaking, scholars of **linguistics** identify three different types of language universal. First, there are so-called absolute universals, which comprise those aspects of language which find expression in every single known (or possible) human language. (For example, vowels have been attested universally in the languages of the world.) The second category consists of so-called implicational universals, whereby the presence of one feature in a given language can be taken as an automatic indicator that certain other features will also be present. Universals of this kind provide an indication of the limitations of natural language, since only certain combinations of properties are permissible. In contrast, distributional universals merely express the relative frequency of certain linguistic characteristics from one language to the next, thus creating a rank order which demonstrates their relative popularity.

When considering absolute universals, an explanation is required for why certain properties of language are indispensable. In this regard, Chomsky's theory of **universal grammar** offers an explanation based on the innate predispositions of human beings. It is argued that language constitutes an independent faculty of the mind which embodies certain highly specific structural properties. The fact that certain aspects of language appear to be manifested universally is thus explained in the context of biological development. In favour of this approach it is often argued that every child manages to acquire a highly complex linguistic system within a relatively short space of time, and comes to demonstrate linguistic knowledge which could not possibly have been acquired on the basis of experience alone. However, the arguments advanced in favour of this approach are rarely supported with convincing empirical evidence, since the task of disentangling the mutually interweaving influences of biology and environment often appears, in our present state of knowledge, insuperable.

It is quite possible that no single theoretical approach will explain the full spectrum of observed language universals. Instead, we should expect a range of possible motivations, applicable within particular domains. Within this framework, innate predispositions might account for some, but not all, observed universals. Competing explanations include the natural limitations of humans in comprehending, producing and memorizing speech; the expression of universal aspects of meaning which are reflected in the syntactic and morphological organization of languages; the perceptual capacities of human beings; and the practical requirements of human communication. It is perhaps too ambitious to expect just one of these competing explanations to account for the full range of observed language universals. For example, a plausible appeal can be made to the pragmatics of **discourse** to explain why all known languages possess a full complement of personal pronouns in the first, second and third persons, in both singular and plural forms (in English, 'I', 'you', 'he', 'she', 'we', 'you' (plural), 'they'). It is argued that the organization of human communication would be impossible unless every language manifested these particular linguistic structures. However, it is equally clear that many universals do not find a satisfactory explanation in pragmatic fac-

tors. One could also ask why a whole range of fundamental pragmatic factors (for example, the expression of a speaker's wishes) have not been universally grammaticalized. **MS**

See also innateness; linguistic typology.

Further reading B. Comrie, *Language Universals and Linguistic Typology: Syntax and Morphology*; W. Croft, *Typology and Universals*.

LASERS

A laser (acronym for Light Amplification by Stimulated Emission of Radiation) is a device which produces a narrow beam of intense radiation. The radiation is produced at a fixed frequency depending on the molecules in the cavity of the laser. The laser has reflecting surfaces at each end. The energy source triggers oscillation between the reflectors at each end and energy transfer corresponds to changes of atomic state in a specialized material in the cavity. The laser energy leaves the cavity through a hole in the centre of one reflector and is generally focused to a narrow beam with a very small angle of divergence. This results in the beam losing very little of its energy while travelling over long distances. The frequency of the laser and thus its colour corresponds to the material present in the cavity. Well known types are the CO_2 laser, the neon, the neodymium YAG (Yttrium Aluminium Garnet), the ruby and the copper laser.

Lasers may function continuously or in a pulsed fashion. The pulsed laser may transmit what are apparently small bursts of energy, for example 10 joules, in times as short as 4 microseconds. This results in an average power level in each pulse of 2.5 million watts! Some of the uses of lasers in cutting or welding utilize these very high rates of power transmission to produce localized reactions or disruptions due to heating.

In medical practice, lasers are used for cutting tissue, and the localized heat which they generate coagulates blood issuing from small vessels and results in a 'bloodless field'. By transmitting the laser through **fibre optics** the energy can be transmitted to the vessels of the heart from an incision in the thigh, the heat developed can be used to convert blood clots into gas or liquid and thus remove the obstruction from the vessel. In opthalmic surgery the small diameter of the laser beam allows the 'welding' of a detached retina to the base structure restoring the function of the eye.

In the same way as all other forms of energy, laser energy effects depend on the frequency of the wave form and the absorption of the energy by a target is governed by the colour and surface condition of the target. A rough black surface absorbs light and heat at almost all frequencies and a smooth silver surface absorbs very little. Laser energy can be targeted at a specific wavelength. For instance, laser energy at a wavelength of 577 nanometres can be used to heat small volumes of blood to near boiling point while the skin and other tissues through which the beam passes take up very little energy. Thus for a patient with a red 'port wine' birthmark the small blood vessels causing the colouration can be obliterated by laser treatment without the overlying skin being burnt.

In large-scale structural civil engineering work the non-divergent beam of the lasers is used for the precise alignment of parts separated by long distances, or in mechanical engineering for aligning the bearing of long rotating shafts such as propeller shafts in ships. At the other end of the scale in the confocal microscope small lasers can be focused precisely to points on a surface allowing microscopic investigation of the roughness and other characteristics of surfaces, even penetrating a few micrometres below the surface.

The introduction of the laser in 1960 in California symbolized modern technology in all its glory. Originally its invention was seen as a solution looking for a problem, as no one was sure what practical purposes it could be put to. But nowadays the laser has become an accepted part of science. Its uses are measurement and energy transfer in military, scientific, engineering and machine operations.

Another exciting development is the use of lasers in nuclear fusion. The idea behind this is to bombard a volume of hydrogen with an intense pulse of laser light and raise its temperature to over ten million degrees kelvin. At this temperature, fusion can take place releasing very large amounts of energy. The major drawback in devising this technique has been the development of sufficiently powerful lasers, and the difficulty of maintaining an intact volume of hydrogen.

It was originally envisaged that the laser would be used as a wonder weapon, and the introducing of the Strategic Defence Initiative, or 'Star Wars' project, by the Americans, has enhanced the laser's warlike image. The idea behind the project was to use high-energy beams to burn holes in ballistic missiles, so rendering them useless. This whole project has become highly controversial in terms of expenditure and technical problems that have arisen, and it seems that the project will be shelved indefinitely. **AA**

Further reading C. Lawrence, *The Laser Book.*

LATE MODERNISM see Modernism

LATE MODERNISM see Modernism

LATENT FUNCTION see Functionalism

LAW

'What is law?' is a question which receives very different answers. In the natural and social sciences laws are understood to be universal truths or regularities (for example, the laws of thermodynamics, or the laws of motion, or the laws of supply and demand). Outside of this context all may agree that laws in post-tribal societies are binding prescriptive rules, enforced by law courts which adjudicate on whether persons have broken the law, and arbitrate decisions between quarrelling parties, However, aside from such banalities there is considerable dissensus on the subject of law.

Historically in Christian, Islamic and Judaic thought law was considered the commandments of God – whether revealed through the Bible or the Qur'an, or interpreted by the Church or religious scholars – and law encompassed private morality as well as public conduct. The theory of **natural law** suggests that all legal systems are attempts by human beings to reach the legal system which would be adopted by rational human beings, a theory which creates more problems than it solves. The theory of **legal positivism**, by contrast, defines a legal system as a set of conventions established by a law-making body: a law is a law if it is (explicitly or implicitly) made by an authorized law-making body; whether the law is moral or is good law is a separate matter.

The domain of law as a subject of intellectual inquiry, and as a set of social practices is enormous. For example, if they make these distinctions at all, legal systems differ among themselves and over time in what they regard as public and private law, in what they deem as criminal or civil law, and in what role they give to the judiciary in reviewing the law-making process. Legal systems also differ in the procedures they use for implementing the rule of law. These variations are the subject matter of comparative law.

Two of the most vexed political subjects are the relationships of law to morality, and of law to politics. For legal positivists it is clear that what the law forbids may be morally permissible, and indeed morally required; and that what is morally wrong may be permitted by the law, or required by the law. Other views of law find such sharp distinctions more problematic. In Western **liberalism** it has been customary to distinguish matters of private moral conduct, which should not be the subject of legal regulation, from matters of public law. This reasoning is the source of the liberal view that the state and the law have no rightful place in the bedrooms of consenting adults. Moral conservatives, whether Christian or Muslim believe by contrast that the law should be used as a guardian of morality, in order to preserve a virtuous social order – a viewpoint shared by many feminists.

The relationships between law and politics are manifold, but the major sources of controversy in liberal democracies are easy to state: they are over the extent to which judges should be able to make public policy, creatively interpret constitutional or other law, and bring judicial regulation to bear on a policy domain previously free of such regulation. **BO'L**

See also rule of law; sovereignty.

Further reading J.M. Finnis, *Natural Law and natural Rights*; H.L.A. Hart, *The Concept of Law*; N. MacCormick, *Legal Reasoning and Legal Theory*.

LAW OF LARGE NUMBERS see
Probability; **Statistics**

LAW OF NATURE

Scientists have discovered an impressive number of laws of Nature. One example is Boyle's law, which states that the pressure of a gas varies inversely with its volume at a constant temperature: so the smaller the volume of a gas the greater its pressure, given that its temperature remains the same.

Philosophers of **science** have attempted to explain just what laws of Nature are. Some have held that laws of Nature are merely true generalizations, stating that whenever an event of one sort occurs, an event of another sort also occurs – that whenever an F event occurs, a G event also occurs. One problem with this is that not all laws of Nature state that all F events are accompanied by G events. Some laws, such as some laws of **physics**, are merely probabilistic and so can only be represented as stating that, for instance, 75% of F events are accompanied by G events.

Further, laws of Nature are not just true generalizations stating that a certain fixed percentage (possibly but not necessarily 100%) of F events are accompanied by G events. They do not just state that, as a matter of fact, x% of F events are accompanied by G events. For it can be accidentally true that x% of F events are accompanied by G events. Suppose that, as a matter of complete coincidence, every time Gail sneezes in London, Pierre sneezes in Paris. Then it is true, but not a law of Nature, that whenever Gail sneezes in London, Pierre also sneezes in Paris. This generalization is not a law of Nature because it is merely accidentally true.

If it is a law of Nature that x% of F events are accompanied by G events, then it is not merely accidentally true that x% of F events are accompanied by G events. Laws of Nature (non-logically) necessitate their instances. Since it is a law that the pressure of a gas varies inversely with its volume at constant temperature, it is (non-logically) necessarily and not just accidentally true that whenever the temperature of a gas remains the same and its volume decreases, its pressure increases.

So laws state not merely that x% of F events are accompanied by G events, but that necessarily, x% of F events are accompanied by G events. Generalizations which are merely accidentally true do not support counterfactuals – they do not tell us what would have been the case if the world had been different from the way it actually was. The accidentally true generalization that whenever Gail sneezes in London, Pierre also sneezes in Paris, does not allow us to infer that if, counter to fact, Gail had sneezed more often in London, then Pierre would have sneezed more often in Paris. In contrast, we can infer from Boyle's law that if, counter to fact, the temperature of a certain gas had remained the same as its volume decreased, then its pressure would have increased.

So laws of Nature state that certain generalizations are (non-logically) necessarily true, and they therefore support counterfactuals. **AJ**

See also modality; philosophy of science.

Further reading D. Armstrong, *What is a Law of Nature?*; C. Hempel, *Aspects of Scientific Explanation*.

LEARNABILITY

Learnability theory, in **linguistics**, is relevant to explanations of how children acquire their first **language**. By means of mathematical modelling, learnability theory takes into account the conditions faced by the language-learning child and examines different classes of languages (both natural human languages and other possibilities), in order to determine which ones are logically possible to learn. Typically, a mathematical model, known as a learning procedure, is set up which substitutes for the language learning capacity of the child. This learning procedure is presented with sentences from a language, one after another, and is faced with the task of identifying the relevant language, in addition to formulating an appropriate grammar. If the procedure is unsuccessful, further guesses are made after the presentation of each new string until success is achieved. In essence, then, the learning procedure is mimicking the eventual achievement of the language-learning child. In fact, the level of mimicry is arguably quite low, since learning procedures often operate on the basis of highly idealized learning conditions, which bear little relation to those actually experienced by the child. For example, the procedure typically has an infinite amount of time available, it is never exposed to ungrammatical sentences, it never makes any errors itself and after the presentation of each new sentence, an entire grammatical system is projected.

Sometimes, the strictures of the learning situation, in conjunction with the characteristics of the particular class of language involved, will result in inevitable failure, since no amount of guessing will allow the language to be identified. Thus, certain types of language are said to be logically impossible to learn. Given the kind of exposure to language experienced by children (the input conditions), learnability models tend to reach the paradoxical conclusion that even natural human languages are unlearnable. The fact that all normal children do in fact learn a language is then normally explained by appealing to the concept of innate linguistic knowledge. It is reasoned that the child must be able to compensate for the paucity of the linguistic input by relying on a genetically determined knowledge of crucial aspects of language. Being innate, the need to learn these features of language, in the sense of deducing what they are by analysing appropriate sentences, is obviated. **MS**

See also innateness; universal grammar.

LEGAL POSITIVISM

Legal positivism is the name given to a theory of **law**, developed by **utilitarian** jurists like Jeremy Bentham and John Austin, and most famously developed in the 20th century by the Austrian Hans

Kelsen and the Englishman Herbert Hart. Legal positivists aimed to develop a theory of what constituted a legal system which was value-free – that is, independent of moral content and amenable to empirical analysis. This theory would establish an analytical foundation for legal analysis autonomous of both political and sociological explanations of legal institutions and practices. Austin believed that law could be defined as the commands of the sovereign, a position which created some difficulties for 'laws' which did not appear to have this character. These difficulties were resolved by Kelsen who argued that any genuine legal system had a *Grundnorm*, or basic norm, which identified the ultimate source of legal authority: Hart's 'rule of recognition' describes the same notion.

Whether in its modern Hartian or Kelsenian variations, the key ideas of legal positivism are straightforward. Legal systems are sets of rules (interpreted in a broad sense) applied by judges as part of societal regulation by states. Laws are laws by virtue of their form, rather than of their moral or political content. The legal system in any state worthy of the name operates under an extra-legal *Grundnorm* (Kelsen) or 'rule of recognition' (Hart). The validity of laws is determined within the empirically relevant *Grundnorm* or rule of recognition.

Applied to liberal democratic states, legal positivism suggests at least three key propositions. First, the formal role of the judicial system is to determine the laws established by the constitution and validly made by the democratically authorized law-makers. It is a matter for empirical investigation by other disciplines to establish whether or not any given judicial system fulfils that role: whether or not judges subvert the laws because of their class, ethnic, religious, gender or ideological backgrounds; whether or not judges defer to (or obstruct) the executive, public agencies, minorities or individuals rather than uphold the laws; and whether or not judges are competently educated, trained and recruited for the tasks they are required to perform. Second, for legal positivists the relevant operational background normative theory for judges and lawyers in a liberal democratic state is the one which establishes the extra-legal source of valid laws. In the case of the US the relevant theory is that the (validly amended) Constitution provides the *Grundnorm*; in the case of the UK the relevant theory is that the *Grundnorm* is provided by the doctrine of parliamentary sovereignty (qualified, perhaps, by the UK's membership of the European Community).

Such background theories, while important, may not, of course, be of much help in deciding judicial 'hard cases' since laws may be ambiguous and conflict. However, legal positivists do not maintain that legal systems are perfectly-integrated hierarchies in which there is no role for debate and argument about the meaning and interpretation of laws; nor that there are no gaps or contradictions in any given country's legal system. It is also a misunderstanding of legal positivism to imply that it means that judges do not, when interpreting the law, have recourse to normative principles. Indeed one merit of legal positivism is that it recognizes that there may be no coherence of a moral or political kind in a given constitutional or administrative order, that rival judicial doctrines may be competing to influence hard judicial decisions, while still maintaining that there is a definite legal system.

Perhaps the strongest merit of legal positivism is precisely that it helps define appropriate boundaries between the subject of law, including its technical interpretation by judges and lawyers, and discussions of the extra-legal determination of law. This demarcation had negative consequences in so far as it apparently established intellectual barriers to entry and enquiry on either side of this division. However, there is no logical reason why legal positivism had to have these consequences. Jules Coleman's book *Markets, Morals and the Law* shows that legal positivism need not be an obstruction to the fruitful intermarriage of law, **economics** and **political science**.

Finally, legal positivism, unlike other approaches to law, is more likely to counsel scepticism on the subject of whether 'international law' actually exists, on the grounds that there is no *Grundnorm* or rule of recognition which can establish the authorized source of 'international law'. **BO'L**

See also justice; natural law; rule of law; sovereignty.

Further reading H.L.A. Hart, *The Concept of Law*; H. Kelsen, *General Theory of Law and the State*.

LEGENDS

Legends (Latin, 'to be read') are **myths** created round historical characters or incidents. Unlike myths, which grow spontaneously, legends often have a specific creator or point of origin, and their purpose is more overtly didactic (usually political or religious). Although in every other way they resemble myths. Legends usually involve (historical) human characters with supernatural beings, and they generalize specific incidents or experiences in a way which, paradoxically, gives it local validity and resonance. At some stage, indeed, legends may well turn into myths. For example we have no way of telling, at this distance, if the Trojan War really happened, if its 'reality' is greater or less than that of Oedipus. King Arthur's Camelot is at the halfway stage between legend and myth, and the death of Julius Caesar is already entering the realms of legend (complete, as in Shakespeare's play, with supernatural overtones). In many legends, there remains a kind of vestigial uneasiness, as if the genre is not entirely stable – and writers who deal in legend, from Livy to the creators of modern commercials (jeans, cars, beer and the Olympic games are all, in their different ways, given a legendary gloss in the interests of consumerism), tend towards a falsely naive swagger – quite unlike the relaxed self-confidence of those who deal in myth. **KMcL**

LEGITIMATION

Legitimation (Latin, 'making lawful'), in **politics**, is the manner and process by which a state or political system receives justification. A political order is legitimate if considered valid by the population. In classical civilization, legitimate power was simply lawful power. In modern discussions of political legitimacy lawfulness and morality have been separated. Governments can have legal authority without having moral legitimacy.

The sociologist Max Weber (1864–1920) made an important contribution to the understanding of legitimacy. Weber stressed the importance of followers' beliefs. He distinguished between legal-rational **authority**, which rests on the belief in the legality of rules on which those with authority act; traditional authority, which rests on the acceptance of those chosen to rule in accordance with the customs and practices of tradition; and charismatic authority, which rests on devotion to an individual leader believed to possess exceptional powers. These three types are 'ideal' or 'pure' types.

Legitimation crisis, a term coined by J. Habermas (see below) refers to the difficulties created for modern political systems, depending as they do on popular 'consent' to maintain their political authority in meeting major social problems. Habermas sees these problems as arising from the need of the capitalist system to accumulate capital on the one hand and increased popular demand for social equality on the other. Failure to reconcile these contradictory pressures leads to a legitimation crisis, he argues. **DA**

See also bureaucracy; capital; charisma; collective action; discourse; dominant ideology; hegemony; ideal type; ideology; power; social construction of reality; social control; social movement; society; sociology of knowledge; state.

Further reading J. Habermas, *Legitimation Crisis*; J.G. Merquior, *Rousseau and Weber: Two studies in the Theory of Legitimacy*.

LEITMOTIF

Leitmotif (German, 'leading theme') is an idea widely used in **music**, especially in such complex works as Wagner's **music-dramas**. A *leitmotif* is a series of notes, or a scrap of melody, harmony or rhythm, embodying a specific idea. In Wagner's operas, for example, each character has a distinctive *leitmotif*, as do objects like castles, rings or swords, not to mention such abstractions as destiny, duty or love. These motifs are woven into the musical texture, enriching the meaning with allusion and suggestion at every point. (The motifs of 'betrayal', 'fate', 'love' and 'magic philtre', for example, underlie the first meeting of a pair of future lovers.)

Wagner's followers claimed that he invented the technique, but it had been used – albeit not so obsessively – in music for centuries, adding motivic richness, for example, to **Renaissance** Christian church music, and being a main resource in Indian art music. European composers after Wagner made extensive use of it, and it is a standard resource in works as distinct as Berg's chamber music, Mahler's symphonies and the **music-theatre** works of Britten, Henze and Stockhausen.

In the other arts, critics have found *leitmotif* techniques analogous to those in music. In Far Eastern nature-painting, specific objects are included to suggest associations or ideas. In film, images are blurred together or recalled to make artistic points. *Leitmotif* adds allusive density to such complex literary works as James Joyce's *Finnegans Wake* or Proust's *Remembrance of Things Past*. In all other arts, however, the technique seems more explicit and contrived than in music – possibly because music, by its very nature, deals in evocation and allusion rather than in assertion. **KMcL**

LEXICOGRAPHY

Lexicography (Greek, 'writing about words'), in **linguistics**, is a practical discipline which deals with the planning and compilation of reference works based on lexical information. Monolingual and multilingual dictionaries are complemented by specialist dictionaries for numerous subjects (for example, medicine, law or navigation) and styles (for example, regional dialects or slang). Other lexically-oriented reference works include thesauri, glossaries and computerized concordance surveys. The information these works contain often takes on a prescriptive character, and contributes to the standardization of a **language** by setting out acceptable linguistic norms. Consequently, dictionaries can illuminate our knowledge of social attitudes

towards language, as much for what is omitted as for the information they contain.

Many dictionaries include information about linguistic form, including spelling, pronunciation, and **morphological** inflections as well as syntactic information about part of speech (noun, verb and so on). The actual definition of a word may comprise several kinds of explanation, including, where appropriate, translation, interpretation in terms of a strictly limited set of defining vocabulary, historical information on word origins, discussion, or an example of the word as it is actually used. Dictionary entries may also provide historical information on origin and earliest recorded occurrences, in addition to **sociolinguistic** data on usage according to region, dialect and style. In recent years, a wide range of texts has been analysed in vast computer surveys, designed so that dictionaries may reflect more accurately how word meanings are partly dependent on the ways in which they are actually used. **MS**

See also computational linguistics; language planning; lexicology; prescriptive grammar.

LEXICOLOGY

Lexicology (Greek, 'the study of words'), in **linguistics**, examines all aspects of the way words figure in human experience, which means that an enormously diverse spectrum of interests is entertained, ranging from the principles guiding dictionary compilation to questions concerning the storage and retrieval of words in the mind (see also **lexicography** and **psycholinguistics**). Until quite recently, the ways in which words combine to form sentences (**syntax**) has received much more attention than the nature of the words themselves. As a result, there has been a tendency to regard the lexicon as little more than a list of words, supplemented by idiosyncratic aspects of word usage.

Of central importance is the issue of how word meaning is represented in the mind. Clearly, words can be used by many different speakers in many different contexts and still convey meaning in a consistent way. This observation led to the idea that words must possess a stable core of meaning which allows them to be identified uniquely. The so-called semantic core of a word comprises a list of essential attributes which together define the meaning of a word. For example, the core meaning of 'bull' is composed of the properties male, bovine and animal. All other aspects of our knowledge about bulls (their aggressiveness, dislike of red rags and so on) are consigned to an encyclopaedic store of non-essential information.

This componential approach is useful because it can account for overlaps in meaning between words. Thus, if man is described as human, male and adult, then an overlap with the meaning of bull is explained, since they both possess the feature male. In addition, synonyms can be described as words which share precisely the same components of meaning, even if their pragmatic meanings vary slightly. However, serious problems arise when we consider that there is no objective method of deciding which components of meaning should be included in the semantic core. Furthermore, for some words it is difficult to find any single feature which is absolutely necessary and applicable to all exponents of the word. A famous example in this regard is the category of games.

A separate approach to word meaning acknowledges that words naturally cluster together according to shared aspects of meaning to form semantic fields. It is suggested that words may be represented in the mind according to the network of links they establish with other words. Word meaning can then be described in terms of the relations between words. Experimental research has revealed that words at the same level of detail are often grouped together: 'rose' and 'poppy', for example, would be more readily associated than 'rose' and 'plant'. Another strong organizing factor is the characteristic association of words known as collocation, as with 'hazel eyes' or 'hot temper' (rather than, for instance, 'hazel hair' or 'lukewarm temper'). A complicating factor, revealed by recent computer analyses, is that the meaning of a word varies according to the particular collocations it enters into, and furthermore, the different senses of an item occur in predictable syntactic patterns. **MS**

See also computational linguistics; prototype theory.

Further reading J. Aitchison, *Words in the Mind*.

LIBERAL ARTS AND LIBERAL SCIENCES

'Liberal arts' (from Latin *liber*, 'free man' and *ars*, 'skill') was an expression coined in 14th-century Europe. It meant aristocratic pursuits and skills, as opposed to 'the mechanical arts': those appropriate to people of lower class. There were seven liberal arts, as defined in universities of the time, and they were divided into two groups. The *trivium* ('triple path') consisted of grammar, **logic** and rhetoric, and the more advanced *quadrivium* ('four-fold path') consisted of arithmetic, **astronomy, geometry** and **music**. By studying these seven subjects, a young European could become a 'master of arts', and was qualified to proceed to the next stage, 'doctor' ('learned'), in a single subject such as **law, medicine** or – the highest ranked – **theology**.

The liberal sciences, as defined in 15th-century Europe, were a variant of the above, and were regarded as a new-fangled aberration unfit for the 'older' universities. They were the basis for an educational curriculum which combined (what we would call) **arts** and **science**; like the liberal arts, they were intended for the education of aristocrats only, and had no connection with the skills required by ordinary working people; they came to underlie the French *baccalauréat* just as the liberal arts once underlay educational systems of other kinds. They were astronomy, drawing, grammar, **painting** and **physics**. KMcL

LIBERAL SCIENCES see Liberal Arts and Liberal Sciences

LIBERALISM

Liberalism (from Latin *liberalis*, 'of a free man or woman') is the name given to a diverse set of political doctrines committed to ensuring **liberty** and **equality** for individuals, within conditions of limited and **representative government**. Liberalisms, in principle, are politically secular, and embrace philosophical **rationalism** and **individualism**. Historically, liberalism originated in western Europe and North America and expressed the political aspirations of those who argued for freedom from state and church control of thought and expression. Liberalism has always stood for tolerance – although liberals are not thereby obliged to display tolerance towards the illiberal, especially those who would seek to abolish liberal arrangements. Liberalism is grounded in the belief that there is no natural moral order which can be confidently known by states or churches; therefore individuals must be free to pursue their own conceptions of the good – consistent, of course, with enabling others to enjoy the same freedom. It follows that liberals support freedom of expression, freedom of association and freedom from governmental 'intervention' in the conduct of private life, and that the institutions of church and state should be separated.

These beliefs explain why liberalism and **democracy** are compatible although historically liberalism has not always been associated with a democratic philosophy. Indeed it was not until the mid–19th century, in the writings of the French analyst Alexis de Tocqueville and the Englishman John Stuart Mill, that liberals came to believe that democracy, individualism, liberty, equality and the **rule of law** could be reconciled. However, this reconciliation of liberalism and democracy had been anticipated in the constitutional republican writings of French- and English-speaking authors of the **Enlightenment** – notably in Rousseau's *The Social Contract* and in *The Federalist Papers*, written by James Madison, Alexander Hamilton and John Jay, which helped shape the American Constitution. American liberals, drawing upon the thought of the French philosopher Montesquieu and the English philosopher Harrington, prescribed checks and balances, and a separation of powers, as ways of preventing the potential for governments to become despotic.

It is possible to distinguish several types of liberalism. In the first place there has been a division between utilitarians and rights-based liberals. **Utilitarians** believe that moral and political philosophy must be based on welfare-maximizing principles: government and public policy must be conducted according to 'the greatest good for the greatest number', on the supposition that each person is to be treated as equally important. On this conception the aim of liberalism is to ensure the maximum degree of want-satisfaction, or alternatively to minimize the degree of suffering experienced by people. The utilitarian foundations of liberalism can be found in the writings of David Hume, Jeremy Bentham and James Mill. By contrast rights-based liberalism, associated historically with John Locke, Immanuel Kant, and John Stuart Mill, emphasizes that individuals have (or should have) inalienable rights or personal autonomy which should not be transgressed by any other individuals, groups, or, most importantly, the state even in pursuit of the greatest good for the greatest number. In this perspective, government should be based upon the consent of individuals who contract with one another to protect their rights; and government should be limited to the protections of these fundamental rights and to the provision of basic services which individuals agree cannot be provided by their own actions.

In the second place we can distinguish between classical or economic liberals, enthusiasts for the *laissez faire* doctrines of Adam Smith and David Ricardo, and new or social liberals, like T.H. Green and J.M. Keynes, who were influenced by **socialism**. Economic liberals emphasize the centrality of private property rights and the free commerce of individuals as the foundations of a free and prosperous society; and reject governmental intervention, except where it is absolutely necessary, on the grounds that governmental monopolies lead to inefficiency and stagnation. Classical liberals believe in maximizing liberty and minimizing government, and in Adam Smith's doctrine of the '**invisible hand**': if agents are left to pursue their economic self-interest they will, unintentionally, produce the best economic consequences. They also embrace methodological individualism. Economic liberals are also likely to see democracy as a threat to the operations of a free market society because democracy permits people to organize against the consequences of market competition and therefore seek to ensure that constitutional provisions can prevent governments from violating property rights.

New liberals or social liberals, by contrast, reject the minimalist role of the state envisaged in classical liberalism. They have a more wide-ranging conception of freedom, positive liberty, which rejects the classical liberal assumption that greater government means correspondingly less freedom. They have historically been influenced by the political theories of the Englishman T.H. Green, which were in turn influenced by the writings of the German philosopher Hegel, by the American educationalist John Dewey, and by the theories of political economy developed by J.M. Keynes. Common to social liberalism is the belief that advanced industrial society requires substantial state intervention in order to offset distortions produced by the free market; and a rejection of the extreme individualism which sees no place for society, community or the state in forging the conditions necessary for individuals to be free and equal. Social or modern liberalism is a friend of benign big government; believing that the welfare state can and should raise the moral and intellectual capacities of citizens, and enable genuine equality of opportunity.

This division within what was liberalism has led classical or economic liberals to be called 'conservatives' in English-speaking countries, while the label of liberalism has been claimed by the new or social liberals, who have often allied themselves with social democrats and socialists. On the European continent, by contrast, liberalism generally retains its classical meaning.

In contemporary political theory, liberalism is criticized by 'communitarians' for having an impoverished, atomistic conception of human beings, which neglects the profound importance of community in shaping individuals' capacities and morality – a criticism common to conservatives, socialists and religious critics of liberalism. Robust defenders of liberalism maintain in reply that it is precisely the virtue of liberalism that it does not take for granted whatever prejudices or values may be bestowed by tradition or communities, but rather requires that they be capable of rational justification. This rationalist impulse explains why liberals are so often in the vanguard of movements to reform societies and states. **BO'L**

See also conservatism; libertarianism.

Further reading G. de Ruggiero, *The History of European Liberalism*; L. Hart, *The Liberal Tradition in America*; D.J. Mannin, *Liberalism*; J.S. Mill, *On Liberty*; M.J. Sandel (ed.), *Liberalism and its Critics*.

LIBERATION THEOLOGY

Liberation theology is a movement mainly found in a Roman **Catholic** context. It developed in the late 1960s and seeks to interpret the Christian faith from the perspective of the poor and oppressed, suffering post-colonial deprivation. The Brazilians Leonardo and Clodovis Boff, for example, speak of a 'chemical reaction': faith + oppression = liberation theology. Gustavo Guttierez talks of 'commitment to the poor, the "non-person"'. Since the 1970s the movement has spread into an African context of racism and apartheid, into black theology, gay theology and so on. **EMJ**

Further reading L. and C. Boff, *Liberation Theology*.

LIBERTARIANISM

Libertarianism (from Latin *libertas*, 'state of being free') is the name given in the **political sciences** to the confluence of **anarchism** and **liberalism**, although the term is often used to refer to any kind of rejection of authority, of whatever kind. Libertarians believe either that 'government is best which governs least', or that 'government is best which governs not at all'. (Since the latter viewpoint is described under the entry on anarchism only minimal-state libertarianism is discussed here). Such libertarians emphasize the inalienable rights of individuals, especially to acquire and maintain private property. The sole legitimate function of government, they say, are to protect these rights, and to enforce contracts made between consenting adults; in other words prisons and courts are the only reasonabl forms of government. Such libertarians regard taxation, especially redistributive taxation, as 'forced labour'.

Contemporary libertarianism owes most to the American reception of the work of the Austrian school of economists (notably Ludwig von Mises, Friedrich von Hayek) which defended the state purely as a 'night-watchman'. The best-known economic, literary, and philosophical exponents of American libertarianism are Murray Rothbard, Ayn Rand and Robert Nozick. The latter's book *Anarchy, State and Utopia* (1974) is perhaps the most lucid statement of the libertarian case, and attempts to establish that a libertarian society would be the most feasible form of a **Utopian** social order – although its author has now repudiated many of its arguments.

Nozick's *Anarchy, State and Utopia* argues against all principles of 'patterned' **justice**: in other words against all attempts to regulate economic prices or incomes to produce specific patterns of income distribution whether they be egalitarian or highly stratified. Justice is purely a matter of establishing whether somebody has properly the rights (or entitlements) to a given set of objects or activities. Libertarians argue that provided the initial allocation of rights in property are just, then any distributive outcomes resulting from the free activities of individuals are for that reason also just.

There are two major problems with this childishly simple argument. First, in most actually existing histories of the world it is plain that existing property rights have stemmed from injustice (sometimes described as conquest, robbery, or exploitation). Second, it would require major governmental activity to establish a régime of just property rights and therefore a consistent libertarian would have to grant to government (or some other agency) a major interventionist role in ensuring that property rights are just.

The key assumption behind libertarian thought is that formal institutions such as governments, formal religions and social organizations are not only poor managers of resources, but are also fundamentally inimical to the autonomy of the individual, the most fundamental libertarian value. It is easy to see why critics of libertarianism

describe it as a rationalization of egoism, but that is a criticism which many libertarians accept with pride. **BO'L**

See also capitalism; individualism.

Further reading T.R. Machan, *Capitalism and Individualism: Reframing the Argument for the Free Society*; R. Nozick, *Anarchy, State and Utopia*; M. Rothbard, *Power and Market*.

LIBERTY

The degree of liberty possessed by the citizens of a state has become the key standard by which liberal democracies are compared with other forms of government. Usually measures of effective **civil rights** and **human rights** are taken to be good indicators of the degree of liberty within a régime. However, there is much less consensus on the meaning of liberty.

In political thought liberty is largely synonymous with freedom, but it is as well to recall that liberty or freedom have not always been valued in Western or other forms of political thought. Indeed religious and political authoritarians, and many conservatives and traditionalists, equate liberty with licence, the absence of control, moral chaos and unbridled relativism. Moreover, many political philosophers, from Plato to Hobbes, have argued that human beings should sacrifice their freedom to ensure order or stability, in the form of strong and/or enlightened government.

Following Isaiah Berlin, many political theorists make a distinction between positive liberty ('freedom to do', or 'self-mastery') and negative liberty ('freedom from' or 'not being obstructed') although others argue that the distinction is not logically sustainable, that it just confuses matters. The concept of liberty, whether positive or negative, or both, evidently means 'not being controlled' or 'not being obstructed'.

The most notable exponents of positive liberty were Rousseau and Kant. They argued that genuine freedom is possessed only by individuals who are autonomous agents – that is, by those whose power of reason is free from manipulation by others, and are capable of exercising **self-determination** in their moral and political choices. We are free only when we act rightly, and vice versa: we are free when our 'real self' is in charge. This thesis can, of course, become a means for suggesting that people are not free even when they claim to be: thus, the Marxist concept of 'false consciousness' is derived from the argument that those who possess the means of production manipulate moral and political thought through their control of the **media**, **culture** and political debate. Of course, those who claim to be able to distinguish between 'true' and 'false' freedom, and 'real' and 'unreal' selves, must assume that they know what genuinely non-manipulated individuals would choose to do in different circumstances – and often their claims to possess such knowledge will be contestable. However, versions of positive freedom have undoubtedly been embraced in **socialism**, social **liberalism** and **Marxism**.

The idea of negative liberty, by contrast, is derived from the doctrine of natural rights which claims that individuals have certain inalienable rights which should not be transgressed by any individual, group or government. Such rights are 'liberties', that is, rights to be free from control, and are most vigorously supported in the doctrine of **libertarianism**. Negative liberty exists where citizens are free to behave in any way which does not harm another citizen or contravene specific laws. Negative liberty is often tested in societies where governments or pressure groups attempt to define what constitutes harm to others: thus the private sexual activities of consenting adults would appear to be harmful to neither the practitioners nor the general public, yet many states prohibit by law certain types of private sexual expression.

In the view of most people the word liberty or freedom is usually an instrument for identifying agents or forces who are allegedly controlling people or obstructing their freedom. Thus libertarians complain that states block freedom; conservatives that liberalism encourages vice and inhibits the virtuous exercise of freedom; socialists that capitalist institutions inhibit human flourishing; nationalists that empires block self-determination; and feminists that the freedom of women is obstructed by patri-archal institutions. In other words arguments about liberty may disguise more fundamental arguments about what constitutes a good society. **BO'L**

See also conservatism; nationalism.

Further reading I. Berlin, *Four Essays on Liberty*; J. Gray and Z. Pelczynski (eds.), *Conceptions of Liberty in Political Philosophy*; A. Ryan (ed.), *The Idea of Freedom*; C. Taylor, *The Sources of the Self*.

LIBIDO

Libido was a word used by physicians in the 18th century (who loosely mixed Latin with their terminology) to mean sexual desire. The first dynamic psychiatrists, Benedikt and Krafft-Ebing, based theories of nervous illness on an undetermined fluid of sexual energies. Sexologists also used the word in the sense of sexual desire. Moll gave it the wider meaning of sexual instinct in a developmental evolutionary sense and Freud adopted this.

Jung identified libido not as sexual energy but as psychic energy which expresses itself through universal symbols. This way of describing libido led to his concepts of the **collective unconscious** and the **archetypes**. For Jung, the first three to five years were a time of pre-sexual libidinal sexual energy; from five to the age of puberty the germs of sexuality appear; then puberty marks the time of sexual maturity. Present difficulties in an adult patient would be seen to be a reactivation of blocked libido in the past Jung's principles of libidinal energy were the same as in the physical sciences: conservation, transformation and degradation They had no cause, only aim, and were unmeasurable. **MJ**

LIFE

Definitions of life have interested philosophers since prehistory and, in many ways technical advances in **biology** have done little to further our understanding of the nature of life. The French anatomist Marie François-Xavier Bichat (1771–1802) defined life as 'The sum total of functions which resist death', but did not attempt to pin down the reasons for this ability. Jean

Baptiste Lamarck (1744–1829) proposed that life was 'organic movement' made possible by organization and external stimulation. The force behind the organization which was clearly a characteristic of life was considered by most 19th-century philosophers to be beyond scientific explanation, though it was widely accepted that many of the processes of life could be explained in physical and chemical terms. Claude Bernard (1813–78) denied that life was the result of complexity of organization, claiming instead that it was the result of directed development. He stated five general characteristics of life which are still useful in modern definitions: Organization; Generation; Nutrition; Development; Death.

Historically, philosophers had reasoned that the vital force resided in certain organs, particularly the heart or the brain; in the 18th and 19th centuries there was a trend to consider the vital force as a property of tissues, cells or organic molecules. The physicist Erwin Schrüdinger (1887–1961), in his book *What is Life?*, proposed that the **genes** held the answer, and the development of an understanding of molecular **genetics** is enabling scientists to explain some of the features of life which were previously considered, because of their inexplicability, to be evidence for a vital force.

Modern biology neither requires, nor permits, the idea of a life force and, as scientists become more specialized, scientific interest in the nature of life seems to recede because experimental science demands that biological functions be interpreted in terms of physical and chemical processes. However, this scientific view of life is disputed by some, largely on theological grounds while there are others, scientists among them, who hold that the idea of a life force and the explosion of life purely in physio-chemical terms are not mutually exclusive. **RB**

See also abiogenesis; biopoiesis; mechanism; organicism; panspermia; vitalism.

Further reading Humberto Maturana, *The Tree of Knowledge*.

LIFE CYCLE

Life scientists use the term life cycle to mean the sequence of development through which an individual organism passes from its first stage as an individual to the point at which it reproduces itself. Thus the life cycle of humans begins with the formation of the single-celled zygote by the fusion of egg and sperm, progresses through embryo, birth, childhood to sexual maturity, and completes the circle when the egg or sperm of the individual contribute to the formation of a zygote. A life cycle is often characteristic of a given group of organisms and is closely adapted to environment and lifestyle. It may include specialized stages for dispersal, reproduction, dormancy, migration, etc. Some organisms, such as the sockeye salmon, may die immediately after reproduction while others may live on to reproduce again or to care for their young. Simple, single-celled organisms, such as bacteria, divide by binary fission and thus have a life cycle which is closely related to the cycle of cell division. **RB**

See also developmental biology; metamorphosis.

LIFE SCIENCES

The life sciences encompass all fields of scientific investigation of living organisms and living processes. The pursuit of life sciences may be described as the application of all of human's scientific disciplines to the elucidation of the processes behind **life** itself. The fields of **medicine** and agricultural science are applied life sciences, while large areas of **geology** and **chemistry** involve the study of the influence of life upon non-living matter.

Prehistoric man, no doubt, had an understanding of living organisms which enabled him to hunt, gather and domesticate those animals and plants which were of use to him. The earliest written records, such as Egyptian papyri from around 1500 BCE, indicate a degree of knowledge about diseases of man and animals, and the preservative and medicinal properties of particular herbs. The Chinese had developed a structured system of medicinal herbs (some of which are today proving useful in Western medicine) by 2800 BCE, and were using the silkworm for the large-scale production of silk. The Hindus in India had developed their own system of herbal medicines, and were knowledgeable about a variety of medical subjects, especially **anatomy**. However, it appears that the pre-Greek civilizations collected their knowledge of living processes primarily because the knowledge could be applied to medicine and agriculture. Furthermore, they believed that natural phenomena were the result of supernatural powers and were therefore often beyond human understanding. The ancient Greeks were the first to search for rational explanations for life; their ideas were based on a mixture of observation, guesswork and superstition, and focused on the question of what separated life from non-living matter, but came to dominate the development of Western **science** for over a millennium. Thales of Miletus, in the 7th century BCE, postulated that all living things were composed of water. This idea was expanded by his student Anaximander, who put forward the idea that life was composed from special mixtures of the four elements (fire, earth, water and air). The Greek philosopher who dominated the study of life was Aristotle (384–322 BCE), who made extensive observations of the living kingdom, classifying and dividing. Aristotle's philosophy was based on his belief that all living processes had a final cause or purpose.

After the decline of the ancient Greek civilization, the ideas of the Greek philosophers were developed by the Arabs, while science lay dormant in the West. When the **Renaissance** arrived, Western **science** was stimulated by the spread of academic ideas and the use of paper and then printing. A questioning environment developed and philosophers were encouraged and patronized by the wealthy; scientific societies, such as the Royal Society in England (founded in 1662), were established for debate between the learned; technical advances, especially the development of the microscope, enabled new fields of inquiry to be opened. Systematic approaches to classification and comparison clarified much existing knowledge, and new ideas were put forward by scientific philosophers which for the first time challenged the dominance of Greek philosophy.

In the 18th and 19th centuries, the progression of the life sciences continued to accelerate, stimulated by expeditions to the New World, such as those made by Captain Cook to Australasia (1768–79) and by Charles Darwin to South America in the 19th century. In the 20th century, progress continued as technology enabled the investigation of the genetic make-up of living organisms and the ultrastructure of their cells. **Ecology** has developed as a major new field of life science and has thrown new light on many older fields. The development of the life sciences continues and the systems which are studied grow increasingly complex along with the techniques used. However, the philosophical questions are little changed. **RB**

See also abiogenesis; biogenesis; biology; botany; science; scholasticism; zoology.

Further reading John Bernal, *Science in History*; Charles Singer, *A Short History of Scientific Ideas*.

LIMIT

Limit, in **mathematics**, is the concept which provides the essential basis for the study of **analysis**. The precise definition of the limit by Karl Weierstrass (1815–97) was the breakthrough which enabled mathematicians to make the **calculus** rigorous in the 19th century, to establish it on an equal footing with other branches of mathematics. Weierstrass's definition of the limit amounted to the following. Suppose f is a **function** and a a point; the limit of f at a is L if for each non-zero epsilon there is a non-zero delta such that if x is less than delta away from a then f(x) is less than epsilon away from L. This rather complicated definition amounts (roughly) to saying that the closer x is to a, the closer f(x) is to L. **SMcL**

LINEAR ALGEBRA see Algebra

LINEARITY

The concept of linearity has two applications in **mathematics**.

(1) In a mathematical structure which has the concept of addition incorporated into it, a linear function f is one for which $f(a + b) = f(a) + f(b)$; in some uses of the term, mainly involving **vectors**, it must also be true that $f(a \times v) = a \times f(v)$, where a is a scalar mul-

tiple (something to make the vector v longer or shorter but not change its direction). Essentially, then, a linear function is one for which it does not matter if addition is calculated before or after the function itself is calculated.

(2) A linear equation is one in which all the terms are raised to only the power 1, such as $ax + by = c$ (which is the general equation for the straight line in **Cartesian coordinates**, hence the name). It is usually much easier to solve linear equations than non-linear ones. This is particularly true of linear differential equations, which can often be exactly solved, whereas non-linear differential equations usually cannot. A linear differential equation will look like $af(x) = bf'(x)$, for example (where f' is the first derivative of the function f), while a non-linear equation might take the form $af(x)f''(x) + bf'(x) = c$ (where f'' is the second derivative of the first derivative of f(x)). Many physical systems are governed by the behaviour of non-linear differential equations (turbulence in liquids, for example), and in the past it has been usual to try to understand these systems by approximating the correct differential equation with a linear differential equation which can be exactly solved. Today, with modern advances in **computer** technology, it has become possible to find approximate solutions to the correct differential equation, which has led to new understandings of many physical theories. **SMcL**

See also chaos theory.

LINGUISTIC RECONSTRUCTION

A major aim in **comparative-historical linguistics** is to trace the developmental paths followed by a **language** as it changes over time, in order to reveal the ancestral forms of language from which current, attested forms have emerged. Typically, the historical linguist is faced with the task of reconstructing extinct language forms on the basis of what is known about the way languages change, supplemented by whatever historical evidence is available.

The process of comparative reconstruction assumes that genetically related languages have developed from a common ancestor. Typically, a set of cognates (words from different languages with similar meanings) is compared to determine the systematic differences in their phonological forms. These differences are then attributed to regular processes which transform the sound patterns of a language over time. If independent evidence for a particular sound change is available from independent, well-attested sources, then it is assumed that the same process is applicable in the reconstruction of extinct languages.

The process of internal reconstruction adopts a similar approach, but in this case, the method is applied to a single language. The aim is to show how a single form develops along two separate pathways until two new forms arise in the language. Changes of this kind generally occur when a language develops more than one way of expressing the same meaning. A third method, typological reconstruction, exploits the observation that the presence of one linguistic feature can sometimes provide a reliable indicator that another feature will also be present (see **linguistic typology**). Consequently, if convincing evidence is found for a particular feature in the extinct language, it is sometimes possible to infer that other specific features must also have been present, even though direct evidence for these latter features may not be available. **MS**

LINGUISTIC RELATIVITY

Linguistic relativity, in **linguistics**, is often referred to as the Sapir-Whorf hypothesis because it came to prominence with the writings of the American linguist Edward Sapir (1884–1939) and his student, Benjamin Lee Whorf. They advanced the idea that the structure of our native **language** has a strong influence on the way we perceive the world. In an extreme version, the linguistic relativity hypothesis proposes that people from different language backgrounds effectively live in separate worlds, because of the disparate experiences provided for them by the structures of their languages. Linguistic relativity is often demonstrated by examining the organization of lexical items in a language. For example, in the Eskimo language, Inuit, there is a range of words used to denote different kinds of snow (though far fewer than was originally believed). According to the precepts of linguistic relativity, Inuit speakers should perceive certain physical distinctions between different kinds of snow, because the various words for snow in Inuit provide the means to do so. By implication, therefore, speakers of English, with the single word snow at their disposal, should be oblivious to subtle perceptual distinctions between different qualities of snow.

The thesis of linguistic relativity, when taken to extremes, compels us to accept the view that we are prisoners of our own language. But common experience informs us that most English speakers are perfectly aware that slushy snow is distinct from frozen snow and so on. Furthermore, skiers have developed terms like powder and corn to describe different types of snow. Evidently, for both Inuit speakers and skiers, the concepts conveyed by the spectrum of snow terms have taken on a special salience. However, it does not inevitably follow that, simply in the manifestation of culturally relevant distinctions, our language will thereby dictate the way we view the world.

Attempts to test the Sapir-Whorf hypothesis objectively have often centred on investigations of colour terms. Languages vary quite widely in the way they segment the colour spectrum. For example, many languages have a term equivalent to the colour yellow, but an object which would be classified as yellow in one language may not be so described in another. Apparently, then, the boundaries of colour terms differ according to the language we speak. However, we must also contend with the discovery that when people are asked to choose, say, the best example of yellow from a selection of objects, then a remarkable cross-linguistic consistency emerges. Evidently, people's perception of a quintessential yellow is the same, regardless of linguistic background.

Establishing the validity of the Sapir-Whorf hypothesis with any empirical certitude has been a notoriously difficult undertaking. Many researchers have, in fact, either rejected the concept of linguistic relativity or have abandoned it as unverifiable.

However, it is possible to distinguish between strong and weak versions of the hypothesis. In its strongest form, sometimes known as linguistic determinism, language determines thought. While the concept of linguistic determinism is probably untenable, a weaker version is more plausible, since it merely suggests that language can influence the way we perceive and think about the world. **MS**

LINGUISTIC TYPOLOGY

The diversity of human **languages** can sometimes appear quite overwhelming, but in fact languages tend to fall into distinct categories according to the underlying structural characteristics they share. Through the classification of vast numbers of languages, the limits within which languages can vary are revealed and interesting conclusions about the nature of language per se can be advanced. One approach to typology, adopted by **Prague School linguists**, classified languages on the basis of their sound systems. In tone languages, like Chinese or Thai, pitch contrasts help distinguish one word from another. Thus, in one dialect of Chinese, if the word-form *ma* is pronounced with a level tone, it means 'mother', whereas a falling tone would alter the meaning to 'reprimand'. In non-tone languages, like English or Japanese, on the other hand, pitch contrasts of this kind are not distinctive and hence contribute nothing to word meaning.

More recently, typological research has focused on aspects of **syntax**, most notably in connection with the ordering of the basic sentence constituents, subject (S), verb (V) and object (O). The simple sentences of a given language display one of six possible configurations: SOV, SVO, OSV, OVS, VSO and VOS. By far the most frequently encountered combinations are SVO (e.g. English) and SOV (e.g. Japanese), followed by VSO (e.g. Welsh) and, lagging further behind, VOS, OVS and OSV. In fact, it is a matter of controversy whether any language actually displays the pattern OSV.

Evidently, 'subject-first' languages predominate, and it has been suggested that this unequal distribution reflects a theme-first principle, in which new or thematic information (normally expressed by the subject) is positioned most naturally at the beginning of a sentence. The so-called verb-object bonding principle also helps explain the distribution of word-order patterns with the observation that the verb of a simple sentence forms a more natural association with the object than it does with the subject. The prevalence of SOV and SVO languages bears witness to the rarity of the subject interceding between verb and object in the world's languages.

Word-order typology has revealed the existence of so-called implicational universals, whereby the presence of one feature in a language allows us to predict that certain other features will also be present. For example, it has been discovered that SVO languages prefer prepositions to postpositions (hence 'in the White House' rather than 'the White House in'), and furthermore that there is a predilection for genitives after the noun rather than before (giving 'the House of Commons' in preference to 'of Commons the House'). There is no obvious or necessary reason why SVO languages should prefer prepositions and genitives after the noun, although attempts are being made to find out if the connection is more than coincidental. This correlation is useful, though, for predicting the form of newly encountered SVO languages. Implicational universals have also been influential recently in **comparative-historical linguistics**, since they provide a valuable predictive device for the reconstruction of extinct languages. Given a bundle of structural features, evidence is only required for one of them in order to project that a language displays the entire range of relevant characteristics. However, caution needs to be exercised since implicational universals represent strong tendencies, rather than cast-iron certainties. Furthermore, many languages do not fit easily into a typological schema based on the simple ordering of S, V and O, since, in some cases, there may be no single, basic word order discernible. **MS**

Further reading B. Comrie, *Language Universals and Linguistic Typology;* W. Croft, *Typology and Universals.*

LINGUISTICS

Linguistics, the scientific study of **language**, has a long historical pedigree, since an interest in language is evident in the works of Greek and Indian scholars more than 2,500 years ago. As a distinct academic endeavour, however, linguistics became established in the late 18th century, with the celebrated discovery, made famous by Sir William Jones, that English bore a reliable and predictable resemblance to many other European and Asian languages, including Sanskrit. The similarities between the various members of this language family were ascribed to their descent from a common ancestor, known as Proto-Indo-European. Linguists attempted to reconstruct this ancestor language by showing how antecedent forms evolved into the patterns observed in attested languages. Until the beginning of this century, linguists were almost exclusively preoccupied by philological questions of language change.

In the early years of this century, a revolution in linguistic science was initiated by the Swiss linguist, Ferdinand de Saussure, who is often referred to as the 'father of modern linguistics'. Saussure drew a distinction between diachronic and synchronic approaches to the study of language. The historical concerns of the 19th century fall under the heading of diachronic linguistics, with their emphasis on processes of language change. Despite his significant contributions to the diachronic tradition, Saussure argued for the primacy of the synchronic approach, in which the focus is on the language system as it exists at a particular point in time. The development of synchronic linguistics coincided with the growing interest in North America to record and describe adequately the numerous languages of native Americans which were under threat of extinction. As a result, the attention of many linguists turned to the study of living languages as systems in their own right, often with little regard for the formative influences which shape languages. After all, as Saussure pointed out, as far as the speakers of a language are concerned, the evolutionary history of words and structures is largely irrelevant. In any event, linguistics in the 20th century has been dominated by the synchronic approach, although historical concerns are still actively pursued.

Another important distinction in linguistic research centres on the difference between describing a particular language as opposed to describing language in general. The general approach recognizes language as a uniquely human phenomenon which distinguishes human beings from animals. A central aim is to reveal the limitations of human language and the characteristics which distinguish it from other systems of communication. In providing the general concepts and terminology with which language may be described, this approach also contributes to the investigation of individual languages. Particular languages have been studied for a variety of reasons, for example, the desire to describe norms of usage in grammars and dictionaries. Insights gained from the study of specific languages can also be of great value for confirming or refuting ideas in the study of language in general. Indeed, it has been argued that the study of a single language in depth can provide insights concerning the universal properties of language. However, the fact that this single language was almost inevitably English probably revealed more about the short-sightedness of certain linguists than about the value of this method. In fact, this extreme view has receded in recent years and now it is common for linguists to explore theoretical issues with data from a much broader spectrum of cross-linguistic data.

The prescriptivist approach to language aims not only to deduce the grammatical rules of a language, but also decrees certain norms and standards of correct usage. However, the reasons for declaring one language variant to be correct, while competing forms are incorrect, often has no basis in linguistic theory at all. Instead, decisions are often motivated by sociological concerns, such as the relative prestige of one form over another. Hence, linguists nowadays generally regard their task as one of describing how a language actually is, as opposed to promoting ideas about how it should be. In other words, modern linguistics is descriptive rather than prescriptive.

It should be noted that a descriptive approach quite properly investigates what is and is not possible in a language, but only from an objective, non-judgemental point of view. Despite neglect by linguists, prescriptive issues continue to generate often heated debates among many people, as testified by the letters page of many newspapers. More seriously, prescriptive concerns are a major consideration in the process of **language planning**, when multilingual nations are faced with the complexities of selecting and promoting an appropriate national language. However, these kinds of issues are more properly the concern of **applied linguistics**, which means that theoretical linguistics generally manages to remain purely descriptive in orientation.

The quest for scientific status was initiated in large part by the American linguist, Leonard Bloomfield (1887–1949). It was his belief that linguistics should confine its theorizing to hypotheses which could be confirmed or refuted using objectively verifiable data. This aim was achieved by gathering a large corpus of language samples and subjecting them to a systematic analysis. This approach suffers from certain drawbacks which were first highlighted in the 1960s by Noam Chomsky, who has also been responsible for a further fundamental shift in linguistic research in the latter half of this century. Chomsky pointed out that no matter how large a language corpus is, it will never contain examples of every conceivable kind of linguistic construction. Rather than pursue this futile aim, attention has shifted towards unearthing the principles of the linguistic system which underlie the actual sentences being analysed. In this way, due consideration is given to the fact that a finite system of grammatical rules can generate an infinite number of novel sentences.

This shift of emphasis allowed large bodies of data to be supplemented by the spontaneous grammatical intuitions of native speakers about what is, and is not, grammatically permissible in a language. Linguists often rely on their own intuitions, or alternatively, make use of an informant. In either case, it is important that intuitions provide a reliable source of information, and fortunately, this is indeed the case in the majority of cases. Intuitions are not infallible, though, since there are many occasions when linguists disagree. Nevertheless, the restoration of linguistic intuitions as an acceptable form of data reveals the importance of tapping the underlying mental system which gives rise to language behaviour. As a result, the last four decades have witnessed a radical reassessment of the goals of linguistic theory. The analysis of language as an abstract object, in and of itself, has given way to the task of characterizing the knowledge of language as it exists in the minds of native speakers. MS

See also comparative-historical linguistics; descriptivist linguistics; generative grammar; lexicography; prescriptive grammar; psycholinguistics.

Further reading J. Aitchison, Teach Yourself Linguistics; J, Lyons, Language and Linguistics: An Introduction.

LITERACY/ORALITY

Literacy/orality (Latin littera, 'letter'; os, 'mouth') is a theoretical opposition that compares the conceptions and practices of literate and preliterate societies. Literacy refers to the social practice of reading and writing while orality describes the transmission of knowledge through stylized or artistic speech, for example in poetry, proverbs, folk tales, myths and legends.

In anthropology, the main use of the opposition has been in the consideration of the effects of introducing writing into preliterate communities. In his works since 1976, Jack Goody elaborated on how literacy acts as an agent of social changes. He considered literacy as the major difference between 'primitive' and 'advanced' societies. Working from the premise that written texts enable the storage of knowledge allowing wider interpretations, innovations and effective administration, Goody identified the defining features of a literate society. These were the development of logic, scientific thought, and specialized educational institutions, the distinction of myth from a historical consciousness, the standardization of cultural crafts and techniques, and the elaboration of bureaucracy and democratic political processes.

Critics of Goody's theories have pointed out that he fails to take account of various types of literacy, for instance the comparisons between forms of literacy present in state or religious institutions. Brian Street called it an 'autonomous model' of literacy in which literacy development, associated with progress, civilization and freedom, is assumed to occur in a single direction. He also pointed out that the differences between literate and preliterate societies are overstated in such 'great divide' theories on literacy. It appears to be another version of the French philosopher Lucien Lévy-Bruhl's controversial distinction between 'pre-logical' and 'logical' societies.

Some anthropologists who have analysed oral traditions in societies argue for a fundamental and psychological continuity between literacy and orality. Amongst the Wana people of Indonesia, for example, oral traditions reveal various genres of text and interpretations, a feature that Goody mistakenly thought characterized literate societies. Similarly, the Hindu Brahmanical tradition privileges the power of the memorized word over written texts. Therefore, the idea of literacy as the master concept that determines the conditions for 'civilization' is very misleading. The question to address is what people do with elements of literacy and orality, not how they automatically affect people. Additionally, ideas related to concepts of literacy and orality are not exclusive, but are often interwoven. Politicians, barristers and priests, for example, even in a modern, literate society, depend a great deal on the memorized and spoken word for their position of authority. RK

See also ethnohistory; language; rationality.

Further reading Jack Goody, The Domestication of the Savage Mind; David R. Olsen and Nancy Torrance (eds.), Literacy and Orality; Joanne Overing (ed.), Reason and Morality; Brian V. Street, Literacy in Theory and Practice.

LITERATURE

The root meaning of literature (Latin, 'written material') causes problems. Novels and short stories are clearly literature in this sense, because they exist primarily as written texts. What of plays, however, and other forms of 'literature' whose primary existence is in speech, not writing? What of the 'literature' of societies that existed before writing, or without the need of writing, but whose verbal artefacts survive in such forms as **myths**, folk tales and traditional **poetry**? There is a second problem of definition. Does 'literature' consist simply, or mainly, of works of what might be called imaginative **fiction**, or does it also encompass factual writing? Essays and oratory have always been regarded as part of the canon – as indeed, nowadays, are biography, travel writing, history and even books on such subjects as cookery and gardening. But where (if at all) does one draw the line? Is a scientific treatise or a car manual 'literature'?

Acknowledging and dealing with these varied and problematical categories has led to a wider definition of what 'literature' is, and means. It is described as a collection of artefacts that use words creatively, much as **music** uses sounds. The artefacts can be spoken or written, fiction or nonfiction, and they can be the work of identifiable authors or anonymous. There is also a qualitative implication in the use of the word. 'Literature' is often taken to mean the kind of work which 'literate' (that is, 'educated') people might be assumed to know or to appreciate: a form of high art, a determinant not so much of **culture** as of social or intellectual status. This was a prevalent view in Europe during the Middle Ages and **Renaissance**, conveniently dismissing from notice all forms of literature of which the 'literate' were ignorant or disapproved. It is an attitude still attributed today to the glitterati.

In the sense of a body of work, 'literature' has also been used as a definer of group character and identity, sometimes historical (Renaissance literature; modern literature), sometimes national or cultural (Mexican literature; Hindu literature). This meaning takes in the entire verbal art of a period or region, lumping together works of the collective imagination (such as myth-cycles) and works of individual creators. Superficially, at least, it seems a more useful form of packaging than some of the others described above, but it can mean crudely grouping Shakespeare, for instance, alongside 'Goosy Goosy Gander' and the legends of Camelot.

If definitions of literature have the quality that each raises more questions and seems more pretentious than the one before, there are fewer problems with 'literary' works themselves. The basic impulse may have been to use heightened language (that is, language not in everyday usage) to speak to or about supernatural forces. **Prayers**, chants and other **ritual** utterances are one fountainhead of literature; another is accounts of miraculous or impressive events, including the origins of things around us. From the start, the distinction was blurred between fact and fantasy. There was no criterion of authorship, individual and accretive creativity being equally valid (and often on the same material). One distinction that does seem to have been made from the beginning is that between prose and verse. Originally, verse was the favoured medium for 'heightened' utterance of all kinds, from prayers to plays. Prose was for everyday use, including such minor heightenings of ordinary speech as anecdotes or maxims. This distinction (which is still followed in most cultures where 'oral literature' is the norm) applied in 'art' literature until prose became a major medium for imaginative writing some 500 years ago. Its use and appreciation was further improved by the anomaly that sacred books were often, and uniquely, written in prose, as if the deity had no need to use the same kind of heightened utterance as human worshippers. KMcL

LITURGY

The word 'liturgy' is derived from the Greek word *leitourgia* ('public service'), used particularly when a public-spirited citizen financed public works or events such as **sacrifices** for the well-being of the city. In the original Greek New Testament it meant community service, but then came to mean actual public **ritual**. Today it now means public worship, the supreme service humankind renders to God. In modern Christian usage, liturgy means a formal order of worship, as laid down since the Reformation in such volumes as the Catholic missal, the Anglican Book of Common Prayer or the Scottish Book of Common Worship. The general pattern followed is directly descended from the ancient traditions of worship in the Early Church. **EMJ**

LOGARITHMS

Logarithms (Greek, 'number-reckoning') were first used in the 18th century; invented by John Napier (1550–1617), they were the first major advance in methods of carrying out complicated arithmetical calculations in a long line leading to modern computational techniques.

In the equation $y = x^m$, the number m is known as the logarithm of y in the base x. The reason that logarithms aid calculations is that if $y = x^m$, $z = x^n$ then $y \times z = x^m \times x^n = x^{m+n}$, so that the logarithm of the product is the sum of the logarithms. Division can also be performed in the same way by subtraction. It is far simpler to work out the sum or difference of two numbers than to do a complicated long division or long multiplication.

Logarithms are published in books. To multiply a by b, you look up the logs of a and b (to give log (a + b)), then look up the antologarithm, which gives you the answer. Slide rules even do the addition for you or, in the case of division, the subtraction of log b from log a. Before electronic calculators, these were indispensable tools of mathematicians, scientists and technologists. **SMcL**

LOGIC

Just as the ancient Greeks were the originators of the tradition of Western logical thought, they were the first people to study the processes of logical thought in any depth. Their work is summed up in Aristotle's treatises on logic (4th century BCE). They were hampered by a lack of any systematic notation for the processes of logic, and so relied on the use of language to explain what they were doing. This approach soon becomes extremely complex

and unwieldy, but Greek logic was the pinnacle of the art for over 2,000 years. Indeed, many of the greatest medieval minds failed even to understand the work of Aristotle, let alone to build on it.

Further great advances of logic only began in the late 19th century. Most mathematical reasoning up to that time was informal, not really based on even the principles of logic that were known. The work of Gottlob Frege (1848–1925), though widely ignored until championed by Bertrand Russell (1872–1970), brought about a revolution in the whole field of mathematics. Like many great advances in mathematics, Frege's was the result of an improvement in notation; he invented **symbolic logic**, the use of symbols to represent ideas. Frege's symbolic logic (and its cousin, **Boolean logic**) meant that mathematical ideas could be precisely written down for the first time, without being dependent on the inconsistencies and vaguenesses of language. (For example, notational vagueness in Newton's time makes it sometimes difficult today to have a precise idea of what he really meant in his various mathematical works.)

Once the significance of Frege's ideas had been grasped, mathematicians were not slow to apply them in as many areas as possible. The greatest exponent of this was Frege's popularizer, Bertrand Russell. Today, the use of symbols in mathematics means that what is being said is crystal clear (at least to those initiated in the subject), with (if used properly) no possibility of ambiguity; it has, however, made the subject among the most incomprehensible of all human knowledge to the layperson.

Today, that logic itself has limitations is more clearly understood than it was in the first flush of excitement at Frege's work; in some cases, the best that can be hoped for is consistency (that is, absence of contradictions) rather than truth. **SMcL**

See also Gödel's incompleteness theorem.

Further reading I.M. Copi, *Introduction to Logic.*

LOGICISM

The logistic school of **mathematics** was the

third school of thought concerning its ultimate basis in the early years of the 20th century: the others were **formalism** and **intuitionism**. The logistic school is very similar to that of formalism. Its basic thesis is that pure mathematics is entirely a branch of **logic** – that all the theorems of mathematics are simply logical statements of the form p implies q. The main exponent of this view was Bertrand Russell (1872–1970), who built on the work of Gottlob Frege (1848–1925) and Giuseppe Peano (1858–1932), to produce with Alfred North Whitehead (1861–1947) the greatest work of the school, the *Principia Mathematica*.

Major problems with logicism began to be seen even at the time. There were problems with the philosophy of logic, and the reduction of mathematics to logic made these also problems in mathematics – an undesirable result. It also became apparent that, although logic is of supreme importance in mathematics, it is by no means necessary as the ultimate basis of mathematical thought. **SMcL**

LONDON SCHOOL OF LINGUISTICS

The approach to language advocated by J.R. Firth is now known as the London School of **linguistics**. Long before the distinction between **semantics** and **pragmatics** had been established, Firth argued for the primacy of the context of situation in the communication of meanings. Social status, setting, level of formality, and cultural traditions all contribute to the **context** in which language is used, and crucially, they affect the linguistic forms we choose when speaking. The linguistic context is also significant, since certain words habitually co-occur, or collocate (for example, 'livid with rage'), an observation which has been enormously influential in latterday **lexicography**.

In the sound system of a language, too, it was argued that at each point in a linguistic construction, there is a range of options available, which are specifically associated with that particular point of choice. The selection of one sound in favour of another alters the meaning conveyed (compare the first sounds in 'man', 'pan', 'ban', 'fan'). As a result, it was proposed that each point of

choice in the sound system is directly relevant to the meanings, or semantic functions, which can be expressed. However, it is doubtful that the choice of *f* at the beginning of the word 'father', for example, says anything about the meaning of the word. The failures of the London School to deal adequately with meaning contributed to its demise as a coherent force within linguistics. However, the London approach to **phonology** has bequeathed many fruitful ideas to current theorizing and the theory of syntax known as systemic grammar also owes its origins to the London School. **MS**

LUTHERANISM

The term 'Lutheran' was first coined by Roman **Catholic** opponents of the 16th-century theological reform movement which adopted Martin Luther's doctrine of 'justification through grace by faith alone, apart from works of law'. Luther himself abhorred the term, fearing that it would lead to narrow denominationalism. Although Lutheranism was mainly a theological movement for ecclesiastical reform it was soon used by German princes as a means to free themselves from papal jurisdiction. Under a principle known as *cuius regio, eius religio* ('states shall have the religion of their rulers'), they established Lutheranism as the religion of their territories. After some 25 years of sporadic fighting and discussion, the Holy Roman Emperor Charles V had to compromise, and the Peace of Augsburg in 1555 tolerated 'the religion of the Augsburg Confession' in areas where the prince was Lutheran. A century later, after the Thirty Years' War (1618–48), Lutheranism was fully accepted as a religion in the Holy Roman Empire. It spread to Denmark, Sweden and Norway and the Baltic cities, but was repressed in Poland and Hungary.

Lutheranism is predominantly Christocentric. Vernacular language is used in worship, with much emphasis on congregational singing and on preaching. Only the two sacraments of baptism (generally infant baptism) and the Lord's Supper are recognized.

Depending as it does for survival on political protection, Lutheranism has frequently suffered from too close an alignment between Church and State. The 17th-century Christian Orthodoxy mixed pure Lutheran doctrine with Christian law, and obedience toward the law became the centre of Lutheran ethics. In the 18th century this gave rise to the pietist reform movement, which stressed the 'religion of the Heart' and not the 'religion of the head'. During the **Enlightenment** Lutheranism once again was compromised; so the 'Neo-Lutherans' (who called for a return to the biblical and confessional norms) made a stand which led to a significant Lutheran revival. At the time of the Third Reich, German Lutheranism succumbed once more to the state's demands. Attempts were made by 'German Christians' to merge Lutheranism with Nazism. Opposition, in the form of the 'Confessing Church', and help from Lutherans outside Germany (especially in the USA) and the ecumenical movement was at hand. They used the old cry of 'Back to the Bible' and the normative Lutheran writings to support their positions as well as the theology of Karl Barth.

The experiences of the two world wars, and unification movements inside the Lutheran Churches, created the desire to establish a body where common interests could be discussed, and this led to the establishment of the Lutheran World Federation (1947) as a 'free association of Lutheran Churches', which had 105 member churches in 1990. **EMJ**

Further reading J.M. Todd, *Luther*.

LYRIC

Lyric verse (from Greek *lurikos*, 'for the lyre') was originally distinguished from such other forms as **epic** or **narrative**. It was short and usually dealt with a single mood or event. It was intended for musical setting, and accordingly (as was common in Greek **poetry**) used one or other of the intricate metres which underlay both words and music. Much of this has persisted. Lyrics are still short poems, often in self-consciously intricate or stylized metres, and deal with specific events or emotions, sometimes in an anecdotal way, sometimes drawing out parallels between the private moment and

wider human experience. In common modern usage, 'lyric' (as an adjective) is used instead of 'lyrical' in such phrases as 'flights of lyric imagination', and (as a noun) has reverted to its roots, meaning verse specifically intended for musical setting and naked without it. **KMcL**

MACHIAVELLIANISM

Machiavellianism, in **political science**, is generally used to describe an amoral political style in which a political objective is achieved without regard to moral consequences. However, this usage is true neither to the spirit nor the content of Machiavelli's writing – even if it is true that Joseph Stalin kept a copy of Machiavelli's *The Prince* by his bedside. Machiavellianism may more properly be described as the view that the conduct of states must be guided by a different morality to that of citizens in their private conduct.

Niccolò Machiavelli (1469–1527) was a Florentine public administrator, political adviser and political theorist whose primary works, *The Prince* and *Discourses on the First Ten Books of Titus Livy* are among the most influential works of realist political theory. He is considered a founding father of political science because of his willingness to develop general maxims about political conduct and behaviour, which are not bound by culture or time. His expressive and vigorous style is best captured by reading him. Among his many claims he contended that in all republics the number of citizens in positions of command is never more than forty or fifty; and that they can be kept quiet with honours or done away with; the rest, who only seek security, pose no problem of control. This particular maxim explains why **élite theorists** are sometimes called neo-Machiavellians.

Machiavelli was not the first proponent of a realist approach to politics, nor was he the first to emphasize the role of *fortuna* (luck), or of boldness, flexibility and cour-

age (political *virtú*). However, the originality of his views can be found in the logical
extension of two premises. First, he argued
that while morality based on either Christian or pagan values is both necessary and
desirable for a functional society, the political sphere is not best governed by the same
morality. Second, as a committed republican, he believed that **sovereignty** should
reside with the people and that government
should be limited by a constitution. From
these two premises Machiavelli concluded
that since it is a leader's duty to succeed in
the public eye and since politics often
requires deceit, it is therefore a leader's duty
to deceive in the attainment and execution
of power. Only after power is secured can
republican society function based upon
morals and laws. Critics of Machiavellianism are numberless, but not many of them
write as well as Machiavelli. **BO'L**

See also republicanism.

Further reading I. Berlin, 'The Originality of
Machiavelli' in *Against the Current: Essays in
the History of Ideas*; J.G.A. Pocock, *The Machiavellian Movement*; Q. Skinner, *Machiavelli*.

MACROECONOMICS

Macroeconomics (Greek *macro*, 'large' +
economics) is the study of what causes the
general level of economic activity in a country's economy to be what it is. It is the study
of such aggregates as **gross national product**
(GNP), employment and price levels to
understand why there are periods of **inflation**, of prosperity and **depression**, of full
employment and unemployment. Macro
issues usually involve government **fiscal
policy** and monetary control. However, as
many economists have pointed out, such
aggregates grow from micro roots: a proper
understanding of unemployment and inflation requires studying labour markets as
well as monetary and fiscal policies. **TF**

See also microeconomics.

Further reading Kevin Hoover, *The Classical
Macroeconomics*; Richard C. Lipsey, *An Introduction to Positive Economics*.

MACROSOCIOLOGY

Within **sociology** there are different levels of

analysis. Macrosociology (Greek, 'sociology in large') is the study of whole
societies, large-scale social groups, organizations or social systems. It focuses on such
areas of social life as the political and economic systems or religious institutions. It
also includes the long-term analysis of
social change. Examples of macrosociology
include **functionalism** and **Marxism**.

Macrosociological analysis provides
insights into the social background against
which people live out their day-to-day lives.
The way that people live their lives is crucially affected by the wider social context in
which they live. Compare, for example, the
different societal contexts against which a
west European carries on his or her life to
that of a Siberian nomad.

Macrosociology is often contrasted with
microsociology which refers to the study of
human behaviour in situations of face-to-
face interaction; though the distinction
between the two is not a rigid one. **DA**

See also alienation; anomie; class; convergence thesis; culture; evolutionism; positivism; social stratification; society; structuralism;
structure; structure-agency debate; suicide;
system; systems theory; theories of modernity; world system.

MAGIC

Magic (Greek, *magika*, 'what wizards do')
is the blanket term for a whole range of
practices and skills supposed to be borrowed from the supernatural world by
favoured mortals or, in its less exalted
form, for the tricks and sleights of hand
used by conjurers, mind-readers and other
entertainers. The sceptic might argue that
the only difference between them is in
degree: that magicians, priests, prophets,
shamans and witches merely perform a
rather elevated form of sleight of hand, and
that their incantations, mystical passes and
potions are just as much hokum as the
'nothing up my sleeve' patter of the stage
magician or card-sharp. Nonetheless, the
idea of magic has persisted throughout
human history, and our willingness to suspend disbelief in it is perhaps a symptom of
our general uneasiness about the super-

natural, and our consequent awe in the face of those who profess to understand its mysteries.

'Magic' skills seem to lie outside the ordinary **laws of Nature**. In different societies and different manifestations, they have included **divination**, **hypnotism**, mindreading, numerology, psychokinesis (making objects move by the power of your thought alone), second hearing (the ability to understand the utterance of every creature on Earth, and the sounds of natural phenomena such as wind in the trees or waterfalls), second sight (seeing outside human time, so that the past and future are as clear as the present), trance (the ability to move in and out of the supernatural world at will), and perhaps most awesome, the power to effect change, whether this is averting disaster and ensuring success, working transformations such as turning water to wine (Christ's miracle has been duplicated, on a mundane level, a million times) or making a pack of cards appear to move from random order to strict suit-order without touching them. Illusions are the stock-in-trade of stage magicians, and have simple explanations. But it is unclear how other astonishing feats are done – walking on red-hot coals or levitation, for example – and until they are satisfactorily and scientifically explained, they will seem to many people to be magical in exactly the same way as once did herbal healing (the origin of the idea of 'magic potions') or palm-reading (in fact a simple process of responding to clues in the subject's body-language and verbal responses as you make your 'analysis').

The overlap between magic and **science** has been of particular interest to anthropologists. Their interest stems from the fact that what a given society regards as magic offers major insights into its patterns of life and thought. But in early **anthropology**, the study of magic was bedevilled by the view that it was an example of a 'primitive' and irrational way of thinking based on the false notion that there was a spatial and temporal relationship between entirely separate phenomena. And if magic is placed in an evolutionary schema, the implication is clear: if ideas about it are illogical, then by extension the people who believe in it are 'primitive'. James Frazer, in *The Golden Bough* (1890) saw magic as a way of influencing events through **ritual** actions, and therefore as something which depended on (and seemed to validate) the belief that symbolic actions could affect the relationship between humans and the natural world – a view cognate with that of **religion**, that symbolic actions affect our relationship with the supernatural. In such a climate of belief, magicians could use sympathetic magic to ensure positive outcomes in the here-and-now drawing a picture of successful childbirth, for example, to influence the outcome of a woman's actual labour. Magic, symbolists claimed, was a way of understanding the principle of causality. Through ideas about the way natural and supernatural forces could be influenced, accidents and misfortunes could be explained as outside individual control.

Such a universe, where nothing happens by chance, seems far more deterministic than the one we are familiar with as heirs to scientific thought. The study of magic contributed to the anthropological debate about whether such modes of thought could be regarded as rational. Such 'primitive' systems of explanation were illogical and in an entirely different mode of thought from that used by modern science. According to evolutionist models, primitive thought would later evolve into scientific thought presumed to be a much more rational way of thinking.

In the mid-20th century, the structuralist Claude Lévi-Strauss joined the debate. He compared magical thought with Western science, and concluded that they involve comparable systems of classification in making sense of the universe. Magic does not reflect utilitarian ideas or causality. It should be examined in structuralist terms, following Lévi-Strauss' theory of a universal way of classifying and understanding the world by sorting through the currently available concepts (which he called *bricolage*). The links are clear between **belief** in magic and religious faith and 'belief' in science can, in these terms, also be viewed as magic, since it has an internal logic which does not necessarily 'make sense'. Belief in science, in short, involves the taking on faith of basic principles which cannot be proved, and thus involves the same kind of suspension of disbelief required of magical thought a view which puts our ideas on magic (and on science) into an entirely different perspective. **CL KMcL**

See also animism; rationality; witchcraft.

Further reading A. Lehmann and J. Myers, *Magic, Witchcraft and Religion*; Claude Lévi-Strauss, *The Savage Mind*; J. Skorupski, *Symbol and Theory*.

MAGIC NUMBERS

Experiments have shown that human beings are the only creatures in the world able to remember and manipulate **numbers**. Other animals can 'count' instinctively: birds, for example, will make up the full complement of eggs in a nest each time one is removed. But calculation, and the awareness it involves of the implications of number, are unique to humans. Perhaps this is one reason for our species' fascination with numbers, and our habit of assigning them properties which are not merely mathematical, but magical.

The fact that each of us has 10 fingers has meant that, in most societies, the first 10 numerals have particular significance. In a few societies only, for example, some Central American aboriginal tribes, each of the first 20 numerals is distinct from all the others, but usually we count to 10 and then begin again. In the 6th century BCE, the Pythagoreans of Greece (who founded an entire philosophical and religious system on numerology), assigned special 'sacred' meanings to each of the first nine numerals. One was Unity, indivisible and unique, and represented the Deity. Two was Diversity and represented the power of Evil. Three was Harmony (formed from the union of Unity and Disorder). Four was Perfection: the first 'square' number (that is, a number formed by another number multiplied by itself). Five was Nature, six was Justice, seven was the climacteric in sickness (the point after which recovery began). Eight was Double Perfection, the octave or 'full chord' in **music**, and also stood for human beings themselves. Nine was Triple Perfection, the trinity of trinities. Similar ideas

were common in the numerology of many cultures, such as ancient Babylon and Egypt, the Indus Valley civilization and the earliest inhabitants of South America. The ancient Chinese evolved number-systems based on complex squares and grids: columns of numbers which added or multiplied up to 'magic' totals.

Throughout history, the odd numbers have always been assigned more magical properties than the even numbers. In many ancient cultures one was a forbidden number, whose use was allowed only to initiates or priests. Nine was associated with the supernatural, and counting to nine, praying nine prayers (or sequences of three times three, as in the *Kyrie eleison* (three times), *Christe eleison* (three times), *Kyrie eleison* (three times) of the Catholic and Orthodox Christian churches), or performing ninefold rituals were ways to solicit the attention of supernatural powers or even to enter their world. (If you twirled round nine times in medieval Germany, you were supposed to depart from 'mortal' time and enter 'fairy' time; whirling dervishes pattern their circles in groups of nine.) Cats (creatures thought to straddle the natural and supernatural worlds) have nine lives in folklore, and the Underworld in Japanese and Greek folklore is said to have nine entrances and nine rivers. Three, the trinity made up of 'beginning, middle and end', is a standard magic number in religious and supernatural systems of all kinds, from the simplest to the grandest, and its numerological 'perfection' seems to be matched both in **mathematics** and in Nature, where three-fold symmetry is commonplace.

The most powerful magic number of all was held to be seven. The origins of this belief may be in the movement of heavenly bodies, and their association in early cultures with gods and other supernatural beings. (In Central American aboriginal **cosmology**, for example, time was a procession, the gods, bearing the days in groups of seven; in Greek and Roman cosmology, each of the seven planets then known was thought to belong to a specific supernatural power, Jupiter, Mars, Mercury and so on.) Medieval European alchemists, drawing on lore from ancient Babylon, assigned seven metals, one to each planet, and maintained that the planet's 'power' was inherent in the metal and that if you worked on a particular metal or combination of metals at particularly propititious planetary times, you would transmute them into the first of all metals, gold, overseen by the first of all heavenly bodies, the Sun. (The other heavenly bodies, and their metals, were Jupiter (tin), Mars (iron), Mercury (quicksilver), the Moon (silver), Saturn (lead) and Venus (copper).) The seven days of the week were similarly given astronomical/religious associations, and most were named accordingly. From them came the idea that seven was a complete cycle (as in the Hebrew creation myth), and that seven was therefore a 'perfect' number. This gave rise in medieval European thought to all kinds of groupings of seven: the **Seven Deadly Sins**, the Seven Virtues, the Seven **Liberal Arts**, the Seven Seas, the Seven Sacraments, and so on. But seven had a significance well beyond Europe: there were Seven Wonders of the ancient Greek world, Seven Gods of Love in Japanese folklore, Seven Sages in Middle Eastern folklore. Still, today, seven is a potent number in **astrology** and superstition.

Examples could be multiplied from all traditions and all historical periods. Our human fascination with numbers is limitless – witness the unceasing efforts, over two millennia and still continuing, to discover the exact (though totally unimportant) value of *pi*. Modern methods of calculation have vastly increased our understanding, and in the process have given folklore, superstition and number-magic generally a huge new supply of symmetries, coincidences and aberrances to add to those which were known in the past, and which still influence the habits of mind and behaviour of even the least credulous inhabitants of the modern world. **KMcL**

MAGIC REALISM

In **literature**, magic realism is a kind of fiction in which supernatural and natural characters and events merge as if there is no distinction between them. It is the method of fairy tale: a way to interrelate the worlds of dream, fantasy and reality. In the 20th century, South American novelists began writing magic realist fables which described harsh political reality in terms of naive, folk-inspired fantasy. Particular masters of the style include Alejo Carpentier, Gabriel García Márquez and Mario Vargas Llosa. Márquez's *One Hundred Years of Solitude* and *Love in the Time of Cholera* are among its masterpieces. Other writers who use personal versions of magic realism include Isabel Allende, Angela Carter, Günter Grass, John Irving and Salman Rushdie.

In **painting**, the term magic realism was used, in a similar way, by a group of 1920s Munich painters – and indeed many artists, from Aboriginal cave-painters to such sophisticates as the sculptors of Hindu temple carvings, Hieronymus Bosch, Marc Chagall, Georgia O'Keeffe and Diego Rivera, have blended realistic depiction and naive fantasy. Their work is often executed in a highly realistic manner, but the subject matter, or incidental details, as in **surrealism**, disrupt a naturalistic reading. For all that, the term 'magic realism', common in literary criticism, is rarely used in art. **KMcL**

MAGNETISM

Magnetism is the term applied to describe the property of a body that experiences a force of attraction or repulsion to another body, without any apparent physical connection between them. These bodies, called magnets, have been known for over 2,000 years, indeed the word magnet was given to a stone noted by the ancient Greeks to show this attraction or repulsion to an iron rod, because it was found near the ancient city of Magnesia. This stone, known as lodestone or magnetite, is an oxide of iron and occurs naturally. It is believed that the ancient Chinese also knew of the 'magical' power of lodestone, and they are credited as the inventors of the magnetic compass. They found that when an iron rod was brought close to a magnet, the rod itself became magnetized and behaved as an individual magnet when it was removed from the original magnet. Later they discovered that if they held the rod in the middle and allowed it freedom to rotate around the centre of its length, the rod would tend to align itself with its length in a north-south direction. This property was soon applied in navigation, particularly for maritime uses, where the absence of landmarks and bad weather obscuring the stars could cause ships to go astray (see **marine compass**).

Characterization of the behaviour of magnets was carried out in the 13th century by Petrus Peregrinus, a French engineer. Using a spherical lodestone and a magnetic compass, he discovered that he could follow lines around the lodestone where the compass remained in a fixed position. All these lines intersected at two points which he called north and south poles, and he showed that like poles repel each other while opposite poles attract each other. It may have seemed logical, in terms of his experimentation, to try to isolate the poles from each other, but Peregrinus found that cutting a magnet in two served only to create two new magnets rather than, as he might have assumed, to give one north pole and one south pole.

It might seem strange, given the benefit of hindsight, that it was not until 1600 that William Gilbert first published the idea that the Earth acts as a huge magnet. It seems obvious, following the work of Peregrinus, as a magnetic compass needle would be attracted to the Earth's magnetic poles – analogous to the spherical lodestone.

By 1785, Charles Coulomb had successfully shown that the force between two magnetized bodies was inversely proportional to the distance between them. As well as creating the first quantitative law for magnetism, Coulomb pre-empted today's molecular theory of magnetism. It is believed today that a piece of magnetic material consists of individual atomic magnets which, internal to the material, may be thought of as cancelling north to south respectively, and that only at the ends of the material would there be no cancellation, giving rise to north and south poles. This would explain why, when a magnet is cut, 'new' north and south poles form to create two magnets from the halves of the original magnet.

Modern magnetic theory may be said to have started with the discovery of **electromagnetism** by Hans Oersted in 1820.

Oersted noted that an electric current flowing in a wire close to a magnetic compass was seen to deflect the compass needle. From this observation he deduced that an electric current produces a magnetic field and several years later in 1831 Michael Faraday proved the converse, that a magnetic field could produce an electric current.

Since the advent of electromagnetism in the early 19th century, and the realization that magnetism and **electricity** are very close relatives, a myriad of applications have used this theory. Magnetism plays a key role in the generation of all our electric power requirements, magnetic tape is used in our computer disks and audio and video cassettes as memory units, and radio uses electromagnetic waves. **AC**

MALTHUSIAN POPULATION THEORY

The Malthusian population theory was developed by the English economist and parson Thomas Malthus (1776–1834). Malthus argued that population growth would always exceed the growth in food supply. The theory states that population tends to grow at a geometric rate (2, 4, 8, 16, 32. . .), while the food supply tends to grow at an arithmetic rate (1, 2, 3, 4, 5. . .). Population growth tends to occur by unrestricted reproduction, while growth in agricultural output is restricted by the law of diminishing returns. The interaction of these two growth ratios will result in a tendency toward poverty and misery for the masses.

Malthus believed that this tendency could be prevented by late marriages, celibacy and moral restraint. He was not optimistic about the practice of what he preached and wrote about other restraints on population growth which included famine, disease and war. His theory was later used to explain the British government policy of maintaining agricultural exports from Ireland during the Great Famine (1845–49) – in which at least 1.5 million people died of starvation or the side-effects of malnutrition, and at least another million immigrated. At that time, Whig government officials appeared to believe that the Irish famine was a beneficial Malthusian disaster. The ensuing loss of population due to starvation was understood in a Malthusian population theory framework as a positive restraint on population growth.

Malthus underestimated the scope for technological progress. He wrote before the development of birth control devices and improvements in agricultural productivity. More important, he failed to anticipate the way in which rising real incomes, not falling ones, would slow down population growth. Latter-day Malthusians still fear that his grim predictions will come true in Africa and India, and many worry about the rate of growth in the world's population relative to the arable land available to feed the population of the future. **TF**

See also population explosion.

Further reading Thomas Malthus, *Essay on the Principle of Population as it Affects the Future Improvement of Society* (1789).

MAMMALOGY

Mammalogy is the scientific study of mammals. It grew from humankind's historic knowledge of animal husbandry. In the 4th century BCE, Aristotle recognized mammals as a group which included whales and dolphins, but the position of humans among the mammals was not accepted until much later. Modern mammalogy is stimulated by this link; the behaviour of mammals is studied in the hope of learning something of human behaviour and a number of mammals are exploited for medical research. Some mammals are thus among the best understood of living organisms yet others have barely been studied. **RB**

See also ethology; homology; primatology; taxonomy.

Further reading T.A. Vaughan, *Mammalogy*.

MANICHAEISM

Manichaeism, named after its founder Manes or Mani (*c.*215–275 CE), is principally remembered today for the effect it had on Augustine of Hippo (354–430) who was a Manichee for nine years before he converted to Christianity. Although he rejected the excessive austerities and dualism of the Manichees, such was Augustine's hatred, after his conversion, of sexuality and women that it is sometimes questioned whether he was fully converted. He might have derived his doctrine of the utter depravity of humankind, which has had such a great influence on Western theology, from them. Like other adherents of **Gnosticism**, Manes taught that particles of light had been stolen by an evil spirit from the World of Light and trapped in the human brain, and that his teaching, a continuation of that of the Buddha and Christ, would liberate human beings from the realm of light. Despite persecution, the sect spread rapidly from Seleucia-Ctesiphon, capital of the Persian Empire, to Rome and Egypt in the 4th century – and from references in medieval Muslim historians, it seems to have persisted in Chinese Turkestan until the 13th century. **EMJ**

Further reading A. Jackson, *Researches in Manichaeism* (1932).

MANIFEST FUNCTION see
Functionalism

MANNERISM

Mannerism, in fine **art**, derives from the Italian word *maniera*, as used by Vasari, meaning style or stylishness. 'Manner', in art, has two main meanings: (1) any style (for all artists must have at least one) without comment as to its nature; (2) 'mannerisms', such as exaggeration of certain characteristics, or affectation, for instance superstructural additions and ornamentations rather than essential elements.

The most specific use of the term Mannerism (with a capital M) is to describe and define European art of the post-High Renaissance period in the 16th century (*c.*1525–1600). The late work of Michelangelo, for example the Laurentian library in Florence, is held to be Mannerist, as is the work of Vasari at the Uffizzi, also in Florence, and of Giulio in Mantua, particularly his Palazzo de Te (1526). The effectiveness of these works is in their deliberate clashes with and contraventions of classical rules: the familiar motif used in the unfamiliar way.

In **painting** and **sculpture**, a Mannerist work will be concerned with style, with the superficialities of appearance rather than profundity of meaning. It will be anti-naturalistic (elongated figures, strange colours), intricate in composition, in love with exotic posture and perspective, and frequently with a heightened, mystical and insistent emotional temperature. Stylishness will be taken to extremes and the subjects will often be fantastic and bizarre. Sir John Summerson aptly categorized the style as 'the art of the *tour de force* of problems undertaken for their novelty and curiosity'. Its complication and cleverness made it suitable to be a court art across Europe, but it shrivelled before the exuberant **naturalism** of the later part of the 16th century, as seen in the works of the Bolognese School and Caravaggio, and the straightforwardness of the **Baroque**. **PD MG JM**

Further reading Walter Friedlaender, *Mannerism and Anti-mannerism in Italian Painting*; J. Summerson, *The Classical Language of Architecture*.

MAP PROJECTIONS

Map projections are systems for transferring patterns from the Earth's surface to maps. They work as if a light inside the globe projected the surface patterns on to a flat sheet, a cone or a cylinder placed against the surface. Since the Earth is a sphere, it is impossible to make this transfer without distortion. Different map projections have different strengths and weaknesses: some preserve shape, others size, others distance or direction, but no projection can do all these things and so no projection is correct for all purposes.

Probably the most familiar projection is that originated by Mercator in the late 16th century. This is convenient for navigation since a straight line follows a constant compass course. It is still used for maps of small areas but it is not suited to long distance navigation (because a constant compass course does not indicate the shortest route),

and it is not suited for atlas maps because of its distortions of size. These result from the stretching of all lines of latitude to the same length as the equator and become extreme in high latitudes, making Greenland, for example, seem larger than Australia though it is actually less than a third as large. In practice, Mercator maps, which were much used for atlases until recent decades, emphasize the mid latitudes over the tropics. They were also popular because, as usually laid out, they put the UK in a central position, so flattering the beliefs of imperial Britain.

Since 1945, several new perspectives have become important. First, the Cold War made strategists look again at relations between the USA and USSR: polar projections show them to be much closer than Mercator suggests, reflecting the new realities of air travel and missile trajectories. More recently, the emergence of Japan has led to questioning of world maps centred on Europe or North America, and to suggestions that the prime meridian should run through the Pacific and not through Greenwich. The desire to eliminate the relics of colonialism has also produced an overtly ideological projection the Peters Projection.

The Peters Projection was stimulated by a desire to give tropical, less-developed countries equal weight by depicting equal areas. At times, the protagonists of the Peters map seem to suggest that it is the only correct projection, but this can only be political correctness and not cartographic correctness. In fact, the Peters preserves equal area by stretching tropical shapes north-south and polar ones east-west. In relation to its own aims, it seems less satisfactory than some other equal area projections, such as the Eckert 4 or Mollweide, where shapes in the tropics were realistic at the cost of deformations in high latitudes as lines of longitude converged. This problem can be reduced by interrupting the projection, dividing it into several segments but that has the problem of reducing visual continuity.

There are now hundreds of map projections, and new ones can be quickly generated by computers, so the topic is detailed and technical. What matters to ordinary map users is not detailed techniques but understanding that all projections distort something significantly if the area covered is more than a few thousand miles across. If the complexities are too daunting, the remedy is to check the maps against a globe, which does preserve shape, area, distance and direction, even though it is not easily portable. **PS**

MARINE COMPASS

The magnetic compass first appeared in China and was probably first used as a fortune-teller's aid (with no purpose except dazzling the customer with what appeared to be magic). The earliest record of it being used at sea was in 1115 by Chinese mariners. It was not long before it was adopted by European and Islamic countries. Its adoption was to transform the economy of the Western world, as its use meant that sailing fleets could take to sea in any weather conditions at any time of year.

The major disadvantage of the magnetic compass is its **magnetism** which means that it may be affected by large masses of ferrous metal in its vicinity and also by electromagnetic machinery or magnetic rocks. The magnetic North Pole is not the true north of the world and the position of the magnetic pole changes with time, requiring corrections to its use on a regular basis.

A more sophisticated instrument is the gyroscopic compass. This depends on the high angular speed of a rotor driven by an electric motor. This will remain with its axis in a fixed direction unless considerable force is applied to it. The shaft is therefore mounted in gimbals which allow it to rotate about axes perpendicular to its axis of rotation. Thus as a ship moves at sea the gyroscope continues to lie with its axis in the same direction. It is this type of instrument which allows accurate navigation of submarines beneath the polar icecaps. **AA**

Further reading Duane Roller, *The De Magnete of William Gilbert*.

MARIOLOGY

Mariology is the systematic study of the figure of Mary, the mother of Jesus, and the theology which has been evolved from her assigned role in human redemption. Three forces have been at work in this. First, in the early centuries of Christendom, the role of Mary as Mother of God was emphasized in order to reinforce the belief that God was literally and historically incarnate in Jesus, that Jesus was fully human, in the face of various alternative theologies. This view was somewhat undermined by the increasing obsession with virginity (for men and women) from the 3rd century onwards, so that Mary herself was said to be 'immaculately conceived' without the agency of a human father.

Mariology is closely linked to the doctrine of papal infallibility, since it was papal pronouncements which established Mary's Immaculate Conception (in 1854) and Corporeal Assumption into heaven (in 1950). Both doctrines had been passionately held by ordinary Catholics for centuries, and celebrated in great works of art since the Middle Ages, being favourite subjects for lay and ecclesiastical patrons in the **Baroque** period.

Mary might almost be called 'the human face of God' because since the 8th century she has been seen as mediatrix, while her obedience to God's plan for redemption has caused her to be called 'co-redemptrix'. Other titles such as 'Star of the Sea' have been appropriated from the worship of the Egyptian goddess Isis, whose character she has also in some respects assumed. Thirdly, there has been the radical reappraisal of Mariology carried out by **feminist theologians** who have reclaimed the docile, smiling heroine and recast her as a brave unmarried mother who rebelled against social customs. **EMJ**

MARKET ECONOMY

A market economy is characterized by decentralized decision-making by private individuals and groups working through markets in which sellers typically produce for unknown and unseen potential buyers. The interaction of buyers and sellers in markets provides the answers to the basic economic questions of what to produce, how and for whom.

The market economy is often contrasted with **centrally planned economies** in which public authorities make the basic economic decisions. **TF**

MARRIAGE

Marriage, in its Western sense, defines the ceremonial and legal union of a man and woman, usually with the aims to live together and reproduce children. However, this definition does not apply to all societies. Whereas the relationship between a woman and her children tends to be similar across societies, there are a myriad of ideas – about **gender** relations and roles, the selection of a mate, marriage ceremonies and residential patterns – to do with the socially acknowledged bond between opposite sexes. A change in social status occurs at marriage, but this need not involve a man's exclusive rights over a woman's **sexuality** or the recognition of the legitimacy of children. In some societies, pregnancy outside of or before marriage may be accepted as the norm.

Many terms have been used to order the varied and complex cultural interpretations of marriage. In 1865, the lawyer John McLennan coined the words exogamy, to describe marriage outside of a social group, and endogamy, for marriage inside a socially distinct group. Along with other social theorists of the time, he believed that marriage patterns evolved from a state of sexual promiscuity to group marriages to one in which monogamy (the culturally approved relationship of one man with one woman) prevailed.

Such evolutionist assumptions were later criticized as speculative and biased against non-Western societies. Instead, anthropologists began to look at how marriage operated as a functional institution of various societies. Types of marriages considered were polygynous marriages, in which the husband marries more than one wife, and the less-common polyandrous marriages, in which the wife marries more than one husband. Usually, these different types of marriages are related to human and land resources. Monogamous families tend to predominate where private property and land are at issue. Polygynous families are prevalent where humans are the most important resources in economic

and political systems such that more children are able to be reproduced. Polyandrous marriages are reported in places like the Himalayas where there is a shortage of land and family size is limited by assigning several males, commonly brothers, to one female.

Marriage payments or gifts take the form of bridewealth (payments, in valuables or estate, from the husband's side to the wife's), or dowry (payment from the wife's group to the husband's or for the couple themselves). In certain marriages, like those of India, the virgin bride is considered as a gift, *kanyadaan*, to be given to the husband's group along with her dowry payment.

There may also be cultural variations in residential and familial organizations after the marriage union. When a wife goes to live with the husband's group, it is called virilocal (Latin, 'in the man's place'). If the husband is expected to live with the wife's group, it is termed uxorilocal (Latin, 'in the woman's place'). Extended family describes the situation in which the married partners are accommodated with an extensive network of kin such as the husband's brother's family or the grandparents. A nuclear family stems from the establishment of a home away from both partners' kin.

As a general rule of thumb, where extended families prevail those with the authority to select mates for their next of kin do so with an expressed interest in the social status and work qualifications of prospective mates. This is usually referred to as 'arranged' marriage. Where nuclear families prevail, the criteria for mate selection depends less on the extended network of kin and sometimes even the parents. Such a marriage is often based upon the concept of a 'love match'. However, the difference between the two forms of arrangement is a matter of degree. Even in 'love' marriages, there is a marked tendency to choose mates from similar cultural, religious and economic backgrounds.

All systems of marriage designate categories of people whom a person may not marry, or may only marry subject to serious disapproval. These stem from two perspectives. One prohibits the marriage of persons who are closely related. This is known as the **incest** rule and may show variations in the categories of kin that are not approved for marriage relationships. Commonly, this takes the form of mother/son, father/daughter and brother/sister. In certain Muslim communities, there is a marked preference for marriage between first cousins related through the father's sister, rather than the father's brother. This serves the purpose of containing property that had been given out as dowry within the original family line.

The other criteria of mate selection prohibits persons from marrying someone from a very different ethnic or economic background. This may be of rigid or adaptable nature according to the social circumstances.

Patterns of marital situations, roles and changes have also formed a part of social enquiry, as have incidents of marriage breakdown and divorce, which also exhibit widely varying features. Whereas divorce may involve highly formalized procedures in Western society, instances such as Hopi divorce involve the less complex practice of putting the husband's belongings outside the house door. Ways of channelling marriage payments and rights of children or other kin after a divorce serve to further outline the way gender rights and status are thought of in society. **RK**

See also caste; ethnicity; evolutionism; exchange; kinship.

Further reading Jack Goody & S.J. Tambiah, *Bridewealth and Dowry*; Lucy Mair, *Marriage*.

MARXISM

The economic and political doctrine known as Marxism was developed by the German theorists Karl Marx (1818–83) and Friedrich Engels (1820–95). Their most famous joint work was the *The Communist Manifesto* (1848), and Engels helped finish Marx's major work *Das Kapital* (1867–94).

There are five key elements in Marxist doctrine. First, Marxists have a theory of **alienation** (and of human nature). They believe that human beings are estranged from their real (creative) selves in non-communist societies because they live in exploitative social relationships. In advanced communist societies this alienation will be overcome and work will become a creative experience for everybody.

Second, Marxists have a theory of history, **historical materialism**. They believe that there is progress in human history, characterized by humankind's progressive mastery of Nature and the accumulation of technological advances. They believe that forms of organizing work and the political and belief systems which accompany them persist as long as they encourage technological progress. Five progressive modes of production existed in human history according to Marx and Engels: primitive communism; Asiatic despotism; slavery; **feudalism**; and **capitalism**. They predicted there would be two more: **socialism** and advanced **communism**.

Third, Marxists have a theory of **class struggle** and **revolution**. Every mode of production, except those of primitive and advanced communism, is characterized by fundamental class division and exploitation. The ruling class owns the means of production (land or capital or people) and extracts 'surplus labour' from subordinate classes. Asiatic peasants, slaves and serfs are exploited by being forced to work for others, whereas workers in capitalist societies are forced to work on pain of starvation. Marx believed that the ruling class of each mode of production, who controlled the **state**, would be challenged and replaced by a new ruling class when its rule ceased to advance progress of production. Thus the feudal nobility in Europe, who were dominant because they owned the land, were replaced with the growth in trade and industrialization by the capitalist middle class (the '**bourgeoisie**'), who gained ascendancy because of their control of capital; while the bourgeoisie in their turn were doomed to be replaced by the industrial working class (the 'proletariat'). Changes in modes of production occur through class struggle and polarization, and are always signalled by revolution.

Fourth, Marxists have a set of economic doctrines, the most famous of which is the **labour theory of value**. Marxists believe that the economic value of products is directly related to the 'socially necessary labour time' which went into producing them, and this theory is used to demonstrate to their satisfaction that capitalism is exploitative because the worker is forced to work for longer periods than he or she is paid for. This theory of exploitation, or of 'surplus value', is also associated with a series of erroneous predictions Marx made about the fate of capitalist economies – in particular his assumption that the class structure of capitalism would simplify into two polarized classes, and his theory that the rate of profit would inevitably fall over time. However, contrary to what one might expect, neither Marx nor Engels had an explicit theory of how a socialist or communist economy might function – they argued that it would be Utopian for them to presume to know how it would operate. In consequence, they bequeathed to their followers no clear vision of the economics of socialism, that is, state ownership and planning the means of production, distribution and exchange, and others had to advocate market socialism the state regulation of capital rather than state ownership and planning.

Finally, Marxism contains a theory of politics. Marx and Engels claimed that they had developed 'scientific socialism' because unlike Utopian socialists they had a theory of history and a critique of political economy, and their theories were grounded in material facts about the world rather then idealist or wishful thinking – not a view with which their critics agreed. They had demonstrated, or so they thought, that the proletariat was coming to be the largest social class, and that its class interests naturally led it to espouse socialism. Marx and Engels also assumed that the state existed merely as an instrument of class domination, and was not amenable to reform: history demonstrated the necessity of a revolutionary break with the past if agents wished to change the mode of production. They also believed that the socialist revolution would be characterized by a temporary 'dictatorship of the proletariat' in which the means of production would be owned by the state which would build the conditions for a classless communist society, with the means of production collectively owned by all members of society, and

goods and services distributed justly according to people's needs. It followed, or so they believed, that after a socialist revolution had abolished the social bases of classes, that is, private property in the means of production, the state would wither away as an unnecessary social institution. To be charitable to Marx and Engels what they thought would wither away was the coercive aspect of state authority rather than its co-ordinating functions. Nevertheless the defects of the Marxist approach to politics, its class-reductionism and revolutionary chiliasm, bear no small responsibility for the forms of **totalitarianism** practised in the name of Marxism in the 20th century. However, it is as well to recall that Marx declared that he himself was not a Marxist, and he can hardly be held culpable for everything that Marxists have done and said in his name.

Through its profound influence on revolutionary communism, and such figures as Lenin, Trotsky, Stalin and Mao Zedong, as well as its lesser influence on evolutionary socialists and social democrats, Marxism has had a great impact on the history of the 20th century. Leninism deviated from orthodox Marxism in assuming the need for immediate and violent proletariat revolution, rather than awaiting the maturation of capitalism, as the orthodox Marxists suggested. Leninism thus gave a voluntarist bias to Marxism, at odds with Marx's theoretical economic determinism. Lenin also adapted Marxism to the conditions of Tsarist Russia – and thereby for all underdeveloped countries advocating and establishing an élite party of professional revolutionaries – to hasten the termination of capitalism, and by arguing for the temporary dictatorship of the Communist party rather than the working class as a whole. Lenin's revolutionary philosophy subsequently codified and canonized as Marxist-Leninism became the guiding doctrine of the USSR and spread throughout the world. It is also known as Bolshevism. In the hands of Stalin, Marxism-Leninism became a crude ideology subservient to the interests of the Soviet state. Indeed, Stalin's Russia was criticized by many Marxists for betraying fundamental Marxist principles: notably by Trotsky who argued that the dictatorship of the proletariat was never meant to be a permanent system, let alone a vehicle for a personalist dictatorship. A range of western Marxist thinkers, notably in France, Italy and Germany, tried to preserve Marxism as a system of thought from contamination by Stalinism, but most western Marxists remained organized in Communist parties which were formally supportive or 'critically supportive' of the Bolshevik revolution and its legacy. Mao Zedong's interpretation of Marxist-Leninism was based on the revolutionary potential of the rural peasantry, and on guerrilla warfare, and adapted Marx and Lenin's ideas to Chinese conditions.

Marxism was once the most widely officially endorsed political ideology in the world. Today it remains the official state ideology of China, North Korea, Vietnam and Cuba – a still very substantial proportion of the world's population. In these countries it is used as a rigid dogma to justify a one-party dictatorship, although it is also used more flexibly with respect to economic management. Nevertheless Marxism is patently an ideology in crisis, which no longer has the same programmatic attraction for intellectuals or workers: Marxist régimes have eventually seen to that. However, Marxism has had an important and pervasive effect on the politics and thought of the advanced industrial countries of western Europe, North America and Japan, influencing intellectuals critical of the prevailing capitalist order, shaping both communist and socialist parties, and forcing conservatives and liberals to justify and improve the workings of liberal democratic capitalism. It has also played an important role in shaping the political protests of anti-colonial and national liberation movements in Africa, Asia and Latin America. Moreover, Marxist ideas, provided they are not employed as dogmatic truths, but rather as potential hypotheses, are likely to remain an important resource in the historical and social sciences. **BO'L**

See also Asiatic mode of production; conflict theory; critical theory; dominant ideology; hegemony; ideology; imperialism; labour process; socialism and social democracy; social movements; social stratification; sociology of knowledge.

Further reading P. Anderson, *Considerations on Western Marxism*; G. Cohen, *Karl Marx's Theory of History: a Defence*; J. Elster, *Making Sense of Marx*; L. Kolakowski, *Main Currents of Marxism* (3 volumes); G. Lichtheim, *Marxism*; D. McLellan, *Karl Marx*.

MARXIST ANTHROPOLOGY

Marxist anthropology emerged primarily from France in the 1960s. It developed out of two motives: the need to evaluate anthropology's historical relationship with **colonialism**, arising out of a discontent with earlier **functionalist** paradigms for the study of societies; and to conduct social enquiry with a greater sense of political and economic perspectives.

In the 19th century, Karl Marx and Friedrich Engels were inspired by anthropological accounts, particularly those of Louis Henry Morgan about North American Indians. A historical development was proposed in which economic factors were seen to be the major dynamic in evolving from 'primitive' hunting and gathering, slave society, feudal society, **capitalism** and ultimately to **communism**. Central to this framework was the concept of 'modes of production', which referred to the forces of production, such as technologies, natural resources and human labour, combined with the social relations of production, such as class or property relations.

By the 1960s, Marxist anthropologists had dropped the evolutionary assumptions underlying Marx's and Engel's theories, but adopted their political and economic analyses to consider social formations and the wider global and historical contexts of precapitalist societies. In this way, Marxist anthropology provided for a critique of the ideologies or the systems of ideas associated with the dominant group, and analyses of historical processes, both in the societies the anthropologists were studying and their own societies in so far as these have played, and continue to play, a large role in imposing these changes.

Marxist anthropology also fitted in with growing areas of concern in the 1960s, such as feminist perspectives (which sought to redress the male bias of conventional anthropological research and literature). Prevalent topics such as **economics** and **power** were given a new lease of life by **Marxism** and **feminism**, particularly in discussions about their relevance to social groups and gender roles in non-Western societies. The concept of 'mode of reproduction' was proposed to take account of the way women's reproductive activities are controlled through social expectations, especially concerning marriage, the care of children and domestic work within the family, and how these act to condition their roles and evaluations in the external labour market.

Other strands of Marxist anthropology include the combination of a Marxist class analysis with theories about the human mind and systems of ideas to concentrate on the philosophical and cultural dimensions of society.

On a geographical scale, the 'articulation of modes of production' takes account of the way different social, economic and political systems interact and affect each other. This phenomena is of significance when capitalism, for instance, has expanded over large sectors of the world to interact with, and often dominate, indigenous ways of organizing social production.

Debate continues as to how far Marxist approaches to the study of society may distort by reducing all social phenomena to a material or economic basis, and whether the notion of class as a social division based on economic means is applicable to all social groupings. **RK**

See also economic anthropology; evolutionalism; gender; political anthropology; structuralism; Westernization.

Further reading Maurice Bloch (ed.), *Marxism and Anthropology*; Maurice Godelier (ed.), *Perspectives in Marxist Anthropology*.

MARXIST ARTS CRITICISM

Marxist criticism takes as its starting point the statement in Marx's preface to *A Contribution to a Critique of Political Economy* (1859): 'The mode of production in material life determines the general character of the social, political and spiritual processes of life.' The point, for critics, is that artistic creators are, consciously or unconciously, affected by the material, economic and social forces of their time and personal circumstances, and that these influences are perceptible in their work. This is readily apparent, and is a major strand in the **criticism** of, **folk** and traditional arts and crafts of every kind. In a sense, the **art** is the society and the society is the art. The application to 'high art', where individual creativity is a major factor, is more contentious, but it is generally accepted, if not exactly axiomatic, that to investigate the circumstances and cultural influences on such creators as Omar Khayyám, Hiroshige or Beethoven, say, is to discover more about their work. **KMcL**

MASCULINE PROTEST

Masculine Protest is a concept of Alfred Adler's **Individual Psychology**, which is partly a theory of psychological hermaphroditism and partly a way of explaining the presence of patriarchal society. Adler's clinical experience showed him a frequency of what he came to call secondary sexual characteristics belonging to the opposite gender among his neurotic patients. This he supposed to be the source of the feelings of inferiority they experienced, and the striving for compensation either in aggression or its opposite passivity. The first was equated with masculinity, the second with femininity. He called this striving masculine protest, and equated it with the need to surpass the father at the Oedipal phase.

Following Bachofen and Bebel, Adler assumes that the superiority of man over woman is a status with a history, a reaction against the ancient period of matriarchy, which men suppressed. Since that time in prehistory, this attitude has been perpetuated and reinforced by education and unconscious suggestion. Adler saw this masculine protest as one of the main causes of neuroses. Sexual perversions and differences were also seen as an expression of increased psychological distance between men and women. **MJ**

Further reading Alfred Adler, *In Freud's Shadow*; P.E. Stepansky, *Adler in Context*.

MASOCHISM AND SADISM

Masochism and sadism were first described by the founder of modern sexual pathology, Richard Krafft-Ebing (1840–1902). Ebing, a forensic scientist, first published his *Psychopathia Sexualis* in 1886; it was an immediate success and was constantly revised and updated. He coined the term sadism in memory of the Marquis de Sade: it describes the act of sexual pleasure in association with afflicting physical pain upon the partner. The word masochism was used in memory of Sacher-Masoch: it described the association of sexual pleasure with humiliation or mistreatment by a woman. (He also pointed out that masochists hated the idea of actual physical pain or flagellation.) **MJ**

MASQUE

The masque was a form of European court entertainment particularly popular around the end of the 16th century in France, England and Italy, which combined the performance of a dramatic text (usually on an allegorical or mythological theme) with **music**, song, **dance** and spectacular scenery and effects. The masque played an important role in the development of **music theatre**, the **proscenium arch** and theatrical machinery. Ben Jonson, whose dispute with Inigo Jones over the relative value of words and spectacle in the masques is a classic example of the **drama/theatre** dichotomy, developed the antimasque in which grotesque characters and humour parody the order of the masque. **TRG SS**

Further reading David Lindley (ed.), *The Court Masque*; Stephen Orgel, *The Jonsonian Masque*.

MASS MEDIA see Media

MASS SOCIETY see Pluralism

MATERIALISM

Materialism, in **philosophy**, is the doctrine that everything is exhaustively physical. Some materialists hold that there are mental phenomena and that they are exhaustively physical. Everything, including the mental, is physical: dualists are wrong to claim that the mental is non-physical. Further, mental properties are not radically different from, and irreducible to, physical properties: the dual aspect theory is wrong to claim that while everything is physical, mental aspects or properties are radically different from and irreducible to physical ones. Rather, the mental is exhausted by – is nothing – over and above the physical.

Other materialists hold that while everything is exhaustively physical, the mental could not be exhaustively physical. They infer that there are no mental things, claiming that we should eliminate the mental from our account of what reality contains. **AJ**

See also double aspect theory; dualism; eliminativism; identity theory; mental phenomena.

Further reading P. Churchland, *Matter and Consciousness*; J. Foster, *The Immaterial Mind*.

MATHEMATICS

Mathematics (Greek, 'what should be learned') is an area of thought basic to the whole of modern civilization. Without the power of **numbers**, finance, commerce, **science**, engineering and technology would all collapse, and we would be faced with a return to barter economies.

Despite the vital importance of mathematics, it is difficult to provide a short definition of it. This is to a certain extent because people's ideas of the nature of mathematics, its content and its aims, have changed throughout history, partly because the contexts in which it has been used have become more and more diverse (as have the methods used in order to keep pace with it), partly because the methods of mathematics change drastically between school and undergraduate levels of education, and partly because there is no longer, in the 20th century, a consensus among mathematicians and philosophers as to the meaning and nature of mathematics.

Despite the diversity of the subject, there are unifying themes within it as taught and researched today. The most important of these is the idea of **proof**. Mathematics at its purest consists of the drawing of conclusions from clearly defined assumptions purely through the use of logical thought. Thus mathematics is closely related to **logic**, though most mathematicians today would deny the claim of **logicism** that their subject is merely a branch of logic.

The difficulty is with the assumptions. These are limited only by consistency, that they should not allow the proof of contradictory statements; however, they may contradict the assumptions made by other mathematicians (the prime example of this being **Euclidean** and **non-Euclidean geometry**). They could, and often are, drawn from scientific observation, but mathematics is not a science, because the exploding of some or all of its hypotheses by new observations does not mean that mathematical research cannot be carried out (on the consequences of the assumptions that are no longer tenable in the real world). They can be creations purely of the mind, interesting ideas that seem to be productive of study, but equally, this does not make mathematics a branch of **philosophy** either.

It is impossible to know when mathematics began in the human past. Cultures all over the world independently seem to have developed counting systems of varying complexity, from Australian aborigines with words for 'one', 'two' and 'many' to the sophisticated Arabic **number system** which is used throughout the business and scientific world today. The crucial point that marks the emergence of mathematics from mere counting is demonstrated even in the simple aboriginal system mentioned above that of **abstraction**.

At the beginning of mathematics stand the numbers. They have formed the basis of a vast number of mathematical systems, and have been subjected to intense scrutiny by philosophers of mathematics (who wanted to know the answers to such questions as 'Why is $2 + 2 = 4$?' and 'What is a number anyway?'). They are still not very clearly understood, and many fundamental questions remain unanswered in the field of **number theory**, the study of numbers. This is also one of the areas of mathematics which impinges most closely on the everyday world; every time we spend money, for instance, or catch a train from the correct platform we practise our expertise in the field of numbers. However, arithmetic gives many people problems – for example, many people are unable to add up a shopping bill or balance a chequebook. It presents a problem educationally which no one seems to have satisfactorily answered; the best way to ensure that school-leavers have the necessary mathematical knowledge to function in today's world is still a matter of great debate in educational circles.

The idea that **zero** was a number sparked off a revolution in mathematics. It led the Indian mathematicians who first realized it to come up with a new system of notation for numbers, on which today's Arabic system with place values is based. This made the operations of arithmetic vastly easier; from the province of the most advanced minds of each generation in the Middle Ages, arithmetic became the (almost) universal property it is today. From the point of view of mathematics, the importance of the greater ease of calculation was the way that investigation of properties of numbers became more possible, leading to the study of **algebra**. There are today two branches of algebra, abstract algebra and linear algebra. Linear algebra concerns itself with the solution of linear equations (see **linearity**). Abstract algebra is the study of properties abstracted from the properties of numbers and arithmetic (the existence of operations mimicking some of the properties of addition and multiplication, for example). Both have become vast fields of study in their own right, and have affected almost every other branch of mathematics.

The other main division of pure mathematics in ancient times was that of **geometry**. This was considered the most philosophically satisfying branch of mathematics by the ancient Greeks; and, indeed, until the end of the Middle Ages, the word 'mathematics' meant geometry. Geometry is the study of the relationship of spatial objects, built up of (idealized) points and lines, to one another. It is an abstraction of the calculations used in building and the measuring of land.

The greatest achievement of Greek mathematics was the creation of the paradigm of an axiomatic system by Euclid (3rd century BCE): a small collection of self-evident rules and definitions from which a vast amount of knowledge can be derived in steps which are apparent to any reasonably intelligent and sufficiently well-trained reader. Euclid **axiomatized** the study of geometry and derived a large number of results from his seven axioms in his book the *Elements*, one of the great classics of mathematics. Various criticisms can today be made of Euclid, and there are a few mistakes in his proofs (most of which were not discovered for well over 2,000 years). His work nevertheless stands as the bench mark against which all subsequent mathematical thought must be measured.

The major problem with Euclid is that one of his axioms, the parallel axiom, was considered questionable. The reason for this is that it involved the possibility of the extension of a given line infinitely. The parallel axiom states that 'Given a line and a point, there is a unique line through the point which does not meet the first line, no matter how far it is extended'. (An easier way to say this is 'Parallel lines do not meet.') How do we know that this holds outside the galaxy, for example? (Euclid himself appears to have had doubts about this axiom; he proved as many results as possible before he first used it.) During the 17th and 18th centuries, many mathematicians attempted to prove the parallel axiom from the other axioms, but their efforts proved fruitless. One method was to assume a contrary axiom instead such as 'Given a line and a point, there are two lines through the point which do not meet the first line, no matter how far they are extended' and use it to deduce an absurdity, a contradiction of one of the other axioms, thus showing that the contrary axiom could not be true: this is an important mathematical method known as **proof by contradiction**. Independent attempts to do this in the 19th century led mathematicians to believe that it was not in fact possible to do so, that the system of geometry with such an axiom was perfectly self-consistent. This discovery led to perhaps the most important mathematical development for many centuries, that of non-Euclidean geometries in which parallel lines

might meet. These seemed to be just an academic curiousity, until Einstein's theory of **relativity**, which relies on non-Euclidean geometry, was verified by physical observation. It is, Einstein showed, only locally that the universe appears to follow a Euclidean pattern.

The two major branches of mathematics, **pure mathematics** and **applied mathematics**, are complementary parts of a whole, rather than divisions, although mathematicians view themselves as 'pure' or 'applied' and sometimes almost despise those in the other part of the subject. Neither could exist without the other. Without the impetus and inspiration provided by physical problems, pure mathematics would wither and die. Without the work done in pure mathematics, often in areas that no one expected to have application, applied mathematicians would be left in the dark. In only one important instance historically has an applied mathematician created a new body of mathematics; this was the development of the infinitesimal **calculus** by Isaac Newton (1642–1727) for application to the problem of determining planetary motion. Newton's work also led to an influential school of philosophical thought, which still affects the way that many people think today: the idea of **determinism**, which states that the path of the universe is pre-determined and can be known in advance.

During the 19th century, the accuracy of many parts of mathematics was called into question. Some parts of mathematics, notably calculus and **probability**, did not seem to rest on sure foundations. Mathematicians began to demand more from a proof than that it was apparently convincing to the intuition. They began to search for greater **rigour**. This meant that every step had to be explicitly stated (or at least be capable of being backed up by a chain of such statements); every supposition had to be laid bare, so that it could be scrutinized by others. The very process of deduction was studied in greater depth, a study which led to the development of **symbolic logic** by Gottlob Frege (1848–1925), which became the accepted basis and fundamental language of mathematics. Simultaneously with this development came the study of **set theory** by Georg Cantor (1845–1918), which became the basic building blocks of every mathematical theory. Cantor defined what mathematics would talk about, in however disguised a form; Frege defined how it should be talked about.

This new concern with the fundamental basics of mathematics came about because of the discovery of non-Euclidean geometry. To philosophers before the 19th century, mathematics represented absolute truth, the very material of thought at its purest, and the system of Euclidean geometry was held up as the supreme example of **a priori** truth (one that follows without the need for assumptions to be made). This view of mathematics was called **Platonism**. However, the acceptance by mathematicians of a body of work contradictory to Euclidean geometry destroyed this whole comforting notion. There were three main responses to this, new ways of defining the meaning of mathematics.

The first is logicism, which seized on the work of Frege and Cantor to assert that mathematics was basically a branch of the study of logic. The second was **formalism**, which said that mathematics was all about the manipulation of symbols under formal rules – for example, saying that $2+2=4$ means that it is always possible to replace the symbols $2+2$ by the symbol 4. The third school was that of **intuitionism**, which said that the basis of mathematics was ultimately on thought and the intuition (and therefore rejected Cantor's work on the concept of **infinity**, for example). All these schools of thought have today been discredited to varying degrees – formalism and its goals by **Gödel's incompleteness theorem**, formalism and logicism by the feeling that they are trivializing the study of mathematics, and intuitionism under its own weight (as proofs became far harder with intuitionistic limitations on what could be said) and because most of the results obtained by intuitionistic means were only confirmations of results earlier obtained by mainstream mathematicians.

The result is that today there is no real consensus about the fundamental nature of mathematics. The subject, however, still goes ahead, even without a philosophical background, because of its uses and because of its internal elegance and the satisfaction it brings to those who study it.

In the 20th century, the role of mathematics in understanding the universe has become more and more apparent. Until the late 19th century, Newton's mathematics ruled supreme in **physics**. The universe ran deterministically, following the rules that Newton had laid down. Towards the end of the century, it became more and more apparent that something was lacking. This lack was filled by two physical theories which relied on more recent developments in mathematics: Einstein's theory of relativity (which relied on non-Euclidean geometry) and Planck's **quantum** mechanics (which relied on statistics) and was directly opposed to a deterministic view of the universe. In quantum mechanics, particles (or waves) are viewed in a totally nondeterministic manner; their position, velocity, mass or whatever is merely statistical.

The first reason that mathematics is important is that of application (see **applicability of mathematics**). This is the way in which mathematics is used by scientists. First, scientists extract what they consider to be the fundamental nature of the problem they are studying in a mathematic form (the process of abstraction). they then use mathematics to manipulate these statements to deduce a conclusion. This is then translated back into the predicted results of an experiment (the process of application), and they will then perform the experiment and check the results obtained against those predicted by the mathematics.

Mathematics has proved so successful in its applications that if the results of the experiment do not tally with what the scientists expect, they will not conclude that mathematics cannot be applied to their problem. They will rather conclude that their measurements are incorrect or that their original abstraction failed to take into account some important factor, or contained an unwarranted assumption, or that their reasoning was flawed. The applications that have been made have proved almost endless. Not only those sciences in which exact measurements can be made (such as branches of physics or engineering) have benefited from the use of mathematics, but also those where measurements cannot be exact (such as sociology or quantum mechanics), where the techniques of statistics and stochastics have proved invaluable. These vast successes have led to the application of mathematics to areas which at first seem far from obvious: **music**, fine **art** and **literature**, for example, have been produced and analyzed according to mathematical models; the methods of logic have been applied to **linguistics**; major philosophical worldviews (determinism for example) have been inspired by mathematics. Advances in technology are daily being made which depend on mathematics in crucial ways, the most obvious being that of the **computer**. But mathematics is not only the underpinning of scientific thought. There are many areas studied in mathematics with no thought of their applicability to the 'real world'; pure mathematics is the study of mathematical objects for their own sake. Many areas of mathematics seem today to bear no possible relation to the real world, particularly some fields of set theory and logic. It must be remembered, though, that this was also true of non-Euclidean geometry until Einstein, or of symbolic logic until Turing. Techniques from pure mathematics have always illuminated applied mathematics. Pure mathematics is the study of objects of human invention, of concepts with no existence necessary outside the human mind; it comprises the most complex imaginative structure ever built by humankind. It can be viewed – indeed, is viewed by many – as an intellectual game, a superior version of chess in which players are limited only by their imagination, but it is also a game which continues to shape the scientific view of the universe around us. SMcL

Further reading P.J. Davies and R. Hersh, *The Mathematical Experience*; P. Hoffman, *Archimedes' Revenge: the Joys and Perils of Mathematics*; M. Kline, *Mathematics in Western Culture*; I. Stewart, *The Problems of Mathematics*.

MATRIARCHY

Matriarchy (Greek, 'rule by the mother') is a concept that has been used by feminists to describe a society or family in which motherhood, rather than fatherhood, is the central principle. Many feminists believe that before the emergence of patriarchal religions (in which there is a male central deity and men are seen to be made in the image of God; for example, **Christianity**, **Islam**, **Judaism** and **Hinduism**) there was a matriarchal, women-centred, religion. Archaeological artefacts such as female figurines and cave paintings, as well as the presence of goddesses in many world folk tales and **myths**, have all contributed to a growing feminist and woman-based spirituality that often worships a feminine or female principle in the form of a **goddess**. In redefining a matriarchal theology, feminist and women-centred spiritualist groups often draw upon the rhythms of female experience, menstruation, pregnancy, and menopause, as parallels to the rhythms of nature – the seasons, tides etc. In recognizing these parallels many feminist spiritualists have taken up radical and activist positions in relation to the misuse and abuse of the planet's resources.

In the visual **arts** many women artists have taken up the theme of women's spirituality and deified the female body. This is often a means of overturning the Christian desexualization of women (exemplified by Mary the 'virgin mother') by representing the role of female sexuality in a spiritual context. Other feminists have sought to create new words to counteract the patriarchal hold on spirituality – an example is Mary Daly's 'Wickedary'. Monica Sjoo, a founder member of Goddess and the feminist arts movement in the UK, has criticized the patriarchal use of matriarchy to express the passive and instinctual primal age that pre-existed the rationality of patriarchy. Mariha Gimbutas also criticizes patriarchal formulations of matriarch or the earth mother passively lying in wait for the reception of the male seed of life. Many feminist spiritualists highlight, instead, the role of women as shamanistic guides who deal with childbirth and death, or priestesses who provide forms of medicine and therapy that have been hidden in patriarchal conceptions of matriarchy. TK

See also patriarchy.

Further reading Mary Daly & Jane Caputi,

The Websters First New Intergalactic Wickedary of the English Language; Marija Gimbutas, Civilisation of the Goddess:The World of Old Europe; Caitlin Matthews (ed.), Voices of the Goddess: A Chorus of Sibyls.

MATTER/ANTIMATTER

The theories of **quantum** mechanics and **relativity** were developed separately in the early part of the 20th century. However, it soon became obvious that a relativistic treatment of quantum mechanics was necessary for a full description of the interactions of elementary **particles**, as they often move at speeds approaching that of light.

The inclusion of relativity required that the non-relativistic **Schrödinger equation**, which describes all non-relativistic interactions, be replaced by a relativistic equation. This equation was discovered by Paul Dirac (1902–84), and named after him.

The solutions to the Dirac equation are found to contain a whole class of new particles in addition to the expected solutions. They correspond to negative energy solutions, and are called antiparticles. At first they were not thought to have a physical existence, but soon experiments showed that antiparticles do indeed exist.

In quantum mechanics, all particles are described by a set of quantum numbers, like spin or charge. Each particle has a corresponding antiparticle which has opposite quantum numbers. Thus the electron, which has one unit of negative charge, has as its antiparticle that positron, with one unit of positive charge. Neutrinos and antineutrinos have opposite spin. In theory, it should be possible to construct anti-atoms, completely composed of antimatter. There are some experiments in progress at this time which are attempting to construct anti-hydrogen.

When a particle meets its antiparticle, they annihilate each other, producing a burst of energy. This means that it is very difficult to store antimatter; as soon as it comes into contact with normal matter, it is violently destroyed.

One of the puzzles of the universe is that it contains far more matter than antimatter. This is not what might be expected, for in all interactions where particles are formed, particles and antiparticles are produced in equal amounts. It is surmised that, near the beginning of the universe, different conditions prevailed which ensured that particles were produced in preference to antiparticles. **JJ**

McCARTHYISM

McCarthyism was named (by the US cartoonist Herblock) after Senator Joseph McCarthy (1908–57), who headed a committee of the US Senate which investigated 'un-American activities' between 1950 and 1954, when McCarthy himself was investigated and censured. The committee was set up as a result of the anti-communist hysteria which gripped the US in the early years of the Cold War. Its purpose was to discover and root out communist sympathizers in every walk of American life: they were thought to be loyal to the 'International Communist Conspiracy' rather than to their country, and to be devoted to subverting national life. McCarthy, supported by J. Edgar Hoover, the FBI chief who had been conducting an anti-left-wing, anti-intellectual campaign of his own for some 40 years, and aided by the future president Richard M. Nixon, hauled hundreds of citizens before the Committee, ranting and blustering at them to reveal their communist sympathies and to betray their friends and colleagues. Rules of evidence were abandoned; guilt was assumed before each proceeding began. No one was immune: politicians, business tycoons, film stars and writers fell victim to McCarthy's witch-hunting methods just as often as ordinary, anonymous citizens.

The Committee hearings were some of the first governmental proceedings ever to be televised, so that McCarthy's bear-pit became a nightly spectacle in millions of homes. In the end this very exposure was McCarthy's own undoing. His methods and his own private life were investigated, and he fell. But it is mistaken to think that McCarthyism was a unique and short-lived phenomenon. It was merely the over-the-top manifestation of a deep-seated feeling in American life, of a kind of national paranoia which is by no means confined to the

US, and McCarthy's basic views were supported by millions who disapproved of his methods. Some modern commentators, not all of them politically left-wing, say that the slow death of **liberalism** endemic to US life in the second half of the century derived an impetus from McCarthyism from which it has never recovered. KMcL

Further reading David Caute, *The Great Fear*.

MEASURE THEORY

Measure theory, in **mathematics**, began as the response to one specific question. Suppose you were given a boundary in space. What is the particular surface which has this boundary and which has the smallest possible area? (The question is usually generalized to higher dimensions.) In three dimensions, the surface is that which would be taken up by a soap bubble given the boundary as a frame. This question is essentially one of **topology**, but from the work in measure theory applications have been found in many branches of mathematics, as well as in **cosmology**. Measure theory has also provided the basis for modern views of the integral **calculus**. SMcL

MEASUREMENT

Measurement is the art or technique of measuring, based upon pre-defined standards: it is a form of the 'abstraction' of reality vital to all scientific and technological activity. It has evolved into a science that has great consequences upon the life of human beings from mathematical theories to the size and weight of goods sold in supermarkets.

The theory of measurement was first studied by the Greek mathematicians Eudoxos of Cnidos and Thaeateros. The theory is based on the use of numbers to represent different objects and physical phenomena. Any measurement theory must involve three basic concepts, those of error, representation and uniqueness.

Errors will always be present; even though scientific experimentation techniques may improve the degree of accuracy the results obtained can always be subdivided to the extent that they are no longer accurate. A kilogram of fruit bought in a supermarket, for example, may actually weight 1.05 kg. This mistake in the degree of accuracy may not matter when fruit is being weighed, but if platinum were measured on the same scales, the error could be costly. Human error may always be present but modern technology can be used to improve accuracy of measurement and identify gross error.

Representation is really the assignment of numbers to such measurements, while uniqueness is the representation chosen for different objects. (Electric current, for example, is not measured in litres, nor is water measured in seconds, and it is this knowledge of the basic framework of measurements that leads to uniqueness.)

Measurement of any object or phenomenon is carried out by comparison. This leads to the need for a reference system from which all measurements are derived. The earliest measurements were based on four standards, those of mass, volume, length and area. The standards first appeared in ancient Mediterranean countries and were based upon what humans saw around them. The first linear measurement, the Egyptian cubit, was based on the measurement from the elbow to the fingertip, while the inch was based on the width of a thumb. These highly inaccurate measurements led to confusion throughout the Western world. The need for standardization was essential if the Industrial Revolution was to succeed. Specialized tools such as borers and lathes could never have worked if measurements were made to such a high degree of inaccuracy.

The adoption of the British Imperial, US Customary and metric system in Europe solved this problem. Nowadays, of course, the standard system in most countries is the SI system (Système d'Unités Internationale) which by standardization has made many parts and components interchangeable throughout the world. This standardization has transformed industry's way of thinking as more and more goods are built on flow-line techniques, so reducing the cost of goods, since assemblers like car manufacturers can rely on the precision of manufacture of components from many different companies and countries.

In the SI system the basic references are the metre (m) for length, the kilogram (kg) for mass, the second(s) for time, the ampere (A) for electrical current, the kelvin (K) for temperature and the candela (cd) for light intensity. The metre was originally defined as the length of a metre bar kept in Paris and the kilogram is the mass of a metallic block maintained there also. While the reference for the kilogram has been unchanged for nearly 200 years the standard for length is related to the wavelength of vibrations of the rare element krypton 86. Similarly the base of time the second is defined relative to the frequency of radiation produced from Caesium 133 under certain conditions.

The English speaking public has difficulties with the units for force, since these are the technically correct ways of expressing weight (the force of gravitational attraction on a body). The reference unit is the newton (N) defined as the force which when applied to a 1 kg mass produces 1 metre per second squared acceleration. This is used in the definition of ampere and the kelvin for temperature is derived from the difference between absolute zero temperature and the freezing point of water.

Instruments to make measurements have required to be developed as technological advances are made. Round-the-world navigation by sea depended on the invention of a reliable time piece, the chronometer. The diameter and lengths of machine components have successfully been measured using wooden then steel rules, vernier calipers, micrometers, comparators using slip gauges and finally lasers. Force or weight is measured by spring balances where displays are mechanical pointers or electrically generated numbers. High technology is available at low cost for time measurement where the markets are stocked with watches whose timekeeping is based on the frequency of oscillation of a crystal of quartz. **AA**

Further reading T.F. and M.B. Gilbert, *Units and System of Weights and Measure, their Origin, Development and Present Status.*

MECHANICS

Mechanics (Greek, 'about contrivances'),

in **physics**, has come to have a multitude of meanings. Its original definition was the study of systems under the action of forces. Today there are different types of mechanics which pertain to different systems.

The most familiar form of mechanics is Newtonian mechanics. This is a description of the physical principles underlying force, mass and motion that holds for all 'classical' systems. Classical systems are those where the scale of the system is too large to make quantum effects noticeable, and the velocity of the system is far less than that of light, making relativistic effects negligible. (Quantum effects can be seen at about 1/1000 of a millimetre, and the speed of light is about 186,000 miles per second.) Thus all familiar systems are covered by Newtonian mechanics. Specializations within Newtonian mechanics include statics, dynamics, fluid mechanics, celestial mechanics and many others.

Quantum mechanics is one of the great achievements of the 20th century. The work of Schrödinger and Heisenberg laid the foundations for this science, upon which all modern computers, electronics, optical communications and other small-scale processes depend.

At the other end of the scale we have relativistic mechanics. This is based on the work of Einstein in the early part of the century, and applies to objects travelling at an appreciable fraction of the velocity of light, or objects subjected to enormous gravities.

See also quantization; quantum theory; relativity.

MECHANISM

In **biology**, the doctrine of mechanism states that organisms are nothing more than self-perpetuating machines which can be broken down into a number of parts, each with a function in the whole and in which each event is entirely predictable from its cause. Since organic matter can be ultimately broken down into basic chemical units, the theory implies that life must conform to the laws of **chemistry** and **physics**. The idea was debated intensely during the 18th century by Cartesian philosophers, and, in the 19th century, Samuel Butler in his satirical work *Erewhon* (1872) examined the idea that man and machine could compete with one another on the same level.

Modern **molecular biology** was hailed as the proof for mechanism and the scientific study of biological systems presupposes that it will conform to mechanistic principles. Yet the control of the whole organism at the genetic (molecular) levels might also be construed as support for **organicism** and, due to the enormous complexity of many biological systems, it is impractical (but in mechanistic terms, not impossible) to attempt to derive certain biological principles from those of physics and chemistry. Thus many biologists would describe themselves as organicists in their philosophical outlook, though attempts to study organisms in a holistic sense do not preclude the application of mechanistic prinicples. **RB**

See also life; metabolism; vitalism.

Further reading Jacques Monod, *Chance and Necessity.*

MEDIA

Media is the plural of medium (Latin, 'middle'), though it is popularly used as both singular and plural. It refers to the whole range of possible channels of **communication** employed in **discourse**: any vehicle or entity through which communication takes place. The word media is commonly associated with the mass media, that is those means by which information, entertainment, **advertising**, and news are transmitted to a general audience. However, its usage is constantly expanding and currently includes public relations, direct marketing and computer networking. A medium is any single vehicle ('channel') through which a message is transmitted to people, and its properties determine the range of **codes** it can transmit and thus will affect the nature of the message and its effect on the receiver.

A channel of communication carries a signal from a sender to a receiver. This signal has been converted from a message in a order that it may be carried. The medium converts the message. Thus a voice, gesture or expression, paper for drawing, television, radio, clothes and books are all types of medium bound by different physical or technological constraints. John Fiske, in *Introduction to Communication Studies*, divides notions of 'media' into three convenient, though not exclusively independent, categories: the presentational media; the representational media; the mechanical media.

The presentational media are the face, voice and body. These make use of such 'natural' languages as speech and gestures. Here the medium *is* the communicator (or sender of the message) and such communication is restricted to the here and now. It produces *acts* of communication where the medium *is* the communicator. Representational media might also be termed creative media. Books, photographs, writing, **sculpture**, **painting**, **architecture**, fashion and other forms of design are representational in that they make use of the conventions, signs and symbols of **culture** and **aesthetics** to produce a 'text'. This text can exist independently of its producer(s), and thus is a *work* of communication. Mechanical media (such as telephones, television, film and faxes) transmit the first two categories. They are subject to technological constraints, including the potential for physical noise.

These categories are marked as much by their similarities as by their differences. They are useful only as a convenient device for the formal analysis of communication process. Apart from its central meaning, the word 'media' is also worth considering in the light of the ideological, sociological and commercially angled prefixes and suffixes it attracts. The most widely used are media control, mass media, media **image**, media coverage, media vehicle, and the phrase 'The Medium Is The Message'.

Media control is generally agreed to be either authoritarian, paternal, commercial or democratic. Authoritarian control is a monopoly of communication channels and therefore control of what messages are sent. (To a certain degree such control could be said to extend to the way such messages are interpreted also.) Raymond Williams, in *Communications*, describes the second type, paternal media, as 'authoritarianism with a conscience'. This means that, unlike the first category, there is evidence that the simple maintenance of absolute power is not the sole concern of the 'paternal' body; values can be held which might contradict those of the body, though not challenge it. The BBC in the UK, for example, might be classed as maintaining a 'paternal' control over its operations. Commercial control is that exerted by market interests. The fourth category, democratic control, is the rarest. Decision-making must be the joint task of all those involved in the production and distribution of its messages. Ideally the recipients of those messages should also be able to feed back their response into the system, and so influence its output.

The general development of media control has been one of a cross-media concentration of corporate ownership. Sophisticated techniques of multi-marketing have grown alongside the centralization of power (sometimes into a very small group of people or even down to one single person), enabling the exploitation of several media in the sale of one prime commodity. The 'star' singer, for example, is created and marketed worldwide via television, makes an album and accompanying video (about which a book might be written). Spinning off from these activities are such things as magazines, posters, T-shirts and television interviews.

Media images are those images which the mass media prefer and relentlessly project, while apparently showing a 'truthful' and 'normal' picture of the world. Most of us receive the bulk of our information about the world through such media and thus our perception of it is to a certain extent formed by its images. The constancy and seemingly 'naturalness' of these images is such that they have become conventional, the yardstick by which we judge 'normality' and any deviation from it. Many would argue that in fact the media offers a mediation of reality while appearing simply to pass on such 'natural truths'.

Media coverage is the percentage of targeted people or households reached by one or more of the media used in a specific advertising campaign. In such a campaign the mass-communications medium used is known as the 'media vehicle'. This is not the same as the channel: that is, the media vehicle for television or radio is the *programme*, and for a magazine or other periodical it would be the *issue*.

'The Medium Is The Message' was the celebrated phrase coined by Marshall McLuhan (1911–80). McLuhan believed, and was one of the first to say, that *what* is said in a message is conditioned by the *way* in which it is said, that is by the medium used. Whatever attributes a medium possesses contributes to the meaning in any communication. The phrase is the title of the first chapter of his book *Understanding Media: The Extensions of Man* (1964). **RG**

Further reading Hartley, Goulden & O'Sullivan (eds.), *Making Sense of the Media.*

MEDIATION

At one level the process of mediation (from Latin *mediare*, 'to go between') refers to the mass **media**'s role in communicating and acting as a medium of image and information to audiences. Implicit here though is the sense in which the media *intervenes* between 'reality' and the audience. This is a process of transformation whereby the media, not necessarily conspiratorially but as an aspect of the everyday technical, economic and cultural processes involved, actively reconstruct and represent the real world. The audience, then receives a mediated version of reality. Television news programmes, for instance, by interpreting reality through selecting, editing, presenting and filming *mediate* between the real world of events and the viewer.

Some media theorists, however, argue that the ability to mediate allows the mass media undue power to present specific values and beliefs. Critics of various political hues have complained that television news, for example, is prone to distortion and camouflage rather than simply mediation. **NC**

See also performing arts; representation.

Further reading P. Schlesinger, *Putting Reality Together.*

MEDICAL ETHICS

Medical Ethics sets out to define the requi

ed code of behaviour between doctor and patient and the regulation of advertising. It has come to include a consideration of the wider social and economic factors which influence the public health.

The Hippocratic Oath has, since the 3rd century BCE, been the defined basis for ethical behaviour of physicians. It is in part an assurance to maintain a family craft-guild. The physician would prescribe drugs and diet, but not wield a knife, leaving surgery to surgeons. Intentional injustice, including sexual relations with members of the patient's household is forbidden. Confidentiality is promised. **Euthanasia** and abortion are both forbidden, although they were morally and socially a part of Greek culture at the time of Hippocrates.

Medical ethics might usefully be considered under the following headings:

Primum non nocere, the classic exortation 'not to do harm'. Although any treatment will be intended to do good to the patient, it has frequently to be balanced against risks of harmful effects.

Respect for the dignity and autonomy of the patient in decision-making about how to proceed in a given situation. This can be made difficult by lack of clear reasons to make choices, and by the attitude of paternalism traditional to, and expected of, doctors.

A regard for the quality of information. The idea of giving true and not false information to patients is desirable but not easy to maintain. Despite the promise and the expectation of the 'scientific revolution' the spectrum of medical knowledge still ranges from scientifically provable, through all points, to folkloric. In order to apear scientific, small fragments of information are often extrapolated into grander, but unsupportable theories.

The Law. The legal code is supposed to provide ethical guidelines but is also guided by fashions, public opinion, investigative journalism, vested interests, etc. **TG**

Further reading L. Edelstein, *Ancient Medicine;* I. Kennedy, *The Unmasking of Medicine.*

MEDICINE

Medicine (from Latin *mederi*, 'to heal') is the body of information and activity related to the alleviation and cure of illness.

Western medicine can be traced to Greek origins, and the Hippocratic oath remains the declaration of Ethical Intent. Until the the last century medicine was the accumulation of observations about the symptoms and signs of illness, and the natural history of the conditions sufficiently consistent to be given the names of particular **diseases**. The practitioners of medicine were able to make a *diagnosis* (to name the illness) and a *prognosis* (to forecast the likely outcome of the illness). The interventions carried out for the benefit of the patient were again based upon the accumulated experience of the practitioners and were, in the main, derived from folklore (for instance, herbal medicine) or craft sources (for example, surgery, bonesetting).

The more scientific aspects of the roots of medicine began with the science of **microbiology**. Particular species of bacteria were linked with specific illnesses. In the 19th century, Robert Koch (the discoverer of Mycobacterium Tuberculosis in 1882) defined the four conditions to be met in order to link a microorganism as the cause of a particular illness. The Koch Postulates, as they came to be known, remain valid to this day. Microbiology enabled preventative medicine either by preventing dangerous organisms from getting into people, or by enhancing the person's mechanisms for dealing with the invading organism (for example, by vaccination). The next step in the establishment of a scientific basis for medicine was the work of Rudolf Virchow (1821–1902). He refined the examination of dead bodies by examining the organs under a microscope and linking observable changes with the illness which led to the death of the patient. This discipline, pathology, remains the scientific grammar of medicine. The third big change was the development of organic **chemistry**;

larger molecules could now be synthesized and tested for possibly beneficial effects on ill people.

The scientific pillars of medicine have continued to be refined. The number and range of known microorganisms have increased almost immeasurably. The causal link of an illness with a microorganism remains a most highly regarded goal, since the search for a useful intervention should become more finite. Pathology, with **biochemistry**, has continued to discover and link more and subtler aspects of illness. Large and elegant pictures have emerged, though the puzzles are not invariably solved. Biochemistry has also widened the range and number of substances which may be useful for the treatment of illness.

At this time Western medicine is a mixture of models or paradigms of somewhat variable scientific quality. Some parts of medicine (that is, some illnesses) are well understood and described, and the model includes a valid and useful intervention which can cure the illness. Other parts have sufficient clarity to enable alleviation of symptoms, or even some limitation of shortening of lifespan. However, there are still parts of medicine in which science has produced insufficient information to be of value to the person with the illness.

The present situation, in which medicine consists of a series of models of variable quality and utility, is severely limiting. Medical practitioners seem loath to differentiate between situations in which their services may be of incomparable value from those in which they may be less so. Furthermore, the high promise of science as the solver of all problems has created expectation and demand which reinforce the problem.

Chinese medicine dates from roughly the 5th century BCE, the same time as the pre-Socratic school of **philosophy**. It derives from a break with the tradition of attributing illness to demons to the linking of health to harmonious coexistence with nature. In classical Chinese philosophy, thoughts and experiences relate by association, correspondences or resonance rather than by the linear cause-effect relationship in Western philosophy. After 1948 – when a primary care system had to be provided

for the Chinese people – it was decided to use traditional Chinese medicine as part of the system. For political and practical reasons it was necessary to 'rewrite' the body of medical knowledge in compartmentalized and linear form, and it was possible to train enough traditional practitioners to provide a useful service. This event provides an interesting example of the utility and the disadvantages of adopting a linear, reductionist and post-Cartesian system of medical thought.

Ayurvedic medicine is a classical Indian diagnostic and therapeutic system which considers people as having different body types and different *doshas* or metabolic principles. It has had substantial influence in East and West, and remains in use. Many other non-Western traditional medical systems have knowledge of procedures and of the use of natural substances in the treatment of illness. Medicine also includes shamanism and other practices which are outside scientific explanation. **TG**

See also Daoism; demonism; disease; health; medical ethics; witchcraft.

MEDITATION

In **religion**, meditation is often mentioned in the same breath as **prayer**, but it is in fact distinct from it, although prayer, especially *mantras* and the constant repetition of formulas such as the 'Jesus Prayer' or 'Ave Maria', may be used to prepare the mind and spirit. Meditation usually involves intense concentration and oblivion to external distraction. As a form of spiritual discipline and a path to enlightenment it is found in all the great religious traditions. There are innumerable techniques, but each has the same goal: to increase the devotee's motivation and devotion. **EMJ**

MEDIUMSHIP see **Parapsychology**; **Pseudoscience**

MEIOSIS

Meiosis (Greek, 'process of lessening') refers to the divisions of the cell nucleus which occur during the formation of gametes (sex cells – eggs and sperm); the parent nucleus, with paired chromosomes, produces four daughters with a single complement of chromosomes each. The genetic make-up of these chromosomes is different from that of either parent, but they consist of components from each because of the exchange of genes which takes place during **crossing over**. These daughters form the gametes which fuse during fertilization their nuclei fuse so that they have paired chromosomes. The division of the chromosome pairs between gametes is a random event so that one gamete receives a paternal and a maternal chromosome; this is the essence of Mendel's law of segregation (see **Mendelism**). **RB**

See also gene; genetic linkage; genetics.

Further reading Bruce Alberts, *Molecular Biology of the Cell*.

MELODRAMA

Melodrama (Greek, 'action with music') originally meant a single scene or monologue played to music. (In this sense it was revived in the 19th century – Tennyson's *Enoch Arden* is typical – but with small success.) From the mid–19th century onwards, its secondary meaning became far more important. In this sense, melodrama is a play or theatre style relying heavily on sensational action, spectacular disasters, and strong emotions. Although scorned by highbrow critics, it was a vigorous theatrical form of wide mass appeal, and melodramatic elements are still to be found in many forms of dramatic activity. Nowadays, melodrama is rarer onstage than in the cinema and television, where its techniques for manipulating and guiding audience response ('tear-jerking', as it was once called) range from the use of music to underline emotional climaxes to the cliffhanging endings of episodes of television **soap** operas. **TRG SS**

See also drama; theatre; tragedy.

Further reading Peter Brooks, *The Melodramatic Imagination*; R.B. Heilman, *Tragedy and Melodrama*.

MEMORY

I can remember that Mrs Thatcher resigned from the post of British Prime Minister in 1991. This is a case, in **philosophy**, of propositional knowledge, of knowing a proposition about the past. I can also remember seeing Mrs Thatcher holding back her tears as her car swept out of Downing Street. This is not a case of propositional knowledge, but a case of personal memory, of remembering an event from my own past experience. Propositional knowledge of the past is not limited by the extent of one's own past experience, whereas personal memory is. I can remember that World War II ended in 1945, but I have no personal memory of the end of World War II, because I was not yet born and therefore not around to experience the event.

In order to have personal memory of a past event one must have experienced the event. One must also currently have a mental representation of the event. But this is not enough for personal memory. Suppose that I have forgotten all about my fifth birthday party, but when asked to imagine what happened at my fifth birthday party, I imagine throwing a tantrum while wearing a blue suit. Further suppose that, as a matter of complete coincidence, I did throw a tantrum while wearing a blue suit at my fifth birthday party. Then I currently have an accurate mental representation of a past event which I did experience at the time. But I am not currently remembering my party it is just that, as a matter of complete coincidence, my imaginings are accurate.

Such considerations have led philosophers to claim that in order to have personal memory of a past event, it is not enough to have a mental representation of a past event which one experienced. It must also be the case that one's past experience of the event is causally relevant to one currently having a mental representation as of it. **AJ**

See also causal theories.

Further reading S. Davis, *Causal Theories of Mind*; N. Malcolm, *Memory and Mind*.

MENDELISM

Gregor Mendel (1822–84), an Austrian

monk, intitiated the modern study of heredity with his observations of the statistical distribution of offspring produced by the breeding of varieties of pea plant, such as dwarf and tall. Although not the first to study heredity, Mendel was the first to record his results in such detail that it was possible to see the significance of the proportions in which each type of individual arose. The only satisfactory explanation for the ratios of offspring types (**phenotypes**) which he observed was that heritable characteristics were particulate. Mendel postulated that 'factors' were responsible for the transmission of discrete features from parent to offspring. These factors were later termed **genes** and their transference between generations as discrete units enables both parents to contribute to the **genetic** make-up (**genotype**) of the offspring without blending of characteristics. Modern laws of heredity have their basis in Mendel's studies, which were published in 1865 but not recognized as important until 1900, when they were rediscovered by the Dutch geneticist Hugo de Vries. Since the beginning of the 20th century, genetics has played an increasingly pivotal role in **biology** and Mendel's original conclusions have been extensively modified, but his principles of heredity have endured. **RB**

See also blending inheritance; meiosis.

MENTAL HEALTH

Mental health is about the well-being of persons as perceived by themselves, and the acceptance of their behaviour by others as 'normal'. It has become the umbrella term for mental, as opposed to physical illness, and everything that has to do with it. An early text *The Anatomy of Melancholy* by Richard Burton (1576–1637) precedes the dividing of body, mind and spirit, and is still a marvellous description of illness with mental, emotional and visceral manifestations.

Mental illness very rarely has a demonstrable organic lesion and the benefits of the advances in pathology, which began in the 19th century, did not benefit the diagnosis or treatment of mental illness. There is large variation from one culture to another about what is acceptable as normal or sane behaviour.

Mental diseases were based upon descriptions of behaviour only, and in the absence of any rational treatments the natural history of the diseases was as much a function of the stigma carried by 'madness' or by the effects of institutionalization. At the end of the 19th century Sigmund Freud challenged the prevailing views, devised a new descriptive 'pathology' and proposed the use of the technique of **psychoanalysis** to deal with the mental illnesses which corresponded to his descriptions. The rationale for this therapy was for the ill person to freely associate ideas and talk until the cause of his or her illness was revealed. Once the cause was understood, it was assumed that the illness would abate. Many styles of psychoanalysis evolved, but all were time-consuming and expensive. To become available to less wealthy people psychoanalysis was tried on groups of patients, and in time it was observed that the interactions of members of the group were at least as important as the work of the analyst. As styles varied more from analysis the term psychotherapy was devised to describe other talking therapies. Most recently the potential value of psychotherapy has been much enhanced by the introduction of the idea of goal orientation in treatment, thereby limiting openendedness. The group evolved usefully into family and other network therapies.

The drug treatment of mental illness has moved from chloral hydrate, the original 'knock-out drops', and barbiturates (downers) and amphetamines (uppers) to antipsychotic drugs like chlorpromazine and various groups of anti-depressive and anxiety reducing substances. The drugs are still linked with disease models which lack a pathological or biochemical basis, and the intent of therapy does not clearly differentiate whether it is to increase the well-being of the ill person, or to make the behaviour of the person more acceptable to society.

In Western culture the confinement of mentally ill people to institutions is relatively recent – 18th to 19th centuries. More recently, attempts have been made to de-institutionalize the care of mentally ill people.

On occasion particular communities have taken on the role of caring for mentally ill people as members of their community. Examples exist in the Netherlands, and in Yorubaland, western Nigeria. **TG**

See also psychiatry.

MENTAL PHENOMENA

Pains, visual and auditory experiences, joy, fear, beliefs, desires and intentions are all mental phenomena. Philosophers often distinguish occurrent mental phenomena or mental events such as pains, gustatory experiences – as of chilli – and thoughts of Paris, from mental phenomena which are not events but dispositions, such as believing that God is good or wanting to read *War and Peace*.

What is the mark of the mental? That is, what is the property that all and only mental phenomena possess? What is it that all and only mental phenomena have in common?

Many mental phenomena are intentional: they are about something and have an object. My desire for a beer, for example, is about something. But (1) many non-mental phenomena are also intentional – consider road signs and picture-postcards. Perhaps such non-mental intentional phenomena are only derivatively intentional; perhaps their object-directedness derives from the intentional mental states of their creators and interpreters. If so, one might claim that mental phenomena are non-derivatively intentional. But (2) not all mental phenomena are intentional. Pains are not about anything, they do not have an object. And perhaps one can be depressed or anxious without being depressed or anxious about anything. So even if all non-derivatively intentional phenomena are mental, not all mental phenomena are non-derivatively intentional. So intentionality is not the mark of the mental.

Many mental phenomena are phenomenological: they feel a certain way. Certainly pains and perceptual experiences are phenomenological. And perhaps undirected depression and anxiety are also phenomenological. But while all phenomenological phenomena are mental, not all mental phenomena are phenomenological. The belief that grass is green and the desire for a cup of tea do not feel a certain way. So phenomenologicality is not the mark of the mental.

Some mental phenomena, such as beliefs and desires, are intentional but not phenomenological. Some mental phenomena, such as pains, are phenomenological but not intentional. And some mental phenomena, such as perceptual experiences and, perhaps, anger are both phenomenological and intentional. But it seems that every mental phenomena is either phenomenological or intentional. And it is plausible that all non-derivatively intentional phenomena and all phenomenological phenomena are mental. So one could claim that what all and only mental phenomena have in common is that they are either non-derivatively intentional or phenomenological. But this suggestion does not explain why we count non-derivatively intentional and phenomenological phenomena as belonging to the same category, the mental. And it is not entirely clear what it is for a phenomena to be 'non-derivatively' intentional. **AJ**

See also consciousness; intentionality.

Further reading C. McGinn, *The Character of Mind*.

MERCANTILISM

Mercantilism (from Latin *mercator*, 'seller in a market') is a descriptive term invented by economists in later years to describe the ideas of some European writers of the 16th and 17th centuries who advocated similar policies, such as an emphasis on manufacture rather than on the production of agricultural raw materials, and protectionist foreign trade measures, both of which would produce an excess of exports over imports, that is, a 'favourable balance of trade'. The central goal was the accumulation of national treasure, to be achieved by exporting as much as possible and importing as little as possible. Net exports would enrich the state when other countries paid off the balance in precious metals, with wealth. Many mercantilists were more sophisticated and looked on the flow of precious metals as a source of purchasing power for such things as navies and standing armies for emerging nation states.

Adam Smith, in the *The Wealth of Nations* (1776), showed that imports bring in useful goods and services while exports send out the nation's goods in return for sterile metals. In this view exports are a necessary evil to finance imports. Smith showed that exports were a sacrifice, desirable only in as much as they allowed a country to import. Although the crudest forms of mercantilism have been banished, contemporary protectionism is motivated by the same beliefs. **TF**

Further reading Eli Hecksher, *Mercantilism;* J.M. Keynes, 'Notes on Mercantilism' in *General Theory of Employment, Interest and Money;*

MESMERISM

The idea of mesmerism was the invention of Franz Anton Mesmer (1734–1815). In his medical doctoral dissertation on the effects of the planets on human behaviour, he put forward the idea of animal gravitation: the force, he claimed, which was responsible for planetary influence on human actions. While Mesmer was working with a patient who had many extreme symptoms (diagnosed a hysteric because her condition did not have an obvious organic cause), a Jesuit astronomer suggested that he use a magnetic treatment by applying magnets to the soles of her feet. This Mesmer did, with immediate effect: after a painful crisis state, seemingly brought on by the magnets, the patient recovered. Mesmer immediately began to publicize 'his' new technique, using the Jesuit's name for it, Animal Magnetism. It also became known as Mesmerism. After other successes Mesmer's theory was published, together with details of the alignment, ebb and flow of magnetic forces within the body. Commissions in Paris were set up to test the theory, but described it as worthless. Nevertheless many people believed in Mesmer and he had enthusiastic supporters, including the French Marquis de Puysegur. Puysegur learned how to induce the crisis state that led to recovery, but he was upset by the discomfort it caused. He tried to induce a calmer state while mesmerizing his subjects, and one day one of his patients, a boy, went into a dream-like state instead of crisis. In this state he did whatever was suggested to him, and when he came out of it he recalled nothing about this. Thus, Puysegur discovered that the changes had to do not with magnetism but with this somnambulist condition. This trance became the basis of all subsequent investigations and treatments.

Patients in a state of mesmeric trance felt no pain. A young English surgeon, James Esdaile, impressed by the mesmeric anaesthesia he witnessed, used it to anaesthetize his patients, reducing their pain and increasing their chances of survival. Another English doctor, James Braid, conducted a scientific investigation and called mesmerism 'Neuro-hypnotism' (nervous sleep). Shortened to Hypnotism, this term has remained with us ever since. **MJ**

Further reading J.E. Gordon (ed.), *Handbook of Clinical and Experimental Hypnosis.*

MESSAGE

In **media** and **communication** studies, the term 'message' is so basic and fundamental that it is often taken for granted rather thn explained. Paradoxically, our understanding of the term has been filtered through a number of different, broad schools of thought whose divergent concerns have led to variations in the ways in which the term has come to be used in academic study.

At its simplest level, a message is a signal from a sender to a receiver, but this omits an essential element in the way we usually understand a message, that is, the meaning encapsulated in the signal. Although for analytical purposes it may be possible to separate out the process of sending and receiving from the element of meaning, in reality we experience the message as a whole.

In communication studies, the two major approaches emanate from, on the one hand, **sociology** and **psychology**, and on the other, from the **semiotic** school influenced by **linguistics**. In the former approach there is an emphasis on the intention of the sender and on the process by which the message is transmitted. So concerns would typically centre on whether or not the message had been successfully received (and if not, what factors might have led to a failure). This approach is also concerned with the possible effects of a given message on the receiver.

In the latter approach the emphasis is more on how meaning is produced. It emphasizes the interaction of **culture** (people sending and receiving) and text (written, visual, aural, musical, etc.), and regards regards the message as consisting of *signs* which can be encoded and decoded. In the process of this interaction, there is the possibility of a range of meanings emerging. Clearly, in this version, the variable cultural backgrounds of receivers figure strongly inasmuch as different messages may be taken from the same text.

In the study of messages it is assumed that there can never be a 'pure' message. All messages are coded in some way; a simple example of this would be the Morse code, but musical notation, slang and the conventions of visual art might be others. Moreover, in the process of sending and receiving a coded message, other factors come into account. How clear is the message? Is the receiver familiar with the code being used? What is the intention of the sender? It is possible for the signal to be recognized but for the meaning to be misunderstood.

A broad consideration of this area was taken up by Marshall McLuhan in the 1960s. McLuhan argued (in *Understanding Media: the Extensions of Man* (1964) that 'The medium is the message' by which he meant that what is said, and our understanding of what is said, are conditioned by the medium through which the message is transmitted. No medium is neutral. **BC**

See also code; context; encode/decode.

Further reading J. Fiske, *Introduction to Communication.*

METABOLISM

In the **life sciences**, the term metabolism (Greek, 'process of change') refers collectively to all the chemical processes which occur within a living organism. Prior to the 19th century little was known about the functions associated with **life**, though philosophers had speculated since the time of the ancient Greeks. Justus von Liebig (1803–73) listed input and excretion, but knew nothing of the processes between; since then, the gaps have been filled quite substantialy for a number of organisms, including man. **RB**

See also biochemistry; cytology; endocrinology; homeostasis; physiology.

METALS AND ALLOYS

Metals and alloys (a mixture of two or more metals) play a fundamental part in the structure of the modern world, but the use of metals by man dates back to pre-biblical times. The first metals used were those that occurred naturally and appeared on the Earth's surface such as gold, silver, iron and copper. These supplies were soon exhausted, and it was not until the Bronze and Iron Ages that it was discovered how to extract metals from their ores, where the metal is chemically combined with other elements such as sulphur and oxygen. As dependency upon metals grew, the techniques to locate and recover the metals from their ores became more sophisticated. Such metals as copper, zinc and lead are extremely rare in the Earth's crust, but they have all become an integral factor in today's society. The availability of ores depends not only on their scarcity but on how easy it is to extract and exploit the ores.

The use of iron and steel account for around 95% of all metal products in the Western world. The process of reducing iron oxides to metallic iron is smelting. This involves heating the iron ores along with carbon to produce carbon dioxide and iron. This process was carried out using charcoal until Abraham Darby (1677–1717) succeeded in smelting iron from coke (which could be easily produced from coal). This raw iron or 'pig iron' (so-called from the shape of the lumps produced by the process) can be melted again to remove impurities and have carbon added to it to produce steel which is much stronger and can deform more before breaking. Cast iron is very brittle and snaps with little deformation. Steel may have other metals added to it, in order to produce alloys that have very useful properties. The addition of nickel and chromium is used in the manufacture of stainless steel, while the addition of cobalt, molybdenum, tungsten or vanadium produces hard-wearing steel for cutting tools.

Although iron has been used for over 4,000 years, the most common metal found in the Earth's crust, aluminium, was only isolated for the first time in 1825 by the Danish physicist Oersted. Aluminium has many uses such as thin foil sheets for food wrapping, the structure of aircraft and in the electrical supply industry as transmission lines.

Another metal in common industrial use is copper and its alloys such as brass and bronze. As well as being a good electrical conductor, it is also used in coinage and in plumbing. Other metals such as gold, silver, tin, lead, chromium, mercury, platinum, magnesium and zinc all have their specific applications, but probably the use of uranium in nuclear power stations causes more controversy than the use of any other metal or alloy.

Metals are being used at an alarming rate as the Third World countries try to catch up with the rest of the world, and the supplies of such scarce metals as silver and platinum are in doubt. A substitute material may be found in order to compensate for such scarcity, but this may not always be possible. Another factor to take into consideration is the fact that as technology becomes more sophisticated the extraction of scarce ores may become viable in the future. **AA**

Further reading W. Alexander and A. Street, *Metals in the Service of Man*; J.E. Gordon, *The New Science of Strong Materials*.

METAMORPHOSIS

Metamorphosis (Greek, 'process of change

of shape') is the term, in the **life sciences**, for the dramatic reorganization of structure which occurs during the **life cycle** of animals which transform from a larval stage to a morphologically different adult stage. It was first studied in insects by Jan Swammerdam, in the 17th century. Subsequently, morphologists used the term metamorphosis to refer to the changes which they proposed occurred when the archetype of a group of organisms changed into a particular form; it was, for example, thought by some that the vertebrate skull was a metamorphosis of several vertebrae.

In the modern sense, metamorphosis is restricted to the description of changes which occur in larvae; such changes are triggered by environmental stimuli and are controlled by hormones. The eggs laid by a frog, for example, hatch as tadpoles and feed and grow as an entirely aquatic stage, complete with gills for extracting oxygen from the water. As it grows the tadpole undergoes a metamorphosis, developing legs and losing its tail until a small frog, complete with lungs, is able to emerge from the water as an amphibian. A more dramatic metamorphosis is seen in the change from caterpillar to butterfly, via the pupal stage during which the radical changes in **morphology** occur. **RB**

See also endocrinology; phenology.

METAPHYSICAL POETRY

The Metaphysical poets were a number of 17th-century English writers, most notably Abraham Cowley, Richard Crashaw, John Donne, George Herbert, Andrew Marvell and Henry Vaughan. They blended description of everyday passions and sentiments with abstract (and sometimes abstruse) philosophizing. Donne, for example, observes a flea that bites him and his mistress, and reflects at length on the mingling of their blood. Herbert, when describing a sunset, launches into a prolonged discussion of the majesty of God. The Metaphysical poets never thought of themselves as a group – the name was coined later by John Dryden – and are very different from one another in style, theme and approach. Not only that, but many other poets similarly blend physical and metaphysical themes without attracting the name. In Japanese and Persian poetry, for example, not to mention most of the the the poetry of European **Romanticism**, this blend is what makes the art. **KMcL**

Further reading Rosemond Tuve, *Elizabethan and Metaphysical Poetry*; F.J. Warnke, *European Metaphysical Poetry*.

METAPHYSICS

Metaphysics (Greek, 'about what is'), in **philosophy**, attempts to characterize all of reality – to say what reality contains and to analyse the concepts we use to think about it. So a metaphysician may both claim that events enter into causal relations and analyse our concept of causation.

So metaphysics attempts to provide a catalogue of the sorts of things reality contains. So, for example, one might hold that reality contains: mental and physical things, entities which have mental properties and entities which have physical properties; events or changes in the properties of things which are and have causes and effects; space, in which things exist, and time, in which changes occur.

Such a catalogue of the sorts of things reality contains does not settle all the questions metaphysicians attempt to answer. Consider the claim that there are both mental and physical things. This claim does not settle the issue of whether everything is of the same fundamental kind or not. Dualists claim that mental things are not physical and that physical things are not mental: there are two fundamental kinds of things. Monists hold that everything, is of the same fundamental kind or not. Idealists hold that the physical world is mental, that everything, including physical objects such as mountains, is mental. Materialists hold that everything including any mental entities is physical. One principle metaphysicians often appeal which seems to support monism is Ockham's razor, which states that entities should not be multiplied beyond necessity.

We said that metaphysics attempts to say what reality contains and to analyse the concepts we use to think about it. Note that the task of saying what reality contains, such as causally related events, is different from the task of analysing the concepts we use to think about reality, such as the concept of causation. For a metaphysician may provide an analysis of the concept of causation and then claim that no events satisfy it: they may examine our concept of causation and yet hold that no events are causally related.

P.F. Strawson distinguished two sorts of metaphysics. Descriptive metaphysics describes the way we actually think about reality. It explores our actual views about reality and the concepts we actually use to think about it. Revisionary metaphysics revises and attempts to improve our views about reality and may also revise and hopefully improve the concepts we use to think about it.

Eliminativists are revisionary metaphysicians. They hold that we should abandon certain ontological claims, that we should eliminate certain claims from our account of what exists. Eliminative materialism, for example, is the view that since everything is physical and the mental could not be physical, there are no mental things. We should revise our common-sense view that there are minds which have pains and intentions, and eliminate the claim that mental things exist from our theory of what reality contains.

Epiphenomenalism is another revisionary view of the relation between mental and the physical. Epiphenomenalists hold that the mental is not physical and that physical events only have physical causes. So the mental, being non-physical, is causally impotent with respect to the physical. Pains and intentions do not have physical effects, such as reaching for aspirin. Our common-sense view that mental events have physical effects is mistaken, and should be revised. **AJ**

See also causation; dualism; eliminativism; epiphenomenalism; essence; essentialism; event; existence; idealism; law of nature; materialism; monism; mental; mind-body problem; Ockham's razor; physical; primary and secondary qualities; properties; reductionism; self; space and time; substance; universals and particulars.

Further reading P.F. Strawson, *Individuals*.

METHOD, THE

The Method is the name (formerly a nick-name) given to a kind of training for actors originated by Stanislavski in Russia in the 1900s, and developed in the USA during the 1930s to 1950s by Lee Strasberg and others (notably at the Actors' Studio in New York). It is still practised, but its ideas are now part of the mainstream of acting theory, subsumed into what most actors do as a matter of course. Debate about the technique – it is often scorned – goes to the heart of what acting actually is. Does an actor create a role from inside, using the psychological theory of emotional memory to project himself or herself into the 'reality' of the person depicted, using his or her own feelings, emotion and experience to help 'become' that person during the performance? Or is a role put on like a suit of clothes, the imitation of action (in Aristotle's phrase) being a matter of technique and illusion only? The dichotomy is present in other **performing arts** – to what extent does a performer in a musical work, or a conductor, 'become' the experience? but acting, because it is essentially representation rather than reality, focuses it most clearly of all.

Stanislavski and the teachers at the Actors' Studio favoured the first approach, absorbing themselves in the background and psychological, emotional and physical nuance of each of the characters they played; 'traditional' actors favoured the second (Olivier used to come offstage, after playing some gut-wrenching and utterly engrossing scene, and take up his crossword puzzle where he had put it down as he heard his cue). It could be argued that neither approach is sufficient in itself, that good acting involves parts of both and certainly many outstanding actors refuse to reveal the inner processes which go to make their art. One reason for the prominence of the Method in the 1950s and beyond was that it seemed especially appropriate not to stage performance, but to the more intimate media of film and television. Many fine film actors (Marlon Brando, Jack Nicholson, Jane Fonda, Dustin Hoffman, Alan Arkin, Meryl Streep) have used Method techniques and have also remained, quintessentially, themselves. Others (Spencer Tracy, Charles Laughton, Bette Davis) have had nothing to do with it and were not noticeably worse or better actors than their Method colleagues. That the Method is precisely what its name states, a method and no more, is demonstrated in the case of one actor who trained in the style and proceeded to make absolutely no use of it whatever in performance: Marilyn Monroe. **TRG KMcL SS**

Further reading Jean Benedetti, *Stanislavski*; Lee Strasberg, *A Dream of Passion*.

METRE

Metre (Greek, 'measure') is a human artistic development of the instinctive response all warm-blooded creatures have to the pulse. The more regular a rhythm, and the closer it is to the heart-rate, the more we are lulled: if the opening chorus of Bach's *St Matthew Passion* (a 12-minute sequence with a regular, repeated pulse) is performed to coincide exactly with one's heart-rate, it has the same effect as stroking a cat or rocking a baby. (Some dentists and surgeons make use of this phenomenon, apparently – the writer has no experience – playing music to their patients rather than using anaesthetics.) Experiments have shown, however, that if the same music is played even two or three beats to the minute faster, it quickens the listener's heart-rate and enlivens his or her response. Possibly brain activity is lessened by regular approximation to the heartbeat, and increased by perceived rhythms which are syncopated or out of phase with the heartbeat.

In music – whether the *St Matthew Passion* or otherwise – composers and performers use this as one of an arsenal of effects. In **folk music**, for example, the simplest of techniques can produce highly sophisticated results. Against a regular pulse, created by one performer or group of performers, other groups set up repeating patterns which cut across across the beat. The hearer's brain is simultaneously lulled by the basic pulse and stimulated by the cross-rhythms and more and more cross-rhythms can be added, to increasingly delirious effect. (In some folk dances, the effect is, precisely, trance.) Similar rhythmic effects are used in all improvised music: Indian and Chinese classical music makes a particularly nuanced use of rhythm, to the point where a single tiny change can electrify an audience. In the West, **jazz** and **minimalist** music both use variants of these techniques: jazz by superimposing complex rhythms on a regular underlying pulse, and minimalist music by introducing minute rhythmic variations to what appears at first to be an unvarying continuum of sound.

In **literature**, still another element is added: the sound of the language, actually heard (as in plays) or in the mind's ear as we read each page. Metre, in prose or verse, consists of sequences of recognizable rhythmic patterns which conform with or syncopate against the natural stresses of the words. In some languages (ancient Greek and Japanese, for example), sounds and syllables also have actual length: in Greek a 'short' vowel-sound (o-mikron, for example) is calculated as just over one-third as long as the corresponding 'long' vowel (o-mega, for example). This means that metrical patterns can be devised which are mathematical: the sounds in a dactyl (DAH-da-da), for example, are in the approximate ratio 8:3:3 (usually simplified in practice to 2:1:1 or 9:3:3). Since the lengths of all syllables are known, a sequence of words can be organized into hugely complicated rhythmic patterns. Over the years, such patterns acquired specific emotional or ritual associations, allowing the artist a subtlety of allusion and overtone hard for non-native speakers to appreciate. (In both classical Greek **tragedy** and Japanese Noh plays, for example, metrical nuance is a major constructional resource.)

In Eastern and Middle Eastern literature, especially that written in languages which have been comparatively stable for millennia (such as Arabic, Chinese or ancient Persian), metrical procedures are often traditional and of extreme antiquity; in a sense, they are organic and innate. In the West, by contrast, where languages tend to be newer, metre is often based on adaptations of ancient Greek or Latin

structures to native sounds; they are artificial and imposed. (A similar generalization could be made about metrical patterns in music.) What the effects on metre will be of the current plurality of world artistic experience, of creative catholicity, is impossible to predict. **KMcL**

METRIC SYSTEM

Until the end of the 18th century no standardization of measurement was used internationally, which led to misunderstandings in measurements across borders as well as from town to town. The French Academy of Sciences proposed a simple logical system based upon decimalisation. They proposed that the basic unit of length was to be one ten-millionth of the distance from the North Pole to the Equator, and this was to be known as the metre. Every other measurement was then based upon the unit of length. The unit of mass, the gram, is the mass of a cubic centimetre of distilled water at 4°C, while the litre was 1,000 cubic centimetres of distilled water. With Napoleon's conquests throughout Europe, the simplicity and logic of the metric system made it the ideal system to adopt. Although its adoption has been accepted worldwide, old measures still live on, such as the hand for measuring horses, and the gallon for measuring liquids.

Since 1971, however, the world has been moving to a revised system based on the original metric system, the 'Système Internationale d'Unités'. **AA**

See also measurements.

Further reading R.A. Lay, *Measuring the Metric Way.*

METRICS

A metric (from the Greek word for 'measure'), in **mathematics** is a generalized idea of the distance between two points. The archetypal metric is the distance function in n dimensional **Cartesian co-ordinates**, which in one dimension is just the absolute value (value made positive by negating if necessary) of the difference between the co-ordinates of the two points; in two dimensions, the sum of the squares of the differences between the x co-ordinates and the y co-ordinates is taken and then square rooted (which gives the answer you would expect, because of **Pythagoras' theorem**).

In general, a metric is a **function** which takes a pair of points and maps them to a positive **real number**; the function maps the pair to zero only when they are both the same point, and satisfies the 'triangle inequality': $d(a,b) + d(b,c) > = d(a,c)$ for any three points a,b,c.

A set with a metric is called a metric space, and such objects continue to have many of the properties of real numbers. This is particularly true of properties involving distance and **limits**. For this reason, metric spaces are important in the study of continuity and other similar properties. The ideas are further generalized in **topology**. SMcL

MICROBIOLOGY

Microbiology (Greek, 'study of small life') is the study of microorganisms, or organisms not visible to the naked eye. The field normally encompasses the study of bacteria, protozoans, single-celled fungi and algae, and may include viruses, though these are not cells and are often considered a special case. The members of these groups are extremely diverse and are usually unlike either animals or plants; they are taxonomically subdivided into a number of distinct groups, many of which have been barely investigated. The scientific study of these organisms has clear beginnings in the 17th century, with the advent of the microscope; microorganisms were first described in the 1670s by Antonie van Leeuwenhoek. However, there was little immediate interest and little experimental study until the work of pioneers in the 19th century, such as Louis Pasteur and Robert Koch who made discoveries concerning the ubiquity of microorganisms and their importance to humans. This was the tip of the iceberg, and enormous interest was aroused.

Throughout the 20th century microbiology has grown to cover a wide range of fields from brewing and **biotechnology** to biological warfare. The subject has also increasingly attracted those who wish to study **evolution**, development and **genetics** because the simpler, single-celled organisms provide excellent models. **RB**

See also abiogenesis; bacteriology; molecular biology; protozoology; virology.

MICROECONOMICS

Microeconomics (Greek *micro*, 'small' + economics) is the study of economics at the level of the individual household or firm, in contrast to **macroeconomics**. Price theory has a central role in microeconomics: how prices emerge and change, and how people respond to them. This brings in issues such as competition and availability of information, both important elements in micro behaviour. The formal distinction between micro- and macroeconomics, though embodied in most textbooks, is often less than helpful. Since the early 1970s economists have renewed attempts to fuse the two, recognizing that certain key macroeconomic questions like **inflation** and unemployment have their roots in the way prices are fixed and labour markets operate. **TF**

MICROELECTRONICS AND INTEGRATED CIRCUITS

Microelectronics and Integrated Circuits continue to revolutionize the **electronics** industry. Following the invention of the point-contact transistor in 1947 at Bell Laboratories in the US, discrete transistor based circuits were found to have several technically limiting application factors. With the advent of the Cold War in the early 1950s, the need for complex and reliable electronic circuits for radar and missile systems, for example, was critical. This led to the development of integrated circuit (IC) technology.

The most significant contribution to IC technology was the planar production process developed by Fairchild Semiconductor in America in 1958. This created several circuit elements, using the recently developed process of diffusion and oxide masking, in a parallel plane to the semiconductor base material (see **semiconductor device theory**). Using this technique complex electrical circuits could be mass manufactured in very small packages, known as 'silicon chips'.

Eventually IC circuits were created that could not be built using discrete devices and offered greatly increased reliability and substantial cost savings.

The introduction of microelectronic devices and ICs relied heavily on advances in material and manufacturing technology, in particular to produce high-purity, defect-free silicon wafers. Since the early 1960s such advances have led to an unprecedented explosion in the use of ICs, which are used in everything from digital watches and personal computers to automatic satellite navigation systems. **AC**

MICROSOCIOLOGY

Microsociology (Greek, 'sociology in small') refers to the level of sociological analysis concerned with the study of human behaviour in the context of face-to-face interaction and interpersonal behaviour in small groups. This type of sociological analysis is often concerned with understanding individual meanings. Examples of this type of sociology include: **ethnomethodology**, **symbolic interactionism** and dramaturgy (see **dramaturgical model**).

Microsociology is often contrasted with **macrosociology** which focuses on large-scale social structures, institutions and whole societies. The distinction between macro- and microsociology, however, is not as well-established or as central as the related distinction of micro and macro in **economics**. **DA**

See also action perspective; generalized other; individualism; naturalism; phenomenological sociology; social self; structure-agency debate; understanding.

MICROTONAL MUSIC

In so-called tonal **music** – for example the classical music of the Western world – the octave is divided into 12 equal semitones. Microtonal music explores smaller divisions than semitones: quarter-tones, sixteenth-tones, thirty-second tones and divisions of less mathematical symmetry 19 divisions or 31 divisions to the octave, for example. To the innocent ear, especially to one used to tonal music, microtones tend to sound merely out of tune; they are, however, common in non-Western music, and in such Western manifestations as 'blue notes' in **jazz**. They are easily sung, and played on string instruments and electronic instruments (where the player can select the pitch of each note); woodwind instruments and keyboard instruments have to be specially built, or tuned, to produce them. For these reasons – and also, some people claim, because tuning by semitones in some way conforms to the 'natural' laws of acoustics – microtones tend to be mainly a colouristic device, and thorough-going microtonal music, at least in the West, is a rare and experimental phenomenon. **KMcL**

MIGRATION

The movement of people from the area of their birth to different parts of the same country, or to different countries has been both the result of **uneven development**, and a major contributor to population change and rates of development. This is not because numbers of migrants are large in comparison with total populations: streams of migrants rarely exceed 10 million as against a world population in the billions. But migration usually involves young adults, with the result that fertility is reduced in the area of origin and increased at the destination. Also, young migrants often seem willing to work extremely hard to create economic success for themselves and the receiving society. Migration can be voluntary or forced, temporary or permanent. Historically, a small number of international migrations have been particularly significant.

The earliest of these was the movement of some 10 million Africans to the Americas between the 17th and 19th centuries to provide slave labour to the European colonists. They were vital in producing precious metals and crops, such as sugar and cotton, which boosted European economies and living standards and strengthened mercantile capital. Later, emigration of Europeans, especially to North America, helped to reduce European birth rates and to consolidate European power in many colonies. At the same time there were substantial movements from India and China into Southeast Asia, Africa and North America.

These 'diaspora' movements were not associated with political power, but led to the establishment of commercial élites in many countries.

During the 20th century, there have been increasing barriers to international migration, but nevertheless there have been large-scale movements of refugees and labour migrants. Refugees are generated in large numbers by wars, revolutions and even natural disasters (for example, the effects of Nazism, Eastern Europe after 1945, the partition of India and Pakistan, the violent régime of the Khmer Rouge in Cambodia, and famine in the countries of the Sahel). In the 1960s and 1970s, millions of migrants were attracted by the booming industrial economies of western Europe and North America, while nearly two million, mainly from Arab countries, went to Saudi Arabia, Kuwait and Libya. Some countries have tried to ensure that 'guest workers' were temporary, but in almost every case the migrants have in fact settled and brought in dependents. As a result, international migration has often been associated with ethnic conflict and racism.

The break up of the Soviet Union and of its east European 'empire' have unleashed ethnic conflicts which have already produced millions of refugees and have also destroyed job prospects for workers with skills which could be valuable in the EC or elsewhere. The prospects are for a period of intense migration activity. The EC is preparing to resist the pressures, but the success of several millions of Hispanics in entering the US, legally or illegally, suggests that immigration is extremely hard to control in anything but a totalitarian society. **PS**

MILLENARIANISM

Millenarianism (from Latin *millennium*, 'thousand years') is a cultic belief stemming from a passage in the Bible Book of Revelation (chapter 22). The verses claim that after Satan has been imprisoned for a thousand years, those martyrs who have 'lived and reigned with Christ' for that time will return to life. This passage seemed to promise an actual date for the Day of Judgement, and the coming of the millen-

nium was an event eagerly awaited by devout Christians in the Middle Ages, who thought that at one minute past midnight on the 1st January, AD 1000 – their trust in human calendar-making was as unshakeable as their faith in scripture – the Last Trump would sound, this world would come to an end and the Kingdom of Heaven would begin. The belief grew ever more intense towards the end of the first millennium, and was reinforced by all kinds of reported portents and prodigies of Nature. It produced on the one hand a feeling of intense and joyful expectation, on the other an upsurge of pessimism and penitential yearning. What happened in the days, weeks and years after the Kingdom of Heaven failed to materialize is not recorded.

If the hysteria surrounding the end of the first millennium after the supposed year of Christ's birth is understandable, its repetition one thousand years later, in the dying years of the second millennium, is much harder to credit, but exists. Almost every kind of evil, from AIDS to the perceived decline in respect of young people for their elders, is blamed on an upsurge of **Satanism** in the world, a kind of last fling of devilment before the final reckoning. In the late 1980s and 1990s, millennial **cults** began mushrooming throughout the world, and expectation of the Day of Judgement even, in some countries, caused a slump in such things as life insurance and fluctuations on the the stock Market (in our capitalist societies, a sign of true panic, not to mention true belief). The discoveries of **archaeology**, **history**, **science** and theology seem to have little effect on these delusions – and indeed, one can see how millennial belief would seem at best asymmetrical and at worst extremely silly if people chose as their date not an exact multiple of one thousand but some scientifically more accurate date such as 1996 (the possible bimillennium of Christ's birth) or 2070 (the bimillennium of the Roman sack of Jerusalem, in the months prior to which the Book of Revelation is thought to have been compiled).

Anthropologists concentrate on one particular manifestation of millenarian cults: those (like the 'cargo cults' of Papua New Guinea) which arose in parts of the world subject to extreme deprivation. In Papua New Guinea, exposure to the material culture of the West, combined with missionary teachings about the coming of a messiah, fired beliefs that dead ancestors would arrive with a cargo of European goods, to usher in the millennium, and that cult adherents would immediately find Utopia: their own immediate prosperity, coupled with the demise of the invaders who were threatening their culture.

In the highlands of South America, millenarianism emerged earlier, as a response to Spanish colonialism. After the abrupt destruction of the Inca empire, the myth of Inkarri arose, promising the violent demise of the colonialists and the return of the Inca king who would restore the Inca state. Even today, those movements in Bolivia, Ecuador and Peru which actively defend indigenous rights identify themselves with the figure of Inkarri, and the millenarian myth, and the hopes that go with it, still have power. **CL KMcL**

Further reading Norman Cohn, *The Pursuit of the Millennium;* P. Worsley, *The Trumpet Shall Sound: a Study of Cargo Cults in Melanesia.*

MIME see **Pantomime**

MIMESIS

The term mimesis (Greek, 'imitation') was first applied to the **arts** by Aristotle, who described it in his treatise *Poetics* as 'the imitation of an action', that is, the process of selection and representation applied to reality by the creative mind to give it forceful artistic expression. Aristotle confined his description to **tragedy**, but clearly mimesis is at the root of every art. All arts involve the ordering of reality to produce a kind of tareality.

The concept has been much discussed by Western critics and artists since Aristotle's time, particularly with relation to **literature**, and two opposing views have developed. On the one side, it is believed that because the arts present images of reality rather than reality itself, they are essentially fraudulent and not worthy of attention. This attitude has been particularly prevalent among **Marxist** artists and critics in this century. The second view maintains that the selected and refracted version of reality which the arts present is more real than real: in effect, a breakthrough into some kind of metaphysical sublimity. This concept was particularly favoured in the Far East in the 17th and 18th centuries, and in the '**art for art's sake**' Western movements of the 19th century.

Another approach, favoured by Western thinkers during the **Renaissance** and by some literary critics of the present century (notably Georg Lukács), is to ask whether questions of what mimesis is, and does, are not rather questions about the nature of reality itself. **KMcL**

MIMICRY

The concept of biological mimicry was introduced by Henry Bates in 1862 to describe the phenomenon in which two or more unrelated organisms resemble each other closely, but where the resemblance is not a **homology** or an **analogy**. Bates observed two butterflies, one of which was distasteful to bird predators and one which was not. He suggested that the butterfly which was good to eat bore similar markings to the inedible species because this would deter predators from eating it. Mimicry thus depends upon an individual (the receiver) being deceived by the similarity between two species, one a mimic, the other a model. Typically the mimetic relationship involves a one-sided benefit to the mimic, the selective pressure being exerted by the receiver.

Although mimicry is commonly based on visual appearance, sound, smell and behaviour may be copied, provided the receiver acts in the same way to both the model and the mimetic signals. Mimicry should be distinguished from the phenomenon of camouflage, which involves seeking not to be noticed at all. Fritz Müller showed in 1870 that two species might mimic one another in a fashion that conferred mutual benefit; this is the case with coral snakes, all of which are similar in appearance, and many of which are poisonous. The predator must attack to discover that the snake is poisonous and, providing it survives, it will subsequently avoid all species in the coral snake group. Mimicry may occur within a species – a male bee, for example, which has no sting, is protected by the knowledge among animals that female bees, which look similar, do sting. **RB**

See also ethology; symbiosis.

Further reading W. Wickler, *Mimicry*.

MIND

Mind encompasses a very wide range of mental phenomena and definitions. Mind, as with psyche, includes in its definition physical and non-physical aspects, the brain, **consciousness**, the **unconscious**, the subconscious and the soul. It encompasses all aspects of **rationality** – **understanding**, intellect, conception, **abstraction** and reasoning as well as the cognitive skills of **perception** and insight. The word personality is also often used synonymously with mind. From a psychodynamic point of view, mind can be described in terms of dynamic processes. These processes are the mental activities of response and adaption which are connected together in sequences.

Psychology, as the science of mind, tends to look at mind as a series of non-physical processes which are separate from the body. This is confused in Freud: he talks of 'mental apparatus' and uses biological models to describe mental activities. Although mind is connected to bodily functions (senses, grey matter, etc.) and is seen to have power over the body, for example in **hysteria**, psychology does not have to be too concerned with the body in its description of the constructions and functions of the mind. (It is challenged in this in examples of aphasia, apraxia and agnosia, and in the physical damage to the function of mind in accidents, strokes, and under the surgeon's knife.)

The model of **artificial intelligence** in **computers** is used to explain the mind's relationship to the body and its ability to control it in hysteria. A robot can 'visualize' the arm and stop its movement; in the case of hysteria, the mind paralyses movement.

Definitions of mind in psychology can be divided into mechanistic and humanistic

views. On the one hand the workings of the mind can be accessed by observing behaviour and exploring a person's cognitive responses; on the other hand they can be understood by making theoretical connections about the unconscious mechanisms. These opposing views roughly correspond to the empiricist/rationalist divide in **philosophy**. **Phenomenology**, as a model of the mind, also tries (as does the computational view) to answer the **mind/body** divide. **MJ**

Further reading Henri F. Ellenberger, *The Discovery of the Unconscious*.

MIND-BODY PROBLEM

Philosophers have long found the relation between mental and physical phenomena problematic. Descartes gave a modal argument for supposing that mental and physical phenomena are distinct. He argued that if it is possible for one's mind to exist without one's body, then one's mind is distinct from one's body. He further claimed that it is possible for one's mind to exist without one's body, for one's mind to exist disembodied. So, he concluded, one's mind is distinct from one's body. There are non-physical minds and non-mental bodies: **dualism** is true.

The most obvious problem for dualism is that if minds and bodies are such radically different things, then it is difficult to see how they could causally interact. How could damage to physical bodies cause **pain** in non-physical minds? And how could perceptual experiences in non-physical minds causally affect the movements of physical bodies? Parallelists respond to this problem by simply denying that minds and bodies causally interact. They hold that physical events have only physical effects, not non-physical mental ones, and that non-physical mental events have only mental effects, not physical ones. Interactionists insist that the non-physical mental does causally interact with the physical. They deny that our difficulty in understanding how the non-physical mental could causally interact with the physical shows that it does not. **AJ**

See also behaviourism; eliminativism; epiphenomenalism; functionalism; idealism; interactionism; materialism; mental phenomena; monism; neutral monism; panpsychism; parallelism.

Further reading J. Foster, *The Immaterial Self*; C. McGinn, *The Character of Mind*.

MINIMALISM

Minimalism is **art** reduced to its minimal elements. In fine art, progenitors of the style included the Russian painter Kasimir Malevich, who in 1913 introduced a movement of his own, Suprematism, with almost identical aims, painted single white squares on white backgrounds and sold the results. But the name 'minimalism', in art, is chiefly associated with a movement which rose to prominence in the 1960s, especially in the USA. More common in **sculpture** than in painting, it eschewed **representation** and narrative in favour of representing, in the first instance, itself. Thus the 'primary structures' of Donald Judd or Carl André, often employing foundry-produced steel cubes or commercially-made housebricks, offer the beholder little information about their purpose beyond the fact of their industrial origin. Such minimalism, in short, embraced the impersonality of industrial production as the vehicle for the artist's expression. In painting, minimalism is characterized by rejection of gestural painting and an emphasis on either the hard-edge abstraction of Frank Stella or Ellsworth Kelly, or on the 'unpainterly' qualities of Morris Louis's understated, stained canvases.

In music, minimalism is a late 20th-century development. Minimalist composers avoid complex counterpoint, harmonies and serial structures in favour of single chords, rhythms or scraps of tune, many times repeated. The effect is suggestive and hypnotic and the result of each minute change in the texture, say a changed note in a chord or a blip in the rhythm, can be like a hammer-blow. Leading minimalist composers, such as Philip Glass, Steve Reich and Terry Riley, work with their own specialist ensembles. Other composers, for example Györgi Ligeti and Krzysztof Penderecki, use minimalist techniques with conventional forces, and have had particular success with works for large symphony orchestra.

The apparent simplicity of minimalist art hides the complexity of its intellectual structure. While the work may exhibit a 'minumum art content', it challenges each beholder to experience a layered and complex aesthetic response based on his or her individual expectations and prejudices. There is a strong hint of **Dada** about minimalism, which (in fine art, for example) allows artists to 'sign' heaps of bricks, strips of cloth or mounted tiles, and (in music) to rely apparently on nothing more than gestures. But perhaps because of the engagement of the beholder, minimalist art of all kinds has an ever-growing popular audience, and may eventually be seen as one of the most fundamental and energetic movements of the late 20th century. **MG KMcL**

MIRACLE PLAY

A Miracle Play is a form of medieval European religious **drama**, retelling Bible stories or events in a saint's life (hence miracle). Often, and confusingly, the phrase has been used as synonymous with **Mystery play**: miracle refers to the content of a play and mystery to the organization responsible for staging a play. **TRG SS**

See also morality play.

Further reading Richard Southern, *The Seven Ages of the Theatre*; W. Tydeman, *The Theatre in the Middle Ages*.

MIRROR PHASE

Mirror Phase is one of the key concepts in the work of the French psychoanalyst Jacques Lacan (1901–81). Lacan re-examined Freud's therapeutic and theoretical systems, using the model of the French linguist Saussure. He explored the language of the **unconscious**, and viewed development as a process which produces **linguistic** structures that make sense of experience for the child and initiate it into society.

Mirror Phase happens during the Imaginary phase at around six to eight months. The Imaginary phase in an infant's life is when it believes itself to be part of the mother and sees no separation between it and the world. During this stage the child develops a body image of itself and what is called a body ego. This is a profoundly alienated entity as at this time it is perceived as an entity separate from itself, with which it merges and identifies. Having this dual identity makes the child vulnerable to its own and others' projections.

The Imaginary phase is brought to a halt by the Oedipal crisis which precipitates the Mirror Phase and facilitates the child's entry into the Symbolic Order of the father (society). In the Oedipal crisis the father's presence splits up the mother and child. The father's possession of the mother and superior strength is represented by the phallus, which causes in the child the fear of castration. This activates the child's recognition of its separate identity and place in society. In the Mirror Phase the infant realizes both 'I am' and 'I am not', the latter being the recognition of the lack of the phallus. The self is constituted as 'difference'. All human life, according to Lacan, is dominated by the Symbolic Order which is acknowledged in the Mirror Phase. As in Freud, the end of the Oedipal phase and Mirror Phase (entry into the Symbolic Order) closes off the unconscious. The unconscious emerges as a result of repressed desire. The desire behaves like a language moving ceaselessly from object to object. Just as language can never fully seize on meaning, so desire, for Lacan, is a driving force with no ultimate satisfaction.

Lacan returned to the unconscious because he was critical of the emphasis on the Ego in **psychoanalysis** (mainly in the US), with its politically-charged notion of making people acceptable to themselves and others. Lacan involved structural linguistic concepts of sign and signifier to explain how the onset of language splits the conscious from the unconscious. As we accept control over thoughts (given by language) we are thereby committed to 'the endless chain of signification'. **MJ**

Further reading D. Archard, *Consciousness and the Unconscious* (chapter 3).

MIXED ECONOMY

A mixed economy is an economic system in which there is some private ownership and management of natural resources and capital goods, together with some public (government) ownership and management of natural resources and capital goods. It is a mixture of **capitalism** and **socialism**. **TF**

MIXED MEDIA see Media

MOCK-EPIC see Epic

MODALITY

Modality (from Latin *modus*, 'measure', 'manner', 'means') is a key concept in **philosophy** and in **music**. In philosophy, it means having to do with necessity or possibility. Some truths and falsehoods are necessary. It is necessarily true that $2 + 2 = 4$; that is, it could not have been false that $2 + 2 = 4$. And it is necessarily false that $2 + 2 = 5$; that is, it could not have been true that $2 + 2 = 5$. (In contrast, some truths and falsehoods are merely contingent. It is merely contingently true that the dog is in its box; that is, it could not have been false that the dog is in its box. And it is merely contingently false that the dog is on the sofa; that is, it could have been true the dog is on the sofa.)

Philosophers have distinguished various forms of possibility and necessity. It is logically necessary that all bachelors are unmarried. That is, it follows from the laws of logic and the meanings of the words 'bachelor' and 'unmarried' that there cannot be a married bachelor. It is not logically necessary that water be H_2O. Simply by reflecting upon the meanings of the words 'water' and 'H_2O', and the laws of logic, one cannot know that water is H_2O, let alone that water is necessarily H_2O. But, if Kripke's discussion of rigid designators is correct, it is impossible for water not to be H_2O. There is no possible situation in which water is not H_2O. So it is metaphysically impossible for water not to be H_2O. That is, there is no possible situation in which water is not H_2O, but this is not due to the meanings of words and the laws of logic alone.

It is not logically necessary that water boil at 100°C. Nor does this seem to be metaphysically necessary. It is possible that water should have a different boiling point but only if the **laws of Nature** are different. So long as the laws of Nature are as they actually are, then it is necessary that water boils at 100°C. It is nomologically necessary that water boils at 100°C. That is, in all possible situations in which the laws of Nature are as they actually are, then water boils at 100°C.

In medieval musical notation, modality originally referred to the various combinations of long and short note values, known as the 'rhythmic modes'. But, more generally, modality in music is a concept involving musical scale and melody. It is important to distinguish between the terms 'scale' and 'mode', which are often confused. Scale is simply a stepwise progression, ascending or descending, of single notes, whereas mode can be defined as a particular scale with its own special characteristics, or as a melodic model or type. To describe a piece of music as modal is to imply the presence of some hierarchy of musical tones and their relationships, or some distinguishing melodic patterns such as closing phrases or cadences. In other words modality is the way a scale is used in an individual melody. In **musicology**, the concept of mode as a type of scale is often used for the classification or grouping of monophonic melodies, particularly folk songs, into theoretical categories.

In Western music history, modality is also associated with the period ranging from early medieval liturgical chant to Renaissance polyphony. During this time, music was based on scale-type modes derived from ancient Greek musical theory. These modes, often inappropriately referred to as the 'church' or 'ecclesiastical' modes, are approximately equivalent to the seven scales that can be made using only the white notes of the piano.

In many Asian musical traditions mode may be interpreted as a melodic model or basis for composition and improvisation. In India, for example, a *raga* is a mode that is identified not only by its characteristic ascending and descending tone patterns and motifs, but also by the ornamentation, embellishment and degrees of emphasis associated with specific tones. These modal elements form the musical material with which a performer will improvise. Furthermore, each *raga* is related to a particular mood, sentiment, time of day, season and other extra-musical factors. These factors, known in advance from tradition, affect both the performers as they improvise on the *raga* and the listeners as they experience the music.

Modality is also a crucial element in melodic recognition. In Western music, the identity of a melody is determined by a unique and invariable succession of tones. However, in the art music of many Oriental traditions the same melody may exist in several different modes, and consequently may comprise several contrasting tone sequences. Its identity, therefore, is related more to its contour than to its precise tonal constituents.

Finally, in **jazz** terminology, 'modal jazz' refers to a style of improvisation that emerged during the late 1950s, and in which melodic improvisation, instead of being conditioned by conventional harmonic structures, is based on modal principles. **AJ KMcL SSt**

See also actuality; rigid and non-rigid designators; scale.

Further reading S. Kripke, *Naming and Necessity*; A. Plantinga, *The Nature of Necessity*.

MODERNISM

Modernism, in all the **arts**, is a term used to describe what critics saw as a characteristic mind-set among European creators at the end of the 19th century and beginning of the 20th. It consisted in a rejection of tradition, a self-conscious determination to reinvent the purposes and techniques of all the arts, and (in some arts) a rejection of **realism** in favour of exploration of the **unconscious** on the one hand and the self-validating image on the other. It would seem that the **avant-garde** of every age appear to 'outsiders' to be iconoclasts or barbarians, and yet 20th-century adherents of new art forms, for instance, **atonality**, the international style or **surrealism**, were doing no more than Latin poets of the 'Silver Age', medieval contrapuntalists or painters who used **perspective** had done before them. What is, perhaps, especially interesting about 20th-century modernism, is that so many creative figures, across such a wide swathe of the arts, all felt the same impulse at the same time. Some writers see this as a response conditioned by historical and social events in Europe, notably World War I and the rise of social equality of all kinds. But again, such momentous events and movements have their parallels throughout history. Perhaps modernism is no more than a critics' convenience, of no use outside **academe**. Certainly the invention of derivative expressions such as 'palaeomodernism' and '**postmodernism**' takes us into the rarefied world of academics, a long way indeed from primary creation.

Modernism is particularly important in **architecture**, and is most properly identified with the Modern Movement; a 20th-century European movement in architectural design, which sought to find an architecture appropriate to modern society, by means of full use of modern technological advance (for example the reinforced concrete frame) and a conscious repudiation of **historicism**, particularly that of the 19th century.

The meaning of 'modern' in this context can be confusing, as when it was first coined it meant only 'contemporary' and now it refers to a period movement which can be dated from the first decade of the 20th century to the late 1970s.

The first wave of the modern movement in architecture was already being defined by a handful of Dutch painters, designers and architects, in their journal *De Stijl*, as a movement dedicated to a clean, uncomplicated abstract purism and rectilinearality in design. The early modern movement can also be closely identified with the setting up of the **Bauhaus** school (Staatliches Bauhaus) in Germany in 1919, which lasted until suppressed by the Nazis in 1933. The first director was Walter Gropius (1833–1969), who taught an ideal of an inspired, committed craftsman, practising a unity of the arts and educated in the principles of formal perception. Architecture became

the chief subject and **functionalism**, particularly under the second director Hannes Meyer, the principal ethic. Functionalism is the idea that the form of a building should be decided by practical considerations and not aesthetics.

The modernists of the earlier generation sought to improve the material conditions of modern society through good, honest design. This aim can be identified with the **Arts and Crafts** Movement of the 19th century. Unlike the Arts and Crafts Movement, modernism did not look to the past for its models, such as the medieval craftsmen, but rather to the possibilities of the present made available by modern technology.

One of the principal ideas behind the activities of modernist architects was a self-conscious reaction to the **revivalist, historicist** architecture of the 19th century and early 20th century. Modernist architecture attempted honesty in construction, and repudiated the practice of concealing structure, particularly with historicist ornament. Many of the active concerns of modernist architects were social; the breaking down of cultural and social barriers which contributed to the alienation of the mass of working people.

From 1928 the Congrès Internationaux Architecture Moderne (CIAM) began to formulate and propagate the tenets of modernism, attempting to bring an international order to the various practitioners of the new architecture across the world. An important forum from this date until the late 1950s, it dominated architectural training in the postwar period.

The devastation of World War II provided the enormous challenge of rebuilding cities devastated by bombing. The rational aspect of modernism was highly adaptable to these tasks, particularly the speedy provision of houses and offices, so that after the war, modernism quickly became the accepted norm, and characterized most architectural and industrial design, from then until the 1960s and 1970s, until seriously challenged by theorists and architects, particularly over the unpopularity of high-rise accommodation, and the issue of the role of history in design and town planning.

Two further 'modernist' trends are defined in architecture: Late Modernism and Organic Modernism.

Late modernism is a term used to define the architecture that can be seen in the continuing tradition of the modern movement: not Postmodern, but a literally late 'modernism' (as one might speak of 'early' or 'late' Renaissance). The suggestion is that 'late modern architecture' takes the forms and principles of the modern movement 'to an extreme, exaggerating the structure and technological image of the building'. An example of which would be the Pompidou Centre (1971–77) in Paris, by Renzo Piano and Richard Rodgers. Such buildings are sometimes referred to as **'high tech'**.

Organic modernism is particularly identified with the work of the US architect Frank Lloyd Wright (1869–1959). It can be seen as an American extension of European **expressionist** architecture of the postwar period following World War I; a rebellion against the purist tyranny of 'right-angle' modern movement architecture.

'Organic architecture' was a term used by Wright to convey his understanding of Louis Sullivan's version of Functionalism 'that every problem...contains and suggests [its own] solution'. Wright interpreted this by stressing the unity of form and function of a building, the relationship of the parts of a building to its whole, and, perhaps most importantly, the close relationship between the building and the natural landscape. In Wright's architecture, buildings are irregular in form and plan, and low in height, so that they appear as if rooted to the ground. Wright believed that the architect's principal inspirations should be the *genius locii* ('spirit of the place'), and the nature of materials to be used. He also drew inspiration from organic forms: for example, the 1956 Guggenheim Museum in New York, perhaps his best-known work, has an internal staircase modelled on the spiral form of a seashell. **PD MG JM KMcL**

Further reading R. Banham, *Architecture in the First Machine Age*; L. Benevolo, *History of Modern Architecture*; B. Bergonzi (ed.), *Inno-*

vations: Essays on Art and Ideas; C. Jencks, *Late Modern Architecture and other Essays*; Frank Lloyd Wright, *An Organic Architecture: the Architecture of Democracy*; Harold Rosenberg, *The Tradition of the New*; B. Zevi, *Towards an Organic Architecture*.

MODERNIZATION

Modernization (from Latin *modo*, 'just now') describes the impact of factory production or industrialization on an economic system with accompanying social and cultural consequences. At the turn of the century, the sociologist Max Weber held that only certain societies contained the seeds of modernization, in particular that of the development of commerce, urban centres and the **Protestant ethic** in the West that extolled the value of work and the modern entrepreneur.

However, Weber's theories are entrenched in a specifically Western history. Modernization has occurred in various societies, without necessarily showing the pattern or consequent effects that characterized Euro-American societies. **Hindu** religious ideas and traditions of relegating work responsibilities within the family have not halted the process of modernization in India. Some of them have used the opportunity to undertake family-run businesses which may act to reinforce bonds between an extended network of kin, rather than transforming into nuclear family units as was the predominant process in the West during the period of industrialization.

By the 20th century, the process of modernization has taken effect in numerous parts of the world. While it may benefit sectors of societies, others may be left worse off. It may also be viewed as a problematic phenomenon in view of the resulting threats to the environment and to established patterns of social and cultural life. **RK**

See also development; Marxist anthropology; syncretism; tradition; urban anthropology; Westernization.

Further reading Milton Singer, *When a Great Tradition Modernizes*; Max Weber, *The Protestant Ethic and the Spirit of Capitalism*.

MODULARITY

The idea that the **mind** is composed of various distinct modules, each with its own structures and capacities, has been advanced most vigorously by the American linguists, Noam Chomsky and Jerry Fodor. The constitution of the mind is envisaged to parallel the heterogeneity of the human body, in which a number of interacting subsystems (for instance, the heart, liver and lungs) are clearly distinct from one another. In a similar way, the uniquely human attribute of **language** is believed to stem from an independent faculty of mind whose constitution and functioning are quite different from other modules of mind. Hence knowledge of language is consigned to a module quite separate from those responsible for perceptual processing, numeracy, or general problem-solving. The uniqueness of language knowledge provides the clearest argument in favour of the modularity hypothesis, although the content and organization of individual modules is still very much a controversial issue. **MS**

See also innateness.

MODULATION

Modulation, applied to communication systems in electrical engineering, is the transfer of information in a low frequency signal, for example speech, to a higher frequency carrier signal for transmission. The carrier signal (so-called because it 'carries' the information) requires demodulation at the receiver to recover the information.

Amplitude modulation (AM) was in use on the telephone networks by the 1920s, and was part of the multiplexed carrier systems which permitted multiple separate communication channels to be used all at once (see **multiplexing**). This enabled the telephone companies to connect more callers to the network at one time and thereby increase their revenue and quality of service.

AM radio broadcasting had also been pioneered by 1915, although problems of unwanted noise affected the transmission. With the invention of frequency modulation (FM) by E.H. Armstrong in 1933, the noise problems were significantly reduced, and at the present time many radio stations have changed from AM to FM broadcasting.

The implementation of modulation techniques required prior advances in the theory of transmission systems, for example J.R. Carson's invention of single sideband transmission. This method of transmitting part of a modulated signal saved electrical power compared to other forms of modulated transmission. Of more importance was the invention of the electrical filter by G.A. Campbell in 1909, which allows selected transmission or blocking of certain signal frequencies, without which modulation schemes could not be practically realized. **AC**

See also transmission line theory.

MOHAMMEDANISM see Islam

MOKSHA

Moksha (*mukti*) means 'liberation', 'freedom' or 'release' from one's individual fate and from the cycles of history. The concept first appears in the Upanishads. In the *Brahaclaranyaka Upanishad*, a distinction is made between the righteous (who rely on faith and so escape from the cycle of rebirth to the 'way of the gods'), those who did no more than their duty, performed austerities and gave alms (who are reborn as mortals), and the ignorant (who are reborn as insects or unclean animals). This doctrine had the advantage of showing how the virtuous would be rewarded and the wicked punished in their next rebirth, but it was difficult to reconcile with the **Vedic** belief. In the Upanishads, it is not just a question of an endless cycle of rebirth until one attains *moksha*, but of cycles of history, of age after age, and the whole universe going through endless phases known as 'the day of the gods'. *Moksha* means liberation from this, too.

If *moksha* is seen as liberation from *samsara*, the endless prolongation of life, and from *karma*, the next step came at the end of the Upanishad period when life itself was seen as evil, something to be transcended, as reason itself must be. The one who has attained *moksha* can see the eternal in the temporal and the temporal in the eternal. However, under the *Samkhya* system, widely accepted in the Middle Ages, *moksha* consisted of separating the soul or self from the world. The temporal and the eternal are not reconciled in the Absolute. (For the consequences of this system, see **yoga**.) Alternatively, under the *advaita* system of Vedantism, *moksha* means that the soul realizes itself as it eternally is, that is as the one *Brahman-Atmam* which is Absolute Being, Consciousness and Bliss. **EMJ**

Further reading R.C. Zahner, *Hinduism* (good bibliography).

MOLECULAR BIOLOGY

Molecular biology is the study of living processes in terms of molecular interactions, and is a modern synthesis of the fields of **biochemistry**, **biophysics**, **genetics** and structural **chemistry**. In the 1930s, interest began to be aroused in biological macromolecules with the discovery of the structure of wool fibre by W.T. Astbury. In 1953, James Watson and Francis Crick proposed the double helix model for the structure of DNA, paving the way for the study of molecular specificity and the molecular basis of individual variation. The idea that differences between species and individuals have a chemical basis had first been suggested in 1909 by E.T. Reichert. It was demonstrated in the 1930s when emerging immunological techniques showed differences in blood groups between humans.

Modern molecular biology is concerned chiefly with the transfer of information from genes to proteins and with the storage of genetic information; vital to this was the elucidation of the **genetic code**, which allows the genetic information to be 'read' in terms of the proteins for which it codes. The field represents the dominance of the mechanistic school of thought in modern biology and is rapidly growing in importance as the techniques available for genetic manipulation develop. **RB**

See also biotechnology; genetic engineering.

Further reading Bruce Alberts, *The Molecular Biology of the Cell*.

MONARCHISM

Monarchism (Greek, 'rule of one alone') is the embodiment of **sovereignty** in one individual. Hereditary monarchy was the normal form of rule in **agrarian societies**, but it is infrequent in tribal societies where 'elected' chieftains are more common, and it is increasingly infrequent in **industrial societies**.

The arguments used to justify monarchical authority have changed considerably throughout history, although there have always been attempts to legitimate monarchical authority through **religion**: the debris of multiple kingdoms and empires bears witness to the idea that monarchs are divine, the idea of the 'divine right of kings', and the idea that the monarch is God's chosen leader. There have also been regular attempts to justify monarchy as the only alternative to **anarchy** (whether the anarchy be denigrated as feudal or democratic chaos). In such reasoning monarchy is justified as the only sure way of ensuring **authority**. Monarchy has been justified also purely by virtue of hereditary property rights: King X owned and ruled this land and its people, and therefore his legitimate heir has the right to rule them now.

The **Enlightenment**, **democratization**, ideas of **representative government** and the development of industrial society served to undermine monarchical authority. From the 17th to the 19th century most European monarchs were either displaced in republican revolutions or transformed into 'constitutional monarchs' – pale shadows of the real thing. In most extant constitutional monarchies the powers of the monarch have been reduced to ceremonial and residual prerogative functions which normally have little if any direct effect on government.

Most modern monarchs are living museum pieces, ancilliaries of the tourist and antiquarian industries, but with considerable popular appeal. On being deposed as King of Egypt King Farouk remarked 'Soon there will only be five kings left in the world: the four in the pack and the King of England'. He was right about the prospects of the four kings found in any pack of cards, but the permanence of the British monarchy is by no means assured. There are though some countervailing trends at odds with the Farouk hypothesis. The Spanish people have established a constitutional monarchy after being re-democratized in the 1970s, and if Kim Il Sung is succeeded by his son as ruler of North Korea the world will witness the novelty of hereditary communist **despotism**.

BO'L

See also absolutism; republicanism.

MONASTICISM

'Monasticism' (from Greek *monos* 'alone') was coined to describe those Christian devotees who lived alone, struggling with themselves and supernatural powers, as John the Baptist and Jesus of Nazareth did. But the tradition stretches back to before the time of the Buddha and the Jain ascetics, being perfected in the legend of the god Siva, the perfect yogi. In all such communities (as indeed in Christian monasticism in later times), there was always a tendency to regard celibate religious life as superior to ordinary family life, no matter how devout the household. (**Hinduism** took a different path with the development of **ashrams**.) Another kind of monasticism, eremitism (from the Greek word for hermit) refers to solitary religious life; 'monasticism' properly describes life in a community.

St Antony of Egypt (?251–365) is credited with being the founder of Christian monasticism when in *c*.305 he organized his disciples and other hermits who had joined him in the desert into a community of hermits living under a common rule of life. This rule discouraged such bizarre austerities as sitting on the top of a pillar for years, and discouraged competitions of hardship. Pachomium (*c*.290–346) founded nine monasteries for men and two for women by the Nile, and these served as a model for later foundations. The sanctity of all such founders contrasted sharply with the worldliness of the church leaders who emerged when persecution of **Christianity**

ceased in 312, and people alienated by the transformation of the Christian Church into a state religion, and by its growing affluence, seized the opportunity to 'flee the world'. Similarly, since martyrdom was no longer available as a rapid route to heaven, many of those earnestly seeking salvation opted for the monastic life. Monasticism in all faiths has always been seen as an accelerated route to heaven or enlightenment.

Monastic life, in Christendom as elsewhere, offered women a degree of freedom and control over their lives that they could never have as someone's daughter, wife or mother. As the movement spread northwards and westwards, it became the vehicle both for evangelism and for development. In the 12th century, for example, Cistercian monasteries introduced commercial sheep farming in northern England; the Orthodox monasteries were oases of Christian culture among the tribes of Russia. As the Roman Empire declined in Europe, monks became the only people who could read, and preserved the classical heritage. In India and Asia, a cultural impact was made by Buddhist monks. Monasteries were also great patrons of the **arts** and their occupants were often a highly subversive element in both church and state, as can be seen in contemporary Sri Lanka.

In Eastern Christianity and **Buddhism**, each monastery is autonomous and adapts the Rule by democratic decision. In the West 'orders' were founded: organizations or movements following a distinctive Rule of Life, sometimes with their own liturgical variations and usually with their own special robes or 'habit'. In addition to the vows of poverty, chastity and obedience, taken by all monks and nuns, the Order may prescribe additional vows. Benedict of Nursia (*c*.480-*c*.550) imposed the rule of enclosure to stop the nomadic habits of monks of his day and create stable communities. Poverty meant holding possessions in common, so although Benedictine abbeys became wealthy, they used their wealth to adorn worship (the monks and nuns' main preoccupation), to give hospitality and to succour the poor. The Cistercians and later the Trappists fled humankind and hospitality, combining worship and agriculture. The Dominicans, founded by St Dominic (1170–1221), are a brotherhood dedicated to preaching, Dominic having devoted his life to winning back heretics. His contemporary, Francis of Assisi (1181–1226), devoted himself to the service of the poor in a way emulated by Mother Teresa today, but hating organization and fund-raising. He rejected the order of 'Little Brothers' which he founded in 1209 and died a hermit. Another successful order was the Augustinian canons, who lived in smaller groups and have been described as 'poor Benedictines'. Martin Luther belonged to a strict house of Augustinians and was educated by them.

When H. Workman concluded his magisterial work on monasticism (see below), he stated that there had been no innovations since the Friars and the Beguines (he did not count Ignatius Loyola's Society of Jesus with their special vow of obedience to the pope). Since Workman's time, however, Charles de Foucauld's Little Brothers of Jesus, George Macleod's Inoa Community and Mother Teresa's Missionaries of Charity have broken in new ground in Christian monasticism, while the French Reformed Taize Community has lifted liturgy to new heights. Other movements such as the Foculari and the Darmstadt Sisters have concentrated on reparations for the suffering caused by World War II, especially the Holocaust. The creation of the Ramakrishna mission, Sri Aurobindo's order, and other new *ashrams* in India and Europe show new life in the monastic practice of other religions, while the importance of Muslim brotherhoods in Egypt and elsewhere cannot be over-estimated. **EMJ**

Further reading H.B. Workman, *The Evolution of the Monastic Ideal from the Earliest Times to the Coming of the Friars* (1913); Helen Waddell, *The Desert Fathers*.

MONETARISM

Monetarism, in **economics**, is the belief that control of the supply of money is sufficient for the attainment of full employment and general economic stability, at least in the longer run. Specifically, monetarists believe in the **quantity theory of money** and see monetary expansion or contraction as only having a transitory effect on 'real' variables like output and employment.

Monetarists applauded when, in 1979, the US Federal Reserve shifted from interest rate targets to money supply targets to try to control inflation and the level of economic activity. Keynesians (see **Keynesian Theory**), on the other hand, emphasize **fiscal policy** for control of the economy, while acknowledging in recent years that money matters, somewhat.

Monetarists differ in their policy recommendations for control of the money supply. Some support the Federal Reserve Board policy of setting money stock targets, which increase or decrease the rate of growth in the money supply to combat **inflation** and the **business cycle**. Many, including Milton Friedman (probably the most famous late–20th-century monetarist), hold that the Federal Reserve should follow a rule of increasing total bank reserves by a constant percentage per year, an increase just sufficient to accommodate the long-run average rate of economic growth. This, in turn, would control the other money supply aggregates which would benefit price stability. **TF**

Further reading Milton Friedman, *Studies in the Quantity Theory of Money; Essays in Positive Economics.*

MONISM

Monism (from Greek *monos*, 'sole'), in **philosophy**, is the doctrine that everything is of the same fundamental kind. **Materialists** hold that everything including any mental things is physical. **Idealists** hold that everything including the physical is mental. And **neutral monists** hold that everything mental and physical is made up of the same neutral stuff; minds and bodies are both made up of the same neutral stuff, and the difference between them is due to the different ways in which it is put together.

In contrast to these three versions of monism is **dualism**, which holds that there are two fundamental kinds of thing. Dualism holds that there is a non-physical mental realm and a non-mental physical realm. **AJ**

MONOPHONY see Polyphony

MONOPOLISTIC COMPETITION

Monopolistic competition, in **economic** terms, is a halfway house between perfect **competition** and **monopoly**. This concept of market structure was developed in the US by Edward H. Chamberlin (1889–1967) for his doctoral dissertation at Harvard in 1933. Also in the 1930s, a similar concept was developed by British economist Joan Robinson (1903–83), who gave her concept the differentiated name 'imperfect competition'. Chamberlin is credited with a more penetrating analysis of advertising and location as well as establishing the need of new theory rather than just a slight modification of the theory of monopoly.

Both Chamberlin and Robinson argued that few firms enjoyed a pure monopoly, that **oligopoly** was more common. Even where there are many competitors, firms enjoyed some discretion in setting their prices because their products were differentiated from those of their competitors. Although this did not result in monopoly profits, their prices were higher and output lower than they would be under perfect competition. A firm in monopolistic competition attempts to differentiate its product from others and acquire consumer loyalty for its particular product in order to gain market power and higher profit. Advertising plays a large role in these efforts, and locational advantage can make a difference. The large number of firms means there is not the degree of interdependence that exists among oligopolists. **TF**

MONOPOLY

Monopoly (Greek, 'sole seller'), in **economics**, is a market condition in which a single seller controls the supply of a product for which there are no close substitutes, and restrictions prevent new firms from entering the market. The single seller is a single, decision-making unit, for example, an individual, a firm, a cartel, etc. The monopolist may set any price, but the quantity sold at any price will be determined by the buyers' willingness to buy.

A natural monopoly is one which exists because two or more firms operating in the market would be grossly inefficient, since a single firm faces a decreasing long-run average cost curve over the relevant range of output. One person's natural monopoly is another's anti-trust suit, but currently accepted natural monopolies would include utilities distributing electric power or telephone service in a local market. Even these 'natural' monopolies, however, may be threatened by future competition.

In practice, monopolies are rarely absolute. A few are enshrined in law – for example, patent and copyright laws grant temporary monopolies. In general, though, the scope for absolute monopoly is limited by near-competitors, international trade and anti-trust laws. **TF**

See also monopolistic competition; monopsony; oligopoly.

MONOPSONY

A monopsony (Greek, 'sole buyer'), in **economics**, is a market dominated by a single buyer, as opposed to **monopoly**'s single seller. A monopsony can have harmful consequences because a monopsonist can change all the prices under its monopsonistic control (for example, prices, raw material, wages, etc.) whenever it wants to vary its purchases by even a single unit. The monopsonist may state any price for purchases, but the quantity supplied at any price will be determined by the sellers' willingness to sell. Under perfect **competition**, by contrast, no individual buyer is large enough to affect the market price of anything.

In practice, monopsony is even rarer than monopoly: perhaps the best example is the Central Selling Organization (CSO), the diamond-buying arm of De Beers. Since the 1930s, it has bought up about 80% of the value of world diamond production and then (acting as a monopoly) regulated the amount of diamonds it sold. Its grip has recently been slightly weakened by recalcitrant producers, notably Zaire and Australia, who have sold some of their diamonds outside the CSO. **TF**

See also oligopsony.

MONOTHEISM

Monotheism (Greek, 'single-god-ism') means belief in one all-powerful God who is distinct from the world but at the same time involved in it. Monotheism is, therefore, different from **animism** (in which natural phenomena are perceived as living beings, with spirits, and are worshipped accordingly), **polytheism** (belief in many gods, with or without a ruling deity), **deism** and **monism** (in which there is no separation between God and the world).

Under the influence of David Hume's views (in *Dialogues Concerning Natural Religion*, 1779), it used to be believed in the West that monotheism was a superior form of religion which had developed from polytheism. Growth of historical knowledge and of scientific **anthropology** has shown that this is not so. The Egyptian pharaoh Akhenaten (15th century BCE) worshipped one god, Aten, with the exclusiveness associated with monotheism. Many so-called 'primitive' peoples believed (and believe) in one supreme god, though he may have under him intermediaries such as the ancestors and local protective deities. This latter view is prevalent even among some overtly monotheistic religions. Christian and Muslim saints, for example, serve a similar purpose and are worshipped in similar ways. **Hinduism** is a particularly interesting case. Some schools of Hinduism are avowedly polytheistic; other Hindus see the various deities as manifestations of one deity; generally each believer worships one deity (for example Siva) as supreme lord, and other deities do not impinge on them.

In **Judaism**, the term monotheism was originally used to describe Israel's perception of its God, who commanded on Mount Sinai, 'I am the Lord your God: you shall have no other gods before me'. This view took many centuries to flower into belief in God as the Supreme Being, creator of all that is, in control of history and ordaining the rise and fall of nations, and

who loves those He has chosen and who obey His will. (This belief finds its classic statement in such prophets of the 8th century BCE as Isaiah. Prior to that the 'god of the fathers', that is of such patriarchs as Abraham, Isaac and Jacob, was simply the protecting deity of a family, tribe and nation. This notion was known as enotheism: there are other deities, but only one God for Israel, whose power had geographical limitations. It took the anguish of the Jewish exile in Babylon in the early 6th century BCE to make Judaism a universalist religion.)

In the Christian New Testament, monotheism and universalism are taken for granted, except that Paul seems to waver between regarding Greek gods as nonexistent or as demons. (The Greek word *daimon* means 'spirit of place': see **demonism**.) Biblical monotheism, both Judaic and early Christian, was hammered out in response to the challenge of surrounding polytheistic worship, and even then, and as late as the 4th century, Christian trinitarianism was castigated by outsiders as a form of limited polytheism. **EMJ**

Further reading John Hick, *An Interpretation of Religion: Human Responses to the Transcendent.*

MORAL SENSE see **Ethical Intuitionism**

MORALITY

Morality is a system of moral (from Latin *mores*, 'customs' or 'behaviour') rules. But what more can we say about morality? One can say at once that it is a set of rules which tell one how to behave, which lay down what one ought to do in certain circumstances. But this does not distinguish moral rules from other sets of practical norms. For instance, there are rules which tell one how to invest money and rules which tell one how to behave at a dinner party. These prudential maxims and rules of etiquette are not normally regarded as forms of morality. So how do they differ from moral rules?

One criterion which might be used to pick out the moral rules derives from Kant. He distinguished between hypothetical and categorical imperatives. A *hypothetical imperative* is one you should obey if you have certain desires. For instance, if you desire to make money, you should buy low and sell high. But if you don't desire to make money, there is no reason to obey this prudential maxim. A *categorical imperative* is one you ought to obey whatever your particular desires. 'Do not kill the innocent' applies to you whatever your desires or interests. However, we cannot say that all categorical imperatives are moral rules since the rules of etiquette are categorical imperatives as well. One should not pick one's nose at the dinner table, whether or not one wants to.

Another criterion which might distinguish morality from etiquette is that moral rules should be overriding where there is a clash between a moral rule and some other practical norm, the moral rule should always win. But this is not how people actually think about morality. To use an example of Phillipa Foot's, a host does not stop serving drinks at a dinner party just because the guests are getting drunk and some have to drive home. Here, the obligation of politeness to one's guests is felt to override one's moral obligation to ensure that people on the road drive safely.

In view of such examples it is difficult to say what makes a set of rules into a morality. **AJ**

Further reading P. Foot, *Virtues and Vices*; R. Hare, *Moral Thinking*.

MORALITY PLAY

The Morality Play was an allegorical form of late medieval/early Renaissance European **drama** in which personifications (for example, Death, Knowledge or Good Deeds) battle over the soul of a representative figure (Everyman or Mankind in the plays of the same names). The plays are powerful moral instruments in serving the **Christian** cause. **TRG SS**

See also miracle play; mystery play.

Further reading Richard Southern, *The Seven Ages of the Theatre*; W. Tydeman, *The Theatre in the Middle Ages*.

MORPHOLOGY

Morphology (Greek, 'study of forms'), in the **life sciences**, is the study of organic form and of similarity in form between different organisms. It was founded in the early 17th century by Johann von Goethe, though previous thinkers such as Aristotle and Pierre Belon, in the 16th century, had compared the shapes of animals and noted similarities in structure. Goethe suggested that all plant parts were derived from a primordial plant organ, which was a leaf. Étienne Geoffroy St. Hilaire (1772–1844) proposed a similar idea in **zoology**: that all animals, including man, are constructed according to the same basic ground plan.

In the 19th century, Karl von Baer proposed that all animals came from a common 'germ' – for example, a chick embryo begins its development with a morphology which is common to any animal embryo, and becomes a general vertebrate and then a specialized (bird) vertebrate before finally differentiating into the chicken morphology. This led to the idea of the archetype, defined by Richard Owen (1804–92) as a hypothetical form with the potential to develop into any of the species in a group. Owen and others applied their ideas of morphology to existing knowledge of **anatomy**, at that time one of the best-studied areas of biology. Georges Cuvier (1769–1832) divided the animal kingdom into four physiological groups, which he called vertebrates, articulates, molluscs and radiates, but only on the basis of functional similarity. In common with the prevailing opinion in the early 19th century, Cuvier would not admit that species which were similar in morphology were of the same type. In 1830, Cuvier and Geoffroy argued their positions before the Paris Academy of Sciences and, though Cuvier was the victor and Geoffroy's ideas of a single, primordial animal were rejected, the unity of type approach endured. Owen used his ideas of archetype to explain the fossil record which showed ancient, simple, general species and more modern complex, specialized species.

The development of morphology set the scene for Darwin, who proposed **evolution** as a mechanism to explain the observed unity of type, in which the archetype was a real, extinct species, the common ancestor of a group. Modern morphology has shifted its emphasis to attempts to relate structure and shape to function.

Morphology, of a different kind, is an important theory in **linguistics**. Each segment of meaning in a word constitutes a separate morpheme, so in the word 'untrue' we can isolate two morphemes: negation (denoted by un-) and true. The fundamental concern of morphology, therefore, is the internal structure of words. Some morphemes can take more than one form, as demonstrated by the morpheme for the simple past tense. In 'walked', the past tense morpheme (spelt ed) is pronounced *t*; in 'smiled' it is pronounced as *d*; whereas in 'shouted' it appears as *id*. In effect, a single unit of meaning is expressible in a variety of ways, which leads to the conclusion that the morpheme is an abstract category which finds physical realization in the form of morphs. It follows then that *t*, *d*, *id* are all allomorphs (associated morphs) of the morpheme for simple past tense. The abstract nature of morphemes is further demonstrated by the refusal of certain words to be neatly segmented into a sequence of distinct parts. Thus 'women' is composed of the separate morphemes woman and plural, which seem to have blended imperceptibly. The synthesis of morphemes in this way is accounted for by so-called morphological processes, whereby separate elements combine to produce a unified word form.

A useful distinction in morphological theory is drawn between free morphs and bound morphs. Free morphs, like 'prawn' and 'alabaster', can exist independently, whereas bound morphs, like '-ed' and '-ing', cannot stand alone and only find legitimate expression as part of a word (for example, 'talked', 'talking'). Morphs can also be distinguished according to whether they are fundamentally lexical or grammatical in nature. Lexical morphs, such as 'non-', 'conform' and '-ist', can be used to build up new word forms (for example, 'nonconformist'), whereas grammatical morphs, like the third person singular marker '-s', only express meaning within a grammatical construction (for example, 'walks').

Categories such as tense, number and gender are often expressed as inflections on word stems and serve to highlight the fuzzy boundary between morphology and **syntax**, since they often affect not only the words they appear in, but the position of the surrounding words also. Inflectional processes of this kind can be distinguished from derivational processes, in which new words are created, by adding affixes to a stem. For example, we can add the suffix '-able' to 'describe' to give 'describable', which can then be prefixed with 'in-', to produce 'indescribable'. One problem in morphology is to explain the constraints on derivational processes which block, for instance, forms like 'indescribe'. A further problem is to describe how derivational processes influence word class membership (noun, verb, adjective and so on). Thus, the derivation of 'denial' from 'deny' is class-changing, since it transforms a verb into a noun, whereas a class-maintaining process leaves word-class membership unaffected, as in the derivation of 'dislike' from 'like' (both verbs). An alternative method of creating new words, known as compounding, involves the conjunction of morphemes which can otherwise occur independently. Examples include compounds – such as 'blackboard', 'bedroom' and 'gearbox' – which have meanings independent of their constituent parts, and which function as single word units. As a result, the individual components are no longer available for inflectional processes, which explains the impossibility of forms like 'gearsbox'. **MS RB**

See also analogy; Darwinism; embryology; homology; palaeontology.

Further reading L. Bauer, *English Word-Formation*; P.H. Matthews, *Morphology*.

MOTIVE

A motive, as its derivation (from Latin *movere*, 'to move') suggests, is that which moves, that is, causes one to act. Many philosophers have held that only the combination of a belief and desire can move one to act. One's desire for water will not cause one to turn the tap unless one also believes that turning the tap is a good way to get water. And one's belief that turning the tap is a good way to get water will not move one to turn the tap unless one desires water. Only in combination can beliefs and desires cause one to act. **AJ**

See also action; morality; volition; weakness of will.

MOVEMENT, THE see **Angry Young Men**

MULTICULTURALISM

Multiculturalism is an attitude towards identity. Do we derive identity from human experience at large, or (in part) from specific national, racial, religious, social or other groupings? Is the diversity of human activity an accident of history, or endemic? Whatever one's answer, the pluralist nature of the modern world has made multiculturalism an important issue, especially in such crucial areas as the **arts**, **politics** and **religion**. (The fact that **science** lies outside the debate suggests that the whole discussion is subjective and not objective, a question so to speak of **style**; it is nonetheless vital for all that.) **KMcL**

MULTIPLES

Multiples are artefacts produced in unlimited numbers without necessary recourse to an artist's prototype. **Pop** art's interest in consumerism made the idea of repetition a key concept in the work of Andy Warhol, who often did little other than oversee the production of his silk-screen prints. Thus a multiple is not synonymous with the limited-edition, fine-art print, where the idea of a limited number of examples helps to boost the value. The true multiple is a consumer article, an industrially-produced fashion accessory, freely available, disposable, and wholly antagonistic to the notion of 'fine art'. **PD MG**

MULTIPLEXING

Multiplexing, in electrical engineering, is the technique of sending multiple signals along a single wire either in one or opposite directions. It was first conceived in USA in the 1850s for use on the developing telegraph network, and was a form of time division multiplexing (TDM). Using this system the signal capacity of the telegraph lines could be greatly increased without the laborious and expensive refitting of new wires.

TDM works on the principle of allocating each signal a specific time slot in a transmission period, and ensuring that each such period is short enough to guarantee coherent communication. The first practical TDM system widely implemented was developed by the Frenchman Baudot in 1874.

A more recent form of multiplexing, frequency division multiplexing (FDM), appeared during World War I due to early work on **radio transmission**. It required the introduction of signal modulation and carrier frequency transmission to become viable, and used signals broadcast at separate and non-interfering frequency bands to achieve an increase in transmission capacity.

At present TDM is widely used in digital communications, while FDM is used each time our radio is tuned to a different frequency and radio station. **AC**

MULTIPLIER EFFECT

The multiplier effect is **economics** shorthand for the way in which a change in spending produces an even larger change in income. For example, suppose spending in an economy is increased by $100 million due to higher investment. The initial effect is to boost the incomes of those who produced the buildings or machinery that make up the extra investment. Those people will in turn spend part of their extra incomes, which puts more money into the pockets of others, who spend it . . . and so on.

In theory, this process could continue indefinitely, in which case the multiplier would have an infinite value. In practice, not all of the extra income is spent. Some of it leaks abroad in the form of imports, and some of it is saved rather than spent. The remainder is defined as the 'marginal propensity to consume' that is, that proportion of an extra dollar of income that is spent. The value of the multiplier can be derived from the simple formula of $1/(1 - \text{MPC})$. If 50 cents of each extra dollar is spent at home, then the multiplier has a value of 2.

The practical value of this knowledge is considerable when governments come to decide their **fiscal policy**. If they want to boost national income by $100 million, and they know that the multiplier is 2, they need inject only 50 million in the form of higher public expenditure or taxation cuts in order to achieve their ultimate target. This, at least, is what Keynesians argue; non-Keynesians, while accepting that spending does have a multiplier effect, argue that the notion (1) gives a misleading impression of precision and (2) implies that the extra spending will produce more real growth whereas it could all dissipate in inflation instead. **TF**

MUSÉE IMAGINAIRE

Musée imaginaire ('museum without walls') was André Malraux's phrase for the vast number of photographic reproductions of works of art available to modern readers – the world's **art** not scattered inaccessibly in buildings, but available between the covers of a book. Malraux teased out the pros and cons of such second-hand availability, and his views have been broadened since to cover the whole weight of past **culture**, which modern reproductive techniques make cheaply available. In fine art, **literature** and **music** especially, it is a more plentiful resource than has been available to any previous generation, and its accessibility affects both the creators of new works, and their audience, in ways which have yet to be assessed. **KMcL**

MUSIC

Music (Greek *mousike*, 'what the Muses know') is the art of organizing sounds, creating relationships and patterns to challenge and stimulate the mind. It is a **performing art**, and (unless the musician is performing for his or her own satisfaction) depends on interaction between performer and listener. The performer creates a sequence of sounds expressing emotion, intellectual ideas, or both, and the listener hears them, responding to their 'meaning'

or assigning new meanings which are his or her own interpretation. A similar process happens with **language**, but there the sounds are fewer and less varied, and the specific meanings assigned to them by convention are more commonly agreed. Musical sounds are suggestive rather than particular, evocative rather than exact, and so offer an enormous range of intellectual and emotional possibility, challenge and satisfaction.

Anthropologists suggest that music's original purpose may have been **magic**: an attempt, using human sounds, to re-create the supposed speech of gods and spirits, and so to communicate with them. In ancient Greece, Pythagoras thought that heavenly bodies made sounds as they moved through space – the **music of the spheres**, which, for him, was an expression of the mathematical harmony and perfection of the universe. In a similar way, native people may have believed that the sounds heard on Earth (animal shrieks and howls, the random noises of infants, the rustling, groaning and gurgling of such inanimate objects as trees, rocks and water) were expressions of contentment or irritation by guardian spirits, and that music was a way to share them, to celebrate or restore the harmony of all created things. In particular, music was often used as part of such 'performances' as funerals, weddings and the enactment of battles and hunts, when the spirits had to be attracted to bring good luck.

Throughout human history, music has continued to play a similar role. However removed they may be in style, the chanting of a Christian archbishop, the humming of Buddhist monks, the cymbal-clashing and trumpet-blowing as Hindu god-statues are carried in procession, are no different in essence from the drumming and ululation of animist religion, and their purpose is the same: to establish communication between natural and supernatural worlds. Music serves a similar function in secular pomp and circumstance: fanfares to herald important personages, marches, drum-rolls for acrobats, all are signals that what is happening is an enhancement of everyday experience.

Nonetheless, all such 'anthropological' or social uses of music are secondary to what rapidly became its primary function: as a performance, intended to satisfy participants and listeners alike. There is more than a hint of show in the performance of a shaman, or in the religious music of a great temple or cathedral – and the show is intended for human ears just as much as, if not more than, for its supernatural audience. Singing and dancing at carnivals, sports matches, weddings and other occasions is primarily for fun. **Dance, music-theatre** and instrumental and vocal performances of all kinds may have originated in religious or social **ritual**, but they have now become primarily entertainment in forms far removed from such origins. Paradoxically, people often still talk of the effect of such performances as if they had superhuman power. Music is heady, we say; it stimulates and entrances; it takes us into other states of being.

As in the other arts, a sharp distinction quickly grew in music between ordinary practitioners and specialists. The trumpeters of King Solomon's Temple in Jerusalem, 3,000 years ago, insisted on being treated as a group apart. Their skills and the music they played were centuries-old hereditary secrets, and they refused to take part in any non-Temple musical activities. Similarly, the skills of Indian classical music, or of Asian temple music, were passed down from teacher to pupil, aloof from possible contamination by the popular traditions beyond the borders of their art. In Europe, medieval musicians formed official guilds and cliques, often conducting lawsuits and fighting battles to preserve their exclusivity. In the modern world, although teaching and knowledge are more widely available, a gulf still exists between the ordinary family or local performer and such huge (and hugely-rewarded) public celebrities as opera singers, pop stars or solo recitalists.

Thus, while the vast majority of the world's music is and always has been folk-based, functional and direct in both expression and appeal, there have also arisen some highly sophisticated, élitist and (it must be admitted) minority forms of music, regarded as among the highest artistic achievements of the human mind. They are not necessarily more sophisticated than popular music – indeed, 'art' music has to work hard to be as complex in effect, and as simple in construction, as the multiple-rhythm drumming of West Africa, Balinese *gamelan* or the harmonic and melodic nuances of Portuguese *fado* or Southern US **blues**. But, perhaps because of their origins as minority entertainments for the rich, some types of music have become cultural jewels, to the point where they are self-referential, self-perpetuating and (it would seem) almost beyond improvement. The traditions of Chinese court music, Indian classical music, Japanese theatre music and Western classical music have become like still-living fossils: on the one hand embalmed in time, on the other as organic and vibrant now as they ever were.

Western classical music is a unique case. All other music – there are no exceptions – is improvised. Its basic ideas may be passed on from performer to performer, in a more or less rigorous way, but each performer adds his or her own ideas in performance, responding directly to the mood of the moment and/or the listeners' response. In pieces of Western classical music, by contrast, a score exists: a detailed notation of what the music's creator had in mind, a blueprint for performance. This began for practical purposes in the early Middle Ages (to ensure that Christian missionaries, everywhere in Europe, used the same musical material in the same services in the same way), and developed over centuries until notes, speed, dynamics and attack (the way the sounds are physically made) are meticulously prescribed, and the performer's job is to realize not so much spontaneous feelings as his or her idea of what the original composer had in mind. In the past, some composers left embellishment of the music to the performers (in the 'divisions' of **Renaissance** music, for example, or the ornaments and cadenzas added in 18th-century music). Some modern composers and performers are experimenting with a blend between notated and improvised music (sometimes enhanced and randomized by computer). But by and large we can be surer of the intentions of past creators of genius in Western classical music, from Palestrina to Mozart, from Handel to Tchaikovsky, than in any other form of the art until the invention of recording.

Recording has had an incalculable effect on our appreciation of music today. First, it has internationalized music in ways impossible on such a scale before. Musical styles and techniques counterpoint, jazz, *gamelan*, *raga* and the work of performers of genius are available everywhere, inspiring new performers in the same or widely differing traditions. Young musicians have access to an enormous archive of the past: not an aural museum but a storehouse of ideas. This has made 20th-century music catholic, tolerant and assimilative in a way scarcely known before. Specialists from one particular tradition or another sometimes deplore this, and recommend retreat into their own stylistic ghetto. But the availability of music of all kinds, the democratization of the art, has liberated it from its past in a unique way. The future of music, its stylistic direction, is unpredictable and creatively open-ended in a way not paralleled in any other art. **KMcL**

Further reading Leonard Bernstein, *The Joy of Music*; Geoffrey Hindley (ed.), *The Larousse Encyclopedia of Music* (one of the best and most comprehensive accounts of all kinds of music ever compiled: in one volume).

MUSIC DRAMA

Music drama was Wagner's name for his own operas: each was a **gesamtkunstwerk** in which music, words, design and production were in perfect balance, contributing equally to the overall effect and meaning. Wagner thought that he had invented a new stage form, but in fact the distinction was only with the more singer-dominated kind of Italian **opera** (of which some Rossini and Donizetti works are typical) and with operetta. 'Music drama' is a standard art form in many cultures of which Wagner was unaware – Indonesian, Japanese, Mogul Indian, for example – and is also a fair description of the operas of Monteverdi, Mozart, Gluck, Verdi, Puccini and a host of others, where we watch a piece of drama articulated through music, and not (as in certain Rossini and Donizetti works) merely a concert of arias and ensembles more or less linked by plot. **KMcL**

See also leitmotif.

MUSIC OF THE SPHERES

The ancient Greeks knew of nine spheres: the Sun and Moon; the planets we know as Mercury, Venus, Mars, Jupiter and Saturn; the 'Starry Sphere' (the fixed stars in the sky); the Crystalline Sphere (the sphere which controlled the procession of the equinoxes). These were all assumed to move round the Earth, in a kind of stately and unvarying procession. Pythagoras' research into sound led him to believe that the spheres, in common with all other objects which move, must vibrate, and that those vibrations must produce sound. As each sphere is a different size from the others, and moves in a different way, the sounds must all be different. However, as all Nature (to Pythagoreans) was a harmonious mathematical whole, the sounds emitted by the spheres must also be harmonious: a kind of glorious universal chord as they made their way through space. The idea of universal harmony and of the discordant chaos when something happens to upset it has persisted in **myth** and **poetry** ever since. **KMcL**

MUSIC THEATRE

'Music theatre' was once the generic name given in the West to theatre shows which were, so to speak, almost **operas**: musical comedies, musicals, cabarets and the like. The essential difference was that in opera the music was generally predominant, whereas in music theatre spoken words took an equal or greater place. English **masques** and Molière's *divertissements* (such as the Turkish ceremony which closes *Le bourgeois gentilhomme*) are characteristically early examples; *The Soldier's Tale*, *The Threepenny Opera* and *Kiss Me Kate* show the form at its mid-20th-century peak; *The Magic Flute* and other operas with spoken dialogue rather than recitative are arguably music-theatre rather than opera (if anyone cares about such categories).

In the second half of the 20th century, Western writers and composers began producing theatre-work of a different kind. Inspired initially by the work of Brecht, it also took in influences from other cultures, such as Noh and Kabuki drama, Balinese dance-drama and 'Peking opera' (that heavily propagandist version of folk opera perfected in Maoist China). In this kind of music-theatre, drama leads and music is one part (though one of the most important) of the total structure. New forms were experimented with – Schoenberg's *Ode to Napoleon Bonaparte* and *A Survivor from Warsaw* are a mixture of declamation and oratorio; Britten's 'church parables' are Noh plays re-created in the Anglican cathedral tradition; Maxwell Davies's *Three Songs for a Mad King* put the singer and musicians onstage, in costume, and has them leaping in and out of character, as performers and as the people or things they are depicting; Henze's *Essay on Pigs* and *El Cimarròn* blend **expressionist** music with harshly political diatribe. Many of these works have and still provoke the uneasiness characteristic of many experimental, hybrid forms of art; even the masterpieces have a feeling of rawness, of succeeding despite rather than because of the means deployed, which argues that music-theatre of this novel kind, as an art form, has still some way to go. **KMcL**

MUSICAL ACCULTURATION

Musical acculturation is a process whereby a society's **music**, or part of it, undergoes changes that are directly attributable to the influence of a foreign culture. One of the study areas for **ethnomusicology**, for example, has been the examination of the impact of Western music on non-Western musical cultures. It is generally accepted that musical acculturation depends on the compatibility or similarity of the two cultures, and on whether the exchange is through essential or non-essential musical characteristics. Essential characteristics concern the musical language itself and may include harmony, **tonality**, modality, rhythm and **metre**. Non-essential characteristics, drawn from the musical context, may include instrumentation, tuning and temperament, amplification, musical notation and the social and behavioural features of musical performance.

Within the broad spectrum of musical acculturation several processes have been identified, of which **syncretism**, **modernization** and **Westernization** appear to be most influential. Musical syncretism occurs when the encounter between two musical systems results in a new, hybrid style. This seems to happen most naturally when there are recognizable musical similarities between the two cultures and, in particular, when they share essential characteristics. The distinction between modernization and Westernization, so crucial in the development of today's so-called **'World Music'**, is less easy to define. Modernization occurs when a society creates a new, adapted, revitalized version of its traditional music by adopting similar but non-essential elements of Western music. On the other hand, Westernization occurs when a society changes its traditional music by taking what it considers to be essential elements from the Western musical system, even though they may be incompatible with that tradition.

Acculturation can occur over an extended period of time as a cyclic, regenerative and reciprocal process. For example, because of the transatlantic slave trade African music was introduced into the New World, where it eventually merged with European and Hispanic elements and created syncretized Afro-American and Afro-Caribbean forms. These new forms, conveyed by the Western commercial recording industry, were reintroduced to Africa as compatible and modernizing influences on its developing urban popular music. This subsequently induced new hybrids of African music in the 1950s and 60s – and these, in turn, were to be vital influences in the development of new Caribbean **pop** and **jazz** forms in the 1970s. The process continues today with African pop music absorbing these new Caribbean styles.

Acculturation also embraces the musical changes within a society brought about by economic, technological and political developments, for example, the effect of urbanization and industrialization on rural and agricultural work songs, or the control of disc or cassette format on the duration and structure of musical performance. The growth of tourism has also had some effect: for instance certain non-Western cultures have accommodated Western preconceptions by exaggerating or distorting their traditions, or by artificially preserving those elements by which they believe Western tourists are attracted. Throughout this century authoritarian regimes, such as some eastern European Communist states, have tried to create national musical identities. This process involved forging together diverse and often incompatible musical elements from the various regions and cultures within the regime's control, without regard to retaining their original identities.

There is some concern that musical acculturation, affected by the rapid technological advances in global communications, can only lead to the contraction and loss of musical diversity, resulting ultimately in what has been described as 'cultural greyout'. SSt

MUSICOLOGY

The earliest documented examples of musicology (academic study of the phenomenon of **music**) are from ancient Greece: Pythagoras' research into the acoustical properties of vibrating strings, and Plato's sociopsychological remarks on the effects of flute music on adolescent boys. Thereafter there is something of a lull, until in the high Middle Ages Guido d'Arezzo did work to codify the notation of plainchant, and Omar Khayyám researched the psychological effects of different categories of sound. More systematic work began in Europe in the 18th century, perhaps triggered by the **Encylopedists**. Attempts were made to discover, and to describe, the various 'national styles' in music, and to write accounts of those composers who used each of them. It was not, however, until the mid-19th century that musicology became a professional discipline, funded by universities – and it was not until the dispersion of European scholars during the **Nazi** period in Germany that the discipline became recognized worldwide. It now has two principal branches: **ethnomusicology**, which is concerned with **folk music** and non-Western music; and musicology itself, which centres on Western art music of the last 1,000 years or so.

Musicology has a number of branches, each largely self-contained. First and foremost are acoustics, the study (predominantly biological and physical) of the nature of sound and how it is produced, and studies (predominantly physiological and psychological) of how we perceive music, of how and why it affects us as it does. A second main branch of musicology is concerned with performance, and involves instrument history, methods of notation, performance practice (historical and contemporary), technology and technique, and the whole place of music in its aesthetic and social environment. Music history is a minor, but crowded, branch of the profession, and there is a profusion of critical writing which is rejected by musicological purists on the grounds that it is not scientific – a besetting problem in a discipline which is attempting to make scientific assessments of a phenomenon which is essentially indefinable and subjective.

Like all academic studies, musicology is internally riven, and its fads and feuds are sometimes as fascinating to its practitioners as their proper work. But because it is concerned with a **performing art**, unlike say the academic study of **literature**, it can be of unique importance (for an academic discipline) on those concerned with primary creation. An example is the late 20th-century fascination with 'authentic' performance. Simple questions like 'Does Bach's music as we experience it today sound anything like it did in his own time?' have led to a flurry of research into instrument manufacture, the nature of halls and audiences, the size of performing groups, and every detail of performance from ornamentation to the bowing of string parts, from speed and attack to the nature and use of vibrato. This research has inspired performers to try to recapture the original sounds and effects, and the result has been that much 'old' music, from pre-**Renaissance** times through to Brahms and Mahler, has been cleaned of the accumulations of practical and theoretical expertise between its date and ours, as an old painting is cleaned of varnish. (After Mahler the task is somewhat different, period recordings adding a direct aural impression of selected pieces – another, and currently eagerly studied, weapon in the musicologist's already bristling arsenal.) **KMcL**

See also academe.

MUSIQUE CONCRÈTE

Musique concrète (French, 'concrete music') was a term invented by the French composer Pierre Shaeffer in the 1940s for his early form of **electronic music**. He recorded 'ordinary' sounds: birdsong, children shouting in a playground, mechanical noise, rustling leaves, traffic and so on. He then snipped the tape and reassembled the sounds to make a collage which followed the 'rules' of music rather than random noise. (The idea was to make an artificial music, analogous to the way concrete is artificial stone: hence the name.) To begin with, recording technology was too primitive to allow any kind of modulation of the sounds. But technical advances soon allowed them to be speeded up, slowed down, played backwards and so on, and increasing sophistication led to the computer manipulation of 'ordinary' sounds, 'sampled' in the same way as instrumental, synthesized or vocal sound. **KMcL**

MUTATION

A mutation, in **genetics**, is a change in a **gene** (or chromosome) which produces a change in **phenotype** as a result of a change in the gene product. Mutations are important in **evolution** because they cause variation within the **gene pool**. They occur at random and are thus nearly all damaging, causing the death of the individual or rendering it unable to survive in the face of competition; such genes are usually deleted from the gene pool as their carriers do not successfully reproduce. Occasionally, a mutation will occur which, by chance, renders the individual better suited to its environment; such a gene can spread through the population at an increased rate, giving rise to variation.

At a molecular level, the term mutation describes a change in sequence of nucleotides in the chromosonal DNA. A mutation can occur in any cell, but those mutations which occur during the production of gametes are of importance in terms of the population and of **evolution**, because they have the potential to be inherited. Some mutations (such as those that result in Down's syndrome) include changes in the number or structure of chromosomes. Most mutations are gene mutations and involve the addition, deletion or, most commonly, the substitution of one or more nucleotides. Since the nucleotide sequence of DNA codes for the amino acid sequence of protein product, the effect of even a single nucleotide substitution can have far-reaching effects upon the development and life of the individual, by altering the structure and function of the protein. Diseases such as haemophilia and sickle-cell anaemia are the result of relatively simple gene mutations.

Mutations can occur as the result of errors in copying during DNA replication, but this process normally has a high level of failure. External factors such as ionizing radiation (x-rays, gamma rays, etc.) and certain chemicals (pesticides, mustard gas) can greatly increase the mutation rate. **RB**

See also adaptation; genetic code; teratology; toxicology.

Further reading Bruce Alberts, *The Molecular Biology of the Cell*; Richard Dawkins, *The Selfish Gene*.

MUZAK

Muzak is a proprietary name, the property of the Muzak Corporation of America. But it is one of those brand names which has passed into popular use throughout the world. It is music (usually recorded) played as a background in factories, shops, restaurants, waiting areas, lifts, stairwells, down telephones while you wait to be connected – even, we are told, in spacecraft and (through loudspeakers in parking meters) in the streets of some towns and cities.

In its wider sense, muzak has existed for millennia. Ancient Greek vase paintings show musicians performing while other people eat or talk; medieval European barons, and the aristocrats of Mogul India and Edo Japan, hired minstrels for a similar purpose. Haydn, Mozart and a thousand lesser composers wrote serenades, divertissements and other pieces to soothe their employers' ears. Early this century, the composer Erik Satie devised 'furniture music' to be played in the foyer during an art exhibition. (It was a failure as furniture, though successful as music: visitors stopped to listen, and forgot the exhibition.) The late 20th-century composer-performer Brian Eno has developed 'ambient music', a kind of discreet, **minimalist** murmur designed to produce feelings of calm and well-being – quite different from the tension and rage engendered by canned music of more assertive kinds. **KMcL**

MYSTERY PLAY

The Mystery Play is a form of medieval European religious drama. Mystery is a term for a craft guild (whose members had skills which were kept from outsiders). In some areas the guilds were responsible for staging plays on religious festivals which might retell the whole of the Bible story from Creation to Crucifixion and beyond to the Last Judgement. Each guild took responsibility for an appropriate story (for example, the nailmakers staged the Crucifixion) and the result was a powerful expression of community theatre reinforcing a religious message. **TRG SS**

See also miracle play; morality play

Further reading Richard Southern, *The Seven Ages of the Theatre*; W. Tydeman, *The Theatre in the Middle Ages*.

MYSTICISM

Mysticism (from Greek *mysterion*, 'password' or 'secret ritual act') is a phenomenon common to all religions. By means of spiritual and/or physical exercises, the mystic experiences transcendent reality and direct contact or even fusion with the divine. The experience makes one see the coherence and unity of all things, natural and supernatural – a unity in which one is oneself involved. In ancient mysticism, and in much Eastern mysticism today, the soul of the mystic is thought to be absorbed into

the divine. In modern **Christian** mysticism, by contrast, devotees retain their human identities, rapt in the beatific vision. **EMJ**

Further reading Evelyn Underhill, *Mysticism*.

MYTH

The Greek word *muthos* means an account: words organized to give specific information or to make a particular effect. It contains overtones of 'fiction' or 'fantasy', unlike, for instance, *logos* which means a rational account of reality. More narrowly, myths are attempts to explain, or at least bring nearer to our comprehension, such matters as the beginning of the universe, the nature and demands of supernatural powers, the hierarchy of creation, the causes of things and the origins of certain social customs and popular beliefs. In a prescientific age, myths were an intellectual binding force, a net of ideas and attitudes which guaranteed social identity. Whether each set of myths reflected its society, or the society reflected its myths, is a moot point; but certainly myths had a defining and enabling power which scientific rationalism has still not begun to equal. By imbuing statements with 'sacred' authority, they could be seen as providing a charter for social action, giving customs an authority and legitimacy they might otherwise lack. By locating traditions in mythical time, contemporary behaviour could be justified by reference to custom.

Recent studies in myth have concentrated on this aspect of their existence. In the 1940s, Bronislaw Malinowski and his fellow-anthropologists saw them not just as explanations of social customs and institutions but as validators, a kind of repository of the status quo. Unlike other such validators, for example codes of **law** or **ethics**, they were not adaptable to changing social conditions, and societies which depended on them tended to collapse or become disorientated after the irruption of the 'modern' world. (Significantly, people from many 'assimilated' cultures are now turning to their ancestral myths as a way of rediscovering and reasserting cultural identity in a pluralist world.)

Claude Lévi-Strauss and his colleagues subjected each myth to a process of **deconstruction**, whose purpose was to reveal the psychological, social, anthropological and other impulses which lay under the simple narrative surface. The argument here was that the structural elements used in myths revealed the basic structures of the human mind, and universal methods of classifying the phenomenal world. Myth's function was to wrestle with the fundamental and irreconcilable contradictions experienced in life. This is to treat myths as direct relatives of **legends** (fantasized history) and **allegory** (fantasized moral or ethical teaching) – the differences being that they are often older, that they arise through accretion rather than through specific composition by single individuals, and consequently that they are less overt, less naive, and therefore more revealing (when suitably 'unpacked') of the society which created them.

While Lévi-Strauss's theories provided rich insights into the analysis of myth, they were incorporated by later anthropologists into an approach which locates myth in its historical and political context. The 1980s saw a renewed interest, among anthropologists, in the relationship of myth to **history**. Whereas **evolutionists** had treated myth as a precursor to history in preliterate societies, contemporary anthropologists argue that all history can be treated as myth. Historical facts, they hold, can never be proven, and in so far as history is the legitimizing narrative constructed by a people, whether family, tribe or nation, it is also myth.

None of this detracts from the direct, primary power of myths as stories and entertainment. They carry on the work of such less-grand relatives as proverbs, riddles, nursery rhymes and folk tales, leading our imaginations, so to speak, from childhood simplicities to larger questions and concerns. They are worked on in two main ways. On the one hand is a vast amount of straightforward collection, literary and anthropological research taking us as closely as possible to each myth's most ancient or most characteristic shape. (In this work, variants are often as fascinating as the basic myths themselves.) On the other hand is almost the entire weight of creative endeavour in the **arts**. No art form is unaffected by myth, at any period and in any society.

Myths are a repository not only of stories, but of themes, attitudes, stylistic strategies and insights. A single example demonstrates the point: the Greek story of Odysseus' homecoming after the Trojan War. This comes down to us originally in the words of Homer, who made a 13,000-line epic poem out of dozens, perhaps hundreds of individual anecdotes and incidents, giving them narrative cohesion and a single authorial 'attitude', drawing out from straightforward adventure the story of a man in quest of his own psychological identity. In the 3,000 years since it was composed, the *Odyssey* has directly inspired novels, poems, plays, operas, ballets, symphonic poems, paintings and sculpture, and has given themes and structure to a host of secondary works from Cervantes' *Don Quixote* or Joyce's *Ulysses* (where the influence is obvious) to Albert Camus's *The Plague*, or Arthur Miller's *Death of a Salesman* (developing the idea of the existential quest). This is *muthos* in the sense used first by Coleridge: a starting-point and a landscape in which the creative journey may be made.

Not all myth-systems are equally fertile. In the arts throughout the world, only ancient Greek myth (predominantly secular) and Hindu myth (predominately religious) have had, and retain, such long-lasting, overwhelming and protean power to inspire new creation. But in large or in small – Inuit sealstone carvings, for example, or the trickster-stories of central Africa – it is not too much to say that for the arts in general, at all periods everywhere, myth has the same validating and energetic power as Malinowski and others have found for it in anthropological terms. **CL KMcL**

See also ethnohistory; language.

Further reading Roland Barthes, *Mythologies;* Robert Graves, *The White Goddess: a Historical Grammar of Poetic Myth;* Carolyne Larrington (ed.), *The Feminist Companion to Mythology;* Claude Lévi-Strauss, *Myth and Meaning.*

MYTHOLOGY

Mythology (Greek, 'study of myth') has two specific meanings. First, a 'mythology' is the corpus of myths, and the study of the myths, of a particular area: Amerindian mythology, Egyptian mythology and so on. Second, mythology is the study of **myth** itself. This is a discipline related to **anthropology**, **language** studies, **literature** and **theology**, and sets out to relate the myths of a given area to those of other areas, and to the beliefs and lives of the people who invented them. An important branch of such study is world mythology, a comparative study of the myths and legends of the entire world, and thus of the human race at one. **KMcL**

N

NAIVE ART

Naive art, not to be confused with **folk art** or primitive art (see **primitivism**), is the work of (usually European) artists without formal training who exhibit a lack of concern with the conventions of representation such as scientific **perspective** or the consistent use of chiaroscuro. Naive artists such as Henri Rousseau in France, Grandma Moses in the US and Alfred Wallace in the UK favour strong colours and literal drawing to express an intensely personal interest in narrative. Not all naive work is by untrained artists, Lowry and Rockwell, for example, have used 'naive' styles to infuse their work with a directness of vision and a 'commonsense' focus on narrative. **PD MG**

NAIVE REALISM

Naive realism, in **philosophy**, is the view that when we perceive objects we perceive them immediately. Our **perception** of objects is not mediated by our immediate perception of sensory experience. I do not perceive the chair by perceiving my sensory experience as of it. The chair is the immediate object of my perception.

This view contrasts with the **representative theory of perception** which holds that,

although we do perceive objects, we do not perceive them immediately. Rather, the immediate object of perception is a sensory experience which represents the object. Our perception of objects is mediated by our immediate perception of sensory experience. **AJ**

See also illusion, argument from.

Further reading A.J. Ayer, *The Central Questions of Philosophy*; J.C. Mackie, *Problems from Locke*.

NARCISSISM

The narcissus is a flower which grows from itself and needs no cross-fertilization. In Greek myth, Narcissus fell in love with his own image and would not accept that it was only his reflection. As a consequence he suffered fits of melancholia and mania until he died of starvation. The baby, like Narcissus, initially has the impression that he is self-satisfying: all his urges are satisfied by the mother who seems to be an extension of himself. This omnipotent appreciation and self-love, in classical Freudian theory, is called primary narcissism. It develops into secondary narcissism when the loss of this position results in introjecting onto and identifying with others as a way of overcoming the loss of a sense of complete control and power. A narcissistic personality would be someone who still felt that all the effects around him were a result of his energies and who was unable to modify his views in relation to reality. Havelock Ellis and Nacke used the word narcissism to describe a sexual perversion where the subject desired his own body in preference to others. The realization that other people's opinions, views, desirability, etc. exist would be a move away from the narcissistic position. **MJ**

NARRATIVE PAINTING

Narrative painting was a form of 19th-century European salon painting in which narrative played the key role. To represent their sentimental and novella-ish themes, narrative painters invariably employed a 'window-onto-the-world' structure (as if the **beholder** is seated in a theatre), with the accent on legibility, academic handling of paint and an attention to circumstantial detail. Narrative painting (which frequently drew inspiration from contemporary **literature**) was the antithesis of the (later) **modernist** interest in surface **abstraction** which draws attention to the processes of painting. Leading exponents of the genre included Baudry, Delaroche, Landseer and Wilkie. **PD MG**

NATIONAL DEBT

National debt is the total outstanding debt of a country's government (usually defined to include local as well as central government). Economists have long pondered whether the national debt is a 'burden', and if so whose burden it is. The consensus opinion is that debt due to foreign creditors is burdensome, because it has to be serviced and repaid out of a country's foreign exchange earnings (themselves a sacrifice, because exports are produced but not consumed). But debt owed to domestic creditors is not a burden for the country as a whole.

Most economists, for example, have not considered the US national debt a major problem until recent years. It was internally held that, as a nation, the citizens owed it to themselves. To pay off the debt to themselves they would tax themselves, so that it should be 'out of one pocket and into the other' for the nation as a whole. At times of repayment there might be a redistribution of income if different people were taxed than held the debt instruments, but there was no 'generation' problem of having future generations pay for current public expenditures. The sacrifice is current, it was argued; it is not passed on. At the time of the deficit people give up private goods for public goods if there is full employment. If there is not, there is no current generation sacrifice either.

Another problem arises when interest on the debt is large as a percentage of the annual budget: it becomes much more difficult to reduce the **budget deficit** because the interest comes off the top and cannot be reduced by simple legislative action to reduce the appropriation, as is a possibility for (say) highways and national defence.

Furthermore, if the deficit is large going into a recession, as it was in 1991, fiscal policy is stymied as politicians fear to pass spending legislation that would increase output and employment but would also make the deficit even larger. **TF**

See also deficit spending.

NATIONAL SOCIALISM see Nazism

NATIONALISM

Nationalism, in the words of Ernest Gellner (see below), is 'primarily a political principle, which holds that the political and national unit should be congruent'. This principle proscribes rule of the nation by non-nationals, but otherwise is variously interpreted. Some take it to mean that each nation should have its own **state**, while others believe that a nation can express its right to **self-determination** within a multinational state. Nationalist conflict emerges when nations and states do not coincide; in particular it occurs because there are far more 'nations' (communities with a common cultural and political identity) than there are states. Therefore, at any time, there are more dissatisfied than satisfied nations. The principle of nationalism threatens most actually existing states only a small minority of which are homogeneous nation-states which is why most states either pretend to be nation-states, or condemn nationalism as chauvinism, ethnocentrism, or racism.

Among many possible distinctions two types of nationalism can be clearly discerned. One, *ethnic nationalism*, assumes that the members of the nation are, or should be, those who share a common ancestral descent; while the other, *civic nationalism*, assumes that the members of the nation are, or should be, those people who are rightful citizens or inhabitants in a given territory. In particular cases these two forms of nationalism may either coincide or clash. Ethnic nationalism is more likely to give rise to racism; civic nationalism is more likely to embrace multiculturalism. However, it is worth observing that there are no purely civic nationalisms as all states adopt culturally discriminatory immigration policies. Nationalist writers hold that all nations are entitled to self-determination including independent statehood if they so desire. They argue that nationalism is democratic, since it embraces popular **sovereignty**: they also maintain that it reduces cultural conflict within states, and encourages a pluralist and diverse world rather than the forms of dictatorial control characteristic of empires or the disguised forms of cultural dominance found in cosmopolitan régimes. They also argue that internationalism, solidarity among free and self-governing nations, is the surest way of obtaining a just political order throughout the world. However, not all nationalists have been democrats, and many nationalists have favoured the political dominance of other nations by their own, sacrificing internationalism for chauvinism and **imperialism**.

Explanations of the rise and preeminence of nationalism in the modern world vary considerably. Nationalists themselves tend to maintain that there have always been nations: it is only the democratization of the world and the collapse of empires which enabled this fact to be clarified. Primordialist and sociobiologically influenced social scientists tend to agree with such nationalists, maintaining that loyalty to kinship groups is a permanent feature of human history. They see nations as extended kinship groups, and nationalism as a form of ethnic nepotism. Idealist historians, by contrast (for example Kedourie: see below), see nationalism as an idea or doctrine with a curious derivation from the principle of self-determination. They consider nationalism a pernicious and regrettable deviation from Western **liberalism**, and maintain that nations are dangerous fictions. Marxists attribute the rise of nationalism to **capitalism**, the **bourgeoisie**, the extension of the market, and the cultural homogenization they bring in their wake. They used to believe that workers were immunme to nationalism and that nationalism would be superseded under **socialism** – beliefs which now have a low market-value. Contemporary social scientists, by contrast (see Gellner and Anderson, below), usually explain nationalism as a by-product of mass literacy and commercial or **industrial** society, which create strong pressures for cultural homogenization, which in turn gives rise to nationalism on the part of both winners and losers. They think that **modernization**, literacy and advanced **media** of communication, both print and broadcasting, forge what are called 'imagined communities', in which people feel solidaristic identification with co-nationals whom they do not know personally. The strongest claim of the modernist interpreters of nationalism is that nationalists create nations rather than the other way around. Their critics (for example, Anthony Smith: see below), while not disputing the modernity of nationalism as a political principle, argue that to explain which nationalisms succeed one must examine the degree to which the relevant societies had strongly developed an authentic sense of national or ethnic consciousness in pre-modern times. Nationalists, in other words, are not likely to be successful unless their nations have some genuine ethnic foundations.

In the **arts**, nationalism is often a fruitful and generative force, the folk traditions and artistic history of a nation inspiring new creativity. A typical case-study is that of European art **music** of the 19th century. At a time when many European countries were searching for, and asserting, national identity, composers wrote works based on the **myths** and history of their country, and began using **folk music** and musical idiom as determinants of style. Previously, when folk-music styles had been brought into art music (as in Haydn's 'Gypsy Rondo' piano trio) it was an exotic, colouristic effect. Now the moods and inflexions of folk music began to affect an artist's entire composing style. Chopin's mazurkas and polonaises, for example, are overt examples of his use of national idioms, but his entire harmonic and rhythmic vocabulary – not to mention turns of piano style – have strong folk roots. Dvořák, Smetana and other Bohemian composers, Grieg in Norway amd Stanford in Ireland, all used folk ideas to edge their vocabulary away from the prevailing Germanic influence, and in Bohemia, at least, this was a political as well as an artistic decision.

By the beginning of the 20th century, research into folk music made a far larger repertoire available, and composers such as Vaughan Williams in England and Bartók in Hungary made full use of it. In fact, many of the harmonic, melodic and rhythmic elements in Bartók's music, which so alarmed traditionally-minded concert audiences in the 1920s and 1930s, were direct transcriptions of Magyar procedures. Nationalism also affected the work of such composers as Sibelius (whose music, even when not based directly on the *Kalevala*, seems to draw inspiration from Finland's very fjords and forests) and the many American composers, for example Bernstein and Copland, whose use of folk legends (such as cowboys and speakeasies) and of the forms of that quintessentially 20th-century folk music, **jazz**, give a nationalist gloss which has now – thanks to film and television imitators – become something of an international style. **DA RK KMcL BO'L**

See also colonialism; democracy; ethnicity; ethnohistory; race; social conflict; tourism, anthropology of.

Further reading Benedict Anderson, *Imagined Communities: Reflections on the Origin and Spread of Nationalism*; Ernst Gellner, *Nations and Nationalism*; E. Kedourie, *Nationalism*; J. Mayall, *Nationalism and International Society*; A. Smith, *The Ethnic Origin of Nations*.

NATURAL HAZARDS

The concept of a natural hazard involves the risk of a natural event which could damage people or property. The term is usually used for sudden events, which can vary from very slight effects to the catastrophic impacts of a major flood or earthquake. It is estimated that 2.8 million people were killed by natural events between 1968 and 1988, with the worst cases, an earthquake at Tangshan city in China and two coastal floods in Bangladesh, each killing more than a quarter of a million people. The puzzling thing about natural hazards is that millions of people continue to expose themselves to risk from natural events which are to some degree predictable. The nature of the risks and the possibilities for reducing them vary from hazard to hazard.

Earthquakes occur where movements of the Earth's crust build up tension which is suddenly released as a fault moves. They occur mainly near plate boundaries, especially where continental plates collide (especially from the Mediterranean to the Himalayas) or move past each other (as in California). Their magnitude is measured on the Richter scale, ranging from just perceptible at force 2 to massive shaking at force 9. Each step on this scale involves a tenfold increase in amplitude and a 31 fold increase in energy released. Damage depends on magnitude, distance from the epicentre, the nature of the underlying rock and the nature of buildings. Casualties tend to be greater in less-developed areas, where planning regulations and building quality are lower. For example, the 1988 Armenian earthquake was magnitude 6.9 and killed 25,000 while the San Francisco event in 1989 was magnitude 7.1 and killed 30. Although the areas most subject to earthquakes are well known, they can occur in other areas and the location and timing of future events are unpredictable. Many millions of people live in areas subject to earthquakes, including the populations of Los Angeles, San Francisco and Tokyo, so it is certain that disasters will occur in future and possible that some could have worldwide economic impact.

Earthquakes under the sea can trigger tsunami, incorrectly known as tidal waves. The worst on record occurred in Japan in 1896, when a wave 24 metres high killed 27,000 people. The wave travels very quickly – crossing the Pacific in less than 24 hours – and is almost imperceptible until it approaches land. Fortunately, the areas at risk are well known and an international warning system allows them to be evacuated, so casualties are much reduced.

Although *volcanoes* are spectacular, they are responsible for fewer recent casualties than floods or earthquakes. They also tend to occur near plate boundaries, indeed, most occur on the sea floor along ocean ridges where they affect people only on islands, such as Iceland and Hawaii. More damaging are the active volcanoes which build steep cones and sometimes explode. Krakatoa, in 1883, was such an explosion and killed 30,000 people, as was Mount St

Helens in 1980, which killed only 50 because it had been predicted and evacuation of the already sparse population had nearly been completed.

Smaller explosions can be dangerous if they trigger landslips. At worst, mudflows can descend river valleys at over 50 km/h and overwhelm settlements, as they did at Nevado del Ruiz, Colombia in 1985, killing 22,000. Lava flows are much slower and can sometimes be impeded or diverted by barriers or pumped water. In many parts of the world people continue to live on volcanoes because they create extremely fertile soils. They may persuade themselves that the volcano is extinct, though vulcanologists now prefer to consider them dormant if not recently active. The prospects for reducing casualties look good as almost all volcanoes give warning signs before erupting.

Although eruptions are a modest hazard in recent history, there are now studies which suggest that some 25 eruptions in the last 10,000 years have had global impacts. Examples are Hekla in 1159 BCE, which blew some 12 cubic kilometres of rock into the atmosphere, and the even larger Thera in 1627 BCE. Deposits of ash and sulphur compounds plus historical records suggest that these eruptions put so much dust into the stratosphere that solar radiation could hardly reach the surface and massive crop failures occurred in one or more seasons. The result was famine and depopulation on the scale predicted for the 'nuclear winter'.

The most serious causes of coastal flooding are tropical *cyclones* or *hurricanes*. These occur over the oceans between 8 and 15 degrees N&S. Cyclones are intense areas of low pressure causing torrential rain and winds which reach some 200 km/h. They quickly lose energy when they reach land, but islands and low-lying coasts can be subject to damage from wind and floods, which can raise sea levels by several metres. Areas frequently affected include the bay of Bengal and the Caribbean. In developed countries, weather forecasts offer enough warning to allow evacuation of coastal areas, though the cost of damage to buildings may be high. In poor countries like Guatemala or Bangladesh mass evacuation is less feasible, and many of the islands of Bengal are so low lying that concrete

cyclone shelters offer the only hope of survival, but the 200 shelters can accommodate only 3% of the population at risk. Yet such is the poverty and pressure on land that people still choose to live in the coastal zone.

Storm surges can occur on coasts far from the tropics. In 1953 a deep depression in the North Sea brought gales which lifted sea level two to three metres above normal and flooded large areas of Holland and East Anglia. Subsequently, very large sums have been spent in an attempt to prevent a recurrence of this flooding, and the Thames Barrier has been built to guard against the possibility of a flood in central London.

Floods are the most common and among the most damaging of natural hazards because the processes that produce the hazard are also the creators of fertile flood plains, which are rich agricultural areas. Major rivers are also the sites of cities, so hundreds of millions of people live on flood plains in the Third World, as do 10% of the population of the US. In principle, river floods seem amenable to rational precautions because past flood records can be used to calculate the probability of future floods of various depths. It should, therefore, be possible to identify and avoid areas at risk. Unfortunately, this has not proved to be true in practice. The US is an extreme case: in spite of spending $10 billion on flood protection, financial losses grew fourfold between the 1920s and the 1980s in real terms. The range of adjustments to floods includes building dams, levees and channels to prevent flooding reaching populated areas, strengthening buildings and evacuation schemes to reduce losses, land use controls to restrict building on flood plains and insurance or disaster relief to compensate victims. In practice, most of these precautions can create further problems: dams have failed, engineering structures and warning schemes encourage the belief that the problem is solved and encourage building on flood plains. Controlling such building is apparently the most cost-effective policy but few governments have been able to enforce it for long. The attractions of flood plains to farmers and developers are usually sufficient to overcome individual and institutional fear of flooding, especially because the risks are usually underestimated.

It seems certain that natural disasters will continue to extract a toll of human life and economic damage, and likely that hazards will do increasing damage. Many Third World citizens face a choice of starvation or farming in areas exposed to floods. Even people with a choice of where to live seem repeatedly to choose hazardous areas – mass immigration into California in the last 90 years or so is an example. In part this is due to lack of public knowledge of the risks, but also it seems that most people deliberately underestimate the risks to themselves. Public authorities are willing to invest in protective works, but few seem able to impose controls on exposure to hazard for long enough periods to have an effect. The best prospect seems to be for more effective systems of evacuation and disaster relief.

If these kinds of response to hazard seem irrational, it is worth remembering that even in California the probability of being killed in an earthquake is only 1 in 500,000 per annum, whereas the probability of being killed in a car crash is 1 in 20,000. **PS**

Further reading K. Smith, *Natural Hazards: Assessing Risk and Reducing Disaster.*

NATURAL LAW

The theory of natural **law**, in **political science**, suggests that all legal systems are attempts by fallible human beings to reach the legal system which would be adopted by rational human beings, a theory which in the eyes of its critics creates more problems than it solves. The theory of natural law is a species of moral **realism**: it implies that there is an objectively discoverable set of principles of right moral conduct. For natural law theorists the test of positive law – the actual set of laws in a given state – is whether or not it matches the obligations or standards set by natural law. They believe that natural law is ultimately normatively superior to positive law. For this reason they may argue that bad positive law is not in fact law – a position contrary to that maintained within **legal positivism** –

although some regard natural law as a standard of evaluation rather than as a test of legal validity.

The most famous adherents of the philosophy of natural law are Thomists – disciples of Saint Thomas Aquinas, who synthesized Catholic theology and Aristotelian metaphysics. Aquinas's view is that the contents of natural law are present in the minds of all human beings through the actions of God and they can be known by rational introspection and dialogue. The principles of natural law, on this understanding, are immutable though the Saint allowed that its doctrines might be variously developed at different times and places. **BO'L**

Further reading J.M. Finnis, *Natural Law and Natural Rights.*

NATURAL RATE OF UNEMPLOYMENT

The natural rate of unemployoment is a politician's and economist's phrase that raises hackles, yet means little more than the equilibrium rate. Like any equilibrium, it depends on the characteristics of its market and the behaviours of those supplying labour and those demanding it. If, for example, people become more selective about the jobs they will take, being prepared for longer spells of unemployment until they find out what they want, the equilibrium will tend to rise.

The notion of a natural unemployment rate is central to the debate about the Phillips Curve: is there a trade-off between **inflation** and unemployment? **Monetarists** (and others who would not call themselves that) answer no: any attempt to steer unemployment below its natural rate will produce not just higher, but accelerating, inflation. For this reason, the natural rate is sometimes known by the acronym NAIRU – the non-accelerating-inflation rate of unemployment. This makes the point that a market is not in equilibrium if the price it is setting (in this case the price of labour) is continuously accelerating. **TF**

NATURAL SELECTION

The survival of individuals in a population is determined by their relative **fitness**;

natural selection is the process that determines which individuals are most likely to survive and reproduce. The theory of natural selection was proposed by Charles Darwin and Alfred Wallace in 1858 as a result of their independent observations that the number of offspring produced by a population is generally far larger than can be sustained by the available resources. The differential survival of these offspring is driven by competition for these resources and determined by the process of natural selection, which is thus central to the concept of **evolution. RB**

See also Darwinism; group selection; kin selection; Lamarckism; sexual selection; speciation.

Further reading John Maynard-Smith, *The Theory of Evolution*.

NATURAL THEOLOGY

Natural theology is the attempt to understand God by means of rational reflection without the use of relevation, such as the Scriptures. In the 13th century, Thomas Aquinas formulated the distinction between natural and revealed theology, as opposed to older Augustinian view that there is no knowledge of God without revelation. There are four different types of argument: (a) the ontological argument which tries to show the logical necessity of God by pure reason; (b) the cosmological argument, that God was the first cause; (c) the teleological argument, that God is the last end of the Word. (These last two were developed in the 'Five Ways' of Thomas Aquinas: see **Thomism**); (d) the moral argument that people of different cultures have the same basic moral values. A contemporary form of natural theology, process theology, has recently been taken up by Roman Catholic feminist theologians, and derives from the view of A.N. Whitehead and others, that God was a factor in the **evolution** of the universe. **EMJ**

Further reading F.H. Cleobury, *A Return to Natural Theology*.

NATURALISM

Naturalism is a key idea in **philosophy**, the social sciences and the **arts**. In philosophy, it is the doctrine that all of reality is natural, that everything that exists is amenable to scientific study. Dualists – who hold that mental phenomena are nonphysical – are often accused of denying naturalism. Since they hold that the mental is not physical – they must, it is said, deny that the mental is natural. But if a phenomenon is natural just if it falls under a **law of Nature**, then dualists can allow that the mental is natural so long as they allow that there are psychophysical or psychological laws. And if **science** is the investigation of the laws of Nature, and the phenomena which fall under them, then dualists who allow that there are psychophysical or psychological laws can also allow that the mental is amenable to scientific study.

In the social sciences, naturalism is a method of study which proposes that the social world should be studied in its 'natural' state, undisturbed by the researcher. For proponents of this view, data should come from 'natural' settings, as opposed to 'artificial' settings such as experiments or formal interviews. In this sense, naturalism contrasts with the approach to study adopted by **positivism**, which has a commitment to the study of social phenomena by applying the methods used in the natural sciences. Naturalism is characterized by the belief that the social researcher should adopt an attitude of appreciation and fidelity for the social world under study: social science has no business in importing research methods from the natural sciences, because social phenomena have a character quite distinct from natural phenomena. Naturalism takes issue with the assumption of positivism that the social world can be understood by means of causal relationships or in terms of universal laws. Naturalists argue that this is not possible because human actions are based upon social meanings, intentions, attitudes and beliefs. Proponents of naturalism maintain that in order to understand people's behaviour an approach must be adopted that gives access to the meanings which guide behaviour.

In the arts, naturalism is of crucial importance in fine **art**, **literature** and

drama. In fine art, it is the attempt to imitate the appearance of the everyday world without the intervention of preconceived ideas or conventions. While much recent thinking has shown that this 'innocent-eye' approach is itself conventionalized and open to the play of the imagination and intellect – simply by making a work of art, even when you take a photograph, you interpose your creative self and your ideas between Nature and the spectator – the concept of naturalism has been part of the occidental way of seeing since the **Renaissance**, when Alberti (writing in 1436) declared that the artist's 'business' is to 'copy Nature'. The idea seems commonplace, but thinking about it is an activity which itself affects the artist's approach to his or her 'business'. In the 17th and 18th centuries, art scholars in Europe had a fine time discussing such matters as whether naturalism was compatible with idealism – they came to the conclusion that it was, arguing that the most naturalistic of all art had been produced by the artists of ancient Greece, but that while those creators had remained close to 'true' nature (that is, had been anatomically correct), they had also shown the limitless potential of the human spirit. By the 19th century, however, Naturalism in art-scholarly circles had taken on its current meaning: that is, referring to art which is (a) representational, and (b) associated by analogy with the empirical procedures of science, the rendering of appearances through minute observation of the natural world (as can be seen for example in the work of the **Impressionists**).

In literature, similarly, 19th-century adherents of naturalism advocated **fiction** which was 'scientifically' accurate. Social and historical settings and material objects should be described with meticulous accuracy, and character-development and interaction should conform to the discoveries of geneticists, psychologists and physiologists. This replacement of fantasy with science as a motor of creativity distinguishes naturalist writers from **realists** (whose work is predominantly descriptive rather than analytical). The chief late 19th-century exponents of naturalism were Dostoevsky and Zola, and their methods (rather than their ideas) influenced other writers of the time, notably Bennett in Britain and Dreiser in the US. In the 20th century, naturalism took its place as one of many 'isms' affecting the writing of fiction; it is a component (one of many) in the work of writers otherwise as distinct as Hemingway, Mauriac, Mishima, Salinger, Simenon and Wells.

In drama, 19th-century naturalism followed similar lines, reflecting the replacement by inquiry and analysis of the earlier view that human life depended on fate or other forces beyond our determination. Playwrights such as Ibsen, Chekhov and Strindberg, and practitioners such as Stanislavski and Antoine, produced plays and performances showing that human beings, while constrained by a material environment which might be difficult to change, still had the possibility of overcoming their condition. (This thought is central, for example, to Chekhov's *Three Sisters*, Ibsen's *A Doll's House* and Strindberg's *The Father*). Through accurate reproduction in sets, costumes and language, the lives as well as the prevailing ideas of characters reflected those of their audience. In the 20th century, by contrast, naturalism waned as a cultural force for change in drama: on stage, in films and on television, naturalistic drama is an entertaining but predominantly mechanical representation of contemporary society, and those dramatists who want to bring about change usually work in other styles. **DA PD MG AJ KMcL JM**

See also action perspective; bourgeois drama; epic theatre; idiographic; individualism; social realism; structure-agency debate; symbolic interactionism; understanding; problem play and well-made play.

Further reading H. Blumer, *Symbolic Interactionism*; Lilian R. Furst, *Naturalism*; E.H. Gombrich, *Art and Illusion*; R. Williams, *Drama from Ibsen to Brecht*.

NATURALISTIC FALLACY

The naturalistic fallacy, in **philosophy**, is the (supposed) fallacy of inferring an 'ought' from an 'is'. From statements only concerning how things actually are one cannot validly infer statements about how things ought to be. From the statement of fact, 'torturing cats causes them unnecessary pain', one cannot validly derive the conclusion that 'one ought not to torture cats'. One can only validly derive the conclusion if one adds a premise which is itself an 'ought' statement such as that 'one ought not to cause unnecessary pain'. **AJ**

See also descriptivism and prescriptivism; fact and value.

Further reading W. Hudson, *The Is/Ought Question; Modern Moral Philosophy*.

NATURE/CULTURE

We commonly make a distinction between nature and **culture**, on the premise that humans differ from animals. Culture is contrasted with nature by referring to the system of social rules which regulate the lives of individuals. This polarity is often seen as fundamental to the organization of human cultural systems.

In an evolutionary perspective, humans were regarded as progressing from a state of nature (seen as something wild and untamed) to that of culture through the institution of social ties based on contractual arrangements rather than kinship obligations. Kinship systems which promoted the exchange of women between communities were supported by the **incest** taboo.

Evolutionary ideas also attempted to provide a natural explanation for **gender** differences. Women were assumed to be 'naturally' closer to nature because of their child-bearing capacities, while culture was considered the province of men because they tended to organize and run society. The anthropology of gender has questioned this **ethnocentric** assumption, and demonstrated that even where these categories have social relevance, they are subject to variable interpretation. In those societies recognizing an opposition between the categories of nature and culture, their associated qualities are sometimes reversed. For instance, children may be associated with nature, and the role of both men and women is therefore to mediate between nature and culture. The concept of nature is by no means universal, and can itself be seen as a cultural con-

struct, in the sense that it is a category created as a product of philosophical speculation. **CL**

Further reading C. MacCormack and M. Strathern (eds.), *Nature, Culture and Gender*.

NATURE/NURTURE see Nature/Culture

NAZISM

Nazi is an abbreviation of the title of the Nationalist Socialist German Worker's Party (NSDAP: Nationalsozialistische Deutsche Arbeiterpartei), led by Adolf Hitler from 1921 until 1945. The **ideology** of the Nazi movement was based on an obnoxious but powerful synthesis of **fascism**, **imperialism**, racism, ethnic **nationalism** and **anti-semitism**.

Attempts to explain the rise of the Nazi party and the appeal of Nazism in interwar Germany focus on seven factors: (1) defeat in World War I and the impositions of the Versailles Treaty injured the collective pride of the German nation, which the Nazi movement offered to restore through reasserting the superiority of 'the Aryan race'; (2) the economic collapse occasioned by the Great Depression (1929–32) which undermined the credibility of the democratic Weimar Republic and created opportunities for an alliance united under the Nazi's programme of 'national socialism'; (3) the economic collapse also facilitated the anti-semitism and racism of the Nazis, encouraging 'scapegoating' of Jews who were accused of dominating the world banking system and the communist movement; (4) the pervasive fear of Soviet and German **communism**, which rallied many conservative traditionalists to the Nazis as the lesser of two evils; (5) the authoritarian and cultural burden of Germany's past which made the Weimar republic a democracy without enough democrats to support it under crisis; (6) the skilful ability of Nazi propagandists to synthesize contradictory ideas with broad appeal (nationalism for conservatives, **socialism** for workers, anti-communism for the bourgeoisie, and anti-semitism for those looking for scapegoats); and (7) the miscalculations of opponents and rivals of

Hitler and the Nazis. Between 1928 and 1932 the Nazi party's percentage of the vote increased from about three percent to over thirty-seven percent. In 1933 Hitler was made chancellor in a coalition government which enabled him to consolidate power with a mixture of constitutional and unconstitutional measures. By the following year he had declared himself the sole leader (Führer) of the official one-party state, under the slogan 'one people, one party, one leader'.

The two infamous legacies of Hitler's dictatorship, World War II, and the genocide of over six million Jews, Communists, Gypsies and others, were extensions of Nazi ideology, as articulated in Hitler's *Mein Kampf*. Hitler attempted to exterminate all the Jews of Europe and other 'degenerate persons' to eliminate the perceived threat to 'racial hygiene'. The territorial expansion of Nazi Germany into Austria, Czechoslovakia and Poland which led to World War II was meant to create sufficient 'living space' for the 'Aryan race' to dominate the rest of the world.

Although unsuccessful in achieving the 'final solution' Hitler's consolidation of power and the extent of the atrocities committed under the influence of Nazi ideology demonstrate the power which ideology and charismatic authority can exert under conditions of political, social and economic uncertainty, and the fearsome possibilities of **totalitarian** government. Neo-nazi movements exist in many parts of the contemporary world, especially where the social strains of massive immigration coexist with economic crises and depressions. While we can be confident that modern Germany has sufficiently strong democratic institutions to withstand the challenges posed by neo-nazi extremism, the same cannot be said about the newly democratized régimes of eastern Europe and the former Soviet Union which are potentially susceptible to domination by charismatic figures spouting nazi-style propaganda, as exemplified by the proponents of 'ethnic-cleansing' in what was Yugoslavia. **BO'L**

See also conservatism.

Further reading A. Bullock, *Hitler: a Study in Tyranny*; J. Noakes and G. Pridham (eds.), *Nazism 1919–45: a Documentary Reader* (3 vols.); E. Nolte, *Three Faces of Fascism*.

NECESSARY AND SUFFICIENT CONDITIONS

One cannot vote unless one is 18. So being 18 is a necessary condition for voting. But being 18 is not a sufficient condition for voting. It is not enough for voting that one is 18. Criminals who are 18 cannot vote, for example. **AJ**

NECESSITY see Modality

NECROMANCY

Necromancy (Greek, 'corpse-prophecy') is prophesying by contacting the dead. It was and in some places still is a standard practice in societies which believed that people's spirits remained part of the community after death, and could be contacted if the right agents performed the appropriate **rituals** in the correct way. (A standard way was for the agent to go into a trance, that is to enter the world of the dead without leaving that of the living, and report back; a rarer way was for the spirits to be encouraged to manifest themselves in the world of the living, either as artificially induced 'natural' phenomena such as wind rustling in leaves or mysterious knockings, or by speaking or otherwise communicating through a medium.)

The point of necromancy is that the dead are thought to live outside human time, and to have access to the past and future which is denied to those still bound by mortality. From the standpoint of scientific rationality, necromancy may seem to belong to the lunatic fringes of superstition. But communication with the dead, and invitations to them to help the living (for example by predicting our future) is standard practice in many societies and religious systems, and is current, in a bastardized, secularized and charlatan-ridden form, in seances and ouija-board sessions throughout the world. It may be possible to draw distinctions between such practices and the ceremonies of voodoo priests or shamans, or between shamans raising dead spirits and Saul in the Old Testament calling up the Witch of Endor, or between all such events and the Roman Catholic evocation of saints and martyrs but it is hard, from outside the belief-systems in question, to be quite sure where exactly those distinctions lie. **KMcL**

NEGATIVE CAPABILITY

'Negative capability' was Keats's phrase for the state of receptivity required for artistic, and specifically literary, creation. The author should open himself or herself up to all experience, become the person or thing being written about. Keats himself named Shakespeare as the prime instance of negative capability in English literature. In Keats's own century, Flaubert and Tolstoy both aspired to the condition, and more recent times have been blessed by Proust's magnificent failure to do so. As to Keats himself, the critical jury is, perhaps, still out. **KMcL**

NÉGRITUDE

Négritude ('blackness') was a literary movement originated in the 1930s by French-speaking black writers who wanted to reassert the cultural values of Africa in place of colonial, European literary culture. The movement (though not the name) has survived, on the one hand taking in the work of writers like Chinua Achebe and Wole Soyinka in Africa itself, and on the other inspiring politico-cultural activism like that in the US during the late 1980s, when students and staff in some campuses proclaimed a reluctance to have anything to do with a culture dominated by DWEMs (Dead White European Males). **KMcL**

NEO-DARWINISM see **Darwinism**

NEO-LAMARCKISM see **Lamarckism**

NEOCLASSICISM see **Classicism**

NEOCOLONIALISM see **Colonialism and Neocolonialism**

NEOEXPRESSIONISM see **Expressionism**

NEOGRAMMARIAN HYPOTHESIS

The Neogrammarians were a group of German linguists working within the field of **comparative-historical linguistics** towards the end of the 19th century. They were notable for their desire to establish a rigorous methodology for investigating how the pronunciation of a language changes over time. An overriding claim was that sound changes take place gradually, but strictly in accordance with phonetic laws which are applicable, without exception, to the entire range of potential targets for change.

The Neogrammarians claimed that sound changes originate in the **language** of one particular speaker and then spread in a regular fashion to other individuals and groups, for reasons of prestige. These changes are said to filter down from the top strata of society towards the bottom. They are initiated, in part, because speakers do not pronounce a particular word in precisely the same way on each occasion of utterance. It was argued that the regular repetition of minor deviations from standards of pronunciation may be cumulative and lead towards the establishment of a new norm. A further source of sound change was said to be the speech of children learning their mother tongue. It was suggested that children are liable to misperceive the speech of adults, with the result that they produce their own, idiosyncratic, versions of linguistic elements which eventually take root and become permanent changes within the language. In fact, there is scant evidence to support this hypothesis, as is the case with many Neogrammarian claims. Yet their desire to place linguistics on a truly scientific footing has exerted a lasting influence. **MS**

NEOIMPRESSIONISM see **Impressionism**

NEOPLASTICISM

Neoplasticism, or De Stijl ('The Style'), was an **art** movement founded by the painter and architect Theo van Doesburg in Leiden in 1917. Founder members of the group included the painter Mondrian, the sculptor Vantongerloo, the architect J.J.P. Oud, and the designer and architect Gerrit Riet-veld. In October 1917 van Doesburg started the magazine *De Stijl*, which took its name from the group. Mondrian's article, *The New Plastic in Painting*, best expresses their ideas for a universal, elemental art divorced from the need to serve representation: 'The new plastic art ... can only be based on the abstraction of all form and colour, i.e. the straight line and the clearly defined primary colour.'

Neoplasticism rejected figuration as the goal of art, and replaced it with the pared-down vocabulary of elemental shapes and primary colours, thereby allowing art to express its own 'plastic' language free of the concerns of representation. The artist in this environment became less the author of a subjective work than the agent of a universal harmony – a goal that leapt the millennia back to prehistoric artists and conformed with the artistic ideals of 'primitive' Greece. The depersonalization of the work of art was carried through into the execution, which was anonymous and impersonal, for example in Mondrian's *Composition with Red, Yellow and Blue* (1930). Nonetheless, many De Stijl paintings are abstractions of natural phenomena, such as van Doesburg's *Rhythms of a Russian Dance* (1918).

In the 1920s, while Mondrian's work adhered to the strict principles of Neoplasticism, van Doesburg sought to broaden the influence of the movement into **architecture**. The austere forms of De Stijl were well suited to the geometric structures favoured by the International **Modernist** movement, while the primary colours favoured by the painters could be used as decorative elements to articulate an otherwise plain facade, for instance in Oud's *Café De Unie* in Rotterdam (1925). Likewise, Rietveld's *Red and Blue Chair* (1917), painted in primary colours and revealing its structure, offers itself for analysis like a Mondrian painting.

The principles of De Stijl art and design had considerable influence on the Bauhaus in the 1920s, and, following Mondrian's emigration to New York in 1940, in the US. **MG PD**

Further reading P. Overy, *De Stijl*.

NETWORK THEORY

The Network Theory, in electrical engineering, permits the mathematical analysis of large electrical circuits (for example the vast network which supplies electrical power to millions of homes). Much early work in Network Theory concentrated on the development of electrical filters, first used in telephony in the 1910s. The theory permits large, complicated systems to be broken down into smaller sub-systems, with known boundary conditions, and solved. The overall system response is then determined by combining the result of the interaction between the sub-systems. A powerful development from network analysis theory is network synthesis, where the process begins with the mathematical equations representing the desired electrical functions, and produces the electrical circuit components and values required.

The main modern use of network theory and synthesis in electrical engineering is in Computer Aided Design (CAD), for example of microelectronic circuits. CAD enables complicated electrical circuits, having many thousands of components, to be designed and tested without having to be physically constructed, and this allows cost-effective, rapid design and development. For instance, development of modern silicon 'chips' was only made possible through the use of CAD simulation programmes which used network theory.

In the **life sciences**, Network Theory is the idea that the immune response is self-regulated by the interaction between antibodies and their idiotypes. The production of specific antibodies against non-self molecules (antigens) is a central function of the immune response and involves recognition at the molecular level leading to binding between antigen and antibody. It has been demonstrated experimentally that antibodies which recognize non-self molecules are seen by the immune system as being antigenic in themselves; this antigenicity is referred to as the idiotype and may stimulate the production of anti-idiotype antibodies which, theoretically, may have structural similarities to the original antigen. Furthermore, the anti-idiotype antibodies are themselves antigenic. Jerne's network theory suggests that such anti-idiotype interactions are responsible for immunoregulation by homeostatic mechanisms and by the amplification of the immune response to specific antigens. Direct experimental evidence for such a role is hard to obtain but the implications of the network theory have been accepted as important. **RB AC**

See also homeostasis; immunology.

Further reading Ivan Roitt, *Immunology*.

NEUROLINGUISTICS

The study of neurolinguistics is concerned with the relationship between **language** and the brain. The ultimate aim in this discipline is to discover the neurological foundations both for our knowledge of language and for our ability to use language. The initial impetus in the field was provided by the study of language pathology, in which language disorders are explained in terms of underlying neurological dysfunctions. Language disorders which have been acquired (either through disease or accident) provided many early insights in the sub-discipline of **aphasiology**. Other disorders can often be traced to difficulties arising from around the time of birth, either due to problems during pregnancy, in the delivery process, or in the postnatal period. Language disorders are commonly classified in terms of a predictable group of symptoms, known as a syndrome, which can often allow the patient's unusual language behaviour to be traced back to specific types and regions of damage to the brain.

A prevalent assumption in neurolinguistics is that language occupies distinct mental faculties, and that individual aspects of language are located in a number of distinct modules, each with a distinct physical and mental realization. However, this concept of **modularity** is by no means an inevitable outcome of neurolinguistic research and it remains somewhat controversial.

Recently, pathological research has been complemented by investigations of language functioning in people with normal, undamaged brains. Several ingenious techniques have been developed which provide the researcher with a window on the relationship between brain and language. For example, it is now well established that the two hemispheres of the brain are specialized for certain cognitive functions. In general, it has been found that the core aspects of language, namely, **phonology**, **syntax** and **semantics**, are located in the left hemisphere of most people. (For a minority of people, these aspects of language are processed in the right hemisphere, but the principle of specialization holds true).

One of the techniques which helped establish this finding is the so-called Wada technique. In this method, sodium amytal is injected into either the left or the right carotid artery of the neck. The result is the temporary immobilization of one side of the brain. And while one half of the brain is inactive, researchers can conduct various tests in order to establish which particular language functions have been lost. Using this technique, the broad discovery of left hemisphere dominance has been supplemented by more subtle findings. For example, it has emerged that the right hemisphere is used in the processing of concrete lexical items whose referents can be easily visualized (for example, table, dog), while more abstract words are processed in the left hemisphere (such as truth or goodness). The Wada technique is just one method which has allowed many startling discoveries to be made in the field of neurolinguistics, although we must acknowledge that huge advances are still necessary in order to fully illuminate the neurological foundations of language. **MS**

Further reading D. Crystal, *An Introduction to Language Pathology*; M.L.E. Espir and F.C Rose, *The Basic Neurology of Speech and Language*.

NEUROPSYCHIATRY

Neuropsychiatry, also once known as organism, emerged in the 19th century. To relieve emotional disorders it searches for biological causes such as chemical or neurological abnormalities and applies drugs, somatic treatments and other physical methods (for example, electroconvulsive therapy and brain surgery).

Inquiries about a patient's thoughts and feelings are made primarily as a basis for making diagnosis. Abnormal states of thought and feeling are regarded simply as manifestations of an underlying physical process, or as possible clues to a disturbance in neurochemistry; they are not explored to provide explanations for abnormal psychological states.

Many neuropsychiatrists, without abandoning their notion of physical causation, prescribe a variety of practical remedies for neurosis including re-education, encouragement and environmental change.

Neuropsychiatry is similar to both **behaviourism** and **psychoanalysis** in believing that the cause of the patient's illness is outside the patient's awareness. **MJ**

NEUROSES

Neuroses have been regarded throughout the history of modern **psychology** to be the result of secrets. Moritz Benedikt published in the mid- to late 19th century cases of **hysteria** and other neuroses, showing that their causes were secrets, usually pertaining to sexual life. **Mesmerism** and hypnotism recognized that hidden aspects cause neurotic illness. In Freud this idea of the pathogenic secret became further developed in the notions of trauma, reminiscences, repression and guilt feelings, and he too saw neuroses as a result of repressed **sexuality**. The Reverend Pfister of Zurich used the cure of souls in his 19th-century practice, uncovering the unpleasant memories that made his patients and parishioners ill or depressed. Adler thought that neuroses were the result of **inferiority complexes** and the resulting **masculine protest**. Jung saw them as a result of an imbalance of types within the self. Types of neuroses have been variously described as traumatic, war neuroses, anxiety neuroses, hysteria, neurasthenia (male hysteria), obsessions, phobias and transference neuroses (in **psychoanalysis**). **MJ**

NEUTRAL MONISM

Monism (from Greek *monos*, 'single') is (roughly) the **philosophical** doctrine that there is really only one sort of stuff. Materialists often claim that mental things are really physical, and that there is really only one sort of stuff, the physical. Idealists claim that physical things are really mental, and that there is really only one sort of stuff, the mental. Neutral monists are also **monists**, but they do not claim that the mental is physical, or that the physical is mental. Rather, both are made up from different arrangements of the same neutral stuff. **AJ**

See also dualism; idealism; materialism.

NEW APOCALYPSE see Apocalyptic Literature

NEW ARTISTIC DANCE see Abstract Dance

NEW CRITICISM

New criticism shifts attention from the author of a work to the work itself. It treats a literary text (any text, but usually a poem) as a freestanding entity with its own style and structure. Close attention to these factors – employing such techniques as statistical analysis – will elucidate its 'meaning', but considerations of its place in its author's output, or even its relationship to other works of the same period or kind, are quite secondary. The notion of the critic-as-connoisseur is replaced by that of the critic-as-scientist: a bracing and still not universally accepted trend.

In **music**, similar techniques of analysis and **deconstruction** are used to give a quasi-objective analysis of how a composition 'works'. The trend began with the rigorous elucidation of the mathematical structures underlying **serial music**, but the methods have since begun to be applied to music of all periods and kinds, from medieval motets to *gamelan*, from Mozart's melodic structures to heavy metal. As with new criticism in **literature**, the movement in music is largely confined to universities, and has had little impact on the art at large. **KMcL**

See also criticism.

NEW DEAL

The New Deal was the name given to the policies enacted by President Franklin Roosevelt from 1933 onwards, to counter the **depression**. The Roosevelt administration adopted largely Keynesian **macroeconomic** policies (see **Keynesian theory**): the federal budget, which balanced in 1930 with spending of $3.6 billion, had a deficit of $5 billion in 1936 (and spending of more than $9 billion). The national debt roughly doubled, from $16 billion to $32 billion.

New Deal **microeconomic** policies were also more interventionist. Trade unions were encouraged; agricultural prices were raised and farmers were paid for the first time to restrict their acreage; the Securities and Exchange Commission was set up in 1934 to regulate American stock exchanges; and the National Industrial Recovery Act of 1933 established the Federal Trade Commission to enforce anti-trust laws.

The results of the New Deal will remain controversial as long as economists have breath in their bodies. Keynesians point to the 8 million rise in employment between 1933 and 1937 (though there were still 7 million unemployed in 1937), and the doubling of industrial production between 1932 and 1937. Non-Keynesians say that recovery was already beginning in 1932, before the New Deal started. Private investment in 1937 was still 8% below its 1929 level because, critics say, entrepreneurs were suspicious of the New Deal and profits were artificially held down. And the recovery ran out of steam in 1937, despite the continuing growth of the **budget deficit**, in the sceptics' view, the fate of all Keynesian recoveries. **TF**

NEW FICTION

New Fiction was a new approach to writing a **novel**, which emerged in France in the late 1950s at much the same time as **New Wave** cinema. Its chief writers were Michel Butor,

Alain Robbe-Grillet and Nathalie Sarraute. Their aim was to abandon the methods of older fiction (such as consecutive narrative, orderly characterization and above all authorial and 'philosophical' comment), and to produce a new fiction suitable for a new age. For the general reader, the **avant-garde** techniques in their work (for instance, dislocated narrative, obsessive attention to apparently trivial or inconsequential details, a feeling of life as ritual or charade) ally it both to the **theatre of the absurd** (Samuel Beckett's and Jean Genet's works, including their novels, are major influences) and to the films of such men as Godard and Resnais. Apart from those mentioned, the finest French New Wave novelist is Marguerite Duras. Outside France – and despite the growth of **new criticism** in universities everywhere – there are few thoroughgoing exponents, though writers as far apart as Jorge Luis Borges, Lawrence Durrell and Günter Grass use some of the new novelists' techniques. **KMcL**

NEW MATHEMATICS

'New' mathematics is the name given to trends in recent **mathematics** to become more dependent on **set theory** and **logic** and, particularly, to attempts dating back to the 1960s to teach mathematics by emphasizing these branches rather than more traditional methods. The idea was to make mathematics more accessible by teaching the ideas that lay at the heart of the subject, and particularly **deduction**. The problem, it became apparent in the 1970s, was that the children failed to understand these concepts and were also unable to carry out the most basic operations of arithmetic. So began the 'back to basics' approach, a return to teaching mathematics by drill and practice of elementary skills. However, it was soon realized that children were memorizing this rote-learning without understanding it, and were therefore unable to apply their knowledge to problems. The approach to mathematical education which has come out of this is to attempt to teach methods of problem solving. **SMcL**

NEW MUSIC, THE

'The New Music' is a phrase regularly used

by European innovators to claim some kind of artistic high ground: Wagner's followers, for example, claimed that his work was 'new music', a reinvention of the art. Perhaps two such claims are more valid than most. In the early 17th century, art music composers such as Caccini (who coined the term 'New Music') used it for work which consisted of a solo line with accompaniment, as compared with the predominantly contrapuntal styles preferred till then. The arrival of a mainly vertical style of music (as against a mainly horizontal style) revolutionized the art. Wagner's work, three centuries later, is merely a refinement and continuation of processes already there. The second claim is late-20th century, and is on behalf of **electronic music**. This again is an entirely 'new music', since both the generation of sounds and the way they are subsequently treated depend on methods, and technical resources, unknown before. **KMcL**

NEW ORLEANS

New Orleans is usually claimed as the original home of **jazz**, and New Orleans jazz as both a style in itself and the matrix for all later styles. It was developed during the 1890s to 1920s from dance tunes and marches. Players took the basic tunes, with their underlying chords, and 'swung' them: syncopating the rhythms, colouring the harmony by adding 'non-essential' notes based on the overtones from the harmonic series on brass instruments (usually suppressed in 'formal' harmony of the time), and inserting 'blue' notes into the melodies (flattenings of the thirds and sevenths of the scale). Choruses (playings of the basic tune) alternated with solo 'breaks': free improvisations by the leading singers or players. The bands usually consisted of trumpet (or cornet), trombone and clarinet, plus a harmony and rhythm section using all or some of piano, guitar, banjo, bass and drums. A feature of the style was the way the players inspired one another, a snatch of improvised tune or rhythm being taken up and developed by the whole band in a kind of controlled inventive frenzy. This method was particularly favoured in the kind of New Orleans jazz played by the first bands to make recordings, and it carried the jazz style

round the world. These bands often called themselves 'Dixieland' bands, perhaps thinking it would be more recognizable than 'New Orleans'. Thus, the most complex kind of New Orleans jazz is still known as **Dixieland**; it is more frenzied, wilder, than pure New Orleans style. In Europe, New Orleans jazz and Dixieland jazz are both popularly called 'traditional'. **KMcL**

NEW RELIGIOUS MOVEMENTS

The New Religious Movements aggressively evangelize on the streets of western Europe and the US, and strongly appeal to young, educated people, who respond with intense commitment.

The question has been raised as to whether these movements are new at all or whether they are not a permanent phenomenon which surfaces in times of social dislocation. Similar movements appeared in Rome in the 1st century CE, in 14th-century France and in Europe during the Reformation – though there were two further elements, popular upheaval and the continual threat of war. One feature common to all such movements, apart from the youthfulness of their adherents and their social mobility, is the degree to which the established social and religious order feels threatened. In the US this has even led to family members kidnapping the young people involved and 'de-programming' them. It is significant that New Movements appear at a time of declining church membership, and, in the case of traditional Oriental religions, when the impact of secularism and consumerism is being felt for the first time.

Although the New Movements are not monolithic, but have fluctuating structures, beliefs and assets, they usually fall into one of three, broad categories: (1) new religious movements originating from within Christianity itself; (2) movements shaped by Western psychology and therapeutic subculture; (3) movements derived from – often distantly – Asiatic religions. The Children of God would be an example of the first, **Scientology** of the second, and the Unification Church of the third. Those in the second category particularly emphasize self-improvement,   self-assertion   and enhancement of life. All offer a way of salvation in a hostile society, in a world of decay and alternative social relationships. Salvation might be achieved, for example, after initiation into the group and satisfying the group of one's commitment by giving away one's property. There is rigorous discipline and members may have to change their jobs or give up regular outside employment altogether. The drop-out rate is high, but (as with numbers leaving the Roman Catholic priesthood) the figures are not advertised. In some movements, celibacy is strictly enforced, while in others (for example the Unification Church or Moonies) the organization arranges all marriages. Many movements have a charismatic leader and there is considerable overlap with **guru movements**.

Another debatable question is whether these movements are new religions in embryonic form and genuinely innovative, or whether they are outbreaks of **fundamentalism** drawing the alienated and secularized back to their roots. The majority of them grew up in the counter-culture of the 1960s and 1970s, achieving peak membership in the late 1970s. Most movements are now in a state of consolidation or crisis as a second-generation leadership is required. Today's new religious movement is often tomorrow's mainline denomination. However bizarre some examples may be their appeal is evidence of the continuing human need for faith to make sense of life, and the creativity of that faith. **KDS**

See also cults.

Further reading Eileen Barker, *The Making of a Moonie: Choice or Brainwashing?*; Allan Brockway and J. Paul Rajashekar (eds.), *Movements and the Churches*; Bryan Wilson, *The Social Dimensions of Sectarianism*.

NEW WAVE

New Wave (*nouvelle vague*) was the name given to a large group of film directors who began working in French cinema in the late 1950s – in 1959–60 alone, principal photography began on 67 individual projects. The New Wave swept aside such established names as Marcel Carné, René Clément and even Jean Renoir. For all the bitterness felt in the profession at the time, the change was salutary: Chabrol, Godard, Malle, Resnais, Rohmer, Truffaut and Vadim created a vigorous new tradition, capable of infinite variety, from the loose, quasi-documentary style of Godard to the imponderabilities of Renais and to Chabrol's Hitchcockian panache. The 'New Wave Style', however, is best exemplified in the films of Truffaut and Malle, and as such has influenced foreign directors from Antonioni to Altman, from Forman to Kubrick. Its main characteristics are a recognizably personal directorial imprint on each film (the director as *'auteur'* of the experience, that is, prime organizer and creative guarantor, is a vital concept in New Wave criticism), a tendency towards understatement and intellectual fastidiousness (very unlike the raucous, ever-bigger and splashier style of Hollywood films of the same period and subsequently), and a loose, fluid style of shooting and montage influenced by television. There have been two subsequent 'New Waves' (the term is a handy critical reach-me-down): one in the US (led by Coppola, Scorsese and the young Spielberg) and one in Germany (led by Fassbinder and Herzog). **KMcL**

See also auteur theory.

Further reading P. Graham (ed.), *The New Wave*.

NEWTON'S LAWS

Everyone has heard the story of Isaac Newton and the apple tree, but the truth behind his laws of gravitation are more complex than a simple story.

Sir Isaac Newton (1642–1727) was born in a small Lincolnshire village. At the age of 19 he was sent to Trinity College Cambridge and by the age of 24 he had made important discoveries in **mathematics**, **optics** and **mechanics**. His book *Philosophiae Naturalis Principa Mathematica*, published in 1687, helped to explain many mysteries about the universe such as the tides.

Newton's work describing the laws of motion were seen as a great advance in the understanding of the physical world. His theories still stand valid today for velocities and dimensions within a person's normal experience, but fail for velocities approaching the speed of light or subatomic dimensions.

Newton's main laws cover kinematics, motion, gravitation and momentum. Kinematics (or the science of motion) is covered by four equations that cover the motion of any body moving in a straight line with uniform acceleration. These equations can be adapted to apply to rotational movement and Newton developed the concept of centrifugal force.

Newton's three laws of motion are as follows:

(1) A body will stay at rest or travel in a straight line at constant speed unless acted upon by an external force.

(2) The resultant force exerted on a body is directly proportional to the acceleration produced by the force.

(3) To every action there is an equal and opposite reaction.

The law concerning the conservation of momentum follows from the third law. The principle states

(4) that before and after a collision, two bodies will have the same momentum, but there is an important rider that there will always be a change in the total energy of the two bodies.

The gravitational force that Newton discovered is one of the **four forces** that occur in nature. (The others are electromagnetic force and the strong and weak interatomic forces.) Newton discovered that every body in the universe attracts every other body. This law applies to the stars in space, but can also be demonstrated by setting up a pendulum beside a large mountain. After thousands of swings the path of the pendulum can be measured to have approached the mountain by a small amount.

Newton's laws have been the basis of most analysis in mechanics and engineering from his time to the present. **AA**

Further reading H. Goldstein, *Classical Mechanics*.

NICHE

Life scientists generally define a biological niche as the status of an organism in its environment, both biotic and abiotic. The niche that an organism occupies is comparable with its habitat, but incorporates ecological variables such as position in **space and time**, and interaction with other organisms. Thus the habitat of a bird may be a particular type of woodland, whereas its niche describes the role which it plays within that habitat; what and where it eats, where it nests, etc. Implicit in the term niche is the conclusion that without the bird the woodland is different. Differences between niches can be subtle, but, by definition, only one species can occupy a given niche. The occupying species is, however, likely to experience competition from other species living in similar niches this is known as the competitive exclusion principle. The idea of the niche is thus rooted in **speciation** and **natural selection**, and is therefore dynamic. Where similar habitats are geographically isolated, each may contain similar niches occupied by very different species these are termed ecological equivalents. **RB**

See also ecosystem; fitness.

NO-OWNERSHIP THEORY OF THE SELF

The no-ownership, or no subject, theory of the self is the **philosophical** doctrine that mental events do not belong to the mental subject who undergoes them. Nothing can be owned by someone unless its ownership can be transferred to another by being given or sold to them, for example. But mental events cannot be transferred in this manner. Therefore, they are not owned by the mental subject who undergoes them. **AJ**

See also self.

Further reading P.F. Strawson, *Individuals*.

NOMINAL ESSENCE see **Essence**

NOMINALISM see **Universals and Particulars**

NON-EUCLIDEAN GEOMETRY

The *Elements* of Euclid, formulated in the 3rd century BCE, for almost 2,000 years seemed to be the last word in **geometry**; they gave a system of **axiomatization** for geometry together with a large number of theorems proved using just these axioms. But one axiom, the parallel axiom (stating that given a line L and a point *a* not on L there is a unique line through *a* which is parallel to L i.e. not intersecting it everywhere) did not seem in the same realm of obviousness as the others, especially as a pair of parallel lines (for example, railway tracks) do appear to meet on the horizon. For this reason, mathematicians spent many years trying to prove that the parallel axiom was a consequence of the other axioms. These attempts led directly to the development of non-Euclidean geometry, because researchers began to try and prove it using **proof by contradiction**, which meant that they were assuming that the axiom was not true and were trying to derive a contradiction from this.

Although none was ever found, it was not until the early 19th century that anyone was daring enough to suggest that this meant that a new kind of geometry had been discovered in which the parallel axiom was not true. Johann Bolyai (1802–60) and Nicholas Lobachevsky (1792–1856) were the two obscure mathematicians who first had the courage to put this idea forward, to establishment derision. It gradually became clear that they were right, and non-Euclidean geometry was established on an equal footing with the Euclidean variety.

Non-Euclidean geometry may appear at first only to be a mental exercise, something that is purely a construct of the imagination. After all, space seems Euclidean and engineering from start to finish. In **architecture**, Euclidean geometry is used with great success in the everyday, and that would seem to be convincing proof.

One of the major predictions of non-Euclidean geometry is that no triangle has the sum of its angles being 180°, whereas Euclidean geometry says that all triangles have the sum of their angles being exactly that figure. Karl Friedrich Gauss (1777–1832) set out to show that the universe was Euclidean, by shining lights between three mountain peaks several miles apart and measuring the angles between them. He discovered that the triangle thus formed was Euclidean up to the limits of his measuring devices. The problems with this approach are that the defect of the triangle could be too small to measure (so that it is never possible positively to prove that the universe is Euclidean by this method), that the tools used assume in their design a Euclidean geometry (so Gauss could have seen exactly what he expected to see), and that it is dependent on the assumption that light rays travel in straight lines. The modern view, the general **relativity** of Einstein (1879–1955), is that light does indeed travel in curved paths which are dependent on the distribution of matter in space. Central to general relativity is the assumption that the universe is non-Euclidean in its geometry (though it approximates to a Euclidean geometry on a local scale). The type of non-Euclidean geometry used by general relativity is more complex than the non-Euclidean geometry of Bolyai and Lobachevsky. Geometry, though, is a mathematical discipline, and so does not need to mirror the real world; to insist that it did so would be to turn it into an experimental science. Instead, we can choose whatever version of geometry we want, whichever is best suited for the purpose for which we wish to use it – Euclidean for engineering and architecture, for example, and non-Euclidean for general relativity.

The destruction of Euclidean geometry as absolute truth was instrumental in bringing about major changes in the philosophy of mathematics. Until the mid-19th century, mathematical truth was assumed to be absolute, **a priori** truth; Euclidean geometry was, for example, held up by Kant as the paradigm of this view of mathematics. Once this idea was shattered, the way was paved for new schools of thought about what mathematics really is: **formalism**, **intuitionism** and **logicism**. Non-Euclidean geometry had a particular influence on formalism; once it was realized that the words 'points' and 'lines' could be replaced in the axioms of geometry by any other pair of words which were not tied down by intuitive ideas of points and lines, and that the theorems were still valid deductions from these axioms (because their derivation did not depend on the diagrams used to make them intuitively plausible in textbook demonstrations), it was only a short step to deciding that all of mathematics consisted merely of the formal manipulations of symbols. **SMcL**

NON-VERBAL COMMUNICATION

Communication is greatly facilitated by the use of **language**, but arguably, certain types of information are conveyed more efficiently and with greater subtlety by non-verbal means. Kinesics is the study of body movements in relation to expressive acts. All communicative events involve kinesic activity, such as the use of hand and eye movements, facial expressions and body posture. Each culture makes use of a unique repertoire of non-verbal communicative events, almost akin to a dialect. For example, the use of space in human interaction (proxemics) varies systematically: in face-to-face interaction, Mexicans tend to stand closer together than British people. And cross-cultural differences in the conventions for non-verbal interaction can sometimes lead to misinterpretation and the breakdown of communication.

Kinesic studies are complemented by a range of non-speech sounds used in communication (paralanguage), including aspects of voice quality, hissing, whistling, and shushing. Non-verbal acts often complement speech, but non-verbal communication can be used to undermine the words being spoken. When there is a conflict of meaning between the words someone uses and their non-verbal actions, the non-verbal message tends to be preferred as a true indicator of the speaker's attitudes. **MS**

NORMS

Norms, in **sociology**, are rules of conduct which provide guidelines for appropriate behaviour in a range of social contexts. A norm may prescribe a type of behaviour or forbid it. All human groups follow definite types of social norm which are supported by a range of sanctions ranging from public disapproval to execution. **DA**

See also assimilation; consensus theory; culture; ethnomethodology; exchange; generalized other; internalization; rational choice

theory; role; social control; social integration; socialization; social order; society; structure-agency debate; subculture; values.

Further reading K. Danziger, *Socialization*; D. Lee and H. Newby, *The Problem of Sociology*.

NOUVEAU ROMAN see New Fiction

NOVEL

Novel (from Italian *novella* (*storia*), 'new history') is a relatively new name (16th century) for an old literary form. Novels – that is to say works of prose **fiction**, of book length, telling a continuous story through a wide variety of character, location and incident, and drawing out philosophical and moral themes as they do so – go back at least 2,000 years, to such classical European works as Apuleius' *The Golden Ass* and Petronius' *Satyricon*. The ancestry of the novel can be traced still further back, even though such older works are written in verse. For example, Homer's *Odyssey*, of some 3,000 years ago, conforms precisely to the specifications of a novel as later perceived. (However, similar **epics** from other countries, and indeed Homer's own *Iliad*, are quite distinct from the 'novel' form, being less unified, less concerned with (human) character, and less interested in using the specific narrative to develop and expound more general themes.)

Murasaki's *The Tale of Genji*, a story in 52 chapters of chivalry and romance in medieval Japan, was written in the 10th century and is generally held to be the first 'genuine' novel in world **literature**. It is also thought to have been composed in imitation of Chinese models, which no longer survive. The word 'novel' itself was first used in 16th-century English translations of the stories of Boccaccio's *Decameron* (called *novelle* in Italian), and came thereafter to be used for longer fiction, replacing the term 'romance' which had been used previously for works by such writers as Chrétien de Troyes, Sir Thomas Malory (with his retelling of the Arthurian legends), Cervantes (*Don Quixote*) and Rabelais (*Gargantua* and *Pantagruel*).

In Europe, though not in any other culture, the novel developed in the 18th century into the major form of prose fiction, literature's equivalent of the **symphony** (which was making equal strides in European art **music** at the same time). Writers in the 18th century favoured three kinds of novel above all: epistolary novels, using letters to tell a developing story from several different points of view; the **picaresque** novel, telling a series of colourful adventures in a lively and often satirical style; the formation novel or **Bildungsroman**, showing cultural, geographical and social influences at work in the maturing of the central character. In 19th-century Europe, epistolary and picaresque novels became less common, and the *Bildungsroman* took its place beside what might be called the 'novel of manners', using extended anecdotes about particular groups of people in specially selected situations to show the customs and attitudes of specific sections of society (particularly the emerging bourgeois society of the time, and the 'underclass' of the sprawling new industrial cities).

By the 20th century, the writing of novels had spread to non-European cultures, and writers now drew on all the established forms of the novel to produce new work. At about the same time, genre novels began to flood the market. Previously, genre subjects (such as **Gothic** or 'old dark house' novels, or romance) had appealed to only a small readership. The rise, however, of mass literacy and cheaper methods of publishing made 'pulp' fiction (so called because the books were printed on pulp paper rather than the more expensive weave) enormously attractive both to readers and writers. Favourite subjects of late-19th-century genre novels were swashbuckling romances (following the model of Dumas' *The Three Musketeers* and best exemplified in the work of Orczy and Sabatini), and exotic adventures (this was the period when 'new' regions were being opened up, in particular Africa, the Dark Continent). Favourite 20th-century genres were, and are, comic novels, crime novels, espionage novels, horror novels, fantasy novels, romance (historical or allied to specific professions, such as medicine), **sf** and war novels. Since Tolkien's fantasy-trilogy *The Lord of the Rings* became a world best seller in the late 1950s, since the arrival of supernatural horror as a popular film subject in the 1970s, and since the rise in popularity of sex-and-big-business **soap** operas in the 1980s, novels in these three genres have dominated world markets.

In some ways, one of the most interesting things about the novel, of all kinds and in all literatures, is its length. Something between 200 and 500 pages seems about right (approximately 50,000–120,000 words). Prevailing tastes have tended to veer between the two extremes of novel length. Long novels, the 'three-volume novels' or 'blockbusters', were extremely popular in the mid–19th century – and are so again today. In between times, 300 pages (80,000 words) were regarded as about right. But novels outside the specifications, from Proust's million-word *In Search of the Past* at one extreme to the 30,000-word novellas (by such writers as Saul Bellow, Gide and Hesse), which were fashionable until just after World War II, seem to arouse suspicion among consumers of fiction, and are more talked about than read. Perhaps the lengths we prefer say something about our concentration span, or our tolerance for fictional narrative, in the same way as a two-hour span in **drama** or a 30-minute span in symphony or **concerto** tell us of our tolerance in other art forms. But whether this is so or not, the 'standard' novel lengths are not solely publishers' conventions (the amount of paper one person can afford, or can hold, on a single occasion), but seem to have some inherent, existential validity which resists analysis. **KMcL**

NUCLEAR FISSION/FUSION

Nuclei are composed of positively charged protons and neutral neutrons. When a nucleus is surrounded by orbiting electrons, we have an atom. Atoms are neutral due to cancellation of the proton charge by the negatively charged electrons.

Early this century, it became obvious that there was something wrong with theories about nuclei. The masses of the free proton and neutron were both accurately known, as were the masses of many nuclei. However, when protons and neutrons were bound together to form a nucleus, the resulting nucleus always had slightly less mass than the total mass of its constituent particles.

This bizarre 'mass defect' was explained by Einstein's famous formula $E = mc^2$. The protons in a nucleus repel each other very strongly as they are positively charged. This repulsion is overcome by the strong force which only operates at short range. However, the energy required to overcome the strong force is enormous, and can only come from the mass of the particles. In effect, some of the mass of the nucleus has been converted into energy in order to keep the protons from flying apart.

The stability of nuclei to fission or fusion is determined by this mass defect. We define the binding energy of a neutron or proton as the mass defect per particle. The more binding energy a particle has, the more stable it will be.

Nuclei fuse or fission to increase the binding energy per particle. The most stable nucleus is iron. Nuclei lighter than iron can gain stability by fusion and heavier nuclei by fission. Thus, it is only the lightest nuclei (hydrogen and helium) that are used in fusion experiments, while very heavy nuclei like uranium and plutonium will fission easily.

The tremendous energy releases that occur in fusion and fission reactions are due to excess binding energy being given off. It is possible to achieve a chain reaction in fission processes, as each fission gives out excess neutrons, which in turn go on to cause more fissions. There is no similar process for fusion, which goes some way towards explaining whay a fusion reactor is far more demanding to build than a fission one. Fusion would produce more energy more efficiently and cleanly than fission; the snag is that to persuade atoms to fuse, they must be subjected to enormously high temperatures and pressures. Designing a reactor with these requirements is proving to be a difficult task. Sustained fusion reactions have only been achieved by humans in the uncontrolled release of energy from a hydrogen bomb. In space, the story is very different. It is nuclear fusion that powers the Sun and all other stars. **JJ**

See also weak force/strong force.

NUMBER SYSTEMS

One of the most important prerequisites for easy manipulation of **numbers** is a system of notation which is easily understood and which is clear and unambiguous. This need is reflected in the whole of **mathematics** (see **symbolism**). The history of the various different ways which human beings have written numbers is complex. The earliest number systems, like the earliest writing systems, consisted of pictorial representations of the numbers – rather similar to the tally marks used until very recently even in official records. This system is extremely cumbersome, but has the advantage of being easy to understand.

It did not take very long before the notation was made more complicated, but easier to use, usually by adopting a new symbol for the number 10. The reason that 10 was picked is not clear; any number could just as easily be used. It is possible that the number is a reflection of the way that hands were used in counting, so that instead of making a mark for every number, you made a mark every time you ran out of fingers to count with. It is also quite easy to recognize how many marks there are in a tally up to some such figure, but differentiating at sight between, say, 15 and 16 marks is quite difficult.

This paved the way for various ancient number systems which had large numbers of different symbols, such as the Roman (with symbols for 1, 5, 10, 50, 100, 500 and 1000 and complicated rules for picking which symbols to use for a given number) and Greek (which used letters of the alphabet for numbers, so had 27 different symbols altogether). All these systems were cumbersome to use and difficult to read – from that point of view they were worse than the tally systems they replaced. The major defect was their lack of perception of the idea that **zero** should have a representation.

This defect was first solved by Indian mathematicians a few hundred years later. They evolved the number system used today (it is known as the Arabic system because the Arabs introduced it to the West). In this system, there are ten symbols: 0, 1, 2, 3, 4, 5, 6, 7, 8 and 9. For numbers larger than nine, the symbols are combined so that the number that is read is (the number on the right hand end) + 10 × (the number on its left) + 100 × (the number on its left) and so on, moving up to a higher power of 10 with each new column used. This system has many important advantages over the ones known previously. It does not run out of symbols as the numbers get too big, or force large numbers of repetitions of the numbers; this makes them easier to read and uses fewer symbols (it is far easier to understand the number 2378 than MMCCCLXXVIII, its equivalent in Roman notation). Arithmetical operations become far easier; once a few tables are learnt, along with the techniques of long multiplication and long division, it is easy to add, multiply, subtract or divide large numbers. (At least, it is easy compared to earlier systems, in which arithmetic was an occult art confined to a few cognoscenti.) These advantages meant that, after an initial period of conservative scepticism, the Arabic system revolutionized mathematics and **science**. The work of such men as Kepler, Newton and the other men of science in the 17th and 18th centuries would have been impossible without the invention of the Arabic number system, as would the work of mathematicians who worked on the beginnings of **number theory**.

As mentioned before, 10 is not the only number which can give rise to a number system like the Arabic one. In fact, any number will do for this; the particular number which is used is known as the base. By far the most used base apart from 10 is 2. This is because there are only two symbols in the base 2, or binary, number system, 0 and 1. The possibility of representing these symbols with electric currents (on for 1 and off for 0) is the only reason why **computers** are capable of performing arithmetical operations, and therefore one of the major reasons for the success of the computer revolution in many areas. SMcL

See also magic numbers.

Further reading John McLeish, *Number*.

NUMBER THEORY

Number theory, in **mathematics**, is the study of **numbers**, and, in particular, of the relationship between the operations of addition and multiplication. Number theory goes right back to the beginning of mathematics, but was hindered from growth by the lack of a clear system of notation for numbers until the end of the Middle Ages. It is an area in which the problems can be very easily stated and understood, but where there are still many unsolved basic questions. After thousands of years of study, the relationship between addition and multiplication remains one of the most mysterious in the whole of mathematics.

One of the key concepts in number theory is that of the prime. A prime number is one which has no divisors (numbers that divide into it exactly, leaving no remainder); the smallest examples are 2, 3, 5, 7, 11, 13 and 17. The ancient Greeks knew that there were infinitely many primes (the reasoning for this is that if there were finitely many, then you could multiply them all together and then add 1 to the product, producing a number which none of the primes divide; this number must therefore be prime, which is a contradiction; so that there must be infinitely many), but many other properties remain unproven. For example, are there infinitely many pairs of primes that differ only by 2, like 11 and 13? Another famous example is the Goldbach conjecture, which has been checked by computer for vast numbers, but which remains unproved, which is that every even number (greater than 2) is the sum of two primes. There are many such conjectures.

One of the most famous number theoretic conjectures is known as Fermat's last theorem. There are numbers x, y and z such that $x^2 + y^2 = z^2$ (x = 3, y = 4, z = 5, for example), but are there any numbers such that $x^n + y^n = z^n$, for any n greater than 2? The conjecture is that there are none, so that 2 is unique in this respect. The reason for the name (which would usually indicate that Pierre de Fermat (1601–65) proved the result) is that in one of the books in Fermat's library, there was a marginal note scribbled to the effect that he had discovered a proof, but it was too long to fit in the margin – a most frustrating state of affairs. (Mathematical journals still receive new 'proofs' of Fermat's theorem every week, but they are all found to be wrong.)

Another major area in number theory is modular arithmetic. This involves doing arithmetic in the normal way, but only looking at the remainders upon division by some fixed number, known as the base or modulus. It is like doing arithmetic in the **number system** based on the modulus and then only looking at the units column in the answer to sums. When looked at in this way, the numbers become far simpler, and properties can be seen which were hidden by all the extra structure there before. For any modulus n, the numbers modulo n form a **ring**, and if n is a prime, this ring is in fact a **field**, so that the powerful weapons of abstract **algebra** can be brought to play against the various problems. **SMcL**

NUMBERS

Numbers are probably the most fundamental of all the objects of mathematical study, yet still remain remarkably little understood. Originally, the idea of a number was among the first concepts which was an **abstraction** from the real world activity of counting. Although a number seems to be an obvious concept, it has proved remarkably difficult (if not impossible) to define exactly what one is, something which perhaps underlines the fundamental nature of the idea. At its most basic, a number is something applied to a set of objects which are being counted. This is not a definition; it has several ambiguous points. With this concept of a number, is **zero** a number? (It was not recognized as necessary, in the West, until the late Middle Ages). Some schools among the ancient Greeks even denied that one was a number.

It soon becomes clear, even without an understanding of what a number is, that the numbers used for counting are not enough for all the purposes for which they are used. In the counting numbers (technically known as the whole numbers, though there is still disagreement among mathematicians as to whether zero is a whole number or not), there are equations of the form $a - b = ?$ which have no solution

(Which whole number is $2 - 4$, for example?). To get around this, the whole numbers were supplemented by the **integers**, which include all the 'owing' numbers of this form (that is, the negative numbers). This turned out to be merely the first step of a process of expansion which led to the **rational numbers, algebraic numbers, real numbers** and **complex numbers**.

Towards the end of the 19th century, mathematicians, who were seeking to bring more rigour into mathematics in general, became somewhat concerned that there was no rigorous definition of number. This problem particularly concerned Bertrand Russell (1872–1970). In his conception of mathematics as a branch of **logic**, he wanted to find a way to characterize numbers as sets, as the basis for the *Principia Mathematica* he was writing with Alfred North Whitehead (1861–1947). It is possible to characterize the idea 'the set y has exactly n elements' with a sentence of symbolic logic; Russell simply defined the number n to be the class of all sets with exactly n elements (this is not a circular definition because the logical sentence does not actually use the number n). Russell's definition, while it is obviously intuitively related to the basis of the concept of number, suffers from several drawbacks which eventually proved fatal. Each number is a class; it is too big actually to be a set itself. This means that a set of numbers is a set of classes – but this is a violation of Russell's own theory of types, as a class is a more complex notion than a set, so that classes can contain sets but sets should not contain classes. Also, it makes the definition of the operations of arithmetic very difficult; the relationship between the sentences for two different numbers is very complex. This meant, for example, that the proof that the *Principia* gives that $1 + 1 = 2$ takes hundreds of pages, hardly a desirable state of affairs.

Russell's definition was finally dropped in favour of a far less concrete way of looking at numbers. Giuseppe Peano (1858–1932), another member of the logicistic school, came up with an **axiomatization** of arithmetic. This requires the notions of 0 and successor (the operation of going from one number to the next) as basic to the concept of number. His axioms mean that in any system where some point can be designated as 0 and where there is a notion of succession can be defined which satisfies the rules he laid down (the most important of which is **induction**), it is possible to define the operations of addition and multiplication in a unique way which means that they behave in exactly the way you would expect. Peano's approach considerably simplifies proofs of the fundamental results of arithmetic in any such system. In effect, they divorce the mathematical concept of number from the intuitive, since all such systems can equally be taken actually to be the numbers. (In modern **set theory**, it is usual to single out one particularly simple such system, where 0 is taken to be the empty set, and the successor of n is the set containing all the members of n, and then n itself as a member.) **SMcL**

O

OBJECT RELATIONS

Object Relations Theory, in **psychoanalysis**, is one in which a person's relations to external and internalized figures are central (as distinct from Freud's instinct theory which concentrates more on the possibility of internal forces controlling the pattern of our lives). The theory was developed by the British School of Psychoanalysis, notably Melanie Klein, D.W. Winnicott, W.R.D Fairbairn and M. Balint.

Object relations are relations with people, parts of people or symbolic representations of one or the other. The word is not used in its sense of 'thing', but instead recognizes the complexity of our relationship to others and the ways in which we psychologically 'construct' other people.

Objects can be 'bad objects': people, aspects or parts of people, or representations which the subject hates and fears. A bad object can be someone in the world or an internalized figure. A 'good object' whom a subject loves is a benevolent figure who is also either a real person or an internalized symbolic figure. These internal

objects are related to as if they are real. 'Object loss' is the loss of a good external figure which is then internalized by the force of introjection and is mourned in this internalized position. **MJ**

Further reading J.R. Greenberg and S.A. Mitchell, *Object Relations in Psychoanalytic Theory*.

OBJECTIVE AND SUBJECTIVE

Something is subjective, in **philosophy**, if its existence is dependent on the existence of mental subjects. Experiences and thoughts are subjective in this sense, since they are dependent on the existence of mental subjects. And something is objective if its existence is independent of the existence of mental subjects. It is natural to think that planets and trees are objective in this sense, since their existence does not depend upon the existence of mental subjects.

Subjective things are no less real than objective things. If reality is everything that is the case, then it is part of reality that I am in pain. For it is the case that I am in pain, even though my being in pain is obviously dependent upon the existence of a mental subject – me. **AJ**

See also intersubjective.

Further reading T. Nagel, *The View from Nowhere*.

OBJECTIVE CORRELATIVE

'Objective correlative' was a phrase coined by T.S. Eliot in a 1919 essay on *Hamlet*. Essentially, he said that if we are to believe in the emotion characters are showing in a work of art, that emotion must be relatable to, in scale with, the situation and events which surround it – what Eliot called its 'formula'. If the emotion seems too much or too little for these externals, we find it unconvincing. The idea is highly debatable (and Eliot himself came to deplore the way his phrase became standard jargon). In much **literature** and **drama**, and particularly in stage **comedy**, it is precisely the disparity between circumstances and emotional reaction which makes the art – and in other works, for example *Medea* or *Madame*

Bovary, it is hard to see how the idea of an objective correlative has any relevance at all. **KMcL**

OBJECTIVISM AND SUBJECTIVISM

Objectivists about a realm, in **philosophy**, hold that that realm is part of objective reality, that it is not dependent on the existence of mental subjects. Subjectivists about a realm hold that that realm is part of subjective reality, that it is dependent on the existence of mental subjects.

Consider the (apparent) fact that murder is wrong. Ethical objectivists hold that the fact that murder is wrong is objective. Ethical subjectivists hold that the (apparent) fact that murder is wrong is subjective, perhaps adding that the claim 'murder is wrong' is not a statement of objective fact, but merely an expression of mental subjects' emotion, of their aversion to murder. So the (apparent) fact that murder is wrong is dependent on the existence of mental subjects.

Idealists are subjectivists about physical objects. For they hold that physical objects are ideas in the mind and, therefore, mind dependent. **AJ**

See also emotivism; idealism.

OBJECTIVISM IN FINE ART see
Imagism

OBLIGATION see **Duty**

OBSESSION

Obsession (from Latin, 'siege') was a word used in **Catholic** ideology for demonic possession which defined two types of possession, somnabulist and lucid. The lucid state remains conscious but speaks of a spirit within: this is obsession. The concept was adopted by **psychiatry**, but here it came to mean that the patient has thoughts and ideas which do not seem to come from themselves, but are experienced through themselves, like possession. If obsessive thoughts like these develop into rituals, then they become compulsions. In practice today these phenomena are now described collectively as obsessive compulsive behaviours.

Freud saw obsessive ideas as self reproaches (for guilty sexual wishes) re-created in a modified form.

Obsessive ideas are an idea or ideas which constantly intrude on a person's consciousness even though he or she recognizes their irrationality. These thoughts differ from ordinary ones in that they are unspontaneous, distracting, repetitive, feel as if they have come from elsewhere and often have absurd, bizarre or obscene subject matter. They can be extended into compulsive acts such as tidiness, handwashing, etc. **MJ**

OCCULTISM

Occultism (from Latin *occultus*, 'hidden') is the study of occult or secret knowledge and the practice of **magic** rituals, which it is believed will harness supernatural powers to do the will of the practitioner or give advance knowledge of events. Typical divisions are **alchemy**, **astrology**, **divination**, **palmistry** and **witchcraft**.

Occultism, in one form or another, has long been a standard part of many religions. The idea is that there are secrets in the universe – numerical sequences, star-patterns, hidden languages – and that human beings can tap into them if the right exercises, formulations and spells are used. In essence, this is no different from the rationale behind much 'mainstream' religious practice. The crucial difference is in intention, since the occultist is not seeking to approach or form a relationship with the divine, but to usurp supernatural prerogatives and to transcend human nature. In the distant past, occult practices were part of many mystery religions. The ancient Pythagoreans, Babylonians and Chinese practised numerology, believing that the secrets of the universe were embodied in numbers, in a series of mathematical codes which could be unlocked and 'read' by diligent research. There is almost no ancient religion which does not use prophecy, often associated with trances and other spiritual exercises designed to carry the priest or devotee beyond human nature and into the supernatural. Attempts to reach transcendental states of being were particularly associated with **rites of passage**, during which propitation of supernatural forces, and their participation in the event, were regarded as essential for the success of human enterprise.

Perhaps surprisingly, many 'mainstream' religions remain tolerant of occult practices. In the East especially, such things as astrology and divination are respectable, indeed often essential, parts of religious practice. Animistic believers, with their close identification of the natural and supernatural worlds, similarly regard 'occult' practices as perfectly normal. It is chiefly in the Christian West that occultism has been at best regarded with suspicion, and at worst savagely oppressed – a mirror image of the oppression which early Christianity (itself then regarded as an occult and dangerous sect) received at the hands of the pagan authorities in Roman times. It was European and American Christians who burnt witches (usually women who practised such innocent activities as herbal medicine), derided alchemists as Satan's cohorts, and generally outlawed any non-Christian practices coming from the feared and hated East.

In the modern era, scientific orthodoxy has replaced religious fervour, and this time occultism has been marginalized as speculative and perverse – a judgement also applied by many scientists to more 'mainstream' religious beliefs and practices. There is, in essence, a standoff between those who believe in the existence of the supernatural and those who do not. This is further compounded by internal wrangling between supernaturalists, with each faction ready to denounce others as deluded, dangerous or ridiculous. However, in the 'real' world – that is, the world of people who live without endless intellectual rationale – occultism and its various manifestations are, and always have been, subjects of endless fascination. Whether benign or malign in their effects they are a central part of our human mental and emotional landscape. **EMJ KMcL**

OCCUPATION

Occupation, in **sociology**, refers to any form of paid employment in which an individual works in a regular way. Work occupies a larger part of people's lives than any other activity. In modern society people work in a large variety of occupations, but this is a fairly recent feature and has accompanied industrial development. In traditional cultures the majority of the population are engaged in one activity only: the gathering or production of food. As improvements in agriculture allow some members of society to be relieved from the task of food production, then permanently employed, waged craftsmen may emerge but they are only a minority of the population.

Occupational structure refers to the **division of labour** within the whole society. Modern societies are characterized by an increasingly specialized division of labour that is single occupations incorporate narrower spheres of work or knowledge. This can be seen in the fragmentation of work in car production, for example, or in the increasing numbers of medical specialities which have emerged as knowledge increases. Variable amounts of status, prestige, and wealth are attached to different occupations. Occupational scales are measures of these characteristics. In modern society occupation is an important determinant of **class** position. **DA**

See also alienation; career; embourgeoisement thesis; labour process; profession; social mobility; social stratification; status; work.

Further reading J.E. Goldthorpe, K. Hope, *The Social Grading of Occupations*; F. Parkln, *Class, Inequality and Political Order*.

OCKHAM'S RAZOR see Scholasticism

OEDIPUS COMPLEX

The Oedipus Complex was discovered by Freud in his own self-analysis. He found that his own memories of wishing to slay his father and possess his mother, and the accompanying feelings of distress, resembled the plot of Sophocles' play *Oedipus Rex*. In this, Oedipus unwittingly murders his father Laius and marries his mother Jocasta, Queen of Thebes, thereby becoming king himself. Discovering this he is so horrified that he puts out his own eyes. He refuses to see what has happened, as

Freud believed we bury deep inside ourselves the memory of our desire for our parents. Several other pieces of evidence from his work with patients suggested to Freud that this was not unique to himself. He concluded that the wish to eliminate the same-sex parent and to possess the opposite-sex parent was the psychic legacy of every child. His hysterical patients frequently invoked incestuous seduction scenes from childhood which fell into the Oedipal pattern, and this was not confined to this particular group of patients. Freud pointed out that children were often very open about wanting to marry their parent of the opposite sex, but also that these wishes were usually covert as the child sees the same-sex parent as powerful. Freud also thought that people's repugnance and disgust that they had lusted after their mother and wished their father dead, confirmed that these were memories too odious to contemplate. **MJ**

OLIGOPOLY

An oligopoly (Greek, 'few sellers') occurs where a few producers dominate an industry. Sometimes they collude in a **cartel**, producing results similar to a **monopoly**: sometimes they are anti-competitive only by default, because they fear that direct competition would damage all of them. Their actions, therefore, try to take account of the reaction of other oligopolists; since that is uncertain, the behaviour of an oligopoly is hard to predict. If a price war breaks out, oligopolists will produce and price much as a perfectly competitive industry would; at other times they act very like a monopoly.

Homogeneous, or pure, oligopoly involves rivalry among a few producers of products which are identical with one another. Differentiated oligopoly involves rivalry among a few producers of products which are similar (in the eyes of the purchasers) but not identical. **Monopolistic competition** is another kind of market which also comprises rivalry among producers of differentiated products, but the market contains a large number of producers rather than just a few.

Oligopoly is considered a common market condition. A localized example of interdependence among a few is the location of three petrol stations on three corners of a rural intersection. If one lowers the price per gallon the others will follow or lose most of their business. Examples in national markets include the automobile industry, the tyre industry, the steel industry and the beer industry. Some small firms may operate at the periphery in national markets dominated by a few, with their actions failing to elicit any reactions, but a giant firm must anticipate reactions from its fellows when it introduces a change. **TF**

See also game theory; oligopsony.

OLIGOPSONY

Oligopsony (Greek, 'few buyers') is a market in which there are so few buyers that they are highly interdependent: each must take into account the reactions of the others when contemplating a change. For example, if one firm offers to purchase at a higher price, it must recognize that the other purchasers will be affected so significantly that they may offer more rather than hold their purchase-price offers constant. **TF**

See also oligopoly.

OLYMPIAN RELIGION

Of all ancient **religions**, the Olympian system is the one most deserving of attention in the modern world. It was the religion of ancient Greece and Rome, and its iconography, ideas and **myths** therefore underlie much of the subsequent thought of Europe, and from there of the Western world. It was the chief religion opposed by the early Christians (who called its adherents *pagani*, 'yokels'), and its ideas thus influence directly, or by deliberate contrast, the whole cast of mind of the early church, and thence of Christendom today.

The Olympian religion centred on a trinity of deities: Zeus ('shining sky'; Roman Jupiter), ruler of the visible world, Hades ('invisible'), ruler of the unseen world, and Poseidon ('giver of drink'; Roman Neptune), ruler of salt and fresh water. They headed an enormous pantheon of gods, spirits and other supernatural beings, each of whom had an assigned function and area of operation. The 12 most senior gods were thought to meet in council in a sky-palace high above Mount Olympus in Greece – hence the name 'Olympian'.

Stability, in the Olympian system, depended on maintenance of balance in the universe. The gods were thought to have human characteristics, magnified to infinity and since these qualities included such things as irritation and jealousy, there were frequent squabbles and wars in the universe, a mirror of human affairs on Earth. Humans were made in the gods' image (by Prometheus, who stole for them the fire of intelligence, hitherto the gods' prerogative and given to no other mortal creature). Gods often desired humans, and mated with them to produce 'heroes', beings endowed with half-human, half-divine natures and powers. The ordinary contract between human beings and the gods or spirits of particular places or phenomena demanded **prayer** and **sacrifice** from the mortal, favours (or absence of hostility) from the immortal. Since the gods were thought to take pleasure in the same activities as delighted humans, they were worshipped in huge festivals incorporating not only prayer but feasting, athletics, dancing, singing, storytelling and the other **arts**, at which their (invisible) presence was assumed. They were also thought to speak to mortals in oracles, by omens, and through inspired prophets, sibyls and other intermediaries.

Like many ancient religions, this system was emotionally and spiritually satisfying without needing an enormous infrastructure of intellectual argument. It was a religion primarily of practice, and offered not only the satisfaction of participation in large occasions, but also the opportunity for private devotion and **ritual** (gods and spirits of place, including the hearth and the home, were fervently worshipped, and were later subsumed in many of the saints and holy places of European Christendom). There was an important mystical element, based in the idea that interpenetration between the mortal and immortal worlds was possible in certain places, at special times, and to favoured people after the correct ceremonies had been carried out. All this practice was adopted, in a more or less modified form, by **Christianity**, and was grafted on to

rites and rituals inherited from **Judaism**. Even the detail of Christian ritual owes as much to Olympian, 'pagan' practice as it does to anything from ancient Israel.

The main religious legacy of Olympianism, however, comes not from what it offered, but from what it lacked. The absence of intellectual rationale led many thinkers in ancient Greece and Rome – people who were often sincere, practising believers in the Olympian system – to ponder those matters which religion did not address, or explained in simplistic, straightforward assertions and imperatives. Ethics and morality, in particular, were regarded as subjects for **philosophy** rather than religion, and were studied and debated without the overtones of partiality and specificity they had in areas subject to religions of other kinds. The result was that, by the time of Christ, there was a vast edifice of 'pagan', secular thought on such matters in Europe, and it was regarded as essential baggage for any educated mind. St Paul, before his conversion to Christianity, was trained in this tradition, and when he came to codify Christian moral and ethical belief, to rationalize what had previously been matters of faith or instruction alone, he drew on the Olympian tradition. For many centuries afterwards, the philosophers of ancient Greece were ranked in a hierarchy of 'proto-Christians': people who, it was claimed, would have been Christians if they had only known about Christ, and to whom the Christian God was thought to have vouchsafed specific revelation, as he did to the pre-Christian prophets of Judaism. Socrates, thanks to his moral and ethical teaching as reported by Plato, was regarded with particular reverence.

In the wider cultural world of early Christendom, this inheritance was matched, in a similarly lateral and unstated way, by the overwhelming prevalence of Greek and Roman styles in the arts rather than those of, say, ancient Israel. The Olympian idea that the gods were like magnified humans led Greek and Roman artists to imagine their appearance and their utterance as idealized forms of those known in everyday existence. Aphrodite (Roman Venus), goddess of beauty, for example, was depicted in **paintings** and **sculpture** as the model of ideal womanhood; Zeus was shown as the embodiment of regality and authority. Myths of the gods and heroes became a vast quarry for intellectual work of all kinds, and often philosophical ideas were grafted on to them, so that they expressed not merely a religious view of life (as do, for example, the myths of ancient Sumeria or Egypt) but a considered human view, putting the supernatural and natural worlds into the same intellectual frame. (Aeschylus' *Oresteia* or Virgil's *Aeneid* are typical: works of art based on ancient myth but putting forward clear ideas about such matters as duty, fate, **guilt**, honour, justice and **law**.) Artists in all fields sought, in their work, to make their creations fit for the ears or eyes of the gods – quality in the arts was a matter of aspiration as well as of satisfying clients in the here-and-now. All these ideas, and the art-styles which arose from them, were part of the continuum of culture throughout the Greek and Roman world – and this legacy of the thought processes depending on Olympianism affected the cultural style and attitudes of Europe, and of areas influenced by Europeans, to an extent shared, among ancient religions in other areas, only by two of those which still survive today: **Hinduism** and **Shinto**. KMcL

OP ART

Op Art (short for Optical Art), as its name suggests, exploits, in an abstract context, visual ambiguities to trick the eye into a misreading of the image. Thus the wavy pinstripes of Bridget Riley's paintings, such as *Drift 2* (1966), seem to shimmer before the eye, while Victor Vasarély, the most successful exponent of Op Art, used various devices, such as positive-negative shapes, to make his paintings flicker like a movie image. Op Art works by focusing interest exclusively on the question of visual perception, while reducing to insignificance any potential interest in subject matter and avoiding a gestural handling of paint liable to draw attention back to the physicality of the painting. It tends to disorient some viewers, while exhilarating others. These unpredictable medical side

effects caused its influence on design and advertising (at its height in the 1960s) to be short-lived. **MG PD**

Further reading Parola, *Optical Art: Theory and Practice.*

OPERA

Opera (Italian, '(dramatic) work') is one of those rare artistic forms which, everywhere it is practised, rapidly reached a mature state and has hardly changed since. In essence, it is a stage show in which the characters sing instead of speak, and in which instruments, instead of merely accompanying, contribute emotional meaning and depth as the spectacle proceeds.

In the East, opera is one of the most ancient forms of theatre show; in China and Japan it was for centuries considered the 'high-art' form of **theatre**, spoken **drama** being a 'lower', more vulgar genre. This may have been because the stories in opera were often elaborated from **myth**, and involved demons, gods and other supernatural characters for whom song (or declamation to music) seemed a more appropriate form of utterance than ordinary human speech. Sometimes, in these operas, the performers onstage mimed and danced silently, while the singers or singer, providing all the voices, performed at the side, with the orchestra in open view. This is also the style of Indian and Indonesian traditional 'opera', where stories from **myth** and **religion** are performed by dancers to the accompaniment of an opera, sung and played alongside in a kind of simultaneous concert. The components of all such shows were traditional, and so intricate that the craft took years to learn, aspirants often starting their apprenticeship as small children.

In the West, opera began in 1598, as the outcome of experiments (by the Camerata) to re-create the performance-style of ancient Greek **tragedy**. Western operas are attributable to named writers and composers; the performers invariably sing (or speak and sing) onstage, and the instrumentalists (except in a few modern operas) are kept separate, in front of or at the side of the stage. Early operas used stories from

Greek myth or Greek and Roman history. In the 18th century a fashion began for setting comic operas, and some serious ones, in contemporary times; in the 19th century, serious operas were often based on **Romantic** novels, grand episodes from European history, or even (in the **Verismo**, 'truth-to-life' school) on newspaper reports of crimes, marriage tangles and other subjects which would once have been dismissed as too 'low-life' for the form. Comic opera, at about the same time, gave rise to a secondary form, operetta, which is essentially trivial, frivolous and tuneful. (In modern times, composers of musicals have reversed this trend: many contemporary musicals are on deeply serious themes, the music being dignified by the subject instead of the other way about.)

Opera has survived experiments of all kinds, from the 'number' style favoured in early 18th-century Europe (where each singer had to have a 'big number', a display piece at least equal to those of his or her rivals, however well or badly such numbers fitted the story) to the overtly propagandist 'Peking operas' of late 20th-century China, where patriotic pageant and political moralizing are grafted on to popular tunes and hollow stage spectacle. Dr Johnson called opera an 'exotic and irrational entertainment'. Its death is constantly being announced, but it remains, both in the East (where it has a heterogeneous audience, both connoisseurs and ordinary people watching local shows) and in the West (where seat prices for live shows appeal more to the affluent and to providers of 'corporate entertainment', but where there is a huge popular appetite for operas recorded on CD and video) one of the most vigorous and thriving of theatre genres. **KMcL**

OPTICS, REFRACTION AND REFLECTION

The science of optics has its roots in the 17th century, when scientists like Galileo, Huygens, Snell and Newton worked to understand the nature of light. Newton's *Opticks* was considered to be the definitive work upon the subject, but it contained one major flaw. Newton believed that light was made of many tiny particles, whereas Huygens believed that light was a wave. Such was Newton's standing that the wave picture of light was not considered for another century, when Young and Fresnel showed that light exhibited wave-like properties. Scientists now believe that both the wave and the particle pictures are valid, but the particles that we know today bear little resemblance to those that Newton envisaged.

Optics in the 20th century has been revolutionized by quantum mechanics. Classical optics reached a triumphant conclusion with the work of James Maxwell, who showed that light was an **electromagnetic** wave and correctly predicted its velocity. Thereafter the work of Einstein, Planck, Bohr, de Broglie and Heisenberg produced the **quantum theory** of light. This work led to the development of the **laser** in the 1960s, which has become a powerful new optical tool.

Two of the more important optical phenomena are refraction and reflection. Refraction occurs when light passes into a medium in which it travels at a different speed. Light travels fastest in a vacuum; this speed cannot be exceeded. In other media, such as air or glass, light travels more slowly. The ratio of its vacuum velocity to its velocity in another medium is known as the refractive index of the medium. Thus we may say that the refractive index of glass is about 1.5, because light travels 1.5 times more slowly in glass than in vacuum. When light passes at an angle into glass, its path is bent, due to the refraction of its wavefront. The diagram on page 530 illustrates what happens. Refraction is not unique to light. All wave-like phenomena, like sound or water waves, can refract under the right circumstances.

Reflection is a very different process. The simplest type of reflection is from a flat or plane, smooth surface, in which case the angle of incidence is always equal to the angle of reflection. Reflection occurs from two types of surface: conducting (usually metallic) and dielectric (usually transparent). With a conducting surface, the reflection is almost total, that is, very nearly all

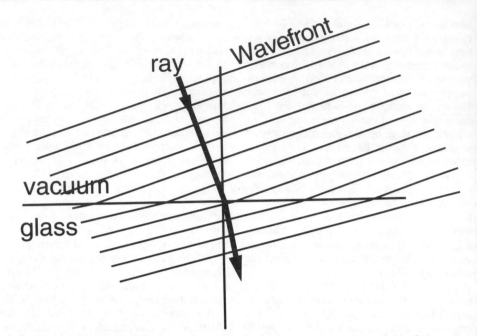

of the incident energy of the wave is contained in the reflected wave. With a dielectric material, the proportion of light that is reflected depends upon the angle of incidence and the refractive index of the material. Thus if the right angle is used, it is possible to have a transparent material reflecting nearly all of the incident light and transmitting none.

Both reflection and refraction also depend upon the frequency of the light. Thus some materials are transparent to one wavelength, but opaque to others. A good example is window glass – it is transparent to visible light but opaque to ultraviolet. **JJ**

ORAL LITERATURE see Literature

ORAL, ANAL AND PHALLIC STAGES

Freud came to believe that, for the infant, sexual pleasure is derived from stroking any part of the body, that the sexual instinct must take some object, but that the specific type of object is not innate but is determined by environmental conditions and learning. He took as a starting point the union of opposite-gender sexual organs as the normal aim; following from that premise, focusing on other parts of the body is seen as a perversion of that aim. Freud recognized that parts of the body other than the genitals were used in sexual practice, particularly the oral and anal cavities; he considered them to be objects of the varied manifestations of the sexual instinct. He called these 'component instincts', and saw that they could totally replace the aim of genital sex.

At different stages of a child's development, different parts of the body would take on a sexual character. They would not only be used for their obvious function but could also be the main sources of physical pleasure and centres of experience. At first Freud thought that an infant could experience pleasure in any part of the body and was what he called 'polymorphously perverse'. Then, through the activities of feeding and sucking the erogenous zone becomes the mouth. Freud saw this as the origin of adult oral sexuality, and called it the oral stage of psychosexual development.

People who are orally fixated, and unconsciously experience the mouth as the primary erotic zone, are, in **psychoanalysis**, seen to be mother-fixated (or breast fixated). Such people engage heavily in talking, eating, smoking and drinking; they are prone to manic-depressive mood swings and to identify with others rather than relating to them as separate people. The reason for this is that survival (keeping the breast) has become equated with identifying with the breast. The manic swing is synonymous with feelings of fusion with the breast and the depressed swing with feelings of loss of the mother. If an infant is overindulged he or she may be cheerful or over-optimistic, if underindulged, prone to pessimism, acquisitive and envious.

The anus is the second erotic zone in the child's developing sexuality. From the point of view of the parents, toilet training is a landmark in a child's development and, from the child's point of view, controlling the anal sphincter is one of the first acts of mastering the body that is rewarded with so much praise from adults, thereby giving the child much pleasure. A child is capable of stimulating the anal region by retention and expulsion of faeces. As this is experienced daily, it gradually takes over the central position that the mouth had in producing pleasurable feelings. Anal ideas such as smearing and cleaning can be central to the anal character. Freud worked out the anal character in more detail than the oral, or later phallic phase, as the idea of this development phase raised such feelings of disgust. If the child had harsh toilet training, the adult retains traits of orderliness, obstinacy and parsimony.

The third phase is the phallic phase when children discover their own genitals as a source of physical pleasure. Despite its name it applies to both sexes around the ages of four to six years when a child's interest in sexual matters is at a peak. This stage moves into latency with the beginning of the Oedipal phase. The phallic character is one who sees **sexuality** as a display of potency. Over-emphasis in terms of curiosity or exhibitionism is the result of trauma at the phallic stage. **MJ**

Further reading Erik H. Erikson, *Childhood and Society*; Sigmund Freud, *Three Essays on the Theory of Sexuality*; B.D. Lewin, *The Psychoanalysis of Elation*;

ORDER

The term order, in common use, suggests sequence and disposition, but in **architecture** it has come to be specifically identified with the classical 'Orders' of Western classical architecture. An 'Order' of this type is a column, with a base, and on the top a 'capital', with an entablature. This Order is the key unit in classical architectural design from Greek antiquity, and therefore makes up the vocabulary of classically inspired architecture from the **Renaissance** onwards.

There are three principal 'Orders', Doric, Ionic and Corinthian, and two further ones which derive from them, Tuscan and Composite. Each Order is principally identified by the different detailing of the capitals, and their different proportions. The origin of the earliest Order, Doric, is thought to derive from primitive timber construction, which became translated into stone – probably in temple construction – the detailing of the entablature reflecting the structural relationship of horizontal and vertical members.

The three principal Orders were described in detail in Vitruvius's treatise *De Architectura* (1st century BCE). Vitruvius describes the proportions and appropriate uses of the particular Orders (for example, the Doric was seen as expressive of power and appropriate to temples of Minerva or Mars). After renewed interest in Vitruvius's text (perhaps the only such discussion to survive from the ancient world) in the Renaissance period, Alberti produced a treatise on architecture which described the Orders with reference both to Vitruvius and to his own observation of Roman architectural remains. There were many other treatises on the subject, of which the most influential in the 17th century were those of Serlio (1537), Vignola (1562), Palladio (1570) and Scammozzi (1615). These provided the source material for architects designing in the classical tradition, and contributed to a process by which the Orders became almost a set of 'canonical formulae embodying all architectural virtue'. From the 17th century until this day in western Europe study of the Orders and their application formed an important part of architectural training. **JM**

See also classicism.

Further reading J. Onians, *Bearers of Meaning: The Classical Orders in Antiquity, The Middle Ages and The Renaissance*; J. Summerson, *The Classical Language of Architecture*.

ORGANELLE

The term organelle (Italian *organella*, 'little organ'), in the **life sciences**, describes each of the discrete parts into which a living cell may be divided. Many organelles are partitioned from the interior of the cell by membranes surrounding them, as membrane surround cells. Organelles have specialized functions within the cells, such as energy transduction or motility. Possession of organelles is a characteristic of the more complex living cells which make up multicellular plants and animals, and single-celled protozoa. Such cells are termed eukaryotic, while the simpler cells of bacteria possess no organelles and are called prokaryotic. Some biologists have suggested that eukaryotic cells may have originated as associations (symbioses) of several prokaryotes and that this **symbiosis**, over time, became permanent, giving rise to organelles. **RB**

See also cytology.

ORGANIC MODERNISM see Modernism

ORGANICISM

Organicism, in the **life sciences**, is an explanation for the nature of the living world, which states that organisms can only be understood in their entirety, not by being broken down into individual components (**mechanism**). To the organicists, a living organism cannot be described merely by the sum of its parts as it possesses qualities which cannot be predicted from the study of those parts, and indeed cannot continue to live fully when physically separated from the whole. Kidney function may thus be studied in isolation from the animal, but its role can only be fully understood in the context of the whole organism. Such a holistic doctrine provides cohesion for the many areas of modern biology and is applicable in other fields where complex

systems may be studied as analogous to the organism, such as **ecology** and **social sciences**. **RB**

See also life; vitalism.

ORGANIZATION

Organizations are social units which are directed towards the achievement of specific goals. The organization comprises a large group of individuals who are linked by a definite set of authority relations and have been brought together for a specific purpose. There are many different sorts of organizations in social life.

Organizations are not new. In preindustrial societies social units were created with the aim of pursuing specific goals. In ancient Egypt, for example, a permanent work force of several thousand skilled workers was formed in order to build the pyramids, and a large-scale organization was created in order to construct and maintain the complex series of dykes, ditches and canals which controlled the flood waters of the Nile and irrigated the fields.

The development of organizations is associated with an increasingly complex **division of labour**. In many societies all members need to be involved in the production of food in order to survive. With developments in agriculture and advances in farming techniques, there is no need for everyone to be employed in food production. Those members of the population who are freed from subsistence activities are able to specialize in particular tasks, which makes possible the emergence of full-time craftsmen. This process is accelerated with the development of modern technology and as more and more members of the population are able to specialize in tasks not related to food production the division of labour becomes increasingly complicated, and requires co-ordination and direction. For example, the specialists employed to construct the ancient Egyptian pyramids included artists, engineers, masons, overseers, quarrymen, scribes, surveyors and toolmakers. All these tasks need to be directed and co-ordinated if they were to produce an end product. This highly specialized division of labour generates a hierarchy of authority and a system of rules, which combine to form an organization.

What is distinctive about modern society is the sheer size, number and scope of organizations – a hospital is a typical example. In modern society organizations are formed for a whole range of purposes, not only production. They are formed for military reasons, to make and enforce legal decisions, to decide upon and administer government policy and to provide health care. A particular organizational form is often associated with modern society: the **bureaucracy**. Sociology owes much to Max Weber who has contributed greatly to our understandings of organizations in general and of bureaucracies in particular. **DA**

See also church; corporatism; labour process; occupation; profession; rationalization; society; work.

Further reading G. Salaman, *Work Organizations*; D. Silverman, *The Theory of Organisations*.

ORIENTALISM

Orientalism is both a term for the body of knowledge that describes the East, and an **ethnocentric** distortion about what the East is like. The Orient has long been portrayed as seductive, exotic and inherently violent. These stereotypes of the Orient were created by Victorian travellers from the West, such as Gustave Flaubert, whose imaginative and subjective accounts influenced early ethnographic accounts of other cultures. As well as reflecting a desire to understand other cultures, Edward Said demonstrated that the dynamics of Orientalism subordinated lives, cultures and societies for the purposes of a Western intellectual rhetoric.

Exotic stereotypes were particularly useful for the paternalistic justifications given by colonialists protecting their interests in the Middle East and India, and explain the enduring fascination and repugnance for the exotic East. Orientalism enabled the British, for example, to think that they knew India better than the Indians themselves. By creating the Orient

as the mysterious 'other' whose otherness was composed of all the things the West was not, the West simultaneously created itself. The notion of a unitary and homogeneous West has been useful in the **hegemony** of Orientalism.

Contemporary **anthropology** is critical of Orientalism as a way of generating knowledge about others, based as it is on ideas of homogeneous cultural and political entities engaged in assymetrical relations of power. **CL**

See also caste; colonialism; primitivism.

Further reading R. Inden, *Imagining India*; Edward Said, *Orientalism*.

ORIGINALITY

Originality (from Latin *origo*, 'source') has two meanings, in the **criticism** and appreciation of the **arts**. In general, it is almost a synonym for 'uniqueness' and refers to the idea that a given creator, or the work created, is one of a kind, exhibiting characteristics shared by no others. This is a Western notion, and one which belongs to the last two or three hundred years only. It is related to the idea of the artist as genius, someone using unique gifts to reach as closely as possible to the 'ideal' form which exists, in philosophical terms at least, for his or her particular form of artistic endeavour. In other traditions, and in the West until the **Renaissance**, this kind of originality was not required: artists, and thinkers of all kinds, were part of a continuum of creativity and invention, and their work was legitimized by its relationship (deferential or hostile) to the whole field. It would never have occurred to Aeschylus, say, or Omar Khayyám, or Hiroshige, to think of themselves as 'originals' or of their work as 'original'. Notions of excellence had more to do with the execution of the work than with its conception; plagiarism, now one of the cardinal artistic sins, was regarded as natural, even a form of flattery: drawing on the common pool of which both your own work, and the work you were borrowing, were part.

In fine art, originality has a second, and far more useful, meaning. Critics in 17th-century Europe, following Neo-Platonist philosophers, defined it as the opposite of the servile copying of nature, and an integral part of the artist's powers of invention. This meaning has been taken up in recent years by those who wish to dissociate originality in art from **authenticity**, thereby widening the parameters of the discipline to include all art, whether 'original' (and indeed 'fine') or not. **PD MG KMcL**

See also connoisseurship; idealism.

ORNAMENT (INDIA AND PERSIA)

Eastern traditions of ornament have long influenced architectural **design** in the West. For example, the complex geometric tiled floors of medieval monasteries and cathedrals in Europe derived from **Islamic** patterns, and such **architectural** details as the 14th-century four-centred arch are now believed to have come from Indian **Buddhist** architecture. However, such influences were sporadic until the 18th century, because architects, artists and designers in the West had access to virtually no printed visual information from Eastern sources. This changed thanks to British trading links with the East, begun by the East India Company. Warren Hastings (1732–1818) encouraged the study of Indian culture, and at the end of the 18th century drawings of Indian buildings became available in Britain for the first time. Indian influence can be seen in the decoration of buildings such as the Royal Pavilion, Brighton. In 1851 a magnificent collection of Indian textiles owned by the East India Company was shown at the Great Exhibition in London, and many examples were subsequently purchased by the Victoria and Albert Museum. This simple event reinforced Indian ornament as the most important non-Western source of design in European art and architecture, supplanted only at the end of the 19th century by the cult of Japan.

Parallel to this 19th-century interest in things Indian was the rise of serious research into Islamic ornament. This began in the 1830s and 1840s with the publication of *Plans, Elevations, Sections and Details of the Alhambra* by Owen Jones and Jules Goury. Jones became the most important

Islamic scholar of his generation, his only real rival being Edward William Lane (who published from the 1830s a series of books on Egyptian architecture and design). Such work encouraged European designers of consumer products of all kinds to explore symmetrical, non-naturalistic geometric designs – a tradition of ornament which continued in the 20th century, particularly in 1930s **Art Deco** and 1980s developments in **postmodernism**. **MG PD**

ORTHODOXY

Although 'orthodoxy' (Greek, 'correct thinking') is used in ordinary speech to mean ideological or theological correctness, when the term is applied to the Eastern Christian churches it means 'right way' (doctrinally) or 'true glory' (liturgically). Orthodoxy is therefore used as a general term to cover every aspect of the life and worship of the Orthodox churches, which trace their history back to apostolic times. The Orthodox world is bound together by the same ancient style of worship, hardly changed since the 5th century, by the same doctrine as defined by the Seven Ecumenical Councils and by a common corpus of canon law. According to the Orthodox, they represent the Johannine tradition in Christendom, while Catholics follow Peter and Protestants Paul.

The exact number of Orthodox Christians is unknown, but it is at least 150 million. Orthodoxy is found in Greece, Russia and Eastern Europe, with significant and vital diaspora churches in France, Geneva and the US. There are so-called monophysite churches in Egypt and Uganda, and Nestorain and Jacobite churches in the Middle East and India. Each national Orthodox Church is autonomous or autocephalous (that is, has its own head, an archbishop or patriarch), but accepts the spiritual leadership of the Patriarch of Constantinople. Some Orthodox churches (for example the Serbian Orthodox Church) are coterminous with language areas rather than with areas of national sovereignty. All have suffered terrible persecution in the course of history, especially under Stalin. Also, having been unable to evangelize in the Western sense of the word, they rely on their worship and lifestyle to be sufficient testimony to the Gospel.

All Orthodox churches see themselves as the guardians of the faith of the Early Church (from the 1st to 4th centuries CE) and of a living tradition of worship, art and scholarship. For them the Church is indefinable, a living body composed of all who gather together around the priest for Eucharistic worship. Beliefs are shaped by experiences in worship as much as by statements of the Ecumenical Councils. Veneration of the Virgin Mary is of great importance, but there are no dogmatic statements to enforce or even define this. Christology centres on the figure of Christ as the union of two natures God and man in one person. Orthodox theology can be summed up in Athanasius's statement, 'God became man in order that man might become God'. For the Orthodox, man is justified by faith and works according to grace. There is no such thing as original sin, only fallen man in his sins, who is rescued not only from sin but also from decay and corruption.

The Orthodox are said to be obsessed with **eschatology**. **Millenarianism** certainly plays a large part, for example, in Russian spirituality. The living pray for the dead, including the saints, as well as for and with sinners awaiting judgement. This is because Orthodox worship is designed to represent heaven come down to Earth. The believer prays surrounded by angels and the communion of saints. **EMJ**

Further reading Kallistos Ware, *The Orthodox Way.*

OTHER MINDS, PROBLEM OF

The problem of other minds is the problem of explaining how, if at all, one possesses knowledge of minds other than one's own.

One possesses knowledge of one's own mental states by introspecting them: I know that I am in pain by introspection. But one cannot introspect the mental states of others: I cannot introspect your pains. So how can one ever know that someone else is in pain? All one can do, it seems, is

infer someone else's mental states from their behaviour: I infer that you are in pain because you are groaning. But this inference is hardly deductive. I could be surrounded by robots who are programmed to behave as though they have minds but are in fact mindless, in which case all my inferences from their behaviour to claims about their minds will take me from truth to falsity.

Some philosophers consider that beliefs about other minds are justified by an argument from **analogy**. I notice that various correlations obtain in my own case, that whenever I groan, I am in pain. I then notice that other bodies behave in the same way as my own, that they groan. And I infer that when other bodies behave in similar ways to my own, other minds have mental states similar to mine, that when other bodies groan, there are minds associated with those bodies that are in pain.

Others argue that beliefs about other minds are justified by an inference to the best explanation. I notice that another body is groaning, and need to explain this phenomenon. There are various possible explanations. One is that the body is a robot programmed to behave as though it has a mind even though it is in fact mindless and, therefore, that it is not in pain. Another explanation of the groaning is that it is caused by a pain, that there is a mind associated with the body, and that its being in pain is causing the groaning. Given that the second explanation is better that its competitors, I can infer that it is true. **AJ**

See also behaviourism; introspection; knowledge; privacy.

Further reading P. Churchland, *Matter and Consciousness*; A. Plantinga, *God and Other Minds.*

OVER-DETERMINISM see Determinism

OVISM

Ovism (Latin, 'eggism') was a biological theory current in the 18th and 19th centuries. It held that the offspring of an individual are preformed within the egg. The theory arose after Regnier de Graaf

(1641–73) observed what he took to be a mammalian egg. When sperm were discovered by Antonie van Leeuwenhoek (1632–1723), the same suggestion was made. Nicolaas Hartsoeker (1656–1725) even went as far as to suggest that each sperm contained a tiny preformed man, a homunculus. These suggestions were, however, not based on scientific evidence and stemmed from the earlier ideas of encapsulation, which stated that all the future generations of offspring were contained within the egg; some literal adherents of this view held that Eve had carried all of humankind. **RB**

See also abiogenesis; embryology; germ layer theory; germ plasm; pangenesis.

PAIN

Medical practitioners and researchers define pain as the sensation perceived in response to a noxious stimulus. It is unique among the senses (for example, touch, hot-cold, spatial position, etc.) or special senses (vision, hearing, etc.) in the lack of clarity of the neurological understanding of the phenomenon.

A description of the pain as perceived by a particular person may be of great value in attempting to determine the cause. The pain may start with a specific event, and it may be in one position or radiate to other places. The pain may be on the surface or within; it may be burning, stabbing, gripping, etc.; it may be continuous or intermittent. It could also be of value to know of aggravating or relieving factors. If the information about the pain points to the cause, and other evidence supports the conclusion, the cause may be removed by medical or surgical means. If the cause cannot be treated the pain may still be alleviated by surgical means (immobilizing a broken bone or wound, for example), or with pain-killing or analgesic drugs. The oldest, and arguably

still the most effective analgesic is aspirin, an extract of willow-bark, acetyl salicylic acid, the first drug ever synthesized.

One of the great mysteries of pain is the variation in perception of intensity of pain between people: the pain threshold. The phenomenon is in part explained by naturally-circulating substances (the opiate-like peptides) which are able to bind to specific receptor sites in parts of the brain known to be involved in pain perception. The phenomenon may be part of a scheme enabling a measured response to noxious stimuli.

Another aspect of pain is the extent to which it may be exaggerated or aggravated by the initial, possibly protective response. A sore joint, for example, is naturally immobilized by contraction of surrounding muscles, and this may result in a more painful spasm. **TG**

PAINTING see **Art(s), Visual**; **Genre Painting**; **Hard-Edge Painting**; **History Painting**; **Landscape Painting**; **Narrative Painting**.

PALAEOBOTANY

Palaeobotany, as its Greek name declares literally, is the study of all aspects of fossil plants. Certain types of plant tissue are well preserved in rock: wood, pollen grains and seeds are all durable plant products, though softer tissues such as leaves are also sometimes found. Palaeobotany is a relatively modern science but has revealed a great deal about the vegetation and climate of prehistoric times. The richest source of information is pollen grains, the outer layers of which are extremely durable and which have peculiarly intricate microscopic structures which allow the identification of the genus or even species of the parent plant (see **palynology**). The construction of pollen profiles showing the relative abundance of different pollen types in deposits of a known geographical age allows an accurate idea of the flora of the time to be established (oak forest, grassland, pasture, etc.). Such information can then be used to draw conclusions about the prevailing climate and land use (palaeoethnobotany), a picture which is of great use to archaeologists. **RB**

See also bioclimatology; dendrochronology; palaeontology.

Further reading Martin Rudwick, *The Meaning of Fossils*.

PALAEONTOLOGY

Palaeontology (Greek, 'study of ancient organisms') is the study of prehistoric animal and plant species by the investigation of their fossil remains, though the term is generally restricted to the study of animal remains (see **palaeobotany** for plant fossil studies). This branch of science was, in effect, founded by the French biologist George Cuvier (1769–1832): previously fossils had been viewed as the leftovers from creation, representing abandoned designs. Although Cuvier believed in creation, he concluded that the quadruped skeletons which he reconstructed from fragmentary fossil remains were not present in the modern world because of extinctions caused by catastrophes, such as the great flood described in the Bible. He was not able to fully explain his observation that older geological strata contained fossils which were less like species seen today than the fossils found in younger strata. In 1812, he published his book *Researches on the Bones of Fossil Vertebrates*, and he went on to introduce fossil animals to zoological classification.

As the title of Cuvier's book suggests, early palaeontology was dominated by the study of vertebrate fossils, as the vertebrate bones are more readily preserved in fossil form than the remains of soft-bodied animals such as worms. Modern palaeontology is still subject to this bias. Although fossilized invertebrates have been found in rocks of great antiquity, and have been instrumental in determining the course taken by **evolution** from the earliest fossil evidence of primitive blue-green algae in the three-billion-year-old Fig Tree Chert fossils, to the remains of early man discovered since the 1970s by Richard Leakey and others. Fossil remains of man, animals, plants and all manner of organic material have been used by palaeoanthropologists and archaeologists to study the lifestyle of ancient societies. **RB**

See also analogy; biogenesis; biopoiesis; homology.

Further reading Martin Rudwick, *The Meaning of Fossils*.

PALLADIANISM

Palladianism is the style of the academic, classically inspired **architecture** of the north Italian architect Andrea Palladio (1508–80), who designed symmetrically planned villas with colonnaded porticoes on the model of temple fronts (features he wrongly believed to be a characteristic of Roman villas). The example of his buildings and his architectural drawings was immensely influential in English country house architecture of the 18th century, and thereafter in the US. **JM**

See also classicism.

Further reading R. Wittkower, *Palladio and Palladianism*.

PALMISTRY

Palmistry, also known as *cheiromancy* (Greek, 'hand-prophecy'), is reading the lines and shape of the palm of a person's hand to make statements about that person's character, past and future. It was practised in ancient China, and from there passed to the Middle East and then to Europe (where it became notably a skill of travellers and immigrants, such as the Gypsies). It is commonly regarded as a joke or a parlour game, but those who believe in it claim that the palm is as unique to each individual as a fingerprint, and that ignorance of why palmistry works is no more reason for dismissing it than is the case with any other mysterious technique from ancient China, for example, acupuncture. **KMcL**

PALYNOLOGY

Palynology (Greek *paluno*, 'I sprinkle' + ology) is the study of pollen structure and its use in the identification of the parent plant. The most important application of palynology is in **palaeobotany**, since pollen grains are among the best-preserved of botanical material and can often be used to identify the parent plant species. **RB**

PANENTHEISM see **Pantheism**

PANGENESIS

Pangenesis (Greek, 'origin of all'), in the **life sciences**, is a theory for the mechanism of inheritance by which particles called gemmules (or pangenes), produced by all the cells in the body, are released into the bloodstream via which they travel to the germ cells, from which offspring develop. Darwin proposed his 'Provisional hypothesis of pangenesis' in 1868, based on the fairly universal pre-Mendelian view that heredity was a property of blood and that parental characteristics were blended in offspring. (Mendel had published work on heredity two years previously, showing that parental characteristics were segregated and subsequently combined, but not blended, but the importance of these findings was not realized for several decades.) The theory of pangenesis satisfied Darwin because it provided a mechanism for the inheritance of acquired characteristics, again the prevailing explanation for variation. However, experiments soon showed that Darwin's hypothesis was incorrect; it was modified by Hugo de Vries in 1889, linking pangenes to chromosomes in the nuclei of all cells and then by August Weismann, in 1892, who proposed that only 'sex cells' bore all the pangenes, somatic cells having only the information required for their differentiation. This chromosome theory allowed no mechanism for the inheritance of acquired characteristics and paved the way for the **gene** theory. **RB**

See also Darwinism; Lamarckism; Mendelism.

PANPSYCHISM

Panpsychism (Greek *pan*, 'all', *psyche*, 'soul' or 'spirit') is the doctrine that everything has mental properties. Even micro-physical particles, it is said, have mental properties. Most contemporary philosophers find panpsychism too incredible to take seriously, but one, T. Nagel, has provided an argument for it. Nagel says that we explain properties of large-scale objects, such as trees and brains, in terms of the properties of their micro-physical constituents. Thus the physical properties of large-scale objects are explained in terms of the physical properties of their constituents. But brains also have mental properties, and their mental properties can only be explained in terms of the mental (and not physical) properties of their micro-physical constituents. Therefore the micro-physical constituents of brains have mental properties. And since the micro-physical constituents of brains are just the same as the micro-physical particles found throughout the inanimate universe, all micro-physical particles must have mental properties. **AJ**

See also mind-body problem.

Further reading C. McGinn, *The Character of Mind*; T. Nagel, *Mortal Questions*.

PANSPERMIA

Panspermia (Greek, 'seeds of all') is the idea that life on Earth was seeded from from elsewhere in the universe. The term was coined by the Swedish chemist Svante Arrhenius in his book *Worlds in the Making* (1908). He proposed that life had arrived on the Earth in the form of spores or microorganisms, which had been carried through space by solar winds and radiation from a distant planet. The theory was initially popular, presumably because it provided a distraction from the controversial ideas of **evolution** and **biopoiesis**, and it has been cultivated by **sf** authors who have proposed that the seed may have been delivered intentionally. It is possible that panspermia could have occurred, and the lack of a fossil record pertaining to the earliest period of life on Earth means that the the theory can be neither proven nor refuted. However, it is difficult to imagine how a living organism, even in the form of a spore, could survive the rigours of radiation and vacuum for the time required to travel to Earth. Furthermore, it seems unlikely that such a seed would have arrived to find suitable conditions for its growth on a world which had previously borne no life. Finally, the concept of panspermia does not provide an alternative for either biopoiesis or evolution because the life which the seed represents must have appeared from non-living matter at some stage and, after arriving on Earth, must have evolved to produce the biodiversity which is extant today. **RB**

See also biogenesis.

Further reading Francis Crick, *Life Itself*; Fred Hoyle, *Lifecloud*.

PANTHEISM

Pantheism (Greek, 'all-god-ism') is used to describe such diverse subjects as the classical **Hindu** belief that the divine is present in everything (which is why the polite Indian greeting is a bow with both hands folded together, as if in prayer: one worships the god within the other person) and the poetry of, for instance, Walt Whitman. The word was coined by John Toland (1670–1722), to mean that the whole universe is divine and God is to be found in everything.

Pantheists fall into two categories. First are religious pantheists, who are to be found in all the major world religions except, theoretically, **Islam**. Second are philosophical pantheists, the most influential of whom was Spinoza in the 17th century, with his formula *Deus sive natura* ('God, otherwise Nature').

Panentheism (Greek, 'everything in God') is the precisely opposite view to pantheism. Instead of God being in everything, panentheism says that everything exists (that is, has reality) *because* it exists in God. **EMJ**

PANTOMIME

The word 'pantomime' (Greek, 'all-imitation') was originally used in ancient Rome of a single performer, who wore a mask representing three separate faces, and performed scenes between them, or who gave a vocal and physical representation of some scene or event (birds singing in a wood, for instance, or the sacking and firing of a city), taking all the parts. (There were equivalent acts in the 19th-century European music-hall: playing a scene between several people using different hats for each, or wearing a double suit of clothes, for example a woman's dress in right profile

and a soldier's uniform in left profile; and the ubiquitous 'farmyard impression' sketch.) But 'pantomime' has two other meanings, quite different and mutually distinct. The first, and most important, describes a theatre practice which dates back to the earliest performances ever given: dumbshow. The performers indicate all feelings, all statements, by movement alone, and the beauty and virtuosity of their body language and gesture are a major part of the show's appeal.

Dance-dramas have always been the most favoured form of pantomime – the range is from a Stone Age re-enactment of a hunt to the sophisticated dance-plays of Far Eastern religion, from Japanese Noh plays to Western **ballet**. Often, in such performances, the actor/dancer is accompanied by offstage music, or by other actors reciting a narration or speaking dramatic words offstage, while he or she remains silent. In Japanese *joruri* theatre, as in Javanese popular theatre and the Karaghiosis plays of the Middle East, the 'actors' are puppets (necessarily silent), and the sound is provided offstage in a similar way. Another derivative from pantomime is mime itself. In its purest form, this is silent, and has a vocabulary of expressive gesture all its own; it is also an ingredient of all kinds of theatre performance, from lampoon to high **tragedy** (for example, the dumbshow in *Hamlet*).

The second, and distinctly secondary, meaning of 'pantomime' is a purely British invention of the last 200 years or so. It is a burlesque show, usually based on a fairy tale or nursery rhyme, and set in some exotic location such as the Middle East of the Arabian Nights, or the giant's castle to which Jack climbs in the nursery story. Topical allusions, slapstick and songs are inserted into the basic story, and there is cross-dressing: the 'principal boy' in traditional pantomime is played by a woman, the 'dame' by a man. Comic animals – eccentric dancers dressed as horses, cows, geese, cats – proliferate. Nowadays, in what some devotees see as a deplorable lapse from tradition, popular comedians, sports personalities and **soap** stars take the lead in pantomimes, often incorporating their own speciality 'business' whether or not it fits the story. A key moment in every pantomime is the transformation scene, using all the techniques of theatre presentation: in the 19th century, gauzes and quick changes, nowadays drum-revolves, lasers and computerized effects. This 'Christmas pudding' of an entertainment drew its roots and star performers originally from the music-hall, and so has links with the **commedia dell'arte** and thence with older forms of pantomime (hence the name). But it has gone its own way since. Although British pantomime rarely appeals beyond British shores, in the UK it is the most popular of all theatre genres except for musicals, and a two-or three-month run of the Christmas pantomime is often what keeps a small theatre solvent throughout the year. **TRG KMcL SS**

PARADOXES

A paradox (Greek, 'against expectation'), in **mathematics**, is a pair of mutually contradictory statements, or apparently contradictory statements, which are both **deductions** from statements which are accepted as true. Paradoxes have cropped up several times in the history of mathematics, and have usually led to major developments as they have been reconciled. There is one interesting exception to this 'rule': the Greeks' discovery of the (to them, paradoxical) fact that there were irrational **numbers** so unsettled them, that they virtually gave up the study of numbers.

One field that paradoxes have played a major part in developing is **set theory**. This is principally because this field was never really given a formal basis until the members of the school of **logicism** wished to give it the status of the most basic part of mathematics. The paradoxes they examined were of two kinds. The first kind was caused because the new set theory developed by Georg Cantor (1845–1918) (and particularly his assertions about **infinity**) ran counter to the prejudices of other mathematicians. They would say that no set could be equinumerous with a proper subset (that is, a subset which is not the whole thing) of itself, but that Cantor had shown that the set of natural numbers is equinumerous with the set of even numbers. The problem was not with set theory itself,

but in the fact that these mathematicians had assumed that a result true of finite sets would also be true of infinite sets.

The second type of paradox was more serious in its implications, particularly as set theory went on to become the basis of mathematics. If there were truly contradictions inherent in set theory, then there were contradictions inherent in the most basic structure of mathematics; and in **logic**, a contradiction means that any result can be proved to be true, a most unsatisfactory state of affairs. There were several different versions of essentially the same paradox, which was to do with the nature of mathematical property.

The best-known version is named after Bertrand Russell (1872–1970). Suppose you consider the set A of all sets which are not members of themselves. (For example, the empty set has no members at all, so is not a member of itself.) Is A a member of A or not? If A is a member of A, then it is not a member of A, by the definition of A; and if A is not a member of A, then it is a member of A, also by the definition of A. This is clearly contradictory, but surely A must either be a member of A or not? The solution to this paradox is to recognize that A is not actually a legitimate set, but what is known as a proper class. Classes have sets as members, but do not themselves have to be sets, though all sets are classes. A class is defined by a formula of **symbolic logic**, and contains all the sets which satisfy that formula. A set is basically a class which can be shown to be a set using the axioms of set theory.

Another similar paradox is to do with numbers. It is clear that the names for numbers in English become longer (in general) as the numbers get larger. So there will be numbers that cannot be described in English in fewer than 250 words. As that is the case, we can define a particular number n to be 'the first number which cannot be described in English in fewer than 250 words'. The problem is that we now have a description of this number in fewer than 250 words, so that we have a contradiction. The key to this paradox lies in the words 'in English'. We have here an indication that English is not the language in which mathematics should be performed – and neither is any other human language. Properties which are to be investigated mathematically should be capable of being expressed in symbolic form, and this one is not. So the nature of properties to be investigated mathematically is limited by paradox to logical sentences. **SMcL**

Further reading E.P. Northrop, *Riddles in Mathematics*.

PARALLEL COMPUTING

Parallel computing is one of the major new directions **computing** has taken since the 1980s. In the past, computers had only one processing unit and processed instructions in the order in which they were received. In the early days of computing, this was a major advance, but by the 1980s it was imposing speed restrictions on computers which became more and more acute. The idea of parallel computing is that several processors, connected together and communicating with each other, carry out several different instructions at once. This makes vast savings in time possible, though development is still in its infancy. **SMcL**

PARALLEL DISTRIBUTED PROCESSING see Connectionism

PARALLELISM

Parallelists, in **philosophy**, are dualists, holding that mental and physical phenomena are distinct. One traditional problem for those who hold that mental and physical phenomena are distinct is the difficulty of explaining how non-physical mental phenomena and non-mental physical phenomena could causally interact. Parallelists respond to this problem by bluntly denying that the mental and physical causally interact. Physical phenomena such as damage to the body do not cause mental phenomena such as pains, and mental phenomena such as pains do not cause physical phenomena such as winces. Rather, mental phenomena are only causally related to other mental phenomena and physical phenomena are only causally related to other physical phenomena. But the mental to mental and physical to physi-

cal causal chains run in parallel, giving rise to the illusion that mental and physical phenomena do causally interact.

An analogy makes clear that two causal chains which run in parallel may seem to be causally related even though they are not. Suppose that the causal chains which run through two time-keeping devices are perfectly correlated. So whenever the traditional clock with two hands shows one o'clock, the electric beeper with no clock face beeps once, whenever the traditional clock shows two o'clock, the electric beeper beeps twice, and so on. This could give rise to the impression that traditional clock's showing the hour causes the beeping. But of course, the two time-keeping devices do not causally influence the other. It is just that some (although not all) of the events in the causal chains which run through each device are so correlated as to give rise to the illusion that they causally interact. **AJ**

See also dualism; epiphenomenalism; interactionism; mind-body problem.

Further reading C. D. Broad, *The Mind and Its Place in Nature*.

PARANOID-SCHIZOID POSITION

The paranoid-schizoid position is, according to Melanie Klein, the way that the infant first experiences the world. In the first year of life the baby shifts between feeling great power over the mother, on the one hand, and feeling persecution by the mother on the other. Klein saw greed and envy as prominent parts of the baby's emotional life at this stage. As Freud discovered the child's phantasy life through his adult patients, so Klein discovered the life of the baby through the phantasies of the children she analysed. Through interpretation of children's play and phantasy she found a picture of the infant as prone to terrible anxieties about annihilation; these were made worse if the mother, because of her own depression or for environmental reasons, was unable to provide consolation and support. Such fears, in an act of defence, split off into the unconscious, but remained potentially active. Thus, unconscious anxieties about murder and madness (directed towards the mother) may remain in the mind, impoverishing the personality. If the mother is able to give good enough support, the baby will find balance between the real and phantasized parts of itself. Anxieties completely split off from consciousness can hinder development. **MJ**

Further reading Hannah Segal, *An Introduction to the Work of Melanie Klein.*

PARAPSYCHOLOGY

Parapsychology (Greek, 'study of what is beyond reason') is what used to be called 'psychic research': the investigation of phenomena not explicable by ordinary sciences. These phenomena include ESP (extra-sensory perception: such things as second sight and second hearing), hypnotism, mediumship, (the ability to communicate with mortals who have passed into the 'world beyond'), precognition (advance knowledge of the future), telekinesis (the ability to move physical objects by the power of thought alone) and telepathy (mind reading). The whole package is sometimes called *psi*, after the Greek letter which begins the word 'psychology', and after the supposed faculty in animals which allows such powers. In prescientific times, most of these powers were taken for granted, as part of the arsenal of ascetics, priests, prophets, shamans and others who claimed direct access to the supernatural. It is only in the last 150 years or so that some people have tried to establish a rational science out of investigating them – and there is still debate about whether parapsychology is real **science** (it has a professorship, unique in the world, at Edinburgh University) or delusion. **KMcL**

See also divination; pseudoscience; spiritualism.

Further reading H.L. Edge, *Foundations of Parapsychology.*

PARASITISM

Parasitism (from Greek *parasitas*, 'eater at another's table'), in the **life sciences**, describes the association between two organisms where one benefits at the expense of the other. Parasitic organisms are found in most parts of the living kingdom, from the viruses, which are all obligate parasites,

to the vampire bat, a parasitic mammal, and parasitic plants such as dodder. Some authorities exclude viruses and pathogenic bacteria from the category of parasites, but this is not justified given the nature of their association with the individuals which they affect. The relationship between parasite and host (the affected individual on which the parasite is metabolically dependent) is usually highly specific and can be damaging by affecting growth rate, reproductive capacity and survival ability; however, it is disadvantageous to the parasite to cause the death of its host (see **parasitoidism**). The host-parasite relationship is highly dynamic in an evolutionary sense, as the host is under intense adaptive pressure to avoid parasitism while the parasite must continually keep up with the host's evolution in order to perpetuate its life cycle. It was suggested by J.B.S. Haldane (1892–1964) that evolutionary pressure imposed by parasites may be a major driving force in **evolution**, and Richard Southwood has recently proposed that parasitic tropical diseases may have been instrumental in driving the development of early man and his migration out of the tropics.

Parasites may live within the body, either inside or in between cells, in the gut, or on the surface of the body; they may themselves bear parasites (hyperparasitism). There also exist various forms of behavioural parasitism, such as brood parasitism (as seen in the cuckoo) and social parasitism (where one species enslaves another). Many parasites have evolved specialized systems of transmission, for instance the use of insect vectors by microparasites such as the protozoan which causes malaria, or complex life cycles involving several host stages. In general, the complexity of the parasite is reflected in the complexity of its association with its host: protozoan and helminth (see **helminthology**) parasites are often implicated in highly adaptive strategies for evasion of the immune response and modification of host behaviour. **RB**

See also amensalism; parasitology; symbiosis; virology.

Further reading Philip Whitfield, *The Biology of Parasitism.*

PARASITOIDISM

Parasitoidism describes a parasitic association (see **parasitism**) in which the host is ultimately killed by the parasite. The phenomenon is most common in wasp species where the female lays her eggs in, on, or in the path of another insect, usually a grub. The wasp larvae hatch and burrow within the host, feeding on its viscera and growing, until they burst out, killing the host. Parasitoids are important insect predators (see **biological control**) and are successful in their aggressive strategy because the host rarely survives and so cannot evolve an immune response, and because the free-living stages allow for efficient transmission. **RB**

See also parasitology.

Further reading Philip Whitfield, *The Biology of Parasitism*.

PARASITOLOGY

Parasitology is the study of the phenomenon of **parasitism**. Parasites, such as fleas, have been an obvious problem since before history and other, less obvious, parasites have been partially understood since the time of the ancient Greeks and Egyptians. However, scientific study of parasites is a relatively new field. The famous pioneer microscopist Antonie van Leeuwenhoek accurately described the flea and its life cycle in the late 17th century, but one of the largest parasites of humans, the tapeworm, remained virtually unknown until its life cycle was elucidated by Pierre-Joseph van Beneden in the 19th century. Modern parasitology ties together a wide range of disciplines from **biochemistry** to **ecology** and from **anthropology** to **genetics**, and is an important source of evidence for **evolution**. **RB**

See also aetiology; bacteriology; helminthology; immunology; protozoology; virology.

Further reading Philip Whitfield, *The Biology of Parasitism*.

PARITY

The parity of a system, in **physics**, is its handedness, or symmetry. An object and its mirror image have opposite parity, as do a left and a right hand.

When a system conserves parity, for every object within the system, there can also exist a similar object with opposite parity. This is the same as saying that every object has a mirror image which would prove physically possible to construct.

The world as we know it appears to conserve parity. It is almost inconceivable that there could exist an object whose mirror image would be impossible to create. And yet, subtle experiments have shown us that this is in fact the case. The universe exhibits a slight, but measurable asymmetry; it does not conserve parity.

This asymmetry may be measured in various ways. It only occurs in processes involving the weak force. The most obvious example is the neutrino. This tiny, neutral particle only exists in a 'left-handed' state; that is, its direction of spin is determined by its direction of motion. If a neutrino is coming towards you, its spin is always clockwise. It can be seen that this does not conserve parity, for if we looked at the neutrino in a mirror, its spin would be reversed but its direction of travel would not. The mirror image, a neutrino with a right-handed spin, is never found in reality.

Another example is atomic parity non-conservation. The weak force at work within the atom produces small, but measurable, effects, which may be seen by passing polarised light through a gas of atoms.

The plane of polarization of the light undergoes a small rotation during its passage through the gas. However, the rotation is always in the same direction, and no system may be set up which looks like the mirror image of the experiment. Thus again, parity is not conserved. **JJ**

See also weak force/strong force.

PARLIAMENTARY GOVERNMENT see
Representative Government

PARODY

Parody (Greek, 'side-road'), in all the **arts**, is basing one's creation on a piece of work (by oneself or by someone else) which exists already. The new piece derives energy from the old as well as adding something of its own. Equally, knowledge of the old adds to our enjoyment of the new, and **irony** may well be an important part of the effect.

At their simplest, parodies simply burlesque their originals. Favourite methods are to treat pompous or pretentious material in a silly way (as in Ibert's send-up of Mendelssohn's *Wedding March* in his music for the farce *An Italian Straw Hat*, or the innumerable burlesques of Shakespeare), or to treat a trivial subject in a bombastic way (as in Pope's mock-Homeric epic *The Rape of the Lock*, or Dochnányi's *Variations on a Nursery Song*, which turn 'Baa Baa Black Sheep' into a grandiose piano concerto). There is, however, a much deeper and subtler use of parody, which is evident in all the arts. This involves taking elements from the work parodied, deconstructing it as it were, and then weaving them into the texture of your own new work, as if they were your own material.

In works of this kind, humour is seldom the intention. Irony is there, but its effect is less to make us laugh than to remind us of other contexts for the piece of work we are experiencing, to add nuances and overtones. In the Middle Ages, Christian church musicians often wrote parody Masses, making popular tunes of the day the basis for complex and deeply serious contrapuntal webs of sound. Virgil's *Aeneid* and Joyce's *Ulysses* parody the *Odyssey*, both in general (the idea of a journey which is also an existential quest) and in particular incidents and details. (Joyce also parodies other writings of every kind, from tabloid journalism and novelettish **fiction** to Jesuit tracts and transcripts of psychoanalytical sessions).

Substantial parody of this kind has been a major resource of all arts in the 20th century. The arts have fed off themselves, and off each other, in a way previously unparalleled. It is as if works of art in general have become a resource, a continuum from which every new work emerges, and with which every spectator is at least marginally familiar. It would be possible to understand the elliptical and jerky narrative of Kafka's *The Trial*, for example, or the **block**

construction in music by Stravinsky or Messiaen, without knowing that both are influenced by Eisenstein's structuring of film narrative by jump-cuts and juxtaposition rather than by developmental flow. But, today, almost everyone is to some degree aware of film cutting, and this enhances our enjoyment of other mediums. (Eisenstein himself acknowledged debts to Büchner's stage-play *Woyzeck*.) This is the sense in which Yeats's chamber plays, Eugene O'Neill's *Mourning Becomes Electra* or Eliot's dramas parody Greek **tragedy** not merely in style, but in specific scenes and themes; in which Picasso's *Les demoiselles d'Avignon* refers to identifiable heads in a particular exhibition of African masks; in which William Golding's *Lord of the Flies* descants unnervingly on Ballantyne's *Coral Island*; in which Berg's violin concerto weaves a half-hour textural web from a Carinthian folk song and a Bach chorale, borrowing not just melody and harmony but a whole aura of emotion and significance. It happens, equally, in the popluar arts. Enjoyment of Peter Bogdanovich's film *What's Up Doc?* is enhanced by our memory of the film it parodies, Howard Hawks's *Bringing Up Baby*; crucial scenes in Kubrick's savage *A Clockwork Orange* parody *Singin' in the Rain*; dozens of bands in the late 1980s made new songs by 'deconstructing' bass lines and riffs originated by such artists as James Brown, Kate Bush and Queen; Tolkien's *The Lord of the Rings* (itself parodying works as disparate as Beowulf and H.G. Wells's *War of the Worlds*) is the matrix from which thousands of **novels**, computer games and roleplaying games have been born. **KMcL**

PARTICLES

Molecules are the building blocks of life. Most of the substance that we meet in everyday life are composed of molecules: our bodies, all plastics, all foods. Molecules are composed of atoms, which are bound together by exchanging or sharing electrons (see below).

Atoms are smaller than molecules, and are composed of a tiny nucleus surrounded by a cloud of orbiting electrons. The negative charge possessed by the electrons is balanced by the nucleus, which has an equal and opposite charge.

The nucleus contains *protons*, which carry the positive charge, and *neutrons*, which, as their name implies, are neutral and carry no charge. The nucleus is bound together by the strong force, whereas the electrons are bound in the atom by the electromagnetic force.

The *electron* and the *positron* are identical in every way apart from the fact that electrons have negative charge and positrons have positive charge. They are 2,000 times lighter than protons and neutrons. Electric current is simply the flow of electrons down wires. The positron is the antiparticle to the electron, which means that if the two meet they will annihilate each other.

Protons and neutrons are each made of three *quarks*, bound together by gluons (see below) – particle physicists were running out of names by this time. There are thought to be six types of quark: the up, down, strange, charmed, bottom and top quark. The top quark has yet to be produced, but its existence is predicted. Each quark comes in one of three **colours**, red, green and blue. These bear no relation to what we know as colours they are just labels for differences between the quarks.

These particles are the constituents of matter. There is another class of particle, called carriers, which are the medium by which forces operate.

Gluons are the field carriers for the colour force, which binds quarks together. The *Z*- and *W-bosons* do the same job for the weak force. The as yet undetected *graviton* is believed to be the field carrier for the force of gravity. The *photon*, while being the particle that light is made of, is also the electromagnetic field carrier.

These field carriers come in very different sizes. The Z-and W-bosons weigh as much as a large atom, while a photon has no mass at all, but is pure energy. It is difficult to place a value on the mass of a gluon, due to the nature of the colour force, but they may weigh as much as a quark. The tiny graviton has little or no mass.

It is believed that at very high energies, all field carriers will look the same, as all fundamental forces are thought to coalesce

into the same force at these energies. **JJ**

PARTY SYSTEMS see **Representative Government**

PASTORAL

Pastoral is an uncomplicated but persistent artistic genre, in which the beauties of the countryside and the perceived simplicities of country life are described and used as a metaphor for natural harmony and calm. (The word 'idyllic' comes from idyl, a favourite pastoral verse form.) In Europe, pastoral dates back to ancient Greece, where the simple life was associated with Arcadia (a mountainous region of the Peloponnese, full of oak woods and inhabited in ancient times chiefly by shepherds). The placid life of farmers and shepherds was taken as a human equivalent of the carefree existence of the gods – a notion paralleled in the Middle Eastern idea of the same period that gardens (for example the Garden of Eden) were models of paradise. Pastoral **poetry** and **paintings** of pastoral scenes spread to the rest of Europe, both in their simple form and, after the **Renaissance**, in more complex **allegories**, in which monarchs and courtiers were depicted as nymphs and shepherdesses. (English and Italian madrigals and the paintings of Watteau are prime examples of this.)

In Europe pastoral styles and forms persisted in **literature** until the **Romantics** began to make more sophisticated use of Nature. The pastoral had a late flowering in **music**, especially the works of Delius, Grieg and Vaughan Williams, which were inspired by folk songs, and the works of Messiaen inspired by bird song. (There was a sub-branch of European pastoral in the US, led by poets resident in New England.) Outside Europe, pastoral has flourished particularly in the Far East, where natural scenes and the events of country life are a favourite subject for artists and writers. In all places where pastoral is favoured, a notable point is that the art made of it has tended to exist for leisured, rich people rather than for country-dwellers themselves. The visions of rural simplicity enjoyed by sophisticates have had little contact with reality, and hence pastoral has tended to have a slightly artificial, ethereal quality which is part of its appeal. This artificiality, in turn, has been set on its head by some creators (for example, in English poetry, by William Blake, the World War I poets and in our own time Ted Hughes), making bitter or ironical use of selected pastoral conventions to articulate distinctly more savage views of human nature and the world we live in. **KMcL**

PATHETIC FALLACY

'Pathetic fallacy' is a phrase coined by the 19th-century critic John Ruskin to describe the way writers and painters ascribe emotion to the phenomena of Nature, or to pretend that such phenomena sympathize with the feelings of the human beings involved with them. Ruskin himself affected to prefer the objective realities of Nature (though he was happier with its beauty or ruggedness – both 'pathetic' adjectives – than with what Tennyson called its redness in tooth and claw). But few imaginative creators have shared this preference, and the pathetic fallacy has been a favourite resource in **fine art**, **literature** and **music**, and not just in **Romantic** times, when it reached, perhaps, its zenith, but from the earliest beginnings to the present day. **KMcL**

PATRIARCHY

Patriarchy (Greek, 'rule by the father') is a family or society dominated by men. Feminists have sought to identify the mechanisms that support patriarchal structures. Different feminisms look at different areas of patriarchal ideologies. Feminist anthropologists and sociologists have challenged the analysis of social structures based on men as head as families. Feminist economists have looked at the way in which **economics** has not accounted for invisible and unpaid work by women. Feminist literary critics have rewritten the patriarchal canon of male authors by rediscovering and republishing forgotten women writers, giving a new criterion for assessing the importance of popular literary genres. Some feminist theorists have used socialist analysis of class structure and psychoanalytic theories of gender construction as methodological tools to help uncover invisible patriarchal structures. Juliet Mitchell, for example, in her influential book *Women's Estate*, uses both these methodologies to identify four main areas in which patriarchy exercises its power: production, reproduction, **socialization** and **sexuality**.

Many feminists contend that the central mechanism of patriarchy is the way in which male domination is disguised as a 'natural' phenomenon. For many women patriarchy is experienced in the form of the father beyond whose authority there can be no further appeal. Patriarchy is often characterized by some feminists as being linear, monolithic and unable to tolerate divergent viewpoints. Feminists have shown that the patriarchal construction of femininity has relied upon a male-defined biological view. Jacqueline Rose describes the female experience of femininity as an injury, because in a patriarchy femininity is used to disable women to secure male power. The power of patriarchy has been identified by feminism in (amongst many areas of life) **politics**, economics, **religion**, **science**, education and **academe**, and in all of these areas the male point of view is invisibly privileged and is taken to be universal. One of the more recent debates that has emerged in **feminism** concerns the possibility of women's participation in these fields without the necessity of adopting a masculinized role (see **tokenism**).

As well as identifying the mechanisms of patriarchy, feminists have also developed different strategies for disrupting and overturning it. Feminists interested in **popular culture** have looked for the contradictions within a text or film showing the foundational flaws of patriarchy. Such feminists have often read texts and film 'against the grain' – celebrating the moments when women break out of the patriarchal order before they are brought back into the family fold. Feminist film-makers, photographers and writers, have in many different ways invented new languages for exposing patriarchal structures in pre-existing texts. Monique Wittig has theorized lesbianism as a strategy for escaping patriarchal conceptions of femininity and female sexuality. Luce Irigaray has categorized power itself as being patriarchal; her books are a rejection of patriarchy and its intrinsic power, a celebration of women as decentred, multiple and contradictory. Other feminists reject the refusal to speak of power and seek, instead, to analyse the historical and economic conditions that maintain patriarchy. Such women, such as Linda Nicholson, often make use of **postmodernism** to fix the location of the patriarchy as a specific viewpoint and to criticize patriarchal theories that try to speak in a transcendent and universal way. **TK**

See also matriarchy.

Further reading Lorraine Gamman & Margaret Marshment, *The Female Gaze*; Juliet Mitchell, *Women's Estate*; *Psychoanalysis and Feminism*.

PEANO ARITHMETIC

Peano arithmetic is the **axiomatization** of the basic operations of arithmetic most commonly used today by mathematicians. It is named after its originator, Giuseppe Peano (1858–1932). It also acts as the basis for modern ideas about **numbers**.

The basic elements of Peano's system are the concepts of **zero** and successor. The successor is a **function** which maps a number to the number which will come after it when counting. These two concepts are the ones for which Peano actually gave axioms; the basic operations of arithmetic are then easily defined. The axioms basically say that every number has a unique successor, that every number except 0 is the successor of some other number, that no number is the successor of two distinct numbers, and, most importantly, the principle of **induction**. Induction is not an axiom, but what is known as an axiom schema, an infinite collection of axioms (in this case, one for every property of numbers expressible using **symbolic logic** and the concepts of 0 and successor). The principle of induction is that if P is a property, such that P(0) is true, and for every number n, if P(n) is true, then so is P(S(n)) (where S(n) is the successor of n); then P(m) is true for every number m.

The operations of addition (+) and multiplication (×) are defined using the principle of **recursion**. This is derived from the principle of induction, and says that we can define a function f by giving its value at 0 (f(0)), and its value at the successor of n in terms of its value at n, for every number n. As examples of this, the operation of 'adding m to a', where a is a fixed number, is defined by saying that $a+0=a$, and $a+S(m)=S(a+m)$; and the operation of 'multiplying a by m' is defined by saying that $a \times 0 = 0$, and $a \times S(m) = (a \times m) + a$ (where, in both cases, S(m) is the successor of m).

With these definitions, it is easy to prove the basic truths of arithmetic, for example that $1+1=2$. (This proof took Bertrand Russell hundreds pages to prove, because of his unwieldy definition of number.) It is important to remember that 1 and 2 are really just shorthand ways to write down S(0) and S(S(0)) respectively, and that neither term has any meaning in the language of logic in which Peano arithmetic operates. The proof goes as follows: $S(0)+S(0)=S(S(0)+0)=S(S(0))$, which is considerably shorter than Russell's. **SMcL**

PENANCE

Penance (Latin *paenitentia*, 'repentance') means the Christian sacrament which includes contrition, confession, satisfaction and absolution. 'Satisfaction', in this context, means the doing of works or acceptance of punishment to atone for the sin in question. Essentially simple, the process of confession was worked up in medieval European **Christianity** to a huge bureaucratic edifice: a hierarchy of sins, each with its appropriate form of 'satisfaction'. The aims were to encompass the whole range of human behaviour, and to make the Church an infallible assessor of guilt and agent of God's mercy. The whole system was an adaptation of the bureaucratic hierarchy of imperial Roman law, appeals being allowed to higher and higher authorities (in Roman law ending with the Emperor, in religious law with the Pope). Acts of confession ranged from private moments with one's confessor-priest to huge public orgies of guilt and self-laceration; 'satisfaction' could similarly involve anything from saying the Rosary to surrender of all one's worldly goods, from small charitable acts to pilgrimages across the whole of Europe. Many masterpieces in **architecture** and the **arts** were the direct results of acts of penance. Whatever its religious importance, in social terms the system was a powerful binding-force throughout the continent for well over a millennium; hardly anyone was untouched by it, and until Luther hardly anyone challenged it. **KMcL**

PENIS ENVY see Castration Anxiety

PENTECOSTALISM

The name for the 20th-century Pentecostal movement is taken from the outpouring of the Spirit 50 days after the Resurrection of Christ. (*Pentecost* is Greek for 'fiftieth day'.) The name reflects the belief that the spiritual gifts listed in Paul's Letter to the Church in Corinth (1 Cor. 12:8–10), as enjoyed by the Early Church, have been rediscovered, especially faith healing, prophecy and speaking in tongues (*glossolalia*). The first Pentecostals, who appeared some 90 years ago, saw their experience as the promised outpouring of the Holy Spirit in the last days before Christ's Second Coming, manifesting Jesus as saviour, healer, baptizer in the Holy Spirit and Coming King.

Although most Pentecostal groups adopt a **fundamentalist** approach to biblical exegesis, and a conservative evangelical theology, their interpretation of scripture is often creative and imaginative, providing a living source of guidance. Pentecostal worship can be described as 'organized spontaneity' with the maximum possible amount of congregational participation. The music is often outstanding, while in many congregations, dancing has great ritual significance. Adult baptism on confession of faith is practised, regardless of whether the convert has been baptized before. Many congregations have no full-time paid clergy, and lay leadership is probably the most important factor in this church's phenomenal growth, particularly in the Third World. **EMJ**

Further reading W.J. Hollenweger, *The Pentecostals*.

PERCEPTION

Perception, in **philosophy**, is the process of apprehending objects by means of the senses. Philosophers have debated whether the immediate objects of perceptual awareness are sensory experiences as of objects or the objects themselves. They have also offered a causal theory of perception. In order to perceive an object it is not enough to have a perceptual experience as of an object which is there. One may have a sensory experience as of a dagger upon the table as a result of taking a hallucinatory drug when, as a matter of complete coincidence, there is a dagger upon the table. If so, one will have a sensory experience as of an object which is there, but one will not be perceiving it. For, it is said, one's sensory experience as of the dagger was not caused by it. According to the causal theory of perception, one perceives an object if and only if one has a sensory experience as of it, the object is there, and the object causes one's sensory experience as of it. **AJ**

See also causal theories; illusion, argument from; naive realism; representative theory of perception.

Further reading D. Armstrong, *Perception and the Physical World*; G. Warnock, *The Philosophy of Perception*.

PERFORMING ARTS

In some **arts** there is direct contact between creator and spectator. Writers of **novels** or painters of pictures speak directly to their audience, on a one-to-one level. The effects and meanings of the work of art are intended to be apparent in the work itself, and to yield themselves to the spectator either immediately or after reflection and consideration. Interventions by third parties – for example, critical exegesis – are handmaids to this process and not essential to it. In the performing arts, by contrast, the performer, the intermediary, is a crucial part of the process. He or she 'realizes' the work of art, and creators take this realization into account when they make the art. A play, for example, exists in its true form only as actors perform it for spectators; when we read it on the page we are missing (or supplying from memory or in imagination) a major part of the experience.

Similarly, the presence of other spectators is often essential to the true experience of a work of the performing arts. Obviously, plays, dances and pieces of music can be performed for single spectators, but usually a larger group of people is involved. Creative collusion between the author and spectator of the work, already modulated by the presence of the performer, thus depends also, in part, on the interaction of a group of people all responding, individually and collectively, to the same work at the same moment. The raptness, enthusiasm or hilarity of one's fellow-spectators can be a major determinant of one's appreciation, and enjoyment, of the show.

These factors raise questions about the exact nature of a given work of the performing arts, particularly nowadays when vast quantities not only of past works, but of past performances, are available to spectators in their own homes. What, for example, is the 'real' *Oresteia* or *Pathétique* sonata – the one witnessed by Aeschylus' or Beethoven's original audience, the one envisaged by the creator, the 'definitive' performance hailed by critics in the past, the one in my mind as I read the work, or the one I hear and see today in the company of other people? Nowadays part of our experience of most works in the performing arts is, precisely, those works' past lives. When I see X's performance in *Swan Lake*, my appreciation may partly depend on my view of Y's and Z's in earlier times (witnessed personally or reported). This raises problems of creative ownership. We hear about 'Karajan's *Otello*' or 'Macready's *Hamlet*', as if these performers had somehow collaborated in the creation of a work of art in a way of which all subsequent interpreters must take account – can this possibly be true? A 'good' performance can reveal, for this or that spectator, the power latent in a work of the performing arts, just as a 'bad' performance can mask it. In this, sense, however, the performer's role is analogous less to the creator's than to that of the critic of a book or painting.

Other questions arise. What is happening when I act out a play for myself, or play the *Pathétique* sonata on my own piano, alone at home? I become two parts of the troika of creation of that work of art on that occasion, the performer and the spectator. How does this differ, if at all, from my collusion with the creator of a work of nonperforming art? Again, is a recording of a performance, whether sound, vision or both, an account of the actual work of art itself – or when I enjoy it, am I not, rather, enjoying a static work of art in its own right: that is, the record of that performance rather than the performance itself?

These philosophical conundrums, interesting though they may be, take us far from the actual experience of works of the performing arts. The enjoyment of all art demands collusion, and it can be argued that because the performing arts require the collusion of so many people, to make and enjoy the performance, they can offer some of the most polyvalent, if not richest, of all artistic experiences. The one thing they lack, in comparison with the static arts, is the opportunity for the spectator to reflect at the moment of perception itself. We may ponder afterwards what we have seen or heard, but unless we drift off into reverie during the show itself, so missing what comes next, our participation in the performing arts, however profound the experience, is of its essence momentary, fleeting and partial – something all creators of works of the performing arts must bear in mind as they plan their effects. **KMcL**

See also ballet; criticism; gesamtkunstwerk; music drama; opera; theatre.

PERIODIC TABLE

Every element corresponds to an assembly of a number of protons forming the core of the atom and a number of electrons situated in one shell or more shells of different diameters round the protons. The number of protons determines the mass of the atom. Each element has its own atomic weight, generally different from every other element. Early **chemistry** recognized that certain elements had similar but slightly different characteristics, for example sodium, potassium and caesium or calcium, barium and strontium, but no general pattern for all the elements was found until Stanislav Cannizzaro (1826–1910) who arranged the 60 elements known at the time (1858). When the elements were arranged in order of increasing atomic weight, a curious repetition of chemical properties at regular intervals was revealed. This was noted by the English chemist John Newlands (1838–98), but his theories were not generally accepted. It was left to the Russian chemist Dmitri Ivanovich Mendeleyev (1834–1907) who in 1869 put forward his theories and was rightly credited as the true discoverer of the Periodic Table.

Mendeleyev wrote the names and some of the main features of the elements on cards. While arranging this pack of cards in different ways he stumbled upon the pattern which we now recognize as the Periodic Table.

The Periodic Table is an arrangement of elements according to the number of electrons in their shell. Travelling horizontally along the table, the next element gains an electron, while travelling vertically downwards means that the next element gains an outer shell. Elements in the same groups (groups run vertically in the table) exhibit similar properties.

Mendeleyev's talent lay in the fact that he knew that there was an underlying trend to the known elements; he did not design the Periodic Table, he discovered it. If his theories were correct, he knew that there were more elements to be discovered where there were spaces in his Periodic Table.

Since Mendeleyev published his table in 1869 a further 40 elements have been discovered or produced by nuclear reactions, and the table has been redesigned in order to accommodate them. **AA**

Further reading I. Asimov, *A Short History of Chemistry*.

PERSON

Different philosophers have given different definitions of 'person'. (The original Latin *persona* means 'mask' or 'character in a play'.) One early definition was 'rational human being'. According to this definition, something is a person just if it is both rational and a member of the species human being. Locke distinguished between the concept 'person' and the concept 'human being', claiming that there could be people who were not human beings. Locke characterized a person as a thinking, intelligent being, that has reason and reflection, and is aware of its own identity over time. So if there were a thinking intelligent parrot, which was aware of its own identity over time, then it would be a person. According to Locke, then, something can be a person without being a member of the species human being.

Many, including Locke, have linked the notion of personhood with the notion of moral responsibility. Only people are responsible for their actions, so animals which are not people are not morally responsible for their actions. And a person can only be responsible for *their* actions, not for the actions of a distinct person. **AJ**

See also no-ownership theory of the self; personal identity.

Further reading J.L. Mackie, *Problems for Locke*; P.F. Stawson, *Individuals*.

PERSONAL CONSTRUCT THEORY

Personal Construct Theory, the work of George Kelly, was first published in 1955. Kelly thought that the most useful way to look at the nature of humankind was as a model scientist. All human beings, whatever the culture, had, he decided, scientist-like aspects. His psychological model of humankind, unlike a biological one, did not look at aims but at a type of attitude towards being in the world: it was an ontological standpoint. Kelly questioned our motivation, and finds us seeking to predict and control the cause of events which are our life; in every human act we make theories, test hypotheses and weigh up experimental evidence. The many differences in personal viewpoints correspond to the differences between the theoretical points of view of different scientists.

Kelly's 'constructs' are the total set of hypotheses about reality that any person holds at one time. A person's aim is to control and predict the environment. The method of enquiry used by a therapist to encourage the use of these tools is a form of **cognitive therapy**. The therapist in turn puts aside his constructs and attempts to enter into the world of constructs belonging to the other person. It assumes that we are all unique and do not construct the world alike. People are seen to experiment with information, to make it meaningful and become master of their own lives. The human baby is dependent for a long period, and has to make sense of its existence using this scientific apparatus. At some point the baby will have to decide what is my body and what is my mother's body. This is a construct: what is and what is not.

Personal Construct theory is a philosophical standpoint (like **phenomenology**), as well as a theory of personality. We are not driven by unconscious forces (as we are in Freud's model), but are agencies whose anticipation looks towards the future. The therapist using Personal Construct Theory will also use tools: grids, questionnaires, drawn models, reflecting the scientific process which goes on in the patient and in the therapy. **MJ**

Further reading G.A. Kelly, *A Theory of Personality: the Psychology of Personal Constructs.*

PERSONAL IDENTITY

We often judge that a certain person at one time is the same person as a certain person at another. The person in the prison cell now is the same person as the person who stole the jewels. But what is it that makes for personal identity, that makes a certain person at one time the same person as a certain person at another?

Those dualists who hold that the mind is immaterial may hold that one person is identical to another just if he or she has the same immaterial soul. One objection to this account is Locke's. Locke claimed that it is possible for a person to transfer from one immaterial soul to another, so that sameness of immaterial soul is not necessary for personal identity. He also claimed that it is possible for one immaterial soul to be associated with one person at one time and then another later on, so, sameness of immaterial soul is not sufficient for personal identity.

Others have held that personal identity is a matter of bodily continuity. One can survive the loss of various limbs. Indeed one could survive a brain transplant operation – I could move from one human body to another when my brain was transplanted from one to the other. So those who hold that personal identity is a matter of bodily continuity hold that personal identity is a matter of the continuity of the brain.

But this suggestion is vulnerable to an objection concerning the possibility of brain bisection. Suppose that the brain of person A is cut in half and that the result is two people, B and C, both of whom have half a brain each of which is continuous with A's brain. (Note that some people do survive with less than half of an ordinary brain.) Both B and C have brains that are continuous with A's brain, but they cannot both be identical to A. For if A is identical with B and B is identical with C, then B must be identical with C. (This is simply a consequence of the transitivity of identity, the logical truth that if x = y and y = z, then x = z.) But B and C, two people existing at the same time, can hardly be identical. So brain continuity is not sufficient for personal identity.

Locke argued that personal identity is a not a matter of sameness of immaterial soul, or of bodily continuity, but of memory. Person A is identical with an earlier person B just if A can remember performing B's action. This suggestion is also open to criticism. We need to distinguish between *genuinely* remembering performing an action and merely *seeming* to remember performing an action. Genuinely remembering performing an action is sufficient for being identical with the person who performed it. But as Butler pointed out, since one can genuinely remember performing an action only if one is the person who performed it, genuine memory presupposes and does not explain personal identity. And seeming to remember performing an action is hardly sufficient for being the person who performed it one can seem to remember doing things which were in fact done by other people, such as paying the bill. Further, neither genuinely nor seeming to remember performing an action is necessary for being the person who performed it, as the existence of amnesia makes clear. **AJ**

See also death; dualism; person; personhood.

Further reading J. Foster, *The Immaterial Self*; J.L. Mackie, *Problems for Locke*.

PERSONHOOD

Marcel Mauss opened the anthropological debate on the nature of 'the person' in 1938 by considering the notion of persona, or mask, and how it was utilized in different societies. In **anthropology**, the individual is generally described as an agent of the institutions in a society. The term personhood is used to refer to the individual as a social actor, often an idealized (sociocultural) state. In the West, 'person' has been contrasted with the 'self' which refers to the individual as the locus of experience. Such notions of agency are typical of a specifically Western view.

Until recently, the nature of the person was taken for granted in anthropology. However, it is apparent that the idea of personhood as a unified self, which experiences things privately, has been reinforced by psychoanalytic theories. According to this view, the experiential realm of selfhood and emotions were thought to be the province of psychotherapy. Other societies do not necessarily make this distinction between a self and social agent. Selfhood may be intimately bound up with social status and identity, where roles and behaviour are prescribed according to one's place in the social order. The Chinese, for instance, have a notion of holism in which the individual is seen as a microcosm of an ordered macrocosm. In **Confucian** philosophy the self is a nexus of possibilities which has to be cultivated. The individual is not fully developed if he or she did not cultivate proper social relations. Notions of individual identity are subsumed to the demands of the group.

The awareness of individuality may also be dissolved in states of trance, possession and mystical experiences. In cases of spirit-possession the body becomes something that is passively acted on by spirits. The topic, opened up by Mauss, has led to wider explorations of **indigenous metaphysics**.

Hindu theories of partibility see the 'individual' as a divisible entity able to take in and give out a variety of influences and essences. For the Hindus, the unstable and composite nature of the person bears little relation to the biological notion of the individual rooted in the physical body, which is prevelent in our own society, and demonstrates the value of examining basic conceptions of personhood. **CL**

See also altered states of consciousness; emotions; transactionalism.

Further reading M. Carrithers, Collins and Lukes (eds.), *The Category of the Person*.

PERSPECTIVE

Perspective, in **painting**, is the deployment of lines on a two-dimensional surface to create the illusion of three-dimensional space. Perspective, however, is not a transcription of how the human eye perceives, but a representational system with specific geographic and temporal associations. Many cultures, such as Australian Aboriginal, Ancient Egyptian, pre-Columbian or Western medieval art, have developed highly sophisticated systems of representation without recourse to a coherent use of perspective.

Linear perspective may be likened to a 'window onto the world'. As the eye of the beholder embraces a scene through a window, so the artist creates the illusion of space by treating the surface of a canvas as a window, tracing outlines which pass 'through' the canvas and so into the eye. The systematic use of such devices makes parallel lines apparently converge as they recede into picture space (until they appear to meet at a given point, often called the vanishing point), and objects of similar size seem smaller the further they are from the picture plane.

In a short space of time in 15th-century Florence a group of **architects** and painters evolved the means to execute architectural plans and paintings in perspective. The architect Brunelleschi is often credited as the inventor of the technique in the early

1420s. His fellow architect Alberti codified many of Brunelleschi's theorems into a treatise on painting, *De Pictura* ('On Painting'), written in Latin in 1435 and translated the following year. Alberti offered an infallible method of drawing in perspective such classics of illusion as a chequerboard floor with both orthogonals and transverse parallels correctly indicated.

Alberti's treatise stated as a truth, 'No one will deny that things which are not visible do not concern the painter, for he strives to represent only the things that are seen'. Thus emphasis on appearance, not essence, became the goal of the painters who strove to apply Alberti's theorems. For example, in such paintings as the *Battle of San Romano* Uccello used a rigorous geometric construction to show fallen soldiers in extreme foreshortening. Most of all it is Piero della Francesca's work that personifies the sense of order with which the humanist values of reason, order and decorum endow the paintings of 15th-century Italy – and all are qualities implicit in perspective. Piero's art also exhibits a clear understanding of the mathematical foundations of Renaissance painting. Later in life he wrote a treatise on perspective.

Northern European artists were also developing perspective. Dürer travelled to Italy in the 1490s and met with artists familiar with the new theorems. A little earlier, van Eyck had employed complex multipoint perspective (that is, where several vanishing points are used instead of one) in paintings such as *The Marriage of Arnolfini and his Wife* (1434). Here perspective is used to facilitate the representation of nature, not, as in Italy, to regulate it. In the 17th century these different roles for perspective erupted into a dispute in the French Academy between the director Charles Lebrun and the Professor of Perspective, Abraham Bosse. The former argued that perspective was a useful servant of the artist, but a tyrannical master; Bosse saw it as a judge to whom no appeal may be made.

Since the early days of **Romanticism**, perspective has been seen as a constraint on artistic freedom. Furthermore **modernism** frequently plays on the difference between 'seeing' and 'knowing': how the laws of perspective alter the reality of a given object such as a plate when seen from an oblique angle. But it is the cubists who are the strongest challengers of the conventions of linear perspective. In breaking up the picture subject into a series of overlapping planes, which must be reconstructed as much in the mind as the eye of the beholder, they deny the validity of perspective as a system of representation. **MG PD**

Further reading E.H. Gombrich, *Art and Illusion.*

PHALLIC STAGE see **Oral, Anal and Phallic Stages**

PHARMACOLOGY

Pharmacology (Greek, 'study of potions') is the study of the effect of chemical substances (drugs) on physiological systems. It is chiefly a 20th-century development because of the **biochemical** level at which drugs act. One of the founding figures in pharmacology was François Magendie who published his *Formulary* in 1821. He investigated the activity of a number of drugs as pure substances, representing a departure from the practice of prescribing complex mixtures of drugs. The Roman physician Galen (129–200 CE) had ascribed properties to various drugs, predominantly botanical in origin, but he prescribed them as mixtures. This practice endures to this day and gives rise to numerous popular, frequently useless or dangerous, 'cure-all' mixtures.

In the 19th century, chemists such as Oswald Schmiedeberg began to study the effects of various drugs upon **physiology**, and it is now routine to perform a wide range of pharmacological studies before a new drug is licensed for use. Paul Ehrlich (1857–1915) proposed that chemicals might be used to treat disease and some of the first examples of this new 'chemotherapy' were chemicals derived from the dye industry. By a process of selective variation of chemical structure these drugs were modified and tested and gradually improved. Substances derived from plants were chemically synthesized and modified in a similar fashion to produce the range of drugs in use today. Most new drug development continues by this process of trial and error, though the new technologies of **biophysics** and **molecular biology** present the possibility of designing drugs to combat specific diseases.

Drugs act on the **metabolism** of the individual or the metabolism of pathogenic organisms which infect the individual. Frequently a single drug affects more than one biological system and two or more drugs together may act synergistically or antagonistically. It is thus vital to carry out comprehensive testing of drugs before they are used for medical or veterinary purposes. The testing typically follows a hierarchical system of simple screening, leading on to more complex and costly testing on animals and finally trials in humans. The study of the effect of drugs at various doses under various conditions is called pharmacodynamics, while biochemical pharmacology involves the study of the action of drugs on the metabolism. **RB**

See also psychopharmacology; toxicology.

Further reading B.G. Katzung, *Basic and Clinical Pharmacology*.

PHASE SHIFTING see **Process Music**

PHASING see **Process Music**

PHENOLOGY

Phenology (Greek, 'study of happening'), in the **life sciences**, is the study of the timing of regular, natural phenomena, such as the flowering of plants and the rutting of deer. Many such phenomena are timed to coincide with cyclic variations which determine resource availability, such as changes in ambient temperature and day length. Thus many organisms time certain events which are important to their life cycles to occur during particular seasons; the production of young in the spring, for example, coincides with warmer weather and the availability of plentiful food, so deer time their rut to occur in autumn, allowing gestation to proceed over the winter. Phenology is concerned with events which occur on a

seasonal basis rather than cyclic phenomena which occur more frequently, such as circadian (daily) rhythms. **RB**

See also biological rhythm; chronobiology.

PHENOMENALISM

Phenomenalism (Greek, 'theory of what appears', 'theory of what is'), in **philosophy**, is the doctrine that statements about physical objects have the same meaning as certain statements about actual or possible sensory experiences. So, for example, the statement that there is a chair in the room might be held to have the same meaning as the statement that if someone is in the room, then he or she will have a visual experience as of a chair. It was in this spirit that J. S. Mill defined material objects as 'permanent possibilities of sensations'.

There are two reasons to doubt that statements about physical objects have the same meaning as certain statements about actual or possible sensory experiences. Consider the suggestion that the statement that there is a chair in the room means the same as the statement that if someone is in the room, then he or she will have a visual experience as of a chair. The second statement is not only about actual or possible sensory experiences, but still contains reference to physical entities to the room. Further, it could be true that there is a chair in the room without its being true that if someone is in the room, then he or she will have a visual experience as of a chair. For the chair will only cause someone to have a visual experience of it if there is enough light to see it and the person's nervous system is working. So the statement about sensory experience which is said to mean the same as the physical object statement must be revised, to refer to yet more physical conditions and objects: in this case to light and to nervous systems. So statements about physical objects do not have the same meaning as statements which refer only to actual or possible sensory experiences, and not to any physical objects. **AJ**

See also idealism.

Further reading A.J. Ayer, *Language, Truth and Logic*; J. Foster, *A.J. Ayer*.

PHENOMENOLOGICAL SOCIOLOGY

Phenomenological sociology is a school of thought which is derived from phenomenological **philosophy** (see **consciousness**), especially from the work of Alfred Schutz (1899–1959). The main focus of this branch of **sociology** is everyday life and its associated states of consciousness. Unlike other schools of thought in sociology (for example **positivism**), phenomenological sociology denies any influence of the wider social **structure** in influencing human behaviour. Proponents of this school take issue with the assumption that human beings are formed by social forces rather than creating those forces themselves in the first instance. Phenomenologists argue that the job of phenomenological analysis is to show how the everyday world, which is ordinarily taken for granted, is made up. Phemonenological study is carried out by 'bracketing off' any assumptions about the causal powers of social structure.

The best-known sociological study, influenced by phenomenology, is Berger and Luckmann's *The Social Construction of Reality* (1967). This argues that knowledge is socially constructed and is directed towards the resolution of practical problems. In this sense, then, no social facts can be thought of as neutral, rather they reflect the purposes for which they were acquired.

Phenomenology has been subjected to extensive criticism. It has been argued that it deals with trivial topics, is purely descriptive and neglects the notion of social structure. Nevertheless it has been influential in certain spheres. The emphasis given to common-sense knowledge has influenced the development of **ethnomethodology** in particular. **DA**

See also action perspective; functionalism; idiographic; individualism; microsociology; naturalism; social construction of reality; sociology of knowledge; structure-agency debate; symbolic interactionism; understanding.

Further reading K.H. Wolff, 'Phenomenology And Sociology' in T.B. Bottomore and R. Nisbet (eds.), *A History of Sociological Analysis*.

PHENOMENOLOGY

Phenomenology (Greek, 'study of what is perceived') is both a method and a standpoint for phenomenological psychoanalysts, psychiatrists and therapists. A **psychology** based on the understanding of phenomenology does not believe in the existence of the **unconscious**. The unconscious is replaced with untransformed experiences, of which we are unaware. The conscious ego is thought to hold all of actual and potential conscious life.

Phenomenology is a **philosophy** developed by Edmund Husserl at the turn of the century. Husserl's philosophical method employed a mental suspension of objects to enable him to take a natural standpoint of pure **consciousness**. By doing this he discovered that all consciousness was tied to objects, whether real or not. Husserl's philosophical method is echoed in the work of phenomenologists like R.D. Laing. Phenomenology is used by psychologists like Laing as a description of our core selves and applies to every conscious waking thought and experience.

It also assumes that we know about the outside world only through **intensionality** and intentional objects. The meaning of experience, from this viewpoint, cannot be located outside experience. Heidegger further developed notions of phenomenology and intensionality by using it to explore ways of describing human experience which avoided the dualism of the mind/body split. **Existentialists** also further explored Husserl and Heidegger's ideas, and this kind of approach to psychology is also known as an existential approach.

Using an intensional model based on phenomenology involves seeing the patient's experience as a complete mental and physical world, which can only be entered through a respect and understanding of its completeness. The analyst or therapist working with this standpoint will try to come to material without presupposition – as Husserl did in his method of appraisal of individual consciousness.

Laing, taking the intensional standpoint with his patients, saw the basis of disturbance as ontological insecurity and a loss of sense of being. This method was very different to the one he had learned in his training as a psychiatrist. He came to the conclusion, after studying schizophrenics, that mental disorders, like schizophrenia, are part of a personal world that includes the 'social events' of that person's family life. The social nexus in the family and the way it is incorporated into the personal mental space of the patient are responsible for the illness, but at the same time there is a belief in an essential self that has become distorted by the internal relationships created by the individual's family bonds. MJ

Further reading R.D. Laing, *Self and Others.*

PHENOTYPE

The term phenotype (Greek, 'kind of manifestation'), in the **life sciences**, refers to the characteristics of an individual, produced by the expression of genetic information and modified by the environment. The phenotype is not inherited and cannot be transmitted genetically to subsequent generations; contrary to the ideas of many 19th-century scientists such as Lamarck (see **Lamarckism**). It can change during the lifetime of an individual in response to environmental changes. An example of a phenotypic characteristic is a suntan: it is produced as a response to the environment, but only the ability to tan is transmitted in the **genotype**. **RB**

PHILOLOGY

Philology (Greek, 'love of learning and literature') was a discipline established at the Library and University of Alexandria in the 2nd century BCE. Until then, knowledge had not generally been kept in written form, but had been passed on and developed in a complex oral tradition. The scholars of Alexandria consciously set out to acquire a written statement of every piece of human knowledge until their time: they talked of the Library as 'the world's memory'. Philology was the discipline of caring for this body of learning. (The

philologists were intellectual curators only; the brute skills of looking after the actual books were left to menial hands.) It involved two activities in particular: study and codification of the niceties of **language** (so that no nuance of meaning in the stored texts would be missed), and systematic critical assessment of the actual contents of the books. From these studies developed such modern disciplines as exegesis, **lexicography**, **linguistics**, textual **criticism** – and in an extension which began with the decoding of ancient Sanskrit in the early 19th century – comparative philology: a study of the history, structure and affinities of all the languages of the world. **KMcL**

PHILOSOPHY

Philosophy (Greek, 'love of wisdom', or more exactly 'love of knowledge acquired by the exercise of the intellect') originally meant a quest for the explanations, origins and nature of things, both actual (snails; thunderstorms) and conceptual (virtue; justice). In ancient times, it was regarded as the occupation of specialists – **Buddhists** called them 'pure souls' – who conducted their quest by discussion with like-minded people, by meditation and by ratiocination, free of the trammels of everyday life. Even when applied to what we would nowadays think of as scientific matters, its method was not research but **scholasticism**, and a major part of that method consisted in the re-evaluation of past ideas. Precedent and authority were thus integral to the discipline, and helped to give philosophy its perceived status as one of the highest and noblest activities of the human mind.

Nowadays, the search for 'wisdom' has become fragmented. **Science** now takes care of enquiries into natural phenomena, and ethics and morality (though still sometimes described as 'philosophy') belong not only to philosophy, but also to such disciplines as **politics**, **psychology**, **sociology** and theology (see below). Philosophy – at least academic philosophy – is a disinterested endeavour to examine human reasoning itself, to take abstract questions and consider their validity not as specific truths but as forms of theory or explanation. The only similarity between this activity and ancient philosophy is that it requires constant back-reference to past ideas and past intellectual precedents. Philosophy is an academic study taught by means of its own history; it is a subject which grows by accretion, the new constantly building on and modifying the old.

One of the main tools of philosophy is **logic**, and a separate branch of the discipline deals with this alone. Logic is the consideration of argument: not of whether an argument is subjectively valid, but whether it is objectively so. Logic removes partiality from the consideration of argument, reducing it to a kind of framework which has consistency and rigour. It is concerned with the structures and principles of reasoning, with the succession and interdependence of intellectual statements. It is related to mathematical logic, in which symbols replace verbal statements; it leads to and facilitates the whole vast area of linguistic philosophy, in which the edifice of meaning and purpose in the use of words is rigorously examined.

Another central concern of philosophy is the nature of reality, and our perception of it. What do we know, how do we know it and are there limits to our knowledge? Investigating these matters is perhaps the overarching agenda of all philosophy, and has been so from earliest times. In the ancient past, throughout the world, the highest branch of such study was *metaphysics*: investigation of the ultimate nature of reality, of such things as the existence of the supernatural, the nature of time, or the relationship between mind and body. In 17th-century Europe, beginning with the work of Descartes, metaphysics gradually gave way to *epistemology*, the investigation of knowledge itself. (Descartes, for example, starting from the famous premise *Cogito, ergo sum*, 'I think; therefore I am', sought to produce a universal system for all human knowledge; Spinoza, Locke, Hume and others examined such matters as where knowledge comes from and what, if any, are the limits of human understanding; modern epistemologists devote themselves to questions of the testing and validation of knowledge, and of its relationship to thought and meaning.)

From earliest times, philosophy has shared two preoccupations with such other disciplines as (what we would now call) politics, psychology and theology. First is the nature of identity. What is personal identity? Is it a material or an immaterial thing? Does it reside in the mind or the body, or in both? Do mind and soul exist, and if so, what are they? Second is our relationship with the world outside ourselves, with the supernatural (if it exists) and with other people. Are morals and ethics – not to mention such things as benefit and harm, duty, good and bad, right and wrong – abstract entities, or human constructs? Are their imperatives innate or learned? It is here, perhaps, that the clear stream of philosophy is most muddied by 'outside' considerations. We all have notions of how we, and others, should behave, of the correlatives (such as the supernatural or the force of **law**) which affect behaviour, and of the moral and ethical status quo. For some people, a 'philosophy of life' is the totality of such notions which governs their approach to everyday living. Some academic philosophers have devoted themselves to such matters. But by and large, academic philosophy has treated them in the same way as all its other concerns: that is, it has attempted to remove the personal from consideration and to discuss each argument in the abstract. **KMcL**

PHILOSOPHY OF LANGUAGE

Language is a natural object of enquiry in **philosophy**, since it is central to the discussion of meaning. On the whole, linguists and philosophers find that their interests overlap to the greatest degree in the domains of **semantics** and **pragmatics**. In addition, philosophers have played an important role in determining what the subject matter of **linguistics** should be.

John Locke's ideational theory of meaning (1690) suggested that a person's meanings are first expressed in the private language of thought and then translated into a linguistic form suitable for communication in words. However, it has been argued that the intrinsic privacy of thought would prevent two speakers from ever being sure that when they use a particular word they are expressing the same meaning thereby. The concept behind the word for each speaker may be entirely idiosyncratic, and the privacy of thought denies the speaker any means for demonstrating to others which particular concept underlies the use of a word.

A further important consequence of Locke's theory is that it propounds the complete separation of language and thought, with the view that language is entirely dependent on **thought**. However, it has been argued that, beyond a very basic level, thought would be impossible without language. Some philosophers of language argue that language furnishes people with a highly sophisticated mode of thinking about the world, although it should be pointed out that this thesis of linguistic relativity finds little favour among many **psycholinguists**.

A theory of meaning which avoids the problem of a private language of thought draws on the notion of reference, which is the action performed by a speaker when referring to something. A form of primitive reference holds that a word is no more than a label, which implies that the meaning of a word is the object it stands for. On this view, the problem of understanding meaning would amount to no more than knowing the object, or referent, for a word. But a problem arises with examples of the following kind: (1) The morning star is the evening star. The sentence in (1) is known as an identity statement, since the two expressions morning star and evening star refer to one and the same referent (the planet Venus). Strictly speaking, it should not be possible for an identity statement to convey new information. However, at one point in the history of **astronomy**, and for many lay people even now, the statement in (1) does in fact express a novel idea. We must therefore distinguish reference from sense, the latter being defined as the sign (word form) which picks out the object being referred to. With this distinction, it becomes clear how a single referent can bear more than one sense. As a result, it emerges that words denote, while speakers refer. A further traditional concern has been to establish the truth value of sentences. Drawing on mathematical systems of **logic**, the conditions under which a sentence can be described as either true or false are determined. More

recent theories on the relationship between language and meaning have attempted to incorporate the role of speaker beliefs and the context of utterance as fundamental factors which affect the interpretation of the actual words uttered on a particular occasion. **MS**

Further reading A.C. Grayling, *An Introduction to Philosophic Logic*; J.J. Katz (ed.), *The Philosophy of Linguistics*.

PHILOSOPHY OF MATHEMATICS see Mathematics

PHILOSOPHY OF SCIENCE

Philosophers of **science** start from two questions above all: Is it possible to understand the universe? and Is natural science the means to reach such understanding? Leaving aside questions of methodology, which constantly ambush the discussion, the quest concerns such things as the nature of universal **truth**, the conflict (if any) between science and other universal explanations (such as **religion**) and the intrinsic identity, nature and validity of 'science' itself. One 20th-century development which would have surprised most previous scientists (and particularly those of the preceding century), is that science now appears to deal more with what we do not know than with what we do: the departure from certainty has been one of the most striking features of its recent evolution. Like all philosophies, that of science is usually studied in terms of its own history; in this, as in its study of such things as the objectivity of evidence and the validity of judgement, it closely parallels religious studies – something else which would have surprised many early scientists. **KMcL**

See also life sciences; mathematics; physics; scientific method.

Further reading R. Harre, *Philosophies of Science*.

PHONETICS

Phonetics (Greek, 'science of voice') is the branch of **linguistics** concerned with the physical properties of the sounds produced in speech. A major concern in phonetics becomes clear if we consider the experience of listening to someone speaking an entirely foreign language. Although we can recognize the stream of sounds as speech, it is extremely difficult to distinguish individual sounds. Even when sophisticated methods of acoustic analysis are employed, it emerges that the boundaries between the contiguous units in speech are not at all easy to define. Even though there are good grounds for arguing that, for instance, the word 'big' comprises three separate speech sounds (b, i, g), in purely physical terms there are no decisive, clear-cut borderlines between the end of one speech unit and the start of the next. There is a clear tension between, on the one hand, an inherently unified and indivisible flow of speech sounds and, on the other hand, the recognition that distinct speech sounds are identifiable as psychologically real events which can be extracted from the speech signal.

A fundamental aim in phonetics is to be able to transcribe the physical properties of human speech with objective accuracy. An effective transcription system must be able to represent acoustic properties which vary over time. Somewhat paradoxically, however, practical constraints necessitate the use of independent symbols, each symbol representing a discrete unit of speech. In fact, these symbols are very often regarded as targets (rather than discrete, separable units) towards which the configurations of the vocal apparatus are directed. In this way, a compromise is reached, and the fluid nature of the acoustic properties of speech remains acknowledged. The International Phonetic Association has arrived at a set of symbols which is designed so that it can be used to transcribe utterances from any known natural language. Not surprisingly, the prescribed set of symbols (the International Phonetic Alphabet, IPA) does not satisfy all phoneticians. Specifically, it has been argued that the IPA symbols are excessively biased towards the specific characteristics of European languages.

It has also been suggested that the IPA list is not sufficiently independent of the way speech sounds are used to convey meaning in languages (see **phonology**). Some phoneticians pursue the ideal of a purely phonetic transcription, in which all the sounds of an utterance are transcribed without reference to the structure of the particular source language. Unfortunately, the perceptually-based judgements of phoneticians do not always correspond to the independently measurable acoustic properties of a speech event. In other words, transcription is essentially a subjective process, despite a generally high level of overall agreement among trained phoneticians.

Beyond the problems of representation, phoneticians are involved with a wide range of questions arising from the physical characteristics of speech sounds. In practical terms, recent years have witnessed a great surge of interest in producing computer systems which can process human speech sounds automatically (see **computational linguistics**). Theoretically, a central interest has been the discovery and explanation of phonetic universals (see **language universals**). The aim is to account for acoustic properties which occur consistently in all known languages. An example is that around 20% of all languages have only five vowels. But more interestingly, those five vowels almost always follow the same pattern, being akin to the Spanish vowels: [i, e, a, o, u]. **MS**

Further reading J.C. Catford, *A Practical Introduction to Phonetics*; P. Ladefoged, *A Course in Phonetics*.

PHONOLOGY

Phonology (Greek, 'study of sound') is a main branch of **linguistics**. The human speech organs have the capacity to produce an extremely diverse range of sounds, but an individual language will only make use of a strictly limited subset of the total in order to convey meaning systematically. By focusing on the way speech sounds are organized as part of the language system, phonological enquiry represents a distinct move away from the study of the purely physical qualities of speech sounds (see **phonetics**). Of great significance was the discovery of the phoneme, an abstract unit which helps account for the way one word can be distinguished from the next. For example, in the word 'shoe', we can recognize two phonemes one consonant / ʃ / and one vowel

/u:/), to give the phonological transcription /ʃu:/. The word 'who' differs phonologically only in the substitution of /h/ in place of /ʃ/, to give /hu:/. These examples also show the importance of disregarding the orthographic conventions of a language in producing a phonemic representation. English spelling conventions in particular are notable for their lack of correspondence to the sounds they represent. Consider, for example, the word 'thing', with five letters but only three phonemes /θɪŋ/.

Many aspects of the acoustic properties of speech are not in fact necessary for conveying meaning. For instance, the [p] sound in the word 'pill' is aspirated, which means that it is produced with a short puff of breath, whereas there is no aspiration in the [p] sound of 'spill'. In a phonetic representation, this information would be included. In a phonological description, however, this information can be omitted, since it is entirely irrelevant when it comes to distinguishing one word from another in English. The two realizations, or allophones, of the /p/ phoneme, although physically different, are treated as the same sound by English speakers, who are not normally even aware of the difference. Allophones often occur in complementary distribution, which means that each is found in a distinct and mutually exclusive range of environments. For instance, only the aspirated version of /p/ is found at the beginning of syllables. Although aspiration is not phonemically distinctive in English, it is important to bear in mind that languages vary greatly in the features of sound which are chosen to convey contrasts in meaning. Thus, in Thai, aspiration does provide a phonemic contrast, such that /phaa/ means to split, whereas / paa / means forest.

The main problem with a purely phonemic analysis is that it presents an image of speech as a series of discrete units of sound strung together like so many beads on a string. However, several aspects of speech sound organization clearly span several segments. Examples of such suprasegmental phenomena include pitch, intonation and the rhythmic properties of speech, which languages also exploit in systematic ways to convey meaning. **MS**

Further reading R. Lass, *Phonology: an Introduction to Basic Concepts*.

PHOTOBIOLOGY

Photobiology (Greek, 'study of light on life') is the study of the effect of light upon living organisms. Photosynthesis, the process by which plants convert the energy of light into chemical energy, plays a central role in **biology** because it is the major energy source in the **biosphere**. But photobiology is also concerned with phenomena such as light detection, and thus vision, and with the biological production of light (bioluminescence). Most organisms modify their behaviour in response to light and the regular cycle of day and night is an important stimulus for a wide range of periodic phenomena in living systems. **RB**

See also biological rhythm; chronobiology; phenology; tropism.

PHOTOGRAPHY

Photography (Greek, 'writing with light'), is the process or art of creating optical images on photosensitive surfaces.

The principles on which photography is based were known to the Greek philosopher and scientist Archimedes who knew that if a small pinhole is made in the wall of a darkened space, then images appear upside down and back to front on the opposing wall. This discovery was not utilized until the early 1800s when, in 1826 or 1827, Joseph Nicéphore Nièpce managed to fix an image upon pewter plates. The picture was formed by the reaction of a thin layer of silver iodide to the light falling on it. In the brightest parts of the picture the silver iodide is decomposed and a thin deposit of silver is laid down. When the excess silver iodide was removed, using mercury vapour, a reverse picture or negative was formed by the silver which in fine powder form appeared to be black. Thus the brighter the image at a particular spot the more black-appearing silver was deposited. When the light was darker then less silver was deposited and the image appeared brighter. Thus the whole picture was formed. He called the process heliography from the Greek *helio* 'the sun'. In 1827, Nièpce met Louis Jacques Mandé Daguerre who was working on a similar project. It was Daguerre and not Nièpce who took the credit for the first practical process of photography, when the Académie des Sciences in Paris in 1839 claimed that Daguerre had discovered a method of permanently recording an image produced by the pinhole camera. His invention, called a daguerreotype, was soon making its impact throughout the world.

Although the daguerreotype was a major breakthrough, it was obsolete within twenty years as other developments superseded it, particularly the introduction by William Henry Fox Talbot of transparent photographic plates which formed the negative image. These could be used to produce negatives of themselves, that is, a positive image. Photography was still unwieldy and awkward as the subject had to remain stationary for minutes on end in order to expose the plates to the right amount of light, since the emulsions used then were not very sensitive.

The introduction in 1871 of 'dry' plates, instead of the wet plates which had been used up until then, transformed photography. Dry plates were made of celluloid or gelatine which provided a transparent, flexible backing for the recording of images. Photography was, by now, a big business as it recorded images of the Victorian age.

The next step was trying to invent a process which could make these images move in synchronization. The first photographs of moving objects were taken in 1877 when Eadweard Muybridge managed to record how a horse gallops by the use of multiple cameras each taking a single image as the horse passed. He invented a 'zoopraxiscope' which animated his pictures giving the impression of movement. This inspired the Lumière brothers in Paris to devise a combined camera and projector. This invention managed to film an event and then have it ready for projection within 48 hours. This was the start of the cinema which first opened in Paris in 1895.

Other innovations such as colour photography and the mass-production of the Kodak camera by George Eastman have made photography one of the biggest businesses in the world. It will remain so as long as people are still influenced by seductive advertisements, the medical profession requires stills of internal scans or the amateur captures moments for his or her own posterity.

Other forms of photography are well known. Most **x-rays** of the human body are recorded on photographic film. A less well-known type of photography uses film which is only sensitive to infrared light and the camera uses filters to keep normal visible light from the lens. Pictures produced in this way show the surface temperature of the target. In medicine this can be used to detect regions of below normal temperature, for example due to blood circulation restrictions or more frequently to show high skin temperatures which may correspond to the start of 'pressure zones' in the disabled who spend their life sitting or lying in bed for long periods. After an injury by burning this kind of picture can direct the kind of treatment required by identifying whether the burn is second degree or third degree of severity. Industrially, such pictures of factories can show regions of high temperature where heat is being lost to the atmosphere and form a guide to the area where energy is being lost. **AA**

Further reading E. Stenger, *A History of Photography: its Relation to Civilisation and Practice* (1939).

PHRENOLOGY see Divination

PHYLOGENY

Phylogeny (Greek, 'evolution of types'), in the **life sciences**, is the history of a living organism in terms of its **evolution**. It provides the basis for phyletic **taxonomy**. Phylogeny is usually very incomplete due to the fragmentary nature of the fossil record and the more than three billion years over which evolution has occurred. Evidence for phylogenetic relationships was traditionally derived from comparative **palaeontology**, **anatomy** and **embryology**, but these days it is supplemented with data from biochemists and molecular biologists. A phylogenetic tree (dendrogram) is used to order species taxonomically, with the species placed at the tips of the branches and the common ancestor represented by the trunk. The distances between species on the tree indicate closeness of relationship in evolutionary terms, though this can be difficult to determine unambiguously. The linking of species with their ancestors in such a rigid (cladistic) fashion can cause taxonomic problems: for example, on a strict phylogenetic tree, crocodiles are separated from lizards as they have a more recent bird ancestor than they do a lizard ancestor. However, crocodiles and lizards are grouped together as reptiles when they are classified according to appearance (phenetic classification). **RB**

See also anatomy; morphology.

Further reading Martin Rudwick, *The Meaning of Fossils.*

PHYSICS

Physics (Greek, 'about nature') is humankind's attempt at understanding the laws of nature. It is our quest to find the physical laws which underpin the workings of the universe. As such, it is concerned only with the truth. A theory is correct if it successfully explains observations, and wrong if it does not.

The principle of experiment is crucial to physics. Two assumptions must be made when performing experiments. The first is that the world is not a figment of the experimenter's imagination. This is not as trivial as it sounds: there is no proof that can be offered to the reader which will prove beyond doubt that the world exists outside of his or her mind! But if we assume that the world exists, we may begin to formulate theories about the nature of that existence.

The second assumption is that the **laws of Nature** do not change from day to day. A simple example is that of gravity. We know that if we let an object fall, it will drop to the ground. We believe that this will happen because it has always happened before: that if an experiment gives a certain result on one day, it will give the same result under the same conditions for all

time. As with the first assumption, we do not know that this holds true; but physics would not get very far without it, and it seems to have been true for all of the history of humankind.

A physical theory is formulated as follows: experiments are performed which give results. These results seem to obey certain laws, for example, for the law of gravity, we may say that the further an object falls, the harder it hits the ground. Then, using the laws that were formulated from the results of the experiment, we may go on to predict the results of other experiments for which the same laws are relevant. It is important to realize that theories contain inherent limitations; they only claim to be true within a range of conditions.

Never at any point do we assume that these 'laws' or theories are anything more than models of the environment, and at any point, if an experiment gives results that contradict the predictions of a particular law, that law is considered to be invalid. A theory is only valid within its limitations; Newton's law of gravitation is only valid for relatively low gravity, and general relativity must be used for very massive objects like neutron stars and black holes.

Each theory enhances our understanding of the universe. The breakdown of a theory indicates that the universe is more complicated than was previously assumed, and that a more subtle theory must be formulated to take its place.

Theory and experiment proceed hand-in-hand; as technical knowledge improves the sensitivity of experiments, theory must keep up with the results and continue to predict further experiments. **JJ**

See also philosophy of science; science; scientific method.

PHYSIOLOGY

Physiology (Greek *phusis*, 'nature' + ology) is the study of the function of the biological processes within living organisms. It is broken down into the study of the function of particular organs: thus **endocrinology** is the study of hormone function. The concept of **homeostasis** is central to the science of physiology. Homeostasis is the regulation of the internal environment within certain parameters, and is not only a requirement for the perpetuation of physiological processes but is their responsibility. Investigation of homoestatic systems involves the biochemical (see **biochemistry**) study of **metabolism** under a variety of conditions to reveal how each system responds, in isolation and in the context of the whole organism. The study of function was of interest to ancient scientists such as Aristotle (384–322 BCE) and Galen (129–200 CE), though their approaches and theories were very different from those of the modern physiologist. The Hippocratic school of medicine proposed the humoral theory of disease (see **humours**) which was influential for 2,000 years, along with ideas such as the tidal flow of blood. These misconceptions, and the willingness of later philosophers to recapitulate the suppositions of the ancient Greeks, held back the development of medicine and ensured that practices such as phlebotomy (bloodletting) remained popular through the Middle Ages.

The publication in 1628 of William Harvey's observations concerning the circulation of blood represented a major step toward the foundation of modern physiology, though all his observations were anatomical. In the 18th century, Albrecht von Haller defined physiology as **anatomy** in motion, and thus established the principle that living organisms must be observed during physiological studies. At around the same time Antoine-Laurent Lavoisier was applying the principles of chemistry to living organisms to reveal the similarities between respiration and combustion. The pioneering French physiologist and pharmacologist François Magendie (1783–1855) studied physiology in living animals and it was one of his students, Claude Bernard, who, in the 19th century, proposed the concept of the internal environment of an organism. Physiology began to be separated from the study of anatomy and grew as an experimental discipline in its own right. **RB**

See also mechanism.

Further reading Margaret Stanier, *Physiological Processes*.

PICARESQUE

Picaresque **literature** (from Spanish *picaro*, 'rascal') is named after two anonymous Spanish **novels** of the 16th century, both dealing with the adventures of the kind of tricksters, living on their wits, who had been a standby of Western stage **comedy** since Aristophanes and Plautus. In a picaresque novel, adventure is strung on adventure as beads are strung on a necklace. The term picaresque is now applied to any episodic novel with a comic or satiric thrust. Characteristic and outstanding examples of such works include Petronius' *The Satyricon*, Rabelais' *Gargantua*, Cervantes' *Don Quixote*, Henry Fielding's *Tom Jones*, Gogol's *Dead Souls* and Thomas Mann's *Confessions of Felix Krull*. As with many similar categories, picaresque strategies have in the 20th century become merely one part of the writer's repertoire, and contribute form and attitude to 'serious' work otherwise as diverse as James Joyce's *Ulysses*, Saul Bellow's *Humboldt's Gift*, Günter Grass's *The Flounder* and (on another level, perhaps) Tolkien's *The Lord of the Rings* and its countless progeny. **KMcL**

PICTURESQUE

Picturesque was an 18th-century concept in Western art, referring to scenes which occupy the mid-ground between the 'ideal' landscapes of the 17th century and the 'sublime' landscapes of **Romanticism**. The leading advocate of the picturesque, William Gilpin, in his *Three Essays on the Picturesque* (1792), defines it as that which stimulates the imagination to reverie or admiration. To call a landscape 'picturesque' was to mean that it had picturesque potential, and many artists used a Claude glass to concentrate the picturesque qualities under observation. In an important departure for English **landscape painting**, Uvedale Price, in his *Essay on the Picturesque* (1794), argued that consideration of the picturesque would bring landscape painting back to a celebration of nature after its involvement with the academic 'ideal'. Outside the English context,

Piranesi's *vedula* ('view') of the ruins of antique Rome obviously calls upon qualities of the picturesque.

The idea of the picturesque influenced not only painting, but also **architecture** and most notably landscape gardening. In the debates between Richard Payne Knight (1750–1824) and Uvedale Price (1747–1829), two theorists of landscape gardening, 'The Picturesque' was defined as a category of aesthetics between the Beautiful (which was made of attractive parts) and The **Sublime** (which induced a feeling of awe). The Picturesque was distinguished by wild ruggedness and irregularity. In landscape gardening this is characterized by variety in texture, the irregular planting of trees in imitation of untrained nature, and in architecture by asymmetry, variety of form and texture, which often found the form of asymmetrical sham castles, with otherwise classical interiors, as well as cottages with the highly decorative features of almost fairy-tale rustic dwellings. **PD MG JM**

PIDGIN AND CREOLE LINGUISTICS

Pidgins and creoles are new **language** systems which are created with amazing rapidity, on occasion within the space of only one or two generations. Very often they arose as the distinctive by-product of European colonial exploits, though it should be stressed that there is a whole range of possible scenarios which might stimulate this kind of language formation. A paradigm case of pidginization arose with the transportation of slaves from a variety of linguistic backgrounds to an isolated plantation, under the domination of a European élite. The resultant linguistic melée created the need for a shared lingua franca, especially as the opportunities for learning a fully-fledged second language became severely limited.

The pidgin created under these conditions is the native language of no one, although it does draw on the linguistic resources of both the (superstratum) European language and the various (substratum) non-European languages. A common pattern has emerged, whereby the vocabulary originates largely with the superstratum language, while the **phonology** and **syntax** normally derive from the substratum languages. The linguistic resources of the resultant pidgin are invariably extremely limited in scope. For example, in the very early stages, the pidgin may operate with fewer than 100 words. The process of creolization is normally described as an expansion in the linguistic potential of the pidgin: the phonology, **morphology**, lexis and syntax of an emerging creole all show signs of elaboration from the original pidgin. Furthermore, the children of pidgin-speaking parents (and subsequent generations) can acquire a creole as a native language.

Numerous pidgins and creoles have arisen, quite independently, in disparate regions of the world, yet, remarkably, they often bear a strong resemblance to one another in terms of their underlying grammatical organization. It is a fundamental research problem to explain how entirely unrelated new language systems could have followed such similar patterns of development. Some have argued that we all share a common ability to simplify language in a uniform way, hence, the similar structure of pidgins in different parts of the world. The similarity of the social contexts in which pidgins occur has also been noted as a significant influence on pidginization. A recent controversial issue has been the extent to which creole studies can illuminate the concept of a genetically determined human language faculty. The problem arises for children born to pidgin-speaking parents, since it is assumed that pidgins provide a model of language which is too degenerate for the purposes of language learning. In order to compensate for the deficiencies of the pidgin, it has been suggested that children draw on the knowledge of language inborn in all humans. In this way, the child has the capacity to expand the linguistic resources of a pidgin into a creole.

Evidently, pidgins and creoles have proven to be highly systematic, and perhaps surprisingly, they exhibit universal characteristics, which cannot be explained by reference solely to historical processes of language change or social contact. Consequently, we must reject the superficial view that they constitute corrupt or haphazard admixtures of linguistic elements, which only merit our interest as wayward curiosities. Instead, the processes of pidginization and creolization have been studied with a view to the more profound questions which can be addressed concerning the nature of language and language learning. **MS**

See also bioprogram; innateness.

Further reading P. Mühlhaüsler, *Pidgin and Creole Linguistics*; S. Romaine, *Pidgin and Creole Languages*.

PLACE

As well as being a common-sense term, place is a key idea in **geography**, and one which has proved hard to pin down. As a result, it has occurred in different forms at different times and has close links to other geographic ideas. Although it may seem anodyne at first sight, the way people behave in relation to place is linked with many bitter conflicts. The initial question is how a place differs from a location or an area. The answers suggest that a place has a distinctive character as a result of the interaction of many factors, from landforms and climate to **politics** and **economics**, over time and in relation to surrounding places. The distinct character may be apparent in the landscape as well as in the culture of the inhabitants. It is usually apparent to outsiders as well as to insiders, though they may well emphasize different aspects. One geographer attempted to clarify what was entailed by arguing that places had authentic local character and that mass processes were producing 'non-places' in our high streets and holiday resorts. Subsequently, it has been argued both that these non-places are made into places by their inhabitants, and that the arbitrary and adventitious nature of development has given the idea of place a whole new set of meanings in the postmodern era.

One strand of the debate about place has focused on the subjective aspect, on the way that people perceive and experience places, especially as insiders. Some have speculated that humans are territorial in the same way that biologists have shown animals to defend territory, either as entitlement to food supply or as a requirement in establishing precedence in mating or for rearing young. Conflict over territory does occur, from the 'turf' of a street gang to the boundaries of states or empires, but for most people affiliation to place is looser and divided between a hierarchy of places, from local to national. Much literature assumes that people relate first to their neighbourhood, and this idea was built into the design of many new towns. Detailed studies have given only qualified support as it seems that people disagree about the boundaries of a given neighbourhood, except where railways or major roads create uniformity, and many people feel at home in a variety of scattered places rather than a distinct area. As mobility has increased, so the old idea of a mosaic of distinct neighbourhoods has seemed less persuasive. More recently a good deal of research effort has been given to studies of localities. These are larger places than neighbourhoods, with populations of tens or hundreds of thousands, and they are seen as held together by contacts between people, most of whom spend most of their time in the locality. Again there are arguments about definition: is it enough to be a labour market area or is it necessary to have a degree of political organization?

At the larger scale that people relate to, the same change has occurred from concepts emphasizing homogeneity to concepts stressing organization. Traditional geographers stressed the importance of regions, sometimes seen as natural regions deriving from a similar environment and sometimes seen as unified by a shared culture. This idea lives on in the practice of collecting official statistics by region, but the subsequent discussion of regions has been contentious in theory and practice. In the UK in the 1970s a Royal Commission was set up to reorganize local government areas and became the focus of bitter dispute. Many people objected to any change to the historic counties, others to the idea of larger areas, others to the idea of moving to city regions areas held together by interaction rather than similarity. The result was a political compromise which pleased few. In many parts of the world, peoples' identification with a region has proved problematic in defining and maintaining the most powerfully entrenched sort of place – the nation state.

The concept of the nation state, which has played such a central role in the history of the last few centuries, matches a nation, a people with shared history, culture and aspirations, with a territory in which they live. At best, for example for Portugal, this is an effective way of administering medium-scale societies, and a shared régime builds up a sense of community over time. Unfortunately, groups of people are often much more mixed and it is often difficult or impossible to match the ideal in reality. This has led to countless conflicts and is currently (1993) causing tragedy in Bosnia and elsewhere in eastern Europe. The dominance of the nation state as the place many people are willing to die for is also a problem for attempts to create new supranational organizations, notably the EC. The contrasts between the global economy, in which we make our living, and the smaller scale places, to which we feel we belong, seem to be becoming stronger rather than weaker as time passes. PS

PLACE NOTATION see Number Systems

PLATE TECTONICS

By the 1950s, the debate about **continental drift** had generated a good deal of evidence that the continents might have moved. This evidence included the fit of coastlines, structures, rocks and fossils and the palaeomagnetic deposits with non N-S orientation. But most geologists remained sceptical because of the absence of a mechanism. Even evidence of high heat-flows at the mid-ocean ridges and of gravity anomalies along the ocean trenches, which seemed to some consistent with the presence of convection cells, was not regarded as sufficiently persuasive. But improved ability to investigate the sea floor brought in dramatic new evidence.

In 1960, an American geologist, Harry Hess, circulated a draft paper suggesting a number of lines of evidence which were consistent with the idea that the oceanic crust might be spreading away from the ocean ridges. In 1961, the Scripps Institute of Oceanography published the results of a magnetic survey which showed the existence of narrow bands of rock with alternating magnetic polarity, the bands being parallel to the mid-Atlantic ridge. In 1963, Vine and Matthews connected the argument to the evidence and presented more detailed evidence to show that the pattern of magnetic reversals in the ocean floor, parallel to the Juan de Fuca ridge in the north Pacific, was exactly consistent with the known timetable of reversals in the Earth's magnetic field which would have been fixed into basalts as they rose, solidified and then spread three cm per year. Over the next few years several similar studies were published, and in 1969 drilling of the ocean floor provided strong support by showing that the age of sediments resting on the basalt layer increased away from the ridges. It was also significant that no ocean-floor basalt had been found to exceed 190 million years in age: this suggested that the oceanic crust must be being destroyed as well as created. Indeed, as South America has ocean ridges on both sides, with crust in the Atlantic moving west, and crust in the Pacific moving east, it is clear that there must be a zone of crust destruction. The volcanically and seismically active range of the Andes and the parallel ocean trench suggested that the Atlantic plate might be being pushed up by the Pacific plate, but the fate of the Pacific plate required another step.

By the mid-1960s the evidence for ocean floor spreading was so strong that the idea of horizontal movement of the crust was becoming generally accepted. The scene was set for the statement of a theory which would account for all the available evidence. This was first attempted by W.J. Morgan of Princeton in 1968 and many other geologists were quick to present similar schemes.

The basic ideas are as follows: the Earth's surface is made up of seven major plates, five minor ones and a small number of smaller ones. Most large plates include both continental and oceanic crust, but the Pacific plate is almost entirely oceanic. These plates are being simultaneously created and destroyed and the crust, including the continents, is moved horizontally in the process. Plates have three kinds of boundary:

Constructive These are mainly the ocean ridges and have the features already described. One such boundary is in the Red Sea, where the Arabian plate is moving away from the African plate. This is a situation similar to that in the South Atlantic 100 million years ago.

Destructive Once the idea of plate movement was accepted, it was realized that it made sense of earlier information, including observations by Wadati and Benioff that near ocean trenches there are zones where earthquakes occur at progressively greater depths. These are now thought to indicate *subduction* of ocean crust – that is, it dips down diagonally below the adjacent plate, which is usually continental, and returns to the mantle. There is also frictional heating causing volcanic activity: thus subduction is the explanation of a phenomenon known for centuries, the 'fiery ring of the Pacific', the concentration of most of the world's great volcanoes in northwest and southeast coastal zones of the Pacific.

Conservative In some parts of the world, adjacent plates are moving past each other without either creation or destruction of crust. These are called conservative because material is conserved, but they are seismically active because friction stops movement for a time until sufficient stress builds up to cause sudden movement and release of shock waves experienced as earthquakes. The San Andreas fault, which parallels the coast of California, is the best-known example of such a plate boundary. As the plates move past each other, rocks from one may be scraped off on to the other to form very complex areas known as 'terranes': this concept explained a number of areas where traditional geology had failed to explain the observed structures.

The theory of plate tectonics is a major revolution in the way we see our world. The resistance to the idea of continental drift is a measure both of its importance and its improbability. The story of its acceptance is a good example of the way **science** works, seeking new evidence and then generating new theories to make sense of the new knowledge as well as of earlier knowledge.

But no theory is perfect and a great deal of work is going on to fill in the detail and to account for evidence which does not seem to fit in. In turn, these exceptions may provoke some future theorist to propose new interpretations. **PS**

PLATONISM

Platonism is one of the main theories in the philosophy of **mathematics**, and is one of the major explanations of what mathematics really is. The question it attempts to answer is whether mathematical **truth** has an independent existence do: mathematicians discover mathematical truths that are, in some sense, out there to be found, or do they invent or create them? The answer to this question will determine the very way in which a mathematician will look at his or her subject, and it is also part of the question of whether mathematics is a **science** or an **art**, or even possibly a game.

The Platonist position, based (as the name implies) on ideas in the works of Plato, is that mathematical truth is discovered. The idea is that mathematics consists of absolute truths, which were **a priori** (needing no other foundation, but being inescapable consequences of logical **deduction**). This position was reiterated by Kant in the 18th century, particularly with respect to **Euclidean geometry**. Unfortunately, the almost immediate discovery of **non-Euclidean geometry** put paid to any such idea, because it showed that the axioms on which Euclidean geometry was based are not all necessarily true. These discoveries, along with that of the **set theory** of Georg Cantor (1845–1918) led directly to the major schools in the philosophy of mathematics of the early 20th century, **logicism**, **formalism** and **intuitionism**.

The problem today is that all these schools have been to some extent discredited as methods by which mathematicians should work, and that many mathematicians have returned to a modified version of the Platonic viewpoint. The idea now is that once all the rules (or axioms) are fixed, then so is the truth or falsity of proposed theorems. There are theorems which are true in one system though false in another; for example, depending on the acceptance or rejection of the **axiom of choice** or the axioms of (say) Euclid or Nicholas Lobachevsky. A dependence on the rules of logic is also recognized. (For Platonism in **philosophy**, see **universals and particulars**.) SMcL

Further reading B. Russell, *An Introduction to the Philosophy of Mathematics* (1919).

PLURALISM

Pluralism is the belief that there are, or ought to be, many things. While not endorsing relativism pluralists defend multiplicity in beliefs and institutions, and criticize **monists**: those who believe that there is, or ought to be only one thing. As a philosophical doctrine pluralism, is the label given to those who think that reality cannot be explained by one substance or principle. This idea still survives in the current, largely political, meanings of pluralism.

Normative pluralism, in **politics**, represents a compromise between **individualism** and communitarianism in the quest for the optimal form of state. The pluralist ideal is of flexible consensus and dissensus: since definitively acceptable definitions of the good are unlikely, if not impossible, it is best to design political institutions which allow for the expression and competition of a plurality of ideals and interests. Normative pluralism developed, especially in Britain, as an assault upon **absolutism**, **sovereignty** and centralized state authority. Political philosophers in Britain, France and America came to advocate institutional pluralism (the fragmentation of state authority) and social pluralism (the development of a vigorous civil society marked by extensive group autonomy, activity and diversity). Although they were defenders of individualism, normative exponents of pluralism, like de Tocqueville in the 1840s, also warned of the dangers posed by societies in which self-interest was paramount and collective social ties were diminished or absent. To this extent normative pluralism is associated with at least one version of social **liberalism**. Pluralists emphasize the merits of exposing individuals to conflicting ideals and interests (through involvement in a variety of social and political associations), the protection of minority rights in law so that the legitimacy of diverse groups is respected, and reducing the amount of influence large, corporately organized interests exercise on political decision-making.

Analytical pluralism, by contrast, is an explanatory approach to the study of the distribution of political **power** in liberal democracies. Modern pluralists, like Robert Dahl and Charles Lindblom, argue that most liberal democracies are actually 'polyarchies' (systems of rule by many) rather than oligarchies or pure democracies. Political power is not held cumulatively, but rather is dispersed throughout society, in political parties, interest group organizations and mass **media**, as well as among individual voters. In principle every interest can get organized and compete for influence. Thus pluralists maintain that 'countervailing power' operates within modern democracies.

Critics of conventional analytical pluralism maintain that it operates with too narrow a conception of power and does not recognize the extent to which the political agenda in liberal democracies is either controlled by the state or by a small number of powerful social interests or a dominant class. The methods of analytical pluralism, according to its critics, blind political scientists to the evidence of systematic domination within modern democracies. Neopluralists, including Dahl and Lindblom, have acknowledged the force of these criticisms, especially the extent to which big business interests distort the workings of polyarchies. In the 1950s and 1960s the pluralist perspective in political science was associated with the right, today it is increasingly the preserve of the liberal left and democratic socialists. BO'L

See also behaviourism; élite theory; representative government; socialism and social democracy; state.

Further reading R. Dahl, *Dilemmas of Pluralist Democracy*; C. Lindblom, *Politics and Markets*.

PNEUMATOLOGY

Pneumatology (from Greek *pneuma*,

'breath' or 'spirit') tends to be used in a rather restricted sense, that of the doctrine of the Holy Spirit in **Christianity**, with reference to the Spirit of God in the Hebrew Scriptures. In the latter case there is no question of a separate deity, or distinct numinous power, but rather of an extension of God's creative power and presence. The Spirit of God broods on the face of the primaeval ocean at Creation. It is responsible for producing courage, wisdom, insight and religious knowledge in the human soul. Because the Hebrew word for Spirit (*ruach*) is feminine in gender, and the imagery is often feminine, especially when the Greek concept of divine wisdom (*sophia*) is absorbed into it, pneumatology has become of great interest to Jewish and Christian **feminist theologians**, and is the subject of much ongoing research. Strictly speaking, the term pneumatology should be used in other religions as well, such as African traditional religions, or certain forms of **Buddhism** and **Hinduism** where belief in supernatural spirits plays an important part in worship and custom, but this is not done, perhaps because they are not seen as part of the godhead.

The Holy Spirit plays a central role in the theology of the early Christian Church, which, since the initial outpouring on the community on the Day of Pentecost, was emphatically charismatic, even after speaking in tongues and the more disruptive phenomena died out. The Spirit was seen as a rushing wind, an advocate and intermediary who scatters gifts to the congregation and inspires qualities or virtues. Orthodox Christianity has always insisted that the Spirit is a person and not a quality or an impersonal force. **EMJ**

Further reading C.K. Barrett, *The Holy Spirit and Gospel Tradition*; J.V. Taylor, *The Go-between God*.

POETRY

Poetry (Greek, 'art of assembling (words)') is verse with cultural affectation. Part of its effect, which verse does not always share, is a kind of self-advertising display, an invitation to us to admire not just what is being said but the 'elevated' manner of the

saying. (Indeed, in bad poetry, manner can be all that is on offer.) There are analogies with counterpoint in **music** – and like counterpoint, poetry is written to a set of elaborate and ingenious rules, which can corset or straitjacket creativity, distil the art or reduce it entirely to hot air. **Dramatic** poems are in the form of dialogue (not all are plays for the stage); **epic** and narrative poems tell stories (epic usually with a grander, less anecdotal sweep); **lyric** poetry explores single moments or moods. Each uses a particular repertoire of forms and procedures to manipulate sound, rhythm and syntax in ways which are analogous to, but essentially distinct from, prose. In the ancient world, poetry was generally regarded as the only fit medium for 'high' literary expression, and prose was reserved for more everyday communication. The modern world has elevated prose writing to an art form, but poetry still keeps its place on the literary high ground, as if its distillation and ritualization of linguistic expression were the Holy Grail of literary craftsmanship. **KMcL**

POINTILLISM

In fine **art**, pointillism is a method of **painting** using innumerable tiny dots of colour. Light is reflected from them to make the picture. The technique was perfected by the 1880s impressionist Georges Seurat. It is analogous both to a method of shading used by earlier painters, and to the process by which photographs were reproduced at the time in books and newspapers. Few other painters have taken it as far as Seurat: his *La Grande Jatte* is at once the justification and the apotheosis of the style.

In **music**, pointillism is a style introduced by Anton Webern in the 1920s, and used by his followers until the late 1960s. Instead of individual notes forming part of recognizable themes or chords, they appear to be isolated, to stand alone in the texture: a single crotchet from a clarinet, a few semiquavers from a flute, a semibreve from violins. In fact, as with all pointillism, this is an illusion: each individual note is part of a carefully ordered and intellectually coherent musical texture, which becomes ever more apparent on repeated hearings. To demonstate this, Webern once orchestrated a Bach fugue in pointillist style, and the result, though like listening to Bach through a kind of aural prism, is still quite clearly Bach. **KMcL**

POLITICAL ANTHROPOLOGY

Political anthropology investigates how **politics** forms a part of social life. It is not exclusively about the study of political structures, processes and representations of formal organizations in the way familiar with in the West, but also extends into considering how power is distributed and relegated in societies that do not appear to be run by formal political organizations.

The earliest contributions to the subject were made by Meyer Fortes and Edward Evans-Pritchard in 1940. Basing their studies on African societies, they suggested three types of political systems. The first was one in which the political structures and kinship organization were fused in such a manner that the kinship system functioned as the major way of disseminating power. This was shown, for example, among the Mbuti pygmies of Congo. Although Pygmies themselves did not regard kinship as performing a political function, authority was dispersed through a grouping of about two hundred people in which there are no acknowledged leaders.

The second type of political system was considered as one determined by lineage frameworks. Lineage defines those people who trace themselves back to a known common ancestor. This system was evident, for example, among the Nuer people of Sudan where lineages were seen to divide and reunite because there was no fixed political identity, but instead one was continually re-created in response to the nature of the opposition.

The third political system was described as one of state societies in which there was an organized political structure with a recognized leader, for example, the Ashanti kingdom in Ghana.

In 1950, Max Gluckman concentrated on aspects of order and rebellion amongst African political systems. He saw rebellion as a process that constantly affected political relations. Rituals were considered as the main means of expressing such conflicts, but ultimately they acted to affirm the unity of the society. Later anthropologists criticized such models of political systems for being static. They seemed to depend more on the anthropologists' presumed theories rather than attempting to account for the actual forms and dynamics of political organizations.

In 1954, Edmund Leach developed these concerns to produce his work on the political systems of Highland Burma. He showed the relative instability of social and political organizations by describing historical alternations between a 'democratic' organization called *gambo*, and an 'aristocratic' type called *shan*. Politics was primarily about competition and confrontation of interests. Therefore, consideration of the contradictions, tensions, and movements both within and outside the society needed to be considered.

Other perspectives have concentrated on the way political hierarchies depend on sacred or religious ideas. In 1960, John Beattie elaborated upon the concept of *mahano* among the Bunyoro people in East Africa. *Mahano* was believed to be a force present in persons, things and events out of the ordinary. The king and his senior chiefs were held to have a lot of *mahano* which acted to confirm their political authority in Bunyoro society.

Since the 1960s anthropologists in a Marxist vein (see **Marxist anthropology**) have suggested that the sacralization of political structures acts to support the interests of a dominant group. They see political structures as dependent upon who has control over economic resources and human labour. This may be between classes, generations, different kin groups or between men and women. From these premises, political discussion has extended into the historical and contemporary relationships between those countries with a history of colonial domination and the countries they formerly ruled, notably in Asia and Africa. **RK**

See also nationalism; power; social conflict.

Further reading John Beattie, *Bunyoro, an African Kingdom*; Meyer Fortes & Edward

Evans-Pritchard, *African Political Systems*; Edmund Leach, *The Political Systems of Highland Burma*.

POLITICAL DRAMA AND THEATRE

Traditionally, Political Drama and Theatre have been used as terms to describe **drama** and **theatre** with an overt political content, which typically encourages its audience to take up a position of struggle against a presented injustice or to ally with a particular political viewpoint. The weakness of such a definition is that it identifies a writer like Brecht or Caryl Churchill as political, while ignoring the operations of **ideology** which mask the political positioning of other apparently unpolitical writers whose ideas are perceived as commonsense, uncontroversial and apolitical, because they reflect uncritically a status quo. Noël Coward, for example, has traditionally not been seen as a political dramatist, but the sexual politics of his drama is highly subversive of commonsense ideas about the family and about heterosexuality. **TRG SS**

Further reading S. Craig (ed.), *Dreams and Deconstructions*; John McGrath, *A Good Night Out*.

POLITICAL OBLIGATION see Political Science

POLITICAL PARTIES see Representative Government

POLITICAL SCIENCE

Political science is an academic discipline, devoted to the systematic description, explanation, analysis and evaluation of politics and power. It might be more accurately labelled 'politology' than political science because the subject is not characterized by one unified body of theory or paradigm (as in some of the natural sciences), and some political scientists reject the idea that their discipline is like that of the natural sciences. The scope of political science is marked by a multiplicity of subfields of inquiry: notably political thought, political history, political theory, political institutions, public administration, public policy, **rational choice**, comparative political analysis, political sociology, and theories of the **state**.

Some political scientists describe themselves first and foremost as *political historians* – albeit with a bias towards **contemporary history**. They tend to be divided into two camps: (a) students of 'high politics', who study élite decision-makers, believe that the personalities and machinations of key élites shape history and cannot be subsumed away as mere by-products of other causes, and generally believe that self-aggrandisement and self-interest will account for most élite behaviour (sometimes such people are denigrated by their colleagues in the profession as mere biographers); and (b) students of 'low politics', or history from below, who believe that the political activities of non-élites, or mass political behaviour, provide the key to explaining major political episodes, rather than the charisma, plots or blunders of political leaders.

The intellectual origins of political science lie in the classics of *political thought*: the accumulated body of texts and writings of great philosophers, especially the 'canon' of Western thinkers from Plato through Machiavelli and Hobbes to Kant, Hegel, Marx and J.S. Mill. Ancient, medieval and early modern political thought shared three common preoccupations, which are still live issues among political scientists: (1) the nature and justification of the state; (2) the nature of **justice**; and (3) the nature of a good political order (see **Utopianism**). Historians of political thought differ over the reasons they advance for paying detailed attention to classical texts. A minority believe that the classics contain permanent truths although they dispute which particular authors and texts contain them. They think that it is the duty of civilized educators to transmit these truths to subsequent generations, and regard empirical political science as a betrayal of 'the great tradition'. Some historians of political thought, by contrast, argue that though the classics address timeless questions, they may be more important for the questions they raise than the answers they provide. For example, the abstract question, 'Would rational persons in a state of nature agree to establish a state, and if so of what type?', helps to clarify the issues underlying political obligation, political legitimacy and our beliefs about human nature. Others argue that the classics, far from being timeless, are texts addressed to contemporaries engaged in political arguments of specific relevance to their own times. They think it is the task of political thought to recover the original meanings and contexts of classical discourses which naturally issues in the question which present debate such historians are themselves addressing.

Political theory has evolved from the history of political thought. It addresses in an analytical vein, often with mathematical and logical rigour, many of the themes raised in political thought and contemporary political science. Political theorists partly see their task as that of conceptual clarification, explicating the possibly contradictory meanings of key political concepts, like **democracy**, **liberty**, **equality**, and justice. However, they also seek to answer major normative questions, such as 'What is justice?': an issue famously addressed in recent times by John Rawls' *A Theory of Justice*, 1971). Much contemporary political theory has a deductive and analytical flavour reflecting the rising ascendancy of rational choice within this field.

The study of *political institutions*, especially the role of constitutions, executives, legislatures, judiciaries and political parties, occasioned the formal establishment of political science departments in most Western universities of liberal democratic states. The concerns of many institutionalists were often indistinguishable from those of constitutional or public lawyers. Contemporary political scientists still spend much of their time monitoring, evaluating, and hypothesizing about the origins, development and consequences of political institutions. They are interested primarily in tracing the origins and developments of political institutions, and providing 'thick' or 'phenomenological' descriptions, normally of the countries in which they reside. (Some of their insulting colleagues claim they engage in 'thick' description simply because they are thick.) They assert, by contrast, that they are real

political scientists: the activities of their colleagues who are area-specialists or knowledgeable about government or public administration in one country, while providing essential data for political science, are not themselves scientific. They maintain that a comparative focus is the only way to be genuinely social-scientific. In their view political science is concerned with establishing 'universal laws' or 'theories of the middle range': that is, generalizations which can provide rigorous and tested time-bound explanations of political phenomena. In its narrowest form 'comparative political institutions' has developed as a discipline which compares constitutions, executives, legislatures and judiciaries either within or across states with a view to explaining differences in the way in which political issues are processed and resolved. However, it can also involve the comparison of militaries, political parties, electoral systems and systems of interest-representation. In its wider form, comparative political analysis, political scientists use general concepts which are not country-specific and are commitment to **positivist** methods. Comparative political analysis developed as part of the **behaviourist** movement in the social sciences which criticized the formalistic and legalistic nature of institutional political science of the 1950s and the 1960s. It sought to test and quantify propositions about political behaviour, arguing that constitutional, legal and formal analyses frequently had little substantiated empirical support. The behavioural revolution was accompanied by rigorous quantitative research on **electoral systems** and electoral behaviour, the functioning of political parties, the role of interest groups, and the making of public policy, with the emphasis often being on studies of decision-making. However, the antithesis between institutionalists and quantitative political scientists has mostly been overcome modern empirical political scientists normally embrace the insights to be derived from both approaches. The marriage between institutionalism and the use of modern empirical techniques such as survey research and statistical testing is perhaps most fruitfully revealed in the testing of cross-national generalizations.

Arend Lijphart's *Democracies: Patterns of Majoritarian and Consensual Government in Twenty One Democracies* (1984) is an exemplary work of comparative political analysis.

Public administration and *public policy* are empirical and normative branches of political science. Whereas public administration focuses on the institutional arrangements for the provision of public services, and historically has been normatively concerned with ensuring responsible and equitable administration, public policy analyses the formation and implementation of policies, and addresses the normative and empirical merit of arguments used to justify policies. Neither public administration nor public policy have one dominant approach: exponents of **pluralism**, behaviourism, rational choice, **Marxism** and **feminism** are to be found engaged in debate with institutionalists who derive their inspiration from the work of Max Weber. The most vigorous intellectual debates in public administration presently centre on the 'new public management' and the validity of economic and rational choice interpretations of the workings of political institutions, especially public **bureaucracies**. Political scientists of a more quantitative bent, especially those with a training in economics, decision-analysis and social policy, have also been developing the field of public policy. The subject matter of this sub-discipline is the formulation, implementation and evaluation of public policies. These political scientists examine who has the power to put policy-proposals on the agenda for example, voters, interest groups, ethnic groups, professional organizations, dominant classes, political parties, mass media, (policy formulation); how policies are made (decision-making) and executed by elected and unelected officials (implementation); and whether or not public policies are effective (evaluation). The distinction between area-specialists, who focus on public policies in one country or one set of institutions (such as the European Community), and specialists in 'comparative public policy' who seek to be genuine social scientists, is also characteristic of the field. In comparative public policy attempts are made to explain both policy-

divergences and policy-convergences both within and across states. Specialists in this field ask and attempt to answer questions such as: 'Does it matter which political parties are in power in explaining policy-outcomes?'

Political economy describes the work of an increasing number of political scientists at the boundaries of politics and economics. Some believe that theories of political behaviour, just like theories of economic behaviour, should start from simple assumptions about human beings and construct predictions about their behaviour from these assumptions. Their critics claim that they share with economists the belief that human beings are simply overgrown pigs: human nature being understood by many of them as the insatiable pursuit of utility. However, for such political scientists the test of a good theory is its predictive power rather than the incontestable truth of its assumptions. The practitioners in this field are specialists in rational choice or in political economy. They generally make the assumption that human beings are rational and self-interested agents, and consequently build 'testable' political hypotheses on the assumption that voters wish to maximize their utility, that politicians are pure office-seekers who wish to maximize the votes they can win at elections, and that utility-maximizing bureaucrats seek to maximize their departmental budgets. However, and confusingly, the label political economy is also used by political scientists working within the Marxist or neo-Marxist tradition, who generally accept the propositions of **historical materialism**.

Political sociology is an important sub-discipline within both **sociology** and political science, and has evolved since the 1950s. Political sociologists reject the firm distinction between the political and the social, and stress the high degree of interaction between the two, which traditional approaches to both sociology and political science under emphasized. Political sociology's original focus upon the relationship between social **structure** (mainly economic class) and political behaviour (mainly voting) has expanded considerably since the mid-1960s to include all aspects of power relations between and within social groups. Debate in this field is often between those who treat political institutions as largely autonomous from social structural determination, those who believe that political institutions are largely reducible to social structural determination, and those who view the distinction between the political and social as fluid and indeterminate. The latter are dominant. For example, theories of political and social movements proposed by Tilly and Gamson distinguish between 'the polity', where formal political influence is concentrated, and 'the external society', but regard the processes of mobilizing social resources in pursuit or defence of interests as essentially similar for both challengers and members of the polity in line with pluralist conceptions of the state and society. Another division within political sociology is between those who espouse **functionalist** theories which treat conflict as an aberration from a 'normal' state of equilibrium, and approaches of a Marxist or pluralist origin which view conflict as a continuous and ubiquitous feature of politics. Subjects studied in political sociology include the influence of childhood socialization on political beliefs; the importance of sex, **ethnicity**, religion and class in shaping and explaining political beliefs and preferences; and the influence of the mass **media** in politics. The subject draws upon arguments developed from the works of the most famous sociologists, notably Weber and Émile Durkheim, but also Karl Marx – now principally known as a falling statue but a key figure in shaping inquiry and debate in political science.

Political science is therefore a multi-theoretical and vibrant field of inquiry, not likely to disappear unless politics is abolished. Many would concur that the subject matter of theories of the state provide the most unified focus for political theory, political thought, political sociology and empirical political inquiry. However, as in politics, so in political science, no judgement of this kind is likely to receive unanimous consent. **BO'L**

See also conservatism; élite theory; liberalism; socialism and social democracy.

Further reading T. Bottomore, *Political Sociology*; P. Dunleavy and B. O'Leary, *The Politics of Liberal Democracy*.

POLITICAL SOCIOLOGY see Political Science

POLITICAL THEORY see Political Science

POLITICS see Political Science

POLLUTION

Pollution of the environment has become a major concern during the 20th century as human society has generated an ever increasing variety and quantity of products and wastes, many of which are released into the environment. Land, water and air are all increasingly affected by a range of pollutants including noise, heat, smoke, chemicals, sewage, manure and radioactive isotopes. Once in the environment, many pollutants are diluted, dispersed or broken down into harmless materials, but others may be concentrated or transformed into more damaging forms. Damage caused by pollution may not be immediately obvious, causing comparatively subtle but far-reaching changes in biological communities which are not of obvious importance to humans and their environment. However, the nature of the **ecosystem** is such that minor fluctuations may be magnified by the interactions between species: for example, the detrimental effect pesticides can have on bird populations. Monitoring pollution pathways and effects is a formidable problem for environmental scientists, but solving pollution problems is more than a technical issue.

Pollution occurs where human activities introduce something into the environment which has harmful effects. The inclusion of harmful effects in the definition means that the concept of pollution is value dependent and hence politically contested. In many cases, values and interests differ: for example, farmers use weedkillers and pesticides and regard the results as beneficial, while conservationists lament the effects on meadow plants or butterflies. In other cases it matters where the substance is: depletion of stratospheric ozone is regarded as a problem, and so is increased low-level ozone. In some cases sulphur dioxide in the air acts as a valuable source of plant nutrients while in others it contributes to acid rain and plant damage. Concentration of pollutants makes a crucial difference: carbon dioxide would not have been regarded as a pollutant a decade ago but now it is involved in one of the most threatening pollution issues. In small quantities, animal manure is beneficial, but in large quantities it can overwhelm the capacity of natural cycles to deal with it. For most chemical pollutants, and even for radioactivity, harmful effects may be difficult to demonstrate at low concentrations so there may be passionate disputes between emitter and affected publics. In many such cases there may be natural sources of the possible pollutant as well as industrial sources so responsibility is difficult to prove. Although governments seem increasingly concerned to regulate pollution, progress is far from simple, which is illustrated by some examples from air, water and land.

Air pollution has changed from a local problem to a global one in the last two centuries. Industrialization caused a huge increase in coal burning for power and in smelting and also involved new chemical processes. Smoke and corrosive gases became serious problems and were subject to regulation by the mid–19th century, but as industry has grown and spread around the world air pollution has usually followed. The use of the internal combustion engine has added to the problems, at first in the form of urban smog but more recently in the regional problem of acid rain. Industrialized areas such as the northeast US and northwest Europe now have such high emissions of sulphur and nitrogen oxides that rain, fog and snow are acidified and lakes and forests are dying. The precise causes of acid rain are still disputed and as a result controls are not strong enough to promise a solution. Acid rain has become an international issue, but ozone depletion is truly global. It was a largely unexpected problem because the cause was a family of chemicals chosen for their safety and stability, and the effect was strongest through a quite unexpected route. The stability of the chlorofluorocarbons (CFCs) was ideal for refrigerators and aerosols, but it allowed them to spread throughout the atmosphere and into the stratosphere where ultraviolet light from the Sun broke them down. The chlorine released proved extremely effective at breaking down ozone, especially in the special conditions of the Antarctic spring, where more than half of the ozone was lost. The surprise at the extent of the damage, plus fear of skin cancer from increased exposure to UV radiation at the surface, has made the international response unusually energetic, but there are still problems in preventing CFC use from spreading into the Third World. The problem of **global warming** is an even more challenging global issue, because its causes are integral to the nature of modern society.

Water pollution has also spread from the local to affect large rivers, lakes and land-locked seas. Perhaps the most pervasive pollutant is sewage, which is broken down by bacteria which use oxygen and may reduce oxygen levels below that required by previously existing plants, fish and insects. Other pollutants which are not themselves toxic, including nitrates from fertilizers and phosphates from detergents, can provide nutrients which trigger algal growth, again taking up oxygen and in some cases releasing toxins which affect animals. Algal blooms are now beginning to affect the Adriatic and North Seas as well as ponds and lakes. Many industrial chemicals find their way into rivers and coastal waters, whether discharged legally, accidentally or illegally. Occasionally, levels of toxic substances, for example, mercury or cadmium, may be high enough to cause acute poisoning, most notoriously at Minamata Bay in the 1950s where at least 46 people died from eating fish which had absorbed mercury wastes. More commonly, industrial rivers carry a cocktail of pollutants, including heavy metals, solvents and PCBs (polychlorinated biphenyl), at levels sufficient to cause concern but not to be demonstrably harmful. Rivers like the Rhine, which flow through several countries, may be a source of international disputes, as are the seas into which they discharge.

Land pollution occurs in three main ways:

(1) Mining and mineral processing may produce large voids and spoil heaps. These are at least unsightly and spoil has the potential to cause significant pollution. The entry of air and water into spoil heaps may cause weathering processes which transform sulphides into dissolved acid. In turn, increased acidity can dissolve metals, some of which are toxic. For example, in acidified water courses it may be dissolved aluminium which kills fish rather than the acid itself.

(2) The sites of manufacturing plants may become contaminated by raw materials, combustion products and wastes over the years they are running. Any attempt to redevelop the site may encounter asbestos, toxic metals or hazardous solvents.

(3) More pervasive, and often less identifiable, are the problems associated with landfill sites. Many old dumps contain chemical and metal wastes as well as household refuse. Water percolating through such dumps may dissolve toxic materials, producing leachates which contaminate water courses. More pervasive still is the decomposition of organic materials to produce methane, a gas which is explosive when mixed with air and which is a very effective greenhouse gas. Modern landfills can be managed to reduce water percolation and to collect methane for use as a fuel, but many old dumps are unrecorded and potentially hazardous.

Pollution control is partly a matter of improving technology, for example, incineration of domestic waste can solve the problem of methane in landfills, as well as generating useful amounts of electricity, but adoption of improved controls may be costly and may require political pressure. Several different principles have been used or proposed. In the UK, the Alkali Inspectorate relied for decades on the principle of Best Practicable Means, that is the use of methods which would reduce pollution but not put the polluters out of business. More recently this has evolved into the Best Practicable Environmental Option and then the Best Available Technology Not Entailing Excessive Cost. Most European countries have preferred to set Emission Limits for pollutants and the EC has moved toward imposing the same limits across its territory to provide a 'level playing field' for competition. The UK, with the advantage of a westerly airflow and rather short rivers, has objected that these limits are unnecessarily tight. A more radical principle of control is currently being discussed. This is the Prevention Principle, which seeks to prevent pollution from ocurring rather than limiting it or coping with the consequences. As this would bear very heavily on industry and face problems of predicting whether or not pollution would occur in particular circumstances its progress will probably be slow. **PS**

Further reading B. Price, *P is for Pollution*.

POLYARCHY see Pluralism

POLYMORPHISM

Polymorphism (Greek, 'many-shapedness'), in the **life sciences**, is the occurrence together in one population of two or more genetically distinct types of individual of the same species. The study of such phenomena is important for an understanding of the mechanism of **speciation**. Polymorphism arises because the forces of selection favour both types equally; if the environment changes, then one or other might be placed in a favourable position and become dominant, or the two types might become still more different, leading ultimately to speciation. Two forms of polymorphism occur: stable and transient. In the former the various forms, known as morphs, exist in stable proportions and all individuals appear to interbreed without preference. Examples of this situation are the maintenance of different blood groups within human populations and sickle-cell anaemia in populations exposed to malaria; individuals who suffer from sickle-cell anaemia are resistant to malaria and are therefore more likely to reach reproductive age and so pass on the gene. Many species exhibit sexual dimorphism, where one or other sex is larger and more colourful, and exhibits behavioural differences – the difference between peacocks and peahens provides a clear example of this. Henry Bates, studying **mimicry** in the mid-19th century, observed that bees exhibit polymorphism with respect to the various castes present in the hive workers, drones and queen. Transient polymorphism is the situation where the balance between forms is not even and one type appears to be increasing in abundance at the expense of the other. **RB**

See also evolution; genetics; natural selection.

Further reading John Maynard-Smith, *The Theory of Evolution*.

POLYNOMIALS

Polynomials (Greek, 'many powers') are among the most fundamental of mathematical objects. Their use originated with the need to solve equations involving powers of numbers (the number multiplied by itself n times is the nth power of the number in question). A polynomial (in one variable) is the sum of multiples of powers of the unknown (usually written x), such as $4x^5 + 3x^2 + x + 2$ (they are usually written with the powers decreasing, for clarity). The 'degree' of the polynomial is the number of the largest power involved in it: 5 in the above example. The smaller degrees have special names: 1 is linear, 2 quadratic, 3 cubic, 4 quartic and 5 quintic. The study of solutions of this kind of polynomial is the inspiration of **Galois theory**.

It is also possible to have polynomials with more than one variable: for example, $xy^3 + 3x^2y + 5$ has two variables, x and y, and degree 4 (because xy^3 is a multiple of a term with degree 1 (x) by a term with degree 3 (y^3), and you add these together). **SMcL**

POLYPHONY

Polyphony (Greek 'having many voices') is a term used to refer to music for two or more instruments or voices, in which most or all of the musical parts move to some degree independently. The antitheses of polyphony are monophony (music that is in one line only) and homophony (music for a single line plus accompaniment). The term tends to be associated with the evolution of European art music from the 13th to 16th centuries, and in particular during the **Renaissance** when the development of vocal polyphony reached its height. The term can also be applied to various techniques of composition that emerged in subsequent periods of European music, such as 'counterpoint', 'fugue' and, in this century, serialism (see **serial music**) or 'twelve-note composition'. All of these techniques involved strict procedural laws, which determined how the musical parts should be melodically and rhythmically related.

When Western **musicology** widened its objectives to include traditional folk and non-Western art music, the understanding of polyphony was extended beyond the European concept. This had emphasized a *conscious* ordering of the musical parts into a unified and law-abiding whole, but was broadened to embrace any music that involved the coexistence of independent contrasting or complementary musical parts, without the necessity of a single organizational principle. Much non-Western music reveals a polyphonic texture, comprising layers, or strata, of homogeneous groups of instruments and voices, each layer possessing its own melodic, rhythmic and timbral identity, and each performing its own musical function. Such polyphonic stratification is a predominant feature in many Southeast Asian orchestral forms, such as Balinese *gamelan*, and in African drum ensembles. It has also been an influential factor in the compositions of so-called **minimalist** or **process music** composers.

There are numerous ways in which the musical parts of polyphonic music may be organized, some according to hierarchical principles and others where they are given equal status. The enormous diversity in polyphonic practice, throughout the world, has prompted musical anthropologists to speculate on whether a society's musical structure is a reflection of its social structure. **SSt**

POLYRHYTHM

Polyrhythm (Greek, 'many rhythms') is the simultaneous use of contrasting rhythmic characteristics by two or more instruments or voices. There is some disagreement between the terminologies used for the discussion of rhythm in Western art **music** and those used to discuss the rhythmic, often percussive music of other cultures, such as African drumming; debate centres on the precise meanings of 'rhythm', 'metre', and 'pulse' or 'beat'.

The most common, albeit diverse, definitions of polyrhythm are: (a) 'rhythmic counterpoint', where simultaneously-performed parts use contrasting rhythmic patterns; (b) 'rhythmic canon', where simultaneously-performed parts have identical or closely similar rhythmic patterns overlapping or displaced in time; (c) where simultaneously-performed parts have different divisors of the same beat: for example when one part with beats divided into three units is set against another divided into four; (d) 'cross-rhythm', where simultaneously-performed parts accent the divisions of the same equally divided bar in different symmetrical combinations (for example, [1-2/3-4/5-6] set against [1-2-3/4-5-6] a favourite device of the composer Brahms); (e) where simultaneously-performed parts have differently accented divisions of the same bar, but where the dominant part shifts the conventional accents off the beat while the subordinate or accompanying part provides the basic regular beat (for example, [1-2-3/4-5-6/7-8] against [1-2-3-4/5-6-7-8]); (f) where simultaneously-performed parts have different accentual patterns, or metres, for example when three bars of four beats are set against four bars of three beats, the cycle recurring every twelve beats; (g) 'polymetric music', where simultaneously-performed parts have different speeds or tempos, with the result that they do not converge on a common beat.

To the nonspecialist, such technicalities may seem abstruse. But in performance, the effect of polyrhythm is easily perceived and is exhilarating and stimulating, the brain simultaneously reacting to the 'reassurance' of a perceived, regular rhythm, and to the 'surprise' of rhythmic variants or contrasts being performed at the same instant. In African **folk music** in particular, and in musics such as **jazz** which make extensive use of syncopation, polyrhythm is a major intellectual and emotional resource. **KMcL SSt**

Further reading Simha Arom, *African Polyphony and Polyrhythm*; Curt Sachs, *Rhythm and Tempo*.

POLYTHEISM

Polytheism (Greek, 'many gods') is the mirror-image of **monotheism**. Monotheists claim that there is only one God, that even in so-called polytheistic religions one god is supreme in the pantheon and the others are subordinate – in other words, that polytheists are monotheists in all but name. Polytheists might equally assert that even the most granitic monotheistic **religions** have their trinities, saints and sages, conforming exactly to the 'minor' deities of polytheism. An atheist might comment that the whole thing is semantic quibbling, that the fact is that humans have always worshipped a diversity of beings, and that whatever the grand intellectual core of a faith, at practical level it is usually fragmented into a variety of local forms involving what seem to be more accessible, more domestic supernatural intermediaries.

The problem, if it is a problem, has been further compounded by the vehement denunciation of polytheistic belief and practice by the large monotheistic religions, notably by adherents of **Judaism** (and from them, **Christianity**) in the West, and by followers of **Islam** in the Middle East after Muhammad's attack on the idolaters in the Ka'aba. The theological tendency of monotheists has been derisively to assert that polytheism is a 'primal' practice, deluded if not evil, and that people evolve from it into monotheism. Are so-called 'primal' religions, the traditional religions of most of the world, including such systems as the **Olympian religion**, the religions of the ancient Egyptians and the medieval Nordic peoples, really of less cultural importance than the so-called 'world' religions? Where do semi-religious systems like **Buddhism**, **Daoism**, **Hinduism** and **Shinto** fit into this pattern? Viewed from outside, it seems high time that the whole nature of world religious belief and practice was re-examined – and a useful starting-point for monotheists might be the attempt to see that polytheism is, and always has been, as valid and as satisfying a human response to the supernatural as their own, not to mention often more widespread and more tolerant. **EMJ KMcL**

POLYTONALITY

Polytonality (Greek, 'in many keys') is a European musical style which involves the use of several keys at once. Some composers use bitonality (the use of two keys at once, as in Stravinsky's *Petrushka*, which derives harmonic energy from the combination of F sharp – black keys on a keyboard – and C major – white keys). In the 1910s and 1920s, the French composer Darius Milhaud wrote several polytonal works, including a setting of the *Oresteia*, in parts of which each voice and instrument is in a different key. The effect, in simpler polytonal music (such as Gustav Holst's *Terzetto* in three keys, or Charles Ives's chorales in four) is often as if conventional harmony had gone inexplicably awry, in the way that some **cubist** paintings look like conventional pictures seen in a distorting mirror. But in the hands of the greatest composers (notably Bartók, Messiaen, Sibelius and Stravinsky), who use polytonality as one component of style and not as a style in itself, the technique produces balanced and expressive results. **KMcL**

See also diatonicism; tonality.

POP

Pop (from popular, Latin *popularis*, 'of the people'), as a cultural label, came into use in the 1950s, and has much the same connotations as 'junk' in 'junk food': that is, those who are not in sympathy with it say that it is manufactured pap for mass consumption, with none of the qualities of taste and variety possesed by their own preferred nourishment; those who enjoy it, however, are entirely satisfied by it and untroubled by critical disparagement. The term is widely applied – there are 'pop' films, 'pop' newspapers, even 'pop' psychologists and holiday resorts – but its main use is in the **arts** and **design**.

The aesthetic of Pop Design had its roots in the activities of the British Independent Group (IG) during the 1960s. The IG challenged the traditions of **modernism** and argued that design need not necessarily be functional and universal, but should reflect the desires of the consumer. They explored areas of **popular culture** such as comics, sf and fairgrounds, and this turnaround of establishment design values came to a head with the youth revolution of the next decade. In the early years of the 1960s, Pop Design reflected these new values with a series of products that explored the throwaway aesthetic in paper furniture and clothes, and brightly coloured surface pattern that drew its inspiration from the imagery of Pop Art and popular culture.

Pop Art, described by the American critic Harold Rosenberg as 'advertising art advertising itself as art that hates advertising', flourished from the 1950s to the 1970s, primarily in the UK and US. It found its imagery and many of its techniques in the realms of advertising and consumer packaging, and in such popular culture as comic books, film stars and pop stars. In the US in particular, Pop Art both fed on and ridiculed the hold consumerism and popular culture had on people's minds. Roy Lichtenstein imitated on a vast scale the subject matter and reproduction techniques of the comic strip in works such as *Whaam!*, while Claes Oldenberg emphasized a **Dadaist** element always implicit in Pop by making giant 'soft' sculptures from vinyl and fabric of such everyday items as hamburgers and telephones. As well as questioning many of the accepted norms of fine art, such works also explored the nature of representation. Their 'minimal art content' relates them to **minimalism**, and questions fundamental notions of the aims of art, of the contextualization of the work, and not least of the role of imitation in the art-making process.

Pop **Literature** covers a huge range of reading material, from 'family' and 'special-interest' magazines and tabloid newspapers to blockbuster novels, from comics to 'pop poetry' (a kind of **poetry** devised in the 1950s, like pop-song lyrics without the music). It feeds off more 'serious' (and perhaps more snobbish) literary forms, but has little in common with them, though critics sometimes tie themselves into knots trying to show relationships. Its chief appeal, in all its forms, is immediacy:

it snags the interest from the first few words, and moves on fast. This is, however, only a trick of style, and brevity and brightness of expression are no barrier (whatever highbrow critics might imply) to profundity or seriousness. Pop newspapers, for example, are often far more on the nerve of events than their stylistic garishness suggests to some, and pop **novels** often have a depth and urgency of appeal which has nothing to do with 'high' literary pretension.

Pop **Music** consists almost entirely of songs. If instrumental solos become pop hits, they are usually novelty numbers. Its style varies round the world. In Arabia and India, pop music tends to be lush and romantic, with a yearning quality quite lacking in Western pop. In Africa and the Middle East pop music is often bouncy and joky, similar in style to the more energetic folk songs and dances. In the pop music of the West – which, nowadays, means the pop music which is gradually colonizing the rest of the world – simple lyrics, usually about teenage love-crises, are sung to plainly-harmonized, catchy tunes over a steady beat suitable for dancing. The Western pop industry is closely tied up with marketing, of everything from the artists themselves to clothes, films, food, games, magazines and videos. Pop borrows extensively from such other musical forms as classical, reggae, **jazz**, rap and **rock music**. As a social phenomenon, it is unique in the arts: a style which hardly existed until the mid-1950s, which spread worldwide in a few months and has never since slackened its appeal. Pop music has reached everywhere. Even remote peoples in Amazonia, the Himalayas and Papua New Guinea, for example, respond to it instantly, as if it is not a created art form at all, but a kind of music somehow natural and instinctive to the human species – something which can be said of none of the kinds of music enjoyed by those who are immune to its appeal. **PD MG CMcD KMcL**

POPULAR CULTURE

Popular culture used to mean the **culture** ordinary people actually made for themselves: activities and habits of mind arising, usually without identified authors, from specific societies and reflecting specific circumstances and world-views. But from the early 19th century onwards, the term has been hijacked by intellectual snobs, to mean what the mass of people enjoy (as opposed to 'high' culture, which is what people of refined taste enjoy). Inverted snobbery now makes some intellectuals affect what they perceive as the styles and manners of popular culture, and makes some critics go into contortions to demonstrate that popular artistic artefacts can be judged (usually with a patter of patronizing applause) by the criteria of 'high' culture. Certainly, comparisons are obligatory between one perceived kind of culture and another, there are points of similarity and influence. It might, however, be argued either that 'culture' (whatever that is) is a single, indivisible phenomenon, or that chalk is chalk and cheese is cheese, and those who simply live and enjoy 'culture', as opposed to analysing it, have the right idea. **KMcL**

See also pop.

POPULATION BIOLOGY

Population biology describes the study of the structure of biological communities as **ecosystems**. The way in which individuals and species interact with one another is dependent upon behaviour and the effect of the environment, and can be studied mathematically in terms of **genetics**. The fluctuations in size and changes in structure which affect all living populations are products of the dynamic equilibrium in which biological communities exist: the population biologist attempts to predict or explain these fluctuations by constructing models which imitate the processes involved. However, such models inevitably oversimplify the situation as population biology is a very complex science. **RB**

See also competition; demography; population explosion.

POPULATION EXPLOSION

The growth of the human population might be seen as an indication of success, but usually it is seen as a problem. From time to time it provokes a near panic, as it did when Malthus wrote *An Essay on the Principle of Population* (1798) and again when the Erlichs wrote *The Population Bomb*. Not only does population grow inexorably, it does so at an increasing rate and the rate of increase is fastest among groups least able to provide for their children. Concern is increased by the fact that wherever such runaway population growth occurs in nature it is followed by a collapse in numbers. Malthus spelt out the problem starkly: populations have the capacity to grow by geometric progression while food supply only increases by arithmetic progression. Unless the growth of population is held back by moral restraint it will be held back by famine, disease or war: the so called 'Malthusian checks'.

The idea of geometric progression is now more commonly known as exponential growth and is most easily understood as growth with a constant doubling time. For most of prehistory there were only a few million people alive. By the time of Christ there were about 300 million. The population took 1,500 years to double, 300 years to double again and only 150 years to double again, reaching 2.4 billion by 1950. In the next 30 years it doubled again, passing 5 billion in 1987. The growth rate peaked at 2.1% per annum between 1965 and 1970, but even at the current growth rate of 1.7% per annum, it would double again in another 40 years. No wonder there is such concern about what will happen in the next century.

Some indication of what might happen can be gained from analysis of current and past variation in growth rates in different kinds of country. At present Africa has the fastest rates of growth, averaging 3% (and in Kenya well over 4%), indicating a doubling time of under 20 years. Then come tropical South America, 2.6%, and South Asia, 2.3%. China and temperate South America have intermediate rates of growth around 1.3%. Lower rates occur in the former USSR, US and the lowest are in Europe, where a few countries have reached zero growth. With the exception of China's draconian population policy, the main influence on these rates seems to be

the length and success of the period of industrialization, though culture also exerts an influence.

A more detailed understanding of population growth requires separate analysis of fertility and mortality. In pre-industrial societies both fertility and mortality rates were high, so life expectancy was short. As Europe industrialized in the 19th century, diet, sanitation and medicine improved and the mortality rate fell, triggering a rapid growth of population. After a few decades, the fertility rate also fell, reducing the rate of growth. This change from high to low fertility and mortality is known to demographers as the *demographic transition*. Unfortunately, it has not proved easy to reproduce this transition elsewhere. Mortality control is relatively easy to achieve, but fertility control relies on a shift in the behaviour of whole populations and has proved much more difficult. Economic prosperity alone is not sufficient, as shown by high fertility in the oil-rich states of the Middle East. Compulsion is only partially successful, as shown by experience in China and India. Provision of contraceptives has limited effects unless people are committed to their use. Education and the changing status of women are part of the pattern. A shift from a way of life where children support their parents in old age to one where parents support their children through a long period of education may be the decisive one. But, such is the variability with which fertility and mortality have changed in different countries, predictions are very difficult. They are even more difficult when many countries have populations growing faster than their rate of economic growth so that income per capita is falling.

The UN publishes population forecasts, with a range from optimistic to pessimistic, but even their optimistic forecast envisages a world population of 7.5 billion in 2025. Even with the assumption that all countries will reduce fertility to replacement levels, the UN envisages world population reaching 10 to 14 billion before stabilization. This will pose a serious challenge to human society and place massively increased pressures on the environment. Achieving sustainable development in these circumstances will require concerted international action, but there is little sign that it will be forthcoming, indeed the opposite seems true. As most of the growth will be in less-developed countries, there will be strong incentives for international migration, and the developed countries seem to be tightening controls in anticipation. The stage is set for internal and international conflicts over migration which may well be a step towards a world dominated by Malthusian checks. **PS**

Further reading Ehrlich, *The Population Bomb*.

PORNOGRAPHY

Pornography (Greek, 'depiction of whores'), in its narrowest sense, is writing or visual images designed to provide sexual stimulation. Debate rages about whether or not this is a morally 'good' thing to do, and also precisely which artefacts could be termed pornographic. For example, are Indian temple carvings, the Kama Sutra, or Persian or Japanese pictures of intercourse pornography? Would it include novels such as *Lady Chatterley's Lover*? Films like *In the Realm of the Senses*? 'Top-shelf' magazines in newsagents? Naked bottoms in television plays? Each person has his or her own definition and national, religious or cultural attitudes also affect the issue: images of women's bare legs are regarded as pornographic by some Muslims, depictions of kissing are pornographic to some Hindus, any depictions of the sexual act at all are pornographic to some Christians. Some feminists (see below) take the view that all heterosexual pornography is an expression of male violence against females; there are, at the other end of this argument, flourishing markets for pornography produced by women for women, or showing homosexual sex.

There is a wider argument, which states that we live in a pornographic society, in which we are bombarded with images not just of carnality but of violence. The assault of such work on the beholder is seen as a kind of rape. Strangely, this is still a minority view, and most campaigners against pornography restrict their opposition to the depiction of nudity and sex (and some-

times to explicit language). It would seem that images of aggression and violence provoke far less systematic rage.

In feminist circles, fierce debate has raged, in both the UK and the US, about the very definition of pornography. There are two distinct issues in feminist analysis of pornography: first, the exploitation of women in the process of making pornography and, second, the way in which different pornographies construct and represent women's **sexuality**.

Andrea Dworkin has argued in her book *Pornography: Men Possessing Women* that pornographic texts reveals men's inherent belief in the right to sexual access to women's bodies. For Dworkin the definition of pornography is all sexual material that shows sexual degradation. Her argument involves the testimony of many women who have been coerced into participation in pornography. Dworkin and Catherin MacKinnon have worked and campaigned to gain stringent laws against all types of pornography in the US. In 1984 an ordinance was drafted by them to enable women to take civil action against anyone involved in the production, distribution or sale of pornography. Although the ordinance was vetoed by the mayor a revised version was passed by Indianopolis City Council which, two years later, was declared unconstitutional by the Supreme Court with the help of the Feminist Anti-Censorship Taskforce. Many contemporary feminists groups, such as Feminists Against Censorship in the UK, would not, as Dworkin does, see pornography as the central agent of women's oppression, but rather as a symptom of oppression. Many anti-censorship feminists argue that the censorship of pornographic images would drive the industry further underground, alienating women who are sex-workers, and also prevent women from creating their own images of sexuality.

Some feminists have further argued that the solution to the problems of pornography is not censorship, and many feminist theorists and artists have engaged different strategies for addressing and defining the problem. Lynne Segal notes that there is much disagreement over the definition and significance of pornography and argues that the disagreements arise from the contrasting political positions from which pornography is seen. In her book *Hard Core* Linda Williams takes a detailed look at heterosexual hardcore pornography on celluloid or video and identifies pornography as a genre with its own formal structure. Susan Sontag's analysis of the 'pornographic imagination' (in her article with that title, republished in *A Susan Sontag Reader*), argues for a reassessment of some written pornographic texts, for example, the works of the Marquis de Sade, to take into account pornography as a subversion of dominant norms.

Many feminists and lesbian independent film-makers have chosen to engage with issues surrounding the representation of women's sexuality and, instead of calling for censorship, have engaged with the task of building a new pornography that does not coerce or exploit women. These film-makers, such as Carolee Schneeman, Barbara Hammer, Monika Treuk, Cleo Ublemann, to name but a few, have sought to build a cinematic space for women's sexuality and pleasure. Feminist and lesbian writers have also taken up this challenge. Kathy Archer and Pat Califa point out that censorship will always foreground a specific world-view and are concerned that prejudice will dictate what can and cannot be seen – asking questions such as: under what criteria can a heterosexual male decide what a lesbian can see? Feminists who do not advocate censorship want sexual speech for women along with free discussion about sexuality so that women can take control of their own sexualities and their representation. **TK KMcL**

See also eroticism; gender.

Further reading Lynne Segal and Mary Macintosh (eds.), *Sex Exposed; Sexuality and the Pornography Debate*.

POSITIVE THEORY OF LAW see Legal Positivism

POSITIVISM

Positivism, in the **philosophy of science**, is a school of thought which asserts that **science** can only deal with observable entities which can be directly experienced. The aim of positivism is to construct general laws and theories which describe and express relationships between observable phenomena.

In **sociology**, positivism refers to the belief, held by a number of the founding fathers of sociology, that it could be scientific in the same way as the natural sciences. Positivist sociologists argued that the behaviour of people could be objectively measured. Just as systems of measurement could be applied to matter, temperature, weight, pressure, etc., so too it was thought that objective systems of measurement could be devised for human behaviour. Positivists considered the measurement of human behaviour to be necessary for its explanation. According to this school of thought, observations based on objective measurement would make it possible to produce statements about the cause and effect of human behaviour. Theories might then be devised to explain social phenomena.

This approach to sociology placed particular emphasis on observable behaviour. Factors that cannot be directly observed, such as meanings, motivations and purposes, are not important. This emphasis within positivism on observable 'facts' is largely due to the belief that human behaviour could be explained in the same way as the behaviour of matter is explained in the natural sciences. Natural scientists do not inquire into the meanings of a given experiment; their purpose is to observe, measure and explain the outcome. Similarly, positivist sociologists assumed that human behaviour is a response to external forces and their job was to explain this.

Émile Durkheim (1858–1917) was a positivist sociologist and his study of **suicide** has now become a classic work of positivist sociology. Durkheim asserted that all social behaviour was the result of observable forces external to the individual members of a given society, even suicide, the ultimate individual act, could be explained scientifically in terms of external social forces. He made a study of the suicide statistics for a number of different societies which he observed varied between different societies but for the same society was remarkably constant over the years. Individual societal members may thus come and go but the suicide rate remains stable. Durkheim concluded that the cause of suicide must therefore lie in social factors external to the individual.

In recent times, positivism has come to be seen as naive. Like other 'sciences' sociology is a scientific discipline in that it involves systematic methods of investigation and data analysis, but the study of human beings has some important differences compared with the study of the natural world. Unlike natural objects human beings are self-aware and confer a sense and purpose to what they do. Many sociologists now believe that it is impossible to describe social life without first understanding the meanings which people apply to their behaviour. **DA**

See also ethnomethodology; individualism; naturalism; phenomenological sociology; social fact; social realism; symbolic interactionism; understanding.

Further reading T. Benton, *Philosophical Foundations of the Three Sociologies*; A. Giddens, *Positivism and Sociology*; R. Keat, J. Urry, *Social Theory as Science.*

POSSIBILITY see **Modality**

POST-SERIALISM see **Serial Music**

POST-STRUCTURALISM see **Structuralism**

POSTFEMINISM see **Feminism**

POSTIMPRESSIONISM see **Impressionism**

POSTMODERNISM

Postmodernism, in the **arts** and **design**, is a phenomenon of the last 25 years, originating in the West but now spreading throughout the world. Whereas **modernism** consisted of dozens of individual 'movements', each with a rigorous artistic dogma and a programme for changing the world, postmodernism is individualistic and anarchic. We live today in a pluralist society, surrounded by images and artefacts from all periods and of all geographical and cultural locations. We are aware of the entire experience of the human race in ways that were not available to previous generations, and we have means and techniques of artistic creation which simultaneously include and beggar all those of the past. We are inheritors of the artistic and personal licence so energetically preached in the 1960s: philosophical, ethical and social libertarianism is the new orthodoxy.

In the arts, this has led to an unprecedented upsurge of eclecticism. Artists are as wary of 'isms' as their great-grandparents were eager to embrace them. 'Doing your own thing' is, for many artists, where creativity begins and boundaries between arts, and between different branches or hierarchic levels of the same art are nowadays of minimal relevance. Stylistic interpenetration is the norm, in particular between what used to be thought of as 'high' art and 'genre' art. Architects are happy to take ideas from all traditions, making buildings in an identifiable 'postmodernist' manner, which would once have been condemned as an incompetent anthology of features. Charles Jencks, whose writings have done much to promote the term, defines a Postmodern building as: 'doubly-coded – part Modern and part something else: vernacular revivalist, local, commercial, metaphorical or contextual'. Postmodernist **architecture** has been particularly identified with **neoclassical** architecture and town planning in Europe and America during the late 20th century; an interesting example of which is the huge housing project known as the Palace of Abraxas, Marne-La-Vallée (1978–83), the work of the partnership of the Spanish architect Ricardo Bofill.

In design, postmodernists took as their starting-point ideas first developed during the 1960s, reviving a whole series of ideas, imagery and materials which had been rejected by the Modern Movement. The furniture of the Italian Memphis Group is typical, mixing unconventional materials such as plastic with expensive wood finishes, reviving historical detailing, combining different decorative patterned surfaces and challenging such conventions as that all the legs on a chair should always be identical.

In a similar way, postmodernist painters and sculptors select from the entire repertory of traditional and experimental techniques, the whole range of folk styles, past styles and themes, confident that their audience will appreciate every nuance of allusion or re-creation. **Drama** bestrides the once-perceived gulf between exclusive and popular traditions: actors are multi-talented first, specialists second; writers produce stage plays one day and soap opera the next; **comedy** and **tragedy** are inextricably combined; improvisation, musical and physical skills (such as juggling or roller-skating) make appearances in performances of even the most 'serious' kind. Musicians write jingles, **pop** songs and **symphonies** with equal panache, and are happy to draw on every kind of creative resource from big tunes to **serial music**, from counterpoint to rap. Writers embrace or pastiche techniques drawn from every period and every level of culture. They import, for example, experimental narrative strategies into popular **fiction**, or genre conventions into more 'serious' work, without feeling the need to declare or explain what's happening.

There is, in short, not a postmodernist movement but a continuum. There are no boundaries save our own individual competence; creator and spectator are locked together in a conspiracy against history, against geography and against specificity, which may be seen as liberating or destructive (the lunatics taking over the asylum), but which is entirely without precedent in the story of the arts. **PD MG JM KMcL**

Further reading Andreas Huyssen, *After the Great Divide: Modernism, Mass Culture, Postmodernism*; Charles Jencks, *What is Post-Modernism?*.

POWER

Power (Old English, derived from the Latin for 'to be able') is conventionally defined as the ability to effect results in an individual or group despite resistance. Methods employed to do so may range from persuasion to physical force. Max Weber (1864–1920) distinguished this concept of power from **authority**, which he defined as the social sanction taking various forms, either on a worldly or spiritual basis, that allowed the individual to control the action or decisions of others in particular situations. These two concepts were further distinguished from coercion which described the application of brute force to overcome resistance.

Marxist approaches use power to describe political and economic dominance as manifest in **class** structures, gender relations, and the imposition of the dominant class's ideas and value systems in society at large. This perspective has been criticized for being too simplistic, neglecting the symbolic or non-material aspects of power relationships. For example, in the Polynesian and Melanesian concept of *mana*, it is the spiritual energies immanent in natural phenomena, places, objects and persons that characterize notions of power.

Recently, anthropologists have concentrated on the many different types of power both within and compared to other societies. For instance, the power of a shaman or priest is quite different from the power of a king over his serfs, which again is quite different from the power of the **media**. Power is not just seen as an ability or attribute of a person, but arising from the kinds of relations and processes between the members. In a democratic nation, the power of politicians is in large part controlled and determined by the people that they represent. Power may therefore be conceived as permeating all kinds of social interactions and relationships.

The theorist particularly associated with this diffuse view of power, Michel Foucault (1926–1984), rejects the view that power is something which can be possessed and used in the interests of a particular individual or group. Foucault argues that power is an invisible force; it is exercised, rather than possessed, it is not the privilege of a ruling class, nobody has power – power simply exists. Foucault stresses the importance of surveillance in many of our social institutions (prisons, schools, hospitals, etc.) and the intricate links of power with knowledge.

The fact that power is one of the most disputed concepts in the political and social sciences should not lead us to believe that it is 'an essentially contested concept', something so value-laden as to be beyond general consensus. The political scientist Keith Dowding helpfully distinguishes 'outcome power' from 'social power'. Outcome power is the ability of an agent to bring about or help to bring about outcomes, whereas social power is the ability of an agent deliberately to change the incentive structures facing another agent (or agents) in order to bring about or help bring about outcomes. Social power is therefore a subset of the more general concept of outcome power.

Debates about the normative question 'Who should have (or exercise) social power?' and the empirical question 'Who actually has (or exercises) decisive social power?' are amenable to empirical testing and evaluation so long as authors can agree on the definition and measurement of power itself. So far, however, such agreement has proven elusive. Three fallacies which frequently accompany the discussion of political power appear to block the prospects of intelligent investigation. The first is the 'blame fallacy'. It asserts that the fact that an agent, call her x, is powerless to bring about an outcome, call it o, implies that there is another agent, call him y, who is exercising power to prevent x achieving o. However, even if y has this potential power it does not follow that y is to blame. In other words, some people fail to distinguish between the ability of one agent to bring about an outcome, and the ability of some other agent to stop them.

The second fallacy, particularly common among sociologists, is to assume that social structures have power. However, describing the distribution of power in society by the structures or relations between people cannot mean that those structures or relations are themselves powerful. One reason why this fallacy is misleading is that the concept of power necessarily implies that power-holders are free to choose to use their power, but there is no way in which we can meaningfully say of structures that they choose or choose not to wield power. One should not confuse 'structures', which are relationships, with institutions which contain agents who can indeed wield power, though it is a much more complex question to address whether or not 'ideas' as opposed to 'structures' have power.

Finally, as Brian Barry (see below) has pointed out, it is common to confuse being lucky with being powerful, that is, to confuse the question of 'Who benefits?' with the question 'Who has power?'. It is true that some people may be more systematically lucky than others, but that does not mean that they are *necessarily* powerful or responsible for making a state and society the way it is. You can be lucky and powerless, powerful and unlucky, lucky and powerful, and powerless and unlucky. **DA RK BO'L**

See also bourgeoisie; capital; charisma; collective action; conflict theory; discourse; dominant ideology; élite theory; hegemony; ideology; pluralism; political science; rational choice; social closure; social control; social movement; social stratification; sociology of knowledge; state; structure-agency debate.

Further reading B. Barry, *Democracy, Power and Justice: Essays in Political Theory*; K. Dowding, *Rational Choice and Political Power*; A. Giddens, *Central Problems in Social Theory*; S. Lukes, *Power: a Radical View*.

PRAGMATICS

Pragmatics (Greek, 'science of use'), in **linguistics**, is the practical study of **language**. Although the arrangement and choice of words in a sentence are crucial to the meaning conveyed, it is also apparent that many aspects of meaning will be missed if we focus only on literal sentence meaning. Being the study of language as it is actually used, pragmatics reveals that the literal meaning of what is said needs to be greatly enriched if communication is to succeed at all. In trying to decipher what someone is trying to say, we supplement the conventional meanings of the words spoken by taking into account the situation, the participants, what has been said before, general background knowledge, and an ability to draw reasonable inferences. Pragmatics, then, aims to bridge the gap between what is said and what is actually understood when language is being used.

The implications of what someone says can sometimes be deduced simply by reference to linguistic factors. For example, when 'and' is used to join two phrases together, there is a literal additive meaning

('I had jelly and ice cream'). Additionally, a more subtle inference is also made, (known as a conventional implicature), whereby 'and' signals that the events are ordered successively in time, as in (1):

(1) The car broke down and I called the breakdown services.

In the following example (2), this convention is violated, and consequently the sentence has an unnatural feel:

(2) I called the breakdown services and the car broke down.

In addition to conventional implications, there are many occasions when our ability to reason and draw non-logical inferences is tested more severely as in example (3):

(3) A: That's the phone.
    B: I'm in the bath.

When (A) says 'That's the phone', it is clearly more than a simple statement of fact. It is, in fact, an indirect speech act which functions as a request for (B) to answer the phone. (B)'s response appears to be a complete non sequitur, but (A) will normally infer that (B) is unable to fulfil the request. This deduction is only possible on the assumption that conversations are more than a random juxtaposition of isolated sentences. Even in the face of seeming gibberish, people will still generally presume that what speakers say is inter-connected and coherent, giving rise to the concept of a co-operative principle to guarantee the success of communication.

A number of factors underlie the assumption of co-operation, and these are traditionally presented as a series of maxims. The first maxim demands that speakers provide just enough information to make their message clear. Second, speakers should only say what they believe to be true. Third, there is a requirement that what speakers say is relevant to the context in which it is produced. And finally, it is incumbent on speakers to be clear, concise and unambiguous in the way they present information. Of course, these maxims can be flouted, as in (3) above, since (B)'s response is not directly relevant. But crucially, people generally continue to assume that their conversational partner is still co-operating. In consequence, the process of inference-making is set in train in order to correctly interpret the speaker's intended meanings. An outstanding problem for pragmatic theory, which is only now receiving attention, is to explain why people should be so indirect in expressing what they mean. **MS**

See also semantics; speech-act theory.

Further reading G.N. Leech, *Principles of Pragmatics*; S.C. Levinson, *Pragmatics*.

PRAGUE SCHOOL LINGUISTICS

The Prague School of **linguistics** was inspired by Vilem Mathesius (1882–1945) and given prominence by one of the most influential linguists of the 20th century, Roman Jakobson (1896–1982). Central to their approach was the belief that linguistic theory should go beyond the mere description of linguistic structure to explain the functions fulfilled by linguistic forms. For example, a great many sentences build on information which is already known (theme) and provide some new information on that topic (rheme). And unless an unusual stylistic effect is required, the functional requirements of the sentence are fulfilled grammatically when the syntax allows the theme to precede the rheme.

(1) Matthew hid the chocolates.
(2) The chocolates were hidden by Matthew.

We would expect to find the active sentence (1) in a discourse in which the identity of Matthew was already established. The phrase 'hid the chocolates', then, provides new information. If, however, the identity of Matthew is novel information, then an English speaker might well resort to the passive structure, as in (2), so as to maintain the theme-rheme order. Not all languages make use of the passive in this way, but the syntactic choice that is made will reflect the functional requirements of the sentence. The Prague School also developed the functional approach to language with notable success in the field of **phonology**, and many of the concepts have been absorbed within linguistic theory in general. **MS**

PRAYER

Prayer, to a heart of lowly love,
Opens the gate of heaven above.

The opening lines of N.V. Tilak's poem sum up the experience of prayer for the devotee, whatever the **religion** or social context. Prayer is generally the means by which one approaches the divine, whether this is understood as reaching out to the beyond, or searching deep within oneself for another dimension. Following Paul in the Christian tradition, it is God's Spirit within one which enables one to pray, though such prayer may be too deep for words, simply a groaning of the spirit.

Prayer is subjective. It can be distinguished from **meditation**, which is objective contemplation of **scripture** or a sacred object, or of a theological concept or image, and is usually practised silently and individually. It should also be distinguished from **mysticism**, when one is rapt, caught up in a divine presence or granted a vision or some other experience for which there is no human means of verification.

There has been considerable debate in modern times as to how prayer 'works' metaphysically, and scorn has been poured on those who appear to have a 'hotline to heaven'. It is felt that God does not intervene personally or directly to grant requests. In most religions, mediators are sought: prayers are addressed, for example, to ancestors, lesser deities, saints and gurus. **EMJ**

Further reading Graham Smith, *Prayer Words.*

PRE-RAPHAELITES

The Pre-Raphaelite Brotherhood (or PRB, as its members signed themselves) was a group of artists and writers in mid-19th-century England which included the painters Holman Hunt and Millais, the writers Christina Rossetti, D.G. Rossetti and William Morris, and the poet and sculptor Thomas Woolner. Their name indicates their artistic aim, which was to model their work on pre-**Renaissance** European styles, to find inspiration beyond the traditions which had ruled in the arts (and especially in the graphic arts) for 300 years. They saw themselves as similar to a medieval artistic guild, and all tried their hand at everything – for example enthusiastically helping, with varied success, to redesign the Oxford Union building. In fine **art** they favoured a flat, perspectiveless style, following that of medieval tapestries or manuscript illuminations, and with clear, bright colours and simple outlines. In **design** they favoured a kind of chunky simplicity, again reminiscent of medieval art. Morris in particular was an advocate of folk styles and the use of folk methods and manner, both to invigorate the machine-design of the early Industrial Revolution and to bring 'fine' style within the reach of ordinary working people.

In **literature**, the Pre-Raphaelites favoured a retreat from the realities of the world into a realm of pure, innocent and unpretentious fantasy based partly on a kind of mock-medievalism (influenced perhaps by the novels of Sir Walter Scott), and partly on memories of nursery rhymes, fairy stories and other schoolroom literature. Christina Rossetti's poem 'Goblin Market' (with its vision of 'little people' hustling and bustling) is typical. There is also a strongly moralizing, pietistic streak, as if the **Metaphysical poets** had abandoned their hard-edged realism for tweeness. The tendency would be little but deplorable were it not for the fact that writers of real ability (such as Hopkins, Tennyson, Yeats) learned much from Pre-Raphaelite ideas, and that one Pre-Raphaelite brother, William Morris, produced literary work of much more robustness, translating **sagas**, rewriting Arthurian **legend** and producing several **Utopian**, socialist novels of distinction. Pre-Raphaelite literature, for adults, hardly survived the ridicule of people like W.S. Gilbert on the one hand, and the flaccidity of the **Decadents** on the other. In children's literature, however, it had a rosy-spectacled influence which has persisted to the present day. **JM KMcL**

PRECOGNITION see **Divination; Parapsychology**

PREDESTINATION

Predestination (Latin, 'ordaining in advance') is the subject of a long-running theological controversy, especially in **Christianity**, **Islam** and **Judaism**. Does God know, and determine, in advance, everything that will happen to each individual and each group in creation, and if so, how does this square with the notion that each human being has free will? The arguments are, first, that God has (or has not) an eternal purpose, which existed long before the creation of the universe and its inhabitants; second, that God has chosen particular individuals or peoples to further this purpose; and third, that God has chosen particular individuals or peoples to be vessels of his grace, and to be given eternal life. The idea of purpose in all this makes it a different view from that of the wheel of life in Indian religions, which is thought of as an objective phenomenon and in which human beings, by their actions in one incarnation, can affect their situation in the next. In Christian theology, predestination was first expounded by St Augustine in the 7th century, and became an important part of **Lutheranism** and **Calvinism** at the time of the Reformation; Augustine was opposed by Pelagius, who supported the counter-doctrine of free will. **KMcL**

PREDICATE CALCULUS see Calculus; Logic; Symbolic Logic

PREJUDICE

Prejudice (Latin, 'prejudgement'), in terms of human thought, is a paradox. Holding a prejudice, for or against, is a willed act of mind – prejudices may be learned, but they are not instinctive – and the sum of our prejudices is a major part of our psychic identity. And yet prejudice is, precisely, the decision not to be open-minded, not to think. It involves value-judgements, and perhaps it is these which we prefer not to consider. Anti-Semitism is prejudice. But if I hate people who are anti-Semitic, is that an equal prejudice? And at what point does moral guilt enter the argument? Are anti-Semitic (or anti-anti-Semitic) thoughts morally neutral? Do they become morally loaded only when uttered, or only when they lead to action? Who decides what moral absolutes are, and how can we be sure that that decision itself is not a form of prejudice? **KMcL**

PRESCRIPTIVE GRAMMAR

Linguists hold that a prescriptive grammar aims to inform a language user whether a particular expression is correct or incorrect. In fact, the native speakers of a **language** possess intuitions about grammaticality which normally allow them to determine the acceptability of a given sentence unequivocally. However, there are many occasions when such decisions are not clear-cut, or where the intuitions of one person clash with those of another. In English, for example, a popular bone of contention has been the distinction between sentences like 'Bill is different from George' and 'Bill is different to George'. A prescriptive approach to this problem is intolerant of variation and hence admits only one version as correct.

An important consequence of this approach is that the legitimacy of dialectal variation is actively denied. Prescriptivists also tend to ignore important differences between spoken and written forms of language, as well as the effects of various speech styles (for example formal versus informal). Prescriptive norms are normally set up by an authoritative élite and justified on pseudo-linguistic grounds, with appeals to logic which conceal the purely social considerations involved. We can contrast the prescriptive approach with the purely descriptive concerns of professional linguists, which preclude decisions about the relative superiority of one language form over another. **MS**

PRESIDENTIAL GOVERNMENT see Representative Government

PRIESTHOOD

The role and nature of the priesthood varies considerably from one religion to another, and from one sect or denomination to another, while in some movements, such as Presbyterianism in **Christianity** or the anti-Brahmin movements of south India, the absence of the concept or aversion to the term reveals as much as its presence within a religious tradition. Since priesthood is about power, often political as well as spiritual, there is clearly great scope for superstition and corruption. However, in various religions the priesthood has at times been responsible for the preservation of culture and learning, or has been the focus for patriotism and resistance to a foreign oppressor.

Generally speaking, a priest is one who operates at the divide between the sacred and the profane, consecrating things, removing impurity, performing sacrifices and representing the people before the god and the deity to the people. This function may be hereditary, or be the result of a sense of vocation, but in either case, and whatever the precise duties and functions, the holder believes God or the the gods have chosen him (hence the term 'clergy', those on whom the lot or *kleros* (Greek) has fallen). In **Hinduism**, such choice is the result of one's *karma*, whereby one is born a Brahman or into one of the families which minister to members of low castes or untouchables.

The word 'priest' itself is a corruption of the Greek word for 'elder', *presbuteros*. Greeks also used the word *hiereus*, meaning a cultic priest, responsible for sacrifices, etc.; the Latin equivalent was *sacerdos* ('one who makes things holy'). **EMJ**

Further reading Hans Kung, *Why Priests?*

PRIMAL THERAPY

Primal Therapy was developed by Arthur Janov in California in the 1960s. It came out of Janov's practice of working with groups. In a particular session a young man was talking about an argument with his girlfriend and in the process of doing this let out an extraordinary, painful wail. In this he seemed to have broken the rules of the group, but he was unrepentant. He said that he felt much better, and that he had touched a place in himself which he had not experienced before.

As a result of this incident Janov began to create 'safe environments' and the therapy became a place to find and re-experience early trauma, for example, birth trauma. The idea of birth trauma came to Janov after several years of research. The key was to trust your impulses and body. There is very little interaction with the therapist until afterwards, when an attempt is made to put the experience into words. The therapist became an enabler and observer. The 'Primals', containing groups of up to 30 people, were encouraged to trust their impulses and bodies in a small room with low lighting and padded floors and walls. A loss of self-consciousness enabled the release of memories, thought and insights. Janov restructured the idea of the primal scene (a term used by Freud to describe the child witnessing its parents having sex) as a term to describe the most painful trauma each individual has, something which is different for every person. Traumas are seen as imprinted on the nervous system. Working within the pain of this enables the experience to resurface and to be exorcised. Without this healing, it will be acted out in ways which are neurotic and far removed from the original traumatic experience. **MJ**

Further reading Arthur Janov, *The Primal Scream*.

PRIMARY AND SECONDARY QUALITIES

Philosophers often distinguish between the primary qualities of objects, such as shape, size and motion, and their secondary qualities, such as colours, sounds and tastes.

One account of the distinction is this. Primary qualities are qualities of physical objects which resemble our perceptual experiences as of those qualities, whereas secondary qualities are qualities of physical objects which do not resemble our perceptual experiences as of those qualities. So squareness is a primary quality because it resembles our visual experience as of squareness. But redness is a secondary quality because there is no quality of objects which resembles our visual experience as of redness: the surfaces of objects are made up of collections of atoms which reflect light of certain wavelengths and not of others, and there is nothing in physical objects resembling our visual experience as of redness.

This way of making the distinction is open to two objections. The first is that it is unclear in what sense some experiences, but not others, resemble the qualities which they represent. What exactly is the notion of resemblance here? The second objection is that if the distinction between primary and secondary qualities is explained in terms of whether our experiences do, or do not, resemble the qualities of objects which they represent, then the distinction presupposes a representative theory of perception. It presupposes that our perceptual experiences of the qualities of objects are distinct from the qualities of objects we perceive. But many philosophers think the representative theory of perception unacceptable.

Another way of making the distinction between primary and secondary qualities avoids these problems. We can say that primary qualities are qualities of objects which (1) are represented by perceptual experiences and (2) figure in the correct explanation of such experiences. Squareness is a primary quality because it is represented by our perceptual experiences of certain objects and the correct explanation of why certain objects appear square to us is that they are square.

In contrast, secondary qualities are qualities of objects which (1) are represented by perceptual experiences and (2) do not figure in the correct explanation of such experiences. Thus, redness is a secondary quality because it is represented by our perceptual experiences of certain objects, and the correct explanation of why certain objects appear red to us is not that they are red, but that the atoms at their surface reflect light waves of a certain length, and these light waves cause us to have experiences as of red.

When philosophers say that redness is a secondary quality do they mean that things are not really red? Error theorists do. Error theorists maintain that when ordinary people clam that pillar boxes are red, they mean that redness figures in the correct explanation of why we have experiences as of red pillar boxes. Further, redness does not figure in the correct explanation of our experiences as of pillar boxes, so when ordinary people say that pillar boxes are red they are in error. Physical objects are not really coloured.

Other philosophers reject the error theory. Some hold a dispositional account of secondary qualities: secondary qualities are dispositions to produce certain sorts of experiences. Further, when ordinary folk say that pillar boxes are red, they only mean that pillar boxes are disposed to produce certain sorts of experiences as of redness. And pillar boxes are disposed to produce experiences as of redness, because they reflect light of a certain wavelength, and light of that wavelength causes experiences as of red in us. So physical objects are really coloured. **AJ**

See also representative theory of perception.

Further reading C. McGinn, *The Subjective View*; J.L. Mackie, *Problems from Locke*.

PRIMATOLOGY

Primatology (as its Greek name suggests) is the study of the **biology** of the primates, the order of mammals which includes humans and our close relatives the monkeys and apes. This relationship to humans has stimulated intensive study of primates over the last century, but the similarity must always have been obvious, even before the relatively recent suggestion of genetic relationship. Galen (129–200 CE) dissected both men and monkeys, and was struck by their anatomical similarity. However, this was accepted by Galen and numerous other philosophers as pure coincidence until the **Renaissance**.

In the 17th century, the English anatomist Edward Tyson was the first European to have access to a true ape, a chimpanzee, which he dissected and compared anatomically with human cadavers. He thought that the ape was a pygmy human and was thus able to conclude that it was very similar to a human, without contradicting the popular view that humans were above classification as animals. In the 18th century, Linnaeus coined the term 'primate' and included humans in this group, along with monkeys, apes, bats and lemurs. However, it was not until some time after Darwin had published his ideas in the 19th century that it became routine to classify humans with the other primates.

During the past century there has been an intensive search for fossil evidence of humankind's primate ancestors – the so-called 'missing link'. Modern primatology is less distinctive and concentrates on behavioural studies, though primates continue to be exploited to test technologies where human-like responses are required, but for which the use of human experimental subjects is considered unethical. **RB**

See also ethology; mammalogy; sociobiology.

Further reading James Else, *Primate Evolution*; Dale Peterson, *The Deluge and the Ark.*

PRIME NUMBERS

The concept of prime numbers is one of the most fundamental in **number theory**, and still provides some of the best-known unsolved conjectures in the whole of **mathematics** (some of which are listed in that article). A prime number is one which has no divisors (numbers that exactly divide into it, leaving no remainder), except for 1 and itself. The smallest examples are 2, 3, 5, 7, 11, 13, 17 and 23 (1 is usually excluded). One of the reasons that prime numbers are so important is that every number has a unique expression as a product of primes (unique, that is, apart from the order in which they are written down). For example, 233577 is 3.3.3.41.211. **SMcL**

PRIMITIVISM

Primitivism (from Latin *primitivus*, 'first of its kind'), in **anthropology**, refers to a body of thought that there exist remote and exotic 'primitive': peoples whose lifestyles and technologies are considered to show marked contrast to those of modern societies.

Historically, anthropologists, among other thinkers, have played a considerable part in imagining that 'primitive' peoples exist as simple, isolated and different societies, as such societies were their designated field of enquiry. Around the 1960s,

anthropologists initiated a critique of the assumptions that underpinned the notion of the 'primitive': assumptions that revealed more about Western thought than so-called 'primitive' societies themselves.

Enlightened ideas since the 18th century (see below) tended to conceive 'primitive' societies in an idyllic way, in order to mourn the loss of communal values in European societies. In the 19th century, 'primitive' was used as a euphemism for 'savage' to describe those societies of comparatively simple technologies. However, 'primitive' continued to carry its pejorative sense particularly when it was thought that those 'primitive' communities of Asia and Africa were from an earlier stage of human and social development. This was emphasized by the 19th-century fashion of constructing evolutionary scales in which 'primitive' societies were compared to those of archaic times. They were deemed to live in an original human condition, and their roles in world history and regional relations with other societies were overlooked.

A typical characterization of 'primitive' societies was that of a communal, nomadic existence, ordered by kinship ties, sexually promiscuous, illogical and given to magical beliefs. In contrast, modern society was characterized by territorial states, monogamous family units, the possession of private property, more sophisticated religious ideas and scientific thought. Such contrasts persist in primitivist ideas today in which communities from the non-Western world tend to be seen through a distorted mirror, representing something that the Western world is not any more. This may be a view that lauds their 'primitive' existence, or one which disparages their 'primitive' condition. Either way, it denies those communities to represent or be represented in a less clouded light.

Anthropologists since the 1960s have tended to critically evaluate primitivist assumptions which see the non-Western world merely in relation to the West. Instead, they have initiated enquiries into the complexities of communities' lifestyles, values and ideas, noting their engagement with others in the region as well as that of the world.

In the **arts** of 18th-century Europe, primitivism was the cult of what Dryden called the 'noble savage'. Rousseau expressed the feeling most clearly in his *Social Contract*, stating that the human race had been born free, but was now struggling in the chains imposed by religion, social custom, law and political oppression. By breaking these chains, we might rediscover the true virtues and true values of our species. Such thoughts led, in one direction, to the scientific and social upheavals of the **Enlightenment**, and in another to an obsession with the lives of actual 'noble savages'. Such people lived supposedly untrammelled lives in places as far distant from 'civilized' Europe as possible. (There was occasionally great public excitement when a 'noble savage' was found in the heart of Europe itself: a child brought up from birth with no company but that of animals, and so thought to be free of human conditioning. Herodotus, over 2,000 years before, had recounted the story of a foolish king who had a baby isolated for several years with no company but that of goats, and who was then convinced, on the basis of the child's cries, that the 'native language' of the human race was bleating.)

The 'noble savage' idea hardly survived either the discoveries of **science** in the 19th century or the savage repression of actual 'savages' by colonial powers in the same century. It was, in essence, a flat-Earth theory but for all that, dynamic and appealing during its years of currency. It also has some interesting offshoots: the notion prevalent in many religions that true knowledge is granted only to God or the gods, and that for human beings to aspire to share it, to reach beyond their own 'primitive' natures, is a dangerous and punishable flaw; the repellent fascination with experiments in remaking the human race, from Frankenstein's monster and his multifarious progeny to 'master race' eugenics and modern medical engineering; exploration and its artistic and entertainment equivalents the **pastoral** and 'pioneer' traditions. We are a sophisticated species, and it is almost as if part of that sophistication involves regretting what we are.

In fine art, the art of 'primitive' cultures has had important effects on the 'high' art of the West. Examples include the influence of Oceanic art on Gauguin, of African **sculp-**ture on pre-cubist Picasso, and of pre-Colombian South American sculpture on Henry Moore. Some artists were once called 'primitive' because their work seemed unsophisticated or naive compared to the prevailing orthodoxy both Italian pre-Renaissance painters and such later artists as Henri 'Douanier' Rousseau and the German **expressionists** were once so designated. But the term, and the implication that 'primitive' somehow means 'inferior', are gradually being squeezed out of critical thinking and vocabulary. **DA PD MG KMcL RK**

See also evolutionism; functionalism; Orientalism; rationality.

Further reading Susan Hiller (ed.), *The Myth of Primitivism*; Adam Kuper, *The Invention of Primitive Society.*

PRINTING

Printing (Middle English *prient*, 'to impress or stamp') is probably the most important invention of the Middle Ages. Printed texts were known to be printed in the Far East as far back as the 8th century. This method of printing was long and laborious, as it involved the printing of texts by woodcut blocks which were immovable and awkward to work with. It was the invention of movable type which constituted a major breakthrough and caused the opening of many networks of communication that revolutionized civilization. The first book using movable type was published in Korea, late in the 14th century; it was quickly followed by printing presses being set up in Europe by such people as Johaan Gutenberg and William Caxton.

Printing using movable type bearing letters, numbers and punctuation marks originated in Germany in the mid-15th century. Monotype and linotype machines producing metal castings of the required lines, or blocks carrying the required letters allowed the automated assembly of the text by an operation at a keyboard similar to that of a typewriter. These machines were developed between 1880 and 1890.

Typewriters were invented in the early 18th century but were not in practical use until the middle of the 19th. The development since the early 1980s of small 'personal' computers with associated dot-matrix, daisywheel, laser and bubblejet printers has allowed the modern office to have facilities for word processing and desk-top publishing. Associated with these are electronic scanners which can read and interpret into computer language text and diagrams for editing and incorporation with other text so that books and magazines can be transmitted from editor to printer in the form of computer disks and cassettes.

With the development of the modern digital computer has come the possibility of E-mail: transmission of text from one computer to another anywhere in the world provided a telephone or even a radio link is available. Few modern offices are now without a fax (facsimile transmission) machine to transmit by telephone line text and diagrams from a paper original for reproduction on paper wherever another fax machine is connected to the telephone system be it in Australia, America or Japan. This saves time, is immediately available and both sender and receiver have a paper copy of the message. **AA**

Further reading F. Denman, *The Shaping of the Alphabet*.

PRIVACY

Sensations are private in the sense that one knows immediately which sensations one has, and one does not need to infer which sensations one has from anything else, whereas no-one else can know which sensations one has immediately, for they must infer which sensations one has from one's behaviour.

Beliefs and desires seem to be unlike sensations in this respect. For one must sometimes infer which beliefs and desires one has from one's behaviour, in the same manner that others must infer what beliefs and desires one has from one's behaviour. **AJ**

See also introspection; mental phenomena.

Further reading A.J. Ayer, *The Concept of a Person*.

PROBABILITY

Probability is the branch of pure **mathematics** which corresponds to **statistics** in applied mathematics. It began as the study of chance, and especially of games of chance, in 16th century France with Blaise Pascal (1623–62), who was paid by a nobleman to find out why he always lost when he made a particular bet (the answer was that he was giving odds of evens on a bet where the odds were really only 47% in his favour). Pascal went on to discover 'his' famous triangle (which was in fact known in other cultures long before), which makes calculations of this sort of probability very easy (calculations of the probability distribution of repetitions of a single event, like the probability of throwing exactly six sixes in twenty-one throws of a die). The problem with Pascal's work, and that of the probabilists who followed him, was that their work was purely empirical; they used 'common sense' ideas of probabilities in mathematical models of real situations (the idea that an unbiased coin should have equal probability of showing heads or tails when tossed, for example), so that what they were doing was not really probability or statistics, but a mixture of both. This dependence on observation made many 19th-century mathematicians reluctant to allow probability a place as a branch of mathematics, rather than part of **physics**.

This did not mean that probability was without its successes. Among these were Bayes's theorem, the basis of **Bayesian statistics**, which was a result long considered controversial. (Because probability was a **science** rather than a branch of mathematics, his results were open to question in a way that no mathematical theorem would be.) Probability also made possible advances in calculation; an analysis of the patterns made by throwing sticks on a floor marked with parallel lines gave a better way, for example, to calculate the number pi than had ever been known before. Advances were made in the applications of probability to the world of insurance, where it was needed to calculate the ratio of premiums to claims needed for companies to make a profit; thus actuarial statistics was born.

Probability was finally given a position in the field of mathematics when it was given an **axiomatization** by Pafnutiy Lvovitch Chebyshev (1821–94). His analysis was quite revolutionary. Probability all takes place within 'probability spaces', which have three parts. There is the 'sample space', which is the set of all possible outcomes, then the set of combinations of events, and the 'probability measure', which assigns a number p(A) between 0 and 1 to each combination A of events from the sample space. The numbers that are assigned have to obey certain rules; for example, the probability that none of the events in the sample space happens is 0, and if A is a set of events, and ~A is the set of all events not in A, then p(~A) = 1 − p(A). Also, if A and B are mutually exclusive events (that is, A and B cannot both happen) p(A or B) = p(A) + p(B). From these simple rules the whole of probability can be derived. As usual in pure mathematics, no questions are asked about the nature of the objects in the probability space: they could be obtained by experiment, they could be given in a problem or be the products of thought and hypothesis; the only important thing is that they obey the rules. (Deciding what the objects in the sample space should be is really the role of statistics.)

One of the most important consequences of the axioms of probability is the Law of Large Numbers, which probabilists had used for many years before Chebyshev without actually realizing that it needed to be proved. In concrete terms, it states that in a large number of identical tests, the proportion of successful results approaches the probability of a successful result in each test. So, for example, tossing a coin two million times will result in about one million heads. (It is not true for small numbers; for nine or ten tosses, seven heads could quite often happen.) This is the result that justifies actuarial statistics, which relies on the data provided by a large number of tests (out of a population of seventy million, for example, the proportion who die in one year from lung cancer) to calculate premiums using the probabilities which are accurate because of the law of large numbers. **SMcL**

Further reading I. Hacking, *The Emergence of Probability*.

PROBLEM PLAY AND WELL-MADE PLAY

The name 'problem' play is generally given to plays which are about social issues, for example, those of such 19th-century European writers as Dumas (*fils*), Ibsen and Shaw, and (in our own century) such authors as Galsworthy, Hellman, Miller and the myriad writers of 'concerned' films and television dramas. Often, though not always, problem plays use the conventions of **naturalism**, depicting ordinary people in everyday clothes and settings, using ordinary speech. Many problem plays also conform to the conventions of the 'well-made' play, devised in 19th-century France. In this, the drama begins with an exposition which sets the scene and gradually reveals the problem or secret at the heart of the plot. There follows a series of alarms, excursions and developments, often involving the revelation of some crucial secret which has so far not been known to one of the central characters. The moment of disclosure of this secret, the turning-point beyond which no lives will be the same again – often the 'problem' is resolved by the destruction or exaltation of the leading character – is a main climax. It is followed by an unwinding of the action, recapitulating and revisiting what has gone before in the light of what the characters (and we) now know, and there is often a further surprise at the moment of curtain-fall. The structure is (consciously) analogous to sonata-form in classical **music**. It can engender **comedy** or **tragedy**: Ibsen's *A Doll's House* and Wilde's *The Importance of Being Earnest* are outstanding examples of the well-made play. The coincidence of the two structures, problem plays and well-made plays, led to some of the finest European drama between 1850 and 1950, as well as to some of the worst, and it is still regarded by some bourgeois audiences as the ultimate theatrical experience: a play about ordinary people with a convincing, and clearly comprehensible, emotional and intellectual structure.

(There is a secondary meaning of 'problem play'. Academics uses the phrase to refer to plays which are 'problematical' because they fail to fit into standard critical categories. Examples are the 'problem plays' of Shakespeare.) **TRG KMcL SS**

PROCESS MUSIC

Process music is a main form of musical **minimalism**, developed in the 1970s by Steve Reich and his followers. In it, the composer sets up a 'process': a pattern of notes or a rhythm which the performers repeat time after time to make the piece. The repetitions are, however, not all they seem. By phasing or phase shifting (the introduction of slight distortions into the pattern) the composer subtly and minutely varies what we hear. The effect is similar to **heterophony**, in that an apparently stable sound-sequence appears to blur and shift even as we perceive it. Process music simultaneously lulls the brain (by repetition) and stimulates it, and in some listeners, the refractions produced by phase shifting induce aural hallucination: they hear secondary melodies, secondary rhythms inside the main texture, aural mirages. **KMcL**

See also metre.

PROCESSORS

Processors form the heart of every **computer**, from small personal computers (PCs) to large supercomputers. A processor generally consists of an arithmetic/logic unit which performs numerical calculations, storage registers for saving calculation values and other information, and a control unit which coordinates all these functions.

The role of the modern processor is to execute a specific set of instructions, a **program**, which will be stored in a computer memory, in the correct sequence of events. A very fast 'clock' is used to time each program operation and ensures all the control functions are synchronized. The first microprocessor, containing an arithmetic/logic unit on only one silicon 'chip', was announced in the US in 1971 by Intel Corporation. This was a result of advances in microelectronics and semiconductor material fields (see **semiconductor device theory**).

Processing theory is increasing the power of computers every day. Modern desk-top PCs, for example, are many times faster and powerful than the first electronic computer ENIAC, finished in 1946 in America, which filled a large room. In the future, parallel processors, which perform several operations simultaneously rather than one after another, will be employed, which will further increase the speed and power of computers and will undoubtedly lead to more applications of computer control and monitoring. **AC**

PROFESSION

A profession (Latin, 'that to which one lays claim') is an occupational group characterized by: the use of skills based on theoretical knowledge; prolonged education and training; professional competence ensured by examinations; a code of conduct; the performance of a service which is for the public good; and a professional association that organizes its members. Professionals normally enjoy considerable social status and prestige derived from their occupation. The traditional professions are: the armed forces, the church, law and medicine.

The term profession continues to be widely debated, as a result of changes in the occupational structure and development of new specialist fields with new groups making claims to professional status: nursing, for example.

Sociologists have traditionally explained the privileged position of the professions in terms of the socially valued service they perform. More recently the self-interest of professional groups has been highlighted. Parkin, for example (see below), has argued that the professions use exclusion strategies to restrict access by means of the high educational requirements they demand, which bear little relationship to the nature of professional work, and these account for their privileges. The increased tendency for professions to be employed in bureaucratic settings has led some to suggest that the autonomy they have traditionally enjoyed is now being eroded. **DA**

See also bureaucracy; career; class; division of labour; occupation; role; social closure; social mobility; social stratification; status; work.

Further reading R. Dingwall and P. Lewis (eds.), *The Sociology of the Professions: Lawyers, Doctors and Others*; F. Parkin, *The Social Analysis of Class Structure*.

PROGRAMME MUSIC

Programme music is **music** (usually instrumental) which is written to illustrate a specific, declared programme: the events of a battle, say, or feelings aroused by walking in the countryside, or the sights and sounds of a particular area. In a few cases (using cowbells or imitating birdsong, for example), music can be directly evocative. But usually the 'programme' of a piece of music is a subjective phenomenon, depending in the first instance on non-musical communication (such as a declarative title or a programme note) between composer and hearer. **KMcL**

PROGRAMS

A program (Greek, 'previous writing') is the set of instructions which tells a **computer** what to do. It is a translation of an **algorithm** for the task which the computer is to be set into a language which the computer can understand (or which the computer can translate into a language it can understand – see **high level languages**.)

Programs are what give computers their flexibility. Most machines can only perform one task, for which they are designed, while computers can perform many, because they are designed to carry out whatever the program tells them to do. This means that programming has become one of the most important skills in today's world, as computers take on more and more roles. **SMcL**

PROGRESSIVE ROCK see Rock Music

PROGRESSIVE TONALITY see Tonality

PROJECTIVE GEOMETRY

Projective geometry is one of the few branches of **mathematics** which had its origins in the Middle Ages. It was developed to serve the needs of artists who wished to draw pictures in more realistic ways. The basic problem these artists faced was the difficulty of representing three-dimensional shapes in only two dimensions, putting the appearance of space onto a piece of canvas. As the **Renaissance** dawned, artists first studied the ways to solve this problem scientifically rather than relying on their instinct and experience.

Projective geometry is obtained from the usual **Euclidean geometry** by adding what is known as the 'point at infinity' to each line. The point at infinity of a given line is the place at which it meets the lines parallel to it, the equivalent of the vanishing point in **perspective**, or the apparent vanishing point on the horizon. This means that the geometry has no parallel lines, because every pair of lines has an intersection, and so the axioms of Euclid no longer hold. A projection of a figure onto a plane from a given point (which may be the point at infinity) is the intersection with the plane of those lines which join points in the figure to the given point. It is what you would see on a projection screen at the plane with the light at the given point. **SMcL**

PROOF

The concept of a proof (from Latin *probare*, 'to show evidence') lies at the very heart of **mathematics**. A proof is a demonstration of a theorem (the result) from the various suppositions which have been made (it may also use results already known). There is some debate about the nature of a proof in mathematics today: for example, does a proof that a **computer** makes which is too long to be checked by humans count as a proof? But basically the idea is to give an explanation of why the result is true which will be convincing to those who read it. The **deduction** of the result should in theory be made using the mechanisms of **symbolic logic**, though in practice, short cuts are usually taken, as formal proofs in symbols are long and difficult to follow. **SMcL**

PROOF BY CONTRADICTION

Proof by contradiction, also known as

reductio ad absurdum (Latin, 'reduction to an absurdity'), is one of the most commonly used methods of proof in **mathematics**. To prove a result using this method, you assume that the opposite is true, and then derive a contradiction, that is, a proof of both a result and its opposite. This means that the original assumption is false, on the grounds that a contradiction could not be derived from true assumptions, and therefore that the theorem that you wish to prove must indeed be true. The proof method relies on the 'law of the excluded middle', that something cannot simultaneously be and not be. Many of the results obtained by this method could also be proved directly, but proof by contradiction is often the quickest means to an end (and mathematicians generally look for the shortest proof, for the sake of elegance and, possibly, out of laziness). The proofs of a large number of existence results (theorems that assert that some kind of object exists) in many areas of mathematics (**set theory** and **logic**, for example) are carried out using proof by contradiction, and it is precisely this use which is challenged by the school of **intuitionism**, which insists on constructive proofs where the object whose existence is asserted is, in at least a theoretical sense, constructed. SMcL

PROPORTION

Proportion is a mathematical concept, important in all the visual **arts**, but most significant in the field of **architecture**, where it is traditionally considered one of the essential variants in a built structure for the creation of visual effect. The proportion, the relationship of one part to another, and of one part to the whole, usually in terms of size, has clearly been a consideration in architecture since Neolithic times. Early built structures, such as Stonehenge, which were built as religious sanctuaries, can be seen to have a careful rhythmic sequence between full and empty spaces, which has been compared to the proportion of the colonnades of archaic Greek temple architecture. In certain examples of early Egyptian tomb architecture it is thought that the proportions were modelled by way of allu-

sion to the symmetrical concepts of the **solar system**, and the relationship of planets and their orbits.

For textual evidence of the significance of the concept of proportion to designers of buildings in the late classical period there is Vitruvius's treatise *De Aedificatoria*. 'Proportion consists in taking a fixed module, in each case for the parts of a building and for the whole, by which method symmetry is put into practice. For without symmetry and proportion no temple can have a regular plan; that is it must have an exact proportion worked out after the fashion of a well-shaped body...in like fashion the members of temples ought to have the dimensions of their magnitude...' In Vitruvius's treatise, and in much subsequent discussion right into this century, most notably in the writings of Le Corbusier, the proportions of a building to its parts were conceived of in terms of the human body, and of the ideal shapes which it was thought could be demonstrated between the whole human body and its parts. These ideal forms were the simple shapes of the square and circle, and by extension the cube and the sphere, based on absolute regularity from the centre: as Vitruvius says: 'If a man lies on his back with hands and feet outspread, and the centre of a circle is located in his navel, then his hands and feet will touch the circumference: a square can be produced in the same way ... the height of a body from the sole of the foot to the crown of the head being equal to the outstretched arms.'

The human analogy can also be used for an analysis of medieval **Gothic** architecture. The historian Frankl (1910–62) observed: 'Even a Gothic cathedral is a system of supports...[in which]...proportion plays a decisive role, but this is precisely the proportion of the skeleton, of the spidery members', he also wisely observes that 'proportions adapted to the human body, in all its variety, range between the extremes of thinness and bloated fatness'.

In the 20th century, an understanding of proportion was seen as part of the search for the pure, mathematical and geometric root of beauty in **functionalist** terms. Le Corbusier and his school within the Modern movement were the most faithful to the notion of a module, part derived by analogy with the human body, which has enormous practical value in modern industrialized societies with the mass prefabrications of parts. **JM**

Further reading G. Raymond, *Proportion and Harmony of Line and Colour in Painting, Sculpture and Architecture*; Le Corbusier, *Le Modulor*.

PROPOSITIONAL CALCULUS see
Boolean logic; Calculus; Logic

PROSCENIUM ARCH THEATRE

The proscenium arch theatre (from Latin *pro scaenium*, 'in front of the stage') is a form of **theatre** in which the stage is separated from the audience by an arch (the proscenium arch) behind which the action is staged. The arch in such theatres is traditionally filled with curtains which part (or rise) at the beginning of the play to reveal a scene which is viewed as though the fourth wall of a room had been removed. Such stages are, therefore, particularly suited to illusionistic and mimetic theatre because the audience can only see the action from the front, and are also hierarchical since the action can be seen more clearly from some seats than from others, whereas theatre in the round can be seen as more democratic. The proscenium arch stage has been attacked by theatre radicals for imposing both physical and metaphysical narrowness of vision on those who write for it, act in it, and watch plays in it. **TRG SS**

See also drama; naturalism; realism.

Further reading Marvin Carlson, *Places of Performance*; George Kernodle, *From Art to Theatre*; Richard Southern, *The Seven Ages of the Theatre*.

PROSTHETICS

Prosthetics (Greek, 'replacement' or 'spare parts') is the artificial replacement of part of the body. This science probably goes back to the emergence of intelligent humans, whose survival depended upon being able to defend themselves and acquire food. With the accidental loss of a leg, he or she would have probably used a tree branch to act either as a crutch or a stump.

Wooden legs were first recorded in 500 BCE. At this time, the limbless were left to fashion crude devices for themselves, commonly known as peg-legs, and it was not until the 15th century that artificial limbs were made to order for knights. The design of limbs improved and some had joints that could move through the use of simple levers and springs.

The American Civil War and the Crimean War in the 19th century, and World War I and II in this century, gave tremendous impetus to the manufacture of limbs and their improvement. It is not only amputees who have benefited from new technology. New hip joints, pacemakers and plastic corneas, to name only a few, have transformed people's lives in a way that was not imagined, even at the start of this century.

A knowledge of the mechanics of walking has enabled the rational design of the socket of the leg prosthesis to be comfortable and transmit the locomotor forces to tissues not adapted to bear pressure. Knee mechanisms are fitted with self-acting brakes to allow the patient to bear load on a flexed knee as in descending stairs. Pneumatic or hydraulic dampers control the movements of the leg in the swing phase of walking. The constant complaint of the amputee is that his prosthesis is too heavy (although it may only be one third of the mass of the parts it replaces!). The use of aluminium and titanium alloys and carbon reinforced plastics have allowed leg prosthesis to be made much lighter. There are as yet no effective power sources capable of developing the loads necessary in leg prosthesis and having sufficient energy to last for an hour. Here is a field for further development.

Hand and arm prostheses pose different problems for the designer. Legs require strength but generally repeat the same movement patterns. Hands and arms tend to undertake a wide range of different function such as feeding, grooming, dressing and also complex functions such as writing or typing. Consequently a unilateral arm amputee will usually undertake most tasks with his or her 'good' arm relegating the prosthesis to simple tasks such as holding the plate while eating or the paper while writing. The major problem of the designer is that the position of the hand in three-dimensional space is defined by three linear dimensions, up, out and forward, and three corresponding angles. This basically requires six motors and twelve control points since each movement must be controlled for far forward and backward directions. Current generations of arm prostheses use either body power from movements of the shoulder or battery power driving one or two miniature electric motors. The control problem can only be dealt with by the amputee looking at his or her limb, since he or she cannot be aware of position, pressure or touch as in the normal way.

Internal prostheses are mostly in the orthopaedic field – exemplified by replacement joints for patients with arthritis. In Europe, in 1992, approximately 300,000 patients received replacement hip joints and about 150,000 replacement knees. The joints usually consist of a metal part moving against a polyethylene part with both being fixed by a kind of cement filler. There are records of patients still using hip joints 25 years after surgery, although at the present time problems seem to be arising due to wear particles in the period 10 to 15 years after the operation. This may require a second session of surgery to fit a new implant, which is usually more technically demanding.

Other prosthetic implants may be in such diverse areas as heart pacemakers, heart valves, cosmetic implants for ear, face or breast, stimulators for paralysed muscle or tubes for arterial replacement or treating hydrocephalus (water on the brain).

For all implants the responsiveness of the material to the body environment, its biocompatibility is of critical importance. Metals currently used involve specific types of stainless steel, titanium alloys and cobalt chromium alloys. Polyethylene and nylon types of plastics and aluminium or zirconium ceramics are also used. **AA**

Further reading A. Bennet Wilson, *Limb Prosthetics*.

PROTESTANT ETHIC

The Protestant ethic is a code of conduct derived from the redirection of Christian asceticism (self-disciplined abstinence from pleasure) by Puritan elements within **Protestantism**, in particular Calvinism. Calvinism embraced the conviction that all everyday, worldly activities are carried out for the greater glory of God, and the whole life of the Calvinist was organized around this idea. There was also a belief in the notion of **predestination**: that is the view that only a select few are chosen by God to be saved, and your future was established by God from the moment of your birth, though there is no way of knowing whether you have been chosen or not.

Max Weber perceived an affinity between Protestant asceticism and a rationalistic economic ethic which embodied the 'spirit' of **capitalism**. He thought that modern capitalism was characterized by a disciplined obligation to work as a duty. He considered that individual capitalists were lifted by a feeling of moral responsibility towards their resources, to increase them without limit by moderate consumption and hard work. He also argued that individuals were not by nature ascetic, rather Protestantism was the incentive behind this transformation of human values.

Weber suggested that Protestant Christian believers suffered from 'salvation anxiety' because there was no way of knowing who had been chosen for salvation. He saw, in this, the psychological link between Protestantism and the spirit of capitalism. He argued that belief in the doctrine of predestination posed a psychological strain on individual believers, which they were unable to live with. Although officially Calvinism maintains there will be no sign as to whether one has been chosen or not, believers cannot cope with this and they look for evidence of God's grace. Weber argues that worldly success was perceived as a sign of salvation. Labour in the material world was highly valued and the accumulation of wealth was thought to symbolize the pursuit of one's duty to God. In this sense wealth was something to be approved of, but it was on no account to be used for idle luxury, rather it should be used for the performance of further good works.

Weber considered the Protestant ethic crucial for the development of capitalism and the resultant accumulation of capital.

He believed that in the modern world the psychological link between Protestantism and capitalism has been broken. No longer does one have to be a Protestant to be a 'this-worldly ascetic'. At the Reformation Calvinism as a style of life was a choice, but now it is all prevailing and everyone is caught up in it. **DA**

See also religion; society; understanding; values.

Further reading G. Marshall, *In Search of the Spirit of Capitalism*; M. Weber, *The Protestant Ethic and the Spirit of Capitalism*.

PROTESTANT POLITICAL THOUGHT

Protestant political thought emerged in the late 15th and early 16th centuries as a *protestatio* against perceived abuses of both temporal and spiritual authority by the Roman Catholic Church (see **Catholic political thought**). **Protestantism**, whether Lutheranism, Calvinism or Zwinglianism, emphasized the Bible as the ultimate source of both spiritual and political authority, rather than the Church, and rejected **hierarchism** in favour of the idea of the 'universal priesthood of all believers'. In these respects, together with its iconoclasm, there is a great deal in common between Protestantism and Islam (see **Islamic political thought**): they are revealed scriptural religions which stress the equality of the community of true believers.

The most influential Protestant thinker of the early Reformation was Luther who argued in favour of the principle of 'Christian liberty' under which all but the most basic temporal matters should be governed by individual conscience. However, to consolidate the Reformation in areas where Catholic influence on secular institutions was strong, and despite the objections of Luther, evangelical authorities encouraged compulsory compliance with the 'true' religion, and in so doing precipitated massive upheaval and violence within the 'Holy Roman Empire' – roughly the area of modern Germany and Austria.

Jean Calvin's political reflections went further than Luther's, envisaging the ideal government as one composed equally of spiritual and civil institutions, but with the spiritual taking precedence over the civil. In short, Calvin's thought was theocratic. The relationship of the individual to the secular authority was to be governed by 'godly discipline' rather than Luther's voluntarist Christian liberty: all citizens had a duty to participate in civil society to achieve religious and moral perfection.

Many important modern historical and political developments can be partially attributed to Protestant political thought. The sociologist Max Weber argued that the Calvinist doctrine of predestination and the **Protestant ethic** were decisive in the development of **capitalism** in western Europe and North America. While this theory has been criticized as overly deterministic, and empirically inaccurate, specific versions of Protestant political thought did exert a strong influence upon bourgeois and liberal political thought, and in the formation of some liberal democratic institutions, most notably the principle of the separation of church and state (pioneered by American revolutionaries on the grounds that to establish any particular church at the federal level of government would provoke a civil war). **Libertarian** notions of the virtues of limited government also have their roots in political Protestantism. It may be fairly said that Protestantism as a set of theological doctrines gave a decisive boost to certain forms of political thinking, especially **individualism** and egalitarianism, although that said Protestants have never been noted for treating Catholics and heathens as individuals or equals.

In our times, Protestantism as a direct basis for a political or party party organization is diminishing. The 'moral majority' in the US – in fact a minority – is a major exception to this trend, and evidence of the continuing vitality of evangelical or fundamentalist or genuine Protestantism in North America. In Scandinavia the Christian People's Parties exist as fringe parties which protest against lax moral standards. In the Far East and Latin America Protestant evangelicalism is making some headway but it is uncertain whether their actions will have long-term political repercussions. **BO'L**

See also Christian democracy; Christian socialism.

Further reading Q. Skinner, *The Foundations of Modern Political Thought vol. 2: The Age of Reformation*; C. Welch, *Protestant Thought in the Nineteenth Century* (2 vols.).

PROTESTANTISM

'In matters which concern God's honour and the salvation and eternal life of our souls, everyone must stand and give account before God for himself; and no one can excuse himself by the action or decision of another, whether less or more.' This statement, from the *Instrumentum Appell-ationis* (25 April 1529) was the bottom line for the signatories of the Protestation of Speyer, a minority led by the Elector of Saxony, the Dukes of Saxony and Brunswick, Philip, Landgrave of Hesse and the representatives of 14 reformed cities who refused to accept the decision of the Second Diet of Speyer. That decision reversed the decree of the First Diet of Speyer (1526) tolerating the reformed faith where it had taken hold, and prohibited the secularization of Church lands. The Protestants, as they came to be called, doubtless wanted to increase their wealth and authority at the expense of the Catholic Church, but their statement was fundamental to the Protestant position. In Protestantism, the individual conscience ultimately decides, though decisions are taken in the light of perceived biblical truth. No decision of pope or emperor can determine one's salvation (which meant an end to the papal indulgences and dispensations), and no bishop or priest can mediate between individuals and their Creator, since there is only one mediator, Christ.

In the next Diet, at Augsburg in 1530, the **Lutherans** had to redefine their position theologically and, in the deteriorating political situation, to defend themselves by force of arms. However, the name 'Protestant' (and hence Protestantism) stuck, and came to be applied to the followers of Zwingli and Calvin as well. Elizabeth I of England abhorred the term, which she saw as synonymous with rebellion against the authority of Church and State, but **Anglicans** are generally counted as Protestants. Today the word is loaded with sectarian overtones, and the original principles are forgotten, especially as Catholics who accept the position of Vatican II (1962–65) have adopted 'Protestant' positions, for example, over freedom of conscience or the centrality of the Bible, which must be in one's mother tongue. **EMJ**

Further reading G.R. Elton, *Reformation Europe*.

PROTOTYPE THEORY

Prototype theory, in **linguistics**, provides an explanation for the way word meanings are organized in the mind. It is argued that words are categorized on the basis of a whole range of typical features. For example, a prototypical bird has feathers, wings, a beak, the ability to fly and so on. Decisions about category membership are then made by matching the features of a given concept against a prototype.

There is, in fact, strong agreement about what counts as the best exemplar of a particular category. For example, most people consider chair to be the most typical instance of the category furniture. Peripheral category members can be accommodated, because it is not necessary for any one member to possess all the features of the prototype. Thus, despite being flightless, an ostrich can still be classified as a bird, since it possesses other bird-like features.

One problem with prototype theory is that each category adopts an idiosyncratic range of criterial features. Furthermore, decisions about the number and type of features to be included in a prototype are by no means straightforward. And although certain features appear to be more central than others, it has often proven difficult to establish which ones take priority when we make decisions about category membership. **MS**

See also lexicology; psycholinguistics.

PROTOZOOLOGY

Protozoology (Greek, 'study of the first living things'), in the **life sciences**, is the biological study of protozoa, the phylum of single-celled animals, which includes many parasitic as well as free-living species. In common with all microbes, protozoa were not seen by humans until the development of the microscope led to studies by Antonie van Leeuwenhoek (1632–1723). The protozoa are an extremely diverse group, containing members which have the plant-like ability to photosynthesize as well as predators, scavengers and species which are some of the most medically and economically important parasites of man and livestock. *Plasmodium*, for example, the malaria parasite, infects hundreds of millions of people and kills millions each year. Certain protozoa, such as the amoeba and paramecium, have been studied extensively by cell biologists and geneticists, revealing much about the organization of these most complex of single-celled life forms. Parasitic protozoa have also been studied intensely but their complexity appears to make the development of vaccines against them more difficult. The protozoan which causes sleeping sickness in millions of people lives in the blood, a site on which most pathogens would be extremely susceptible to attack by the immune system. Yet this parasitic protozoan is able to change its appearance so frequently that the immune system cannot mount an effective attack. **RB**

See also cell biology; microbiology; parasitology.

PROVABILITY

Provability, in **mathematics**, is the study of what results can be proved (under various conditions). This study is reliant on an understanding of the nature of what **proof** actually involves, which is still a point of controversy in mathematics. The followers of different schools of thought (**formalism**, **intuitionism** and **logicism**) have different views of what a proof is and, since proof is fundamental to mathematics, any different ideas of what the nature of mathematics really is will affect the ideas of what a proof really is, and vice versa. Intuitionists, for example, would deny that many results proved using the classical mechanisms of mathematics (**proof by contradiction** in par-

ticular) are really proved, and would set about to prove then by the restricted means at their disposal.

Within particular mathematical systems, more can be said about what can be proved than can in general. In any particular mathematical system which is strong enough for the idea of provability to be encoded within it (as is the case with **Peano arithmetic**), then **Gödel's incompleteness theorem** shows that there are results which are true but which are not provable within that particular system. This result itself has had an impact on the concepts of what mathematics really involves: see **Hilbert's programme**.

In recent years, a further facet of proof has become a controversial issue. In **topology**, there is a famous result, the four colour theorem (which states that with only four colours it is possible to colour the regions of a map on a flat surface in such a way that no adjacent regions share the same colour), which was finally proved fairly recently after many years. The problem with the proof is that it involved splitting the problem up into a large number of possible cases (thousands of them) and then checking each possibility with a computer. To check them all by hand would be beyond the lifespan of any person. So does this count as a proof, when it requires trust in the work of the computer? This problem becomes more acute as the problems to be solved become more complex, and as mathematicians rely ever more increasingly on computers to help them solve them. **SMcL**

PSEUDOSCIENCE

Pseudoscience (Greek *pseudo*, 'false', Latin *scientia*, 'knowledge') is a controversial term. It is applied to all those disciplines and belief-systems which are not rational **science**, and thus takes in, at one end of the spectrum, **alchemy**, **astrology**, **divination**, **myth**, **spiritualism** and some would argue **religion**, and at the other such practices as alternative medicine and **meditation**. While it is convenient to lump together in a kind of lunatic fringe anything which hardly fits the 'rules' of rational science, and while some activities and beliefs (for example, research into the Bermuda triangle, or the notion that our human belief in the gods arose because we were once visited, and taught all skills, by benevolent astronauts from other galaxies) do seem more eccentric than others, it remains uncomfortably true that practices once condemned as irrational or fraudulent (for example, acupuncture or hypnotism) do seem to work, and that many of the ideas of 'real' science once seemed just as far beyond the pale. **KMcL**

PSYCHE see Mind

PSYCHIATRY

Psychiatry, the medically-based practice of **psychology**, draws on a wide range of sources including clinical practice itself and the many different psychological models of the mind. A psychiatrist is a medical doctor who takes further training in psychology. Some medical schools favour a purely clinical approach, based on traditional diagnosis, treatment and prognosis. They will be particularly concerned with a person's pathology, abnormal mental thoughts and their connection to symptoms. Others favour early inroduction to psychological principles showing how human behaviour may be governed by unconscious processes, and relating these to interpersonal relationships and their consequences in people's lives and behaviour, where the patient is seen not just as a collection of mechanical systems, but more as a human being with his or her own social history.

Many disorders treated by psychiatry have a clinical, physical component; dementia, organic brain disease and the delirium tremens suffered by alcoholics. In other cases, classification in psychiatric illness is based on observable features of the mental illness (that is, of the **depression** or **anxiety**). The main areas of psychological disturbance dealt with in psychiatry are schizophrenia, affective disorders such as anxiety, depression, mania and hypomania, organic states like delirium and dementia, hysteria, the personality disorders of people who are psychopaths or have abnormal personalities, obsessional disorders, addiction and subnormality. Clinical **psychology** is the study of disease as it relates to mental illness. **MJ**

Further reading W. Mayer Gross, E. Slater and M. Roth, *Clinical Psychiatry*; James Willis, *Lecture Notes on Psychiatry*.

PSYCHOANALYSIS

Psychoanalysis is Freudian **psychology**. This form of treatment was invented by Sigmund Freud in the 1890s and was thereafter developed by him, his collaborators and subsequent followers. The key concepts are the **unconscious**, **free association**, **resistance** and **defence mechanisms**, **transference** and **interpretation**.

The existence of an unconscious, the idea that mental activity exists of which the individual is unaware, is not new. Poets and writers, in particular, had alluded to forces underlying human action. But Freud was the first person to formulate these into a psychological system and a therapeutic approach.

Freud's work, and the work of all subsequent Freudian analysts, aids the process of free association, starting from the problem or question the patient brings and free associating from there without any form of censorship. The analyst looks for key elements or indications of unconscious processes, and gives these back to the patient in the form of interpretations. These include interpretations of the resistance (in the form of defence mechanisms) which the patient has to this activity, and analysis of the patient's relationship with the analyst through the transference (unconscious feelings and attitudes that are part of past relationships, but still used in the present as ways of relating to others including the therapist or analyst).

The Freudian analyst expects that if the patient free associates for long enough in daily contact with the analyst, repressed thoughts will eventually present themselves. Freudian analysis is usually a fulltime commitment of five 50-minute sessions a week. This regular contact with the analyst is designed to aid the transference by making the analyst a central figure in the patient's life for the duration of the therapy.

Historically, free association replaced **hypnosis** as a technique and interpretation replaced suggestion. Freud formulated theories on the dynamics of neuroses based on his experience of his patients' free associations, their resistance to interpretations and their transference. He went on to formulate a theory of development using his clinical material (which included his own analysis of himself). **MJ**

Further reading Raymond E. Fancher, *Psychoanalytical Psychology: the Development of Freud's Thought*; Peter Gay, *Freud a Life for our Time*; Ernest Jones, *The Life and Work of Sigmund Freud*; Charles Rycroft, *A Critical Dictionary of Psychoanalysis*.

PSYCHOANALYTIC THEORY OF ART

The Psychoanalytic Theory of Art focuses on the psychic life, not of whole societies or periods, but of individuals (albeit seen as part of societies). Art critics and historians attempt to discover the particular neuroses, sexual preferences, repressions and desires of a given individual in order to explain his or her creative work. In studying factors as ineffable as **creativity**, psychoanalysts and critics speak of the 'sublimation' of desire into a socially acceptable activity. A difficulty with the approach is that its theories cannot be tested, and its methodology tends to determine the outcome – a fact not lost on those, like the philosopher Karl Popper, who are antagonistic to prescriptive theorizing.

Freud's interest in the **unconscious** – he wrote an admired, and seminal, study of Leonardo – was enthusiastically taken up by the **surrealists**, who saw his studies of the **dream** as central to their own desire to disrupt the norms of perception. But their difficulty, namely that of articulating the unconscious, is shared by a psychoanalytic theory of art in general, which finds difficulty in proving the connection between psychosis and the form it takes in art. For example, are the acidic colours and tortuous contours of van Gogh's paintings a manifestation of the artist's madness or of **expressionism** (with which he shares many stylistic conventions)? Are Schoenberg's tortured harmonies in *Die Glückliche Hand*, or Dostoevsky's or Gorki's nightmare descriptions of the underbelly of Tsarist Russia, the artist's own memories, or objective evocations of madness and historical veracity respectively? **PD MG KMcL**

PSYCHOANALYTICAL CRITICISM

Psychoanalytical criticism is the application to literary texts of analytical methods similar to Freud's techniques for unlocking his patients' repressed emotions. It starts from the premise that an author's repressed emotions affect the way he or she writes, and that examination of particular stylistic methods will reveal more about those emotions and therefore about the work. Particular stylistic techniques involved are displacement (refocusing emotion from one person or object to another: Thomas Mann's story *Death in Venice* is a notable example of this) and condensation (combining of several ideas into one, as in metaphor or metonymy).

Psychoanalytical criticism has general value, in the consideration of writers as varied as Frank Herbert and Franz Kafka, Murasaki and Gabriel García Márquez. But its principal claim on the attention, at least of literary critics, is that it was one starting point for the theories of Jacques Lacan, in which – as applied to **literature** – the hidden meanings and agendas of a text are assumed to have a philosophical existence almost independent of (and certainly capable of study apart from) the person who created it. **KMcL**

Further reading E. Wright, *Psychoanalytical Criticism*.

PSYCHOLINGUISTICS

Psycholinguistic research (Greek *psyche*, 'mind' and Latin *lingua*, 'tongue') investigates the way knowledge of **language** is acquired and represented in the mind. There is a natural overlap with current **linguistic** theory, which aims to develop a theory of grammar that explains language as it exists in the mind. It is, however, extremely difficult to assess the plausibility of competing grammatical theories when considered as models of psychological phenomena. An immediate problem is the widespread assumption that language knowledge can be distinguished from language use. If the validity of this distinction is accepted, then the amazing speed and efficiency with which humans produce and understand speech would implicate quite separate mental capacities from those required to function as a 'storehouse' of language knowledge per se. Psycholinguistic enquiry seeks to characterize the content of individual components of the human linguistic capacity, and furthermore, to establish the ways in which knowledge and use of language are linked within the mind.

Problems concerning the ways in which we comprehend and produce speech have been a major preoccupation of psycholinguistic research. It has been discovered, for example, that the ability to understand speech is partially dependent on powerful perceptual strategies which provide people with expectations about what they think they will hear. As a result, the listener can guess with considerable accuracy what a speaker is going to say on the basis of the first portion of an utterance. However, these short-cuts to comprehension operate in tandem with more systematic processes, which begin constructing an interpretation of the utterance as it progressively unfolds.

A further topic of fundamental importance arises from the fact that all normal children learn to speak a language in a relatively short time and in much the same way. Children achieve the remarkable feat of language acquisition despite a conspicuous lack of explicit attempts by parents to teach their children. It has been suggested, therefore, that in certain crucial respects, language is a feature of the human genetic endowment. As a result, children would not have to learn language in the normal sense of the term, since the essential features of language are inborn.

Certainly, language is often described as the single most distinctive characteristic of human beings, which sets them apart from other animals. Attempts to teach language to intelligent animals, including chimpanzees and gorillas, have invariably produced disappointing results compared to the intricate knowledge even very young children possess about language. It has become clear that human beings do not learn a given language, be it Finnish or Swahili, simply by treating it as a puzzle to be solved

via the powers of general intelligence. Most researchers accept, therefore, that human beings must be innately predisposed to acquire language. But it remains a challenge to specify precisely what aspects of language are innate. An extreme position, adopted by Chomsky, asserts that all of the essential syntactic and conceptual structures characterizing the language knowledge of an adult are present in the mind at birth. Less controversially, many researchers prefer to stress that we have an inborn predisposition to process language. In this way, infants find it easier to cope with the extraordinary complexities of language than to learn simple arithmetical operations such as multiplication and division. **MS**

Further reading J. Aitchison, *The Articulate Mammal: An Introduction to Psycholinguistics,* 3rd edition; A. Garman, *Psycholinguistics.*

PSYCHOLOGY

Psychology (Greek *psyche*, 'soul', 'mind' + *logos*, 'a discourse'), the attempt to understand and conceptualize the workings of the **mind**, goes back to the time of the shamans and primitive healers. It was a subject given consideration by the ancient Greeks and connected to **rituals**. Psychology was a branch of **philosophy** until breakthroughs in the 19th century enabled it to lay claim to being a scientific study with practical application and to develop a professional class working with the established schools of thought.

Research has revealed that among 'primitive' and ancient peoples there were aspects not dissimilar to modern psychologies. The shaman undergoes a long initiation as an introduction into the spirit world, inhabited by the forces believed to be creators of psychological disturbance. Treatments for finding the lost soul, in exorcism, or for extracting disease 'objects' (the cause of symptoms and malaise) contained many ritual elements: the actions themselves were manifestations of a belief system. This operated on the basis of the individual reacting to or being affected by forces from outside only, none (except parasitic demons) from within. Modern psychopathology, the study and theory of abnormal mental functioning looks at mental dysfunctioning and its relation to physical symptoms. Modern psychologists and therapists also require long training in psychological concepts. They are initiated into complex belief-systems which encompass all aspects of mind and its behaviours, and they set up practices which reflect these different sets of ideas in their day-to-day work, that is, the couch (transference), length of session (boundaries), method of reply (interpretation).

Also important both for the shamans of the past and for psychologists and therapists today is the healer's faith in his or her abilities after long training in special secret or difficult knowledge and traditions. It is also essential for all the traditions that the definition of mental disease and the acknowledged method of healing are recognized by the social group and that the patients have faith in the healers' abilities. **Psychiatry** (medical psychology), **psychoanalysis** (Freudian psychology), analytical psychology (Jungian psychology), or psychotherapy (drawing on different schools) deal with mental disturbances and illnesses unexplained by physical examination.

The Christian church used what could, by hindsight, be described as psychological ideas and methods to address mental disturbance, which they named obsession and possession. Mental disturbance was seen as a struggle in the individual between opposing divine forces. Ritual, based in a belief in exorcism, and the power of the healing confessional were used to combat evil.

The ancient Greeks were concerned with psychology in their search to define the ideal society and the ideal citizen. The Roman thinker Quintilian (1st century CE) thought it best to look at the actual nature of developing individuals and to pay attention to their needs and abilities; to beat them less and let them learn through play. This was a precursor of modern developmental psychology, an area of modern research which has produced many different conceptual models of childhood development, drawing on sociological ideas as well as the concepts of the various schools of psychology that have developed since the work of Sigmund Freud (1856–1939).

Modern psychology starts with the discovery of **mesmerism** (animal magnetism) which in turn led to the discovery of **hypnosis**. The phenomenon of hypnosis pointed the way to the scientific discovery of the **unconscious** and marks the beginning of the great psychodynamic therapies which concieve mind as a dynamic interplay between conscious and unconscious mental processes.

Hypnosis was discovered by a French nobleman Puysequr who investigated the experiments of F.A. Mesmer. By the mid-19th century investigations in hypnotism had established a number of genuine hpnotic effects including amnesia, suggestion, paralysis and anaesthesia. These were later discovered to have a marked similarity to the condition of mental patients suffering from paralysis and hysteria, and this connection was later investigated by the French neurologist Jean Charcot and by Sigmund Freud, the architect of psychoanalysis and the father of all modern psychodynamic, psychological movements.

Psychoanalysis is Freudian psychology. Freud developed its key concepts in the course of fifty years' work. These concepts are the **defence mechanisms, free association, interpretation resistance, transferemce** and unconscious. He discovered that dreams are the 'royal road' to the unconscious and was the first person to understand the nature of infantile sexuality found in the reminiscences of his adult patients. Freud's model of mind is a scientific, mechanistic one which therefore has elements of **determinism**. Later theories like those of Jacques Lacan (1901–81) reinterpreted Freud using linguistic models of thought.

Carl Jung (1875–1961) was a pupil of Freud who widened the concept of the unconscious to that of the **collective unconscious**. He broke with Freud because of Freud's adherence to the exclusively sexual nature of the **libido**, or psychic energy. Jung saw psychology, not as a struggle with the unconscious but as a process through history which creates **archetypes** representing the primitive and instinctual self that are experienced through **dreams**. Other important Jungian concepts are the **anima and animus** (the male and female parts of the psyche), the development of the **self** through **introversion and extraversion**, and the presence of the **shadow** self.

Alfred Adler (1870–1937), another pupil of Freud, broke off in another direction, regarding human beings as socially oriented and human behaviour as only understandable in the context of the group. He also had a teleological view, identifying people's long- and short-term goals. His view was holistic and **individual psychology** stresses the importance of the **mind-body** relationship. He maintained that the **inferiority complex**, which describes a sense of no-place being replaced by a striving for superiority to be behind much **neurosis**. Adler developed a theory of **masculine protest** which placed the inferiority complex and other mental problems into anthropological as well as psychological perspective.

The work of Freud and his disciples has been developed by many followers, notably Melanie Klein (1882–1960) whose work in child psychoanalysis led her to develop the concepts of the **depressive position** and **paranoid-schizoid position**, which she believed to be the experience of every young infant. Anna Freud (1895–1982) also worked in child analysis, but came to different conclusions and developed an ego psychology, a theory of stages of development.

Behaviourism, a complete departure from the psychodynamic theories of Freud, Jung and Adler, was formulated at the beginning of this century and sees mental disturbance as a form of faulty learning and conditioning. It does not believe in unconscious mental forces, but works instead with behavioural patterns.

Cognitive therapy, which was developed in the 1950s, focuses on the individual as a conscious being, at the mercy neither of unconscious drives nor of the environment. Another major movement was in existential psychology, where psychiatrists such as R.D. Laing used **phenomenology** as an underlying philosophy to his psychological work.

All these and many other conceptual psychologies, such as **gestalt**, make up the various conceptual models that inform modern psychology and psychotherapy, and are used in practice both as separate schools and eclectically. **MJ**

See also anger; anxiety; autism; autonomy; castration anxiety; character analysis; compulsion; counselling; depression; ego psychology; fantasy; fixation; id, ego and superego; infant sexuality; oral, anal and phallic stages; personal construct theory; primal therapy; regression; spiritualization.

Further reading Elliott Aronson, *The Social Animal;* Henri F. Ellenberger, *The Discovery of the Unconscious;* H.J. Eysenck, *Psychology is about People;* L.S. Hearnshaw, *The Shaping of Modern Psychology;* E.R. Hilgard and R.C. Atkinson, *Introduction to Psychology.*

PSYCHOLOGY OF PERCEPTION

While a formalist approach to **art** analyses the work in terms of objectively measurable factors, such as volume, mass and colour, the psychology of perception recognizes the limitation of this approach: namely that such reductivism fails to consider the reactions of each individual viewer, which will always 'colour' perception of the work. Placing the onus of perception upon the eye rather than the brain of the viewer may suggest that the response to works of art must always be eternal, because it is dependent upon physiology rather than upon **ideology**. Not so, says E.H. Gombrich, whose influential book *Art and Illusion* demonstrates that, while the eye will of course respond mechanically, perception in a broader sense is not mechanical, but is culturally determined. **MG PD**

Further reading R.N. Haber, *The Psychology of Visual Perception.*

PSYCHOPHARMACOLOGY

Psychopharmacology, as its name suggests, is the study of drugs which modify behaviour. It is a modern science despite historical knowledge of mind-altering drugs. Great advances in the care of the mentally ill have been made possible by the development of drugs such as antidepressants and tranquillizers, though they are often used inappropriately to alleviate symptoms in cases where the cause could be treated without resort to drugs. It is certain that modern drugs are an improvement over sedatives and their use is often highly successful in conjunction with psychotherapy. Research into the mode of action of psychopharmacological substances has been hampered by a limited understanding of the relationship between the **biochemistry** of nerves and their function. This is largely due to the complexity of the brain and the limited uses of animal models in psychological studies. **RB**

See also ethology; pharmacology; toxicology.

PSYCHOSIS

Psychotic individuals, faced with their own particular history, escape it by taking on a private reality of delusions and hallucinations, a reality which has its own internal logic. Psychotic patients, as well as those who are borderline and **narcissistic**, have a severely damaged sense of self. There are three major psychoses: schizophrenia, manic-depressive illness (now known as reversal syndrome) and paranoia (often regarded as a variety of schizophrenia). There is a tendency to use the word psychosis interchangeably with insanity, but otherwise insanity (and sanity) are only used by psychiatrists, analysts and therapists as legal terms. **MJ**

PURE MATHEMATICS

Pure mathematics is one of the two main branches of mathematics, the other being **applied mathematics**. The latter is about relating mathematical concepts and results to the real world; pure mathematics is about obtaining these results in the first place, in a context which is divorced from the distractions of the real world. Although mathematics is truly a unity, and the two branches rely on one another, the real world often gives the wrong impression about what is really going on in general, and so pure mathematics tries to ignore the assumptions which the real world puts into our minds and which seem intuitively obvious, in case they turn out not to be generally true, (The obvious case in point is that of **Euclidean geometry**, where the conclusions that were reached that seemed to be based on idealization of the properties of lines and points in the real world were not

challenged until the 19th century, and today it is even thought to be only an approximation on a small scale to the **truth** in the universe.)

Pure mathematics is, by its very nature, an extremely abstract study, with its own language of **symbolic logic** being more fully developed than most technical vocabularies. It is not, however, only a game, as many have thought; it has again and again found results and invented areas of study which, though apparently divorced from any connection with the world, have had applications found for them. It is a field studied for its own sake, with no thought given to the application of the results, and, indeed, pure mathematicians often look down on their applied counterparts, feeling that they alone do the truly original work. This feeling is not really justified; many of the most fertile branches of pure mathematics would have never come into being without the existence of the applied variety; no-one, for example, would have studied non-linear differential equations without the spur of **chaos theory** and chaotic behaviour in the physical world. The main branches have grown up around such applications, and from the urge to understand the earliest systems abstracted from Nature. **SMcL**

See also algebra; analysis; geometry; numbers; set theory.

Further reading J.H. Panlos, *Innumeracy: Mathematical Illiteracy and its Consequences.*

PYTHAGORAS' THEOREM

Pythagoras' theorem is one of the best-known results in **Euclidean geometry**, but the theorem attributed to Pythagoras (*c*.560-*c*.480 BCE) was in fact known throughout the world before he introduced it to Greece. For a right-angled triangle (one where the largest angle is 90 degrees), the sum of the squares of the lengths of the two shortest sides is equal to the square of the length of the longest side. This result was discovered by Egyptian and Chinese mathematicians, and is an example of the way in which the same mathematical results were developed independently throughout the world, thus demonstrating that mathematics is not purely a development of Western culture. This is something important to those mathematicians who feel that logical thought is universal, and that the language of **symbolic logic** is not culturally based. The result has also formed the basis of the definition of length used in co-ordinate geometry in two dimensions. **SMcL**

QUAKERISM

The Society of Friends (Quakers), as it is known today, has had an influence out of all proportion to its numbers. As with many other religious movements, an insulting epithet, in this case describing the way they were alleged to 'quake' before God in their meetings, has become an honourable name. They themselves maintained they were a Religious Society (originally called the Society of the Friends of Truth), partly because they abhorred all the theology, pomp and ceremony of churches ('steeple-houses') and especially of the Church of England, and partly to try and evade crushing 17th-century legislation against Nonconformists. Addressing each other as 'Friend' and using the familiar 'Thee/Thou' form, and eschewing all the social customs and formal etiquette of the day, they took **Protestantism** to its ultimate conclusion. However, they also developed a positive theology based on believers finding 'inner light' within themselves, prayer, meditation and reading the Scriptures without the use of any sacraments, clergy or music. They are distinguished by their integrity, complete tolerance, absolute pacifism and support of 'green' issues. **EMJ**

Further reading W.C. Braithwaite, *The Beginnings of Quakerism;* R.M. Jones, *The Faith and Practice of the Quakers.*

QUANTITATIVE HISTORY

Quantitative history is the application of statistical methods to the analysis of historical data. Influenced by **positivism** and by the behavioural movement in the social sciences

(see **behaviourism**), 19th- and 20th-century historians began to adopt quantitative approaches to analyse existing historical statistics as well as to convert non-numeric forms of data into numeric forms. The approach can be used as a means of adding rigour to traditional historical description, and indeed to refute previous conventional wisdom.

Before quantitative history developed, the incorporation of **demography**, based primarily upon the analysis of census data, was under-utilized by historians. It was also rare for historians to count or systematically analyse votes in legislatures, or to analyse economic and social data informed by bodies of social scientific theory. Considerable benefits have also been derived from the formal content analysis or lexicometry, studying the frequency of key words or themes in historic texts. Quantitative methods are now applied to test hypotheses in support of specific theories. For example, Snyder and Tilly used historical records of agricultural and protest data in France to argue against a 'relative deprivation' theory of the causes of collective violence. Critics of the quantitative approach to history argue that apart from the inherent problems of reliability and validity, statistical records are of limited use when analysed outside the social and political context of the era. They in turn are rightly accused of an obscurantism which masks their own mathematical incompetence. Used properly, quantitative methods are an indispensable tool for a rigorous historian. **BO'L**

See also history; historicism.

Further reading R. Floud, *An Introduction to Quantitative Methods for Historians;* L. Haskins, *Understanding Quantitative History;* C.H. Lee, *Social Science and History: an Investigation into the Application of Theory and Quantification in British Economic and Social History.*

QUANTITY THEORY OF MONEY

The quantity theory of money, in **economics**, is the foundation stone of **monetarism**. This theory maintains that the level of prices in a country is determined by the quantity of money in circulation. It was developed into an equation by Irving Fisher (1867–1947) as $MV = PT$, where M is the money supply, V is its velocity of circulation, P is the price level, and T is the volume of transaction in goods and services. If V is constant and T changes very little over a short period of time, then the price level (P) depends upon the money supply (M). Other economists, such as Alfred Marshall and Milton Friedman, have developed their particular versions of the quantity theory of money.

Critics argue that V is neither constant nor predictable and that T can change in critical amounts in short periods of time. A second dispute is that even if there is a link between M and P, it need not be a causal link, still less one that leads from money to prices.

These controversies have raged since the 1930s, when **Keynesians** began to challenge the orthodoxy represented by the quantity theory. The theoretical debate has been supplemented by a mass of empirical research into the value of V and into the timelag between changes in M and changes in P. Modern monetarists recognize that the relationship is complicated but continue to hold that the quantity of money is key to controlling the price level and the level of economic activity in the longer run; Keynesians believe that they are vindicated. The argument continues. **TF**

Further reading Milton Friedman, *Studies in the Quantity Theory of Money*; J.M. Keynes, *The General Theory of Employment, Interest and Money*.

QUANTIZATION

The concept of quantization, in **physics**, is difficult to assimilate, since it only occurs on a very small scale, and thus we have no direct experience of it. In essence, it means that certain basic quantities, like energy and angular momentum, may only have certain values. The first ideas about quantization come from ancient Greece. The Greeks reasoned that a substance cannot be divided into smaller parts indefinitely: the smallest possible part of the substance will be reached, which cannot be further divided and still retain its nature. The ancient Greeks named these indivisible objects atoms ('uncuttable elements'). The word was taken up by early chemists who discovered their existence.

In modern physics, quantization has a slightly different meaning. Energy itself is not quantized, but a system like an atom may only accept or emit quanta of energy. The atom can only exist with certain definite amounts of energy, and not with any energy in between these levels.

The basis of quantization is the wave nature of matter. If we accept that all particles have a wave-like nature, then it may be seen that this nature imposes quantization upon them. An example of how waves imply quantization is to be found in the behaviour of a vibrating string.

A string fixed at both ends has only certain modes of vibration. The easiest of these to excite has its maximum amplitude of vibration in the centre, with no movements at the ends. The next mode of vibration has a still point at the centre (a node) and a maximum amplitude of vibration (antinode) at points one quarter and three quarters of the way along. The next mode will have two nodes and so on.

What may be noticed is that any modes of vibration that do not have nodes and antinodes in exactly the right place do not exist upon the string: they are not allowed. We can see that they would not be very successful; a mode with an antinode at a fixed end will not get very far! As the energy of a vibrating string depends upon its mode, the allowed energies of the string are quantized.

A particle confined within a certain area (like an electron orbiting an atom) is now considered to be strongly analogous to a wave on a string fixed at both ends. Thus its allowed energies are not continuous but only occur at certain values. This is found to be true in experiments; atoms only have certain energy levels.

Energy is not the only quantity that is quantized in confined systems. Other quantized quantities are velocity, angular momentum and magnetic moments. **JJ**

QUANTUM THEORY

The theory of quantum mechanics is one of the great achievements of 20th-century **physics**. It has been rigorously tested and shown to be valid in a huge variety of situations. Modern computers and electronics are designed using quantum mechanics.

Quantum mechanics involves **mathematics**, and cannot properly be understood without it. Central to the theory are the concepts of wave functions and operators. The motion of a quantum mechanical particle is described by a wave function Ψ, which is analogous to the amplitude describing the motion of a wave, providing we accept the wave nature of matter and transfer from a wave to a particle concept. The probability of finding the particle in a certain place is given by Ψ^2.

All properties of a particle have corresponding mathematical operators. These can be simple or complex the operators for momentum and position are $\dfrac{d}{dx}$ and x respectively. The operators and wave functions are combined to give matrix elements, which correspond to observable properties of the particles. Thus, to find an equation describing a property of a particle, we first find its wave function (not usually a simple process!) and then use the operator corresponding to the property of interest in to produce the matrix element which we may observe.

An important part of quantum theory is the **uncertainty principle**. This is a natural consequence of the wave nature of matter, and means that it is impossible to measure both the position and the momentum of a particle at the same time with perfect accuracy. **JJ**

See also quantization; Schrödinger equation; wave-particle duality.

QUARREL OF THE ANCIENTS AND MODERNS

The quarrel of the ancients and moderns was a running dispute, active in European fine-art circles for most of the 17th and 18th centuries, on the relevance and relative worth of antique and modern art. The difference revolved around the excessive reverence accorded by some to the ancients (who held it as an article of faith that modern art might and should seek to match that of classical antiquity, but could never surpass it)

and the confidence of the others in contemporary achievements which, as they reminded their adversaries, were unknown in antiquity. 'The Quarrel' (for example between Diderot and Falconet) may seem silly today, but it affected attitudes not merely to Renaissance art and the classical tradition, but also to the teaching of art in the academies. Some sought to strike a balance: 'Speak of the moderns without contempt', wrote Lord Chesterfield to his son in 1748, 'and of the ancients without idolatry; judge them all by their merits, but not by their age.' **MG PD**

Further reading Stanley Rosen, *The Ancients and the Moderns: Rethinking Modernity.*

QUIETISM

Quietism is the belief that God touches only those people who are totally passive and quiet, who empty their whole personality so that God can (even must) fill them with his spirit. Quietism is an extreme form of Christian **mystical** theology, but in a more general form it can be found at any period in many religions, for example *bhakti*, **Sufism** and **yoga**. **KDS**

R

RACE AND RACISM

In prescientific times, the term 'race' was used to classify any group or type of species in the natural world: people spoke, for example, of the 'race' of monkeys or 'the canine race'. From the early 19th century onwards, however, the word began to be applied specifically to human beings, to describe what were (wrongly) perceived as mutually distinct groups of *Homo sapiens*. It is still commonly assumed that different 'races' of human beings can be distinguished, and that the distinctions reveal themselves in such things as bone construction, common descent, hair form and skin colour. But unbiased genetical and statistical data provide no evidence for such views; rather, they disprove them. To take a single example: the defining characteristics of the 'negroid' race were once claimed to include dark skin and tightly curled black hair. Yet Australian aborigines, to choose one group among many, tend to have dark skin but wavy and sometimes blonde hair. Advances in **genetics** have also shown that the differences within breeding populations who share certain physical characteristics are as great as those between such groups. Findings like these have led to the discreditation of 'race' as a scientific term, and to its replacement in **anthropology** and **sociology** with such concepts as **ethnicity** and 'ethnic group'.

The so-called scientific study of race, as a biological feature of human beings, was a typical activity of 19th-century Europe, during the period of nationalist and imperialist expansionism. Typologies of humans were constructed, in which cultural and psychological characteristics were equated with perceived physical characteristics. Common distinctions in such 'scientific racism' were 'caucasian', 'mongoloid' and 'negroid'. Each of these groups was considered to be distinct from the others, and to have come from different ancestry. (Some authorities identified the ancestors quite specifically, as Noah's sons Shem, Ham and Japheth in the Old Testament flood story.)

Once the idea of distinct races was accepted, the next step was to claim that the differences between them were not merely biological but indicated different levels of 'elevation' on the ladder of evolution, and that each population group had a unique set of characteristics, whether negative or positive. Beliefs about the inferiority of 'negroid' peoples were particularly rampant, and were used to legitimize discrimination against them, especially in the context of the expansion of **capitalism** which required the use of cheap labour. If, for example, the equality of black people with white could be denied on 'scientific' grounds, this legitimized the practice of whites treating black labour as a commodity. In India, British colonialist administrators engaged in the practice of 'anthropometry', in which selected physical features were measured to form a typology of caste groups. Not unnaturally, such practices appeared, to those who used them, to reinforce and 'prove' the perceived superiority of the white man, and to

justify their presence in countries within their colonial dominion. It also served to construct a hierarchy of orders in which people could be allotted according to so-called 'natural' characteristics.

Such historical perspectives on race continue to have their legacy in contemporary times, in which political and economic factors persist in structuring perceptions of race. Ideas about race go hand-in-hand with forms of racism: the **ideology** and practice of discrimination against conceived racial groups, such as the Blacks, Jews and Irish. Racism need not necessarily be a visible brute force, but it could manifest itself as institutional racism in which a climate of discrimination against particular social groups permeates in a range of overt or covert ways.

Although race is a socially constructed phenomenon, it is a powerful motivating force behind people's thoughts and behaviours. Contemporary social theorists assess the extents and effects of racism on people, whilst some have engaged in political struggles against its iniquities. Historical analyses that explain the colonial conditions which underly contemporary thoughts about race have been considered in relation to how capitalist economies mediate these situations. For example, a gulf between black and white workers may act to undermine working class solidarity, which would be largely in the interests of those who seek to control the labour force. Such perspectives are complicated by a range of other social considerations, particularly when there is a diffusion of people and ideas across class and racial divisions. **DA RK**

See also assimilation; caste; colonialism; culture; dependency theory; ethnocentrism, evolutionism; Marxist anthropology; nationalism; orientalism; power; primitivism; social closure; social biology; stratification; typifications.

Further reading Michael Banton, *The idea of Race*; J.G. Gabriel, *The Concepts of Race and Racism: an Analysis of Classical and Contemporary Theories of Race*; Paul Gilroy (ed.), *The Empire Strikes Back*.

RADICAL CHIC

Radical chic was the phrase coined by the

New York writer Tom Wolfe to describe an upsurge of artists from the First World giving performances or producing work for **Third-World** causes during the 1970s and 1980s. The best-known example was Band Aid in the mid-1980s: **pop** singers round the world uniting to raise money for famine-stricken Africa. But the urge is much older: Wolfe himself was writing of a 1970s concert by Leonard Bernstein in aid of black rights in the US, and in earlier times artists had raised funds in similar ways for Spain in the 1930s, for the victims of the Paris Commune in 1871, and no doubt for many other causes. The phrase 'radical chic' expresses the sniffiness some of the chattering class feel towards such endeavours, as if it were somehow smarter to mock people who do good works than to roll up the sleeves and get down to it oneself. **KMcL**

RADIO TRANSMISSION

Radio Transmission is a generic term applied to wireless electricity, that is electricity transmitted without the use of wires. It was a dream of the pioneers of telegraphy, the first form of communication achieved using electrical means, to dispense with the expensive, time-consuming and unreliable method of installing electrical cables to facilitate communication. The birth of radio transmission to fulfil this need can be traced to early experiments of H. Hertz in 1888 and to James Maxwell's electromagnetic theory in 1873 (see **electromagnetism**).

Hertz had shown that electrical power created in one circuit could be transmitted and detected in a second circuit, although the two circuits were not connected to each other and were indeed separated by a distance of several metres in air. This experiment was used by Hertz to prove some of Maxwell's early mathematical theories that had predicted this effect, although Hertz failed to recognize the potential of his work for communication purposes.

The credit for radio transmission for communication belongs in the main to the Italian, G. Marconi. Marconi was inspired by the work Hertz had performed and also had the vision to realize the application of this new technology. At this time, around 1897, other developments in radio came

together to form the first practical radiotelegraphy demonstration. An adequate receiver for the early spark-generated radio waves, the coherer, had been discovered by E. Branly, and was demonstrated in lectures by O. Lodge. Lodge had also shown the effects of tuning in radio transmission: that is, making the transmitter and receiver circuits resonate and therefore work at the same frequency. Marconi applied these principles and realized that by using a larger antenna a greater separation distance between transmitter and receiver could be achieved. He succeeded in achieving radio communication over a distance of several miles. In 1900, he successfully used his radiotelegraphy sets to provide ship-to-shore and ship-to-ship communication for the British Admiralty, an obvious use for wireless telegraphy. A few years later he created another milestone in radio transmission by establishing the first radio communication across the Atlantic Ocean.

Further advances in radio transmission followed, for example, speech transmission was greatly helped by the development of early **electronic** devices. The first diode, invented by T. Edison in 1880, was used in radio receivers from around 1904 and its electronic successor, the triode, was implemented as both an amplifier and oscillator in the transmitter and receiver of electronic radios.

The use of the triode as an oscillator, capable of producing a single high frequency signal, was invaluable in enabling the various modulation schemes devised for radio transmission to be realized. In particular, frequency modulation (or FM as it is better known today), developed in 1933 by E. Armstrong, reduced noise on radio sets and set the standards for transmission quality.

By the 1920s radio broadcasting was under way, for instance from the British Broadcasting Corporation (BBC) in 1927, and radio transmission has since expanded into fields such as radiotelephony, using cellular phones, television broadcasting and the use of radio waves in radar. The radio pioneers' dream of wireless electricity is today a very well-established and useful reality. **AC**

RADIOACTIVITY

Radiation (Latin *radiare*, 'to emit beams') is the emission of waves or particles. The three types of radiation are alpha ray particles, beta ray particles and gamma rays emitted from the nuclei of radioactive elements.

Alpha rays consist of a stream of helium nuclei, that each contain two neutrons and two protons. The penetrating power of alpha ray is small and it can be stopped by thin sheets of paper.

Beta rays consist of emitted electrons or positrons (which are identical to the electron but with a positive charge). The penetrating power of beta particles is greater than alpha particles, and it may need several millimetres of aluminium to stop such particles. Both beta and alpha rays can be deflected by a magnetic field.

Gamma rays on the other hand are electromagnetic waves (photons), and can only be stopped using many centimetres of lead. Since gamma rays have no charge they are not deflected by a magnetic field.

The time for half the atoms initially present in a sample to decay is known as the half life. Decay can result in a series of new elements being produced which may themselves in turn decay. Half lifes can last from seconds to years (protactinium has a half life of 72 seconds, while carbon has a half life of 5,730 years). It is carbon's half life that is used to date organic material, using the process of **carbon dating**. AA

Further reading Harald Enge, *Introduction to Nuclear Physics*.

RADIOBIOLOGY

Radiobiology, in the **life sciences**, is the study of the interactions between radiation and living systems. The area was opened in 1895 by Wilhelm Röntgen's (1845–1923) discovery of the x-ray and its diagnostic value in medicine. The use of x-rays spread rapidly and it was soon observed that they had deleterious and occasionally fatal effects upon those regularly exposed to them. Radiobiology grew from these first observations and expanded as it was discovered that other forms of electromagnetic radiation, such as gamma rays and ultraviolet rays, could affect living cells as could particulate radiation such as that emitted by radioisotopes. Such ionizing radiations can cause chemical changes where they interact with atoms and molecules and are thus distinguished from radiations such as visible light and microwaves, which generally cause heating effects. Ionizing radiation delivers energy to atoms with which it interacts causing chemical reactions to occur; in the controlled environment of a living cell this is likely to be destructive, though the effect on the individual depends greatly upon species, insects being capable of surviving far greater doses than mammals.

The effect of ionizing radiation on a cell is to produce random mutations in the DNA. Typically, radiation causes cell death or effects the rate of cell division as a result of damage to DNA, possibly resulting in cancer. A number of early radiation workers, such as Marie Curie, died from cancers caused by the materials they were investigating, and cancers are more common among individuals exposed to high levels of ultraviolet radiation or to nuclear weapons used in warfare or in tests. Cells which are actively dividing (such as cancer cells) are more sensitive to the effects of radiation; this is the basis for the use of radiotherapy in the treatment of cancer, and also explains how sub-lethal doses of radiation can reduce the immunity of an individual by destroying the stem cells which produce white blood corpuscles. Hereditary effects of radiation are confined to instances where the germ cells are exposed and are thus only seen with penetrating radiations such as gamma and x-rays. The mutations produced are almost always harmful and frequently fatal, though the naturally occuring radiation in the environment may be important in the induction of a low-level of **mutation** which is important in **evolution**. RB

See also biophysics; teratology.

Further reading Eric Hall, *Radiation Biology*.

RAGTIME

Ragtime was a style of music popular in the US from the 1890s to 1920s, and a precursor of **jazz**. Its name is a contraction of 'ragged time', and refers to the contrast between a regular, unvarying pulse in the accompaniment (usually left hand of piano) and the syncopations (anticipations and delays of the beat) in the melody (usually right hand of piano). The best-known ragtime composer was the American Scott Joplin (who in the 1910s even wrote a ragtime opera), and the best-known ragtime piece not by him is Irving Berlin's song 'Alexander's Ragtime Band', which became a jazz standard. Bohuslav Martinu, Ravel, Stravinsky and other 'serious' composers in the 1920s were attracted by the jerky perkiness of ragtime, and used it as a component of **neoclassical** pieces of their own. KMcL

RATIONAL CHOICE

Rational choice is the label given to a methodology now common across the **social sciences**: the method of modelling social behaviour on the supposition that individuals are rational agents who optimize subject to constraints. In politics and **sociology** the rational choice approach is sometimes called public choice, to distinguish collective decisions from the individual or private decisions more characteristically studied in **economics**. The use of **game theory** and formal decision theory is very common among social scientists using rational choice methods, but they are best known for their work in four domains of **political science**.

First, rational choice theorists have examined the logic of voting rules. Controversial discussion still centres on certain alleged paradoxes of collective choice identified in 'Arrow's theorem' which demonstrates that no system of voting which seeks to aggregate preferences from knowledge of individual preferences can avoid logical inconsistencies when five apparently reasonable conditions are required not to be violated.

Second, rational choice theorists have explored the logic of treating voters as utility maximizers and political parties as pure office-seeking organizations intent on maximizing their votes. These assumptions have been used to explain the convergence of parties on similar policy platforms in plurality-rule election systems, and the sharp policy-differentiation between parties in proportional representation systems. They have also been used to explore the logic of **coalition** behaviour.

Third, rational choice theorists have examined the logic of assuming that bureaucrats can be modelled as budget-maximizing individuals, predicting that government services will be 'over-supplied' and inefficiently supplied because of the monopolistic advantages of bureaucrats – at least as compared with politicians and voters.

Finally, rational choice theorists have examined the extent to which constraints on collective action prevent some interests from getting organized while others find it easy to organize. The product of an interest group is a 'public good', that is a good which is non-excludable (people will get the benefit from it even if they do not contribute to it) and non-rival (that is, individual consumption of the good is not affected by other people's consumption of it). Therefore, it is reasoned, rational individuals may calculate that the benefit they receive from the production of a public good (multiplied by the probability that their contribution will be decisive to the good being advanced) is less than the costs of their contribution. In short, in many cases individuals have the incentive to 'free ride' rather than to contribute towards public goods. This 'logic of collective action' has been invoked, controversially, to explain many different phenomena, including why some interests are better represented than others in a **democracy** and why some countries have higher economic growth rates than others.

The critics of rational choice usually condemn it on the grounds that they disagree with the realism of its assumptions. More rarely, but more effectively, critics show how the methodology can be used to make political analyses and predictions at odds with the classical **liberalism** or **libertarianism** espoused by most rational choice theorists. BO'L

Further reading P. Dunleavy, *Bureaucracy, Democracy and Public Choice*; J. Elster (ed.),

Rational Choice; L. Lewin, *Self-Interest and Public Interest in Western Politics*.

RATIONAL NUMBERS

A rational number, in mathematics, is one which can be represented by a fraction, the ratio of two **integers** (the one which does the dividing, the denominator, cannot be 0). The rational numbers were introduced to solve the problem that there were equations of the form a/b=? with no solutions. It is usual to write rational numbers 'in their lowest terms', meaning that the two numbers in the fraction cannot have any integers which divide both of them. One of the problems which most distressed the Greeks was that there are still equations with no rational number solutions (the example they discovered that there was no rational number whose square is 2, which means that there is no solution of the equation $x^2 - 2 = 0$). This problem, which the Greeks did not attempt to solve, was overcome by the introduction of the **algebraic numbers** (this was not possible until systematic notation for **polynomials** was introduced).

It may seem to be difficult to think of numbers which are not rational, but in fact, very few numbers really are. One of the first controversial results of the **set theory** of Georg Cantor (1845–1918) was that the number of rational numbers was not the same as the number of **real numbers**. (This was controversial because mathematicians felt that any idea that there were different sizes of **infinity** was impossible to consider.) Cantor showed that the rational numbers were countable (that is, could be counted or written in a list) whereas the real numbers were not. The proof that the rational numbers were countable relies on a famous 'diagonalisational argument', in which he gave a way in which they could be listed. The rationals are written in an infinite square by writing all those with denominator 1 in the top row, as 0/1, 1/1, 2/1 and so on, then all those with denominator 2 on the next row, and so on. The way to list them is to start at the top, left-hand corner, to go one to the right (to 1/1), then diagonally down and to the left (to 0/2), then down (to 0/3) and then diagonally up and to the right (to 1/2) and again (to 3/1); then to 4/1 and diagonally down and right again and so on. Every number will at some point be included in such a list. **SMcL**

RATIONAL-EMOTIVE THERAPY see Cognitive Therapy

RATIONALISM

Rationalism is the philosophical view that reason is the source of all knowledge, a view attributed to Descartes, Spinoza and Leibniz. (It contrasts with **empiricism**, the view that all knowledge derives from experience.) So, for example, some rationalists have held that, simply by using reason, we can know that God exists: revelation is unnecessary. If reason is the source of all knowledge, then everything that can be known including the natural world must be intelligible and rationally explicable. **AJ**

See also knowledge.

RATIONALITY

Rationality (from Latin *rationari*, 'think', 'calculate'), which is usually considered to refer to the realm of logic or reason in achieving certain aims, has raised a specific debate within **anthropology** since the turn of the century. It may be traced back to the sociologist Max Weber's theories on 'rational man'. Weber argued that those pursuing the path of maximum benefit for the minimum input of resources demonstrated a rational decision. Rational behaviour was, therefore, associated with the prevalent ethos of capitalist society.

Anthropologists of Weber's time supported his ideas, simultaneously asserting that so-called 'primitive' societies were orientated by 'non-rational' institutions, such as **kinship**, **religion** and supernatural beliefs. Where such 'non-rational' elements were noticed in Western society, it was considered that they were survivals from an earlier epoch.

Lucien Lévy-Bruhl, a French philosopher noted for his 1923 work *The Primitive Mentality*, advanced the view that 'primitive' thought was collectively different from the logical thought characteristic of Western society. 'Primitive' thought was considered 'pre-logical' or mystical, demonstrating the 'law of participation' which stated that the subject and object were believed to fuse into each other. Although such features may be noticed in the West, it was the objective pursuit of knowledge and the 'rule of non-contradiction' stating that two things could not logically occupy the same place, that dominated collective thought of the West.

From the 1950s, Claude Lévi-Strauss challenged such views, arguing that all human beings were 'rational'. They all ordered and classified phenomena in a fundamentally similar manner. Apparent differences were the result of surface appearance due to the kinds of relationships that existed between thought, action and the environment. This he characterized with the notion of the *bricoleur* in 'primitive' societies: that is, he dealt with concrete items in the manner of an engineer creating a 'science of the concrete'. Western thought was described as 'domesticated' and in which abstract **science** and **history** were the prominent organizing principles.

In 1975, Dan Sperber developed Lévi-Strauss' theories to deal with symbolic systems. He argued that the keys to understanding symbols were symbols themselves. If we do not have familiarity with these symbolic enmeshments, then we will continue to judge peoples' thoughts and conducts by our own Western assumptions on rationality. Western views, in turn, are dependent on the symbolic complex of technology, progress and **economics**.

This brief outline of the rationality debate is underpinned by the universalist and relativist dimensions. The universalists argue that all human beings are 'rational' because we are ultimately able to communicate and understand each other's values and lifestyles. The relativist viewpoint is that human societies are differently organized, so that varying definitions and views of what is 'rational' apply.

The problem with this universalist/rationalist debate is that in the process of identifying what defines 'rationality' for any particular community, their actions and thoughts may be over-rationalized. Statements do not need to be strictly logical in order to have intended effects. Nor do all people run their lives according to 'rational' motives, however one defines it. The issues of social contradictions, inconsistencies or absurdities also need to be taken into account.

Most contemporary anthropologists accept the view that in order for a society to be organized, a degree of 'rational' ordering is necessary which may be particular to the society. On the other hand, there is a universalist dimension present in the ability to transcend cultural parameters and relate to others on mutual grounds of agreement. **RK**

See also cultural relativism; emotions; ethnocentrism; magic; primitivism.

Further reading Claude Lévi-Strauss, *The Savage Mind*; Dan Sperber, *Rethinking Symbolism*; Brian Wilson (ed.), *Rationality*.

RATIONALIZATION

The term rationalization (from Latin *ratio*, 'reckoning') has two separate meanings. It was used by Pareto (1848–1923) to refer to the justification of an act, seeking to present it in a favourable light after it has been carried out. Pareto believed that rationalization involved the use of less than genuine explanations in order to justify actions. He considered that most social accounts, including most social and political theorizing, involved rationalization in this sense.

In its second usage in **sociology**, rationalization refers to the **organization** of social and economic life according to principles of efficiency on the basis of technical knowledge. It was a concept first used by Max Weber in his analysis of modern **capitalism**. For Weber, whole societies could be characterized by the typical forms of action they contained within them. He believed that there was a general tendency in modern capitalist society for all institutions and most areas of life to become subject to calculation, measurement and control: that is, rationalization. He maintained that progressive rationalization had in fact been occurring throughout history and that once the process had occurred it was irreversible. For Weber, rationalization was a master process which underlay the transformation of the economic, political and legal institutions of Western societies. He believed that this process would restrict individuality and create an 'iron cage' which would ultimately separate the individual from the community.

Weber argued that the process of rationalization would affect all areas of social life and would be manifested in a number of ways. For example, rationalization in **science** involved the decline of the individual innovator and replacement by the development of research teams, coordinated experiments and state-directed science policies; in **law** it meant the replacement of *ad hoc* law making and case-law with the application of universal laws; and in society as a whole it implied the spread of **bureaucracy**, state control and administration; it would also involve a waning of the influence of **religion**. For Weber, the development of the form of social organization known as the bureaucracy was the essence of the spirit of rationality.

Historical developments in the **labour process**, namely the system of **assembly-line production** associated with Henry Ford, illustrate the extent to which processes of rationalization can be pushed. Ford rationalized the production process by producing a standardized product (the Model T Ford), which enabled the purchase of specialized machinery. Work was subdivided into routine constituent parts. One of the most famous innovations was the assembly line. Workers were tied to their position and the rate and pace of the work were dictated by a machine. Although Ford maximized his production, he soon found that control over the productive process did not mean control over the workers. Rationalization of work processes to this degree resulted in problems of absenteeism and high levels of worker turnover. **DA**

See also authority; division of labour; secularization; state.

Further reading A. Giddens, *Capitalism and Modern Social Theory*.

RATIONALIZATION see Defence Mechanism

REAL ESSENCE see Essence

REAL NUMBERS

The real numbers represent almost the final step in the various expansions of the number system from the **integers** to the **rational numbers** to the **algebraic numbers** to the real numbers and the **complex numbers**. The real numbers form a **field**, they have an ordering, and they also have the property of 'completeness'. This means that if there is any set X of real numbers such that they have an upper bound (a number that is bigger than everything in X), then they have a least upper bound (an upper bound which is smaller than any other). For example, suppose X is the set of numbers whose square is greater than 2. This has an upper bound (3 is bigger than anything in the set) and so has a least upper bound, which will be the square root of 2. The real numbers are (apart from just renaming the numbers) the only mathematical structure which is a complete ordered field.

The real numbers represent a considerable increase in size from the **algebraic numbers**. The algebraic numbers are countable (can be counted, or written in a list), whereas the real numbers cannot. This fact was first discovered by Georg Cantor (1845–1918), and was controversial because mathematicians felt that saying a set was infinite was all that could be said, there were no degrees of infinite (see **set theory**).

Why can the real numbers not be listed? Suppose that there is a way that they can be listed. Then there is a way of listing the numbers between 0 and 1 (as infinite decimals). But then there is a number which is not on the list: the one which in the nth decimal place has 1 if the nth decimal place of the nth number on the list is 2, and 2 if it is not. It is different from every number on the list, in the nth decimal place, and so no such list can be complete. So there is no way of listing the real numbers. **SMcL**

REALISM

In **philosophy**, realism is the doctrine that some things exist independently of any mind: it is the antonym of philosophical **idealism**. Sceptics about realism ask the kind of question beloved of philosophers:

'Can one believe in realism about the mind if no mind can exist independently of itself?' One reply is that realism is not necessarily the view that things can exist independently of minds in general, but rather that they exist independently of any specific beliefs we might have about them. In other words realism emphasizes that truth is possible: beliefs are testable against 'reality', and that reality is 'knowable'. Scientific realism is the belief that scientific theories and hypotheses, even about unobservable entities, are theories and hypotheses about real entities that is, entities that are independent of our theories about them. It rejects the sloppy reasoning found in contemporary relativism which says that all knowledge is 'theory-dependent' and concludes that 'therefore' all knowledge is a matter of opinion. Scientific realism does not deny that theories are dependent on minds (or languages or judgements) if only because such theories have to be expressed by minds and in languages – it just denies that the world would be other than it is without such theories.

In **politics** realists are analysts who claim to be able to understand the world as it is, rather than as others might wish it to be. They are vehement critics of **Utopianism**, and condemn political idealism for judging matters according to moral criteria, and for not knowing that **power** and self-interest are what explain political events and developments. Critics observe that it is not realistic of political realists to think that people are never motivated by ideals or moral values. Yet because realism counsels caution and pessimism about the principled nature of one's opponents and one's friends, its sage-like charms are never likely to disappear from the political lexicon. Realism is especially prevalent in **international relations**, partly because the absence of a world state make an analysis focused on power and self-interest more plausible than one grounded in the claims of morality and duty.

Realism is an important concept in fine **art**, **drama** and **literature**. In fine art, critics use the term loosely, redefining it constantly in light of the work in question. For example, it is not a synonym for **naturalism** or **illusionism**, nor does it describe a mirror image of the world. Nor is Realism (the movement, signified by the use of the capital 'r') synonymous with 'realism' (the quality). Historically, Realism is the offspring of the **Romantics**' interest in finding beauty in the bizarre or the conventionally ugly, and is epitomized by the work of the mid–19th-century artist Gustave Courbet. The Realists focused on scenes of workers and peasants depicted in a gritty or earthy manner: Courbet's *Burial at Ornans* (1849) is typical, both in the scene it depicts and the way its composition and application of paint match the down-to-earth nature of the subject. But 'realism' anticipates this kind of Realism by many centuries. Giotto is 'realistic' in the sense that his compositions are psychologically plausible; Caravaggio is a 'realist' because he represents Bible characters as 'real' people. In this sense, realism is the opposite process to idealization, and may be applied to works as diverse as Greek statuettes of grimacing slaves, Japanese paintings of beggars and crones, and European works as aparently remote from them as Rembrandt's *Jewish Bride* (1669). More recently, critics have used the term to designate the work of those, like Lucien Freud, whose figurative paintings tacitly oppose abstract impressionism. But this last use clearly shows the term's inadequacy as an artistic concept, since the works in question are 'realist' only in the sense that they are not abstract.

In literature, realism was a movement in European fiction whose intellectual origins lay, first, in the political egalitarianism proclaimed during the French Revolution, and second, in the rise of the bourgeoisie during the early 19th century – a reading audience with an enormous appetite for descriptions of people and events similar to those they saw around them. (At the time, this was for most writers an untapped resource.) Realist writers set out to describe, in unaffected language, the 'reality' of life and people, to give fiction as it were a documentary dimension. Artificiality of style and fanciful invention of character and incident were both eschewed. Notable adherents of the style were Balzac and Flaubert (who said that he worked to make his own authorial presence in his work as unobtrusive as possible), and its main monument is Tolstoy's

War and Peace. But to say that is to reveal the innate flaw of realism as a literary theory, and it is similar to the problem in fine art. All writing is an assemblage, the result of authorial **attitude** and choice, and Tolstoy's novel (for example) no more represents the 'reality' of the historical events and society it depicts than (for instance) Austen's *Pride and Prejudice* does the reality of life in middle-class Regency England. In Balzac, the principles of realism are sometimes taken too far, until the work becomes both grandiose and otiose. The old man in *Père Goriot*, for example, stands out not because he is 'photographed' in prose, but because he is a magnificently-imagined individual character (that is, realism is selectively deployed) and because the other characters in the novel are too many and too relentlessly described to escape boring us. In later fiction, thorough-going realism has tended to be the practice of such comparatively minor writers as (in English) Margaret Drabble, Mrs Gaskell, C.P. Snow and Jerome Weidman; the finest authors who have used realist techniques – they include Dickens, George Eliot, Joyce and Proust, not to mention a host of 'moderns' from Grass to Roth, from Samuel Beckett to Patrick White – have made them part of much wider fictional strategies.

In theatre, the distinction between realism and naturalism is important but blurred. In naturalism and classic realism, the effacing of artifice is imperative, and is achieved through a system of conventions. The idea of realism as a mimetic representation of life has informed theatrical practice, and responses to it, from the **Renaissance** to the present day. Naturalism, while utilizing the characteristics of realism, developed from, and sought to represent, specific 19th-century concepts. The transparent function of realism as a 'window' to meaning was made concrete by the idea of the 'fourth wall' in theatres with a **proscenium arch**, through which spectators look at the 'meaning' of the play. The challenge to the Aristotelian concept of **mimesis**, which had a direct effect on theatrical representation, came from what has been identified as the 'Brecht/Lukács' debate in the mid–20th century. In this debate, Brecht defines realistic drama as that which is not fixed in a specific historical moment, but which allows the spectators at a particular time and place to understand and to change the conditions of their existence. In practice, this means that the spectators do not lose themselves in the detailed reproduction of a fictional world, but are constantly reminded of the artifice of the play being performed: so that, for example, while Mother Courage's cart has to look as though it has covered many miles over several years, there is no attempt to create a setting for it other than a stage. Classic realism is the dominant form of most film and television (**media** which are much more able to reproduce the illusion of the real), but theatre has been more able to respond to formal and conceptual challenges to the fixed form of classic realism. **PD MG TRG KMcL BO'L**

See also materialism; objective and subjective; reduction and reductionism.

Further reading J. Foster, *The Case for Idealism*; Damian Grant, *Realism*; H. Putnam, *The Many Faces of Realism*; C. Rosen and H. Zerner, *Romanticism and Realism: the Mythology of Nineteenth Century Art*; Raymond Williams, *Modern Tragedy*.

RECEPTION THEORY

Reception theory, in literary criticism, concerns the way readers respond to the texts they are reading. A text exists in two ways: absolutely, in its own right, with no contact except between it and the reader who is reading it at that moment; and second it is 'equipped' with an aura of meaning derived from its place in the literary and social canon, from its reception by other readers since it was first produced. It is this second phenomenon with which reception theory is concerned the cloud of external significance which is generated by a text, but which is not entirely implicit in that text itself, and may be considerably different from what the original author had in mind. **KMcL**

See also semiotics.

RECIPROCITY

Reciprocity (from Latin *reciprocus*, 'alternating'), in **sociology**, describes a situation in which an item or service is returned. It demonstrates a mutual exchange between persons or a social group that acts to unite them while, at the same time, differentiating them as separate members in the exchange relationship.

Marcell Mauss is the first prominent theorist on the subject of reciprocity. In his 1925 work, *The Gift*, he comments on how reciprocity entails a moral obligation to return the value of the **gift** to the donor, either immediately or in the distant future.

Later critics said that there is little clarity in Mauss's use of reciprocity. They questioned whether it refers to something that is visibly returned, a social ideal or human nature: that is, where gifts are not returned visibly, could a different kind of return (for instance, emotional, spiritual or religious) be envisaged? Such would be the case with the Christian practice of giving alms with the view to gain merit in the next kingdom.

K. Polyani identifies reciprocity in an economic idiom claiming that reciprocity is the dominant mode of distributing goods and services in certain societies. The other two modes of distribution were redistribution when goods are pooled together at the political centre to be distributed out later, as in feudal society; and market exchange as present in capitalist society.

Marshall Sahlins identifies three kinds of reciprocity in precapitalist society, depending on the kinds of materials exchanged and the social distance between the participants. *Generalized reciprocity* is characteristic of people in intimate relationships like that of the family. This creates greatest solidarity, there is no strict obligation to return the item, but reciprocity is still apparent when it is viewed in a moral way, such as when close kin are expected to support and help members in need. *Balanced reciprocity* marks an equivalence between goods and services exchanged. It is characteristic of trade relationships and is more economic than moral in character. *Negative reciprocity* applies to those situations in which attempts are made to make gains at the expense of the other side as instanced in theft, raiding and warfare.

Reciprocity may also be considered in the light of **marriage** arrangements where women are regarded as symbolic gifts. All these areas demonstrate how reciprocity is a many-sided organizing principle in the lives of people in societies. **RK**

See also economic anthropology; exchange.

Further reading Claude Lévi-Strauss, *The Elementary Structure of Kinship*; K. Polyani, *Primitive, Archaic and Modern Economies*; Marshall Sahlins, *Stone Age Economics*.

RECORDING

With the introduction of Thomas Edison's (1837–1941) phonograph (Greek, 'sound-writer') in 1877, the world of recording was born. His system used a diaphragm at the end of an amplifying horn to move a stylus in synchronism with the sound, cutting fine grooves on the circumference of a rotating metal drum. When the stylus retraced the groove, sounds were produced through the horn. These metal drums proved to have poor reproduction qualities and it was not until 1888, when wax cylinders were introduced, that recordings became clearer.

The next advance in sound reproduction came in 1888 with Emile Berliner's invention of flat discs with a long spiral groove. His invention opened up the way for the mass-production of recordings, as master discs could now be used to cut as many copies as were required. Recordings further improved in the 1920s when the sounds were captured by microphone, electrically amplified and the electric signal used to cut the master disc.

Other innovations, such as the introduction of stereo by EMI in 1933, and the development of magnetic tape by Telefunken and Farben in 1935, all helped to improve the quality of reproduction. Recording was also helped by better and more reliable reproduction equipment as the valve was superseded by the transistor.

During the 1970s, work was carried out that transformed people's way of thinking about recording. The introduction of the video and the compact disc have increased our expectations of sound and visual reproduction. The video is a magnetic tape recording of the signals necessary to produce picture and sound in a television set. The compact disc, however, uses laser light to interpret digital coding on a flat disc and translate it into speech and music. Since the sound is digitally recorded the quality of the original is retained much more effectively than by mechanical grooves or magnetic tape. **AA**

Further reading John Eargle, *Sound Recording.*

RECURSION

Recursion (Latin, 'running back over'), in **mathematics**, is a method of constructing **functions** from ones which already exist, and is related to the idea of **induction**. It is the way in which many important functions are defined, including addition and multiplication in **Peano arithmetic**. Suppose that f is a function from some set X to itself, and that a is a member of X. Then there is a function g from the natural numbers to X defined by $g(0) = a$, and for each number n, $g(n + 1) = f(g(n))$. (Addition is defined using the successor function, the function of counting, as f, and multiplication is defined using addition as f.)

Recursion is also used in **computability**, where it is used to define the set of recursively enumerable functions, which turn out to be those which computers can calculate. **SMcL**

REDEMPTION/REDEEMER

The origin of this powerful imagery in the Judaeo-Christian tradition is that of the benefactor who pays off someone else's mortgage or debts (particularly when the debtor or members of his or her family were in danger of being sold into slavery to settle those debts), or who ransoms them from slavery. One's 'redeemer' could also be one's advocate, as when Job tells his friends he will be vindicated ('I know that my Redeemer liveth..'). Running through the Hebrew Scriptures and liturgy is the refrain of the God of Israel redeeming his people form bondage in Egypt. By early Christian times a redeemer was one who paid a ransom for a captive or a slave, or among Greeks and Romans arranged manumission. Hence many longed for a heavenly redeemer who would redeem them from sin and death, a theme found in

other religions as well, especially where, as in **Hinduism**, redemption from the misery of this world is so ardently desired.

Jesus spoke of giving his life as a ransom for many, and the image became part of the **Christian** theology of **atonement**. For St Paul redemption involved not only release from bondage to sin and death, but the restoration of all creation to what God intended it to be. The early church fathers drew not only on Hellenistic concepts of a heavenly redeemer, but developed the vision of God's mercy and love in restoring humanity to divine status and the world to incorruptibility. Since there could be not limits on God's love, even the inmates of Hell would in the end be redeemed. In an agreeable mixture of theological and the original practical meaning of 'redemption', several groups saw it as their Christian mission to 'redeem' people from hardship in the temporal world. During the Crusades, the Redemptionists bought back Christians captured as slaves; in 1732 the Society of Redemptionists was formed, to 'buy back' the poor and the heathen from Satan, by doing good works. **EMJ KMcL**

REDUCTIO AD ABSURDUM see **Proof by Contradiction**

REDUCTION AND REDUCTIONISM

Within **philosophy**, there are various forms of reduction and, therefore, of reductionism. Phenomenalists claimed that sentences about physical objects could be translated without loss of meaning into sentences about actual or possible experiences. Sentences about physical objects were analysed into sentences about actual or possible experiences. Physical object concepts were said to be dispensable. So phenomenalists were analytical or conceptual reductionists. *Analytical* or conceptual reductionists analyse one set of statements or concepts in terms of another.

Metaphysical reduction involves the reduction of one part of reality; one part of reality is said to be nothing over and above another part of reality. So, for example, idealists (see **idealism**) argue that the physical part of reality is nothing over and above the mental part of reality. They need not consider that our talk about physical objects can be analysed in terms of talk abut actual or possible experiences. They need not be phenomenalists. Metaphysical reductionists do not require analytical or conceptual reduction. But they do attempt to reduce the physical part of reality to the mental part of reality.

Nomological reduction involves the reduction of one set of **laws of Nature** to another. For example, the laws of thermodynamics can be reduced to in the sense of derived from the laws of statistical mechanics. **AJ**

See also phenomenalism.

Further reading J. Foster, *A.J. Ayer*; E. Nagel, *The Structure of Science*.

REFLEXIVITY

Contemporary **anthropology** is characterized by reflexive self-scrutiny. In this process it submits its own motives and methods to scrutiny. Anthropologists, critical about power imbalances related to the historical imposition of Western conceptual models on other societies, have tried to restore the balance between the power relations of the discipline and those it studies.

The methodology of anthropology has created a reliance on constructing the world-view of other societies through a long and close interaction with a few, selected, indigenous informants. **Interpretative anthropology** since the 1970s placed extra importance on the way, and the precise terms, in which indigenous peoples described their lives. Yet the attempt to understand others' world-views in their own terms is inevitably hampered by our own assumptions about the way the world is ordered. The best **ethnography** can hope for, with such a methodology, is to try to understand what informants perceive. A reflexive approach in ethnographic writing attempts to articulate the relationship between anthropologist and informant as one of dialogue. This involves the anthropologist self-consciously locating his or her own perspective in academic writings.

The **hermeneutic** principle, which describes the way in which the observer participates in the creation of a new reality, has thrown light on the problem of the role of the observer. It is now recognized that ethnographers can never claim to perceive as the indigenous people perceive. Their observations can ultimately only be an individual interpretation.

The **postmodernist** influence in Western culture fractures preconceptions and denies any possibility of objectivity, or finding an ultimate truth. Anthropologists responded to this general disenchantment by experimenting with the style and form of their writing. Some have perhaps become over-reflexive, lapsing into totally subjective self-indulgent experiments, where the society under investigation comes across as a mere incidental. **CL**

See also language.

Further reading V. Crapanzano Tuhami, *Portrait of a Moroccan*.

REGRESSION

Regression and **fixation** were Freud's words for what Darwin had called arrests in development and reversion. Freud also saw **dreams** as a regression of the level of language to thinking in pictures.

Regression theory, prior to Freud's, included that of mental decadence, a popular psychiatric theory in the 1850s. Lombroso, in the early 1880s, put forward the theory of the born criminal whose psychic make-up regressed back to a primitive man. Infantile characteristics in somnambulists were called regression by Flournoy. The French School of the late 19th century, notably Moreau de Tours and then Pierre Janet, saw mental illness as a world full of delusion and hallucination that brought about regression in intellectual functions.

Jung assumes that psychic energy is directed either in the form of regression or progression. Regression, for him, was inward movement, an increase in introversion and a move towards the **unconscious**. A stop in the process of **individuation** (growth) brings about regression (introversion) and then progression (linked to extroversion); it is here seen as part of a cycle. **MJ**

REICHIAN THOUGHT see **Character Analysis**

REINCARNATION

Reincarnation (Latin, 'being clothed again in flesh') is a theory in **tribal religion** and in many Eastern religions (notably those of India), and was a feature of many ancient religions and philosophical systems (it was, for example, known to Pythagoras and Plato as *metempsychosis*, 'transmigration of the soul'). The idea is that the body is a temporary home for the soul, and that when the body dies the soul transmigrates to a new body. In Pythagoreanism, the process was thought to be haphazard, so that you had no idea 'whose' soul was contained in any given body at any given time; Platonists, by contrast, believed that unborn souls could choose their future existence on the basis of their previous character; the philosophical implications for personal identity in the first case, and for behaviour in the second, were zestfully teased out.

In **Buddhism, Hinduism, Jainism** and **Sikhism**, the idea is linked to the views that there is a cycle of birth, death and rebirth, and that we suffer the consequences of our behaviour. The soul is continuously reincarnated, and the body it takes on each incarnation depends on actions in the previous incarnation. We strive to escape from the cycle by winning enlightenment or bliss for intermediate periods prior to rebirth, until we cease to be reborn at all. A few 'great souls' (such as the Buddha) deliberately opt to return in order to help suffering humanity. (The successive incarnations of Vishnu should also be seen in this light, since he comes at times of disaster to restore *dharma*.)

To some thinkers, the ethical and moral imperatives inherent in this belief imply a continuity of personal identity from incarnation to incarnation: we are aware of our actions in previous incarnations, and can reflect on their consequences in the present. Others hold that there is no continuity of identity, or at least of awareness of identity. The soul's identity is independent of that of the body, and we can only assume, never know, what our present situation implies about the nature or behaviour of the body which 'our' soul inhabited in its previous incarnation. Others again say that ethical implications of the doctrine of reincarnation are secondary, and probably came from the reforming zeal of the Buddha, since in earlier times the souls of the departed were thought simply to be absorbed into the elements – and indeed, in some areas of south India belief in ghosts and spirits dwelling in stones still prevails over that of rebirth. **EMJ KMcL**

Further reading W.D. O'Flaherty, *Karma and Rebirth in Classical Indian Traditions*.

RELATIVITY

Albert Einstein (1879–1955) developed the theories of Special Relativity and General Relativity. Both demand that, to understand them, we discard familiar concepts about time and space.

Special relativity is the simpler theory of the two. It became obvious at the turn of the century that something was wrong with our ideas about space and time, when a series of experiments proved that the speed of light in air never changes, no matter whether the source of the light or the observer of the light are moving. This is not the case with something like sound. The measured speed of sound emitted by a moving car is equal to the normal speed of sound plus the speed of the car. However, a person inside the car measures just the normal speed of sound.

If we used light in this experiment rather than sound, then both we and the person in the car would measure the speed of light as being the same. This paradox was resolved by Einstein, who developed his theory using two axioms, or postulates. These were that the speed of light is always the same, regardless of the speed of the source or the observer, and that it is impossible to tell the difference between standing still and proceeding at a constant velocity.

The remarkable consequences of these assumptions include: (1) A person travelling close to the speed of light ages more slowly. This effect has been tested with a very accurate clock in Concorde – it had lost time after travelling around the world when compared to a clock that was kept on the ground. (2) It is impossible to exceed the speed of light if you try, you just get heavier! This has been shown to be true in particle accelerators, where electrons are accelerated up to 40,000 times their normal mass. (3) Moving objects grow shorter along their direction of motion.

We do not notice these effects, as they are very small at speeds less than a few percent of the speed of light, which is 300,000 kilometres per second.

General Relativity is a far more complex theory, involving tensor mathematics. Special Relativity only describes objects travelling at a constant speed, that do not turn, accelerate or decelerate. General Relativity includes all these phenomena. It has one basic postulate; that it is impossible to tell the difference between gravity and acceleration. Thus, an observer in a box, who feels what seems to be gravity acting downwards, cannot perform any experiment that will tell him whether he is in fact on the Earth, or in space accelerating upwards at a certain rate.

The consequences of this theory include: (1) The presence of a massive body (like a planet) slows down time in its vicinity. (2) Time stops at the surface of a black hole, that ultimate producer of gravity. (3) Even light will fall into a black hole. **JJ**

See also gravity; space and time.

Further reading H. Bondi, *Relativity and Common Sense*.

RELIGION

Humankind, it seems, has always felt the need to search for **God**, whether to survive in a hostile environment at a time when good weather, good hunting and the safe delivery of healthy children were crucial, or to explain the sense of awe and wonder inspired by particular events or sacred places, or to assuage the anguish in the human soul. The etymology of the word 'religion' (Latin, *religio*) is disputed, but the most logical is that it is a combination of *res*, 'a thing', and *ligare*, 'to bind'. Religion is thus what binds things together (such as families, societies, the world), and which enables humankind to live in harmony with the animal world and with the gods. In most societies it is the basis for morality and for all human relationships, especially where it is believed that there is a divine law controlling all things, and it gives meaning to life. Inequality and injustice in this life can be rectified by appeal to either divine intervention now, or to another dimension to which one can escape. Many religions promise personal transformation and/or that of society, in this life or the next, but essentially religion is concerned with this life.

To sociologists at least, one of the best ways of thinking about religion is in terms of what it is not. It is not necessarily the belief in one god (religions can involve many deities). It is not identifiable with moral prescriptions for human behaviour (the idea that gods are interested in behaviour on Earth is alien to many religions). It is not necessarily concerned with the origins of the world (some religions have myths of origin but many do not). It cannot be identified as intrinsically involving a belief in the supernatural (some beliefs and practices conventionally thought of as religious – **Buddhism**, for example – do not correspond to this definition).

What, then, is religion? The sociologist Émile Durkheim (1858–1917) defined religion as a system of **beliefs** and **rituals** which binds people together in terms of social groups. This certainly seems to include features that all religions have in common. Whether or not a religion involves a belief in god or the gods, there are virtually always objects which inspire awe. Religions practise diverse rituals and all religions involve ceremonials practised collectively by believers. Critics have pointed out, however, that such a definition is rather inclusive, since almost all public activity has an integrative effect on human groups. (Football matches are an example).

In Europe, after the wars of religion which followed the Reformation, the price for peace was the increasing secularization of society. The trend among monarchs in Roman Catholic countries was to keep the church at arm's length and drastically curtail its temporal power. In Protestant countries, this was paralleled by the demand that all denominations be treated equally. This coincided with the rise of modern science, and with the Evangelical revivals, with their heavy emphasis on personal piety. The result was that with the exception of events such as coronations, Remembrance Sunday, etc., religion became a private affair rather than a societal concern. In global terms, this was and is an aberration. In most countries outside the West, religion is viewed as embracing the whole of life (as **Christianity** does theoretically). In Islamic countries, for example, one sees clearly the effect of governing all life by religious practice; everything is done in response to the divine will. In India, there is no word for 'religion', only *dharma*, which could be translated as one's religious duties but also means the faith prescribed for each person, the duties one has to family, society and the gods, and above all the obligation to fulfil one's function in society to the best of one's ability. (This is the Latin concept of *pietas*, often misleadingly translated as 'piety'.) Neglect by one person threatens the well-being of the whole of society.

In other words, religion is not just something believers do; it defines what they are. Many scholars hold that religion involves not only the performance of rites, but also inner experience of an extra-personal reality. For this reason there is debate as to whether Buddhism is a religion or a **philosophy**, since no such reality was acknowledged until Buddhism had absorbed elements of **tribal religion**. In **Judaism** the same tension is resolved by the saying 'The fear of the Lord is the beginning of wisdom', and the command (shared with Christianity) to love the Lord God with heart and mind, soul and strength.

There would seem to be no authoritative answer to the question of whether religion is an innate quality of the human personality, or whether it is implanted by society and experience. But there is no denying the quality of the lives of saints of every faith, or of the fine **art**, **drama** and **literature** religion has inspired. In some faiths the answers are that there is within every person an element of the divine, or that the believer can become infused with God's spirit. In an uncertain and unstable world, religion offers many people security, marks the transitions from one stage of life to another, and offers an assurance of continuing existence after death. **DA RK EMJ KMcL**

See also animism; charisma; church; Confucianism; Daoism; Hinduism; Islam; secularization; Shinto.

Further reading S.S. Acquaviva, *The Decline of the Sacred in Industrial Society*; É. Durkheim, *The Elementary Forms of Religious Life* (1912); Mircea Eliade, *Patterns in Comparative Religions; A History of Religious Ideas* 3 vols; R. Robertson, *The Sociological Interpretation of Religion*; B.S. Turner, *Religion and Social Theory*.

RELIGIOUS ART

Religious **art**, in all traditions, from aboriginal cave paintings to Mantegna, from Cycladic figurines to carvings of Shiva dancing in the circle of fire, raises one immediate question: what is it for? The same can be asked of religious examples of the other arts: Indonesian dance-dramas, for instance, or Bach's B minor Mass. Are they created for the purposes of devotion and religious instruction, for aesthetic enjoyment, or for both at once? Clearly, a large proportion of religious art is mainly functional: a temple statue or Lutheran chorale exists, or at least was created, primarily to guide and aid worship. The ornate images in many Christian churches sequences, showing the Stations of the Cross, for example, or the Miracles of St Francis, were made to be what the Church called a *Biblia Pauperum* ('paupers' Bible'); a version of Scripture for those unable to read. There is also the matter of glorifying the divine: religious art is often rich and aesthetically satisfying because both the commissioning authorities and the craftsmen and women wanted it to be the best they could provide. Devotional purposes were not hindered by lavishness; indeed, they might even be enhanced.

The tendency to lavishness has, however, led in many cases to religious art becoming an object of wonder in its own right, divorced from its original purpose. Christian Books of Hours, for example, originally texts to assist private devotion, became so beautifully illustrated that by the late

Middle Ages in Europe they were among the most sumptuous possessions an aristocrat might own. Krishna images, or bracelets engraved with the opening of the Qur'an, similarly, began to be appreciated, and traded, for their beauty alone, with religious function playing a decidedly secondary role. It was as if people liked to own art which reminded them of their religious beliefs, rather than channelling or expressing them and once this happens, the gate is wide open for secular appreciation of the objects for their own sakes, and for commerce. Nowadays statues of Lord Buddha are owned and 'enjoyed' worldwide, by people who have no idea what Buddhism means or is; Palestrina's Masses are more often sung in concert halls, to paying audiences, than they are heard in church; Far Eastern sacred dramas, or the ceremonies of aboriginal peoples, are danced and sung for tourists. Religious art has taken its place in that huge museum of the world's treasures round which we cultural tourists all process – and the questions remain: is this what the art is really for, is true religious art really 'art' at all, and if we bastardize its true function by the use we now make of it, does this matter, and if so how and why? **KMcL**

RENAISSANCE

Renaissance ('rebirth', French translation of Italian *rinascimento*) was an artistic and intellectual movement in Europe during the 14th to 16th centuries. Its name comes from the idea, put forward originally by the 14th-century poets Petrarch and Dante, that it was time for the glories of the ancient classical **culture** to be reborn, that Europe could emerge from the slumber of the Middle Ages and remake itself in the image of (what seemed to them) the two noblest civilizations which had ever been. Three events crucial to the Renaissance, all in the early to mid–15th century, were to the development of printing, the fall of Constantinople to the Christians (which sent a flurry of scholars and a flood of classical manuscripts west, in some cases for the first time), and the Reformation in the Christian church.

In general terms, this last event is perhaps the most emblematic. The Middle Ages in Europe (taking their cue, perhaps, from the Roman Empire which preceded them) had been a time of monolithic prescriptivism in ideas, **law**, **politics**, **religion** and social life. The old (distantly Platonic) notion that there was, in every field of thought or endeavour, a single ideal had been corrupted into a dogmatism of power, and heterodoxy of any kind, from religious dissent to herbalism, from the writing of plays to the use of sixths and thirds in church music, had been debated (at best), discouraged, and sometimes punished with death. There had, to be sure, been a measure of artistic, intellectual and political activity, but by contrast with what preceded and followed it, and for all its (often considerable) technical and aesthetic quality, this now seems both uneventful and unadventurous.

From the 14th century onwards, by contrast, pluralism and experimentation became norms. Printing was crucial to this process, making ideas universally available instead of the property of a select and initiated few. One by one, the old certainties were re-examined. Some survived (political movement, for example, was far slower than any other); others were reinvigorated or junked. Ptolemy's model of the universe was totally discredited; systematic methods of diagnosis and treatment began to make their way into medical practice in place of a kind of *guru* approach to healing; in all the arts, from **architecture**, **painting** and **sculpture** (where the results were, perhaps, most noticeable) to **poetry**, **music** and **drama** (virtually reinvented overnight), the discovery that classical models existed and could be imitated and developed caused an explosion of the new activity whose reverberations can still be felt throughout Western culture. Most important of all, the idea of the dignity of Man (not to mention of every individual man and woman) replaced former notions of religious and social hierarchy, with devastating effects in law, learning, **philosophy** and eventually politics. It is this change that accelerated momentum for a challenge to the monolithic Roman Catholic view of Church and State: **humanism** and **Protestantism**, no less than the cathedral domes of Brunelleschi or the plays of Shakespeare, are the most glorious achievements of the Renaissance.

Europeans are perhaps prone to make too much of the Renaissance. It was, after all, the greatest period in their continent's history since the cultural dominance of ancient Rome. To outsiders, the Renaissance may seem no more important, globally speaking, than (for instance) the Heian period in Japan or the years of Mogul rule in India do to most Europeans. But for Europe, it was the time the continent reinvented itself: a true renaissance. The mercantile enterprise which had been increasing in previous centuries now led to exploration and expansion of trade worldwide (helped by improvements in chartmaking consequent on the abandonment of Ptolemy's fanciful geographies, and by the invention of the multi-sailed galley). This in turn triggered an increase in importance for the cities and countries of northern Europe, whose attitudes and practices were different from those of the previously-dominant south. New riches, spread among the bourgeoisie as well as the aristocracy, led to artistic patronage, and to an artistic efflorescence, on an unprecedented scale. **Science** shook itself free from the shackles imposed by Christian dogma and began seeking rational explanations for universal phenomena. The divine right of princes (whether of Church or State), a crucial medieval notion, began to be challenged: a first, small step on the on the long road to **democracy** and **equality**.

There is a dark side to almost all of this. In the arts, for example, new dogmatisms quickly began to replace the old ones: they were, perhaps, more numerous than before (a dozen ways to write plays or poems; a hundred 'isms' in architecture or painting) but they were just as programmatic. In religion, the rise of Protestantism led to Christian sectarianism on a massive scale, a development which was to have (and still has) catastrophic and bloody consequences throughout the world. In political life, the rise of individual towns and rulers all over Europe – at one stage there were 300 individual princedoms in Germany alone – led to persistent squabbles, uneasy alliances and often wars which were protracted as

they were pointless. The self-confidence Europeans had rediscovered, coupled with their new mobility beyond the continent, led them to regard other parts of the world not as the home of equals, but as places to be 'discovered', colonized and plundered. To some extent, this Eurocentric view of the world still persists – with justice, Europeans sometimes claim in their Eurocentric way – but in today's pluralist, multicultural world it seems an idea well past its time. **KMcL**

See also arts; academies of Western art; Catholic political thought; Christian art; Machiavellianism; perspective.

REPARATION

Reparation is the word Melanie Klein used for the healing, in **psychiatry**, of imagined and received injuries in infancy. It manifests itself in a desire for reconciliation and the ability to identify with other people in a caring and sensitive way. It is the time when the patient can let go of painful frustrations and suffering in the past. It results in the ability to love and be loved.

In Kleinian analysis the patient is seen to be the victim of persecutory and depressive anxieties which reduce the patient's relationship to the external world. This is finally worked through in the mourning period of analysis, the termination of therapy. Reparation takes place when there is an understanding of the patient's dependence on, and idealisation of, the internal objects that represent mother and father (the imagos). **MJ**

Further reading Hannah Segal, *An Introduction to the Work of Melanie Klein.*

REPRESENTATION

Representation, in communication studies, means the way in which signs are used to convey meaning, and refers to the construction of meaning within any system of communication: speech, writing, television, film, newspapers, video or academic discourse. It is through systems of representation that ideologies formulate and frame the things which concern them. The meanings within a particular system alter over time to accommodate change and challenge. As such, **feminism** is itself a system of representation with a matrix of meanings that pivot around the central notion of equality for women.

In the past, representation (in the form of speech and writing) was taken to be an objective measure of 'reality': a device mediating between our experience and the external world. This notion was overturned by, among others, Ferdinand de Saussure, Wittgenstein and Jacques Derrida, who in different ways argued that representation does not mediate between experience and 'reality', but, instead, that systems of representation categorize and determine our experience. In collapsing the distinction between 'inside' and 'outside' they considered that notions of truth were the product of particular systems of representation.

Theories of representation are particularly important in feminism. One of the main projects for feminisim was, and is, the task of uncovering hidden negative representations of women in **language** and in the **media**. But after the work of de Saussure and Derrida, especially, Elizabeth Cowie posed the question: how should we deal with representations of women if no fundamental truth could be accessed under patriarchal misrepresentations of women? Cowie and other feminists chose to deal with this question by highlighting the way in which representations are produced, and the way in which they formulate themselves as truth.

Many feminist theorists have used **psychoanalysis** to help explain how women are positioned within systems of representations. Jacqueline Rose, for example, argues that within the 'phallic' order 'woman', as a sign, represents difference and loss a usage which underpins the 'phallic' representational order. She argues that the representation of women as archaic and primordial, which often appears within feminist texts as a means of escaping the patriarchal construction of feminity, secures instead the 'phallic' order by replicating its representation of women as 'other'. Rose emphasizes, as does Cowie, the role of **fantasy** and the **unconscious** as one of the means by which we acquire gender identity within a representational system in which the phallus is

the primary signifier. The unconscious factor, they suggest, has been left out of many feminist explanations of sexual difference, which see sexual difference only in terms of external forces. **TK**

See also Marxist criticism.

Further reading D. Lusted, *The Media Studies Book.*

REPRESENTATIONAL ART see
Figurative Art

REPRESENTATIVE GOVERNMENT

In politics representatives 'stand for', 'act for', or symbolically represent others who are not, or cannot be, present: that is the root meaning of the Latin word. Representative government developed in most agrarian empires and kingdoms where estates, classes, castes and religious clergy were 'represented' by selected or elected agents. The election of agents lays the foundations for the modern idea of representative government, which has become a synonym for the systems of indirect **democracy** through which all advanced industrial societies are governed.

Under modern systems of representative government elected officials 'represent the people', who, though sovereign, cannot be in continuous assembly deliberating over public policy. Aside from specific arrangements enabling popular initiatives to mandate referendums, or specific procedures requiring referendums before constitutional change, citizens do not directly determine the **law** or public policy under systems of representative government. In effect representative government applies the principle of the **division of labour** to democracy. Specialists in politics make policy, and the people reject their services if they prove incompetent.

The idea of representative government has always been variously interpreted. Conservative thinkers, suspicious of the capabilities of the mob, like Edmund Burke, emphasize the benefits of autonomous representatives who, once elected, are required only to do what they think is best for their constituents: representatives are not, and should not be, delegates. By contrast, radical democrats, like Rousseau and Karl Marx, argue that representatives should be delegates, subject to a right of recall by their constituents, otherwise, as Rousseau remarked, the people are free only on the day they elect their representatives.

There are two basic forms of representative government in the contemporary world: parliamentary and presidential government. Under *parliamentary government* executive and legislative powers are held by the members of a representative assembly. The Westminster parliament was the earliest and prototypical form of parliamentary government, though considerable variations have subsequently emerged in continental European and Commonwealth governmental systems. The executive in a parliamentary system is chosen either by the majority party, or through negotiation among minority parties when no majority party exists. The executive consists of a prime minister (or chancellor) and a cabinet of ministers responsible for individual departments or ministries. Strong executive powers to form public policies and shape legislation are granted to the cabinet through the customs of parliamentary privilege, privacy and collective cabinet responsibility. These apparently arbitrary powers are counterbalanced by the principle of *responsible government* which requires individual ministers to be fully accountable for the performance of their ministries, and mandates that failure in the performance of duties should lead to the resignation of the responsible minister (a principle now more honoured in the breach than the observance). According to the same principle of responsible government the failure of the executive to maintain the confidence of a majority of the members of parliament usually leads to the government's resignation.

Parliamentary assemblies are either one chamber (unicameral) or bicameral, composed of an upper and a lower house. The form of representation varies from one system to another. The members of the upper house may be appointed by the lower house (in systems where the upper house is limited to residual and supervisory powers) or they may be elected representatives (where the upper house is responsible for the passage of legislation). Members of the lower house are traditionally meant to be representative of 'the people'; members of the upper house are normally representatives of regions, states or provinces though in the eccentric British case the descendants of aristocrats sit in the House of Lords. The primary functions of a parliamentary assembly are to choose the government, provide a forum for public debate, to create and pass legislation, to authorize the collection and allocation of public finances, and to act as a means through which citizens' grievances can be raised and remedied. Legislation is normally created in committees and then presented to the whole house for debate before a vote is taken to pass or reject it.

Parliamentary government is often contrasted with *presidential government*, in which executive and legislative powers are more sharply separated, and the executive is directly elected by the people rather than by an elected assembly. Presidential government is necessarily found in a republic. The president is the head of state, and may also be the head of the executive. However, it is only in the latter case that most people speak of presidential government. Republics with parliamentary systems, like India, Ireland, Italy, and Germany, have presidents whose duties and powers are largely ceremonial. Under a dual executive system, like that in France, the president has considerable potential power in foreign affairs and domestic policies, but day-to-day conduct of the government is under the authority of the prime minister: such systems are often called 'semi-presidential'. The most common form of presidential government, found especially in the US and in Latin America, is the limited presidential executive who is simultaneously the head of state and the head of government. Such presidents are directly elected, and independent of a separately elected congressional assembly (consisting of one or two houses). They are checked and balanced by that assembly, and by judicial review. The president can veto congressional legislation, but such a veto can be overturned by an extraordinary congressional majority. Such presidents usually require congressional approval for declaring war, making foreign treaties, and appointing cabinet members and supreme court justices. (There is also a considerable number of states which operate with an 'unlimited' presidential executive, i.e. dictatorships, which are not authentic systems of representative government.)

Presidential systems of government are usually criticized for three reasons: (1) temporal rigidity, (2) majoritarianism, and (3) creating crises of dual legitimacy. The first criticism focuses on the fact that a presidential term is usually fixed. Such provisions may make a president insensitive to public opinion (especially because impeachment is difficult). Conversely, presidents nearing the end of their terms of office lose much of their authority, and the limits on presidential terms (two in the US) seem inflexible when there is a highly popular and competent president. The second criticism is based on the fact that a presidential system appears to be necessarily majoritarian: the winner must get 50% + 1. It is argued that this trait makes presidents less likely to be sensitive to minorities and makes electoral contests into divisive 'winner takes all' disputes. (However, this criticism depends on the idea that presidentialism requires one president. This is the normal case, but there can be collective presidencies). Finally, presidents and assemblies have dual legitimacies, which can create political crises if there is a deadlock. Both can claim to be representatives of the people, even though they are elected in different ways. For these reasons, among others, many have argued that presidentialism is inferior to parliamentary government, and more likely to lead to a breakdown of a democratic system. Defenders of presidentialism argue that if we look at the breakdown of democratic régimes (in states of more than 200,000 people) in the 20th century the evidence is mixed: 50% of presidential systems have broken down compared with 44% of parliamentary systems. They also argue that presidentialism, by contrast with parliamentary government, assists accountability, enables the electorate to identify clearly who will be responsible for executive government, creates a useful system of checks and balances which promotes consensual government, and establishes an institution with the capacity to arbitrate conflict.

In all systems of representative government *political parties* have become the primary indirect mechanism of representation: literally representing 'parts' of society. Political parties are formal voluntary organizations which attempt to gain control of government to represent the ideas and interests of one or more groups within society. Formal political parties emerged in Europe and North America in the 18th and early 19th centuries when social processes associated with industrialization led to the enlargement of electorates, greater democratization, and then to the development of formal organizations to represent the ideas and interests of those electorates.

In modern democracies political parties may organize around social **cleavages**, ideas and **ideologies**, or they may attempt to be 'catch-all' parties which, in principle, can appeal to everybody. In most political systems there is a left-right, conservative-liberal, or conservative-liberal-socialist spectrum of parties, but this left-right spectrum may not be the defining or dominant feature of the party system. Other cleavages and ideas, singly and in combination, also play important roles in the formation of parties (for example, religion, ethnicity, nationalism, language, and region); while more mundane factors, like faction-fights and clientelism, may lead to the fragmentation of leftist, centrist and rightist political parties. In countries which are relatively religiously, linguistically and ethnically homogeneous it is common to find catch-all parties which represent a wide range of diverse interests. In states with **election systems** based on proportional representation it is more common to find small, single-issue parties, or parties which seek to represent 'communities of belonging' rather than appealing to as many people as possible.

Party systems in representative democracies are distinguished primarily by the size and effective number of parties which compete in elections. Political scientists and politicians regularly debate the merits of two-party systems and multi-party systems.

The advantages of the two-party system are alleged to include: a clearer choice for the electorate; alternation between two dominant parties which guarantees accountability of the party in office and prevents one-party dominance; a guaranteed majority which leads to effective government; and incentives for parties to be responsive and pragmatic rather than ideological. Each of these claims is contested: two-party systems may create centrist parties which fail to represent non-mainstream views; neither pragmatism nor alternation are guaranteed by a two-party system (as exemplified by continuous Conservative rule in the UK since 1979); a two-party presidential system may lead to stalemate between the executive and the congress if one party each has control of one institution (as in the US from 1980 until 1992). The advantages of multi-party systems are said to include: a wider array of political opinion being represented in parliament or congress; the absence of a majority party obliges the leaders of minority parties and coalitions to explore fully the merits and pitfalls of diverse policies; and the stable representation of non-mainstream or minority views discourages extra-constitutional challenges to the political order. However, critics argue that multi-party systems may be less stable and less effective because coalition governments must accommodate diverse political interests; in the limiting case of postwar Italy the average life span of a government has been less than 10 months. But other multi-party systems are more stable. In the Scandinavian countries and Germany where multi-party systems are comprised of one dominant party and two or three minor parties, stable and effective government has been achieved through varying coalitions, thus combining effectiveness and stability with continued representation for minor parties. **Consociationalism** represents a form of multi-party representative government in societies which are linguistically, religiously or ethnically divided, and, where it works, shows that the engineering skills involved in designing effective representative government are some of the most important social tools of our world.
BO'L

See also conservatism; federalism; liberalism; socialism and social democracy.

Further reading A. Lijphart, *Democracies*; A. Lijphart (ed.), *Parliamentary Versus Presidential Government*; G. Sartori, *Parties and Party Systems: a Framework for Analysis, vol. 1*; M.S. Shugart and J.M. Carey, *Presidents and Assemblies*; A. Ware, *Political Parties: Electoral Change and Structural Response*.

REPRESENTATIVE THEORY OF PERCEPTION

This is the theory, in **philosophy**, that when one perceives an object, the immediate object of one's awareness is a sensory experience which represents the object. One is not immediately or directly aware of the object itself. The main motivation for the representative theory of perception is the argument from illusion.

Adherents to the disjunctive theory of perception are unimpressed by the fact that when one hallucinates the immediate object of one's awareness is a sensory experience which represents a object, and not the (nonexistent) object itself. They insist that when one perceives an object the immediate object of one's awareness is the object, and not merely a sensory experience as of it. So when one seems to see a dagger, the immediate object of one's awareness is either the dagger which one really is seeing, or a sensory experience as of a dagger which one is merely hallucinating.

Many suppose that the representative theory of perception must be false, because if it were true then we would be stuck behind a veil of appearances, never having direct contact with objects in the external world. Since one could directly perceive objects in the external world, one would never be able to check that the world really is as it seems to be.

But the disjunctive theory of perception also seems vulnerable to sceptical worries. Since it also allows that hallucinating an object is phenomenologically indistinguishable from (feels exactly the same as) perceiving it, advocates of the disjunctive theory are vulnerable to the worry that, for all one knows, whenever one seems to be perceiving an object one is really the victim of a massive perceptual illusion. Their claim that if one is perceiving an object, then one is directly perceiving it and not just one's sensory experience as of it, does nothing to block this sceptical line of thought. **AJ**

See also idealism; illusion, argument from; naive realism; scepticism.

Further reading A.J. Ayer, *The Central Questions of Philosophy*; J. Dancy, *Perceptual Knowledge*.

REPRESSION see Defence Mechanism

REPRODUCTION

Many feminists consider that the capacity to conceive and give birth to children are pivotal to **patriarchy**'s oppression of women. Juliet Mitchell, for example, identifies reproduction as one of the four main areas of women's oppression. Feminists have looked at how patriarchy controls reproduction and the care of children, and have sought strategies for transforming the ways in which motherhood and child-care are conceptualized. They have fought for women's right to control their own reproductive function through the use of contraception and the right to abortion. The right to choose is still an important issue in contemporary political campaigns such as the National Abortion Campaign and within women's health groups. In some countries these rights still do not exist and in other countries these rights are continuously in danger of being eroded.

Some feminist theorists have separated the reproductive function from **sexuality**, seeing this as a means of breaking down the identification of women with bringing up children. This separation enables some feminists to talk about female sexual pleasure and **eroticism** in social terms rather than as an extension of biological function. Other feminists have seen reproduction and child-care as being intrinsic to women's experience and do not wish to separate the reproductive function from sexuality.

As the project of feminism is to establish a critical re-examination of male-dominated systems of knowledge, medical methodology and science have come under a great deal of scrutiny. An example of male control of medicine has been found by feminist historians in the case of midwifery, where documented evidence shows that the role of women as midwives was consciously diminished and displaced by the male, medical professional. Shulamith Firestone criticizes medical science for its lack of interest in making the process of child-bearing external to the body. She also argues that both child-bearing and child-rearing should be a social responsibility and not seen as an exclusively female task. Julia Kristeva laments the rejection of motherhood by some radical feminists and asks for a new understanding of the physical and psychic agony of childbirth and child-rearing (see **representation**). Adrienne Rich has distinguised between a patriarchal view of motherhood and women's actual experience of motherhood. **TK**

Further reading Boston Women's Health Collective, *Our Bodies, Ourselves*; Shulamith Firestone, *The Dialectic of Sex*; Adrienne Rich, *Of Woman Born: Motherhood as Experience and Institution*.

REPRODUCTION IN FINE ART

Reproduction, in fine **art**, is the multiplication of an original work of art or **design** by mechanical means. It may be either in three dimensions (for example, plaster casts) or two dimensions (for example, images made by the techniques of woodcutting, engraving or etching). While a bronze made from a maquette by Rodin, for instance, is a kind of reproduction, allowing a foundry to make any number of 'copies' of the original, most commonly reproduction serves to make multiple copies of an independent work, for example the six engraved scenes of Hogarth's *Marriage à la Mode* (1742–44). Engravings of this kind are called reproductive engraving. A similar kind of reproduction would be a plaster cast of the Laocoön group.

The invention of the printed book provided an impetus for the production of illustrations for the book trade. These early prints were woodcuts: that is, a relief print where a raised surface receives the ink. The invention of the technique of intaglio printing (where the ink is held in a groove cut into a metal, usually copper, plate) improved the precision of the image, allowing more detail. As a means of reproduction, the engraving enabled engravers to publicize the work of fine-artists: a good example is Marcantonio Raimondi's engravings after the work of Raphael. Indeed, Raphael in part owes his pre-eminence among artists to the quality and availability not of his own work, but of reproductions.

Reproduction techniques changed little until the 19th century. Works of art continued to be reproduced by engraving, aided by the development of new techniques such as etching (where the copper plate is bitten back with acid to provide the vehicle for the ink); mezzotint (where the plate is roughened to accept the ink); and aquatint (where the surface is treated with powdered resin). The invention of lithography early in the 19th century meant that an artist was able to draw directly onto stone. This was important, as the lithographic print did not express the artist's ideas at second hand, but directly. But all of these mechanical means of reproduction shared an inability to reproduce the material properties of the original. In response to this failure manual copies offered a reproduction imbued with the human touch. Museums of these copies, such as the Musée des Copies, Paris and the Cast Courts at the Victoria and Albert Musuem, London, offered the public surrogate originals. But the advent of **photography** (seen erroneously as translating an original without interposing its own processes) cost the manual copy its constituency.

The invention of photography led to the development of photo-mechanical reproductive processes such as photo-engraving, in which the original to be copied is photographed onto a sensitized zinc plate which is then immersed in acid in the same way as in the intaglio methods of printing noted above. Modern colour printing, such as we see every day, is a reproductive process based on the successive overprinting of three, sometimes four, colours to give the reproduction a full range of lifelike tones. But no more than the woodblock are these prints able to transcribe the true material aspect of the original; nor can they possess what Walter Benjamin has called the 'aura' of the work of art: its lived presence in space and time. Following Benjamin, John Berger based an important chapter of his *Ways of Seeing* on the impact of reproductions on our perception of art. Today colour slides and colour illustrations are the tools of art historians, students of art history and a large number of the public; but while a reproduction facilitates access to any number of images, it also distorts (and, if Benjamin and Berger are right, impairs) our ability to experience directly the authentic work of art. **PD MG**

REPUBLICANISM

Republicanism is the antonym of **monarchism**, and is the political doctrine that political **sovereignty** should reside with the citizens of a state, bound by a **social contract** to obey laws, and whose rights as are guaranteed by a constitution. Early forms of republicanism, as established in ancient Greece, ancient India and the Roman city-state, replaced the arbitrary (and often tyrannical) rule of monarchs or despots, either with a directly sovereign popular assembly, or, as in Rome, with a 'mixed' form of government, based on a **separation of powers** between elected generals or consuls, a senate, representing the aristocracy, and a forum representing the citizens. In classical republican thought participation in government was meant to inspire public virtue, whence the expression 'civic republicanism'.

The merits of mixed government and citizen participation was echoed by **Renaissance** republican thinkers, like Machiavelli, who emphasized the centrality of patriotism in preserving civic virtue. Republicanism, especially as prefigured in James Harrington's *Oceana* (1656), and Rousseau's *Social Contract* (1764), later inspired 18th-century revolutionaries in America and France. The establishment of the USA and the writing of its constitution significantly advanced republicanism because it firmly established the principle of the separation of powers and included a bill of rights to protect the liberty of the citizenry (see **civil liberties** and **civil rights**). Most importantly the USA represented an extension of republican government beyond the unit of the city-state, to that of a larger entity. The fact that republicanism could be exercised at the level of the nation-state, in a federation or confederation (see **federalism**), through a system of representative government, immensely increased the plausibility of republican government as an alternative to monarchism or dynastic rule.

Today, formally republican forms of government are firmly established in most states of the world: that is, most states are not *ancien régime* monarchies. Although the last king or queen has not yet been beheaded many constitutional monarchies are in fact disguised republics in which sovereignty rests with the people and the monarch is purely a symbolic head of state: though in some countries, notably the United Kingdom and Australia, full-blooded republicanism is being revived. However, many formal republics are in fact tyrannical dictatorships bereft of the elements of constitutionalism, popular government, the rule of law and civic participation which are integral components of the authentic republican vision. The genuine civic republican emphasis on the virtues of political participation and the merits of social equality as ways of energizing political institutions remains vibrant in the thinking of liberal and democratic socialist writers. **BO'L**

See also liberalism; socialism and social democracy.

Further reading A. Hamilton, J. Madison and J. Jay, *The Federalist Papers* (ed.) I. Kramnick; J.A.G. Pocock, *The Machiavellian Moment: Florentine Political Thought and the Atlantic Political Tradition*; Q. Skinner, *The Foundations of Modern Political Thought: Volume 1; The Renaissance*.

RESISTANCE

Resistance, in **psychoanalysis**, is the power possessed by an individual to deny self-knowledge. Freud's hysterical patients put up resistance to remembering scenes which precipitated their symptoms. They denied the existence of the traumatic incidents responsible for their illness. In Freud's own self-analysis he realized that he resisted forming certain conclusions about himself in the same way as his patients because the facing of repressed material was painful. Overcoming his patients' resistances became a key part of the psychoanalytical work. Dreamers did not wish to accept wish-fulfilling interpretations of their dreams, and were reluctant to look at their latent content. Freud also found that a large number of cases of resistance related to sexual ideas dating from childhood. Incest and wishes involving the sexual, 'perverted acts' of the mouth, anus or genitals often occur in free association. Resistance has come to be used as a general term for a patient's or client's resistance to formulations in psychodynamic analysis. **MJ**

RESONANCE

Physical scientists describe many varied examples of resonant phenomena. One example often quoted is the playground swing, which must be pushed at the correct intervals to attain a good amplitude of swing. Another is the behaviour of water in a vessel – the water in a bath slops out if it is swished back and forth at the right frequency. A diver bounces on the board at the correct frequency to build up a good 'spring'. All such events depend upon resonance.

All objects have what is known as a natural frequency. This is the frequency at which they will happily oscillate, and which, if given a sudden impulse, they will settle down into. An excellent example of this is a pendulum: given a push, it will begin to swing at its natural frequency.

Resonance occurs when we push or strike an object at or close to its resonant frequency. Pushing a swing at random intervals will not achieve very much, but as soon as we find the resonant frequency, the swing responds and goes much higher. The closer the applied or driving frequency approaches to the resonant frequency, the more the object responds and oscillates.

Resonance is vital to musical instruments. Sound boxes are designed to resonate at the frequencies produced by the strings within them, thus producing a better sound. Strings will vibrate if a note at their natural frequency is played close to them.

The resonant frequency of buildings and similar structures must be investigated carefully to avoid damage, as a building may shake violently if a force is applied to it at the right frequency. The best-known example of this was the Tacoma Narrows bridge, in the state of Washington. The wind, gusting at a steady rate, caused the bridge to twist like a piece of ribbon until it was totally destroyed. Bridges nowadays have shorter spans to alter their natural frequency and prevent similar disasters. **JJ**

RESOURCE DEPLETION

Depletion of vital resources is often put forward by environmentalists as one of the principal ways that environment influences human society. The idea was most spectacularly presented in *The Limits to Growth*, a book which used computer models to argue that current rates of increase in consumption of vital resources would lead to disastrous shortages within a few decades. The methods used to make these predictions were subsequently discredited, but the concern over resources remains.

Resources are natural products or processes which are used to provide materials or energy for human use. Their effective abundance depends on the natural processes that make them available and the social processes which decide which are actually used. Natural materials can only be used if they are identified and if technology is capable of extracting them and transforming them into useful products. In the modern world, they tend to be used only if they are cheaper than alternatives, though politics can also influence whether or not a resource is used.

Resources are categorized into two types. *Stock* resources are those which exist in finite quantities, usually as a result of geological concentration over very long timescales. *Flow* (or continuous or renewable) resources are those which can be used

and reused as long as they are not damaged by over use. Resource depletion has different meanings for the two types.

The obvious examples of stock resources are metal ores and fossil fuels. In fact modern society uses much larger quantities of building stone or aggregate, but with rare exceptions such stone is of low value and is only transported short distances. The concept of an ore is tautologous because metals exist in almost all rocks, but only those with the highest concentrations of the most suitable chemical composition are regarded as ores. Different metals are exploited at very different concentrations. Iron, which is abundant in nature and makes up 95% of all metal traded, is only exploited when ores contain more than 25% iron; copper is extracted from ores with only 0.5%; metals like gold, uranium and mercury are extracted at much lower concentrations. In no case are ores likely to be exhausted: if the most concentrated ores are used up, the response will be more intensive prospecting, and even if that fails less-concentrated sources will be available. However, lower grade ores will be more expensive, will require more energy to refine and will produce larger voids and more spoil. Increasing cost may stimulate efforts to recycle metals or to substitute alternative products, and so it is unlikely that, with a few exceptions like silver, tungsten and tin, metals will be the most acute resource problem.

The stock resource most likely to cause problems of depletion is fossil fuel, especially petroleum and natural gas. During this century consumption has increased exponentially until more than half of commercial energy comes from these two sources. Unfortunately, they are geologically rare and it is proving more and more difficult to find new fields. Even optimists calculate that oil and gas will be acutely scarce in a few decades if current trends continue. Although coal has been used over a longer period, there appear to be sufficient reserves for a century or more. Given the dominant role of fossil fuels in energy supply, dramatic changes will be needed to conserve them even if the **pollution** impacts are ignored. It is also significant that oil is potentially more valuable in the long term as a source of raw materials for the chemical industry than it is as a fuel. There are thus several lines of argument which indicate a need to reduce use of fossil fuels for energy and hence a need to become more energy efficient and/or to use renewable energy resources.

Renewable energy is one of three kinds of continuous resource. *Solar radiation* is both a continuous resource in itself and also the motive power of *natural cycles* which supply air and fresh water as well as wind, hydro and wave energy. Natural *ecosystems* offer a harvest of animal and vegetable products or can be cleared to use the soil to grow agricultural crops. The throughput of energy through these systems is enormous: only 0.2% of the solar energy entering the atmosphere is used in photosynthesis, but this is 30 times as much as the total consumption of fossil fuel and nuclear energy. So the resource base exists for a move to renewable energy and the economics are competitive. What seems to be lacking at present in most countries is the political will, perhaps because renewable energy technologies are still seen as 'low-tech' or 'alternative', and therefore suspect. Also, a move to the use of continuous resources may require a move to a more dispersed supply, and so raise problems of organization and ownership in sustaining the resource and distributing the benefit. These problems are not easy to overcome, as shown in the case of the other flow resources. Human activities cannot significantly affect solar radiation or the wind and waves, but they can lead to soil erosion and desertification.

The technical problems of managing continuous resources are not all that difficult, but the social problems are harder to overcome. A particularly problematic situation is that of managing resources held in common. Garret Hardin crystallized the problem in his description of 'the tragedy of the commons'. If many people live on the produce of a common resource, such as an area of grazing land or the fish from a lake, each individual may gain by exploiting the resource more intensively. But if everybody does so the result is overuse and reduction of the output. Some

mechanism is required to regulate exploitation to a level that does not damage the resource. Some experts advocate private ownership, though it is easier to achieve for the land rather than the lake and hard to contemplate for atmosphere or ocean, while others press for co-operative arrangements, whether between villagers or between countries. However, the continuing disputes over fisheries and whaling are an indication that sustainable management of common resources is an intractable problem. It is particularly so where the individuals or groups concerned are poor.

Deforestation is a particularly emotive resource-management issue, with widespread criticism by the First World of destruction of tropical forests and of trees in the semiarid tropics. But this is not a black and white issue: the effects of deforestation of hills, with soil erosion in the uplands and floods and deposition of stones and boulders in the lowlands, has been known in Mediterranean countries for 2,000 years. Massive deforestation has occurred in the old world and the eastern US, some producing productive farmland, but not always without flooding and erosion. Clearance of trees in the tropics is more hazardous than in temperate areas because the heavy rain makes erosion more likely. The potential benefits are often small because tropical soils are typically infertile. But most of those involved in clearance have pressing short-term reasons: demand from the First World gives logging companies the incentive, ranchers may get government subsidies for clearance to produce meat for export, landless peasants need land to grow food to survive, or have no other fuel to cook with. The solutions may lie, as the tragedy of the commons suggested, in changing patterns of land ownership and in international agreements on the terms of trade. Like the management techniques themselves, the social organization of resource management needs to take a long-term perspective, but such a perspective is hard to achieve when individuals are concerned with survival and companies are concerned with short-term profits rather than long-term assets. **PS**

RESPONSIBILITY AND MORAL LUCK

One is responsible for one's actions just if one can be held accountable for them, and so can be praised or blamed for them. One is responsible for one's actions only if they were within one's control. Nagel has argued that the notion of moral luck is incoherent. This is the idea that one's moral status, that one's being worthy of blame or praise, can be affected by factors beyond one's control, by one's luck.

Suppose that two drivers get drunk and crash onto a pavement. One is lucky: no one is on the pavement. The other is unlucky: a child is on the pavement and is killed by the collision. There were thus two very different outcomes. The first outcome was a car crash in which no one was hurt. The second outcome was the death of a child. But the two drivers' contributions to these outcomes were exactly the same. They both got drunk. The difference between the outcomes was determined by a factor beyond the drivers' control, whether or not someone was on the pavement they mounted. The difference between the outcomes was determined by luck. So, Nagel argues, the drivers must be equally culpable. **AJ**

See also freedom and determinism.

Further reading T. Nagel, *Moral Questions*; B. Williams, *Moral Luck*.

REVELATION

In the Greek New Testament the word for 'revelation' is *apocalypsis* ('uncovering'), the word which gives us the English word 'apocalyptic'. This is an indication of the import of revelation: the unveiling of God's purpose for the end of the age. It involves seeing God as he really is.

The concept of revelation gives authority to **scripture** in the world religions of **Christianity**, **Islam**, **Judaism** and **Sikhism**, since their scriptures are held to be the vehicle of the revelation of the truth. However, conflict arises between those who see revealed truth as a set of propositions on a sliding scale, some of which can be comprehended by reason (which means that revelation can also be found in natural **philosophy**) and some which can be grasped only by **faith**. This leads to a distinction between **natural theology** and revealed theology and to a debate about the extent to which human reason can comprehend divine truth. Another controversy, between **Catholics** and **Protestants** in Christianity and between certain traditions in Judaism, is whether God reveals truth beyond what is set down in scripture. Does extra-scriptural tradition contain revelation? For Christians, at least, the answer has been to find everything necessary for salvation in the Bible (as 'special revelation'), and to label everything else as 'general revelation', accessible to all humankind, indeed what makes people human. This position has been maintained despite the collapse of the idea of scriptural inerrancy in the face of modern biblical criticism: religions which forbid the textual criticism of their scriptures do not have this problem. Belief that general revelation is possible means for some that their God can communicate through the belief systems of other faiths, and thus that inter-faith dialogue is possible. Such dialogue is likely to be even more meaningful if one perceives that revelation is not confined to one set of scriptures, and that God is still revealing his truth in world history. **EMJ**

Further reading Emil Brunner, *Revelation and Reason*; H.R. Niebuhr, *The Meaning of Revelation*.

REVENGE TRAGEDY

Revenge Tragedy is a form of European **drama** in which the protagonist is called to right a wrong done to him (historically, rarely her) or a member of his family in the absence of means of legal redress. Revenge is a staple element of drama in general, from the *Oresteia* to Alan Ayckbourn's *The Revenger's Comedies*, but Revenge Tragedy as a specific form is particularly associated with the love and duty tragedies of Corneille, Calderón and Lope de Vega, and with English **Renaissance** drama. In English Revenge Tragedy the ingredients often include a heady mixture of ghosts, skulls, macabre deaths, madness, poisoning and political, social, physical and metaphysical corruption. *Hamlet* is the best-known of revenge tragedies. Tragedy of Blood is a term used as virtually synonymous with Revenge Tragedy. **TRG SS**

Further reading Fredson Bowers, *Elizabethan Revenge Tragedy;* Northrop Frye, *Anatomy of Criticism.*

REVISIONISM

In **historical** studies, revisionism (Latin, 'seeing again') is a 20th-century phenomenon: either (politely put) the revising of particular views of events in the past or (less politely put) the rewriting of history. It first appeared in the 1890s, when orthodox Marxists used it as a term of ideological abuse for those in the movement who sought to challenge, or reinterpret, Marx's views in ways which deviated from the official line. In the 1930s it was applied in a completely different context, to attempts by countries in central and eastern Europe to rewrite the geography of their areas following World War I. In the 1960s, finally, it was one side of an argument among US historians, about who was to blame for World War II and then the Cold War: revisionist historians blamed the economic policies and (what they perceived as the) imperialistic ambitions of the USA.

In the **arts**, revisionism is often the work of historians engaged, sometimes in a confrontational manner, in the re-establishment of neglected or derelict reputations; an example is the rediscovery by 20th-century feminist critics of many female European painters of the last 500 years. Such revisions are not always accepted by those holding what they take to be more orthodox opinions, usually on the grounds that the creators involved have earned their obscurity by lack of talent rather than the malignancy of outside forces. The revisionist answers are: (1) that the construction of any history is an exercise in value-judgement; and (2) that the work under consideration has aesthetic as well as political claims on our attention. Revisionism is most contentious among scholars of the visual arts; in the other arts, it is both less controversial and more successful, those benefiting include such writers as Svevo

and Trollope, and such composers as Alkan, Telemann and even Bach (whose 'rediscovery' by Mendelssohn in the 1830s was one of the first and most dazzling 'revisionist' coups in any of the arts). **KMcL**

REVIVALISM

Much of Western **art** history is the story of revivals, of the resurrection of forms and ideas slightly or radically adapted to suit new contexts and horizons. Eastern art, by contrast, being traditional and assimilative in nature, has tended to follow a course of continuous evolution – or, at times, centuries-long stagnation – rather than the fits-and-starts, leapfrogging process implied by revivalism in the West.

Most artistic revivals have an intellectual rationale and are not simply stylistic. They often originate directly from or reflect developments in **literature**. Nor is revivalism always a protest against the prevailing taste of a particular period. It is, instead, complementary, succeeding if it fills a need and failing otherwise. The **Renaissance** was a revival of classical ideas and themes, as were Fascist art and architecture under Mussolini. In both, a programme is identifiable, and such assimilation of the past is not necessarily a bar to originality and innovation.

Revivalism seems to occur throughout history (for example, the medieval revivals of Early Christian styles, the **Baroque** interest in Hellenistic antiquity and the 19th-century **Gothic Revival**: see below), but in the 18th and 19th centuries the phenomenon was especially strong and varied. Because of trade, travel, scholarship and conquest, a whole series of extra-European revivals occurred, including Indian, Chinese and Persian. However, these were short-lived because they were of interest to only a few, and impractical to apply thoroughly except in the decorative arts. The Greek and Etruscan revivals are much stronger because they were part of the classical tradition, which is a constant in European arts.

Strongest of all, throughout Europe, were the medieval revivals, such as the **Romanesque** but especially the Gothic Revival. They were successful not only because there was a developing interest in history, but because they served specific yearnings to reinvigorate national pasts (the same applies to the Colonial revival in the USA). France, England, Scotland, Wales and the German states all had their own particular forms, bolstered by medieval literature (some of it recent forgeries) and by the sentiment that Gothic was a suitable language for church architecture, matching a classicism largely accepted for the civic life. **PD MG JM**

Further reading K. Clark, *The Gothic Revival: an Essay in the History of Taste.*

REVOLUTION

A political revolution is a systemic transformation in the political institutions of the state, involving a change in the powerholders and the system of government. Jack Goldstone distinguishes three major processes which make up a complete political revolution: the breakdown of the control of the central state; competition for control after the development of a 'power vacuum'; and the formation of new institutions. A fully blown social revolution additionally requires a systematic transformation of property relations.

A revolution may occur primarily in a peaceful way, as with the breakdown of communist rule in much of eastern Europe and the Soviet Union, but has more usually been thought to require the use of violence on the part of revolutionaries: as in the Bolshevik Revolution or Cuban revolutions. While liberal revolutions have often been peaceful, communist revolutions have never been peaceful.

The earliest theories of revolution were probably those expressed by Plato and Aristotle who differed in their view of the inevitability of a progression from good to tyrannical forms of government. However, most classical and medieval political thinkers focused on the issue of whether or not, or when, rebellion against tyranny might be justified, rather than on the properties of revolutions, or systematic explanations of their occurrence. The exception was the richly political and sociological account of revolutions in the Islamic world found in the writings of Ibn Khaldun (see **Islamic political thought**), and which some have found helpful in interpreting the recent Iranian revolution.

Explanatory theories of revolution can be broken down roughly into state-centred and society-centred approaches, as preferred by political scientists and sociologists respectively. Following the paradigmatic French Revolution of 1789 Alexis de Tocqueville in the 19th century, Crane Brinton in the early 20th and Samuel Huntington in the second half of the 20th century all focused on the inability of the state to meet rising societal expectations, and its institutional incapacity to manage political demands produced by rapid economic growth and a fiscal crisis. In this perspective revolutions occur not because they are willed, but because states and their institutions break down. Society-centred explanations, by contrast, emphasize the effects of changing social structures and modernization as catalysts of revolution. Marx and Engels argued that the evolution of **capitalism** would produce severe inequalities between workers and capitalists. The 'crisis of capitalism' would lead to a revolution which would enable the proletariat to wrest control of the means of production (see **Marxism**). Revisionist Marxists subsequently developed less deterministic theories, allowing for the possibility of non-violent revolution, or focusing on the revolutionary capacities of peasants, as opposed to urban workers. In the 1960s, political sociologists like Ted Gurr shifted the focus to the motivational aspects of individuals and groups. He argued that 'relative deprivation' led to aggressive responses to the frustration of felt needs, and if sufficiently organized against a weak or inept state such motivations could lead to revolution. In the 1970s, Charles Tilly argued that the 'mobilization of resources' was more important than deprivation in explaining revolution. Deprivation is ubiquitous but rebellion is rare. As Trotsky once put it 'poverty is not the cause of revolution, if it was the masses would always be in revolt'.

The most ambitious theories of revolution attempt to combine state-centred and society-centred approaches. Barrington Moore sought to explain the patterns of the major revolutions of the modern world through a comparative focus on the class and political structures of **agrarian societies**, while his student Theda Skocpol argued that a combination of over-extension in international conflicts and internal social and fiscal crises explained the French, Russian and Chinese revolutions. However, both have been criticized, especially for downplaying the active role played by revolutionaries in bringing about revolutions especially in the Russian and Chinese cases.

Presently much of the literature devoted to explaining revolutions is less ambitious. McAdam's 'political process' model focuses upon patterns of interaction between groups challenging state authority and the effect of the state's response upon further mobilization; while Goldstone has been examining the relationship between population growth and the ability of states to meet increased demands for food production. This reversion to 'under-deterministic' approaches is an admission of the failure of existing overarching accounts of the complexity and diversity of modern revolutions. The position of the general theorist of revolution is like that of Chairman Mao: when asked for his judgement on the French Revolution of 1789 Mao replied that it 'it was too early to tell'. **BO'L**

Further reading Alexis de Tocqueville, *The Ancien Régime and the French Revolution*; J. Goldstone (ed.), *Revolutions: Theoretical, Comparative, and Historical Studies*; J. Goldstone, T. Gurr and F. Moshiri (eds.), *Revolutions of the Late Twentieth Century*; B. Moore, *The Social Origins of Dictatorship and Democracy*; T. Skocpol, *States and Social Revolutions*.

RHYTHM-AND-BLUES

Rhythm-and-blues was the name invented by record-industry executives in the 1940s to publicise music which had hitherto been sold under such politically incorrect names as 'race music' or 'sepia music', or even, briefly, 'nigger music'. It was a form of **jazz** combining the rhythmic bounce of **Dixieland** with a vocal style of melodic playing

(often on saxophone) derived from and influenced by **Blues**-style singing. In the later 1940s and 1950s, as big bands increasingly took up jazz, rhythm-and-blues became a main entertainment form for small groups, and itself evolved into **pop** and later **rock**. **KMcL**

RIGID AND NON-RIGID DESIGNATORS

A rigid designator, in **philosophy**, designates the same thing in all possible worlds. The word 'water', for example, is a rigid designator: it actually designates water. That is, it designates water in the actual world, and (unless its meaning is changed) there is no possible situation in which it designates anything other than water. That is, it designates water in all possible worlds.

A non-rigid designator does not designate the same thing in all possible worlds. The description 'the first woman Prime Minister of Britain' is a non-rigid designator. It actually designates Mrs Thatcher; it designates Mrs Thatcher in the actual world. But it could have designated someone else, for someone else might have been the first woman Prime Minister of Britain. That is, there are possible worlds in which it designates someone other than Mrs Thatcher.

Saul Kripke introduced the distinction between rigid and non-rigid designators. It is important because, Kripke argues, identity statements – statements that one thing is identical with another – conjoining rigid designators are, if true, necessarily true.

The word 'water' is a rigid designator, it designates the same thing in all possible worlds. The term 'H_2O' is also a rigid designator, since it too designates the same thing in all possible worlds. Further, 'water' and 'H_2O' refer to the same thing: water in the actual world. So 'water' and 'H_2O' refer to the same thing: water in all possible worlds. The identity statement 'water is H_2O' is not only true, it is *necessarily* true. It is impossible for the statement 'water is H_2O' to be false.

By contrast, identity statements – statements that one thing is identical with another – in which one or more non-rigid designator occurs are, if true, merely contingently true. 'Mrs Thatcher' is a rigid designator. But 'the first woman Prime Minister of Britain' is non-rigid. It does not designate the same thing in all possible worlds, for someone else might have been the first woman Prime Minister of Britain. So although the identity statement 'Mrs Thatcher was the first woman Prime Minister of Britain' is true, it is merely *contingently* true. For it is possible for someone else to be the first woman Prime Minister of Britain; it is possible for 'Mrs Thatcher was the first woman Prime Minister of Britain' to be false.

Kripke's claim that identity statements conjoining rigid designators are, if true, necessarily true is extremely important. Philosophers have long held that the distinction between the **a priori and a posteriori** and the necessary and contingent coincide. A statement is a priori just if it can be known to be true or false independently of experience, a posteriori just if it cannot be known to be true or false independently of experience. A statement is necessarily true just if it cannot be false, necessarily false just if it cannot be true. And a statement is contingently true just if it is true but could have been false, contingently false just if it is false but could have been true.

Philosophers, then, have long held that a statement is a posteriori just if it is contingent. But if Kripke is right, then some statements are a posteriori and necessary. Consider the identity statement 'water is H_2O'. As we have seen, this statement is not merely true but necessarily true. Further, it is a posteriori. One cannot know that water is H_2O independently of experience. One can only know that water is H_2O if one has an experience such as an experience of a chemical experiment or of a chemistry lesson. **AJ**

See also modality.

Further reading S. Kripke, *Naming and Necessity*.

RIGOUR

The property of rigour (Latin *rigor*, 'unbendingness') is considered by mathematicians to be the greatest virtue. It is applied to arguments and proofs. It has been the main goal of mathematicians since the early 19th century, when the haphazard results and arguments of earlier mathematicians began to be systematized and questioned, following the uncertainty caused by the discovery and acceptance of **non-Euclidean geometry**. Rigour means arguing with the strictest application of the principles of **logic**, and not using any assumptions which are not explicitly stated at the outset. The reason that mathematicians sought rigour is that the results it gives cannot be questioned, whereas results which rely on intuition, your ideas about what should happen, can often be mistaken.

The search for rigour has led to **pure mathematics** becoming increasingly dependent on logic and **set theory**; some have even viewed mathematics as only a part of logic. The reason these two areas were chosen to be the basis of mathematics is that logic is supposed to be universal and to be the arbiter of a correct argument (though both those statements are open to question), and that set theory is sufficiently general and powerful for every mathematical concept to be defined in terms of sets. **SMcL**

RINGS

Rings are among the fundamental structures studied in **algebra**. They are an intermediate stage between **groups** and **fields**, though they have a rich theory of their own. A ring, like a field, has two operations, addition and multiplication; the structure, again like a field, is a group under the operation of addition. The difference is in the operation of multiplication; in a ring, the elements do not have to have multiplicative inverses (another element which when multiplied by the original one gives the answer 1). This is because the **integers** form a ring but not a field, and much of the work in rings has been inspired by work in **number theory**. **SMcL**

RITES OF PASSAGE

Rites of passage are **rituals** that mark changes in the social status of an individual passing through the 'developmental cycle' of birth, puberty, marriage and death. Rites of passage give communal recognition to social relationships which are altered or newly formed. The influential anthropologist Arnold van Gennep, in his book *Rites de Passage* (1909), demonstrated that the life-cycle rituals of birth, marriage and death followed the pattern of initiation rites. In small-scale societies, elders generally inducted a group of initiates of the same sex into social roles during a period of time in which the initiates were also tested by undergoing privations. Van Gennep's model demonstrated that rituals of passage have a tripartite structure: a rite of separation, followed by a transitional state he termed liminal (from the Latin *limen*, 'threshold'), and concluded by a rite of reincorporation into the everyday realm of living, but with a different status.

A great deal of anthropological attention has been paid to the liminal state, during which the individual is 'betwixt and between' social roles. It can also be called marginal, because the person may be considered dangerous or polluting and therefore subject to **taboos**. A good example of van Gennep's model are those mortuary rites characterized by a second burial, where the bones of the deceased are dug up and then reburied. In Potamia in rural Greece, for example, this happens after five years, at which time the liminal status of the relatives of the deceased (who have been in mourning all this time) is resolved, and they are reincorporated into normal social life while the spirit is sent to its new abode. Funerary rituals, generally, are rites of passage by which the deceased is converted into an ancestor, and the social positions of the living are redefined.

The ambiguity of the liminal state means that social norms are often turned on their head, and during this phase people are given licence to behave in ways that flout social conventions. Many festivals can be seen as liminal: for example, during the Catholic carnival preceding Lent gender roles are often reversed and there is much sexual revelry. In India, during the Hindu festival of Holi high caste Brahmins might ride on donkeys, women initiate sexual liasons and men dress as women. In this upside down world, people are showered with coloured water and powdered dyes, an action which expresses goodwill and social solidarity between people.

In most societies, rites of passage are marked by religious celebration and ritual. Indeed, the rite itself is often regarded as a religious experience, the deity accepting and validating the individual's change in human status. Main rites of passage, from the religious point of view, are the postnatal acceptance of a baby into the community of faith (by such activities as baptism, circumcision or name-giving), coming of age, when the child takes responsibility for its own religious observances (for example in such ceremonies as adult baptism, Bar Mitzvah, confirmation or thread-giving), marriage and death (committal to the afterlife and separation from the living). These transitions may be perceived as dangerous because of the exposure to divine power, and may be hedged in with taboo. But they are also **sacraments**, where Earthly symbols denote a divine reality; they are a means of communion with the supernatural, eternal world, and they are acts of personal commitment of profound theological significance. For example, marriage may appear to be principally a social contract, involving the financial and social linkage of two families and questions of succession and inheritance; but in many religions perpetuation of the family is a duty sacred to both the living and the dead, and marriage ceremonies also reflect the theological understanding of the relationship between man and woman. **DA EMJ CL**

See also death.

Further reading Jean la Fontaine, *Initiation: Ritual Drama and Secret Knowledge Across the World*; James Frazer, *The Golden Bough*.

RITUAL

Rituals (from Latin *ritualis*, 'following solemn procedure') are stylized, formulaic patterns of behaviour frequently conducted in a religious context. Participants often see them as celebrating, maintaining and renewing the world. Rituals both assert and renew basic social values; they deal with relationships between individuals, and between humans and the environment, including the supernatural world. They have, therefore, psychological, social and symbolic dimensions.

Early anthropologists generally assumed that rituals were concerned with beliefs and religious sentiments, that they were attempts to influence supernatural forces. A **phenomenological** perspective sees such religious ideas as heightening personal experience: the experiential realm of ritual derives its intensity from collective participation.

Anthropologists study three levels in ritual: indigenous interpretations, which often reflect ideals; actual behaviour; and the relationship of ritual elements and symbols. Ritual is seen as a grouping of symbols (including objects, sequences of movement, gestures and costumes) which have to be understood in relation to each other. The nature of symbols allows for the existence of a multiplicity of interpretations of meaning.

Although those who practise rituals generally understand them in relation to supernatural 'other worlds', anthropologists and social scientists also interpret them in relation to society, focusing on the interaction between ritual and society. Debate about the meaning of rituals has led to an emphasis on ritual as a system of communication: they express values in dramatic form and communicate them to spectators as well as participants. Functionalist analysis examines the underlying and instrumental purposes of ritual, for example the way in which ritual acts reinforce collective sentiments, or the way ritual is used to challenge or negotiate with those in positions of power. In political terms, ritual tends to underline differences in status, validating respect for the status quo by reference to tradition. In such circumstances, ritual often symbolizes the power of political authority. Even where it threatens to subvert the authority of political and social systems, it ultimately tends to validate it. For example, during the harvest first-fruits festivals of some Bantu kingdoms in southern Africa, the king was publicly humiliated and the world of established authority was turned upside-down for the duration of the ritual but afterwards social order returned immediately to normal.

Religious ritual is an expression of one's religious identity (for example when a Christian makes the sign of the cross or a Muslim bows to pray in the direction of Mecca). It is a way of reinforcing one's convictions and controlling one's relationship with the divine. Rituals are used to regulate time (as in worship), as a way of giving meaning and order to daily life (by sanctifying it for God), and to change states of being (for example in ceremonies of initiation, purification or passage). In some religions ritual is thought actually to affect the change in status during a **rite of passage**: the new-born child is accepted, the journey is made from childhood to adulthood, two people marry, a soul departs from this life or incarnation to another.

Ritual in religion is also used to establish the presence of the divine, for example in the commissioning of a new temple idol, in the consecration of a mosque or synagogue, or in the Christian eucharist. Ritual can be used as a form of **magic**, that is as a way of controlling supernatural (or even natural) forces, as in exorcism, healing or rain-making. It is crucial in matters of purity and **taboo**, for instance in the *mikva* or ritual bath whereby an orthodox Jewish woman cleanses herself after menstruation, or in the innumerable ceremonies, worldwide, surrounding childbirth.

The idea that ritual is a form of magic is picked up in the Judaeo-Christian prophetic tradition: it is believed that by performing acts proleptically, or symbolically, one can actually make things happen or bring them closer. In the **Protestant** tradition, the faith of the participants is necessary to make ritual effective; in Catholic canon law, by contrast, sacraments are held to have validity *ex opere operato*, 'by virtue of having been performed'. In many religions, to be valid a ritual must be performed by a member of the priestly order or group, and must follow a specific formula down to the last detail. (In ancient Rome this was sometimes carried to ludicrous lengths: in the time of the stammering Emperor Claudius, who also served as High Priest, some ceremonies had to be repeated as many as a dozen times, from the beginning, until they were word-perfect.) **DA EMJ CL**

See also interpretative anthropology; political anthropology; prayer; sacraments.

Further reading M. Bloch, *From Blessing to Violence*; Joan La Fontaine (ed), *The Interpretation of Ritual*; V. Turner, *The Ritual Process*.

ROBOTS

Robots are among the most well-known applications of **computers**, made so by the many words written about them by **sf** authors. The word robot is derived from the Czech word *robota*, meaning 'work', and a robot is in essence a machine which carries out work under the guidance of a computer.

Before robots were developed industrially, stories full of the menace of robots were the vogue in sf magazines. In fact a rampaging robot is virtually impossible, under the guidance of a **program** written to prevent such ocurrences. Indeed, the robots that are used today are mainly specialist machines designed to do one task (such as spot welding) efficiently; they are unable to perform other tasks, and are immobile or unable to sense their surroundings. The main menace of the robot perceived today is that of jobs being taken over the menace of all technological progress since the very earliest days of civilization. This menace has led to contrasting views by those who favour the introduction of robots (thinking that this will lead eventually to humans being able to live lives of luxury and ease, their every need catered for by efficient robots) and those who are against it (seeing a society of immense poverty and unemployment, full of people unable to reap the benefits of the introduction of robots, which will be reserved for the very rich).

Much research is being undertaken today to increase the versatility of robots. This work includes the development of perception, which is still largely unsuccessful in realizing its more long-term aims (perhaps due to their ambitiousness), and is really yet to produce a robot that can cope with a non-laboratory environment containing those unpredictable objects, human beings. SMcL

See also artificial intelligence.

Further reading F.H. George and J.D. Humphries, *The Robots are Coming*.

ROCK CYCLE

The idea of the rock cycle is used by geologists to show that different types of rock are related by geological processes. It is an abstraction rather than a description of the way any particular rock will change. It is a more powerful concept than a classification as a way of discussing differences between rock types precisely because there is an element of process explanation.

The rock cycle is best illustrated by a diagram (see below). The diagram can be read from any starting point, but the most logical place to start is with igneous rocks because they are the first rocks to form. Igneous rocks are those which form by the cooling of magma: molten rock originating in the mantle. The nature of igneous rocks depends on their chemical composition and on the speed at which they cool. Chemical composition varies from acid to basic, and the rocks from granitic, through intermediate to basaltic. Some igneous rocks reach the surface, where they form volcanoes, others do not reach the surface but solidify at depth. Slow cooling at depth allows large crystals to form and may give time for selective crystallization and/or mobility, which means that different parts of the cooled mass will have different compositions. Granite bathyliths are the extreme form of this. Where molten magma reaches the surface it cools quickly and cannot be chemically separated, but the form of the volcano depends on the chemical composition: basalt is extremely runny and forms wide horizontal lava flows, while acid lava is more sticky and forms more conical volcanoes. Acid lavas are more prone to explosive eruption, and can throw large boulders and ash high in the air and across substantial distances. So volcanoes may vary in shape and in the degree of consolidation of the deposits.

When any rock is exposed at the surface, it will be subject to heating and cooling and to wetting and drying, and so to physical and chemical weathering processes which weaken it and sometimes wash away some components. Weathered rock may then be

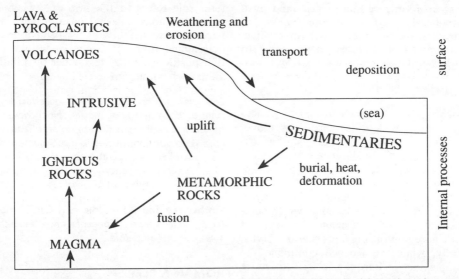

LAVA &
PYROCLASTICS

Weathering and
erosion

VOLCANOES

transport

deposition

surface

INTRUSIVE

uplift

(sea)

SEDIMENTARIES

IGNEOUS
ROCKS

METAMORPHIC
ROCKS

burial, heat,
deformation

Internal processes

fusion

MAGMA

eroded, or broken down into particles or
into solution, and can then be transported
down slopes or by rivers or glaciers. At
some point, usually when slopes lessen or
streams flow into lakes or sea, rock particles are deposited, commonly as sand or
clay, more rarely as a chemical precipitate.
In some circumstances, especially in a shallow sea in a geosyncline, sediments can
build up to depths of thousands of metres.
Its own weight then consolidates it into
sedimentary rocks. Often, the processes of
mountain building will raise sedimentary
rocks to high altitudes and expose them to
weathering and erosion, so making another
loop around that part of the cycle.

In other cases, sedimentary rocks can be
deeply buried, subjecting them to further
heating and pressure. Sometimes, they can
be exposed to further heating by igneous
intrusions and be greatly altered in physical
form. So sandstone can be turned into
quartzite or limestone into marble. Rocks
whose character has been changed in this
way are called metamorphic rocks.

If heating is extreme, igneous, sedimentary or metamorphic rocks may be
remelted, only to cool and solidify as
igneous rocks. So the cycle is closed,
though the new igneous rock may be different from those which first formed. As
explained under **composition and structure
of the Earth**, the first igneous rocks were
basaltic while the continents were built up

of intermediate, andesitic rock and eventually formed acid granitic rocks. This process required the operation of **plate
tectonics** over thousands of millions of
years. **PS**

ROCK MUSIC

Rock music began in the 1960s, as a fusion
of earlier **jazz** styles (especially **rhythm-and-
blues**) with those of newly-emerged **pop**
(especially rock 'n' roll). Like jazz, it is as
often instrumental as vocal, and is intensely
virtuosic. Like pop, it interacts with **popular culture** in general and fashion in particular, to the point where artists can cross
over from one style to the other without
undue compromise. Rock makes extensive
use of electronic instruments, notably
drums, guitars and keyboards. Rock
musicians are at the forefront of development in this field, and their enormous
popularity has had incalculable effect on
the spread of new instruments and new
playing techniques. The main branches of
rock include folk rock (close to folk, with a
serious-mindedness about its lyrics and a
reticent musical style), glam rock (the nearest to pop, with a dependence on light
shows, high-fashion clothes, extravagant
make-up and dance and a corresponding
fining-down of complexity in the music),
hard rock (and its coarser derivative heavy
metal), which often favour aggressive

images of violence and protest, and push amplifiers, instruments and voices to extremes, and progressive rock (innovative, experimental and closest in technique to both jazz and **electronic music**). **KMcL**

ROCOCO

Rococo (from French *rocaille*, '(fancy) rock-work') was a European **arts** movement of the early 18th century. In fine art, the amalgam of the **Baroque** with elements of **classicism**, which in France had characterized the court of Louis XIV, gave way, on his death, to the lighter, more playful and private art of the Rococo, which demonstrated a need for elegance and comfort quite absent in the previous century. Stylistically, while the Rococo continued the complexities of Baroque surface structure, it treated it as pure decoration, justified only insofar as it charmed the eye and amused the senses. Although such art was essentially decorative, the Rococo period produced some magnificent painters, such as Boucher, Fragonard and Watteau in France, Guardi and Longhi in Italy and Gainsborough and Hogarth in England. While stylistically these painters differ greatly, they all share the common traits of the period: a move away from the grandiloquent history painting of the 17th century towards a smaller, more intimate art, a love of decorative effect, a brightness of touch often revealed by a bravura and sparkling application of paint and – though this is not universal – erotic or amorous subject matter, typified in the *fêtes champêtre* of Watteau.

In **music**, 'rococo' is sometimes used to describe the highly-ornamented, formal style of such 17th- and 18th-century French composers as Couperin, Lully and Rameau, and the music of composers who occasionally affected French styles, for example, Bach and Telemann. **MG KMcL**

Further reading A. Schönberger and H. Sochner, *The Age of Rococo*.

ROLE

In sociological terms, a role is a collection of socially defined attributes and expectations associated with social positions. The term role refers to the fact that when a person occupies a social position such as parent or teacher his or her behaviour is determined more by the expectations of that position than by his or her own individual behaviour. **DA**

See also action perspective; bureaucracy; culture; dramaturgical model; functionalism; generalized other; institution; internalization; norms; occupation; profession; social integration; socialization; social order; status; structure; structure-agency debate; symbolic interactionism; typifications; values.

Further reading B.J. Biddle and E.J. Thomas (eds.), *Role Theory: Concepts and Research*; J.A. Jackson (ed.), *Role*.

ROMAN À CLEF

Roman à clef ('story with a key') is a form of writing in which real people are presented, accurately or otherwise, as characters with their names changed. Sometimes the purpose is satirical, as in Somerset Maugham's novel *Cakes and Ale*, in which the literary feuds of 1930s London were given a waspish working over. However, the allusions can be subtler. In Rabelais's *Pantagruel*, for example, or Swift's *Gulliver's Travels*, the parodies are of specific politicians and thinkers of the day, but they are so subsumed into the general narrative that real identities are now a matter of largely antiquarian interest, and a reverse situation exists to the one intended by the author: the characters in the *roman à clef* flesh out real identities and behaviour rather than the other way about. **KMcL**

ROMANESQUE

Romanesque **sculpture** and **architecture** have features derived from Roman antiquity. The style flourished especially in those regions where the influence of Roman art and culture had been particularly strong, such as Provence, Sicily and central Italy. Also, the great size and longevity of the Roman Empire meant that the Romanesque found favour from Spain to Britain and from Germany to the Holy Land.

In architecture, the characteristics of the style are the use of rounded barrel vaults, with large expanses of wall pierced by slit windows, and often a wall decoration which imitates the classical **Orders**, and acanthus friezes and inhabited scrolls. In large-scale sculpture (which itself revived after the millennium largely due to the influence of antique examples) the figures take on an antique elegance after the dumpy, earlier medieval mannequins (cf. the figures of the Arch of Constantine). They frequently have faces and hair modelled after classical figures, and flowing classical dress also reappears.

As is so frequently the case, the readoption of antique styles in the Romanesque is not just a valueless, stylistic exercise. In most instances a conscious desire to tap into the prestige of the antique can be assumed, though rarely proven, along with an awareness of the value and power of traditional forms. **PD MG JM**

Further reading Meyer Shapiro, *Romanesque Art*.

ROMANTIC COMEDY

Romantic Comedy, in **drama**, is a form in which the main impetus of the action is the protagonists' attempts to find an appropriate sexual partner, in the face of either external opposition (for example, patriarchal fathers who want their daughters to marry for money, not love), or internal misunderstanding (for instance, lack of self-knowledge leading to an inability to recognize true feelings), or a mixture of both. Many Romantic Comedies rely on elements of **Comedy of Manners**, while the complications which ensue when there are two pairs of would-be lovers can be close to **farce**. The enduring popularity of Romantic Comedy owes much to the near-universality of its subject matter, and to the opportunities it offers audiences to share vicariously the triumphs of true love, since in a typical Romantic Comedy there is seldom room to doubt that the concluding marriages are anything but a happy ending. **TRG SS**

See also comedy.

Further reading Northrop Frye, *Anatomy of Criticism*; Elder Olson, *The Theory of Comedy*; Wylie Sypher, (ed.), *Comedy*.

ROMANTICISM

There were two kinds of romanticism in Europe. The first, in the 16th and 17th centuries, was an almost exclusively literary phenomenon. 'Romantick' writers and their readers were fascinated by the exotic and the supernatural. The *Odyssey*, the *Arabian Nights*, Ovid's *Metamorphoses* and Apuleius' *The Golden Ass* were particularly potent influences. Most thoroughgoing Romantick works are long forgotten, but elements of the style can still be seen, for example in Shakespeare (heroes and heroines shipwrecked on the coasts of magic countries; statues that come to life; enchanted woods; ghosts) and in the **masques** and **operas** of many nations. In the 18th century the Romantick style survived principally in puppet-plays (where 'Turks' and 'genies' were favourite characters) and in operas (for example, Mozart's *The Abduction from the Seraglio* and *The Magic Flute*), and its subsequent manifestations were in children's literature (the folk tales collected by the Grimm brothers are full of it) and in music hall and **pantomime**.

The second, and more significant, kind of European romanticism began midway through the 18th century and ran wildfire until the rise of **modernism** some 150 years later; indeed, in such manifestations as neo-romanticism, it still persists today. This was a philosophical and intellectual movement – or rather, since it was not confined to the arts, a climate of opinion – based on the ideas of individual freedom and self-expression. Thinkers of the **Enlightenment** had proclaimed that humankind could shake off the darkness of superstitious ignorance thanks to a kind of mass awakening produced by universal education. The Romantic view was that each person possessed individual freedom, and would find it by being true to his or her own individuality. Assertion of self would open the individual to a kind of transcendental reality, the sublimity (not necessarily religious) which is all round us and of which we aspire to be part.

These ideas led to a vast upsurge of libertarian theory and activity. The period from the 1770s onwards saw philosophers grappling with the ideas of individual identity and responsibility, with concepts of freedom, the nature and duties of the state, and the implications of all such matters for ethics and morality. In **religion**, 'free-thinking' Christian sects burgeoned. There was discussion, if not much actual movement, towards true **democracy** and the emancipation of women. Agitation began for prison reform and the end of slavery. In **science**, the consensus was increasingly challenged, and individual thinkers, from Hutton to Linnaeus, from Berzelius to Darwin, from Lamarck to Mendel, produced radical new ideas in every field, so that this period, even more than the time of Galileo and Newton, is where 'modern' science starts. 'New' intellectual disciplines burgeoned based on the scientific model: **anthropology**, **archaeology**, **sociology** all sharing the premise that every human experience was valid, and that 'modern' people were the point to which all human history had been laboriously progressing.

In the **arts**, romanticism was a convulsive force. Until the end of the 18th century, the prevailing European view was that of the Middle Ages: that artists were craftsmen and that what they did floated on an enormous raft of tradition and experience. You might extend or redefine the rules, apply individual genius, but in every case tradition was what validated present practice. (To take examples at random: neither opera nor the **novel**, two of the most significant 'new' artistic forms of the post-**Renaissance** era in Europe, sprang fully-formed from nowhere. Each grew gradually, as creator after creator worked on previous ideas. The origins of opera lie in attempts to re-create the style of ancient Greek **tragedy**; the origins of the novel are the romances of medieval chivalry on the one hand, and on the other the character-rich, moralizing or ironical narratives of such people as Boccaccio and Chaucer, who were inspired in turn by writers of the more distant past.) By the 1780s, practitioners of all the arts were beginning to assert individuality, the claims of their own creativity. Artists were increasingly rebelling against the demands of patronage, taking the money but kicking against the servant status their patrons often assigned to them, and against the need to produce the kinds of work their employers preferred as opposed to the kinds their own individual inspiration prompted. When, in the early 19th century, a new bourgeois market arose for works of art, large numbers of artists abandoned their aristocratic patrons altogether, producing instead for mass publication, public performance, civic commissions and the marketplace at large. This in turn fostered the view of the artist as some kind of creative paladin, storming the bastions of convention and struggling heroically to impose his (more rarely her) will on recalcitrant material.

In fine art, Romanticism rejected the universalizing rules of **classicism** in favour of an emphasis on the imagination, the expression of emotion, the relationship of the individual to the cosmos and a profoundly subjective approach to beauty. Romantic artists showed a taste for, and identifaction with, the wilder manifestations of Nature and natural disaster. In Turner's painting *Hannibal Crossing the Alps* an Alpine storm threatens to rout Hannibal's army. In Caspar David Friedrich's *Arctic Shipwreck* a ship is implacably crushed by great ice floes. Such paintings represent a break with the ideal landscapes of classicism, in which humanity is seen to be in harmony with Nature, in favour of a model where the individual and the environment are in conflict. Another disaster, that of a shipwreck, allowed Géricault to make an association between the individual's conflict with Nature and political conflict: his *Raft of the Medusa* depicts the story of the ship Méduse, wrecked with tragically high loss of life due to the incompetence of a Royalist captain. Likewise Delacroix represents conflict, this time revolution, in *Liberty Leading the People*, while Goya's *Third of May 1808* portrays the suffering shared by all victims of unrest.

In **literature**, artists were happy to develop existing forms, particularly the novel and the various kinds of lyric **poetry**. In poetry, a favourite idea was, in Blake's phrase, to show 'the World in a Grain of Sand' – a version of the earlier concern of

Metaphysical poets to draw out 'sublime' resonances in commonplace experience. Fascination with Nature (often as a metaphor for the **Sublime**), combined with concentration on individual feeling, meant that it was often a human being who was seen as Blake's grain of sand, a focus for the surrounding, inarticulate immensity. The 19th century also saw a rise in poetry about character: exposition or revelation of personality being used in an anecdotal way. **Lyric** poems in particular were often an emotional equivalent of snapshots (this period also saw the beginning of photography): fleeting moments, thoughts or feelings frozen on the page, and given resonance (like photographs) because of the feeling that here was an instant of reality, forever captured.

In novels, writers focused their work on individual 'cases' (or, in late-Romantic, post-Freudian times, 'case-studies'): individuals whose existence was not just interesting in itself (as, for example, Tom Jones' existence is in Richardson's quintessentially pre-Romantic novel), but was also emblematic of wider concerns. Goethe showed individual characters experiencing and reacting to all kinds of emotional, philosophical, social and above all intellectual ideas current at the time; Dickens and Zola showed characters against the background of the social conditions about which they (the authors) had urgent opinions to impart; Tolstoy and Flaubert were concerned, in a kind of literary **pointillism**, with building up pictures of real life (both external and emotional) from a myriad of tiny incidents, meticulously described. As the 19th century progressed, psychological and social themes began to predominate in character-drawing and the invention of incident respectively. This was the case at least in more ambitious fiction, though genre novels returned to the superficial swashbuckle (emotional or physical) of pre-Romantic forms. Any collection of quintessential novels of the Romantic age would include *Oliver Twist*, *Madame Bovary*, Goethe's 'Wilhelm Meister' novels, *Wuthering Heights* (also notable for its stylistic experimentation – neurotic emotional states rendered in dislocated or allusive prose), *Crime and Punishment*, *Moby Dick* and *The Hound of the Baskervilles*.

In **music**, one of the main innovations of Romanticism was the rise of the virtuoso – whether as performer (Liszt, Melba, Paganini) or composer-genius (Beethoven, Wagner). Concert music broke away from 18th-century decorum, either by exploding previous notions about form, harmony and scoring or by innovation. When Mendelssohn writes a symphony, it is only superficially 'like' those of Haydn or Mozart: intellectual rigour is replaced by mood-painting and a slightly self-conscious feeling of 'beauty' as some kind of existential force. When Berlioz writes a 'symphony', it is entirely unintellectual and subjective, showing dream-states induced by Romantic passion and by opium (in the *Symphonie fantastique*) or a human being reacting to the immensity of Nature (in *Harold in Italy*). Beethoven worked largely with traditional forms, but gave them a grandeur, a spacious interiority, which is not less powerful for being indefinable. Liszt and Wagner tirelessly redefined every aspect of music, inventing new forms (symphonic poem; **music drama**), new organizational techniques (block construction; **leitmotif**), radically new ways of managing harmony and counterpoint, new ways of performing (Liszt makes demands, and not only on pianists, unprecedented in earlier music), new ways of scoring (vastly increased demands on such 'Cinderella' instruments as harp, viola, piccolo and timpani; newly-invented instruments such as the 'Wagner' tuba). Naivety in music became a ploy, not (as previously) a product of genuine freshness and genuine simplicity. When an 18th-century composer uses a folk tune, for example, it is usually unaffected and charming, but when a 19th-century composer does the same, it is usually with irony (for example Berlioz or Mahler), or as part of some nationalist or other overtly idealistic programme. There are very few genuinely unaffected romantic musicians and those there are (such as Dvořák and Wolf) are partly interesting because they cut (or in Wolf's case struggled) so much against the spirit of their times.

To give an impression of the Romantic attitude to buildings one can quote the well-known passage from Goethe, who wrote of his sensations as he stood before the medieval cathedral at Strasbourg in 1772: 'It rises like a most sublime, wide arching tree of God who with a thousand boughs, a million of twigs and leafage like the sands of the sea, tells forth to the neighbourhood the glory of the Lord, His Master...'. In this passage Goethe refers to qualities not recognized as in the classical canon for the critical judgement of beauty in architecture. In the Romantic mind what is held uppermost is the appeal to the senses, and to the emotions. **PD MG JM KMcL**

Further reading M.H. Abrams, *The Mirror and the Lamp*; H. Honour, *Romanticism*; H.G.A.V. Shenk, *The Mind of the European Romantics*.

RULE OF LAW

The rule of **law** is frequently little more than a rhetorical phrase, although it does embody a widely valued ideal. Enthusiasts for the rule of law emphasize the certainty and predictability of legal rules, their generalizability and lack of scope for discretion, and their durability and absence of contradiction. Whether any set of legal rules contain these properties may be sensibly questioned by anybody who is cognitively competent.

However, most importantly the ideal of the rule of law holds that what is fundamentally important about the ideal of the rule of law is its universal application both to law-makers and those subject to legal rules. Where rulers are not themselves subject to the rule of law then **absolutism**, **authoritarianism**, **despotism** or **totalitarianism** are facilitated. The requirement that both rulers and the ruled be accountable to the law is of unquestionable value especially for modern democrats. However, many democrats are sceptical about whether all societies necessarily benefit from other facets of what is invoked under the rule of law. They may be constrained by the rule of law from doing what is right; they may be constrained by 'juridification' (judges entering an area previously left to politicians or others); and they may be impaired by 'legalism'; that is, excessive veneration of the law and its procedures which inhibits independent assessment of the merits of a given policy proposal. **BO'L**

See also democracy; legal positivism; liberalism; natural law.

Further reading J.W. Harris, *Legal Philosophies*.

S

SACRAMENT

Originally *sacramentum* in Latin meant a soldier's oath of allegiance, but in **Christian** worship loyalty to the Roman emperor was replaced by commitment to Christ. The word 'sacrament' was then applied to anything from a creed or the Lord's Prayer to the **rituals** of baptism and the Eucharist. However, it was also taken as the equivalent of the Greek *musterion* ('mystery') and hence to mean a ceremony which was not for unbelieving eyes. The definition given in the Anglican Book of Common Prayer was 'an outward and visible sign of an inward and spiritual grace', and from the 4th century a sacrament was held to be the sign of a divine reality or grace which sanctifies humankind. In the 12th century, Peter Lombard enumerated seven sacraments universally accepted in Catholic churches: baptism, confirmation, the Eucharist, penance, unction (anointing with oil), marriage and ordination. The Orthodox churches retain the original combined baptism/ confirmation order. Interestingly, the taking of monastic vows is not a sacrament, though full of sacramental actions in **Buddhism** and **Hinduism**, as in Christianity. A distinction is made between baptism and the Eucharist (The Lord's Supper), believed to have Christ's special authorization and 'necessary of salvation' in the **Protestant** tradition, and those sacraments such as marriage which are essentially **rites of passage** or signs of a God-given vocation (for example ordination). **EMJ**

Further reading O.C. Quick, *The Christian Sacraments*.

SACRIFICE

The concept of sacrifice (Latin, 'to make

holy') is difficult for the Western secular mind to understand. Not only is the colloquial usage 'making a sacrifice' far removed from the original practice of making something sacred by setting it apart for the divine (for example by offering it to God), but the theology of sacrifice has become divorced from its original context of worship. Nevertheless, the idea of sacrifice is still both a powerful psychological symbol and a key to understanding central **Christian** and **Judaic** doctrines such as **atonement** – and in many religions which spring from the primal vision the unity of worship and theology is maintained, and sacrifice is crucial to the community of human and divine.

From earliest times, sacrifices (in the form of offerings left on altars, by graves and beside sacred trees, streams, etc., and as libations or liquid offerings) were considered an appropriate response to the numinous and a means of venerating the dead. The oldest form of sacrifice was as fulfilment of a vow, whether by an individual or the community, to obtain the help or avert the displeasure of supernatural forces, or in gratitude for favours received. In essence, sacrifices were tokens or offerings paralleling the tribute made to powerful mortal rulers, but the attitude that the gods need the sweet odours of sacrifice to survive was deep-rooted. (It is satirized by Aristophanes in his play *Birds*, in which the birds build a wall between heaven and earth and starve the gods by blocking the passage of sacrifice.) An element of that feeling persists in the daily temple ritual in **Hinduism**, where the idol is bathed, clothed and fed in a manner reminiscent (at least to Westerners) of the *grand levée* of the 'Sun King' Louis XIV of France. In Hindu practice, however, offerings have a spiritual significance, and the ashes received back (smeared on the forehead) symbolize God's grace.

When God (or the gods) was perceived as creator of all and sustainer of the natural world, he could not very well be offered what he created or controlled, as if it were something he needed. But the belief persists that the ancestors do have need of such offerings. Indeed, anthropologists observe that sacrifice was originally associated less

with belief in gods than with **totemism** and ancestor-worship. The symbolic statements made about relations between human and spirit realms meant that sacrifice could be interpreted in terms either of expiation or communion, the offering establishing a temporary connection between the natural and supernatural worlds, and the donor making symbolic contact because of his or her association with the offering.

In Old Testament Israel, slaughtering an animal was a sacramental act: people believed that life, contained in the blood, was returned to its source. In many ancient religions, and in some religions today, meals with meat had and have special significance, for establishing fellowship in the community and bonding it with the god. This is why God was given his portion in a sacrifice. In different societies, different hierarchies of offering existed. The **Olympian religion** prescribed specific creatures for sacrifice on particular occasions; in **Vedic** India the horse was the supreme sacrifice; in Aztec society humans were the ultimate victims. (Some anthropologists claim that this was merely a convenience, religious practice both facilitating and cloaking **cannibalism**. The theory is disputed, and in any case does not apply to human sacrifice in other communities.) Since the entrails of sacrificed creatures were regarded as auspicious, they were often used for **divination**.

Since sacrifice is seen as a means of reconciliation with and manipulation of cosmic forces, it was inevitable that the first **Christians** should interpret Jesus' death (involving, they believed, victory over death) as the supreme sacrifice. Christians see Christ's sacrifice as different in nature from the self-immolation of gods in other religions (for example, Prometheus in the Olympian system, or the creator-mothers in Polynesian and early Japanese religion.) The writer Frances Young summarizes the developments in Christian thinking on the matter in the first centuries CE as follows: 'The sacrifice of Christ was God's act of salvation, a sacrifice offered by God to expiate sin, to avert the devil, and to reconcile God with himself; to this Christians responded with sacrifices of praise and thanksgiving.' Such ideas of sacrifice lie at the heart of Christian theology, and it is through the influence of Christian **asceticism** on society in general that the phrase 'making a sacrifice' (that is, giving something up for the sake of a higher good) has come to have its present meaning. **EMJ CL KMcL**

Further reading W. Arens, *The Man-eating Myth*; H. Hubert and M. Mauss, *Sacrifice, its Nature and Function*.

SADISM see **Masochism and Sadism**

SAGA

Saga (Old Norse, 'story') is a a form of medieval Icelandic **literature** and, with the exception of two or three Latin **novels**, is the oldest prose fiction in Europe. Most sagas are heroic **legends**, concerned with the (part real, part fictional) battles, jealousies and love affairs of real people living in the centuries before and including the 13th century. Fine examples include *Njal's Saga* and *Laxdaela Saga*. A few sagas involve the supernatural: notable among these are the swaggering *Grettir's Saga* (analogous to *Beowulf* or *Gawain* without the moralizing) and the *Volsung Saga*, parts of which reappear in Wagner's *Ring of the Nibelungs*. *Heimskringla*, by Snorri Sturluson, is not a saga but a history, in the style of a saga, of the ancient kings of Norway.

In modern usage, saga has come to mean a set of novels telling the history of a family. John Galsworthy's *The Forsyte Saga* (1906–28) was the progenitor, and the form has become an especially popular genre in the last two decades, with family and big-business alliances and feuds being treated as literary **soap** opera. **KMcL**

SAIVA SIDDHANTA

Saiva Siddhanta is the theology of the Saivite saints, systematized by Maykandar Karulturai and his pupil Arulananti (Arunandi) Sivacarya in the 13th century CE from the *Agamas* the sacred books of the movement. The movement is permeated so much by devotion to the God of love, that it comes very close to **Christianity**, and reinforces the Tamil belief that St Thomas brought Christianity to India. It certainly represents the highest form of **theism** in **Hinduism**. God (Shiva) is wholly other and transcendent, yet throughout the ages he loves each human soul and desires its good. Through grace the soul responds by entrusting itself to God. The soul is never God, nor God the soul, as in *advaita*. God acts in the world to release the soul and transform it, but even when in union with God, each soul retains its identity. God is never impersonal and immovable. Although always at peace, he is active through **Sakti**, his creative power and eternal consort, with whom he is co-substantial and co-eternal but always distinct.

Saiva Siddhanta claims that by responding to God's grace with worship, personal discipline and **yoga**, the soul can go beyond the liberation offered by other schools to union with God, transformed but not annihilated through enlightenment. **EMJ**

Further reading Dhavamony, Mariasusai, *Love to God according to Saiva Siddhanta; a study of the mysticism and theology of Saivism.*

SAKTI

Sakti (or Shakti, Sanskrit for 'power') is the feminine element or creative force in God, the means by which he is immanent in the world. Originally this force was depicted in anthropomorphic terms as the god's consort (Uma; Parvati; Kali) and relates to Shiva, or to the male deity being venerated in a particular temple, as a shaft of sunlight does to the Sun. In popular form it merged with the ancient worship of the mother goddess. In the Sakta cults, the female power is worshipped rather than the male Shiva, who is felt to be too remote from this world, in his perfect yogic trance, to be able to hear human prayers. (The principle is somewhat similar to the appeal of the Virgin Mary in **Christianity**, as a mediating force more accessible than God or Christ.)

Sakta families often worship the mother goddess in her fearsome form as Durga ('Inaccessible'), as Kali ('the black one', originally a tribal goddess of pre-Brahmanic times, though attempts have been made to link *kali* ('black', a Dravidian word), with the Sanskrit word for time, thus producing the idea of the controller of time, death), or as Candi ('the fierce one'). But she is really the mother defending her vulnerable children. As the consort of Shiva she is shown as a young and beautiful woman. She is also worshipped in the *yoni*, female counterpart of the *lingam*. She is Mata, 'mother', and Mahadevi, 'the great goddess', often popularly referred to just as Devi, 'the goddess'. **EMJ**

Further reading Narendra Bhattacharyya, *A History of the Sakta Religion*.

SAMPLING see **Electronic Music**

SANITY AND INSANITY see **Psychosis**

SATANISM

Satanism (from Hebrew *shaitan*, 'adversary') was a development, in **Judaic** and **Christian** areas, from straightforward **demonism**. The monotheists of early Judaism characterized all non-God gods and spirits as evil, as adversaries of good, and postulated the existence of a single, chief Adversary, all-evil in the way that God was all-good. (This was a characteristic view of many ancient religions: **Zoroastrianism**, for example, saw existence as a permanent battle between the powers of Light and Dark, with the universe as its battleground.) Christians developed this idea into a complex **myth** about the Serpent, Fallen Angel, Son of the Morning: its best-known exposition in English is Milton's *Paradise Lost*. Satanism itself soon followed: the worship of Satan, of the Prince of Darkness. Initially the cult was a reaction against Christianity, and its practices were mirror images of Christian practices: the Mass said backwards, for example. On to it, partly as a result of European Christian persecution of pre-Christian beliefs and practices, were grafted a whole set of ideas from **animism**, druidism and **witchcraft** – and they in turn, though often perfectly innocent, were tainted by association and became part of the 'dark side' of the human psyche which Satanism was supposed to explore. When Tutankhamun's tomb was opened in the 1920s, and garbled accounts of Egyptian ideas of the afterlife filled the popular press, a whole set of ideas from Egyptian myth was added. Satanism, in short, seems to the ordinary person to be an eclectic mishmash of perverted supernatural beliefs and orgiastic practices, and its modern adherents react by trying to 'purify' it, to go back to the innocent forms of demonism from which it sprang. **KMcL**

SATIRE

Satire comes from the Latin word *satura*, 'stuffing', and its popular links with Greek satyrs are mistaken. It uses mockery or imitation to reveal the perceived folly or evil of what is being satirized. **Irony**, distortion and insult are typical satirical weapons, deployed in work otherwise as disparate as Juvenal's *Satires*, such films as Altman's *M*A*S*H or The Player* and stand-up **comedy**. Most satire, from political cartoons to comic mimicry and literary **parody**, deflates by ridicule. But there is no need for satire to be comic: Swift's *Gulliver's Travels*, Hogarth's *Rake's Progress*, Kafka's *The Trial* and Orson Welles's film *Citizen Kane* are all satirical. **KMcL**

SCALE see Modality

SCARCITY

Scarcity (from Latin *escarpus*, 'picked out') is used in **anthropology** to describe a community in a state of hardship and material impoverishment. Until well into this century, scarcity had been characteristically associated with hunter-gatherer societies. They were considered to lie at the bottom of a social and economic developmental scale that placed Western industrial society at the top. Those living in apparent scarcity were seen as perpetually burdened by the task to collect necessities of food and water leaving little opportunity for leisure pursuits.

Anthropologist Marshall Sahlins challenged these assumptions in *The Original Affluent Society* (1972). He argued that affluence could be arrived at through desiring little as well as producing a lot of material items. The hunter-gatherer societies' predilection was described as the 'Zen road to affluence', one that is characterized by people having limited wants and little concern with the accumulation of material goods. Therefore, the concept of scarcity is of little relevance to them. It is a concept by which Western societies evaluate standards of social life.

Critics of Sahlins have pointed to his too rosy portrayal of hunter-gatherer lives. He tends to select only those communities that support his ideas. However, his argument serves the valid purpose of reflecting on one's own cultural presumptions, influenced by theories of social evolution progressing in an ascending line to Western capitalism.

From the other perspective, social theorist S.B. Linder argues that it is capitalist society that institutes notions of scarcity, for it encourages the desire to acquire things even if they are not within reach. It is from this anxious vantage point that we look back at hunter-gatherer societies. Time has become scarce, a precious commodity increasingly difficult to find. Considerably more hours are spent in productive activities of various kinds and leisure, in concentrated forms, has become a necessity to compensate for this phenomena. **RK**

See also authenticity; economic anthropology; evolutionism; primitivism.

Further reading R.B. Lee and I. De Vore (eds.), *Man the Hunter*; Marshall Sahlins, *Stone Age Economics*.

SCEPTICISM

Scepticism (from Greek *skepsis*, 'questioning'), in **philosophy**, is the doctrine that one cannot attain knowledge. There are various limited versions of scepticism, which claim that one cannot possess knowledge of certain limited kinds. Scepticism about other minds is the doctrine that one cannot possess knowledge of minds other than one's own; scepticism about **induction** is the view that one cannot acquire knowledge of the unobserved; sceptics about memory believe that one cannot know anything about the past; sceptics about the external world think that one cannot know whether physical objects (rather than one's sensory experiences as of them) exist.

Global scepticism is the view that one can know nothing, or at least the view that one can know almost nothing. Global sceptics may allow that one may know a very few things such as: (1) that one currently exists; (2) what one's own current mental states are; (3) that one knows nothing else. Global scepticism is made plausible by the point that the evidence one has for almost any of one's beliefs is compatible with the falsity of that belief. Assuming that we do know what we think we know, then we know that our senses can be unreliable. The tower in the distance seemed to be square but when we approached it turned out to be round. So maybe our senses are misleading us now. More worryingly, assuming that we know what we think we know, then we know that dreams can seem like waking reality. One can dream that one is reading, wake up, and discover that one was not reading but asleep. So maybe you are not reading this, but tucked up in bed having a convincing dream. And even more worryingly, the entire course of one's experience may be misleading. Perhaps an evil demon is fooling you into thinking that you are reading this, and has been fooling you since the day you started having experiences. Or perhaps a mad scientist extracted your brain from your body just before you were born and is using a computer to stimulate your brain so as to give you the experience as of reading this book when in fact this book and your hands on the page do not exist. You have no justification for thinking that this book exists which excludes the possibility that it does not and that you are a brain in a vat. Indeed, for nearly all of your beliefs, whatever evidence you might give in an attempt to justify them, that evidence is compatible with their falsity. So those beliefs cannot count as knowledge. **AJ**

See also epistemology; knowledge; other minds, problem of.

Further reading J. Dancy, *An Introduction to Contemporary Epistemology*; B. Stroud, *The Significance of Philosophical Scepticism*.

SCHOLASTICISM

Scholasticism (Greek, 'studiousness') was a

method of analysis developed in pre-scientific societies, particularly in ancient Greece. It assumed that truth about any matter from the existence of God to the life cycle of the mosquito could be determined by thought alone. If enough people gave enough time to thinking about and discussing the issue in all its aspects, they would reach a consensus, and that would be truth. There was no need for examination, research or experiment; brainpower was all that was needed. The scholastic idea (it was hardly a method) bedevilled philosophical, religious, scientific and social thought for millennia, and still survives in the legal and religious thinking of many societies. In Europe, it degenerated into disputations about such matters as the size of angels or the nature of the soul of a butterfly until it was sliced down by the principle which is known in Jewish logic as *sebhara*, which was nicknamed 'Ockham's razor' (after William of Ockham, who enunciated it in the 14th century) and which is now known in **science** as the principle of economy. This states that 'entities should not be unnecessarily multiplied', that is that generalizations should be based on observed facts, not on other generalizations, and that all irrelevancies in an explanation should be pruned away. **KMcL**

See also logic; scientific method.

SCHRÖDINGER EQUATION

It is impossible to talk of the Schrödinger equation without some recourse to **mathematics**, in order to understand the concepts involved. The equation was proposed as a quantum mechanical version of the classical equation of conservation of energy. This is

$$E = \frac{p^2}{2m_0} AV(x,y,z).$$

This classical equation states that the total energy E of a system is equal to the kinetic energy $2\frac{p^2}{m_0}$ plus the potential energy $V(x,y,z)$. p is the momentum of the particle, while m_0 is its mass. The transfer from the classical equation to the quantum mechani-

cal one is achieved by replacing p and E by mathematical operators and allowing them to operate upon a wave function . The equation becomes

$$i\hbar \frac{\partial \Psi}{\partial t} = -\frac{\hbar^2}{2m_0}\nabla^2\Psi + \nabla\Psi$$

It is important to realize that this is a process of **induction**, where a known result (the classical equation) is generalized to include quantum mechanics, rather than **deduction**, where a specific result is derived from generally known properties. As such, it must be, and has been, rigorously tested in a variety of situations and shown to be valid.

There is no pretence that the introduction of Schrödinger's equation is anything other than mysterious. But the initial postulates of a theory, by their nature, are not derived from anything else. One can only present them in their most plausible form and find justification for them in the validity of their application to physical problems.

The postulation of a wave function can only be understood in a rather abstract manner Ψ, the amplitude describing the motion of a quantum mechanical particle, is analogous to the amplitude describing the motion of a wave, provided we accept the wave nature of matter and transfer from a wave to a particle concept. **JJ**

SCIENCE

'Science' is derived from Latin *scientia*, a complicated word whose apparently simple meaning, 'knowledge' conceals an origin in the idea of finding out about things by subdividing them and sorting the pieces. But to call science 'knowledge', with the implication of certainty, is an idea long past its prime: modern science is far more a form of enquiry into natural phenomena, a consensus of information held at any one time (all of which is, so to speak, on loan, and may be modified by new discoveries and new interpretations at any moment), and, most loosely of all, a community of people engaged in enquiry into the natural world.

The word 'science' was not used, even in these senses, until the mid–19th century. Until then, it simply meant the study or skill of any field of **knowledge** at all: there was a 'science' of playing the viol, another of baking bread, another of parliamentary government, and so on. 'Scientists' in our modern sense were at this time called 'natural philosophers' (as opposed to moral philosophers: see below). The first person to describe a 'natural philosopher' as a 'scientist' was William Whewell, in 1840, and the name has stuck. The separate 'sciences' of the time (that is, areas of enquiry into the natural world) were **astronomy**, **biology**, **chemistry** and so on. These were ordered, in the mid-20th century, into two large groupings, **life sciences** (concerned with the animate world) and physical sciences (concerned with the inanimate world). **Technology** is science applied to the practical world, and there is also a group of other disciplines which use **scientific method** to a greater or lesser extent and which are often called 'sciences', though some prefer the word 'studies': **anthropology**, **psychology**, the **social sciences** and others. **Pseudosciences**, as the name implies, are disciplines which claim (or once claimed) the same kind of rigour as the natural sciences, but which on investigation seem (at least to non-devotees) not to live up to those claims: **astrology**, **parapsychology**, **spiritualism** and so on.

The quest of science begins with the human attempt to come to terms with the universe. It takes a different path from such approaches as **myth** or **religion**. In these, the power in the universe, sometimes even the universe itself, is personalized, assumed to have character and identity (usually on the human model). With such a universe, with such powers, it is possible to form a relationship (again on the human model), but objective understanding is neither possible nor the point. If, by contrast, you treat the universe as non-arbitrary, non-controlled, as an impersonal machine, it is as pointless trying to form a relationship with it as it would be with a kettle or a wall-clock. Instead, understanding is a possible, even desirable, endeavour, on the assumption that the governing principles of the universe are not the whims or grand designs of gods and demons, but a number of unchanging, objective and discoverable rules. (The idea that the rules do not change, that the 'laws' of the universe are

fixed and are the same everywhere, literally 'universal', is as fundamental to this approach as faith is to religion. It is, in modern science, undergoing some shocks.)

If the universe is assumed to be governed by gods and spirits, an accepted way to describe it is to explain natural phenomena (such as lightning flashes or the cycle of the seasons) with stories. Storms are caused by irritation among the heavenly powers; the Sun needs to be helped by humans (for example by worship or sacrifice) to return each morning from the world of dark to the world of light; whatever is or happens in the universe is there because some god or other personalized power decided that it should be there. Such ideas can be extremely simple (like the myths described above), and they can also act as the basis for elaborate, beautiful and satisfying systems of **arts**, **belief**, civilization and custom. If, by contrast, the universe is assumed to be impersonal, to be controlled by laws which can be discovered and understood, the method is to look at natural phenomena, find their points of similarity or difference (if any), ponder them objectively and reach logical conclusions about them. The quest is not organic, like that of a tree (as is the proliferation of myths and religious belief-systems); it is a progression, step by logical step – there may be side-paths and detours, but the progression continues nonetheless.

In such a model, it is necessary to start somewhere. Each journey, in the cant phrase, has to begin with the first step. This step cannot be assumed to lead from any other, or it could not be the first step. Therefore it must in some way be so obvious, so self-evident and simple, that it is impossible to disagree with it. The ancient Greeks, who (so far as is known) first started the systematic investigation of natural phenomena, called such steps 'axioms'. If something is axiomatic, it does not need proof: it is itself the basis for a system of logical proof of other things. For example, the Greeks would have claimed as axiomatic that fire is hot and ice is cold, that rock is harder than water, that the shortest distance between two points is a straight line, that parallel lines never meet.

All such ideas depend on observation of Nature – and indeed it is possible to live one's life comfortably and securely simply by accepting them, without bothering about explanations or derivatives. There is a continuum of common-sense 'knowledge' about the natural world which is enough for most people. Just as one knows that to buy food one needs goods or money to exchange for it, without bothering to go into all the complexities of economic theory and fiscal management, so one knows, without needing to swallow a scientific textbook, that if water is heated it boils (and scalds), that clay left in the Sun hardens, that horse-manure used as a mulch for roses makes them grow better, and so on. The 'scientific' thinkers of most ancient societies, most notably the Greeks, left all such practicalities to others. They assumed that the logical systems which could be built on such axioms were of no particular interest in daily life, that they were a preserve of the mind alone, and therefore of specially trained or talented individuals who gave their attention to such matters – 'natural philosophy' – as others gave their attention to human character, belief or behaviour, extrapolating logical systems from axioms in exactly the same way, calling the resultant activity 'moral philosophy'.

This method of enquiry is **deduction**. Its appeal is almost entirely intellectual, and its rigour and beauty led to its being regarded, in ancient times, as one of the highest achievements of human thought. Its beauty is the vastness and elegance of the structures which can be built on the original axioms: for example, if you take as axiomatic that the most perfect form of curve is a circle, and that the heavens (as opposed to the brute Earth) are perfect, then you deduce that the bodies visible in the heavens, and their movement, are patterned in circles. If you further assume that the Earth is stationary in the heavens (and it does not, apparently, move under one's feet except in earthquakes), then you assume that it is the still centre of the universe, and that the other heavenly bodies move round it – they can be perceived to move – in circles. Another elegance of the system, as an intellectual construct, is that it seems to be finite. When you reach the end of all deductions possible from a given axiom, however complex the system created, you stop: all know-

ledge in that particular area has been achieved. Euclid's book *Elements* is one of the most impressive achievements of the process. It takes the axioms of **geometry**, one by one, and deduces from each a logical edifice each part of which is directly traceable back to the original axiom, and seems to reach a logical conclusion, as if there were no more to say on the subject. To 'know' geometry, therefore, might simply be to 'know' Euclid's *Elements*: this is what intellectuals in the West believed for some 2,000 years. In all human history, few books except religious sacred writings have had such long-lasting and widespread authority.

The essential flaw in this kind of 'science' is that it assumes that the axioms are infallible. If this or that phenomenon in Nature, or the deduction made from it by this or that observer, fails to 'fit' the theory, then the theory is right, the natural phenomenon is an aberration and the observer has made a mistake. There is no need for continuous practical observation: deductive systems depend on thought alone. This view was accepted throughout the Western world, and led to the elevation of **scholasticism** as a form of intellectual exploration, and to the marginalization of observation and experiment, for some 2,000 years. Christian divines, notably St Thomas Aquinas in the 13th century, even sought to produce a whole system of belief and practice by deduction, a kind of 'scientific' **Christianity**. Others of the same period, for example Albertus Magnus, set out to synthetize and intellectualize all knowledge about the divine, human and natural worlds, to make all experience part of the same deductive system. Those who sought other ways of explaining the perceived phenomena of the universe, and tried to explore them by observations and experiment, were at best tolerated by the Christian establishment (Roger Bacon is a case in point), or were demonized, denounced and persecuted with a kind of mechanistic rigour (for example practitioners of **alchemy**, rational **medicine** and **witchcraft**). In the East, by contrast, natural philosophy and religion were kept apart, and practical observation was never excluded, so that 'science' was able to make progress, and to keep its relationship with the natural world (for example in heavenly observation and **mathematics**) in a way impossible in the West.

The second major problem with early investigation of the natural world was the absence of instruments of any kind more substantial than the plumb-line and abacus. Natural philosophers had no need of them, as their investigations were remote from the real world; in realms where practicality was essential (for example building-work and commerce), technology was sufficient for need, or if not, need was tempered to technology. The most important developments in 'scientific' thought, in the first millennium of the modern era, were all in the area of calculation (that is, mathematics excluding geometry, which had, in *Elements*, its own sacred text), and its comparatively advanced state was due entirely to need: making charts of ever-increasing complexity for such things as the inundations of the Nile, the mating-sequence of the Chinese Emperor and his various wives and concubines, or the commercial, financial transactions brought about by the burgeoning of international trade. There were no microscopes, no telescopes, no accurate timepieces, no tables or mechanical means of calculation; all observation was limited by the human eye, all manipulation by the skill of the human hand. The miracle is that despite this, astronomers in particular made huge strides in charting the heavens, at first in the Middle East, and then in Europe, where in 1543 Copernicus, on the basis of naked-eye observation and interminable calculation, suggested that one of the most fundamental axioms of the astronomy of the last 3,500 years was mistaken: the Sun, not the Earth, was the centre of the universe. (Lacking instruments, he had no concept of a universe beyond the solar system.)

When Brahe, a couple of decades later, showed that the planets' orbits were elliptical and not circular, and when Galileo, at the end of the 16th century, first used the newly-invented telescope to prove Copernicus correct and then, by rolling balls down ramps (not, as legend has it, by dropping balls from the top of the Leaning Tower of Pisa), shattered another of the major axioms of ancient Greek physics, that a given weight of some 'heavy' material (such as lead) falls to the ground faster than the same weight of some 'light' material (such as feathers), science, in the modern sense, at last was born. The basis now was that the universe was true, not the axioms, and therefore that if there was a conflict between observed fact and theory, the theory should be modified. The method became not deduction but **induction**: starting from observations and elaborating principles from them, and being prepared to fine-tune the principle each and every time a new observation challenged existing ideas.

It is impossible to overstate the importance of this 180-degree turn in our view of how to study the natural world. The rise of observation and experimentation had been prefigured in the previous few centuries – in the work of Roger Bacon, for example, or in Paracelsus' experiments with diagnosis and treatment in medicine – but now it became the central plank of all scientific work. Its rise coincided with other intellectual movements, notably Descartes' demonstration that it was possible to believe in a universe which was mechanistic rather than deterministic, the suggestion, by the **humanists** among others, that human beings and not God might be the 'measure of all things', and, not least, the feeling that it was not enough to accept the view of the world's **geography** propounded since ancient times, but that physical exploration, backed by maps based on observation rather than imagination, was possible. In 1605, Francis Bacon propounded what has become known as the 'scientific method', setting the pattern for inductive science just as Aristotle's methods had established deductive science some 2,000 years earlier. In the following decades Boyle and Hooke began a systematic exploration of chemistry, removing it far from its mumbo-jumbo image in **alchemy**; Newton began studying the properties of light and the movement of physical objects in the universe; Newton and (separately) Leibniz developed the **calculus**, the most sophisticated method of mathematical calculation yet devised; measuring devices, from barometers to chronometers, from mechanical calculators to marine compasses, were invented, refined, and turned to the purposes of scientific exploration as well as the 'practical' uses for which they were created.

From this moment on, at first in the West and then (from the 1900s onwards) in the East and eventually worldwide, science has grown at an exponential rate. At the beginning of the 19th century (the time of Priestley's work on oxygen and the first thorough-going experiments to harness electricity), a single individual could, with application, learn all available scientific knowledge. By the mid-century, each branch of science had grown so fast, and become so complex, that even experts had to rely on libraries, assistants and *aides-mémoires* even in their own fields. As investigation proceeded, instrument-making kept pace, often itself triggering new directions in research. There was another fundamental change, in place by the end of the 19th century (and signalled, perhaps, by the presentation of the first Nobel prizes). Instead of science being an esoteric and hermetic discipline, conducted by cult-like groups (such as the Pythagoreans in ancient Greece) or by intellectual gurus whose thoughts were considered to elevate them far beyond ordinary mortal understanding (Ptolemy in his day, and Newton in his, spring to mind) scientific knowledge came to be regarded as the property not of individuals but of the entire human race. Discoveries and research-methods were shared; investigation became the work of teams. This co-operative approach (not, it must be admitted, shared by all scientists: there were, and are, a few determined hermits) was matched by the rise of rationalism, the collapse of the consensus that God had anything to do with the creation, ordering or maintenance of the universe. We may or may not, nowadays, retain our religious beliefs, but for better or worse we live in a world which is perceived in scientific and secular-scientific terms.

There remain many problems. Scientific activity is perceived by many as dangerous, polluting and potentially disastrous. Business considerations have distorted some scientific areas (for example, dictating directions in drugs research or suggesting the patenting of plant or human genomes). Science has become esoteric again, so that there is often little mutual understanding between scientists from different disciplines, let alone between scientists and non-scientists. And most important of all, perhaps is the thought (alarming to many, both in and out of the 'scientific community') that there is, now, no such thing as 'truth' in science. **Non-Euclidean geometry** (discovered in the early 19th century), **quantum** mechanics and the **relativity** theories of Einstein in the early years of the 20th century, not to mention current discoveries in every area from astrophysics to **genetics**, suggest that the best we have at any moment, the best we have ever had, is a temporary working model of the way things are, and that exploration, investigation, are endless. Once again, the earlier consensus about the universe and its laws has been turned on its head, and one of the main questions philosophers of science seek to answer is, if (as is now apparent) induction from observation, considered as a method of reaching logical 'truth', is as flawed as deduction, where does science go next? **KMcL**

See also chaos theory; philosophy of science; scientific laws; two cultures.

Further reading Colin A. Ronan, *Science: its History and Development Among the World's Cultures*; K.R. Popper, *The Logic of Scientific Discovery*; R. Harre, *Philosophies of Science*.

SCIENTIFIC HUMANISM see Humanism

SCIENTIFIC LAWS

In **science**, enquiry proceeds on the basis that some principles are universally applicable and valid. They may be added to (as for example Euclid's principles of **geometry** were supplemented in the 19th century by the system known as **non-Euclidean geometry**) or they may be modified (as for example Newton's laws of motion were modified in the light of the theory of **relativity**), but by and large they are not rejected. It is, for example, a scientific law (Boyle's Law) that, at a constant temperature, the volume of a given mass of gas is in inverse proportion to its pressure. This seems different from a theory, such as that when substances burn they give off a substance called phlogiston: an idea totally destroyed by Priestley's discovery of oxygen and its properties. Perhaps, as some modern scientists and philosophers of science are claiming, all laws of science are theories which have not, so far, been disproved. **KMcL**

See also philosophy of science; scientific method.

SCIENTIFIC METHOD

If 'scientific method' is taken to mean 'a way of reaching the **truth** about natural phenomena', there is no such thing. There are many 'truths', and many 'methods'. Nothing can be taken for granted. Even the view, put forward by Francis Bacon in the 16th century, that logical inference based on observation is better than guesswork, does not hold true in every instance. It used to be believed that there was a fixed body of truth about the universe, and that if we used the right method and the right amounts of effort and sophistication, we might one day discover, own, all of it. This no longer seems to be the case; in fact the more scientists discover, the more evidence they find for chance, randomness and unpredictability. Statistically, the amount of such things is still minute but we have to remember two things, first that one aberrant result in a billion billion identical tests of a theory is enough to cast doubt on the theory, and second that we only know, have only probed, a tiny fraction of what is there to be investigated. Laws and paradigms (models, such as **physics**) are useful in helping us to make sense of natural phenomena, but their value lasts only until we start taking them, in whole or in part, as absolute truths. (Darwin's theory of **evolution**, for example, does not match the paradigm of physics. Newton's laws of motion failed to explain the orbit of the planet Mercury, and it was only with the development of the theory of **relativity** that it was seen that the problem was not that Mercury's orbit was an aberration, but that Newton's laws were wrong. The theory of relativity itself is incompatible

with **quantum** mechanics; eventually some discovery will be made which resolves the inconsistencies, but in the meantime the two ideas cover enough ground, and enable enough work to proceed, for us to accept their incompatibility and study it.)

In ancient intellectual investigation of the natural world, the method used was deductive reasoning (see **deduction**). Starting from simple premises (ones regarded as self-evident, such as that parallel lines never meet), one proceeded by logical steps, each dependent on the one before, until a conclusion was reached. The assumption was that if the initial premise was true, and the **logic** was properly carried out, the conclusion must also be true.

This is the method of mathematical calculation, and underlies much work in the physical sciences, where behaviour and relationships can be precisely measured and quantified. But it suffers from two major flaws. First, someone must decide on the truth of the initial premise of a line of reasoning, and if that decision is wrong, then the whole line of reasoning is invalidated. (Parallel lines, for example, may never meet in Euclid's two-dimensional **geometry**; but in the real, curved universe they do.) Second, the method tends to advance under its own intellectual impetus, the steps following the processes of logic and sidestepping the real world. This is fine so long as the real world does not throw up examples which conflict with the logic. Failure to relate the intellectual rationalization of science to practical observation, the belief that if observed phenomena conflicted with the events in a logical progression it was the phenomena which were 'wrong', hindered the development of science for two millennia.

Since the **Renaissance**, the deductive method in science has been replaced by (or gone hand in hand with) the method of **induction**. Here one starts from an observation (such as that the Sun has risen every day, in human experience, so far), and induces the conclusion that the Sun will rise tomorrow. From a large set of particular statements one goes to a single general statement. The chief flaw in this method is that, once again, it depends on the ability and application of the person doing the work. From a given set of observations, I may induce one general statement, you may induce quite another. The problem is that, unlike the conclusion in a deductive argument (which is, so to speak, 'contained' in the original premise), that in an inductive argument is not, and could in theory be anything at all. In practice, the scientist must spend time gathering evidence to support the thesis (the assumption, or theory, he or she makes based on the original observation).

In the 18th century, David Hume pointed out that the inductive method, though attractive and useful, was logically entirely invalid; in the 20th century Karl Popper said that the way to restore rigour was to seek not to confirm theories, but to refute them. This has led to general and healthy **scepticism** in science. Nothing is taken on trust, all experiments are repeated and repeated, and everything we 'know' is taken to be, as it were, a temporary acquisition based on information at present available and a useful basis for speculation and analysis, but by no means absolute truth. This means that science is now two-headed. In speculation it is imaginative, intuitive, a matter of inspiration; in execution it is methodical, mechanical and unimaginative, a matter of perspiration. Its incarnation as a speculative enterprise which uses analytical methods as accurate as can be devised is, some argue, a departure from the real world almost as remarkable as that of the ancient Greek 'natural philosophers' who saw no need to test their reasoning by observation, and a very long way indeed from the simple 'Start with a hypothesis, do experiments to test it, and then announce a conclusion' of the average school exercise-book. **KMcL**

See also mathematics; philosophy of science; science; scientific laws.

SCRIPTURE

It is now recognized that the earliest Hebrew Scriptures were transmitted for hundreds of years before being committed to writing, and that even when the writing process began, about the time of King Solomon in the 10th century BCE, the living tradition continued in prophecy and psalm until collections of these were made at the time of the Exile in Babylon, and books (the section known as 'The Writings') were directly written down. This period, from the initiation of the oral tradition to the point when it was written down, is very short compared with the Hindu Scriptures, composed in a sacred language, Sanskrit, and handed down with remarkably little deviation from generation to generation of Brahmin priests.

The point when tradition becomes scripture is clearly a landmark in the history of a religion. The point of scripture is that the original revelation is preserved for all time, giving a norm by which conduct and teaching can be judged. In the early Christian Church, this was not initially deemed necessary because the world was expected to end imminently, and it was only when the eye witnesses of Jesus' life and resurrection began to die that oral teaching was set down definitely for the worship and education for the second generation. The Vedas, the oldest Hindu scriptures, were set down to ensure that rites were correctly performed and the gods propitiated; later when sacrifices alone failed to satisfy the human spirit, the Upanisads record the quest for **truth**.

If the reason for scripture varies from one religion to another, so does the decree of authority vested in it, especially in relation to tradition and interpretation. But always at some point a *canon* (Greek, 'rule', 'measure') is established which permits neither of addition nor subtraction to the collection. **EMJ RM**

SCULPTURE

The making of objects in the round or in relief has been practised since prehistory. Current evidence suggests that Australian aborigines were carving designs into rockfaces at least 45,000 years: ago an estimated 13,000 years before such art appeared in Europe, and 19,000 years before the first paintings on rock. Whether bas-relief sculptures were made in the estimated 15,000 years between the arrival of humans in Australia and such petroglyphs is not yet known.

The purposes of prehistoric sculpture are difficult to determine with precision, but were perhaps connected with **magic** and **ritual**, as well as with aspects of society and perhaps politics and 'art' as well. The subject-matter of sculpture has, until the past century, been remarkably consistent, in a balance established by the ancient Egyptians and confirmed by the Greeks and Romans. Decorative work, iconic or aniconic depending on religious and cultural preferences, must always have filled the largest part of most sculptors' days. The largest proportion of sophisticated and surviving work is dedicated to funerary sculpture connected with mortals, with the stelai, statues, bas reliefs and even complete tombs and funerary temples surviving in enormous quantities. Less populous, but more important, are representations of the lives, images and deeds of gods, goddesses and heroes, and heroized monarchs as well, often focused in mythological stories. Next comes portraiture, much used in funerary work, and an anchor for the modeller of coins, which are of course the widest-spread of all sculptural creations, often of very high quality, and demonstrably the most influential as well, not only for their 'original' artwork, but also for their valuable role in spreading knowledge of large-scale works. An important nexus in the history of sculpture is between works for public and those for private display. While the prestige lies frequently with imposing public displays, the often smaller works for private consumption should not be forgotten: statuettes as religious offerings or for table decoration, jewellery and other personal adornment. A constant theme is of utilitarian items raised to the status of art by their materials and craftsmanship, from Cellini's famous saltcellar to complete table-settings in silver, gold or porcelain.

A continuing thread in the historiography of sculpture is the lifelike nature of the statue: according to Greek legend, Pygmalion fell in love with the ivory statue of a maiden he had made, and implored the gods to give it life. Similarly, legends abound of miraculous statues of the Virgin or of saints: some cry real tears, or drip blood; others walk around their domain at night. The legend lives today in stories of computerized robots.

Depending on the material employed, the sculpting process is subtractive or additive: the sculptor carves away unwanted marble, stone or wood with appropriate chisels or knives; or models (with the hands) wax, clay or plaster. Beautification may be needed to enhance poor-quality or unsuitable materials: wood and stone may be painted after covering with gesso to ensure a smooth surface. Support and protection may also be required: large-scale works in clay, a common and useful material, require an internal armature for support, and protection if they are to withstand the weather (hence the popularity of Della-Robbia, a technique for enamelling terracotta developed by the Florentine sculptor Luca della Robbia in the 15th century). Wood has probably always been the most popular (if far from the most prestigious) material for sculptors, but large quantities have been lost through decay and disaster. Today, even marble cannot often withstand our polluted atmosphere, and the surface detail crumbles away. Wax and plaster are usually intermediates, the former for delicate surface modelling of work to be translated into bronze, the latter for making casts. Frequently, small-scale models are produced by the master, and transferred to full-size (in a different material, usually marble) by an assistant. The master then adds the finishing touches. Sheet materials (such as gold, silver, brass, copper or bronze) are often employed to cover a cheaper armature, and given detail by being worked from behind (*repoussé*); to these may be added ivory, useful because it approximates both to the tint and the 'depth' of flesh.

Available materials have naturally influenced the complexion of production, with marble traditionally restricted to the Mediterranean basin, and other centres using stone of varying quality: granite and sandstone for the ancient Egyptians, and volcanic tufo for Borobodur (Java, Indonesia). Working methods – abrasives, rasps, chisels, punches and mallets – have changed little over the centuries, although some scholars ascribe the stylistic caesura in Greece of about 500 BCE to newly available steel and iron tools, both sharper and more robust than the bronze ones they replaced.

Unlike marble, the use of bronze is widespread, from China and other parts of Asia to Africa and Europe; an unrepresentative selection of works probably survives, because the material is so useful, being easily recast. Bronze is an alloy largely or exclusively of copper and tin, used since about 2000 BCE. Because of its lower melting point, it is easier to cast (using some kind of mould or supporting core) than copper, and also wears better because it is harder. Hence it was early recognized as an ideal material for sculpture: lighter than marble, able to be duplicated (not to mention repaired), and sturdy enough to survive outdoors. Just as attractive to sculptors was the material's ability to take fine detail. Casting was a specialized business, sometimes experimented with by the adventurous (such as Donatello), but often left to professionals, such as bell-casters. Sculptures would usually be made around a core (apparently wooden in archaic Greece), and this might be left in place in the case of small statuettes or even lifesize pieces; larger sculptures would have the core removed, and then be given a skeleton ('armature') so that the metal could be cast suitably thin and therefore not cost too much. Colossal statues, like their smaller fellows, would conveniently be cast in sections, and then fitted together, with drapery or armour perhaps concealing the joins. Bronzes could therefore be more adventurous than marble: better suited, for example, to large-scale equestrian statues, or to figures in energetic action with wide-flung limbs. The very finest bronzes employed the lost-wax technique, employed in the Mediterranean since at least archaic Greek times, and long before by the Chinese; it is known throughout the world. Ordinary casting can be a copying process, often for transferring work in one medium into another. Taking a mould of an existing bronze is possible, and this has the advantage that the original is not damaged; the disadvantage, however, is that the surface modelling cannot fully be reproduced. Lost-wax casting entails making the sculp-ture in wax, supported by some central core or armature. The wax makes possible very fine modelling, faithfully taking every hint of the artist's hand. The finished work is bundled up in a fine plaster package, suitably adorned with vent-holes, and heated. The wax escapes, leaving its negative impression on the plaster. Molten bronze is then poured in, taking the place of the wax, and faithfully adopting all its surface features. The technique is, as it were, a mirror image of moulding: although the quality is excellent, the original wax model is perforce destroyed in the process itself.

Such a luxurious medium has always been popular, and statuettes especially so, not just among collectors, but also with artists, for whom they provided portable models, as it were. Ghiberti, for example, probably had antique statuettes in bronze and terracotta to inspire his work on the Gates of Paradise (the bronze doors of the baptistry of Florence Cathedral). **Renaissance** collectors avidly sought not only the antique statuettes themselves, but also modern versions and imitations inspired by the antique. Large-scale bronzes suffered when fashion changed, especially when war came, for their material was intrinsically precious and they were easily melted down.

Marble (metamorphized limestone) occurs in many varieties, some single-colour, others striated. Characteristics can include large or small crystals; no apparent 'grain'; opacity, translucency and luminosity in varying degrees; ability to take a polish which 'deepens' the surface effect; ability to stand slicing into thin veneeers, or excavating into truly large blocks; and, very importantly, the ability to withstand ordinary atmospheric conditions and retain its surface detailing. Not all countries have marble: the UK has none, whereas fine marbles are to be found in Italy, Greece, Asia Minor and North Africa. Having suitable marbles locally did not prevent the importing of others: whereas the classical Greeks were content with nearby supplies, the Romans had a vigorous import trade, especially with North Africa and Asia Minor. Indeed, the beautification of ancient Rome (and that of innumerable cities, corporations and private individuals since) is often dependent upon the prestige and rarity of the marbles used.

In the Mediterranean basin, the material has been prized since the second millenium BCE for small-scale sculpture, then for pieces of increasing size; and since Hellenistic times the colour ranges and luminosity of the stone have made marble a luxury furnishing material for floors, walls and columns – and an index of quality and luxury, so much so that in centuries when quarries were closed (for instance, during much of the Middle Ages) make-and-mend and reuse of existing veneers, sarcophagi, etc. was rife. In Greek and Roman times, it is not unusual to find whole buildings (and their associated sculptures) made out of marble: a notable example is the Parthenon.

Marble has been the primary sculpting material in the West from Greek times through to the Renaissance and into the 19th century. If it cannot usually mimic flesh tones, it can approximate to the luminosity and 'depth' of skin, especially when tinted. The different colours available allow whole multicolour statues to be pieced together – white marble for the head and other flesh parts, perhaps grey for some clothes and black for others. Few other materials possess the same beauty, revealed through detailing and polishing; and the possibility of quarrying very large blocks adds monumentality to the list of its attributes. Although wooden statues were surely made in far larger numbers, marble assigns 'aristocracy' to the artist, in much the same way as true fresco painting did (as compared to panel painting) in the Italian Renaissance.

A medium especially useful for flesh tones is bone. Objects for ritual, domestic and decorative use have been made of bone since prehistoric times, for bone is readily available in large quantities, sufficiently hard even to make needles, is white or whitish, and takes detail well. Elephant ivory has the same qualities, together with the cachet of being a luxury item, traded at high cost from as early as the second millenium BCE, and avidly used by Persians as well as Greeks. The cost and quality of ivory, as well as the restricted dimensions of tusks, made it suitable for small works,

especially statuettes, jewel or cosmetic caskets, tablets of various kinds, or as coverings for furniture. During the Middle Ages, it was especially popular for statuettes of the Virgin and Child, or for portable altars. Islam, being closer to the areas of production and trade, captured part of the market, and caskets of ivory, sometimes with classical friezes of putti and/or vine scrolls, found a ready market in medieval southern Europe.

Since Greek times, ivory had been used in small plaques to plate wooden furniture, its best-known Christian counterpart being the 'Chair of St Peter' in St Peter's basilica, an ivory chair possibly made in the 9th century, and subsequently encased in a shrine by Bernini. Another use was the late-antique Consular Diptych, two panels of ivory with scenes indicative of the power of the Consul, sent out throughout the Empire from the 5th century CE, which much later was sometimes included in Church treasuries and even used for calendars. Ivory carving was at its height during the Middle Ages in East and West, with some influence from former to latter. It survived as a luxury item during the Northern Renaissance, especially in Germany.

Relief sculpture, where the designs or figures are anchored to a determinable planar surface (a door, wall, or piece of furniture) exists in bronze, marble, stone and wood. It is often modest in scale (in the West, it is sometimes the work of goldsmiths), although the Egyptians covered large walls with 'inverse relief', where the designs are incised rather than standing proud. In marble low relief, sensitive atmospheric effects and a suave delicacy may be achieved; high relief is equally skilful, as the nearly–3D figures (which are sometimes given metal accoutrements to increase verisimilitude) must be carefully worked if they are to remain intact. Relief sculpture is a mainstay of architectural decoration (cf. the Parthenon, or Borobudur), but sometimes the figures are worked separately and then attached to the marble, bronze or stone backing.

An important aspect of sculpture in East and West is a fascination with large-scale works: colossal statues sometimes many times human scale. Usually representing gods, kings and heroes, these are frequently in relief, using whole rock-faces for support. When free-standing, they are sometimes pieced together from various materials over an armature. The genre was adopted during the Middle Ages in the West for architectural sculpture (which would have seemed insignificant if placed high in a cathedral at only lifesize); and antique horizons reopened with a vengeance during the Renaissance, when the colossal manner was widely adopted. Indeed, it became (as a visit to Italy or Korea will indicate) a mode as important for sculptural credibility as, perhaps, fresco work for a painter.

The great majority of all sculpture, worldwide, is and always has been polychromatic: that is, painted in many colours, usually to enhance lifelikeness. (Real hair, ivory teeth, pearl eyes, and so forth were not unusual.) Sculpture in wood (the cheapest and most readily available material) was usually painted on top of a coating of plaster, which helped fill in the grain. Greek sculpture, even in marble (such as the Elgin Marbles), was routinely painted, and this tradition continues down into the Middle Ages, so that the great portals of the Gothic cathedrals might to our chaste Renaissance-influenced taste have seemed garish if not vulgar with their multicoloured stone figures. Plenty of traces remain from all periods: see, for example, the tympanum of the Puerta de la Gloria at Santiago de Compostella, or Sluter's Well of Moses in Dijon. Polychromatic multifigure wooden altarpieces, often gilded, adorned Spanish and northern altars until well into the 17th century, when canvases usually took their place. It seems to have been a misunderstanding by the Renaissance of Roman sculpture which encouraged them to promote plain marble for their works. In other words, the Roman material they studied had long since lost its colour, or perhaps they chose to ignore it.

The Renaissance taste for 'pure' marble sculpture was broken virtually completely by Bernini, who observed and wished to imitate the Roman use of different coloured stones and marbles to produce composite busts or even complete groups, as can be seen from his funerary monuments in St Peter's.

The Renaissance 'interlude' was, however, reconfirmed in the 18th century, when the neoclassical quest for purity came up against incontrovertible proof of polychromy amongst the admired ancients and yet won. There are a few dry examples of the technique in the 19th century, especially in the various revivals; but a renewed interest in the natural beauty of materials meant that our century has not been well disposed to hiding it under layers of polychromy. **MG PD**

Further reading Rudolf Wittkower, *Sculpture: Processes and Principles.*

SECONDARY QUALITIES see **Primary Qualities**

SECT/SECTARIANISM

A sect (from Latin *secare*, 'to cut off') is a small, voluntary, exclusive religious or (occasionally) secular group, which demands total commitment from its followers. Sects typically emphasize their separateness from, and rejection of, orthodox religious and/or secular institutions, doctrines and practices.

In the 17th century, during the English Civil War and the religious upheavals, a 'sectary' was someone who was considered to put the interests of his or her religious community above all else. Sectarianism came to embody the attitude of 'my church right or wrong'. The tragic consequences of this attitude can still be seen in Northern Ireland today.

Where there is a majority faith established by law, such as the Church of England, or the churches recognized by the Treaty of Augsburg (1555) in different constituent states of Germany, minority groups are labelled as 'sects', and are often legally disadvantaged. (For example, in the British House of Lords no representatives of other churches hold equivalent status to the **Anglican** bishops.) This discrimination diverts attention from an important theological and sociological difference. The 'established' churches or churches which claim to be catholic, that is universal, accept as members all who are born and baptized within their territory. They embrace, potentially, the entire population of a country and accept pastoral responsibility on that basis. Sects, by contrast, are free of any connection with the state, and are 'gathered' in the sense that members elect to join, sometimes by adult baptism, or by public statement of faith. **DA EMJ**

See also charisma; church; religion; secularization; state.

Further reading B. Wilson, *Religion in Sociological Perspective.*

SECULARIZATION

Secularization (from Latin *secularis*, 'of the age') is the process in modern societies whereby religious ideas, practice and organizations lose their influence in the face of scientific and other knowledge.

Tracing the extent of secularization is a complex process and the extent of secularization across Western societies varies considerably. In the US, for example, religious membership has remained high and the formation of new **cults** or **sects** has continued in many modern societies. That secularization cannot be assumed to be an automatic feature of modernity is indicated by the resurgence of religion in some modernizing societies (for instance, recent Islamic revolutionary movements). In Northern Ireland, Protestants and Catholics keep alive a deep-seated religious divide.

Despite the continued significance of religion in modern society, with the exception of the US, industrialized countries have all experienced considerable secularization when measured by level of membership of religious organizations. Secularization also concerns how far religious organizations have been able to maintain their social influence, wealth and prestige, and this has progressively waned. Religion continues to be of significance but the hold of religious beliefs is far less than it was even 20 years ago. **DA**

See also church; culture; ideology; rationalization; religion; theories of modernity.

Further reading T. Luckmann, *The Invisible Religion: the Problem of Religion in Modern Society;* Martin, *A General Theory of Secularization.*

SEDUCTION THEORY see **Child Abuse**

SEISMOLOGY

Seismology (Greek, 'study of quaking') is the modern science of studying the action of shock waves from underground explosions (natural or human-made). It allows a picture to be constructed of the nature and behaviour of the Earth's interior, and leads to predictions of earthquakes and other such significant events on the surface. The work is now done with the help of measuring instruments and computers, and seismology is a formal science. In ancient times the ability to predict earth movements was regarded as a psychic gift analogous to second sight or mediumship. In earthquake-prone areas, those sensitive to earth movements were often made the guardian-presences of prophetic shrines – and since animals are as sensitive to these movements as humans, such 'guardians' might just as easily be horses or cattle, thought to be party to the purposes of the gods. In ancient Greece, one shrine was tenanted by a flock of prescient hens, and in ancient Japan, carp in a pool predicted earthquakes. **KMcL**

SELF

For centuries, philosophers and psychologists have puzzled out the nature of the self. In simple terms, it is the 'aware subject', the subject of mental activity, the thing that thinks, feels and wills; above all, it is the subject as he or she experiences himself or herself. But this is only the platform for more complex (and more subjective) thought. In the 17th century, Descartes wrote of the self as non-physical and immortal, and said that thinking is essential to it. A century later, Hume denied that there is a subject of mental activity (a thing which feels, sees, thinks and wills, distinct from and something over and above occurrent events of feeling, thinking and willing), and noted that when we introspect, we find various mental items – events of feeling, thinking and willing – but no distinct 'thing' that has them.

Writing in the 19th century, Josiah Royce made the psychological distinction between self and non-self: the beginning of distinctions between **ego** and subconscious or **unconscious**. Pierre Janet, a French contemporary of Freud, distinguished between *individu, personnage* and *moi*. William James in his *Principles of Psychology* (1880) makes a distinction between self as object and self as subject. The philosopher G.H. Mead, developing the idea at the same time, made a similar distinction between I, Me and Self.

Jung's theories on the self were derived from his own personal crisis, as a result of which he talked about the self with enormous conviction of its psychic reality. He described the journey of the psyche as one which led to the **individuation** of the self. **AJ MJ**

See also death; dreams; no-ownership theory of the self.

SELF-DECEPTION

Self-deception, deceiving oneself is, in philosophical terms, extremely puzzling. When two people are involved, deception involves the deceiver intentionally making another person, the deceived, believe what the deceiver knows to be false. Thus a husband may intentionally get his wife to believe what he, the deceiver, knows to be false: that is, that the two of them have a monogamous relationship. But it is difficult to see how one person could manage to deceive themself in this way. How could one intentionally get oneself to believe what one believes to be false? How could one intentionally get oneself to believe that one's partner is faithful when one believes that he or she is not? For how could one intend to deceive oneself?

One attempt to resolve this conundrum is to split the self into sub-systems. Just as ordinary deception involves two people, one of whom intentionally deceives the other, self-deception is said to involve one part of the self intentionally deceiving another part of the self. The sub-systems of the self are both person-like in that they have beliefs, desires and intentions, and they causally influence each other. And no sub-system of the self ever intends to deceive its self, but one sub-system may intend to and succeed in deceiving another. **AJ**

Further reading R. Wollheim and J. Hopkins, *Philosophical Essays on Freud.*

SELF-DETERMINATION

The idea of self-determination originated with philosophers of the **Enlightenment**. For the individual the idea implied that a morally autonomous person was one who freely and rationally chose the right course of action, that is, was self-determining. Analogously for a community the idea of self-determination implied that for a people to be genuinely free they must determine their own government and the form of that government – a doctrine enunciated in the American Declaration of Independence and in the French Declaration of the Rights of Man. This idea of self-determination dovetails neatly with **nationalism**, the belief that the national unit, or the national people, and the unit of government should be congruent, and nations should be free to establish such congruence.

Self-determination has therefore been associated with the democratization of the world and the arguments used to undermine illegitimate empires, and consequently has a rightly honoured place in the lexicon of political freedom.

However, there are multiple difficulties with the idea of self-determination, which are the subject matter of many contemporary national and ethnic conflicts. Who are the people who have the right to self-determination? Are they self-defining, or are they the people of the existing unit of government? Who decides who are the people? Those in revolt say they do so themselves, the **state** says that the definition of the people is its prerogative, as does so-called 'international law' (although it does recognize the right of colonies to self-determination). What if the people are not one people, but several peoples? Who then has the right of self-determination: all, the largest or none? How is self-determination to be implemented: through revolution, secessions, partitions, referendums, and/or plebiscites? What is the scope of self-determination? Need it extend to seeking full statehood and **sovereignty** for one's nation? The degree of autonomy pursued by a stateless nation can range from the partial devolution of legal and fiscal responsibilities (as in home rule arrangements) to more complete autonomy (as in **federalism**), to accepting arrangements for shared sovereignty over a given territory, through to demands for outright **independence**. These difficulties with the idea of self-determination do not mean that it is worthless, or indeed pernicious as many often suggest, but rather that it must be carefully handled. Perhaps the right to self-determination is like the right to **liberty**: something which people should be free to exercise providing they do not cause demonstrable harm to the rights of others to enjoy self-determination. **BO'L**

See also colonialism; consociationalism; democracy.

Further reading B. Barry, 'Self-Government Revisited' in D. Miller and L. Siedentop (eds.), *The Nature of Political Theory*; A. Cobban, *National Self-Determination*; D.P. Moynihan, *Pandaemonium: Ethnicity in International Politics*.

SELFISH GENE

In the **life sciences**, the selfish gene theory is the Darwinian concept of **natural selection** broken down to the level of individual genes as the units upon which natural selection acts. This approach was expounded by Richard Dawkins in *The Selfish Gene* (1976) and *The Extended Phenotype* (1982). In Darwinian terms, natural selection acts upon the individual organism, but Dawkins considered the individual as a collection of self-replicating genes together coding for, and carried by, a self-preserving survival machine (the body). In this context it is possible to reconcile natural selection with behaviour, which appears, at the level of the individual, to be altruistic (see **altruism**). Thus a gene might sacrifice some copies of itself in order to promote the survival of other copies. **RB**

See also group selection; kin selection.

SEMANTICS

Semantics (from Greek *semantikos*, 'significant'), in **symbolic logic**, is the task of reading meaning into sentences. In pure **logic**, it is always emphasized that the symbols are merely symbols, and that words like 'true' and 'false' are no more than labels which persist for historical reasons. In the wider field of **mathematics**, and even more so in the applications of mathematics to other areas, these terms are taken at their face value and are interpreted by using semantics.

In **linguistics**, semantics deals with the way meaning is organized and interpreted within languages. A perennial theme is the need to account for the relationship between the two central concepts, reference and sense. Reference can be thought of as the relationship between a language expression and the actual thing which is being talked about. An immediate problem arises with the realization that a single language expression can very often be used to refer to several quite different things (for example, the phrase 'Queen of England' refers to a different person when uttered in 1890 as against 1990). A further complication is that separate expressions may refer to the same object, or referent. A well-known example is provided by the phrases 'Morning Star' and 'Evening Star', both of which refer to the planet Venus. It is clear that very few expressions in a language bear a fixed reference. Most referring expressions can only be interpreted by taking into account the **context** in which they are uttered.

In contrast with reference, sense relations are not derived through allusion to the external world or context of utterance. Instead, the sense of an expression is akin to the dictionary definition of a word, in so far as words are typically defined in terms of other words. Meaning is often considered to be compositional, since the sense of a complex expression can be worked out by combining the senses of its constituent elements. It has been suggested that certain concepts are semantically basic, or primitive, since their sense cannot be broken down any further into separate subcomponents (for example, 'I', 'you', 'want', 'think', 'this'). However, if certain concepts cannot be defined in terms of any other constituent, the possibility is raised, unpalatable to some, that we are born ready-equipped with these meanings. If they are not innate, it is difficult to conceive how they could otherwise be defined or understood.

The sense relations of natural language expressions can be dealt with more rigorously within the framework of a metalanguage, or semantic representation. Formal systems of logic are often used to represent meaning in this way since they are especially useful for revealing the conditions which establish whether a sentence is true or false. However, the psychological status of semantic representations is highly controversial, since not all semanticists accept the idea that they describe how meaning is actually represented in the mind.

A complicating factor in syntactic theory is that the **syntax** of a sentence can exert a profound influence on the way its meaning is interpreted, as the following examples demonstrate: (a) Sarah hates David. (b) David hates Sarah. Despite being composed of identical words, these two sentences clearly have different meanings. Hence, the order of words in the sentence, a syntactically-controlled phenomenon, can exert an influence on its meaning. This kind of interaction between syntax and semantics is extremely complex and continues to present semantic theory with some of its greatest challenges. **SMcL MS**

Further reading G.N. Leech, *Semantics: the Study of Meaning*; F.R. Palmer, *Semantics*.

SEMICONDUCTOR DEVICE THEORY

Semiconductor Device Theory, in electrical engineering, is based on the principle that the conductivity of the semiconductor material – how well it allows electricity to flow – can be controlled over wide limits by varying the concentration of impurities added to the pure semiconductor. Semiconducting materials, as their name implies, have conductivities between those of good conductors (such as metals) and good insulators (such as most plastics).

The real semiconductor revolution did not occur until 1947 when J. Bardeen and W.H. Brattain invented the transistor. The transistor, or 'transfer resistor', could be used as both an electrical amplifier and oscillator and offered greater reliability and performance over the electronic valve devices it replaced. **AC**

SEMIOLOGY see Semiotics

SEMIOTICS

Semiotics (originally semiology or semeiology: Greek, 'study of signs'), in **linguistics**, is concerned with the mechanisms of communication, with signs and the way they function systematically to convey meaning. The exact nature of the sign relationship is controversial, but almost all theories recognize at least two components, sometimes referred to as the *representamen* ('sign vehicle'), and the *object* (what the sign stands for).

The founder of semiotics, the US philosopher C.S. Peirce (1839–1914), showed how the communicative purpose of a sign is dependent on the kind of relationship between representamen and object. He identified three kinds of signs: 'iconic', 'indexical' and 'symbolic'. 'Iconic' signs represent what they refer to: an example is the sign showing a ferocious dog and meaning 'Beware of the dog'. 'Indexical' signs can only be interpreted by reference to what is being 'pointed at' in a given context: the word 'me', for example, means something quite different when I use it and when you use it.

It has been argued that iconic and indexical relationships dominate our ordinary use of language. However, the recognition of language as a unique sign system is in some large measure due to the symbolic functions words embody. 'Symbolic' signs, Peirce's third category, are quite independent of the objects (any objects) to which they refer; their meaning is established by convention, and nothing in the nature of the sign resembles or refers to any specific object. Numerals and letters of the alphabet are obvious examples, but most words in a language clearly do come into this category.

Peirce's original categories applied principally to language. It was the Swiss philosopher Ferdinand de Saussure (1857–1913) who broadened semiology (as he called it) to include methods of communication of all kinds. His ideas are not only crucial to modern linguistics and to such literary-critical disciplines as **psychoanalytic criticism** and **structuralism**, but play an important part in modern **anthropology**, **media** studies and **sociology**. **KMcL MS**

Further reading Umberto Eco, *A Theory of Semiotics*; Terry Eagleton, *Literary Theory: an Introduction*.

SENTIMENTAL DRAMA

While sentiment, in its modern sense, may be found in all forms of **drama** and **theatre**, Sentimental Drama was a specifically 18th-century European form in which, as Oliver Goldsmith put it, 'the virtues of private life are exhibited, rather than the vices exposed'. ('Sentiment' at this period meant 'feeling' or 'sensibility'.) While many of the plays were nominally comic, the characters tended to be dull and priggish, the plots bathetic and the language stilted. Despite this, it was popular with the rising middle-class audience, especially in Germany, France and Britain, because it tended to treat them seriously in ways which neither **comedy** nor **tragedy** did. For all its dramatic ineptness (at least from today's perspective) it is important in theatre-historical terms, as it marks an important stage in the development of serious prose drama. **TRG SS**

See also bourgeois drama; carnival; domestic drama; tragicomedy.

Further reading A. Sherbo, *English Sentimental Drama*.

SEPARATION OF POWERS see **Representative Government**

SERIAL MUSIC

Composers of serial music seek to remove randomness from their art by subjecting some or all of its elements – pitch, duration, volume – to external mathematical discipline. In twelve-note music, for example, the twelve notes of the octave (C, C sharp, D, D sharp, etc.) are arranged in a series (for example, 2,5,8,9, etc., where C is 1, C sharp is 2 and so on); no note may be repeated until the whole series has been played. (This style, developed by Schoenberg in the late 1910s, and formalized by him in 1923, is the single most radical innovation in 20th-century European art music, as fundamental to it as the development of **cubism** was to **fine art**.) The series can be used vertically to produce chords and harmonies, or horizontally to produce melodies and counterpoint; it can appear backwards and upside-down, and can begin on any of the twelve chromatic notes – 48 permutations are thus available. In addition to pitch, many composers have experimented with rhythmic series. Olivier Messiaen used Greek poetic metres and the *talas* of Indian art music, Boris Blacher used irregular, rigorously repeated patterns of crotchets and quavers, Pierre Boulez, Karlheinz Stockhausen and Iannis Xenakis serialized duration according to imposed mathematical rules, using, for example, number systems like the Fibonacci series, or systems generated by computer. The difficulty of playing music in which every note is a different length and pitch from all the others, and needs a different kind of attack – in some Boulez piano works, each finger is playing in a different way – led, in the 1950s and beyond, to the development of **electronic** and computer-played music, which eliminates the fallible humanity of the players. This art, though enthusiastically enjoyed by its devotees, has remained that of an **avant-garde** minority; only twelve-note serialism has proved a serious influence on music at large.

Post-serialism is a movement of the 1970s and beyond. Composers began to make selective use of serial techniques, and of the sounds and ideas of serialism, without subjecting their works to rigid mathematical organization. Serial methods, in fact, became one resource among many, instead of the chief determinant of all the material. This style has now displaced strict serialism, and is the predominant mode of 'classical' art music composition throughout the world. **KMcL**

Further reading A. Whittall, *Music Since the First World War.*

SET THEORY

Sets are among the most fundamental and general objects in the whole of **mathematics**. At the most basic level (in what is known as naive set theory), sets are collections of objects (numbers, points, other sets, apples), though they are subject to certain restrictions (see **paradoxes**). The objects contained in a set are known as members or elements.

The originator of the subject, Georg Cantor (1845–1918), did not really have a clear, rigorous idea of what was meant by the term. Sets are general enough to be used as the basic mathematical object; in modern views of mathematics, everything is a set (or possibly a class, which is a group of sets too large to be a set itself). A number is a set; a group is a set; and anything that mathematics can effectively talk about should be a set or a collection of sets.

Today, the concept of a set has been given a more rigorous definition, mainly by the **axiomatization** of set theory by Ernest Zermelo (1871–1953) and Adolf Abraham Fraenkel (1891–1965). There are twelve axioms, which assert the existence of various sets (the empty set, containing no members; an infinite set), which allow the construction of new sets from old ones (the union of a set, which is the set of all things in members of the set; a subset for each sentence of **symbolic logic**, consisting of all the things in the set for which the sentence is true; the set which is a pair of given sets and so on) and which define properties of sets (the axiom of foundation, banning infinite chains of the form A1 containing A2 as an member, which contains A3, which contains A4 and so on; and the

axiom of choice). Sets, in this view, are any classes which can be proved to be sets using the axioms. Some of the axioms can be dispensed with; alternative set theories have been developed in which the axiom of choice is false.

Set theory in its modern context, with the inclusion of infinite sets in its domain of discourse is set against the views of the **infinite** held by the **intuitionists**, who claimed that Cantor's results about infinite sets were against common sense. Intuitionistic versions of set theory have been developed, but they have not been very successful, because they are necessarily limited in scope by their avoidance of direct use of the infinite. Today's set theory is very much the product of **logicism**, and, to a lesser extent, of **formalism**. However, it is now independent of such philosophical backgrounds, and takes its place in today's mathematics, which is so confused about the philosophical meaning of what is actually being done in the subject. **SMcL**

SEVEN DEADLY SINS

The Seven Deadly Sins much occupied the minds of medieval Christian thinkers. They were held to be sins that guaranteed the death not of the body but of the soul, unless it could be rescued in time by penitence and holy works. Distantly derived from the Ten Commandments, the seven sins were Avarice, Envy, Gluttony, Lust, Pride, Sloth and Wrath. The 'magic' number seven was also applied to counterbalancing qualities. The Seven Gifts of the Holy Ghost were Counsel, Fear of the Lord, Fortitude, Knowledge, Righteousness, Understanding and Wisdom, and the Seven Virtues were Charity, Faith, Fortitude, Hope, Justice, Prudence and Temperance.

Even in medieval times, such lists as these were regarded (except by those who compiled them or sermonized about them) as fanciful wordplay, with as little relevance to life as speculation about angels dancing on the points of pins. The idea was, however, of interest to artists and writers. Chaucer's *Canterbury Tales* gleefully go through the catalogue of sins, and Malory's *Morte d'Arthur* weaves the idea of sins and virtues into the whole ethical and moral framework of the society it depicts. Satirists and comedians, not unexpectedly, have fallen on the sins, keeping them vigorously alive right to the present day. **KMcL**

SEVEN GIFTS OF THE HOLY GHOST
see **Seven Deadly Sins**

SEVEN VIRTUES see **Seven Deadly Sins**

SEX

The function of sex was debated intensely by life scientists (among others) in the 18th and 19th centuries (see **ovism**). The discovery of sperm by Antonie van Leeuwenhoek (1632–1723) and the (erroneous) discovery of the female egg brought the suggestion from the ovists that the function of sperm was to activate the egg so that its preformed contents might grow. With the advent of cell theory and the discovery of the true mammalian egg, the observation that sperm and egg fuse during fertilization was accepted and led, naturally, to the assumption that characteristics of each parent were blended as a result. The true situation, that sets of chromosomes from both parents are paired to form a diploid zygote, was not realized until the early 20th century when the work of Gregor Mendel (1822–84) was rediscovered. This explained how sexual reproduction could lead to variation in the offspring. **RB**

See also gene theory; pangenesis; sexual selection.

SEXUAL SELECTION

When individual organisms select mates for sexual reproduction, their choice is based upon certain characteristics in the opposite sex. This leads to competition for mates. The term sexual selection was coined by Charles Darwin to describe his theoretical ideas concerning the influence of **natural selection** on the choice of mating partner. He suggested that competition could exist between the sexes of a species for the opportunity to mate with the fittest individuals, that is, those with the best genes. This strategy would give offspring the best genes and thus enhance their **fit-**ness. A consequence of this phenomenon is that certain characteristics, called secondary sexual characteristics, are selected because they play a role in sexual selection. Thus peacocks have evolved oversized, colourful tail feathers as a secondary sexual characteristic, and are chosen by peahens on the basis of their ability to produce an impressive display. The phenomenon of competition for mates is seen in a wide variety of animals and the time, energy and risk which it involves suggests that there is an important issue at stake. Secondary sexual characteristics such as stag antlers require large amounts of energy to develop and may increase visibility to predators, while the energy expense and risk of injury during the rut (the battle between stags for dominance and the right to mate) can result in death.

It is difficult to quantify the link between sexual selection and fitness of offspring because of the great number of factors involved. Natural selection will result in the accentuation of any characteristics which infer fitness, so that a characteristic may be selected because it is attractive to the opposite sex. Thus male walruses may have become very large in order to attract females; however, they may also have become large in order to win fights with other males and gain mates in this way. Studies in the laboratory have shown that there is a correlation between the ability of the male fruitfly to perform a courtship dance and his fertility. **RB**

Further reading Richard Dawkins *The Selfish Gene*; John Maynard-Smith, *The Theory of Evolution*.

SEXUALITY

Sociologists use the term 'sexuality' to refer to those attributes, desires, roles and identities which are concerned with sexual activity and behaviour. It may also refer to an orientation towards, or preference for, particular forms of sexual activity and expression. This sociological understanding of the term contrasts with its normal usage, which tends to regard sexuality as something that is intrinsic to the individual. It is commonly supposed that human sexual behaviour is mainly determined by biology. Sociologists, by contrast, emphasize the social basis of the **norms** (accepted rules for conduct) which surround sexual behaviour.

The fact that expression of sexuality varies between periods and cultures has led sociologists to conclude that sexual behaviour is not genetically determined, but is almost all learnt. For example, kissing is a sexual practice accepted in some societies, and yet in others it is either not done or is considered disgusting. In the majority of countries notions of sexual attractiveness focus more on the looks of women than they do on men, though this is beginning to change in the West. The features that are considered sexually attractive vary enormously between different cultures.

Christianity has influenced Western attitudes towards sexuality for nearly 2,000 years. Generally speaking the prevailing view was that all sexual behaviour was suspect and should be kept to the minimum necessary to produce children. Religious presumptions about sexuality were replaced in the 19th century by medical ones. Many early writings on sexual behaviour differed little from those of the church. Masturbation, for example, was said to bring on blindness, insanity and heart disease. There was enormous sexual hypocrisy in Victorian times. A virtuous woman was believed to be indifferent to sex and to tolerate it as a wifely duty. 'Respectable' men regularly visited prostitutes and kept mistresses, and this was accepted. If a respectable woman behaved in a similar manner it would have been scandalous. The 1960s saw the development of more liberal attitudes towards sexuality many of which continue today; for instance, premarital sexual activity is widely accepted, and a range of different sexual practices are increasingly tolerated. Nevertheless, more traditional attitudes towards sexuality undoubtedly remain.

Although homosexuality exists in all cultures the idea of a homosexual as someone clearly distinct from the majority of the population in terms of their sexual tastes is a relatively recent development. The term itself was only coined in the 1860s, while use of the term lesbian dates from a slightly

later time. In the West, it has only been a few decades since homosexuality was decriminalized. In many non-Western cultures, however, homosexual relations are tolerated or even encouraged. The Batak people of northern Sumatra, for example, permit male homosexual relations before marriage.

Feminists use the term 'sexuality' not just to refer to sexual acts, but also to refer to desires, fantasies and **eroticism** which occur in conjunction with or outside of sexual behaviour. The word has many different meanings within different feminisms. For many feminists sexuality and the meanings that are ascribed to it are central to women's oppression. Feminist critics have argued that oppression occurs in the way that female sexuality has been theorized by **patriarchy**, and also in the way that women experience male sexuality. Feminists have in a variety of ways sought to understand the sexual differences between men and women. They have also attempted to uncover what is hidden in the meanings that we assign to different forms and theories of sexuality.

Josephine Butler, a feminist campaigner against the Contagious Diseases Act of the 1860s, argued that male sexuality was not biologically driven but was, instead, a social construction and that therefore prostitutes were not 'necessary'. Butler also spoke out against the definition of women's sexual 'natures' as 'fallen, or 'pure', becuase these categories were governed by male sexuality. In 1974, feminist film theorist Molly Haskell wrote that the representation of women in Hollywood films is dictated by their relation to sexuality – they are either excessively sexual (fallen) or without any sexuality (pure), Haskell's work shows that Butler's insight is still relevant in the analysis of male notions of female sexuality.

Feminists have, from different perspectives, criticized sexologists and psychoanalytic theories for using male sexuality as the norm and then measuring the difference of female sexuality against it; some psychoanalytic feminists refer to this as 'phallocentricism'. The identification of this conceptual model has enabled feminists to show that female sexuality has either been theorized as a riddle or problem, or is seen merely in terms of the process of procreation. Feminists often argue that the male medical establishment uses 'science' to control and legislate against women's sexuality. In politicizing sexuality feminists have taken it out of the realms of personal and placed it in the domain of the social and the ideological; thus allowing them to expose the male model of female sexuality. Michèle Barratt criticizes some of the major theories of female sexuality for being either too simplistic or a negative subset of male sexuality. Another major criticism levelled at early psychoanalytic conceptions of female sexuality is the location of the female orgasm. Anne Koedt, for example, has disputed the notion of both Freud and Masters & Johnson that the location of the female orgasm is not the clitoris but the vagina. Adrienne Rich has disputed many theories of sexuality for their narrow definition of sexuality, pointing out that motherhood can be a source of libidinal pleasure. Luce Irigaray argues that female sexuality, being multiple and diffuse, is qualitatively different from male sexuality.

One of the major projects for contemporary feminist theorists is to challenge assumptions of **gender** characteristics in relation to sexuality, to challenge heterosexuality as a norm. Another major strand of enquiry for contemporary feminism, which has often been marginalized in favour of looking at the effect of male sexuality on women, is the exploration of female desires. **DA TK**

See also community; culture; norms; socialization; society; sociobiology.

Further reading Michèle Barrett and Mike Brake (ed.), *Female Sexuality in Human Sexual Relations*; M. Foucault, *The History of Sexuality*; Anja Meulenbelt, *For Ourselves*; J. Weeks, *Sexuality and its Discontents*.

sf

sf (the lower-case letters are obligatory) is short for science fiction and, with fantasy **literature** (its derivative), is one of the dominant genres of 20th-century fiction. Its ancestors were stories of human beings visiting strange worlds (in such collections as the *Arabian Nights*), and the **Utopian** literature of **Renaissance** and post-Renaissance Europe. But it came into its own only at the end of the 19th century, when **science** and **technology** took a firm hold on the popular imagination. The earliest sf writers, Jules Verne and his imitators, wrote of visits to the Moon, under the sea, to the centre of the Earth and so on. H.G. Wells, the other chief parent of the form, broadened its scope to include genetic engineering, time travel, transformation and war between beings from mutually alien environments.

In the 20th century, space travel and the exploration and colonization of alien worlds have provided plots for one main strand of sf. Writers have concentrated on technology, the **sociology** and ethics of alien societies (and of the Earth people who visit them), and (in an ingenious variant) on the Utopian, or more often dystopian, future of our own planet, depleted by the **greenhouse effect**, nuclear warfare, overpopulation, and remorseless technological and social engineering. The other major strand, particularly since the 1960s, has been psychological sf, exploring states of altered consciousness, 'alternative' philosophies and the interface between hallucination and the supernatural. Fantasy literature (which sprang into being, almost fully-formed, with the publication of Tolkien's *The Lord of the Rings* in the late 1950s) sets heroes and antiheroes to battle for the health of worlds populated by demons, monsters, samurai warriors, wizards and supernatural beings of every conceivable kind.

sf is one of the first literary genres to have an almost simultaneous impact on readers throughout the world. Its universal popularity, especially among younger readers, is parallelled only by that of **pop** music or junk food. Although to equate it with either is to patronize, there is junk in plenty in sf, as in any other form of literature. Its leading authors (such as Isaac Asimov, Philip K. Dick, Frank Herbert, Walter Miller, Stanislav Lem and Gene Wolfe – interestingly, most are from the UK or the US) have produced work of quality, and radicalized the thinking of a whole generation worldwide, in a way readers resistant to the genre may find hard to recognize. **KMcL**

SHADOW

The shadow is a Jungian term for the dark side of the personality. Jung thought that people were afraid of the idea of the **unconscious** because of the presence of this shadow self. We can plainly see this shadow in other people in egotism, laziness, sloppiness, unreal fantasies, cowardice things obvious to others but unnoticed by the subject. Jung believed that overwhelming rage at criticism of some aspect of ourselves probably indicated that part of our shadow selves had been touched upon.

The shadow plays a vital role in Jung's analytical **psychology** because it contains the hidden, repressed and unfavoured aspects of the personality. But the shadow is not just the converse of the conscious **ego**; it has good aspects as well. Nevertheless the ego is in conflict with the shadow. The theme appears frequently in dreams as a mysterious figure or the true hero. This battle Jung called the battle for deliverance and saw it as symbolized by heroes and monsters. Shadow selves, representing these unacknowledged attributes, usually appear in dreams as members of the same sex. Jung noted that, possibly as a consequence of this, that we are more tolerant of the shadow in the opposite sex than in people of the same sex. He believed that this shadow side was vulnerable from what he called the collective infections which are part of mob activities. **MJ**

Further reading Jolande Jacobi, *The Psychology of C.G. Jung.*

SHAIVISM

Shaivism (Saivism) derives from the worship of the Lord Shiva, who is identified with the Vedic god Rudra, and who has become for many Hindus the supreme God, the creative power inherent in nature, and eternal spirit. Yet he can be known within the human heart, since he transcends the infinite and is more intimate to the human soul than the soul itself. This insight was developed in the philosophy of **Saiva Siddhanta**.

Shiva can never be domesticated or internalized in any form of **yoga** or devotion, though he himself is the supreme **guru**, the ultimate yogi. He remains wrathful as well as benevolent to his devotees, and though the name Shiva means 'mild' or 'auspicious' he is associated with the terrible goddess Kali and her Earth-shaking dances. Himself the Lord of the Dance, Shiva is both creator and destroyer. It is in that form that he has inspired the most outstanding classical sculptures and bronzes, especially from the Tamil kingdoms of the 9th to 13th centuries.

Shiva is essentially an **ascetic**. His austerities threaten the power of the other gods, and his wife can only capture his attention by austerities. In contrast to Vishnu/Krishna, he is chaste. Shiva's temples today are full of pilgrims emulating his austerities. He is also worshipped as Lord of the animals, especially of cattle, and in the form of a bull. **EMJ**

Further reading R.C. Zaehner, *Hinduism.*

SHI'ISM

Shi'a, from which the word *Shi'ism* derives, means 'party', that is the party of 'Ali, a cousin, son-in-law and close companion of the Prophet Muhammad. Muhammad's unexpected death led to uncertainty as to who should be his caliph or 'deputy'. Shi'ites believe that it should have been 'Ali, followed by 'Ali's descendants. However, three others preceded 'Ali, and after his death, his son Hussain died in a massacre at Karbala. This martyrdom is important to all Muslims, but at the time it precipitated an unbridgeable gulf between Shi'ites and Sunnis. A distinctive feature of Shi'ism today is the festival of 'Ashura in commemoration of the martyrdom. In Iran and southern Iraq in particular, plays are enacted depicting the events, and processions take place in which men whip and cut themselves in a heightened atmosphere of identification with the martyr.

Shi'ites also differ from Sunni Muslims (the majority) in believing that Muhammad instituted a succession of inspired leaders, Imams. Iranian Shi'ites are 'Twelvers', accepting a particular succession of 12

Imams, the last of whom disappeared and is known as the Hidden Imam. He is expected to return prior to the Day of Judgement as a messianic figure. (Ayatollah Khomeini was often called Imam Khomeini, but only as a sign of the reverence in which he was held, not because he claimed to be the Hidden Imam.) 'Ayatollah' is an honorific title in Twelver Shi'ism, which again differs from Sunnism in having a structured hierarchy of *ulama* (or mullahs), with a Grand Ayatollah at the apex of the pyramid. He has usually resided in southern Iraq, where the towns of Karbala (with the tomb of Hussain) and Najah (with the tomb of 'Ali) are the holiest centres of Imamism.

The other main group of Shi'ites are the Seveners, who accept a particular succession of seven Imams. They have further subdivided into several groups, one of which is led by the Aga Khan. There is also a group of Fivers known as Zaidis, and a number of other sects such as the Alevites and 'Alawis, Babis, Yazidis and Druzes, but these have moved outside Islam proper. Shi'ism, in its varying forms, represents about 10% of the Muslim world population. **JS**

SHINTO

Shinto is a Chinese corruption of the Japanese expression *kami no michi* ('way of the kami'), and is a descriptive rather than prescriptive name for the **religion** of Japan. *Kami* is often translated as 'gods' in the West, but in fact derives from the word for 'higher', 'lifted up' or 'more special' beings, with no particular supernatural implications. *Kami* refers to the power in everything in creation which makes it uniquely itself, the immanence of each object. There are thus *kami* of places, stones, natural phenomena such as storms, and qualities such as mercy or anger. Ancient Shinto teachers said that there were eight million million *kami*, and that each deserved respect if not reverence. Thus, in worshipping the *kami*, a human being is in fact responding to and helping to sustain the harmony of the universe, in which everything has its allotted place and function.

Although Shinto is bound up with the gods and spirits of the most ancient Japanese religion, of itself it has no founder, specific creed, sacred scripture or prescribed system of worship. (Its festivals and ceremonies are either adapted from other systems, particularly **Buddhism** and **Daoism**, or are 19th-century creations intended both to evoke and to codify traditional religious practices of the past.) In essence, since *kami* are everything and everywhere, simply to accept the world as it is is a form of worship. In practice, there are innumerable shrines, each with its own indwelling *kami*, and prayer and sacrifice are offered at each of them. Three particular kinds of *kami* are worshipped in particular. First are the *uji-gami* ('clan-ancestors'). The oldest of these are Amaterasu, the Sun-goddess, and Izanami and Isanagi, the male and female creator-spirits. Second are the *takami-musubi* and *kami-musubi*, creative powers responsible for such things as growth, 'straightening', 'twisting' and so on, the *omoikani-kami* which gives wisdom, and the *kami* of natural objects, animals and insects. Third are the souls of past leaders and sages: human beings who because of their outstanding powers have become important figures in the spirit world, and who take an interest, benevolent or malevolent, in events of the here-and-now.

Although Shinto, as an essentially personal religion, is fluid and undogmatic, its philosophy and public practice are subject to periodic reassessments and recodifications. The most important took place in the 8th century, when two books, the *Kojiki* ('Records of ancient matters') and *Nihongi* ('Chronicles of Japan') were compiled. These set out the earliest myths and beliefs of Japan, and hence of Shinto, with an aura of comment and speculation which set, so to speak, the philosophical and intellectual agenda of Shinto. The books, though not canonical, are still regarded as the most important of all Shinto writings. A second major reassessment of Shinto occurred in the 19th and 20th centuries, when it was hauled into line not merely as a religion but as the foundation of the entire Japanese state. Central to this process was a belief that each emperor was divine, a direct lineal descendant of Jimmu, the (mortal) great-grandson of Amaterasu herself. Thus, the Imperial family, and through it every person in the state, was directly linked to the most vital force in the universe, in a way which lent itself to hierarchies and forms of etiquette of every kind. Continuity and order in human affairs had always seemed a paradigm of harmony in the universe, and when this idea was married to precise forms of ritual, centred on the Emperor's person and to specific holy places, sacred and secular became inextricably entwined – or so it seemed. The possibilities in such a belief for social structuring are obvious, and go a long way to explain the huge public sense of despair when Emperor Hirohito was stripped of divine status, and state and religion were divorced forever, after World War II.

Japan is now officially a pluralist society, and Shinto fulfils a largely ceremonial and theatrical role in public affairs. But at a local and personal level, the sense of cohesion which Shinto gives to families and to the people in general, no less than the prayers and visits to shrines which are so much part of ordinary Japanese life, make it still a major and a vital force in Japanese life. **KMcL**

Further reading W.G. Aston, *Shinto: the Way of the Gods*; Jean Herbert, *Shinto: at the Fountainhead of Japan*.

SIKHISM

Sikhism is a faith espoused by some 15 million people worldwide. Nearly all Sikhs are of Punjabi ancestry and, following the Partition of India in 1947, 80% of them live in the present Indian state of Punjab. The most widely accepted definition of Sikhism came in 1945 from the Sikhs' most authoritative elected committee, the Shiromani Gurdwara Parbandhak Committee, in the opening statement of the *Rahit Maryada* (*A Guide to the Sikh Way of Life*): 'A Sikh is any woman or man whose faith consists of belief in one *Akal Purakh* (immortal God), in the ten Gurus, and in the teachings of the Guru Granth Sahib (the Sikh Scriptures) and of the ten Gurus, and who has faith in the *amrit* (initiation by water) of the tenth Guru and who professes no other **religion**.'

One of the grievances behind the current unrest in Punjab is the refusal to grant Sikhism recognition as a separate religion under the Constitution of India. Most Sikhs reject the assertion that they are a **Hindu** sect.

Sikh teaching about God is **monotheistic**. It was encapsulated by Guru Nanak (1469–1539) in the words *ek onkar*. This is written as the Punjabi digit for one (since the word, consisting of more than one stroke, would not convey oneness so emphatically), followed by a syllable which has long been used in the Indian spiritual tradition as a representation of the ultimate reality. *Ek onkar* is used to open the first composition in the Guru Granth Sahib, where God is defined as *Satnam* ('whose name is truth'), *karta purakh* ('the immanent creator'), *nirbhau* ('without fear'), *nirvair* ('without emnity'), *akal murat* ('immortal in form'), *ajuni* ('never taking birth'), *saibham* ('self-existent') and *gurprasad* ('known by the Guru's grace'). This definition, repeated daily by Sikhs, avoids gendered language and denies the concept of incarnation. God is transcendent and can be experienced, but is beyond full human comprehension. Sikhs believe that revelation is a continuing process to which the Gurus made a unique contribution. Fundamental to the Gurus' teaching about God is the concept of *hukam* ('will', 'order'). Everything in creation exists by God's *hukam*. To obtain truth, one should submit to this divine order.

In the Sikh tradition, a Guru is more than a teacher, but rather one who reveals knowledge of the divine, a dispeller of the darkness of spiritual ignorance. The supreme Guru, God, is often referred to as *Satguru* ('true Guru') and *Vahiguru* ('wonderful Guru'). According to Sikh doctrine, there have only been 10 human Gurus. Their lives spanned the years from 1469 (birth of Guru Nanak) to 1708 (death of Guru Gobind Singh). They are believed to be one in spirit; a favourite analogy being the lighting of wicks from a single flame. Any apparent inconsistencies in teaching, such as Guru Nanak's eirenic approach and the sixth and the tenth Gurus' call to take up arms, is attributed to the demands of a changing context, not to a fundamental difference of message.

The last Guru, Gobind Singh, did not appoint a successor, but indicated that the Scriptures, henceforth to be referred to as Guru Granth Sahib, were to be regarded as taking his place. Sikhism is, in a unique sense, a 'religion of the book', since the Scriptures are upheld as the Gurus' body made manifest. This belief entails having the Guru Granth Sahib present and consulting it at all ceremonies, and having it installed with appropriate symbols of authority: a canopy, a special stand and a fan made of white yak hair.

Guru Gobind Singh also passed authority on to the *panth* (the Sikh community). In 1699 he dramatically actualized the concept of *khalsa*, which means both 'pure' and 'owing allegiance to no intermediaries' and therefore refers to those Sikhs who observe the Sikh *dharma* more strictly. He called for volunteers who would be ready to lay down their lives. His five followers who accepted the challenge became the nucleus of the *khalsa*, a community of men and women formally initiated with *amrit* (sweetened water stirred with a two-edged sword). They eschew **caste** divisions, observe a strict diet (often vegetarian), and maintain the five signs of their commitment at all times. These are uncut hair, a comb and cotton shorts to signify cleanliness and restraint, and a steel wristband and sword. They also commit themselves to keep four cardinal rules of conduct: not to cut hair anywhere on the body, to refrain from tobacco and other intoxicants, not to eat meat or commit adultery.

Essential to the understanding of *khalsa* is the concept of *sant-sipahi*, the 'saint-soldier'. The Sikh is to protect the defenceless and, if necessary, fight for right to prevail. Yet it is right to draw the sword only when all efforts to restore peace prove useless.

Guru Nanak taught that 'highest is truth but higher still is truthful action'. Human life must demonstrate the quality of truth in action. The Gurus took for granted the Hindu concepts of *karma* and successive rebirths (see **Dharmic religion**) as well as liberation from this system (see **moksha**). One barrier to this freedom is believed to be *maya*, ignorance of one's true nature and a false, materialistic view of the world.

Through the Guru's grace one can perceive the truth and live accordingly.

Nam japan or *nam simran* are sometimes translated as meditation. *Nam* refers to the total reality of God, encapsulated in the divine name. If one is constantly centred upon *nam*, in the midst of one's duties, spiritual progress takes place. Daily worship, after rising early and bathing thoroughly, consists of reciting set prayers morning and evening. Voluntary service (*seva*) to the community is a key principle. In particular Sikhs are exhorted to serve in the *gurdwara*, the place of worship which doubles as a community centre. Here the principle of equality is demonstrated by the community meal, provided free, with no distinction on the basis of caste or social status. Community discipline is also meted out here, one penalty being to clean members' shoes.

Sikhism acknowledges no priestly caste, and women, like men, can and do carry out the tasks required in the *gurdwara*, reading the Scriptures, singing, distributing the sweet mixture called *karah prashad* and preparing and serving the corporate meal, the *Guru-ka-langar*. In practice fewer women than men serve on *gurdwara* management committees and women cook more often than men. Women never act as *panj piare*, the five Sikhs respected for their strict adherence to *khalsa* discipline, who initiate candidates at the *amrit* initiation ceremony. **EN**

Further reading Max Arthur Macauliffe, *The Sikh Religion: its Gurus, Sacred Writings and Authors.*

SILVER AGE see Golden Age

SIN

A crude distinction between sin and crime is that sin is an offence against God, whereas crime is first an offence against society and may be only indirectly sin as well. For example, in some faiths, touching a menstruating woman or breaking the rules of **caste** are sins, but no crimes are involved. Contraception, abortion and **suicide** are regarded as sins by the Roman **Catholic** Church but are not controlled by law in every 'Catholic' country. Because of the Judaeo-Christian tradition that to harm a fellow human being is not only to damage the community but to offend God, it is hard to imagine a crime which is not also a sin. However, this does not mean that all laws are to be obeyed. The state can sin in passing unjust laws, making it a duty to rebel; but clearly without belief in God sin has no meaning. It is only in a theocracy that crime becomes coterminous with sin.

In the Christian tradition a further distinction is made, between a sinful act and the state of sin of which sins are only an outward symptom. In the West, following Augustine, sin is seen as a state of utter depravity inherent in the human condition (though few nowadays would agree that it is the very act of procreation, which being sinful, re-creates the sin of Adam in the child). Reinterpretation of the myth sees humankind in a state of total **alienation** from God, the concept of alienation itself being derived from modern **psychology** and **existentialist** philosophy, but consistent with biblical texts. Many of Jesus' healings were of people who had made themselves ill with guilt and *angst*. In the East, the original Greek word for sin, *hamartia*, meant a failing, a falling short, as when an arrow falls short of the target. Compared with the righteousness and glory of God, humankind was sinful, but it was a deprivation of good, a negative rather than a positive state of evil. This sense of inadequacy before God is a common feature of mystics in all religions, as is the conviction that however redemption is achieved, humankind is rescued by the grace and love of God.

It was a commonplace of the old Christian evangelism that other religions lacked a sense of sin, but this idea owed more to the need for a moral justification for colonialism than an accurate reading of non-Christian **scriptures**. There are different ideas of what constitutes a sin in different cultures; infanticide and female circumcision (for instance) can be justified by theological sleight of hand just as easily as were slavery and the Inquisition in Christendom. In all faiths sin is in essence disobedience to God, however the numinous is perceived: by direct defiance of divine law, by breach of one's *dharma* or by stifling the potential

for enlightenment. In some faiths, such as African traditional religions, sin is always social, against the tribe and the ancestors (for example, abortion is wrong because it deprives the ancestors of descendants), and it can be overcome by propitiation, usually a **sacrifice**. EMJ

Further reading Sören Kierkegaard, *The Concept of Dread* (1844); C.S. Lewis, *The Screwtape Letters;* Reinhold Niebuhr, *Moral Man and Immoral Society.*

SLAVERY

The institution of slavery, in which some people are legally recognized to be the property of other persons or institutions, pre-dates the development of the Western liberal canon of **human rights**, in which the right of 'self-ownership' is considered central and inalienable. Slavery used to be considered part of the natural order, or at least was defended as such by thinkers like Aristotle. The argument for slavery was that slaves somehow deserved to be slaves either because they were either naturally inferior to free people or they had lost the right to be free through defeat in war.

Slavery is now supposed to be illegal throughout the world, although whether its global abolition owes more to its alleged economic inefficiency or to the success of the egalitarian and humanitarian arguments of abolitionists is still a moot point among historians. Moreover, many liberals would argue that state slavery exists in **totalitarian** régimes where states compel people to work (forced-labour camps are, after all, slave labour camps); and many **feminists** would argue that the institution of marriage, especially when it confers property rights for husbands or patriarchs over wives (and sons and daughters) is the most enduring and ubiquitous form of household slavery; and anti-slavery societies argue that what is conventionally understood by slavery exists in some Islamic societies and they argue that many forms of prostitution rackets amount to informal slavery.

We can distinguish crudely between three types and uses of slavery: household slavery, clerical or administrative slavery and slave labour for production (or extraction). The use of slaves, whether in households, administration or production, was characteristic of régimes and empires built by conquest, as in ancient Athens, Rome, and some modern European empires. Slavery appears to have been historically ubiquitous, although its scale and significance in given societies varied: it has been argued that Australia is the only large land mass of the world in which conventional slavery never occurred. The use of some kind of non-economic compulsion to force people to work for others was characteristic of most precapitalist societies, but not everybody agrees that serfdom and corvée labour should be classified as forms of slave labour, and many have observed that **capitalism** and slavery have co-existed in many parts of the world (for example in the deep South of the US). Slaveholding economic systems, that is, societies in which slave labour played a major role in production, existed in ancient Greece, ancient Rome, colonial and independent America and the Caribbean.

The institutions of slavery, and the extent to which slaves were mere (rightless) chattels of their owners, have varied considerably across slave-holding societies. For example, slaves in the Iberian colonies of America and in ancient Rome had more opportunities to achieve freedom (manumission), than in some states of the US where laws prevented this possibility. **BO'L**

Further reading D.B. Davis, *Slavery and Human Progress*; G.E.M. de Ste Croix, *The Class Struggle in the Ancient Greek World*; M. Finley, *Ancient Slavery and Modern Ideology*; J. Walvin, *Black Ivory: a History of British Slavery*.

SMART STRUCTURE

A smart structure, in electrical engineering, is one which can adapt to its environment by altering its physical characteristics in response to information from sensors embedded within it. Exciting applications of such an idea range from civil engineering to automobiles and aeroplanes, where the structure could change, for example, its shape, colour, stiffness or thermal conductibility. **AC**

SOAP

Soap (short for 'soap opera') is a popular form of radio and television **drama**, and of **literature**. It gets its name from 1930s daytime radio shows in the USA, which were 'soap' because they were financed by detergent manufacturers, and were 'opera' because of the melodramatic acting style and the feverish intensity of characterization and plotting. Soaps are serials, usually about the interlocking lives of a group of people in a single situation. They may live in the same street, work in the same business, or be members of the same extended family. Ambition, apathy, hate, love, treachery, trust – the whole of human life is there, and in some soaps (notably those of India and South America, where radio soaps have their largest following), demons, ghosts, gods and witches also play their parts. In North American soaps, the setting is usually a family (sometimes rich and bitchy, sometimes not rich and stickily 'together against the world'). European soaps (the UK and Spain are the major consumers) are usually set in a business or a neighbourhood. Australian television gained enormous worldwide success during the 1980s with soaps set in an ordinary, suburban street and a women's prison. In the UK the longest-running soaps (both over 40 years old) are *The Archers*, a radio soap set among farmers, and *Coronation Street*, a television soap set in a working-class town in northern England.

Soaps are treated with self-conscious enthusiasm or self-righteous contempt by highbrow critics, and with a kind of amused obsession by their devotees. The essence of the form is familiarity, and its success depends on the strength of its characters and, in the plotting, a blend of familiarity and incessant surprise. Soap styles – fluid narrative, relaxed and unpretentious dialogue, unembarrassed use of sentimentality, short scenes and rapid cutting – have influenced much 'serious' drama, and in particular have softened the edge of popular films (for example those of Steven Spielberg). Soaps are also a major influence on literary fiction. There are innumerable blockbuster **novels** in soap style, dealing with the trials and tribulations of ordinary people coping with life or with ruthless waifs making their way in big business. In 'serious' literature, soaps are an important influence on the content and style of **magic realism**, and have also given themes and a manner to novelists as diverse as Margaret Atwood, Heinrich Böll, Colette, Alison Lurie, François Mauriac, Iris Murdoch, Cesare Pavese and John Updike. **KMcL**

SOCIAL CLOSURE

Social closure is a term first used by Max Weber and later by F. Parkin (in an analysis of **class**) to describe the actions of social groups to maximize their own advantages by restricting access to certain social rewards (usually economic) to their members, and thereby closing access to those rewards to outsiders. **DA**

See also ethnicity; power; profession; race; social stratification; status.

Further reading F. Parkin, *The Social Analysis of the Class Structure.*

SOCIAL CONFLICT

The concept of social conflict, in **anthropology**, covers various aspects of social disintegration involving individuals, groups or social classes. It is a general feature of human relationships and exists when two sides wish to carry out acts which are mutually inconsistent. These may be of various forms personal violence, rebellions, industrial strikes, warfare and perhaps even sport (in which there is an institutionalized and constrained form of conflict). Measures to resolve issues of conflict may be termed conflict management and regulation, or rules of law.

Conflict theories in the **social sciences** emerged around the 1960s as a result of criticism of **functionalist** theories, which stressed the integration of societies. Conflicts when interpreted by the functionalists was represented as a structural part of societal integration, such that conflicts between groups related to each other by ancestry acted to confirm the social structures in society. Other functionalists interpreted incidents such as rebellions as discharging social tensions, which ultimately served to reintegrate the existing social order. Conflict theorists argued that functionalists played down the dynamic nature of internal conflicts, while those who worked in colonized areas, such as Africa and Asia, overlooked the tensions and conflicts between ruler and ruled. Instead, later theorists worked from the premise that conflicts of values and interests are inherent in all societies and sought to analyse their particular characteristics.

Two basic kinds of conflicts arise: intersocietal, referring to conflicts between societies as in warfare; and intrasocietal, locating conflicts within society such as ethnic rivalry or the Marxist notion of class struggle inherent in capitalist societies. Either types of conflicts may occur as a result of competing interest groups, or be stage-managed by the powers-that-be in order to promote their interests of cohesion on another level. For instance, warfare between communities may be initiated to relieve conflict within the communities, or, alternatively, a policy of 'divide and rule' as encouraged by colonial powers in order to separate those they ruled and to divert antagonism away from the rulers.

Some societies engage in armed aggression or warfare more often than others; while others manage conflicts in a nonaggressive way. Attempts have been made to link such observations to factors of overcrowding: conflict is a safety valve to discharge psychologically aggressive tendencies, a means to promote solidarity between groups, or even a result of calorie-intake availability (in which groups engage in conflicts when their ecological and energy needs are exceeded). However, symbolic, ideological and political dimensions of particular societies are far more significant in motivating people to engage in conflicts. Concepts of male bravado, religious values or patriotism are a few examples of how social forces, rather than psychological or environmental reasoning, compels one to engage in conflicts of various kinds. **RK**

See also ethnicity; Marxist anthropology; nationalism; political anthropology; power; transactionalism.

Further reading Anthony Giddens and David Held (eds.), *Classes, Power and Conflict: Classical and Contemporary Debates*; Michael Nicholson, *Conflict Analysis*; David Riches (ed.), *The Anthropology of Violence*.

SOCIAL CONSTRUCTION OF REALITY

A division exists within **sociology** between those who stress the externality and independence of social reality from individuals and those who emphasize that individuals participate fully in the construction of their own lives. Following Émile Durkheim, some argue that societies possess social realities of their own which cannot be reduced to the aggregate effect of individuals' actions. According to this school of thought social phenomena have an objective existence outside of individual members of society and exert a force which shapes individual behaviour. It is assumed that it is possible objectively to measure such phenomena.

Sociologists on the other side of the theoretical divide stress the fact that social reality is actively constructed and reconstructed by individual actors. Sociologists working from within this perspective argue that social phenomena do not simply have an unproblematic objective existence, but have to be interpreted and given meanings by those who encounter them: they have to be socially constructed. From this perspective, all knowledge of the world is a human construction rather than a mirror of some independent reality. The 'objective' measurement of social phenomena is actually a social construction grounded on the subjective meanings given to a situation by those doing the measuring. **DA**

See also critical theory; discourse; ethnomethodology; individualism; phenomenological sociology; positivism; social fact; sociology of knowledge; structure-agency debate; symbolic interactionism; understanding; values.

Further reading T. Bottomore and R. Nisbet (eds.), *A History of Sociological Analysis*; P.S. Cohen, *Modern Social Theory*.

SOCIAL CONTRACT THEORY

Social contract theory, in the **social sciences**, explains the formation and maintenance of states or societies (or both) as the outcome of tacit or explicit contracts between individuals or groups. Thus some social contract theorists envisage a state being formed by individuals as the best way of advancing their interests: they contract with the state to protect and enforce the terms of this bargain, and to do no more than that.

Social contract theory developed in medieval and early modern Western political thought, although it is not without antecedents in Greek thought or without analogues in the political thought of ancient India. It is common to see social contract theory as an intellectual expression of European **feudalism**, in which contractual obligations between king, lord and vassal were central to the organization of military, political and legal affairs. Social contract theory began in discussions of the duties of various status groups (kings, princes, nobles, bishops, commoners) but much later, notably in the writings of Hobbes, Locke and Rousseau, centred on what rights rational and equal individuals would seek to have protected by society or the state. In some authors social contract theory was presented as if there had actually been a genuine historical social contract, in which a constitutional convention of kings, nobles and commoners had met, debated and hammered out the terms of a collective bargain. However, with most authors social contract theory was employed as a fictional device or parable, or as a method for framing arguments about what would constitute a just state.

Having been long discredited, social contract theory has made a major comeback in the social sciences in the last three decades. This intellectual revival has been especially strong among **rational choice** theorists who have focused on problems of collective choice (for example, Kenneth Arrow's *Social Choice and Individual Values*, 1951, and James Buchanan and Gordon Tullock's *The Calculus of Consent*, 1962) and among moral and political philosophers. Indeed, for the last twenty years most political philosophy has been a set of footnotes and commentaries on John Rawls's *A Theory of Justice* (1971), a work of 'ideal contractarianism'. Rawls's book asks what just political, legal and economic institutions would agree to be rational individuals behind a 'veil of ignorance' (that is, people who do not know what positions they will occupy in society but do have a good knowledge of how societies operate)? Rawls's way of framing arguments about justice and his answers, and the controversies they have invoked, have thoroughly revitalized social contract theory. **BO'L**

See also game theory; justice; liberalism; libertarianism; political science.

Further reading J.J. Rousseau, *The Social Contract* (1762); J.A. Rawls, *Theory of Justice*.

SOCIAL CONTROL

Social control refers to the practices, developed by all social groups, through which social behaviour is kept within certain limits. Most sociologists agree that social control is achieved through a combination of compliance, coercion and commitment to social values. **Values** and **norms** are internalized through the process of **socialization**, and in this way individual group members come to learn and take for granted certain limits of acceptable behaviour. Sanctions may be used against rule-breakers. These may be positive sanctions which reward conforming conduct, or negative sanctions which punish non-conformist behaviour.

The legal and the prison systems are obvious elements of the formal institutions of social control within society. Sociologists have also suggested that such social phenomena as mental institutions, **medicine** and scientific knowledge serve similar functions. A number of sociologists have pointed out that one of the most subtle forms of social control is through the control of ideas. The status quo is not challenged because the power of the ruling **ideology** in a given society leads societal members to

accept it as given, or natural. Similarly, the dominance of certain ways of thinking about social phenomena, or of certain forms of knowledge may act to close off other possible interpretations or explanations of reality. **DA**

See also conflict theory; consensus theory; critical theory; discourse; dominant ideology; hegemony; internalization; power; social construction of reality; social integration; sociology of knowledge; state.

Further reading S. Cohen, *Visions of Social Control: Crime, Punishment and Classification*; M. Foucault, *Discipline and Punish: the Birth of the Prison*.

SOCIAL FACT

The term social fact was first used by Émile Durkheim to describe social phenomena which were external to the individual yet constrained his or her actions. He thought that societies had their own objective realities, which could not be reduced to the actions of individuals. For Durkheim, the task of sociology was to study these objective social realities (or 'social facts' as he called them) which he believed could be treated in the same way as 'things' were in the natural sciences. He considered that the subjective thoughts or motivations of individual members of society had no place in sociological explanations.

Sociologists remain divided between those who stress the externality and independence of social facts from individuals, and those who say that individuals participate fully in the construction of their own social lives. That Durkheim saw little place in sociological explanation for the ideas and meanings of individual members of society has been subject to considerable criticism. Social phenomena, for example **suicide**, cannot be fully understood unless the variable meanings attached to social activities by different individuals is fully appreciated. **DA**

See also action perspective; individualism; naturalism; positivism; social construction of reality; social realism; society; structure; structure-agency debate; understanding; values.

Further reading A. Giddens, *Durkheim*; A. Giddens (ed.), *Positivism and Sociology*.

SOCIAL INTEGRATION

Integration, the question of how the various elements in society hold together, is one of the central problems of classical **sociology**. It is a particularly salient concept for the branch of sociology known as **functionalism**. The term is used in a number of ways. In one sense it is used to refer to the extent to which an individual experiences a sense of belonging to a social group as a consequence of sharing its **norms**, **values** and beliefs. Integration, used in this sense, was a key concept in the sociology of Durkheim, it was particularly important for his study of **suicide**.

Integration is also applied to the functionalist analysis of social institutions. Here it refers to the extent to which the activities or functions of social institutions complement rather than contradict each other. Functionalist sociology believes that societies are social systems of interdependent parts, and should be studied in terms of the contribution the various parts make to the smooth running of the whole.

Integration may also be used to refer to the process by which different races come to have closer social, economic and political relationships. **DA**

See also assimilation; community; consensus theory; culture; ethnicity; internalization; rationalization; religion; social control; socialization; social order; society; state; urbanism/urbanization.

Further reading D. Lockwood, 'Social Integration and System Integration', in G.K. Zollschan and W. Hirsch (eds.), *Explorations in Social Change*.

SOCIAL MOBILITY

Social mobility, in **sociology**, is the movement of people between social positions. Lateral mobility is the geographical movement of individuals or groups from one region to another. Vertical mobility is movement up and down a hierarchy of stratification. Those who gain in property, income or status are said to be upwardly mobile, while those who move in the opposite direction are said to be downwardly mobile. Intergenerational mobility compares the present social position of individuals with their parents. Intragenerational mobility compares the position of the same individual at different moments in the course of his or her working life.

A further important distinction made in studies of social mobility is between structural and nonstructural mobility. Structural mobility is movements made possible by changes in the occupational structure in society. Nonstructural mobility is any movement which does not involve such changes.

In sociology, the major focus of study has been on the character of intergenerational mobility within different societies. Different societies have different systems of stratification which will affect social mobility. The amount of vertical mobility in a society is a measure of its 'openness', this indicates the extent to which individuals will be able to move up and down the socioeconomic ladder. In principle at least, social mobility within a **caste** system of stratification is impossible as individuals are born into a caste. In modern societies movement is measured in terms of social **class** which is linked to occupation. It is generally accepted that modern society permits more social mobility than traditional societies though this in part reflects changes in the occupational structure which has witnessed the growth of professional, technical, managerial and clerical occupations and the contraction of manual jobs.

On the whole, sociologists have conceived of social mobility as performing vital social functions. Lipset and Bendix (see below) believed that mobility was essential for the stability of modern industrial society, since open access to élite positions would allow talented and ambitious people to rise up from lower social levels, acting as a safety valve by reducing the likelihood of revolutionary action by the lower classes. Blau and Duncan have argued that the efficiency of modern society requires mobility if the most able people are to perform the most important jobs.

Many people in modern society believe that it is possible to reach the top if they work hard and persistently enough. Statistics indicate that in reality few succeed. The socioeconomic order is shaped like a pyramid with very few positions of power and wealth at the top. Those in positions of power have many opportunities to perpetuate their advantages and to pass them on to their children. Their children will have the best education enabling them to secure good jobs, and ways are found of passing on their wealth. **DA**

See also career; division of labour; embourgeoisement thesis; feminism; occupation; power; profession; social closure; social stratification; society; status; structure; urbanism/urbanization; work.

Further reading A. Heath, *Social Mobility*; S. Lipset and R. Bendix, *Social Mobility in Industrial Society*.

SOCIAL MOVEMENTS

Social movement is a term used by political theorists and sociologists to describe various forms of collective action aimed at accomplishing or blocking social change within a society.

There are considerable variations between social movements. Many social movements are very small, amounting to no more than a few dozen members, and others might incorporate thousands, even millions, of people. Some movements carry on their activities within the framework of the law of the society in which they operate, others function as illegal or underground groups. In general, however, they tend to be loosely organized and operate outside of the established political framework of a society.

Social movements are usually distinct from formally organized political parties or pressure groups. Although they may have links with political parties, and they can, in time, go on to form a political party. Thus the distinction between the two can become blurred. Social movements can gradually become formal organizations. The Salvation Army in the UK, for example, began as a social movement but has now taken on the characteristics of a more permanent organization.

Sociologists distinguish four main types of social movements: (1) *Transformative movements* are directed at far-reaching social changes of the societies of which they are a part. (2) *Reformative movements* have limited objectives aspiring to alter only certain aspects of the existing society. They may focus on a specific type of injustice or inequality. (3) *Redemptive movements* are concerned to rescue people from a life they see as corrupting. Many religious movements belong to this category. (4) *Alternative movements* aim at securing partial change in individuals. A good example of a movement of this type is Alcoholics Anonymous.

Sociological research on social movements has tended to focus on the social and psychological characteristics of their participants, the relations between the leaders and the led, and the social and political outcomes of their activities.

An example of a social movement that has been influential over the last few decades is the Women's Movement. The Women's Movement has not only provided subject matter for sociologists to study, but it has also changed the ways in which sociologists think about certain areas of social behaviour and identified weaknesses in established frameworks of sociological thought. The feminist movement is a good example of the ways in which social movements can help to bring about social change. **DA**

See also collective behaviour; feminism; legitimation; religion; sectarianism.

Further reading A. Giddens, *The Nation State and Violence*; N.J. Smelser, *Theory of Collective Behaviour*; J. Wilson, *Introduction to Social Movements*.

SOCIAL ORDER

The concept of social order refers to the stable patterns of social expectations and social structures that exist in any society, and to the maintenance of these patterns. The problem of what makes societies cohere, and how social order is sustained, is a central one in **sociology**.

Utilitarian approaches to social order locate its origins in individual self-interest and the interdependence that this generates. Thomas Hobbes questioned this position in the 17th century when he raised the question that if everyone pursued their own self-interest would it not end with a state of what he called a 'war of all against all'? At the beginning of the 19th century, this vision of chaos and anarchy started to acquire an ominous ring and an alternative solution to the problem of social order was sought.

Cultural approaches to social order stress the importance of shared **norms** and **values** which create a consensus within society. Approaches of this type can be found in the work of Durkheim and Parsons. Others, however, have emphasized the importance of power and domination in the maintenance of social order, though they do not deny the role of values and norms also. Marx and Weber are exponents of this approach. **DA**

See also authority; conflict theory; consensus theory; dominant ideology; functionalism; generalized other; hegemony; ideology; internalization; Marxism; power; social control; social integration; socialization; structuralism; structuration; structure.

Further reading N. Abercrombie, S. Hill, B.S. Turner, *The Dominant Ideology Thesis*; P.S. Cohen, *Modern Social Theory*.

SOCIAL REALISM

Social realism, in **sociology**, refers to the assumption that social reality, social structures and related social phenomena have an existence over and above the existence of individual members of society, and independent of our conception or perception of them.

Social realists consider that science is an empirically based, rational and objective enterprise, the purpose of which is to provide explanatory and predictive knowledge. For the realist, there is an important distinction between explanation and prediction. Social realists believe that explanation should be the primary objective. They claim that explanation in both the natural and social sciences should entail going beyond simply demonstrating that phenomena are instances of some observed

regularity, and uncovering the underlying and often invisible mechanisms which causally connect them. Frequently, this means postulating on the existence of types of unobservable phenomena and processes which are unfamiliar to us, but realists believe that only by doing this will it be possible to get beyond the mere 'appearance' of things to their very nature and essence.

Sociologists make a distinction between social realism and **positivism**, which asserts that science can only deal with observable entities known directly to experience.

In the **arts**, social realism is the truthful, objective and unpartisan depiction in works of art of society as it actually exists (and particularly of the disadvantaged in society). Its main forms have been 'documentary novels', 'faction' plays and films, war poetry, and such fine art as Henry Moore's drawings of miners or people sheltering from the Blitz. It is not the same as **Socialist Realism**. **DA PD MG KMcL**

See also individualism; naturalism; structuralism.

Further reading R. Keat and J. Urry, *Social Theory as Science*; D. Shapiro, *Social Realism: Art as a Weapon*.

SOCIAL SCIENCES

The social sciences are a group of disciplines concerned with the study of human behaviour. The 'standard' social sciences are **anthropology**, **economics**, **political science**, **psychology** and **sociology**, but the sphere of interest also includes parts of such other disciplines as **archaeology**, **geography**, **history**, **philosophy** and theology, even **ethnomusicology**, **linguistics** and literary **criticism**, and more recent areas of study (notably **feminism**, **ecology** amd **media** studies) are acquiring bodies of work and methodologies which make their claims to inclusion ever more clamourous.

It is a matter for debate whether human behaviour can be studied at all in the same way as the phenomena of the natural world, whether 'science' is in any sense the correct term for all these disciplines. Adherents once vehemently claimed that it was, that any form of study using scientific methods of hypothesis, experimentation nd analysis was a 'science'. This was certainly the view taken in 18th- and 19th-century Europe, when many of the disciplines first became individually established (instead of being part and parcel of wider topics like religious studies or philosophy). But of late, as the disciplines have burgeoned and begun to interpenetrate one another, sharing techniques and combining evidence, there has been strong impetus towards counting the whole study of human behaviour as a single entity and calling it 'social studies'. **KMcL**

SOCIAL SELF

Social self, in **sociology**, refers to the basis of self-consciousness in human individuals according to the theory established by G.H. Mead in his work *Mind, Self and Society* (1934). The social self is the identity conferred upon an individual by the reactions of others. A person achieves self-consciousness by becoming aware of his or her social identity, this cannot happen without society.

Mead believed that children develop as social beings by imitating the actions of those around them. In their play children often imitate what adults do. He referred to this process as 'taking the role of the other', that is, learning what it is like to be another person. It is only at this stage that children acquire a developed sense of self. Children reach an understanding of themselves as separate agents – as 'me' – by seeing themselves through the eyes of others. According to Mead, when we learn to distinguish the 'me' from the 'I', then we achieve self-awareness. The 'I' is the unsocialized infant a collection of unbridled wants and desires; the 'me', as used by Mead, is the social self.

The concept of social self is important to the developmental and humanistic branches of **psychology**, and to **symbolic interactionism** within sociology. **DA**

See also action perspective; dramaturgical model; generalized other; microsociology; socialization.

Further reading P. Rock, *The Making of Symbolic Interactionism.*

SOCIAL STRATIFICATION

Social stratification, in **sociology**, refers to the existence of inequalities between groups on the basis of wealth, power, race, income, age, prestige or some other characteristic which are built into the fabric of society. Social stratification is not simply the existence of social inequalities it is a peculiar sort of social inequality. It refers to the presence of social groups which are hierarchically ranked. Those who belong to a particular group (or social stratum) have some awareness of their common interests and a common identity. They share a similar style of life and social habits, which distinguish them from members of other social groups above and below them in the hierarchy. Sociologists have distinguished three types of stratification: **caste**, estate and **class**. There is a certain amount of debate as to whether stratification is universal.

The Indian caste system is one example of social stratification. Hindu society in traditional India was divided into five main strata: four castes (*varna*) and an outcaste, the untouchables. They are ranked in a hierarchy of ritual cleanliness which derives from the lifestyles and occupations permitted to members of a particular caste. This hierarchy of prestige, grounded in notions of ritual purity, is mirrored by a hierarchy of power. The upper castes are the Brahmins (priesthood), followed by the Khasatriyas (secular and military rulers and landlords), the Vaishyas (entrepreneurial middle classes) and the Shudras (workers and slaves). The Harijans stand outside the hierarchy as outcastes or untouchables who perform only those degrading tasks which are considered unclean. So polluting is the presence of the untouchables that if their shadow falls across that of a Brahmin then it renders it unclean. Within the different castes themselves thousands of subdivisions (*jatis*) exist and these determine occupation.

In modern society it is generally assumed that class is the basis of social stratification. The major classes in the West are:

an upper class (the wealthy, employers and industrialists, plus top executives – those who directly own productive resources); a middle class (which includes most white-collar workers and professionals); and a working class (those in blue-collar and manual jobs). In some industrialized countries, such as France and Japan, a fourth class peasants (people engaged in traditional types of agricultural production) has until recently been important. Some have argued that American society does not fit this class system of stratification: other attributes such as **race** and **gender** are often identified as important sources of social inequality.

Sociologists have drawn attention to the importance of stratification for the life chances of those who occupy different positions in the strata. In the UK, for example, despite the introduction of a National Health Service, the health of the population, in almost every respect, is directly related to class. **DA**

See also bourgeoisie; capital; embourgeoisement thesis; ethnicity; feminism; Marxism; occupation; power; profession; social mobility; structure.

Further reading F. Parkin, 'Social Stratification' in T. Bottomore and R. Nisbet (eds.), *A History of Sociological Analysis*; J. Westergaard, H. Resler, *Class in Capitalist Society*; E.O. Wright, *Classes*.

SOCIAL/SOCIOLOGICAL PROBLEM

In **sociology**, there are tremendous difficulties involved in the definition of a social problem. Cultural differences mean that what is a social problem for one group may not be for another. Historically, social problems can change over time with changes in the law, ethics and social standards. Finally, sociologists have pointed out that there is a political component involved in the definition. The identification of a problem may involve the exercise of **social control** of one group over another. Sociologists clearly reject the commonplace notion that social problems somehow have an objective status, rather they stress their socially constructed character.

An important criticism made within sociology is that many official definitions of social problems contain the assumption that they derive from the personal characteristics of individuals rather than from the structural features of the social system over which the individual has little control. The assertion, for example, that unemployed people are work-shy diverts attention from the broader causes of unemployment. Similarly, schemes aimed at 'better equipping individuals to secure jobs' imply that it is the unemployed individual who is at fault rather than the job market. **DA**

See also culture; discourse; dominant ideology; ideology; norms; power; social construction of reality; sociology of knowledge; values.

Further reading R.K. Merton and R. Nisbet (eds.), *Contemporary Social Problems*.

SOCIALISM AND SOCIAL DEMOCRACY

Socialism and social democracy (both derived from Latin *socius*, 'one to whom I am bound') are the names of political doctrines and movements. The expression social democracy is now preferred by those socialists who wish to distinguish their political beliefs from classical socialist doctrines, especially those associated with **Marxism** and Marxism-Leninism. The four core values of **democracy**, **liberty**, **equality** and community are the easiest way to understand the numerous forms of socialism and social democracy, as they lie at the centre of their historical evolution. And the tensions between democracy, liberty, equality and fraternity help explain much of the internal debate and fragmentation within socialist and social democratic movements.

Liberty and Democracy Socialists and social democrats alike believe in 'positive' as well as 'negative' liberty, that is, in the importance of people being free to achieve their objectives and realize their talents. Mere 'negative' liberty, or freedom from government, is insufficient to build a good society. Historically, all socialists and social democrats, organized in socialist, social democratic or labour parties, have been distinguished by their fundamental commitment to democracy, understood as government based on popular consent and popular participation in the formation and exercise of political authority. Since human freedom requires democratic freedom to choose the government and to dissent from it, and civil rights of assembly, expression and participation, democracy is considered necessary to ensure liberty.

Socialists have always been divided, however, over the scope and means to greater democratization, and as a way of advancing political liberty. Social democrats now unambiguously embrace the institutions of representative government (the periodic election of parliaments and/or of presidents under universal suffrage) and the rule of law (the regulation of all social activity by constitutional and other legislation). They have more rarely sought to extend democratization to non-governmental organizations. In contrast, classical socialists (and communists) have emphasized the merits of 'workers' control', 'industrial democracy', 'economic democracy' or more generally 'participatory democracy'. They have also believed in the merits of politicizing such formally neutral institutions as state bureaucracies, the police and the judiciary. And **libertarian** socialists, who resemble anarchists in their political beliefs, would entrust ultimate authority to 'mass meetings' of active people rather than to 'laws or constitutions which give power to élites. In part these differences reflect conflict among socialists over the relative importance of liberty and equality. Socialists generally believe that greater equality requires radical democratization of all institutions, whereas social democrats think that too much democratization may threaten other left-wing values, like liberty, and may not necessarily produce stable democratic institutions.

Socialists and social democrats have also been divided over how to achieve their commitment to liberty. Social democrats or democratic socialists have been reformists: they believe that they should work within the institutions of liberal democracy to extend support for their values (see **Fabianism**). They usually

organize themselves in mass socialist, social democratic or labour parties for these purposes. By contrast the classical socialists and Marxists were often revolutionaries, believing that liberal democracy or **representative government** was a sham: a façade for 'bourgeois' or 'capitalist' democracy. They believed that 'true democracy', that is, proletarian or working-class democracy, can only be achieved through insurrectionary means. They have usually organized themselves in élite, or cadre parties to achieve these purposes, using the example of the Russian Bolsheviks as their model. However, the Marxist-Leninist or Communist (with a capital 'c') commitment to democracy has been fundamentally compromised since the 1917 Russian Revolution, associated with the 'dictatorship of the proletariat', which in practice meant the dictatorship of the Communist Party. Such parties have monopolized state power in the USSR and eastern Europe (until 1989), in China, Southeast Asia and Cuba.

Equality Socialists and social democrats alike believe that liberty can only flourish in a society of equals. Indeed they are best known for their commitments to 'equality'. Egalitarianism requires opposition to hereditary privilege, especially aristocratic but also kin-based patronage, on the grounds that such privilege has nothing to do with merit. This principle is indispensable to the socialist vision of a 'classless society'. Social democrats believe that equality of opportunity requires governmental regulation of private property and family rights to ensure that equality of opportunity is meaningful. Thus a redistributive welfare state, based upon progressive taxation of income and wealth, and which ensures equality in access to basic social goods, such as education, health care and insurance, is vital to enable people to have a fair chance of benefiting from equality of opportunity.

Social democrats and socialists also believe that inequalities between people in income, wealth or resources have to be justified by the benefits such inequalities generate for the rest of society. This requirement sets limits to the differentials in income and wealth which can be accepted within the principles of **social justice**. Here socialists and social democrats part company with economic liberals, who believe that equality of opportunity means equality of opportunity to achieve unequal rewards.

Socialists and social democrats have progressively extended the principles that all adults should be treated as meriting equal respect and possessing equal rights before the law, because of their equal humanity. Thus they have been hostile to **imperialism**, the conquest and coercive domination of some ethnic groups by others; to racism, the belief that some races are generally superior to others; and to sexism, the belief that men are generally superior to women (and vice versa). Moreover, they generally seek to rectify discrimination against ill-treated groups, whether defined by their race, ethnicity, religion, gender, sexual preference or physical traits, by advocating **affirmative action** to ensure that members of such groups are properly integrated into modern society as equal citizens.

Most controversially, socialists and social democrats have historically been associated with an egalitarian philosophy which opposed the free market and private property rights in production, distribution and exchange. Thus many early socialists and Marxist-Leninists favoured the complete replacement of the free market by a planned economy, and state or 'social' as opposed to private ownership of the means of production, distribution and exchange. They argued that such policies were necessary to control the anarchy and inequalities of capitalist markets, to abolish class privileges, and to create the genuine solidarity which they believed should characterize a socialist society. This 'state socialist' tradition has been the dominant one on the left, especially the Marxist Left, and was applied in the USSR from the late 1920s, and after 1945 in places as diverse as eastern Europe, China, Southeast Asia and Cuba since 1945.

However, the 'state socialist' tradition has never been universal among socialists and social democrats. Western social democrats like British Fabians, French Proudhonists, Christian socialists and numerous other socialist groups have argued that capitalist markets can be regulated to achieve socialist ends (i.e. egalitarian and fraternal outcomes) without supplanting them completely by state planning. They have agreed with some liberals that monopolistic state ownership and planning endanger liberty and reduce efficiency, without necessarily producing either greater equality or solidarity. In the 1980s the 'state socialist' tradition became totally discredited as Gorbachov's programme of *perestroika* revealed the fundamental failures of the planned economies of the Communist bloc. This discrediting has permitted the democratic socialist Left in western Europe, such as the Swedish and German social democrats, the British Labour party, and the French socialists, to clarify their commitment to economic pluralism, that is, to a **mixed economy** in which capitalist markets should be regulated (rather than terminated) by governments to maximize liberty, equality and community. There has also been 'a third way' in socialist economic thought, 'market socialism', which advocates combining social ownership of the means of production with a very considerable role for the market in making allocative decisions through basing production in workers' co-operatives. This third tradition, which has never been extensively experimented with outside Yugoslavia tries to merge the efficiency of the market mechanism with democratic principles in the organization of work and property rights.

Community Community – or 'fraternity' to use what is now a sexist expression – is the least precise of socialist values and has been interpreted in various ways. It has been understood first as a commitment to 'internationalism', that is, to the rejection of the idea that political activity should be bound within the confines of one nation, and support for global political co-operation between nations. It has also, and to the contrary, been understood as a commitment to **nationalism**, the emotional solidarity of all citizens of the self-governing nation. Finally, it has been understood as a generalized commitment to 'collectivism' or 'communitarianism' which is opposed to the egoistic **individualism** espoused by some liberals. This understanding of community as 'collectivism' is very prevalent on the Left, and is obviously linked to its egalitarian commitments. Historically the socialist commitment to fraternal solidarity was associated with an exclusive commitment to the interests and aspirations of the (manual) working class, but today social democrats extend their conception of 'community' to the people as a whole. More recently a green socialist tendency has emerged, which argues that the commitment to solidarity and equality with other humans must also be extended to 'Nature' itself if human existence is to be preserved in a tolerable form.

Rationalism The socialist and social democratic values of democracy, equality, liberty and community are usually expressed in rationalist political argument. Those who hold them believe that the world can be understood through, and only through, the powers of human reason – although this belief is challenged by some socialist feminists. They also believe that all political institutions must be justified by reason, rather than by appeals to traditions, emotions, religions, intimations or instincts. Unlike conservatives, socialists and social democrats do not regard human beings as unimprovable or inherently evil. They believe that most, if not all, political problems and conflicts are soluble through the application of human reason. Such rationalism, which entails optimistic conceptions of human nature and the human condition, distinguishes socialists and social democrats, whatever their many internal differences over the relative importance of democracy, liberty, equality and fraternity, and the ways in which these values can be practically implemented. **BO'L**

See also conservatism; guild socialism; liberalism.

Further reading R.N. Berki, *Socialism*; G.D.H. Cole, *A History of Socialist Thought: Volumes 1–7*; C.A.R. Crosland, *The Future of Social-*ism; G. Lichtheim, *A Short History of Socialism*; A. Nove, *The Economics of Feasible Socialism*.

SOCIALIST REALISM

Socialist Realism was a doctrine first approved at the Congress of Socialist Writers in 1934, at the instigation of Stalin. Until then, Soviet artists had been allowed to associate political radicalism with artistic revolution. However, after Stalin's rise to power the Soviet régime developed a dislike of 'bourgeois' avant-gardism, and replaced it with the idea of Socialist Realism. This stated that the role of the artist was to serve the people by producing positive, upbeat and accessible works of art. The social function of art was to elevate and educate. Experimentation, negativism and an adherence to 'bourgeois values' were forbidden. In the name of this doctrine, some appalling rubbish was hailed (and lavishly rewarded) as art, and some creators of the highest ability, from Mayakovsky to Shostakovich, from Malevich to Pasternak, were vilified. In the former USSR, the writer A.A. Zhdanov was made commissar in charge of creativity – a position which gave him power over patronage, and a stranglehold on artistic innovation, which persisted in the country's artistic life well into the 1980s.

Socialist Realism is not the same thing as **social realism**. **KMcL**

Further reading C.V. James, *Soviet Socialist Realism: Origins and Aims*.

SOCIALIZATION

Socialization is the term used by sociologists and anthropologists to refer to the process by which a individual member of a society acquires its **culture**. Through the process of socialization culture is passed on from generation to generation and new members of a society learn appropriate ways of behaving. An important aspect of culture that is passed on through socialization is **language**.

An infant is not born instinctively knowing how to behave in a given society; this has to be learnt. Without socialization, an individual would bear little resemblance to any human being defined as normal by the standards of society. It is reported that the Indian emperor Akbar (who ruled from 1542 to 1602), ordered a group of children be brought up without any instruction in language, to test the belief that they would eventually speak Hebrew, the language of God. The children were raised by deaf mutes. They developed no spoken language and communicated solely by gestures.

It is through socialization that individual members of a society acquire the social **norms** (rules and guidelines which direct conduct in a number of situations, for example, norms governing dress) and **values** (more generalized notions of what is important and worthwhile) of that society. Socialization also provides guidelines for behaviour considered appropriate for certain social roles (for instance, parenthood or spouse). A number of agencies of socialization can be identified: the family, peer relationships, school, the mass **media**, and work. In all cultures it is the family which is the principal socializing agency of the child during infancy. Formal schooling diminishes the influence of the family. In school the child is deliberately taught skills and knowledge but much more is learnt besides via the 'hidden curriculum'. The development of mass communications has greatly extended the range of socializing agencies. Television exerts a particularly powerful influence.

Socialization continues throughout the life cycle. Three forms of socialization are distinguished by sociologists: primary, secondary, and adult socialization. Primary socialization refers to the socialization of the young child within the family; secondary socialization refers to the socialization that occurs once a child enters school; and adult socialization relates to the fact that socialization is a process which continues throughout adult life as new roles and situations are encountered.

In some circumstances, involving a marked alteration in the social environment of an individual or group, people may undergo processes of resocialization – in prisons, concentration camps or religious sects for example.

Since the cultural setting into which one is born comes to influence one's behaviour it would be easy to assume that there is no room for individuality or free will in society. Within **sociology** some have written about socialization as if society placed its members into a pre-set mould; but they have been accused of treating people as if they were merely puppets with 'society' pulling the strings. Others have pointed out that it is through socialization that we are able to develop a sense of self-identity, and the capacity for independent thought and action. **DA**

See also assimilation; consensus theory; ethnicity; gender; generalized other; internalization; role; sexuality; social integration; social self; society; sociobiology; sociolinguistics; structure-agency debate; subculture.

Further reading K. Danziger, *Socialization*; C. Jenks (ed.), *The Sociology of Childhood*.

SOCIETY

Society (from Latin *sociare*, 'to join together') is one of the key concepts in **sociology**. In everyday usage the term society is normally applied to nation-states and political boundaries. Within sociology the concept of society is also used in this sense, but this is not always the case as societies do not necessarily correspond to political boundaries. For sociologists, the term has a broader application which incorporates the totality of human relationships.

In essence, a society is a system of interrelationships which binds individuals together in a social group. Individual group members occupy a relatively bounded territory, sharing a common **culture** and way of life. Different societies may have a distinctive language, patterns of dress, social institutions, customs, traditions and systems of government. Each individual is aware of a common identity shared with other members of the society.

The notion of society is intimately bound up with that of culture. No society could exist without culture, but equally no culture could exist without society. A society's culture embraces the whole way of life shared by group members and includes modes of dress, customs and traditions, **language**, patterns of work, family life, religious beliefs and ceremonies, and leisure pursuits.

Culture also includes **norms** and **values**. Values are shared abstract ideas about what is desirable, proper, good and bad. Norms are definite principles and rules which group members are excepted to observe. For example, in Western societies a prominent value is being faithful to a single partner. In many other cultures a person may be permitted to have several wives or husbands simultaneously. It is the cultural variations between human groups which distinguishes different types of society.

The culture of a given society is passed on from generation to generation through the process of **socialization**. The main agencies of childhood socialization are the family, the school and peer groups. Socialization is, however, a continuous process throughout adult life as new experiences and social situations are encountered.

Sociologists have distinguished between different types of society. It should be noted, however, that while the different categories are broadly similar, considerable variations exist within each group.

In *hunter-gatherer societies*, the people do not grow crops or keep livestock, rather they live by gathering plants and hunting animals. *Tribal societies* are held together socially, culturally, and physically by blood relations, and they may be pastoral or agrarian. In *pastoral societies*, the raising of domesticated animals provides the major source of livelihood. *Agrarian societies* depend on the cultivation of fixed plots of land. Larger, more developed agrarian societies may form *traditional states*. A distinct type of agrarian society is *feudal society* in which unfree peasants hold land on condition of payment of rent in labour, in kind or in cash. In western Europe, between the 15th and 18th centuries, feudal societies were succeeded by *capitalist societies*. Capitalist societies are based on the private ownership of the means of production and an economy geared to making profit. In eastern Europe, for most of the 20th century, feudalism was succeeded by *communist societies*, based on the principle of the absence of private property. In *industrialized societies* (which may be capitalist or communist), industrial production is the main basis of the economy industrial techniques are also used in food production.

Sociologists also refer to *postindustrial society*, a concept formulated by D. Bell in the 1960s to describe the result of social and economic changes in the late 20th century: the declining dependence on manufacturing industry, the rise of new service industries, and a new emphasis on the role of knowledge in production, consumption and leisure. On the whole, however, there is generally little acceptance that modern societies have moved beyond industrialism in any of the senses Bell suggested. Modern societies tend to be culturally diverse embracing a wide range of different **subcultures**, whereas small societies tend to be culturally quite uniform.

Although the concept of society is a basic one in sociology it is not without its difficulties, and disputes surround its use. Critics have pointed out that although the concept can be quite readily applied, in its common-sense meaning, to well-established nation-states, the identification of societal boundaries is more problematic in the case of traditional states, which were usually comprised of fairly loose assemblies of different peoples with little conception of a collective identity.

A further issue that can create difficulties is the question as to the point at which an historically changing society should or should not be treated as the same society.

Increasingly, social and economic relationships are stretching worldwide, and many aspects of people's lives are influenced by organizations and social networks thousands of miles away from the societies in which they live. This has led some theorists to caution against an over-emphasis on the concept of unitary societies, which may lead to a failure to give sufficient attention to the importance of global connections.

Within sociology, the term society is also used in a slightly different sense. Émile Durkheim, one of the founding fathers of sociology, conceived of society as a distinct object. As the object of study in sociology, society in this sense was distinct from and greater than the sum total of the individuals who comprised it. For Durkheim, society was a 'moral power' which was external to its individual members and constrained and shaped their actions and behaviour. The use of society conceptualized in this way has been a source of contentious debate within sociology, and contemporary sociologists are increasingly reluctant about conceptualizing society in this way. **DA**

See also assimilation; capital; community; convergence thesis; dependency theory; diffusionism; evolutionism; functionalism; generalized other; globalization; historical sociology; internalization; religion; role; social integration; social self; state; structuralism; structure; structure-agency debate; suicide; theories of modernity; world system; urbanism/urbanization.

Further reading R. Benedict, *Patterns of Culture* (1946); P. Worsley, *The Three Worlds: Culture and World Development*.

SOCIOBIOLOGY

Sociobiology, a discipline which straddles **anthropology**, the **life sciences** and **sociology**, is the study of interaction in biological systems. It concentrates on explanations of how instances of social behaviour have evolved, and to what extent social behaviour is prescribed in the genes. It has been of interest since the early 1970s, and in particular since the publication, in 1975, of *Sociobiology: the New Synthesis*, by the US zoologist Edward Wilson. Until this time, although an evolutionary continuity between other animals and human beings had long been recognized, most biologists had tended to emphasize the distinctive qualities of the human species. Wilson and others challenged this assumption, claiming by contrast that there are innumerable parallels between human behaviour and that of other animals. For example, some species of animals have elaborate courtship rituals, leading to sexual union and reproduction – and according to sociobiologists, human courtship and sexual behaviour involve similar rituals, similarly based on inborn characteristics.

The aspiration of sociobiology is to bring together aspects of anthropology biology and sociology into a single scientific discipline, studying (for example) social insects and social primates with an emphasis on particular types of behaviour (such as **aggression** and **altruism**). Genetic determinants are one area of study; others are the behaviour of a given group and the elements which make it up: age, communication, division of labour, organization, sex ratio, size and so on. But although scholars with biological training tend to be sympathetic to its claims, anthropologists and sociologists are usually more sceptical. There is also a fundamental (and perhaps less territorial) objection: that the discipline is inescapably **anthropomorphic**, that it is impossible for human observers to avoid colouring their researches with reference to their own societies. Sociobiologists have begun to address this issue, but the discipline is too recent, and perhaps too controversial, for an agreed methodology to have become established. **DA RB RK**

See also ethology; gender; sexuality; social construction of reality.

Further reading K. Bock, *Human Nature and History: a Response to Sociobiology*; Richard Dawkins, *The Selfish Gene*; J.F. Eisenberg and W.S. Dillon (eds.), *Man and Beast: Comparative Social Behaviour*.

SOCIOLINGUISTICS

Sociolinguistics is an area of study informed by both sociology and psychology, and concerned with the social and cultural aspects and functions of language, with the enormous diversity of issues arising from the interaction between language and society. Topics like **dialectology**, **pidgins and creoles**, **language planning**, **bilingualism** and **accommodation theory** all demonstrate how groups of people influence the forms of language spoken, and vice versa. Important contributions have been made in this field in relation to language and social class in particular.

As an academic discipline, sociolinguistics often appears highly heterogeneous and dissipated, owing to the many kinds of data gathered, the variety of analyses performed, and the broad spectrum of theories developed. However, one factor which unites almost all sociolinguists is their rejection of linguistic studies which entirely divorce language from the social influences which shape it. The latter approach, most closely associated with Noam Chomsky, argues that linguistics should be concerned solely with revealing the system of grammar, or competence, known by every native speaker.

In contrast, the bulk of sociolinguistic enquiry falls under the heading of performance, since it deliberately highlights the great heterogeneity within people's speech. For example, it is pointed out that even speakers who nominally speak the same language do so in a wide variety of ways. For example, the differences between speakers caused by dialectal variation are compounded by variation within the speech of a single person, as with the switch from formal to informal styles, according to the social context. In fact, there are many sources of linguistic variation which depend on numerous social factors, including social class, geographical region, sex, age, social and physical setting, and level of formality.

The English sociologists B. Bernstein suggested that the speech patterns of the working classes and the middle classes were different, and that this in part accounted for the different educational achievements of middle- and working-class children. Bernstein believed that working-class speech was characterized by a 'restricted language code' and middle-class speech by an 'elaborated language code'. He argued that formal education was carried out by use of the elaborated code, and that working-class children were consequently placed at a disadvantage. Bernstein has, however, been criticized for implying that middle-class speech patterns were in some way superior. The American linguist W. Labov conducted a study of speech patterns of lower-class black children in Harlem. He argued that these speech patterns were not inferior to standard English: they were simply different.

For Chomsky, working from a purely linguistic perspective, all sources of variation constitute unhelpful distractions from the task of describing the homogeneous system of grammatical competence. However, a leading opponent of this view, Dell Hymes, has argued that knowledge of grammar is useless without a knowledge of how to use language. Hymes's notion of communicative competence describes language as a rule-governed phenomenon,

integral to the language system. This stance is partly motivated by the belief that studies of how language is used can provide relevant insights for the purely linguistic theories of **syntax**, **morphology** and **phonology**.

If linguistic variation is systematic, then it follows that there must be natural limits to the observable variation. That is, although there may be a range of linguistic alternatives within a given domain, it is not the case that 'anything goes', since the result would be gibberish on many occasions. Defining the limits of variation provides an idea of the prevailing linguistic norms in force and provides a basis for discovering how these norms are acquired and maintained. A prevalent view is that social factors somehow shape, or at least interact with, language and the way it is used. The contrary view, **linguistic relativity**, whereby language influences, or determines, social behaviour and thought, has also been given serious consideration, though it is no longer widely accepted. **DAMS**

See also class; culture; dominant ideology; socialization; social mobility; social stratification; subculture.

Further reading B. Bernstein, 'A Socio-Linguistic Approach to Social Learning', in P. Worsley (ed.), *Modern Sociology: Introductory Readings*; W. Labov, 'The Logic of Non-standard English', in N. Keddie, *Tinker Taylor ... The Myth of Cultural Deprivation.*; P. Trudgill, *Sociolinguistics*; R. Wardhaugh, *An Introduction to Sociolinguistics*.

SOCIOLOGY

The term sociology (from Latin *socius*, 'companion' and Greek *logos*, 'study of') literally means the study of the processes of companionship. The word was originally coined by Auguste Comte (1789–1857), and in its early usage meant the scientific, and more specifically, the positivistic study of **society**. Since then the term has gained much wider currency, and is used to refer to the systematic study of the functioning, organization and development of human social life, groups and societies. Sociology characteristically embraces a wide range of competing paradigms and approaches. It has also remained open to ideas imported from other disciplines.

Sociology is one of a group of social sciences which includes: **anthropology, economics, political science** and human **geography**. The divisions between the various social sciences are not well-defined they all share a range of common interests, concepts and methods. Some argue that what distinguishes sociology from the other social sciences is its peculiar interest in the problems of modern industrial societies. While this is certainly a central interest of the discipline, the concerns of sociology are far more wide-ranging and incorporate all aspects of all types of society.

The scope of sociology is extremely wide, stretching from the study of a passing encounter between two individuals to the analysis of global social processes. The subjects covered by the discipline include: the sociology of development (the examination of social change from agrarian to industrial societies and in particular the Third World); the sociology of deviance (the study of behaviour which departs from that regarded as 'normal' within a society, including crime, mental illness and sexual behaviour); the sociology of health and illness (the study of the experience, distribution and treatment of illness); the sociology of the family and kinship (the study of how sexual reproduction is organized and of the social relations deriving from blood ties); the sociology of art (a sociological concern with the visual **arts, music, theatre**, cinema, and **literature**); the sociology of education (the sociological analysis of educational processes and practices); the sociology of knowledge (the study of the social processes involved in the production of knowledge); the sociology of **law** (the sociological study of the social context, development and operation of law and the legal system); the sociology of housing (the analysis of different patterns of housing provision and housing tenure, historically, comparatively and within societies); urban sociology (the study of social relationships and structures in the city); the sociology of industry (the study of work as paid employment and of industry); the sociology of mass communications (the study of the mass **media** of communications); the sociology of organizations (the study of the factors which affect organizational structure and the social behaviour of people in organizations), the sociology of **religion** (the sociological analysis of religious phenomena); the sociology of **science** (the study of social processes involved in the production of scientific knowledge as well as the social implications of this knowledge); the sociology of sport (a subdiscipline within sociology which focuses on the relationship between sport and society), the sociology of the built environment (a recent emphasis in sociology which brings together a number of special studies previously handled separately: the sociology of housing, urban sociology, **architecture** and **town planning**); the sociology of work (the sociological analysis of work and its organization, especially, but not solely, in terms of paid work); the sociology of **gender** (the study of the ways in which the physical differences between men and women are mediated by culture and social structure); and the sociology of **race** (the study of the historical, social and cultural bases of contemporary inequalities between different ethnic groups).

The practice of sociology involves the abilities to think imaginatively and to detach oneself from preconceived ideas about social relationships. Within sociology there are some broad divisions as to the assumptions that can be made about the nature of social reality, and these crucially influence the approach to analysis that is adopted, the research methods employed and, ultimately, the theories that are generated.

A central question within sociology concerns the basis of **social order**. Why do societies exhibit certain stable patterns and regularities of social behaviour and structure? What are the factors that make societies cohere? The classical answer to these questions was provided by the functionalist, Émile Durkheim (1858–1917), one of the founders of sociology. He believed that society was more than just the aggregate product of its individual members, rather, he argued, society pre-exists human beings and exerts a moral force over their behaviour. For Durkheim, it is the external constraining effects of the society that directs human behaviour and it is to society and not individuals that one should look for explanations of social phenomena. Other social theorists have also emphasized the importance of social structure in explanations of social life: two notable figures were Karl Marx (1818–1883) and Talcott Parsons (1902–1979). Others – ethnomethodologists and phenomenologists, for example – argue that this approach to social reality ignores the fact that for the members of a society, social reality is meaningful and that individuals act on the basis of this meaning, purposefully directing their activities towards the accomplishment of certain goals, and in so doing construct and reconstruct social reality. In practice, most sociologists accept that social structure and individual action both play a part in the creation and re-creation of social reality though there are differences in emphasis. A further major division within social theory is that existing between those who stress the importance of a consensus of social values as the basis of social order (**consensus theory**), and those who emphasize the role of conflict and opposed interests (**conflict theory**). **DA**

See also action perspective; critical theory; dependency theory; dramaturgical model; ethnomethodology; evolutionism; exchange; functionalism; historical sociology; holism; individualism; interactionism; macrosociology; Marxism; microsociology; naturalism; phenomenological sociology; positivism; rational choice theory; social/sociological problems; social realism; society; sociology of knowledge; structuralism; structuration; structure-agency debate; symbolic interactionism; system; systems theory; understanding.

Further reading A. Giddens, *Sociology*; D. Lee and H. Newby, *The Problem of Sociology*.

SOCIOLOGY OF KNOWLEDGE

The sociology of knowledge, as its name suggests, is a branch of **sociology** which studies the social processes involved in the production of **knowledge**. Its subject matter may include ideas and beliefs in addition to knowledge as it is more usually thought of,

such as **science**. It is concerned with the relationship between knowledge and the wider social **structure** – the effects of knowledge and the social processes which might condition either the form or the content of knowledge.

The sociology of knowledge developed as a reaction to Marx's analysis of the relationship between the economic structure and culture – the values, ideas, art forms, etc. of a society. In Marx's work (or rather that fraction of it) available to inter-war sociologists, he claimed that all knowledge was a reflection of **class** interests, a partial understanding of the world called he an 'ideology'. Only the proletariat, the class with no material interest of its own, had a true vision of society.

As more of Marx's work has been published, it has become clear that his ideas were more complex than this. Nevertheless, his apparent challenge to traditional assumptions about the objective nature of reality and the possibility of obtaining unbiased knowledge provoked a powerful reaction. The idea that the proletariat had privileged access to the truth was quickly discredited, but the notion that what counted as knowledge in any given time and place was strongly influenced by the interests of the people involved was widely accepted as the basis for an important area of sociological research.

Karl Mannheim (see below) distinguished two tasks for sociologists: the critical examination of particular ideologies; and the study of the total ideology of a society, which was the particular mission of the sociology of knowledge. He argued for the study of all ways of thinking and knowing available to people in particular social and historical situations. What was accepted knowledge? Who decided this? What procedures were used to resolve disputes about truth and error, bias and objectivity, personal beliefs and collective interests?

These questions have been taken up in studies of institutions responsible for creating and transmitting knowledge in modern societies: science, **religion**, education, the professions, mass **media**, the **arts**. Thomas Kuhn, for example (see below), showed the way in which science did not progress by small incremental changes but by periodic revolutions. In 'normal' times, powerful cliques defined what counted as scientific truths, incorporated these in textbooks and curricula and denied funding and publication opportunities to anyone who did not share their views. But sometimes their position became intellectually unsustainable and there were brief periods of intense conflict over jobs, money and students before a new orthodoxy was established. The winners inherited the power and the privilege; the losers were written out of the official history of the field.

In recent years, the sociology of knowledge has become absorbed in the general movement of social constructionism, the view that all knowledge of the world is essentially a human creation rather than a mirror of some independent reality. **DA**

See also critical theory; discourse; dominant ideology; hegemony; ideology; phenomenological sociology; power; social construction of reality; values.

Further reading T.S. Kuhn, *The Structure of Scientific Revolutions*; K. Mannheim, *Ideology and Utopia*; M.F.D. Young (ed.), *Knowledge and Control: New Directions in the Sociology of Education.*

SOLAR SYSTEM

The solar system consists of the Sun and its orbiting planets. The Sun, vastly larger than any of the planets, is a small star, similar to many of the stars in the night sky. Its light is generated by hydrogen fusion. This process occurs because the gases in the star (mostly hydrogen) are subjected to incredibly high pressures and temperatures, due to the gravitational field of the star. These conditions force the hydrogen atoms into close proximity, whereupon two hydrogen atoms fuse to form one deuterium atom. Energy is released by this process, and much of it is emitted as visible light.

The rest of the bodies which make up the solar system, the planets, are indistinguishable from stars to the naked eye. However, with a telescope it may be seen that they have surface features and sometimes moons, whereas stars remain point-like,

due to their distance. Patient observations reveal that the planets move against the background of stars as they orbit the sun.

The closest planet to the Sun is Mercury, an airless ball of rock about the size of our Moon. The temperatures on its night side and day side differ by 670 degrees centigrade – the largest such contrast in the solar system.

Next is Venus, similar to Earth in size and distance from the Sun. Venus has a daytime temperature of 450 degrees centigrade, and an atmosphere of 90% carbon dioxide. It is covered with a thick layer of sulphur clouds, which have recently been penetrated by spacecraft which have sent back information about its surface.

The next planet out from the Sun is Earth, whose oxygen-rich atmosphere and small temperature variations combine to support life. Earth has one moon.

Mars is the next planet out; slightly smaller than Earth and with similar daytime temperatures, it offers the best hope of supporting human life. However, it has a carbon dioxide and carbon monoxide atmosphere, and the night time temperatures are about -100 degrees centigrade. Mars is orbited by two moons, Phobos and Deimos.

After Mars we find the asteroid belt, a huge ring of orbiting rocks. Many of the meteorites that we see burning up in our upper atmosphere as shooting stars come from here.

Jupiter, the largest planet, lies beyond the asteroid belt. This gas giant could fit 1,000 Earths within it, but is still small compared to the sun, which has 1,000 times the volume of Jupiter. Jupiter has a tiny solid core surrounded by a dense atmosphere of hydrogen, helium, methane, ammonia and a little water. Its swirling cloud systems produce distinctive patterns including the Great Red Spot. Jupiter has 12 large moons and many smaller ones, which lie in the same band as Jupiter's faint ring system.

Further out is Saturn, a gas giant similar to Jupiter but smaller, with 10 large moons and extensive ring systems. Beyond Saturn we find Uranus and Neptune, both gas giants with five and two large moons respectively. Uranus has a highly unusual mode of rotation in that its axis points toward the sun, unlike all the other planets whose axes are at 90 degrees to the plane of the solar system.

Last of all is tiny Pluto, a system of two frozen rocks orbiting each other. Due to its eccentric orbit, Pluto is sometimes closer to the Sun than Neptune.

All of the planets and the asteroid belt lie in a plane, so that the solar system has a disc-like appearance. This indicates that the cloud of gases from which it formed had an overall rotation. **JJ**

See also astronomy; nuclear fission/fusion.

SOLIPSISM

Solipsism (Latin, 'for-oneself-ness'), in **philosophy**, is the theory that only oneself and one's experiences exist. If the only immediate objects of awareness are one's own sensory experiences, then it is difficult to see how one could ever establish that one's sensory experiences are experiences of a world whose existence is independent of one's own, rather than just a dream generated by one's own unconscious mind. But solipsists go further than sceptics. Sceptics hold that while one cannot know whether or not there is a world whose existence is independent of one's own, there may be such a world. Solipsists assert that nothing other than one's own mind and experiences exist. They claim to know that there is no world independent of oneself and one's own experiences. **AJ**

See also scepticism.

Further reading B. Russell, *Our Knowledge of the External World.*

SOVEREIGNTY

Sovereignty (ultimately derived from Latin *super*, 'above') is a concept which was developed in early modern political and legal theory especially in the writings of the French and English scholars Jean Bodin, Thomas Hobbes, Rousseau and John Austin. Its meanings and significance are the subject of much rhetorical and symbolic warfare. It is generally agreed that sovereignty is possessed by the supreme source of authority within a political system: it can therefore be vested in a person (a sovereign monarch), a parliament (a sovereign parliament), a people (a sovereign people).

Sovereignty possesses both external and internal dimensions. Externally a sovereign **state** is formally recognized by others as possessing full authority over a given territory and its population. Naturally the factual sovereignty (or autonomy) of many formally recognized states may be meaningless as in the case of client states. Within a state, internal sovereignty is possessed by that person, organization or body of people who have ultimate authority. Naturally there can be debate as to whether the formal source of *de jure* sovereignty is in fact the *de facto* sovereign: for example although the Queen in Parliament is the *de jure* sovereign in the UK most agree that *de facto* sovereignty is held by other persons or institutions (for example the cabinet, or the government, or, in the view of some optimists, the people).

Four major debates surround sovereignty. The first is whether it is divisible. Some maintain that it is indivisible, pointing that the concept originated in the claims made on behalf of jurists who favoured absolutist monarchs having a monopoly on legislation. Others argue that the separation of executive, legislative and judicial powers in written constitutions divides sovereignty vertically, whereas the autonomous powers of federal and provincial governments within a federal political system fragments sovereignty horizontally. There is a second and similar debate over whether or not sovereignty can be 'pooled' or 'shared'. Traditionalists maintain that sovereignty implies monopolistic possession and therefore cannot be 'shared'; in this view treaties are exercises of sovereignty and not allocations of shares in sovereignty. Revisionists suggest that in political systems where political organs are constitutionally obliged to share responsibility and authority they must be thought of as sharing sovereignty; in this perspective international treaties are allocations of shares and duties in pooled sovereignty. In turn traditionalists maintain that in federal systems it is the constitution which is the sovereign, to which the reply is then made that such constitutions specify how sovereignty is to be divided and shared, to which the riposte is given that any legal system must be unified and cannot be parcelled out amongst various bodies, and so on *ad infinitum*. The best resolution of these arguments is that of Preston King (see below) who argues that the hallmark of sovereignty is not indivisibility, but rather the finality of authoritative decision: that is, that there is some formal way of determining the source of authorized action. Third, some argue that law is the command of the sovereign and therefore that the sovereign is not subject to legal challenge, while others maintain that this viewpoint confuses legal and political sovereignty: the legal sovereign is that which authorizes valid law, while the political sovereign is that which has the ability to make valid law. Finally, there is controversy over whether the concept of sovereignty is historically outmoded, redundant or culturally parochial. Some argue that the term is a leftover from the age of monarchs who owned lands and peoples, that its useful meanings can be conveyed as well by other notions, like authority, **power** and responsibility, and that it is only a complex notion in countries where legislatures possess unlimited right to make laws (as in the UK before it joined the European Community) and where there is no formal constitutional recognition that the people are the ultimate source of legitimate authority. **BO'L**

See also confederation; federation; independence.

Further reading F.H. Hinsley, *Sovereignty;* P. King, *The Ideology of Order: a Comparative Analysis of Jean Bodin and Thomas Hobbes;* P. King, *Federalism and Federation.*

SPACE see Space and Time

SPACE AND ARCHITECTURE

'Space' ideas must be considered the characteristic quality of **architecture**, distinguishing it from the arts of the painter or sculptor. Our impression of architecture is more than the sensation created by the mere treatment of surface elevations, or even the modelling of mass, in terms of the outward form. The departure in architec-ture is the experience of enclosed space, through which we might pass with a multiple series of visual and physical impressions. **JM**

Further reading P. Frankl, *Principles of Architectural History,* chapter 1 'Spatial Form'; N. Pevsner, *An Introduction to European Architecture.*

SPACE AND TIME

Space is the three-dimensional expanse in which all material objects are located. Time is the fourth dimension in which all events are located.

Various philosophical questions arise concerning space and time. Are space and time real? Do the past and future exist? Places which are not here exist. But do times which are not now exist? Do space and time have a reality independently of objects and events? Is it possible for there to be an empty space (a space which contains no objects), or an eventless time (a time in which nothing changes)? And do space and time have a reality independently of observers? Does time flow? Is the asymmetry of time necessary or contingent? Are space and time finite? Do they have boundaries? Some have held that space is infinite and unbounded, others that it is finite and unbounded, in the sense in which the surface of a ball is finite and unbounded. (As the example of the surface of a ball makes clear, being finite is not the same as having a boundary.)

Some philosophers have advocated absolute theories of space and time, while others adhere to relational theories. Absolute theories hold that space and time are both real, existing independently of objects and events, and of observers. Things move or are at rest, and this is not a matter of their changing or unchanging relations with other things: even if something were the only thing in the universe, it could move, or be at rest.

Relationalists hold that space or time are merely matters of relations between objects or events. There is no more to space or time than relations between objects or events.

Einstein's theory of **relativity**, to some philosophers, seems to cast doubt on absolute theories, suggesting that whether or not one event is judged to occur before, after or simultaneously with another is always relative to an observer's position. Suppose that there are two clocks, A and B, which are millions of miles apart and appear to be synchronized to an observer millions of miles from both. This observer will judge that clock A and clock B strike 12 simultaneously. An observer standing next to A, however, will judge that A strikes 12 before B, for light from A reaches her long before light from B does so. And an observer standing next to B will judge that A struck 12 after B, for light from B reaches him long before light from A does so. This not only suggests that whether or not one event is judged to occur before, after or simultaneously with another is always relative to an observer's position. It also indicates that space and time are not independent of each other, but interwoven in a single space-time.

In modern **physics**, the speed of light, gravity, space and time are all dependent upon each other. We define speed as being the distance travelled in a given time interval hence miles per hour, or metres per second. Originally, time was thought to flow at a perfectly constant rate for all objects, with speed being a less fundamental quantity. Experiments performed in the early part of this century showed that this was not the case for light, and Einstein's theory of relativity revealed that the speed of light was of far greater significance than had previously been realised.

We now know that it is the speed of light that is the fundamental constant, not space or time. Both will warp in order to preserve the value of the speed of light. Thus all theories which assume a constant view of time or space have been physically invalidated. Einstein's theory has been shown to hold in many different situations, and tested up to speeds very close to that of light in particle accelerators.

The closer an object travels to the speed of light, the slower its internal clock goes. The very highest energy particles that we know of take 5 minutes of their own time to traverse the width of a galaxy, while an observer at rest with respect to the galaxy sees them take several thousand years. To the particles, space and not time has been distorted they see the whole enormous width of the galaxy compressed by a factor of a billion.

Gravity can also have a dramatic effect upon space and time. The tremendous gravity produced by **black holes** and neutron stars means that time slows down in their vicinity, and light no longer travels in straight lines but bends to follow the warped curvature of space.

Philosophers also have difficulties with the notion of the passage of time. We find it natural to think of time as flowing, of ourselves as moving through time. But this suggests that time could flow quicker or slower than it actually does, that we might move more or less quickly through time. But with respect to what could time flow quicker or slower? One unpromising suggestion is that there is a second-order time, within which time flows more or less quickly.

To anthropologists, space is an element of all social organizations, but it is conceptualized, ordered and used in widely diverse ways. It is to this phenomenon that anthropologists have looked. Some combine it with considerations of its counterpart, time that is, to think of space one must also think of time and vice versa.

Broadly, there are two interdependent senses in which societies take on spatial form. First, space is arranged by means of buildings, boundaries and zones – which, in a circular manner, are dependent on, as well as affect, cultural conceptions about space and its uses. Second, space arranges people in relation to each other. Their distribution and uses of space may reflect a host of features including social and economic position, philosophical or cosmological conceptions, population numbers and environmental considerations.

Related to such ideas is the consideration of personal space, or how the space surrounding the body is adjustable according to the social context and degree of engagement with the participants. The notion of private space or privacy appears to be a feature of modern 'objective' societies in the West, where a premium is placed on the desire to preserve one's personal space and property from others. In most societies, deployment of both personal and social space is closely related to the status of the person. The status of a person in authority is enhanced by a separated and raised platform in certain contexts. Similarly, the spatial separation between men and women in society reflects cultural conceptions and evaluations about the respective **genders**.

From the 1960s onwards, structuralist anthropologists (see **structuralism**) have attempted to trace the relationship between the geographical and physical expressions of space in societies to models of conceptual ordering in the human mind. Central to this is the distinction between **nature** and **culture**, or how human-made divisions of 'raw' space act to socialize the natural environment. Structuralists argue that even though space may show varying physical expressions the underlying logic to its organization is the same for societies everywhere.

While illuminating, structuralist theories on space attempt to offer grand, universalizing models to the neglect of personal and practical uses of space. It is also underpinned by scientific and geometrical metaphors characteristic of organization in Western society. The Pintupi people, an Australian Aboriginal group, for example, conceive of space in a different way: most aspects of their life, including persons, customs and geographical features are based on the 'Dreaming' in which mythological creatures, representing another level of being, created the world through actions such as turning into natural phenomena or going underground. Space is conceptualized on a qualitive, cosmological basis rather than something to be divided, covered and measured typical of predominant views of space in the West.

After Émile Durkheim's distinction between sacred and profane in 1912, discussion has also ranged around how sacred space is kept apart from mundane space for everyday usage. Durkheim regarded the sacred as something that was deeply revered, bonding people together. Similar feelings have been associated with sacred spaces, for instance with pilgrim locations like Lourdes, Mecca and Varanasi. Recent social theorists have applied this distinction of sacred and profane spaces to special places visited by the tourist. More generally, it is impossible to think of any geographical location in the 'raw' without our ideas moulding our perceptions of it. Space, therefore, is constituted by a continual dialogue between our imaginations, our social and cultural experiences and the actual physical landscape.

So far as time is concerned anthropologists argue that it can be grasped only through the uses and metaphors we apply to its description, rather than simply as a part of an objective experience of the world. We may consider the passing days and seasons, and the process of ageing, as an experience of reality, but these processes through time are also described according to particular sets of social codes. For instance, in Western societies, age is quantified according to the number of years, and these revolve around a set of seasonal markers. Western industrial societies standardize time by measurement with devices such as clocks and calendars. The precise measurement of time is a crucial factor in the rise of **capitalism**, where ideas of time as a commodity and of time-discipline govern people's lives. In some other societies, time appears to be experienced on a more qualitative basis – that is, more directly dependent on the seasons or on personal recollection of past events. Anthropologists have generally referred to this as 'human time'.

Edward Evans-Pritchard was one of the earliest anthropologists to concentrate on concepts of time in other societies. He did this in relation to the Nuer people of Sudan in 1940, arguing that their notions of time were determined by social structures, principally through the individual's passage through age-grades. Studying the Navaho people of North America, Benjamin Whorf concluded that their concepts of time were determined by their language, and were therefore unique and distinct from other societies. Both anthropologists argued that, essentially, notions of time in such societies were cyclical (as opposed to the linear model of past, present and future following one another in a progressive line typical of Western societies).

Such propositions have sparked off anthropological debates on, first, whether concepts of time are cyclical and repetitive or linear and irreversible and, second, whether time is relative to a particular community or the same for people in all societies. Some have proposed that in **ritual** contexts time is experienced as cyclical, whereas in mundane situations time is conceived as a linear progression. Others have criticized the terms of the argument itself for being reliant on two geometric metaphors to describe time, which are largely a construct of Western society.

Recent anthropologists, acknowledging that there are some aspects of time that are universal features of all peoples' lives, have turned their attention to the various metaphors and methods of organizing time in societies, instead of trying to attempt the impossible in cracking a code about experiences of time. Such perspectives consider how time is codified, how time reflects religious and cultural values, how it organizes and is organized by daily social routine, and how it relates to other concepts such as space, **history**, **death** and **personhood**. Time is a defining part of our sense of reality and raises some very fundamental concerns, the most important of which is to be vigilant about our culturally learnt assumptions of time. The standardization of Greenwich Mean Time was a key component in spreading the dominance of the Western ethos around the globe, confirming that a Western notion of time or reality is, to a large extent, also conflated with a universal notion of time. **AJ JJ RK**

See also cultural relativism; ethnohistory; indigenous metaphysics; language; primitivism; rite of passage; tourism, anthropology of; Westernization.

Further reading R. Gale, *The Philosophy of Time*; Bill Hillier and Julienne Hanson, *The Social Logic of Space*; James Middleton, *Myth and Cosmos*; Fred R. Myer, *Pintupi Country, Pintupi Self: Sentiment, Place and Politics Among Western Desert Aborigines*; J.J.C. Smart, *Problems of Space and Time*; Michael Young, *The Metronomic Society*.

SPECIATION

Speciation (from Latin *species*, 'kind') is the evolutionary mechanism by which a species, the basic unit of biological classification, is formed. Most species are distinguishable from others because members have a high degree of similarity with one another and produce offspring which are similar to both parents. This similarity exists because it is inherited, while differences between species are retained because interspecies mating is rare if not impossible. Humans have long been capable of recognizing those species which are important to them, but an understanding of the evolutionary mechanism and significance of speciation is relatively modern. The process of speciation cannot be observed as it takes place over a period of time which far exceeds the duration of human civilization. However, it is a continuous process, and the evolutionary process by which populations change are observable and fairly well understood.

It is probable that a new species arises as a result of the reproductiove isolation of a group of individuals from an existing population. The most obvious, and possibly most common, type of isolation is geographical, and speciation which occurs by such a mechanism is termed *allopatric speciation*; that which occurs by other means is termed *sympatric speciation*. Two geographically isolated groups of a single species will evolve independently because no two habitats are identical, and because **evolution** involves the appearance of variation by random **mutation**. Thus two isolated groups will eventually lose the ability to mate with each other and will subsequently diverge still further as separate species. In geological terms, events which might divide populations are very frequent and need not be cataclysmic; changes in sea level result in bodies of water and land being subdivided, along with the organisms they are home to. Sympatric speciation is less readily envisaged but is theoretically possible where, for example, a species forms two loci of population around two similar food sources. The individuals in each sub-population may tend to breed with nearby individuals: and this effect, coupled with evolutionary pressure to become more specialized to the chosen food, may eventually lead to the two groups becoming separate species. **RB**

See also biogeography; hybridization; niche.

SPEECH ACT THEORY

Speech act theory, in linguistics, describes how words are often used to do things, rather than merely to comment on a state of affairs in the world. For example, the person who says 'I name this ship Titanic', is actually performing the action of naming a ship by uttering those words. However, even sentences which seem to be merely describing a situation can also be used to accomplish actions, and in so doing they function as indirect speech acts. Someone who says 'It's rather hot in here' could well be conveying a request, indirectly, for a window to be opened.

The actions performed with words are often described in terms of their illocutionary force, which refers to the conventional social functions they fulfil, such as greeting, praising, complaining, and the like. Speech acts can be categorized according to the kind of illocution transmitted by an utterance. Thus, directive acts involve the speaker trying to get the hearer to behave in a particular way, as happens when giving an order or making a suggestion. In order for an utterance to succeed in conveying a particular illocution, a number of so-called felicity conditions must be fulfilled. For example, an offer will only be felicitous if the hearer does not yet possess what is being offered. MS

See also pragmatics; semantics.

SPEED OF LIGHT

All experiments show that light travels at a constant velocity through a vacuum, and that more importantly that this speed is finite, and that nothing travels faster than light. The speed of light is approximately 300,000,000 metres per second. A light year is the distance light will travel in one year, and this distance – using the above approximation – is 9,460,800,000,000,000 metres in one year. This is equivalent to 5,913,000,000,000 miles.

White light is a mixture of light of different colours, each colour having its own wavelength. The extreme red end of the visible spectrum has a wavelength of 0.4 millionths of a metre and violet at the other end 0.8 millionth of a metre. Since the velocity v of all radiation corresponds to the equation $v = n$ where n is a constant it will be clear that light of different colour travels at different speeds. AA

See also astronomy; relativity.

SPIRITUAL

As early as the 16th century the word 'spiritual' was used to denote Christian religious texts sung to folk or popular secular tunes. Later, it was used to distinguish these religious songs from traditional psalms and hymns. The white-American spiritual flourished in the southern states during the revivalist religious movements of the 18th and 19th centuries, particularly in the camp-meeting an open-air service involving huge congregations and lasting several days. The use of folk melodies was regarded by many dissenting denominations as a revolt against the staid psalmody of the established doctrines. The texts and tunes of the camp-meeting spirituals were characteristically simple and repetitive, using stock phrases and responsorial refrains. Although the white spiritual emerged from, and belonged essentially to, an oral tradition, many were published using an elementary teaching notation called 'shape-note', in which each pitch was given its own individual shape.

The belief that the black spiritual evolved exclusively among black slaves transported from Africa to America, and that it retained identifiable African traits, has now been displaced by substantial evidence suggesting that both black and white spirituals shared common origins in the inter-racial camp-meetings. However, the musical and textual similarities between black and white spirituals and the work songs of the black slaves, with their recurring themes of death, salvation and liberation, nurtured the independent growth of what can be regarded as the first, truly syncretic Afro-American music.

During the 1870s, a black, university-based ensemble called the Fisk Jubilee Singers took the black spirituals to a wider, international audience by performing them in arrangements harmonized according to the European art music tradition. Their popularity was soon followed by the publication of many collections with piano accompaniment. It is these mediated, urbanized versions that most will recognize as the so-called Negro spiritual. **SSt**

Further reading Dena J. Epstein, *Sinful Tunes and Spirituals: Black Folk Music to the Civil War*; George Pullen Jackson, *White Spirituals in the Southern Uplands.*

SPIRITUALISM

Spiritualism was a kind of industrial-society equivalent of the belief common in all religions and at all periods that our spirits survive the death of the body, and pass into another world in which (with luck and the right rituals) they can be contacted. The spiritualist movement began in North America in the 1840s, and was rapidly taken up in Europe. 'Experiments' were set up in contacting spirits, at seances, through mediums, by such means as table-tapping and the Ouija board. Spiritualism became a favourite after-dinner pastime among the middle class, and mediums and other experts – for example the many 'investigators' who set up 'scientific' experiments to test spirits or record them on film or cylinder – made fortunes. Freud's and Jung's investigations of the **unconscious** gave spiritualism a boost in the 1920s, and the present writer can still remember going 'ghost-hunting' in the 1950s with a group of perfectly sane scientists (geologists, physicists and psychologists). The Society for Psychic Research, set up in Britain in 1880, still exists, and although spiritualism has nothing like the profile it did 100 years ago – its supporters deserted en masse to the various New Age and mystic cults of the 1960s – it still occasionally makes news. **KMcL**

Further reading Oliver J. Lodge, *Raymond, or Life and Death, with Examples of the Evidence for the Survival of Memory and Affection after Death* (1916).

SPLITTING see **Defence Mechanism**

SPONTANEOUS GENERATION see **Abiogenesis**

STAMMBAUM THEORY

The 19th-century, German linguist August Schleicher examined the ways in which languages are related to one another in distinct language families. Schleicher was the first to propose a family tree structure (*Stammbaum*) which can be used to reveal the common ancestors of related languages. Of particular interest was Schleicher's application of Darwinian concepts of evolution to his Stammbaum theory. Schleicher suggested that languages are living organisms, subject to the laws of **natural selection**. In the UK, for example, the domination of English over minority languages such as Gaelic and Welsh would be taken as an example of the survival of the fittest. The inherent nature of English as a strong language ensures its selection and propagation. Political and social pressures on the spread of one language at the expense of another were not entertained. Although no longer influential, as an early attempt to incorporate the study of language within the biological sciences, Stammbaum theory was far in advance of its time. **MS**

STARS

Stars are huge compared to the Earth; the Sun, a relatively small star, could contain one million planet Earths within its volume.

Stars are born when a cloud of primordial hydrogen begins to coalesce. This happens for several reasons. If there is a slightly greater density of matter in one part of the cloud, then gravitational attraction will cause other matter to drift towards it. Also, there will be light from surrounding sources but not from within the cloud. Light exerts a perceptible force upon small particles, and thus the cloud would condense.

Once the process has started, it speeds up, as the central core of matter becomes denser. The hydrogen atoms are forced into close proximity, and eventually gravity is strong enough to cause fusion of two hydrogen atoms into helium. This fusion releases energy in the form of radiation, containing some visible light. The gas cloud has become a star.

The star is now in its first phase. What happens to it next is entirely determined by how much matter the original cloud contained. It will burn hydrogen by fusion for millions of years – our Sun is in this phase. But eventually the hydrogen will run out, leaving the star with helium, which it cannot burn. Then the star will begin to collapse, since previously radiation pressure had balanced the force of gravity, and now only gravity remains.

If the star is small, about the mass of our Sun, it will not collapse far. Its outer layers will expand, enveloping and destroying any planets it may possess. It is now a red giant, and when the gas envelope dissipates, the small remaining core will be a white dwarf. White dwarf matter is very dense by Earth standards, weighing several tons per teaspoonful.

A heavier star will collapse much further, until the helium begins to fuse. The star will have a kind of rebirth, called a nova. Depending upon the size of the star, this cycle of collapse and ignition may continue, forming many other elements. All elements that we know today were formed in the interiors of stars. Eventually the star will begin to form iron and the elements heavier than iron. However, energy is absorbed rather than released when these heavy elements are formed, and thus their formation hastens the star's collapse. The star collapses swiftly, until the collapse is brought to an abrupt halt as a neutron core is formed. All the particles in the star have been forced into a single conglomerate with the density of a nucleus, and will not collapse further. This causes a huge explosion as the collapse rebounds, and about half of the matter of the star is lost to surrounding space. This explosion is known as a supernova, and for the few weeks that it burns, a supérnova will be brighter than its entire galaxy.

The usual remnant is a neutron star, an incredibly dense object. One teaspoonful of neutron star matter weighs several million tons. But an even heavier star will collapse further than a neutron star, to form the enigmatic **black hole**, from which not even light can escape. **JJ**

See also nuclear fission/fussion; relativity.

STATE

The political world is now constituted by states, and will remain so for the foreseeable future. However, the world has not always been comprised of states. The state is a set of governmental institutions of relatively recent historical origin. Until very recently parts of the world were either unclaimed by states or under the control of stateless nomads, but that is no longer so. Government, in the sense of rule-making and decision-making, has been characteristic of all societies, even tribal societies, but the state has not. There have been stateless societies. What then defines a state?

There is no universally agreed answer. All those who define the concept organizationally accept that a state is special type of government which must exercise sovereign authority over a specified territory and population, and have that **sovereignty** recognized by other states. Internally, a state is differentiated from its society by the fact that it is the formal source of law, the claimed monopolist of civil force, and the final extractor of taxation. Its activities are normally administered and managed by authorized bureaucracies. Externally, a state exists in a world of other states. To be an authentic state a polity must be capable of autonomous diplomacy and organized war-making. Thus understood, states vary in the extent to which they are effectively sovereign both in international relations and within their territories. They vary in the extent to which they are centralized, bureaucratized, internally co-ordinated, and autonomous from (or free from control by) their societies; and they vary radically in the extent to which they are democratic, that is, subject to the control and direction of the free choices of their citizens.

States are also, and confusingly, defined *functionally* either by their alleged goals or by their alleged consequences. For example, it is sometimes said that the central function of the state is to preserve order which can have the odd implication that all institutions which preserve order (for instance, the family) become part of the state.

Finally, states are sometimes defined *normatively*, that is, they are discussed as models of how political systems should behave. In these discussions states are usually characterized as operating according to the **rule of law** (as opposed to lawless régimes), or more broadly according to rational principles. Thus Hegel's *Philosophy of Right* presents the modern state – as the objective realization of the subjective freedom latent in the human spirit.

Understood organizationally it is widely agreed that the modern state emerged in late medieval Europe, through the supersession of **feudalism**. It is, however, a moot point, whether any of the ancient empires of the Mediterranean, the Middle East, pre-Columbian America, India or China should be described as states. There has been an enduring temptation on the part of all historians and political scientists to read back into history the presence of many core features of the modern state – sovereignty, centralization, territoriality and bureaucratization. The alternative temptation has been to draw a sharp distinction between the 'city states', 'feudal polities' and 'empires' of **agrarian societies**, and the states of commercial and industrial societies.

The rise of the state in modern Europe was reflected in 16th-and 17th-century political theory, notably in Machiavelli's *The Prince*, Jean Bodin's *Six Books of the Republic* and Thomas Hobbes' *Leviathan*. Bodin and Hobbes, theorists of sovereignty, shared a common hostility to feudalism, and the belief that states were essential for the preservation of order. In their writings the idea of the state emerges for the first time as an abstract and impersonal set of offices, in principle independent of the particular officials who occupy positions within it. The absolutist implications of Bodin's and Hobbes's defences of states were not universally accepted, and in response liberal political thought, notably in the work of John Locke, sought to ensure that the modern state would be governed with the consent of the governed, through principles of **representative government**. Liberals, and subsequently democrats, have sought to limit the autonomy of state power through ensuring citizens have

rights against the state, and in limiting the scope of the doctrine of *raison d'état* ('reason of state'), which permitted public dishonesty, the violation of treaties and the illegal use of violence.

Although states vary considerably in their forms and official doctrines and ideologies almost all of them, leaving aside some residual traditional monarchies, seek to legitimate themselves in two reinforcing or contradictory ways. Modern states invariably claim to be legitimate emanations of their peoples. They claim on the one hand to be expressions of popular or democratic sovereignty (even dictators go through the motions of legitimating their rule through plebiscites). On the other hand they usually claim to be nation-states, embodiments of the rule of the nation, emanations of the **self-determination** of the people of X. These two claims explain two of the fundamental political dynamics of modern states. On the one hand competition for control and use of the state centres on claims to represent the popular will. On the other hand competition for definition and control over the territorial boundaries of the state centres on claims to represent the national will. The sometimes reinforcing and sometimes conflicting projects of 'state-building' and 'nation-building' stem from these dynamics.

Much recent **political science** has focused on interpreting the organizational nature of the state in liberal democracies. In part these interpretations are responses to the growth of state activities in the capitalist democracies of the West, which in the 20th century have seen the liberal state's functions expand beyond those of the defining features of government (defence, civic order and law-making), to include extensive involvement in economic management and regulation and the organization of social and individual welfare.

Five distinct schools of thought on the workings of the democratic state are evident in political science: **pluralism**, **Marxism**, **rational choice**, **élite theory** (now sometimes called 'new institutionalism' or 'statism') and neo-pluralism. Some claim to be able to detect novel feminist and green theories of the state, although these claims are disputed. Each of these bodies of thought is internally divided over the extent to which they believe that states are controlled by their citizens or societal collectivities or vice versa. Simplifying matters drastically three different interpretations of the way in which the state operates can be discerned in the political science literature: (1) in *cipher* models states (or their officials) are understood to be controlled by their societies (or the most powerful agents in their societies); (2) in *guardian* models states (or their officials) are considered sufficiently autonomous to be able to redirect and reshape the pressures placed upon them by their societies (or the most powerful agents in their societies); and (3) in *partisan* models states (or their officials) are considered sufficiently autonomous to act directly against the pressures emanating from their societies. Thus a Marxist who believes that the democratic state is in fact controlled by the capitalist class illustrates the employment of a cipher model; a pluralist who believes that the democratic state acts to look after the unorganized as well as the organized illuminates the guardian model; while a rational choice theorist who argues that public bureaucracies oversupply public services uses a partisan model.

Most political thinkers regard the state as an ineluctable feature of modernity, a necessary part of the landscape of industrial societies, an indispensable source of public cohesion and power. Only a minority of anarchists, libertarians, and Marxists wish to smash the state, or promise to make it wither away into historical memory (so far only Marxist revolutionaries have had the chance to break this promise). However, among those persuaded that a state is an indispensable feature of modern life there is passionate disagreement about the appropriate scope and limits on state power.

One crude distinction differentiates friends and enemies of state intervention on three dimensions. One dimension, the preservation of defence, law, order and property rights, is warmly extolled by conservatives, but disliked by anarchists, pacifists and libertarian socialists. Another dimension, the redistribution of wealth and income, is endorsed by social democrats, socialists and social liberals, but opposed by conservatives and economic liberals. A third dimension, the maintenance of traditional moral values, finds liberals and libertarians opposed to state regulation of private morality, with moral conservatives taking the converse position. **BO'L**

See also absolutism; anarchism; conservatism; democracy; liberalism; nationalism, socialism and social democracy.

Further reading P. Dunleavy and B. O'Leary, *Theories of the State: the Politics of Liberal Democracy*; C. Tilly, *The Formation of National States in Western Europe*.

STATISTICS

Statistics (Greek, 'reckoning'), in **mathematics** and elsewhere, is the study of the application of **probability** to real world situations. The difference between pure and applied mathematics is easily seen in the difference between probability and statistics. In probability, one of the most important results is the 'law of large numbers', which states that in a large number of experiments, the proportion of successes approaches the probability of success. In the theoretical study of probability, that result is satisfactory, since all the experiments carried out are purely theoretical, so that as many as needed can be carried out. However, statisticians are interested in knowing such information as how many experiments would be needed before the probability can be established with a certain accuracy, because their work is aimed at practicable studies of real world phenomena. (This particular interest has led to the development of statistical confidence.)

Statistics influences most, if not all, of modern society. No new products are put on the market today without a great amount of research into the market and the statistical question of whether people would buy at particular prices; no politician stands for election without statistical analysis of the trends in voting intention and the perceived importance of various issues; no insurance premium is set without statistical analysis of the risks involved; no roads are built without statistical analysis of the probable flow of traffic.

As well as its effects on society, statistics is also used to probe the most fundamental structure of the universe. **Quantum** mechanics uses statistical determinations of the positions of particles (that is, the ability to say that a particle is in a particular area with a certain probability) rather than the exactly defined analytical positions of earlier mechanics. The universe does not seem to be exactly determinable; and the death of **determinism** at the hands of modern **physics** is dependent on the use of statistics by its theoreticians. **SMcL**

Further reading D. Huff, *How To Lie With Statistics*.

STATUS

Status (Latin, 'standing' or 'condition'), from one sociological perspective, has a specific legal sense in that it defines the rights and duties of a particular person, for instance in the term marital status. This is the sense that the lawyer and social theorist Henry Maine made of the word in his noted work of 1861, *From Status to Contract*. In this, he argued that in 'primitive' societies relations and statuses based on kin formed the fabric of social and legal life. This was seen to evolve into modern industrial societies where relationships were formed by individuals in a more flexible way through voluntary contracts.

The more general sense of status referring to social rank was proposed by Max Weber in the late 19th century. Weber was critical of Karl Marx's notion of **class** as being too restrictive. In his view, status described a position occupied in society based on a variable **hierarchy** which was nonetheless definite for any particular instance. It also implied the ideas of respect and self-respect, and various symbols may be displayed or acquired to demonstrate this. Associated with the sense of status is the more recent idea of status denoting a kind of lifestyle which may be acquired in a consumer society.

In 1945, K. Linton (see below) proposed a much-used distinction between that of ascribed and achieved status. Ascribed status designated a position that a person assumed through no effort of his or her own, such as that based on gender, age and kinship relationship. This was believed to be predominant in preindustrial societies. Achieved status was based on an individual's efforts or ability to attain a position such as that based on occupation and economic means. This was considered predominant in modern industrial societies. However, even here factors such as age, gender or ethnic group may have a considerable bearing on what kind of status a person can actually achieve in this apparently egalitarian society.

Status may also attach to social groupings rather than to individuals. This is illustrated in societies that hold the honour/shame complex, in which the status of the family depends to a large extent on what the female members do – if she is not chaste, it is the family's status that goes down in the eyes of society.

Status considerations may reveal a host of complexities and sometimes contradictions. Among the Muslim *pirzade* community of New Delhi, for example, women have a low status in the patriarchal (male-dominated) society. But if a woman is married, and in relation to her sons, she may be held to have a high status. Within the course of marriage arrangements she has a very important role to play. In this case, the status of a woman through the developmental cycle of girl, wife and mother counteracts to varying degrees the ascribed status of women in the larger society. **DA RK**

See also caste; developmental cycle; kinship; marriage; Marxist anthropology; power; social stratification.

Further reading Patricia Jeffrey, *Frogs in a Well*; K. Linton, *The Cultural Background of a Personality*.

STEAM ENGINE

A steam engine converts the heat energy of pressurized steam into mechanical energy. This usually consists of steam driving a piston inside a closed cylinder. Its development was to spark one of the greatest changes that have occurred in human history.

A major fallacy that has arisen with the steam engine is that James Watt (1736–1819) invented it totally on his own, and that his idea stemmed from watching a kettle boil. His steam engine was, in fact, an adaptation of earlier inventions. In 1698, Thomas Savery devised a steam pump that was used to lift water from mines. His pump was very inefficient and because it never had a safety valve, it tended to blow up. His invention was improved by Thomas Newcomen in 1712, whose ideas were reliable and safe. Newcomen allowed the steam from the boiler to enter the lower part of the cylinder, so driving the piston upwards. At the top of the stroke, the cylinder was then cooled and the steam was condensed back into water. This created a partial vacuum which forced the piston down to its original position. The piston was attached to a beam which was connected to a pumping rod at the other end. Although his engine worked well, it was highly inefficient, and it was not until Watt saw a model of Newcomen's engine that vast improvements were made.

Watt's first major concept was to design a separate condenser. This meant that the cylinder did not need to be heated and cooled during every cycle so reducing dramatically the fuel consumed. He also invented the so-called 'sun and planet' gearing system that allowed the crossbeam to drive a large flywheel instead of a pumping rod. His discoveries led to the double-acting steam engine which used both the upstroke and downstroke, which again was more efficient that Newcomen's engine which only acted as a pump during the downstroke.

Steam engines, as well as being used in the mining industry, were also used in other industries, such as the iron manufacturing and textile industries. One large engine was used to drive a shaft running through a factory and belt drives delivered power to individual machines. Its implications were vast, as the heavy toil of working using manpower alone was superseded.

Steam power meant that factories could now be set up instead of manufacturing items on a cottage industry scale, as vast amounts of power were available to drive machinery. This revolutionized the way people lived, as more and more were forced to live in cities near their places of work. This led to a rapid expansion in population growth within these industrial zones, as villages became towns and towns became cities.

Steam power also revolutionized **transport**, as shipping and then railways adapted the steam engine. As well as the transportation of goods becoming cheaper and more reliable, the new transport opened up one of the biggest industries in today's modern society, that of tourism.

Although reciprocating steam engines are no longer a major power source, their development and use was one of the pioneering factors in the Industrial Revolution, that changed the world forever.

The thermodynamic properties of steam are, however, vital in the operation of most electrical power generating stations, coal-fired boilers and nuclear reactor heated boilers produce superheated steam to drive the turbines which deliver power to the electric generators. A typical power station turbine will have a large diameter shaft passing through the turbine carrying multiple rows of discs on which blades of complex form are mounted. Steam is introduced at one end of the turbine through a ring of nozzles and it impinges on the blades on the first disc developing force on each blade to make the disc rotate and thus the shaft. The steam coming from the first row of blades is deflected by fixed blades secured to the casing of the turbine so that it impinges on the blades on the next disc at the correct angle, and this process is repeated at each disc. A large turbine may have as many as 20 discs, each one being of larger diameter than its predecessor as the steam travelling through the turbine expands in volume. After the last set of blades the steam is directed downwards onto the set of pipes which comprises the condenser. The steam passes over the outside of the pipes and cooling water is pumped through them. **AA**

Further reading J.D. Storer, *The History of the Steam Engine*.

STEP-TIME COMPOSITION see **Electronic Music**

STIJL, DE see Neoplasticism

STOCHASTIC MUSIC see **Electronic Music**

STOICISM

Stoicism was a philosophical system named after a building, the Painted Stoa in ancient Athens, where its founder Zeno taught in the late 4th century BCE: originally Zeno simply called his school 'Stoa'. As a philosophical and educational system, Stoicism had enormous influence on the aristocratic thinking of Hellenistic Greece and early Imperial Rome (Brutus, the friend and assassin of Julius Caesar, and Seneca, the tutor of Nero, were prominent adherents); St Paul was trained in it, and its ideas influenced his own teaching, and from there the moral and ethical thought of the early **Christian** Church and the whole of Western Christendom.

The Stoics divided their teaching into three disciplines: Logic (theory of knowledge, logic and rhetoric), Physics (ontology, physics and theology) and Ethics. They held that all virtue is based on knowledge, and that knowledge is the harmony of one's intellectual ideas with reality. The virtuous person is therefore one who lives in harmony with Nature, in awareness of its guiding principle *logos* (reason), which is one of the attributes of God. Nothing else matters but virtue (as defined): death, love, pain, power, wealth are all illusion or distraction from the true path of virtue, and the true philosopher will be indifferent to them. Later Stoics modified this last belief, saying that although the true philosopher may be independent of worldly concerns, he or she has a duty to become involved in the world, in order to help those who are aspiring to virtue but have not yet reached it. **KMcL**

STREAM OF CONSCIOUSNESS

As part of his therapy, Freud encouraged his patients to speak freely and (so far as possible) without conscious control: to verbalize their unconscious thoughts. He published transcriptions of several of their monologues, in whole or in part, with his commentaries on what they revealed of the subjects' psychological state. These monologues, and the idea of the 'stream of consciousness', the extra revelation of personality and behavioural motivation granted by unguarded utterance, had a profound effect on 20th-century **drama** and **literature**.

In drama, asides and monologues had always existed, but they usually included a component of collusion between speaker and audience: Shakespeare's Edmund (in *King Lear*) or Richard III, for example, speaking soliloquies directly to the audience, or the comedians making asides in 19th-century French **farce**, are giving us information and are conscious of themselves doing so. Stream-of-consciousness monologues, by contrast, give us the feeling that we are eavesdropping on a character's inner self, hearing things of which the character may well not be aware or may prefer concealed. In 20th-century drama, therefore (for example the plays of Tennessee Williams or Harold Pinter), the technique is an important part of **irony**.

In literature, passages of overt stream-of-consciousness range from Molly Bloom's soliloquy at the end of Joyce's *Ulysses* to the overlapping monologues of Faulkner's *The Sound and the Fury* (one of the most outstanding books to use the technique) and Woolf's *Mrs Dalloway*. The technique, and the ironical detachment it appears to give, are vital to many first-person novels of this century, from Svevo's *Confessions of Zeno* to Heller's *Something Happened*, and underlie writings as varied as Beckett's novels, the books of Kerouac and Burroughs, and such works of **magic realism** as Roa Bastos' *I, the Supreme*, Vargas Llosa's *The Perpetual Orgy* (a highly self-conscious pastiche of stream-of-consciousness) and Marquez's *No One Writes to the Colonel* and *The General in his Labyrinth*. **KMcL**

See also consciousness; novel.

STRUCTURALISM

The system of ideas now referred to as structuralism (from Latin *struere*, 'to build') was first advanced by the Swiss linguist Ferdinand de Saussure (1857–1913).

The first application of structuralist ideas was aimed at completely redefining the object of enquiry in **linguistic** science. In the 20th century, however, Saussure's theories have been applied not only in **language** studies, but in **anthropology, sociology** and throughout the **arts**.

Linguistics in the 19th century was essentially historical, or diachronic, in orientation, with demonstrations of how certain aspects of language changed over time (see **comparative-historical linguistics**). However, Saussure suggested that the history of a language is entirely irrelevant to the speakers of that language. The linguist, too, has the option to ignore what has gone before and adopt a synchronic approach, which concentrates on the language system as it exists at a particular point in time.

In a synchronic approach, individual linguistic elements cannot be defined in isolation, but can only find their meaning in relation to other elements within the system (or structure). For example, the meaning of 'blue' can only be derived by contrasting it with other members of the system. Thus a blue object can be defined as one which is not red, not brown, not purple and so on. In Japanese, the term blue is conventionally translated as *aoi*, but we cannot assume equivalence of meaning. In fact, Japanese speakers also use *aoi* to refer to objects which would be described as green in English. So clearly, the term *aoi* occupies a different range of meaning in the colour system to that occupied by blue, and the meaning of each term derives from the contrasts with other members in their respective systems.

Saussure described the linguistic sign as the fusion of a 'signified', or concept, together with a 'signifier', or word, which is the physical manifestation of a sign. Saussure argued that there is no compelling reason why the sequence of sounds in the word blue should necessarily stand for the concept which it represents. This lack of any inherent relationship between 'signified' and 'signifier' reveals the fundamentally arbitrary nature of the linguistic sign. The language system as a whole is considered to be an abstract phenomenon: one cannot, after all, touch or see a language. The words we hear or read on the page are examples of what Saussure called *parole*, that is, the concrete deployment of the system on a particular occasion of use.

The brand of European structuralism advocated by Saussure emphasizes paradigmatic relations, in particular. That is, the focus is on elements which can substitute for one another in the same slot, or linguistic paradigm. In linguistic studies in the US, however, the 20th century has witnessed a heavier emphasis on syntagmatic relations, that is, the way linguistic elements combine into longer constructions (sentences). The concern with syntactic structures, independent of the meanings they convey, was spearheaded by Leonard Bloomfield, and is also, on occasion, described as structuralism. In a superficial sense, almost all 20th-century linguistics has been structural in nature, but there is clearly a distinction to be made between European and American versions of structuralism. Saussure's ideas often seem perfectly obvious and straightforward to a latter-day audience, yet the revolutionary importance of turning the attention of linguists towards the systematic aspects of language should not be underestimated.

As a theory in anthropology, structuralism is primarily associated with the works of Claude Lévi-Strauss since the late 1950s. It describes theories attempting to explain what characterizes us all as human beings living in society. As language is one of the key elements separating us from animals, linguistic theories were adopted as tools to get to the bottom of cultural systems and the structures of the human mind.

Lévi-Strauss's view was that all humans had a tendency to order and classify, in the same fundamental manner, whatever phenomena they perceived. He relied upon computer logic and the linguistic model of 'binary oppositions' that operated by ordering two elements into a relationship of opposition or contrast like raw/cooked, male/female and **nature/culture**. From his earlier work on **kinship** and **marriage** systems, to his later work on **myth** and **symbolism**, he attempted to systematize cultural phenomena according to such 'binary oppositions'. Cultural elements such as myths were not considered on their own, but treated with others as part of a total system built up from these basic contrasts.

Lévi-Strauss had enormous influence on other anthropologists, each of whom interpreted and contributed to the body of structuralism in his or her own manner. Edmund Leach considered how language terms and social mores acted to construct conceptually distinct compartments in a field that is otherwise continuous. (For instance, the English language discriminates between seven colours in the light spectrum. These are not real as such but artefacts of human thought imposed on external reality.) Mary Douglas concentrated on Jewish rules of food prohibition as mentioned in the Old Testament for her work *Purity and Danger* (1966). She concluded that those animals not falling into the set classification system were considered polluting and not eaten. Lord Chesterfield's saying 'Dirt is matter out of place' was borrowed to illustrate how it is that something not fitting into category systems is considered polluting rather than it being dirty in itself. Using a familiar example, she remarked how shoes are not dirty in themselves but are considered so when placed on the dining table.

Criticisms of structuralism in anthropology centre on its essentially static nature, which make it inadequate in explaining historical changes and the disregard for the active role of the individual in creating cultural patterns. Others have challenged its ambitions to explain the universal operations of the human mind through the analysis of social and cultural phenomena. They question why structuralism has not been satisfactorily applied to the fields of politics and economics. Instead, later anthropologists have tended to critically adapt and incorporate elements of structuralism into their approaches without entirely subsuming their methodologies to it.

In sociology, scholars use the term 'structuralism' in two ways. At the general, it refers to a perspective based on the concept of social structure and the view that society exists prior to its individual members. In a more specific sense, it refers to a distinctive style within sociology concerned with the identification of underlying structures in social or cultural systems. Structuralism also refers to any assumption that

social analysis should be concerned with the exploration beneath surface appearances in order to discover the deeper structures which are believed to determine social relationships. Certain Marxist sociologists (such as Althusser) adopted a structuralist framework in seeking to explain social phenomena by reference to the underlying structures of the type of production in a given society. These contemporary structuralist positions in sociology have been criticized for being ahistorical, impossible to verify, and dismissive of human creative activity.

The importance of structuralism for the arts is that it cuts through much **Romantic** rambling on the ineffable qualities of genius, leaving the artist as the animator, not of new thoughts and images, but in the words of Roland Barthes of the 'already written'. But this is not to remove all volition. The study of **painting** and **sculpture** in particular is the study of a 'poetic' sign system which self-consciously separates itself from other outwardly similar sign systems, such as traffic signals or road maps. The study of structuralism has advanced art history towards the 'science' of signs, but has by no means ended the debate surrounding the origins and nature of art.

In **literature**, structuralists use techniques such as **deconstruction** to examine not the meaning of a piece of writing – anything from a bus ticket to a creation myth – but the structures which produce meaning. It is concerned above all with the mechanisms (often subconscious) by which meaning is put into a piece of writing meant as communication, and with the mechanisms (not necessarily the same ones) by which that meaning is actually communicated.

Post-structuralism takes the critical analysis back to each specific text, and examines the way the specificity of that text collaborates with or resists the structures which produce meaning, in order to achieve the specific communication it exists to make. **DA PD MG RK KMcL MS**

See also exchange; Marxism; Marxist anthropology; social realism; society; structure; structure-agency debate.

Further reading Ferdinand de Saussure,

Course in General Linguistics; E. Kurzweil, *The Age of Structuralism: Lévi-Strauss to Foucault;* Edmund Leach, *Culture and Communication; Lévi-Strauss;* D. Robey, *Structuralism, an Introduction.*

STRUCTURATION

Structuration is a concept introduced into **sociology** by Anthony Giddens in the 1980s. It expresses the mutual dependency, rather than the more commonly assumed opposition, of human agency (individual activity and action) and social **structure** (the more enduring and regular features of social life which provide the background against which all social activity is carried out).

Within sociology the debate is centred as to the relative importance of individual action and social structure in determining social phenomena. Some schools of thought emphasize the importance of social structure over individual actions, while others reverse this emphasis. Most tend to accept that structure and agency are complementary. Giddens attempts to articulate the nature of the relationship between social structure and human agency, and in so doing accords primacy to neither.

Within sociology social structure has been seen by some schools of thought as exerting a constraining influence on human behaviour. Giddens suggests that social structures should not be seen as barriers to individual activity, but as intimately involved in the production of human action. It is the structural properties of social systems, argues Giddens, that provide the means by which people act and which, at the same time, are the outcome of these actions. **DA**

See also action perspective; social order; structuralism; structure-agency debate.

Further reading A. Giddens, *The Constitution of Society: Outline of the Theory of Structuration.*

STRUCTURE

Social structure, in **anthropology** and **sociology**, refers to any arrangement of social phenomena into a definite pattern. To refer to the structure of a society is to refer to those enduring and patterned aspects which provide the context and background against which people live out their daily lives. Examples of social structure include: the class structure, economic structure, education and the occupational structure.

Social structure is a concept over which there is much debate in sociology. Some branches of the discipline (for example **functionalism**, **Marxism** and **structuralism**) assume that social structure pre-exists individuals and plays a leading role in shaping social reality and creating social order. Others (for example supporters of **ethnomethodology**, **phenomenological sociology** and **symbolic interactionism**) dispute this and accord a greater role to individual action in the creation and re-creation of social structure.

The term structure is used in a second sense in structuralism. This use of the term has its origins in **linguistics**, but has been developed in anthropology and sociology. Supporters of this perspective hold that there exists a set of social structures that are unobservable, but which generate observable social phenomena. A distinction is drawn between surface and deep structures. It is believed that analysis of social phenomena should involve getting beyond surface appearances and discover the deeper structures which are believed to govern social relationships. **DA**

See also action perspective; class; generalized other; holism; individualism; macrosociology; microsociology; norm; role; social construction of reality; socialization; social order; social realism; social stratification; society; structuration; structure-agency debate; values.

Further reading T.B. Bottomore and R. Nisbet (eds.), *A History of Sociological Analysis;* R. Keat and J. Urry, *Social Theory as Science;* C. Lévi-Strauss, *Structural Anthropology* vols. 1 & 2.

STRUCTURE-AGENCY DEBATE

The issue of **structure** and agency is central for **sociology**. Sociologists recognize two main determinants of social phenomena, social structure and individual actions (human agency); what is contested is their relative importance. Social structure refers to those larger and relatively enduring features of **society** which provide the background against which social life is carried out: for example, the **class** structure. It highlights the fact that human societies have certain regularities in the social relationships which people engage in. Agency, on the other hand, refers to the volitional and purposeful nature of human activity. Social structure is believed to exert a constraining effect on human activity; agency refers to the ability of individuals to act independently of this.

It is possible to identify three main standpoints in the debate. (1) Some branches of sociology (such as **structuralism**, **functionalism** and **Marxism**) assert that social life is largely determined by social structure, and that individual activities can be explained mostly as an outcome of structure. (2) Other branches (for instance, **phenomenological sociology**, **ethnomethodology** and **symbolic interactionism**) reverse this emphasis, stressing the ability of individuals to construct and reconstruct and give meaning to their world. Proponents of this view emphasize the need to provide explanations for social phenomena which reflect the views of the individuals they study. (3) Other approaches stress the complementarity of structure and agency. Social structure influences human actions, but individual activities can similarly influence social structure.

Most forms of sociological theory highlight the complementarity of structure and agency, though different theories exist about the nature of the relationship between the two. Berger and Luckmann suggest that the relationship between structure and agency is one in which society forms the individuals who create society in a continuous dialectic. Giddens has offered a formulation of structure which is both constraining and enabling. The debate is likely to be an on-going one. Whatever the sophistication of general theories of the structure-agency relationship, disputes are nonetheless likely to persist in their application to particular cases.

See also action perspective; exchange; gen-

eralized other; holism; idiographic; individualism; internalization; macrosociology; microsociology; norms; rational choice; social integration; socialization; social order; social self; structuration; values.

Further reading T. Bottomore, R. Nisbet (eds.), *A History of Sociological Analysis*. **DA**

STÜRM UND DRANG

Stürm und Drang (German, 'storm and stress') was the name given to some works of art made in Germany in the mid-18th century. The style was a kind of prototype **Romanticism**, inserting into works of otherwise limpid 18th-century decorum an element of violent contrast and passionate utterance. The chief difference between the two styles was that in Romantic works passion and violence were concerned with emotion, and were at the root of the work's meaning, whereas in *Stürm and Drang* works the tension often seems perhaps by hindsight external and contained, a colouristic effect rather than a depiction of truth.

In **fine art**, *Stürm und Drang* was chiefly concerned with the depiction of stormy seas and skies, rugged Nature (especially mountain scenery) and battle-scenes Goya's paintings are a late, non-German flowering of the style. In **literature**, it was chiefly shown in **drama**, in a breakaway from Greek-inspired orderliness to unruly plays based on real people and real historical incidents or dilemmas, and inspired by Shakespeare: for example the work of Schiller and the young Goethe. In **music**, its main manifestations are works (by such composers as C.P.E. Bach) depicting battles, domestic quarrels or storms at sea, and a series of passionate minor-key **symphonies** and string quartets by Haydn (those numbered 40–60, including such evocatively-nicknamed works as the 'Mourning', the 'Passion', the 'Fire' and the 'Distracted'). **KMcL**

STYLE

Style (from Latin *stilus*, 'pointed stick') is a specific way of behaving, and of creating or presenting material. Specificity can be either to oneself or to a group. Like all forms of identification, as opposed to identity, style is a subjective phenomenon and is both superficial and ephemeral; like all matters of choice or **taste**, it tends however to be discussed as if it were fundamental and had objective rules. Fussing about style, whether one's own or other people's, has primarily been an activity of the pedant or the insecure; it defines not the essence of things, but our attitude to things – and in that sense, to some extent, ourselves. **KMcL**

STYLISTICS

In common with **discourse** analysis, stylistics is an area of language study which goes beyond the study of sentences to consider more global, textual phenomena. The fundamental concern in stylistics is with the aesthetic uses of language. By analysing the language forms employed by an author, the stylistician tries to explain the aesthetic responses of the reader to certain texts. Stylistic analysis is not restricted only to those texts which have been designed to exploit the aesthetic potential of language. In addition to novels, poems, letters and the like, one could also conduct a stylistic analysis of more routine texts such as instruction manuals or business letters. Furthermore, stylistics is not restricted to written texts; spoken texts, such as radio announcements, speeches and even ordinary conversations can be subjected to stylistic examination.

It is commonplace for certain stylistic effects to be associated with a particular author. In this way, the Dickensian style of writing contrasts with the Joycean style. It is the task of the stylistician to propose a framework of analysis which will allow these kinds of intuitions to be confirmed on the basis of a careful study of the way linguistic forms are manipulated, organized and exploited by the author. A tightly constrained framework for analysis will also allow hypotheses about certain stylistic effects to be properly formulated and tested. In general, it has been argued that an aesthetic response is evoked when linguistic forms are used in a novel way. Our surprise at the unique and unexpected patterning of language forms leads us to focus on some aspect of the language per se rather than on simply the message being conveyed.

Several aspects of linguistic form can contribute to the stylistic effects in a text, from the physical qualities of the speech sounds to the configuration of the syntactic forms deployed. For example, the phonetic qualities of the words chosen, and the patterns created thereby, can be important in conveying a particular aesthetic effect. It has even been suggested that the physical aspects of speech sounds possess intrinsic symbolic qualities quite separate from their arbitrary occurrence in words. Thus, Otto Jespersen, a pre-eminent linguist of his day, argued in 1922 that so-called back vowels symbolize dislike, scorn or disgust in English. Hence the frequent occurrence of back vowels in words such as 'blunder', 'clumsy', 'dull' and 'slum'. Although it is not difficult to find counter-examples (for example, 'snug', 'cuddle' and 'hug'), the belief in sound symbolism has persisted in various forms and is not as easy to dismiss as might first appear. In some cases acoustic properties can be cited which correlate with the symbolic qualities commonly ascribed to them. For example, the common description of sounds like t, k, p as hard or sharp can be traced, at least in part, to the timing of vocal cord vibrations and the particular configuration of muscular tension in the vocal apparatus which feature in the production of these sounds. The study of sound symbolism is but one branch of stylistics, demonstrating the value of a methodical approach to the influence of language use on the aesthetic qualities of a text. **MS**

Further reading G. Turner, *Stylistics*.

SUBCULTURE

The term subculture signals a reaction against mainstream **culture**, a system of ideas, beliefs, attitudes, modes of behaviour and styles of life distinct from, but related to, those held by the majority of the population in a society. Small societies tend to be culturally uniform but modern societies incorporate a great diversity of subcultures. In modern cities, for example, there are a great many subcultures living side by side. Groups as diverse as Punks, Freemasons and Rastafarians could be classed as subcultures, and in this context they have been the subjects of much research by sociologists and cultural historians.

The relationship of the subculture to the dominant culture is generally identified as one of subordination and powerlessness. Power relations are thus an important aspect of the analysis of subcultures. What is interesting is the interaction of subculture groups within a larger established culture. For example the style, speech, dress codes and attitudes of gay subcultures have influenced high street fashion for 'straight' men. In the UK, for example, the word has come to have a particular meaning applied to Britain's postwar, white, working-class youth movements, including Teddy Boys, Skinheads and Punks. Their energy and style impacted on the world of mainstream culture influencing **music**, **advertising**, fashion, film and television.

Critics have pointed out two main problems with the concept of subcultures. First, it is unclear what the main determinants are, and second, the concept assumes the existence of an identifiable dominant culture, but the cultural diversity of modern societies makes the identification of a dominant culture difficult. **DA CMcD**

See also assimilation; dominant ideology; ethnicity; hegemony; ideology; internalization; norms; power; social control; social integration; socialization; society; values.

Further reading M. Brake, *The Sociology of Youth Culture and Youth Subcultures*; S. Cohen, *Folk Devils and Moral Panics*; G. Suttles, *The Social Order of the Slum*.

SUBJECTIVISM See Objectivism and Subjectivism

SUBLIMATION

Sublimation (from Latin *sub*, 'under' and *limen*, 'threshold') was a theory in 19th-century aesthetic criticism, taken up and developed by Freud. Writers such as Nietzsche, Novalis and Schopenhauer had suggested that sublimation of sexual instinct might go some of the way to explaining the creation of work of genius; Freud's systematization of their ideas echoed his theories on human mental and sexual development. In the growing adult, he said, the sublimation of **sexuality** happens in the following way: infant sexuality is suppressed by the **Oedipal complex**; there follows a period of latency, after which the sexual instinct is revived in puberty, in a reorganized form. So, too, in the case of genius, the sexual instinct is sublimated, repressed and redirected into creative work.

Nietzsche applied the idea of sublimation to aggressive instincts as well as sexual ones, saying that 'Good actions are evil actions sublimated'. Sublimation of instincts is the result of inhibition or rationalization by intellect; sexuality, however, is always still connected to the sublimated forms of behaviour. In 1903 the psychologist C.S. Myers published his notion of the 'superior function' of the sublimated **self**, and said that works of genius come from a storehouse of reflected knowledge and understanding that lies behind consciousness. This 'superior function', he claimed, also connects us to the spirits of the dead and has the unconscious task of weaving fantasies. **MJ**

See also creativity; defence mechanism; taste.

Further reading F.W. Nietzsche, *The Birth of Tragedy*; Sigmund Freud, *Three Essays on the Theory of Sexuality*.

SUBLIME, THE

The term the Sublime (Latin, 'what is under the threshold [of experience]') was first named by the literary critic Longinus (?2nd century CE), and received much currency in Europe when his treatise *On the Sublime* was translated by Boileau in 1674. The Sublime is a conglomerate name for anything for which human beings feel wonder: the divine, natural phenomena, outstanding or inspirational human qualities. Implicit in its recognition is a somewhat self-congratulatory feeling that humankind, alone of creation, is able to experience it, and to articulate that experience in words, writing or images.

The idea had enormous currency among 18th-century European thinkers, and influenced the **arts**, **philosophy** and **politics**. Edmund Burke, in his *Philosophical Enquiry into the Origin of Our Ideas of the Sublime and the Beautiful* (1757), said that the Sublime, in contrast to the ordered universe of the **Enlightenment**, contains the potential to fire the imagination. Immanuel Kant, in *The Critique of Judgement* (1790) described the feeling of humanity confronted with something of limitless power, and defined 'sublime' qualities as those which transcend understanding. Characteristic of such thinking is the way, in fine art, the painters of the time, and for generations later, showed the immensity of Nature: for example in Turner's *Snow Storm: Steamboat off a Harbour's Mouth* (1842), humanity is not at one with Nature, as in a **pastoral**, but in danger of being overwhelmed by its limitless power. The impulse of such thinking was always towards a broad-brush emotional assertion, sometimes inarticulate but always grandiose.

The idea of the Sublime had a crucial effect on the rise of **Romanticism** in the arts and the notion of the 'superman' in 19th-century philosophy. Because such ideas were the antithesis of scientific **rationalism**, they helped to create the standoff between science and the arts which did not exist until the 18th century, but which has, some say, been prevalent ever since. **MG KMcL**

See also scientific method; two cultures.

Further reading P. Crowther, *The Kantian Sublime: from Morality to Art*; M.D. Paley, *The Apocalyptic Sumblime*.

SUBSTANCE

The word 'substance' (from Latin *substantia*, 'essence', derived from *substare*, 'to stand underneath') has been used in various different ways by different philosophers. In one sense, a substance is a thing which has properties and qualities, but is not itself a property or quality of some-

thing else. In another, a substance is something which is capable of existing independently of anything else.

We can distinguish between (1) properties or qualities and (2) the things or substances which have properties or qualities. The issue is not so simple, however, since properties and qualities can themselves have properties and qualities. So, for example, the quality redness can have the further property of being bright. So if we are to distinguish between (1) properties or qualities and (2) the things or substances which have them, we will have to say that there are (1) properties or qualities and (2) the things or substances which have properties and qualities, but are not themselves properties and qualities of something else.

In another sense, substances are that which can exist apart from anything else (except perhaps God). So, for example, Descartes held that mind and matter are distinct substances. For minds can exist without bodies – minds can exist disembodied. And matter can exist without minds. Neither depends upon the other for its existence, each depending only upon God for its existence. **AJ**

Further reading D. Wiggins, *Sameness and Substance*.

SUCCESSION

Succession, in **ecology**, is the process by which biological communities respond to environmental disturbance. A common pattern of succession is a progression from simple, transient beginnings towards a more complex, stable **climax** community. Thus a newly exposed bare rock provides a **niche** for simple plants such as lichens and mosses; as these plants contribute to the effects of weathering and the rock begins to break down to form a thin, patchy soil, other plants such as grasses can begin to grow. The weathering process is accelerated and still larger plants such as shrubs and trees colonize the habitat. Thus the community evolves through a succession of phases, each characterized by certain species types. Ultimately, a dynamic equilibrium is attained where the community is stable until an environmental shift or disturbance occurs. The process of succession may be seen in a situation where the human activity has caused environmental disturbance – thus if a building plot is left derelict, the first plants to colonize will be weeds, appearing within days. Provided the land remains undisturbed, shrubs and then trees begin to grow. **RB**

See also competition.

SUFISM

The name 'Sufi' comes from the Arabic word *suf* ('wool'). In the 8th century, the century following the death of Muhammad, an Islamic empire was established under a ruling dynasty, the Umayyads, which became associated with moral laxity and corruption. Some believers reacted against this decline in standards by practising a more austere lifestyle, including the wearing of garments made of rough wool (hence the name), partly in imitation of Christian monks and **ascetics** in Egypt and Palestine at that time.

Sufis are generally known as Muslim mystics, but Sufism is much more varied than that, even if **mysticism** has been a central strand. Its influence, especially in the spread of **Islam**, has been enormous, though the forms in which Sufism is found have not always been acceptable to either the *ulama* or modern reformers. The deep personal piety of these first Sufis caused them to concentrate on the inner life. At one level this led them to meet in groups for prayer, and in contrast to the routines of mosque worship they developed their own routines of rhythmic chanting, singing and dancing. This is still a feature of Sufi gatherings today. In particular, they chant repeatedly the 99 'names of God' contained in the Qur'an.

At another level, complex theories were developed about different states of the soul and how to attain them. The highest state was union of the soul with God. This is the basis of the claim that Sufis are mystics. The goal of union with God was controversial and to those outside the Sufi movement it was regarded as blasphemous. In one notorious case, in 922, a Sufi, al-Hallaj, was crucified for blasphemy. (As a result of his mystical experiences he had allegedly claimed, 'I am the Truth'.) Eventually, partly under the influence of the great Muslim thinker, al-Ghazali (d. 1111), Sufism became tolerated at least as long as the Sufis moderated their more extravagant claims and remained within the framework of the *shari'a*. At the same time Sufism took on the institutional form, which it retains today, of the Sufi orders or brotherhoods.

Certain individuals gained great prestige as spiritual teachers or guides. They are referred to as *shaikhs*. Their followers passed on their particular teachings and techniques, which then continued to be handed down to succeeding generations in a particular line of spiritual heritage called a *silsila*. Adherents of a particular *silsila* had their own meeting places, and gradually these came to form networks which could be purely local, regional or even international in scope. These are the Sufi orders, of which there are more than a hundred. On occasion an English nickname encapsulates a distinctive feature of a particular order, and this is certainly so with the 'Whirling Dervishes', the Mawlawiyya in Turkey.

Sufi centres often provided education, health care and accommodation for travellers. These could become large and socially powerful complexes, especially if built around the tomb of the order's founder, as in Konya. Others might be small, but associated with the tomb of a local spiritual leader, a person referred to in English as a 'Sufi saint'. Some of these centres have become pilgrim shrines (see **cult**) with great annual festivals being held to commemorate the saint. **JS**

SUICIDE

The sociologist Émile Durkheim believed that suicide rates and different types of social context are related. Durkheim attributed the rate of suicide to the level of **social integration** (the extent to which individuals have adopted the dominant social values and ideas) in a given society. Using official statistics he first eliminated various environmental and psychological factors previously proposed as explaining suicide.

He then proposed four distinctive types of suicide: egoistic, altruistic, anomic and fatalistic, each corresponding to a particular condition of society.

A major criticism of Durkheim's theory, and the use of official statistics in particular, has been made by J.B. Douglas. Douglas demonstrates that official statistics are inaccurate and biased in ways which support Durkheim's case. For example, highly integrated groups may be more likely than loosely integrated groups to conceal suicides by ensuring that other causes of death are recorded. Suicide statistics are socially constructed and a whole range of factors can influence whether a death is interpreted and labelled as a suicide.

More recently, however, it has been demonstrated that regularities in the incidence of suicide recur across cultures, for example, among the widowed and divorced, among the unmarried and childless; official statistics then may not be quite as unreliable as Douglas has suggested. **DA**

See also anomie; culture; internalization; positivism; social construction of reality; social fact; social/sociological problem; socialization; society; structuralism; structure; structure-agency debate; symbolic interactionism; understanding.

Further reading J.M. Atkinson, *Discovering Suicide*; J.B. Douglas, *The Social Meanings of Suicide*; Émile Durkheim, *Suicide: a Study in Sociology* (1897).

SUPEREGO see **Id, Ego and Superego**

SUPERVENIENCE

The aesthetic properties of objects, in **philosophy** *supervene* upon their physical properties. That is, if two objects have the same physical properties then they must have the same aesthetic properties. If two objects have exactly the same physical properties and one is beautiful, then the other object must also be beautiful.

Similarly, the ethical properties of actions supervene upon their non-ethical properties. That is, if two acts have exactly the same non-ethical properties, then they must have exactly the same moral properties. If two actions are exactly alike in all non-moral respects and one is wicked, then the other action must also be wicked.

Materialists often claim that mental properties supervene upon physical properties. They claim that if two creatures have exactly the same physical properties, then they must have exactly the same mental properties. If two creatures are exactly alike in all physical respects and one is in pain, then the other must also be in pain. In contrast, dualists hold that mental phenomena are non-physical, and therefore allow that there could be two creatures exactly alike physically, one of whom has a non-physical mind and is in pain, the other of which does not have a mind and so is not in pain. **AJ**

See also dualism; materialism.

Further reading S. Blackburn, *Spreading The Word*; C. McGinn, *The Character of Mind*.

SUPPLY-SIDE ECONOMICS

Supply-side **economics** is a focus on variables that affect the supply of goods and services rather than on demand, in a search for policies to stabilize the economy. Supply-siders are particularly concerned with tax reforms, regulatory reforms, and other policies to stimulate supply by promoting such activities as savings, work effort, education and training, investment in plant and equipment.

Economists have long recognized the importance of the productive capacity of an economy, its stock of capital and labour, and the incentive needed to get the best out of them. However, these elementary points may have been obscured by the Keynesian emphasis on managing demand (see **Keynesian theory**). Attention to the supply side is a reaction to what many consider to be an overemphasis on the demand side by Keynesians and neo-Keynesians. As part of this reaction, some politicians and economists began stressing the need to encourage supply instead. This became trivialized by the belief that cutting taxes would release new energy into the economy. The reduction *ad absurdum* of this view was the **Laffer curve** – cutting tax rates would raise tax revenues is a supply-side concept which some economists thought was relevant to the US economy of the 1970s, while others laughed. In the 1980s, supply-side became a politically-charged term, used by either left or right to abuse the other. In reality, it is politically neutral. For example, because of Marx's emphasis on the means of production and the relationship between capital and labour, he was in many respects a supply-side economist. **TF**

SUPREMATISM

Suprematism was an early 20th-century form of geometric **abstraction**. The aim was to avoid representing the visible world, in favour of non-objective abstraction in which the work of art would stand only for itself – in other words as 'pure art'. Malevich, the movement's founder, published a manifesto explaining his aims in 1915. Stylistically, Suprematism uses simple geometrical shapes, such as the circle, square or cross, disposed across the picture plane with little or no suggestion of recession into depth, as in Malevich's *Suprematist Composition: White on White* (1918). The movement, which reached its apogee in Revolutionary Russia, had a significant influence in the development of **constructivism**. **PD MG**

SURREALISM

A child of **Dada**, surrealism was christened by Guillaume Apollinaire in 1917, and defined by André Breton in 1924 as 'pure psychic automatism, by which it is intended to express...the real processes of thought'. Inspired by Freud's theories of the **unconscious** and especially his interest in **dreams**, the Surrealists tried to explore the irrationality of the subconscious, to smash the barriers imposed on the **arts** by the need to conform at least to some extent to the 'realism' of life. Their ambition was to break through into the 'superior realism' of the subconscious, unhindered by such **objective correlatives** as the trappings of everyday existence, and they hoped that this activity would liberate the subconscious not only of artists, but also of spectators. The various

subconsciouses would then unite in the face of everyday reality, and so purge it of show and sham.

For a time in the 1910s and 1920s, surrealism held sway in every art save **architecture** (which needs firmer ground to build on than the subconscious). But it soon proved a sterile form in **music** – even Cage, the greatest surrealist composer, wrote his best works when he disciplined his random plinks and plunks and became associated chiefly with fine art, **literature** and **theatre**. In literature, surrealism is a combination of cuteness and hallucination. Sentences, words, even single syllables and letters disengage themselves from syntax and float free, producing in readers either the feeling that they, too, have been liberated into new spheres of meaning, or bafflement. Surrealist **poetry** (whether by Hans/Jean Arp, Paul Éluard, David Gascoigne or the **imagists**, **objectivists** and **Beat** poets they influenced), and surrealist prose (where the range is from Gertrude Stein to William Burroughs, and those influenced include James Joyce, Virginia Woolf and the exponents of **magic realism**) is pretty more often than beautiful, entertaining more often than meaningful. Surface, in short, can sometimes be all, and style can gobble form. In fine art, a similar problem arose. The difficulty was finding a means to represent the subconscious in conscious terms, and the chosen solutions (for example juxtaposing unrelated objects) often meant that the images (whether de Chirico's piazzas and mannequins, Magritte's room-filling apples or Oldenburg's floppy toilets) tended to absorb the attention for a moment only, and to provide clues to the artists' sense of humour and (often dazzling) technique rather than to the 'superior reality' they were seeking to reveal. Surrealism in both literature and fine art was like talking with spirits in a seance: good fun while it lasted (if you believed in it), but no substitute for genuine person-to-person dialogue.

In the theatre, and particularly in film, where the element of performance essential to surrealism could be allowed full scope, the style had its greatest success and led to work of true substance. Antonin Artaud began as surrealism's 'Director of

Research', was 'expelled' from the movement by Breton and founded his own movement, **Theatre of Cruelty**. Early surrealist drama (its ancestor was Jarry's *Ubu roi*, and its chief 1920s creator was Jean Cocteau, who continued to use it for 40 years, notably in his films) was inconsequential, shocking and delightfully ridiculous. Apollinaire's play *The Breasts of Tiresias*, Dali's and Buñuel's short film *The Andalusian Dog* or Cocteau's and Satie's ballets *Parade* and *Relâche* ('Theatre Closed') are typical examples: soapbubbles which only the most earnest ever took for art. But the seeds were sown which 30 years later blossomed into the work of directors such as Fassbinder and Fellini, and their myriad admirers and acolytes, and into the **theatre of the absurd**, a genre which transformed the art – and incidentally transformed surrealism, by letting the spectators into the secret (philosophical, moral or otherwise) for which the work itself is just a metaphor. **PD MG KMcL**

Further reading D. Ades, *Dada and Surrealism Revisited*; André Breton, *Manifestoes of Surrealism*; M. Nadeau, *The History of Surrealism*.

SUSTAINABLE DEVELOPMENT

The concept of sustainable development was advocated by the Brundtland Report. This was the first report of the World Commission on Environment and Development, which was set up by the United Nations in 1983 to propose solutions to the world's problems of environment and development. Even the terms of reference of this report were an important advance: previously it had been usual to regard environment and economic development as inherently contradictory. The Commission's own analysis was equivocal, emphasizing that some environmental problems (notably deforestation and desertification) were in large part caused by poverty, and that economic development could produce the knowledge and wealth to overcome environmental problems, though it often tended to cause problems in the short term. So the Commission, led by Gro Brundtland, sought to define a form of

development which could solve the problems of poverty without increasing the problems caused by affluence.

Sustainable development is defined as 'development which meets the needs of the present without compromising the ability of future generations to meet their own needs'. In terms of environmental values this is an argument based on stewardship, but in effect the Commission put even more emphasis on meeting the needs of poor people, especially in the less-developed world, so equity was at least as important as environment. The Brundtland Report analysed current problems and proposed policy changes in six linked areas: population and human resources; food security; species and **ecosystem** conservation; energy; industry; urban settlements.

In each case they were able to show how the international economy created problems which national and international institutions were unable to overcome. The worst case was the debt crisis affecting much of Africa and parts of Latin America, and leaving the populations of these areas with diminishing income per capita and worsening environmental and economic problems. The idea of sustainable development involved new priorities as well as institutional and legal change.

The concept of sustainable development has been both widely welcomed and bitterly criticized. Environmentalists have complained that it does nothing to reduce human society's impacts on Nature, while more mainstream critics have denounced it as a conspiracy against growth and the free market. In principle, many governments have been willing to support the idea, and heads of state flocked to the 1992 Earth Summit in Rio de Janeiro which was the second major result of the 'Brundtland Process'. But in practice few developed countries have been willing to reduce their own environmental impacts and none have even contemplated doing so to a sufficient degree to allow the less-developed countries to increase their standards of living and calls on environmental resources. Unless problems like the **population explosion** and **global warming** make more developed countries realize that solving problems in the less-developed world is in everybody's interest, the problems diagnosed by the Brundtland report will continue to worsen. **PS**

Further reading P. Sarre and P. Smith, *One World for One Earth*; UNCED, *Our Common Future*.

SYMBIOSIS

The term symbiosis was coined (from Greek) by Heinrich de Bary in the 19th century, to mean 'living together of dissimilarly named organisms'. In the modern context, a symbiosis is a mutually beneficial association between different types of organism (where the organisms are not intimately associated in space, the term mutualism is sometimes used). A lichen, for example, is a symbiotic association of algae and fungus, allowing both organisms to colonize habitats in which they could not survive without their symbiotic partners. Symbiotic relationships pervade all levels of biological systems. Most animals, including humans, harbour symbiotic microorganisms which aid the digestion of food, while many plants provide shelter to symbiotic bacteria and fungi which enhance their ability to extract nutrients from the environment. It seems probable that symbiotic relationships played a key role in **biogenesis** (the development of life) and in **evolution** itself.

Multicellular organisms such as plants and animals, and many single-celled organisms, such as protozoa, have cells which are described as eukaryotic and are distinguishable from prokaryotic cells such as bacteria because they possess **organelles**. These are bodies, surrounded by membrane, which are found within the eukaryotic cell and which are generally specialized in function. The observation that these organelles can divide independently of the cell, and that they appear to possess their own nucleic acid, has led to the suggestion that eukaryotic cells may have originated in a symbiotic relationship of several prokaryotic cells. This idea remains an unproven hypothesis, but there exists substantial evidence that many living organisms are based upon a primeval symbiosis. **RB**

See also niche.

Further reading Lynn Margulis, *Symbiosis in Cell Evolution*.

SYMBOLIC INTERACTIONISM

Originally named in 1937 by Herbert Blumer, symbolic interactionism is a theoretical approach within **sociology** which seeks to explain human action and behaviour as the result of the meanings which human beings attach to action and things. In the 1970s, symbolic interactionism was seen as a major alternative to the then dominant ideas of **functionalism** and **systems theory**. For symbolic interactionists, the meaning of a situation or object is not fixed and unproblematic, rather it has to be constructed and arrived at by the participants in the scene. Meanings are the product of social processes. Emphasis is given to the active, interpretive and constructive capacities of individuals in the creation of social reality. This contrasts with those approaches in sociology which have given emphasis to the constraining effects of social **structure** in determining human behaviour and minimize the importance of individual activity.

Symbolic interactionism has its intellectual roots in the concept of 'self' developed by G.H. Mead. Mead argued that social life depends on the ability of individuals to observe themselves from the standpoint of others. The concept of self develops by placing oneself in the position of others and looking back at oneself with an objective stance. With an awareness of self individuals are able to see themselves as others see them. This provides the basis for co-operative action in society. The individual will become aware of what is expected of him or her and will modify his or her actions accordingly. This view of human action sees the individual actively creating the environment and also being shaped by it.

The aim of symbolic interactionism is to discover the meanings of the individuals involved in a given social situation. This leads to the adoption of methods of research which yield qualitative rather than quantitative information. Students in the field tend to focus on face-to-face interaction in the context of everyday life. A feature of this approach is that it has often adopted a more socially radical stance by exploring the position of the underdog. Studies employing this perspective have made major contributions to the study of socially deviant behaviour, **socialization**, criminal behaviour and communication.

Although symbolic interactionists reject those approaches to sociology and **psychology** which seek deterministic universal laws, they nonetheless see a place for generalizations within sociology. Symbolic interactionism maintains that generalizations should be appropriate to the subject matter of sociology.

Symbolic interactionism has been criticized for concentrating too much on small-scale situations, and because it has difficulty in dealing with larger social structures and processes. The approach is further criticized for ignoring historical factors. Those who favour an ethnomethodological approach to the study of social life, have voiced the criticism that symbolic interactionism does not examine social life in sufficient depth. **DA**

See also action perspective; dramaturgical model; ethnomethodology; generalized other; idiographic; individualism; macrosociology; microsociology; phenomenological sociology; social self; structure-agency debate; understanding.

Further reading H. Blumer, Symbolic Interactionism Perspective or Method; P. Rock, The Making of Symbolic Interaction.

SYMBOLIC LOGIC

Symbolic logic was principally the work of Gottlob Frege (1848–1925), building on the ideas of George Boole (1815–64) (see **Boolean logic**). Apart from the symbols used by Boole, a second type of symbol is now used, the quantifier. The commonly used quantifiers translate the phrases 'for every' and 'there is a', and are known as universal and existential quantifiers respectively. With these additions, symbolic logic becomes the language of mathematics. Indeed, those who held to the school of **logicism** dominated by the work of Ber-

trand Russell (1872–1970) believed that **mathematics** was in fact just the study of a branch of symbolic logic.

Symbolic logic has had such a great impact on mathematics because it provides a notation which is extremely flexible yet, to the initiated, simple to use. All the different ideas expressed throughout mathematics can be written in this language with only a few different 'words'. However, like any language, it takes a long time to become familiar with it, to use it in its full expressiveness and even to think in it. Symbolic logic has had the unfortunate consequence of giving mathematics a completely incomprehensible appearance to the nonmathematician: it is written in a language as foreign to the average English speaker as Russian or Greek. All fields have their own technical vocabulary; mathematics has perhaps the most developed and alien one of all. **SMcL**

Further reading G. Boole, The Laws of Thought (1854); J.N. Crossley et al., What Is Mathematical Logic?.

SYMBOLISM

Symbolism was a European movement from the mid–1890s through to World War I. The Symbolists reacted against the view that the aim of **art** was to portray the appearance of things. The poet Jean Moréas (in 'Le Symbolisme', a manifesto published in Figaro littéraire in 1886) claimed, by contrast, that the goal of art was to find an adequate language to express ideas.

In fine art, the movement was loose-knit, attracting artists of different kinds united only in their distaste for the prevailing belief in **science** and **naturalism**. Within this broad-based movement there were two main groups. The confusingly named 'literary' symbolists, led by Gustave Moreau (teacher of Matisse) and including Puvis de Chavannes and Odilon Redon, favoured jewel-like paintings of the more fantastic episodes drawn from the Bible and the classics; this tendency led in 1888 to the foundation of the Rosicrucian movement. Historically more significant was 'pictorial' symbolism, with its origins in the work of Paul Gauguin. After a visit to Brittany, Gauguin simplified his hitherto **impressionist** palette into broad areas of pure colour enclosed by a black line. Maurice Denis, the theorist of the movement, commented on this approach, 'Remember that a painting, before being a warhorse, a nude or an anecdote, is essentially a flat surface covered with colours disposed in a certain pattern'. Such ideas freeing colour and form from the referent of Nature facilitated the development of true **abstraction** in the 20th century.

In **literature**, as in art, Symbolism was predominantly French. The Symbolists sought to replace direct description with evocation, to use words less because they stood for specific objects or ideas than because of their 'musical' qualities: sound, rhythm and evocative overtones. The chief Symbolists were Huysmans, Laforgue, Maeterlinck (who wrote *L'aprés-midi d'un faune* and *Pelléas et Mélisande*, two of the quintessential and most lasting Symbolist works because they inspired Debussy), Rimbaud, Verlaine and Villiers de l'Isle Adam.

Although all **theatre** uses symbolic elements, critics of **drama** use the term specifically to refer to works from the end of the 19th century in which a reaction to Naturalism and **realism** led to an attempt to do justice to the unconscious and the transcendent. Maeterlinck was probably the most notable Symbolist dramatist. Although the Symbolists' interest in the unconscious points to affinities with **expressionism**, **surrealism** and **Theatre of the Absurd**, their emphasis on the transcendental is a significant point of difference. **PD MG TRG KMcL**

See also vorticism.

Further reading A. Robinson, *Symbol to Vortex: Poetry, Painting and Ideas* (1885–1914); J.L. Styan, *Modern Drama in Theory and Practice 2: Symbolism, Surrealism and the Absurd*.

SYMBOLS

Symbols are signs that are generally regarded as representing something else. They were once assumed to have a definite and unambiguous relationship with the ideas they stood for, in the same way that words were thought to have an intrinsic meaning associated with the objects or ideas they represented. Later the influence of the structural **linguistics** of Ferdinand de Saussure on **anthropology** demonstrated that the relationship of words to what they stood for was totally arbitrary, and was instead defined by systematic relationships between the words themselves.

The symbolist Victor Turner challenged the notion that symbols unambiguously stood for the 'real' world, because symbols can possess different interpretations in the same way that words can have multiple meanings. There is no one correct interpretation; it is their inherent ambiguity which lends them to multiple interpretation. An example is the way in which the the mudyi tree, which oozes milky sap when cut, stands for a nexus of ideas among the Ndembu of Zambia. Whether its use refers to breast milk, purity, dependency, or matrilineal descent depends on the specific context in which it is used, and the level of interpretation the individual wishes to make.

The interpretative anthropologist Clifford Geertz argued that there are two sorts of relations between symbols and reality: they provide an explanatory model of reality, as well as a prescriptive model. However, this approach has been criticized for being over-reliant on linguistic parallels.

Dan Sperber argued against making too much of native explanations over other ways of relating symbols, because of the limitations of using semantic explanations for a conceptual system that is not located in the realm of words. Symbols are symbolic precisely because they are inexplicable through normal modes of explanation. He argues that symbols cannot simply be made to stand for something else. They have different meanings for different individuals. By rejecting Western assumptions of symbols standing for something else in a straightforward manner, anthropology can explore the various and complex ways meanings within a social discourse are conveyed. **CL**

See also interpretative anthropology; language; rationality; taboo; totemism.

Further reading Mary Douglas, *Natural Symbols*; Edmund Leach, *Culture and Communication*; Dan Sperber, *Rethinking Symbolism*; V. Turner, *The Forest of Symbols*.

SYMPHONY

Symphony (Greek, 'sounding together') originally was used to describe any group of instruments playing together. In medieval European paintings, for example, a 'symphony' is a group of angels playing instruments in Heaven, the exact equivalent of a choir. In 16th-century Europe, the word was used in this sense, to mean the musicians accompanying **opera** or religious **music**. It was not till the 18th century that the word began to refer not to the players but to the music itself. The first symphonies of this kind were short pieces based on the styles of the music used to introduce operas at the time: a busy fast movement, a gentle slow movement and a dance movement. In the 1730s, composers began to write more substantial symphonies, adding a fourth movement and giving each work overall unity, so that symphonies were indivisible wholes, in contrast to the looser, multi-movement suites (or 'overtures', as they were confusingly then known).

The 18th-century symphony was predominantly a German and Austrian form, perfected at the many small courts of central Europe (and at some large ones, notably Mannheim with its magnificent orchestra, and Esterhazy where Haydn was Music Director). By the end of the century, in the hands of composers like Haydn and Mozart, it had become a large-scale, substantial form, second in importance in a composer's output only to opera and church music. This importance was enhanced by Beethoven, who added a feeling of sublimity and striving, making the symphony seem a statement almost of philosophical as well as musical identity. Such an interpretation appealed to 19th-century **Romantics**, many of whom used the symphony to give abstract expression to their most lofty thoughts and aspirations – as Mahler said, at the end of the century, a symphony should 'contain the world'. (Other composers, for example Mendelssohn and his followers, wrote less grand, more 'entertaining' symphonies – a tradition which has continued to the present.)

Because of the closely argued, developmental style of symphonic writing perfected by such composers as Brahms and Mahler, 20th-century composers at first felt that the form was unsuitable for experimental and **modernist** styles. Symphonies went on being written, but they were usually by composers seen as 'traditionalists' rather than innovators: Nielsen and Sibelius in Scandinavia, Shostakovich in Russia, Vaughan Williams in the UK, and Hanson and Harris in the USA. **Concerto**, opera and symphonic poem were the main orchestral forms which appealed to experimentalists, and a host of new forms were developed exploring the possibilities of **chamber music** and **music theatre**. The imminent death of the symphony was proclaimed by musical jeremiahs as often as that of the **novel** in literary circles. But all that has happened is that the symphony is no longer the predominant large orchestral form. It continues to thrive, and young composers no longer blush to write its name at the head of complex scores. Indeed, the symphonies of Witold Lutoslavski, Bohuslav Martinu, Peter Maxwell Davies, Igor Stravinsky, Michael Tippett and others, though markedly different in style and aims both from each other and from the symphonies of (say) Bruckner and Dvořák in the previous century, are among this century's most fully-achieved, most durable orchestral works. **KMcL**

SYNCRETISM

Syncretism (Greek, 'binding together') is the process of mingling different philosophies, religions or traditions of belief and practice, resulting in hybrid forms. (It is distinct from eclecticism: choosing elements from different philosophical and religious systems and combining them in a new system, usually with the personality of the founder strongly imprinted upon it: for example **Sikhism**, in which Guruk Nanak combined elements from **Hinduism** and **Islam** with his own powerful vision.) Syncretism can be seen as a process of osmosis, such as occurred in the Mediterranean civilization of the Hellenistic or Roman periods, or as a more formal event, such as the establishment of the 'syncretic' churches in colonial Africa, a fusion of **Christian** and indigenous traditions. In the religious context, the word is also used when a thinker attempts to unite two systems or to explain one system in terms of another: in Roman **Catholic** theology, for example, it describes attempts to combine Thomist and Molinist teaching.

Anthropologists also use the word syncretism to describe the general cultural changes which result when different cultural traditions appear to be blended together. In the 19th century, examination of such matters was known as 'acculturation studies'. But in the first half of this century, the term 'acculturation' began to be used in a negative way, to describe what was considered as cultural decline. The anthropological method here was to establish a picture of two cultures before they came into contact with one another – 'the cultural baseline' – and then to draw out the processes of change. Usually, such scholars emphasized only the influence of industrial societies on non-industrial communities, failing to recognize both influences from elsewhere and processes of change within the community. Their models were static and too dependent on the idea that there exist discrete units of culture which were fixed and static before coming into contact with each other. When this view was tied up with that of 'native' culture, it affirmed the 'myth of the primitive' (in which so-called 'primitive' societies were thought to live in a timeless, uncontaminated state before Western contact). For this reason, modern anthropologists studying social and cultural change have tended to replace the word 'acculturation' with such terms as syncretism, hybridization or creolization, which seem more adequate descriptions of the continuous and diverse merging of social and cultural processes. (Creolization also has a specific linguistic meaning: the development of a pidgin language formed from communication between two different communities but subsequently adopted as the mother-tongue of a particular speech community, for example in modern Jamaican and Haiti.)

In theological systems where salvation depends on faith alone, and/or on holding the 'right' beliefs, syncretism is seen as a particularly insidious factor, one which undermines the uniqueness of the faith. **Lutheran** Christians, for example, are particularly wary of the process, as *reine Lehre* ('pure doctrine') is essential to their theology, and syncretism is too close to **relativism** (the view that all religions are equally true). For all that, it could be argued that early Christianity, and the **Judaism** from which it arose, are themselves in part the results of syncretic processes. Hindus say that all religions are rivers which flow into the same sea, and their beliefs are quintessentially syncretic, drawing on and welcoming elements from many traditions. **RK KDS**

See also culture; diffusionism; evolutionism; modernization; primitivism; Westernization.

Further reading Bede Griffiths, *The Marriage of East and West*; Felix M. Keesing, *Cultural Anthropology: the Science of Custom*; I.M. Lewis, *Syncretism and the Survival of African Islam*.

SYNERGISM

Synergism (Greek, 'working-together-ism'), in the **life sciences**, describes a co-operative interaction between two systems such that their combined action exceeds the sum of their actions in isolation. The phenomenon is most commonly encountered in **pharmacology** when two drugs exert a synergistic effect – alcohol and sleeping pills together have a far more profound effect than comparable doses of each taken alone. **RB**

SYNTAX

Syntactic theory, in **linguistics**, deals with the constraints which govern how words are put together to create grammatical sentences. Of paramount importance has been the influence of Noam Chomsky, whose writings since the 1950s have reinvigorated and revolutionized the previously neglected topic of syntax. Chomsky stressed the need for syntactic theory to describe the systematic knowledge of grammar every native speaker has about their language. Every normal speaker knows many thousands of words plus a number of syntactic principles (or rules), which enable an explicit judgement to be made about the grammaticality of a given string of words. Modern syntactic theory is not, therefore, confined to writing rule systems for generating correct sentences. There is also a keen interest in what makes certain sentences ungrammatical, since a unique insight is gained into the bounds of possibility for natural human languages.

The data which a linguist works with are sentences, which naturally originate in the mind of a speaker/writer. However, people's speech is often syntactically fragmented and ill-formed, owing to such deviations as false starts, slips of the tongue and hesitations. The vagaries of language production, though, are not the concern of the syntactician. Therefore, Chomsky distinguished between competence (the system of grammatical knowledge in someone's head) and performance (the use of the language system on a particular occasion). The terms competence and performance enjoy wide currency, being inspired by the **structuralist** terms *langue* and *parole*, although Chomsky has recently modified and rechristened them I-language and E-language, respectively. For Chomsky, syntactic theory should describe native-speaker competence, which means revealing the state of language knowledge in the brain. Not all linguists share Chomsky's urgency to relate their analyses of words and sentences to matters of psychology and cognition. However, most linguists do acknowledge the importance of describing the pure, underlying qualities of the syntactic system, which are captured by the concept of competence.

Despite their great diversity, all theories of syntax deal with a common set of basic phenomena (see **theories of grammar**). At a basic level, an adequate theory must account for the constituent structure of a sentence, which provides an analysis of a sentence into its constituent parts (noun, verb, adjective and so on). A so-called distributional analysis reveals the patterns which particular constituents form within sentences. However, all syntactic theories agree that basic constituent structure analyses are very limited, since nothing is said about the systematic links between sentences of related types, including active and passive, declarative and interrogative and so on (see **transformational grammar** for one approach to this problem). A further major problem is subcategorization, which reveals how particular subclasses of words are strictly confined to certain types of syntactic structure only. Compare the acceptable 'George seems to be depressed' with the ungrammatical 'George seems'. These examples show that the verb 'seem' cannot occur without some kind of complement (in this case, 'to be depressed'). Particular theories handle these and other problems in strikingly different ways, to produce highly intricate and abstract analyses. Although Chomsky's current theory of **universal grammar** receives most attention at present, competing theories testify to the vigour of research in this area of linguistics. **MS**

See also generative grammar; psycholinguistics.

Further reading R.D. Borsely, *Syntactic Theory: A Unified Approach.*

SYSTEM

The notion of system (from Greek *syn*, 'together' and *histemi*, 'set up'), in **sociology**, is a widely used analytical tool. The concept of a social system is vital in all social theory. Broadly speaking a system is any collection of interrelated parts, where a change in one part would affect some or all of the other parts. A system is often seen to be purposeful or functional in that it exists to satisfy some objective or goal in relation to an external environment. Social scientists have treated social relations, groups or societies as a set of interrelated parts which function to maintain their boundaries within a wider environment. A further aspect of the concept of a system is the assumption of a tendency towards equilibrium. Social scientists have drawn an analogy between society and a biological organism each comprised of interdependent parts performing essential functions contributing to the smooth-running of the system as a whole.

The notion of a system has been used in social science since the 19th century though most explicitly by **functionalism** in the 1950s and 1960s. Although the approach has been subject to immense criticism the concept has been developed and remains important. **DA**

See also evolutionism; holism; social integration; society; structuralism; structure; systems theory; theories of modernity; world system.

Further reading W. Buckley, *Sociology and Modern Systems Theory*.

SYSTEMS THEORY

Systems theory is the belief that the general concept of a 'system' can be applied to naturally occurring systems of many types: social, biological and mechanical.

Within **sociology**, systems theory is traditionally associated with the work of the US sociologist Talcott Parsons, which was fashionable in the 1950s and 1960s. Parsons produced a model of the 'social system' and of 'action systems' which comprised the nucleus of the branch of sociology called structural-functionalism. A further objective for Parsons was to integrate the study of different social sciences under an overarching general systems theory. In Parson's model, every social system has four subsystems – adaption, goal-attainment, integration and pattern maintenance – which correspond to four basic needs essential to the social system's survival. In adapting to the external and internal environment social systems have to solve these four problems in order to ensure its continuance.

Parsons' efforts have been subject to much criticism, but systems theory remains an important influence within social science today. Any social theory that treats social relations, groups or societies as a set of interrelated parts which function to maintain some boundary or unity of parts is based implicitly or explicitly on the concept of a social system. **DA**

See also evolutionism; functionalism; holism; society; structuralism; structure; system; theories of modernity; world system.

Further reading Alexander, *Theoretical Logic in Sociology* vol. 1; W. Buckley, *Sociology and Modern Systems Theory*; W.L. Wallace, *Sociological Theory: An Introduction*.

T

TABOO

Taboo comes from the Polynesian word *tapu* which means 'marked off'. Taboos are actions that are prohibited by custom, but they can also be people, places or objects. The ritual quality of taboo means that any contact with forbidden persons or things is seen as fraught with mystical danger. They are regarded as imbued with either overwhelming or dangerous powers. Menstruation is an example of a condition subject to widespread taboos. The assumed possibility of contamination means that complex avoidance procedures often have to be observed. Restrictions on sexual intercourse, contact with food and objects, or physical segregation are extremely widespread.

Structuralists suggested that taboos can be seen as categories which help to exclude objects or conditions that do not fit into a particular society's scheme of the universe. If categories cut up the continuum of the world around us, taboos are the uncategorized areas that fall in between. In this way taboos order the universe in the same way conceptual categories do.

There is broad agreement among anthropologists that the taboos current in any society are those that relate to objects and actions most significant for social order. Each form of ritual avoidance can be related to the context in which it occurs, as part of systems of social control. **CL**

See also cannibalism; caste; incest; structuralism.

Further reading M. Douglas, *Purity and Danger*; Edmund Leach, *Culture and Communication*.

TACHISM

Tachism (from French *tache*, 'blot' or

'spot') was a name given in the late 19th and 20th centuries to European, particularly French, non-geometric abstract painting. (Tachism is used interchangeably with a series of other terms: *Art informel* ('Art without Form'), *Art autre* ('Other Art') and *Abstraction lyrique*. While the adjective 'tachist' had been used, pejoratively, as early as 1889 by Félix Fénéon with reference to Impressionism. *Art informel* and *Art autre* were coined by Michel Tapi for an exhibition and book, *Un art autre*, in 1952. The aims of the artists working under these appellations paralleled those of the American **abstract expressionists**. They laid emphasis on the value of the spontaneous expression of the artist's emotions, which they saw best communicated through the use of the unpremeditated, gestural stroke. Principal practitioners of the movement were Jean Dubuffet, Jean Fautrier, Hans Hartung, Georges Mathieu, Henri Michaux, Antoni Tapiss and Wols. **MG PD**

TANTRISM

Tantrism (from *tantra*, 'rule' or 'ritual') is the blanket term for a welter of sects based on occult practices, the development of psychic powers by special yogic disciplines, and the recitation of secret texts or *mantras*. Its origins lie in non-Vedic popular religions, with the need to tap into spiritual power in a hostile world, and it is, therefore, not surprising that Tantric worship also flourishes in **Buddhism**. The most notorious were based on worship of *kali* or 'the goddess', who traditionally stands on the left hand of 'the god'. Members ritually broke all **taboos**, for example, they drank alcohol, ate meat and some indulged in group sex.

Tantrism has always been an esoteric, minority movement, though strong in Bengal, and sharing the features of other sects with the emphasis of self-mortification and yoga. Practitioners of Tantrism keep their identity secret. Since Tantrism is based on worship of the goddess, Tantric Scriptures often consist of dialogues between Shiva and his spouse (Shakti or Durga), and cover such subjects as creation, the destruction of the world, worship of the gods and modes of union with the supreme spirit. Sexual intercourse between the god and his consort, and between the worshippers, was felt to have cosmic and supernatural power, which the believer could cultivate to gain power. Hence the erotic element in Hindu religious sculpture. **EMJ**

TAOISM see Daoism

TASTE

The word 'taste' is ultimately derived from Latin *tangere*, 'to touch'. Its technical meaning (one of the five senses) has been broadened and metaphorized. Lord Shaftesbury, for example, writing in 1714, called taste 'Relish in the concerns of Life', and Kant, in *Critique of Judgement* (1790), more narrowly but more loftily defined it as 'the completely disinterested faculty for judging an object or a manner of representation, and judging it pleasing or displeasing; the object judged pleasing is beautiful'. Both these statements reveal one of the main problems with thinking or writing about **aesthetics**. Shaftesbury's implication that taste is innate, and Kant's statement that it can be exercised objectively, are disingenuous. Who is to say what 'relish in the concerns of life' is, except for oneself? The concerns I relish may displease you; yours may disgust me. And who is to judge what constitutes a 'disinterested faculty of judging', and to whom should such a faculty be entrusted? In truth, taste – especially in the narrower meaning of 'good' taste which both definitions also take for granted – is neither objective nor innate. It is a cultural determinant: some people perceive others or themselves to possess it; it defines groups of like-minded people both to themselves and to outsiders. Taste is not a faculty but a construct; of its nature it is not constant but fugitive.

In the broader view, it might be argued that all human **civilization**, all **culture**, depends on taste, that all the customs and beliefs which hold society together, from sumptuary laws to social **taboos**, from **myth** to etiquette, reflect a kind of taste-consensus, which defines the group and makes its continued existence possible. Certainly we react to people who offend against this consensus – depending on the society, their offences might range from religious nonconformity to a fondness for **incest** – in a way different only in degree from the way we chide or ostracize those who wear the 'wrong' kind of clothes or entertain themselves in ways of which 'we' disapprove. In aesthetic theory, such confusion of the shallow and the deep is endemic. From antiquity, writers like Plato or Cicero in the West, or the anonymous authorities who codified the 'Confucian' system of life and lifestyle in China, tried to define such concepts as **beauty** and moral excellence, and proceeded from definition to prescriptions about behaviour and **attitude**.

The aura of philosophical objectivity which surrounds such writings has infected thoughts about taste in the entire civilized world: in fact our very idea of 'civilized' now contains overtones of aesthetic sensitivity (or snobbery, depending on your point of view). Those aspiring to what they see as cultural 'betterment' are often as obsessed with the taste-minutiae of the admired society as with (say) its material or technological advantages. In reality, taste concerns a shallow, narrow range of options, and the only mystery is why, when so many of the perceptions and ideas it involves are vain and frivolous, they are promoted and adhered to as eagerly as if they were, precisely, essential for survival. There are many people – and not just style gurus in Western Sunday newspapers – for whom taste is a major factor of every moment of existence, not so much the frame as the skeleton of what they are.

There are tastes in taste itself. In **Renaissance** Europe, for example, taste in the arts and **design** – a prerogative, as so often, of those rich enough and absorbed enough with self-image to bother about such matters – depended on imitation of models from ancient Greece and Rome, from hairstyles to literary forms, from **sculpture** to garden-design. In the early 20th century, by contrast, **modernism** saw taste as an area closely linked to form and function (see **functionalism**), the purity of machine production and the new materials of technology. The arrival of **postmodernism** raised difficult questions about how concepts of 'good' or 'bad' taste are linked to **class**, social conditions, **race** and **gender**. Contemporary ideas on taste largely ignore traditional canons in favour of an eclectic aesthetic, which takes what it wants from cultures of every kind and every level in the world, and which is constantly squabbled over and redefined by 'experts' whose influence is often out of all proportion to their credentials.

The ephemerality of taste, particularly in an age of mass consumerism, can be a depressing phenomenon, at least to those whose 'disinterested faculty for judging' leads them to find the current taste-consensus itself distasteful. Such people might argue that we are given too limited a selection of options on which to exercise judgement, that the 'taste' which society exhibits at any given moment is not for the best of everything, but merely for the least worst of what is available. Discrimination, such people might claim, depends on education. But this is merely another form of Shaftesbury's and Kant's intellectual and cultural snobbery. No one can know, can experience, everything; all choices must be made from the options available. In the final analysis, taste is a manifestation of closed-mindedness, and therefore (it can be argued) not the result, but an enemy, of human thought. **KMcL**

See also criticism; kitsch.

TAXONOMY

Taxonomy (Greek, 'naming groups') is the science of biological classification and involves the organization of related species into hierarchical groups (*taxa*) that are related to one another, and which may themselves be organized along the same lines. The relationship between these species and groups need not be genetic, though most taxonomic systems are based on **phylogeny** and therefore attempt to reflect evolutionary relationships. The chief alternative to this phyletic taxonomy is a taximetric classification, which attempts to reduce subjectivity of judgement by measuring quantifiable taxonomic features and, using a computer to collate the data, to produce a classification based on total similarity. This is most effectively done by composing the DNA of separate species, though this strategy can only be applied where the DNA sequence has been ellucidated.

The first attempt at classification of living organisms was made by Aristotle (384–322 BCE) and his pupil Theophrastus (c.371–287 BCE) who described plants and animals in ranked groups based on their apparent complexity according to Aristotle's system of logic. The principles of this system endured until the 19th century when phylogenics appeared. During the **Renaissance**, interest grew in the idea of imposing order on man's knowledge of nature. Botanical gardens were being established and **anatomy** was an expanding field, providing much new material for classification. In the 17th century, John Ray determined that the species was the basic unit of taxonomy and summed up many of the previous attempts at classification, but the 18th-century, Swedish botanist Linnaeus, author of the *Systema Naturae*, is generally considered the founder of modern taxonomy. He developed a system which was important because it could be standardized. Species were given binomial names which indicate the genus (the group of immediate relatives) and the species (for example, *Homo sapiens* and his extinct but close relative *Homo erectus*) and these were arranged into hierarchies. He published many books which could be used to identify species because he used systematic, consistent taxonomic keys.

The Linnaean system is the basis for the taxonomic system in use today, which divides life into kingdoms (such as the animal kingdom) and each kingdom into hierarchically arranged groups (phylum, class, order, family and genus) according to perceived evolutionary closeness. The subjective nature of such a system means that it is in dynamic equilibrium and, as new techniques to investigate phylogeny become available (for example, **immunology** and **molecular biology**), the taxonomic positions of many species are continually being reinforced or undermined. However, the *sine qua non* of taxonomy is that it imposes order on living species: thus a classification system should be reliable and consistent above all else. **RB**

See also homology; morphology; palaeontology; speciation.

Further reading Salvador Luris, *A View of Life.*

TECHNOLOGY

Technology (Greek *techne*, 'skill with hands' + ology) is the application of scientific principles to the problems of everyday living. It is an ability of no other species but humans: a weaver-bird's nest or a honeycomb, for example, is constructed but not planned, and there is a perceptible difference in Nature between a finch using a twig to gouge insects out of bark and a human being devising a tool for the same purpose. Technology requires analysis of a practical problem, pondering of the principle(s) involved in solving it, and a combination of practical and intellectual inventiveness in devising means to applying that principle in the most elegant and least expensive way. (This last point explains why even the simplest gadgets, hammers, for instance, or bottle-openers are constantly being redesigned.)

Since the beginning of human history, technological activity has been a measure of the process of civilization. One can imagine a society without technology, but it could hardly be 'advanced' or long-lived. Some results of technology – ploughs, guns, the harnessing of electricity – are concerned with brute survival; others, writing is a prime example, more concern the intellectual environment. Of itself technology is morally and ethically neutral: modern 'technofear' is a projection on to inanimate systems of our incomprehension of how this or that gadgetry works, and our anxiety about controlling it. But the uses of technology can be bad as well as good. It is hard, for example, to make absolute judgements about the benefits or disbenefits to the human race of such things as the invention of high explosives, the **internal combustion engine** or television. Good or bad, however, technology is a central activity of human thought, a main function of human curiosity and ingenuity, and therefore one of the core activities that makes us, 'Humans the Toolmakers', what we are. **KMcL**

See also aerodynamics and aircraft; civil engineering; gearing systems; measurement; photography; prosthetics.

Further reading James Burke, *Connections*.

TELEKINESIS see **Parapsychology**

TELEOLOGY

Teleology is, literally, Greek for the study of ends, goals or purposes. In **philosophy**, certain phenomena can be explained in terms of their ends, goals or purposes. Plants grow roots with the aim of absorbing water and minerals from the earth. Animals flee with the purpose of avoiding danger. People drive to supermarkets because their goal is to get food. Each of these explanations are teleological, explaining phenomena in terms of their goals or purposes.

Teleological explanations, explanations in terms of attaining a goal in the future, contrast with explanations in terms of prior causes. But teleological explanations do not exclude explanation in terms of prior causes. Animals flee with the purpose of avoiding danger, but their behaviour also has a prior cause their fear. **AJ**

Further reading J.L. Mackie, *The Cement of the Universe*.

TELEPATHY see **Parapsychology**

TEMPLE

The temple is perhaps most simply defined as a building erected for the purpose of ritual or worship of the divine. Such buildings are a feature of the built environment of most developed societies. The Latin word, *templum*, from which the word derives, originally signified a staked out piece of land which belonged to the people or the deity and was used for the reading of the stars; use of the term to include structures built for religious purposes came later.

In most cultures, the temple appears to have been treated as the dwelling place of the deity, and the character and style of the architecture reflected his or her importance. The 'house' would resemble a palace, and the activities of the priests were modelled on those of a royal household. The presence of the deity was often signified, as in for example **Hindu** temples, by images or symbols, secluded by a structural barrier in what might be called a 'sanctuary'.

The significance of a temple site was often by association with the real or supposed history of the deity. The great **Buddhist** centres, for example, were constructed on sites that had been significant in the life of the Buddha. In the **Christian** religion, shrines and churches were often on the sites of miraculous events. In early aboriginal nomadic tribes tents would be pitched around a pole which was treated as the sacred centre of the settlement, and in the pueblo architecture of Mesa Verde in North America, a subterranean room was carved out for the purpose of **ritual** under the centre of the grouping of mud huts which constituted the pueblo itself: the deity's 'home' thus, literally, underlay the homes of his or her worshippers, and was part of the settlement.

The form, design and layout of temples was influenced by the rituals performed, by the nature of the acts of worship and their inclusion or exclusion of the secular. The form of the temple was also often influenced by other matters of belief, and was symbolic in origin; Christian churches, similarly, were cross-shaped.

In many cultures, temple architecture has had an enormous influence over secular architecture. The temple style of ancient classical Europe, for example, has significance beyond its contemporary religion as it became the focus in later centuries for revivalists of classical prototypes who regarded the colonnaded temple as in some ways the archetype of good architecture. In certain ways, Buddhist temple styles in Asia, Hindu temple styles in India, and the style of **Shinto** shrines in Japan, all had their influence on secular architecture, and gave a distinctive vernacular style first to grand buildings in public places, and then to the more domestic houses and workplaces which drew on their styles. **JM**

Further reading G. van der Leeuw, *Sacred and Profane Beauty: the Holy in Art.*

TERATOLOGY

Teratology (Greek, 'study of freaks'), in the **life sciences**, is the study of abnormal growth and development resulting in individuals with biochemical or anatomical abnormalities. The term was coined in 1822 by the French zoologist Isidore Geoffroy St Hilaire, who, continuing the work of his father Étienne, proposed that they were caused by changes in the environment of the embryo. It has subsequently become clear that the causes of abnormalities in both animals and plants are attributable to both environmental and genetic factors. Teratogenic agents include drugs such as thalidomide and alcohol, infection with pathogens such as rubella (German measles), dietary deficiencies and ionizing radiations such as X-rays.

The development of the foetus is a complex, synchronized series of processes which can easily be disrupted by environmental factors, particularly during sensitive periods; the drug thalidomide, for example, causes abnormality in babies if the mother takes the drug between the 38th and 42nd days of pregnancy. The vast majority of cases result in spontaneous abortion, usually before development has progressed very far.

In man, modern medical techniques often permit the survival of individuals who would otherwise have died in infancy as a result of abnormality; it is variously reported that between 0.3 and 4% of live human births are of abnormal infants. Yet the definition of abnormal is inherently subjective and attempts must be made to distinguish between normal variation and abnormality. In the past, abnormal animals, human in particular, were often considered to be the result of curses or unnatural matings – and 'freaks', both living and preserved, were eminently collectable in 19th-century Europe. **RB**

See also embryology; hybridization; pharmacology; radiobiology; toxicology.

TEXT LINGUISTICS

Text linguistics falls into the tradition of language studies which look beyond individual sentences to consider the ways in which entire texts are organized (see also **discourse** analysis and **stylistics**). A central aim is to provide a principled account for the intuition that texts fall into distinct categories. An attempt is also made to highlight those factors which determine the success or failure of a text, and in this regard, the words of a text are but one part of an overall communicative occurrence. For it is assumed that texts can only be interpreted relative to the situation in which they occur and the responses they evoke in the receiver.

The textuality of a text comprises a number of interweaving factors which contribute to its communicative value. Language-based factors include the cohesive forces which help link sentences together, as below:

George moved out of the White House. He left the keys for Bill.

The pronoun 'he' cannot be interpreted without referring back to George in the previous sentence, and so a cohesive link is established between the two sentences. Among other important factors, textuality is also dependent upon the intentions of the text author, the attitudes of the text receiver, the density of information in the text, and the situation in which the text occurs. **MS**

THEATRE

Theatre (from the Greek 'seeing-place') has extended from being a reference to the buildings or space within which **drama** can take place to encompass the range of phenomena which constitute the relationship between an audience and a performance. Theatre is a social institution which operates on social interaction in its production processes. It is also a social activity which includes those involved in the production process as well as with the spectator/spectator and spectator/performance exchange.

The social nature of Western theatre, which derives from the Greek pattern of celebration and demonstration of the ties of a community, has become more complex in contemporary society and, since the **Renaissance**, has a more economic base in both mainstream and alternative theatres.

The earlier concept that theatre was to entertain or instruct was beginning to be challenged towards the end of the 19th century by the concept that theatre should experiment and analyse. Theatre should no longer have a moralizing or didactic role but should operate as detached scientific investigation. Influenced by Émile Zola's essay 'Naturalism and the Art of Theatre' (1880), which was in turn indebted to Darwin's theories of **evolution**, the theatre should reproduce day-to-day reality exactly and objectively. The idea that environment and heredity condition behaviour initially effected a reformation of the stage environment, action and language and subsequently affected playwriting, notably the work of Ibsen, Strindberg and Chekhov, though their illusionistic dramas extended beyond the thesis of scientific **naturalism**.

The Aristotelian concepts of **tragedy** and **comedy** began to be challenged and blurred. The directional and design ideas of Appia, Craig and later Reinhardt, Copeau and Meyerhold, which began to move towards the concept of 'total theatre', emerged very soon to counter the stultifying nature of an increasingly narrow illusionism, but it was not until Bertolt Brecht developed his concept of **Epic Theatre** that the role of the audience was seriously addressed. Epic Theatre focuses rational and objective audience-attention on the social and historical questions embodied in the performance by revealing the illusionistic aspects of theatre which created empathy and thus dulled the critical sense. Brecht used theatrical means such as masks, back-projection, songs and music, visible lights and *gestus* to distance the audience so that they could more appropriately interrogate the meanings of the performance.

Antonin Artaud rejected the concept that theatre must mirror the surface reality of life by abandoning spoken language and putting in its place the idea of theatre as a 'double' (rather than a reflection) of existence. He proposed the use of highly stylized theatre forms, such as the Balinese dance-drama, to provoke in the audiences the profound symbols of consciousness beyond the intellectual, and developed a '**Theatre of Cruelty**' which influenced a diverse range of later practitioners from Peter Brook to environmental theatre.

The study of theatre has generally started from an empirical and chronological position, recording the material spaces and conditions of theatre, study of the texts or historical investigations of the work of various practitioners, such as theatre directors. Historical or critical approaches to theatre disregarded aspects of performance, and in the UK it was not until Raymond Williams began to investigate the relationship between text and performance in the 1950s that a need was articulated for a critical language for the examination of the whole theatre process, including performance and audience. European practitioners and theorists, such as Artaud and Brecht, had earlier begun to establish their essentially different, but wide-ranging concepts of theatre.

The idea of theatre is approached from a broader base than the traditional **literature**-grounded perspective, which deals with the drama text, to one which is able to deal with the simultaneity of experiences that constitute the theatrical response. Although predominantly theatre has, through its long history, created meanings verbally, it also uses space, movement, colour and sound which interrelate to create a synaesthetic or multiple medium. Critical approaches deriving initially from **semiotics** and later from **structuralist**, post-structuralist and **psychoanalytic** theories, have enabled the development of an academic study of the network of elements of theatre. These moves are very much in process, but are an attempt to establish a 'poetics' of theatre which is discrete yet affiliated to that of drama, together with the development of the understanding of theatre as a cultural institution. The ephemeral nature of the stage spectacle has meant that, historically, the written text has necessarily been prioritized.

Thus a study of theatre, until the mid–20th century, has been seen only as a subsidiary and supportive reference to the study of drama. With new approaches, the theatrical processes are seen to be crucial in the understanding and study of drama, and have developed as an interdependent but discrete discipline. The key to the difference is to do with the relationship of the audience to the drama. This is not to do with questions of the 'ideal' audience, which has been hypothesized in some Shakespeare studies, but rather the significant role the spectator plays in the production of meanings in the theatre, both as functionaries and features of performance analysis. Theatre does not take place unless the spectator is actively engaged in meaning-production. In drama, the reader/spectator's concern is with an interpretation of the written text or script through the performance which has to be based on two assumptions: that the text is a constant which can be interpreted or communicated through performance and second, that the audience is a constant. This is impossible when dealing with performance, and can only be reproduced by a single reader of a single text, and even this is arguable as conditions of reading may differ. In theatre, the role of the spectator is more concerned with the communication of meaning in the performance, which is itself mediated through the performers' production of the text and the conditions of performance, such as the physical conditions of theatre architecture and the constituency of the audience. TRG SS

Further reading Artistotle, *Poetics*; A. Artaud, *The Theatre and its Double*; E. Bentley (ed.), *Theory of the Modern Stage*; P. Brook, *The Empty Space*; R. Williams, *Drama in Performance*.

THEATRE OF CRUELTY

The French theorist, actor, and director Antonin Artaud coined the term Theatre of Cruelty to refer to his idea of a theatre that should communicate to its audiences at a visceral level like a plague, rather than through words. His aim was to address the **unconscious** and liberate the imagination through a form of total theatre. His influence on directors from Brook and Barrault to Grotowski and Marowitz has been

widespread, and his work, deriving from **surrealism** has affinities with the **Theatre of the Absurd**. TRG SS

Further reading A. Artaud, *The Theatre and its Double*; M. Esslin, *Artaud*; J.L. Styan, *Modern Drama in Theory and Practice 2: Symbolism, Surrealism and the Absurd*.

THEATRE OF THE ABSURD

Theatre of the Absurd is a term coined by the critic Martin Esslin to draw attention to apparent similarities of approach and subject matter in plays by a number of mid–20th century dramatists, notably Samuel Beckett, Jean Genet, Eugene Ionesco, Edward Albee and Harold Pinter. In his influential book *The Theatre of the Absurd* (1961), Esslin was following Albert Camus's philosophical use of the term 'absurd' (from Latin *absurdus*, 'out of tune') to refer to the meaninglessness of the universe; but journalistic usage has blurred the issue by seizing on those elements which are absurd in the more limited sense of 'comic'. Although there never was an organized movement of Absurdists, the term has become shorthand for a type of drama which rejects determinism, linear causality, logic, and the trappings of **naturalism** in favour of more associative and allusive dramatic strategies. TRG SS

See also Dada; epic; existentialism; expressionism; Surrealism.

Further reading Enoch Brater and Ruby Cohn (eds.), *Around the Absurd*; J.L. Styan, *Modern Drama in Theory and Practice 2: Symbolism, Surrealism and the Absurd*.

THEISM

Theism (from Greek *theos*, 'god') is the belief in one personal creator-God who is distinct from the world but constantly active in it. Theism is therefore distinct from **deism** (which does not accept the revelations of a God active in the world) and from **pantheism** (which holds the position that all is God and God is therefore not distinct from it). **Christianity**, **Islam** and **Judaism** are identified as the three major theistic religions.

While theism, as a philosophical position, can be traced back to Plato, it was the theologians of the major theistic religions who developed the arguments which support the theistic position. The ontological argument for God states that every mind, independent of all environmental influences, has some idea of a highest being, a fact that points to his existence. The cosmological argument states that God can be seen in the order which rules all things while the teleological argument goes further and states that this order can be better understood in view of a goal (God). (Taking the theory of **evolution** into account, F.R. Tennant in his books *Philosophical Theology* (1928–30) developed the wider teleological argument by stating 'if Nature evinces wisdom, the wisdom is Another's'.) The moral argument takes moral consciousness into account and states that a person's value judgements do not originate in that person and point, therefore, to another, higher being. **EMJ**

Further reading A.O. Lovejoy, *The Great Chain of Being: a Study of The History of an Idea.*

THEORIES OF GRAMMAR

In the field of **linguistics**, there has been a huge upsurge of interest in syntactic theory in the latter half of this century, largely due to the dominating influence of Noam Chomsky. Almost every major recent innovation in syntactic theory has either originated with Chomsky or in reaction to particular ideas of his. There are, though, numerous competing theories of **syntax**, whose diversity is matched only by their volatility. Indeed, Chomsky's own thinking has resulted in three quite distinct phases, each of which has marked a dramatic reappraisal of the goals of syntactic theory.

The earliest version of Chomsky's theory is notable for an interest in the mathematical properties of human languages, in particular the capacity for a finite set of grammatical rules to generate an infinite number of different sentences. An important conclusion from this period was that phrase structure (PS) rules, which specify how words can combine into sentences, cannot by themselves deal with certain kinds of syntactic phenomena. The shortcomings of PS rules were initially compensated for by so-called transformational rules, which dealt with the necessary movement of elements within sentences, in addition to describing how certain sentence types are related (for instance, active and passive; declarative and interrogative). Several other theories which have risen to prominence in the 1980s, including Lexical Functional Grammar (LFG) and Generalized Phrase Structure Grammar (GPSG), also commonly acknowledge that PS rules need to be modified in some way.

The latest version of Chomsky's theory (now often referred to as **universal grammar** or UG), has restricted the role of transformations enormously. The constraint of transformational rules has been carried to its logical conclusion within GPSG, since transformational rules have been abolished altogether. Instead, the phrase structure of a sentence permits the flow of information from one part of the sentence to another, in a tightly constrained manner. LFG has also abandoned transformational rules, and relies instead on the properties of lexical items to explain the connections between sentence types. For example, the relationship between active and passive sentences is established via the lexical properties of active and passive verb forms (for example, eat/is eaten; see/was seen).

While the interest in mathematical **formalism** has diminished within UG, it has been applied even more rigorously within GPSG. However, GPSG disputes Chomsky's early belief in the autonomy of syntax and instead explores the links between the structural form of a sentence and the meanings conveyed thereby. LFG, on the other hand, shares Chomsky's interest in the psychological reality of syntactic theory. On this view, a syntactic theory is adequate only if it describes the language system that a native speaker actually has in his or her mind. LFG is notable for asserting that grammatical functions, such as subject and object, are of primary importance.

Despite many fundamental differences between competing syntactic theories, there are many common assumptions. For example, a significant shift in emphasis is emerging, which asserts that the meanings of individual words determine to a large extent what kinds of sentence structures they can occur in. With this shift towards lexical determination of sentence structure, the role of purely syntactic phenomena in determining grammaticality may prove ultimately to be quite limited. **MS**

See also generative grammar; transformational grammar.

Further reading P. Sells, *Lectures on Contemporary Syntactic Theories.*

THEORIES OF MODERNITY

Modernization theories, in **sociology**, are those theories which attempt to explain the global process through which traditional societies achieved modernity. More specifically, modernization theory refers to a model of development associated with the structural-functionalist branch of sociology developed in the US in the 1950s and 1960s.

Modernization refers to the overall societal process by which previously agrarian and contemporary societies have become developed. The term includes industrialization but incorporates a wider range of processes besides. Changes towards modernity are seen as the result of an increasing differentiation of social structures. Thus, in traditional societies many different areas of life are merged, for example home and work. In modern societies, it is argued, different areas of social life become increasingly separated from each other.

While there are important variations between different authors, there are some main threads in theories of modernity. Modern society is contrasted with traditional society which is seen as hindering economic development. Changes occur through evolutionary stages which are broadly similar for all societies. Political modernization entails the development of key institutions – political parties, parliament, voting rights and secret ballots – which support participation by all in decision making. Cultural modernization typically involves the decline of religion as an

explanation for events and the rise of secular scientific explanations. Modernization is believed to involve the development of **nationalism**. Economic modernization is seen to involve profound economic changes an increasing **division of labour,** the use of management techniques, and improved technologies. Social modernization is believed to involve increasing literacy and **urbanization**, among other things.

A number of criticisms have been made of modernization theories. It is based on the model of development in the West and is thus a culturally arrogant model of development, which ignores the possibility of the development of novel societal forms in the Third World. Further it is argued that modernization does not necessarily lead to industrial growth and equal distribution of social benefits since it does not occur evenly and has resulted in the underdevelopment and dependency of some areas. Modernization theories have also been criticized for only examining processes which occur within a society rather than factors outside of it. Thus, they ignore **colonialism** as an important factor influencing the development of many Third World countries.

Critics point out that behind modernization theories lay both political and ideological concerns. Many of the main theorists were from the US and involved in governmental advisory roles, and explicitly committed to the curtailment of Socialism or Communism in the **Third World. DA**

See also bureaucracy; community; convergence thesis; culture; dependency theory; diffusionism; evolutionism; functionalism; globalization; historical sociology; labour process; organization; postmodernism; rationalization; secularization; society; state; world system; values.

Further reading D. Lerner, *The Passing of Traditional Society;* W. Rostow, *The Stages of Economic Growth.*

THEOSOPHY

Theosophy (Greek, 'wisdom about God') was a pan-religious **cult** founded in 1875 by Helena Blavatsky (1831–91) and Colonel H.S. Olcott. It proclaimed the unity of all religions, and drew beliefs and practices from a variety of sources, both religious and psychic. Theosophists believed in *karma*, **reincarnation** and communion with spirits, and practised **Christian** ethics and morality. From **Buddhism** they developed the idea of 'great souls', calling them 'world teachers' who would manifest themselves to end the human race's ignorance of and blindness to the divine. Blavatsky herself claimed to be one of these 'world teachers', and held seances and 'miracle' meetings (sometimes before as many as 100,000 people). The cult was investigated in 1884, and declared fraudulent, but in its day it attracted a huge following, worldwide. **KMcL**

Further reading Helena Blavatsky, *The Key to Theosophy* (1889); Peter Washington, *Madame Blavatsky's Baboon*.

THERMODYNAMICS

Thermodynamics (Greek *thermai*, 'heat' + *dunamikos*, 'powerful') is the study of heat and temperature in relation to the mechanical power produced. The distinction between heat and temperature is that heat is a form of energy and temperature is the measure of hotness. For example, a pot of water placed on a stove receives energy and this increases its temperature.

Kinetic Energy is the form of energy corresponding to movement. For a body of mass m moving a velocity v the kinetic energy is $0.5\,mv^2$.

Potential Energy corresponds to height above a base line: that is, the energy required to raise a body of mass – to a height h above base line is mgh where g is the acceleration due to gravity. Another form of potential energy corresponds to deformation – as in stretching an elastic band or putting gas under pressure.

There are two laws which have been established to explain the nature of thermodynamics. The first law states that if an interaction occurs between two bodies then energy is neither created nor destroyed. In other words if a quantity of heat is absorbed by one body this energy is equal to the sum of the increase in internal energy and any external work done by the body. This law is a direct consequence of the law of conservation of energy. This change in internal energy will be made up of an increase in both the kinetic and potential energy of the body. This change of energy may take any form, that is, thermal, mechanical, etc. This law states that it is possible to convert all work totally into a thermal change, such as heat.

The second law is that the reverse is not true; that is, all heat cannot be turned back into work. In other words, energy will not be transferred from a cooler body to a warmer body. This law was established by the French engineer Sadi Carnot (1796–1832) who worked on trying to establish the most efficient engine possible. This engine, the Carnot engine, established the upper limit of efficiency for turning thermal energy into mechanical energy. His sole publication, called *Réflexion sur la Puissance Matrice de Feu*, explains his concepts that became known as the Second Law of Thermodynamics. **AA**

Further reading M.W. Zemansky and Richard Dittman, *Heat and Thermodynamics*.

THIRD WORLD

The concept of the Third World was initially a political idea and has subsequently been used, rather inappropriately, as an economic one. In the 1950s, there were two opposed geopolitical blocs: the NATO alliance of liberal democracies (the First World) versus the Soviet bloc of state socialist countries (the Second World). There was also a growing number of newly independent countries eager to separate themselves from the colonial powers. The idea of the Third World was at first used to describe those countries which were not part of either bloc, but there was also an active 'non-aligned movement' intended to promote the interests of the Third World. This movement was a loose one, partly because leading members tended to fall into one or other of the opposing camps, partly because the Third World was very heterogeneous and partly because decolonization quadrupled the number of countries from the initial 30.

Although the initial definition was in terms of political affiliation, it was also true that the countries of the First World were economically the most developed, that those of the Second were industrialized, though at a lower level of prosperity, and those of the Third were much poorer. The term soon began to be used, along with rough equivalents such as underdeveloped, less developed or developing, to refer to economic status. As the Cold War reached its height and then began to thaw the term Third World became primarily a description of economic development.

The division into three worlds was always problematic: for instance some countries were difficult to classify and, as already mentioned, the Third World was and is culturally and economically very diverse. China, with a fifth of the world's population, was initially counted as part of the Second World, but after its split with the USSR it was simultaneously communist, undeveloped and non-aligned, and consequently differently classified by different people. More serious were the internal variations, which grew as some Third World countries developed in certain ways. Again, there are different classifications, but there are now huge differences between oil-exporting countries (some of which have an income per capita similar to the First World), newly industrializing countries (some of which began to close the income gap in the 1970s), middle developing countries (those neither conspicuously successful or unsuccessful), and least developed countries (countries with an average income of only a few hundred dollars sometimes known as Fourth World countries). The 30 or so countries in the latter group, including China and India, comprise half the world's population and produce about a twentieth of its wealth. Even omitting the dubious case of China, the Third World as a whole has half the world's population and half its land surface, but produces only a fifth of its wealth,

It has long been argued that the term Third World is outmoded. If a broad description of economic development is needed 'more versus less developed' is a preferable term, because it suggests a continuum rather than sharply separated groups and accords more comfortably with the concept of **uneven development**. The collapse of the Second World makes the original concept of three worlds a nonsense and provides an ideal opportunity to adopt different terminology. However, there are still great differences between more and less-developed countries, and there could be a renewed emphasis on the division between North and South, as defined by the Brandt Report. Divisions between North and South have been apparent in recent negotiations over GATT and global warming, but the concept of **sustainable development** is designed to reduce the differences between countries as well as to solve environmental problems. **PS**

Further reading B. Crow and A. Thomas, *Third World Atlas.*

THOMISM

Thomism is the Christian theological tradition based on the thinking of Thomas Aquinas. The substance of Aquinas's teaching was accepted as the official doctrine of the Roman **Catholic** Church and his influence can be seen in all branches of theology.

In April 1244, Aquinas defied his aristocratic family (the name Aquinas comes from his father, Count Landulf of Aquina) and entered the new Dominican order of friars. His theology provided the underpinning for the key Catholic doctrine of transubstantiation. After considerable controversy in his lifetime, especially with the Franciscans, his teachings were widely adopted by individuals and groups, and he was canonized in 1323.

Aquinas followed Augustine by grounding faith on God's revelation in the Scriptures. Faith, he said, is never founded on reason, but believers should use reason to elaborate and defend doctrine. Faith is so sharply distinguished from reason because, whereas all knowledge begins with experience, there are fundamental Christian concepts – such as the nature of the Trinity, heaven and hell – of which we can have no direct experience. Further fundamental ideas are: there is nothing in our mind which has not been sensed before (except the mind itself) because we are born with an **a priori**, the inner capacity to know. God alone is pure existence, 'Being'. Everything else 'has' being whilst God's essence is to exist.

Because the limited can not express the unlimited, all our language is 'pure act', in whom every possible perfection is realized. He created the world out of nothing. The human being consists of body and soul; the soul survives death and awaits reunion with the body at the resurrection of the dead.

Following Aristotle, Aquinas takes as the basis of his **metaphysics** a distinction between matter and form. His teaching on the incarnation was significant, and he denied the Immaculate Conception of the Virgin Mary.

By the 16th century Thomism had become normative in the theology and ethics of the Catholic Church; it was adopted by the Jesuits and permeated the language of the decrees of the Council of Trent (1545–63). However, Thomism declined in the 18th century and gradually fell into disuse. It was revived in the 19th century when its value became evident in confronting the dehumanization of the Industrial Revolution in Europe. In 1879 Pope Leo XIII commended Thomism, so giving rise to the 20th-century movement of Neo-Thomism, with the maxim that 'existence precedes essence': the human being knows by intuition that something exists before it knows what it is. **EMJ**

Further reading E. Gilson, *The Christian Philosophy of St Thomas Aquinas*; Mary Grey, *Redeeming the Dream*; A. Walz, *Saint Thomas Aquinas: a Biographical Study*.

THOUGHT

It is only recently, with the development of computers, that a plausible model has arrived of how we think. Down the centuries, the question provoked a vast amount of speculation and quasi-philosophical **scholasticism**, which is fascinating – intellectual narcissism is a characteristic of the 'thinking ape' – but which lacks scientific verisimilitude. The development of artificial brains may have cleared a path through all this undergrowth though 'may' is all one can say, as scientific investigation of the processes of thought is difficult and contentious.

Computers work by turning each piece of information they receive into digital code, and then manipulating it according to preset programmes. The basic processes are simple and mathematical; the programmes elaborate them into cat's-cradles of complexity. It is possible to make a crude analogy with the process of human thought. Our brains make an abstract model of each piece of information they receive, and then manipulate it according to such pre-stored 'programmes' as comparative analysis, **logic** and **memory**. It is open to question whether thought is possible without such 'programmes' and without any input of information and at what age such thought begins. The ancient Chinese conducted crude experiments, separating children from their mothers immediately after birth and bringing them up with animals, or in total seclusion, to see what languages they would talk or how they would describe the world when they grew up. (The children brought up with animals behaved like animals; those deprived of all stimulus became apathetic and died, or reacted to their first contact with the outside world, the first onslaught of experience, by going mad. The pathetic results of a similar kind of intellectual stunting filled the world's television screens in the early 1990s, when reporters were allowed into orphanages set up by the former Rumanian dictator Ceausescu.) In the abstract, one can imagine experimenting to find out when a child begins to think, and what its first thoughts are, but it is hard to work out what form such experiments might take.

The **nature/culture** debate of which the above is a form is one of the most absorbing problems facing students of human thought. A related question is the matter of child prodigies. Leaving aside how a child can play chess, solve mathematical problems, speak languages, make music better than most adults, where does he or she acquire the experience and knowledge required for such abstruse activities? They are forms of learned behaviour, and the child's prodigious ability must therefore consist in learning the basics, and seeing their potential for development, in a fraction of the time it takes most people. Another related matter is (what we call) inspiration. What exactly is it, and does everyone have it? Is it innate but latent (so that when it appears, in the work of a 'genius', it seems astonishing), or is it, like the ability of a prodigy, merely an enhanced skill at manipulating intellectual stimuli, and therefore learnable by anyone?

Such questions take us back from **science** to scholasticism. Theory is far more abundant than proof. Perhaps surprisingly, the same is true of something which at first glance seems much easier: the question 'What happens physiologically, in the brain, each time we think?' If the crude analogy with computers holds up, then the synapses of the brain are like the 'gates' on microchips, and we think by sending impulses along preselected paths. One problem with this analogy is that the brain is organic whereas computers are mechanical. There is no way, as yet, to build a computer which is anything but reactive, to make a machine which genuinely 'thinks' on the human model. Computer 'thought' is also unaffected by emotion; computers never tire or feel 'inspired'. Another problem is that the brain's capacity, compared to that of any existing computer, seems to be infinite (or at least unmeasurable): a thought which has led some experts to make analogies not with machines but with the universe itself. This seems to move us into the realm of **poetry**, not science. But it is nevertheless possible that such ideas as **chaos theory** may provide useful, if mind-boggling, insights into the workings of the brain. **KMcL**

See also artificial intelligence.

THREMMATOLOGY

Thremmatology (Greek, 'study of nurslings'), in the **life sciences**, is the controlled breeding of plants and animals to accentuate desirable characteristics at the expense of those which are undesirable. Early man, for example, domesticated animals such as dogs and horses, and plants such as wheat and oats. By selecting those individuals from the wild populations which had useful features he formed sub-populations, which, over time, became new species so that modern domestic plants and animals may bear little resemblance to their wild ancestors. Most of these domesticated varieties would not survive without human care.

Thremmatology became a science in the 18th century in Britain when agricultural stock began to be exhibited and prize examples were sold or lent for breeding. In the 20th century, worldwide demand for food grew and new technologies enabled breeding to be controlled more efficiently so that the process of selection could be accelerated. Artificial insemination revolutionized livestock breeding and **genetic engineering** has great potential in breeding, though ethical considerations must be taken into account. **RB**

See also hybridization; speciation.

TIME see **Space and Time**

TIME-SPACE COMPRESSION

Time-space compression is a term used by geographers to indicate the apparent compression of geographic space by faster means of transport and communication. At one level, this is an obvious idea and most people must be aware that a few centuries ago the fastest means of transport covered only a few miles per hour. Great technical progress 150 years ago made it possible to envisage a voyage around the world in only 80 days. Today, the same journey can be made in fewer hours. This idea has a long history in geography as a reduction in the 'friction' of distance. However, the idea of time-space compression indicates more than an even reduction in friction in all directions because most transport media are confined to routes which vary in speed (between motorways and lanes, main-line railways and branch lines) and which often vary in cost in a way which relates to speed. So the compression is uneven over space and different people have different degrees of access to fast travel.

The complexity is increased by the expanding role of electronic communication, from telegraph to computer networks. Here the speed is so great that space has apparently collapsed. But different media have very different properties, some broadcasting to millions, others available to one or a few, some one way and others two way. Again, a key difference is in access to the **media**: not for nothing was the portable phone the status symbol of the 1980s. The difference is not just between individuals but between organizations: the international cable and satellite networks used by financial institutions were highly significant in changing the world economy, including changing the form of **uneven development** and the **international division of labour**. A particular feature has been the emergence of world cities, such as New York, London and Tokyo, as the major centres of financial power in an economy where prices and exchange rates vary instantaneously in response to electronic messages. **PS**

TONALITY

Tonality, in **music**, is the convention of anchoring a piece aurally in the same tonal centre, or key: that is, as it were, in C major or E flat minor throughout. The notes and harmonies of the chosen key dominate, and excursions into other keys reinforce this dominance by contrasting with it and producing a marked feeling of completion when the music returns from them. This is one of the main structural devices in Western symphonic music. Even in music not written in keys, for example the **folk music** of Africa or Eastern Europe, or the art music of Indonesia and India, tonal centres are established and the music stays in them, sometimes from intellectual choice (for example, because each Indian *raga* uses certain notes only, in a clear relationship to one another), or because of the restricted tuning of the instruments (such as in a *gamelan*). In the 20th century, some Western composers have sought to abandon tonality (for instance by writing atonal or **serial music**), or to stretch tonality by such devices as bitonality, **polytonality** and 'progressive tonality' (in which a piece starts in one key and ends in another). Such ideas are, however, the exception rather than the rule. Throughout history and the world, in music of every kind, a sense of tonality, of a 'home base' for the sound, has been such a strong principle that some musicians even claim that it is endemic to the physics of sound, that the relationships are mathematical as well as aural, and that to use other systems flies in the face of Nature. (This is scientific and aesthetic nonsense, no more valid today

than it was when Pythagoras first put forward his views on universal harmony and the **music of the spheres**.) **KMcL**

TOPOLOGY

Topology (from Greek *topos*, 'place'), in **mathematics**, began as a generalization of the results of **analysis**. Part of this generalization is the use of **metrics**, which take the idea of distance and **axiomatize** it. Topological spaces are one step further, and lose the idea of distance totally while still making it possible to show some of the most useful results of analysis. Topology takes the basic notion to be that of the 'open set', which can be defined using distances (it is a set in which around every point, all the other points within a certain distance are also within the set), and axiomatizes the relationships between collections of open sets. (This means that anything can be called an open set provided the collection of 'anythings' satisfies the conditions laid down for relationships between open sets.) The conditions are that the empty set and the whole set of points are both open sets, that the set of points in both of a pair of open sets is also an open set, and that the set of points in at least one of the members of any collection of open sets is also an open set. Any system of open sets which satisfy these axioms is called a topological space.

The reason that many of the results of analysis are true of topological spaces in general is that the concept of **continuity** can be easily defined for topological spaces. A continuous function is one where given an open set X, the set of points mapped by the function to points in X is also an open set. (So it preserves the open set structure in a sense.)

Topology is a subject which has many applications, reflecting its generality. Another way of looking at it (or, more strictly, at one particular topological space, that of three-dimensional space) is that a continuous function is one which stretches and bends spatial objects without tearing them. For example, a mug and a doughnut are the same as far as topology is concerned, because it is possible to continuously deform one to give the other; a ball and a doughnut are not, because it is impossible to get rid of the hole in the doughnut without tearing it.

One of the most famous questions in topology, the 'four colour theorem', about the ways to colour regions on a map, has recently been solved, but its solution has led to controversy about the nature of proof (see **provability**).

Another famous result in topology is the 'hairy-ball theorem', which states (when put into non-technical language) that it is impossible to comb the hair on a ball that is covered with it without leaving tufts or ridges. (This result does also have serious consequences.) **SMcL**

TORAH see Judaism

TOTALITARIANISM

The concept of totalitarianism was first invoked by fascist ideologues in 1930s Italy. Since then it has been used, and abused, as a comparative concept in **political science** and political argument. Totalitarian régimes are conceived by political scientists as the limiting case of modern **despotisms**, only possible in industrial or industrializing societies. Totalitarian régimes are far more organizationally capable, ruthless and centrally dictated than the absolutist forms of rule found in **agrarian societies**. A totalitarian political system is dominated by a monopolistic political party suffused with the ambition to transform society, gripped by a single chiliastic and 'totalistic' ideology which pulverizes all rival and local belief systems, and which uses organized terror systematically to crush its opponents, maintains a monopoly of the mass media of communications, subordinates the legal system to political imperatives, presides over a centrally controlled economy, and is territorially expansionist. These are the key elements of the totalitarian syndrome. Others include slave labour camps, death camps and the deliberate 'checks and balances' and 'separation of powers' between the party, the bureaucracy and the secret police which enable the totalitarian dictator (or collective leadership) to maintain overall hegemony through organized fear.

Argument once raged over the usefulness of the term in describing or explaining the political systems of Nazi Germany, fascist Italy and the Marxist-Leninist régimes established after 1917. The argument used to be made that these were radically different political orders, and that to label them as structurally similar was a Cold War attempt to tarnish communist systems through associating them with fascist and nazi régimes. These arguments have diminished considerably as the merits of the totalitarian description of the USSR and Communist China became more and more transparent especially in light of the criticisms made of the Soviet and Chinese systems by those who tried to reform them. However, Western Cold War analysts of totalitarianism showed how the term could be radically abused. They dogmatically supposed that totalitarian systems could not be democratized, whereas **authoritarian** systems could. In the hands of people like Jeanne Kirkpatrick, adviser to Ronald Reagan, this argument was used to excuse American support for right-wing dictatorships – a bizarre irony given that totalitarianism was originally constructed to show what modern left- and right-wing dictatorships had in common. In history the main abuse of the term lies in its anachronistic employment to describe régimes in the ancient and medieval world. However, because a concept is abused does not mean it is thereby worthless. The concept of totalitarianism captures one dreaded configuration in modern political systems. **BO'L**

See also absolutism.

Further reading B. Barber, 'Conceptual Foundations of Totalitarianism' in C. Friedrich, M. Curtis, and B. Barber (eds.), *Totalitarianism in Perspective*; C. Friedrich and Z. Brzezinski, *Totalitarian Dictatorship and Autocracy*.

TOTEMISM

The word totemism comes from the Amerindian Ojibwa word *ote*, which means 'belonging to a local group'. In many tribal societies animal names and emblems were identified with social groups such as clans groups related by descent. Clans are often associated with animal species, plants and natural forms, which clan members take care not to injure. Early anthropologists assumed that totems represented the divinities of the clan, often ancestors of the group.

In the 19th century, theoretical debate concerning totemism was intense. Evolutionists used the belief in a mythical ancestor to explain animal emblems, sacrifices and avoidance **taboos**. Other anthropologists were concerned with understanding why particular objects of animal species were chosen as totems, and used a number of **utilitarian** and later psychoanalytic perspectives to investigate the phenomena.

In the 20th century, the functionalist Radliffe-Brown noted that in Australia exogamous (outmarrying) groups were named after birds. The rule of exogamy meant, for example, that eaglehawk men married crow women, and vice versa. He argued that totemism referred not to the mystical beliefs, but to the way humans conceived the relationship between the social and natural world.

The structuralist Claude Lévi-Strauss developed the idea that totemism resulted from a universal mode of human classification that created homologies between the natural and cultural spheres. The important factor was not the way an individual totem related to an individual clan, but how relationships between totems reflected relations between social groups. Totemism, according to Lévi-Strauss, was part of a broader cognitive system of classification, which involved divisions between **nature/culture** and female/male. The relationship posited between natural species became a way of talking about the relationship between social groups. The use of totemism as a classifying system naturalized these differences. **CL**

Further reading Adam Kuper, *The Invention of the Primitive Society;* Claude Lévi-Strauss, *Totemism.*

TOURISM, ANTHROPOLOGY OF

Tourism (from Greek *tornos*, 'lathe', 'compasses'), both domestic and foreign, is a key feature of modern societies across the world. It is a leisure phenomenon that has proliferated this century due to the increasing travel, communication and tourism industry networks, but it has had its historical antecedents as far back as recorded time in the form of explorers and merchants. Also included in the records are pilgrimages, journeys to spa-towns, the activities of colonial administrators and missionaries in Asia and Africa, and those pursuing tours for the enhancement of their own education and status, for instance the 'Grand Tours' of the 17th and 19th centuries by the sons of aristocratic or wealthy European families, who visited the great Classical and Renaissance sites, particularly in Italy.

Tourism began to receive theoretical attention in the 1970s. One school of thought considers all tours as essentially the same, likening them to **rites of passage**. This view envisages travel as a separation from the normal place of residence and familiar acquaintances. This leads to a social and spatial displacement in which everyday responsibilities are either suspended or reversed, and tourists share a sense of community in their common goals and activities while on vacation. Afterwards, there is the return home when the tourist resumes his or her mundane activities, but usually at a higher social status in view of the prestige attached to travel in the modern society.

Others claim that there is a distinctiveness about modern-day tourism due to factors such as industrialization, the availability of relatively cheap and comfortable transport, the development of paid holidays, and the re-evaluation of leisure activities as worthwhile pursuits.

In 1976, Dean MacCannel argued that as meaningful structures are 'smashed' in modern societies there is an accompanying sense of alienation. Tourism fulfils the need to search, experience and gain something authentic, a kind of nostalgia for something that is felt to be missing in the tourist's own society. Tourism is, therefore, a modern sociological version of a sacred journey, characterized by a search for something that is symbolically 'sacred', such as tourist sites, souvenirs and other tokens of travel.

More political theories suggest that tourism on a global scale is more often from the industrially-developed nations to less-developed nations. A modern form of **imperialism**, in which ideas of conquering space and subjecting other countries to the demands of the 'developed' nations continue to persist.

In 1978, Valene Smith argued against a uniform way of considering tourism and proposed different types of touristic experiences. These different experiences include cultural tourism, which has its roots in the Grand Tours, historical and ethnic tourism. There is also natural tourism (the 'sun, sea and sex' variety) and environmental tourism, for example, recreational and camping holidays. A more recent development is that of 'green' tourism, a term applied to measures and tour packages geared to preserve the environment. Similarly, Eric Cohen argued for a typology of different types of tourists. These range from tourists who continue to identify with their own society and go on holiday primarily to raise their own status back home, to those who acquire a new spiritual centre on their travels, choosing to identify with the society they have travelled to.

Further themes in the anthropology of tourism centre on how host societies accommodate tourism and the ways they interact with the tourists. The study involves considering links between sex and tourism, developmental and economic aspects of tourism, tourism's part in creating a cultural or national industry, and a focus on the visual factors of tourism, for instance in the decoding of brochure images, advertising and photography, and how together they may condition the 'tourist gaze' to concentrate only on certain aspects of tourist locations. **RK**

See also authenticity; development; status; space; visual anthropology; Westernization;

Further reading Dean MacCannel, *The Tourist: a New Theory of Leisure Class*; Valene Smith (ed.), *Hosts and Guests*; John Urry, *The Tourist Gaze: Leisure and Travel in Contemporary Societies*.

TOWN PLANNING

Town Planning in the modern world is, precisely, the preparation of plans which will be used to control the enlargements of urban areas, and contribute to the creation of a healthy, efficient, well-serviced community.

The problems of dealing with the growth of towns is a challenge to urban administrators in most organized societies; indeed, as soon as towns are developed at all, some thought must go into their organization, even if this is no more than provision for, say, fortification.

Aristotle wrote of Hippodamus of Miletus (*fl.*500 BCE) a political theorist who considered particularly the issue of towns and their organization. Hippodamus argued against the haphazard layout of Greek cities up to that time, and devised a gridiron plan for an ideal city, where the land was carefully divided into sacred, public and private spaces. In the 1st century BCE Vitruvius (architect-surveyor to the Emperor Augustus) dealt, in the first section of his treatise *De Architectura*, with the site of the city, the construction of city walls, the direction of the streets; he also commented on the importance of wind-direction and the choice of sites for public buildings.

In medieval Europe, interest was taken in fortification and in great public buildings such as cathedrals and market halls. But it was not until the **Renaissance** that there was a serious renewed interest in classical discussions of the ideal city. From this period until the 19th century the changing layout of cities and towns was largely influenced by classical example and theory, and was concerned with symmetrical and formal layouts relating to public and important ceremonial public spaces.

The modern understanding of town planning arises out of the poor conditions of housing and sanitation in the 19th century. This period had seen enormous population booms in the industrialized countries (some cities like Glasgow increasing their population tenfold between 1800 and 1900). The appalling conditions of the mass of the working population caused serious epidemics, and a variety of social and sanitary reforms led to an awareness for the need for overall strategies for towns, particularly their rapid growth and the health of their population. As a result in the late 19th century, legislation provided for public authorities to organize roads and sewerage, refuse collection and water supplies.

The improvement of housing and road systems could be used to ensure a degree of social control, such as the grand designs of Baron Haussmann in Paris in the late 19th century, sweeping away the old slums, and replacing them with wide elegant boulevards, which might allow the police and army more effective control of the populace. In the Western world, in the later 20th century, such plans have in theory come under much greater scrutiny in the democratic process.

The problems of dealing with the needs of a population and of machine and service industry simultaneously have led to different attempts to separate the population from the worst effects of insanitary overcrowded accommodation and industry. One important late–19th-century movement was the garden city ideal, of which the best examples in England, built in the early 20th century, are Letchworth and Hampstead Garden Suburb, providing humane housing in a semi-rural environment, and influencing much subsequent suburban development.

In the latter half of the 20th century, the damage caused by bombing in World War II also required a massive campaign of urban renewal throughout Europe, involving the rebuilding of housing, as well as industry and office accommodation. In the 1960s and 1970s, the continuing social challenge to public authorities to improve the quality of life for the mass of the urban population (by providing sanitary housing on a mass scale) led to the development of the tower block, described by Le Corbusier as 'the garden city on its side', and of zoning: the development of industry and commerce in separate areas. From the late 1970s both these signal tenets of modern town planning have been criticized by theorists such as the postmodernist Robert Krier, and indeed generally, as inhumane; but no one alternative seems to have been developed. JM

See also urbanism/urbanization.

Further reading W. Ashworth, The Genesis of Modern Town Planning; C. Paris, Critical Readings in Planning Theory.

TOXICOLOGY

Toxicology (Greek, 'study of poisons'), in the life sciences, is the study of the harmful effects of substances upon biological systems. The techniques of toxicology have much in common with pharmacology when the poison concerned is of chemical origin. Biological poisons (toxins and venoms) may also act as drugs, but are usually also antigenic they are bound by specific antibodies and can be sequestered within the body by the immune system. This is how antisera against poisons such as snake venom work. Toxicology involves the isolation of the agent and the elucidation of its mechanism of action. Generally, precautions can be taken to protect against exposure in the environment, as has been the case since it was discovered that asbestos was toxic. The toxicologist is also concerned with finding a treatment and an antidote for specific poisons; often it may be noted that the harmful effects could be of use in a different context. The paralytic poison curare, for example, is used in the production of poison darts by South American indians, but it also has important medical uses.

Where man develops poisons for use in pest control, it has been realized that great care must be taken to ensure that species beneficial to man are not harmed at the same time. Historically, a knowledge of poisons dates back to the first discovery that certain potential foods were best avoided. From this grew the arts of using known poisons for suicide and murder, and the detection of their use; though these sciences became highly advanced because of the rewards which were available to experts, it was not until the early 19th century that the effects of poisons on animals were systematically studied: Matthieu Orifila pioneered this field with experiments using dogs to investigate the effect of poisons in various quantities. RB

See also immunology; pharmacology; teratology.

TRADITION

Traditions (from Latin tradere, 'to hand down'), in anthropology, refer broadly to beliefs, customs and values passed down through successive generations. The ethical and moral connotations of traditions have three primary functions: to establish social cohesion; to legitimize forms of behaviour; to inculcate beliefs.

The terms 'great' and 'little' traditions were introduced in 1956 by Robert Redfield, to show that there could be local alternatives to a tradition invested with authority by the custodians of **culture**. In the case of a **world religion**, such as **Islam**, 'great tradition' referred to the textual orthodoxy of the élite, while 'little tradition' referred to folk practices often informal and orally transmitted. This distinction was useful because it illustrated the way alternative interpretations could coexist with formal, established traditions.

The concept of great and little traditions has been replaced with Michel Foucault's notion of **discourse**: a multiplicity of coexistent interpretations, rather than just two. Traditions are not always rooted in the past, though their initiators may claim that they are. Traditions may be invented as a response to new situations, legitimizing their significance in the present by recourse to the past. As an adaptive attempt to situate current solutions in some kind of cultural continuity, invented traditions are often utilized by groups such as immigrants who are concerned with maintaining a defined identity. The importance of tradition is often elevated at times of great social change or to promote a political cause. **CL**

See also authenticity; ethnohistory; religion.

Further reading E. Hobsbawn and T. Ranger (eds.), *The Invention of Tradition*.

TRADITIONAL JAZZ see **Dixieland**

TRAGEDY

'Tragedy' is Greek for 'goat-song', and no one has satisfactorily explained how the word came to have its more (or perhaps less) technical meaning. Whatever the origin of the word, tragedy is one of the two main groups into which Aristotle divided **drama** in his *Poetics* of the 4th century BCE. (The other was **comedy**.) These groups are not apparent in non-Western drama, and hardly cover the range of plays written in Europe since Aristotle's time. Nonetheless, Aristotle's account of the form and purpose of Greek tragedy (his notes on comedy are lost), and his comments on the complex of beliefs which underlie it, have crucially influenced Western drama. For Aristotle, tragedy was the imitation of reality, intended to purify its spectators by arousing 'pity and terror'. (For more on this, see entry on drama.) Basing his analyses on a few plays by Sophocles, notably *King Oedipus*, he said that the central character of a tragedy should be a noble person who is brought low because of some flaw in his or her own nature. (In Oedipus' case the flaw is persisting in seeking out a truth which he knows will destroy himself.) The hero's fall (*peripeteia*) is the nub of tragedy, and is the chief means of achieving **catharsis** (purification). At some point in the action, there should be recognition (*anagnorisis*) by the hero of his or her flaw, and of the inevitability of suffering; this is the turning-point of the play. The action of the play is structured to articulate these themes.

Although these ideas apply to only a fraction of surviving Greek tragedies – for example, they are relevant neither to Aeschylus' extant plays nor to the greatest surviving works of Euripides – they influenced the writing of Western drama for two millennia. However, epistemological shifts brought about by historical, social and religious change meant that by the **Renaissance**, Aristotle's idea of tragedy had become somewhat blurred and remote from practice. (It was closer to **opera**, the art form invented in the late 16th century to reconstruct the methods and practices of ancient tragedy.) Renaissance tragedy still sometimes dealt with the fall of kings and princes (as in Shakespeare's *King Lear*), but was equally concerned with the effect its theatrical strategies might have on audiences (Calderón's plays are excellent examples.) One of the main concerns behind this idea was the 'pity and terror' which Aristotle claimed the tragic action evoked in the spectator. The main distinction in ideas is between the religious basis for Greek tragedy and the increasingly secular nature of tragedy from the Renaissance onwards: even the *auto da fé*, the principal philosophical and stylistic influence on Calderón, was secularized in what he made of it. Increasingly, the dilemmas and suffering of ordinary human beings were seen to be possible subjects for tragedy and by the 19th century (in the **naturalistic** plays of such writers as Ibsen) they had become a far more potent subject than the downfall of the mighty. Nonetheless, and although cross-cultural forms such as those from Asian theatre practice, are beginning to be used and adapted by Western playwrights, the 'rules' postulated by Aristotle for the structure of Greek tragedy, and said by him to be intrinsic to the plays' original religious function, continue to dominate much theatre practice, and to underlie most scholarly analysis of the nature and function of tragedy, and of 'literary' theatre of every kind. **TRG KMcL SS**

Further reading Aristotle, *Poetics*; C. Leech, *Tragedy*; J. Orr, *Tragic Drama and Modern Society*.

TRAGEDY OF BLOOD see Revenge Tragedy

TRANSACTIONAL ANALYSIS

Transactional analysis, in **psychology**, is a model of mind and human interaction developed by Eric Berne. He built on Freud's model using Paul Federn's idea of ego states, that is, 'distinct states in which the ego is manifest at any time'. Berne was at pains to point out the difference between his ego-state model and the **id, ego and superego** of Freud. According to Berne there are three ego-states: Parent, Adult and Child. These are always denoted with a capital letter to separate them from other uses of the same words. A small letter refers to the real life of the parent, adult and child, but the Parent, Adult and Child ego-states refer to an internal reality. The Child ego-state uses strategies, responses and behaviours replayed from childhood; the Parent ego-state uses strategies, responses and behaviours copied from parents; and the Adult ego-state responds to the here and now, using all the skills a person has learnt so far and all the resources available to the grown-up person. Transactional analysis regards every person as moving constantly from one state to another in every phase of their lives. The Parent ego-state is not necessarily the correcting conscience of the Superego and

the Child ego-state does not describe the unconscious state of the id, but sets off feelings, thoughts and behaviours. The Adult ego-state is a purer state of response to reality, which may free itself of the Child and Parent. It is the Adult which transactional analysis wishes, as a therapy, to enlist, to help diminish the disabling other internal ego-states if they have too strong a hold on the psyche.

Communication is always seen to come from one of the ego-states and each communication is called a 'transaction', and in this methodology the sequences of these transactions are analysed, hence the name 'transactional analysis'. Because the communications often contain the strategies we learnt as children, which may no longer be working for us, transactional analysis aims to move out of what the therapy calls a fixed lifescript into **autonomy**, and the tools the adult uses for this purpose are awareness, spontaneity and a capacity for intimacy. **MJ**

Further reading Eric Berne, *Games People Play*; Ian Stewart and Vann Jones, *TA Today: a New Introduction to Transactional Analysis*.

TRANSACTIONALISM

Transactionalism (from Latin *transigere*, 'to drive through', 'to accomplish'), in **anthropology**, was a theory first advanced by Frederick Barth in 1959 to consider social processs and interactions. Barth was critical of earlier functionalist models that portrayed an overly cohesive and collective picture of society without paying due attention to the roles, relationships, decisions and innovatons of the individual. Using the examples of the Swat Pathan people in Pakistan and, later, in 1966, organization among Norwegian fishermen, Barth set out to demonstrate that social forms like kinship groups, economic institutions and political alliances are generated by the actions and strategies of the individuals deployed against a context of social constraints. By observing how people interact with each other, an insight could be gained into the nature of the competition, values and principles that govern individuals' choices, and also the way resources are allocated in society.

Barth acknowledged that transactionalist models could not be used to explain all kinds of human behaviour. Even so, criticism has been levelled at his over-reliance on economic principles, a Western perspective in which individuals are viewed as self-interested actors wishing to get the best value in exchange relationships. Individuals are thereby characterized as autonomous, independent and essentially non-social beings. This model of individualism may be incompatible with other ideas about the person and social practices. For instance, in Japanese society, it is the corporate group model that is conventionally stressed rather than individualism. It is also important to acknowledge the symbolic, cultural and religious ideas that might govern peoples' choices and decisions in their social interactions. Other anthropologists point out that Barth's transactionalist models ignore long-term historical processes while some have criticized transactionalist theories for paying insufficient attention to the structures of class and property relations in society.

However, supporters of transactionalism claim it to be a productive tool in social analyses and have adopted transactionalist models to consider the interactions between individuals as manipulations to gain power. This acts to weaken transactionalism's dependence on economic models, and allows for the investigation into how power is conceived, systematized and gained in particular communities. **RK**

See also economic anthropology; exchange; functionalism; personhood; power; social conflict; symbols.

Further reading Frederick Barth, *Models of Social Organisation*; Richard Fardon (ed.), *Power and Knowledge*; Brian Kapferer (ed.), *Transaction and Meaning*.

TRANSCENDENTAL ARGUMENTS

A transcendental (Latin, 'climbing beyond') argument, in **philosophy**, begins with certain assumptions we make, or experiences we have, and then attempts to establish the preconditions of the truth of these assumptions or of the occurrence of those experiences. So, for example, Kant begins with the experience of being aware of one's own existence, and then attempts to establish that this experience can occur only if there is an objective world: so 'the mere consciousness of my own existence proves the existence of objects in space outside me.' **AJ**

Further reading P.F. Strawson, *The Bounds of Sense*.

TRANSCENDENTALISM

Transcendentalism was an idea put forward in 1840s New England by Ralph Waldo Emerson, Henry David Thoreau and others, and promoted in Emerson's book *Nature*. Its essential statement was that there was no need for organized **religion**, for intercessors between humankind and God. Everything humankind achieved was a part of the divine: the creation of great works of art, scientific research, ordered societies, rationality itself. Self-improvement, the attempt to perfect one's human abilities, was therefore also an expression of the divine. Although the **Utopian** communities founded by the transcendentalists were themselves short-lived, the idea rooted itself deeply in the self-awareness of immigrant Americans, and led, some historians say, to the feelings of drive, self-help and organization which have been ever since claimed as unifying virtues of the USA. **KMcL**

TRANSFERENCE

Transference (Latin, 'carrying across'), in **psychoanalysis**, means the displacement on to the analyst or therapist of feelings and ideas which have been part of past relationships. When Freud's patients started to project their feelings in this way, he felt that it interfered with the analysis, as it moved him away from the exploration of repressed memories and affected the patient's ability to be objective. But by 1912 he had come to see transference as part of the process of **free association** and as an acting out of the past in the consulting room. People readily transfer and project expectations from the past onto other people, but transference in analysis is heightened by the analyst's refusal to reveal anything of himself or herself. This makes him or her a figure onto which many projections can be made by the patient: in the course of treatment the analyst will become mother, father, sister or brother of the person involved. The transference relationship and the analytic relationship are seen as separate but part of a totality of interactions.

Detailed accounts of transference usually include reference to the patient's early life with his or her parents, or as a baby and the possible object-relations in infancy that he or she had with early caring figures. All analysts now agree that the work done by the analyst on the patient's transference directly addresses situations which have arisen in childhood and infancy, and resolving these conflicts has a profound effect.

Within therapies other than analysis, transference can also mean any feelings that the patient may have for the therapist, or any feelings that are neurotically based, or feelings that are derived from infantile life. **MJ**

TRANSFORMATION

Transformation (Latin, 'shaping across'), in **mathematics**, is a type of **function**. In origin, it is an idea from **projective geometry**, based on the examples of rotations (which turn a figure about a point without altering the lengths of lines or the angles between them) and translations (which move a figure along a line without altering the lengths of lines or the angles between them). The concept proved important in linear **algebra**, where linear transformations were developed: transformations which preserve the operations of addition of vectors and multiplication by scalars.

In **genetics**, a transformation is a change in the genome of a microorganism brought about by the introduction of nucleic acid by physical or chemical means, such as microinjection of genetic material into the nucleus of an individual cell. Where the same event occurs as a result of a vector, for example a virus, the phenomenon is termed transduction. **RB SMcL**

See also gene therapy; genetic engineering.

Further reading J. Singh, *Mathematical Ideas*.

TRANSFORMATIONAL GRAMMAR

The study of transformational grammar is a linguistic enterprise which revolutionized the study of **syntax** when it first appeared in the 1950s. Noam Chomsky proposed that grammar is an independent system, quite separate from other components of language such as **phonology** or **semantics**. The grammatical component was held to comprise various sub-components, each interrelated and each characterized by the operation of rule systems which conjoined to determine those sentences which were permissible, and those sentences which were not allowed in the language (ungrammatical).

A central aim in transformational grammar was to capture the insight that certain sentence types are clearly related to one another. Consider the case of active and passive sentences:

a. Matthew drank a lot of wine. (active)
b. A lot of wine was drunk by Matthew. (passive)

Theoretically, it would be desirable to acknowledge this relationship within the grammar, rather than leaving it as an arbitrary, ungoverned linguistic artefact. This aim can be achieved by first recognizing that the sentences we hear or read are merely the end product of more abstract, underlying syntactic processes. In transformational grammar, each sentence is first characterized as an abstract deep structure, which is then passed on to the transformational component. Among other rule systems, the transformational component contains rules which deal with related sentence types. The relationship between active and passive sentences can therefore be explained in terms of their originating from a single, underlying, deep structure.

In effect, a transformational rule converts one syntactic form into another, and consequently there must be an input to the rule (known technically as a structural analysis) which contrasts with a (transformed) output (known as a structural change). Transformational rules include such operations as the movement, deletion, copying and adjoining of elements within the sentence as appropriate. Once all the relevant transformational rules have applied, the result is the so-called syntactic surface structure, which still requires the operation of the phonological component to realize the sentence as we know it in its written or spoken form. In the most recent version of Chomsky's syntactic theory, the concepts of deep and surface structure have been redefined and rechristened D- and S-structure respectively.

Throughout the 1960s, there was an explosion of research in the field of transformational grammar. Eventually, it became apparent that there was, in fact, an unhealthy proliferation of transformational rules, which raised the question of what the fundamental rationale for certain rules should be, especially if they were to retain any truly explanatory (as opposed to merely descriptive) power. There was, too, an excessive concentration on the vagaries of a single language, English, rather than on the stated ambition to discover and explain aspects of syntax common to language per se. Currently, the concept of transformation is still an axiomatic feature of the Chomskyan approach to syntax, but it is now much more heavily constrained and also more relevant to the concerns of **universal grammar**. MS

Further reading A. Radford, *Transformational Syntax*.

TRANSLATION

Translation (Latin, 'carrying across'), at one level, is a machine activity. Electronic notebooks are available which instantly render handy words and phrases in half a dozen languages, and larger computers can cope automatically with the translation of more sophisticated material (such as computer instruction manuals) with few problems. At a more complex level still, human translators stand beside dignitaries at international meetings, translating a few seconds behind their employers. Like simultaneous translation at conferences or international parliaments, this work requires an ability to do two things at once (listening and talking), but absolutely no creative skill. The translator must be as self-obliterating as the electronic notebook.

Thanks to a centuries-long bias, in the European teaching of classical languages,

towards grammatical and syntactical exegesis, it was (wrongly) assumed for generations that this kind of mechanical exactness was all that was required for literary translation. Indeed, the view was prevalent until only about 30 years ago, among academics specializing in foreign languages and literatures, that unless you were prepared to learn the language in question, you did not 'deserve' its literature. Fortunately for the majority of readers and theatre-goers, this extraordinary view has not been shared by literary translators. Fine works of **literature** from other cultures are available in a plethora of versions, and in most cases their inherent individuality and quality are perfectly apparent.

Paradoxically, because the literary translator is dealing not just with superficial meaning but with nuance, the freer the translation the more successful it can often be. An academic specialist in Goethe, for example, is likely to be expert in German and in German literature but not necessarily in the creative writing of his or her own native language. The translator of Goethe, by contrast, needs to be more of a specialist in such writing than in Goethe or Goethe's original: it is easier to find out what Goethe wrote, and meant, than it is to render that meaning in another language in a way which Goethe himself might have used, or of which he might approve. Expertise all round is the most desirable qualification, but even then, 'fidelity' to the original is a far less definable matter than it is in technical translation, and (perhaps especially) in the translation of sacred texts, where rendering of nuance has doctrinal, not to say propagandist, overtones. (This is the heart of the debate about translations of the Bible. The argument is less about language, sonorous or otherwise, than about clarification or distortion of interpretation.)

With a few outstanding exceptions (for example, among English literary translations, Urqhart's Rabelais or Rieu's Homer) translations are mainly for their own time, and should be regularly replaced. Even the literary stature of the writer is no guarantee of lasting quality: Browning's and Lowell's versions of Aeschylus, Archer's versions of Ibsen and Burton's *A Thousand Nights and One Night*, once peaks of the art, now seem laboured and obsolete, neither faithful nor with literary stature of their own. The finest 'translations' of all, perhaps, are works like Plautus' reworkings of Menander, or Shakespeare's reworkings of just about everybody (including Plautus): one powerful creative mind engaging with another. In the gaps between such lightning-strikes, the best we can hope for is an author of genius being rendered, for one generation only, by a translator of talent, or vice versa, and for a steady continuum of hackwork of real excellence, such as the translations into English of current South American or European modern fiction which obtrude the translator's personality so gently that we seem to be reading the original. **KMcL**

TRANSLATION THEORY

The problems encountered when translating a message from one language into another have concerned linguists for centuries. The knowledge and skills required to translate both written and spoken texts do not differ markedly. The so-called **semiotic** status of texts does vary, though, since written texts are held in much higher regard than their spoken counterparts. Consequently, fidelity to the author's original communicative intentions is more likely to be preserved in the case of written texts.

Linguistic theories of translation, influenced by **transformational grammar**, argue for a three-phase translation process. First, the surface form of the source language message undergoes a back-transformation into a set of kernel structures. The relatively simple kernel structures at this deep level of analysis are then translated into kernel structures in the target language (TL). Finally, a forward-transformation converts the kernel structures into recognizable TL surface forms.

Linguistic theories of this kind have been criticized for neglecting many other factors, beyond the transliteration of words and structures, which contribute to the meaning of a message. Other theories have emphasized that the overall effect of the words in a message are at least as important as the words themselves. Additionally, consideration must be given to the potential conflict between the cultural assumptions of the message-producer and the intended recipients. **MS**

See also translation.

TRANSMIGRATION OF SOULS see
Reincarnation

TRANSMISSION LINE THEORY

Transmission Line Theory, in electrical engineering, allows the analysis and design of electrical communications and power transmission systems, for example telephone lines or electric pylon lines. The theory permits transmission systems to be created that are efficient with respect to integrity of information exchanged and ensure maximum power transfer between transmitter and receiver.

The foundation of transmission line theory lies in the workings of **electromagnetism** as detailed by James Maxwell in 1873. By this time telegraphy (communication by a series of electrical pulses) was well established and growing; indeed a telegraph undersea cable had been laid across the Atlantic Ocean as early as 1858. From the telegraphers' point of view, long-distance transmission only affected the transmitted signal by attenuating it, consistent with elementary **circuit theory**, and could be tolerated. However, following the discovery and introduction of telephony in the 1870s using the existing electric cables, long-distance telephony could not be achieved due to severe distortion of the transmitted signal making speech unintelligible.

The solution to this problem appeared following the recognition and use of inductance in long cables by the Englishman O. Heaviside. Previously W.T. Kelvin had identified that a cable had a certain capacitance distributed along its length, the effect of which was to distort an electrical pulse. At the time of its discovery the effect of capacitance did not greatly perturb the telegraphers, but caused despair among those developing long-distance telephony. Heaviside's work correctly identified that proper use of inductance could cancel the effect of the capacitance and greatly reduce distortion of speech signals. This led to M.

Pupin receiving the patent in 1899 for the use of inductive coils as Heaviside had suggested, to increase the distances that telephony could be achieved over.

These newly acquired electrical concepts of capacitance and inductance were to influence many other areas of electrical engineering. Circuit theory was updated to include these two components and high frequency circuits could now be correctly analysed. Electrical filters could be produced from these two new components and were widely used in **modulation** and **multiplexing** schemes later used in radio and other communication systems.

The theory of transmission lines also introduced new mathematical methods to the study of electrical engineering, such as **complex numbers** and Laplace **transformations**. These proved to be useful in studying electric power transmission lines, defining conditions to achieve maximum power transfer while maintaining stability of the electrical generators, and implying that efficient transmission of large amounts of power should be done at high voltage. Results such as these have led to today's high voltage power network, or 'supergrid', which uses large pylons holding high voltage wires to transmit huge quantities of power from one end of the country to another.

Transmission line theory and the use of Maxwell's equations also led to other transmission systems such as microwave communications and the use of other **waveguides**. In essence this theory helped create the communications age of today, where a person takes for granted the technology to talk with someone on the other side of the planet, or indeed far out in space. **AC**

TRAUMA

Trauma is a word (originally Greek) used in **medicine** for wounds, fractures and burns, but in **psychology** it is used to describe an unexpected experience which the subject is unable to assimilate, the response being one of shock rather than physical injury. Psychodynamic therapies deal with early life traumas which have been blotted out. Trauma equals any experience mastered by mental **defence mechanisms**. Cut off from

consciousness in this way, trauma can become anxiety and develop into neurosis. In psychoanalysis, infantile trauma (deprivation and separation) can cause adult neuroses; this is a causal concept, against the will of the subject. According to Freud all neurotic illness is the result of infantile trauma. In **cognitive therapies** early trauma is seen to lead to idiosyncratic beliefs and attitudes. In **Transactional Analysis** the trauma is seen to produce a 'scripting' process whereby the person limits their own capacity for intimacy, spontaneity and awareness. **MJ**

TRIBAL RELIGION

The term 'tribal religion' is applied today to religion previously called **animism**. While 'animism' is rightly felt to be pejorative (for reasons outlined in the article on that subject), to call this complex cultural and religious phenomenon 'tribal' is to reduce it to one aspect only, and other names for it (for example 'culture of non-literate peoples' or 'religions of nature') can be equally partial and misleading. It is difficult to see, for example, why the worship of the millions of Yoruba in Nigeria and the diaspora should be classified as 'tribal' when they outnumber the adherents of **Sikhism**, classified as a **world religion**. Use of the word 'tribal' refers to the fact that all such religions began as the practice of small groups, extended families, clans or tribes, and were originally confined to the ancestral lands of these groups. The religion becomes an identifying feature of members of the group, so that even when exogamy is practised, they remain bound together by symbols and practices as well as by blood relationships.

Although the matter is complicated for scholars by the way in which tribal religion is often subsumed into so-called 'higher' religions (for example early **Christianity** or **Hinduism**), it nevertheless has a number of features which distinguish it from 'world' or 'universal' religions. There are clearly very different experiences behind religions as diverse as those of native Americans, the peoples of Africa, the indigenous peoples of Australia, Indian tribals and so on. However, certain common features can be seen. Each tribal religion is based on a particular area – often a sacred space, or containing sacred places dear to the ancestors. It has a spiritual homeland, as it were – not disembodied (like the heavenly Jerusalem of **Judaism**) but an actual geographical area. Adherents have one language, one culture, and one code of behaviour, usually governed by the fact that the members of one tribe or village do everything together (that is, hunt, farm, make tools and so on), and depend on one another for survival. The religion makes no claims to universal validity, and there is no question of mission and evangelism.

Such religions are essentially conservative, directed to preserving the stability and continuity of society. Relationships are of central importance, expressed and reinforced by **ritual** relationships between individuals, villages, the living and animals (on which the humans depend for survival) and the living and the living-dead. There are no **scriptures**: oral tradition has authority, but direct experience is considered more imporant than the word of another. A spirit-filled person, such as a diviner, prophet, priest or shaman, may speak with authority, to explain dilemmas, heal illnesses (seen as diseases of the family or of malfunctioning relationships rather than as mere physical afflictions) and resolve conflicts.

Since in such societies all life is religious, there are seldom exclusively 'religious' functionaries. The chief, the householder, the mother have sacred status, but equally the elders of either sex and the sexually immature have special access to divine wisdom, or may be used to channel it. Every action has religious meaning, and care must be taken to conform to custom and to please the ancestors. **Myth** and **legend** are used to explain the existence of the world, the gods and divine reality, and their truth is never questioned. (What we call) 'theology' is expressed in parable and proverb. Generally, religion is focused on the preservation and improvement of this present life, the here-and-now, though there is a sense of community with the ancestors who have gone before and the generations still to come. Religion is life-affirming, and a means of harmonizing humankind with the natural world.

Tribal religion makes demands on its adherents as total as those of any 'world' religion. It is in no sense expansionist, and is tolerant of other religions. One is either born into the faith or not, though some adaptation from one cult to another may come about because of marriage. In the modern world, adherents of tribal religion are vulnerable to evangelism from the world religions, but in many areas the rediscovery and renewal of ancient tribal religious belief and practice can be a major step in the assertion of individual, cultural and political identity. **EMJ**

See also tribalism.

Further reading E.B. Idowu, *African Tribal Religion, a Definition*; John B. Taylor, *Primal World Views.*

TRIBALISM

The term 'tribe' (Latin *tribus*) was originally used for territorially defined political divisions in the Roman state. In general usage, tribe is a grouping of people under a chief or headman. They were small-scale, food-producing societies categorized as 'primitive' because of their rudimentary political organization. Social relations within a tribe were based on kinship groupings.

Evolutionists, in **anthropology**, placed tribes in a schema which traced the emergence of complex states from simple hunter-gatherer societies, through tribal agriculturalists organized under chiefs. They were seen as isolated, though tribes have always bartered with outsiders and often commanded large territories through which they had easy access. Tribal societies were not primitive precursors of the modern state, but always existed together with other complex forms of society as an alternative way of life. Anthropology tended to create an image of a tribal world consisting of a mosaic of self-sufficient communities before the intrusion of European influences. Whether tribes existed as forms of social organization, except in relation to national political organizations, is debated.

Geographical boundaries are important to the concept of tribalism, which is now used to designate a demarcated group with a common ethnic identity. Tribalism is a form of identity connected with geographical and ethnic attributes of a tribe. Whether real or invented, tribalism has now become a way of making a statement about identity, in the face of attempts to control or coerce on the part of the state. **CL**

See also ethnicity; nationalism; primitivism; tradition.

Further reading P. Khouri and J. Kostiner (eds.), *Tribe and State Formation in the Middle East*; Richard Tapper (ed.), *The Conflict of Tribe and State in Iran and Afghanistan*.

TROPISM

Tropism (Greek, 'faculty of turning [towards the Sun]'), in the **life sciences**, is the phenomenon of a plant's involuntary response to an environmental stimulus which has directional orientation. The response of plants to gravity was the first tropism to be scientifically investigated, but the subject was expanded to include responses to light and wounds by Charles Darwin and his son Francis, who demonstrated that the mechanism of tropism was a curvature produced by differences in the growth on each side. Plants respond to touch and to chemicals by the same mechanism, which is co-ordinated by certain auxins (plant hormones). The term tropism has also been used to refer to bacteria, which may be motile; it has been shown that bacteria can exhibit tropism in response to magnetic forces. The use of the term in the context of animal movements is more controversial and, while simple animals, particularly single-celled animals, may respond involuntarily to stimuli such as light, ethologists prefer to use the term taxis for such animal movements. **RB**

See also endocrinology; ethology.

TRUTH

Although truth might seem to be an absolute concept, in the disciplines which need or seek to define it exactly, **mathematics** and **philosophy**, it has proved more elusive than might have been thought possible. For example, until the early 19th century mathematicians accepted that **Euclidean geometry** was a paradigm of the absolute truth of their discipline, but then the work of Bolyai and Lobachevsky demonstrated that there was more to geometry than had been suspected, and the idea of mathematics as absolute truth became invalid overnight. In modern mathematics, the **axiom of choice** involves acceptance of the fact that many results are true in one system but not in another; equally, **Gödel's incompleteness theorem** shows that 'true' and 'provable' are not always the same thing in mathematical terms, as had previously been believed.

In **logic**, truth has a restricted meaning, and is really a label with no content at all. A sentence of the propositional **calculus** is either true or false, and its truth value depends on whether the individual particles that make it up are true or false. (For example, the sentence 'A and B' is true if A and B are both true, but false if either of them is false.)

Such ideas underlie the various philosophical theories which attempt to answer the question 'What is truth?'. According to the correspondence theory of truth, a statement is true just if it corresponds to the facts, to how things are. Thus the statement that the cat is under the table is true just if the cat is in fact underneath the table, and is false just if the cat is not in fact underneath the table. A statement is true just if it stands in a certain relation – the relation of correspondence with the facts, with how the world is independently of whatever statement may or may not be made about it. One difficulty here is to say exactly what the relation of correspondence is supposed to be.

According to the coherence theory of truth, a statement is true just if it is a member of the most coherent set of statements. Thus the statement that the cat is under the table is true just if it is a member of the most coherent set of statements about the cat, the furniture and, indeed, anything else. And a statement is false just if it is not a member of the most coherent set of statements. So a statement is true just if it stands in a certain relation – the relation of coherence – with the most coherent set of statements. Truth is not a matter of the relation between statements and something else – the facts – but a matter of the relation between statements. The most obvious objection to the coherence theory is that there could be two equally coherent sets of statements, both of which are more coherent than any other sets, but which contradict each other. But two contradictory sets of statements could not both be true.

According to F. P. Ramsay's redundancy theory of truth, when one says that a certain statement is true one is doing no more that making that statement. When one says that the statement that the cat is under the table is true, one is doing no more than stating that the cat is under the table. So it is redundant to say of any statement one makes that it is true. **AJ SMcL**

See also semantics.

Further reading S.F. Baker, *The Elements of Logic*; F. Palmer, *Semantics*.

TSUNAMI see Natural Hazards

TURING MACHINES

Using the concept of the Turing machine, Alan Turing (1912–54) investigated the theoretical limits of what **computers** could do – an amazing feat, considering the primitive state of computers at the time. The Turing machine, a simple model of the computer, provided one of the main ways in which the study of **computability** could be approached, and was perhaps the easiest to comprehend intuitively because the Turing machine concept was related to the concrete idea of the computer.

A Turing machine consists of a device that will carry out a **program** with an infinite strip of paper running through it. On this piece of paper are boxes, each of which is blank, or contains a 0 or a 1. The Turing machine can read the paper and write on it, putting 0 or 1 into a blank space or erasing a written figure. The Turing machine is programmed with instructions of the form 'if you read the sequence 01001 then move six boxes to the right and erase the symbol

in this box'. The Turing machine, like a computer, uses the binary **number system**, so only needs 0 and 1.

This is very close to the way a real computer works. The actual machine represents the Central Processing Unit of the computer, where the calculations are carried out, and the paper represents the memory store, where the memory locations are either blank (unused) or contain 0 or 1. However, the Turing machine is only a theoretical device, because it is impossible to build a computer which has an infinite memory capacity.

One of the most surprising results in computability is that the main approaches to discover what a computer can do all came up with the fact that the same functions are computable, whether based on concrete models of the computer like the Turing machine or on theoretical considerations of functions. **SMcL**

TWELVE-NOTE MUSIC see Serial Music

TWO CULTURES

Two cultures was the name given in a 1959 lecture by the novelist C.P. Snow to the parties in a long-existing standoff between **science** and the **arts** (or in earlier times, science and such subjects as **religion** and **philosophy**). The problem, as stated, is that scientists have no understanding of anything outside science, and non-scientists are scientifically illiterate and innumerate. The situation is many centuries older than Snow's statement of it, and its existence has always been more a subject for chatter than an imperative to change perhaps an indication that it is less of a problem than it seems. **KMcL**

Further reading Matthew Arnold, *Literature and Science*; C.P. Snow, *The Two Cultures and the Scientific Revolution*.

TWO KINGDOMS DOCTRINE

From the inception of Christianity believers had to define the relationship between the reality of the civil authorities and the claims of faith. When the Roman Empire became officially Christian, in the 4th century, this problem became acute as bishops became embroiled in political intrigue. Constantine's heirs in Byzantium deposed patriarchs at will, while in the West, following the sack of Rome in 410, it became clear that the Church was the only stable institution in an age of turbulence and transient government. Augustine of Hippo responded in a classic work of 22 books, *The City of God*, which contrasted the *civitas Dei* ('city of God') with the *civitas terrea* ('earthly city') or *civitas diaboli* ('city of the Devil'), and it was to his writings that Martin Luther turned when rejecting the medieval alliance between emperor and pope as two forces within Christendom.

In formulating the Doctrine of Two Kingdoms (Augustine thought in terms of the city state, Luther of the new nation states of western Europe), Luther duplicated the division between Law and Gospel. Since Christian believers are justified by faith alone, they belong to the kingdom of grace and faith, and obey the law of Love. Yet they must also obey the secular ruler. 'The Gospel ... does not overthrow worldly authority, civil force and order of marriage, but rather desires that all these should be accepted as the true order, and that every one should show Christian love and good works according to his own calling and vocation.' The order of Government is in fact one of the divinely ordained orders of creation, and 'the godly prince' has a duty to intervene and reform the Church if the ecclesiastical authorities fail to correct abuses. Conversely the Church can refuse obedience if the State becomes tyrannical. Later Luther sharply distinguished the heavenly kingdom of grace and faith from the earthly kingdom of sin and death. In the kingdom to the right of God, God and Christ rule without the law through the Word and the sacraments. In the kingdom to the left of God, not Christ but the emperor with the sword rules, and all moral and civil law are placed. For Luther the Church, as the invisible community of believers, has no legal character. He used the Two Kingdom Doctrine to condemn the peasants of Saxony who rebelled in the name of Christian freedom against oppressive feudalism and extortionate taxes. **KDS**

Further reading W.A. Visser't Hooft and J.H. Oldham, *The Church and its Function in Society*.

TYPES AND TOKENS

Tokens, in **philosophy**, are particular instances of a type of thing. Types are sorts or kinds of things. Suppose that, overcome with regret, I say 'I'm sorry', pause and then repeat, 'I'm sorry', then I have said the same thing twice. I have made two utterances of the same type, but I did make two utterances. I produced two tokens of the same type.

The distinction between types and tokens is often important. For example, it enables us to distinguish between two forms of the **identity theory**, the theory that mental events are physical. The type identity theory holds that mental types are physical, that, for example, the mental type pain is identical to the physical type C-fibre stimulation. This entails that all pains are C-fibre stimulations. A weaker and perhaps more plausible version of the identity theory is the token identity theory. This states that every token mental event is physical. Every pain is physical, but while some may be C-fibre stimulations other may be D or E type stimulations. **AJ**

See also universals and particulars.

TYPIFICATION

Typification, in **sociology**, refers to the fact that the bulk of life-knowledge refers not to the individual or unique qualities of things or persons, but to their typical or broad features. A stereotype is a one-sided, exaggerated and normally prejudicial view of a group which is usually associated with **racism** or **sexism**. **DA**

See also assimilation; ethnicity; ethnomethodology; feminism; gender; phenomenological sociology; role; social closure; social construction of reality; sociobiology; status.

U

UNCERTAINTY PRINCIPLE

The uncertainty principle is one of the most

important consequences of quantum mechanics. In its most general form, it states the accuracy with which we may carry out a measurement of two properties of a system. This will be determined by a mathematical relationship between the two properties. The most common pair of measurable properties that we apply this principle to are position and momentum.

We may understand the position-momentum uncertainty principle if we think about trying to accurately measure the position of a particle. If we wish to see where the particle is, we must shine light on it. Only by detecting the light which is reflected from its surface may we know its position. However, light may be thought of as being composed of particles itself, called photons. Each photon possesses momentum of its own, and when it strikes the particle, it gives the particle a small 'kick'. Thus by measuring its position accurately, we have altered its momentum. We can never measure the position of the particle without imparting an uncertain amount of momentum to it. It is possible to show by similar arguments that we cannot measure momentum withtout increasing the position uncertainty.

The mathematical statement of the positino-momentum uncertainty principle is the equation

$$\Delta x \Delta p_x \geq \tfrac{\hbar}{2}$$

Here x is the uncertainty in position, px the uncertainty in momentum, and h is a very small number, 6×10^{-34}, known as Planck's constant. The fact that Planck's constant is so very small is the reason that we never come across the effect in our everyday lives.

Recently it has been proposed that it may be possible to do better than the uncertainty principle in some parts of a system, at the expense of greater uncertainty in other parts of the system. This process is known as 'squeezed states', and initial results are promising. **JJ**

See also de Broglie waves; quantum theory; wave-particle duality of light.

UNCONSCIOUS

The unconscious, the idea that not all ideas must be conscious to effect mental life, was proposed by Johann Herbart, an influential philosopher of the early 19th century. He also wrote that ideas could vary in intensity and energy, and that those with a certain level of energy could become conscious. His writings had an important influence on Freud's thinking.

Freud thought that the unconscious was not only a large area of stored experience and thought, but also an active mental area. This was shown by the fact that his patients could not explain, consciously, many aspects of their behaviour, except by **free association** which could eventually get back to the unconscious input. These Freud called the unconscious determinants of human behaviour. When he used the word unconscious he meant it in a dynamic sense: it is entirely unconscious and cannot be accessed directly, but only through interpretation of behaviours which result from unconscious pressures. The unconscious is ideas incapable of entering into the conscious part of the mind, but which nevertheless exert an enormous influence on our actions. **MJ**

Further reading Sigmund Freud, *The Ego and the Id* chapter 1; Merton M. Gill, *Topography and Systems in Psychoanalytical Theory.*

UNDERGROUND

The Underground was a 1960s movement whose members were concerned to drop out of advanced industrial **society**, using its artefacts but rejecting its philosophy and values. The movement was part of the general feelings of protest and liberation current at the time, and became associated with such phenomena as flower power, the adoption of Eastern religious and meditative practices in the West, and advocacy of such ideals as universal equality, an end to war and a rejection of every kind of complexity in human existence. Characteristic underground art forms were protest songs (whose musical style hybridized folk song and **pop**, and which covered the range of expression from nursery-rhyme-like innocence to the wished-for ruderies of Punk Rock); **poetry** (also using folk styles) which was philosophical, ironical or both; 'adult comics' and a huge variety of manuals on how to survive on the margins of society. We now live in a post-underground age, in which the ideal of a free-living, free-swinging lifestyle has been absorbed by young people worldwide (fostered by advertisements and consumer-manipulation of every kind), and 'mainstream' fine artists, designers, musicians, performers and writers have assimilated and worked on underground ideas to such an extent that they are part of the mainstream: chief signifiers, not to say modifiers, of what we are. **KMcL**

UNDERSTANDING (OR VERSTEHEN)

When used in **sociology** *verstehen* (German, 'understanding') normally means 'meaningful understanding', that is the procedure by which individuals in society and sociologists interpret and are able to appreciate the meanings of others.

The concept of *verstehen* formed part of a critique within sociology of those who asserted that human actions could be studied from the outside, using the same methods as those used in the natural sciences. It was introduced into sociology by Max Weber (1881–1961), who believed that the job of sociology was to gain access to and recognize the meanings that people gave to their actions. *Verstehen* refers to the procedure by which sociologists can have access to the meanings of a situation for the individuals they study. It involves placing oneself in the position of those one wishes to study in order to appreciate the meaning they give to their action, what their purposes are, and the ends they believe will be served by their action.

Weber wished to take *verstehen* further by combining interpretation of action with causal explanation. Within sociology, however, there is some debate as to what he actually meant by this. Some have suggested that Weber meant that the meanings in themselves could function as causes of behaviour, others have suggested that he intended *verstehen* to be a way of generating universal causal laws. Weber does in fact seem to make references to 'causes' in both these senses. This has led some to conclude that within sociology as a whole Weber's approach represents a half-way location between a purely 'positivist' position, which has no place for the meanings of individuals in explanations of social behaviour, and 'interpretative' sociology, which has no place for causal analysis. For Weber, sociology should go as far as it could in making sociology a science, but not so far that the meanings of the individuals studied becomes lost. **DA**

See also action perspective; agency-structure debate; ethnomethodology; functionalism; idiographic; individualism; naturalism; phenomenological sociology; positivism; social realism; structuralism; structure; suicide; symbolic interactionism; values.

Further reading W. Outhwaite, *Understanding Social Life*.

UNEVEN DEVELOPMENT

The existence of dramatic differences in levels of economic development, whether at a world scale (in the form of differences between developed and less-developed countries), or at a continental scale (such as the north-south divide in Europe), or at a subnational scale (for example the differences between the southeast and the rest of the UK) are debated by geographers and economists as examples of uneven development. Even as a descriptive concept, there are debates about how best to characterize unevenness, but the most profound disagreements are about explanations.

According to neoclassical **economics**, uneven development should be self-correcting because less-developed areas will have low costs for land and labour and hence attract investment from high-cost areas. There are some examples of this, especially the appearance of the newly-industrializing countries in the 1970s, but often unevenness seems extremely persistent over time. This point is emphasized by Marxists, who stress that more developed status at one time tends to lead to a concentration of economic and often of political **power**, which can be used to ensure that future investment largely favours the more developed area, and so that advantage becomes cumulative. This fits well with the

UK government's adoption of policies which favour the southeast and with US domination of the World Bank and IMF.

However, there are some exceptions to the perpetuation of advantage. British capital, for example, has been keen to invest abroad and the West Midlands region of England has plummeted from privilege to deindustrialization. Conversely, economies in the Far East have advanced rapidly in relation to Europe and the US. A third set of arguments, under the title 'spatial divisions of labour', suggests that the pursuit of profit and growth uses the differences between places in different ways at different times to produce changes which are neither self-correcting nor self-perpetuating. This argument is more difficult to refute than the two earlier positions, and has the merit of directing attention to the detailed reasons for persistence and change in unevenness. But its critics object that it is more a detailed description than a general explanation. **PS**

Further reading D. Massey, *Spatial Divisions of Labour*.

UNIFIED FIELD THEORY

This theory, in the physical sciences, is concerned with showing that all forces and interactions, though they may seem very different, are in fact aspects of one fundamental force, which existed at the beginning of the universe. This idea, attractive though it may seem, has no guarantee of being true. But present theories appear to indicate that it may well be the case.

In order to test ideas about the early universe, scientists attempt to re-create conditions at that time in high-energy particle accelerators. The early universe contained **particles** possessing enormous energies, and only by imparting similar energies to particles today can we hope to approximate those conditions.

All forces, for example **gravity** or **electromagnetism**, act by interchange of field particles. Unified field theory attempts to show that all these forces and their respective field carriers are the same at high energies. The first example of unification of forces was James Maxwell's equations, which combine the phenomena of electricity and magne-

tism in one elegant theory, and show that electricity and magnetism are just different aspects of the electromagnetic interaction.

As the universe cooled, the forces began to separate. First to branch away was gravity, which is perhaps why gravity is so very different from all the other forces. The next was the strong nuclear force, followed by the weak nuclear force, leaving the electromagnetic force. It was shown in the 1960s that the electromagnetic and weak nuclear forces are essentially the same energies that may be achieved in modern accelerators, and that at these energies, their field particles, the photon and the Z boson, are the same. Grand unified theories attempt to do the same for the strong nuclear force, but these theories are hampered by the fact that no accelerator is large enough to test them. Gravity is proving to be very difficult to include, and its field carrier, the graviton, has never been detected. **JJ**

See also weak force/strong force.

UNIFORMITARIANISM

Uniformitarianism was a theory put forward by James Hutton in 1785, to explain how the Earth's rocks, continents and mountains had been formed. Until then, most people had accepted the idea that they were created instantaneously, by God or the gods, at a fixed moment in time – one 17th-century Christian prelate, James Ussher, even identified the year as 4,004 BCE – or had explained geology in terms of catastrophes like Noah's flood. However, Hutton, believed that his approach was consistent with the existence of a divine designer, though one working over very much longer timescales than that envisaged by the book of Genesis. Given the slow rate of processes, such as erosion and deposition, let alone that of evolution, uniformitarianism implies a much longer timescale than anyone had previously contemplated: hence Hutton's dictum 'no vestige of a beginning, no prospect of an end'.

Hutton argued that many natural processes are cyclical. For example, land is uplifted to form hills which are then eroded to produce particles, which are transported and redeposited as soil or sediment. Indeed, he recognized that continuous destruction was needed to produce the soil which forms the necessary basis for plants and animals. In the longer term, he recognized that marine sediments could be uplifted to form new mountains.

A dispute that for a time overshadowed that between Uniformitarians and Catastrophists concerned the origins of granite. Hutton argued that this had formed by solidification from molten rock, but recognized that some granites were geologically quite recent. He was opposed by the so-called Neptunists, led by Werner, who argued that all rocks, including granite, had formed by precipitation from the universal ocean. Although it is now clear that Hutton was right, the Neptunists were more widely influential for decades after his death.

Such controversies, however, hardly affected the widespread acceptance of Hutton's views at the time among scientists in general, and the feeling that rationality (as opposed to superstition) was at last entering discussions of the origin of the Earth. Uniformitarianism inspired research in other areas, and led to even more radical proposals such as Darwin's theory of **evolution** by **natural selection**. They caused an uproar, nonetheless, among **fundamentalist** Christians and began a standoff between science and some Christian sects which persists today.

One interesting 20th-century development in the field is the realization that the 'normal processes' described by Hutton include occasional catastrophic events, such as meteorite impacts and huge volcanic eruptions. Modern thinking, therefore, although it still dismisses the need for divine intervention, has moved back some of the way towards catastrophism. **PS**

Further reading James Hutton, *The Theory of the Earth*; James Ussher, *Annals of the Old and New Testament.*

UNITIES, THE

In the 17th century, neoclassical critics elevated and distorted Aristotle's discussion (in *Poetics*) of some aspects of theatrical verisimilitude into a set of rigid prescriptions, called the Unities of Time, Place, and Action. According to these rules, the represented action of a play should not be longer than a day, it should have unity of action with no digressions, and it should take place in one location (sometimes interpreted to mean one town, thus permitting different locations within the town). Although the Unities made a considerable impact on European critics and on some French dramaturgy between the 17th and 19th centuries, they did not offer the universal model of playwriting that their supporters claimed for them. **TRG SS**

See also drama; epic theatre; naturalism; tragedy.

UNIVERSAL GRAMMAR

Universal grammar (UG), in **linguistics**, is the syntactic theory developed by Noam Chomsky and his followers in the 1980s. The ultimate goal of UG is to explain how all normal children manage to learn the complexities of their native language in such a short time. This achievement is made more remarkable with the assertion that each child comes to know certain linguistic facts which could not possibly have been learned from the limited samples of language he or she is exposed to. This so-called poverty of the stimulus, nevertheless, does not prevent successful language acquisition, which leads Chomsky to assert that specific aspects of linguistic knowledge must be genetically determined. A note of caution is necessary here, since the presumed poverty of the stimulus is more an article of faith in UG theory than a proven fact.

The child does not inherit knowledge of a particular language, such as Chinese or Swahili, but instead inherits a system of universal grammar, comprising syntactic principles, which underpin the organization of all known (or possible) languages. Although UG principles account for the underlying similarities among human languages, there is nevertheless a manifest wealth of linguistic diversity which also requires explanation. A great deal of this diversity, including details of lexical differences, are described by Chomsky as superficial and unlikely to cause significant problems for the language-learning child.

Other aspects of variation, though, are explicable in terms of UG, through the operation of parameters of variation. An example is provided by comparing the order of words in English phrases such as 'near the post office', with the Japanese counterpart, in which the word order is reversed to give, literally, 'post office near' (*yuubinkyoku-no-chikaku*). This and many other facts about word order are all explained by a single parameter of variation. English chooses one option for word order, Japanese an alternative option. Crucially, the differences between the two languages stem from a single, universal characteristic of human language. Principles and parameters aim to capture what is syntactically possible in human language. As a result, language-specific rules of grammar, which generate particular sentences, can be abolished. Instead, strings of words are judged to be grammatically well-formed as long as they do not violate any of the precepts of universal grammar. **MS**

See also learnability; modularity.

UNIVERSALIZABILITY

Kant held that any moral judgement about a particular is universalizable to all similar particulars. That is, if I judge that 'Tom ought to keep his marriage vows', then I commit myself to the universal judgement that 'everyone in the same position as Tom ought to keep their marriage vows'. R. M. Hare has claimed that a judgement is a moral judgement only if it is universalizable. **AJ**

See also morality.

Further reading R.M. Hare, *The Language of Morals*; Kant, *Groundwork of the Metaphysics of Morals*.

UNIVERSALS AND PARTICULARS

Universals, in **philosophy**, are the features or qualities which many objects may share. Redness and squareness are both universals, since they are features or qualities which many objects share: all red objects possess the former universal, all square objects possess the latter.

Particulars are the things or objects which possess universals. This pillar box is a particular and so is that scarf, and they both possess the universal redness: they are both instances of the universal redness.

Realists about universals hold that universals have a reality distinct from their instances that universals exist distinct from the particulars which possess them. Platonists treat universals as having an existence independent from their instances: not merely are there things which possess the quality of being red, but the universal redness also exists. Advocates of this view can thus hold that those universals of which there are no instances nevertheless exist. The universal leprechaunhood exists, even though there is no particular individual which possesses – it even though there are no leprechauns.

Conceptualists hold that universals are in the first instance ideas or concepts in the mind. Unlike realists, they hold that universals have no reality or existence independent of the mind. We have an idea or concept of redness and any object which resembles our idea, or satisfies our concept of redness, has the universal redness. One problem here is that it is seemingly arbitrary which ideas or concepts minds form in the first place. We group together certain objects as red because they resemble our idea or satisfy our concept of redness, but the concept we form is not constrained by any universals existing independently of particulars or by any resemblances between particulars.

Nominalists claim that objects which possess the same universal do resemble each other. Universals do not exist independently of their instances. But it is not simply arbitrary that we group certain things together as being red. Rather, we group certain things together as being red because they resemble each other in respect of their colour. **AJ**

Further reading D. Armstrong, *Universals and Scientific Realism*; B. Russell, *Problems of Philosophy*.

URBAN ANTHROPOLOGY

Urban (from Latin *urbs*, 'city') **anthropology** emerged as a sub-discipline during the 1960s in order to concentrate on issues to do with people living in or moving to urban environments. There were two factors that led to the formation of urban anthropology. One concerned the need to shake off the myth, both in popular and anthropological imagination, that anthropology is solely about the study of small, isolated and 'primitive' communities. The other focused on the need to consider people everywhere, particularly when the transition from rural to urban forms of **society** (urbanization) was becoming a widespread global phenomenon.

The Chicago school of urban anthropology took the lead in considering rural and urban forms of society. In 1956, its most prominent theorist, Robert Redfield, developed the theoretical construct of a folk-urban continuum from his studies of Mexican communities. This was intended to account for the differences between folk society and urban society. A folk society was ideally small in size, isolated, homogeneous, preliterate and one in which kinship ties and sacred beliefs organized social and cultural life. Urban society was considered to involve the opposite of all these features. Redfield believed that any community could be placed along this continuum from folk to urban depending on the kinds of characteristics it had. Implicit within this scale was the idea that simpler or folk forms of society would evolve to complex social forms with time.

Later anthropologists held that Redfield's idea of folk and urban societies did not correspond to any actual community. They also pointed out that it was more useful to consider the way folk and urban societies are part of a larger social, political and economic environment, rather than considered as separate poles on a continuum. Debate has also focused on what is meant by the term 'urban' or its synonym, city. Whether it should be a reference to population sizes and densities, an industrial or market-based economy, or ideas about social complexities, little consensus has been reached in defining the terms for considering societies worldwide. It has been noted that Western ideas about the city as a major commercial centre are not applicable to all types of cities. Some cities are con-

sidered primarily as the loci for government and religion. Cosmological ideas attached to the geographical space of a city may also mark it off as an important place. City planning internally may show divisions that one normally associates with rural places. For instance, in several Indian cities, spatial segregation of caste groups and other traditions usually associated with rural societies continue to be found.

Recent trends in urban anthropology have looked at migration patterns to urban centres, the social and cultural dimensions of communities within an urban setting, and how ties may be retained with the home village. Attention has also been given to slum settlements or shanty towns that have developed around non-Western cities because of the large influx of people. Within urban settings, inter-ethnic relations both in Western and non-Western societies have been considered. Finally, studies on leisure activities and changes have lent insights into the lifestyles, values and ideas of urban populations. **RK**

See also caste; development; modernization; scarcity; space and time; tourism; Westernization.

Further reading U. Hannerz, *Exploring the City*; Aidan Southall (ed.), *Urban Anthropology*; P.D. Wiebe, *Social Life in an Indian Slum*.

URBANISM/URBANIZATION

Urbanization, in **anthropology**, refers to the development of towns and cities, and more specifically to a growth in the proportion of a country's population living in urban centres. The world's first cities appeared in about 3500 BCE. In traditional societies cities were small and only a small proportion of the population lived in them; in industrial societies between 60 and 90 per cent do. The urbanization of the Western industrialized societies in the 19th century was very rapid. In this century the urban population increased as a result of migration from the countryside. Urbanization is occurring very rapidly in the Third World also, though this is due to the sheer increase in the size of the population rather than solely to migration from rural areas. In Europe, urbanization and industrialization did occur generally at the same time, but there is some debate as to the exact nature of this association. Urbanism was used by Louis Wirth to denote the distinctive characteristics of urban social life: the loss of primary (kin) relationships, weaker social control, an increased **division of labour**, greater importance of the mass **media** and the tendency for people in urban areas to treat each other instrumentally.

Urbanism, in **architecture**, is a term used to describe both the phenomenon of urbanization in modern industrialized societies (that is, the concentration of the working population into urban areas) and more specifically the rational school of **town planning**. This sense of the term, fashionable in architectural circles in the 1980s, seems to have derived from the French word *urbanisme* and has taken on connotations of '**neoclassical**' town planning: formality of layout focused on clearly defined public spaces. It can also be identified with the notion that life in a town has a quality distinct from that in a suburb or a country village.

The term 'Urbanism' is frequently used in the discourses of late–20th-century neoclassical theorists, such as the Belgian Krier brothers. They argue for a radical approach to town planning, for a unity of design, whole streets and squares being laid out on the classical model, as opposed to the individualistic architecture of **modernism** (impressive buildings designed either without attention to context, or specifically to challenge the existing context). The Kriers argue against some of the principal tendencies of modern town planning which has been (for reasons of efficiency, transport, health and administration) to separate cities into different zones for different functions, such as residential and industrial. One of the principal effects of such zoning in the 20th century was the provision of housing in multi-storey tower blocks of gigantic scale. The Kriers' view draws much of its inspiration from town planning of the Georgian era in England, itself neoclassical in inspiration, and seeks to create environments of mixed use, made up of buildings of human scale, in consistent materials, with a common style.

This **postmodernist** brand of Urbanism might be called '**Utopian**' in a traditional, even ideological sense, associated with traditional philosophical speculation on the subject of an 'ideal city' which dates back to the earliest theorizing on the subject. **DA JM**

See also community; contextualism; convergence thesis; globalization; social mobility; society; theories of modernity.

Further reading A.N. Cousins, et al., *Urban Life: the Sociology of Cities and Urban Society*; J. Friedmann, R. Wulff, *The Urban Transition*; P. Hall, *The World Cities*; R. Hertz, and N. Klein, *Twentieth Century Art: Theory: Urbanism, Politics and Mass Culture*; C. Jenks, *Architecture Today*.

UT PICTURA POESIS

Ut Pictura Poesis (Latin 'as is painting, so is poetry') is a tag from Horace's didactic poem *Ars Poetica* ('The Art of Poetry'). Horace's intention was to point up a similarity between the arts of painting and **poetry**, especially with regard to **imitation**. They both not only represent the appearance of the world and the actions of beings in it, but also improve on Nature through the means of **art**. Its importance is primarily for fine art and rests principally on the justification it gives the painter on two points: (1) to be regarded as the practitioner of a liberal art (poetry was so considered by the ancient world); (2) to establish **history painting**, that is, painting which most closely resembles the subject matter of classical poetry, as the preeminent genre.

In the 16th to 18th centuries especially, the notion provided the principal starting point for discussion of the arts in Europe, notably in the 17th-century French Academy. A closer study leads one to suspect that part of the complexity is based on nothing more than semantic laxity. In the 18th century Gothold Lessing argued, in *Laokoön*, that the doctrine had caused unnecessary confusion in the arts – a point that was taken up in the 20th century by the modernist Clement Greenberg in *Towards a Newer Laocoön*, when he argued that each art should address concerns proper to it, and not those of another art form. **MG PD**

UTILITARIANISM

Utilitarians (from Latin *utilis*, 'useful') believe that we ought to do whatever will maximize well-being. In **philosophy**, therefore, it is a form of **consequentialism**, with the desired consequence being happiness. Recently, utilitarians have divided into two camps: act utilitarians and rule utilitarians. Act utilitarians wish to maximize the happiness generated by each individual act, while rule utilitarians are concerned to choose the best pattern of action or behavioural disposition. (They often claim that they can thereby avoid the act utilitarians' ruthless conclusion that 'ends justify the means'.)

To illustrate, we can imagine a situation in which I promise my father on his deathbed that I will use all his money to build a mausoleum for him, even though the money is needed to educate his grandchildren. The act utilitarian would advocate breaking this promise so as to maximize happiness, especially if the promise was secret and my breaking it will go unnoticed and so won't undermine the system of promising. The rule utilitarian would insist that what I ought to do is to cultivate a disposition in myself to keep promises, a disposition which is, on the whole, extremely beneficial to all concerned, though it may not be so in this particular case. If I start breaking promises when I think it advantageous, this will undermine the disposition, open the way for mistakes, and remove the social benefits which derive from my automatically keeping promises.

As a form of consequentialism utilitarianism is open to the objections which face all consequentialists. However, further objections apply particularly to the utilitarian's moral theory. They centre on how one should construe the notion of the greatest happiness of the greatest number. First, it is difficult to see how to measure happiness or well-being. How, for example, does one weigh the pleasure derived from an hour of creative writing against the pleasure derived from an hour of television watching? Which is worse, the pain of arthritis or the pain of an unsatisfactory marriage? Secondly, even if we have some way of quantifying well-being, surely we should make an effort to ensure that it is equitably distributed. A society in which 50% of the population is in ecstasy while 50% are thoroughly miserable is less desirable than one in which none is either. But if we are simply after the greatest quantity of happiness and are unconcerned with its distribution, this kind of consideration will not matter. **AJ**

See also deontology.

Further reading R. Hare, *Utilitarianism and Beyond*; B. Williams and J.J.C. Smart, *Utilitarianism For and Against*.

UTOPIANISM

Utopianism (from Greek *outopia*, 'nowhere', or more likely *eutopia*, 'good place' – and sometimes called Atlanteanism, after the mythical Greek kingdom of Atlantis) is the imagining of ideal societies. It has been a common literary and philosophical activity, and takes in works as diverse as Plato's *Republic*, Thomas More's *Utopia* (which gave the activity its name), and Samuel Butler's *Erewhon*. Much travel writing and even anthropological writing (for example, Margaret Mead's books about Samoa) is also tinged with it: the urge to find excellence in places and societies unlike our own. As this implies, Utopianism often draws comparisons with the state of the writer's own society, usually to its disadvantage – Swift's *Gulliver's Travels* is a notable example. Many 20th-century writers, both mainstream (such as Anthony Burgess, Aldous Huxley and George Orwell) and **sf** (J.G. Ballard, Frank Herbert and George Turner) have imagined alternative societies which are terrible rather than seductive, and this kind of literature has been named dystopian (from Greek *dystopia*, 'bad place').

The writings of political Utopians, whether theoretical or **fiction**, can be differentiated in two ways. First, the Utopian vision can be ascetic, like that of Plato, Moore and Rousseau: frugality and simplicity are considered virtues, and the institutionalization of these traits removes the corrupting possibilities of greed and egoism. Alternatively the Utopian vision can be materialist: plenty, abundance, indeed cornucopia characterize the perfect society, and the abolition of scarcity resolves the problems of politics. Ascetic Utopias had great appeal in agrarian societies – although they are making a comeback in green and 'postindustrial' political thought, and they have never disappeared from Christian-inspired and monastic social thinking. Materialist Utopias, by contrast, are characteristic of industrial societies, and have been particularly common among writers inspired by **anarchism** or **socialism**, though there have also been libertarian Utopias.

Second, the Utopian vision can be either egalitarian or hierarchical. Thus as regards the functional division of labour William Morris's *News from Nowhere* is egalitarian whereas Plato's *Republic* praises a **caste**-like order; while relations between the sexes are feminist in Plato's *Republic* Rousseau's writings are now considered sexually 'incorrect'.

The technique of the Utopian author is to extrapolate some principle, ideal or trait of an existing society, and to work through the consequences of its full expression; or, alternatively, to elaborate the repercussions of abolishing some social institution (like private property , or monogamy) or radically transforming it. Utopian thought is considered by some to be purely fanciful, mere entertainment. For others its virtue lies in its capacity to extend the range of what is considered possible or thinkable and to provide regulative ideals for the conduct of political activity. The converse position, common among conservatives, condemns Utopianism because it encourages people to believe in the prospects of heroic or large-scale re-engineering of society: given that axiomatic belief in the imperfectibility of humans and the human condition is the hallmark of conservatives, it is not surprising that Utopianism attracts their ire.

In the centuries following the first European explorations of America and Australasia, a few hardy souls set out to form real Utopian communities. Unfortunately, in every social, intellectual and ethical Eden,

the serpent of human nature sooner or later reappeared. Nonetheless, the vision remained, and still remains. As that great socialist and satirist Wilde once put, 'A map of the world that does not include Utopia is not even worth glancing at.' **KMcL BO'L**

Further reading B. Frankel, *The Post-Industrial Utopians*; B. Goodwin and K. Taylor, *The Politics of Utopia: a Study in Theory and Practice*; F.E. Manuel and F.P. Manuel, *Utopian Thought in the Western World*; J. Passmore, *The Perfectibility of Man*.

V

VAISHNAVISM

Vaishnavism springs from the worship of the god Vishnu. In the *Rig-Veda* he is only a minor god, but already he is striding across worlds. Worship of Vishnu was greatly expanded when he was associated with a series of *avatars*: 'For the promotion of the good and the destruction of evildoers, and for the re-establishment of *dharma* I come into being in successive ages.' These incarnations are generally held to be fish, boar, man-lion, dwarf, Parasu-Rama (who terminated the Kshatriya class), Rama (the hero of the *Ramayana*), Krishna and **Buddha**. Finally, he will appear as Kalki, to inaugurate a new age.

Vaishnavism also involves worship of Lakshmi, Vishnu's popular consort, the goddess of good fortune whose festival Divali (or Deepavali) is a feast of lights joyously celebrated by all Hindus. **EMJ**

VALUES

The concept of values is a term used by **social scientists** to refer to generalized, abstract ideas held by human individuals or groups about what is desirable, proper, good or bad. Differing values are an important aspect of the diversity of human **cultures**. What individuals value is strongly influenced by the culture of the **society** in which they happen to live. The concept of values is particularly important for the **functionalist** school of thought within the social sciences. Proponents of this school believe that through the process of **socialization** values become internalized (see **internalization**) by individual members of society, and these values are used to guide their activities. According to this perspective, it is this value consensus which provides the basis of **social order**.

In **Marxist** sociology, value has an entirely different meaning: it refers to the quantity of labour power, measured in units of time, which on average is necessary to produce a commodity. Marx recognized that value in this sense did not correspond to actual prices. It was this discrepancy that Marx believed best revealed the social relations underlying the capitalist economy.

Another sense in which the concept of values is used within social science is with reference to ethical ideals and beliefs about how things ought to be, in particular where such views are held to be unscientific. Value freedom is the view that sociology can and should conduct research scientifically excluding any influence of the researchers' values. Max Weber argued that even if sociologists were unable to exclude all biases introduced into their work by their own values they could at least make clear what these values are and how they affect their work.

The notion of value freedom, or neutrality as it is sometimes called, also operates at an institutional level. It is argued that academic sociologists should not use their professional status as teachers to dictate values to students. On the issue of value freedom a number of objections have been made. It is argued that even if researchers personally declare value neutrality, it is still possible for values unwittingly to intrude into research. Indeed, it is argued, that it is not clear whether value neutrality, even in principle, is actually possible. Finally, some suggest that maybe value neutrality is not always desirable and that on some questions at least nobody should be neutral. **DA**

See also consensus theory; norm; positivism; role; social integration; social stratification; society; sociology of knowledge.

Further reading P.S. Cohen, *Modern Social Theory*.

VARIATION THEORY

Variation theory, in **linguistics**, as pioneered by William Labov in the late 1960s, is concerned with the fact that languages possess a whole range of resources for producing a given linguistic expression. The spectrum of variation exists at every level of the linguistic system, from the way we pronounce certain words to the syntactic forms we choose. Geographical variation is apparent, even in monolingual countries, from the various dialects which characterize particular regions. And social variation is evident when the particular forms of language used are influenced by the social class of the speaker.

Linguistic variation between groups of people is compounded by the variation which exists within the speech of each individual. For example, English speakers in New York sometimes pronounce the *r* sound in words like 'car', 'floor' and 'fourth', and at other times they omit it. Beyond the finding that all speakers fluctuate between the inclusion and omission of *r*, Labov showed that speakers from a high socioeconomic level tend to pronounce *r* relatively often. However, *r* inclusion is more frequent in the speech of all speakers when they are paying careful attention to their speech in a formal setting. Evidently, the influence of social class interacts with the particular setting to determine which speech variant is chosen. In this way, Labov provided the crucial insight that linguistic variation is not at all random, but is in fact both predictable and systematic. **MS**

See also sociolinguistics.

VEDIC RELIGION

The Vedas are the Hindu sacred **Scriptures**. Although interpretation has varied, their authority is unchallenged. The question of authenticity does not arise because they do not derive their authority from authorship but from their contents, and are seen as the vehicle of divine revelation.

The oldest of the Vedas is the *Rig-Veda*, a collection of 1,017 hymns made for the benefit of the priests responsible for invoking the gods at sacrifices. They reveal an optimistic people seeking divine favour in the form of material advance. The *Sama-Veda* is a collection of chants for the cantor, and the *Yagur-Veda* a group of rules for sacrifice. All have the *Brahmanas* commentary and explanation interleaved. The *Artharva-Veda* is completely different, being a collection of spells which may have originated from the Sudra classes.

The Vedas merge into the Upanishads via the 'Discourses in the Forest'. **Religion** now becomes internalized, speculative and deeply devotional. Classic Hindu pantheism emerges. Already the late-Vedic hymns refashion older poems to give answers to burning questions. The ideas of intellect (*buddhi*) and of the soul emerge. (Originally soul was 'breath', as in the Old Testament.) The immortality of the soul is simply asserted in beautiful **poetry**. There are no philosophical arguments.

In later times, the Vedic gods declined, and minor gods became more important, most notably Vishnu. Almost all are male and benign. The most important Vedic gods are Varuna, the Supreme Being, the celestrial Brahman *par excellence*, Agni, god of fire and sacrifice (now only invoked at weddings and funerals), and Indra (god of the storm). Indra is the supreme Aryan warlord; he has Maruts, storm gods, to assist him, and prefigures Krishna with his exploits. He is king by right of conquest, and gradually takes on Varuna's attributes. Another Vedic god, Rudra, Lord of cattle, was later identified with Siva.

There have been various 'Back to the Veda/Upanishads' movements since Ram Mohun Roy (d. 1833) began translating them, but as **Hinduism** is not a legalistic religion, and allows much flexibility in practice, the effect is different from **fundamentalism** among **Christians** and **Muslims**. **EMJ**

Further reading G. Parrinder, *The Wisdom of the Forest*.

VEGETARIANISM

Given the biological fact that human beings are omnivores, it seems illogical that large numbers of us should choose to remove meat (or in extreme cases, all animal products) entirely from our diet. Vegetarianism has always been practised as a form of religious abstinence (the range is from Catholics giving up meat-eating for Lent to Hindus giving it up altogether), and the rationale in each case is perfectly comprehensible. Others give up meat-eating on health grounds, claiming that vegetarians have less cholesterol in the blood, that they are less prone to rage and other excessive emotions, and that they live longer. In the Western world in the last quarter of the 20th century, vegetarianism has been widely practised: it was calculated in 1989, for example, that 11% of all girls in the US below the age of 15, and 8% of all boys, were vegetarians. Whatever the reasons distaste for modern methods of farming, slaughtering and preserving meat-animals, ecological concern (there is a correlation, for example, between hamburger sales and the amount of rainforest being cut down to make pasture for cattle), the fashion for slimness, health worries the statistic is extraordinary, without precedent in any society which is meat-eating by custom. Perhaps vegetarianism is a function of human fancy rather than of human thought; but (as with **cannibalism**) its wide spread and its very incoherence as a principle, tell us something about what we are as a species, and what we (or at any rate some of us) would like to be. **KMcL**

Further reading Colin Spencer, *The Heretic's Feast: a History of Vegetarianism.*

VERIFIABILITY AND FALSIFIABILITY

A sentence is verifiable just if there is a procedure for determining whether it is true or false. The sentence 'there are one hundred pages in this book' is verifiable because there is a procedure for determining whether it is true or false. A sentence is falsifiable just if there is a procedure which could determine that it is false. Some sentences are falsifiable but not verifiable. For example, the sentence 'all swans are white' can not be verified, because no matter how many swans one examines and finds to be white there is always the possibility that the next one will not be white, that not all swans are white. But the sentence 'all swans are white' can be falsified by the discovery of a non-white swan.

Some have endorsed the verification principle, holding that a sentence is meaningful only if it is analytic (that is, true solely in virtue of its meaning) or empirically verifiable (that is, there is an empirical test determining whether it is true or false). Popper rejected this principle, and argued that a hypothesis is scientific only if it is falsifiable. **AJ**

See also verification principle.

Further reading A.J. Ayer, *Language, Truth and Logic.*

VERISMO

Verismo ('realism') was a late–19th century European arts movement. **Novels, plays** and **operas** were made from ordinary lives and incidents, the kinds of story reported by newspapers. The aim was to democratize the arts, as it were, showing that human suffering and passion were the same regardless of social status. In practice, the dichotomy between domestic surroundings and high-tragic expression made the style seem melodramatic and somewhat ridiculous. Pirandello's plays about housewives and prostitutes have a phoniness of utterance quite unlike the seriousness and urgency of (for instance) Ibsen before him and Arthur Miller after him. Mürger's and Dumas *fils'* stories and novels about students indulging in grand, doomed passion similarly suffer from an excess of manner over matter. The most successful pieces of *verismo* art, the operas of Puccini and his followers, tend to work because the ennobling power of the music obliterates rather than enhances the tawdriness of the surroundings. Picasso's pictures of acrobats and other performers similarly find human truth in grubby circumstance. But *verismo* was rather a short-lived parasite on **realism** than a fully-fledged movement in its own right. It betrayed and patronized its subjects rather than revealing the human truth in them. **KMcL**

VIROLOGY

Virology, in the **life sciences**, as its Greek name suggests, is the study of the structure and function of submicroscopic particles, collectively termed viruses. The existence of viruses as agents of infection was first demonstrated in 1892 by Dmitry Ivanovsky when he used a porcelain filter to show that tobacco mosaic disease could be transmitted between plants by a bacteria-free filtrate. At the turn of the century, foot and mouth disease and yellow fever were shown to be caused by filterable viruses, but the viruses themselves could not be visualized until the development of the electron microscope in the 1940s. Prior to this, the tobacco mosaic virus had been crystallized in 1935 from thousands of pure particles; this development enabled the first work on the structure of virus particles by X-ray crystallization.

It is now known that viruses are simple particles which do not grow and which can only replicate by parasitizing a living cell and redirecting its activity to produce many virus copies. A viral particle consists of a package of nucleic acids surrounded by a coat of protein, which protects the nucleic acids from the environment. The virus cannot be considered alive outside its host cell; it is merely an inert dispersal stage. The core of nucleic acids carries the information necessary to commandeer the cell and to instruct it to replicate the virus; for this reason most viruses infect only specific cell types. This form of parasitism must have a cost to the host cell and, where changes are observed, the virus is said to be cytopathogenic. It is not clear how many viruses infect cells without causing obvious pathology, though these may be in the majority. The protein coat is antigenic: it is this which stimulates immunity after exposure to the virus, or vaccination with an attenuated form. Many viral diseases have been effectively controlled by vaccination; smallpox has been eradicated and poliomyelitis is now extremely uncommon. Others such as the common cold and influenza have proved difficult to control because there are many types of virus responsible, all of which have different surface coat proteins.

Virology has advanced rapidly over the past decade as a result of the intense international effort to control the human immunodeficiency virus (HIV), which causes acquired immunodeficiency syndrome (AIDS) in humans. Despite this, there is no vaccine or successful treatment so far.

Recent evidence suggests that a class of infective agents may exist which have no nucleic acids; these largely hypothetical agents called prions, may be the cause of diseases such as bovine spongiform encephalopathy (BSE). The possibility of replication in living cells without nucleic acids is a radical concept in biology; in this case the material which is responsible for carrying genetic information appears to be protein. The implication of this is that the prions, once within a host cell, must use protein to encode a nucleic acid sequence so that the cell may replicate the prion. If this is the case, then an important assumption of biology, that information flow between nucleic acids (DNA/RNA) and amino acids (protein) is unidirectional, is no longer valid. Beside the pathogenic viruses, there is another group of great importance to humans. These are the bacteriophages, which parasitize bacterial cells, inserting their genetic information and thus altering the genotype of the organism (transduction). This feature has been turned to advantage by molecular biologists who use such viruses in **genetic engineering**. RB

See also aetiology; microbiology; parasitism; parasitology.

Further reading Scientific American, *Microorganisms from Smallpox to Lyme Disease.*

VIRTUES AND VICES

To the philosopher, a virtue is an ethically desirable character trait, such as honesty, courage, generosity or kindness. A vice is an ethically undesirable character trait, such as cruelty, cowardice or selfishness. To have a virtue is not to follow or apply any kind of rule. A generous person will constantly ponder what generosity requires, but will simply behave in a generous manner. Indeed, if someone gives money away because he or she thinks that this is what generous people do, the action is not done out of generosity. A truly generous person simply sees someone who needs something and feels inclined to satisfy this need, if possible. In general, the virtuous person is someone who has certain emotional reactions to various situations, reactions which lead him or her to behave in a virtuous fashion.

An ethical system based on the cultivation of virtue can be contrasted with a system of deontological ethics. In **deontology** it is a set of rules which defines right and wrong, and the good person is one who consults them and acts in accordance with them. It doesn't matter whether this person feels naturally inclined to obey the rules – what matters is that he or she actually does obey them. Indeed, one deontologist, Kant, argued that someone who is tempted to behave badly, but resists temptation, is morally better than someone who feels no temptation at all, but naturally does the right thing. By contrast, someone who feels inclined to be selfish is not fully generous and therefore does not have the virtue of generosity, however well he or she may behave. So a system of ethics or virtue disagrees with Kant on this point.

Furthermore, virtue theorists are sceptical about whether the behaviour characteristic of a virtuous person can be captured by any set of rules. What rule could describe the behaviour of a generous person? Presumably the rule would have to mention things such as responding to human need, so that anyone capable of applying the rule would have to be sensitive to human need (something which is characteristic of a generous person). So a rule prescribing generous behaviour could be applied only by someone who already had part of that virtue. Hence ethical knowledge cannot be captured in a set of rules. AJ

Further reading P. Foot, *Virtues and Vices*; A. Rorty, *Essays on Aristotle's Ethics.*

VISUAL ANTHROPOLOGY

Visual (from Latin *visus*, 'sight') **anthropology** includes a number of relatively recent and diverse interests concerning the visual dimensions of human behaviour: it is generally agreed by anthropologists that vision is not simply about the objective sense-experience of the world. It is customary to think of vision as being patterned by the brain, but this is dependent on learned codes which themselves are determined by cultural ideas about vision. Anthropologists have approached this topic in other societies through a number of inroads: an investigation into how sight may be culturally encoded; in terms of what people say about vision; through a consideration of visual media, such as drawings, paintings, sculptures, architecture, personal decorations, masquerades, films and so forth. Such artefacts are vehicles of social ideas and values that inform on the aesthetic domains of a particular person or community, as well as serving some practical usage within it, such as political and ritual purposes.

Visual culture within the Abelam community of New Guinea, for example, centres on the elaborately painted façades and panels of ceremonial house fronts associated with the *tambaram* cult. Only initiates of the cult are tutored into recognizing the forms and their significance. On the other hand, the anthropologist Anthony Forge remarked on how he had to instruct Abelam people to interpret photographs – not a visual medium that they were familiar with. The visual arts for the Abelam people meant a different way of seeing related to their experiences with the *tambaram* cult. This example serves to illustrate the point that vision involves elements of socialization of learned codes.

The Hindu idea of *darshan* in devotional cults interprets vision as an objective force, which can mingle both the god's and the devotee's vision. Vision is conceived as so powerful that it can leave the body and, if combined with malicious sentiments, which need not always be conscious, could do harm to the person the gaze is directed at.

The concept of the 'evil eye' appears in various forms around the world. Among the Muslim people of North Africa, amulets of the hand of the daughter of the Prophet Muhammad or pieces of decorated blue glass are used to avert the invidious gaze of the 'evil eye'. In the Mediterranean countries, the 'evil eye' can be diverted if it is tempted by sexual desire, and an appro- priate gesture is believed to deflect its force. To this end, a phallic amulet was once worn as a protective talisman.

Other interpretations of artefacts or symbols may be more complex, for they do not always signify a particular meaning in a straightforward manner. Whereas different senses of aesthetic appreciation and a series of styles in particular artefacts may be noted, they are articulated in a different register to the language we use to describe them. Various theories seek to address this central problem concerning the relationship between the visual realm and its meaning articulated in language. Some have likened the visual **arts** to **poetry** or **music** for they all avoid literal descriptions.

The visual medium of film has now become an established part of anthropological enquiry. Pioneering work was done by Robert Flaherty, who screened his film on North American Eskimos, *Nanook of the North*, in 1922. Ethnographic film is usually the name given to the genre of films in which anthropological films about another community are made. But this is a restrictive term, for anthropologists have employed a wide range of films and film techniques that defy attempts at categorizing. Films made by indigenous members of a society are particularly illuminating if one wishes to find out about their social lives and thoughts, provided within which is an arena for considering concepts of visuality. Hindi popular film is a prime example of indigenous film-making that provides an insight into different visual conventions, informing on such themes as religious views, kinship relations – particularly that between the mother and son – archetypes about women, **caste** issues, **urbanization**, **nationalism** and ambivalent views about the West – a place admired for its technological achievements, but also characterized as morally licentious. **RK**

See also beauty; nature/culture; space and time; symbols; tourism; Westernization.

Further reading Karl Heider, *Ethnographic Film*; Robert Layton, *The Anthropology of Art*; P. Mayer (ed.), *Socialisaton: the View from Social Anthropology*.

VISUAL ARTS see Art(s), Visual

VITALISM

Vitalism, in the **life sciences**, is the doctrine that life cannot be explained purely by the application of the principles of **chemistry** and **physics**.

The concept of a vital force has ancient roots in **religion** and began to impinge upon scientific thought with Aristotle (384–322 BCE) who, with other ancient Greek philosophers, considered that the heat produced from an animal was associated with its life force. They suggested that this 'vital heat' had its source at the centre of the body, often in the heart, from whence it spread around the body before being expelled by the lungs. Although such ideas seem far removed from the today's scientific study of life, they do represent an attempt to separate the living from the non-living. Aristotle's ideas of a vital force were set in the context of the existence of a continuous chain or series in which supposedly similar organisms could be arranged adjacent to one another; the definition of 'organism' was rather different from our modern understanding and stones were thus placed at one end of the chain.

The nature of the vital force was debated by numerous philosophers, who fall into two main groups according to whether or not they felt that the force was an internal property of living organisms or an external. The Swiss chemist Paracelsus (1493–1541) used the term *Archeus* to describe his ideas of an externally derived power which confers life upon all things, including animals, plant, stones and spirits. Others, epitomized by the French anatomist François-Xavier Bichat (1771–1802), believed that life was a spontaneous event.

Vitalism, in one form or other, was the philosophy of most, scientists or otherwise, until the late 19th century when reductionist ideas began in Germany with the development of cell theory and the idea that the mechanism behind life itself could be explained. In retrospect, it seems that vitalism received its death blow with the synthesis of urea in 1828 by Friedrich Wöhler – this was the first time that such an organic compound had been produced by inorganic means and was a process which most vitalists considered impossible. As the new science of **biochemistry** developed, more such evidence accrued and new theories ceased to draw on vitalist precepts. However, the teleological aspects of vitalism held on, and even flourished, outside reductionist scientific thought. Hans Driesch (1867–1941) proposed the existence of a soul-like force, to which he applied the Aristotelian term *entelechy* (movement from potentiality to actuality: originally a philosophical concept, and an abstraction), which guides the development of an embryo. The French philosopher Henri Bergson (1859–1941) argued for the existence of a single, unique vital impulse which is continually developing; he thus implied that **evolution** was creative rather than mechanistic.

In the context of modern science the concept of vitalism is defunct, if for no other reason than it appears to be of no use in providing an explanation for the processes of life. Research throughout the 20th century has shown that biological systems, when studied in a controlled way, are entirely predictable from physical and chemical principles. This is the doctrine of **mechanism** and applicable at all levels of biological organization, though **quantum** mechanics suggests that the chemical processes which underpin life may not themselves be truly predictable. **RB**

See also biopoiesis; life; organicism.

Further reading Henri Bergson, *Creative Evolution* (1907).

VOLITION

A volition is an act of will. Some philosophers argue that an event is an **action** only if it is appropriately caused by a prior volition. One problem for this theory is that if volitions are themselves acts of will, if volitions are mental actions, and an event is an action only if it is appropriately caused by a prior volition, then every volition must itself be appropriately caused by a prior volition. When I act upon the physical world, perhaps by opening a door, my physical movement is appropriately caused by a prior volition. And that volition must be appropriately caused by a prior volition. And that volition must be appropriately caused by a prior volition. And so on, in an infinite regress.

Others hold that volitions are tryings or attempts to perform an action. They argue that since there is always the possibility that one will fail to perform the action one wants to perform (my arm may always be suddenly paralysed just as I am about to reach for my cup) one must always attempt to perform the action one wants to perform. **AJ**

Further reading B. O'Shaughnessy, *The Will*; G. Ryle, *The Concept of Mind*.

VON NEUMANN MODEL

In the earliest days of **computing**, the instructions in a **program** and the data it used to perform calculations on were considered to be totally different kinds of information. This meant that the instructions to the **computer** were given in a completely different way from the input of data. For instance, the data could be stored in cards with holes in them while the instructions were implemented by manipulating levers. In particular, it meant that instructions had to be entered individually as they were needed, which in turn meant that the same instruction might need to be given thousands of times.

John von Neumann (1903–57) realized that because the instructions were given in the form of symbols, the computer itself could process them in the same way that it processed data. This had major consequences for computing; von Neumann has even been called the father of computing as a result. One of its important consequences is that programs can be stored within the computer itself and implemented with only one instruction, which saves operator and computer time, and which makes possible the large programs used today (even the simplest word processing system, for example, would be far beyond the reach of computing in the 1930s or 1940s).

It was not until the 1980s that computers began to move beyond von Neumann's ideas. By this time, the von Neumann architecture (in which an individual instruction is read in from the memory and then processed, then the next and so on) had become the major brake on the speed at which computers could work. The computers which are being developed today employ parallel processing, where there are several processing units connected together in particular ways, implementing different instructions all at the same time. **SMcL**

VORTICISM

Vorticism was a European fine-art and literary movement of the early 1910s, founded by Wyndham Lewis and Ezra Pound (who christened it after what he called the 'vortex' which was his name for the **modernist** spirit in the **arts**). Its aims were to assault bourgeois expectations in the arts, to be aggressive, dynamic and innovative. In fine art, Vorticist works were characterized by brusquely angular, overlapping planes which commented on (or, as Lewis insisted, rejected) both the **futurist** obsession with dynamism and the static nature of **cubism**. Apart from Lewis, the major Vorticists were David Bomberg, Jacob Epstein and C.R.W. Nevinson.

In **literature**, the Vorticists favoured broken syntax, single words hurled at the reader, even a jangle of typefaces and sizes as if snipped from different magazines and glued together. The movement's energy was dissipated by the outbreak of World War I, and its energy was transformed from negative to positive by many of the artistic movements which followed it – not least in the work of both Pound and Lewis when their iconoclastic arteries hardened and they moved on to more considered creativity. But in its brief heyday, Vorticism summed up, better than most other isms, exactly what modernism in the arts was all about. **PD MG KMcL**

VULCANISM

Vulcanism (named after Vulcan, the Roman god of fire, who was thought to make thunderbolts for Jupiter in a smithy under Mount Etna), in lay terms, is the study of volcanoes (including the prediction of possible eruptions). Scientifically speaking, it has two meanings. Vulcanists (also called Plutonists, after Pluto, Greek god of the Underworld) hold that most geological phenomena are the result of heat in the Earth's interior, and the process of vulcanism is the convective flow of hot materials from the interior to the surface of a planet. Vulcanism of the second kind is common on Earth (where it is the venting of hot gases and molten materials from the radioactive decay which causes the planet's internal heat), and has also been observed on the Moon, Venus, Jupiter's moon Io and Neptune's moon Triton but nowhere else in the universe. **KMcL**

W

WAVE THEORY

Wave theory, in **linguistics**, provides an explanation of how languages gradually change. Like the concentric rings created when a stone is thrown into a pond, linguistic changes are thought to spread outwards in all directions. In any speech community there will be different configurations of waves intersecting with one another. Linguistic innovation tends to arise in the middle of the social **class** range, although a number of social factors can affect the rate and direction of change, including age, sex, social class and region. Change can spread along any one of these social dimensions, typically via people who have contacts with more than one social group. **MS**

See also comparative-historical linguistics; dialectology.

WAVE-PARTICLE DUALITY

The principle of wave-particle duality is that all waves have a particle nature, and that, conversely, all particles have a wave-like nature. There are extremes of each: water waves are almost completely wave-like particles, like electrons and neutrons, and, even in some cases, atoms, may be shown to behave like waves under the right conditions.

The wavelength of a particle is determined by its mass and its velocity (see **de Broglie**

waves). A snooker ball has such a tiny wavelength that it is completely indetectable. We could, in theory, increase this wavelength to a measurable distance by allowing the ball to move only very slowly, but if it was moving slowly enough, it would take more than the age of the universe to do anything interesting.

Electrons, which are undoubtedly charged particles, may act as waves. Crystals may be examined by passing an electron beam through them, and the wave pattern that is detected in the emerging electrons will give us information about the interior of the crystal. Many experiments can be performed which show particles travelling like waves but being finally detected as particles. Sound waves may be shown in some circumstances to act like particles, which have been given the name phonons. **JJ**

See also quantum theory; wave-particle duality of light.

WAVE-PARTICLE DUALITY OF LIGHT

The nature of light has long been of absorbing interest to humankind. Newton, in the mid–17th century, was the first person to apply serious thought to the problem, concluding that light was made up of many tiny particles. However, Huygens later proved that light is far more easily explained as a wave. The wave-like behaviour of light is exhibited in phenomena such as diffraction and refraction.

To illustrate the difference between wave-like and particle-like behaviour, we may consider the behaviour of water waves. If a series of waves hits a barrier with a small gap in it, they will spread out on the far side of the gap in a series of circular ripples (a process known as diffraction). If, however, a beam of particles passes through a small gap, they will not spread out, but continue in a straight line.

If a beam of light is shone upon a small hole, it diffracts exactly like water waves. This behaviour, both in light and in water waves, is seen when the gap is of a similar size to the wavelength. Thus light, which has a very small wavelength, only exhibits this behaviour when the hole is very small.

This would appear to show that light is a wave. But other evidence says otherwise. If the energy of a light beam is detected, it is not deposited smoothly, as a wave would be. Instead, it is detected in separate quanta, the size of which are determined by the colour or frequency of the light. It is, in fact, impossible to detect light other than in discrete packages: it is quantized. The packages are called photons.

This would appear to suggest that light is composed of particles. Scientists may conclude, from these two modes of behaviour, that light travels as a wave (diffraction), but interacts as a particle (quantized energy).

Current theories lead to various ways of resolving this problem. One way of thinking about it is to say that light is neither purely a wave nor a particle. We may model it with waves for some situations, and with particles for others, but it is a thing different from either, possessing the properties of both.

A different formulation of the behaviour of light has been given by Feynman. He describes mathematically the whole range of properties of light by assuming that it is a particle with phase properties, in his theory of quantum electrodynamics. **JJ**

See also de Broglie waves; optics, refraction and reflection; quantization.

WAVEGUIDE THEORY

Waveguide Theory, in electrical engineering, is used to predict and analyse propagation of high frequency electromagnetic waves in a variety of media. It can be thought of as an extension of **transmission line theory** applied to high frequency electricity, and like transmission line theory was formed from the basis of **electromagnetic** theory. The impetus behind the research and application of waveguide theory was the need for ever faster and more numerous means of communication, whether it be more telephone lines or higher radio frequencies to permit transmission of more television stations.

Since the 1890s it had been shown theoretically possible to propagate electromagnetic waves inside a hollow tube of conducting material. At this time, however, it was thought a physical impossibility as electricity required two conductors in order to flow, one to allow current to flow to the object and the second to allow the current to return to the source, thereby completing an electrical circuit. Around the 1930s it had been shown experimentally that such propagation was physically possible, at this time along water-filled pipes, and shortly afterwards the theory was devised to characterize these effects more accurately.

The theory predicted a relationship between the frequency of electromagnetic wave propagated and the dimensions of the waveguide or pipe. Whereas conventional electrical wires would conduct from zero frequency to large frequencies, where the signal was attenuated, waveguides were found to propagate waves only from a certain cut-off frequency and upwards, the opposite to convention. The cut-off frequency in most instances was considerably higher than the upper working frequencies of electrical wires. It was the fact that such frequencies could be propagated that offered the possibility of communicating much greater amounts of information and at faster speeds. This form of metal pipe waveguide was microwave communication.

Although a microwave radio link between Dover and Calais was in use in 1934, applications of microwaves were primarily in radar until the end of World War II, because microwave radar used smaller antennae and transmitters than previously, and equipment was therefore lighter and easier to transport and provided greater directional resolution.

The theory of waveguides has produced other propagation media. Coaxial cable (where one conductor is located in the centre of the hollow second conductor space being filled with an insulator) was also being used in the 1930s. This offered increased performance and greatly reduced interference from neighbouring conductors than conventional parallel wire cables.

The latest use of waveguide theory is in the area of optical fibres, where light, an electromagnetic wave of very high frequency, is propagated along a very small glass fibre. Due to the use of higher frequencies even than microwaves, vast amounts of information can be propagated along a single fibre. Development of practical optical fibre systems has only occurred since the late 1960s following the invention of **laser** light sources and light-emitting diodes, and with the solution of certain problems in the manufacture of glass fibre. AC

WEAK FORCE/STRONG FORCE

These two forces, which are very different, are often linked together by physical scientists because they both operate within the nucleus. The strong force prevents the positively charged protons in the nucleus from flying apart; it is stronger than the repulsion, but only acts at short distances. The weak force is responsible for a particular decay mode of nuclei, beta decay, which involves the emission or capture of electrons or positrons. At high energies, such as inside particle accelerators, the weak force becomes much more important.

The strong force is due to gluon exchange between the quarks that the protons and neutrons in the nucleus contain. This exchange only occurs within the protons and neutron, however, and does not bind the nucleus together. This is done by the 'leakage' from the gluon exchange in the form of the exchange of another particle, the pion, between the protons and neutrons themselves. The strong force is very different from the other three forces in that it grows stronger with distance, like stretching a piece of elastic. Thus, if we attempt to separate two quarks, all we do by pulling them apart is increase the attractive force and the interaction energy between them. If they are pulled apart until the interaction energy is equivalent to the mass of two new quarks, then two new quarks will immediately be formed, and we will have two pairs rather than the one that we started with. This property of the strong force leads to confinement of quarks, which means that it is impossible to find a single quark: they only come in pairs or threes.

The weak force involves other exchange particles, the Z and W bosons. They are can interact with the orbiting electrons and the protons and neutrons within the nuc-

leus. This force has the property of not conserving parity, or mirror symmetry, in its interactions. **JJ**

See also four forces; parity.

WEAKNESS OF WILL

Weakness of will, also known as *akrasia* (Greek, 'impotence'), is acting against one's own better judgement. A person manifests his weakness of will when sincerely judging that it would be best to perform one action, such as paying his debts, but performs another, such as going shopping.

Some philosophers doubt that weakness of will is possible. If an agent seems to judge that it would be best to perform one action, but performs another, then his or her judgement about what it would be best to do is not sincere. One cannot sincerely judge that it would be best to perform one action, but perform another.

Other philosophers argue that weakness of will is possible. They insist that one can sincerely judge that it would be best to perform one action, but intentionally do something else. So, they hold, intending to perform an action is different from sincerely judging that it would be best to perform that action. For one can sincerely judge that it would be best to perform one action, and yet intend to do something else. **AJ**

Further reading D. Davidson, *Essays on Actions and Events.*

WELFARE ECONOMICS

Welfare **economics** is the study of conditions in an economy that will maximize general economic well-being, that is, achieve all of those changes that will make one or many people better off without making anyone worse off. (It is not the study of public welfare systems in support of the poor.) More precisely, maximization of economic welfare occurs when two conditions are achieved: (1) no further change in the economy is possible that could make one person better off without an adverse effect on another person; (2) no further change is possible that can make one person better off and one worse off, but yet provide sufficient gain to the former to compensate the latter fully and still leave some gain to the former.

These two conditions in welfare economics are an attempt to avoid consideration of shifts of resources that would require a value judgment. A value judgment would hold that the condition of person x ought to be improved at the expense of y without full compensation to y. On the other hand, when an equilibrium is reached which conforms to these conditions, the economy is at what is known as a 'Pareto optimum'.

The phrase 'Pareto optimum' was named after an Italian economist, Vilfredo Pareto (1848–1923), and is used to describe circumstancs in which nobody can be made better off without making somebody else worse off. If an economy's resources are allocated inefficiently, a Pareto improvement ought to be possible: that is, making one person (or more) better off without harming anybody else. In practice, such uncontroversial opportunities are rare: change usually involves losers as well as winners, and the Pareto criterion has nothing to offer on how the balance should be judged. **TF**

See also game theory.

WELTANSCHAUUNG see Ideology

WESTERNIZATION

The term Westernization describes the cultural influences of the developed nations of Europe and America on other parts of the world, such as with the **arts**, **literature**, **media** and **music**. It is a phenomenon that is greatly enhanced by the travel and communication networks of the 20th century, leading to a kind of 'global shrinkage'. But Westernization does not follow a predictable pattern for all societies. A varied and complex range of responses may occur with any one community. They may adapt certain features of Westernization or fuse them with their own traditions. Sometimes, Westernization may be resisted in an active way and initiate a revival of one's own cultural traditions.

Marxist perspectives on Westernization consider the historical, political and economic dimensions. They claim that the present situation, in which there is a stronghold of influences in Western, 'developed' nations and a periphery of non-Western 'undeveloped' or 'developing' countries, has largely arisen out of a colonialist relationship in the past. This relationship was (and as some would argue, still is) one of a predator and its prey. The spread of capitalist institutions into colonial and post-colonial countries provides the means to appropriate cheap labour and raw materials from the tropical periphery in order to bulwark the prosperity and global control of the Western metropolitan nations. The cultural aspects of Westernization are no more than ideological mechanisms to dominate on political and economic grounds.

Critics have argued that this is too sweeping and mechanistic a view. It fails to consider the internal dynamics of how non-Western countries manage their own cultural and economic affairs, accomodating principles of Western culture and capitalism but not being subsumed by it. **BO'L**

See also ethnomusicology; colonialism; evolutionism; Marxist anthropology; modernization; syncretism.

Further reading Mike Featherstone (ed.), *Global Culture*; Anthony D. King (ed.), *Culture, Globalisation and the World System*.

WHORFIAN HYPOTHESIS see Linguistic Relativity

WILLING SUSPENSION OF DISBELIEF, THE

In **theatre**, 'Willing Suspension of Disbelief' is a crucial part of the implied contract between theatre audiences and theatrical practitioners. Although the term itself was invented by Coleridge, the phenomenon is far older, since audiences must always agree to a whole series of potentially counter-factual propositions in order to make sense of theatrical events. An audience does not have the right, for example, to intervene to convert the action of *Othello* into comedy by informing Desdemona of what is going on; if you refuse to believe in fairies, at least for the duration of the performance, your enjoyment of *A Midsummer Night's Dream* is likely to be severely curtailed. This issue has been little discussed (perhaps because it strikes many critics as blindingly obvious); but it lies at the heart of what theatre is, and does. To take one point at random, for example: what sort of suspension of disbelief, willing or otherwise, happens to the 'spectators' of religious drama (such as those of Far Eastern dance-plays)? Is this the same suspension of disbelief as felt by the audience of (say) a Feydeau farce, a Beckett play or a television **soap**? TRG KMcL SS

See also drama; naturalism; unities, the.

Further reading E. Aston and G. Savona, *Theatre as a Sign-System*; K. Elam, *Semiotics of Theatre and Drama*.

WIT

Wit (old English, 'knowledge') used to mean quite simply the quality of intelligence or understanding, a meaning which survives in such phrases as 'He doesn't have the wit he was born with'. Its use in this way suggests a kind of intellectual alertness and articulacy, and these qualities led to its secondary meanings in the 18th century, a faculty for relating concepts, for understanding and clearly expressing intellectual ideas, and from the 19th century onwards, a specialized kind of humour.

The last meaning is the only one which still persists today. Writers on comedy and jokes often make a distinction between 'wit' and 'humour'. 'Humour', they say, derives from the medieval European idea that all created things were made up of different combinations of the four elements air, earth, fire and water, and that our individual temperament depended on the proportions of each element in our makeup. Humour is thus an innate quality, something we have and are. Wit, by contrast, is an **attitude** to life: it is extrovert and declarative, a form of show (and often, a mask). It seldom shows gentleness or warmth, as humour does; whether verbal or physical, it tends to play to the gallery, to solicit admiration, and fairness and truthfulness are secondary considerations. Wit often has victims; it deflates and wounds; it is a form of **irony**, requiring collusion between two people (the witty person and the admirer) against a third person (the butt) or an object or situation. In some societies – ancient Rome and the modern Middle East are notable cases – this hardness in wit has been one of its most prized features, and has made it a main form of **discourse**. In other societies – the English-speaking peoples are examples – it has been approached more gingerly, so that witty people tend to be regarded as dangerous, to be admired rather than loved (at least in the way that humorous people are loved), and so that self-deprecation (irony against oneself) is the only really favoured form. **KMcL**

WITCHCRAFT

Witchcraft (from Old English *wiccian*, 'to practise sorcery') is using esoteric skills and occult knowledge to manipulate the natural world. It includes such benign activities as **divination** and healing, and such malign ones as causing disaster and communion with evil spirits. Witches can be of either sex, and they use 'familiars' (spirit-slaves which take the form of animals, usually birds or cats) and 'talismans' (inanimate objects invested with magic powers).

Such is the popular view of witchcraft: and it is an outsider's view, coloured by the hostility of some religions (notably **Christianity**) to practices which seem to involve the supernatural but which lie outside their control. In Europe, at least, actual practitioners of witchcraft see what they do as beneficent and harmless, as a holistic system of **belief** and practice which bypasses formal religion and which has existed since prehistoric times. By invocations, **ritual** and spells, witches assert their community with Nature and with the supernatural world; this identity gives them no special powers or prerogatives, but may enhance understanding. To 'real' witches, what they are and what they do are utterly remote from the witch-stereotypes of folk tale and the popular imagination stereotypes – whose persistence and vigour nonetheless seem to speak of a need, in societies and artists of all levels, to embody the Other and so, perhaps, control and demystify it.

Anthropological studies of witchcraft have tended to look at it not from the insider's point of view, but from that of the society in which witches operate. In particular, anthropologists have examined how societies allocate blame in cases of witchcraft – on the individual, the supernatural, or in some cases on a physical substance. (Among the Azande of Sudan, for example, witches are believed to inherit witchcraft in the form of a substance, *mangu*, which lies dormant until activated by grudges against neighbours. Blame is not attached to the person inadvertently causing witchcraft, but to the person thought to have caused offence, usually by excluding the person identified as a witch from full social relationships.)

A pattern of accusations and blame has emerged in societies ranging from the Azande to Tudor England, which has resulted in the theory of witchcraft as a gauge of 'social strain'. Those accused are usually people in the weakest positions in society, such as old women living alone. The threat of witchcraft serves as a double-edged means of social control. As well as controlling the weak, it also attempts to ensure that proper social relations are maintained.

While Westerners make a distinction between intention and the actual outcome of an evil act, in other societies evil is seen as part of an object or a person. The widespread belief in the evil eye (one of the main powers attributed to witches everywhere) conceptualizes evil as a force associated with the act of looking, capable of harming children or animals. Closely related to feelings of envy, it is a voluntary power associated with the destructive force of individual envy, but it can also be considered involuntary with certain socially excluded classes of people (old women or disabled persons). The notion of the evil eye serves to explain why misfortunes or illness happen to particular people at particular times.

The embodiment of spirits often provides a means of negotiating with their negative aspects as in the case with possessionary spirits in the *zar* spirit-possession cult of Egypt and Sudan. Sometimes the spirit is assumed to be completely outside moral control. On the other hand, witchcraft can be seen as an integral part of moral systems, in the way that is is used as a social sanction. The question of attribution of responsibility reveals a great deal about how good and evil are seen in relation to personal responsibility.

Feminist studies of witchcraft concentrate on activities in 15th-century Europe, in Britain in the 16th and 17th centuries and 17th-century New England. In these three areas thousands of people, 90 per cent of them women, were accused of witchcraft and in many cases were tortured, imprisoned or burned. Feminist historians and theorists have tried to discover the reasons for this persecution. Some maintain that these women belonged to a witch cult that was woman-centred and at odds with the dominant, male-centred Christian religion. Others argue that these women were persecuted because they had special knowledge of healing and midwifery that challenged the new all-male professional doctor. One of the main ideas that underlies most feminist views of witchcraft is that the women who were single with children, spinsters or widows were outside the control of the patriarchal family, and that the threat and terror of an accusation of witchcraft were used as a method of containing them.

Many different strands of feminism, including psychoanalytic feminism, have shown that masculinity includes fear of the woman's body as Other. This is important for feminist studies of witchcraft, for witches – as fairy tales and horror films make abundantly clear – can be seductively beautiful as well as hideously ugly, and sometimes both as once. Many Eastern religions also feature women (dakinis) who seduce men and during intercourse suck away their vital juices. The eroticisation of witches as seductive and bewitching reveals, for many feminists, an unconscious male fear of the difference of the female sexual body. French feminist theoretician Helene Cixous proposes that witches are model women who exist on the edge of **language** and **culture** and, together with madwomen and hysterics, resist patriarchal structures.

Witchcraft has another aspect in some kinds of feminism. During the late 1960s and 1970s feminists began to 'reclaim' witchcraft or *wicca* as a woman-centred religion. Feminist spiritualists worship a **Goddess** and celebrate the connection of the rhythms of the body and world. The feminist study of witchcraft is part of a greater trend to construct histories of women that have been left out of the 'official' history books, centred as they are on male, ruling-class views of the world. **TK RK CL KMcL**

Further reading Mary Daly, *Gyn/Ecology*; M. Marwick (ed.), *Witchcraft and Sorcery*; Margaret Murray, *The Witchcult in Western Europe*; D. Parkin, *The Anthropology of Evil*.

WORK

Work (Old English *wyrcan*) refers to the activity through which human beings produce from the natural world in order to survive. Work is the exertion of physical and mental effort, which has as its objective the production of goods and services which cater to human needs. For most people, in all types of society, work occupies a larger part of their lives than any other type of activity. In all societies work is the basis of the economic system.

When sociologists use the term work they do not simply associate work with paid employment. Employment is any activity which one is engaged in for wages or a salary. Wage-labour is only a particular form of work associated with **capitalism**. In traditional societies, there was often only a elementary monetary system, and very few people worked for money payments. In modern societies housework and the informal or black economy (transactions carried on outside the sphere of orthodox paid employment) are major spheres of non-waged work which make a major contribution to the overall production of wealth. Nevertheless in modern society a woman running a house and

bringing up children is still likely to be distinguished from a woman who works in paid employment. **DA**

See also alienation; career; class; division of labour; feminism; gender; labour process; Marxism; occupation; profession; Protestant ethic; role; social stratification; society; status.

Further reading C. Littler (ed.), *The Experience of Work*; A. Oakley, *The Sociology of Housework*; K. Thompson (ed.), *Work, Employment and Unemployment*.

WORLD BANK

World Bank is the colloquial name for the International Bank for Reconstruction and Development (IBRD). Established at the 1944 **Bretton Woods** Conference, it opened for business at its Washington DC headquarters in 1946, with 38 members. By 1960, the number of members had risen to 68 and to 150 in 1986. The bank's aim is to provide low-interest, long-term loans to people and governments for economic development when such loans are not available from private sources. Originally intended to finance Europe's reconstruction after World War II, the bank's first loans were to France, Holland and Denmark, and then it quickly started to concentrate on loans to poor countries. It is now the largest single source of development aid.

Loanable funds are provided from subscription for capital stock from member nations according to economic importance. The bank can also raise funds by selling bonds. It makes loans for economic development projects that are expected to produce a return to pay back the loan, such as cattle ranching in Spain. It also makes loans to governments for social overhead capital that increases the productivity of enterprise in a country, such as roads, schools, labour training, etc. **TF**

WORLD MUSIC

The expression 'world music' has been used by ethnomusicologists to mean all living **music**, and to emphasize the universal nature of this aspect of human social behaviour, distinguishing their academic concern from the narrow ethnocentric approach of European **musicology**. The term embraces the orally-transmitted folk music of the world as well as the art music of all non-Western societies. In Western music education, since the 1960s, not only has the number of world music programmes in university music degree courses steadily grown, but also the introduction to world music has begun to feature in secondary school curricula, reflecting a more enlightened approach in our multi-racial society.

However, recently a different meaning of world music has entered the vocabulary. It has become a term used, somewhat arbitrarily, for marketing various kinds of non-Western music as commercial **pop** commodities. In 1987, the label 'World Music' was chosen by a group of representatives from the independent recording industry to overcome the problem of categorizing the increasing amount of modern, non-Western music appearing on the European market. Some regard this World Music as an indigenous, modernized, urban popular music, emerging as a direct result of technological advances in non-Western cultures and the growth of independent broadcasting and record-producing companies. Others consider it a product of **Westernization**, as a contrived hybrid of traditional, non-Western forms with elements of Western **rock** and **jazz**. There is also the sceptical view that the Western recording companies have promoted World Music as a 'Third World' phenomenon, to exploit younger consumers' increasing awareness of a global identity, and at a time when the state of Western pop music seemed to be at its most stagnant and technologically synthetic.

Since the mid–1960s, when the Beatles developed an interest in north Indian classical music and used the sitar in some of their songs, an increasing number of Western pop-music composers have looked beyond their own cultural traditions for alternative sources of inspiration. Probably one of the most influential factors in convincing the industry of the potential for a World Music market was the unprecedented international success of the American singer-songwriter Paul Simon's album *Graceland* in 1986. On this album Simon coupled Western with South African popular and traditional music styles. There has always been to some extent a commercial market for World Music, from the time when the first recordings of Afro-American jazz were introduced to Europe, to the international popularity of Jamaican reggae in the early 1970s. The establishment in 1981 of the International Association for the Study of Popular Music (IASPM), concerned with all forms of popular music from an intercultural viewpoint, has bestowed academic respectability on what was once an inconceivable topic in music education and research.

The World Music market has become firmly established, and appears to be gradually broadening its scope to return world music to its original ethnomusicological meaning, permitting such forms as Indian art music, Bulgarian diaphonic song, Japanese Shinto drumming and Andean panpipe music to pervade its pop music menu. Whether the living music traditions of the world are being enriched or impoverished by the commercial manipulation of world music remains to be seen. **SSt**

Further reading Simon Frith (ed.), *World Music, Politics and Social Change*; Peter Manuel, *Popular Musics of the Non-Western World*; Philip Sweeney, *Virgin Directory of World Music*.

WORLD RELIGIONS

'World' religions (also known as 'universal' religions) are so called because they claim to possess universally valid truths and/or experience of a deity or deities who demand the obedience of all humankind. The term 'world' also distinguishes them from **tribal religion**, which is restricted to a particular family, tribe or society originally living in an area sacred to it. Nonetheless, the majority of the adherents of world religions are born into their faith, not converted to it, and some so-called world religions have become so identified with the patriotic aspirations of particular minorities that it is unthinkable to convert across that line. **Shinto**, for example, is so strongly identified with the Japanese nation that it is questionable whether a non-Japanese would adopt it.

All world religions have gone through phases of mission and evangelism, though this may occur less for religious reasons than because political leaders see the advantages of expanding a faith community, and exploit its claims to increase their power. (The Crusades are a notorious example of this, but doubtless rulers and leaders who used methods of forcible conversion, such as Philip II of Spain, would declare themselves convinced of the rectitude of their conduct.) World religions are never really 'dormant': revival can break out unexpectedly and lead to startling expansion, as in the case of **Islam** in the last decades of the 20th century, a major contrast to its position a hundred years ago. In some world religions, for example, **Buddhism**, **Christianity** and Islam, propagating the faith, or evangelism, is an imperative written into their 'constitution', as it were.

All world religions possess sacred **scriptures**, though these do not hold the same degree of authority in each faith. Except for **Hinduism**, each religion has an identifiable founder, who by his life and teaching laid down a pattern for his followers to emulate, and whose transparent holiness is thought to give his followers access to the divine beyond and within themselves. World religions can be divided into two categories according to whether this 'enlightenment' is attained by divine grace through faith (as in Christianity), or as a result of the believer's personal efforts (as in Buddhism); one can also see the two responses in a single faith community, for instance in Hinduism.

Since each world religion has a different set of perceptions of the human predicament and the way to salvation, comparisons are difficult, but sometimes it seems that certain religions (for example Hinduism) emphasize more who God is, and others (for instance Christianity) what God does. This distinction is underlined by the fact that the religions where God is creator and intervenes in history (Christianity, Islam, **Judaism**) are also 'religions of the book' with a scriptural tradition which describes these acts. Buddhism and Hinduism, by contrast, are seen as 'mystical'

religions where **meditation** and **mysticism** predominate. All world religions have strong ethical traditions, though this is often not recognized by adherents of other faiths, and all have inspired sophisticated philosophical systems, **art**, **drama** and **music**.

The growth of international travel, trade and political alliances on the one hand, and migration and settlement on the other, has greatly increased the amount of contact between members of the different world religions. This has not only demanded changes of the migrating religion (especially in Hinduism and Islam) but has challenged claims to exclusive truth. Multi-faith worship is no longer uncommon but generally it is a question of one community inviting members of another to share special occasions. The challenge of religious pluralism is one of the most acute theological problems today. **EMJ**

Further reading Ronald M. Green, *Religion and Moral Reason*; Geoffrey Parrinder, *Encountering the World's Religions*; Ninian Smart, *The World's Great Religions*.

WORLD SYSTEM

The term 'world system', originally developed by the sociologist I. Wallerstein, refers to a conception of the modern social world which views it as a single, interlinked entity. **DA**

See also convergence thesis; dependency theory; diffusionism; division of labour; globalization.

Further reading I. Wallerstein, *The Modern World System: Capitalist Agriculture and the Origins of the European World-Economy in the Sixteenth Century*; *Historical Capitalism*.

X-RAYS

X-rays are electromagnetic radiation with a wavelength between 0.4 and 100 nanometers. They consist of relatively high energy photons that are used for their penetrating powers to produce images of the interior of bodies or structures. They were first discovered by Wilhelm Röntgen in 1895. He was able to show that they were able to penetrate bodies to varying degrees depending on the density of the substance. Their discovery was taken up immediately by the medical profession to locate foreign bodies and broken bones within the human body. Early experiments with x-rays were sometimes far fetched, such as a textile company who tried to market x-ray-proof underwear for the modest woman. This fatuous attempt has reflections at the present time since we now know that exposure to even small amounts of x-ray radiation to be hazardous to health and workers using x-rays require to take special precautions to avoid receiving any excessive amounts. Hospital patients generally have their reproductive organs screened during x-ray imaging since even low levels of exposure may induce abnormalities in the unborn child.

As well as being used in medicine, x-rays also have a wide range of industrial and scientific uses. In industry they are used to detect the cracks associated with metal fatigue and fissures in such items as aircraft wings and pressure vessels such as boilers or nuclear reactors.

In the field of **astronomy**, x-ray emissions from stars and constellations give valuable information relating to their nature and dynamics. At the other end of the dimensional spectrum, in the electron microscope the x-rays scattered from the specimen give signals which can be analysed to determine the chemical elements which are present. **AA**

See also wave-particle duality.

Further reading G.L. Clarke, *Applied X-rays.*

YOGA

There are six schools in orthodox Hinduism which offer ways of salvation. The first three, *nyaya* ('analysis'), *vaisesika* ('school

of individual characteristics') and *sankhya* ('the count'), consist of philosophical systems of knowledge. *Yoga*, the fourth system, may be translated as 'spiritual discipline' or 'application'. The word itself is cognate with 'yoke' in English, and is used loosely to cover all kinds of religious exercises and asceticism. The practitioner is known as a *yogi.*

The eight stages of yogic training, which are similar to **Buddhism**'s eightfold path, are: (1) self-control, including nonviolence and continence; (2) observance of the rules of purity and austerity; (3) posture, the most famous of which is the 'lotus position'; (4) breath control; (5) restraint, whereby the sense perceptions are ignored; (6) steadying the mind by focusing on one object; (7) meditation; (8) deep meditation; when the whole personality is dissolved this is known as 'royal yoga'.

The whole methodology has been exploited to gain control over feelings of pain and for bizarre contortions of the body. It is based on the idea that by yoga one can release psychic energy, the serpent power in a mystical experience which brings spiritual strength and salvation. Yoga has been adapted by Westerners as a means of relaxation and physical wellbeing, but it is doubtful if the methodology can really be separated from the philosophy behind it. **EMJ**

Z

ZERO

Numbers first developed from the needs of counting, from the need to ensure that you were not being cheated in a deal, from the need to have some idea of the size of your possessions. Obviously, if you had none of something, there was no need to count it. Why would anyone list 'no elephants' with the rest of their possessions? For this reason, there was no number representing none of something.

For counting alone, the lack of a representation for nothing is not important. However, for more complicated transactions, the concept becomes more vital. Even so, although there were words for none of something, the 'none' did not reach the status of a number itself. In English, the answer to a question of number is still usually 'none' rather than 'zero'.

Indian mathematicians were the first to recognize zero as a number. This recognition lay at the basis of their invention of the place notation for numbers (see **number systems**). Without zero, it is impossible to distinguish, for example, the numbers 2190 and 2019 using place notation – this is probably the reason why no-one developed such systems earlier. The recognition of zero as a number in its own right lay at the basis of one of the most fundamental changes in the way that numbers are used, and, through the way that calculation was eased, paved the way for subsequent developments in **mathematics**.

Today, zero is often considered the most important number. It lies at the basis of the **axiomatization** of arithmetic by Peano; it is the number which is the most important in the **integers** looked at as a **group** or a **ring**, being the identity for addition (that is, you can add it to any number without changing the value of the number). SMcL

ZIONISM

Zionism is the doctrine and movement which seeks to bring Jews together in Palestine to establish and maintain their own state. 'Zion' is the name of a hill in Jerusalem and also signifies the 'Promised Land'. The doctrine's founding text is Theodor Herzl's *The Jewish State* (1896); its author was a Viennese journalist. The first Zionist World Congress was held in 1897, and led to the creation of an organization dedicated to buying land in Palestine and encouraging colonial settlements. Following the formation of the state of Israel in 1948, through war and the expulsion of Palestinian Arabs, Zionism become an official state ideology.

In its origins Zionism is a species of political **nationalism** and settler **colonialism** rather than a theological movement. It has four key premises: (1) the present-day Jewish people are the descendants of the Jews who originated in Zion before being dispersed throughout the world (following the Roman assault on the Jews in the 2nd century BCE); (2) Jews cannot be assimilated into other societies; (3) Jews have the right to return to Zion; and (4) Ottoman Palestine was 'a land without people for a people without a land'. Each of these key articles of Zionist faith is hotly disputed, both by Jews and non-Jews. The fourth is palpably false: Palestine was not a land without people when Zionists embarked upon their schemes of colonization in the early 20th century; it had an extensive Arab-speaking population, and adherents of three religious faiths, **Islam**, **Christianity** and **Judaism**, lived in Jerusalem and elsewhere.

Zionism succeeded in winning support among the Jewish populations of Europe and the USA because of their fears of **anti-semitism**, and the pogroms launched against Jews in central and eastern Europe from the 1880s onwards. Zionists were also astute in winning backing from the governments of the British Empire, Tsarist Russia, Wilhemite Germany and the Ottoman empire, who were persuaded to back the Zionist project for a diverse set of narrowly instrumental motives. However, Zionism received decisive impetus only after the genocide of six million European Jews during the **Nazi** dictatorship (1933–45). Creating a separate state in Palestine made sense to many Jewish survivors of the genocide, and in response the USA and the European powers agreed to support the establishment of a Jewish and an Arab state in Palestine. A Jewish state has been established in Palestine, the state of Israel, but to date no Arab state.

Whether Zionism's doctrinal objectives have been successfully realized in the state of Israel is a matter of debate. The central objective, the creation of a safe state for Jews, has not been established: the state of Israel, founded and expanded through colonial conquest, does not live in peace with its neighbours. The second objective, the creation of a Jewish homeland in which most Jews would live, has only been partially realized: only a minority of the world's Jewish population lives in Israel. Moreover its critics maintain that although Zionism was an understandable reaction to

European anti-semitism in the hands of many of its proponents, it has become a species of anti-Arab racism. **BO'L**

Further reading W. Lacquer, *History of Zionism*; E. Said and C. Hitchens (eds.), *Blaming the Victims: Spurious Scholarship and the Palestinian Question.*

ZOOLOGY

Zoology (Greek, 'study of living things') is the study of all aspects of the biology of animals. It was originally used to describe the study of the medical uses of animals and their products, and it was not until the 17th century that zoology began to be used to describe animal studies in their own right. However, human knowledge of animals is presumably as old as humans, and the original hunters must have known much about the ecology and behaviour of their prey animals and of potential predators. When humans began to develop animal husbandry, they came into close contact with various animals and, in the course of caring for valuable livestock, must have learnt much about their biology. The ancient Greeks studied many animals, largely in a descriptive sense, and the Roman writer Pliny the Elder (23–79), in his encyclopaedic work *Natural History*, devoted 5 volumes out of 37 to animals.

In the medieval period bestiaries were popular, listing animals in various orders according to similarities which were often superficial, and often illustrated with a significant degree of artistic licence. The first recorded scientific investigations of animals were made during the **Renaissance** by anatomists such as Vesalius, and during the 17th and 18th centuries progress was made with studies of biogeographical distribution of animals, stimulated by the exploration of the New World. Taxonomic systems became popular as humans attempted to describe the natural world in a systematic fashion.

The 19th century was a period of great expansion in zoology as broad areas of study such as **morphology** and **physiology** appeared; this expansion has continued throughout the 20th century, though the trend has been towards specialization of disciplines and away from general natural history and zoology. **RB**

See also anatomy; embryology; life.

ZOROASTRIANISM

The prophet Zarathustra, better known by the Greek version of his name Zoroaster, gave his name to Zoroastrianism. He is usually said to have lived in the north-eastern part of Persia (Iran) *c.*588–541 BCE, but recent research has suggested an earlier date within the period 1700–1400 BCE. Zoroastrianism was the state religion of the Persian dynasties for 1,000 years, until in CE 644 Muslim Arabs conquered Persia and enforced adherence to **Islam**. In the 10th century a considerable number of Zoroastrians emigrated to the west coast of India, where they became known as Parsees or Persis. The largest modern community of Parsees is found in and around Bombay, but there are small settlements even as far inland as Madurai. Some 17,000 live in Iran, and about 4,000 in the UK.

Although Zarathustra was a monotheist, he is chiefly remembered for the **dualism** of his theology, 'a dualism of spirit, postulating two principles, two twin-spirits at the origin of the universe: the spirit of truth or *Spenta Mainyu*, and the spirit of the lie, or *Angra Mainyu*'. In later Zoroastrianism the spiritual battle in the universe is waged by Ahura Mazda on the one hand and by Ahriman, his opponent, on the other. In Zarathustra's teaching Ahura Mazda, though father of both twins, is not responsible for *Angra Mainyu*. The spirits exercised complete freedom of choice and the outcome was entirely due to their choice. Men and women likewise cannot escape, he taught, from making moral choices, and by virtue of their choice and conduct they identify themselves with one of the two spirits in the universe, light or darkness, truth or lie, order or chaos, good or evil.

The *Gathas* also reveal Zarathustra as a fiery prophet, indignantly rejecting the enemies of truth. Initially he expressed hope for the victory of the forces of good over evil and the establishment of the kingdom of righteousness on Earth. The concept of kingdom or dominion (*Xshathra*) is one of the six attributes of Ahura Mazda's divine power. The others are: good mind, good order, devotion, welfare and immortality. Together they form the *Amesha Spentas*, which are either Ahura Mazda's divine attributes or companion spirits. The notion of angels and archangels in later Zoroastrianism, also adopted in post-exilic **Judaism** and hence **Christianity**, may have developed from the idea of these spirits.

Another ancient Iranian concept, of Indo-European origin, used by Zarathustra in his theology is the principle of cosmic order as opposed to chaos. This principle is at work in the natural world, in the regular rhythm of night and day, in the flow of rivers from their source to the sea, and in the movement of the stars. There was order in the service of the gods through **liturgy** while the moral law created order in human affairs.

Towards the end of Zarathustra's ministry, he developed the supernatural dimension of immortality. His idea of the 'bridge of the separator' over which each individual's soul must pass before he or she can enter eternal life was taken from earlier times, but he gave it a distinctive moral significance. Ahura Mazda, he said, had designed the bridge as an instrument of divine judgement of the dead. It represents a dreadful ordeal for the wicked: the followers of the lie will fall off the bridge into a pit of everlasting torment, whereas, assisted by Zarathustra's presence, 'powerful in immortality shall be the souls of the followers of truth'. Life beyond death was seen essentially as life in the body. Zarathustra's teaching, therefore, included a doctrine of the resurrection of the body. In later Zoroastrianism the concept of a restored physical world appears, a world 'most excellent, unaging, undecaying, neither passing away nor falling into corruption'. Associated with this was the doctrine of the coming of a saviour, Soashyant, who would appear at the end of time when all the evil forces in the universe would finally be overcome.

Zoroastrians today are also known as 'fire-worshippers'. This practice goes back also to ancient Indo-Aryan times when fire was worshipped as the god Agni (see **Vedic religion**). Today temples provide the shrine, the sanctuary for the sacred fire which signifies the presence of God, and there are two such temples in Iran and eight in India.

Another distinctive feature of later Zoroastrianism is the elaborate cult of the dead, still practised today. The practice of burial or cremation of the dead is rejected by the Parsis on theological grounds: the purity of the earth and of fire must be strictly preserved from the pollution of death. Instead the corpse is exposed to vultures and birds of carrion on the top of 'towers of silence', with accompanying rituals.

Zoroastrians share with the Indo-Aryans the god Mithra, who was popular in Vedic times. The Mithra cult, as the champion fighting for the victory of good over evil, light over darkness, was taken up by Roman soldiers and brought to Britain. The image of the triumph of light over darkness clearly appealed in northern lands, and was taken up in Christian hymns and prayers. **RW**

Further reading S.G.F. Brandon, *Man and His Destiny in the Great Religions*.